San Diego County
Bird Atlas

SAN DIEGO COUNTY BIRD ATLAS

© 2004 San Diego Natural History Museum
P. O. Box 121390
San Diego, California 92112-1390
www.sdnhm.org

Library of Congress Catalog Number pending

ISBN 0-934-797-21-8

ISSN 1059-8707

San Diego County Bird Atlas

by

Philip Unitt
PROJECT MANAGER AND AUTHOR

Ann E. Klovstad
PROJECT ASSISTANT

with contributions by
William E. Haas
Patrick J. Mock
Kirsten J. Winter

photographs by
Anthony Mercieca
Jack C. Daynes
Kenneth W. Fink
Kenneth Z. Kurland
Brian L. Sullivan
Richard E. Webster

No. 39
31 October 2004
Proceedings of the
San Diego Society of Natural History

San Diego
Natural History Museum

Ibis Publishing Company

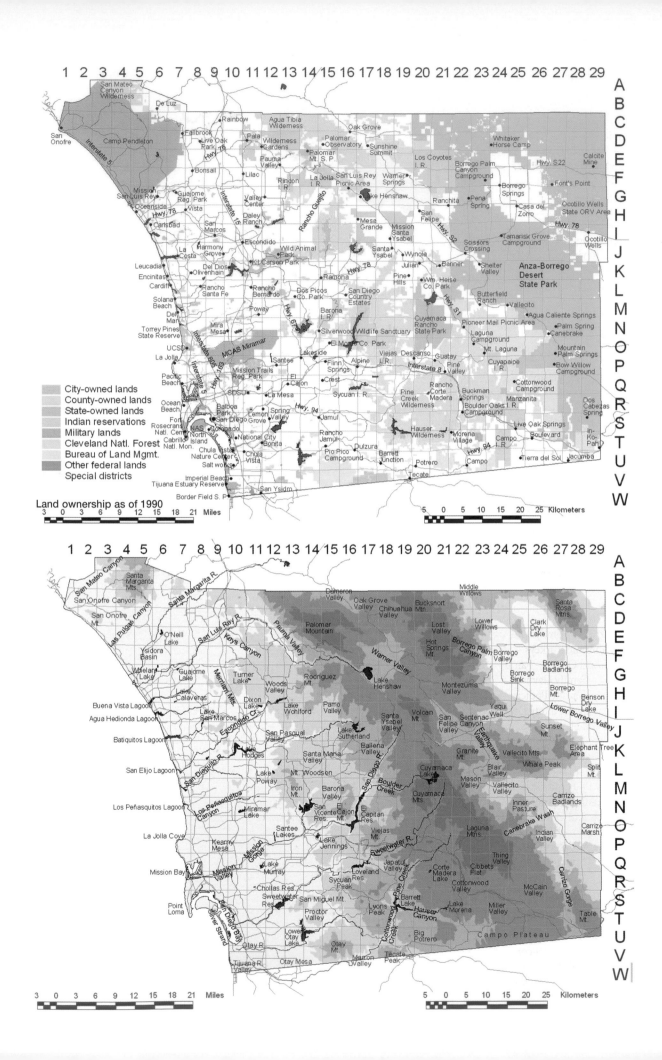

CONTENTS

DEDICATION

Brilliant, passionate, adventurous, and disciplined, Margaret McIntosh was an outstanding birder, an inspiration and an ideal to many. When we initiated the bird atlas in 1997 Margaret and her husband Bert became enthusiastic participants, spending over 700 hours in the field. Her death from pancreatic cancer on 28 August 2001 was a terrible blow to the bird atlas, to the museum's department of birds and mammals (where she had volunteered for 10 years), and to all of us who knew her as a friend. Especially in her last few weeks, Margaret told me many times how proud she was of the project's amazing accomplishments. In recognition of her steadfast support, unwavering loyalty, and tireless effort on its behalf, right up to the very end, this atlas is dedicated to Margaret.

PREFACE

Why does an area smaller than the state of Connecticut merit a bird atlas on a scale as ambitious as the one you're looking at? The people of San Diego County are passionate about the quality of their environment, the factor that brought many thousands of them here in the first place. This bird atlas is an expression of that passion.

Biodiversity is a fundamental element of environmental quality. Coastal or cismontane California, the "California floristic province," is the hotbed of biodiversity in the contiguous United States. San Diego County straddles this hotbed completely. Indeed, it may be considered the core of the southern half of this region, extending along the Pacific coast from Point Conception to El Rosario. This subset, the "San Diegan District" of Miller (1951), is a realm of unique biology, with many plants and animals found nowhere else. Other groups of organisms exemplify this uniqueness more strongly, but at least 23 subspecies of birds are endemic to the region (Table 1). Within the county, conditions are far from uniform. They change radically over short distances. Rugged topography and diverse geology have led to biological diversity on a remarkably fine scale. At no two spots is the biota identical. With the extra boost of a position astride the Pacific Flyway and a long history of birders searching for vagrants, San Diego County boasts the biggest bird list of any county or of any area of equal size in the United States: 492 species as of June 2004 (Appendix 1). On purely biological reasons alone a comprehensive bird atlas for San Diego County is well justified.

Though small on a global scale, an area the size of San Diego County can make a major contribution to world biodiversity. Compare San Diego County's 4235 square miles with some other biologically important areas of similar size worldwide:

Yellowstone National Park, 3458 square miles
Jamaica, 4244 square miles
Lebanon, 3927 square miles
Panay Island, Philippines, 4446 square miles
Sumba Island, Indonesia, 4306 square miles
Viti Levu, largest of the Fiji Islands, 4053 square miles
Hawaii (the "Big Island"), 4021 square miles

Two hundred years ago, San Diego was a tiny mission settlement, at the farthest edge of the world's consciousness. Today, it is the crucible of social and environmental change. Immigration, multiculturalism, economic globalization, air and water pollution, water importation, fire management, automobile traffic, affordable housing, urban sprawl, habitat conservation … the list of contentious issues of which San Diego is at the forefront seems endless. The gate at San Ysidro is the busiest international border crossing in the world. Clandestine immigration and drug smuggling tear at both the fabric of society and the natural environment. Virtually all food, energy, and water are imported. The people clamor for quality of life while buying homes in the suburbs and clogging the roads. The population increases at third-world rates while consuming resources at first-world rates (Figure 1). The San Diego Association of Governments projects that in 2020 San Diego County will be home to over one million more people than in 2000, an annual rate of increase of 1.6%, the same as that of Indonesia, Kenya, India, and Bangladesh, and slightly greater than that of Mexico. Can

Table 1   Endemic birds of the southern part of the California Floristic Province

Southern Mountain Quail, *Oreortyx pictus confinis*
Light-footed Clapper Rail, *Rallus longirostris levipes*
Southern White-headed Woodpecker,
    Picoides albolarvatus gravirostris
Greater Olive-sided Flycatcher, *Contopus cooperi majorinus*
Belding's Western Scrub-Jay, *Aphelocoma californica obscura*
San Pedro Mártir Mountain Chickadee,
    Poecile gambeli atratus
San Diego Oak Titmouse, *Baeolophus inornatus affabilis*
Blackish-tailed Bushtit, *Psaltriparus minimus melanurus*
White-naped Pygmy Nuthatch, *Sitta pygmaea leuconucha*
San Pedro Mártir White-breasted Nuthatch,
    Sitta carolinensis alexandrae
San Diego Cactus Wren,
    Campylorhynchus brunneicapillus sandiegensis
San Diego Bewick's Wren, *Thryomanes bewickii charienturus*
Mary Clark's Marsh Wren, *Cistothorus palustris clarkae*
Coastal California Gnatcatcher,
    Polioptila californica californica
Colonet California Gnatcatcher, *Polioptila californica atwoodi*
San Pedro Mártir Western Bluebird, *Sialia mexicana anabelae*
Grinnell's Loggerhead Shrike, *Lanius ludovicianus grinnelli*
Anthony's California Towhee, *Pipilo crissalis senicula*
Ashy Rufous-crowned Sparrow, *Aimophila ruficeps canescens*
Belding's Savannah Sparrow,
    Passerculus sandwichensis beldingi
Laguna Hanson Dark-eyed Junco, *Junco hyemalis pontilis*
Townsend's Dark-eyed Junco, *Junco hyemalis townsendi*
San Diego Red-winged Blackbird,
    Agelaius phoeniceus neutralis

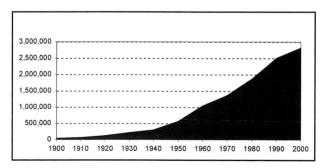

FIGURE 1. San Diego County population growth 1900–2000, based on U.S. census data.

the region's natural heritage sustain such an onslaught? San Diego County already has more threatened species, plants and animals combined, than in any area of similar size in the conterminous United States. Coastal wetlands, native grasslands, and vernal pools have already been reduced to a small percentage of their former extent.

Though much has been lost, much still remains. San Diego is fortunate in that a substantial fraction of its hinterland has already been conserved in state and local parks, national forest, and even military bases. But these areas miss many critical habitats, and society has realized that many more will be lost without an aggressive effort toward further conservation. Yet the economic forces consuming these habitats—these nonrenewable resources—are relentless, and time is short. Thus the advent of the multiple-species conservation plan for metropolitan San Diego and similar projects elsewhere in the county, which seek to accommodate this conflict. What will be the outcome of these gigantic experiments? Evaluating an experiment requires a control group. The San Diego County Bird Atlas, representing conditions at the time the plans were adopted, is a standard against which future generations will gauge these efforts' success or failure. Quick to respond, rich in species, diverse in ecology, near the top of the food chain, and readily accessible to human eyes, birds are with good reason the organisms ordinarily used in ecological and environmental monitoring.

What are the San Diego County Bird Atlas' goals? To describe and depict each species' distribution and relative abundance, in both the breeding season and winter, as it stood during our five-year data-recording period, 1997–2002. To put our atlas results in the context of each species' biology. To put each species into its historical context, to identify trends in ranges and numbers, and to search for the factors responsible for these trends.

Why is the San Diego County Bird Atlas necessary, when my *Birds of San Diego County* was published just 20 years earlier, in 1984? Between 1980 and 2000 the county's human population increased by over 51%, adding almost one million people—to bring the 2000 figure to 2.814 million. The status of at least 50% of the county's bird species has changed. The atlas incorporates data from many areas simply unexplored in the early 1980s. And the atlas reaches a level of detail impossible 20 years ago, a level far more relevant to conservation planning. Twenty percent of the county's surface burned in 2002 or 2003, making the atlas a basis for assessing the effects of these firestorms without precedent in recorded history. It is my hope that the San Diego County Bird Atlas will be useful to the policy makers who are making irrevocable decisions about our future. I hope it will be useful to birders at all levels familiarizing themselves with this remarkable area. I hope that it will be useful to scientists attempting to understand and predict the effects of urbanization on birds. And I hope it will be useful to the people of San Diego County, who need to understand their natural heritage if that heritage is to have any future.

ACKNOWLEDGMENTS

An effort with the scope of the San Diego County Bird Atlas was possible only because of the cooperation and generosity of many people and organizations. First I must thank our many volunteer observers. Their energy and diligence in the field—over 55,000 hours—were the atlas' cornerstone. Their faith and trust drove the project from start to finish.

Because of the talents and dedication of project assistant Ann Klovstad, the San Diego County Bird Atlas reached a far higher level of achievement than it could have without her. Her professionalism shaped every phase of the project, and it is only because of that professionalism that the San Diego County Bird Atlas can serve as a model for similar efforts. She did the vast majority of the data entry, orchestrated our semiannual "wingdings" to thank and recognize our volunteers, figured out how to generate the charts of nesting schedules, oversaw our complex finances, and compensated for many shortcomings, especially mine. To recognize her accomplishments adequately would take a book in itself. Thank you, Ann. And Ann thanks Cheryl Mann and Frank and Betty Scheible, whose support kept her going through the entire project.

The organizations and agencies sponsoring the project were vital to its success. The California Department of Transportation was our earliest sponsor and stuck with us faithfully through the entire life of the project. Many thanks to Pam Beare, Sue Scatolini, Darlene Alcorn, and Chris White for their kind support, and many thanks to Barbara Kus for overseeing the grant as it was funneled through San Diego State University Foundation, and looking out for us at the turn of each fiscal year.

The U.S. Forest Service supported the project for several years under challenge-cost share agreements through its Partners in Flight program. Forest biologist Kirsten Winter not only assisted with funding and access and served as a member of the atlas advisory group, she was one of our most dedicated field observers. I owe many thanks to Kirsten and to Cleveland National Forest supervisor Anne Fege for their unflagging support.

The California Department of Fish and Game generously supported the project with a grant though its Natural Community Conservation Plans Local Assistance Program. This grant enabled me to focus exclusively on the San Diego County Bird Atlas in the final year of data analysis and writing. Thanks to Lyann Comrack and Dave Lawhead for their kindness in overseeing this grant.

The atlas' coverage of Anza-Borrego, Palomar, and Cuyamaca Rancho state parks was thorough, thanks to the sponsorship of California State Parks. Funding through the parks enabled us to deploy field assistants to even the most remote and difficult wilderness areas. Park resource ecologist Paul D. Jorgensen helped coordinate our coverage of the Anza-Borrego Desert and served as an advisor from the project's beginning. Paul, ranger Robert Thériault, and park supervisor Mark Jorgensen were among our most active field observers in the park.

The Zoological Society of San Diego supported the project from its Conservation and Research Fund, sustaining its operation for two years. This grant provided the computer capable of managing the databases and handling the programs the project entailed. Many thanks to Bill Toone for his faith and support in facilitating this grant.

The National Fish and Wildlife Foundation also helped support the San Diego County Bird Atlas' operation for two years. Thanks to Greg Elliott and Alexandra Rose of the foundation, and to Barbara Kus, Jim Sulentich, Liam Davis, John Lovio, and Michael R. Smith for their support of our application.

A contract with the U.S. Navy assisted with funding, in exchange for data and copies of the atlas itself. Thank you to Tim Burr for helping to arrange this contract.

For funding for the print version of the atlas, I have many generous donors to thank. The San Diego Unified Port District provided a grant covering nearly a third of the cost. Thanks very much to environmental services director David Merk, assistant director Eileen Maher, port commissioner Frank Urtasun, and port staff Melissa Mailander, Allison Gutiérrez, Rita Vandergaw, and Bruce Hollingsworth for their support in making the port's grant a reality.

The San Diego County Water Authority kindly authorized a grant, thanks to the support of Tim Cass.

Similarly, the Sweetwater Authority also contributed to our publication fund; I thank Peter Famolaro for arranging this grant, as well all the data he contributed.

Many individual donors contributed generously to operation and publication costs from the inception of the project. At the end of the field work, Bert McIntosh proposed a "Century Club" of donors of $100 or more to support publication, and a large proportion of our participants contributed. Many others contributed in memory of Margaret McIntosh, one of the project's most enthusiastic supporters, and one of my dearest friends, to whom this atlas is dedicated. Table 2 is the list of all these generous individual donors. Michael G. Mathos contributed the funds enabling the purchase of GIS software ArcView 3.2.

Thanks to Michael R. Smith for getting us started with the geographic-information system, networking our computers, setting up the GIS files of the grid system, and directing our takeoff on the information superhighway. Thanks to Richard Wright and John Kaiser of San Diego State University's geography department for allowing us to take the training course in ArcView 3.2 offered to SDSU faculty and staff.

TABLE 2 Individuals and Societies Contributing Financially to the San Diego County Bird Atlas

Paulette D. Ache*, Donald K. Adams*, Janet A. Anderson*, Iola Arakelian†

Richard L. Barber*, Joseph R. Barth*, Mona Baumgartel & John DeBeer*, Frederick A. Belinsky*, Adeline L. Black†*, Suzanne I. Bond*, Katie Boskoff†, Richard & Susan L. Breisch*, Dorothy Burns†

Stephen D. Cameron*, Patricia A. & Kurt F. Campbell*, Elizabeth A. Castillo*, Sunny Christiansen*, Lucie Clark†, James L. Coatsworth

Joyce M. & Andrew S. Dart, James Determan*, John A. Dietrick*, Paul & Joan Dudley†*

Claude G. Edwards*, Richard A. Erickson*, Michael U. Evans*, Anne D. Ewing

William & Charlotte Fairbairn†, Samuel L. & Sandra J. Farrow*, Meryl A. Faulkner*, Roberta A. Fischer*, Friends of Blue Sky Canyon*, Patricia Fry†

Melvin L. Gabel, Gamma Phi Beta Alumnae†, Emily Garnica*, Donald P. Geiger*, Patricia Gerrodette*, Ted A. & Margaret A. Godshalk*

Michael W. & Denise Hager†*, John M. & Beverly Hargrove*, Lori J. Hargrove*, Anne Hegwer*, Donald & Jane Hensel†, Joan M. Herskowitz*, Dorothy S. & Arthur W. Hester*, Cliff B. Hewitt*, Dorothy V. Hill*, Mark David Hoefer*, Harrison & Jackie Hollywood†*, Linda M. Holt*, J. Dennis Huckabay*

Linda D. Johnson*, Virginia P. Johnson†*

Ann P. & Thomas E. Keenan*, Kerrie L. Kirkpatrick*, Gerard & Anja Kroon*, Ellen E. Kuhns*, Barbara E. Kus*

Nola E. Lamken*, Jeffrey L. Lincer*, Brian D. Loly*, LSA Associates, Inc., Michael Lubin*

Clark R. Mahrdt†, Carol McKie Manning*, Michael G. Mathos*, Andrew & Kathy Mauro*, Mary & Glenn McHeffey†, Bert McIntosh†*, Janet H. McLaughlin, Esther Jane McNeil†*, M. J. & Frances Mehling†, Edith Helen Monsees*, Virginia S. Moran*, Arthur G. & Jean H. Morley*, Joanne T. Moore*, Mary B. Mosher*

Philip K. and Heather L. Nelson*, Christine M. Nyhan*

Ruth A. O'Rourke*, Barbara J. Orr*, N. (Oz) Osborn*

Palomar Audubon Society*, Carol M. Parker*, Grace Bell & Will Parsons*, Robert T. Patton*, James A. & Barbara J. Peugh†*, Jack & Grace Pletcher†, Philip R. Pryde*

Nancy Owens Renner†, Joan M. Roberts*, Norman C. Roberts*, Charlotte L. Ryde*

San Diego Audubon Society*, Conrad Sankpill, Luis R. Santaella*, Kathleen Satterfield*, Frank W. & Betty R. Scheible*, David G. Seay*, Betty Siegel*, Robert & Sharlott Small†, James H. Smith†*, Thomas & Ona Smith†, Glen E. Spencer*, Ruth Stalnaker, John & Barbara Stokley†, Herb Stone*, Mary Beth Stowe*, Norma Sullivan, Melvin & Ellen Sweet†

Melba M. Taylor†*, Robert Thériault*, Carl & Anna Marie Thompson†, Mary Toomey*, William & Anita Tumlin†

Lou Ann Unger†

Charles E. Van Tassel*

Alison & Ronald Weiss†, Herbert H. & Katherine Williams*, James K. Wilson*, Doretta Winkelman†, Annette & Wade Winner†*, Carol H. Winter*, Kirsten J. Winter†*, Shauna M. Wolf†*, Catherine Woodruff*, Joseph C. Worley*

Herbert L. Young*, Mary M. Yount*

---

*Members of the "Century Club" proposed by Bert McIntosh.
†Contributors in memory of Margaret McIntosh.

Ogden Environmental and Energy Services offered computer-generated habitat maps and aerial photos of the county by atlas square. Thanks very much to Patrick Atchison for this service, enabling atlas participants to cover the diversity of habitats in each square.

The San Diego County Department of Planning and Land Use offered to digitize the thousands of point localities for rare and sensitive birds that atlas observers plotted on paper maps. Thanks to Melanie Casey, Dan Henderson, Bob Asher, and Tom Oberbauer for their support with this aspect of the project, among the most critical to its applications in conservation.

Advisory group members Michael U. Evans, Paul D. Jorgensen, Ann E. Klovstad, Barbara E. Kus, Karen Messer, Conrad Sankpill, Michael R. Smith, Kenneth L. Weaver, and Kirsten J. Winter deserve many thanks for their steadfast support and kind guidance throughout the project (see also Organization).

San Diego County's birding organizations, the San Diego Audubon Society, Buena Vista Audubon Society, Palomar Audubon Society, and San Diego Field Ornithologists supported the atlas enthusiastically from start to finish, setting aside programs for recruiting meetings and progress reports, featuring the project in newsletters, and providing the backbone of our corps of participants. Grants from the Palomar and San Diego Audubon societies were substantial additions to our publication fund. Thanks to the many members of these societies, and to their leaders Kathie Satterfield and Jim Coatsworth of San Diego Audubon and Richard Barber and Clark Mahrdt of Palomar Audubon for initiating these grants.

Thanks to the compilers of San Diego County's Christmas bird counts: Richard and Susan Breisch, Claude G. Edwards, Robert T. Patton, Robert Thériault, Kenneth L. Weaver, and Dennis Wysong. Christmas bird counts were a major contribution to the winter phase of the atlas. Coordinating them with the atlas grid system was difficult but critical to maximizing the use of this source of information. As a result of the effort of both compilers and participants, the coordination of the county's six Christmas bird counts with the atlas ranged from good to perfect.

Access to many sites not typically open to the public was vital to the thorough coverage the atlas achieved. Many managers and landowners kindly went out of their way to facilitate such access. I fear the following list far from complete, but I must thank Slader Buck, Jim Asmus, Deborah Bieber, and Christine Mukai of Camp Pendleton, Paul Dorey of the Vista Irrigation District, Jim Brown, lakes program manager, and all the staff of the city of San Diego Water Department reservoirs, Greg Hill of the Bureau of Land Management, Los Coyotes Indian Reservation, La Jolla Indian Reservation, Helix Water District, Bobby Curo,

Richard Day, Fritz Hartung family, "Doc" Holmes, Don Madison, Mr. & Mrs. Ralph Nunnery, Melody O'Driscoll, Nick & Lucretia Stehly, and Gemma Thornburn.

Dale Clark supported the project in many valuable ways. As the founder and mastermind of the San Diego Natural History Museum's website, she played a critical role in bringing the project into the 21st century: getting the quarterly newsletter on the website, enabling on-line submission of data, and making the website a primary means of communication about the project. She kindly arranged access to Rancho Corte Madera. I thank her deeply for more contributions than can be listed here.

Publication of the atlas as a website was made possible by grants from the San Diego Foundation, in part under its Environment Program, in part through its Blasker-Rose-Miah Fund for science and technology, and in part through the recommendations of anonymous individual donors. Thanks very much to Bill Kuni, Emily Young, Carolyn Colwell, Ted Case, Tom Oberbauer, Mike Kelly, and everyone among the San Diego Foundation's staff and volunteer proposal reviewers.

I thank Patrick J. Mock for contributing the account of the California Gnatcatcher and William E. Haas for contributing much or all of the accounts of the Long-eared Owl, Spotted Owl, Willow Flycatcher, Cassin's Vireo, Black-throated Gray Warbler, and Black-throated Magpie-Jay. Bill and Pat have much more first-hand experience with these species than do I, so their contributions make the accounts for these species much superior to what I could have written on my own.

Many reviewers contributed to ensuring that the accounts were as accurate and as readable as possible. I am especially indebted to Michael A. Patten, who read and reviewed the entire text. Kenneth L. Weaver also read the entire text and commented on many accounts. Amadeo M. Rea reviewed the accounts of most of the land birds. Philip R. Pryde and Barbara E. Kus reviewed the introductory sections. The following persons reviewed one or more species accounts in his or her realm of expertise: David Bittner, Peter Famolaro, Christine Fritz, Kimball L. Garrett, William E. Haas, William J. Hamilton, Barbara E. Kus, Jeffrey L. Lincer, Jeffrey A. Manning, John A. Martin, Guy McCaskie, Patrick J. Mock, Kathy C. Molina, Robert T. Patton, Bonnie L. Peterson, Mary F. Platter-Rieger, Abby N. Powell, Brian L. Sullivan, and Richard Zembal. Finally, many participating observers read the accounts in which their observations were cited and made many corrections. I thank all these reviewers for their kind assistance; the quality of this atlas is far higher as a result of their suggestions and corrections.

The photographs illustrating this atlas were all generously donated by San Diego's leading bird photographers. I am especially grateful to Anthony Mercieca, and it is an honor to be able to feature his legendary work as the primary source of photos in this book. Jack C. Daynes made numerous field trips to photograph species whose images we were missing, and he helped with the scanning of the photos. Brian L. Sullivan and Kenneth Z. Kurland also kindly contributed photos to fill some gaps. Kenneth Fink and Richard E. Webster donated substantial collections of slides to the San Diego Natural History Museum, another valuable resource I have drawn upon. Suzanne I. Bond, Alan M. Craig, Brian Foster, Dave Furseth, Joseph R. Jehl, Jr., Alden Johnson, Peter LaTourrette, John S. Luther, Jerry R. Oldenettel, Matt Sadowski, Jack W. Schlotte, Mary Beth Stowe, and Scott Streit each contributed one to three photos, either directly or through the museum's photo archive. I thank Suzanne I. Bond for spending many hours at the computer processing the scanned images to ready them for publication, as well as for reading and correcting page proofs.

Many thanks to typographer Tim Brittain; Tim's rigorous professionalism and good-humored cooperation made this atlas a work of art as well as a work of science.

James F. Clements of Ibis Publishing Company kindly donated his expertise and help with publication. He proofread the entire text, and he negotiated and orchestrated the printing of the book, critically valuable contributions for which I am deeply grateful.

Many staff members at the San Diego Natural History Museum assisted the project in diverse ways. The expertise of computer managers Gabriel Virissimo and Bridget Milliken was essential to a project as data-intensive as the San Diego County Bird Atlas. Graphic designers Nancy Owens-Renner, Erik Bolton, and Shar Huston produced our quarterly newsletter *Wrenderings*, the project's primary means of communication with participants and supporters. Website manager Debbie Walden sustained what Dale Clark had begun, ensuring the working of this critical component of the project through its end. The skill and sincere interest of grant writers Katie Boskoff and Elizabeth Castillo were essential to securing the backing enabling the project to be run at the level it was. Finally, the enthusiasm of the museum's executive director, Michael W. Hager, ensured the institutional backing needed to make the project a success.

METHODS

The San Diego County Bird Atlas resembles other bird atlases in that it is based on data recorded in the framework of a grid system over a five-year period, March 1997–February 2002. It differs in that it addresses winter distributions as well and presents substantial data on migrants, especially spring migrants. It is founded on databases of nearly 400,000 records, supplied by hundreds of observers (Table 3). At the outset of the project, I defined coverage goals for each of the 479 squares of the grid, and these goals were met in 97% of the squares for both winter and the breeding season. Thus the birds of San Diego County are now among the best known in the world.

ORGANIZATION

The idea of proposing a bird atlas for San Diego County first came to me over Memorial Day weekend in 1996, as the San Diego Natural History Museum reformulated its research division as the Biodiversity Research Center of the Californias. A bird atlas is about as fundamental as biodiversity research gets. The concept was also an outgrowth of some ideas Michael A. Patten, Richard A. Erickson, and Kurt F. Campbell and I addressed in a commentary in *Western Birds* in 1995 (Patten et al. 1995a). Of course, breeding-bird atlases had been around for years, so there were many models. I believed, however, that the method could accomplish much more with a level of investment higher than it usually received. Examples of failure haunted me as much as examples of success encouraged me. I was certain that both institutional backing and broad community support were vital to success. Therefore, I sought and won the confidence of the San Diego Natural History Museum administration. I recruited a group of key advisers from the community of leading birders and professional biologists. Initially, the group consisted of Michael U. Evans (then with the U.S. Fish and Wildlife Service), Paul D. Jorgensen (California State Parks), Karen Messer (Buena Vista Audubon Society and California State University, Fullerton), Conrad Sankpill (San Diego Audubon Society), Michael R. Smith (then with the U.S. Fish and Wildlife Service), and Kenneth L. Weaver (Palomar Audubon Society). Conrad and Mike Smith left San Diego during the project, but Ann Klovstad (project assistant and San Diego Audubon Society), Kirsten J. Winter (U.S. Forest Service), and Barbara E. Kus (U.S. Geological Survey and San Diego State University) joined us. Each of these served as an ambassador for the project to a key constituency and supported the effort in diverse and vital ways (see also Acknowledgments), as well as keeping me firmly focused on the goal and grounded in reality.

During the fall and winter of 1996–97, I scheduled several meetings for recruiting participants, speaking to the San Diego Field Ornithologists, all three San Diego County Audubon societies, U.S. Fish and Wildlife Service biologists, and at the Salton Sea bird festival. The word was circulated through these organizations' newsletters as well, and over 100 prospective participants attended a kickoff meeting at Mission Trails Park in February 1997. By this time, we had established the grid system and the coverage goals, and each participant received a packet of maps, lists, forms, and instruction handbook.

The initial concept was that one observer or team "adopt" one or more squares, committing to covering it until the criteria for completeness were met (see Coverage). This technique was the backbone of our effort, and many squares were covered by this method. After the first breeding season, though, it became clear that certain regions of the county remained poorly covered, and we instituted a supplementary strategy, "blockbuster weekends." In these, we targeted a region, recruited observers for one or both days of the weekend, reserved a convenient campsite for Saturday night, and divided into teams to survey usually 10 to 12 squares over the two days. Besides covering areas that would otherwise go unvisited, these events attracted some observers who preferred this mode of participation, helped train less experienced birders by teaming them with the more experienced, and built team spirit, a factor vital to our success.

In 2000, Conrad Sankpill suggested an additional strategy, the "attack squad." In this, attack squad members notified Ann and me when they were able to go into the field, or how many days they could devote in a season, and we directed them to the squares most needing attention for our coverage goals to be met. Because we kept data entry current with incoming reports, and because our facility with the databases had reached the point where we could extract lists of species recorded and confirmed breeding in each square, and usually e-mail the lists to the observers, by summer 2001 we could send our observers to where attention was most needed day by day. Thus the attack squad proved extremely effective in speeding us to the coverage goals.

Funding from the California Department of Transportation, California State Parks, and U.S. Forest Service enabled us to hire part-time field assistants for the last three and a half years of the project. Joseph R. Barth, Lori J. Hargrove, M. Brennan Mulrooney, Geoffrey L. Rogers, and David C. Seals helped us in this capacity at various times. Each had proved his or her skills as a volunteer. The field assistants proved critical, especially in remote areas of the Anza-Borrego Desert and in squares that were entirely private property, requiring that we befriend landowners to achieve adequate coverage. Thus by the end of the project our strategy had four comple-

TABLE 3 **Observers Contributing Data to the San Diego County Bird Atlas**

All observers are listed here, whether they contributed directly or indirectly to the atlas database. Indirect contributors include those reporting to the San Diego rare bird hotline (compiled since 1999 by Michael U. Evans). Principal participants, reporting 10 or more hours in the field for the atlas or contributing a substantial block of data, are in **bold**. The list of participants in Christmas bird counts follows the main list.

Paulette D. Ache, **Donald K. Adams**, R. J. Adams, Douglas W. Aguillard, **Judy Aguirre**, Eva Aiken, Daniel Aklufi, **Kathy Aldern**, Andrew Aldrich, Lisa Ale, **Frank Aleshire†**, Matthew Alexander, Monica Alfaro, Amy Allen, Chuck Allen, D. W. Allen, Larry Allen, Linda Allen, Jake Allsop, Marian Alter, **Barbara Anderson**, **Candy Anderson**, Pat Anderson, **Caron Andregg**, Frances Armstrong, B. Arnold, **Evelyn Ashton**, Jim Asmus, **David W. Au**, Terri Ayers

Maryanne Bache, Lee Backstrand, Nancy Backstrand, Hank Baele, Jane Baele, David Bainbridge, C. Bandy, **Richard L. Barber**, Brad Barker, **James D. Barr**, Lariann Barretta, **Joseph R. Barth**, **Cyndee Batzler**, **David Batzler**, Jim Bauer, **Mona Baumgartel**, Michael Beck, **Peter P. Beck**, Frederick A. Belinsky, **Barbara E. Bell**, Susan Bell, J. Benet, **Jemila Bennett**, Tom Benson, Jim Berg, **Sue Berg**, Paul Bergford, **Ruth Bergstrom**, **Erik Berndes**, **Jon Berndes**, **Kai Berndes**, Faith Berry, Eric Bertic, Deborah Bieber, Mark Billings, **David Bittner**, Mitch Bixby, C. D. Black, Lynn Blackman, Richard Bledsoe, David V. Blue, John Boaz, Steven Bobzien, Beth Boekel, Josh Boggs, Sean Bohac, John Boland, Suzanne I. Bond, Brian Bonesteel, Jane Booth, Chuck Border, Dave Born, Katie Boskoff, Chloe Bostic, **Brian Bothner**, Randy Botta, Larry Bottroff, Bill Bourdeau, C. W. Bouscaren, Cheryl Boyd, **Steve Brad**, Terry Brashear, Thad Braun, **Richard Breisch**, **Susan L. Breisch**, Kevin Brennan, Terry Brewer, Dan Brimm, Maury Brucker, **Sean Buchanan**, Slader Buck, Andy Burbaugh, Milo Burcham, Carl Burgess, Jim Burke, Doug Burley, **Kevin J. Burns**, **Timothy A. Burr**, Ken Burton, Gale Bustillos, Karen Butler, Peter Butler, **Dan Bylin**, **Debi Bylin**, Dick Byrne

Nigel Calder, Donna Calvao, **Stephen D. Cameron**, **Alan Campbell**, Bruce Campbell, Kurt F. Campbell, Patricia A. Campbell, **Rita Campbell**, Sonia Cardinal, David Carlson, John Carson, Nigel Carter, **Orval Carter**, Michelle Carvana, Therisa Cash, Tim Cass, **Michael Cassidy**, **Susan Cassidy**, Joanne Casterline, Bob Cazin, Richard Cerutti, Frank Cervantes, Paul Chad, Matt Chadwick, Elsie Chan, George Chaniot, Bob Chaney, Kay Charter, Jim Charter, Janet Chenier, Amie Childs, **Sunny Christensen**, Ross Christie, R. Church, **Joni Ciarletta**, Mary Clark, Dale Clark, Sandy Clark, Therese Clawson, **James F. Clements**, **James L. Coatsworth**, Coralie Cobb, **Jeff Coker**, Luke Cole, Shane Coles, Jim Colclough, **Andrea Compton**, Robert Compton, Lyann Comrack, Heath Conkle, **Tammy Conkle**, Virginia Conway, Craig Cook, Jason Cook, **Daniel S. Cooper**, Elizabeth Copper, Chris Cornett, Maureen Corrigan, Stephanie Costelow, Warren Cotton, George Courser, Susan Coyne, **Allen Craft**, Ed Craven, William Craven, Matt Cuny

Evelyn Dalby, Amanda Dall, Sharon Dall, **Wendy Dallas**, Bernard Dambron, Jeannette D'Angelis, Joyce M. Dart, Jonathan Daubin, **Cory Davis**, Liam Davis, James Dayberry, John DeBeer, **Alice DeBolt**, **Joe Decanio**, Bill Decker, Ann Dempsey, Bill Denton, **James Determan**, Henry Detwiler, Cheryl DeWitt, Anna Dietrick, **John A. Dietrick**, Monique Digiorgio, James Dineen, **Vesta Dineen**, Jeannie Dolan, Joe Donner, Leroy Dorman, **Thomas W. Dorman**, Rod Dossey, Darlene Dougan, **Maxine Dougan**, Bill Doyle, Jeanine Dreifuss, Kyle Drob, Joan Dudley, Doug Dunn, James Dunn

Dick Eales, Nancy Eales, Bettina Eastman, Bob Ebersol, Karen Ebersol, Harry Eckstein, Peggy Eckstein, Nancy Ede, Steve Ede, **Claude G. Edwards**, Alan M. Eisner, **Lisa Ellis**, Rosemary Emberger, Judy Endeman, Norman Engvall, Leonard Enos, **Kathy Estey**, **Jane Evans**, Jordan Evans, **Michael U. Evans**, William T. Everett, Exequiel Ezcurra

Peter Famolaro, Matt Farley, **Samuel L. Farrow**, **Sandra J. Farrow**, **Meryl A. Faulkner**, Mike Feighner, Corey Ferguson, Erica Fielder, Elizabeth Fink, Dee Finkbinder, John Finkbinder, **Roberta E. Fischer**, Kylie Fischer, **John Fitch**, **Pat Flanagan**, Amber Fogarty, Karin Forney, Ron Forster, Ken Fortune, Brian Foster, **Joan Fountain**, Ed Fox, **Nova Fraser**, Jim Freda, **Marjorie Freda**, Steve Fretwell, Julie Frietas, Mike Frietas, Bob Frishman, Christine Collier Fritz, **Michael Fugagli**, **Sachiko V. Fukuman**, Terry Fulcher, Erik Funk, Dave Furseth

Melvin L. Gabel, Terri Gallion, **Laurie Gammie**, **Emily Garnica**, P. Galvin, **Anna Gateley-Stanton**, **Donald P. Geiger**, Ivan Getting, Bud Getty, Justine Gibb, Dan Gibbs, Judy Gibson, Tom Gilleland, June Ginger, **Peter A. Ginsburg**, Lori Gleghorn, Enid Gleich, Margaret A. Godshalk, **Ted A. Godshalk**, David Goldberg, Scott Golden, Mike Goldhamer, Jerry Golub, Kelly Goocher, Alice Goodkind†, **C. C. Gorman**, Carole Gormley, **Donna Gould**, **Bill Graffius**, Irja Graham, Lloyd Graham, **Shirley Grain**, Ruth Gransbury, **Gary Grantham**, Ed Greaves, **Dorothy Green**, Juan Green, Jane Griffith, John Griffith, **Donald R. Grine**, Joan Grine, Jesse Grismer, Mary Grishaver, Judy Guilmette, Jim Gustafson, Andy Guss

William E. Haas, Steve Haber, Alan Hagen, **Charity Hagen**, Kem Hainebach, **Robin Halford**, **Edward C. Hall**, **Freeman Hall**, Steve Hall, Worth Hall, Barbara Hallman, **Robert A. Hamilton**, Jeanne Hammond, **John Hammond**, Pat Hanley, **James Hannan**, Ann Hannon, Bruce Hanson, George Hanyo, **Beverly Hargrove**, Jim Hargrove, **John M. Hargrove**, **Lori J. Hargrove**, Wayne Harmon, Georgia Harper, **Jan Harrell**, Michelle Hartmann, **Don Hastings**, **Marjorie Hastings**, Bob Hatch, Nancy Hawkins, Steve Hayden, Ruth Hayward, **Gjon C. Hazard**, Bob Hazen, G. Heck, M. Heilbron, Patricia Heinig, Steve Helm, Eleanor Henchy, Tom Henchy, Holly D. Henderson, Charles Hendew, **Bonnie Hendricks**, Larry Hendrickson, Linda Henry, **Penny Hernandez**, Michelle Herring, Diana Herron, **Joan M. Herskowitz**, Charles Herzfeld, **Arthur W. Hester**, **Dorothy S. Hester**, Cliff B. Hewitt, Robert Hewitt, Patty Heyden, Mel Hinton, Ruby Hjorth, Linh Hoang, Richard Hodges, **Mark David Hoefer**, Gus Hollenbeck, Bill Holst, **Linda M. Holt**, David Holway, Irene Horiuchi, Pierre Howard, **J. Dennis Huckabay**, Ron Huffman, Lauren Hughes, Debbie Hui, **Ruth Hummel**, Bill Hunter, John E. Hunter, **Laura Hunter**, Liz Hutson

Yasuhiro Ikegaya, Marshall Iliff, **Hank Ingersoll**, Chuck Inman, **Nancy Inman**, Ben Innes, M. Ireland, John Irvine, Pam Isaacs

Diane Jadlowski, Robert James, Hal Jameson, L. Louise Jee, G. T. Jefferson, Sue Jobe, Stefan Johansson, Arvilla Johnson, Larry Johnson, **Linda D. Johnson**, Paul Johnson, **Ron Johnson**, Ruth Johnson, **Virginia P. Johnson**, Willard Johnson, Andy Jones, Bernice Jones, **Cindy Jones**, Deborah Jones, Robert Jones, **Evan Jorgensen**, Jack Jorgensen, Kelley Jorgensen, **Mark C. Jorgensen**, **Paul D. Jorgensen**, **Steve Jorgensen**, **Doug Julian**, Joann Julian

Terese Kastner, Isabelle Kay, **Ann P. Keenan**, **Thomas E. Keenan**, Joanne Kellogg, Liz Kellogg, Keith Kendall, **Bonnie Kenk**, **Kerry Kenwood**, Nancy Kenyon, Abby King, **Steve Kingswood**, David Kisner, **Michael W. Klein**, Deirdre Klevski, **Ann E. Klovstad**, Brian Knott, Jamie Knowles, Peter Kochevar, John Konecny, Sandy Koonce, Jeremy Krefft, **Anja Kroon**, **Gerard Kroon**, Jason Kurnow, **Barbara E. Kus**

(continued)

TABLE 3   *(continued)*

Ed Lamb, **Phillip Lambert**, **Nola E. Lamken**, Dale Laney, Ken Lange, Dan Langhoff, **Dick Lantz**, Leslie Lara, **Jane Larson**, Marilyn Lawry, Mark Lawry, Jamie R. Lawson, Andy Lazere, Mike LeBuffe, Eugene Lee, **Lucy Lee**, Paul E. Lehman, Vic Leipzig, Jesse Lenaker, Joan Lentz, **Margaret Lesinsky**, Jayne Lesley, Tom Leslie, John Lewis, Karina Leyva, Pam Libby, Alisa Light, Jim Lightner, Jeffrey L. Lincer, Roger Linfield, Terri A. Lisman, Ilene Littlefield, Brian Loly, Peter Lonsdale, **Kim Lopina**, Aaron Lotz, Paul Lovehart, **John C. Lovio**, Michael Lubin, Erik Luedeke, Lynn Lunceford, Carolyn Lundberg, Jeff Lyon

Gerald MacNamera, Kevin Maconbrie, Andrew MacRae, Connie Madia, Frank Madia, **Clark R. Mahrdt**, **Cheryl L. Mann**, Marcia Dustin Mann, **Carol McKie Manning**, Jeff Manning, Jerry Manning, **Barbara Marino**, **Viviane Marquez**, Cindy Martel, Barry Martin, John A. Martin, Linda Martin, Scot Martin, Corrie Martinez, Mike Martinez, Paul Marvin, Barbara W. Massey, **Michael G. Mathos**, Kim Matzinger, **Andrew Mauro**, **Kathy Mauro**, Dave Mayer, Scott McArthur, William McBlair, John McCarthy, Jim McCarty, **Guy McCaskie**, Jack McCleod, Bill McCausland, Gerard J. McChesney, Peter McDonald, Dave McFarland, John McGowan, Vernie McGowan, **Bert McIntosh**, **Margaret McIntosh**†, Sharon McKelvey, Mike McNew, Mac McWhorter, **Esther Jane McNeil**, Chris Meador, Jim Meier, Jim Melli, Cheryl Melban, A. J. Mercado, Anthony Mercieca, Gary Meredith, **Karen Messer**, Sara Meyers, Tom Meyers, Linda Michael, Ed Midsey, Barbara Middlebrode, **Bob Miller**, Laurie Miller, Nancy Miller, Ray Miller, **Ed Mirsky**, Stella Mitchell, **Bill Mittendorff**, Patrick J. Mock, Joann Mockbee, Marie Molloy, **Edith Helen Monsees**, Jean-Pierre Montagne, David Mooney, **Barbara Coffin Moore**, Bob Moore, Joanne T. Moore, Lynette Moore, **Virginia S. Moran**, Earl Moree, Don Moreland, **Gillian Moreland**, Rosalyn Moreland, Amy Morice, Joseph Morlan, **Arthur G. Morley**, Jim Morris, Gretchen Morse, **Mary B. Mosher**, Jon Muench, **Kamal Muilenburg**, **M. Brennan Mulrooney**, Tim Murray, Barry Mussen, Jean Murton, Mike Muse, **Tom Myers**, Leif Myklebust

Patricia Nance, Laura Nass, Lucinda Navarre, Jerusha Matsen Neal, **Karlene Neal**, Heather L. Nelson, Michael Nelson, **Philip K. Nelson**, **Nancy Nicolai**, Joan Nimick, Julie Nin, Richard Norgaard, Garry Norris, Bob Norton, Dick Norton, R. J. Norton, Sue Novaks, Zach Nowak, Bill Nutter, Christine Nyhan

John Oakley, Thomas Oberbauer, Fergal O'Doherty, Diane O'Keeffe, **Bryan O'Leary**, Cliff Oliver, **Barbara J. Orr**, Regena Orr, Brock Ortega, **N. (Oz) Osborn**, Quinn Osborn, Chris Otahal

Patricia Page, Joyce Page-Breyer, Melody Padget, Amber Pairis, Eugenia Palmer, Carol Paquette, Jenny Park, Carol M. Parker, Dennis M. Parker, Robert Parks, Patricia Parris, Caryl Parrish, Grace Bell Parsons, Will Parsons, **Michael A. Patten**, Cam Patterson, **Robert T. Patton**, Sharon Paulin, Ann Payne†, **Richard Payne**, Evelyn Peaslee, Rachel Pence, Todd Pepper, Grady Perkins, **Nicole Perretta**, Kaaren Perry, Shannon Peters, **Andrea Peterson**, **Bonnie L. Peterson**, Mary Peterson, Stan Peterson, **Barbara J. Peugh**, **James A. Peugh**, Susan Morse Pfaff, Jialin Phillips, Roberta Phillips, Reed Pierce, James E. Pike, Kelly Pinion, Mary F. Platter-Rieger, **Tim Plunkett**, Pavana Plunkett, Aaron Polichar, **Leslie Polinsky**, **Mark Polinsky**, Al Ports, **Ed Post**, Mary Post, Susan Potts, Dave Pound, Geoff Pouwels, **David W. Povey**, Rob Power, **Wayne Pray**, Jason Price, Jennifer Price, Jennifer Prichett, Mike Pritzl, **Philip R. Pryde**

David Quady, **Ingri S. Quon**

Patti Raffelson, Russ Railsback, Ruben S. Ramirez, Judy Ramirez,

Kesler Randall, G. Randolph, George Ravenscroft, **David Rawlins**, Nathan Ray, Carolyn Raynesford, Amadeo M. Rea, Jon Rebman, **Ginger A. Rebstock**, **Craig H. Reiser**†, Paul Remeika, John Reseck, **Carol Reynolds**, Bill Ridell, **Christine Rideout**, Douglas Rideout, Katie Rideout, Royce B. Riggan, Don Riley, Jim Roberts, **Joan M. Roberts**, Steve Roberts, Joe Robinson, Mary Ann Robinson, Tina Robinson, Mark Rochefort, Joyce Rodgers, Raymond Rodgers, **Richard Roedell**, **Geoffrey L. Rogers**, Jon Rogers, Lindsay Romo, Kim Ronin, Rob Ronin, **David Rorick**†, Jorge Rosales, Joan Rosen, Curtis Ross, Danny Russen, Jim Rowoth, Ced Ruano, Betsy Rudee, John Rudley, Dennis Ruggles, Ann Rumsey, **Jim Russell**, Will Russell

Gail Sabbadini, Scott Sabbadini, **Matt Sadowski**, Tanja Sagar, Bonnie Salbach, Ron Saldino, Donna Sams, James R. Sams, Marty Samse, Mike San Miguel, **Gerald Sanders**, Al Sandlin, Carol Sandlin, **Robert C. Sanger**, **Conrad Sankpill**, Paul Saracini, Kathleen Satterfield, Julie Savary†, Bill Savory, Sue Scatolini, Betty Scheible, Bill Scheible, Frank Scheible, Vince N. Scheidt, **Rick Schiller**, Dianne Schilling, Jeanne Schinto, Jack W. Schlotte, Annette Schneider, John Schneider, Julie Schneider, **Claudine H. Schork**, Casey Schroeder, Brad Schram, Suzanne Schultz, Elizabeth Schweizer, Lou Schweizer, Tina Scruggs, **David C. Seals**, **David G. Seay**, Carolyn Secor, Mike Sellors, Pat Sena, **Lisa Seneca**, Leigh Sevy, Leslie Sewell, Erik Sgariglia, David Shaari, K. Shank, Paul Sharman, Bryan Sharp, **Frances Shaw**, Joe Shelton, Gaynell Schenk, Linda Shipman, Tom Shipman, Phil Siefert, **Betty Siegel**, Barbara Simon, **Jamie Simmons**, Ann Sixtus, Fran Skillman, John Skirgandas, Pam Skirgandas, **Keith Smeltzer**, Holly Smitt, **Carrie Smith**, Chris Smith, Gary Smith, **Jerry Smith**, Jim Smith, **Margaret Smith**, **Michael R. Smith**, **Mike Smith**, **Susan E. Smith**, Tricia Smith, Winona Smith, Vic Snider, Craig Snortland, Mark K. Sogge, Liz Sorenson, Steve Sosensky, John Spain, Larry Spann, Susan Spann, Caleb Spiegel, Markus Spiegelberg, **Fred Sproul**, Mike Spurrier, J. St. John, Mike Stalder, **Todd Stands**, **David Stanton**, Peter St. Clair, Barbara Stegman, Linda Stehlik, Nick Stehly, Jr., Greg Steinbach, Bill Stepe, Gregg Stiesberg, Deborah Stilman, Drew Stokes, Barbara Stone, **Herb E. Stone**, Ralph Stone, **Mary Beth Stowe**, Carol Strilich, Dianne Strzelinski, Brian L. Sullivan, Gary Sullivan, Norma Sullivan†, Carol Sunlight, Sage Swain, Larry Sward

Victor Talbott, Ed Tandelfino, Claudia Taylor, **Lee E. Taylor**, Naomi Taylor, Scott Taylor, Stacey Tennant, Jill Terp, **Robert Thériault**, Patricia Thompson, **Kemer Thomson**, Don Tomlinson, Chris Tratnyek, **Brian Travis**, Scott Tremor, Tres Trestrail, David Trissel, Rich Trissel, M. Trotter, Andy Truban, Joe Trudel, Tommy Tucker, **Jennifer Turnbull**, **Robert Turner**

Philip Unitt, **Frank L. Unmack**

Charles E. Van Tassel, Dean Vanier, Tom Vaught, Bob Vinton, Paul Vircsik, **Phoenix M. von Hendy**

E. Waardenburg, Robyn Waayers, Don Waber, Dorothy Wadlow, Edge Wade, John Wagoner, Stan Walens, David Waller, **Ed Wallace**, Kyle Wallace, Lauren Wallace, **Pat Walsh**†, **John F. Walters**, Brian Walton, **Ron Warren**, Paula Watson, Donna Weaver, Kaitlin Weaver, **Kenneth L. Weaver**, **Richard E. Webster**, Ian Weeks, **Jeffrey M. Wells**, Mike Wells, Pat Wells, Roy Wells, Randy West, David S. Wheeler, Rick Wheeler, Paula White, Pete Wickham, Harold A. Wiert†, Dan Williams, **Herbert H. Williams**, Katherine Williams, **Kathy S. Williams**, Doug Willick, Peter Willmann†, Teresa Wilks, Ken Wilson, **James K. Wilson**, Jeff Wilson, Julie Wilson, Michael Wilson, Mike Wilson, Jerry Wilson, Mark Wimer, Clark Winchell, **Kirsten J. Winter**, Rami Wissa, **Shauna M. Wolf**, A. Wolfe, Rachel Woodfield, Bruce Wollitz, **Catherine Woodruff**, John Woodward, **Joseph**

(continued)

TABLE 3 *(continued)*

C. Worley, Keith Wrestler, **Gail Wynn**, **Roger Wynn**, **Carol Wysong**, **Dennis Wysong**

Susan Yamagata, Emiko Yang, Tim Youmans, Crystal Young, **Arnold Young**, **Herbert L. Young**, Rebecca Young, Ruth Young, Matt Yubas

Sheldon Zablow, Jimmie Zabriskie, Dave Zeiss, Richard Zembal, Jeri Zemon, Barbara Zepf, Paul Zepf, Nancy Zevallos, Barry Zimmer, **James O. Zimmer**, Carolyn Zuker, **Paul Zucker**, Bambi Zuehl, Jimmie Zuehl

ANZA–BORREGO DESERT, COMPILED BY ROBERT THÉRIAULT

Paulette Ache, David W. Au, Maryanne Bache, Joseph R. Barth, Peter P. Beck, Tom Belzer, James Berg, Sue Berg, Carol Black, Harlan Boucher, Helen Boucher, Dahlia Boyarsky, George Breunig, Kathy Bussey, Ted Caragozian, Jan Clark, Phil Clark, Mike Clayton, Hal Cohen, Joanne Cohen, Jeff Coker, Evelyn Dalby, Alice DeBolt, Phil Decker, Jim Determan, Marilyn Dickson, Marilyn Dudley, Claude G. Edwards, Ron Forster, Melvin L. Gabel, John Guelke, Valerie Guelke, Robin Halford, Lori J. Hargrove, Fiona Harrison, Marjorie Hastings, Chuck Hatch, Tootie Hatch, Joe Hopkins, Bill Hunter, Laura Hunter, Nancy Inman, Don Irwin, L. Louise Jee, Linda Johnson, Ron Johnson, Jack Jorgensen, Mark C. Jorgensen, Paul D. Jorgensen, Steve Jorgensen, David Kisner, Michael W. Klein, Chuck Knight, Barbara E. Kus, Nancy Lee, Kurt Leuschner, Bonnie Loizos, Carol McKie Manning, Donalee Mattson, Mac McNair, Anne Mendenhall, Bob Miller, Virginia Moran, Gretchen Morse, Mary Mosher, M. Brennan Mulrooney, Heather Nelson, Philip K. Nelson, Bonnie Nielson, Ruth Olsen, N. (Oz) Osborn, Verlene Ota, Ann Payne, Paula Payne, Richard Payne, Barbara Perdue, Doug Perdue, Bonnie L. Peterson, Ed Post, Mary Post, Allan Power, Priscilla Price, Philip R. Pryde, Raylene Remeika, Royce B. Riggan, Royce P. Riggan, Geoffrey L. Rogers, Judy Rose, Curtis Ross, Patricia Ruston, Tom Ruston, Tarja Sagar, Weena Sangkatavat, Conrad Sankpill, Jack W. Schlotte, Tom Schwend, Erik Sgariglia, Bryan Sharp, Betty Siegel, Tom Simpson, Marjorie Sinel, Keith Smeltzer, Susan E. Smith, Winona Sollock, Alexander Spacek, Ed Spacek, Jackie Spacek, Deborah Sperberg, Catherine Stone, Geoff Stone, Herb E. Stone, Joe Stone, John Strong, Robert Thériault, Homer Townsend, Tina Townsend, Philip Unitt, Don Waber, Harold A. Wier, Peter Willmann, Tiffany Woznicki, James Wycoff, Julie York, Herbert L. Young.

ESCONDIDO, COMPILED BY KENNETH L. WEAVER

Lisa Ale, Barbara Anderson, Steve Anderson, Richard L. Barber, Joseph R. Barth, Cyndee Batzler, Dave Batzler, Peter P. Beck, Barbara E. Bell, Paul Bergford, Ruth Bergstrom, Deborah Bieber, Crystal Bingham, Justin Box, Timothy A. Burr, Orval Carter, Michael Cassidy, Susan Cassidy, Sunny Christiansen, Jim Coatsworth, Jeff Coker, Maureen Corrigan, Ruth Cramer, Susan D'Vincent, Alice DeBolt, Joe Decanio, Vesta Dineen, Marilyn Dudley, Claude G. Edwards, Lisa Ellis, Don Evans, Michael Falina, Tracy Falina, Sam Farrow, Sandy Farrow, Elizabeth Fink, Mel Forman, Eleanor Foulke, Jim Freda, Marj Freda, C. C. Gorman, Shirley Grain, William E. Haas, Edward C. Hall, Jeanne Hammond, John Hammond, Doug Hansen, Lori J. Hargrove, Charles Harman, Sue Harman, Ann Harmon, Penny Hernandez, Donna Hilliard, Kay Hubson, Dennis Huckabay, Lauren Hughes, Ruth Hummel, Liz Hutson, Pamela Isaacs, Pat Jensen, Linda Johnson, Ron Johnson, Priyantha Karunaratne, John Klavzar, Michael W. Klein, Chuck Knight, Susan LaJoie, Cheryl Learn, Emerson Learn, Mike LeBuffe, Janet Lipham, Tom Loeber, John C. Lovio, Nancy MacGillivray, Clark R. Mahrdt, Julie Manglicmot, Michael G. Mathos, Jim McCarty, Bill McCausland, John McColm,

Esther Jane McNeil, Karen Messer, Barbara Middlebrook, Dan Miller, Gillian Moreland, M. Brennan Mulrooney, Ben Nasserly, Ellie Newcomb, Barbara Orr, N. (Oz) Osborn, Bonnie L. Peterson, Wayne Pray, Kristine Preston, Maren Preston, Melissa Preston, Priscilla Price, Philip R. Pryde, Ingri S. Quon, Linda Rasmussen, Christine Rideout, Doug Rideout, Robin Ronin, Jim Russell, Conrad Sankpill, Jack W. Schlotte, Suzanne Schultz, Cecelia Secor, Ed Sher, Betty Siegel, Shari Sitko, Keith Smeltzer, Susan E. Smith, Tina Somers, Margie Stinson, Mary Beth Stowe, Brian Swanson, Lee E. Taylor, Kemer Thomson, Chuck Tralka, Andy Truban, Robert Turner, Philip Unitt, Andrea Vedanayagam, Phoenix von Hendy, Kenneth L. Weaver, Herb Williams, Kirsten J. Winter, Kathy Wohlhieter, Mike Wohlhieter, James O. Zimmer.

LAKE HENSHAW, COMPILED BY CLAUDE G. EDWARDS AND GRETCHEN MORSE

Donald K. Adams, Daniel Aklufi, Julie Alpert, Byron Anderson, David W. Au, Leticia Azala, Maryanne Bache, Richard L. Barber, Lariann Baretta, Joseph R. Barth, Mike Barton, Barbara E. Bell, Jemila Bennett, Fred Beretta, Sue Berg, Hank Bower, Bill Box, Justin Box, Eleanor Briefer, Nelson Briefer, Timothy A. Burr, Gale Bustillos, Dan Carlton, Orval Carter, Robin Church, Jeff Coker, Evelyn Dalby, Alice DeBolt, Thomas W. Dorman, Kathi Dudgeon, Claude G. Edwards, Charlotte Farrell, Sam Farrow, Sandy Farrow, Kylie Fischer, Ron Forster, Brian Foster, Jim Freda, Marjorie Freda, Melvin L. Gabel, Laurie Gammie, Ivan Getting, Peter A. Ginsburg, William E. Haas, Edward C. Hall, John Hammond, Lori J. Hargrove, Chip Hatch, Susan Hector, Wendy Hein, Art Hester, Dorothy Hester, Annie Hollenbeck, Gus Hollenbeck, Bill Hunter, Laura Hunter, Hank Ingersoll, Pam Isaacs, Linda Johnson, Ron Johnson, Robert Jones, Ann Keenan, Tom Keenan, Michael W. Klein, David Kniffing, Chuck Knight, Adam Koltz, Jason Kurnow, Dale Laney, Kathy Lapinsky, Tom Leslie, Joe Liebezeit, Jeffrey L. Lincer, Eileen Littlefield, Brian Lohstroh, Brian Loly, Clark R. Mahrdt, Julie Manglicmot, Pauline Matthews, Rich Matthews, Jim McCarty, John McColm, Judy McIntosh, Thane McIntosh, Esther Jane McNeil, Bill Mittendorff, Gretchen Morse, M. Brennan Mulrooney, Thomas Myers, Doug Nail, Bryan O'Leary, N. (Oz) Osborn, Marjorie Oslie, Dennis M. Parker, Robert T. Patton, Nicole Perretta, Ed Post, Mary Post, Clint Powell, Wayne Pray, Priscilla Price, Philip R. Pryde, Ingri S. Quon, Jeanne Raimond, Anita Reith, David Reith, Christine Rideout, Royce B. Riggan, Royce P. Riggan, Claire Roberts, Ron Roberts, Geoffrey L. Rogers, Robert C. Sanger, Juliette Savary, Jack W. Schlotte, Betty Siegel, Susan E. Smith, Fred Sproul, Mary Beth Stowe, Robert Thériault, Lee Thornton, Earl Towson, Philip Unitt, Don Waber, John F. Walters, Kenneth L. Weaver, Mark Webb, James K. Wilson, Lynn Wilkinson, Kirsten J. Winter, Shauna M. Wolf, Gary Wood, Janet Worts, Stephanie Worts, James O. Zimmer.

OCEANSIDE–VISTA–CARLSBAD, COMPILED BY DENNIS WYSONG, FREEMAN HALL, AND CHRISTINE RIDEOUT

Donald K. Adams, Allen Alexander, Doug Alexander, Jane Alexander, Richard L. Barber, Joseph R. Barth, Cyndee Batzler, Dave Batzler, Mona Baumgartel, Barbara E. Bell, Deborah Bieber, Hank Bower, Curt Bruce, Timothy A. Burr, Alan Campbell, Rita Campbell, Orval Carter, Michael Cassidy, Noby Cederholm, Joni Ciarletta, Jim Coatsworth, Ron Collins, Warren Cotton, Allen Craft, Dan Daniels, Alice DeBolt, Jim Determan, Vesta Dineen, Claude G. Edwards, Nancy Ferguson, Pete Fitzpatrick, Scott Fleury, Ken Fortune, Joan Fountain, Jim Freda, Marj Freda, Steve Fretwell, Michael Fugagli, Sachiko Fukuman, Emmy Garnica, Donald Geiger, C. C. Gorman, Carol Gormley, Irja Graham, Lloyd Graham, Shirley Grain, Ruth Gransbury,

(continued)

TABLE 3 *(continued)*

Andy Guss, Edward C. Hall, Freeman Hall, Gjon C. Hazard, Ann Hegwer, Linda Holt, Darold Holten, Virginia Holten, Robert Hoover, Rachel Hopkins, Dennis Huckabay, Liz Hutson, Linda Johnson, Ron Johnson, Taryn Johnson, Michael W. Klein, Chuck Knight, Michael LeBuffe, Mary Patricia Lemon, Margaret Lesinsky, Jayne Lesley, Ilene Littlefield, Eric Lodge, Brian Loly, John C. Lovio, Clark R. Mahrdt, Carol McKie Manning, Jerry Manning, Andrew Mauro, Roxanne McAndrew, Jim McCarty, Josh McLean, Esther Jane McNeil, Melissa Mersy, Karen Messer, Dan Miller, Nancy Miller, Gillian Moreland, M. Brennan Mulrooney, Herbert Nierman, Bryan O'Leary, N. (Oz) Osborn, Jan Owen, Caryl Parrish, Robert T. Patton, Brandon Percival, Andrea Peterson, David W. Povey, Allan Power, Terri Reinhard, Carol Reynolds, Christine Rideout, Geoffrey L. Rogers, David Rorick, Conrad Sankpill, Tara Schoenwetter, Jack W. Schlotte, Claudine H. Schork, Brenda Senturia, Betty Siegel, Vic Snider, Bob Stephenson, Marlin Stephenson, Debra Stillman, Don Stillman, Ralph Stone, Mary Beth Stowe, Pete Suffredini, Naomi Taylor, Andy Truban, Robert Turner, Philip Unitt, Stan Walens, Norman Walker, Kenneth L. Weaver, Peter Willman, Kirsten J. Winter, Shauna M. Wolf, Carol Wysong, Dennis Wysong, Arnold Young, Herbert L. Young, James O. Zimmer, Paul Zucker.

RANCHO SANTA FE, COMPILED BY ROBERT T. PATTON

Kathy Aldern, Monica Alfaro, Jeff Allen, Barbara Anderson, Stan Arnold, Maryanne Bache, Richard L. Barber, Joseph R. Barth, Mona Baumgartel, Timothy A. Burr, Orval Carter, Sunny Christiansen, Joni Ciarletta, Maureen Corrigan, Alice DeBolt, Joan DeCarli, Jim Determan, Claude G. Edwards, Audrey Elliott, Kathy Estey, Michelle Evancho, Matt Farley, Neil Fergusson, Brian Foster, Ed Fox, Emmy Garnica, Anna Gateley-Stanton, Dorothy Green, William E. Haas, Edward C. Hall, Freeman Hall, Worth Hall, Lori J. Hargrove, Gjon C. Hazard, Susan Hector, Penny Hernandez, Joan Herskowitz, Liz Hutson, Linda Johnson, Ron Johnson, Taryn Johnson, Oliver Jones, Julie Jones-Putnam, Isabelle Kay, Michael W. Klein, Chuck Knight, Gerard Kroon, Jayne Lesley, Joe Liebezeit, Brian Loly, Clark R. Mahrdt, Carol McKie Manning, John A. Martin, Andrew Mauro, Scott McCarthy, Bert McIntosh, Margaret McIntosh, Alden Miller, Barbara Coffin Moore, Bob Moore, Cindy Moore, Gillian Moreland, Bonnie Mulrooney, M. Brennan Mulrooney, Brian O'Leary, Brock Ortega, William Ostheimer, Dennis M. Parker, Robert T. Patton, James Peugh, Wayne Pray, Ingri S. Quon, Joan Roberts, Richard Roedell, Martin Rosen, Jim Russell, Luis Santaella, Jack W. Schlotte, Brenda Senturia, Frances Shaw, Linda Shipman, Thomas Shipman, Betty Siegel, Jonathan Snyder, Todd Stands, David Stanton, Denise Stillinger, Tim Stillinger, Ralph Stone, Philip Unitt, Phoenix von Hendy, Stan Walens, Ron Warren, Kirsten J. Winter, Shauna M. Wolf, Paul Zucker.

SAN DIEGO, COMPILED BY CLAUDE G. EDWARDS, ANN E. KLOVSTAD, AND PHILIP UNITT

Donald K. Adams, Douglas W. Aguillard, Marya Ahmad, Daniel Aklufi, Kathy Aldern, Monica Alfaro, Doug Allen, Jake Allsop, Fred Andrews, Maryanne Bache, Mike Barbee, Joseph R. Barth, Patricia Beard, Ruth Bergstrom, Richard Bledsoe, Andrea Bond, Andy Bradvica, Richard Breisch, Susan L. Breisch, Sarah Brooks, Tom Carnes, Orval Carter, Lisa Chaddock, Ross Christie, Therese Clawson, Jim Coatsworth, James Colclough, Elizabeth Copper, David Crabb, Evelyn Dalby, Bernard Dambron, Alice DeBolt, Bev Detrez, Anna Dietrick, John Dietrick, Thomas W. Dorman, Penny Drozd, Claude G. Edwards, Fred Esparza, Michael U. Evans, Peter Famolaro, Ruth Finnegan, Kylie Fischer, Joyce Forester, Ron Forster, Brian Foster, Nova Fraser, Jack Friery, Anna Gateley-Stanton, Marc Gehr, Ivan Getting, Peter A. Ginsburg, Paul Gobel, Ted Godshalk, Wendy Goldfinger, Mike Goldhamer, Debbie Good, C. C. Gorman, Judith Guilmette, William E. Haas, Lori J. Hargrove, Peggy Harmon, Wayne Harmon, Don Hastings, Marjorie Hastings, Gjon C. Hazard, Bonnie Hendricks, Annette Henry, Art Hester, Dorothy Hester, Mel Hinton, Richard Hodges, Anna Hollenbeck, Gus Hollenbeck, Lauren Hughes, Liz Hutson, Yasuhiro Ikegaya, Linda Johnson, Ron Johnson, Virginia P. Johnson, Bernice Jones, Deborah Jones, Ann Keenan, Tom Keenan, Kerry Kenwood, Jan Kitchel, Michael W. Klein, Ann E. Klovstad, David Kniffing, Chuck Knight, Debbie Knight, Fernand Kuhr, Chuck Lapinsky, Kathy Lapinsky, Bob Laymon, Brian Lohstroh, Shannon Lounsbury, Connie Madia, Frank Madia, Cheryl Mann, Viviane Marquez, John A. Martin, Michael G. Mathos, David Mayer, Guy McCaskie, Bill McCausland, Judy McIntosh, Esther Jane McNeil, Anthony Mercieca, Bob Miller, Ed Mirsky, Bill Mittendorff, Joann Mockbee, Anne Monsees, Edith Helen Monsees, Barbara Coffin Moore, Joanne Moore, Gillian Moreland, Gretchen Morse, M. Brennan Mulrooney, John Murphy, Ed Myers, Tom Myers, Gretchen Nell, Philip K. Nelson, Bryan O'Leary, Jerry Oldenettel, Ruth O'Rourke, Barbara Orr, N. (Oz) Osborn, Carol Parker, Holly Parker, Robert T. Patton, Josephine Payne, Barbara Peugh, Jim Peugh, Leslie Polinsky, Mark Polinsky, Ed Post, David W. Povey, Allen Power, Wayne Pray, Priscilla Price, Philip R. Pryde, Susie Qashu, Ingri S. Quon, Jeanne Raimond, Kesler Randall, Craig H. Reiser, Christine Rideout, Royce B. Riggan, Clare Roberts, Ron Roberts, Geoffrey L. Rogers, Allison Rolfe, Diane Rose, Curtis Ross, Phil Rouillard, Jay Rourke, Jorge Sanchez, Weena Sangkatavat, Conrad Sankpill, Kathie Satterfield, Jack W. Schlotte, Carrie Schneider, Valerie Schwartz, David C. Seals, David G. Seay, Dennis Selder, Frank Siebenborn, Betty Siegel, Arsenio Sierra, Ann Sixtus, Keith Smeltzer, Gary Smith, John Spain, Peter St. Clair, Anna Stalcup, Todd Stands, David Stanton, Mary Beth Stowe, David Sweig, Jill Terp, Earl Towson, Sharon Towson, Sally Trnka, Philip Unitt, Stan Walens, Ed Wallace, Lauren Wallace, David Waller, John F. Walters, Kristen Ward, Samantha Weber, Richard E. Webster, Peter Willman, James K. Wilson, Mayda Winter, Shauna M. Wolf, Catherine Woodruff, Joseph C. Worley, Betty Wotton, Bob Wotton, Susan Yamagata, Pete Yingling, Arnold Young, Herbert L. Young, Paul Zepf, James O. Zimmer.

mentary prongs; we maintained a spreadsheet tracking how each method would serve to reach the goal for each square.

GRID SYSTEM

Bird atlases are commonly based on a grid system of squares 5 kilometers or 3 miles on a side. With a grid of this scale, I estimated that the resulting number of squares could, in concept, be covered adequately by San Diego County's birders over the projected five years. Therefore, we adopted this system, basing the grid on the public land survey of townships, ranges, and sections. This survey has been used heavily for defining property boundaries; roads often follow section boundaries, and the lines are represented on U.S. Geological Survey topographic maps, the Cleveland National Forest map, and the Thomas Brothers road atlas. Therefore it was convenient for our observers to use in the field. An additional benefit was that township lines correspond with the county's boundary with Imperial and most of Riverside County. Thus most of the atlas squares represent one-quarter township or nine sections and average three miles on a side. Along the coast and along the Mexican border, some grid cells that would have been much smaller than nine square miles were combined with neighboring cells (usually the one directly north) to make the size of our sampling units more uniform. Another complication was that the ranchos and pueblo lands granted during the era of Mexican rule in California were never part of the public land survey. Michael R. Smith interpolated the atlas squares in these areas for us by means of a computerized geographic information system (GIS). The atlas grid thus consists of 479 cells averaging 8.84 square miles or 22.9 square kilometers each. Each square was designated by an alphanumeric code (alphabetically north to south, numerically west to east) and by a name recalling the best known or most colorfully named location in the square (Table 4).

COVERAGE

How to balance the conflicting goals of breadth and depth of coverage has vexed organizers of bird atlases since their inception. Another challenge was finding a workable balance between the uniformity of standards needed for a scientific study and the flexibility needed for a study relying largely on volunteers. After studying the standards set by various other atlases, I decided on a threshold defined by multiple criteria, all of which needed to be met for the threshold in that square to be cleared. I figured it was best to set the bar high initially, because it could be lowered if necessary, but raising it would be impossible. Fortunately, only minor fudging of the criteria proved necessary (see below).

For the breeding season, I originally established five criteria constituting the goal for each square:

1. Minimum 25 observer-hours from March to August (could be satisfied in one year or spread over the 5-year life of the project at the participating observers'

discretion). There was no maximum; observers gave some squares far over the minimum.
2. Every accessible habitat be visited at least once (observers received a computer-generated habitat map courtesy of Ogden Environmental and Energy Services; evaluating accessibility was left to the observers' judgment).
3. At least two visits in June for the coastal slope, two visits in May for the desert slope. This criterion was meant to encourage observers to schedule time in the field in the month when they would be most likely to encounter fledglings and to ensure they got into the field after all summer visitors had arrived. As it proved cumbersome to track and not essential to criteria 4 and 5, I did not maintain this criterion through the study. Nevertheless, 84% of the squares were visited at least twice during the target month, and 97% were visited at least once during that month.
4. At least 90% of the number of species on a "target list" tailored for the square be identified as at least possibly breeding. I devised the target lists by outlining on a digital map of the county an estimate of each species' breeding range; a program devised by Michael R. Smith then converted these maps into a database containing the lists by square. Note that the criterion for the threshold was based on the number of species, not the composition of the list. Nevertheless, the observers received the lists so as to call their attention to species likely in the area. Sometimes the target numbers proved low; in these cases, I did not revise the number upward but relied on the 25-hour criterion to ensure the comparability of these squares with the others. In desert squares that lacked oases or developed areas, though, the original target lists soon proved unrealistically high and were reduced by a uniform factor to 75% of the original.
5. At least 50% of the number of species on the target list actually be confirmed as breeding. For most species this meant by observing nest building, distraction displays, aggressive defense, active or used nests, fledglings still dependent on their parents, adults disposing of nestlings' fecal sacs, or adults carrying food to young. For some species, these behaviors needed to be interpreted more narrowly, especially for the terns, whose dependent young follow their parents many miles from their natal colony. Observations of pairs, courtship displays, or copulation counted only as probable breeding and thus did not contribute to satisfying this criterion.

For the winter, the criteria were parallel to those for the breeding season:

1. Minimum 25 observer-hours in December, January, or February.
2. The square be surveyed in at least three of the project's five winters. This criterion was an attempt

to encompass the irregularity of some winter visitors, amply demonstrated between 1997 and 2002.

3. Every accessible habitat be visited at least once.
4. At least 90% of the number of species on the target list be identified. I devised target lists for each square for the winter by the same procedure I used for the breeding season. The 90% could include early spring migrants like swallows or *Selasphorus* hummingbirds. The same desert squares whose original breeding target numbers were reduced had their winter target number reduced by the same 75% factor. A few other squares that were covered almost entirely by chaparral also proved to have inappropriately high initial goals for winter; here the winter target was reduced to either 75% or 90% of the original.

Results of San Diego County's six Christmas bird counts were integrated into the winter database, thanks to the coordination of the count compilers, all of whom were key atlas participants. Each count circle has a diameter of 15 miles (Figure 2) and was covered by about 20 to 30 parties of observers. Each count was run annually on one date between the third Saturday of December and the first weekend of January. Count participants generally recorded their observations by atlas square, and the goals for winter coverage were met in several squares largely through Christmas bird counts.

All the criteria for the breeding season threshold were met in 465 squares, 97% of the total (Figure 3). In four squares (M13, S12, S13, U10) the number of hours formally reported was under 25, but observers living and/or working in these squares sent data sufficient to demonstrate that they had spent well over 25 hours observing birds there. The 25-hour criterion could not be met in

seven other squares (C17, C23, D13, G14, H14, O25, S28) as a result of difficult access. In six squares in the Anza-Borrego Desert (C25, C26, F22, O26, O28, Q29) the goal for number of confirmed breeding species could not quite be met in spite of at least 25 hours of effort. In one square with extremely difficult access (O25) the goals for numbers of possible and confirmed breeding species were met with under 25 hours field time. Only one square (C4, lying entirely within bombing range on Camp Pendleton) went completely uncovered.

All the criteria for the winter threshold were met in 467 squares, 97.5% of the total (Figure 4). In four squares (D13, G14, H14, N18) with poor access neither the goals for number of hours or number of species could be achieved. In two squares (I14, I19) the goal for number of species could not be reached in spite of at least 25 hours. Three squares with difficult access (C26, C27, O25) had all the criteria for their thresholds met but were visited in only two winters. Again, only square C4 was unvisited in winter.

Nevertheless, the results have limitations and biases. For a project based largely on the dedication and judgment of volunteers, standards had to be flexible. Because observers determined their own field schedules within the guidelines of the project, we did not capture year-to-year variability uniformly for each square. Some squares thus missed being covered in the wet El Niño spring of 1998 or in winters when Mountain Bluebirds or Cassin's Finches invaded. Thus the observed nesting schedules of more localized species may be skewed. We had no standards for nocturnal coverage, so the distributions we recorded for night birds are considerably less complete than those for diurnal species. As always, observers' ability to detect a species varies with experience and acuity of eyes and ears—the reason for establishing coverage criteria based on number of species as well as number of hours. Each square was covered to a varying degree beyond the minimum 25 hours—sometimes far beyond. Therefore the distribution of some rare species, especially winter visitors, still reflects observer effort to some extent.

REPORTING

Participants submitted their observations primarily on forms designed for the project, which asked the observers to supply a number of individuals estimated or counted on a specific date, as well as any breeding behavior observed on that date (see below). Our procedures thus differed from those of some atlas

FIGURE 2. San Diego County Christmas bird count circles.

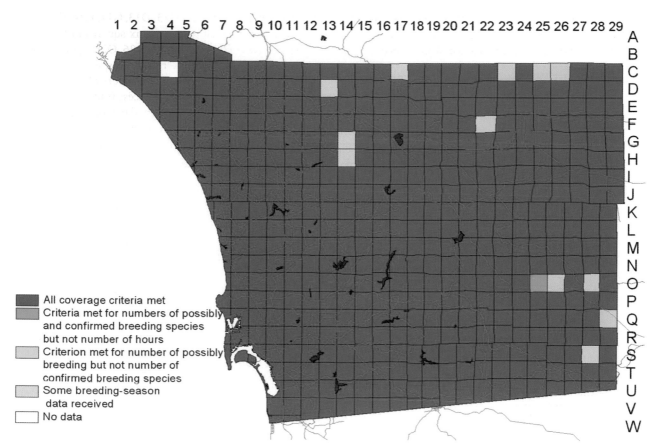

FIGURE 3. San Diego County Bird Atlas coverage achieved during the breeding season.

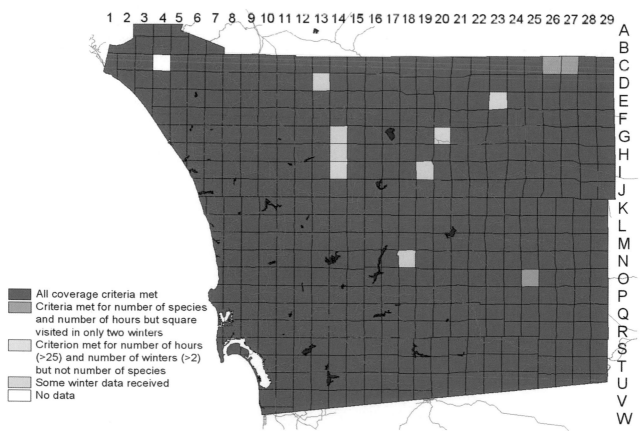

FIGURE 4. San Diego County Bird Atlas coverage achieved during winter.

projects, which ask observers for only a summary of what they observed over a season. Some have called our procedures overkill, but they are no different from what any responsible birder does in his field notes. This level of detail was essential in distinguishing migrants from birds on breeding territory, especially relevant in an area like San Diego County where much of the breeding season for local birds overlaps with spring migration for those breeding farther north. Some observers nevertheless sent composite lists, but these were a tiny fraction of the total.

The forms for the breeding season asked for time in the field and had columns for both numbers of individuals observed and breeding behaviors. Observers could enter as many behaviors as were relevant for that species. The behaviors were coded in a system similar to those used for other bird atlases, especially that for Los Angeles County.

SH, species observed in habitat suitable for breeding during its breeding season.

SM, singing male in suitable breeding habitat during the species' breeding season.

JV, juvenile bird independent of its parents, in species where the young do not migrate or disperse while still in this plumage.

MM, multiple singing males in suitable breeding habitat within the square on a single day. Observers were asked to estimate a number of such birds. Unlike all the other behavior codes, which were represented in our database by true/false fields, the MM field contained a numeric value.

AB, agitated behavior or anxiety calls from adult birds.

PR, pair in suitable breeding habitat during breeding season.

TB, territorial behavior such as a dispute or chase by two individuals of the same species.

CB, courtship behavior such as courtship feeding, breeding displays, or copulation.

PN, probable nest, for use in cases where a nest was suspected but for some reason, such as accessibility, could not be confirmed.

PB, probably building a nest, for species like some wrens and the Verdin, which build roosting or dummy nests, or woodpeckers, which maintain holes as roost sites. If these species were paired while engaged in apparent nest building at the proper season, though, we used the following code.

NB, nest building or carrying nest material.

DD, distraction display by injury-feigning or aggressive defense of an unseen nest against predators such as corvids or raptors.

UN, used nest or eggshells found.

ON, occupied nest but contents unknown (nest inaccessible or brooding bird not disturbed).

FL, fledglings still dependent on their parents, in species where the family remains on its territory.

FS, adult carrying fecal sac.

FY, adult feeding young or carrying food to them.

NE, nest with eggs.

NN, nest with nestlings seen or heard.

Observers who "adopted" a square also received a block-summary form allowing them to track their progress toward the coverage goals for that square, for both hours and species. As our capabilities with the databases improved, we were able to get the answers for which the block-summary forms were devised directly from the databases.

For winter the forms were simpler than for the breeding season, asking only for time in the field and number of individuals observed. Breeding behavior observed from December through February resulted in records entered in both the breeding and winter databases. The winter forms comprised a 12-column form for use in one square over the entire project and a 3-column form for use on blockbuster weekends, by the attack squad and field assistants, and for casual observations.

Participants also received incidental-observation forms, encouraging them to report observations apart from field trips made specifically for the atlas. We cast our net as widely as possible, attempting to draw in even casual birders, reasoning that such involvement could generate reports that could be checked out by experienced observers if necessary, could facilitate access, and could spark enthusiasm for the project in the broader community.

The forms were also available on the San Diego Natural History Museum's website, and an increasing fraction of observers submitted their results via this medium. Data transmission over the Internet became more important toward the end of the project when continuous updating of the database became critical to ensuring that the coverage goals were met in the largest possible percentage of squares. Nevertheless, reports via the website were treated the same as reports on paper, being reviewed and entered by Ann Klovstad and me rather than going directly into the databases.

In addition to forms, participants received maps. Varying according to availability and appropriateness for the area, these included topography, vegetation communities, roads, and/or land ownership. The availability of topographic maps on compact disks enabled us to generate such maps by atlas square. Using GIS files based on mapping done in the early 1990s, Ogden Environmental and Energy Services kindly generated vegetation maps by atlas square, the vegetation types simplified from the originals for appropriateness for birds. Michael R. Smith kindly provided a GIS file outlining publicly owned lands as of 1990. Observers also received enlarged photocopies of 1:100,000-scale topographic maps for plotting the areas they covered on each field trip and the locations of rare or sensitive species. Species for which we requested plotted locations were designated with asterisks on the forms. In addition to generating more precise locations for species of conservation concern, the mapping helped ensure that observers knew where they were with respect to our grid system and that they reported their results in that framework. Although not all observers followed the mapping procedures completely, the effort still generated several thousand point localities for the targeted species.

DATA REVIEW

The quality of observational data is always a concern. Especially when habitats surveyed may be degraded or destroyed, getting the story right the first time is essential to using the data as a standard for gauging changes. I reviewed all reports as they came in, before Ann Klovstad entered them in the database. Ann caught further errors as well. I contacted the observers for clarification, or arranged for independent verification, if reports deviated from established patterns. Another round of editing took place at the end of the five years of data recording. As I generated the maps, I looked for outlying records that might be suspect. The common error picked up by this means was the coding of a species as in suitable breeding habitat when it was recorded in the square during the species' migration period only. A parallel procedure with the charts of breeding behavior by date also revealed some misinterpretations needing correction. My standards were conservative, and I believe all the extensions reported in this atlas are well founded. I refer to specimen data frequently: specimens are the skeleton, sightings the flesh of our understanding of bird distribution.

My conservatism risked our nearly missing some notable discoveries. On 6 May 2001, during a "blockbuster weekend" to southeastern San Diego County, Ginger Rebstock and Jim Determan reported in the Manzanita Indian Reservation agitated behavior of a Brewer's Sparrow, suggesting a possible nest. Because the species had never been found nesting as far south as San Diego County, and because in 1999 migrants had remained until the end of May, I brushed this idea aside. The following weekend, I found a Brewer's Sparrow nest myself at Ranchita and had to eat crow. Shortly thereafter, Joe Barth saw a Brewer's Sparrow carrying a white object, in retrospect an insect, in upper McCain Valley just east of the Manzanita Reservation; on 11 and 13 June 2001 Joe and I saw two independent juveniles.

HISTORICAL DATA

Because one of the most important roles of a bird atlas is to address change, the distribution maps illustrate past distributions where these differ appreciably from those we observed from 1997 to 2002. The data on which these historical distributions are based are far from complete, consisting primarily of the San Diego Natural History Museum's specimen collection, the Western Foundation for Vertebrate Zoology's egg collection, published literature, and my own field notes. An exhaustive search of all sources, especially environmental impact reports, proved impractical. Many early locations are too imprecise for the location to be fixed to the proper square of our atlas grid. No matter how exhaustive a historical database could have been assembled, it would have been far patchier than the database we amassed during the atlas' term. Despite these shortcomings of the historical data, I believe they are vital to putting the current view in proper context.

TABLE 4

Square		Breeding Season			Winter		
		Species[a]	Hours	Primary observer(s)	Species[b]	Hours	Primary observer(s)
A-3	White Oak Springs	60	36.25	L.J.Hargrove, J.M.Wells, K.J.Winter, P.Unitt	50	36.00	L.J.Hargrove, B.E.Bell, J.M.Wells, K.J.Winter, P.Unitt
A-4	Cold Spring Canyon	53	75.00	J.&B.Hargrove, J.R.Barth, K.J.Winter	49	44.00	J.R.Barth, J.M.Wells, K.J.Winter, C.Ferguson, J.&B.Hargrove
A-5	Tenaja	61	26.50	K.J.Winter	60	25.58	K.J.Winter, J.R.Barth, J.&B.Hargrove
B-2	Talega Canyon	64	44.50	S.V.Fukuman, P.Unitt	69	32.00	P.Unitt, S.V.Fukuman, B.E.Bell
B-3	San Mateo Canyon	64	37.91	J.R.Barth, P.Unitt	55	29.83	J.R.Barth, P.Unitt
B-4	Case Spring	79	52.80	P.A.Ginsburg	76	23.50	P.A.Ginsburg
B-5	Margarita Peak	58	32.67	E.C.Hall, J.O.Zimmer, J.R.Barth, L.J.Hargrove	72	28.75	W.E.Haas, E.C.Hall, J.O.Zimmer, J.&B.Hargrove, L.J.Hargrove
B-6	De Luz	75	27.90	K.L.Weaver	77	30.01	K.L.Weaver, W.E.Haas
B-7	Ross Lake	76	25.45	K.L.Weaver	82	26.71	K.L.Weaver
C-1	San Mateo Point	74	89.50	M.Lesinsky, L.Ellis	128	100.25	M.Lesinsky, L.Ellis, J.&B.Hargrove, M.B.Stowe
C-2	San Onofre Creek	65	36.25	S.Brad, L.J.Hargrove, L.Lee	73	32.25	S.Brad, L.Lee, L.J.Hargrove, J.R.Barth
C-3	Jardine Canyon	64	28.50	P.Unitt, J.R.Barth	69	26.42	P.Unitt, J.R.Barth, L.J.Hargrove
C-5	Roblar Creek	69	161.08	J.M.Wells, J.Turnbull, P.P.Beck, L.J.Hargrove, D.C.Seals, J.R.Barth	62	25.50	B.E.Kus, L.J.Hargrove, D.C.Seals
C-6	De Luz Creek	74	27.05	K.L.Weaver	67	25.15	K.L.Weaver
C-7	Sandia Canyon	85	58.80	K.L.Weaver	81	27.10	K.L.Weaver
C-8	Upper Santa Margarita	91	101.55	K.L.Weaver	79	32.60	K.L.Weaver, L.Ale, E.Ashton
C-9	Rainbow	73	30.80	K.L.Weaver, D.C.Seals, P.Unitt	72	25.70	K.L.Weaver, D.C.Seals, J.Ciarletta
C-10	Mt.Olympus	66	32.85	K.L.Weaver, D.C.Seals, P.Unitt, J.Ciarletta	61	26.15	K.L.Weaver, L.J.Hargrove, D.C.Seals
C-11	Trujillo Creek	69	111.25	J.&B.Hargrove	53	40.75	J.&B.Hargrove
C-12	Agua Tibia	62	66.00	J.Determan	50	30.56	J.Determan
C-13	Eagle Crag	70	93.83	J.&B.Hargrove, K.J.Winter, L.Hoang, J.M.Wells	53	41.00	J.&B.Hargrove, R.C.Sanger, K.S.Williams, J.M.Wells
C-14	Cutca Valley	64	174.83	J.&B.Hargrove	51	43.00	J.&B.Hargrove
C-15	Dameron Valley	86	51.40	K.L.Weaver	79	26.44	K.L.Weaver
C-16	Oak Grove	85	29.60	K.L.Weaver	103	25.60	K.L.Weaver, J.K.Wilson, P.Unitt, L.&M.Polinsky
C-17	Dick Spring	38	18.75	J.&B.Hargrove, J.K.Wilson	59	27.75	B.&M.McIntosh, H.E.Stone, P.D.Jorgensen, P.Unitt, J.&B.Hargrove, L.J.Hargrove
C-18	All One God Faith Rainforest	72	38.66	B.&M.McIntosh, J.&B.Hargrove, A.Mauro, P.K.Nelson, J.K.Wilson, P.Unitt	65	31.45	J.K.Wilson, B.&M.McIntosh, A.Mauro, H.Ingersoll, N.Fraser, P.Flanagan, J.R.Barth, P.Unitt
C-19	Chihuahua Valley E	54	43.34	J.R.Barth, R.C.Sanger, K.S.Williams, P.D.Jorgensen, P.Unitt, K.J.Burns, K.L.Weaver, J.Hargrove	54	39.00	J.R.Barth, K.J.Burns, E.C.Hall, C.R.Mahrdt, P.Unitt, J.&B.Hargrove
C-20	Bucksnort Mt.	51	53.83	L.J.Hargrove, P.Flanagan, G.A.Rebstock	37	53.66	L.J.Hargrove, P.Flanagan, R.C.Sanger
C-21	Alder Canyon	57	48.50	G.A.Rebstock, L.J.Hargrove, P.D.Jorgensen, B.Bothner	47	54.50	L.J.Hargrove, J.Determan, R.C.Sanger, P.D.Jorgensen, B.Bothner
C-22	Collins Valley	52	60.50	P.D.Jorgensen	53	26.00	P.D.Jorgensen
C-23	Box Canyon (Coyote Cr.)	26	21.25	D.C.Seals, M.B.Mulrooney, J.R.Barth	33	31.33	J.R.Barth, K.J.Winter, C.Van Tassel, D.C.Seals
C-24	Butler Canyon	23	25.00	K.J.Winter, C.Van Tassel	26	25.50	K.J.Winter, C.Van Tassel, R.Thériault, D.C.Seals, S.Peters
C-25	Clark Valley N	20	40.80	D.C.Seals, S.Peters, H.E.Stone, J.R.Barth	23	38.67	H.E.Stone, M.B.Mulrooney, J.R.Barth, D.C.Seals, P.D.Jorgensen
C-26	Santa Rosa Mts.NW	19	25.00	H.E.Stone, J.&B.Hargrove	18	37.58	J.&B.Hargrove, H.E.Stone
C-27	Villager Peak	32	57.31	R.Thériault, P.Unitt, P.D.Jorgensen	30	50.25	P.Unitt, R.Thériault
C-28	Santa Rosa Mts.NE	24	34.00	R.Thériault	21	30.75	R.Thériault
C-29	Travertine Palms Wash	24	31.00	R.Thériault	29	25.25	R.Thériault

D-2	San Onofre Beach	64	35.50	R.Fischer, L.Ellis, P.D.Jorgensen	89	52.67	R.Fischer, J.R.Barth, P.D.Jorgensen, L.J.Hargrove, L.Ellis, P.Unitt
D-3	Horno Canyon	66	58.25	R.&S.Breisch, D.Gould, K.Perry, D.C.Seals	70	55.45	R.&S.Breisch, D.Gould, K.Perry, G.L.Rogers
D-4	Horno Summit	63	37.25	B.O'Leary, P.Unitt, P.A.Ginsburg, B.E.Bell	74	37.00	B.O'Leary, L.J.Hargrove
D-5	Upper Las Pulgas Canyon	65	48.25	R.Fischer, J.R.Barth, P.Unitt, D.C.Seals	69	38.83	D.Gould, R.&S.Breisch, G.L.Rogers
D-6	Middle Santa Margarita	78	206.75	B.E.Kus, J.M.Wells, J.Turnbull, P.P.Beck, W.E.Haas, D.C.Seals	72	25.25	B.E.Kus, P.A.Ginsburg, G.L.Rogers, P.Unitt
D-7	Fallbrook	89	51.30	K.L.Weaver	104	36.35	K.L.Weaver
D-8	Live Oak Park	77	61.75	M.Freda	86	34.75	M.Freda, E.Ashton, K.L.Weaver
D-9	Monserate Mt.	70	25.00	E.C.Hall	75	25.00	E.C.Hall
D-10	Gomez Creek	87	58.75	K.Aldern, M.Bache, E.C.Hall, J.O.Zimmer	73	29.50	K.Aldern, M.Bache
D-11	Pala	81	28.25	V.Dineen, K.L.Weaver, L.J.Hargrove	108	37.50	V.Dineen
D-12	Wilderness Gardens	84	56.95	K.L.Weaver, G.Moreland, V.Dineen	74	39.90	B.Orr, K.L.Weaver, G.Moreland, W.E.Haas
D-13	Frey Creek	31	7.83		32	16.75	R.C.Sanger
D-14	French Valley	71	116.50	P.D.Jorgensen	61	51.00	P.D.Jorgensen, K.J.Winter, J.Hargrove
D-15	Palomar Observatory	70	66.90	K.L.Weaver	60	27.50	K.L.Weaver, J.M.Wells, K.J.Winter
D-16	Rattlesnake Creek	72	64.60	J.R.Barth, K.L.Weaver, J.Fitch, K.J.Winter, G.L.Rogers, J.Hargrove, J.M.Wells	60	26.50	R.C.Sanger, K.S.Williams, M.G.Mathos, P.Unitt, J.M.Wells, K.J.Winter, J.K.Wilson
D-17	Sunshine Summit	69	29.16	J.K.Wilson, A.Mauro, P.K.Nelson, P.Unitt, M.B.Stowe	60	25.00	J.K.Wilson, H.Ingersoll, J.Fitch
D-18	Cow Canyon	55	45.00	M.B.Stowe, E.C.Hall, C.R.Mahrdt, L.J.Hargrove, J.Determan, P.Unitt	42	38.00	M.B.Stowe, A.Craft, L.J.Hargrove, P.Unitt, B.O'Leary
D-19	Indian Flats	63	42.58	K.J.Burns, L.J.Hargrove, J.R.Barth, J.Determan, K.J.Winter	49	62.33	K.J.Burns, J.M.Wells, J.R.Barth, J.Determan, J.K.Wilson, L.J.Hargrove, K.J.Winter
D-20	Lost Valley	73	52.25	J.&B.Hargrove, W.E.Haas	50	27.75	J.&B.Hargrove
D-21	Shingle Spring	61	25.00	L.J.Hargrove, W.E.Haas	50	31.50	L.J.Hargrove, J.&B.Hargrove, P.D.Jorgensen, R.C.Sanger, J.Determan
D-22	Sheep Canyon	36	27.50	P.D.Jorgensen, P.Famolaro	39	37.00	P.D.Jorgensen, E.Jorgensen, A.G.Morley
D-23	Lower Willows	61	138.25	M.L.Gabel, B.L.Peterson, R.&S.Breisch, A.G.Morley, P.D.Jorgensen	55	60.16	B.L.Peterson, M.L.Gabel, P.R.Pryde, A.G.Morley
D-24	Alcoholic Pass	35	63.70	R.&S.Breisch, E.C.Hall, J.O.Zimmer, K.L.Weaver, K.J.Winter, M.B.Mulrooney, D.C.Seals, P.Jnitt	39	25.41	M.B.Mulrooney, K.J.Winter, C.Van Tassel, M.&D.Hastings, P.R.Pryde, R.B.Riggan
D-25	Clark Valley W	25	23.80	K.J.Winter, C.Van Tassel	33	26.57	K.J.Winter, C.Van Tassel, E.Post
D-26	Clark Valley Central	21	26.92	P.K.Nelson, J.R.Barth	37	28.77	E.Post, P.K.Nelson, M.B.Mulrooney
D-27	Santa Rosa Mts. SW	25	27.25	R.Thériault, L.J.Hargrove, J.R.Barth	29	26.00	R.Thériault, L.J.Hargrove, J.R.Barth
D-28	Santa Rosa Mts. SE	27	31.25	L.J.Hargrove, R.Thériault, J.R.Barth	24	34.25	L.J.Hargrove, R.Thériault, P.D.Jorgensen, J.R.Barth
D-29	Wonderstone Wash	23	31.00	R.Thériault, P.D.Jorgensen	27	31.75	P.D.Jorgensen, R.Thériault
E-3	Agra	83	97.90	R.&S.Breisch	95	37.40	R.&S.Breisch
E-4	Lower Las Pulgas Canyon	70	57.70	P.A.Ginsburg, P.Unitt, S.Brad	69	26.50	P.A.Ginsburg, B.E.Bell, P.Unitt, L.J.Hargrove, C.Smith
E-5	Camp Pendleton Airfield	83	57.65	P.A.Ginsburg, B.E.Bell	100	27.50	P.A.Ginsburg, B.E.Bell, S.Buck
E-6	O'Neill Lake	101	201.95	P.A.Ginsburg	145	99.50	P.A.Ginsburg
E-7	Morro Hill N	86	79.75	P.A.Ginsburg	101	37.70	P.A.Ginsburg
E-8	San Luis Rey Heights	84	72.60	P.A.Ginsburg	114	47.80	P.A.Ginsburg
E-9	Pala Mesa	81	54.75	D.&C.Wysong, C.M.Manning	94	29.25	D.&C.Wysong, C.M.Manning, E.C.Hall, P.Raffelson
E-10	Couser Canyon	85	49.75	M.Bache, K.Aldern	94	26.33	M.Bache, K.Aldern
E-11	Pala Mt.	68	30.50	D.C.Seals, E.C.Hall	69	25.00	D.C.Seals, M.Bache, K.Aldern
E-12	Pauma Valley	70	25.75	A.Mauro, L.J.Hargrove, J.O.Zimmer, J.Determan, P.Unitt, E.C.Hall	78	25.33	R.T.Patton, S.M.Wolf, A.Mauro, M.Mosher, K.Fischer, J.R.Barth

(Continued)

TABLE 4   (Continued)

Square		Breeding Season			Winter		
		Species[a]	Hours	Primary observer(s)	Species[b]	Hours	Primary observer(s)
E-13	Nate Harrison Grade	79	96.50	C. Sankpill	75	51.25	C. Sankpill, E. C. Hall, P. D. Jorgensen, R. Breisch, J. M. Wells, K. J. Winter, J. O. Zimmer, P. Unitt
E-14	Boucher Hill	77	70.25	K. Messer, R. Turner, D. S. Cooper, O. Carter, E. C. Hall, J. R. Barth, G. & A. Kroon, M. Sadowski, P. Unitt	74	32.33	J. & B. Hargrove, A. Mauro, J. K. Wilson, G. L. Rogers, E. C. Hall, P. Unitt
E-15	Mendenhall Valley	78	66.08	E. C. Hall, C. R. Mahrdt	68	25.00	E. C. Hall, C. R. Mahrdt, D. C. Seals, K. J. Winter
E-16	Barker Valley	61	89.75	D. Rawlins, R. Bergstrom, J. M. Wells, J. Turnbull, P. Unitt	55	50.75	J. O. Zimmer, E. C. Hall, R. B. Riggan, R. Bergstrom, J. M. Wells, K. J. Winter
E-17	Aguanga Ridge	73	45.75	J. O. Zimmer, E. C. Hall, C. R. Mahrdt, J. D. Barr, J. R. Barth, J. M. Wells, K. J. Winter, G. L. Rogers	54	34.75	J. D. Barr, J. M. Wells, A. Mauro, J. R. Barth, E. Wallace, E. C. Hall, J. O. Zimmer
E-18	Puerta La Cruz	67	27.75	P. K. Nelson, A. & T. Keenan, P. Unitt, L. J. Hargrove	69	32.75	A. & T. Keenan, P. K. Nelson, R. & S. Breisch, N. Fraser, M. B. Stowe, E. Wallace, J. M. Wells
E-19	Ward Canyon	59	59.30	O. Carter, W. Pray	60	61.35	W. Pray
E-20	Hot Springs Mt. W	58	55.60	K. L. Weaver, C. R. Mahrdt	43	26.50	K. L. Weaver, C. R. Mahrdt
E-21	Hot Springs Mt. E	70	34.65	K. L. Weaver, C. R. Mahrdt	63	44.35	K. L. Weaver, C. R. Mahrdt, P. D. Jorgensen
E-22	Palm Mesa	55	29.16	J. R. Barth, D. C. Seals, M. B. Mulrooney, P. Unitt	48	31.82	P. D. Jorgensen, M. B. Mulrooney, J. R. Barth
E-23	Henderson Canyon	31	40.25	R. Thériault, L. J. Hargrove	28	48.50	R. Thériault, M. B. Mulrooney, M. G. Mathos, J. R. Barth, P. D. Jorgensen, P. Unitt, C. Border
E-24	Borrego Valley N	45	41.50	P. Ache, J. Fitch, P. D. Jorgensen, P. K. Nelson, L. & M. Polinsky, R. & S. Breisch	76	34.16	J. Fitch
E-25	Coyote Mt.	29	24.30	P. Ache, K. L. Weaver, P. K. Nelson	49	26.12	P. Ache, P. K. Nelson, P. D. Jorgensen
E-26	Clark Valley SW	17	37.10	J. Fitch, D. C. Seals, M. B. Mulrooney, K. L. Weaver	29	30.27	E. Post
E-27	Clark Valley SE	24	35.75	R. Thériault, P. D. Jorgensen, D. C. Seals, J. R. Barth	39	25.53	R. Thériault, A. & K. Mauro, J. R. Barth
E-28	Palo Verde Canyon	22	29.00	P. D. Jorgensen	22	28.00	P. D. Jorgensen, H. E. Stone
E-29	Big Wash	16	25.50	J. R. Barth, H. E. Stone, P. D. Jorgensen	17	31.05	J. R. Barth, H. E. Stone, P. D. Jorgensen
F-4	Aliso Creek Mouth	78	54.25	B. C. Moore, K. Estey, B. Anderson, J. Roberts, D. Green, A. E. Klovstad, C. L. Mann	101	30.50	B. C. Moore, B. Anderson, K. Estey, D. Green, J. Roberts, A. E. Klovstad, C. L. Mann
F-5	Ysidora Basin	89	123.00	R. Fischer, J. Morlan	98	29.50	P. A. Ginsburg, R. Fischer, E. Garnica, B. C. Moore
F-6	Pilgrim Creek	77	23.75	B. E. Bell	88	35.25	B. E. Bell
F-7	Morro Hill S	80	74.20	A. Peterson, P. A. Ginsburg	96	41.00	A. Peterson
F-8	Bonsall	85	79.80	P. A. Ginsburg, L. Gammie	121	64.20	P. A. Ginsburg, L. Gammie
F-9	Moosa Canyon	71	29.25	J. Evans, E. C. Hall	122	57.50	J. Evans, E. C. Hall
F-10	Lilac	65	26.00	P. Unitt, M. McIntosh, L. J. Hargrove, J. K. Wilson	76	42.00	J. & B. Hargrove, P. K. Nelson, J. Ciarletta, B. O'Leary, S. Berg, P. Unitt
F-11	Keys Creek	65	25.00	J. O. Zimmer, P. Unitt	70	34.00	J. O. Zimmer, P. K. Nelson, B. & M. McIntosh, P. Unitt
F-12	Cool Valley	72	49.42	E. C. Hall, Jamie Simmons, J. R. Barth, O. Carter	83	25.00	E. C. Hall, A. Mauro, P. Unitt, S. M. Wolf, R. T. Patton, J. & B. Hargrove
F-13	Rincon	74	58.50	S. Berg, M. Mosher, E. Wallace, B. & M. McIntosh, J. Determan, J. R. Barth	71	32.00	S. Berg, M. Mosher, J. R. Barth, G. L. Rogers
F-14	Rancho Cuca	74	45.50	S. & J. Berg	67	29.00	S. & J. Berg
F-15	La Jolla Amago	66	109.50	M. Dougan, S. Berg, D. C. Seals	71	31.91	S. Berg, I. S. Quon, W. E. Haas, J. R. Barth, D. C. Seals
F-16	Dyche Valley	74	32.33	L. J. Hargrove	79	42.58	L. J. Hargrove
F-17	West Fork San Luis Rey	68	25.75	S. E. Smith, K. J. Winter, G. A. Rebstock, J. R. Barth, L. J. Hargrove	76	38.25	P. Unitt, J. R. Barth, T. Myers, K. J. Winter, C. G. Edwards, G. L. Rogers, R. L. Barber

F-18	Swan Lake	64	27.25	C.G. Edwards, G.A. Rebstock, M.G. Mathos, P.Unitt, P.K.Nelson	82	47.50	G.L. Rogers, D.K. Adams, J.R. Barth, M.G. Vlathos
F-19	Warner Springs	77	30.25	C.G. Edwards, P.R. Pryde, D.G. Seay, A. Mauro, P.K. Nelson	103	115.00	C.G. Edwards, M.W. Klein
F-20	Eagles' Nest	80	52.20	B.&M. McIntosh, K.Thomson, S.D. Cameron, D.C. Seals, P.Unitt, K.J. Winter, P.R. Pryde	66	42.21	M. Bache, J.&B. Hargrove, B. O'Leary, P.Unitt, J.R. Barth, K.Thomson, F. Sproul, K.L. Weaver
F-21	Los Coyotes	69	123.50	J.&B. Hargrove, M.& M. Smith	54	41.50	J.& B. Hargrove
F-22	San Ysidro Mt.	54	51.33	J.R. Barth, D.C. Seals, M.B. Mulrooney	49	52.25	J.R. Barth, D.C. Seals, M.B. Mulrooney, P.D. Jorgensen
F-23	Borrego Palm Canyon	52	127.50	L.J. Hargrove, A.G. Morley, P.D. Jorgensen, P. Famolaro	60	75.16	H.L. Young, Alice DeBolt, P.D. Jorgensen
F-24	Borrego Springs N	42	27.25	M.L. Gabel	109	149.83	M.L. Gabel
F-25	Borrego Airport	40	89.00	P. Ache	61	59.50	P. Ache
F-26	Peg Leg E	18	39.65	B. Siegel, P. Ache, S.M. Wolf, D.C. Seals, M.B. Stowe	31	25.25	B. Siegel, R. Payne, P.D. Jorgensen, P. Unitt
F-27	Font's Point	21	71.20	G.A. Rebstock, K. Forney	22	38.95	G.A. Rebstock, K. Forney
F-28	Ella Wash	19	25.00	D.C. Seals, L.J. Hargrove, K.L. Weaver	23	25.41	J.R. Barth, S.M. Wolf, P.Unitt, P.D. Jorgensen
F-29	Microwave Relay Sta.	20	32.00	C. Hagen	25	34.75	C. Hagen, J.R. Barth, P.D. Jorgensen, G.A. Rebstock
G-4	Santa Margarita Estuary	76	56.50	P.A. Ginsburg, B.L. Peterson, B. Foster	143	46.25	P.A. Ginsburg, B.L. Peterson
G-5	Wire Mt.	82	51.50	R. Fischer, J. Morlan	111	31.75	R. Fischer
G-6	San Luis Rey	86	84.00	M.R. Smith	137	80.75	M.R. Smith, D. Rorick
G-7	Guajome	86	131.40	D. Wysong, S. Grain	133	93.83	D. Wysong, S. Grain
G-8	Vista NE	71	69.00	M. Lesinsky, C.G. Edwards, E.C. Hall, J.O. Zimmer, L.J. Hargrove, O. Carter, J. Ciarletta	101	59.00	M. Lesinsky
G-9	Merriam Mts.	64	46.50	J.F. Clements, L. Holt, O. Carter, C.M. Manning, J. Ciarletta	71	36.50	M. Baumgartel, B.& M. McIntosh, C.M. Manning, L. Holt, J.F. Clements
G-10	Oat Hills	68	25.00	E.C. Hall, J.O. Zimmer	72	25.00	E.C. Hall, J.O. Zimmer, G.L. Rogers
G-11	Valley Center W	75	61.75	S.& S. Farrow, L. Seneca, V. Dineen	92	65.50	S.& S. Farrow
G-12	Valley Center E	64	26.67	J.R. Barth, P. Unitt, A.& D. Stanton	68	26.00	A. Mauro, T. Stands, S. Yamagata, P.K. Nelson, P. Unitt
G-13	Lower Hellhole	67	46.75	G. Moreland, A.& T. Keenan, R. Breisch, L.J. Hargrove, P. Unitt, E.C. Hall	71	33.73	G. Moreland, B. Orr
G-14	Rodriguez Mt.	44	10.50	P. Unitt, P.K. Nelson	47	18.25	P. Unitt, J. Ciarletta, J.K. Wilson, W. Pray
G-15	Pine Mt.	56	35.50	K.J. Winter, J.M. Wells	54	29.00	K.J. Winter, J. Ciarletta
G-16	San Luis Rey Picnic Area	75	65.75	W.E. Haas	93	27.50	W.E. Haas, J. Ciarletta, L.J. Hargrove, R.L. Barber, M.B. Stowe
G-17	Lake Henshaw	81	33.08	R.& S. Breisch, P. Unitt, C.G. Edwards	124	70.23	C.G. Edwards
G-18	Matagual Creek	69	31.73	P.K. Nelson, M.U. Evans, T. Stands, S. Yamagata, G.L. Rogers, C.G. Edwards	68	34.25	C.G. Edwards, B.& M. McIntosh, P. Unitt
G-19	Warner Ranch	65	26.60	J.D. Barr, J.R. Barth, E.C. Hall, A. Mauro, M.U. Evans, P. Unitt	66	37.00	R.& S. Breisch, M.B. Stowe, P. Unitt, I.S. Quon, R.T. Patton, J.K. Wilson
G-20	Upper Warner Valley	61	57.55	A.& T. Keenan, P. Unitt, M.G. Mathos, L.J. Hargrove, J.R. Barth	62	75.00	A.& T. Keenan, T.W. Dorman, M.L. Gabel, J.K. Wilson, M.B. Stowe
G-21	Ranchita	68	36.46	J.R. Barth, D.C. Seals, L.J. Hargrove, E.C. Hall, B.E. Bell	74	26.50	R. Thériault, A.& T. Keenan, P. Unitt, T.W. Dorman, M.L. Gabel, B.E. Bell
G-22	Chimney Rock	58	68.65	P.D. Jorgensen, J.R. Barth, G.L. Rogers	51	39.17	P.D. Jorgensen, M.L. Gabel, J.R. Barth, G.L. Rogers
G-23	Hellhole Canyon	48	43.50	M.L. Gabel	63	46.92	M.L. Gabel
G-24	Borrego Springs S	42	54.00	P. Ache	110	117.21	P. Ache
G-25	Borrego Sink	36	56.25	R. Thériault	63	81.00	R. Thériault
G-26	Borrego Sink Wash	28	26.50	J. Fitch, P.D. Jorgensen, M.B. Mulrooney, D.C. Seals	31	25.20	J. Fitch, J.K. Wilson, M.B. Mulrooney

(Continued)

TABLE 4 (Continued)

Square	Breeding Season			Winter		
	Species[a]	Hours	Primary observer(s)	Species[b]	Hours	Primary observer(s)
G-27 Hills of the Moon Wash	20	36.80	J.R.Barth, G.L.Rogers, G.A.Rebstock, D.C.Seals	23	27.00	D.C.Seals, J.R.Barth, P.K.Nelson, J.K.Wilson, P.D.Jorgensen, P.Unitt
G-28 Fault Wash	17	30.00	D.C.Seals, M.B.Mulrooney, P.Unitt	18	26.25	J.R.Barth, M.B.Mulrooney, P.Unitt, P.D.Jorgensen, G.A.Rebstock
G-29 Five Palms Spring	20	46.75	G.A.Rebstock, K.Forney	23	31.50	G.A.Rebstock, K.Forney
H-5 Oceanside	78	108.00	J.Determan	136	80.13	J.Determan, J.Ginger
H-6 Buena Vista Lagoon E	83	68.50	L.E.Taylor, J.Ginger	122	98.00	L.E.Taylor
H-7 Vista SW	67	32.50	L.Holt, E.C.Hall, J.O.Zimmer, P.Unitt, D.Huckabay, J.Ciarletta	85	37.50	D.Huckabay, M.Fugagli
H-8 Vista SE	58	32.35	J.O.Zimmer	82	32.25	J.O.Zimmer
H-9 Twin Oaks	72	30.30	J.O.Zimmer, L.J.Hargrove	78	32.25	A.Craft
H-10 Jesmond Dene	60	28.75	D.&D.Bylin	73	26.00	D.&D.Bylin
H-11 Burnt Mt.	69	39.75	D.&D.Bylin	79	28.00	A.Mauro, M.B.Stowe, B.E.Bell, L.Hunter, B.C.Moore
H-12 Lake Wohlford	74	29.25	P.Hernandez, S.Christiansen, E.C.Hall, D.C.Seals, W.E.Haas	105	52.10	P.Hernandez, S.Christiansen
H-13 Bear Valley	68	35.25	O.Carter, P.Unitt, E.C.Hall, B.&M.McIntosh	82	41.83	W.Pray, C.Rideout, L.&R.Johnson, N.Osborn, L.Hunter, R.Forster, W.Hunter
H-14 Rancho Guejito	52	9.00	K.L.Weaver, P.Unitt	51	14.33	A.Mauro, P.Unitt, J.R.Barth, W.Pray
H-15 Pamo Valley N	58	28.00	O.Carter, W.Pray	61	33.42	O.Carter
H-16 Gem Hill	79	25.65	E.C.Hall, J.O.Zimmer	78	28.33	E.C.Hall, J.O.Zimmer, J.McColm
H-17 Mesa Grande	75	25.37	M.McIntosh, P.Unitt, C.M.&J.Manning	85	36.94	K.L.Weaver, B.&M.McIntosh, L.J.Hargrove, E.C.Hall
H-18 Moretti's Junction	68	27.90	C.G.Edwards, J.R.Barth, P.Unitt	62	42.00	P.Unitt, B.&M.McIntosh, J.K.Wilson, W.E.Haas
H-19 Matagual Valley	64	32.50	D.C.Seals, B.E.Bell, M.Baumgartel, A.Mauro, P.Unitt, S.E.Smith	65	41.67	R.B.Riggan, R.T.Patton
H-20 San Felipe	81	56.00	A.&T.Keenan	79	61.50	A.&T.Keenan
H-21 Lithia Springs	52	39.16	B.E.Bell, P.Unitt, J.O.Zimmer, E.C.Hall, G.A.Rebstock, M.McIntosh	61	27.75	B.E.Bell, P.Unitt, R.Thériault, W.E.Haas
H-22 Camel Rock	50	57.75	P.D.Jorgensen, J.R.Barth, P.Unitt	46	25.00	P.D.Jorgensen, J.R.Barth, P.Unitt
H-23 Pinyon Ridge	42	29.00	M.L.Gabel	51	34.92	M.L.Gabel
H-24 Yaqui Meadows	24	25.00	P.K.Nelson	32	25.75	P.K.Nelson
H-25 Casa del Zorro	39	43.00	H.L.Young, M.Mosher	91	64.75	H.L.Young, M.Mosher
H-26 Sleepy Hollow	30	27.00	M.L.Gabel	41	26.50	M.L.Gabel, H.E.Stone
H-27 Borrego Mt. West Butte	24	27.00	M.L.Gabel	27	29.25	M.L.Gabel, H.E.Stone
H-28 Borrego Mt. East Butte	19	25.55	J.R.Barth, P.D.Jorgensen, G.A.Rebstock	19	27.25	J.R.Barth, P.D.Jorgensen
H-29 Squaw Peak	15	29.24	J.R.Barth, P.Unitt	18	26.48	J.R.Barth, J.Determan, P.Unitt
I-6 Agua Hedionda	76	50.10	W.E.Haas, P.A.Ginsburg, J.Ciarletta	142	53.76	P.A.Ginsburg, J.Ciarletta
I-7 Palomar Airport	70	73.00	E.Garnica, D.Geiger, G.G.Edwards, M.Baumgartel	91	71.00	E.Garnica, D.Geiger
I-8 Green Oak Ranch	70	114.75	C.H.Schork, I.Graham, S.Grain, N.Taylor, B.&M.McIntosh	96	30.25	C.H.Schork, I.Graham, S.Grain
I-9 San Marcos	64	80.25	P.Zucker, G.L.Rogers, J.Ciarletta, K.L.Weaver	95	44.50	P.Zucker
I-10 Escondido NW	69	25.00	E.C.Hall	69	25.00	E.C.Hall
I-11 Escondido NE	65	31.50	O.Carter, R.Hummel, D.C.Seals, P.Unitt	90	48.75	L.Hunter, C.Rideout, M.Baumgartel, O.Carter, B.C.Moore, J.Russell, E.C.Hall

Cell	Location						
I-12	Bottle Peak	75	38.95	C. Rideout, J.O. Zimmer	97	46.82	C. Rideout
I-13	Rockwood Canyon	66	25.58	O. Carter, C.R. Mahrdt, E.C. Hall	65	27.00	O. Carter, C.R. Mahrdt, P. Unitt, L. & R. Johnson
I-14	Boden Canyon	59	54.25	R.L. Barber, C.R. Mahrdt	59	55.70	R.L. Barber, C.R. Mahrdt
I-15	Pamo Valley S	70	38.25	O. Carter	102	77.41	O. Carter
I-16	Black Canyon	60	38.50	K.J. Winter, S. McKelvey	53	53.80	K.J. Winter, O. Carter, M. Baumgartel, J. DeCanio, T.A. Burr, P. Unitt, R.C. Sanger, M.B. Stowe
I-17	Bloomdale Creek	70	31.15	D.C. Seals	64	25.83	D.C. Seals, L. & R. Johnson, A. & T. Keenan, K.L. Weaver
I-18	Santa Ysabel Mission	76	32.10	S.E. Smith, D.W. Au	74	31.25	E.J. McNeil, L. & R. Johnson, M.B. Stowe, C. Rideout, J. Coatsworth, S.E. Smith
I-19	Upper Santa Ysabel Creek	65	62.95	S.E. Smith, D.W. Au	48	28.50	D.W. Au, P.R. Pryde
I-20	Volcan Mt.	76	56.75	A. & T. Keenan	81	82.00	W.E. Haas, A. & T. Keenan, R.T. Patton
I-21	San Felipe Valley N	72	42.30	J.O. Zimmer, W.E. Haas	88	50.00	J.O. Zimmer
I-22	Grapevine Canyon	38	36.50	P.K. Nelson	40	26.25	P.K. Nelson, A. & T. Keenan
I-23	Yaqui Flat	45	47.00	P.K. Nelson	39	25.50	P.K. Nelson
I-24	Tamarisk Grove	40	124.75	P.K. Nelson	59	45.50	P.K. Nelson
I-25	San Felipe Narrows	23	26.50	P.K. Nelson	30	33.50	P.K. Nelson, P. Ache, A. Mauro
I-26	Sunset Wash	24	31.50	L.J. Hargrove	29	30.25	L.J. Hargrove
I-27	Cactus Garden	16	25.00	P.K. Nelson, D.C. Seals	27	25.58	P.K. Nelson, A. & K. Mauro, J.R. Barth, P. Unitt
I-28	Ocotillo Wells	26	26.16	J.R. Barth, L.J. Hargrove, B. Miller, P. Unitt	37	25.09	J.R. Barth, P. Unitt, P.K. Nelson, J.K. Wilson
I-29	Ocotillo Badlands	27	26.24	P. Unitt, J.R. Barth, B. Miller	32	25.09	J.R. Barth, P. Unitt
J-6	Batiquitos Lagoon	65	109.00	M. Baumgartel	118	90.00	M. Baumgartel
J-7	La Costa	85	351.50	M. Baumgartel, C.C. Gorman	145	133.00	M. Baumgartel, C.C. Gorman
J-8	Questhaven	82	53.50	J.O. Zimmer	134	78.95	J.O. Zimmer
J-9	Harmony Grove	85	56.40	J.O. Zimmer	97	46.20	J.O. Zimmer
J-10	Escondido SW	67	61.75	O. Carter	104	50.25	O. Carter
J-11	Escondido SE	68	52.00	W. Pray	108	66.83	W. Pray
J-12	Wild Animal Park	91	48.45	D. & D. Bylin	154	134.75	D. & D. Bylin
J-13	San Pasqual	71	38.75	D. & D. Bylin, B. & M. McIntosh	89	43.18	D. & D. Bylin, M. Fugagli
J-14	Tim's Canyon	72	50.25	C.R. Mahrdt, R.L. Barber	82	45.85	C.R. Mahrdt, R.L. Barber
J-15	Valle de los Amigos	71	62.58	L.E. Taylor	99	76.00	L.E. Taylor
J-16	Sutherland Lake W	78	46.87	B. Travis, G. Warneke, J.R. Barth	87	28.00	K. Thomson, J.C. Lovio, J.M. Wells, J. Cia-letta
J-17	Sutherland Lake E	70	26.50	J.O. Zimmer, E.C. Hall, B. Travis, G. Warneke	77	29.00	J.O. Zimmer, E.C. Hall
J-18	Santa Ysabel	73	32.90	S.E. Smith	82	40.25	S.E. Smith
J-19	Wynola	95	76.10	S.E. Smith, D.W. Au	84	60.05	S.E. Smith, D.W. Au
J-20	Julian N	84	67.30	M.B. Stowe, E.C. Hall, J.O. Zimmer, A. & T. Keenan, J.R. Barth, O. Carter	92	55.10	M.B. Stowe
J-21	San Felipe Valley S	48	29.75	P.K. Nelson	63	28.25	P.K. Nelson
J-22	Scissors Crossing	85	73.83	E.C. Hall	65	28.00	E.C. Hall
J-23	Sentenac Canyon	67	67.00	R. Thériault	61	25.50	R. Thériault
J-24	Chuckwalla Wash	32	35.20	L. & M. Polinsky, S.D. Cameron, J.R. Barth, G.L. Rogers	30	44.99	J.R. Barth, J.K. Wilson, S.D. Cameron, A. & T. Keenan
J-25	Mescal Bajada	26	41.00	B. & M. McIntosh	27	40.20	B. & M. McIntosh
J-26	Sunset Mt.	27	33.75	A.G. Morley, M.B. Mulrooney	27	32.17	P.D. Jorgensen, M.B. Mulrooney, J.R. Barth, J. Determan, M.D. Hoefer
J-27	Vallecito Mts. NE	21	27.50	A.G. Morley, J.R. Barth, D.C. Seals, P. Unitt	22	25.74	J.R. Barth, D.C. Seals, P. Unitt
J-28	Bendire's Thrasher	26	27.75	J.R. Barth, G.L. Rogers	30	25.67	J.R. Barth, P. Unitt
J-29	Halfhill Dry Lake	30	29.50	L.J. Hargrove	36	27.17	L.J. Hargrove

(Continued)

TABLE 4 (Continued)

		Breeding Season			Winter		
Square		Species[a]	Hours	Primary observer(s)	Species[b]	Hours	Primary observer(s)
K-6	Moonlight Beach	40	30.75	J. Ciarletta, C. C. Gorman, P. Unitt	77	39.50	J. Ciarletta, E. Garnica
K-7	Encinitas	64	65.75	C. C. Gorman, R. & A. Campbell, J. Ciarletta	70	51.75	C. C. Gorman, R. & A. Campbell
K-8	Olivenhain	64	60.25	J. Determan	100	49.57	J. Determan
K-9	Elfin Forest	68	75.75	L. E. Taylor	79	45.75	L. E. Taylor
K-10	Lake Hodges	84	194.91	R. L. Barber	145	154.00	R. L. Barber
K-11	Kit Carson Park	104	100.75	E. C. Hall	164	135.32	E. C. Hall, R. L. Barber
K-12	Highland Valley	80	44.75	E. C. Hall	100	57.50	E. C. Hall
K-13	Bandy Canyon	91	32.50	P. M. von Hendy, M. McIntosh	98	34.50	P. M. von Hendy
K-14	Ramona NW	65	46.75	G. & A. Kroon, G. L. Rogers, B. & M. McIntosh	79	30.99	K. Smeltzer, G. & A. Kroon, J. L. Lincer
K-15	Ramona NE	77	29.50	B. & M. McIntosh	109	51.78	B. & M. McIntosh
K-16	Hatfield Creek	70	32.75	G. & A. Kroon	76	34.45	G. & A. Kroon, G. L. Rogers, R. & S. Breisch, J. Ciarletta
K-17	Ballena Valley	70	50.25	O. Carter, J. DeCanio, D. C. Seals	81	28.00	O. Carter, J. DeCanio, D. C. Seals
K-18	Dye Mt.	57	41.33	R. C. Sanger, L. J. Hargrove, J. R. Barth, K. J. Winter	54	25.50	R. C. Sanger, K. S. Williams, J. M. Wells, K. J. Winter
K-19	Pine Hills	74	35.95	S. E. Smith, J. R. Barth, L. J. Hargrove, R. Breisch, M. B. Stowe	71	31.00	M. B. Stowe, S. E. Smith, A. & T. Keenan, R. Warren, J. Ciarletta, V. Moran
K-20	Julian S	73	40.95	E. C. Hall	81	26.50	E. C. Hall
K-21	Banner	72	35.25	P. K. Nelson	77	22.25	P. K. Nelson, J. K. Wilson, P. D. Jorgensen
K-22	Granite Mt.	47	45.00	A. & T. Keenan, L. J. Hargrove, J. R. Barth, D. C. Seals	49	26.00	A. & T. Keenan, M. B. Mulrooney
K-23	Earthquake Valley W	43	105.75	G. Sanders, P. K. Nelson, L. & M. Polinsky	53	30.00	G. Sanders, A. & T. Keenan, J. R. Barth
K-24	Earthquake Valley E	34	40.00	B. Graffius, D. C. Seals, M. B. Mulrooney, L. J. Hargrove	28	40.25	B. Graffius, S. M. Wolf, N. Fraser, M. B. Mulrooney, P. Unitt
K-25	Pinyon Mts.	32	38.00	R. Thériault, D. C. Seals, J. R. Barth, M. B. Mulrooney	31	25.50	R. Thériault, M. B. Mulrooney, J. R. Barth
K-26	Pinyon Canyon	27	44.00	M. D. Hoefer, E. Jorgensen, M. B. Mulrooney, D. C. Seals	28	25.67	M. D. Hoefer, M. B. Mulrooney, P. Unitt, J. R. Barth
K-27	Harper Flat	23	24.88	J. R. Barth, P. D. Jorgensen, D. C. Seals	20	26.58	J. R. Barth, D. C. Seals, M. D. Hoefer
K-28	Starfish Cove	29	38.00	L. J. Hargrove, A. & T. Keenan	27	35.00	L. J. Hargrove, M. Bache, G. A. Rebstock, R. C. Sanger, J. O. Zimmer, M. D. Hoefer, D. C. Seals, K. S. Williams, J. Determan, P. Unitt
K-29	Elephant Tree	24	41.00	M. D. Hoefer, L. J. Hargrove, A. & T. Keenan	31	61.50	M. D. Hoefer, L. J. Hargrove
L-7	San Elijo Lagoon	80	127.33	A. Mauro	151	123.50	A. Mauro
L-8	Rancho Santa Fe	68	37.00	A. Mauro	101	48.75	A. Mauro
L-9	Lusardi Creek	71	37.00	A. Mauro	108	50.00	R. T. Patton, A. Mauro
L-10	La Jolla Valley	72	28.00	K. J. Winter, C. Van Tassel	71	36.00	K. J. Winter, R. Warren
L-11	Rancho Bernardo	55	59.00	E. J. McNeil	79	41.25	E. J. McNeil
L-12	Blue Sky Ranch	73	48.00	B. & M. McIntosh	101	38.80	B. & M. McIntosh
L-13	Mt. Woodson	68	55.25	P. M. von Hendy, C. G. Edwards, K. J. Winter	96	65.00	P. M. von Hendy
L-14	Ramona SW	67	64.25	G. Moreland, F. Sproul, G. L. Rogers, E. C. Hall	88	58.63	F. Sproul, B. Orr, G. Moreland
L-15	Ramona SE	70	46.50	A. Mauro	86	27.00	A. Mauro, P. Unitt
L-16	San Vicente Valley	74	54.40	J. D. Barr, M. & S. Cassidy	79	25.75	J. D. Barr, M. & S. Cassidy, B. & M. McIntosh, R. & S. Breisch
L-17	Mt. Gower	82	99.33	R. C. Sanger, K. S. Williams	83	35.25	R. C. Sanger, K. S. Williams
L-18	Mildred Falls	65	27.75	W. Pray, O. Carter, K. J. Winter, L. J. Hargrove, R. C. Sanger	59	33.50	W. Pray, O. Carter, J. K. Wilson
L-19	Inaja/Cosmit	75	36.50	O. Carter, W. Pray	62	28.50	O. Carter, W. Pray
L-20	North Peak	72	70.75	A. Young, A. Mauro, R. Breisch, K. Satterfield, D. C. Seals, J. R. Barth, V. Moran	72	56.50	A. Young, R. Breisch, V. Moran
L-21	Chariot Canyon	74	88.85	J. K. Wilson	76	47.50	J. K. Wilson

Code	Location						
L-22	Oriflamme Canyon	50	52.00	R.Thériault, J.R.Barth, M.B.Mulrooney, P.Unitt	51	26.50	R.Thériault, P.D.Jorgensen, J.R.Barth
L-23	Box Canyon (Hwy. S2)	35	67.35	D.Lantz, B.Siegel, P.K.Nelson	35	36.32	D.Lantz, S.D.Cameron, B.Siegel, J.R.Barth
L-24	Blair Valley	30	31.75	R.Thériault	46	29.50	R.Thériault
L-25	Whale Peak	32	42.50	R.Thériault	33	26.00	R.Thériault
L-26	Hapaha Flat	28	35.25	J.R.Barth, D.C.Seals	30	29.66	J.R.Barth, W.T.Everett
L-27	Mud Palisades	21	27.75	D.C.Seals, M.B.Mulrooney	26	26.83	J.R.Barth, D.C.Seals, M.B.Mulrooney
L-28	Mollusk Wash	20	32.25	D.C.Seals, L.J.Hargrove, M.B.Mulrooney	17	35.42	D.C.Seals, J.R.Barth, B.Bothner, M.B.Mulrooney
L-29	Split Mt.	20	30.67	M.D.Hoefer, G.A.Rebstock, K.Forney, J.R.Barth	19	29.33	D.C.Seals, J.R.Barth, P.D.Jorgensen
M-7	Del Mar	71	88.00	D.R.Grine	138	114.75	D.R.Grine
M-8	San Dieguito Valley	64	43.58	P.Unitt, L.& R.Johnson, B.& M.McIntosh	122	45.75	R.T.Patton
M-9	McGonigle Canyon	56	29.00	K.J.Winter, C.Van Tassel, F.Hall	67	32.50	K.J.Winter
M-10	Rancho Peñasquitos	68	40.50	K.J.Winter, C.Van Tassel	76	37.75	K.J.Winter
M-11	Poway W	77	40.00	K.J.Winter	72	33.00	K.J.Winter
M-12	Poway E	64	48.25	P.M. von Hendy, B.& M.McIntosh	67	27.00	P.M. von Hendy, B.& M.McIntosh, K.J.Winter
M-13	Iron Mt.	68	2.00	R.Payne, K.J.Winter, C.Van Tassel	66	25.33	K.J.Winter, B.& M.McIntosh
M-14	Fernbrook	62	69.00	B.Hendricks, D.C.Seals, J.Savary	81	36.75	W.E.Haas, B.Hendricks, D.C.Seals, M.McIntosh, P.Unitt
M-15	Cañada de San Vicente	83	93.82	J.R.Barth, J.Smith, J.K.Wilson, P.K.Nelson, C.H.Reiser	76	28.92	P.Lambert, J.Smith, W.E.Haas
M-16	San Vicente Mt.	68	82.92	J.D.Barr, R.C.Sanger, J.R.Barth, E.C.Hall, M.Farley, M.B.Mulrooney	62	31.00	J.D.Barr, M.B.Mulrooney, G.L.Rogers, J.M.Wells
N-17	Isham Creek	78	91.58	R.C.Sanger, K.S.Williams	75	37.50	R.C.Sanger, K.S.Williams, D.C.Seals
N-18	Devil's Punchbowl	62	107.75	R.C.Sanger, Kathy Williams	52	30.00	R.C.Sanger, K.J.Winter, L.J.Hargrove, P.Unitt
N-19	Sill Hill	64	30.00	K.J.Winter, S.McKelvey, C.Jones	56	25.00	K.J.Winter, J.R.Barth
N-20	Cuyamaca Peak	97	195.85	A.& T.Keenan, R.E.Webster, G.L.Rogers	107	51.25	A.& T.Keenan
N-21	Upper Green Valley	69	72.50	P.D.Jorgensen	66	28.00	P.D.Jorgensen
N-22	Oriflamme Mt.	49	48.90	P.D.Jorgensen, J.R.Barth, D.C.Seals. D.& C.Batzler	47	32.75	P.D.Jorgensen, J.R.Barth, G.L.Rogers
N-23	Butterfield Ranch	53	59.03	H.Williams, R.Thériault, P.K.Nelson, R.Or. B.O'Leary	65	34.00	H.Williams, P.K.Nelson
N-24	Vallecito Valley	50	48.60	P.K.Nelson, B.Siegel, J.Aguirre, J.R.Barth, R.Thériault, P.D.Jorgensen	52	28.58	P.K.Nelson, B.Siegel, J.Aguirre, P.Unitt
M-25	Vallecito Stage Station	50	36.30	M.C.Jorgensen, P.D.Jorgensen, R.Thériault	62	30.08	M.C.Jorgensen, P.D.Jorgensen, A.E.Klovstad, C.L.Mann, R.Thériault
M-26	Agua Caliente	39	43.95	E.C.Hall	58	34.25	E.C.Hall
M-27	June Wash	20	26.25	R.Thériault	24	25.83	R.Thériault
M-28	Fish Creek Wash W	17	33.08	D.C.Seals, J.R.Barth, M.B.Mulrooney, P.Unitt	16	25.82	J.R.Barth, M.B.Mulrooney
M-29	Fish Creek Wash E	18	28.50	J.R.Barth, D.C.Seals	19	26.92	J.R.Barth, P.Unitt, P.D.Jorgensen
N-7	Los Peñasquitos Lagoon	86	160.75	D.K.Adams	169	190.58	D.K.Adams, K.Estey, B.C.Moore
N-8	Carmel Mt.	77	158.00	D.K.Adams	101	172.00	D.K.Adams, L.& R.Johnson
N-9	Los Peñasquitos Canyon	65	45.00	A.& D.Stanton	82	52.25	A.& D.Stanton
N-10	Miramar Reservoir	79	79.50	K.J.Winter, C.Van Tassel, G.& A.Kroon	105	83.25	K.J.Winter, G.& A.Kroon
N-11	Beeler Canyon	69	35.01	K.J.Winter, C.Van Tassel	87	38.75	K.J.Winter, Brock Ortega
N-12	Goodan Ranch	72	29.26	W.E.Haas, B.& M.McIntosh	61	27.40	B.& M.McIntosh, W.E.Haas
N-13	Slaughterhouse Canyon	69	107.00	R.& S.Breisch, C.G.Edwards, K.J.Winter	94	103.30	R.& S.Breisch, N.Osborn
N-14	San Vicente Reservoir	75	26.25	N.Lamken, P.R.Pryde	93	42.75	N.Osborn, R.& S.Breisch, P.Lambert
N-15	Barona	76	63.50	R.C.Sanger, P.Unitt, D.C.Seals	91	34.25	N.Lamken, R.C.Sanger, J.Smith
N-16	El Cajon Mt.	64	41.58	J.R.Barth, D.C.Seals	80	41.66	J.R.Barth, D.C.Seals, J.M.Wells, K.J.Winter
N-17	Sand Creek	65	33.83	D.C.Seals, J.R.Barth	60	29.83	J.R.Barth, D.C.Seals, P.Unitt
N-18	Tule Springs	54	36.33	J.R.Barth, E.C.Hall, A.& T.Keenan, P.Unitt, J.O.Zimmer	30	5.50	J.R.Barth
N-19	Sheriton Valley	68	40.17	G.& R.Wynn, P.D.Jorgensen, J.R.Barth	67	27.58	G.& R.Wynn

(Continued)

TABLE 4 (Continued)

Square		Breeding Season			Winter	
	Species[a]	Hours	Primary observer(s)	Species[b]	Hours	Primary observer(s)
N-20	Cuyamaca West Mesa	75	139.75	B. Siegel, D. Jadlowski	57	80.25	B. Siegel, D. Jadlowski
N-21	Cuyamaca East Mesa	65	36.50	J. Fitch, P. D. Jorgensen	65	27.00	J. Fitch, P. D. Jorgensen
N-22	Filaree Flat	70	118.50	G. L. Rogers, D. C. Seals	56	66.67	G. L. Rogers
N-23	Garnet Peak	57	34.00	B. Graffius, K. J. Winter, D. C. Seals	43	36.50	K. J. Winter, B. Graffius, J. M. Wells
N-24	The Potrero	25	24.75	J. R. Barth, P. Unitt, N. Nicolai	32	39.25	N. Nicolai, E. C. Hall, J. O. Zimmer, G. L. Rogers, R. T. Patton, V. Moran, R. Breisch, P. Unitt, J. R. Barth
N-25	Inner Pasture	26	46.25	A. & T. Keenan, D. C. Seals, J. R. Barth, M. B. Mulrooney	30	27.33	A. & T. Keenan, J. R. Barth, M. B. Mulrooney, G. A. Rebstock, S. M. Wolf, R. T. Patton
N-26	Tierra Blanca	28	39.32	J. R. Barth, L. J. Hargrove, D. C. Seals	28	38.25	J. R. Barth, M. G. Mathos, P. Unitt, R. T. Patton, P. D. Jorgensen, M. B. Mulrooney
N-27	Palm Spring	41	25.60	R. & S. Breisch, D. C. Seals	37	26.15	R. & S. Breisch
N-28	Arroyo Seco del Diablo	21	77.00	R. & S. Breisch	24	26.37	R. & S. Breisch
N-29	Deguynos Canyon	21	30.17	J. R. Barth, P. Unitt	20	25.25	J. R. Barth
O-7	Torrey Pines	50	47.75	D. G. Seay	102	44.65	D. G. Seay
O-8	Golden Triangle	60	55.50	D. K. Adams	90	57.75	D. K. Adams
O-9	Miramar W	64	33.92	N. Osborn, T. Conkle, G. L. Rogers, P. Unitt	68	56.75	D. K. Adams, T. Conkle
O-10	Miramar Central	69	40.50	G. Grantham, T. Conkle, G. L. Rogers	102	46.50	G. Grantham, W. E. Haas, J. R. Barth
O-11	Miramar E	73	112.33	G. L. Rogers	74	43.25	G. Grantham, G. L. Rogers
O-12	Sycamore Canyon	86	55.92	W. E. Haas, I. S. Quon, T. Conkle, G. L. Rogers, P. Unitt	117	29.25	I. S. Quon, W. E. Haas, R. & S. Breisch, M. B. Stowe
O-13	Eucalyptus Hills	60	41.50	N. Osborn, D. C. Seals	79	25.25	D. C. Seals
O-14	Wildcat Canyon	73	26.50	M. B. Stowe	105	28.50	M. B. Stowe
O-15	El Monte Park	75	77.75	D. C. Seals, S. Peters	77	38.25	D. C. Seals, S. Peters
O-16	El Capitan Reservoir	86	85.00	S. Kingswood	94	46.66	S. Kingswood, J. K. Wilson
O-17	Viejas Mt.	55	36.50	J. R. Barth, D. C. Seals, L. J. Hargrove, P. Unitt, C. G. Edwards	60	25.09	P. Unitt, J. R. Barth, C. G. Edwards, J. M. Wells
O-18	Poser Mt.	55	27.00	K. J. Winter, L. J. Hargrove	54	28.00	K. J. Winter, L. J. Hargrove
O-19	Hulburd Grove	79	52.67	J. R. Barth	67	29.75	C. Anderson, K. J. Winter, L. J. Hargrove, P. Unitt
O-20	Oakzanita	70	44.25	D. W. Povey, A. & T. Keenan, L. Polinsky, P. D. Jorgensen	83	47.00	D. W. Povey
O-21	Upper Pine Valley Creek	62	49.00	P. Unitt	55	30.50	P. Unitt
O-22	Noble Canyon	71	73.50	P. Unitt	63	25.00	P. Unitt
O-23	Mt. Laguna	77	134.25	A. E. Klovstad, C. L. Mann, C. G. Edwards	58	18.25	A. E. Klovstad, C. L. Mann, E. C. Hall, J. O. Zimmer, P. Unitt
O-24	Stephenson Peak	48	25.00	P. Unitt, L. J. Hargrove, N. Nicolai	47	25.33	N. Nicolai, J. R. Barth
O-25	Red Top	28	15.50	J. R. Barth	31	27.58	J. R. Barth, J. Determan
O-26	Canebrake Canyon	31	43.08	J. R. Barth, P. Unitt	33	43.92	J. R. Barth, L. J. Hargrove, J. Determan
O-27	Well of Eight Echoes	35	43.58	P. R. Pryde	43	36.17	P. R. Pryde, G. L. Rogers, P. K. Nelson, L. J. Hargrove
O-28	Bow Willow	30	87.08	P. Famolaro, P. D. Jorgensen, R. & S. Breisch, D. C. Seals, J. R. Barth, L. J. Hargrove	40	33.25	P. D. Jorgensen, E. C. Hall, P. K. Nelson, P. Famolaro, A. & T. Keenan
O-29	Carrizo Marsh	37	36.67	M. C. Jorgensen, P. D. Jorgensen, P. Unitt, M. G. Mathos, F. Belinsky	42	25.25	M. C. Jorgensen, P. D. Jorgensen
P-7	La Jolla	54	58.05	L. & M. Polinsky	123	62.08	L. & M. Polinsky, M. G. Mathos, F. Belinsky
P-8	San Clemente Canyon	57	49.00	A. Compton, B. Marino, K. Muilenburg, K. Neal, M. Mosher, Joanne Moore, C. G. Edwards	65	26.25	A. Compton, B. Marino, K. Muilenburg, P. Unitt, L. & M. Polinsky, M. Mosher
P-9	Kearny Mesa	62	25.93	K. Kenwood, G. L. Rogers, L. & R. Johnson, R. Breisch	77	25.25	T. Myers, T. Conkle, K. Kenwood

Code	Location			Observers	Observers		
P-10	Murphy Canyon	57	25.77	D.K. Adams	D.K. Adams	72	43.75
P-11	Mission Gorge	79	52.80	E. Post	E. Post, G. Grantham, J. Harrell	90	28.00
P-12	Santee	83	35.75	E. Post, N. Osborn, C.G. Edwards, B.C. Moore, M.B. Mulrooney, F. Shaw	E. Post	139	37.00
P-13	Winter Gardens	78	151.00	D.C. Seals	D.C. Seals	86	29.00
P-14	Lakeside	81	65.00	M.B. Stowe	M.B. Stowe, C.G. Edwards	109	41.50
P-15	Harbison Canyon	75	113.50	R. Roedell, N. Osborn, E. Wallace, C.G. Edwards	N. Osborn, R. Roedell, C.G. Edwards, P. Unitt	71	41.50
P-16	Galloway Valley	73	60.00	G. & S. Sabbadini, P. Unitt, M. McIntosh, M.3. Stowe, D.C. Seals, C.G. Edwards, J.K. Wilson, R. Breisch	G. Sabbadini, P. Unitt, K.J. Winter	64	25.00
P-17	Alpine	70	54.50	C.G. Edwards, K.J. Winter, M. McIntosh, P. Unitt	C.G. Edwards, K.J. Winter, M.B. Stowe, P. Unitt	90	25.75
P-18	Viejas Valley	73	32.50	K.J. Winter	K.J. Winter	60	25.00
P-19	Descanso	69	35.50	B. & M. McIntosh, R. Schiller, D.C. Seals, P. Unitt	P. Unitt, J.M. Wells, K.J. Winter, M.B. Stowe	66	25.25
P-20	Guatay Mt.	66	25.42	P. Unitt, J.K. Wilson, J.R. Barth, L.J. Hargrove	P. Unitt, J.K. Wilson, P.K. Nelson, L.J. Hargrove, N. Osborn, B. Siegel, M. Sadowski, L. Polinsky	81	32.75
P-21	Pine Valley/Guatay	77	95.00	J.K. Wilson	J.K. Wilson	66	57.50
P-22	Scove Canyon	72	44.75	P. Unitt	P. Unitt	61	25.00
P-23	Wooded Hill	69	48.50	E.C. Hall, J.O. Zimmer	E.C. Hall, J.O. Zimmer	58	27.12
P-24	Cuyapaipe	57	38.25	D.C. Seals, P. Unitt	D.C. Seals, E.C. Hall, J.O. Zimmer	45	27.00
P-25	Pepperwood Trail	38	34.66	J.R. Barth, L.J. Hargrove, G.L. Rogers, M.B Mulrooney	L.J. Hargrove, M.B. Mulrooney, J.R. Barth	41	34.16
P-26	Sombrero Peak	40	72.75	P.R. Pryde, M.B. Mulrooney, L.J. Hargrove	P.R. Pryde, A. & T. Keenan, M.B. Mulrooney, P.K. Nelson	38	30.25
P-27	Egg Mt.	33	80.00	D.G. Seay	D.G. Seay, P.K. Nelson, J.K. Wilson, F.L. Unmack, M.B. Mulrooney, P. Unitt	32	46.00
P-28	Sweeney Pass	24	37.75	P.K. Nelson, J.K. Wilson, D.C. Seals, J.R. Barth	B. & M. McIntosh, A. Mauro, F.L. Unmack, M.B. Mulrooney	25	26.00
P-29	Canyon sin Nombre	21	38.66	D.C. Seals, J.R. Barth, M.B. Mulrooney, P.D. Jorgensen, M.G. Mathos, F. Belinsky, P. Unitt	G. & A. Kroon, J.R. Barth, R. Breisch	27	25.17
C-7	Pacific Beach	46	58.00	J.C. Worley	L. & M. Polinsky, E. Wallace	120	25.00
Q-8	Bay Park	71	66.75	E. Wallace, J.C. Worley	E. Wallace, J.C. Worley	145	74.25
Q-9	Linda Vista	58	99.50	T. Plunkett, D. & A. Hester	T. Plunkett, D. & A. Hester	62	96.75
Q-10	Grantville	63	29.25	N. Osborn, P. Unitt	P. Unitt, N. Osborn	90	25.75
Q-11	Lake Murray	86	165.50	N. Osborn	N. Osborn	117	114.00
Q-12	Grossmont	55	87.25	J. Bennett	J. Bennett	64	62.50
Q-13	El Cajon	37	26.75	K. Neal	K. Neal	64	26.75
Q-14	Singing Hills	69	58.75	J., E., & K. Berndes, T.A. Oberbauer	J., E., & K. Berndes, T.A. Oberbauer	81	69.00
Q-15	Dehesa	84	49.07	H.L. Young, A. Young, P. Unitt, G.A. Rebstock, J.R. Barth, W.E. Haas, N. Osborn	P. Unitt, A. Young	96	27.25
Q-16	Loveland Reservoir	76	64.75	J.K. Wilson, L.J. Hargrove, R. & S. Breisch, P. Famolaro	J.K. Wilson, L.J. Hargrove, R. & S. Breisch	90	84.80
Q-17	Hidden Glen	81	89.25	P. Famolaro	P. Famolaro, R. & S. Breisch, M.B. Stowe	86	32.00
Q-18	Japatul Valley	68	28.00	K.J. Winter, L.J. Hargrove, D.C. Seals, P. Unitt	K.J. Winter, J.K. Wilson, M. Sadowski, P.K. Nelson, N. Osborn, P. Unitt, R. & S. Breisch	92	36.75
Q-19	Horsethief Canyon	62	37.74	D.C. Seals, P. Unitt, M.G. Mathos, P.K. Nelson, J.K. Wilson, J.R. Barth	P. Unitt, M. McIntosh, D.C. Seals, N. Osborn	60	25.00
Q-20	Pine Creek Wilderness	59	29.00	K.J. Winter, G.A. Rebstock, G.L. Rogers	G.L. Rogers, W.E. Haas, R. & S. Breisch, R.T. Patton, J.R. Barth	87	30.33
Q-21	Long Valley Creek	69	51.25	L.J. Hargrove, E.C. Hall, J. Determan, J.K. Wilson, M.U. Evans, P. Unitt, P.D. Jorgensen	A. & T. Keenan, B.C. Moore, P. Unitt, G.L. Rogers, F.L. Unmack	78	33.75
Q-22	Glen Cliff	69	158.50	J.K. Wilson	J.K. Wilson	53	73.00
Q-23	Cibbets Flat	63	51.00	C.G. Edwards, E.C. Hall, J.O. Zimmer, J.R. Barth	C.G. Edwards, J.R. Barth, L.J. Hargrove, J.M. Wells	51	87.50

(Continued)

TABLE 4 (Continued)

	Breeding Season			Winter		
Square	Species[a]	Hours	Primary observer(s)	Species[b]	Hours	Primary observer(s)
Q-24 Thing Valley	57	39.49	J.R.Barth, P.Unitt, R.C.Sanger, D.C.Seals	63	27.50	J.R.Barth, J.M.Wells, P.Unitt
Q-25 Cottonwood Campground	47	42.00	N.Nicolai, E.C.Hall, J.O.Zimmer, A.&T.Keenan, J.R.Barth	43	39.08	N.Nicolai, B.&M.McIntosh, G.L.Rogers
Q-26 Rockhouse Canyon	44	40.66	R.C.Sanger, J.R.Barth, D.C.Seals, P.Unitt, L.J.Hargrove, B.O'Leary	47	25.41	P.Unitt, M.G.Mathos, A.&T.Keenan, J.R.Barth
Q-27 Carrizo Canyon	35	39.00	L.J.Hargrove, F.L.Unmack, D.Julian	29	42.30	D.Julian, R.Breisch, A.Mauro
Q-28 Jojoba Wash	23	35.00	G.&A.Kroon	26	40.00	G.&A.Kroon, P.D.Jorgensen, H.E.Stone
Q-29 Volcanic Hills	22	56.00	G.&A.Kroon, D.C.Seals, P.Unitt, J.K.Wilson, J.R.Barth	24	28.00	G.&A.Kroon
R-7 Ocean Beach	33	162.80	V.P.Johnson	109	41.00	V.P.Johnson
R-8 Old Town	63	36.85	A.E.Klovstad, C.L.Mann, C.Hewitt, J.&B.Peugh	147	28.33	A.E.Klovstad, C.L.Mann, B.C.Moore
R-9 Mission Valley	64	99.50	J.K.Wilson, H.L.Young	107	151.75	J.K.Wilson
R-10 East San Diego	48	112.33	J.Dietrick	51	81.25	J.Dietrick
R-11 Lemon Grove	46	29.75	P.Unitt, F.Shaw	82	30.00	D.&A.Hester, M.B.Stowe, E.Wallace
R-12 La Mesa	49	32.10	N.Inman, M.&D.Hastings	75	41.75	N.Inman, M.&D.Hastings
R-13 Casa de Oro	82	88.05	M.&D.Hastings, J.R.Barth, A.Mercieca	89	32.00	M.&D.Hastings, J.R.Barth
R-14 Jamacha	79	26.50	N.Perretta, P.Nance	80	27.25	N.Perretta, S.D.Cameron, R.&S.Breisch
R-15 McGinty Mt.	65	40.25	P.Unitt, G.A.Rebstock, J.R.Barth, N.Osborn, T.A.Oberbauer, W.E.Haas	60	26.27	P.Unitt, W.E.Haas
R-16 Sycuan Peak	67	37.04	P.Unitt, J.R.Barth	57	27.41	P.Unitt, J.R.Barth, M.B.Mulrooney
R-17 Lawson Valley	64	48.03	J.R.Barth, P.Unitt, A.Mauro, G.A.Rebstock	65	26.18	J.R.Barth, M.B.Stowe, K.Thomson, P.Unitt
R-18 Japatul Fire Station	62	36.75	M.Sadowski, J.K.Wilson, J.R.Barth, D.C.Seals	60	25.99	D.W.Povey, R.&S.Breisch, J.R.Barth
R-19 Espinosa Creek	55	42.50	L.J.Hargrove, J.R.Barth, G.L.Rogers	47	35.13	J.R.Barth, G.L.Rogers, L.J.Hargrove, R.&S.Breisch, A.&T.Keenan
R-20 Corte Madera	67	51.66	J.R.Barth, D.Herron, A.E.Klovstad, C.L.Mann, G.L.Rogers, J., E., &K.Berndes, D.Clark	88	28.00	L.&M.Polinsky, P.Unitt, R.&S.Breisch, A.E.Klovstad, C.L.Mann, D.Herron, D.Clark
R-21 Long Valley	54	33.25	L.J.Hargrove, J.K.Wilson, B.&M.McIntosh, P.Unitt	67	26.00	P.Unitt, B.McIntosh, G.Bustillos, E.C.Hall, W.E.Haas, B.C.Moore, F.L.Unmack
R-22 Cottonwood Valley	66	25.50	L.J.Hargrove, A.&T.Keenan	63	26.00	P.Unitt, J.M.Wells, R.&S.Breisch, M.U.Evans
R-23 Kitchen Creek	60	66.60	L.J.Hargrove	62	27.99	L.J.Hargrove
R-24 Simmons Canyon	71	34.25	J.Larson, A.&T.Keenan, P.K.Nelson, D.C.Seals, J.R.Barth	74	29.42	J.Larson, A.&T.Keenan, B.&M.McIntosh, J.R.Barth, J.M.Wells
R-25 Manzanita Reservation	56	27.17	J.R.Barth, G.A.Rebstock, J.Determan	75	25.25	A.Mauro, K.J.Winter, J.R.Barth, J.K.Wilson, L.J.Hargrove, G.L.Rogers, T.Cass
R-26 Lost Valley	69	42.08	P.Unitt, A.Mauro, J.R.Barth, G.A.Rebstock, L.J.Hargrove, R.Orr	55	25.00	J.&B.Hargrove, L.J.Hargrove, J.K.Wilson, F.L.Unmack, S.M.Wolf, R.Breisch, A.Mauro, J.R.Barth
R-27 Redondo Flat	45	30.75	L.J.Hargrove, P.D.Jorgensen, G.A.Rebstock, R.C.Sanger, B.O'Leary	38	32.00	L.J.Hargrove, J.R.Barth, G.A.Rebstock, P.Unitt, M.B.Mulrooney, E.C.Hall, J.O.Zimmer, S.M.Wolf
R-28 Indian Hill	32	33.65	J.O.Zimmer	39	30.75	J.O.Zimmer
R-29 Dos Cabezas Mine	31	42.00	G.A.Rebstock, P.K.Nelson, M.B.Mulrooney, D.C.Seals, J.R.Barth, L.J.Hargrove	22	51.83	J.R.Barth, P.Unitt, L.J.Hargrove, R.C.Sanger, E.C.Hall, J.O.Zimmer
S-7 Point Loma	52	134.25	V.P.Johnson	124	77.00	V.P.Johnson, J.C.Worley
S-8 North Island	31	40.49	R.T.Patton	128	93.00	R.T.Patton
S-9 Downtown San Diego	41	42.50	Y.Ikegaya	114	119.25	Y.Ikegaya
S-10 Greenwood/Mt.Hope	44	30.75	P.Unitt	90	37.00	P.Unitt
S-11 Encanto	43	25.08	P.Unitt	58	25.25	P.Unitt

S-12	Sweetwater Reservoir	77	21.75	P.Famolaro	127	30.07	P.Famolaro,T.W.Dorman
S-13	San Miguel Mt.	98	2.75	P.Famolaro	112	56.12	P.Famolaro,T.W.Dorman,P.Unitt
S-14	Steele Canyon	69	53.75	S.D.Cameron,N.Osborn,P.Unitt	62	25.50	S.D.Cameron,P.Unitt
S-15	Jamul	73	63.25	C.Woodruff,A.&T.Keenan,B.&M.McIntosh,P.Unitt	70	31.50	C.Woodruff,P.R.Pryde,J.&B.Hargrove,M.G.Mathos,P.Unitt, E.Post,D.Hastings,A.Mercieca
S-16	Lee Valley	62	27.75	J.R.Barth	65	25.07	J.R.Barth,P.Unitt,C.Rideout
S-17	Lyons Valley	62	60.85	J.R.Barth,P.K.Nelson,D.C.Seals	59	31.25	J.R.Barth,D.W.Povey
S-18	Wilson Creek	76	64.50	R.&S.Breisch,J.Hannan	83	25.30	R.&S.Breisch,J.M.Wells,J.Hannan
S-19	Barrett Lake	74	70.42	R.&S.Breisch,J.Hannan	92	25.30	R.&S.Breisch,J.Hannan
S-20	Hauser Wilderness	55	53.83	E.C.Hall,J.O.Zimmer,R.C.Sanger,D.C.Seals,J.R.Barth, L.J.Hargrove,R.&S.Breisch	51	36.00	J.R.Barth,D.C.Seals,J.M.Wells,R.&S.Breisch
S-21	Morena Creek	80	56.58	S.E.Smith	103	38.00	S.E.Smith
S-22	Boulder Oaks	90	155.75	R.&S.Breisch	103	47.90	R.&S.Breisch
S-23	La Posta	71	33.25	L.J.Hargrove,B.&M.McIntosh	80	25.00	L.J.Hargrove,E.C.Hall,C.R.Mahrdt,O.Carter
S-24	Miller Valley	72	28.25	L.J.Hargrove,B.&M.McIntosh	75	25.00	L.J.Hargrove,B.&M.McIntosh
S-25	Live Oak Springs	58	43.00	D.C.Seals,B.Siegel,B.&M.McIntosh,R.&S.Breisch, J.K.Wilson,J.R.Barth	56	26.25	W.Dallas,R.Vinton,R.&S.Breisch,B.O'Leary,P.Unitt,D.C.Seals
S-26	McCain Valley	59	34.83	F.L.Unmack,J.K.Wilson,G.L.Rogers,P.Unitt,M.U.Evans	55	26.50	F.L.Unmack,J.K.Wilson,P.K.Nelson,D.C.Seals
S-27	Sacotone Spring	45	50.25	E.C.Hall,J.O.Zimmer,M.Sadowski,J.K.Wilson, B.&M.McIntosh,P.Unitt,R.Orr	40	25.16	J.K.Wilson,F.L.Unmack,D.C.Seals,A.Mauro,G.L.Rogers,J.R.Barth
S-28	Carrizo Gorge	30	13.75	R.Breisch,A.Keenan,J.R.Barth	38	39.90	R.Breisch,F.L.Unmack,P.K.Nelson,J.K.Wilson
S-29	Dos Cabezas Spring	34	40.99	A.Young,A.&T.Keenan,J.R.Barth,A.Mauro,P.Unitt	37	28.50	A.Young,A.&T.Keenan,P.Unitt
T-9	Silver Strand	20	29.75	Y.Ikegaya,J.Coatsworth	102	83.75	J.Coatsworth
T-10	National City	45	31.50	P.Unitt,R.T.Patton,T.Godshalk,W.E.Haas	118	44.00	T.Godshalk,P.Unitt
T-11	Bonita	69	52.74	P.Unitt	121	97.56	P.Famolaro
T-12	Sunnyside	67	124.50	T.W.Dorman	114	102.14	T.W.Dorman
T-13	Upper Otay Lake	76	100.83	T.W.Dorman,J.F.Walters	119	85.99	T.W.Dorman,J.F.Walters
T-14	Proctor Valley	59	27.50	P.Unitt	67	25.58	P.Unitt
T-15	Rancho Jamul	70	36.00	J.K.Wilson,F.L.Unmack,V.Marquez,P.Unitt	81	37.50	P.K.Nelson,B.&M.McIntosh,J.K.Wilson,J.Determan,P.Unitt
T-16	Dulzura	65	49.41	D.C.Seals,T.Stands,S.Yamagata,P.Unitt,A.&D.Stanton, D.&A.Hester,A.&T.Keenan	78	50.71	R.&S.Breisch,D.W.Povey,A.Mauro,M.B.Stowe
T-17	Mother Grundy Peak	69	26.75	P.K.Nelson,D.C.Seals,L.J.Hargrove,S.M.Wolf,P.Unitt	60	33.72	S.M.Wolf,A.&T.Keenan,J.K.Wilson,H.Ingersoll,J.R.Barth, L.J.Hargrove
T-18	Rattlesnake Canyon	61	25.25	P.Unitt,L.J.Hargrove	53	27.50	P.Unitt,J.R.Barth,L.J.Hargrove,J.M.Wells
T-19	McAlmond Canyon	73	28.91	J.R.Barth,P.Unitt,J.K.Wilson,E.C.Hall	72	26.50	J.R.Barth,J.&B.Hargrove,E.C.Hall,R.&S.Breisch
T-20	Round Potrero	77	30.75	J.M.Wells,J.R.Barth	75	27.00	L.J.Hargrove,D.C.Seals,J.M.Wells
T-21	Lake Morena	82	145.20	R.&S.Breisch	91	46.70	R.&S.Breisch
T-22	Morena Village	67	43.25	R.&S.Breisch	86	29.13	R.&S.Breisch
T-23	La Posta Microwave	64	25.25	L.J.Hargrove,J.Larson,P.Unitt	72	33.00	L.J.Hargrove,B.Siegel,E.C.Hall,C.R.Mahrdt,O.Carter,R.&S.Breisch
T-24	Clover Flat	65	40.83	P.Unitt,J.R.Barth,D.C.Seals,B.Siegel	66	25.92	J.Larson,G.A.Rebstock,M.B.Stowe,A.Mauro,J.R.Barth,P.Unitt
T-25	Hill Valley	64	30.83	P.Unitt,E.C.Hall,J.Determan	75	25.41	E.C.Hall,J.O.Zimmer,C.R.Mahrdt,P.Unitt,R.B.Riggan
T-26	Boulevard	61	55.38	J.K.Wilson,F.L.Unmack	64	27.50	F.L.Unmack,D.C.Seals,P.Unitt
T-27	Bankhead Springs	69	41.88	J.K.Wilson,F.L.Unmack	82	35.00	F.L.Unmack,J.K.Wilson
T-28	Arsenic Spring	55	45.50	F.L.Unmack,J.K.Wilson	49	36.80	F.L.Unmack
T-29	In-Ko-Pah	30	32.25	B.Siegel,D.C.Seals,P.Unitt	32	36.00	B.Siegel,F.L.Unmack,L.J.Hargrove
U-10	South Bay	55	20.75	B.C.Moore,M.R.Smith,R.T.Patton	139	73.00	B.C.Moore

(Continued)

TABLE 4 (Continued)

Square		Breeding Season			Winter		
		Species[a]	Hours	Primary observer(s)	Species[b]	Hours	Primary observer(s)
U-11	Chula Vista	51	72.57	T.W. Dorman, P. Unitt	78	88.98	T.W. Dorman
U-12	Telegraph Canyon	59	136.83	T.W. Dorman	82	207.00	T.W. Dorman
U-13	Lower Otay Lake W	68	34.74	V. Marquez, P. Walsh, T. Stands, S. Yamagata, P. Unitt	103	62.75	V. Marquez, P. Unitt, B. & M. McIntosh, T. Stands, J.R. Barth
U-14	Lower Otay Lake E	82	61.53	S. Buchanan, N. Osborn, P. Unitt	108	43.63	S. Buchanan, N. Osborn, T. Stands, P. Unitt, B. & M. McIntosh
U-15	Otay Mt. N	54	40.50	A. & T. Keenan, P. Unitt, G.L. Rogers, L.J. Hargrove, J. Hammond	44	26.09	J.R. Barth, J. Hammond, K.J. Winter, A. & T. Keenan
U-16	Donohoe Mt.	61	66.58	J.R. Barth, R. Breisch, J. Hammond, P. Unitt, D.C. Seals, L.J. Hargrove, A. & T. Keenan, E.C. Hall, K.J. Winter	53	35.25	A. Mauro, S.D. Cameron, J. & B. Hargrove, L.J. Hargrove, J.R. Barth, J. Hammond
U-17	Engineer Springs	71	42.75	D.W. Povey	79	55.95	D.W. Povey, S.M. Wolf, R.T. Patton
U-18	Barrett Junction	70	28.00	P. Unitt, L.J. Hargrove, N. Fraser, D.C. Seals	66	25.25	P. Unitt, J. & B. Hargrove, G.L. Rogers, V. Marquez
U-19	Potrero Peak	59	25.50	B. & M. McIntosh	63	25.65	B. & M. McIntosh
U-20	Potrero	71	55.75	R. & S. Breisch, P. Unitt	86	30.15	R. & S. Breisch
U-21	Hauser Mt.	60	34.00	D.C. Seals, J.R. Barth, K.J. Winter, R.C. Sanger, P. Unitt	55	25.25	P. Unitt, J. Determan, R. Breisch, L.J. Hargrove, A. Mauro, S.M. Wolf
U-22	Campo W	69	25.00	E.C. Hall, C.R. Mahrdt	66	26.00	E.C. Hall, C.R. Mahrdt
U-23	Campo E	70	53.42	D. & A. Hester, B. & M. McIntosh, P. Unitt	83	30.33	D. & A. Hester, B. & M. McIntosh, D.C. Seals
U-24	Shockey Truck Trail	58	26.16	J.R. Barth, P.K. Nelson, L.J. Hargrove, F.L. Unmack	49	28.50	P.K. Nelson, F.L. Unmack, J.R. Barth, L.J. Hargrove, G.L. Rogers
U-25	Tierra del Sol	62	36.16	J.R. Barth, G.L. Rogers, E. & L. Wallace, D. Gould, S. Jorgensen	56	25.58	E. Wallace, J.R. Barth, R. Breisch, J. & B. Hargrove, G.L. Rogers, T. Cass
U-26	Lake Domingo	59	54.66	J.K. Wilson, F.L. Unmack	67	36.70	F.L. Unmack
U-27	Boundary Creek	64	104.75	F.L. Unmack, J.K. Wilson	72	66.25	F.L. Unmack
U-28	Jacumba	69	58.11	F.L. Unmack, J.K. Wilson, P.K. Nelson, C.G. Edwards, P. Unitt	71	27.00	F.L. Unmack
U-29	Jacumba Airstrip	38	51.75	F.L. Unmack, J.K. Wilson, P. Unitt	40	41.45	F.L. Unmack
V-10	Imperial Beach	70	32.50	C.G. Edwards, B.C. Moore, R.T. Patton, M.R. Smith	183	157.00	C.G. Edwards
V-11	Otay Valley	76	25.25	P. Unitt, G. McCaskie	143	50.00	G. McCaskie, P. Unitt
V-12	Otay Mesa W	68	94.25	P. Walsh, P. Unitt, G.L. Rogers	68	32.75	P. Walsh, W.E. Haas, P. Unitt
V-13	Otay Mesa E	62	25.75	P. Unitt, G.L. Rogers	97	25.00	P. Unitt, W.E. Haas
V-14	O'Neal Canyon	61	49.00	S.D. Cameron	63	34.75	S.D. Cameron
V-15	Otay Mt. S	45	47.00	P. Unitt, D.C. Seals, G.A. Rebstock	41	25.25	J.R. Barth, L.J. Hargrove, P. Unitt
V-16	Mine Canyon	64	39.00	D.C. Seals, A. & T. Keenan, B.E. Kus, P.P. Beck	66	32.50	D.C. Seals, J.K. Wilson, M.G. Mathos, P. Unitt
V-17	Little Tecate Peak	70	48.50	D.C. Seals, P.P. Beck, A. & T. Keenan	66	29.00	E.C. Hall, J.O. Zimmer, C.R. Mahrdt, G.L. Rogers, A. & T. Keenan
V-18	Tecate Peak	45	46.00	D.C. Seals, A. & T. Keenan, P. Unitt	34	42.00	D.C. Seals, A. & T. Keenan, P. Unitt
V-19	Tecate	55	24.25	B. & M. McIntosh	51	25.05	B. & M. McIntosh, D.C. Seals, A. & T. Keenan
W-10	Border Field	80	40.33	W.E. Haas, P. Unitt	142	45.75	S. Walens, G.L. Rogers, K. Aldern
W-11	San Ysidro	61	25.00	P. Unitt	95	25.50	P. Unitt

[a]Species possibly, probably, or confirmed nesting within the square; migrants and nonbreeding visitors excluded.
[b]All species recorded December–February; early or late migrants included.

RESULTS

The San Diego County Bird Atlas led to discoveries on many levels, from species new to the county to new insights in ecology. I hope that I have only opened the door to further discoveries. Many types of analysis of the atlas data remain possible but still to be done.

NEW SPECIES

Because San Diego County had a long history of bird study before the atlas period, the only species new during the period were four vagrants, the Yellow Rail, Upland Sandpiper, Belcher's Gull, and Northern Wheatear, and one pioneer, the Brown-crested or Wied's Flycatcher. Twenty-nine species have been added to the county list since the 1984 publication of my earlier *Birds of San Diego County* (Table 5). Of more relevance to our atlas effort were the 11 species confirmed nesting in the county for the first time from 1997 through 2001. The Purple Finch, Crissal Thrasher, and Fox Sparrow had been known as regular during the breeding season for some time previously; their breeding had been inferred but not reported before 1997. The Sooty Tern, Allen's Hummingbird, Red-naped Sapsucker (hybridized with the Red-breasted), Brown-crested Flycatcher, Hermit Thrush, Brewer's Sparrow, Summer Tanager, and Yellow-headed Blackbird were new discoveries. Whether they represent pioneers (especially likely for the hummingbird, flycatcher, and tanager) or ephemera only time will tell.

RANGE EXTENSIONS

We found many species in areas where they were unknown previously. Some of this resulted from covering areas that had seldom or never been visited previously by ornithologists or birders. Some areas, like much of Camp Pendleton, had been surveyed for endangered species but not for birds in general. Species whose ranges are extended probably for this reason include the Violet-green Swallow (found breeding at scattered lowland sites and in the Santa Rosa Mountains), Steller's Jay (found resident in several areas of oak woodland far from conifers, especially in southeastern San Diego County), and the Gray Vireo (found wintering in the elephant trees near Alma Wash in the Anza-Borrego Desert). Some extensions resulted from birds actually moving into new areas concurrently with the project. Examples of these are the Purple Finch, found through the breeding season over much of northwestern San Diego County, Cassin's Kingbird, spreading to higher elevations and beginning to show up in the Anza-Borrego Desert, and the Great Egret, establishing new colonies. Some range extensions, like those of the Western Flycatcher, Orange-crowned Warbler, Black Skimmer, and Gull-billed Tern, probably reflect forces acting over regions broader than San Diego County, though facilitated by local habitat changes. Distinguishing among

multiple causes is often not possible or will require further study. Especially interesting are species expanding in spite of habitat loss or a history of population decline; clear examples of these are two new colonists, the Summer Tanager and Brown-crested Flycatcher. The forces governing bird numbers and distributions can easily pull in different directions.

MARGINAL SPECIES

One of the many interesting things about ornithology in San Diego County is that so many species come to a limit of their range here. The east side of the mountains, in a rain shadow, differs radically in biology from the west side. The difference corresponds to a major biogeographi-

TABLE 5   Birds added to the San Diego County list since 1982

White-eyed Vireo, *Vireo griseus*, 7 June 1982
Mississippi Kite, *Ictinia mississippiensis*, 18 June 1982
Sooty Tern, *Sterna fuscata*, 27 September 1982
King Eider, *Somateria spectabilis*, 3 December 1982
Laysan Albatross, *Phoebastria immutabilis*, 31 March 1983
Pyrrhuloxia, *Cardinalis sinuatus*, 26 May 1983
Golden-winged Warbler, *Vermivora chrysoptera*,
    6 October 1984
Tufted Duck, *Aythya fuligula*, 18 February 1985
Dusky-capped or Olivaceous Flycatcher,
    Myiarchus tuberculifer, 8 March 1985
Gull-billed Tern, *Sterna nilotica*, 15 July 1985
Yellow-throated Vireo, *Vireo flavifrons*, 13 November 1985
Gray-cheeked Thrush, *Catharus minimus*, 1 October 1986
Xantus' Hummingbird, *Hylocharis xantusii*, 27 December 1986
Ruddy Ground-Dove, *Columbina talpacoti*, 12 October 1988
Spotted Redshank, *Tringa erythropus*, 19 May 1989
Louisiana Waterthrush, *Seiurus motacilla*, 9 February 1990
Brown Booby, *Sula leucogaster*, 2 April 1990
Little Bunting, *Emberiza pusilla*, 21 October 1991
Inca Dove, *Columbina inca*, 16 February 1992
Lesser Black-backed Gull, *Larus fuscus*, 22 February 1996
Rufous-backed Robin, *Turdus rufopalliatus*, 16 March 1996
Red-footed Booby, *Sula sula*, 24 May 1996
Violet-crowned Hummingbird, *Amazilia violiceps*,
    3 November 1996
Cook's Petrel, *Pterodroma cookii*, 13 June 1997
Belcher's Gull, *Larus belcheri*, 3 August 1997
Yellow Rail, *Coturnicops noveboracensis*, 16 December 1998
Upland Sandpiper, *Bartramia longicauda*, 19 October 1999
Brown-crested or Wied's Flycatcher, *Myiarchus tyrannulus*,
    26 August 2000
Northern Wheatear, *Oenanthe oenanthe*, 18 October 2001
Masked Booby, *Sula dactylatra*, 30 December 2001
Curve-billed Thrasher, *Toxostoma curvirostre*, 28 April 2002
Gila Woodpecker, *Melanerpes uropygialis*, 25 September 2003
Yellow-bellied Flycatcher, *Empidonax flaviventris*,
    28 September 2003
Magnificent or Rivoli's Hummingbird, *Eugenes fulgens*,
    11 October 2003
Manx Shearwater, *Puffinus puffinus*, 28 April 2004

cal boundary, with many species restricted to one side or the other. The 6500-foot range of elevation in the county leads to much altitudinal zonation, with rainfall increasing and temperatures decreasing with increasing elevation. Several species have disjunct ranges on mountain tops. On the coastal slope, there is also a gradient of decreasing rainfall from north to south. Perhaps as a result of this, several birds reach the southern limit of their ranges in San Diego County. This difference has been accentuated as a result of the difference in water use on either side of the international border. North of the border, water and woodland birds have been able to colonize and spread in the wake of the installation of reservoirs, massive importation of water, and planting of water-loving trees. In Mexico, far less water is available, and it is not used with such profligacy. Species or subspecies reaching a southern limit of their breeding ranges along the Pacific coast in or near San Diego County are the Eared, Western, and Clark's Grebes, American Bittern, White-faced Ibis, Gadwall, Redhead, Band-tailed Pigeon (subspecies *monilis*), Spotted Owl, Belted Kingfisher, Downy and White-headed Woodpeckers, Red-breasted Sapsucker, Willow Flycatcher, Barn Swallow, Steller's Jay, Mountain Chickadee (subspecies *baileyae*), Red-breasted Nuthatch, Brown Creeper, American Dipper, Cactus Wren (subspecies *sandiegensis*), Marsh Wren, Swainson's Thrush, California Gnatcatcher (subspecies *californica*), Dark-eyed Junco (subspecies *thurberi*), and American Goldfinch. Some of these nest very locally or irregularly in Baja California; edges of birds' ranges are seldom sharp. Some of these species' ranges are expanding and may extend farther south in the future. Hardly any birds, however, reach the northern limit of their range here. The Vermilion Flycatcher nests farther north in the desert but not normally so on the Pacific slope. The colonization of a pair of Harris' Hawks marks a tenuous addition to this list.

URBAN ADAPTATION

We commonly think of development and urbanization as detrimental to wildlife, and indeed it is to most. A surprising and growing number of birds, though, are adapting to these artificial habitats. Some, like the House Finch, Northern Mockingbird, Brewer's Blackbird, Hooded Oriole, and Anna's Hummingbird, have long been fixtures of the domesticated landscape. But others have only begun to make an adaptive shift.

Buildings and bridges offer nest sites to some birds like the White-throated Swift and Black Phoebe that were once localized to rock faces. Irrigation leads to lush gardens, then urban runoff, facilitating the spread of birds like the Song Sparrow that prefer more humid habitats. Planting of trees has allowed certain arboreal species to spread into what was once treeless scrub. The most obvious recent beneficiary is the American Crow, a species that nests in dense-foliaged trees. It has spread out of its historic range and increased so conspicuously as to draw the attention of the general public. Eucalyptus trees are

prime nest sites for birds of prey, allowing the spread of those like the Red-shouldered and Cooper's Hawks that do not need wide-open spaces for hunting. The eucalyptus' loose slabs of bark offer niches perfect for Western Flycatcher nests. In the late 1980s Nuttall's Woodpecker started adapting, moving into the city wherever it was landscaped with woodpecker-friendly species like liquidambar, birch, alder, and even agave. This cavity excavator paved the way for two secondary cavity nesters, the House Wren and Western Bluebird. In the late 1980s, I told people inquiring about birdhouses to forget about putting them up in metropolitan San Diego; no native species along the coast would use them. Enough people ignored my advice to make birdhouses an increasing factor in the spread of the House Wren and Western Bluebird. Further adapters can be expected. A pattern is emerging: many arboreal species that can live in a stratum above us people on the ground ultimately adapt to urbanization, while terrestrial and undergrowth species retreat.

Adaptation to the city is even more evident among wintering birds than among breeding species. Lush irrigated vegetation, offering a diversity of fruit and flowers through the winter, has allowed some species wintering primarily in the tropics to extend their winter ranges north. The first such example was the Western Tanager, first reported in 1922. Subsequently it has become annual in small numbers. Other increasing wintering species in this category include Cassin's and Plumbeous Vireos, Yellow, Black-throated Gray, Black-throated Green, and Black-and-white Warblers, Bullock's and Baltimore Orioles, and Summer Tanager. All of these are rare (though now annual), and most occur in native riparian woodland as well as urban parks, but they would be far less regular without the boost of exotic vegetation.

RANGE CONTRACTIONS

Early detection of population declines is a central goal of many bird studies. How to identify changes in populations accurately is a vexed topic in ornithology, difficult but critical to conservation policy. A bird atlas is a tool primarily for detecting changes in ranges, which are likely to lag behind changes in numbers. Much of the use of the San Diego County Bird Atlas will come in the future as our heirs look back to evaluate changes in their own time.

Nevertheless, at least 70 species, close to 15% of San Diego County's bird list, have decreased or contracted noticeably at some point in recorded history. For some, like the Short-tailed Albatross and Peregrine Falcon, the changes happened long ago and may have been halted or reversed. Other declines, like that of the Burrowing Owl, Grasshopper Sparrow, and Tricolored Blackbird, are happening as I write these words. Many changes are due to local habitat loss. Our atlas results demonstrate range retractions to varying degrees as a result of urbanization and habitat fragmentation for the California Quail, Greater Roadrunner, and Rufous-crowned and Sage Sparrows, among others. Colonial species that nest on or near the ground, like the Tricolored Blackbird and Least Tern, are especially vulnerable. In general, terrestrial and undergrowth species are ill adapted to cope with urbanization, which leads not only to habitat loss and fragmentation but to increased disturbance, proliferation of exotic plants and animals, and an increase in certain predators. The Northern Harrier, Lesser Nighthawk, Western Meadowlark, Grasshopper Sparrow, Horned Lark, and Burrowing Owl are all examples of terrestrial species in decline.

The scale of many retractions is broader than just San Diego County. The breeding range of the Bank Swallow and Swainson's Hawk retracted out of all of southern California, that of the Yellow-billed Cuckoo nearly so. From 1987 to 1994 Sooty Shearwater numbers off southern California decreased by 90%, with an increase in ocean temperature and a decrease in zooplankton (Veit et al. 1996). San Diego County was part of the sad story of the California Condor. Often we see changes resulting from local habitat loss combined with negative forces elsewhere. Species exemplifying this include the Mountain Plover, now only a former winter visitor to San Diego County.

Winter habitat and stopover sites for migrants are just as critical to bird conservation as breeding habitat. Though diminished by more than 90%, San Diego County's coastal wetlands remain important to waterbirds. But their use in the context of the entire Pacific flyway needs continuous monitoring so the functioning of these fragile habitats can be maintained. I hope the winter phase of the atlas will be a first step in addressing conservation of winter habitat. Many spring migrants coming north from the Gulf of California or along the west coast of mainland Mexico use San Diego County, with its comparatively low mountains, as a corridor for crossing those mountains and reaching the Pacific coast. The easiest of the passes, up San Felipe Valley, is now revealed as important a corridor for migrating birds as it was for early human travelers.

The formal designation of certain species as endangered has been critical in slowing or reversing their declines. The Least Tern, Clapper Rail, Bell's Vireo, and Peregrine Falcon have all benefited from this status. The process of listing itself is just a start, the opening of a door, on the road to recovery. Listing helps focus public land acquisition on listed species' habitat and helps guide management in areas already in public ownership. Even if multiple-species conservation plans prove successful, the federal Endangered Species Act, however flawed, remains the most powerful tool for stemming the loss of biodiversity.

Even vagrants can suffer declines, and these can be instructive. Some decreases appear due to the local disappearance of the habitats these migrants select, like the shallow freshwater ponds sought by Baird's Sandpiper. Some decreases appear due to changes affecting populations in the breeding and/or winter ranges, as

with several warblers originating in the boreal forest of Canada—especially the Tennessee, Cape May, Blackpoll, and Bay-breasted. And some decreases are undoubtedly due to both types of factors acting simultaneously, as with the Bobolink and Chestnut-collared and McCown's Longspurs.

ANNUAL IRREGULARITY

Many species of birds are known for their irregularity. Nomadism to take advantage of ephemeral food supplies and to avoid adverse conditions is a part of many species' biology, especially in arid regions. Winter visitors are especially known for their irregularity, some species invading in large numbers in some years, going elsewhere in others. Species feeding mainly on fruit or conifer seeds like thrushes, finches, and corvids are most susceptible to irruptions. Sometimes invasions of certain species coincide, sometimes not. The atlas' five-year term captured one significant invasion year, 2000-01. In that winter, numbers of Mountain Bluebirds and Cassin's Finches were exceptional, a flock of Pinyon Jays, the first in the county in 11 years, drew birders to Lake Cuyamaca, and a couple of Steller's Jays made it to the coast. An even greater invasion, featuring especially the Red Crossbill, Pine Siskin, and Red-breasted Nuthatch, took place the winter before the project started. Thus winter distributions for these species are highly dependent on the time over which the distribution is recorded and on conditions outside the area studied.

Our study revealed irregularity among certain species in which it had not been reported previously. Scott's Oriole, for example, was reported twice as frequently in 1999-2000 than in any other winter of the atlas period. The causes of many examples of irregularity remain to be identified.

Irregularity within San Diego County, as a result of local weather, also emerged from our atlas results. In four of the project's five years rainfall was below normal, but in 1997-1998 El Niño arrived, bringing above-normal precipitation well spread through the season (at San Diego, eighth wettest year since 1851). In the Anza-Borrego Desert birds responded immediately. That winter the White-crowned Sparrow, Brewer's Sparrow, and Sage Sparrow (pale migratory subspecies *nevadensis*) were exceptionally numerous and widespread throughout the desert. Northern Mockingbirds and Lesser and Lawrence's Goldfinches spread into marginal nesting habitat in spring of 1998. But the effect was transitory. The next winter, Brewer's Sparrows remained abundant but Sage Sparrows decreased and White-crowned Sparrows withdrew to oases. The following winter, Brewer's Sparrows took their turn in decline. By the end of the project, in February 2002, San Diego County was in the grip of the driest year in recorded history. In the bleakest parts of the Anza-Borrego Desert, even "common" birds had become rare.

The effects of rainfall variation emerged on the coastal side as well. Poor-wills were reported far more often in the wet winter of 1997-98 than in the remaining four winters of the project combined. On the coastal slope, the effect was most noticeable in the schedule of breeding. In 1998 many species began nesting earlier in the spring and continued later into the summer than in the other years of the period. Evidently drought compels a contraction of breeding seasons in both directions, not a shift earlier in the year. After the conclusion of the five-year recording period, the record drought of 2001–02 led to pervasive nesting failure—usually failure even to attempt nesting—among birds dependent on naturally dry habitats.

Cowbirds and Their Hosts

The invasion of the Brown-headed Cowbird, first record-ed in coastal San Diego County in 1911, confronted many insectivorous songbirds with a new threat. Coming at the same time as—and probably as a result of—irrigation, agriculture, and other new types of land use, the cowbird played a major role in the collapse of the populations of several riparian host species. How much was due to cowbird parasitism and how much to riparian habitat destruction are impossible to evaluate since these factors operated in tandem. And the degree of effect on the hosts can be assessed only very grossly, because data on their populations before the arrival of cowbirds are so limited. Nevertheless, when one compares writings from the early 20th century with these species' abundance in the 1970s and early 1980s, it appears that the Willow Flycatcher, Blue-gray Gnatcatcher, Bell's and Warbling Vireos, and Yellow Warbler, at a minimum, suffered steep declines. In the case of the Bell's Vireo and Willow Flycatcher, the areas of decline covered the range of entire subspecies, leading to the formal listing of *Vireo bellii pusillus* in 1986 and *Empidonax traillii extimus* in 1995 as endangered by the U.S. Fish and Wildlife Service. As a result, cowbird trap-ping was introduced widely for management of the vireo and as mitigation for vireos displaced by developments. The vireo responded spectacularly, increasing through the 1990s by a factor of approximately six. Unfortunately, only for the endangered species was there sufficient data on their numbers before trapping for changes to be assessed. And, unfortunately, this experiment in wildlife manage-ment has been carried out with no coordination. There is no central office in charge of tracking how many traps are out, how long they are operated, how many cowbirds are trapped, trends in the return for effort, and how the effort might be made more cost-effective. So evaluating cowbird trapping's general effect is almost as difficult as evaluating the effect of the cowbird invasion in the first place. Countywide, the Blue-gray Gnatcatcher, Yellow Warbler, Orange-crowned Warbler, and Yellow-breasted Chat also appear to have increased substantially over the same period in which Bell's Vireo increased. Yet one of the few sources of quantitative data, a banding station on De Luz Creek in Camp Pendleton, implies a decline of the Yellow-breasted Chat from 1995 to 2001 (Kus and Sharp 2002). Since 1986, the Willow Flycatcher popula-

tion in Camp Pendleton, trapped heavily for cowbirds, has remained static, so the response of various host species varies greatly. If this management practice is to be used efficiently and effectively, better-controlled experiments are needed of the effects of cowbird trapping at multiple scales on all hosts. The future of riparian songbirds along the entire Pacific coast of the U.S. may hinge in part on policy toward cowbirds.

Exotics

The introduction and spread of plants and animals outside their native ranges has become an accelerating plague in the age of the globalized economy. Among birds, the House Sparrow was San Diego County's first recorded alien invader, first reported in November 1913. The European Starling was first reported in winter "1948 or 1949" but did not arrive in numbers until 1962-63. These "old" exotics have now passed their exponential growth phase and are likely increasing now only at the rate new development creates new habitat for them.

The "Wild" (actually, self-domesticating) Turkey was introduced at least in 1959 but died out by the early 1980s. Another strain of turkey introduced in 1993 has increased rapidly and spread aggressively, by 2004 almost throughout the county's mountains and foothills—con-tradicting claims by the proponents of the introduction that the birds would remain in the private ranches where they were released. Another exotic game bird, the Ring-necked Pheasant, is on the verge of dying out, possibly surviving only near De Luz, Guajome Regional Park, north Escondido, and Pine Hills. Other sightings are like-ly of escapees or males (one sex only) released for hunt-ing on California Department of Fish and Game land at Rancho Jamul and San Felipe Valley. The origin of two species of waterfowl, the Canada Goose and Wood Duck, could comprise both introductions and colonization of wild birds. The spread of the latter has been encouraged by nest boxes installed at Cuyamaca and Santee lakes. Mute Swans may have originated from birds released at the Del Mar racetrack; they have spread as far afield as Fallbrook and Lakeside.

A new wave of exotics has begun arriving from the south, escapees from captivity brought in from Mexico or flying across the border. The Red-crowned Parrot is the best established, reported in increasing numbers through the 1990s in Ocean Beach and El Cajon, then spreading from there elsewhere in metropolitan San Diego. Successful nesting was confirmed in both the Ocean Beach/Point Loma area and El Cajon beginning in 1997. The similar Lilac-crowned Parrot is less numer-ous but also confirmed nesting beginning in 2000. The Red-masked Parakeet, a native of southwestern Ecuador and northwestern Peru, is also proliferating in the beach areas. Several other parrots were recorded over the atlas period but were less certainly breeding.

The Tijuana River valley is the front line for exotics. Black-throated Magpie-Jays and Northern Cardinals are both nesting in small numbers there, and a group of the former has settled in Bonita as well. Telling what Mexican species might be reaching San Diego as natural vagrants rather than escapees has become almost impossible. Sightings of the Painted Bunting, Gray Silky-Flycatcher, and Black-backed Oriole lead to more questions than answers. Just as with human immigrants, birds from not only Mexico but all over the world may reach San Diego by this route, as suggested by a Rufous Treepie (*Dendrocitta vagabunda*), a native of southern Asia, on Otay Mesa. We recorded all escapees in our atlas databases, never knowing when this year's escapee could be next year's colonizer.

CLIMATE CHANGE

Possibly overshadowing even the effects of runaway population growth on the San Diego environment is the specter of global climate change. Though San Diego, through Scripps Institution of Oceanography, has been at the forefront of research on this issue, the effects of climate change on the local environment have been little discussed. Global warming is being expressed in San Diego County, as over much of the North Temperate Zone, by an increase in winter low temperatures; summer temperatures as yet show no clear trend here. Since 1914, the average January minimum temperature at Lindbergh Field has increased at an average annual rate of 0.041 degrees Fahrenheit per year or 3.67 degrees total from 1914 to 2002. Although cities generate their own warmth, which might be thought to account for this increase, the temperature increase appears even steeper at higher elevations, in areas of minimal development. For example, from 1949, the earliest year on record, the average January minimum temperature at Cuyamaca has increased at an average annual rate of 0.089 degrees Fahrenheit per year or 4.83 degrees total from 1949 to 2002.

Thus the effect of climate warming is most likely to be seen in winter visitors and year-round residents than in summer visitors. Winter visitors and year-round residents may spread upslope, as the House Wren and Cassin's Kingbird are doing. Some species at the northern end of their winter range may increase, as the Barn Swallow is doing. Winter visitors from farther north may decrease or even fail to reach San Diego County at all, as migrating so far south becomes unnecessary. Possible examples of these are the White-winged Scoter, Purple Finch, Bohemian Waxwing, Bonaparte's Gull, and migratory subspecies of the Horned Lark (Patten et al. 2003).

Because climate warming is still in an early stage, the winter phase of the San Diego County Bird Atlas is all the more relevant as a standard for gauging future changes.

Nevertheless, summer visitors are far from immune, though no changes due to climate warming are obvious among them in San Diego County yet. A shift in the time of peak abundance of their insect prey could throw their food supply out of phase with their migration schedule, as has been found for the Pied Flycatcher (*Ficedula hypoleuca*) in the Netherlands (Both and Visser 2001).

A decrease or more irregularity in rainfall is also a great concern in an arid region like San Diego County. From 1997 to 2002, we saw how birds respond to swings in rainfall. Longer droughts could eliminate some species at the margins of their ranges, especially in the Anza-Borrego Desert. Shorter wet spells could give them insufficient time to repopulate, resulting in permanent contraction of ranges. The effects of longer droughts could be indirect. The pines of San Diego County's mountains have already been stressed enough by drought that some have been killed by bark beetles. Many trees of other species of conifers have died from insufficient water. Drought also leaves vegetation more susceptible to fire, an inevitable force in San Diego County's chaparral-dominated landscape. After a fire or beetle epidemic, drought could leave the forest unable to regenerate itself. By promoting fog drip and retention of water in the soil, forests often maintain the conditions that make their own growth possible. The birds inhabiting these forests could see their ranges reduced. Those that are in low numbers or at the southern tip of their ranges in San Diego County, like the Spotted Owl, Saw-whet Owl, White-headed Woodpecker, Olive-sided Flycatcher, and Brown Creeper, are the most likely to be affected.

In the firestorms of 2002 and 2003, 24.8% of San Diego County's area covered in natural vegetation burned— 19.9% of the county's total area. The effect of fires on this unprecedented scale cannot be predicted, but the San Diego County Bird Atlas stands as a benchmark against which the recovery from these fires can be gauged.

One of the greatest calamities that global warming may induce is an increase in sea level. A rise of just a few feet would eliminate San Diego County's coastal wetlands. With development crowded up to their edges, there is no opportunity for these habitats to shift inland, as they could during past climate cycles. A rise in sea level would be even more disastrous to all of San Diego County's coastal water birds than it would to its human inhabitants.

PLAN OF THE SPECIES ACCOUNTS

TEXT

Each account begins with a brief introduction, including the species' habitat and general status in San Diego County. Each covers the species' breeding distribution, nesting, migration, and winter distribution in the county, with the species' primary role in the county generally being addressed first. Plants used by birds are generally indicated with an English name only, unless the botanical name is in wider local use, but the scientific names of all plants mentioned in text are listed in Appendix 2.

Breeding distribution interprets the maps, addresses geographical and elevational ranges within the county, abundance, annual irregularity, and habitat use in greater detail where needed. It illustrates these topics with specific records. Locations are indexed to the square of the atlas grid system. Whenever possible, the place names used are those on commonly available maps. I hope this level of specificity is adequate to compensate for this book's lack of a gazetteer.

Three areas referred to regularly are too large for their atlas squares to be given in every account in which they are mentioned:

Campo Plateau: elevated region of southeastern San Diego County, extending from Potrero (U20) east to the Imperial County line near Jacumba (U29) and straddling the divide between the coastal and desert slopes. Though it is crossed by many granite ridges, it is less rugged than much of inland San Diego County.

Tijuana River Valley: floodplain of the Tijuana River in southwestern San Diego County (V10/V11/W10/W11). The historic "Myers Ranch," site of Guy McCaskie's discovery that vagrants from the eastern United States are regular in California, lies along Hollister Road at the convergence of the four atlas squares. It is now part of the Tijuana River County Open Space Preserve.

Warner Valley: San Diego County's largest block of grassland, encompassing the basin north and east of Lake Henshaw. It covers all or part of atlas squares E17, E18, E19, F17, F18, F19, F20, G17, G18, G19, G20, H17, and H18.

Nesting provides information on the species' nest, nest placement, and nesting season, emphasizing original data recorded during field work for this atlas. It compares recent data to earlier data published or accompanying the egg collection of the Western Foundation of Vertebrate Zoology, Camarillo (WFVZ), a resource vital to understanding change in the temporal, geographical, and habitat distribution of bird nesting.

Migration addresses arrival and departure dates, migration routes and peaks if known, and variation in migration within the county. This section emphasizes data on spring migrants recorded during field work for this atlas. More details on fall migrants may be in my 1984 *Birds of San Diego County*.

Winter interprets the maps, addresses geographical and elevational ranges, abundance, annual irregularity, and habitat use for that season.

Conservation points to trends in the species' range and abundance, possible reasons for these trends, and makes suggestions for improving the species' conservation outlook.

Taxonomy lists the subspecies occurring in San Diego County. If a species has more than one subspecies in the county, the section covers the status of each subspecies, the characters distinguishing them, and what the subspecies reveal about the direction and schedule of the bird's migration. For rare birds, it lists the specimens preserved in museums. Acronyms used for museums are these: AMNH, American Museum of Natural History, New York; CAS, California Academy of Sciences, San Francisco; CMNH, Carnegie Museum of Natural History, Pittsburgh; CSULB, California State University, Long Beach; DEL, Delaware Museum of Natural History, Greenville; FMNH, Field Museum of Natural History, Chicago; LACM, Natural History Museum of Los Angeles County, Los Angeles; MVZ, Museum of Vertebrate Zoology, University of California, Berkeley; SBCM, San Bernardino County Museum; SBMNH, Santa Barbara Museum of Natural History; SDNHM, San Diego Natural History Museum; SDSU, San Diego State University; UCLA, University of California, Los Angeles; USNM, National Museum of Natural History, Smithsonian Institution, Washington, D.C.

Subspecies of birds are a useful tool for learning about migration and evolution. Joe Marshall's explanation (in Phillips et al. 1964) is still the best ever: subspecies or races (the words are synonyms) "constitute whole populations which are 'marked' by their peculiarities of color, size, and proportions. By carefully identifying a bird to race, we can tell from which general breeding area of the species it originated, just as surely as if it were banded." Among birds, a subspecies may be defined as a population that is morphologically distinguishable, and has a breeding range that is geographically distinct, but is not reproductively isolated from, other populations of the same species. The usefulness of subspecies among birds arises because migration may take different populations—subspecies—of a species in different directions at different times, giving us a view into migration and dispersal deeper than if we could identify the birds to species only. Though some ornithologists attack the concept of subspecies because some subspecies do not differ in some genes of mitochondrial DNA, these researchers do not study bird distribution and migration. The usefulness of the category in illuminating these aspects of bird biology cannot be refuted.

MAPS

The distribution of every regular breeding or wintering in San Diego County is illustrated by at least one map appropriate to its season of occurrence. Sedentary species may have the winter and breeding-season distributions combined onto one map; if the species' distribution during the two seasons differs substantially, there is a map for each. The level of certainty of breeding is shown in the three levels standard for bird atlases: confirmed, probable, and possible, corresponding on the maps to three shades of green. "Confirmed" breeding is generally based on nest building (code NB in the database), distraction display (DD), used nest (UN), occupied nest (ON), fledglings (FL), adult carrying a fecal sac (FS), adult feeding young (FY), nest with eggs (NE), or nest with nestlings (NN). "Probable" breeding is generally based on multiple singing males in suitable breeding habitat on a single day (MM), agitated behavior of adults (AB), pairs in suitable breeding habitat during the breeding season (PR), territorial behavior (TB), courtship behavior (CB), or probable nests (PN, PB). "Possible" breeding is generally based on observations of the species in habitat suitable for breeding during its breeding season (SH), a singing male in suitable breeding habitat during the species' breeding season (SM), or observations of juveniles independent of their parents, in species where the young do not migrate or disperse while still in this plumage (JV). The application of these criteria had to be modified if they were inappropriate to the species' biology (see under Reporting). Squares in which a species was observed during the breeding season but is unlikely to breed, occurring only as a migrant or disperser, are shown in gray, often lacking a border so as to put these squares in the background. In cases where the species' distribution has contracted significantly through recorded history, sites of known or presumed breeding before 1997 are shown in red. "ND" in square C4 signifies no data.

Winter distributions are based on observations December–February unless spring migrants arrive before 1 March. Examples of species whose mapped winter distributions are based on shorter intervals are the Turkey Vulture, Sage Thrasher, and Tree Swallow. If the winter distribution is based on an interval ending before 28 or 29 February, the defining dates are specified. For species represented by a winter map only, additional squares in which the species was recorded as a migrant are shown in orange. For most species the orange squares represent spring migration only, but for the shorebirds, arriving in midsummer, they include some fall migrants as well.

Because atlas participants counted or estimated bird numbers, the maps also show relative abundance. This may be based on a calculation of numbers reported versus time spent in the field (for species dispersed widely through their habitat), or it may be based on the maximum number reported in the square per day (for localized, flocking, or colonial species). In some cases either means of portraying abundance could have been used, requiring an arbitrary decision. Because for most species these figures give just a rough idea of a bird's abundance, the maps show no more than three levels of abundance. Only in the case of intensively studied species is any bird's numbers known with any accuracy; the goal of portraying relative abundance on these maps is to point out where a species is most concentrated. For both the breeding season and winter the estimates of relative abundance are for periods when migrants are few or none, as appropriate for each species.

For the breeding season, the three levels of abundance are shown with diagonal lines layered over whatever shade of green specifies the degree of certainty of breeding. Cross or double hatching represents the highest level; single hatching represents the intermediate level; no hatching over a green background represents the lowest level. If one or two levels are not used, "N/A" in the legend specifies that these

Except for the red squares in maps of selected species, the distributions shown are for the five-year atlas period 1997–2002 exclusively. No records after 28 February 2002 are included, though a few species have been reported nesting in a few additional squares subsequently.

CHARTS OF NESTING SCHEDULES

Atlas participants recorded a vast amount of new information on birds' nesting schedules. This is portrayed by charts showing the daily distribution of nesting activity by behavior code (listed under Maps). Each mark on the chart corresponds to a single date (regardless of year). If the behavior was recorded for that species multiple times on the same date, the chart still shows only one mark for that date. The number of records for each type of behavior is in the legend. The scale varies to fit the season appropriate to the species. Behaviors absent from a species' chart were not recorded for that species. In the case of intensively monitored species such as the Golden Eagle, Least Tern, Willow Flycatcher, or Bell's Vireo, biologists studying those species have far more data on those species' breeding than is portrayed in these charts.

PHOTOS

The photos were kindly donated by Anthony Mercieca primarily, with further contributions from Jack Daynes, Ken Fink, Ken Kurland, Richard Webster, Brian Sullivan, and others. Selecting photos was a balancing act. I preferred photos taken in San Diego County when possible but went with ones taken elsewhere if clearly superior in quality. I preferred photos showing plumages most typically seen in San Diego County when possible. Fortunately, Tony has an amazing archive of many species, and I thank him for his indulgence and guidance during the process of selection.

San Diego County as Habitat for Birds

San Diego County's wondrously diverse biota is the product of diverse topography, climates, and soils, besides its position along the coast and astride a pathway for migration. Here I can offer only a brief overview. For information in greater depth, see Philip R. Pryde's book *San Diego: An Introduction to the Region* (Pryde 2004).

GEOGRAPHY

San Diego County's rugged and varied topography (Figure 5) is one of the main reasons for its biological diversity. The county may be divided into several regions useful for interpreting bird distribution. From west to east, the first is the open water of the Pacific Ocean. Since 1980, with oceanographic changes, numbers of many ocean birds off San Diego have plummeted, led by the Sooty Shearwater. Nevertheless, the species characteristic of the California Current can still be seen, even though a pelagic birder may spend hours of cruising the sea by boat with little return. Strong west winds, though, concentrate ocean birds nearer the coast, and on good days remarkable numbers can be

seen (with a spotting scope) from La Jolla. The distribution of birds over the ocean is strongly influenced by distance from shore. The continental shelf is only 2–10 miles wide off San Diego County. Ocean birds are usually most abundant within 10 miles of shore, and several species seldom or never venture farther out. Other species, such as the Black-footed Albatross, Leach's Storm-Petrel, and Xantus' Murrelet prefer to stay out of sight of land, however, so there is a substantial difference between the birdlife 5 or 50 miles offshore.

The coastline is a vital resource to a great number of birds. In many places, the littoral habitat is only a narrow sandy beach or sandstone bluff. Only small numbers of a few species frequent bare sandy beaches, but the clumps of giant kelp (*Macrocystis pyrifera* and *M. angustifolia*) that often wash up afford good foraging habitat for many shorebirds. With the rivers dammed and delivering little sediment to the beaches, though, erosion of sand is a continuing problem. Around La Jolla and Point Loma, the shoreline is bare rock, except for algae and sessile inver-

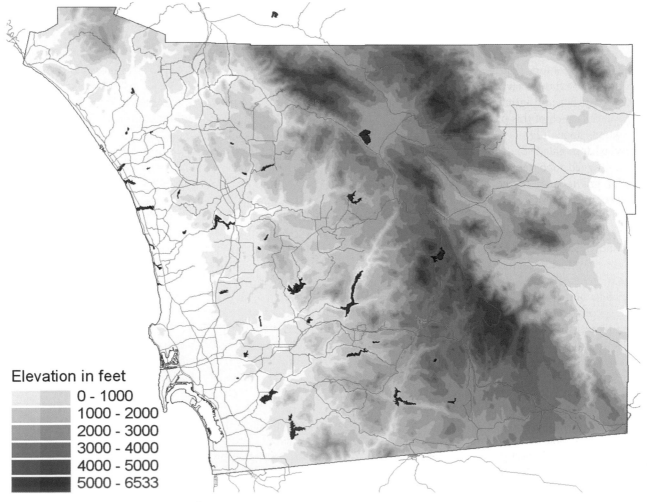

Elevation in feet

- 0 - 1000
- 1000 - 2000
- 2000 - 3000
- 3000 - 4000
- 4000 - 5000
- 5000 - 6533

FIGURE 5. San Diego County topography.

tebrates. Birds like the Snowy Egret, Wandering Tattler, Surfbird, and Black Turnstone seek the tidepools here.

The outstanding features of San Diego's coastline are the 17 wetlands, the estuaries and lagoons, and bays. Each of these has its own unique features that result in a different combination of bird species frequenting each wetland. San Diego and Mission bays are fully open to the tides and offer large surfaces of water, a habitat sought by many ducks, loons, and grebes. Tidal mudflats are found in San Diego County primarily around San Diego and Mission bays and at the San Diego and Tijuana River mouths. As a result, species that prefer tidal mudflats, like wintering Red Knots and Short-billed Dowitchers, are restricted to those localities. The mouths of some lagoons are often blocked, so they may dry up or be flooded by high tides or winter rains only irregularly. Sedimentation of the lagoons, accelerated by the development of their watersheds, is a serious problem. Restoration is expensive, but without it these irreplaceable habitats will only degrade further. The Tijuana River estuary is of prime importance because it, of all the county's wetlands, remains most nearly in its natural condition.

The lowland region inland from the coast is characterized by a series of marine terraces or mesas. Through time, streams cut canyons and valleys through the mesas. The result is a mosaic of habitats: riparian woodland or sycamore groves in the valleys, coastal sage scrub on south-facing slopes, denser chaparral on north-facing slopes, and sparser chaparral with scattered vernal pools on the few mesa tops that remain undeveloped. In some places soil conditions favor grassland rather than scrub. Extensive urban and agricultural development has altered or replaced much of this pattern.

Above about 1200 feet elevation the marine terraces and clay-dominated soils of the coastal lowland give way to the rugged topography of the Peninsular Range geological province. Here the soil is composed primarily of decomposed granite, and in many areas large granite boulders or outcroppings form a conspicuous feature of the landscape. In some areas, though, the base rocks are a metamorphic gabbro, which weathers into a deep red soil with few large rocks. Both granite and gabbro soils support chaparral, but the plants composing it differ substantially. The effect of the soil type on birds is less evident from the species composition of plants than from the lower, more open growth of shrubs on the gabbro soils, a condition that favors the Sage Sparrow. The foothills are separated by canyons and valleys. The flatter valley bottoms are vegetated with grasses (now overwhelmingly nonnative) and low herbaceous plants, while the narrower canyon bottoms and the margins of the valleys usually support a woodland of coast live oaks. In some places, such as near Santa Ysabel, oaks are scattered in grassland to form an oak savanna. The largest grassland in San Diego County is that in Warner Valley, from Lake Henshaw to Warner Springs and east nearly to Ranchita.

In some places above about 4000 feet elevation, temperature and rainfall permit the growth of coniferous trees. So distinct a combination of bird species inhabits coniferous woodland that the mountains supporting it may be considered a separate montane zone. This zone is broken into five ranges. Hot Springs Mountain (6533 feet) and Palomar Mountain (6140 feet), in northern San Diego County, support "islands" of coniferous woodland, isolated from other tracts of this habitat by expanses of chaparral and grassland. In central San Diego County, the Volcan (5719 feet), Cuyamaca (6512 feet), and Laguna (6378 feet) mountains are more intimately connected with each other. The montane woodlands of San Diego County are isolated from similar habitats both to the north in the San Jacinto and Santa Rosa mountains and to the south in Mexico's Sierra Juárez. The highest mountains of the Anza-Borrego Desert, the Santa Rosa Mountains (up to 6000 feet at the Riverside County line) and the Vallecito Mountains (5349 feet) support small stands of pinyon pines but few birds characteristic of more heavily forested mountains.

The eastern slopes of the mountains are steep and rocky. As they descend into the Colorado Desert, they open into broad alluvial fans or bajadas. Farther into the desert there are broad sandy washes, rocky hills, sandy valley floors, and dry lake beds. Another desert landform is found in the Borrego and Carrizo badlands, where the sedimentary substrate has been deeply carved by the rare heavy rains, producing a contorted land surface. The ground here is almost devoid of vegetation and in dry years the area supports very few birds. A few oases are scattered along the east base of the mountains and at Carrizo Marsh along Carrizo Creek near the Imperial County line.

CLIMATE

The ocean temperature off San Diego varies only from about 55° to 72° F. The ocean constrains variation in air temperature along the coast from an average low of about 45° F in winter to an average high of about 78° F in summer. Rainfall distinguishes the seasons more sharply than does temperature (Figure 6). Almost all rain falls from November to April; the months from May to October may be completely dry. Within the rainy season, precipitation is quite irregular. Long dry spells may occur even in February, on average the rainiest month. Often two or three stormy periods account for the bulk of the year's precipitation at San Diego, which averages 9.91 inches. Along the coast, average rainfall decreases from north to south (12.70 inches at Laguna Beach in southern Orange County; 9.28 inches at Chula Vista).

There is also great variation in rainfall from year to year, from a high of 25.97 inches at San Diego in 1883-1884 to a low of 3.01 inches in 2001-2002 (as measured from 1 July to 30 June). The San Diego County Bird Atlas' five-year term thus captured a wide range of variation in rainfall. As measured at Lindbergh Field:

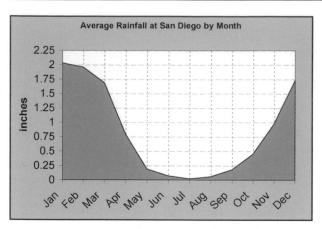

FIGURE 6. Average rainfall at San Diego by month, based on records maintained by the U.S. Weather Service.

1996-1997: 5.11 inches
1997-1998: 17.78 inches, eighth highest recorded since 1851
1998-1999: 6.72 inches
1999-2000: 5.78 inches
2000-2001: 8.61 inches
2001-2002: 3.01 inches, lowest since at least 1851

A relatively wet period that began in 1978 came to an abrupt end in 1998. These variations affect birds enormously. Breeding begins earlier and lasts later in wet years, and birds are able to spread into drier habitats than they can inhabit in dry years.

An outstanding feature of the dry season is the marine layer, the fog or low clouds that often cover the coast during the night and morning hours. This layer is caused by warm air being cooled over the colder ocean water, resulting in condensation. It has an appreciable local effect on bird migration since birds cannot use their celestial navigation when the sky is hidden, and the fog often obscures terrestrial landmarks as well. As a result, migrating land birds tend to concentrate along the coast if the fog is persistent. The fog may account for the absence or rarity of certain breeding birds like the Western Kingbird, Bullock's Oriole, and Lark Sparrow that are widespread and common except along the coastal strip.

Variation in temperature increases with distance from the coast. In the inland valleys summer highs average 88°

to 94° F. The rainfall regime in these areas is similar to that along the coast, but totals are higher, 12 to 20 inches annually, and summer thundershowers are possible.

The higher mountains are the coolest and most humid region of San Diego County. In winter freezing temperatures are the rule (lows average 28° to 32° F), and precipitation often falls as snow. Average annual precipitation is 20 to 34 inches. The severity of the dry season is relieved by occasional thundershowers.

The Anza-Borrego Desert lies in the rain shadow of the Peninsular Ranges, so precipitation is very sparse and irregular, with an annual average of only 6.09 inches at Borrego Springs and probably under 3 inches at the Imperial County line (average 2.6 inches in the Imperial Valley). Eastern San Diego County and western Imperial County make up one of the driest regions of the United States, second only to Death Valley.

VEGETATION

Plants and vegetation communities are so important to the distribution of so many birds that it is worthwhile to understand them in some detail (Figure 7). The following account is based primarily on the summary prepared for the earlier *Birds of San Diego County* by Thomas A. Oberbauer, one of the county's leading botanists.

Coastal strand vegetation grows on the beaches and sand dunes separating the bays, lagoons, and estuaries from the ocean. Its plants are small, herbaceous or succulent, often prostrate. They cover the ground sparsely, leaving wide areas of bare sand. The most common species are the exotic sea rocket (*Cakile maritima*) and the native beach evening primrose (*Camissonia cheiranthifolia*), beach bur (*Ambrosia chamissonis*), beach morning glory (*Calystegia soldanella*), and various rattleweeds (*Astragalus* sp.). The Snowy Plover, Least Tern, and Horned Lark are the only regular nesting birds, but the vegetation provides critical shade for the young chicks. The Killdeer, Black-bellied Plover, Least Sandpiper, American Pipit, Western Meadowlark, and House Finch visit to forage, and other shorebirds, gulls, and terns loaf on the strands.

Coastal wetlands that are at least occasionally flooded by the tides support salt marshes. The marshes' composition varies with how frequently they are inundated.

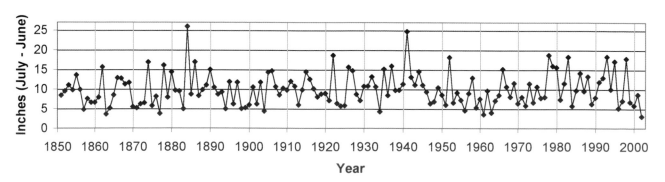

Figure 7. Annual rainfall at San Diego 1850–2002, based on records maintained by the U.S. Weather Service.

California cordgrass (*Spartina foliosa*) forms nearly pure stands in places covered by shallow water for long periods. On higher ground, flooded only by the highest tides or strong winter storms, the vegetation is dominated by low-growing succulents. Pickleweed (*Salicornia* spp.) is the most abundant plant; other common species are the alkali heath (*Frankenia salina*), fleshy jaumea (*Jaumea carnosa*), saltwort (*Batis maritima*), western marsh rosemary (*Limonium californicum*), saltgrass (*Distichlis spicata*), shoregrass (*Monanthochloe littoralis*), and dodder (*Cuscuta salina*). Among breeding birds, daily flooding of the habitat is challenged only by the Clapper Rail. In the higher zones of the marsh, the Mallard, Gadwall, Northern Harrier, Black-necked Stilt, American Avocet, Western Meadowlark, and Belding's Savannah Sparrow nest. The coastal salt marshes are essential to the Clapper Rail and Belding's Savannah Sparrow. They sustain the many herons, waterfowl, and shorebirds that forage in the coastal wetlands.

Freshwater marshes grow in shallow standing water or on perennially saturated ground. Their dominant plants are cattails (*Typha domingensis, T. latifolia*), bul-

rushes (*Scirpus* spp.), smartweed (*Polygonum* spp.), and dock (*Rumex* spp). Their characteristic birds include the Least Bittern, Cinnamon Teal, Ruddy Duck, Virginia Rail, Common Gallinule or Moorhen, American Coot, Black Phoebe, Marsh Wren, Common Yellowthroat, Song Sparrow, and Red-winged and Tricolored Blackbirds. In an arid and rugged region like San Diego County, freshwater marshes are naturally small and scattered. Patches lie at the upper ends of Buena Vista, Agua Hedionda, Batiquitos, and San Elijo lagoons, where they are often mixed with saltmarsh plants. Small freshwater marshes grow around many lakes and ponds on the coastal slope. A surprising number lie on the Campo Plateau in arid southeastern San Diego County.

The upland vegetation community nearest the coast is the coastal sage scrub. It is found mainly on south-facing slopes below about 1500 feet elevation where the rainfall is under 15 inches per year. The plants of the coastal sage scrub are mostly shrubs 2 to 4 feet high. They cover most of the ground but leave enough openings that a person can walk through the scrub easily. Many of the shrubs are summer-deciduous in response to the long dry

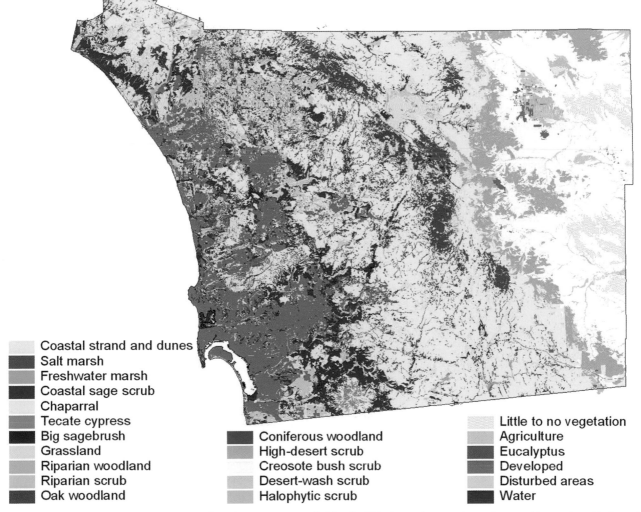

Coastal strand and dunes
Salt marsh
Freshwater marsh
Coastal sage scrub
Chaparral
Tecate cypress
Big sagebrush
Grassland
Riparian woodland
Riparian scrub
Oak woodland

Coniferous woodland
High-desert scrub
Creosote bush scrub
Desert-wash scrub
Halophytic scrub

Little to no vegetation
Agriculture
Eucalyptus
Developed
Disturbed areas
Water

FIGURE 8. San Diego County vegetation, based on maps compiled by the U.S. Forest Service, Anza–Borrego Desert State Park, and the San Diego Association of Governments.

season. The dominant species are California sagebrush (*Artemisia californica*), flat-top buckwheat (*Eriogonum fasciculatum*), white sage (*Salvia apiana*), black sage (*S. mellifera*), lemonadeberry (*Rhus integrifolia*), and laurel sumac (*Malosma laurina*). The Greater Roadrunner, California Gnatcatcher, Rufous-crowned Sparrow, and subspecies *sandiegensis* of the Cactus Wren prefer this habitat, and some species of chaparral inhabit sage scrub as well. Most of San Diego County's original acreage of coastal sage scrub is now lost, converted to houses. Multiple-species conservation plans focus primarily on coastal sage scrub, but these still allow further loss, and the viability of the fragments that will remain is an open question.

Chaparral is the most widespread vegetation community in San Diego County, covering nearly 35% of the land surface. Chaparral is composed of shrubs with hard evergreen leaves and stiff woody stems. The shrubs grow generally 5 to 12 feet high and have such dense foliage that the habitat is almost impossible to walk through. Its composition varies greatly from region to region within the county, and the community can easily be subdivided into finer categories, but the birds are not much different among the various types of chaparral. The most abundant and widespread plant is chamise (*Adenostoma fasciculatum*). Among the many other chaparral components, manzanitas (*Xylococcus bicolor* and *Arctostaphylos* spp.), *Ceanothus* spp., toyon (*Heteromeles arbutifolia*), coast spicebush (*Cneoridium dumosum*), holly-leaf redberry (*Rhamnus ilicifolia*), *Yucca whipplei*, San Diego mountain mahogany (*Cercocarpus minutiflorus*), redshank (*Adenostoma sparsifolium*), and scrub oaks (*Quercus* spp.) are some of the important species. The California and Mountain Quail, Anna's Hummingbird, Western Scrub-Jay, Wrentit, Bewick's Wren, California Thrasher, Spotted and California Towhees, and Sage and Black-chinned Sparrows are prominent and characteristic breeding birds of chaparral. More reflected in the makeup of the birds of a tract of chaparral than the component plant species is the habitat's maturity—the time since it last burned. Chaparral and the animals inhabiting it are adapted to fire. Certain birds, like the Lazuli Bunting, Lawrence's Goldfinch, Lark Sparrow, and Costa's Hummingbird, move in the first year after a fire, when the habitat is dominated by herbaceous plants that proliferate while the ground is still largely bare. In the next couple of years, as the shrubs resprout, the semiopen chaparral is ideal for Rufous-crowned, Black-chinned, and Sage Sparrows. Within a few years of the fire, the shrubs crowd together, the species of the earlier seral stages drop out, and the birds differ little from those in old, dense chaparral.

Occurring largely as scattered patches in the chaparral, on flatter topography, are stands of the Great Basin or big sagebrush (*Artemisia tridentata*). Though this habitat resembles that in the Great Basin, in a different biogeographic region, in San Diego County the birds of these stands are basically a subset of those in chaparral.

Both the Sage and Black-chinned Sparrows use them. San Diego County's few breeding Brewer's Sparrows were found in this sagebrush.

Habitats dominated by low-growing herbaceous plants are grouped under the term grassland. In the lowlands and foothills, grasslands are composed largely of nonnative grasses such as wild oats (*Avena* spp.), red brome (*Bromus madritensis* ssp. *rubens*), soft chess (*B. hordeaceus*), ripgut grass (*B. diandrus*), hare barley (*Hordeum murinum* ssp. *leporinum*), and fescues (*Festuca* spp.), and herbaceous dicots such as filarees (*Erodium* spp.) and mustards (*Brassica* spp.). These species originating in the Mediterranean region had largely replaced the native grassland species before San Diego County was well explored ornithologically, so we have no way of knowing what effect this ecological calamity had on the native birds. Native perennial bunchgrasses (*Nassella* and *Achnatherum* spp.) are now uncommon and localized, persisting mainly where the soil is undisturbed. Patches of grassland habitat are scattered on rolling hillsides and valley floors. The largest tract in San Diego County lies in Warner Valley, the broad plain extending north and east of Lake Henshaw. In the higher mountains, moist meadows represent another grassland habitat. The plant species here, rushes (*Juncus* spp.) and sedges (*Carex* spp.), are different from those in grassland at lower elevations, but the birds are rather similar. Grassland has few breeding birds, principally the Horned Lark, Western Meadowlark, and Grasshopper Sparrow, but many other species that nest in trees or shrubs adjacent to or scattered in grassland depend on the grassland as foraging habitat. Quite a few nonbreeding visitors, especially birds of prey, seek grassland.

Riparian woodland covers barely one half of one percent of the county's area, yet is of major importance to birds. This vegetation community grows in strips along rivers in damp sandy soil. The dominant plants are willows (*Salix* spp.), cottonwoods (*Populus fremontii*, *P. trichocarpa*), western sycamore (*Platanus racemosa*), white alder (*Alnus rhombifolia*), and velvet ash (*Fraxinus velutina*). In addition to these canopy trees and large shrubs, dense undergrowth is an important part of the riparian community. Mulefat (*Baccharis salicifolia*), mugwort (*Artemisia douglasiana*), stinging nettle (*Urtica dioica* ssp. *holosericea*), California blackberry (*Rubus ursinus*), and wild grape (*Vitis girdiana*) are among the common riparian undergrowth plants. Riparian woodland is outstanding for its rich diversity of breeding birds. These include, among many others, the Green Heron, Downy and Nuttall's Woodpeckers, Willow and Western Flycatchers, Swainson's Thrush, Bell's Vireo, Orange-crowned and Yellow Warblers, Common Yellowthroat, Yellow-breasted Chat, Bullock's Oriole, Black-headed Grosbeak, American Goldfinch, and Song Sparrow. Much of the habitat has been destroyed for agriculture, residential and commercial developments, and flood-control, though the pace of this loss has been slowed with regulations governing wetlands and the formal designation of the Least Bell's Vireo as an endangered species. Nevertheless, the damming of most streams has disrupted the cycle of flood and recovery that sustains riparian woodland. Exotic plants, especially the giant reed (*Arundo donax*), continue to proliferate in flood-plains, displacing the native woodland.

Stream courses that do not have enough permanent water to support the full variety of riparian woodland often contain open groves of sycamore trees or riparian scrub. Riparian scrub is usually sparser than the jungles in riparian woodland, and mulefat is the most prominent plant. The blue elderberry (*Sambucus mexicana*) is also typical of riparian scrub and a food source for frugivorous birds like the Phainopepla. Most birds of riparian scrub, like the Lazuli Bunting, Lesser Goldfinch, and Lark Sparrow, are equally at home along the interface between riparian woodland and grassland. Sycamore trees are used heavily by large tree-nesting birds like the Red-tailed Hawk, Common Raven, and Great Horned Owl, by cavity-nesting species like the American Kestrel, Northern Flicker, and Ash-throated Flycatcher, and by the Black-chinned Hummingbird, which typically builds its nest with the fuzz from sycamore leaves.

In canyon bottoms, on north-facing slopes, and around the edges of valleys, groves of live oaks form another major habitat. Coast live oak (*Quercus agrifolia*) is the dominant species, but the Engelmann oak (*Q. engelmannii*) is widespread in the foothills, the canyon live oak (*Q. chrysolepis*) in the mountains. Undergrowth plants common in oak woodland are poison oak (*Toxicodendron diversilobum*), skunkbrush or pubescent basketbush (*Rhus trilobata*), currants and gooseberries (*Ribes* spp.), and creeping snowberry (*Symphoricarpos mollis*). In many places oak woodland is mixed with or adjacent to riparian woodland, but oaks do not grow along the coast. The Western Screech-Owl, Acorn and Nuttall's Woodpeckers, Western Wood-Pewee, Western Scrub-Jay, Oak Titmouse, House Wren, Western Bluebird, Hutton's Vireo, and Black-headed Grosbeak are some of the typical breeding birds of this vegetation community. Sparse woodland or savanna of the Engelmann oak grows in some parts of the foothill zone that have hot summers but receive over 17 inches of rain per year. Originally, the ground cover was white sage (*Salvia apiana*), but over two centuries of cattle grazing have resulted in its replacement in most places by the introduced grasses. Most of the birds that inhabit broken woodland or woodland edges show no special preference among deciduous trees, live oaks, or conifers.

In San Diego County, coniferous woodland is largely restricted to the higher mountains in places that receive over 18 inches of rain per year. Besides the conifers, the deciduous California black oak (*Quercus kelloggii*) and canyon live oak are also important members of this community. The composition of the coniferous woodland varies with humidity and exposure. In drier, flatter areas, the trees are more widely spaced, there is little ground cover, and Jeffrey (*Pinus jeffreyi*) and Coulter (*P. coulteri*) pines dominate. In more humid, steeper areas, incense cedar (*Calocedrus decurrens*), white fir (*Abies concolor*), sugar pine (*P. lambertiana*; Cuyamaca and Hot Springs mountains only), and big-cone Douglas fir (*Pseutotsuga menziesii*; Palomar and Volcan mountains only) also grow. Characteristic breeding birds of this habitat include the Band-tailed Pigeon, Northern Saw-whet Owl, Hairy and White-headed Woodpeckers, Olive-sided Flycatcher, Violet-green Swallow, Steller's Jay, Mountain Chickadee, White-breasted and Pygmy Nuthatches, Brown Creeper, American Robin, Western Tanager, Purple Finch, and Dark-eyed Junco. Most of the species of oak woodland also occur in these coniferous woodlands.

On the east side of the mountain crests, the chamise-dominated chaparral abruptly gives way to a high-desert scrub. This varied habitat includes some components of the chaparral to the west and the creosote bush scrub to the east as well as several distinctive plants. The most prominent of these are the California juniper (*Juniperus californica*), the Mojave yucca (*Yucca schidigera*), and the yucca-like *Nolina bigelovii*; also common are the turpentine broom (*Thamnosma montana*), desert apricot (*Prunus fremontii*), lotebush (*Ziziphus parryi*), sugarbush (*Rhus ovata*), catclaw acacia (*Acacia greggii*), blackbush (*Coleogyne ramosissima*), and desert scrub oak (*Quercus cornelius-mulleri*). Also mapped as part of this community is the vegetation of the higher outlying mountains of the Anza-Borrego Desert, the Santa Rosa and Vallecito mountains. In those mountains grow stands of pinyon pines (*Pinus monophylla* and *P. quadrifolia*), but the stands are not large enough to support many birds different from those in high-desert scrub without the pinyons. The Mountain Quail, Ladder-backed Woodpecker, Western Scrub-Jay, Bushtit, Bewick's and Rock Wrens, California Towhee, Black-throated Sparrow, and Scott's Oriole are characteristic birds of this habitat.

Most of the Anza-Borrego Desert, in fact, about 16% of the entire area of San Diego County, is covered with a sparse scrub in which the creosote bush (*Larrea tridentata*) is the most common shrub. This creosote bush scrub community covers the most arid regions of San Diego County, and the density of plants is much lower than in other vegetation types. Other important desert plants include the ocotillo (*Fouquieria splendens*), brittlebush (*Encelia farinosa*), jumping or teddy-bear cholla (*Opuntia bigelovii*), barrel cactus (*Ferocactus acanthodes*), and bur-robush or white bursage (*Ambrosia dumosa*), desert agave (*Agave deserti*), and desert lavender (*Hyptis emoryi*). The abundance of birds in this habitat varies greatly with rainfall; after several dry years it is very low. The Lesser Nighthawk, Costa's Hummingbird, Loggerhead Shrike, Cactus Wren, Black-tailed Gnatcatcher, House Finch, and Black-throated Sparrow are the most typical birds here.

Desert washes are able to support denser stands of shrubs and small trees up to 15 feet tall. The most common plants are the cheesebush (*Hymenoclea salsola*), catclaw acacia (*Acacia greggii*), smoketree (*Psorothamnus spinosus*), ironwood (*Olneya tesota*), mesquite (*Prosopis glandulosa, P. pubescens*), blue paloverde (*Cercidium floridum*), and desert "willow" (*Chilopsis linearis*). The mesquite bosque in the floor of the Borrego Valley (G25/G26), a habitat unique in San Diego County, is also mapped as part of this desert-wash scrub. Characteristic birds of desert-wash scrub include those of the creosote bush scrub plus the California and Gambel's Quail, White-winged and Mourning Doves, Northern Mockingbird, Bewick's Wren, Verdin, and Phainopepla. The Borrego Valley's mesquite bosque is San Diego County's only site for the Crissal Thrasher and Lucy's Warbler. Native California fan palms (*Washingtonia filifera*) grow at oases in a few canyons draining into the desert; these appear on the vegetation map as riparian woodland.

On the desert floor where drainage is poor, mainly on the floors of Borrego and Clark valleys, a scrub of salt-tolerant shrubs grows. These are plants of the family Chenopodiaceae: the iodine bush (*Allenrolfea occidentalis*), bush seepweed (*Suaeda moquinii*), and various saltbushes (*Atriplex* spp.). Bird diversity in this habitat is very low, especially in the breeding season. But this is prime habitat for LeConte's Thrasher. In winter, the Vesper, Brewer's, and pale migratory subspecies (*nevadensis*) of the Sage Sparrow invade.

Faced with land prices rocketing upward, agriculture is on the retreat in San Diego County. Nevertheless, it remains a billion-dollar business here, sustained mainly by avocados, citrus fruits, cut flowers, and nursery stock. Eggs, milk, and beef cattle remain important agricultural products, but pastures and rangeland are mapped here as grassland. Orchards are used by a limited variety of birds,

such as the Northern Mockingbird, House Finch, and Lark and Chipping Sparrows. The Dark-eyed Junco may be starting to colonize.

Urban development offers suitable, even preferred, habitats for some birds. Because of cultural attitudes, historical accidents, and climate, certain exotic plants useful to birds are a common feature of the urban environment. Eucalyptus trees offer nest sites to birds of prey, kingbirds, and the Western Flycatcher. Flowering eucalyptus trees as well as many others offer nectar to hummingbirds and passerines. Native birds are quickly learning to feed on the lerp psyllid (*Glycaspis brimblecombei*), an insect pest of eucalyptus trees that first appeared in southern California in the 1990s. Many horticultural plants bear berries that sustain frugivorous birds such as the Northern Mockingbird, American Robin, and Cedar Waxwing. The crevices among the leaf bases of the Canary Island date palm (*Phoenix canariensis*) are nest sites for birds that originally used cavities in trunks or branches. Fan palms (*Washingtonia* spp.), used for nest material and placement, are the main reason for the Hooded Oriole establishing itself as a common urban bird. The density of urban trees has reached the point where some woodland birds, the Cooper's Hawk, Nuttall's Woodpecker, House Wren, Western Bluebird, and above all the American Crow are moving into the cities. Other native birds that have adapted well to the suburban landscape include the Bushtit, Western Scrub-Jay, Mourning Dove, Lesser Goldfinch, Anna's Hummingbird, and House Finch. One study, based on a single 8-minute count per site, reported significantly greater numbers of the last three species, plus the mockingbird, along the urban fringe than in larger stands of native habitat (Bolger et al. 1997).

CONSERVATION CONCERNS

The hope of many of us investing our energy toward the San Diego County Bird Atlas is that it be used as a tool for effective bird conservation. How might this happen? How might such a tool be used? The answer to these questions comes through understanding of the role of levels of scale.

One can look at a range map in a field guide or read the American Ornithologists' Union Check-list of North American Birds to get a fairly accurate idea of a species' general status in San Diego County—the coarsest level of scale. On the other hand, a regulator may require a developer to hire a consultant to delineate the territory of a single pair of endangered Bell's Vireos—the finest level of scale. Each of these levels has its uses. Between these extremes, however, lie the answers to many questions that can be addressed only at intermediate levels of scale. Our bird atlas grid represents the finest scale on which it is possible to achieve thorough coverage of all of San Diego County, with the time, money, access, and number and expertise of the participants available.

Here are some questions most appropriately addressed at this level of scale:

What areas support greatest bird diversity? (See Figures 8 and 9.) If the goal is to conserve maximum diversity, such areas would logically be targeted first. What areas support low bird diversity? What factors have operated to lead to this outcome?

Where are the biggest populations of species X? Do they lie in areas already managed as wildlife habitat or are they in areas subject to development or degradation? Which populations lie adjacent to the urban growth front and which are more secluded, possibly allowing more time and greater flexibility for effective management?

Is species X adapting to the urban environment? Does it persist in enclaves of natural habitat within cities or only in broader expanses beyond?

Is species X of legitimate conservation concern or not? Our effort has already shown that some native species (Nuttall's Woodpecker, Western Flycatcher, Cooper's Hawk) are thriving in nonnative environments. Some species (Downy Woodpecker, Tree Swallow), even though scarce and requiring rare habitats, are faring well in spite of themselves. But others (Grasshopper Sparrow, Chipping Sparrow, Snowy Plover, Burrowing Owl) are

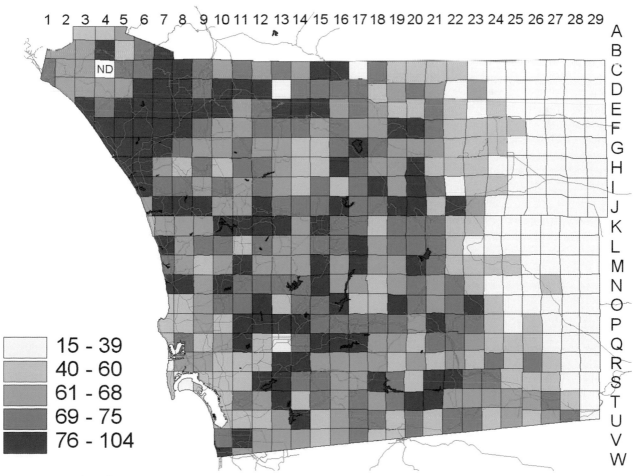

FIGURE 9. Number of breeding species (confirmed, probable, and possible) by atlas square, 1997–2001.

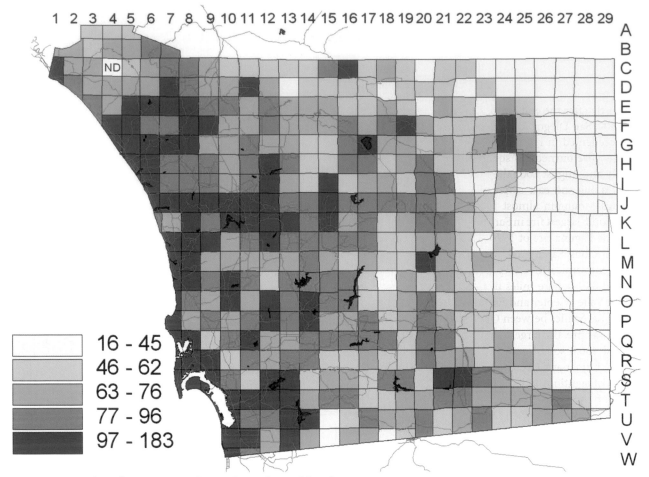

FIGURE 10. Number of winter species (December–February) by atlas square, 1997–2002.

revealed as, if anything, even more rare or restricted than I suspected before the project began.

What factors affect the distribution of species X? Is habitat type or vegetation community sufficient to explain it or are less conspicuous factors important too? Elevation, slope gradient or aspect, soil type, rainfall, fog versus sun, minimum winter temperature, maximum summer temperature, postfire succession, nearness of surface water may all play a role. Even if the exact role of various factors isn't clear, there will be enough to alert us that there may be more than meets the eye.

Some applications will be farther into the future. Twenty, 50, 100 years from now our successors will be able to look back at our results and compare them with current conditions. They will be able to ask whether multiple-species conservation plans are working for species X but not for species Y—and possibly respond in time to make a difference. No one will be able to claim that the species had already been extirpated from an area before the management plan went into effect if our data show otherwise.

In San Diego County natural ecosystems face an especially difficult challenge: a human population grow-

ing at third-world rates but consuming resources at first-world rates. Despite all the wrangling over endangered species and conservation plans, grading for new developments continues at a frightening pace. Our wildlife is destined to compete for fewer and smaller patches of open space. Will the species living in these patches in 2000 still be surviving in 2050 or 2100? Will we have to accept an environment without Sage Sparrows, Roadrunners, and California Quail in exchange for getting one with California Gnatcatchers? Questions like these look back at me as I look into the maps our effort generates.

The analysis of our data in this atlas barely scratches the surface of what is possible. By making more information available via a website, by making the database searchable, by offering as many maps of environmental variables as possible, and by enabling those maps to be overlaid with the distribution of any species, I hope to unleash the power of the atlas method. I hope this tool will help lead to new insights in ecology and will help identify conservation needs that can be met while there is still time.

WILDFIRE

Kirsten J. Winter and Philip Unitt

Shortly after the end of the field surveys for this atlas in 2002, San Diego County was swept by fires of a scope unprecedented in recorded history. In February 2002 the Gavilan fire burned 9.0 square miles north of Fallbrook. In July and August 2002 the Pines fire burned 51.4 square miles along the east slope of the mountains from Hot Springs Mountain almost to Mount Laguna—making it the second-largest fire in San Diego County history, behind only the Laguna fire of 1970. Then in October 2003, during ferocious Santa Ana winds, the Roblar fire burned 7.6 square miles in Camp Pendleton, the Paradise Fire burned 88.1 square miles in northern San Diego County east of Valley Center and Escondido, the Otay fire burned 69.9 square miles between Otay Mountain and Jamul, and the Cedar fire, the largest single fire in California history, burned 436.4 square miles of central San Diego County from Miramar and Crest east to Julian and Mount Laguna. The conflagrations killed 17 people, compelled the evacuation of thousands, burned 2454 houses, and shut the business of the city of San Diego down for two days. From a human perspective, the firestorm was the most pervasive disaster in San Diego County history. Was its effects on birds and other components of the natural environment just as great? Only time—and adequate study—will tell. Nevertheless, ecological succession following smaller fires suggests that long-lasting effects are likely only among the most localized and specialized species.

Southern California's ecology implies a long history of evolving with fire. Few places in San Diego County remain unburned through recorded history (Figure 11). After a fire, the native vegetation grows back quickly. For many plant species, fire is required to break their seeds' dormancy and allow germination. Most annual plants respond vigorously to fire, and the increased minerals and nutrients in the ash often allow them to grow to extra-large sizes. There are dozens of wildflowers that are "fire-followers," especially in the poppy and waterleaf families. Shrubs and trees may grow back from seed after fire. Many woody species also have the ability to resprout from stems or burls. In most cases, vegetative cover is

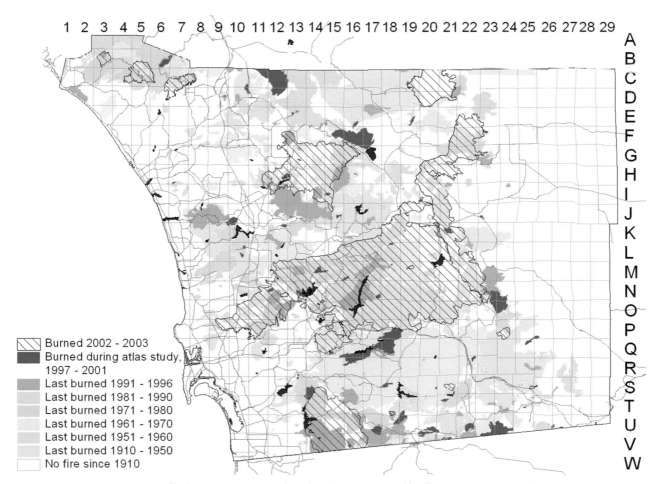

FIGURE 11. San Diego County fire history, 1910–2003, based on data maintained by the U.S. Forest Service's Remote Sensing Lab.

fully re-established after three to five years (no additional erosion expected). Within 10 to 15 years the vegetation structure is similar to, though usually less dense than, the structure before the fire. Chaparral usually will not burn again until it is 25 to 30 years old. Coastal sage scrub, however, may reburn after only a few years, before shrubs have become large enough to survive another fire. This is a major concern, as too-frequent fire can rapidly convert coastal sage scrub to non-native grassland, particularly at drier inland sites. Such a conversion can be seen over large areas of the San Jacinto basin in western Riverside County. Next to development, fire is likely to emerge as the greatest threat to coastal sage scrub.

Adaptations for recovery after fire are not limited to chaparral plants. Even species that may burn less often, such as riparian trees, are able to recover from fires. Coast live oak trees have very thick bark and are extremely resilient. Even trees that have been severely burned are usually able to resprout from their crowns. Other oak species that grow as trees (black oak, canyon live oak, Engelmann oak) may be "top-killed" by fire but resprout from the base. Sycamore, willow, and cottonwood trees resprout vigorously from their roots.

What about the animals? Hawks, ravens, and vultures congregate to feed on animals that were burned in the fire. In a fast-moving fire, rabbits, woodrats, and other animals may become confused and run into the flames. Birds too may be killed or injured. Fires may reduce animal populations substantially for one to several years, depending on the species' reproductive rate. In the first few years after the fire, the abundant flowers, new growth, and resprouts are highly nutritious and very attractive to Costa's Hummingbirds, deer, and quail. The effect on Costa's Hummingbird is especially dramatic because some of the plants that proliferate after fires, like the sticky nama or poodle-dog bush (*Turricula parryi*), showy penstemon (*Penstemon spectabilis*), and woolly blue-curls (*Trichostema lanatum*) attract feeding and nesting Costa's Hummingbirds in numbers far higher than in mature chaparral. Recently burned areas may be favored by birds that prefer sparser vegetation, such as the Sage Sparrow and Rufous-crowned Sparrow. The seeds of fire-following fiddleneck (*Amsinckia intermedia*) and popcornflower (*Cryptantha* sp.) plants are a major food for Lawrence's Goldfinch. Often Lazuli Buntings colonize recovering chaparral in large numbers. Although bird densities in burned areas are typically higher than those in older chaparral, nesting success may be lower, as nests are more easily detected by predators.

In spite of these adaptations by plants and animals, the fires may have a long-lasting effect if they are a symptom of a shift to a warmer, drier climate. Cool, moist habitats like coniferous forests are likely to show the results first. With the burning of the entire Cuyamaca Mountains in October 2003, some species could see their ranges cut back permanently. With southern California's latest drought—the most severe in recorded history—further large-scale wildfires seem almost inevitable.

Waterfowl — Family Anatidae

Fulvous Whistling-Duck *Dendrocygna bicolor*

A population collapse that eliminated the Fulvous Whistling-Duck from San Diego County in the 1950s was on the verge of eliminating it from all of California by the beginning of the 21st century. The species is kept commonly in captivity—or as an ornamental waterfowl in free flight—so for decades sightings have been assumed to be due to escapees. Since 1997 even that source has largely dried up.

Breeding distribution: The status of the Fulvous Whistling-Duck in San Diego County was poorly documented before the species was extirpated. The only specific record of breeding is J. B. Dixon's of small young in the San Luis Rey River valley on 18 May 1931 (Willett 1933).

Migration: Stephens (1919a) wrote of the Fulvous Whistling-Duck, "Rather common spring migrant. Rare winter visitant. Stragglers may remain through summer and breed." Yet two of the three SDNHM specimens were collected in fall: Mission Bay (Q8), 10 September 1922 (11313), and Warner Springs (F19), 21 October 1956 (30051). The last represents the most recent presumed wild Fulvous Whistling-Duck in San Diego County.

In the 1970s and 1980s free-flying Fulvous Whistling-Ducks kept at Sea World and the Wild Animal Park resulted in many sightings nearby, especially in the San Diego River flood control channel (R8). Since 1997, however, the only reports were of one at the Tijuana River

Photo by Anthony Mercieca

mouth (V10) 26 June 2003 (R. T. Patton, J. R. Barth) and three in the nearby estuary 2 August 2003 (M. Billings).

Winter: One specimen was collected 5 miles west of Santee (P11) 14 December 1954 (SDNHM 30023), another at San Diego in December, year not cited (Salvadori 1895).

Conservation: The reasons for the Fulvous Whistling-Duck's extirpation remain unclear. The species is not dependent on natural habitats; in the southeastern U.S. rice fields are its principal habitat. Draining of marshes and development of floodplains likely affected it, yet other ducks like the Mallard and Gadwall have proliferated under the same conditions. The threat to the Fulvous Whistling-Duck in California may lie in the birds' presumed Mexican winter range.

Greater White-fronted Goose *Anser albifrons*

Like southern California's other geese, the White-fronted was a common winter visitor in the 19th century, before uncontrolled hunting took its toll. Another steep decline of the Pacific coast population took place in the 1970s and 1980s (Ely and Dzubin 1994), and no recovery from it is evident in southern California. The White-fronted remains scarce and is now the goose least often seen in San Diego County.

Winter: The Greater White-fronted Goose is noted in San Diego County every year, but its numbers may be low—only four in 2001–2002. It is more likely to be seen in San Diego County in a small flock than as scattered individuals. Most occur on lakes with grassland or marsh vegetation adjacent to them, but a few visit lawns or salt marshes (one at Kendall–Frost Marsh, Mission Bay, Q8, 29 December 2001–7 January 2002, M. Billings). Locations are mainly in the coastal lowland but scattered over the coastal slope. From 1997 to 2002, the only sites where the species showed up repeatedly were Guajome Lake (G7; up to three on 4 January 2001, S. Grain), Lake Henshaw (G17; up to 15 from 9 to 24 December 2000, R.

Photo by Anthony Mercieca

Linfield), and Sweetwater Reservoir (S12; up to 17 from 18 December 1999 to 1 January 2000, P. Famolaro).

Migration: Even within Alaska, different populations of the White-fronted Goose follow different migration schedules. In both spring and fall, those breeding around Bristol Bay and wintering in northwestern mainland Mexico migrate much earlier than those breeding in the Yukon–Kuskokwim delta (Ely and Dzubin 1994). The

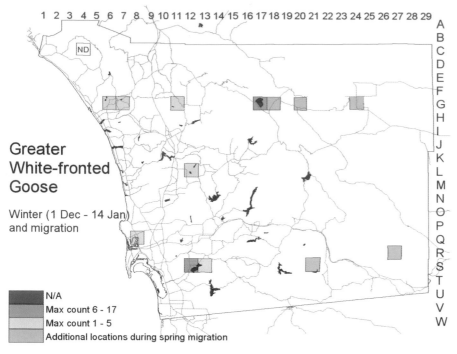

Greater White-fronted Goose

Winter (1 Dec - 14 Jan) and migration

- N/A
- Max count 6 - 17
- Max count 1 - 5
- Additional locations during spring migration

along the Silver Strand (T9) 20 April 1974 (J. L. Dunn), and one at Santee Lakes (P12) 13 April–5 May 2003 (M. B. Mulrooney, M. Hastings).

Conservation: The White-fronted Goose's first population crash probably took place largely by the end of the 19th century; Stephens (1919a) wrote that the species was only "formerly common." Through the second half of the 20th century numbers seen in San Diego County remained at about the same meager trickle. The 6 and 17 at Sweetwater Reservoir in 1997 and 1999, respectively, gave the San Diego Christmas bird count its largest totals ever.

Taxonomy: A definitive treatment of the subspecies of the Greater White-fronted Goose in North America has still not been published. One question is whether the size and color differences between the small geese breeding in western Alaska (*A. a. frontalis* Baird, 1858) and the larger ones breeding in northern Alaska and Canada are sufficient to define two subspecies. Another question is the application of the oldest name for a North American White-fronted Goose, *A. a. gambelli* Hartlaub, 1852. Because the type locality for this name is Texas, logically it represents the northern (and only eastern) population, but because the original description emphasized the bird's large size, the name is often used also for the Tule Goose, the very large, dark subspecies breeding around Cook Inlet, Alaska, and wintering in the Sacramento delta, designated *A. a. elgasi* by Delacour and Ripley (1975). Whatever name is applied to them, the birds migrating to and through southern California are from the western Alaska populations of relatively small geese.

former are presumably responsible for records in San Diego County as early as 22 September (1985, 15 flying south at Point Loma, J. O'Brien, AB 40:158, 1986). Sightings of 50 over Palomar Mountain 29 January 1978 (B. Cord), 50 flying west over Warner Valley (G18) 15 January 1999, and two flying west out of Carrizo Gorge (R27) 11 February 2001 (P. Unitt) match this population's northward migration schedule in midwinter and suggest that, to some extent, the White-fronted Goose uses San Diego County as a route to cross to the Pacific coast, paralleling the Black Brant. A flock of geese heard at night flying north over the intersection of highways S2 and S22 (G20) 22 January 2002 were most likely migrating White-fronted as well (J. R. Barth). Late for spring were one at the Borrego Springs Country Club (G24) 28 March 1999 (P. D. Ache; only record for the Anza–Borrego Desert), one

Snow Goose *Chen caerulescens*

The Snow Goose is a rare winter visitor to San Diego County with about 25 to 50 individuals occurring each year. Most of these associate with flocks of Canada Geese. The steady growth of the wintering population of the Snow Goose at the Salton Sea, and the explosive growth of the population rangewide, have hardly touched San Diego County.

Winter: The Snow Goose's distribution in San Diego County is an echo of that of the Canada Goose. From 1997 to 2002 our higher numbers of the Snow Goose were usually near large flocks of Canada Geese: eight at Bonsall (E8) 14 December 1999 (P. A. Ginsburg), eight at Lake Hodges (K10) 15 February 2000 (G. Grantham), eight in San Dieguito Valley (M8) 5 February 1998 (P. A. Ginsburg), and 11 at Sweetwater Reservoir (S12) 16

Photo by Anthony Mercieca

December 2000 (P. Famolaro). The Snow Goose also occurs rarely in coastal wetlands, e.g., three in the Santa Margarita River estuary (G4) 27–29 January 1999 (P. A.

Ginsburg), up to eight at San Elijo Lagoon (L7) 26 December 1999 (R. T. Patton), and two in the Tijuana River estuary (V10) 24 December 2000–13 January 2001 (H. L. Young). In southeastern San Diego County our only records were of two at the upper end of Lake Morena (S22) 5 December 1999 (R. and S. L. Breisch) and two at Jacumba (U28) 1–5 February 2000 (F. L. Unmack). In the Anza–Borrego Desert there are three records from Vallecito (M25), including one of a flock of 50, presumably spring migrants, 5 February 1975 (P. D. Jorgensen), and three from the Borrego Valley, including two at Borrego Springs (G24) 15 January 1999 (P. D. Ache) and seven flying over it 1 January 1991 (M. C. Jorgensen).

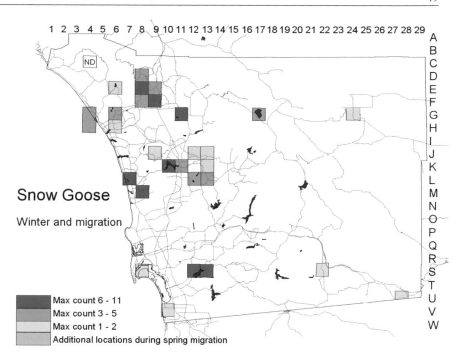

Snow Goose

Winter and migration

■	Max count 6 - 11
▨	Max count 3 - 5
▢	Max count 1 - 2
▨	Additional locations during spring migration

The Snow Goose does not use any site consistently. Though San Diego County's six Christmas bird count circles encompass the county's best Snow Goose habitat, no count gets the goose annually. The Rancho Santa Fe circle, including San Dieguito Valley, has the Snow Goose most often, recording it on 18 of 22 counts 1980–2003. The Oceanside count, however, has had larger numbers, up to 59 on 26 December 1993.

Migration: The Snow Goose occurs in San Diego County primarily from November to February. Two records for October (100 at Pauma Valley, E12, 4 October 1951, AFN 6:37, 1952; one at Corte Madera Lake, Q20/R20, 20 October 1929, SDNHM 12501) have not been paralleled recently. Spring departure takes place in February. Three were flying north over Fallbrook (D8) 16 February 1999 (M. Freda). The latest winter visitors were seven at Bonsall (E8) 25 February 2000 (P. A. Ginsburg) and three that departed Turner Lake (G11) 28 February 1998 (V. Dineen).

The only records of stragglers are of one at Jacumba 26 April–5 June 1964 (G. McCaskie) and one in the east basin of Buena Vista Lagoon (H6) 9 March–13 July 1999 (P. A. Ginsburg, J. Ginger).

Conservation: In the 19th century the Snow Goose wintered in coastal southern California in immense numbers (Belding 1892). Uncontrolled hunting rapidly depleted the population, which apparently continued to dwindle gradually through the first half of the 20th century. In the second half, the population rebounded over much of the range, including the south end of the Salton Sea (Patten et al. 2003). But in San Diego County the species remained more or less stable at the current low level. King et al. (1987) detected a decrease at San Elijo Lagoon from 1973 to 1983. The birds shifted, becoming less frequent at Whelan Lake (G6) and Lake Henshaw (G17), their principal sites in the 1970s.

Taxonomy: The subspecies of the Snow Goose reaching California is the Lesser Snow Goose, *C. c. caerulescens* (Linnaeus, 1758). The blue morph has been recorded in San Diego County only once, a sighting of an adult with two immatures at Whelan Lake 3 December 1983–16 January 1984 (R. E. Webster, AB 38:357, 1984). The genus *Chen* is commonly merged with *Anser*.

Ross' Goose *Chen rossii*

With the steep increase of Ross' Goose's population through the second half of the 20th century, this species has become an annual winter visitor to San Diego County. By the beginning of the 21st century, about 10 were being found each year, making the ratio between Ross' and Snow Geese in San Diego County similar to the 1:5 to 1:3 seen at the Salton Sea. Ross' Geese are often found with their larger relative but also occur in developed areas with little but lawns nearby for foraging habitat, keeping company with American Coots and domestic Mallards.

Photo by Anthony Mercieca

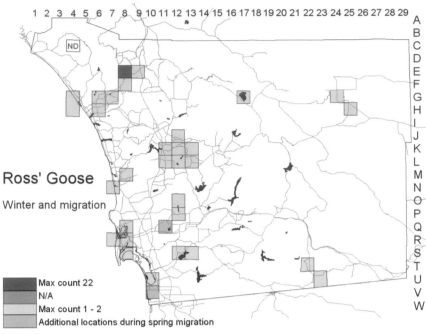

Ross' Goose

Winter and migration

Max count 22
N/A
Max count 1 - 2
Additional locations during spring migration

period were of migrants, not wintering birds.

Migration: Like the Snow Goose, Ross' Goose arrives in November. The earliest date is 8 November (1991, one found dead on the beach at Scripps Institution of Oceanography, O7, SDNHM 48060). Spring departure, however, is sometimes later than that of the Snow Goose. Migrants have been recorded as late as 28 March–2 April (2001, one at the Tijuana River mouth, V10, R. T. Patton) and 5–7 April (1985, one at Lake Henshaw, R. Higson, AB 39:349, 1985). The largest number of Ross' Geese found in San Diego County, 22 at Bonsall (E8) 25 February 2000 (P. A. Ginsburg), were clearly migrants, as only a single individual had been at this site earlier in the winter.

One Ross' Goose at Buena Vista Lagoon (H6) failed to migrate north in the spring of 1998 and remained there, with the domestic Mallards, until its death on 12 November 2000 (SDNHM 50494).

Winter: The distribution of Ross' Goose in San Diego County shows both similarities to and differences from that of the Snow Goose. Like the Snow, Ross' often shows up in the San Luis Rey River valley from Oceanside to Bonsall, in the San Pasqual Valley, and near Ramona. But there are records from numerous other sites in the coastal lowland south to Nestor (V11), where a pond now filled in was the site of the county's first known Ross' Goose 15 November 1966 (AFN 21:77, 1967). Farther east, Ross' Goose has been found on several occasions at Lake Henshaw (G17), with up to six on the Christmas bird count there 3 January 1987, and twice on the Campo Plateau, with one at Lake Morena (T22) 23 January 1999 (S. E. Smith) and one at Campo (U23) 3 February 1999 (D. C. Seals). In the Borrego Valley, Ross' Goose has been noted at both golf courses (G24; up to two from 21 November to 25 December 1999, one on 27 February and 25 December 2001, P. D. Ache) and at the sewage ponds (H25; two on 20 December 1999, H. L. Young, M. B. Mosher).

Whereas Snow Geese often show up in San Diego County in small flocks, records of Ross' Geese are primarily of single birds or pairs. From 1979 to 1988 flocks of up to 11 were seen occasionally at Whelan Lake (G6), but the only sightings of more than two during the atlas

Conservation: In the 19th century Ross' Goose likely occurred in San Diego County with the Snow Goose but was overlooked. Willett (1912) wrote that he had "seen many of these birds in the Los Angeles markets, brought in from the surrounding country," in the days when the once vast grasslands of the Los Angeles basin were a major center for wintering geese. But he reported no specific location for Ross' Goose south of Orange County. Overhunting decimated the population, and by 1931 the species' total numbers were estimated at only 5000–6000 individuals. Significant recovery did not begin until the 1950s, when the birds in the Central Valley shifted from wintering in native grassland to agricultural fields. By the 1990s the species' total population was about 300,000 (Ryder and Alisauskas 1995), and the number of winter visitors (migrants excluded) in San Diego County from 1998 to 2002 was 9 or 10 individuals annually. Ross' Goose could become a common winter visitor to parks and golf courses, provided society continues to devote imported water to such extravagances.

Canada Goose *Branta canadensis*

Roughly 5000 to 8000 Canada Geese spend the winter in San Diego County, visiting habitats that combine fresh or brackish water with low grass or succulent leaves on which the birds graze. Most of the geese congregate in a few large flocks that frequent the same areas year after year. Urban sprawl has displaced some, and continued development of pastures and floodplains could leave the geese with little habitat but golf courses, inviting the conflict between

man and goose seen elsewhere in the United States. Though the nuisance of the goose's nesting in developed areas is notorious, captives have been released in San Diego County and have begun nesting here.

Winter: By the late 1990s, San Diego County's largest flock of the Canada Goose was that in the San Pasqual Valley. Counts here in a single atlas square ranged up to 2083 near the east end of Lake Hodges (K11) on 2 January 1999 (E. C. Hall), and the entire flock, with annual variation, may number about 1500 to 3000. Another major site for the species is the Santa Maria Valley around Ramona, where our single-square counts ranged up to 549 southwest of Ramona (L14) 21 January 1998 (F. Sproul). In central coastal San Diego County another flock (up to 450 on 10 January 1998, R. T. Patton) focuses on the San Dieguito Valley (M8), where it moves among the remaining natural floodplain, horse pastures, and golf courses. In northwestern San Diego County pastures in the San Luis Rey valley continue to be a center for the Canada Goose, especially near Bonsall (F8; up to 350 on 18 December 1998 and 5 January 1999, J. Evans).

At Lake Henshaw (G17) and nearby in the Warner Valley numbers in the low hundreds are regular; during the atlas period our maximum on the lake was 510 on 12 December 2000 (J. R. Barth). Numbers on Lake Henshaw Christmas bird counts have varied much more than at the goose's other regular sites, from a high of 2581 on 3 January 1987 to lows of one on 18 December 2000 and zero on 16 December 2002. In the south county the goose's main site is Sweetwater Reservoir (S12), with up to 806 on 16 December 2000 (P. Famolaro). On the Campo Plateau the Canada Goose occurs in only small numbers, up to 40 at Campo (U23) 22 January 2000 (D. S. and A. W. Hester) and 36 in Hill Valley (T25) 10 February 2001 (E. C. Hall). The installation of golf courses in the Borrego Valley has allowed the Canada Goose to winter regularly there, with up to 98 on the Anza–Borrego Christmas bird count 31 December 1988 and 100 on 27 December 1992 (A. G. Morley).

The geese probably move freely among all the main wintering sites. Flocks are sometimes seen in flight far from them, such as 100 over El Monte Park (O15) 9 February 1998 (D. C. Seals) and 17 over Presidio Park (R8) 10 December 1997 (P. Unitt).

Migration: Mid November to late February is the Canada Goose's main season in San Diego County. In 2002 and 2003 the species arrived two weeks earlier than previously recorded with 23 at San Elijo Lagoon (L7) 14 October 2002 (R. T. Patton et al.), two there 13 October 2003 (A. Mauro), and six at the San Dieguito River estuary (M7) the same day (R. T. Patton). At Turner Lake, Valley Center (G11), a wintering flock of 400 departed on 25 February 1998 (V. Dineen). Few geese remain after 1 March; those left after mid March are likely sick, injured, or released captives. Some individuals have remained year round, such as one at El Capitan Reservoir (O16), still present in 2001, that had stayed for six or seven years, according to reservoir employees. Three records from the Anza–Borrego Desert, however, suggest migration until mid April: one in Culp Valley (G23/H23) 8 April 1996 (M. L. Gabel), one with a broken wing in San Felipe Wash 15 April 1964 (ABDSP database),

Photo by Anthony Mercieca

and 11 flying northwest of Ocotillo Wells (H28) 16 April 1998 (M. Vaught). Some February records from the desert are clearly of migrants, but others, such as 33 heading west over Mason Valley (L22) 27 December 1991 and 35 heading west over Blair Valley (L24) 15 January 1998 (R. Thériault), suggest a more local commute between the Salton Sink and the coastal slope of San Diego County.

Breeding distribution: The Canada Goose had not been reported nesting in San Diego County before we initiated field work for this atlas. None of the nesting we observed was in natural habitats. In most cases the birds were known or presumed to have been planted, though some could have been joined by wild geese that failed to migrate. Sites of confirmed nesting were the east basin of Buena Vista Lagoon (H6; young on 8 June 1999, M. Freda), La Costa Meadows Business Park (J7; two goslings with 20 adults 10 May 2000, C. C. Gorman), San Marcos Creek at Questhaven Road (J8; young on 8 June 1997, J. O. Zimmer), Wynola (J19; two released captives with a nest and eggs 11 April 2000, D. Brimm), and the Princess Resort, Vacation Isle, Mission Bay (Q7; pair on nest with

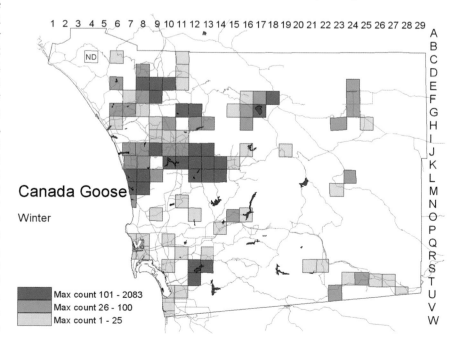

Canada Goose

Winter

Max count 101 - 2083
Max count 26 - 100
Max count 1 - 25

eggs 21 April 2000, L. Polinsky). Other places with several summering Canada Geese, more or less domesticated, were Mendenhall Valley (E15; 20 on 21 July 2001, J. R. Barth), San Marcos (I9; 10 on 23 June 2001, P. Zucker), Valley Center (G11; 20 on 30 June 2000, S. L. and S. J. Farrow), and the San Diego River near Boulder Creek (M17; five on 18 May 2000, K. J. Winter).

Conservation: Like other geese, the Canada was abundant in the 19th century, then decimated by overhunting. With hunting regulated the numbers stabilized but, in San Diego County, loss of habitat remains a threat. A change is most evident in the San Luis Rey River valley of Oceanside, where Whelan Lake (G6) was formerly one of the goose's main sites in San Diego County (Unitt 1984). From 1976 to 1980 the Oceanside Christmas bird count averaged 2809 Canada Geese; from 1997 to 2002 it averaged only 107. Even if many of these birds simply relocated to other wintering grounds within the county, the change was a response to rapid urbanization. Nevertheless, Christmas bird counts suggest the total number in the county remained fairly steady from at least 1985 through 2002.

In other parts of the United States the goose has adapted to suburbs and golf courses, domesticating itself. The establishment of nonmigratory geese in such places elicits human complaints about the birds' copious droppings, fear over the spread of disease, and the growth of an industry in goose repellent. San Diego County could save itself from this conflict by curbing the proliferation of golf courses, where geese can graze year round, and leaving floodplains in their natural state, attractive to geese only during the winter rainy season. Release of captive geese should be forbidden, as these may form a nucleus around which wild birds settle. Better to preserve the goose's natural migration, which inspires awe, than to encourage self domestication, which inspires contempt.

Taxonomy: Of the many subspecies of the Canada Goose, the primary winter visitor in San Diego County is the large *B. c. moffitti* Aldrich, 1946, which originates largely in the intermountain region and to which this account as a whole applies. Four San Diego County specimens have been preserved from Point Loma, Lake Henshaw,

and Warner Ranch. One specimen from Lake Henshaw (SDNHM 42132) had been banded as a chick at Willard, northern Utah.

While this atlas was in press, the American Ornithologists' Check-list Committee split the Canada Goose into two species, the large Canada Goose (*B. canadensis*), including *moffitti*, and the small Cackling Goose (*B. hutchinsii*). At least two subspecies of the Cackling Goose are known from San Diego County. The smallest subspecies, the Cackling Goose proper, *B. c. minima* Ridgway, 1885, is a rare winter visitor, usually keeping to itself rather than flocking with *moffitti*. Records since those listed by Unitt (1984) include one at Famosa Slough (R8) 25 October 1985 (D. Patla), one at Ocean Beach (R7) 2 November 1995 (SDNHM 49432), and one in Mission Bay (Q8) 6 December 2000 (L. Johnson). Also, two Cackling Geese visiting spots with domestic geese failed to migrate: one in the east basin of Buena Vista Lagoon (H6) 11 February 1998–21 July 2001 (P. A. Ginsburg) and one at Lindo Lake (P14) 26 May 2000 (C. G. Edwards). The primary winter range of the Cackling Goose is shifting north from the Central Valley of California to the Willamette and Columbia River valleys of Oregon and Washington (Mowbray et al. 2002), so the frequency of this subspecies in San Diego County may decrease.

The Aleutian Cackling Goose, *B. c. leucopareia* (Brandt, 1836), has been reported twice, on the basis of sightings of a flock of 13 photographed in the Tijuana River valley 13–14 November 1981 (G. McCaskie, J. Oldenettel, AB 36:217, 1982) and up to seven in San Dieguito Valley 16 December 1990–21 January 1991 (L. Santaella, AB 45:320, 1991). This formerly endangered subspecies, which winters largely in the Central Valley, has been restored, so it may become more frequent, unless its range shifts north like that of the Cackling.

Under the name *hutchinsii*, A. W. Anthony (in Belding 1892) reported the Lesser Canada Goose—presumably *B. c. parvipes* (Cassin, 1852) or *B. h. taverneri* Delacour, 1951—to be numerous in parts of San Diego County. But in lack of a specimen to identify the subspecies definitively the Lesser Canada Goose is best omitted from the list of San Diego County birds.

Brant *Branta bernicla*

San Diego and Mission bays were once two of the Brant's major wintering sites on the Pacific coast of North America. With uncontrolled shooting, then development of most of the bays, the Brant's numbers collapsed. Since the 1970s they have increased again, so that by the end of the 20th century about 750 to 1500 Brant were wintering annually around San Diego. Eelgrass in the bays is the key food source sustaining the birds. In the mid 20th century many of the Brant shifted to new winter quarters in the Gulf of California, establishing a new migration route over the mountain passes of eastern San Diego County.

Photo by Anthony Mercieca

Winter: South San Diego Bay is currently the Brant's primary habitat in the county. Within the bay the birds are concentrated strongly along the Chula Vista bayfront and in Emory Cove (U10), sites of the largest stands of intertidal eelgrass (Macdonald et al. 1990, Manning 1995). Covering virtually all of the Brant's habitat in San Diego Bay weekly from April 1993 to April 1994, Manning (1995) found a December–January average of about 350 and a maximum of about 550. From 1997 to 2002 numbers were somewhat higher: Barbara C. Moore estimated 500 along the Chula Vista bayfront repeatedly through the atlas period. Totals on San Diego Christmas bird counts reached 1118 on 15 December 2001 and 1292 on 14 December 2002. Relatively few Brant use central and northern San Diego Bay; our highest count there was of 53 around North Island Naval Air Station (S8) 15 December 2001 (R. T. Patton).

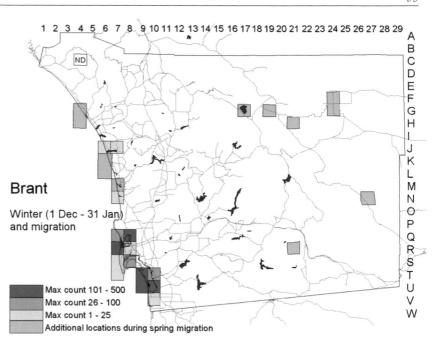

Brant

Winter (1 Dec – 31 Jan) and migration

Max count 101 – 500
Max count 26 – 100
Max count 1 – 25
Additional locations during spring migration

Brant have used the San Diego River flood-control channel (R7/R8) for decades. Counts of 50 to 200 are regular here, with a maximum of 260 on 20 December 2000 (G. Grantham). Counts of 100 to 200 are now regular on Mission Bay, with a maximum of 230 on 7 December 1998 (J. C. Worley). Elsewhere along San Diego County's coast, however, wintering Brant are rare. Our only December–January records during the atlas period were of one at Batiquitos Lagoon (J6/J7) 10 and 30 December 1998 (M. Baumgartel, R. T. Patton) and two at Los Peñasquitos Lagoon (N7) 3–4 January 1998 (K. Estey, D. K. Adams). The Oceanside and Rancho Santa Fe Christmas bird counts record the Brant rarely, just one or two individuals, except for 50 on the Oceanside count 31 December 1977.

Migration: Fall migrants may arrive as early as 28 October (1972, one at the San Diego River mouth, G. McCaskie), but the third week of November appears to be the typical arrival schedule. The earliest date Preston and Mock (1995) recorded on central San Diego Bay was 22 November 1994 (43 birds). Southbound migrants usually pass through unnoticed, offshore or at high altitudes, but northbound migrants are conspicuous and often outnumber wintering birds—most Black Brant winter in Baja California. On San Diego Bay Manning (1995) recorded higher numbers in February and March than in December and January, up to 714 on 29 March 1994. Some birds are moving north as early as 2 February (1992; 75 flying past Los Coronados Islands, P. Unitt). By April most have departed, but some are seen through early May. A few stragglers fail to migrate. Numbers of such oversummering birds range up to six near the Chula Vista Nature Center 30 May–5 June 1999 (B. C. Moore) and 10 in the Tijuana River estuary (V10) 27 June 1998 (C. G. Edwards).

The principal spring migration route for Brant leaving the Gulf of California crosses eastern San Diego County. The heart of the corridor parallels Highway S2 from the Anza–Borrego Desert up through San Felipe Valley to Lake Henshaw (G17). Most of the birds make the trip nonstop, noted only when they pause on Lake Henshaw because of storms or the fierce headwind so frequent at this season. Counts on the lake range up to 754 on 4 March 1983 and 688 on 16 March 1984 (R. Higson, AB 37:912, 1983; 38:958, 1984). Occasionally, however, Brant can be seen in flight headed northwest up the corridor, such as 15 near Canebrake (N27) 17 April 1998 (P. D. Jorgensen) and 40 in San Felipe Valley (H21) 26 April 2001 (P. Unitt). Spring migrants have been recorded widely elsewhere in eastern San Diego County, with up to 38 at Lake Cuyamaca (M20) 22 April 1967 (AFN 21:540, 1967), 50 flying up Banner Canyon (K21) 13 March 1977 (AB 31:1047, 1977), 75 at Yaqui Well (I24) 19 April 1984 (B. Wagner, AB 38:958, 1984), and 31 on the golf-course pond at Club Circle, Borrego Springs (G24), 19 April 1999 (P. D. Ache). Several have been found exhausted or dead, such as one near Canebrake 11 March 1989 (R. Thériault, SDNHM 47503).

The passage overland takes place mainly in March and April. In 1983, when El Niño generated repeated storms, Roger Higson monitored Lake Henshaw regularly and noted the Brant from 4 March to 29 April. Extreme dates are 18 January (1993, one on the Borrego sewage pond, H25, J. Dougherty) and 1 May (1992, one dead and one exhausted along Highway S2, R. Thériault), except for five at the Roadrunner Club (F24) 24 May 1988 (T. Hatch) and one at the Borrego sewage pond 1 June 1988 (A. G. Morley). Such records parallel the regular summer stragglers at the Salton Sea (Patten et al. 2003). It seems likely that southbound migrants follow the same route but are not detected because of the lack of headwinds impeding them.

Conservation: Nineteenth-century writers commented on the fabulous abundance of the Brant on San Diego Bay, but the only specific estimate is of 50,000–100,000 at Spanish Bight (now filled) between Coronado and North Island in the 1880s (McGrew 1922). By the 1890s these numbers were already being depleted (Belding 1892), and by the early 20th century the Brant was rare (Stephens 1919a). "Reckless, idiotic shooting…reft the bay of one of its chief attractions" (McGrew 1922). Through the middle of the century Brant numbers on San Diego Bay varied from zero in the early 1930s and late 1970s to 1100 in 1942 and 1573 in 1961 (Moffitt 1938, 1943, Christmas bird counts). In 1952, Leopold and Smith (1953) omitted San Diego and Mission bays from their rangewide survey, considering numbers there negligible and writing, "pollution, dredging, and other developments, plus continued disturbance by boats and airplanes, have rendered this area of less use to Brant." The increase since the late 1970s may be due to improved water quality and recovery of eelgrass. By 2000, eelgrass covered the maximum possible remaining available habitat in San Diego Bay (M. Perdue pers. comm.). The Brant feeds also on sea lettuce, apparently relying on this plant when eelgrass is not available (Moffitt 1943). Slow regrowth of aquatic plants in Mission Bay after the dredging and development of the late 1950s has allowed some Brant to return there. At the Brant's low point in the 1970s the San Diego River flood-control channel was the species' only consistent site (Unitt 1984).

The shift of the Brant's main wintering population to Baja California and the spread of the winter range to the Gulf of California may have been a response to the disturbance and loss of habitat at San Diego. In Sonora, the Brant was first noted in 1958 and increased rapidly to about 25,000 birds (Russell and Monson 1998).

Taxonomy: The Black Brant is the subspecies of Brant migrating along the Pacific coast and regular in San Diego County. There are seven sight records of the light-bellied Atlantic subspecies *B. b. hrota* (Müller 1776), all summarized previously by Unitt (1984). Because there is no specimen, however, it is possible that some or all of these were of the gray-bellied population breeding in the western Canadian arctic, wintering mainly in Puget Sound, and reported from Baja California (Reed et al. 1998). Delacour and Zimmer (1952) and Buckley and Mitra (2002) suggested that the name *B. b. nigricans* (Lawrence, 1846) applies to these birds and that *B. b. orientalis* Tugarinov, 1941, should be used for the Black Brant.

Tundra Swan *Cygnus columbianus*

California's Central Valley is the southern end of the main winter range of the Tundra or Whistling Swan. Farther south, as in San Diego County, the swan is rare. In the five years of the atlas study only a single individual turned up.

Winter: Most Tundra Swans reported from San Diego County have been on the north county lagoons, such as San Elijo (L7; two records, King et al. 1987) or Buena Vista (H5/H6; three on 5 December 1991, M. Johnson, AB 46:314, 1992), or on inland lakes, such as Hodges (K10; three on 29 November 1981, K. L. Weaver, AB 36:217, 1982) or Lower Otay (U14; four from 3 to 5 January 1991, P. Unitt). But the only report from 1997 to 2002 was of a migrant in flight over south San Diego Bay (U10) 16 February 2002 (D. M. Parker, NAB 56:223, 2002). These examples also include the maximum numbers reported in San Diego County since 1958; most records are of single individuals. Though Tundra Swan records are well scattered over the coastal slope of San Diego County there are none from the Anza–Borrego Desert.

Migration: Most Tundra Swans found in San Diego County have been found in December and January. The extreme dates are 12 November (1926, two at Lake Morena, T21, SDNHM 11307–8) and 18 March (1984, two near Escondido, K. L. Weaver, AB 38:357, 1984).

Conservation: The Tundra Swan was always rare in San Diego County, but its frequency is on the decline. Contributing factors may be climatic warming allowing the winter range to shift north and a decline in the population of western North America as a whole (Serie

Photo by Anthony Mercieca

and Bartonek 1991). The largest number ever reported in San Diego County was "a flock of over 75…a few days" previous to 21 December 1918 at Warner Springs (F19; Stephens 1920a). The numbers in the winter of 1956–57, 15 at Del Mar (M7) and up to 12 at the San Diego River mouth and on Mission Bay (R8/Q8; AFN 11:60, 290, 1957), have not been approached since.

Taxonomy: The Whistling Swan, the North American subspecies *C. c. columbianus* (Ord, 1815), has little or no yellow at the base of the bill. Bewick's Swan, the Eurasian subspecies *C. c. bewickii* Yarrell, 1830, with extensive yellow on the bill, has been noted a few times as a vagrant to northern and central California.

Wood Duck *Aix sponsa*

The Wood Duck is one of America's best-loved waterfowl. The primary expression of this affection is the providing of nest boxes for this species, which originally nested in tree cavities. Such boxes have allowed the Wood Duck's breeding range to spread into southern California. Once only a rare winter visitor to San Diego County, the Wood Duck is now also a local breeding resident, helped in part by releases of captive-reared birds.

Breeding distribution: The primary center for the Wood Duck in San Diego County is Santee Lakes (O12/P12), where counts in summer range as high as 32 on 23 July 1999 (F. Shaw). From there the ducks have spread to borrow pits in the San Diego River between Santee and Lakeside (P13; up to 12, including chicks, on 30 April 1998, W. E. Haas) and Lindo Lake, Lakeside (P14; female with four chicks 9 May 2001, N. Osborn). The Santee Lakes population is presumably the source of Wood Ducks dispersing west to Lake Murray (Q11; up to two on 26 April 2000, M. Billings) and east as far as the upper end of Loveland Reservoir (Q16; three on 13 June 2001, J. K. Wilson). From Santee Lakes Wood Ducks have been seen repeatedly flying northwest, far up West Sycamore Canyon, in the direction of no nearby water (P. Unitt).

The Wood Duck's other San Diego County nesting sites are Cuyamaca Lake (M20; up to 14, including young, on 6 August 1999, A. P. and T. E. Keenan) and Wynola (J19; up to five, including a pair, on 8 May 1999; chick on 19 June 1999, S. E. Smith). At Cuyamaca the birds have raised about 80 chicks since they were introduced in 1994, but by 2003 the population was only about 12 individuals, their nesting success and survival being low through successive years of drought (H. Marx pers. comm.).

Wood Ducks near human habitation elsewhere in late spring and summer may have been domesticated: three in Valley Center (G11) 15 May 1997, one at Ramona (K15) 25 May 1998 (M. and B. McIntosh), and two at Pacific Beach (Q7) 7 May 2000 (L. Polinsky). But individuals at or near the Santa Margarita River mouth (G4/G5) 12 July 1998, 16 July 1999, and 13 May 2000 (P. A. Ginsburg) and along the San Luis River near the Forest Service picnic area (G16) 31 May 1999 (W. E. Haas) and 21 May 2001 seem more likely to have been natural pioneers.

Nesting: Primitively, Wood Ducks nested in cavities in trees over or near water. Nest boxes have been used widely in the effort to increase the species' population, and the species' establishment in San Diego County was dependent on them. Our sightings of chicks suggest the Wood Duck lays

Photo by Anthony Mercieca

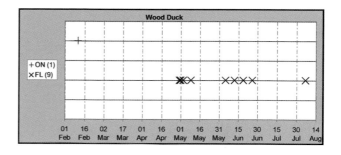

from about 1 April to about 1 June, though the birds have been seen around nest boxes at Santee Lakes as early as 11 February.

Migration: With the Wood Duck's establishment as a breeding bird in San Diego County, its migration schedule here is no longer well defined. But all, or almost all, migrants occur from October through March. The 13 records for the Anza–Borrego Desert range from 16 October (1994, one at Lower Willows, D23, L. Clark et al.) to 21 January (1998, one at Scissors Crossing, J22, E. C. Hall).

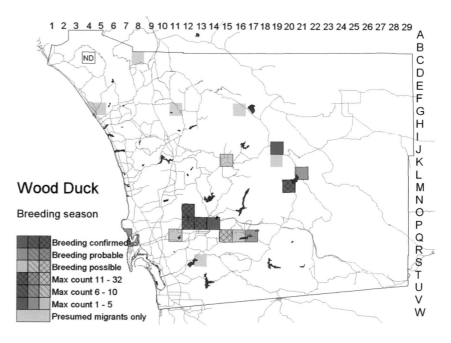

Wood Duck

Breeding season

- Breeding confirmed
- Breeding probable
- Breeding possible
- Max count 11 - 32
- Max count 6 - 10
- Max count 1 - 5
- Presumed migrants only

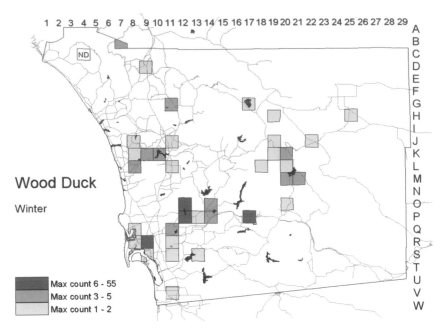

Wood Duck

Winter

■ Max count 6 - 55
▨ Max count 3 - 5
□ Max count 1 - 2

Alpine (P17), 8 February 2000 (M. B. Stowe), and 10 in Mission Valley (R9) 11 January 1999 (J. K. Wilson). The only reports of greater concentrations are from Lake Henshaw Christmas bird counts 23 December 1985 (13) and 19 December 1988 (30).

Except for the two cited under Migration, all records from the Anza–Borrego Desert are from artificial ponds from the Borrego Valley and are of no more than two birds.

Conservation: After being nearly extirpated from California in the early 20th century (Grinnell et al. 1918), the Wood Duck has enjoyed a renaissance throughout its range. A federal ban on hunting Wood Ducks from 1918 to 1941 allowed the recovery to begin, and the provision of nest boxes has contributed since. In San Diego County the species was introduced at Cuyamaca Lake. Six birds raised at Sea World were released in 1994, another six in 1995, and another five in 2002 (H. Marx pers. comm.). At Santee Lakes, on the other hand, there may have been no deliberate introduction. Wood Duck enthusiasts noticed the birds, put up boxes, and the birds colonized, as they have also in the Prado Basin and at Lake Elsinore, Riverside County (J. Brown pers. comm.). At ponds with domestic ducks Wood Ducks often become tame and remain year round, planting a nucleus for a breeding population if nest boxes are provided. If lacking such boxes the birds may prospect for nest sites in unsuitable man-made structures: near Viejas Creek a female Wood Duck came down a chimney (H. Marx pers. comm.).

Winter: The Wood Ducks at Santee Lakes remain year round, in numbers up to 55 on 28 December 1998 (E. Post). Some, at least, remain at Cuyamaca Lake and Wynola through the winter as well. Our high winter counts at those sites were four on 14 December 1999 (A. P. and T. E. Keenan) and two on 27 December 1999 (A. Young), respectively. Most of the Wood Ducks at Cuyamaca, however, move to other sites for the non-breeding season (H. Marx pers. comm.).

Wood Ducks originating farther north are widely but sparsely scattered over San Diego County. The largest flocks noted during the atlas period were five at Ross Lake (B7) 18 February 2002 (K. L. Weaver), five in Escondido Creek near Elfin Forest Lake (K9) 9 January 1999 (L. E. Taylor), 12 in a pond along Viejas Creek,

---

Gadwall *Anas strepera*

Like other puddle ducks, the Gadwall prefers shallow fresh and brackish water. Since the 1960s, it has increased greatly as a wintering bird, becoming abundant in the coastal lagoons, and has colonized as a breeding species. This colonization represents a southward spread of the Gadwall's breeding range, which continued on to northwestern Baja California after covering San Diego County (Erickson et al. 2002).

Breeding distribution: San Diego's Gadwalls are strongly concentrated in the coastal lagoons of the north county. During the breeding season our peak counts in this area, often including young, were 60 at the Santa Margarita River mouth (G4) 26 July 1998 (B. Peterson), 100 in the west basin of Buena Vista Lagoon (H5) 14 July 1998 (C. C. Gorman), 80 in the west half of Batiquitos Lagoon (J6) 15 May 1998 (M. Baumgartel), and 50 at San Elijo Lagoon (L7) 26 June 1999 (J. Ciarletta). In south-coastal San Diego County the Gadwall breeds at least in the

Photo by Anthony Mercieca

Tijuana River estuary (V10/W10; up to 20 on 16 May 1998, B. C. Moore) and the San Diego Bay salt works (U10/V10; seven nests in 1997, M. R. Smith; average of 12 and maximum of 50 individuals in June 1993, Stadtlander and Konecny 1994).

Breeding or summering Gadwalls occur also at many ponds and well-vegetated reservoirs inland, especially in the lower Santa Margarita and San Luis Rey River valleys (up to 20 at O'Neill Lake, E6, 4 July 2000, P. A. Ginsburg; 25 at Whelan Lake, G6, 17 June 1997, D. Rorick). Warner Valley proved to be a minor center for the Gadwall, with the birds using ponds and marshy areas throughout the valley as well as Lake Henshaw (G17), which had up to 13, including young, 17 July 1998 (C. G. Edwards). Gadwalls summer, apparently irregularly, at San Diego County's highest lakes, Cuyamaca (M20; up to two on 26 May 1998, B. C. Moore) and Big Laguna (O23; two on 24 July 1998, E. C. Hall, and 7 July 2001, J. R. Barth). The summer range extends slightly onto the east slope of the mountains in McCain Valley (R26, two on 6 May 2001; S26, two on 9 June 2001, P. Unitt) and at Tule Lake (T27; up to 10 on 6 June 2000, J. K. Wilson).

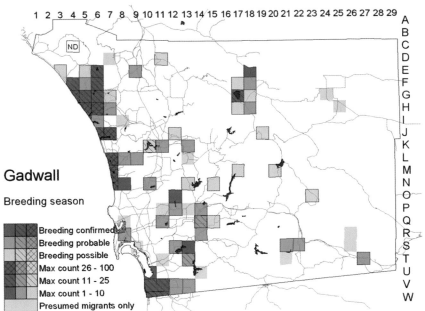

Gadwall

Breeding season

- Breeding confirmed
- Breeding probable
- Breeding possible
- Max count 26 - 100
- Max count 11 - 25
- Max count 1 - 10
- Presumed migrants only

1997), though the species winters there commonly. On the basis of monthly surveys done in the early part of each month, King et al. (1987) found Gadwall numbers at San Elijo Lagoon to be at low summer levels in October but at high winter levels in November. Records for the Anza–Borrego Desert range from 26 October (1988, four at the Borrego Springs sewage pond, H25) to 15 March (1983, one at Lower Willows, D23, A. G. Morley). Spring departure is largely in April: numbers are at high winter levels early in that month but then drop quickly.

Winter: In winter as in the breeding season, the Gadwall is most abundant in northern San Diego County's coastal lagoons. Our counts there ranged up to 450 in the west basin of Buena Vista Lagoon 22 December 2001 (J.

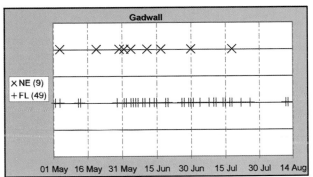

Gadwall

X NE (9)
+ FL (49)

01 May 16 May 31 May 15 Jun 30 Jun 15 Jul 30 Jul 14 Aug

Nesting: Gadwalls nest on the ground, hiding the nest in dense low vegetation near water. In coastal San Diego County stands of pickleweed are the usual nesting habitat. Our dates for nests with eggs ranged from 1 May to 18 July, but we saw chicks as early as 2 May, implying egg laying as early as about 6 April.

Migration: With the Gadwall's increase as a breeding species in San Diego County, its migration schedule is less distinct than formerly. Nevertheless, fall arrival is in late October or November, later than that of other puddle ducks. Quarterly surveys at Batiquitos Lagoon in 1997 found no Gadwalls at Batiquitos Lagoon on 27 and 28 October (Merkel and Associates

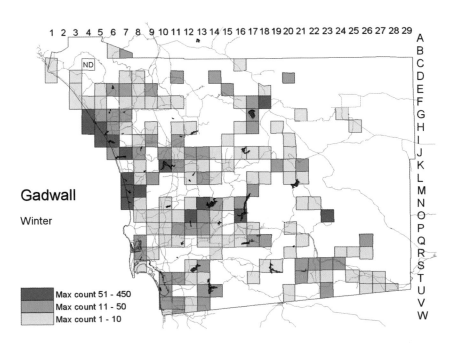

Gadwall

Winter

- Max count 51 - 450
- Max count 11 - 50
- Max count 1 - 10

Determan), 227 at San Elijo Lagoon 26 December 1999 (R. T. Patton), and 138 at the San Dieguito River estuary (M7) 13 February 1999 (D. R. Grine). In the tidal salt water of Mission and San Diego bays the Gadwall is irregular, generally uncommon, and restricted to shallow marshy areas. Inland, it is considerably more widespread and abundant in winter than in summer, with up to 117 in the upper ponds of Santee Lakes (O12) 13 February 1999 (I. S. Quon) and 100 at Swan Lake (F18) 29 December 1997 (G. L. Rogers). We found it wintering repeatedly as high as 5400 feet elevation at Big Laguna Lake (O23; up to 60 on 24 December 2001, P. Unitt). In the Anza–Borrego Desert the few winter records are all from ponds in the Borrego Valley and of no more than four individuals, as at the Roadrunner Club (F24) 15 December 1991 (A. G. Morley).

Conservation: Through the second half of the 20th century, over much of North America, the Gadwall increased and spread (LeSchack et al. 1997). In San Diego County,

the species was just a winter visitor until 1971, when Alice Fries discovered a brood of chicks at Buena Vista Lagoon (AB 25:906, 1971). It spread rapidly over the next two decades, throughout the county's coastal slope. Winter numbers also increased over this period. King et al. (1987) observed an increase at San Elijo Lagoon from 1973 to 1983. From 1961 to 1980 the San Diego Christmas bird count averaged 5.6 Gadwalls and sometimes missed the species. From 1989 to 1996 the average was 221. Similarly, the Oceanside count averaged 56 from 1975 to 1979 but 323 from 1989 to 2002. Though the Gadwall takes advantage of many artificial bodies of water, the change seems less likely due to local habitat changes than to broader forces such as regulation of hunting. The increase could reverse, too: from 1997 to 2002 numbers on the San Diego Christmas bird count were on the decline, averaging 63 during this interval.

Taxonomy: Gadwalls in both North America and Eurasia are nominate *A. s. strepera* Linnaeus, 1758.

Eurasian Wigeon *Anas penelope*

Of the birds with a primarily Eurasian distribution that reach southern California, the Eurasian Wigeon is the most frequent. In San Diego County several are found each winter, always with flocks of American Wigeons.

Winter: The Eurasian Wigeon may turn up wherever the American Wigeon flocks in large numbers. Locations for the species are well scattered over the coastal slope, both along the coast itself and well inland. Usually only a single Eurasian Wigeon is noted among a flock of Americans, but there are many records of two individuals together and a few of three, as in the Tijuana River valley 11 March 1989 (J. O'Brien), at Mesa Grande (H17)

Photo by Kenneth W. Fink

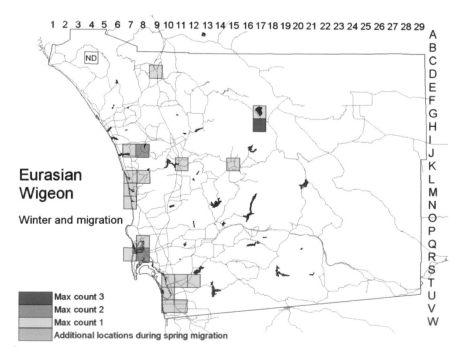

Eurasian
Wigeon

Winter and migration

Max count 3
Max count 2
Max count 1
Additional locations during spring migration

27 December 1999 (K. L. Weaver), and at Lake Henshaw (G17) in 1983, 1985, and 1986 (R. Higson, AB 27:337, 1983).

The Eurasian Wigeon is now an annual visitor to San Diego County. During the five-year atlas period the number found each winter ranged from four in 2001–02 to nine in 1999–2000. It is likely that many of the birds return to the same wintering site year after year. Such returnees presumably accounted for the repeated observations along San Marcos Creek near Rancho Santa Fe Road (J8; up to two 26–28 December 1999, W. E. Haas, E. C. Hall), in the San Diego River flood-control channel (R7/R8; often two individuals), and the Sweetwater River flood-control channel (T10/T11; one on four consecutive San Diego Christmas bird counts).

Migration: November through March is the main season for the Eurasian Wigeon in San Diego County. A somewhat increased frequency of sightings in February and March may reflect spring migration. Extreme dates are 29 September (1985, San Elijo Lagoon, L7, J. L. Coatsworth, AB 40:158, 1986) and 29 April (1996, Batiquitos Lagoon, J7, P. A. Ginsburg, NASFN 50:332, 1996).

Conservation: By the turn of the millennium the Eurasian Wigeon was being found considerably more often than in the 1960s and 1970s. It is unclear whether this apparent change is the result of more observers looking in more places or of the Eurasian Wigeon's sharing in the increase of the American Wigeon.

Taxonomy: The Eurasian Wigeon hybridizes with the American regularly. California may be a likely area for such hybrids to be seen if they result from Eurasian Wigeons straying into the breeding range of the American, crossing with Americans, then migrating south with flocks of Americans along the Pacific coast. Sightings of hybrids in San Diego County are from Lake Henshaw 24 February 1985 (G. McCaskie, AB 39:210, 1985) and south San Diego Bay 10 December 1988 and 5 December 1992 (G. McCaskie, AB 43:365, 1989; 47:300, 1993).

American Wigeon *Anas americana*

Though usually classified in the same genus as the dabbling ducks, the American Wigeon differs somewhat in its behavior. It spends considerable time out of the water grazing on terrestrial vegetation. In San Diego Bay it feeds principally on eelgrass. Because of these habits the wigeon is more widely distributed in San Diego County than related ducks. It is preadapted to that novel habitat now so widespread here—the golf course.

Winter: After the Mallard, the American Wigeon is San Diego County's most widespread duck. It often occurs in numbers in places where other ducks are few or none, especially golf-course ponds (e.g., 60 at the Shadowridge Country Club, Vista, I8, 2 March 2001, C. H. Schork; 420 at Singing Hills, Q14, 5 December 1999, N. Perretta). Nevertheless, coastal wetlands with natural vegetation remain important to the wigeon: our high counts in these habitats ranged up to 387 at San Elijo Lagoon (L7) 26 December 1999 (R. T. Patton), 500 in the San Diego River flood-control channel (R8) 24 December 1997 (P. Unitt), and 500 along the Chula Vista shore of San Diego Bay (U10) 16 December 2000 (B. C. Moore). This last area supports San Diego's most extensive remaining beds of eelgrass.

Some other sites wigeons use heavily are Lake Henshaw (G17; up to 450 on 21 December 1998, J. O. Zimmer), the Wild Animal Park (J12; up to 500 on 30 December 1999, D. and D. Bylin), and Lake Hodges (K10/K11; up to 400 on 11 February 1998, R. L. Barber). Even small lakes in the mountains attract small numbers of wigeons (e.g., 16 in Lower Doane Valley, D14, 7 January 2000, P. D. Jorgensen; up to 40 at Big Laguna Lake, O23, 23 February 2002, K. J. Winter). Because of its use of golf-course ponds, the American Wigeon is the

Photo by Anthony Mercieca

most numerous waterfowl in the Borrego Valley, as judged on the basis of Anza–Borrego Christmas bird counts. The count has yielded as many as 109 on 19 December 1999; the highest number at a single site was 85 at the Roadrunner Club (F24) 30 January 2000 (P. D. Jorgensen).

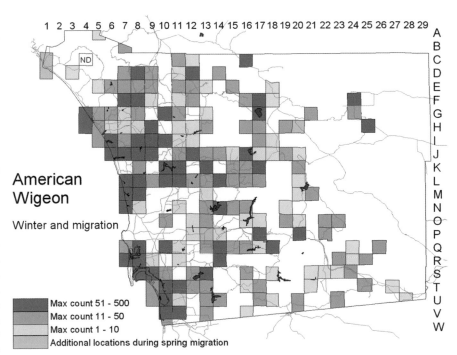

American Wigeon

Winter and migration

Max count 51 - 500
Max count 11 - 50
Max count 1 - 10
Additional locations during spring migration

Migration: The American Wigeon arrives slightly later than most other dabbling ducks that occur in San Diego County as winter visitors. The earliest arrivals are at the end of August, exceptionally 15 August (2003, one at the Sweetwater River mouth, T10, J. R. Barth), but few birds arrive before late September. Maximum numbers are not reached until November. Spring departure may begin in February; it continues through the first half of April, with numbers as high as 200 at the upper end of Sweetwater Reservoir (S13) as late as 10 April (1997; P. Famolaro) and 60 in the San Diego River flood-control channel as late as 15 April (1999; J. R. Barth). Almost all depart soon after this date, but a few migrants may still be seen in the first week of May (13 near Mesa Grande, I17, 5 May 1999, D. C. Seals).

During the atlas period, from mid May through early July, we recorded summering stragglers of the American Wigeon on 10 occasions—an unexpectedly high number for a species not known to nest anywhere in southern California. These records were well scattered from the coast to just over the mountain crest in upper San Felipe Valley (H20; one on 23 May 1999, A. P. and T. E. Keenan). Our largest concentration of summering wigeons was five at Whelan Lake (G6) 19 July 2001 (J. Smith). King et al. (1987) found summering wigeons at San Elijo Lagoon three times 1973–83, maximum 15 on 7 June 1981.

Conservation: Over the long term, it is unclear, from the American Wigeon's point of view, how the gain of lawns and artificial ponds has balanced the loss of natural wetlands. The chemicals used on golf courses may pose a threat to wigeons as well as to other wildlife around them. The organophosphate insecticide Diazinon, used on golf courses, was responsible for at least three mass die-offs of American Wigeons in southern California (Littrell 1986). Sale of this chemical after 2004 has been banned, but other pesticides have been invented to replace it.

Recent trends in American Wigeon numbers on Christmas bird counts have been approximately flat in the Oceanside, Rancho Santa Fe, and Lake Henshaw circles but definitely up in the San Diego, Escondido, and Anza–Borrego circles. In the last two cases, the birds' use of artificial habitats is clearly responsible for the increase. King et al. (1987) observed an increase at San Elijo Lagoon from 1973 to 1983. Improved water quality in San Diego Bay allowed the extent of eelgrass there to increase from at least the mid 1980s to 2000 (M. Perdue pers. comm.). In the latter year the coverage of eelgrass reached 1600 acres, the maximum currently possible. The wigeon's increase on San Diego Bay likely followed the increase in eelgrass.

Mallard *Anas platyrhynchos*

The Mallard is San Diego County's most widespread duck. Over the final third of the 20th century its population exploded, the birds taking advantage of any water from large reservoir to intermittent creek. As a result, the Mallard is now a common, locally abundant, year-round resident. It provides a counter example to the general principle that birds nesting on the ground retreat from urbanization.

Breeding distribution: The Mallard has by far the widest distribution in San Diego County of any breeding duck. Hardly any pond on the coastal slope now lacks the species. The largest numbers are seen where domestic Mallards have been released, as at O'Neill Lake (E6; 200 on 30 July 2001, P. A. Ginsburg), Miramar Lake (N10; 212 on 5 July 1999, A. and G. Kroon), and Sweetwater County Park, Bonita (T12; 300 on 14 June 1999, T. W. Dorman). But there is no longer a clear-cut distinction between domestic and wild Mallards. Many Mallards nesting in urban areas bear no sign of domestication and fly strongly. Every evening, speeding over the traffic clogging Highway 163, flocks commute from Balboa Park to Mission Valley.

A few Mallards nest where the only water available is salt, as at the Chula Vista Wildlife Reserve and salt works in south San Diego Bay (U10/V10), regular sites for the species (Stadtlander and Konecny 1994, M. R. Smith, R. T. Patton). Most Mallards, though, nest around brackish or fresh water. Some are in urban settings where the only possible nest sites are under ornamental shrubbery, such as a cement-lined channel near Goodland Acres Park,

Photo by Anthony Mercieca

Spring Valley (R12; female with chicks 12 July 1998, P. Unitt). Some are along creeks deep in the wilderness, such as San Mateo Canyon (A3; family of five on 18 June 1998, J. M. Wells, J. Turnbull).

The breeding range spills onto the desert slope in San Felipe Valley (H20/I21; young on 27 July 2000, J. O. Zimmer) and in southeastern San Diego County, where the birds range east to Jacumba (U28; up to five on 22 April 1999, F. L. Unmack). Our most interesting Mallard nesting was in the wet spring of 1998, when San Felipe Creek flowed farther than usual, reaching the mouth of Sentenac Canyon (I23). Here P. K. Nelson found a female and five downy ducklings on 26 May. The Mallard has never been confirmed nesting in the Borrego Valley, though such nesting is possible around golf-course or sewage ponds. Occasional birds occur in this area late in the spring, as late as 27 May (2001, four at the Roadrunner Club, F24, M. L. Gabel). Three records from the riparian oasis of Lower Willows along Coyote Creek (D23) include a bird there 4 July 1999 (K. Wilson, B. Getty). Three juveniles at Butterfield Ranch (M23) 22 May 2001 (P. K. Nelson) had likely already dispersed from elsewhere, as this was our only breeding-season record from this site.

Nesting: Mallards nest in a depression on the ground, using surrounding or overhanging vegetation to screen the nest from predators. Nevertheless, predation is frequent. The chicks follow the female to water soon after hatching. Our dates for nests with eggs ranged from 29 March to 7

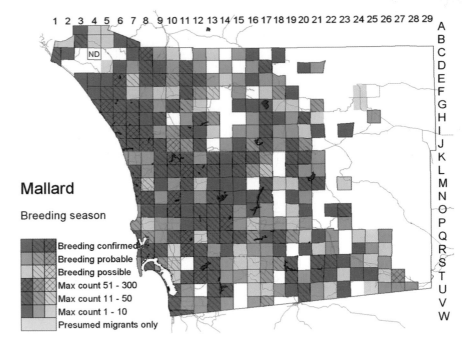

Mallard

Breeding season

- Breeding confirmed
- Breeding probable
- Breeding possible
- Max count 51 - 300
- Max count 11 - 50
- Max count 1 - 10
- Presumed migrants only

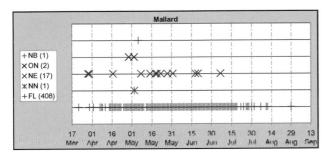

June, but on the basis of several sightings of chicks as early as 30 March, laying as early as the first week of March is not rare. One sighting of chicks as early as 22 March (1997, Lake Murray, Q11, N. Osborn) suggests occasional laying in mid February.

Migration: Though the Mallard is highly migratory over much of its range, it is unclear how much of this migration reaches San Diego County. Just to the east, around the Salton Sea, the Mallard is largely a winter visitor, occurring primarily from September to April (Patten et al. 2003). But in San Diego County Mallard numbers at many localities form no clear seasonal pattern. At some places the species is more numerous in winter, but at others, including those best studied with regular counts—San Elijo Lagoon (King et al. 1987) and the salt works (Stadtlander and Konecny 1994)—it is somewhat more numerous in summer.

Winter: The Mallard's winter distribution in San Diego County is similar to its breeding distribution but slightly less extensive. We recorded the species as at least possibly breeding in 44 squares where we missed it in winter, versus only 15 for the reverse comparison. It is likely that wintering Mallards are drawn to places where domesticated—or self-domesticated—ducks reside. Our highest winter counts were from such sites: the Wild Animal Park (J12; 1000 on 30 December 1999, D. and D. Bylin; 679 on 2 January 1999, K. L. Weaver), Balboa Park (R9; 368 on 15 December 2001, V. P. Johnson), and Bonita (T12; 400 on 18 December 1999, E. Mirsky). The Mallard winters as high in the mountains as Big Laguna Lake (O23; up to 25 on 24 December 2001, P. Unitt) and in the desert at ponds in the Borrego Valley (up to 56 in Borrego Springs, G24,

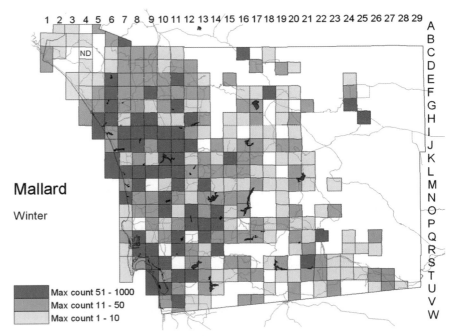

Mallard

Winter

- Max count 51 - 1000
- Max count 11 - 50
- Max count 1 - 10

17 December 2000, S. and J. Berg) and at Butterfield Ranch (up to seven on 18 February 2000, H. H. Williams).

Conservation: Over most of North America, the population of the Mallard was fairly stable through the second half of the 20th century, though there was a spike upward from 1993 to 1999 (Drilling et al. 2002). In San Diego County, by contrast, from the 1960s to the 1990s the Mallard population increased exponentially. From 1960 to 1969 the San Diego Christmas bird count averaged 6.4 Mallards; from 1992 to 2002 this average was over 100 times greater at 732. For the Oceanside count the averages over the same intervals were 13.2 and 800. Over their shorter terms the Rancho Santa Fe and Escondido counts show similar trends.

Nesting in the 19th century, recorded by Cooper (1880), Sharp (1907), and Willett (1933), shows that San Diego County has long been part of the Mallard's breeding range. Stephens (1919a) called the species an "occasional" summer resident; Sams and Stott (1959) said "resident in small numbers." The rapid increase is likely due to a combination of factors: importation of water, creation of ponds, cessation of hunting at many sites, release of domestics, and self-domestication.

Taxonomy: *Anas p. platyrhynchos* Linnaeus, 1758, is the only subspecies of the Mallard in San Diego County, although there are three equivocal records of the Mexican Duck, *A. p. diazi* Ridgway, 1886, from elsewhere in California (Patten et al. 2003).

Blue-winged Teal *Anas discors*

Though the Blue-winged Teal is regular in San Diego County in small numbers, at least from October to April, it is scarce enough that the species can never be expected—except at Famosa Slough and the San Diego River flood-control channel. The Blue-winged is very closely related to the Cinnamon Teal, and in San Diego the Blue-winged is almost always seen in the company of the Cinnamon.

Winter: Because the Blue-winged Teal's spring migration apparently starts in late January, the map shows for wintering only locations where the species was noted 1 December–20 January; later records are mapped as migrants.

The San Diego River flood-control channel and nearby Famosa Slough (R8) are by far the primary spots for wintering Blue-winged Teals in San Diego County. Typical numbers at both places are from five to ten, but up to 60

Photo by Anthony Mercieca

have been noted in the flood-control channel (9 January 2001, R. E. Webster, NAB 55:227, 2001), and up to 20 have been noted at Famosa Slough (1 and 6 January 2000, J. A. Peugh). Occasionally the birds extend to nearby Mission Bay (Q8; six on 16 January 2000, J. C. Worley).

Elsewhere wintering Blue-winged Teals are rather rare; at other sites counts during the atlas period did not exceed four. Their locations include south San Diego Bay, the coastal lagoons, and lakes and ponds scattered through the coastal lowland. Though we did not encounter any wintering at higher elevations from 1997 to 2002, there are two records each of two individuals on Lake Henshaw Christmas bird counts, 23 December 1985 and 31 December 1989. There are also three winter records from the Borrego Valley: one at the Borrego sewage ponds (H25) 18 January 1993 (A. G. Morley), one on the Anza–Borrego

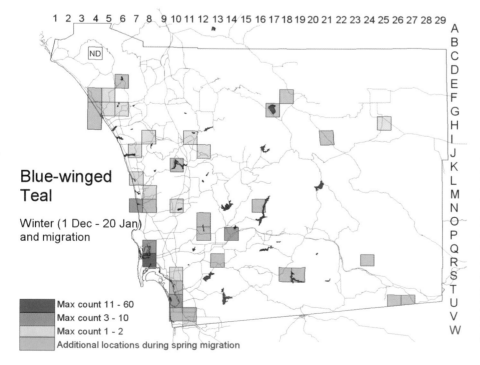

Blue-winged Teal

Winter (1 Dec - 20 Jan) and migration

- Max count 11 - 60
- Max count 3 - 10
- Max count 1 - 2
- Additional locations during spring migration

Christmas bird count 20 December 1987, and two on the count (on ponds at Ram's Hill, H25) 21 December 1997 (R. Halford)

Migration: Spring migration of the Blue-winged Teal follows closely behind that of the Cinnamon Teal. The birds are probably on the move by late January (four at Crestwood Ranch, R24, 22 January 2000, A. P. and T. E. Keenan, J. S. Larson), certainly by early February (14 on Barrett Lake, S18/S19, 5 February 2000, R. and S. L. Breisch). During the atlas period we did not find the Blue-winged Teal noticeably more numerous in spring migration than in winter, but we did find migrants occasionally at ponds isolated in dry regions such as Lake Domingo (U26; two on 9 February 2000, F. L. Unmack) and San Felipe Valley (I21; five on 26 April 1999, J. O. Zimmer). Wintering birds or migrants evidently remain to late April (nine in the San Diego River flood-control channel 27 April 1999, M. B. Stowe).

The Blue-winged Teal's fall migration is poorly known because of the species' close similarity to the Cinnamon Teal when in eclipse plumage. But fall migrants evidently begin returning as early as 23 July (Unitt 1984).

Breeding distribution: The Blue-winged Teal has never been confirmed breeding in San Diego County, though it has been as near as Bolsa Chica, Orange County (Hamilton and Willick 1996). Such breeding is quite possible in San Diego County, however, as the species remains occasionally through the summer. From 1997 to 2001 we noted the Blue-winged Teal seven times from May through early July. All these birds were along or near the coast, except for one at Swan Lake (F18) 24 June 2000 (C. G. Edwards). Only one of these records, however, is of more than one individual (two at Los Peñasquitos Lagoon 2 June 2001, K. Estey).

Conservation: By the end of the 20th century the number of Blue-winged Teals wintering in San Diego County had increased over that in the 1970s. The change equalized the formerly noticeable difference between the species' status in winter and in spring migration.

Taxonomy: The Blue-winged hybridizes occasionally with the Cinnamon Teal, and such hybrids have been noted in San Diego County during spring migration.

Cinnamon Teal *Anas cyanoptera*

Unlike the Mallard and Gadwall, the Cinnamon Teal has enjoyed no great population increase in San Diego County. Instead, the population may be slipping with the loss of the shallow natural wetlands that the teal favors. Deeper reservoirs without a fringe of low wet vegetation are inferior habitat. Currently, the Cinnamon Teal is common as a spring migrant, generally uncommon as a breeding summer resident, and fairly common as a fall migrant and winter visitor.

Breeding distribution: Nesting Cinnamon Teals are widely scattered on the coastal slope of San Diego County and extend east over the divide on the Campo Plateau and possibly in San Felipe Valley. But they are seldom common. During the narrow interval from mid May to early July when migrants are not expected, our high counts were of 16 (including young) at O'Neill Lake (E6) 4 July 2000 (P. A. Ginsburg), 15 (including young) on Sweetwater Reservoir (S12) 8 June 1998 (P. Famolaro), 16 at the upper end of Lake Morena (S22) 2 July 2000, chicks there 31 May 1998 (R. and S. L. Breisch), and 20 at Tule Lake (T27) 21 June 2000 (J. K. Wilson). Other known nesting sites include Lake Henshaw (G17), the Mesa Grande area (I17), Cuyamaca Lake (M20/M21), and Big Laguna Lake (O23), so in San Diego County the Cinnamon Teal is just as likely to nest well inland as in the coastal lagoons and lowland. Even intermittent ponds can support the species: at a pond 2 miles south of Bankhead Springs (U27), empty in dry years, the Cinnamon Teal has nested repeatedly (F. L. Unmack). Nesting is not confirmed in the Borrego Valley but possible. In 1998, at the Borrego sewage ponds (H25), six were in courtship

Photo by Anthony Mercieca

display 5 April 1998 (P. D. Jorgensen) and one remained until 23 May (H. L. Young, M. B. Mosher).

Nesting: Like other dabbling ducks the Cinnamon Teal nests on the ground near water, in and often under dense vegetation. From 1997 to 2001 almost all our confirma-

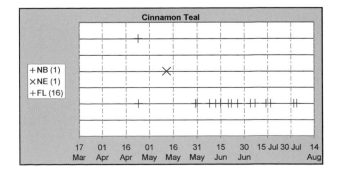

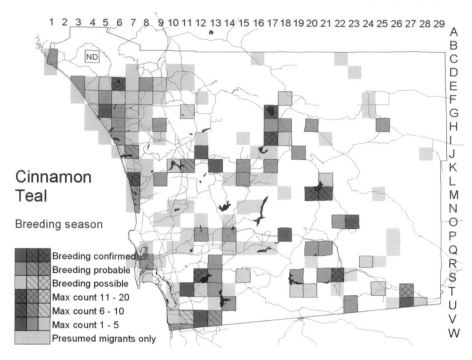

Cinnamon
Teal

Breeding season

Breeding confirmed
Breeding probable
Breeding possible
Max count 11 - 20
Max count 6 - 10
Max count 1 - 5
Presumed migrants only

lower Santa Margarita River (G5) 25 January 1998 (B. C. Moore). During migration, Cinnamon Teals visit salt water, which they avoid at other seasons. Quarterly surveys of south San Diego Bay outside the salt works 1988–89 found the species only in early spring (maximum 22 on 7 February 1989, Macdonald et al. 1990). Weekly surveys within the salt works 1993–94 found it February–April and in September almost exclusively (maximum 27 on 24 February 1993, Stadtlander and Konecny 1994).

In the Anza–Borrego Desert the Cinnamon Teal is noted most often from February to early April, with high counts of 20 at the Borrego Springs sewage ponds 9 February 1993

tions of the species' breeding were sightings of chicks, on dates ranging from 24 April to 3 August. This interval suggests the species lays at least from late March to June. Cooper (1880) collected a female with an egg in her oviduct near San Luis Rey (G6) 22 June 1861, and G. McCaskie found a nest with eggs at Lake Cuyamaca (M20) 25 June 1978.

Migration: In San Diego County the Cinnamon Teal is considerably more widespread and numerous as a migrant than as either a breeding bird or winter visitor. It is also one of the area's earliest migrants. Its numbers increase rapidly in late January, and our highest count during the atlas period was of 300 on ponds near the

(A. G. Morley) and 4 April 1997 (H. L. Young, M. B. Mosher). Eleven in Borrego Springs (G24) 4 May 2000 (P. D. Ache) suggest the teal's spring migration extends into early May. Away from artificial ponds, the birds stop occasionally at natural oases and even in the shade of boulders, far from water, to wait out the day. To their great surprise, atlas observers encountered Cinnamon Teals in rocky waterless desert twice: 15 were in Bow Willow Canyon (P26) 19 February 2001 (A. P. and T. E. Keenan); three were 3.5 miles southwest of Ocotillo Wells (J28) 4 April 2000 (J. R. Barth).

Fall migration extends mainly from mid July (40 at Lake Henshaw 17 July 1998, C. G. Edwards) to October. Four fall records from the Anza–Borrego Desert range from 15 August to 30 September.

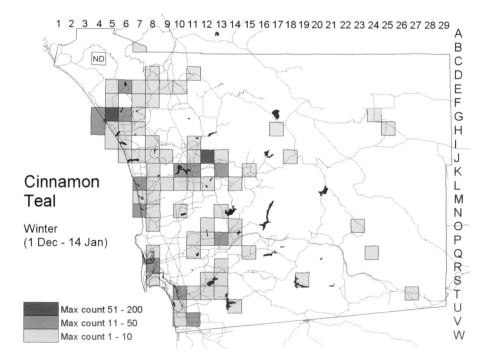

Cinnamon
Teal

Winter
(1 Dec - 14 Jan)

Max count 51 - 200
Max count 11 - 50
Max count 1 - 10

Winter: Because of the species' migration schedule, the map of the Cinnamon Teal's winter distribution shows only records from 1 December to 14 January. The Cinnamon Teal winters mainly in the coastal lowland, on fresh or brackish water. Sites of exceptional concentration are the Wild Animal Park (J12; up to 200 on 30 December 1999, D. and D. Bylin; 72 on 30 December 2000, K. L. Weaver) and sewage ponds near the Santa Margarita River mouth (G5; up to 150 on 8 January 2000, R. E. Fischer). Elsewhere we found fewer than 50 and seldom more than 20. A few appeared in the foothills and mountains, twice even as high as 5400 feet elevation at Big Laguna Lake (O23; one on 6 December 1999, D. S. Cooper; four on 24 December 2001, P. Unitt). Wintering Cinnamon Teals also show up rarely on ponds in the Borrego Valley. The species has been recorded on five of 19 Anza–Borrego Christmas bird counts 1984–2002, with a maximum of six on 22 December 1996.

Conservation: The status of the Cinnamon Teal in San Diego County seems not to have changed greatly through history. Loss of shallow natural wetlands, ideal Cinnamon Teal habitat, may have been offset by the importation of water. Numbers on San Diego Christmas bird counts have gyrated, from a low of two in 1971 to a high of 219 in 1992 and back down to nine in 2000 and 2002. But these changes are likely due to variations in water levels and habitat changes within that circle; other counts in the county have been more stable. Nevertheless, there could be some broader decline: the numbers King et al. (1987) reported as averages at San Elijo Lagoon 1973–83 were seldom equaled anywhere in the county 1997–2002. The 42 young with 5 adult females at the east end of Lake Hodges (K11) 19 June 1982 (K. L. Weaver) were not equaled 1997–2002.

Taxonomy: All Cinnamon Teals in North America are *A. c. septentrionalium* Snyder and Lumsden, 1951. In addition to hybrid Cinnamon × Blue-winged Teals, a hybrid between the Cinnamon Teal and Northern Shoveler was reported from near Imperial Beach 1 March 1984 (E. Copper, AB 38:357, 1984).

Northern Shoveler *Anas clypeata*

The Northern Shoveler is primarily a winter visitor to San Diego County, abundant in shallow water over a muddy bottom. Here the shovelers can use their spatulate bills to filter the water for seeds, snails, and plankton. Small numbers remain through the summer, but the shoveler is known to have nested in San Diego County only once.

Winter: The Northern Shoveler winters widely in San Diego County's coastal wetlands and on its inland lakes. Certain lakes and lagoons, however, are sites of consistently large concentrations. The most important of these are O'Neill Lake (E6; up to 1000, as on 4 December 2000, P. A. Ginsburg), Windmill Lake (G6; up to 763 on 27 December 1997, P. Unitt), Whelan Lake (G6; up to 593 on 21 January 1998, D. Rorick), Lake Hodges (K10/K11; up to 655 on 22 December 2000, R. L. Barber), San Elijo Lagoon (L7; up to 2000 on 20 January 1998, A. Mauro),

Photo by Anthony Mercieca

and Sweetwater Reservoir (S12/S13; up to 800 on 14 January 1999, P. Famolaro).

Though most common on fresh or brackish water, the shoveler also uses tidal mudflats and salt marshes, with up to 330 in south San Diego Bay (U10) 16 December 2000 (G. Moreland). If water is adequate, shovelers exploit seasonal wetlands and intermittently filled lakes such as Big Laguna (O23; 30 on 23 February 2002, K. J. Winter), Corte Madera (Q20/R20; 75 on 20 February 1999, G. L. Rogers), and the upper basin of Lake Morena (S21; 550 on 16 February 1998, S. E. Smith). In the Anza–Borrego Desert the shoveler is a rare visitor reported only from artificial ponds in the Borrego Valley (maximum five in the north Borrego Valley, E24, 5 December 1976, P. D. Jorgensen).

Migration: Northern Shovelers begin arriving in San Diego

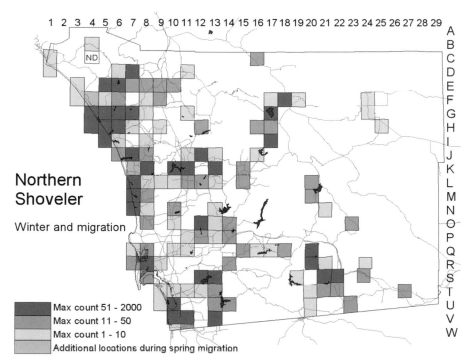

Northern Shoveler

Winter and migration

Max count 51 - 2000
Max count 11 - 50
Max count 1 - 10
Additional locations during spring migration

County in mid August, and their numbers increase through December (Unitt 1984, King et al. 1987). Yet, in weekly surveys of the south San Diego Bay salt works through 1993, Stadtlander and Konecny (1994) did not find shovelers in numbers until November. Spring departure is in March and April. Substantial numbers may remain as late as mid April (84 at Buena Vista Lagoon 13 April 1999, M. Freda), but almost all depart soon after that.

Breeding distribution: From May to July the Northern Shoveler is rare in San Diego County, but from 1997 to 2001 we noted it during these months in 11 areas. Summering birds were most frequent at Whelan Lake and Buena Vista Lagoon (up to seven on 29 May 2001, R. Gransbury). Particularly surprising were three on the Campo Plateau at Tule Lake (T27) 27 June 2001 (J. K. Wilson). Shovelers at Sweetwater Reservoir (S12/S13) 1–3 May 2000 (P. Famolaro) appeared paired, but otherwise we saw no suggestion of the species' breeding in San Diego County. Alice Fries' observation of five ducklings following their mother in the sewage pond at Camp

Margarita (E5) 6 June 1978 is still the county's only confirmation of shovelers nesting.

Conservation: The evidence for trends in shoveler numbers in San Diego County is contradictory. At San Elijo Lagoon, King et al. (1987) found no trend from 1973 to 1983, and the numbers we recorded there 1997–2002 seem consistent with the high levels of that earlier study (winter average 600 birds). The Rancho Santa Fe Christmas bird count, including San Elijo, shows no clear trend in shovelers. On the San Diego count, however, shovelers have increased, from an average of 161 from 1960 to 1985 to an average of 870 from 1997 to 2002. Yet on the Oceanside count the trend looks negative. On that count shovelers went from an average of 3105 from 1975 to 1984 to an average of 758 from 1997 to 2002. Unfortunately, the historical record is too poor to illuminate the species' history further. But, with the development of most of the coastal floodplains and Mission and San Diego bays, many of the shallow and seasonal wetlands ideal for shovelers have been lost.

Northern Pintail *Anas acuta*

The Northern Pintail was once the county's most abundant dabbling duck, but its numbers have dropped behind those of the American Wigeon and Northern Shoveler, while those of the Mallard have surged past it. But the pintail is still a locally common winter visitor to shallow water both inland and along the coast. In late spring and early summer it is uncommon. San Diego represents the southern tip of its breeding range, but it has been confirmed nesting in the county only a few times, none during the five-year atlas period.

Photo by Anthony Mercieca

Winter: Pintails are widespread in San Diego County but concentrate at rather few places. These include some of the north county lagoons, especially Batiquitos (J6/J7; 660 on 6 January 1997, Merkel and Associates 1997; 352 on 2 January 1998, C. C. Gorman). In the southern half of the county the principal sites are northeastern Mission Bay (Q8; up to 165 on 21 December 1998, J. C. Worley), the San Diego River flood-control channel (R8; up to 500 on 24 December 1997, P. Unitt), south San Diego Bay (U10; 467 on 16 December 2000, D. G. Seay; V10; 400 on 18 December 1999, J. L. Coatsworth), and the Tijuana River estuary (V10/W10; 350 on 20 December 1997, S. Walens).

Major inland sites are the Wild Animal Park (J12; up to 582 on 2 January 1999, K. L. Weaver), Lake Hodges (K10/K11; up to 300 on 5 and 11 February 1998, R. L. Barber), Sweetwater Reservoir (S12/S13; up to 150 on 2 January 2002, P. Famolaro), and Sweetwater County Park, Bonita (T11; up to 150 on 19 December 1998, L. D. and R. Johnson). Pintails occur in smaller numbers at other lakes, provided their shores are not so steep as to minimize aquatic vegetation. We found no pintails in reservoirs installed in deep canyons, such as San Vicente

and Loveland. The pintail winters at elevations as high as 5400 feet at Big Laguna Lake (O23; up to 30 on 23 February 2002, K. J. Winter) but is one of the scarcer ducks in the Anza–Borrego Desert. Christmas bird count, state park, and atlas databases contain only 10 records, all of single individuals except for an incongruous flock of 100 flying over the Carrizo Badlands 15 January 1971 (M. C. Jorgensen).

Migration: At north San Diego County's coastal lagoons, pintails arrive in August and depart largely in March (King et al. 1987). In 1978, Batiquitos Lagoon was a major migration stop, with numbers reaching 2000 on 26 August (P. Unitt). In 1993, however, in the south San Diego Bay salt works, Stadtlander and Konecny (1994) found none before October and few before November. Dates for the Anza–Borrego Desert range from 5 August (1973; one at Pena Spring, G23, ABDSP database) to 5 March (1991; one at the Borrego sewage pond, H25, A. G. Morley). On the coastal slope enough pintails summer that the schedule cannot be defined exactly, but atlas data suggest that few wintering birds remain after 1 April.

Breeding distribution: The Northern Pintail summers in San Diego County in small numbers. From 1997 to 2001 we noted it on 21 occasions between 15 April and 10 July. Some of these summering pintails were in coastal lagoons, up to two at San Elijo Lagoon (L7) 3 May 1999 (A. Mauro). On their monthly counts at San Elijo 1973–83, King et al. (1987) had a May–August average of 4.1 pintails. Other summering birds were at inland lakes, up to six in the southeast corner of the Lake Cuyamaca basin (M21) 16 June 1998 (P. D. Jorgensen). Though we saw pairs at Lake Cuyamaca (M20) 8 July 1998 (A. P. and T. E. Keenan), at the northeast corner of Lake Morena (S22) 31 May

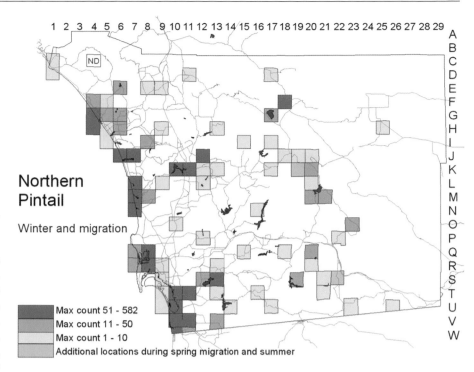

Northern
Pintail

Winter and migration

Max count 51 - 582
Max count 11 - 50
Max count 1 - 10
Additional locations during spring migration and summer

1998 (R. Breisch), and at Sweetwater Reservoir repeatedly (P. Famolaro), during the atlas period we found no nests or chicks. The only published records of actual nesting in San Diego County are from Lake Henshaw (G17; "many hundred" young raised in 1926, fewer in 1927, Abbott 1928a), the Santa Margarita River mouth (G4; broods of chicks 16 June 1973 and 28 June 1974, A. Fries, AB 28:948, 1974), and the south San Diego Bay salt works (nest with eggs 9–29 May 1978, Unitt 1984).

Conservation: From the 1970s to the early 1990s the North American population of the Northern Pintail fell by over 50% (Austin and Miller 1995). There is evidence for change in San Diego County as well. The numbers King et al. (1987) recorded at San Elijo Lagoon from 1973 to 1983 (fall/winter average of 470) were not matched from 1997 to 2002 (maximum count 141 on 26 December

1999, R. T. Patton). The Rancho Santa Fe Christmas bird count, which includes San Elijo Lagoon, averaged 1300 pintails from 1983 to 1988 but 197 from 1997 to 2002. Numbers on the Oceanside count dropped precipitously with the new millennium. They averaged 538 from 1975 to 1993 but only 17 from 2000 to 2002. Some of this change, however, may be due to the birds shifting to a new wintering site. Numbers on the Escondido Christmas bird count have increased almost continuously since that count was established in 1986, as a result of pintails adopting the Wild Animal Park as winter habitat. Although the birds use these artificial ponds, conservation of natural shallow wetlands is as critical to the pintail as to many other water birds. Note the pintail's absence from Agua Hedionda Lagoon (I6), which differs from the north county's other lagoons by having been dredged.

Green-winged Teal *Anas crecca*

California's smallest duck, the Green-winged Teal is a winter visitor to San Diego County. It is less numerous than most other dabbling ducks but still locally common. It shares both coastal wetlands and inland lakes with the other ducks, favoring shallow fresh and brackish water over salt. There are a few records of stragglers remaining through the summer but only one old record of nesting.

Winter: The Green-winged Teal is widely distributed in San Diego County but at most sites the numbers are rather small. Flocks seldom number over 50 individuals. Along the coast, the species' primary sites are the Santa Margarita River estuary (G4; up to 200 on 15 January 2001, P. A. Ginsburg), Batiquitos Lagoon (J7; up to 115

Photo by Anthony Mercieca

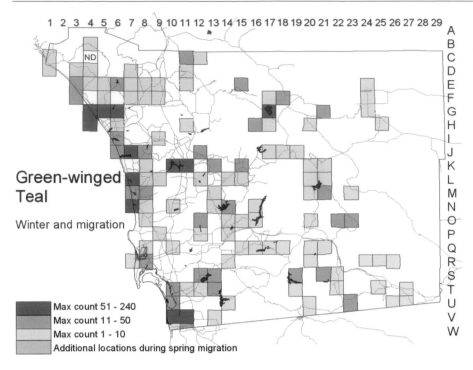

Green-winged Teal

Winter and migration

- Max count 51 - 240
- Max count 11 - 50
- Max count 1 - 10
- Additional locations during spring migration

on 6 February 1998, C. C. Gorman), San Elijo Lagoon (L7; up to 170 on 26 December 1999, R. T. Patton), and Los Peñasquitos Lagoon (N7; up to 102 on 3 February 2002, S. E. Smith). Important freshwater sites in the coastal lowland are Lake Hodges (K10/K11; up to 240 on 26 December 1999, E. C. Hall) and the pond along Dairy Mart Road in the Tijuana River valley (V11; up to 150 on 20 December 1997, G. McCaskie).

Farther inland the Green-winged Teal is irregular, as attested by its great variation on Escondido and Lake Henshaw Christmas bird counts. During the atlas period our highest numbers in the foothills and mountains were 110 at Lake Henshaw (G17) 29 December 1997 (J. O. Zimmer), 50 in the southeast corner of the Lake Cuyamaca basin (M21) 11 February 1998 (P. D. Jorgensen), and 40 at Barrett Lake (S19) 29 December 2000 (R. and S. L. Breisch).

In the Anza–Borrego Desert the Green-winged Teal is rare but more frequent than the Gadwall, Northern Shoveler, or Cinnamon Teal. Most records are from ponds in the Borrego Valley, with up to 10 at the Roadrunner Club (F24) 28 February 1999 (P. D. Jorgensen) and 12 at the Borrego sewage ponds (H25) 9 February 1993 (A. G. Morley).

At any one site in San Diego County the numbers of Green-winged Teals wintering vary much from year to year. But comparison of the results of San Diego County's Christmas bird counts suggests little if any correlation among the counts.

Migration: The Green-winged Teal begins arriving in mid August but does not reach full abundance until December (Unitt 1984, King et al. 1987). Sightings at desert oases in the latter half of February show that spring migration begins by then (25 at Lower Willows, D23, 18 February 1982, P. D. Jorgensen; one at Butterfield Ranch,

M23, 26 February 2000, E. C. Hall; one along Vallecito Creek between Mason and Vallecito valleys, M24, 27 February 1988, Massey and Evans 1994). Most Green-winged Teals depart in March and early April. From 1973 to 1983 King et al. (1987) found the species regularly into early May, but from 1997 to 2002 our only sighting later than 16 April was of one at Los Peñasquitos Lagoon 3 May 1998 (D. K. Adams, K. Estey).

Breeding distribution: King et al. (1987) noted the Green-winged Teal at San Elijo Lagoon on four occasions in June or July 1973–83, with a maximum of five individuals on 3 July 1983. During the atlas period we found no summering individuals. J. B. Dixon's report of a "nest containing 11 pipped eggs" in the San Luis Rey River valley 18 May 1931 (Willett 1933) is still the only record of the Green-winged Teal nesting in California south of Kern County.

Conservation: Christmas bird count results suggest that in San Diego County the Green-winged Teal could be going into decline. From 1975 to 1984 the species' average on the Oceanside count was 427, but from 1997 to 2002 it was 137. The Rancho Santa Fe count averaged 502 from 1981 to 1990 but 253 from 1997 to 2002. King et al. (1987) recorded a winter average of 220 on their monthly surveys of San Elijo Lagoon 1973–83, but our maximum count there during the atlas period was only 170. Over the species' range as a whole, however, the Green-winged Teal increased through the second half of the 20th century (Johnson 1995).

Taxonomy: *Anas c. carolinensis* Gmelin, 1789, is the subspecies of the Green-winged Teal resident in North America. The nominate subspecies of the Old World, *A. c. crecca* Linnaeus, 1758, also reaches California as a rare visitor, being more frequent farther north. There are nine records from San Diego County, from Bonita (T11; 29 January–24 February 1962, AFN 16:364, 1962), San Elijo Lagoon (18–24 March 1973, AB 27:662, 1973), Batiquitos Lagoon (12 December 1973, AB 28:692, 1974), Lake Cuyamaca (M20; 11 March 1979 and 16 March 1980, AB 33:312, 1979 and 34:306, 1980), Lake Henshaw (5–12 February 1982, R. Higson, AB 36:330, 1982), and the San Diego River mouth (4 February–12 March 1989, G. McCaskie, AB 43:365, 1989; 17–19 February 1990, J. O'Brien, AB 44:328, 1990; 13 January–5 March 2001, P. E. Lehman, NAB 55:227, 2001). Also, an apparent hybrid *crecca* × *carolinensis* was at Bonita 4 January–1 February 1963 (AFN 17:358, 1963); it showed both the vertical white stripe of *carolinensis* and the horizontal white stripe of *crecca*.

Canvasback *Aythya valisineria*

Unlike many wintering ducks, which return to the same sites year after year, the Canvasback is rather irregular. Almost everywhere it occurs it is usually uncommon, yet large flocks appear from time to time on some lakes and lagoons. Though the brackish lagoons of northern San Diego County are some of the Canvasback's most consistent sites, the species is rare on the salt water of San Diego and Mission bays.

Photo by Anthony Mercieca

Winter: From 1997 to 2002 O'Neill Lake, Camp Pendleton (E6), was by far the principal site for the Canvasback in San Diego County. Counts there exceeded 150 every year of the atlas period and reached a maximum of 600 on 4 December 1999 (P. A. Ginsburg). The next most important site was Buena Vista Lagoon, where counts were at least 20 in the west basin (H5) in all five years and reached a maximum of 232 on 27 December 1997 (D. Rorick). Large numbers were fairly frequent at the Santa Margarita River mouth (G4; up to 250 on 8 February 2000, P. A. Ginsburg) and in the east basin of Batiquitos Lagoon (J7; up to 120 on 26 February and 18 December 1999, M. Baumgartel). The Canvasback is often found on lakes elsewhere in northwestern San Diego County, making this region the nucleus of the species' distribution in the county.

Elsewhere the Canvasback is more scattered and less consistent. Lake Cuyamaca (M20) is one of the more regular sites, with up to 50 on 14 December 1999 (A. P. and T. E. Keenan). We also found the Canvasback repeatedly in southeastern San Diego County with up to 42 at Corte Madera Lake (Q20) 21 February 1999 (W. E. Haas), 76 in Round Potrero (T20) 23 December 1999 (L. J. Hargrove), and 40 at Tule Lake (T27) 5 January 2000 (F. L. Unmack). With the installation of ponds in the Borrego Valley the

Canvasback has become a rare visitor in that area, with up to three individuals on golf courses in Borrego Springs (G24) 21 February 1999 (P. D. Ache) and 17 December 2000–21 January 2001 (S. and J. Berg).

Atlas participants saw one or two Canvasbacks on Mission Bay only twice and did not find any on San Diego Bay. Various intensive surveys of San Diego Bay 1988–95 yielded only a single sighting, of three in the bay's southeast corner (U10) 26 November 1988 (Macdonald et al. 1990).

Migration: The Canvasback begins arriving in San Diego County in early November (Unitt 1984); arrival in October could be expected because the species has been found as early as 7 October at the Salton Sea (Patten et al. 2003). Spring departure is in March and early April. A count as high as 100 at O'Neill Lake 26 March 2001 (P. A. Ginsburg) was exceptionally late. Our latest spring migrant was one at Round Potrero 16 April 2000 (P. Unitt).

Summer stragglers have been recorded at Carlsbad 14 June 1982 (T. A. Meixner, AB 36:1015, 1982), Batiquitos Lagoon 29 July 1989 (J. Oldenettel, AB 43:1367, 1989), and Lake Cuyamaca (16 May 1964, G. McCaskie; 8 June 2000, J. D. Barr; 24 August 2002, J. R. Barth, P. Unitt).

Conservation: The Canvasback's population rangewide, monitored closely because of the species' popularity with duck hunters, has fluctuated considerably. It decreased from 1982 to 1995 but then rebounded (Mowbray 2002). The Canvasback's decline at the Salton Sea has not been reversed (Patten et al. 2003). Any trend in San Diego County is obscured by the species' irregularity.

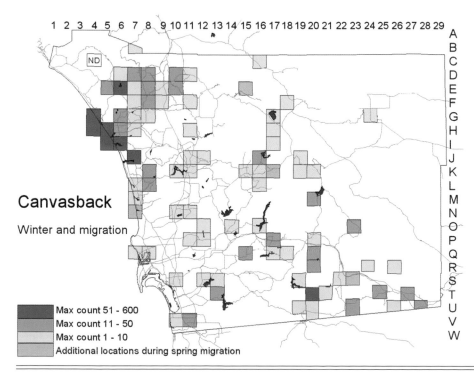

Canvasback

Winter and migration

- Max count 51 - 600
- Max count 11 - 50
- Max count 1 - 10
- Additional locations during spring migration

Redhead *Aythya americana*

Hundreds of Redheads winter in Mission Bay. Flocks appear occasionally on lakes and lagoons elsewhere, but nowhere away from Mission Bay is the species consistently common. Though a diving duck, the Redhead prefers rather shallow water. It is mainly a winter visitor but also breeds in small numbers along the county's north coast. San Diego County represents the southern tip of the species' breeding range along the Pacific coast of North America.

Photo by Anthony Mercieca

Breeding distribution: From 1997 to 2001 the only sites where we confirmed Redheads nesting were sewage ponds along the Santa Margarita River between Pueblitos Canyon and Rifle Range Road (F5; 19, including chicks, 28 June 2000, R. E. Fischer, J. Morlan) and at Stuart Mesa Road (G5; 24, including chicks, 20 June 1999, R. E. Fischer). Other sites where the species is known to have bred are Whelan Lake (G6; chicks photographed 18 May 2003, J. C. Daynes), "San Luis Rey Valley" (eggs collected 11 May 1933, Willett 1933), Guajome Lake (G7; eggs collected 11 May 1936, WFVZ 2564), Santa Margarita River estuary (G4), Buena Vista Lagoon (H5/H6), Batiquitos Lagoon (J6/J7), San Elijo Lagoon (L7), and Los Peñasquitos Lagoon (N7; Unitt 1984). During the atlas period we saw Redheads, often in pairs, through the breeding season at all these sites except Los Peñasquitos. O'Neill Lake (E6; up to six on 2 July 1999, P. A. Ginsburg) and the mouths of Las Flores (E3; up to four on 17 May 1998, R. and S. L. Breisch) and Aliso (F4; pair on 1 July 2001, B. C. Moore) creeks are new sites of possible breeding. Numbers at all sites of possible breeding were usually five or fewer. The records with chicks excluded, our highest counts during the breeding season were of 15 in the east basin of Buena Vista Lagoon 16

May 1999 (L. E. Taylor) and 20 in the San Dieguito River estuary (M7) 10 July 1999 (D. R. Grine). The Redhead appears to be irregular at many of these sites.

A few late spring records elsewhere suggest the Redhead could nest occasionally in other parts of San Diego County. Two were at Turner Lake, Valley Center (G11), 15 May 1997 (L. Seneca), one was at Wynola (J19) 12 March–19 July 1999 (S. E. Smith), one was at Sweetwater Reservoir (S12) 4 May 1998 (P. Famolaro), and three were at Tule Lake (T27) 6 June 2001 (J. K. Wilson).

Nesting: Redhead nests are usually within dense marshes, often over water. Besides the two egg sets collected on 11 May, evidence for the Redhead's nesting schedule in San Diego County comes from sightings of chicks, which range from 24 May to 27 August (A. Fries in Unitt 1984).

Migration: In fall, Redheads return in numbers by late October (68 at Batiquitos Lagoon 27 October 1997, Merkel and Associates 1997). In spring, they depart in March and early April. Forty were still in the San Diego River flood-control channel (R8) 15 April 1999 (J. R. Barth). Sixteen in northwest Mission Bay (Q7) 21 April 2000 (L. Polinsky) and three at Miramar Lake (N10) 26 April 1998 (P. Unitt) were late stragglers. Ten records from the Borrego Valley range from 11 November (1990, two at the Roadrunner Club, F24, E. H. Monsees) to 28 March (1999, one at Borrego Springs, G24, P. D. Ache).

Winter: Currently, Mission Bay is the center for wintering Redheads in San Diego County. Often the birds congregate in

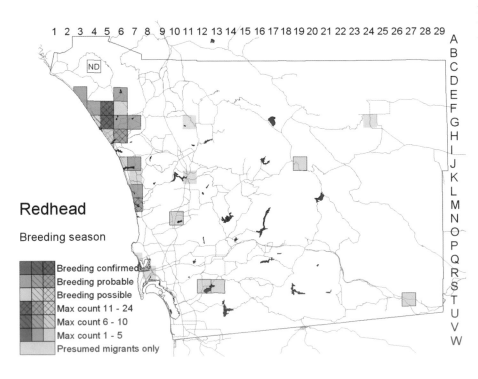

Redhead

Breeding season

- Breeding confirmed
- Breeding probable
- Breeding possible
- Max count 11 - 24
- Max count 6 - 10
- Max count 1 - 5
- Presumed migrants only

the low hundreds in the southeast corner of the bay at the mouth of Tecolote Creek (R8). But they move around. Our highest count, of 1915 on 7 December 1998, was in the northeast quadrant of the bay (Q8; J. C. Worley). Sometimes the birds move across Sea World Drive to the San Diego River flood-control channel (up to 450 on 9 December 2000, P. A. Ginsburg).

At other places numbers of wintering Redheads vary wildly. Buena Vista and Batiquitos lagoons are among the more regular sites, and numbers there are sometimes large, with up to 722 at Batiquitos 7 January 1997 (Merkel and Associates 1997). But numbers on Oceanside Christmas bird counts, which

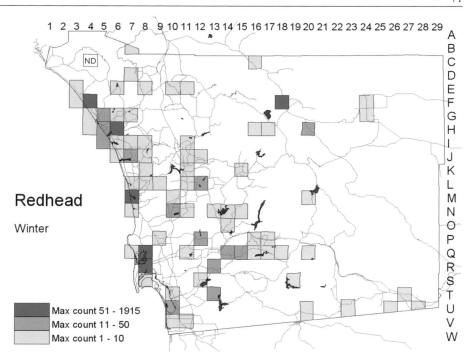

Redhead

Winter

██	Max count 51 - 1915
▓▓	Max count 11 - 50
░░	Max count 1 - 10

include both these lagoons, have varied from a high of 442 in 1996 to a low of two in 1979. Similarly, numbers on the Rancho Santa Fe count, which encompasses San Elijo, San Dieguito, and Los Peñasquitos lagoons, have varied from 97 in 1987 down to one in 1980 and 2001.

Farther inland the Redhead is even more sporadic. Miramar Lake (N10) was the only inland site where we found the species regularly (up to 25 on 1 February 2000, G. Grantham). Since the inception of the Lake Henshaw Christmas bird count in 1981, the Redhead has been recorded on fewer than 50% of the counts. Yet our largest inland flock during the atlas period, 100 at Swan Lake

(F18) 21 December 1998 (G. L. Rogers), gave this count its only total greater than ten.

Conservation: The sharp fluctuations from year to year in numbers of Redheads on San Diego County Christmas bird counts are not coordinated among the counts. The variations could thus be due as much to flocks shifting from site to site within the county as to annual variation in the numbers migrating into the county from the north. The breeding population has remained at a low level for decades without conspicuous change.

Ring-necked Duck *Aythya collaris*

The Ring-necked Duck differs from other diving ducks in its preference for small ponds and avoidance of coastal bays and lagoons. It is a common winter visitor at some inland lakes and ponds but rare or absent at others. A few individuals remain into the summer each year, but the species has never been found nesting in southern California.

Winter: Because the Ring-necked Duck uses both small ponds and larger lakes, it is more widespread than most diving ducks. Sometimes it is common on large lakes such as Cuyamaca (M20; 120 on 22 February 1999, A. P. and T. E. Keenan), Loveland (Q16; 70 on 31 January 2001, J. K. Wilson), and Sweetwater (S12; 60 on 16 December 2000, P. Famolaro). But numbers can be just as large on small ponds such as one at the mouth of Beeler Canyon, Poway (N11; 100 on 17 December 1999, K. J. Winter) and another in Rancho Santa Fe (L8; 1000 on 22 December 2000, A. Mauro). Ornamental ponds in cemeteries are often good Ring-necked Duck sites: Greenwood Cemetery (S10) is the most consistent site for the species within the San Diego Christmas bird count circle. From 1997 to 2002 the

Photo by Anthony Mercieca

largest flocks were at O'Neill Lake (E6), where numbers are usually 10–50 but were 150 on 18 February 1998 (P. A. Ginsburg), and the Wild Animal Park (J12), where numbers are usually 75–130 but were 400 on 30 December 1999 (D. and D. Bylin).

Besides the Ruddy Duck, the Ring-necked is the most frequent diving duck at artificial ponds in the Borrego Valley. It has been recorded on 11 of 19 Anza–Borrego

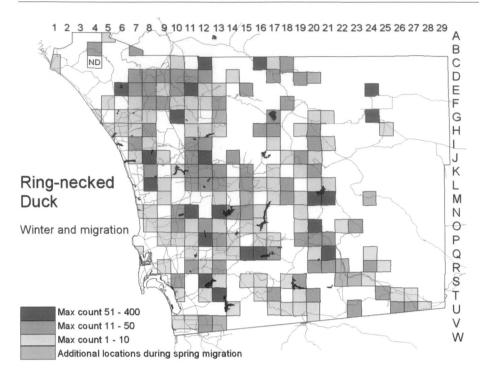

Ring-necked
Duck

Winter and migration

Max count 51 - 400
Max count 11 - 50
Max count 1 - 10
Additional locations during spring migration

only two records from the salt works, with a maximum of six birds 5 January 1994. King et al. (1987) reported only one record from San Elijo Lagoon (L7) with none on 10 years of monthly surveys 1973–83.

Migration: In fall the Ring-necked Duck arrives rarely as early as late September but does not become common until November. In spring it remains common through March and departs largely in April. Small numbers persist through May. The end of spring migration is indistinct because of the regularity of summering individuals. We found at least one Ring-necked Duck from June to August in each of the five years of the atlas period; 1999 and 2000 each yielded five. Our maximum count of summering birds at one site was four at Pine Hills (K19) 10 June 2000 (L. J. Hargrove).

Christmas bird counts 1984–2002. High numbers for the desert are 60 in the north Borrego Valley (E24) 17 December 2000 (P. R. Pryde) and 52 at Club Circle (G24) 16 December 2001 (D. Waber).

Along the coast the Ring-necked Duck is rare. From 1997 to 2002 we found it only eight times in coastal wetlands, with maxima of five in the Santa Margarita River estuary (G4) 22 January 1999 (P. A. Ginsburg) and four in the northwest corner of Mission Bay (Q7) 21 January 2001 (L. and M. Polinsky). Various systematic surveys of San Diego Bay (Macdonald et al. 1990, Manning 1995, Mock et al. 1994, Stadtlander and Konecny 1994) yielded

Conservation: Christmas bird counts show no clear trend in Ring-necked Duck numbers in San Diego County. But it seems likely that the species is now more numerous and widespread than before so many reservoirs were built and so much water was imported. Stephens (1919a) called the Ring-necked Duck only an "occasional winter visitant," suggesting numbers lower than today's. The species may be on the increase range wide, and its breeding distribution is spreading (Hohmann and Eberhardt 1998).

Tufted Duck *Aythya fuligula*

An Old World relative of the Ring-necked Ducks and scaups, the Tufted Duck is a rare annual winter visitor to the Pacific coast of North America. Few of these birds make it as far south as southern California. In San Diego County there are only three records of the Tufted Duck, the southernmost in the New World, plus three of hybrids with scaups.

Winter: San Diego County's pure Tufted Ducks were a female in south San Diego Bay (V10) 18 February 1985 (R. E. Webster, Roberson 1993), a male at Miramar Lake (N10) 13 January–9 February 1992 (P. A. Ginsburg, Patten et al. 1995b), and a male at Famosa Slough (R8) 5 February–1 March 1998 (B. R. Zimmer, FN 52:256, 1998).

Apparent hybrid Tufted Ducks × scaups were at San Elijo Lagoon (L7) 20 February–22 March 1987 (S. Ranney-Gallagher, King et al. 1987) and 18–24 February 1996 (E. L. Mills, NASFN 50:222, 1996) and at the San Luis Rey River mouth (H5) 16–29 February 1992 (T. Clawson, Patten et al. 1995b).

Photo by Anthony Mercieca

Taxonomy: The frequency of Tufted Duck × scaup hybrids suggests that some Tufted Ducks straying across the Bering Sea to Alaska mate with their closest available relatives, in lack of mates of their own kind.

Greater Scaup *Aythya marila*

In San Diego County, near the southern tip of its winter range, the Greater Scaup is uncommon to rare. It is found with Lesser Scaups and easily overlooked among the large flocks of the more common species. The two scaups' close similarity has led to their numbers being pooled in many studies and has left the Greater's exact status in San Diego County poorly known.

Winter: The Greater Scaup occurs in San Diego County primarily in south San Diego Bay, where it mingles with the large flocks of the Lesser Scaup. Rarely are more than three or four individuals identified, but 35 were along the Silver Strand between Crown Cove and Coronado Cays (T9) 6 December 1988 (Macdonald et al. 1990), and 53 were in south San Diego Bay (U10) 3 March 1993 (Stadtlander and Konecny 1994). The Greater occurs at least irregularly on Mission Bay (up to 10 near Crown Point, Q8, 10 December 2000, E. Wallace) and in the San Diego River flood-control channel (R8; up to five on 12 February 2002, M. B. Mulrooney).

Elsewhere along the county's coast the Greater Scaup is even scarcer. It has been reported on 8 of 22 Rancho Santa Fe Christmas bird counts 1980–2003 with a maximum of 35 on 18 December 1988. It has been reported on only 2 of 28 Oceanside Christmas bird counts 1976–2002, with a maximum of two on 28 December 1980. On fresh water wintering Greater Scaups have been reported only from the lower Otay River just east of San Diego Bay (V10), with one on 17 December 1977 (G. McCaskie), and Santee Lakes (P12), with two from 10 January to 2 February 1978 (J. L. Dunn) and one each

Photo by Anthony Mercieca

on 20 January 1998 (E. Post) and 4 February 2002 (J. C. Worley).

The skeleton I previously reported (Unitt 1984) as a Greater Scaup was actually a mislabeled Lesser Scaup, but J. R. Barth found a recently dead Greater Scaup at the Chula Vista Wildlife Reserve, south San Diego Bay (U10), 13 April 2003 (SDNHM 50696).

Migration: The Greater Scaup's typical season in San Diego County extends from 5 November (1977, one at Border Field State Park, W10, L. Bevier) to 21 March (1977, three on San Diego Bay, E. Copper). In 1978, a year of apparently exceptional abundance, the species remained as late as 19 May (four at the San Diego River mouth, AB 32:1054, 1978). Two Greater Scaups were on south San Diego Bay 30 May 1963 (AFN 17:434, 1963) and one was there 15 September 2000 (G. C. Hazard). Late stragglers are probably unhealthy; the one picked up 13 April 2003 had failed to molt properly.

One at Lake Henshaw (G17) 2 March 1985 was presumably a spring migrant crossing from the Gulf of California to the Pacific coast (R. Higson, AB 39:349, 1985).

Conservation: There is no evidence for historical change in the Greater Scaup's status in San Diego County. Though the numbers reaching San Diego may vary from year to year, the species has never been common.

Taxonomy: Banks (1986b) ascertained that *A. m. nearctica* Stejneger, 1885, is the proper name for the North American subspecies of the Greater Scaup.

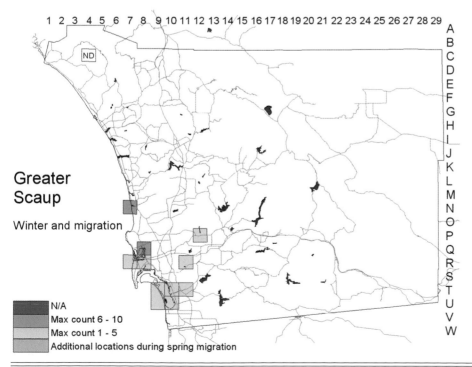

Greater Scaup

Winter and migration

N/A
Max count 6 - 10
Max count 1 - 5
Additional locations during spring migration

Lesser Scaup *Aythya affinis*

San Diego Bay is a major wintering site for the Lesser Scaup: about 3000–5000 converge there each year, the largest concentration in all of southern California. On south San Diego Bay, the scaup is second only to the Surf Scoter as the most abundant bird. Mission Bay has become important too, with about 1000 wintering scaups. Other coastal wetlands have relatively few, but some inland lakes host flocks of dozens. An occasional Lesser Scaup straggles through the summer, but the species is not known to nest south of San Francisco Bay.

Photo by Anthony Mercieca

Winter: Regular thorough surveys of San Diego Bay 1988–89 (Macdonald et al. 1990) and 1993–94 (Manning 1995, Mock et al. 1994, Stadtlander and Konecny 1994) are the soundest basis for estimating the Lesser Scaup's numbers. Macdonald et al. (1990) and Manning (1995) both found about 2000 in south San Diego Bay outside the salt works. Within and near the salt works, Stadtlander and Konecny (1994) found a maximum of 4409 in February 1993. Preston and Mock (1995) found up to 867 in central San Diego Bay 25 January 1994, and Mock et al. (1994) found up to 301 in the north bay (northwest of the bridge) 12 January 1993. From 1997 to 2001 our less systematic counts ranged up to 3100 on south San Diego Bay (U10) 18 December 1999 (J. L. Coatsworth), suggesting that similar numbers continue, at least in some years.

In Mission Bay our counts ranged up to 1170 in the northeast quadrant of the bay (Q8) 26 January 1999, 1016 there 16 January 2000 (J. C. Worley), and 300 in the southeast corner 24 December 1997 (P. Unitt).

Along the coast away from San Diego and Mission bays the Lesser Scaup is widespread but far less abundant. At the other coastal wetlands the scaup's greatest concentrations are at the Santa Margarita River mouth (G4; up to 150 on 8 February 2000, P. A. Ginsburg), San Elijo Lagoon (L7; during the atlas period, up to 50 on 14 January 2000, A. Mauro), and the San Dieguito River mouth (M7; up to 150 on 26 December 1999, M. Baumgartel).

Inland, the Lesser Scaup occurs in small numbers on most lakes, in large numbers on a few. For no clear reason, particularly large numbers of scaup frequent Dixon Lake (I11; up to 190 on 3 January 1998, J. Russell), Lake Ramona (L12; up to 88 on 25 January 1998, M. and B. McIntosh), Lake Miramar (N10; up to 200 on 3 January 1998, P. Unitt), and Santee Lakes (P12; up to 56 on 5 December 1997, E. Post).

The Lesser Scaup is a rare visitor to the Borrego Valley, recorded on 6 of 19 Anza–Borrego Christmas bird counts 1984–2002. All records for this area are of three or fewer, except for 13 at Ram's Hill (H25) 20 December 1998 (R. Halford).

Migration: In some years Lesser Scaups begin arriving in early October (Unitt 1984, King et al. 1987), but surveys of San Diego Bay suggest that in others they do not arrive until mid November. Their abundance peaks in January and February. Most Lesser Scaups depart in mid March, but some remain to mid April (20 in the San Diego River flood-control channel, R8, 15 April 1999, J. R. Barth) and a few to mid or late May (three at Buena Vista Lagoon, H5, 11 May 1999, M. Freda; four at Dixon Lake 17 May 1999, A. G. and D. Stanton; one

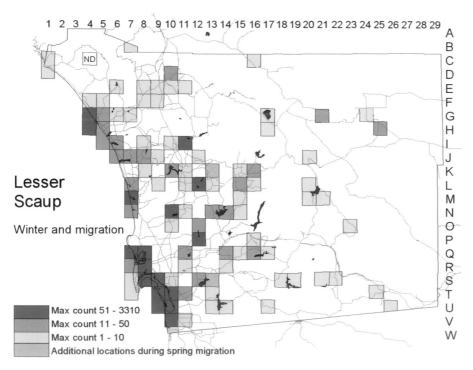

**Lesser
Scaup**

Winter and migration

■ Max count 51 - 3310
▨ Max count 11 - 50
□ Max count 1 - 10
▨ Additional locations during spring migration

west of Ramona, K13, 26 May 2000, P. M. von Hendy).

Birds grounded at Vallecito (M25) in early April 1966 and at Angelina Spring (I22) 3 April 1966 (Banks 1967) suggest that the Lesser Scaup, like the Brant and Surf Scoter, uses eastern San Diego County as an overland migration corridor. But no parallel occurrences have come to light since.

A few Lesser Scaups fail to migrate and remain to summer both along the coast and inland. From 1997 to 2001 we noted three such stragglers, at Lake Cuyamaca (M20) 20 June–8 July 1998 (A. P. and T. E. Keenan), at Barrett Lake (S18) 22 June 1997 (J. Hannan), and on south San Diego Bay 11 August 2000 (G. Grantham).

Conservation: The number of the Lesser Scaup on San Diego Bay, though difficult to monitor, is one of the primary gauges of the bay's biological viability. Because intensive surveys have followed the same procedure for only a single year, the San Diego Christmas bird count is the only basis for assessing long-term changes. This count is inconsistent because of variation in coverage, the variable availability of a boat, and, possibly, temporal variation in the birds' arrival. The scaup's abundance does not reach its peak until January, though the count has long been scheduled for the third Saturday of December. Numbers have been higher in some past years, up to about 11,800 on 3 January 1965 and 15 December 1979. They have not exceeded 4000 since 1984. So a decline seems likely, but better monitoring is called for. Just a single-day survey by boat about 1 February would be adequate, if coordinated with coverage of the salt works.

Factors that could affect the scaup include water pollution, chemical contamination of its foods, disturbance by boats, and bayshore development. Among 14 species of water birds studied in San Diego Bay, the scaup avoids developed shorelines the most strongly (J. A. Manning).

King Eider *Somateria spectabilis*

Eiders are birds of the far north, rarely reaching even northern California as winter vagrants. The single record of the King Eider for San Diego County is the species' southernmost along the Pacific coast of North America.

Winter: San Diego County's King Eider was an adult male, found at the Imperial Beach pier (V10) 4 December 1982. It later moved up the Silver Strand to Glorietta Bay (T9), where it remained to 25 January 1983 (M. B. Stowe, Morlan 1985). Seven King Eiders, more than in any year before or since, reached southern California during the winter of 1982–83, a year of El Niño.

Photo by Mary Beth Stowe

Harlequin Duck *Histrionicus histrionicus*

More typical of rocky coasts farther north, the Harlequin Duck is only a casual visitor to San Diego County. Here, in atypical habitats at the southern extreme of its winter range, the Harlequin Duck does not do well—several of the birds have failed to return north on their proper schedule. Our five-year atlas period, 1997–2002, saw a spate of Harlequin Ducks, 6 of the 12 recorded in San Diego County.

Winter: During the atlas period, Harlequin Ducks were found at Agua Hedionda Lagoon (I6) 16 February–14 March 2001 (E. Wade, NAB 55:227, 2001), Torrey Pines State Reserve (N7) 26 December 1999 (S. Walens), La Jolla (P7) 20 February 1998 (G. McCaskie, FN 52:257, 1998), De Anza Cove, Mission Bay (Q8), 4–18 March 2001 and 28 October 2001–27 February 2002 (D. G. Seay, NAB 55:227, 2001; 56:106, 223, 2002), the power plant in Chula Vista on San Diego Bay (U10) 22 January–26 May 1998, Chula Vista, R. T. Patton, FN 52:257, 503, 1998), and the Imperial Beach pier (V10) 7 November 1999–17 May 2000 (G. Moreland, T. Stands, NAB 54:104, 220, 326, 2000). One in the San Diego River flood-control channel (R8) 18–30 December 2001 (R. E. Webster) was presum-

Photo by Anthony Mercieca

ably the same bird spending most of its time at De Anza Cove. Unitt (1984) listed earlier records, three from San Diego Bay and one from Agua Hedionda Lagoon, except for one on the Rancho Santa Fe Christmas bird count 26 December 1982. The records for San Diego County were the southernmost for the Pacific coast until the first for Baja California in 2003 (NAB 57:407, 1983).

Migration: The Harlequin Duck's return to De Anza Cove 28 October 2001 is the species' earliest arrival in San

Diego County. One on San Diego Bay 5 October 1983 had more likely summered (AB 38:246, 1984). The latter bird included, 4 of the county's 12 Harlequin Ducks have overstayed their expected departure time in March. One found

at Agua Hedionda Lagoon 31 December 1977 remained there continuously for over five years until last reported 28 February 1983 (AB 27:338, 1983).

Surf Scoter *Melanitta perspicillata*

San Diego Bay supports probably the largest concentration of Surf Scoters in the species' entire winter range: 8000 to 10,000 birds in the mid 1990s. It remains one of the scoter's key winter habitats in spite of numbers in the 1990s being no more than a third of what they were in the 1960s. Because of its dependence on mollusks as food and its sensitivity to disturbance by boats, the Surf Scoter is the most critical indicator of the biological health of San Diego Bay. San Diego County plays another major role in the Surf Scoter's life cycle by being the route through which birds wintering in the Gulf of California cross overland to the Pacific Ocean.

Winter: The Surf Scoter is the most abundant bird on San Diego Bay. The birds have a preference for water 5 to 35 feet deep and are concentrated largely from the Naval Amphibious Base south (Preston and Mock 1995). Because they feed largely on mollusks, especially mussels, they concentrate where these animals colonize. Rocky ocean bottom and the pilings for piers are habitats secondary to the bed of San Diego Bay.

The systematic surveys of the bay from 1993 to 1995 give us the most current picture of the species' status in this critical habitat. In the north bay, from the entrance to the bridge, in weekly surveys through 1993, Mock et al. (1994) found a maximum of 757 on 19 January. In the central bay, from the bridge to Crown Cove and the

Photo by Anthony Mercieca

Sweetwater River, in monthly surveys through 1993 and weekly surveys through 1994, Preston and Mock (1995) found yearly maxima of 6583 on 20 January 1993, 5708 on 8 March 1994, and 8945 on 28 December 1994. In the central and south bay combined, in weekly surveys from April 1993 to April 1994, Manning (1995) found a maximum of 7458 on 28 December 1993. The combination of these results suggests the figure of 8000–10,000 for San Diego Bay's total winter population in the 1990s. Counts during the atlas period from 1997 to 2002 were largely from shore and not systematic. But numbers of up to 5000 on San Diego Bay near the Chula Vista Nature Center (U10) 15–21 December 1997 (B. C. Moore) and 3500 by boat on San Diego Bay 15 December 2001 (M. Bache) suggest the scoters sustained something close to that level to the beginning of the 21st century.

In Mission Bay Surf Scoters are generally absent. But hundreds congregate on the ocean just off shore, especially off Imperial Beach and the Tijuana River estuary (V10/W10; up to 782 on 19 December 1998, R. B. Riggan) and Point Loma (S7; up to 415 on 18 December 1999, J. C. Worley). Elsewhere along the coast Surf Scoter numbers are highly variable. Results of Oceanside Christmas bird counts range from 1040 in 1987 to 10 in 2001 and 2002. Those of Rancho Santa Fe counts range from 1026 in 1986 to two in 2001.

Except for the outer basin of Agua Hedionda (I6), Surf Scoters avoid the lagoons of

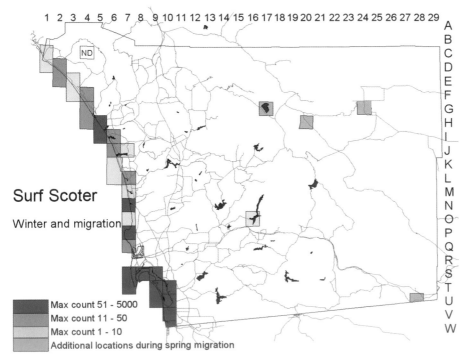

Surf Scoter

Winter and migration

Max count 51 - 5000
Max count 11 - 50
Max count 1 - 10
Additional locations during spring migration

northern San Diego County. As a result of the deepening of Batiquitos Lagoon, ordered as mitigation for loss of subtidal habitat in the Los Angeles harbor, the scoter visited that lagoon in small numbers, occasionally reaching the east basin (J7; up to eight on 15 February 1998, R. Campbell).

The Surf Scoter uses inland lakes as a migration stopover only, not as normal winter habitat. But nine on El Capitan Reservoir (O16) 20 December 1998 (S. Kingswood) were outside the main migration periods.

Migration: Fall arrival of Surf Scoters ranges from mid October to early November. In their weekly surveys of central San Diego Bay in 1994, Preston and Mock (1995) found no scoters summering, then two on 11 October and 131 on 19 October. But parallel surveys of the north bay in 1993 yielded no increase over summer numbers until 26 October with six, and 2 November with 17. Fall migration continues into early December: over 1000 were streaming south over the ocean at La Jolla (P7) 6 December 1998 (G. McCaskie). Numbers on San Diego Bay peak from mid December to early March.

Spring departure takes place mainly from March to mid April. No date can be given for final departure because small numbers remain through summer, at least in some years. In their studies of north and central San Diego Bay, Mock et al. (1994) and Preston and Mock (1995) found up to six on 6 June 1993. Atlas observers found up to 31 at Los Peñasquitos Lagoon (N7) 6 June 1998 (D. R. Grine), 30 along the Silver Strand (T9) 25 August 1998 (B. C. Moore), and 25 in south San Diego Bay 19 June 1998 (Y. Ikegaya). Earlier counts of summering birds ran as high as 85 (Unitt 1984).

The most interesting aspect of Surf Scoter migration is its use of San Diego County as a corridor for crossing between the Gulf of California and Pacific coast. Many of the birds make the trip nonstop, but storms may compel them to stop on lakes or, rarely, crash on land. The principal route parallels county Highway S2, the historic route of least resistance over the mountains for man and bird alike. Because Lake Henshaw (G17) lies just beyond the pass at the head of San Felipe Valley (H20), most records and the largest numbers have been on that lake, up to 1000 from 16 to 18 March 1983 (R. Higson, AB 37:912, 1983), over 1000 on 21 March 1992, and 900 on 23 March 1997 (G. McCaskie, AB 46:480, 1992; FN 51:927, 1997). Records elsewhere along the route are too numerous to list, but notable during the atlas period were two on a small pond in San Felipe Valley (H20) 22 March 1998 and 17 April 1999 (A. P. and T. E. Keenan). The passage is not restricted to this narrow corridor, however. With the establishment of ponds the Surf Scoter has begun to stop occasionally at Borrego Springs (G24; up to two on 30 March 1998, P. D. Jorgensen), and other records are scattered south to Jacumba (U28; Sams and Stott 1959, one on 4 April 1999, P. Unitt).

Extreme dates for spring migrants inland are 21 January (2001, one at Borrego Springs, P. D. Jorgensen), the only record for January, and 12 May (1995, 60 on Lake Henshaw, G. McCaskie, NASFN 49:309, 1995). In 1983, when storms associated with El Niño brought many Surf Scoters down on Lake Henshaw, Roger Higson monitored the lake regularly, noting the species from 4 March to 1 May. The Surf Scoter's use of this route in fall is less clear than in spring, perhaps because the rarity of storms at this season means the birds are seldom obliged to stop. Nevertheless there are five fall records on dates from 12 November (1985, 238 on Lake Henshaw, R. Higson, AB 40:158, 1986) to 6 December (1986, one on Lake Cuyamaca, C. G. Edwards, AB 41:328, 1987)

Conservation: Because of its diet of mollusks, which concentrate contaminants in the water, the Surf Scoter is vulnerable to pollution and a possible indicator of water quality. Like other diving seabirds, it is highly susceptible to oil spills. Yet in spite of water quality in San Diego Bay improving since the 1960s, Surf Scoter numbers have declined over the same period. Guy McCaskie attempted to census scoters on San Diego Bay in the 1960s, and the results are reflected in totals of Christmas bird counts: an average from 1962 to 1967 of 24,084 and a maximum of 30,097 in 1962. Subsequent counts have not sampled scoters consistently, but the results of the surveys in the 1990s show that the numbers had dropped to about one third of the former figure. Two of the count's four lowest totals since the 1950s fell within the five-year atlas period, 1997–2002. The decrease may not be restricted to San Diego Bay alone. In spite of huge annual variation, totals on the Oceanside and Rancho Santa Fe counts, which represent scoters on the ocean, both reached their lowest ever in 2001. Taken together, all three species of scoter are on the decline in their breeding range in Alaska (Hodges et al. 1996).

One negative factor on San Diego Bay is disturbance by boats, which Macdonald et al. (1990) proposed as the primary reason for the scoter's decline. Preston and Mock (1995) found the scoter to be the water bird most sensitive to such disturbance, fleeing a boat at a distance greater than other species and concentrating in regions of central San Diego Bay with less boat traffic.

White-winged Scoter *Melanitta fusca*

The White-winged Scoter was once a common winter visitor to San Diego County, especially to San Diego Bay. Its almost complete disappearance since the 1970s, in lack of reports of a catastrophic decline in the species as a whole, suggests that the winter range has shifted north, few individuals bothering to migrate this far south.

Winter: From 1997 to 2002 we noted the White-winged Scoter only 13 times in San Diego County. Only three sightings were of more than a single individual: eight at La Jolla (P7) 21 January 1999 (L. and M. Polinsky), three in the west basin of Batiquitos Lagoon (J6) 6 February 1998 (C. C. Gorman), and 20 at San Onofre (C1) 27 February 1999 (L. Ellis). At least the last, and possibly all three records, were of spring migrants rather than wintering birds. Surprisingly, only four of the birds were within

San Diego Bay, the traditional site for the species. More intensive surveys of the bay in the 1990s also yielded few White-winged Scoters. In spite of weekly or monthly surveys of north and central San Diego Bay 1993–95, Mock et al. (1994) and Preston and Mock (1995) found only a single individual in the north bay 4 April 1995. On the basis of weekly surveys of the central and south bay 1993–94, Manning (1995) recorded a cumulative total of 13 in the south bay, which could have included repeated sightings of the same individual(s).

Migration: The White-winged Scoter's migration schedule is similar to that of the Surf Scoter, with fall arrival beginning in late October (18 October 1969, three on San Diego Bay, J. L. Dunn; 28 October 2000, one on the south bay, E. Wallace) and spring departure completed in early April. Since 1970, two summer stragglers have been recorded on San Diego Bay, one near the Naval Amphibious Base (T9) 30 June 1988 (Macdonald et al. 1990) and one near the D Street fill (T10) 9 June 1999 (R. T. Patton).

In spite of being a regular if rare migrant at the Salton Sea (Patten et al. 2003), the White-winged Scoter does not use the migration corridor across San Diego County as does the Surf Scoter. There is only a single inland record, of one at Lake Henshaw (G17) 2 April 1982 (R. Higson, AB 36: 893, 1982).

Conservation: The White-winged Scoter was apparently always irregular in abundance in San Diego County, but over the long term its history has been one of sharp decline. Stephens (1919a) called the White-winged Scoter a "common winter resident," and Sefton (1939) reported about 500 on San Diego Bay 11 November 1938, saying this was the largest concentration he had seen. Decline had apparently begun by the 1950s, as Sams and Stott (1959) called the species "regular but moderately sparse." From the inception of regular San Diego Christmas bird counts in 1953, the White-winged Scoter was recorded annually through 1971. From 1955 through 1971 totals

Photo by Anthony Mercieca

ranged from 5 to 200, except for 2000 on 3 January 1960. The last winter with any substantial influx was 1979–80, when the San Diego Christmas bird count yielded 170. Since 1981 the count has not exceeded four, and from 1987 through 2002, the species was recorded on only 6 of 16 counts. The White-winged Scoter has not appeared on an Oceanside Christmas bird count since 1987 or on a Rancho Santa Fe count since 1988.

Though local factors like water pollution, disturbance by boats, and contamination of the mollusks on which they feed could all have affected the White-winged Scoter on San Diego Bay, unknown larger-scale factors are probably more important. The numbers of scoters (all species combined) breeding in Alaska declined through the latter half of the 20th century, but not to the degree the White-winged Scoter has declined in San Diego. The southern edge of the White-winged's breeding range on the northern Great Plains has retracted northward (Brown and Frederickson 1997), and some of the birds originating in this region migrate to California (Houston and Brown 1983). Climatic warming could result in the scoter's failing to migrate as far south as formerly.

Black Scoter *Melanitta nigra*

The Black is the scarcest of the three scoters in San Diego County, reaching the county as a winter visitor at a rate of about one per year. Like those of the White-winged and Surf Scoters, its numbers have declined, but unlike the others, it was never common. Like the other scoters, it occurs usually on San Diego Bay or on the ocean near shore, especially near piers, where it can feed on mussels.

Winter: Only six Black Scoters were found in San Diego County during the five-year atlas period, 1997–2002. Their distribution appears representative. Only one was on San Diego Bay, near the J Street marina, Chula Vista (U10) 21 February–2 March 2002 (M. B. Mulrooney). Other sites were the Oceanside pier (H5; 16 November 1997, C. Jones), the ocean off Oceanside (26 December 1998, D. W. Povey), the Imperial Beach pier (V10; 8 November 1999, B. Foster, NAB 54:104, 2000), the

Photo by Kenneth Z. Kurland

Tijuana River estuary (V10; 20 December 1997–1 January 1998, W. Mittendorff, FN 52:257, 1998), and Border Field State Park (W10; 18 December 1999, S. Walens).

Migration: Dates for the Black Scoter in San Diego County range from 31 October (1984, AB 39:102, 1985) to 18 April (1928, Helmuth 1939), except for the two credible records of summer stragglers: two on San Diego Bay 21 June–24 July 1962 (AFN 16:507, 1962) and one there June–July 1985 (G. McCaskie, AB 39:962, 1985). The only inland record for the county is of a spring migrant at Lake Henshaw (G17) 18 March 1983 (R. Higson, AB 37:912, 1983).

Conservation: Although the Black Scoter was recorded only once in San Diego County before 1950 (Helmuth 1939), it was reported on nine consecutive San Diego Christmas bird counts, 1954–62, with an average of 6.2 and a maximum of 17 on 26 December 1954. Even if some of these birds were misidentified Surf Scoters, the numbers suggest the Black was considerably more frequent in the 1950s and 60s than at the beginning of the 21st century. The decline has been essentially continuous. In the 20 years from 1963 to 1982 the San Diego Christmas bird count averaged 1.15 Black Scoters per year, whereas in the 20 years from 1983 to 2002 it averaged 0.25 per year.

Long-tailed Duck or Oldsquaw *Clangula hyemalis*

The Long-tailed Duck is rare but of nearly annual occurrence on San Diego Bay, which represents the southern tip of the species' winter range. In good years up to seven individuals have been found, but in others there have been none at all. The Long-tailed Duck is less frequent in Mission Bay and only casual elsewhere in San Diego County.

Winter: San Diego Bay is the primary site for the Long-tailed Duck in San Diego County, though it is irregular even there. From 1997 to 2002 its numbers varied from at least seven in 1998–99 to zero in 2000–01, the only one of the five years of the atlas period in which it was missed. It has been recorded on 18 of 45 San Diego Christmas bird counts 1958–2002. Systematic surveys of San Diego Bay 1993–95 found the species occasionally in all parts of the bay, with no concentration in the south bay, as for so many other ducks. These studies yielded no more than two individuals per day (Manning 1995, Mock et al. 1994, Stadtlander and Konecny 1994). From 1997 to 2002 the largest numbers were five in north San Diego Bay at Harbor

Photo by Anthony Mercieca

Island (S8) 4 February 1999 (E. C. Hall) and six, probably the same individuals, at the submarine base on the east side of Point Loma (S7) 17 April 1999 (P. A. Ginsburg). No larger numbers had been reported previously.

Though the Long-tailed Duck occurs occasionally in Mission Bay, during the atlas period we found only one there, in the bay's northeast quadrant (Q8) 7 January 1999 (E. Wallace). There have been a few sightings in the Tijuana River estuary and at the Imperial Beach pier (V10), including one at the pier 18 December 1999 (G. McCaskie). Along the coast from La Jolla to Oceanside the species is reported only about once every three or four years and was missed entirely during the atlas period. Inland there are only three records, of one at Santee Lakes (O12/P12) 6–8 November 1991 (C. G. Edwards, AB 46:148, 1992) and 12 March 2003 (M. B. Stowe), and one at Lake Murray (Q11) 10 January–28 February 1999 (J. Morris, N. Osborn, NAB 53:208, 1999).

Migration: The Long-tailed Duck begins arriving in November, with an earliest date

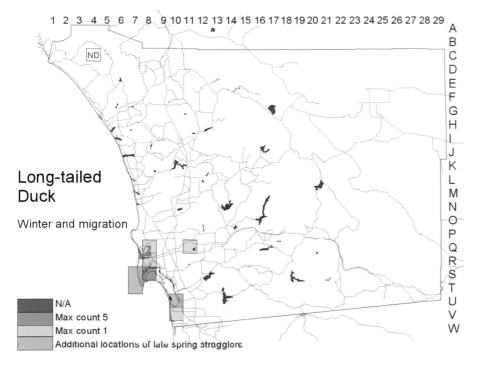

Long-tailed Duck

Winter and migration

1 2 3 4 5 6 7 8 9 10 11 12 13 14 15 16 17 18 19 20 21 22 23 24 25 26 27 28 29

A B C D E F G H I J K L M N O P Q R S T U V W

ND

- N/A
- Max count 5
- Max count 1
- Additional locations of late spring stragglers

of 1 November (1979, one at Oceanside, AB 34:200, 1980; 1990, one at Point Loma, R. E. Webster, AB 45:151, 1991). Most individuals depart in March; those at the submarine base in 1999 were unusually late (three remaining on 22 April, one on 9 May, P. A. Ginsburg). There are 10 records of later stragglers, in poor plumage from failure to molt, including one that summered in south San Diego Bay (U10) in 1998 (R. T. Patton, FN 52:503, 1998).

Conservation: At the source, in Alaska, the Long-tailed Duck population is in decline. Aerial surveys of the arctic coastal plain found numbers decreasing at an average rate of 2.5% per year from 1986 through 2002 (Mallek et al. 2003), and the decrease over the period 1977–94 was even sharper (Hodges et al. 1996). But San Diego has received its dribble at the same rate for at least 40 years and probably longer—Stephens (1919a) called the species an "occasional winter visitant."

Bufflehead *Bucephala albeola*

About 2000 Buffleheads winter on San Diego Bay, making the species the third most abundant diving duck on the bay, behind the Surf Scoter and Lesser Scaup. The Bufflehead is a common winter visitor in other coastal estuaries also. It is widespread on lakes and ponds inland but common on just a few of these. Stragglers remaining through the summer are only occasional.

Winter: South San Diego Bay is the center for the Bufflehead in San Diego County, as for so many other ducks. Weekly counts of the salt works and adjacent bay from February 1993 through February 1994 disclosed a maximum of 976 on 3 March 1993 and a steady level of about 300 through the winter of 1993–94 (Stadtlander and Konecny 1994). These numbers remained fairly consistent through the beginning of the 21st century: the San Diego Christmas bird count 15 December 2001 yielded 478 within the salt works (D. C. Seals) and 397 just outside them in southwestern San Diego Bay (P. R. Pryde). The Bufflehead is also common elsewhere in the bay: systematic counts 1993–95 recorded up to 375 in the north bay 21 December 1993 and 480 in the central bay 3 January 1994 (Mock et al. 1994, Preston and Mock

Photo by Anthony Mercieca

1995). Substantial numbers of Buffleheads winter also in Mission Bay, with up to 150 in the bay's northwest quadrant (Q7) 8 January 2000 (L. Polinsky) and 133 in the northeast quadrant (Q8) 16 January 2000 (J. C. Worley).

The Bufflehead uses all other substantial coastal wetlands as well, being most numerous in Batiquitos Lagoon (J6/J7; up to 120 on 22 December 2001, R. and A. Campbell) and the San Dieguito River estuary (M7; up to 114 on 16 December 1997, D. R. Grine). The most consistent inland sites are Dixon Lake (I11; up to 40 on 6 January 2001, L. Hunter), sewage ponds in San Vicente Valley at the base of Spangler Peak (L15; up to 60 on 2 February 2001, A. Mauro), and the upper ponds of Santee Lakes (O12; up to 53 on 18 February 2001, R. Breisch). Smaller numbers are regular elsewhere on the coastal slope, including the higher mountains and the Campo Plateau. On ponds in the Borrego Valley the Bufflehead is rare. Most records there are of just one or two individuals and none is of over five, as at the Roadrunner Club (F24) 15 December 1987 (A. G. Morley) and at Club Circle (G24) 5 December 1998 (P. D. Ache).

Migration: Buffleheads arrive occasionally in late October (four in the San Diego River flood-control channel, R8, 22

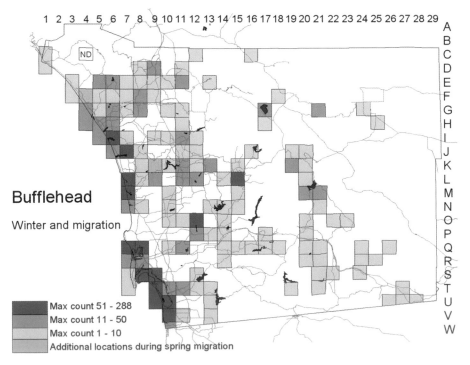

Bufflehead

Winter and migration

Max count 51 - 288
Max count 11 - 50
Max count 1 - 10
Additional locations during spring migration

October 1985, D. Patla; two there 25 October 1981, P. Unitt). But weekly surveys of San Diego Bay 1993–95 did not have any before 2 November (Mock et al. 1994, Preston and Mock 1995). Manning's (1995) weekly surveys of San Diego Bay found the Bufflehead's numbers there steady from December through March. Departure is largely in April. Late stragglers were four in Batiquitos Lagoon (J7) 4 May 2001 (C. C. Gorman) and two in central San Diego Bay 9 May 1994 (Preston and Mock 1995).

Summer stragglers average less than one per year in San Diego County. During the atlas period there were three, near Ramona (K13) 26 May 2000 (P. M. von Hendy), at Big Laguna Lake (O23) 2 June 2001 (C. G. Edwards), and along the lower Sweetwater River (T11) 2 July 1998 (P. Famolaro).

Conservation: In contrast to the decreases evident in the Surf Scoter and Common Goldeneye, the Bufflehead appears to have maintained its numbers through the second half of the 20th century. Christmas bird counts suggest much annual variation but no consistent trend.

Common Goldeneye *Bucephala clangula*

The Common Goldeneye is far from common in San Diego County. It is an uncommon winter visitor only in the salt works of south San Diego Bay and rare elsewhere. The species is on decline in San Diego Bay, probably more because of a shift in the species' winter distribution than because of a decline in total numbers.

Winter: The south end of San Diego Bay is the only current regular site for the Common Goldeneye in San Diego County. From 1997 to 2002 numbers here ranged up to only eight individuals, except for 13 on 16 February 2001 (G. Grantham). Weekly surveys of the salt works from February 1993 to February 1994 yielded a maximum of 17 in February 1994 and monthly averages of no more than eight (Stadtlander and Konecny 1994). Surveys of south San Diego Bay outside the salt works 1988–89 revealed no more than five per day. Other regular studies throughout San Diego Bay outside the salt works 1993–95 did not find any (Manning 1995, Mock et al. 1994, Preston and Mock 1995).

Elsewhere along the coast of San Diego County the goldeneye is seldom seen. During the atlas period only

Photo by Anthony Mercieca

about 10 individuals showed up along the coast away from south San Diego Bay. All sightings were of single individuals, except for two in the east basin of Buena Vista Lagoon (H6) 23 December 1998 and up to three in the Santa Margarita River estuary (G4) 27 January 1999 (P. A. Ginsburg). Inland, the species is even scarcer but shows up occasionally on small ponds as well as larger lakes. Inland sightings during the atlas period were of one at 3.3 miles southeast of central Escondido (J11) 29 December 2001 (P. Hernandez), two in Boden Canyon (J14) 18 January 1999 (R. L. Barber), one at the east end of Lake Hodges (K11) 27 December 1998 (O. Carter), four on Sweetwater Reservoir (S12) 17 January 2002 (G. Chaniot), one on Upper Otay Lake (T13) 14 February 1999 (J. R. Barth), and one on Lake Domingo (U26) 13 January 2000 (F. L. Unmack). In the Anza–Borrego the only record is of three on a golf-course pond at Club Circle, Borrego Springs (G24), 23 December 1967 (ABDSP database).

Migration: Dates for the Common Goldeneye in San Diego County extend from "October" 1919 (Mission Bay, SDNHM 2168) and 9 November

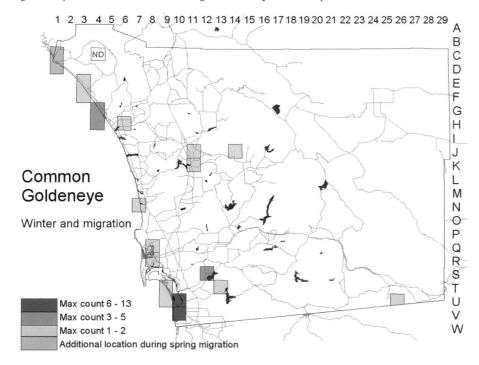

Common Goldeneye

Winter and migration

■ Max count 6 - 13
▨ Max count 3 - 5
▢ Max count 1 - 2
▢ Additional location during spring migration

(1962, three on San Diego Bay, AFN 17:67, 1963) to 21 March 1999 (one in the Santa Margarita River estuary, P. A. Ginsburg) and 7 April 2000 (eight in the salt works, R. T. Patton), except for the three summer stragglers listed by Unitt (1984).

Conservation: Numbers of Common Goldeneyes in San Diego County have declined almost continuously since the early 1960s. The peak on the San Diego Christmas bird count was 94 on 31 December 1961. From 1963 to 1982 the count averaged 19.1 goldeneyes, from 1983 to 1992 it averaged 13.1, and from 1993 to 2002 it averaged only 3.5.

Eadie et al. (1995) reported that the Common Goldeneye's population, taken as a whole, was approximately stable through the late 20th century. Therefore, it seems likely that the birds have simply shifted, perhaps not needing to migrate as far south as San Diego as the climate warms. Also, since the 1980s, Common Goldeneyes have begun wintering in large numbers on the Colorado River below Glen Canyon Dam (Rosenberg et al. 1991, LaRue et al. 2001). These birds presumably abandoned other sites where they had wintered previously.

Taxonomy: The Common Goldeneye is usually divided into an Old World and a New World subspecies; *B. c. americana* (Bonaparte, 1838) is the one in North America.

Barrow's Goldeneye *Bucephala islandica*

The four records of Barrow's Goldeneye in San Diego County are the species' southernmost on the Pacific coast. The bird is unknown in Mexico, though it has become regular in small numbers below the large dams on the Colorado River above Parker.

Winter: One Barrow's Goldeneye was at Otay (V11) 7 March 1964 (McCaskie and Banks 1966), one was in San Diego Bay along the Silver Strand (T9) 15–20 February 1975 (AB 29:741, 1975), one was at the south end of San Diego Bay (V10) 7 January 1979, and possibly the same individual was at this locality again 9 March 1979 (AB 33:312, 1979).

Photo by Anthony Mercieca

Hooded Merganser *Lophodytes cucullatus*

Finding the ornate and striking adult male Hooded Merganser in San Diego County is an uncommon delight. Males and females combined, only 30 to 40 Hooded Mergansers are noted countywide each year. Though it occurs occasionally on larger lakes and coastal wetlands, this winter visitor prefers small freshwater ponds.

Winter: The Hooded Merganser is widely scattered through San Diego County, but it has a few favored sites: a private business park along San Marcos Creek at Questhaven Road (J8; up to 14 on 27 January 1998, J. O. Zimmer), Santee Lakes (O12/P12; up to 12 on 19 January 2000, G. Chaniot), and a pond in La Posta Creek 1 mile northeast of La Posta Ranch (S24; six on 9 December 1998 and 23 January 2000, L. J. Hargrove).

Though the Hooded Merganser avoids San Diego Bay and occurs in most other coastal wetlands only rarely, it is regular in the flood-control channel at the mouth of the San Diego River and in adjacent Famosa Slough (R8), where numbers ranged up to three on 22 January 2001 (P. R. Pryde). With records from Palomar Mountain (D14; three from 31 December 1999 to 9 February 2000, P. D. Jorgensen) and Lake Cuyamaca (M20; one on 7 December 2001, R. Ronin), the Hooded Merganser is as likely to occur in the higher mountains as at most places along the coast. In the Anza–Borrego Desert there are

Photo by Anthony Mercieca

just four records of single individuals, all from ponds in the Borrego Valley.

Migration: From 1997 to 2002 dates for the Hooded Merganser in San Diego County ranged from 3 November (1999, one at Borrego Springs, F24, R. Thériault) to 24 March (2000, two at the San Diego River mouth, R7, M. Billings). Extreme dates recorded are apparently still the same as reported by Unitt (1984), 25 October and 30 March, except for a straggler at Santee Lakes 28 May 1977 (AB 31:1041, 1977).

Conservation: The Hooded Merganser has never been common in San Diego County. Christmas bird counts

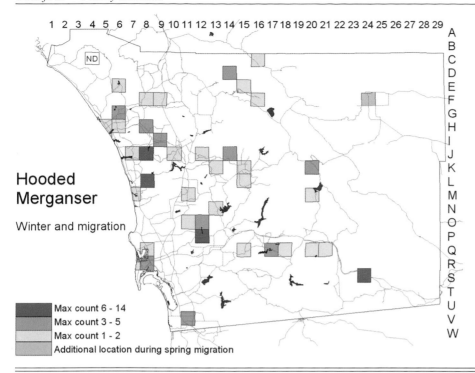

Hooded
Merganser

Winter and migration

- ■ Max count 6 - 14
- Max count 3 - 5
- Max count 1 - 2
- Additional location during spring migration

suggest the number reaching this area stayed at about the same low level for decades. An increase, however, may have started about the time the atlas study was initiated in 1997. The Rancho Santa Fe Christmas bird count, for example, averaged only 0.6 Hooded Mergansers from 1980 to 1996. But from 1997 to 2003 it averaged 6.2. The Escondido count, though initiated in January 1986, did not record the Hooded Merganser until 2000, yet in 2002 it yielded 10. The Hooded Merganser, with its preference for small lakes, is a logical beneficiary of the importation of water and installation of reservoirs.

Common Merganser *Mergus merganser*

The Common Merganser's distribution in San Diego County is the converse of the Red-breasted's. Both species are winter visitors, but the Common frequents inland lakes and only rarely visits coastal wetlands. It prefers lakes in the foothills and mountains over those in the coastal lowland.

Winter: The lakes on which the Common Merganser winters in greatest numbers are Wohlford (I112/I12; up to 160 on 29 December 2001, N. Osborn), Cuyamaca (M20; up to 42 on 18 February 1999, A. P. and T. E. Keenan), and Henshaw (G17). At the last, our highest count from 1997 to 2002 was of 60 on 29 February 2000 (J. L. Coatsworth). The median on Lake Henshaw Christmas bird counts 1981–2002 was 18, but large flocks are occasional. The count on 23 December 1996 yielded an exceptional 800. Smaller numbers are regular on El Capitan (N16/O16; up to 12 on 6 February 2001, D. C. Seals, 16 January 2002, J. R. Barth) and Morena (T21/S21/S22; up to 12 on 16 February 1998, S. E. Smith) and less frequent on other foothill and mountain lakes. Even minor ponds in the mountains get the occasional flock of Common Mergansers, such as 10 at Wynola (J19) 17 January 1999 (S. E. Smith) and 10 at the Lucky 5 Ranch, Laguna Mountains (N21/N22), 12 January 2002 (G. L. Rogers).

In the coastal lowland away from the steeper hills the Common Merganser is rare. During the atlas period we noted only a few scattered individuals in this zone. In coastal wetlands the species is even scarcer, with just four sightings 1997–2002 and only one of more than a single bird (three in the Tijuana River estuary, V10, 19 January 1998, R. B. Riggan). The various systematic surveys of San Diego Bay yielded only five in the intake channel for

Photo by Anthony Mercieca

the power plant at Chula Vista (U10) 7 February 1989 (Macdonald et al. 1990) and single birds near the south end of the Silver Strand (U10) 29 December 1993 and 5 January 1994 (Stadtlander and Konecny 1994).

Records for the Anza–Borrego Desert are all from ponds in Borrego Springs (F24/G24): three or four from 3 to 31 March 1991, one on 18 December 1992 (A. G. Morley), and one from 11 December 1999 to 18 February 2000 (M. L. Gabel)

Migration: The Common Merganser occurs in San Diego County primarily from 12 November (1978, 10 at Lake Henshaw, D. W. Povey) to March. One at Lake Cuyamaca 14 April 2001 (M. Billings) and two at Lake Morena 26 April 1998 (S. E. Smith) were exceptionally late. The only summer straggler recorded was one at Lower Otay Lake (U13/U14) 15 June–26 September 1983 (R. E. Webster, D. W. Povey, AB 37:1027, 1983; 38:246, 1984).

Conservation: The variation from year to year on Escondido (including Lake Wohlford) and Lake Henshaw

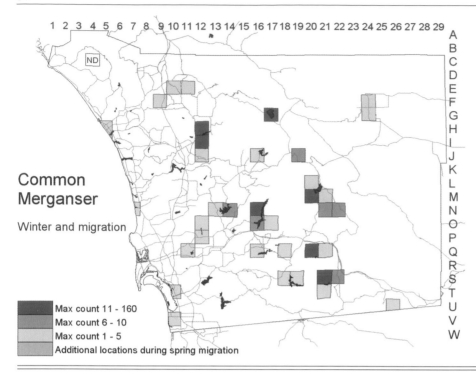

Common
Merganser

Winter and migration

Max count 11 - 160
Max count 6 - 10
Max count 1 - 5
Additional locations during spring migration

Christmas bird counts is so great that any trend in Common Merganser numbers through the 1980s and 1990s is unclear. The flock on Lake Wohlford, however, was no more than 75 from 1986 to 2000 but reached 160 in 2001 and 101 in 2002. In any case, before the building of dams and the stocking of reservoirs with fish, the Common Merganser would have found practically no habitat in San Diego County.

Taxonomy: The New World subspecies of the Common Merganser is *M. m. americanus* Cassin, 1852.

Red-breasted Merganser *Mergus serrator*

Of California's three mergansers, the Red-breasted is the only one with a preference for salt water. The Red-breasted Merganser is a common winter visitor on San Diego Bay but much scarcer at other coastal wetlands and rare on inland lakes. Almost all Red-breasted Mergansers reaching San Diego County are females or immatures with white breasts and rusty heads.

Winter: San Diego Bay is by far the principal site for the Red-breasted Merganser in San Diego County. In weekly surveys of the central and south bay from April 1993 to April 1994 Manning (1995) recorded an average of about 70 in January, the peak month, and a maximum of 117 on 21 January 1994. In weekly surveys of the salt works and adjacent south bay from February 1993 to February 1994 Stadtlander and Konecny (1994) recorded an average of about 100 in December, the peak month in that study, and a maximum of 184 on 29 December 1993. From 1997 to 2002 the maximum reported in a single atlas square was 45 in southwestern San Diego Bay (U10) 18 December 1998 (P. R. Pryde). Numbers in the central and north bay are smaller than in the south bay. In weekly surveys of the central bay (National City to bridge) Preston and Mock (1995) found a maximum of 32 on 20 December 1994, whereas in weekly surveys of the north bay (bridge to mouth) Mock et al. (1994) found a maximum of 44 on 10 February 1993 and 7 December 1994.

Elsewhere along the coast the merganser is less numerous and less consistent but occurs both within estuaries and on the ocean near shore. Numbers as high as 30 along the beach at Encinitas (K6) 1 January 1999 (J. Ciarletta) and 18 in the west basin of Batiquitos Lagoon (J6) 28 December 1999 (R. and A. Campbell) are unusual. From

Photo by Anthony Mercieca

1976 to 2002 the Oceanside Christmas bird count averaged 9.1 Red-breasted Mergansers; from 1980 to 2003 the Rancho Santa Fe count averaged 8.8.

Though the Red-breasted is by far the commonest merganser along the coast, in San Diego County it is by far the scarcest inland. Nevertheless, atlas observers noted at least 14 individuals inland, with up to six at Lake Hodges (K11) 13 December 1999 (B. C. Moore) and three at the upper end of Lake Morena (S22) 20 December 1997 (R. and S. L. Breisch). Repeated sightings of one at Lake Murray (Q11) in 1997–98, 1998–99, and 1999–2000 (N. Osborn) were possibly of one individual returning for successive winters. Winter records for the Borrego Valley are of single birds at the Roadrunner Club (F24) 25 January 1990 (A. G. Morley) and 30 January 2000 (P. D. Jorgensen) and at Club Circle (G24) 4 January 1995 (M. L. Gabel).

Migration: Fall arrival of the Red-breasted Merganser has been recorded as early as 4 October (1978, Unitt

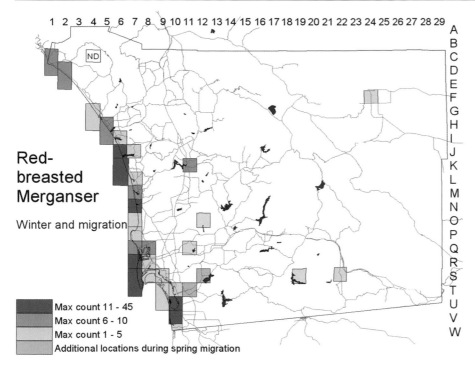

Red-breasted Merganser

Winter and migration

■ Max count 11 - 45
▨ Max count 6 - 10
□ Max count 1 - 5
▣ Additional locations during spring migration

San Diego Bay to 16 August 1994 (Preston and Mock 1995), one at the Santa Margarita River mouth (G4) 19 July 1995, and nine at the Tijuana River mouth (V10) 14 August 1978 (P. Unitt).

Because the Red-breasted Merganser is so frequent a spring migrant at the Salton Sea, on par with the Black Brant and Surf Scoter (Patten et al. 2003), one might expect that the merganser uses the same migration corridor across eastern San Diego County. But there are only three records suggesting this, of 12 at Lake Henshaw (G17) 8 April 1981, five there 16 April 1982 (R. Higson, AB 36: 893, 1982), and one at Lower Willows, Coyote Creek (D23), 26 March 1993 (ABDSP database).

1984), but regular surveys of San Diego Bay 1993–95 found no arrival until November. In both 1993 and 1994 the earliest date on which Mock et al. (1994) and Preston and Mock (1995) recorded the species was 9 November. Spring departure is in March and early April, with a few stragglers remaining later. From 1997 to 2001 our latest was one at Batiquitos Lagoon (J7) 4 May 2001 (C. C. Gorman). Birds that fail to migrate and remain through the summer were not reported during the atlas period but can be expected occasionally, such as two on central

Conservation: With a high of 526 in 1975 and a low of 21 in 1994, results of San Diego Christmas bird counts suggest that the numbers of Red-breasted Mergansers on San Diego Bay vary considerably from year to year. But there is no clear trend. Because of its diet of fish, the Red-breasted Merganser is susceptible to concentration of contaminants as they rise up the food chain and is a species suitable for monitoring the biological health of San Diego Bay.

Ruddy Duck *Oxyura jamaicensis*

The Ruddy Duck, North America's only representative of the stiff-tailed ducks, is locally common as a breeding bird and abundant as a winter visitor in brackish lagoons and freshwater lakes and ponds in San Diego County. Indeed, at many places, it is the most abundant wintering duck, though less conspicuous than others because of its small size, reluctance to fly, and, in winter, drab colors.

Breeding distribution: Nesting locations for the Ruddy Duck are scattered throughout San Diego County's coastal slope but are most concentrated in the northwest, in the coastal lagoons and in the valleys of the lower Santa Margarita and San Luis Rey rivers. The largest concentration is at Buena Vista Lagoon, with up to 150 in the east basin (H6) 25 April 1999 (L. E. Taylor) and 113 in the west basin (H5) 12 August 1997 (D. Rorick). Among other important sites are the Santa Margarita estuary, including nearby sewage ponds (G4/G5; up to 50, including juveniles, 1 August 1999, R. E. Fischer), Whelan Lake (G6; up to 77 on 16 July 1997, D. Rorick), and Batiquitos Lagoon (J6/J7; up to 37 on 10 July 1997, Merkel and Associates 1997).

Photo by Anthony Mercieca

Away from the north coastal area breeding Ruddy Ducks are more scattered and less common. High counts were up to 22 on Lake Murray (Q11) 1 May 1998 (N. Osborn), 21 at Upper Otay Lake (T13) 13 May 2001 (T. W. Dorman), and 27 at Barrett Lake (S19) 19 May 2001 (R. and S. L. Breisch). In southeastern San Diego County breeding sites extend a short distance onto the desert slope, east to Tule Lake (T27; up to 20 on 6 June

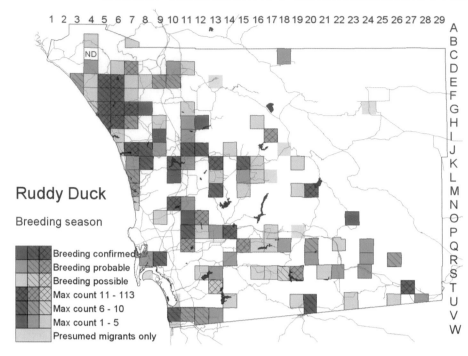

Ruddy Duck

Breeding season

- Breeding confirmed
- Breeding probable
- Breeding possible
- Max count 11 - 113
- Max count 6 - 10
- Max count 1 - 5
- Presumed migrants only

Migration: Wintering Ruddy Ducks arrive in October and November and depart in March and April. In the south San Diego Bay salt works, Stadtlander and Konecny (1994) found dozens to hundreds from November to March but few or none from April to October. King et al. (1987) found large numbers remaining at San Elijo Lagoon (L7) into April, recording their 10-year maximum of 970 on 6 April 1975. During the atlas period we found the same at many sites such as Lake Hodges (50 at the lake's east end, K11, 27 April 1997, E. C. Hall) and the flood-control channel at the San Diego River mouth (R8; 100 on 15 April 1999, J. R. Barth; 50 on 27 April 1999, M. B. Stowe).

Although tens of thousands

2000; chicks on 6 June, J. K. Wilson) and Jacumba (U28; up to four, birds paired, on 19 May 1999, J. K. Wilson). Ruddy Ducks nest at San Diego County's highest lakes, Cuyamaca (M20; up to 12, including chicks, 26 June 1999, A. P. and T. E. Keenan) and Big Laguna (O23; up to five, including chicks, 24 July 1998, E. C. Hall).

Nesting: Ruddy Duck nests are well hidden in marshes; many are screened by a canopy built above them. The chicks leave the nest, however, within a day after hatching, swimming with their mother but feeding themselves. As a results, all our breeding confirmations of the Ruddy Duck were of chicks. These range in date from 1 May to 28 August, suggesting egg laying from about 7 April to about the third week of June.

of Ruddy Ducks winter on the Salton Sea a few miles to the east, in the Anza–Borrego Desert the Ruddy Duck is uncommon, occurring on artificial ponds in the Borrego Valley. The only one reported elsewhere was found on the ground with an injured leg at Tamarisk Grove Campground (I24) 6 November 1960 (ABDSP database). Anza–Borrego records range from 30 September (1992, two on the Borrego Springs sewage ponds, H25, A. G. Morley) to 9 May (2001, four on golf-course ponds

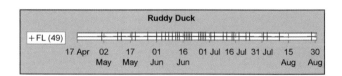

Ruddy Duck

Winter

- Max count 51 - 500
- Max count 11 - 50
- Max count 1 - 10

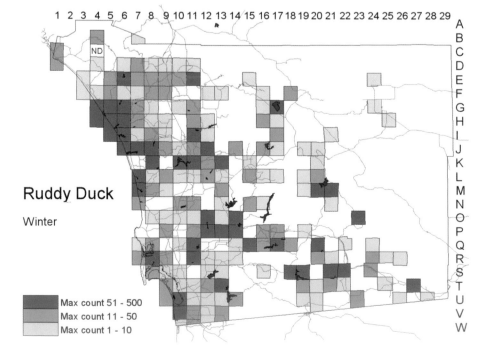

in Borrego Springs, G24, P. D. Ache). Twenty in the Ram's Hill development (H25) 3 October 1987 (P. R. Johnson) were the only recorded desert flock of more than eight.

Winter: San Diego County's population of the Ruddy Duck is augmented greatly in winter by migrants from the north and northeast. Winter counts during the atlas period ranged as high as 500 at O'Neill Lake (E6) 4 December 1999 and 20 January 2000 (P. A. Ginsburg), 417 at San Elijo Lagoon 26 December 1999 (R. T. Patton), 440 at Corte Madera Lake (Q20) 21 February 1999 (R. T. Patton), and 430 at Barrett Lake

(S19) 5 February 2000 (R. and S. L. Breisch). Wintering birds are uncommon on the salt water of Mission Bay and most of San Diego Bay but abundant in the salt works, presumably because of the concentration of invertebrates in the hypersaline water. Weekly censuses there 1993–94 averaged about 240 in January and occasionally reached about 430 (Stadtlander and Konecny 1994). Wintering Ruddy Ducks occupy many lakes and ponds where breeding birds are absent and are not restricted by elevation, sometimes occurring in large numbers on Cuyamaca Lake (up to 300 on 28 January 1999, M. B. Stowe) and Big Laguna Lake (up to 75 on 18 January 1998, P. Unitt). They are regular in small numbers in the Borrego Valley (maximum eight in Borrego Springs 21 January 2001, P. D. Jorgensen).

Conservation: Across North America, Ruddy Duck numbers through the second half of the 20th century were on an increase, punctuated by many peaks and troughs (Brua 2002). In San Diego County Christmas bird counts suggest no consistent trend in the numbers wintering here. During the atlas period, however, we recorded no counts approaching the 2000 at Lake Henshaw 1 April 1978 (G. McCaskie) or 1100 at the upper end of Lake Hodges 11 December 1983 (K. L. Weaver). The installation of reservoirs created much new habitat for Ruddy Ducks, but the lakes must have adequate fringing marshes to support the birds. Where marshes are essentially lacking, as at San Vicente and El Capitan reservoirs, the duck is rare to absent.

Taxonomy: *Oxyura j. rubida* (Wilson, 1814) is the subspecies of the Ruddy Duck throughout North America; its distinctness from nominate *O. j. jamaicensis* (Gmelin, 1789) of the West Indies has been questioned.

PHEASANTS AND TURKEYS — FAMILY PHASIANIDAE

Ring-necked Pheasant *Phasianus colchicus*

A native of Asia, the Ring-necked Pheasant has been introduced widely in North America as a game bird. It thrives best in grain-growing regions, which no longer include San Diego County. The pheasant's status in the county is tenuous; the birds may not be breeding in the wild and are seen with any consistency at only two sites. For hunting, the California Department of Fish and Game currently releases only males at Rancho Jamul and San Felipe Valley, guarding against the possibility of a feral population establishing itself from that source. Escapees or releasees from private breeders are also seen occasionally.

Photo by Anthony Mercieca

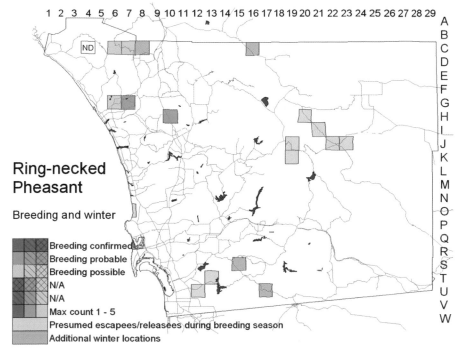

Ring-necked Pheasant

Breeding and winter

Breeding confirmed
Breeding probable
Breeding possible
N/A
N/A
Max count 1 - 5
Presumed escapees/releasees during breeding season
Additional winter locations

Breeding/winter distribution: From 1997 to 2002, the Ring-necked Pheasant was seen most regularly in and near Guajome Regional Park (G7), with up to five near the junction of Melrose Drive and Bobier Drive 10 and 12 April 2001 (C. Andregg) and ten in Guajome Park 23 December 2000 (C. G. Edwards). Another site was in north Escondido near Jesmond Dene Park and in the surrounding valley (H10), where Dan and Debi Bylin noted one or two individuals regularly, including a male and female together 8 April 1999, our closest suggestion of pheasants breeding in the wild in San Diego County. Also, a male found struck by a car here 16 March 1998 had enlarged testes (SDNHM 50023). Three observations between De Luz and Fallbrook (C6/C7/C8; K. L. Weaver) may mean a small population persists in that area. Six sightings of up to two individuals from Wynola (J19) to Pine Hills (K19) were likely the result of releases by, or escapes from, exotic pheasant breeders in Wynola (S. E. Smith).

On a few occasions we saw the birds released for hunting at Rancho Jamul (S15) and San Felipe Valley (I21) and noted their dispersal as far as Dulzura (U17; one on 30 January 2001, D. Povey) and Sentenac Ciénaga (J23, one on 10 April 1999, D. Tomlinson). The few scattered sightings elsewhere were all likely of escaped captives.

Conservation: No history of the Ring-necked Pheasant's introduction into San Diego County has been preserved, and, until the beginning of the releases at Rancho Jamul

and San Felipe Valley in the late 1990s, may have been done by private individuals or clubs only. The earliest published records are from Christmas bird counts, on the Oceanside count beginning in 1952 and on the San Diego count beginning in 1955. The species was never more than uncommon and local and declined as urban sprawl spread over the pastureland and agricultural land where it was formerly seen. The number reported on the Oceanside Christmas bird count peaked at 18 in 1963. On the San Diego count, the pheasant was last reported in 1968, on the Escondido count in 1989, and on the Rancho Santa Fe count in 1990. The introduction of the Ring-necked Pheasant into San Diego County appears to be on the verge of failure early in the 21st century. The current release program consists of "put and take" rather than an introduction intending to establish a self-sustaining population.

Wild Turkey *Meleagris gallopavo*

Though native to North America, the Wild Turkey is not native to California. Early efforts to introduce the species to San Diego County failed, then in 1993 another attempt took root. By 2002 the birds had spread from two points of release in central San Diego County north to the Riverside County line and south to within ten miles of the Mexican border. The name "Wild" Turkey is a misnomer as far as San Diego County is concerned; far from remaining in wild areas where they would offer real sport to hunters, the birds accumulate in parks and around human settlements where they can't be hunted—domesticating themselves.

Breeding distribution: From January to March 1993, the California Department of Fish and Game released 234 turkeys on private ranches near Sutherland Lake (J18) and at Pine Hills (K19). From these sites, the birds spread over most of the oak woodland of central San Diego County. They had begun nesting by 1997 and probably earlier. By 1999 the county population was estimated at 1500. During the breeding season our counts ran as high as 25 in La Jolla Indian Reservation (F15) 17 May 2000 (S. Berg), 25 in Cañada Verde, Los Coyotes Indian Reservation (F20), 12 May 2001 (D. W. Au, K. J. Winter), 25 in the Edwards Ranch northeast of Santa Ysabel (I19) 16 March 2001 (D. W. Au), and 30 north of Julian (J20) 26 June 2001 (O. Carter). Most of the birds have remained in the mountains and foothills, but a few have spread down to the coastal lowland, where noted west to Wilderness Gardens (D11; one on 6 April and 18 May 2000, V. Dineen), Escondido (J11; up to two on 27 June 1998, W. Pray), and upper San Clemente Canyon, Air Station Miramar (O11; one on 18 May 2000, G. L. Rogers). During the atlas period turkeys spread east toward the desert as far as Scissors Crossing (J22; one on 17 March 2001, R. Thériault), and afterward even farther, far outside suitable habitat: up to 11 at the north end of

Photo by Anthony Mercieca

the Borrego Valley (E24) 13 May 2002, four in the Ram's Hill development of Borrego Springs (H25) 7 April 2002, and two at Tamarisk Grove (I24) 4–11 April 2002 (M. C. Jorgensen, P. D. Jorgensen).

Nesting: Turkeys nest in a scrape on the ground. Our two dates of nests with eggs are 26 April and 5 May. On the latter date, the incubating hen was found killed by a bobcat, as attested by tracks around the nest (R. Botta). Our

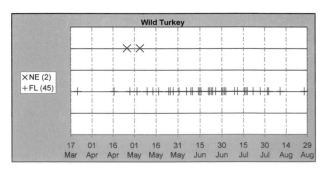

observations of turkey chicks, however, show the species has a long breeding season in San Diego County. The earliest date for chicks, 22 March 1998 in upper San Felipe Valley (H20; A. P. and T. E. Keenan), means that incubation of the clutch began by 22 February in this wet year. Otherwise our earliest date for chicks is 17 April 1999. Several records of chicks extend into August; the latest was of young only one quarter grown near Descanso (P20) 27 August 1998 (D. W. Povey).

Migration: The turkey is non-migratory but capable of dispersing considerable distances over a short time, as the birds' spread demonstrates. One bird fitted with a radio transmitter and released near Sutherland Lake moved 12 miles north, as far as the west fork of the San Luis Rey River (R. Botta).

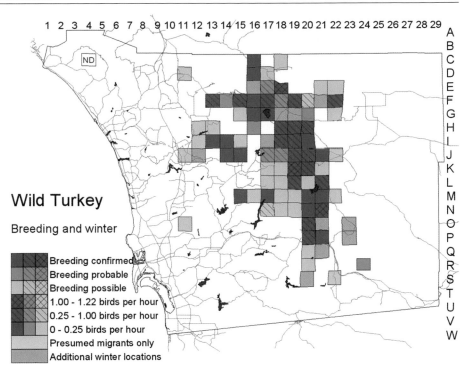

Wild Turkey

Breeding and winter

Breeding confirmed
Breeding probable
Breeding possible
1.00 - 1.22 birds per hour
0.25 - 1.00 birds per hour
0 - 0.25 birds per hour
Presumed migrants only
Additional winter locations

Winter: We encountered turkeys in winter in flocks even larger than during the breeding season, up to 75 in the Edwards Ranch 8 January 2000 (D. W. Au).

Conservation: The turkey was first introduced into San Diego County on Palomar Mountain in 1931, but that attempt, using domestic birds from a game farm, failed. Another introduction, in 1959 of 57 turkeys from the King Ranch, southern Texas, released at Corte Madera Ranch, resulted in numbers estimated at 200–300 by 1965. After San Diego County's second-biggest recorded fire, the Laguna fire of October 1970, the population was much reduced, never recovered, and apparently died out by 1985 (Calif. Dept. Fish and Game 1995). Releases in Camp Pendleton in 1978 and on Palomar Mountain in 1990 were likewise unsuccessful.

The more ambitious introduction in 1993 was controversial from the beginning, promoted by hunting interests, opposed by the California Native Plant Society, Save our Forests and Ranchlands, California State Parks, and some private landowners. A lawsuit brought by the first two organizations blocked further releases beyond those in 1993, but the initial introduction proved sufficient to populate much of the county. Much of the better turkey habitat, oak woodland with broken shrubby understory, is on private property and in Cuyamaca Rancho State Park where hunting is prohibited. Comparatively little good habitat is in the chaparral-dominated lands of the Cleveland National Forest, where hunting is permitted. On one of our field trips to cover north-central San Diego County, 1 May 1999, we encountered turkey hunters searching in vain for the birds in Blue Canyon (E17), within the national forest. The same day, we encountered

the turkeys themselves just 2 miles away at Puerta La Cruz Conservation Camp (E18), where they walk around the prison grounds with no regard for people. Concern has been expressed over the turkeys' possibly depleting the food supply (especially acorns) on which native wildlife relies, their preying on rare reptiles and amphibians, and over their possibly degrading the habitat of certain rare plants. California State Parks have as their goal conserving native wildlife and preventing the spread of exotic organisms, so the California Department of Fish and Game, at the instigation of park authorities, has trapped and removed over 160 turkeys from Cuyamaca Rancho State Park since 1995. The park had become one of the sites of greatest turkey concentration in San Diego County, but in spite of the trapping the numbers both inside and outside the park continue to increase. Similarly, the U.S. Forest Service expressed concern over the likelihood that the turkeys would spread into designated wilderness areas, where introductions of nonnative plants and animals are forbidden.

One argument in the debate was that the turkey is not a truly exotic species in California because it is known here from Pleistocene fossil remains. The fossil species, *Meleagris anza* Howard, 1963, and *M. californica* (Miller, 1909), however, are not the same as the extant *M. gallopavo*. *Meleagris anza*, found in the Carrizo Badlands, dates from the early Pleistocene when the environment was far different from today's.

Taxonomy: The turkeys released in San Diego County in 1993, of intermediates between *M. p. intermedia* Sennett, 1879, and *M. p. gallopavo* Vieillot, 1817, were trapped in the wild in eastern Texas (J. Massie, California Department of Fish and Game).

NEW WORLD QUAIL — FAMILY ODONTOPHORIDAE

Mountain Quail *Oreortyx pictus*

Even though it often passes unnoticed by birders unfamiliar with its calls, the Mountain Quail is one of the commonest birds in San Diego County's higher foothills and mountains. The dense chaparral clothing these mountains is the quail's preferred habitat. In April and May the slopes echo with the Mountain Quail's ventriloquial calls, yet only the hiker on the trail at dawn has a good chance of actually seeing the birds. In spite of its preference for dense vegetation, the Mountain Quail recolonizes recovering burned chaparral quickly, ahead of some other seemingly more mobile birds.

Breeding distribution: The Mountain Quail occurs in all of San Diego County's mountains, up to near the summit of Hot Springs Mountain (11, including a brood of chicks, 3 June 2000, K. L. Weaver, C. R. Mahrdt). Most of our higher counts are from the higher elevations, with as many as 34 per day on the north slope of Palomar Mountain (D15) 14 May 1999 (K. L. Weaver) and 30 in the Laguna Mountains from Oasis Spring to Garnet Peak (N23) 24 May 2001 (K. J. Winter). But the quail is not a bird of coniferous forest, except where an understory of chaparral grows near the trees, and it ranges well below the county's higher mountains. On the coastal slope of southern San Diego County it extends down to about 2000 feet elevation, but in the county's northwestern corner, in the Santa Margarita Mountains, it ranges down to the bases of the steep hills, to about 450 feet elevation along San Mateo Creek (B3; up to five on 12 June 2001, M. Fugagli). The Mountain Quail is rare along the Santa Margarita River in Temecula Canyon (C8; only record 1997–2002 is of one

Photo by Jack C. Daynes

on 24 May 1997, K. L. Weaver), and the range is broken between there and the west base of Palomar Mountain.

In central San Diego County outlying localities on the west are Orosco Ridge (I14; 14 on 12 May 2000, R. L. Barber) and El Capitan County Open Space Preserve (N15; one on 14 April 2001, R. C. Sanger). In southern San Diego County the Mountain Quail ranges west to Lyons (S17) and Mother Grundy (T17) peaks, with isolated populations on the east slope of McGinty Mountain (R15; five on 11 March 2000, J. R. Barth) and near the top of Sycuan Peak (R16; one on 30 April 2001, P. Unitt) and over most of Otay Mountain (U15/U16/V15; up to five on the north slope, U15, 25 May 1999, G. L. Rogers) and Tecate Peak (V18; three on 10 May 2001, D. C. Seals). The population on Otay Mountain is not completely isolated from the main range of the species, as shown by an adult with four chicks about 1600 feet elevation near Dulzura Summit on Highway 94 (U17) 11 July 2000 (D. W. Povey, his only record of the species at this site in 17 years).

On the east side of the mountains, the Mountain Quail occurs in desert-edge scrub, though more sparsely than in dense chaparral. Probably to drink at springs, the birds come rarely all the way to the base of the mountains, where we recorded them at 2050 feet at Mortero Palms (S29; two on 18 April 1999, P. Unitt, A. Mauro) and at 1000 feet elevation near Whitaker Horse Camp (D24), site of three observations in April 2001 (maximum four birds on 4 April, J. O. Zimmer).

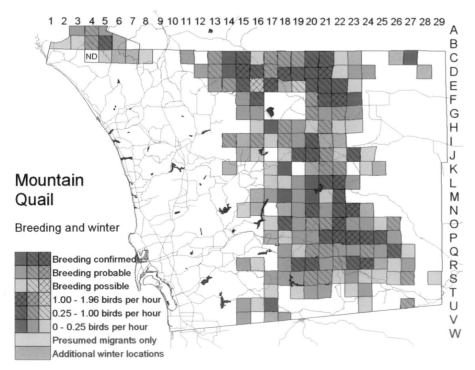

Mountain Quail

Breeding and winter

- Breeding confirmed
- Breeding probable
- Breeding possible
- 1.00 - 1.96 birds per hour
- 0.25 - 1.00 birds per hour
- 0 - 0.25 birds per hour
- Presumed migrants only
- Additional winter locations

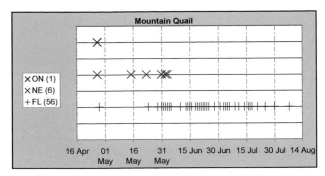

Mountain Quail

X ON (1)
X NE (6)
+ FL (56)

16 Apr 01 16 31 15 Jun 30 Jun 15 Jul 30 Jul 14 Aug
        May May May

Small outlying populations live in the Pinyon Mountains (J23/J24/K24) and in the Santa Rosa Mountains (C27/D27/D28).

The Mountain Quail is common in the mountains of northern Baja California, but there is a partial break in the range along the Mexican border on the Campo Plateau, perhaps due to the region's flatter topography. According to Brennan et al. (1987), rugged terrain is not a prerequisite for the Mountain Quail, but the association between the quail and steep slopes is as strong in San Diego County as elsewhere.

Nesting: The Mountain Quail nests on the ground, sheltered by a shrub, branch, or rock. One nest we found was protected on all sides by being wedged between an overhanging rock and a small yucca. Our observations imply the species lays from early April to at least early June.

Winter: The Mountain Quail is less vocal and so more easily overlooked in winter than in spring. Nevertheless, large flocks are seen occasionally in winter, up to 40 in Barker Valley (E16) 21 February 2001 (J. O. Zimmer), 40 in Banner Canyon (K21) 7 February 1999 (A. Mauro), and 60 near Shingle Spring (D21) 23 December 2000 (L. J. Hargrove). The Mountain Quail migrates altitudinally in the Sierra Nevada but there is as yet no evidence for such a migration in San Diego County. The birds occur as high as the summit of Hot Springs Mountain (E20), at least in some winters (up to two on 9 December 2000, K. L. Weaver, C. R. Mahrdt). Comparison of snowy winters with dry ones might reveal some annual variation. The few atlas squares where we recorded the Mountain Quail in winter but not summer are probably all areas where it is resident in small numbers year round.

Conservation: Though the Mountain Quail has declined in abundance at the northern end of its range, in San Diego County it remains common with no suggestion of change. Its preferred habitat is little disturbed, and much lies within the Cleveland National Forest and Palomar, Cuyamaca, and Anza–Borrego Desert state parks. The primary factor affecting the Mountain Quail's habitat is fire, yet the species seems little affected by fires. A study comparing mature and young (average age six years) chaparral near Pine Valley found the Mountain Quail to be the eighth commonest bird in the young chaparral, the sixth commonest in the old. The quail was more numerous in the mature chaparral but the difference was not statistically significant (Cleveland National Forest unpubl. data). The abundance of food in the young chaparral, still dominated by herbs, may compensate for the reduced cover that may expose the birds to greater predation.

Taxonomy: Because Friedmann (1946) questioned the validity of *O. p. eremophilus* van Rossem, 1937, to which San Diego County Mountain Quail have long been assigned, I investigated the species' variation in color with a Minolta CR-300 colorimeter. *Oreortyx p. eremophilus* (type locality Argus Mountains, Inyo County, California) may be valid after all, distinguished from nominate *O. p. pictus* (Douglas, 1829; type locality confluence of Willamette and Santiam rivers, Oregon) by its paler back and from *O. p. confinis* Anthony, 1889 (type locality Sierra San Pedro Mártir, Baja California) by its paler breast. Colorimeter readings of the darkness (L) of the lower back range from 24.1 to 28.7 in 14 October–January specimens from eastern Oregon (nominate *pictus*) but from 30.4 to 32.0 in four October specimens from the Argus Mountains (*eremophilus*). Readings of the breast range from 33.8 to 37.7 in 19 specimens from the Sierra San Pedro Mártir (*confinis*) but 38.1 to 39.6 in the four specimens from the Argus Mountains.

Twenty specimens from San Diego County are much closer to *confinis* than to *eremophilus*; they range in breast darkness from 33.3 to 38.4. A *t* test revealed that the mean of the San Diego County sample (36.4) is not significantly different from that of the Sierra San Pedro Mártir sample (36.0; $p = 0.16$)

California Quail *Callipepla californica*

Over much of San Diego County, the California Quail remains common, occurring year round in sage scrub, broken chaparral, open woodland, and desert oases. In rural areas where buildings are scattered amid natural vegetation the quail persists. But once the natural areas are surrounded by development the quail begins to disappear. Habitat fragmentation is accompanied by an increase in disturbance, exotic weeds, predators, and other negative factors still to be identified, bad news for all birds, like the California Quail, that nest on the ground.

Photo by Anthony Mercieca

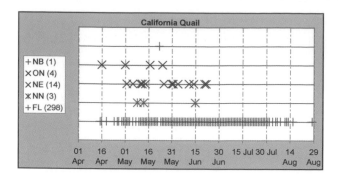

Breeding distribution: The California Quail is found throughout San Diego County's coastal slope except in extensively forested areas and where it has been eliminated by development. Our daily counts on the coastal slope ran as high as 200 in Boden Canyon (I14) 13 April 2000 (R. L. Barber) and 136 at Barrett Lake (S19) 18 June 2000 (R. and S. L. Breisch). The quail is at least as abundant on the desert slope, concentrating in large numbers around water (up to 200 around Scissors Crossing, J22, 22 March 2000, E. C. Hall; 150 at Vallecito County Park, M25, 12 May 1999, M. C. Jorgensen). It does not reach the summits of Hot Springs Mountain or Cuyamaca Peak but ranges uncommonly up to nearly 6000 feet in the Laguna Mountains (two near Wooded Hill, P23, 21 June 1998, A. E. Klovstad, C. L. Mann).

The California Quail extends onto the floor of the Anza–Borrego Desert, where it overlaps the range of Gambel's Quail. From 1997 to 2001, we found the species to be even more widespread than reported and mapped by A. G. Morley (in Massey 1998). The distributions of both species are dynamic, changing over rather brief periods, probably as a result of cycles of wet and dry years and in response to the artificial availability of water at human settlements. During the atlas period, we found the California Quail regularly east to Coyote Creek, to all developed areas in the Borrego Valley (male with six chicks at the Borrego sewage ponds, H25, 25 May 1998, P. D. Jorgensen), Tamarisk Grove, and Vallecito and Carrizo creeks east to Carrizo Marsh (O29, up to 25 on 25 April 2001, M. C. Jorgensen). Occasional birds occurred slightly farther east even in the breeding season: one on the north side of Clark Dry Lake (D25) 19 April 1998 (P. K. Nelson), 20 at San Felipe Narrows (I25) 10 April 1999 (P. K. Nelson), one in Harper Canyon (J26) 18 April 2000 (M. B. Mulrooney), and one along Pictograph Trail (L25) 21 June 2001 (R. Thériault).

Nesting: The California Quail nests usually on the ground, concealing the nest in leaf litter, a clump of grass, or a hollow under a shrub. Its nesting season varies with rainfall. The quail usually begins nesting about the end of March, as chicks are seen regularly from the last week of April. In most years the last clutch is laid around the end of June, but in wet years the birds continue later. In 1998 we noted chicks still flightless near Iron Mountain (M13) as late as 28 August (M. and B. McIntosh), implying egg laying near the end of July. The quail occasionally nests at other times of year, as reported by Belding (1890). From 1997 to 2001 our only record of unseasonal breeding was of fledglings along Forester Creek (Q14) 3 March 1999 (J., E., and K. Berndes).

Winter: The California Quail's pattern of abundance in winter is much the same as in the breeding season, as expected for a sedentary species. The birds can be seen in large coveys from the time the young fledge through the winter. Our highest winter count was of 160 in Thing Valley (Q24) 25 December 2001 (J. R. Barth).

Conservation: Though the California Quail comes into backyards in residential areas if these are adjacent to native vegetation, it is unable to adapt to urbanization. Furthermore, it suffers from habitat fragmentation, disappearing from patches of native scrub surrounded by development. This sensitivity was shown well by Crooks et al. (2001), who found the quail in 13 of 30 isolated canyons in San Diego surveyed in 1987 but only four of these canyons when they were resurveyed in 1997. No canyon where the quail was absent in 1987 was recolonized ten years later. Crooks et al. (2001) projected that the quail has a 95% chance of surviving 100 years only in habitat fragments of 173 hectares or larger. The quail persists on Point Loma (S7), where about 365 hectares of scrub remain, isolated for decades. Outside San Diego, atlas

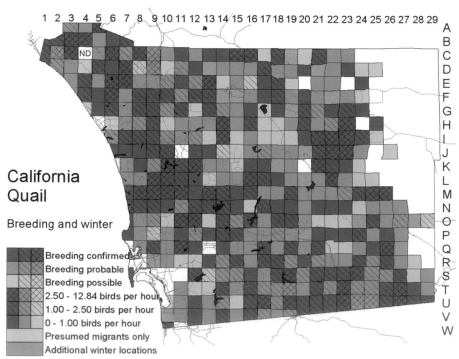

California Quail

Breeding and winter

Breeding confirmed
Breeding probable
Breeding possible
2.50 - 12.84 birds per hour
1.00 - 2.50 birds per hour
0 - 1.00 birds per hour
Presumed migrants only
Additional winter locations

results show the California Quail already gone from areas as large as an atlas square in El Cajon (Q13), Escondido (J11), and Oceanside (H5).

In contrast to its retreat from urbanization along the coast, the quail has evidently benefited from settlement in the Anza–Borrego Desert. The species' spread through the developed areas of the Borrego Valley may be quite recent. In the 1970s only Gambel's Quail was known in this area (Unitt 1984), though the California has always occurred down to the eastern bases of the county's mountains.

Taxonomy: The subspecies of the California Quail in San Diego County is *C. c. californica* (Shaw, 1798), intermediate between a darker, browner subspecies in coastal northern California and a paler one in Baja California.

Gambel's Quail *Callipepla gambelii*

By and large, Gambel's Quail replaces the California Quail in the desert Southwest, but in San Diego County the situation is far more complex. Both species occur in the Anza–Borrego Desert, leading to considerable hybridization. Gambel's is always common in the Borrego Valley, in mesquite thickets, saltbush, orchards, and residential areas alike. But elsewhere its distribution is unstable, perhaps varying with rainfall. Its occurrence in San Diego County at all may be a recent colonization.

Breeding distribution: The Borrego Valley is the core of the distribution of Gambel's Quail in San Diego County. The species is found throughout the valley but during the breeding season appears most numerous in the mesquite bosque in the center of the valley (G25), with up to 30 on 11 March 1997 (R. Thériault). Mesquite seeds are a major component of the quail's diet (Brown et al. 1998). The birds also occur in mesquites on the west and north sides of Clark Dry Lake (D25/D26), with up to 15 in D26 on 11 March 2000 (P. K. Nelson). From there they extend in a narrow zone around the base of the Santa Rosa Mountains, where they are sparse except in the northeastern corner of the county (C29; up to 24, including 17 juveniles, on 23 June 1998, R. Thériault). On the east side of the Vallecito Mountains Gambel's Quail is rare and irregular; the only records from this area are of one calling male in Cactus Garden (I27) 26 April 2000 (P. K. Nelson) and three at the mouth of the canyon of Alma Wash (K28) 4 May 1999 (L. J. Hargrove).

In other parts of the Anza–Borrego Desert the California is the predominant or exclusive species of quail. Gambel's, however, colonized the area of Yaqui Well (I24) apparently beginning in 1982 (ABDSP database). We found it in this area in the breeding season regularly, with up to eight on 25 April 1999 (P. K. Nelson), as well as just to the southeast on Mescal Bajada (J25), with up to eight on 12 June 1998 (M. and B. McIntosh), and once just to the west on Yaqui Flat (I23), with a pair on 26 May 1998 (P. K. Nelson).

Gambel's Quail has also invaded the range of the California by spreading up into the canyons draining into the Borrego Valley, going as high as 3400 feet at Peña Spring (G23; up to five on 10 April 1999, M. L. Gabel; one photographed 6 November 1999, L. J. Hargrove). It has occurred in small numbers in Culp Valley (G23/H23) at least since 1992 (M. L. Gabel). One had cleared the mountain crest by about 0.5 mile and was at about 4100 feet elevation at the east edge of Montezuma Valley (H22) 26 May 2000 (P. D. Jorgensen).

Photo by Anthony Mercieca

In the southern Anza–Borrego Desert Gambel's Quail is apparently irregular, though its history could be clouded by misidentification. There is no record in the state park database from this area earlier than 1978. From to 1993 to 1995 Paul and Mark Jorgensen found both the California and Gambel's Quails common at Carrizo Marsh (O29), with up to 80 Gambel's 2 May 1993. Yet from 1997 to 2002 the same observers found only the California here. Smaller numbers were noted, perhaps irregularly, to 1995 at Vallecito (M25), Agua Caliente Springs (M26), Palm Spring (N27), Indian Gorge (O27), and Bow Willow Campground (P27), but from 1997 to 2002 the only reports by a reliable observer were from Vallecito in 2000, of a remarkable 60 on 31 January followed by two on 30 March 2000 (R. Thériault).

Nesting: Like the other quails, Gambel's nests usually on the ground, under the protection of a shrub. Nearly all of our confirmations of Gambel's Quail breeding were of chicks following their parents. Dates of these observations extend from 10 May to 12 July, suggesting egg laying

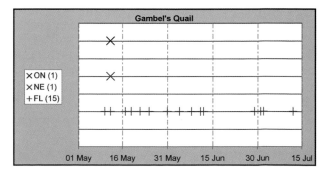

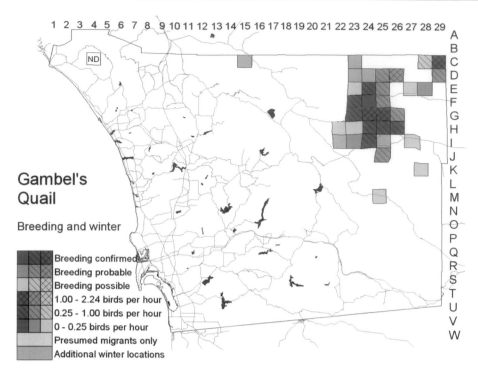

Gambel's
Quail

Breeding and winter

Breeding confirmed
Breeding probable
Breeding possible
1.00 - 2.24 birds per hour
0.25 - 1.00 birds per hour
0 - 0.25 birds per hour
Presumed migrants only
Additional winter locations

before about 1980 may all represent misidentified California Quail, as none came from well-known reliable observers; all county specimens are from the Borrego Valley only. At some popular birding spots like Yaqui Well it is certain that Gambel's Quail is a recent colonist. The record from Temecula Creek recalls the occurrence of other desert birds like the Black-tailed Gnatcatcher, Ladder-backed Woodpecker, and Black-throated Sparrow in the Aguanga/ Dameron Valley area. It may reflect range expansion west through Riverside County not detected until it reached San Diego County, an expansion paralleling that of the Ladder-backed Woodpecker and possibly a response to a drying climate. On the other hand, Gambel's Quail has been transplanted outside its native range as a game bird, and the record from Temecula Creek could have resulted from some unreported introduction.

In spite of an apparent trend of expansion, Gambel's Quail clearly retracted from some marginal areas in the mid 1990s. This may have continued into the atlas period, as implied by our finding the species along Alma Wash on the first visit in 1999 only. In desert wildernesses, the fluctuations are likely due to variations in rainfall and possibly to interactions with the California Quail, which are still not understood in detail. Population cycles of boom and bust are typical of Gambel's Quail (Brown et al. 1998).

from about mid April to early June. Both the latest and earliest dates were in 1998, suggesting that nesting begins earlier and lasts later in wet years than in dry ones.

Winter: Gambel's Quail is nonmigratory, but we found it in winter in a few places where it was lacking in the breeding season. Most notable among these were the Coyote Creek region (C23/D23/D24), where we had only three reports from 1997 to 2002, even though A. G. Morley and K. Smeltzer (in Massey 1998) found it a common breeding resident at Lower Willows (D23) from 1993 to 1995. Thus the situation at Lower Willows parallels that at Carrizo Marsh, a range expansion followed by a contraction.

In the San Felipe Creek drainage P. K. Nelson noted Gambel's Quail in winter twice at outlying localities, Angelina Spring (I22; 15 on 2 December 1999) and San Felipe Narrows (I25; 11 on 4 February 2000). By far our most remarkable Gambel's Quail record, however, is from the coastal slope, along Temecula Creek just west of Dameron Valley (C15). On 3 February 2001 K. L. Weaver studied three Gambel's loosely associated with a flock of California Quail. There are no previous records of Gambel's Quail on the coastal slope of California.

Conservation: Gambel's Quail was first reported from San Diego County in 1927, when local residents told Abbott (1928a) that the species was common in the Borrego Valley and collected two specimens. The Anza–Borrego Desert was barely explored ornithologically before then, so whether the discovery represented a recent colonization is uncertain. Reports outside the Borrego Valley

Taxonomy: Hybridization between the California and Gambel's Quails is routine. Up to 11 hybrids have been reported on Anza–Borrego Christmas bird counts. Massey (1998) reported hybrids from numerous sites including Chariot Canyon (K21), well outside the known range of Gambel's Quail. Atlas observers noted mixed pairs in Borrego Palm Canyon (F23) 1 July 1998 (L. J. Hargrove) and in the Borrego Valley (E25) 24 April 2000 (P. D. Ache). Just to the north of San Diego County, in Deep Canyon in the Santa Rosa Mountains, Gee (2003) found that 60% of 500 quail trapped in a zone of overlap were hybrids. She observed mating of the two species to be random in the wild yet species-specific when tested with birds in captivity.

Nominate *C. g. gambelii* (Gambel, 1847) is the only subspecies of Gambel's Quail in California.

Loons — Family Gaviidae

Red-throated Loon *Gavia stellata*

The Red-throated is the smallest and scarcest of the three loons known from San Diego County, an uncommon winter visitor both on the ocean close to shore and in San Diego Bay. There are only a few records inland, suggesting the Red-throated Loon uses San Diego County as an overland migration route far less than does the Common Loon.

Winter: The Red-throated Loon occurs rather uniformly in low density all along San Diego County's coastline. There may be some concentration off Torrey Pines State Reserve (N7), site of several of our higher counts 1997–2002, including the highest, of 31 on 23 December 2001 (S. Walens). On San Diego Bay, the Red-throated, like the other loons, is more numerous in the north bay. During the atlas period our maximum count there was 15 near North Island (S8) 18 December 1999, while weekly surveys through 1993 returned a January–March average of 10 and a maximum of 18 on 2 February (Mock et al. 1994). We found only a single individual in Mission Bay, at the southeast corner (R8) 8 February 2001 (P. Unitt).

The one found inland during the atlas period, at Sweetwater Reservoir (S12) 15 December 1998 (P. Famolaro), may have been a late fall migrant, though a bird evidently wintering remained at Santee Lakes (P12) 27 January–19 February 1978 (AB 32:393, 1978).

Christmas bird counts suggest considerable variation from year to year in the number of Red-throated Loons in San Diego County. Since 1970 the San Diego count has varied from a low of two in 1974 and 1993 to a high of 117 in 1983; that year yielded high numbers of Red-throated Loons on all three of the county's coastal Christmas bird counts.

Photo by Anthony Mercieca

Migration: The Red-throated Loon may arrive in October (one at Point Loma, S7, 25 October 1976, J. L. Dunn; two on central or south San Diego Bay in October 1994; Manning 1995). But the species' earliest date on the weekly surveys of north San Diego Bay (Mock et al. 1994) was 7 December. Spring departure is largely or entirely completed in April. During the atlas period our latest date was 2 April (2000, two at Torrey Pines State Reserve, D. K. Adams). The various systematic surveys of San Diego Bay recorded the species up to 14 April, except for one on the north bay 18 May and 18 June 1993 (Mock et al. 1994), one of the few records of a summer straggler.

Inland, the Red-throated Loon has been found in fall twice at Lake Henshaw (G17), one on 12 November 1978 (AB 33:213, 1979), two from 12 to 17 November 1985 (AB 40:157, 1986), and once at Borrego Air Ranch (H26), one picked up 21 November 1996 and released on a pond in Borrego Springs the next day (R. Thériault, NASFN 51:119, 1997). Inland spring records number six, from 8 March (1964; one at Lower Otay Lake, U13/U14, G. McCaskie) to 26 April (1983, one at Lake Henshaw, R. Higson, AB 37:912, 1983). One of the birds at Lake Henshaw in spring 1983 stayed into summer, noted on 8 August (R. Higson, AB 37:1026, 1983).

Conservation: Groves et al. (1996) reported that the number of Red-throated Loons breeding in western Alaska fell by 53% from 1977 to 1993, but this change is not paralleled in the number wintering in San Diego County, as suggested by Christmas bird counts.

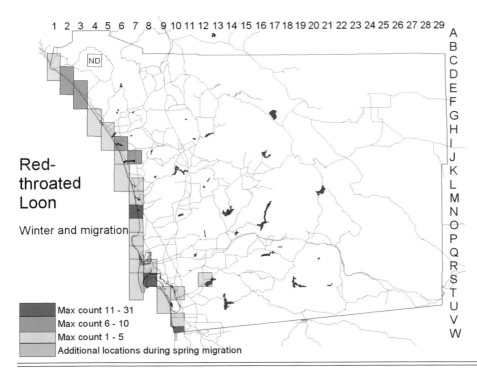

Red-throated Loon

Winter and migration

Max count 11 - 31
Max count 6 - 10
Max count 1 - 5
Additional locations during spring migration

Pacific Loon *Gavia pacifica*

The Pacific is the most abundant but also the most oceanic of San Diego County's three loons. As a winter visitor it is often common on the ocean 1 to 10 miles offshore but uncommon to rare in the bays and lagoons. Because of the concave shape of the southern California coast, most of the hundreds of thousands of Pacific Loons that migrate past California take a short cut closer to the Channel Islands and so miss San Diego County. But strong northwest winds sometimes drive fall migrants close to shore even here.

Winter: The bight between Point Loma and Imperial Beach is the Pacific Loon's prime habitat in San Diego County, used by as many as 679 on 18 December 1976 and 421 on 20 December 1997 (D. W. Povey). The numbers in this area vary greatly, however: in spite of Povey's consistent coverage of it on San Diego Christmas bird counts 1975–2002, the figures for the Pacific Loon on the count have been as low as 8 in 1975 and 18 in 1994, averaging 141. Along the coast of northern San Diego County Pacific Loons are usually fewer. On 22 counts 1980–2003 the Rancho Santa Fe circle has averaged 65, with a maximum of 583. On 28 counts 1976–2002 the Oceanside circle has averaged 38, with a maximum of 214. Presumably the birds shift up and down the coast with schools of fish. Variation in Pacific Loon numbers on San Diego County's three coastal Christmas bird counts is only slightly if at all coordinated. For example, 1995 and 1997 generated the highest totals since 1976 on the San Diego count but totals well below average on the Oceanside count.

Inside San Diego Bay the Pacific Loon is uncommon in the north bay and becomes scarcer farther south. In weekly surveys of the north bay through 1993, just

Photo by Anthony Mercieca

once did Mock et al. (1994) count more than 10 (20 on 5 January). Weekly surveys of the central bay in 1994 yielded no more than six (Preston and Mock 1995). Covering all of San Diego Bay south of the bridge weekly from April 1993 to April 1994, Manning (1995) found no more than five per day. In Mission Bay the Pacific Loon is inconsistent; from 1997 to 2002 our maximum number there was four on 20 January 1998 (B. C. Moore). The only north county lagoon inside which we found the Pacific Loon was Batiquitos (J6/J7), undoubtedly as a result of the deepening of the lagoon carried out 1994–96. Four sightings at this site included a maximum of four individuals 27 December 1997 (F. Hall).

Migration: Most of the Pacific Loon's population migrates along the California coast. In central California the birds hug the shoreline, but between Point Conception and the Mexican border they take a more direct route over the ocean, out of sight from the mainland (Russell and Lehman 1994). As a result the huge numbers seen at places like Point Piedras Blancas and Pigeon Point are rarely seen at San Diego. Russell and Lehman (1994) found that northbound migrants halted when headwinds were too strong, but southbound migrants may take advantage of northwesterly tailwinds (rare in fall), even if they have to fight their way around bends in the coast. On 6 December 1998, during a strong northwest wind, the loons were streaming past La Jolla (P7) in flocks of up to 100, and thousands passed by over the course of the day (G. McCaskie).

Fall arrival has been recorded as early as 8 October (1973, two at Point Loma, S7, J. L. Dunn), but the weekly surveys of San

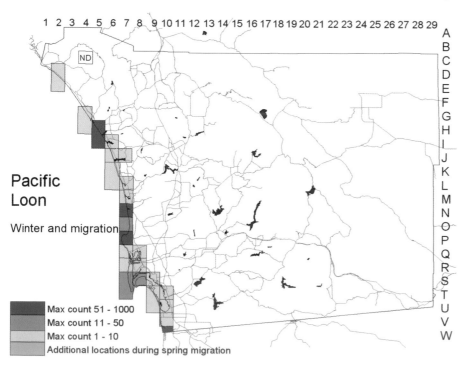

Pacific Loon

Winter and migration

Max count 51 - 1000
Max count 11 - 50
Max count 1 - 10
Additional locations during spring migration

Diego Bay did not detect the species until 9 November in 1993. Spring migration lasts from late March to early June, as attested by 25 off San Diego 3 June 1972 (G. McCaskie), three at Torrey Pines State Reserve (N7) 3 June 2001 (P. A. Ginsburg), and one on north San Diego Bay 6 June 1995 (Preston and Mock 1995). Stragglers remaining to summer are rare; the only one during the atlas period was at the San Diego River mouth (R7) 20 July–11 August 2000 (C. G. Edwards).

Pacific Loons wintering in the Gulf of California evidently make their overland crossing south of the international border, in Baja California (Huey 1927). As a result, the species is only casual inland in San Diego County. In spring there are only two records, listed by Unitt (1984). In fall there are three records from Lake Henshaw (G17),

each of two birds: 19 October 1983, 12–15 November 1985 (R. Higson, AB 38:245, 1984; 40:157, 1986), and 7–8 December 1996 (C. G. Edwards, NASFN 51:801, 1996).

Conservation: In San Diego County any trend in the Pacific Loon's numbers is obscured by the great variability from year to year. Daily counts of migrants in central California through the entire spring yielded about 1,000,000 individuals in 1979 but only about 450,000 in 1996; the difference could be due to a population decline, a northward shift of the winter range, or both (Russell 2002). Because of the Pacific Loon's funneling in migration through narrow bottlenecks, it is especially vulnerable to oil spills at those points.

Common Loon *Gavia immer*

The Common Loon is at best a fairly common winter visitor to San Diego County, widespread along the coast both on the ocean near shore and in tidal bays and estuaries. But the number of individuals wintering rarely if ever exceeds 150. The Common is the only loon likely to be seen inland, a few wintering, exceptionally summering, on the larger lakes. Migrants presumably headed to and from the Gulf of California cross San Diego County regularly but seldom stop unless compelled by storms.

Winter: The Common Loon occurs all along San Diego County's coast. On the ocean, the birder walking the beach or scanning from a lookout seldom sees as many as 10 in a day; 20 at Oceanside (H5) 27 December 1997 (D. Rorick) is a maximum count. The birds may prefer the calm water within the bays. Our numbers in Mission

Photo by Anthony Mercieca

Bay ranged up to eight in the northeast quadrant (Q8) 7 December 1998 (J. C. Worley). Various studies of San Diego Bay found that the Common Loon, unlike many other water birds, is more numerous in the deeper water of the north bay and becomes less numerous farther south. In weekly surveys of the north bay (bridge to mouth) through 1993 Mock et al. (1994) found an average of 10.4 from December through March and a maximum of 24 on 26 January. In monthly surveys of the central bay through 1993 and weekly surveys there through 1994 Preston and Mock (1995) found an average through the same months of 8.5 and a maximum of 18 on 22 November 1994. In weekly surveys of central and south bay April 1993–April 1994 Manning (1995) found no more than 10.

The Common Loon also winters occasionally on inland lakes, at a rate of less than one

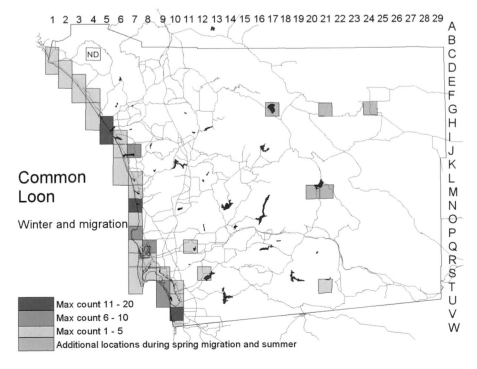

Common Loon

Winter and migration

Max count 11 - 20
Max count 6 - 10
Max count 1 - 5
Additional locations during spring migration and summer

per year. Our only such records from 1997 to 2002 were of one at Lake Murray (Q11) 7 January 1998 (N. Osborn), one found dead at Sweetwater Reservoir (S12) 19 December 1998 (P. Famolaro), and one at Lake Morena (T21) 27 December 1998 (R. and S. L. Breisch). Over 18 Christmas bird counts from 1986 to 2002, the Escondido count recorded single Common Loons twice; over 22 counts from 1981 to 2002, the Lake Henshaw count recorded only one, on 31 December 1990.

Migration: A Common Loon heading south has been seen in San Diego County as early as 26 September (1976, one over Point Loma, S7, G. McCaskie), but the regular surveys of San Diego Bay did not detect arrival before 13 October and found that numbers were still building into November. Spring departure is largely in late March and early April, but some remain until May and occasional birds remain through the summer. From 1997 to 2001 only one was found summering along the coast, at Los Peñasquitos Lagoon (N7) 2 June 2001 (K. Estey).

The Common Loon migrates inland over San Diego County, primarily using the same route along Highway S2 and over Lake Henshaw (G17) as the Brant and Surf Scoter. It is seen less frequently inland in fall than in spring, but there are several fall records extending from 1 October 1983 (14 at Lake Henshaw, R. Higson, AB 38:245, 1984) to 24 November (one stranded alive in the north fork of Fish Creek Wash, L28/L29, ABDSP database). The only large flock reported in fall was of 211 on Lake Henshaw 12 November 1985 (R. Higson, AB 40:157, 1986). In

spring, migrants have been found at Lake Henshaw from 21 March (1983, R. Higson, AB 37:912, 1983) to at least 12 May (2000, G. Grantham), but occasional individuals coming down inland remain through the summer. During the atlas period we found four on Lake Henshaw 17 July 1998 (C. G. Edwards) and up to three on Lake Cuyamaca (M20/M21) 28 May–3 September 1998 (A. P. and T. E. Keenan, P. D. Jorgensen)—note that these followed El Niño with its repeated spring storms that can interrupt the loons' overland journey. Another year of El Niño, 1983, yielded the largest flock of Common Loons ever recorded in San Diego County, 317 at Lake Henshaw 18 April (R. Higson, AB 37:912, 1983).

Conservation: Because of its habit of diving and diet of fish, the Common Loon is susceptible to oil spills, other types of water pollution, and contamination of its food. But Christmas bird counts suggest no long-term trend in the number wintering in San Diego County through the late 20th century. Stephens' (1919a) and Sams and Stott's (1959) assessment of the species as "common" suggest it may have been more numerous in the past.

Overland migration is a hazard for a bird that can take flight only from water and is doomed if it crashes on land. On 11 April 1989 an estimated 200 died when they landed along Highway S2 (R. Thériault). Casualties of that fallout are preserved as specimens from 3 miles east of Borrego Springs (F25), 1 mile southeast of Scissors Crossing (J23), and near Canebrake (N27; SDNHM 45700–2).

GREBES — FAMILY PODICIPEDIDAE

Pied-billed Grebe *Podilymbus podiceps*

Strange loud noises like choking, emanating from a marsh, are most likely coming from a Pied-billed Grebe. Large lakes, small ponds, and brackish lagoons offer habitat to this species year round as long as they support patches of marshes. Some birds disperse for the fall and winter onto protected salt water. The Pied-billed Grebe is adopting some of the habits of the megapodes of the Australasian region, using the heat and insulation from rotting wet nest material as an aid to incubation.

Breeding distribution: The Pied-billed Grebe occurs throughout San Diego County's coastal slope wherever it can find suitable habitat. The largest numbers are in the coastal lagoons, especially Buena Vista Lagoon, site of up to 46 in the lagoon's west basin (H5) 13 June 1999 (J. Ginger) and 30 in the east basin (H6) 18 June 1999 (L. E. Taylor). The birds are also numerous on lakes well equipped with fringing marshes; for example, daily counts at O'Neill Lake (E6) ranged up to 25 (21 August 1997, P. A. Ginsburg), those at Lake Murray (Q11) to 18 (N. Osborn).

In the foothills and mountains there are fewer suitable ponds and lakes, but the grebe nevertheless occurs

Photo by Anthony Mercieca

at many of these, some quite isolated, such as Twin Lakes in Cooper Canyon (C18; three, including one chick, 15 June 2000, M. and B. McIntosh). It is confirmed breeding as high as 4600 feet elevation at Lake Cuyamaca (M20; up to ten, including fledglings, 26 June 1999, A. P. and T. E. Keenan) and recorded as high as 5400 feet at Big Laguna Lake (O23; up to two on 24 July 1998, E. C. Hall). The Pied-billed Grebe is also found at a few spots a short distance over the divide on the east slope of the mountains. Among these places, only at Tule Lake (T27) did we find more than two individuals and confirm breeding (up to 20 on 6 and 21 June 2000, adults feeding young 6 June 2001, J. K. Wilson).

Nesting: The Pied-billed Grebe builds a floating platform of marsh vegetation, tying it to emergent plants. Research in San Diego County, among other places, demonstrated that the grebes regulate the temperature and humidity of the incubating eggs by covering them with damp nest material, partially substituting it for the body of the adult (Davis et al. 1984). Sometimes the nest is at the edge of a marsh where it can be seen by a human observer, but often it is hidden within dense vegetation. As a result, the great majority of our confirmations of Pied-billed Grebe breeding were of observations of chicks. The young leave the nest and climb aboard the adult's back shortly after hatching.

Almost all of our records of Pied-billed Grebe chicks fell between 11 April and 22 September. An abandoned newly hatched chick was picked up in Rancho Santa Fe (R8) 15 September 2001 (SDNHM 50574). These data show that in San Diego County the Pied-billed Grebe lays mainly from the third week of March to the third week of August. The species also nests occasionally in winter, as we noted once during the atlas period, with two young several weeks old but still begging from an adult at Wilderness Gardens (D11) 20 January 2001 (K. L. Weaver).

Migration: The degree to which movement of Pied-billed Grebes reflects arrival of migrants from the north versus shifting of the local population is unclear. On salt water, the species occurs mainly from September to March, only rarely in late spring and summer (no more than one per monthly survey of central San Diego Bay 3 May–13 October 1993–94, Mock et al. 1994; no more than one per weekly survey of the San Diego Bay salt works April–July 1993, Stadtlander and Konecny 1994). The latter authors found a max-

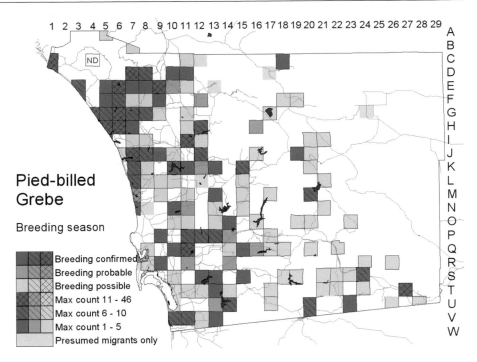

Pied-billed Grebe

Breeding season

- Breeding confirmed
- Breeding probable
- Breeding possible
- Max count 11 - 46
- Max count 6 - 10
- Max count 1 - 5
- Presumed migrants only

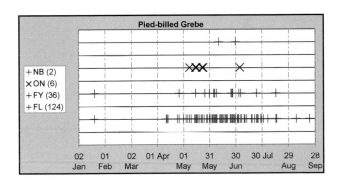

Pied-billed Grebe

+ NB (2)
X ON (6)
+ FY (36)
+ FL (124)

02 Jan | 01 Feb | 02 Mar | 01 Apr | 01 May | 31 May | 30 Jun | 30 Jul | 29 Aug | 28 Sep

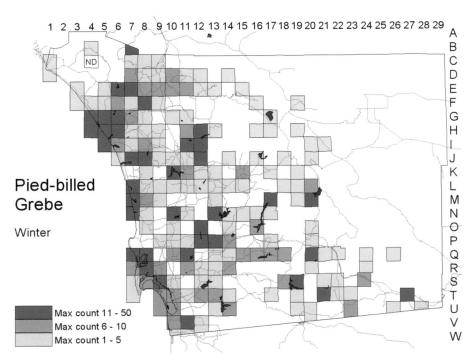

Pied-billed Grebe

Winter

- Max count 11 - 50
- Max count 6 - 10
- Max count 1 - 5

imum of 20 on 13 October 1993 and a monthly average peaking in December and January.

Juveniles may disperse soon after fledging while still retaining some of the chicks' striped head pattern. Such a juvenile on a small pond in Greenwood Cemetery (S10) 31 May 1997 was not raised there (P. Unitt).

In the Anza–Borrego Desert the Pied-billed Grebe is a rare visitor. There are five records in the Borrego Valley in fall from 5 September (1998, one near Borrego Springs Country Club, F24, P. D. Jorgensen) to 15 November (1984, one at the Roadrunner Club, F24, A. G. Morley). In late spring there are two records, of two in Borrego Springs (G24) 22 May 2001 (P. D. Ache) and one at a pond in an orchard near the mouth of Coyote Creek Canyon 15 June 1973 (ABDSP database).

Winter: In winter the Pied-billed Grebe ranges more widely than it does in spring and summer. Salt-water sites where it winters but does not breed are Agua Hedionda Lagoon (I6; up to six on 27 December 1997 and 26 December 1998, C. Sankpill), Mission Bay (up to 20 in the northwest quadrant of the bay, Q7, 21 January 2001, L. Polinsky), the San Diego River flood-control channel and Famosa Slough (R8; up to 20 on 6 January 2000, J.

A. Peugh), and San Diego Bay (up to 20 between downtown San Diego and Coronado, S9, 15 December 2001, Y. Ikegaya). Numbers on the lagoons of northern San Diego County are little changed from those in the breeding season, but on some inland lakes they can be considerably higher, e.g., up to 49 at Dixon Lake (I11) 2 January 2000 (C. Rideout) and 50 at Lake Cuyamaca 15 January 1998 (A. and. T. Keenan). In the Anza–Borrego Desert the only winter record is of one on the small pool at Butterfield Ranch (M23) 20 January 1973 (ABDSP database).

Conservation: There is no clear evidence for any trend in Pied-billed Grebe numbers in San Diego County, and data from other parts of the range are contradictory (Muller and Storer 1999). As an aquatic bird the grebe is exposed to water pollution, though it nests successfully in sewage ponds. In San Diego County, the grebe benefits greatly from the mass importation of water and the creation of the many reservoirs and ponds used to manage this water. The stocking of these ponds with fish and the introduction of the crayfish, not native to southern California, have supplied the grebe with its staple foods.

Taxonomy: All Pied-billed Grebes in North America are nominate *P. p. podiceps* (Linnaeus, 1758).

Horned Grebe *Podiceps auritus*

A winter visitor, the Horned Grebe is small and easily overlooked among the many other swimming birds along San Diego County's coast. Even though San Diego is near the southern tip of the species' winter range, the Horned Grebe is fairly common on San Diego and Mission bays, though outnumbered by the similar Eared Grebe.

Winter: In San Diego County, the Horned Grebe occurs most numerously on San Diego and Mission bays. Our highest count on San Diego Bay from 1997 to 2002 was on the Christmas bird count 15 December 2001, when 54 were found, 47 in the south bay, seven in the north bay. A high count for a more limited area was 38 in San Diego Bay off Crown Cove (T9) 9 December 1988 (Macdonald et al. 1990). Regular surveys of north and central San Diego Bay 1993–94 yielded no daily count higher than 17 on 1 February 1994 (Mock et al. 1994). Within the salt works Horned Grebes are fewer; Stadtlander and Konecny (1994) found no more than five there per weekly survey 1993–94. In Mission Bay, numbers ranged up to 12 in the northwest quadrant of the bay (Q7) 8 January and 12 February 2000 (L. Polinsky).

Elsewhere in the county the Horned Grebe is at best uncommon. A few occur on the ocean near shore (up to eight between La Jolla and Torrey Pines State Reserve, O7, 11 December 1997, S. E. Smith), in the Oceanside harbor, and the lagoons open to the tide (up to 11 in Batiquitos Lagoon, J7, 26 December 1998, R. Stone; four in Agua Hedionda Lagoon, I6, 23 December 2000, R. T. Patton). In lagoons with intermittent or no tidal input, such as San Elijo and Buena Vista, the Horned Grebe is rare.

Photo by Anthony Mercieca

There is considerable variation in the number of Horned Grebes found in San Diego each year, but it seems chaotic. The peaks and troughs on San Diego and Oceanside Christmas bird counts do not coincide. The highest total on an Oceanside count was 57 on 1 January 1977; since 1960 the highest total on a San Diego count was 176 on 26 December 1966.

Our finding wintering Horned Grebes a few times on inland reservoirs was unexpected because all but one of the few previous inland records for San Diego County were of spring migrants. Six at Lake Miramar (N10) 3 January 1998 dwindled to one by 12 February (P. M. von Hendy, P. Unitt, M. B. Stowe). Eight were on El Capitan Reservoir (O16) 20 December 1998 (S. Kingswood). At Loveland Reservoir, the species was found in two winters, with three on 31 January 2001 and 20 on 12 January 2002 (J. K. Wilson). The earlier record is of one in a borrow pit in the San Diego River (Q10) 1–9 January 1975 (J. L. Dunn).

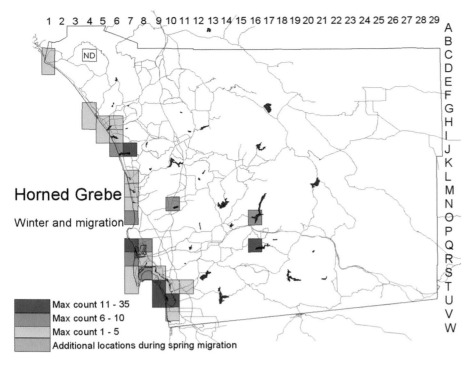

1 2 3 4 5 6 7 8 9 10 11 12 13 14 15 16 17 18 19 20 21 22 23 24 25 26 27 28 29

A B C D E F G H I J K L M N O P Q R S T U V W

Horned Grebe

Winter and migration

Max count 11 - 35
Max count 6 - 10
Max count 1 - 5
Additional locations during spring migration

when the many rainstorms associated with El Niño were an obstacle for migrants and Roger Higson monitored Lake Henshaw (G17), where many migrating water birds came down. That year, Higson noted at least 15 Horned Grebes from 4 March to 29 April, with a maximum of three on 31 March (AB 37:912, 1983). The only other records of inland migrants are of two at Lake Henshaw 7 March 1978 (D. W. Povey), one there 20–26 February 1979 (AB 33:312, 1979), and two at Lake Cuyamaca (M20) 1 March 1980 (AB 34:815, 1980).

Conservation: The Horned Grebe appears to be experiencing a slow decline in numbers and a contraction of its breeding range (Stedman 2000). In San Diego County, which lies near the southern end of the species' winter range on the Pacific coast, possible evidence of change comes from totals on Christmas bird counts in the 1950s, up to 661 in 1956 and 428 in 1957, that have not been approached since. These could, however, have been misidentified Eared Grebes. Siltation of the coastal lagoons degrades them as Horned Grebe habitat; conversely, the dredging of Batiquitos Lagoon in the mid 1990s led to the grebes using this site, where they had been absent previously.

Migration: The Horned Grebe occurs in San Diego County mainly from November to March, sometimes arriving in the last few days of October (earliest, one at Batiquitos Lagoon 27 October 1997, Merkel and Assoc. 1997). Surveys of San Diego Bay in 1993 and 1994 (Mock et al. 1994) recorded the species from 18 November to 6 April; Macdonald et al. (1990) recorded it as late as 17 April. From 1997 to 2001 our only record later than the third week of March was of one at Batiquitos Lagoon 16 April 1998 (C. C. Gorman). The only records later than 5 May are of one on San Diego Bay 25 May 1957 (AFN 11:376, 1957), two there 13 May 1984 (R. E. Webster, AB 38:957, 1984), one there 4 June 1967, and one on Mission Bay 11–18 July 1967 (G. McCaskie, AFN 21:604, 1967).

Horned Grebes migrate overland over southern California but rarely stop inland. In San Diego County, such migration has been noted mainly in spring 1983,

Taxonomy: Parkes (1952) upheld the distinction of the Horned Grebe of the Old and New worlds as subspecies, with *P. a. cornutus* (Gmelin, 1789) in North America. But Cramp and Simmons (1977) reported too much individual variation for the subspecies to be valid.

Red-necked Grebe *Podiceps grisegena*

Uncommon as a winter visitor even in coastal northern California, the Red-necked Grebe is casual as far south as San Diego County, where there are three well-supported records. These are the southernmost for the species along the Pacific coast; the Red-necked Grebe is unknown in Mexico.

Winter: One was at Sweetwater Reservoir (S12) 20 December 1969–2 January 1970 (AFN 24:538, 1970), one was at the south end of San Diego Bay (V10) 14 March 1977 (AB 31:372, 1977), and one was at Santee Lakes (P12) 30 December 1984–6 January 1985 (D. and N. Kelly, AB 39:209, 1985). Other published reports from the 1950s and 1960s are more likely of misidentified Horned Grebes (Unitt 1984).

Eared Grebe *Podiceps nigricollis*

Though highly migratory, the Eared Grebe is also flightless for much of the year; its breast muscles atrophy except when needed for migration. Breeding birds use ponds and marshes with fresh to brackish water, but nonbreeders concentrate in water that is hypersaline. In San Diego County, such conditions are found in south San Diego Bay, where the Eared

Grebe winters by the thousands. Though the grebe is still common on both fresh and salt water elsewhere, the numbers are much smaller. As a breeding bird the Eared Grebe is rare and irregular in San Diego County, which lies near the southern tip of the breeding range.

Winter: The salt works at the south end of San Diego Bay are the center for the Eared Grebe in San Diego County.

Numbers recorded here on San Diego Christmas bird counts range as high as about 4100 on 19 December 1998 and are almost always several hundred. Because this count takes place in the third week of December and wintering grebes may not finish arriving until January (Jehl 1988), the count may not always represent the species' peak abundance. Weekly surveys of the salt works from February 1993 to February 1994 yielded a maximum of 2359 on 17 March (Stadtlander and Konecny 1994). The Eared Grebe occurs in all other coastal wetlands, too, in lagoons and estuaries (up to 60 at the Santa Margarita River mouth, G4, 27 December 1999, P. A. Ginsburg, 50 in the west basin of Buena Vista Lagoon, H5, 22 December 2001, J. Determan), on Mission Bay (up to 30 in the northwest quadrant, Q7, 8 January 2000, L. Polinsky), and throughout San Diego Bay (up to 262 in the central bay 10 March 1993, Mock et al. 1994).

The Eared Grebe can be quite common as well on large reservoirs, with up to 85 on El Capitan Reservoir (O16) 11 January 1998 (S. Kingswood), 102 on Barrett Lake (S18/S19) 2 February 2001 (R. and S. L. Breisch), and an exceptional 465 on Lake Hodges (K10/K11) 27 December 1998 (R. L. Barber, O. Carter). A few winter sometimes as high as Cuyamaca Lake (six on 15 January and 11 February 1998, A. P. and T. E. Keenan). One at Big Laguna Lake (O23) 6 December 1999 (D. S. Cooper) was likely a transient. In the Borrego Valley the Eared Grebe occurs rarely on artificial ponds, in most cases as a migrant but a few times in winter (G24; up to three on 9 February 1998, P. D. Ache).

Migration: The Eared Grebe's migration pattern is unique: after breeding, most of the North American population gathers on Mono Lake and Great Salt Lake, remains through the fall, then migrates to the Salton Sea and Gulf of California. Thus, even though a few birds begin arriving in mid September, most arrive in October and

Photo by Anthony Mercieca

November, and some arrive as late as January (Jehl 1988). In spring, most Eared Grebes depart in March and early April. Records from the Borrego Valley (Roadrunner Club, F24) range from 30 September (1986) to 28 April (1982; A. G. Morley).

Breeding distribution: The Eared Grebe breeds mainly in the intermountain region and northern Great Plains; southern California is marginal to its breeding range. During the atlas period, we confirmed the species' breeding at three sites: the Ramona Water District's pond 4.1 miles west of Ramona (K13; three young on 15 June 2000, W. E. Haas), in a borrow pit along the San Diego River in Santee (P13; young on 30 April 1998, W. E. Haas), and at the northeast corner of Lake Morena (S22; young two-thirds grown on 31 May 1998, R. and S. L. Breisch). In 2003, a pair with chicks was at Lake Murray (Q11) 27 April (N. Osborn). Typically, the Eared Grebe is colonial, and a few of the earlier records of nesting in San Diego County are of ephemeral colonies. In 1989, for example, 25 were on nests at Batiquitos Lagoon (J7) 8 July 1989 (J. Oldenettel, AB 43:1366, 1989). Unitt (1984) summarized other nesting records.

Nonbreeding birds are widespread through late spring and summer in small numbers; we recorded the species in 38 atlas squares in May, June, and July. These summering birds occur on both freshwater lakes (up to nine at Whelan Lake, G6, 17 June 1997, D. Rorick) and San Diego Bay (seven on the north bay, S8, 26 May 2000, R. T. Patton). The grebes are likely to nest irregularly at some of the freshwater sites, especially Sweetwater Reservoir (S12; up to six on 12 May 2000 and 16 May 2001, P. Famolaro), Loveland Reservoir (Q16; pair on 13 June 2001, J. K. Wilson), Lake Cuyamaca (M20; pair on

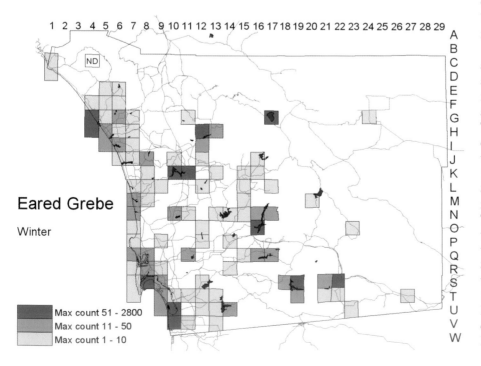

Eared Grebe

Winter

Max count 51 - 2800
Max count 11 - 50
Max count 1 - 10

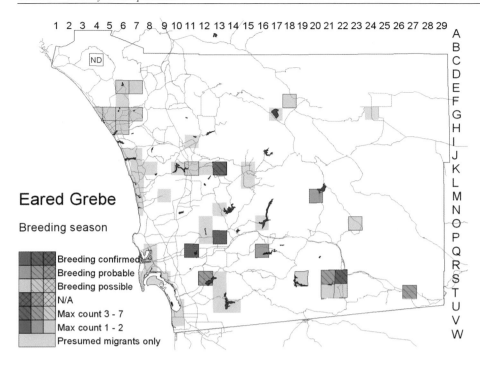

Eared Grebe

Breeding season

- Breeding confirmed
- Breeding probable
- Breeding possible
- N/A
- Max count 3 - 7
- Max count 1 - 2
- Presumed migrants only

American population (Cullen et al. 1999). An increase at the Salton Sea is likely due to the birds' shifting to this lake to take advantage of an increase in pile worms (Jehl and McKernan 2002). The grebe's reliance on three lakes for staging during migration, however, makes it vulnerable at these bottlenecks; Owens Lake, formerly a major site, was eliminated by water diversion (Jehl 1996a), and the remaining staging sites are all foci of environmental controversy. The Eared Grebe has suffered some mass die-offs as a result of disease or migrating birds being downed by storms (Jehl 1996b, Jehl et al. 1999). A die-off along the coast of San Diego County in January 1983 (Jehl and Bond 1983) was most

28 May 1998, A. P. and T. E. Keenan), and Tule Lake (T27; up to seven on 6 June 2000, J. K. Wilson).

Nesting: Like other grebes, the Eared nests on a platform of aquatic vegetation. And, like other grebes, it does not have a sharply defined breeding season. The family at Lake Murray implies egg laying as early as the beginning of April, yet R. A. Erickson noted a nest with eggs at the Stuart Mesa ponds, Camp Pendleton (G5), as late as 18–22 August 1978.

Conservation: With a total population of about 4 million, the Eared is the world's most abundant grebe, evidently because of its unique ability to exploit the superabundant brine shrimp, alkali flies, and pile worms in salt lakes (Jehl 2001). There is no demonstrable trend in the North

likely due to food shortage during El Niño (Jehl 1996b)

In San Diego County, the Eared Grebe doubtless benefited from the installation of reservoirs and sand mining that left borrow pits. The building of the salt works, more than anything, created prime wintering habitat for the Eared Grebe. With the salt works now a national wildlife refuge, it has become a question of public policy how much of this artificial habitat will be maintained for the sake of the Eared Grebe and other water birds that have capitalized on it.

Taxonomy: *Podiceps n. californicus* Heermann, 1854, is the subspecies of the Eared Grebe in North America, differing from those in the Old World by lacking white in the primaries.

Western Grebe *Aechmophorus occidentalis*

In the middle of the 20th century, the Western Grebe was just a winter visitor to San Diego County, common on salt water along the coast. It continues as one of the most abundant winter visitors on San Diego Bay and the ocean near shore. Since the 1950s it has taken on an additional role as a locally common breeding species, colonizing an increasing number of lakes and lagoons with fringing marshes. The Western Grebe is an outstanding example of a bird that has taken advantage of the need for San Diego County's human population to import and manage vast quantities of fresh water.

Breeding distribution: As of 2001, the Western Grebe was up to six nesting sites in San Diego County. At O'Neill Lake, Camp Pendleton (E6), the birds were summering by 1997 and first confirmed breeding in 1999. The numbers there are still small, maximum 12, includ-

Photo by Anthony Mercieca

ing a fledgling, 30 July 2001 (P. A. Ginsburg). At Buena Vista Lagoon (H5/H6) the grebes have nested since at least 1997 (K. Messer), both east and west of Interstate 5. Numbers in spring and summer are sometimes large,

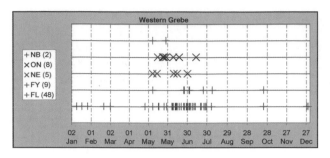

up to 132 on 11 May 1999 (M. Freda). San Dieguito Reservoir (K8) was a new breeding site discovered as a result of the atlas effort in 1997. The maximum count there in summer was at least 40 on 21 June 1997, including five adults with chicks. The birds nested there in winter as well, with up to 50, including three chicks, on 28 December 1997 and 18 January 1998 (J. Determan). Lake Hodges (K10) has become a major population center for the Western Grebe, with up to 400, including chicks, 14 June 1999 (R. L. Barber). Sweetwater Reservoir (S12/S13), site of San Diego County's first Western Grebe colony in 1956, continues to be important, with up to 40 on 4 May 1998 (P. Famolaro). Finally, a new but large colony is at Lower Otay Lake (U13/U14), with up to 60, including young, in square U13 on 25 June 1999 (V. Marquez) and 150 in U14 on 2 April 2000 (S. Buchanan).

From 1997 to 2001, we found Western Grebes summering at least irregularly on most of San Diego County's other reservoirs. On Lake Henshaw (G17) the numbers were large, up to 150 on 17 and 18 June 2000 (P. Unitt). On other lakes where the species was not confirmed breeding the numbers were much smaller, with no more than ten from May through August. Because of the Western Grebe's history, however, further increases and colonizations may be expected.

Nesting: For its nest, the Western Grebe makes a pile of cattail leaves and other aquatic vegetation, normally in the water if not actually floating. Some nests are visible from lakeshores, but most of our confirmations of Western Grebe breeding were of chicks, often riding on their parents' backs. Shortly after hatching, Western Grebe chicks leave the nest and climb onto the adults' backs.

The peak of the Western Grebe's nesting in San Diego County lasts from May through early July, but observations of chicks show that this species perhaps more than any other breeds year round. Small chicks have been noted at Lake Hodges 23 October and 30 December 1998, 27 January and 2 March 1999, and at San Dieguito Reservoir 28 December 1997, 10 and 18 January 1998, and 21 February 1998. Winter breeding of the Western Grebe at Sweetwater Reservoir was noted as long ago as 1966 (Lee 1967).

Migration: Winter visitors from the north and northeast arrive in October and November and depart mainly in April. In the spring of 2000, however, unusually large numbers remained late into the spring, with 675 on the ocean off North Island Naval Air Station (S8) 26 May (R. T. Patton) and 160 off Torrey Pines State Reserve (N7) 4 June (S. E. Smith). In the other four years of the atlas period, records of late stragglers after 2 May were of eight or fewer individuals. In weekly surveys of north San Diego Bay 1993–94, Mock et al. (1994) found the Western Grebe year round but fewest in August (no more than 12 per day).

In the Borrego Valley, there are five records of single fall migrants, 15 October–29 November, and one record of a spring migrant at Lower Willows (D23) 15 April 1974 (ABSDP database).

Winter: As a winter visitor, the Western Grebe is most numerous on the ocean within a mile or two of the shore, especially in the bight extending from Point Loma to Imperial Beach. The birds are here each winter by the hundreds, and in some years by the thousands. On 18 December 1999, the total estimated here on the San Diego Christmas bird count was 5440 (D. W. Povey, R. B. Riggan, S. Walens). Large flocks are regular elsewhere along the coast as well, with up to 1100 off San Onofre (D2) 27 December 2001 (P. D. Jorgensen) and 1840 off Oceanside (H5) 26 December 1998 (S. Walens).

The Western Grebe is common on San Diego Bay, too, with up to 536 in the central and south bay 26 January 1994 (Manning 1995). Mock et al. (1994) found it to be the sixth most numerous bird in north

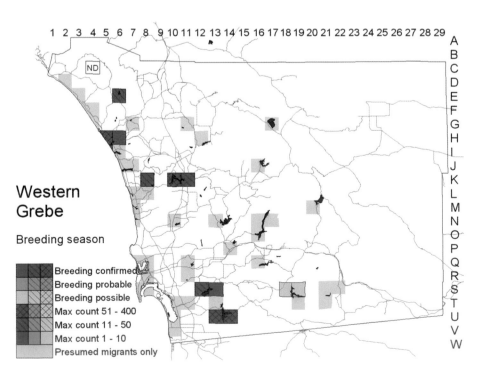

Western Grebe

Breeding season

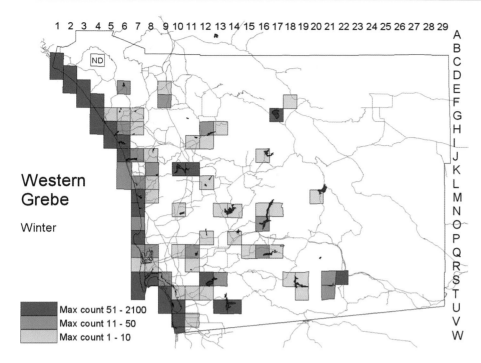

Western
Grebe

Winter

Max count 51 - 2100
Max count 11 - 50
Max count 1 - 10

San Diego Bay even when counts throughout the year were pooled. Their weekly counts peaked at 399 on 19 January 1993.

In winter, the grebe is found on inland lakes even more widely than in summer. Even where it breeds in large numbers, its numbers are even larger in winter, up to 918 on Lake Hodges 27 December 1998 (R. L. Barber) and 900 on Sweetwater Reservoir 16 December 2000 (P. Famolaro). On lakes that the grebe has not yet colonized winter counts run up to 115 at Lake Henshaw 12 December 2000 (J. R. Barth) and 62 at Lake Morena (S22) 20 December 1997 (R. and S. L. Breisch). Above 3000 feet, the elevation of Lake Morena, the only winter record is of two at Lake Cuyamaca (M20) 4 December 1998 (A. P. and T. E. Keenan).

Conservation: The Western Grebe has long been common as a winter visitor along San Diego County's coast;

there has been no clear change through history in its status in that role. As a breeding species, however, the Western Grebe is a newcomer. It was found nesting first at Sweetwater Reservoir, long the only breeding site in the county, in May 1956 (AFN 10:409–410, 1956). All other colonies have established themselves since the mid 1980s. The numbers of nonbreeding birds on inland lakes have increased greatly since that time.

Clearly the building of dams, the filling of reservoirs, and the reservoirs being stocked with fish were prerequisites for the Western Grebe's colonization and spread. Most of these were established, however, decades before the grebe began nesting. Sweetwater Reservoir, closed to the public, provided an undisturbed refuge and nucleus for the colonization. Lakes Hodges and Lower Otay, however, are open to small boats, so the grebes can adapt to some level of disturbance. Some factors not yet identified must be facilitating a population increase. The Western Grebe still faces threats, however, most notably coastal pollution. Because San Diego County's coast is in the core of the Western Grebe's winter range, a large oil spill here could kill many thousands. The effects of pollution on a small scale can be seen in the dead grebes contaminated with spots of oil that wash up regularly on the county's beaches.

Taxonomy: Both the Western and Clark's Grebes consist of two subspecies, a small one on the Mexican Plateau and a larger one farther north. The northern subspecies of the Western Grebe is nominate *A. o. occidentalis* (Lawrence, 1858).

Clark's Grebe *Aechmophorus clarkii*

Long considered a color morph of the Western Grebe rather than a distinct species, Clark's Grebe is only barely over the threshold of being a species. In San Diego County hybridization is frequent. In biology, so far as is known, the differences between the two grebes are trivial. The two occur in the same habitats, breed in mixed colonies, and flock together in winter. As a breeding bird in San Diego County, the Western tends to be somewhat more numerous than Clark's, but the difference is not great. As a winter visitor, however, the Western far outnumbers Clark's.

Breeding distribution: The distribution of Clark's Grebe is closely similar to that of the Western. At O'Neill Lake (E6), Clark's occurs in numbers similar to those of the

Photo by Anthony Mercieca

Western, counts in summer ranging up to seven on 4 July 2000 (P. A. Ginsburg). A pair nested there apparently

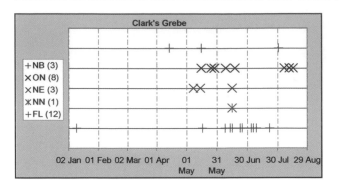

Clark's Grebe

+NB (3)								
×ON (8)								
×NE (3)								
✳NN (1)								
+FL (12)								

02 Jan 01 Feb 02 Mar 01 Apr 01 May 31 May 30 Jun 30 Jul 29 Aug

chick was at the east end of Batiquitos Lagoon (J7; M. Baumgartel). In 1998, up to eight adults were at the east end of Loveland Reservoir (Q17) 29 April, but on 22 June, when one was on a completed nest with no eggs, it appeared to be the only bird left (P. Famolaro).

We noted just a few Clark's Grebes summering at lakes where they did not breed. The only records of more than single birds were of two on Lake Murray (Q11) 16 July 1999 (N. Osborn) and three on Lake Wohlford (H12) 14 July 1999 (D. C. Seals). Some Clark's, however, may have been overlooked among Western Grebes.

Nesting: No differences in nesting biology between the Western and Clark's Grebes have been reported (Storer and Nuechterlein 1992). From 1997 to 2002, we noted winter breeding of Clark's Grebe only once, at San Dieguito Reservoir. The other records correspond to egg laying from about mid April to early August.

Migration: The migration schedule of Clark's Grebe appears to be the same as that of the Western. Migrants have departed largely by mid April though a few may straggle to early May. Six at Agua Hedionda Lagoon (I6) 20 April 1999 (P. A. Ginsburg) made our latest spring coastal count of more than two individuals. Two in Mission Bay (Q8) 28 June–8 July 1999 (J. C. Worley) and one in the Santa Margarita River estuary (G4) 30 June 2000 (P. A. Ginsburg) were the only summering Clark's Grebes reported from salt water away from breeding sites.

Winter: In winter, Clark's Grebe is considerably more numerous than in summer on Sweetwater Reservoir (up to 500 on 18 December 1999, P. Famolaro) and Lake Hodges (up to 83 on 23 December 2001, R. L. Barber), sometimes on Buena Vista Lagoon (70 on 27 December 1997, D. Rorick). Winter counts at other sites were of 15 birds or fewer. On salt water especially, Clark's makes up a small minority of grebe flocks; for example, on 18 December 1999, when D. W. Povey and M. B. Mulrooney recorded 1500 Western Grebes off Coronado they noted only 15 Clark's. During their weekly census of the salt works 1993–94, Stadtlander and Konecny (1994) recorded a maximum of 73 Clark's on 17 February 1993, but this was their only count of more than 25. Ratti (1981) found 13% of the 332 wintering *Aechmophorus* grebes he observed around San Diego in January 1977 to be Clark's. Part of the apparent difference between the species by season, however, may be due to the plumage difference between them being less well marked in winter and to the difficulty in distinguishing the birds at a distance in the large flocks seen offshore.

unsuccessfully in 1997, then successful nesting began in 1999, the same year as the Western. Indeed, many of the pairs at this site have been mixed. At Buena Vista Lagoon (H5/H6), by contrast, Clark's Grebe is much less numerous than the Western and not confirmed nesting; our high count here during late spring or summer was only three on 2 May 1999 (J. Determan), and we did not confirm the species' nesting. At San Dieguito Reservoir (K8), our only records were in winter, but the birds bred there in 1997–98, with up to ten individuals including one pair with two nearly grown young and others in courtship display 10 January 1998 (K. Aldern). Lake Hodges is as major a site for Clark's as for the Western; counts here in spring and summer ranged up to 35 in square K10 on 16 April 1997 (V. P. Johnson) and 35 in K11 on 13 June 1998 (E. C. Hall). At Sweetwater Reservoir (S12/S13) Clark's breeds regularly but in numbers smaller than the Western (eight on 4 May 1998, P. Famolaro). At Lower Otay Lake (U14) Clark's is also confirmed breeding (young on 4 July 1999, S. Buchanan) but occurs usually in small numbers; the only count of more than ten was of 55 on 29 May 2001 (N. Osborn).

We confirmed nesting of Clark's Grebe at two sites where the Western did not breed. On 17 May 1997 a

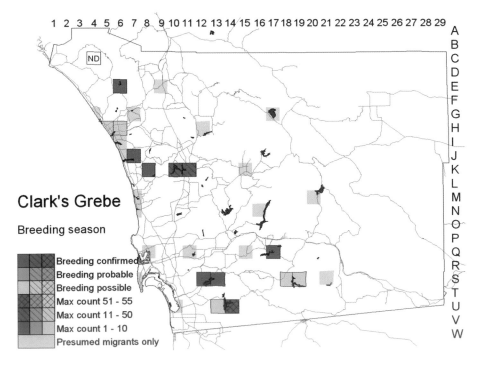

Clark's Grebe

Breeding season

Breeding confirmed
Breeding probable
Breeding possible
Max count 51 - 55
Max count 11 - 50
Max count 1 - 10
Presumed migrants only

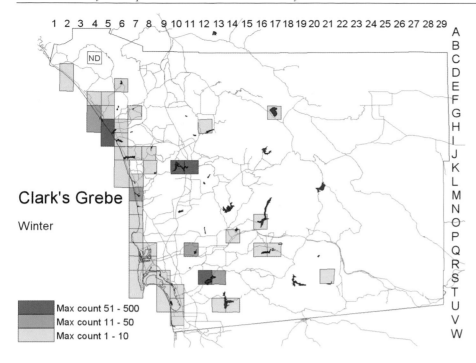

Clark's Grebe

Winter

Max count 51 - 500
Max count 11 - 50
Max count 1 - 10

Western and Clark's Grebes in San Diego County appears to be considerably higher than in the areas furnishing the data on which the decision to split the species was based (Ratti 1979). At Lake O'Neill mixed pairs are frequent, perhaps just as frequent as if the birds were selecting their mates without regard to species (P. A. Ginsburg). Of three nests at Sweetwater Reservoir observed by A. Mercieca in 2003, two belonged to mixed pairs. Possibly each grebe's preference for its own species emerges only where the number of each in a colony is large. Possibly the degree of reproductive isolation between them varies regionally. The situation in San Diego County suggests that the relationship between these grebes could use further study.

Conservation: Because Clark's Grebe was widely recognized as a species distinct from the Western Grebe only in the early 1980s there are no substantial historical data on its status. In San Diego County the careers of the two grebes appear to be progressing in tandem.

Geographic variation in Clark's Grebe parallels that in the Western, with a small subspecies on the Mexican Plateau. The larger subspecies of Clark's found in the United States is *A. c. transitionalis* Dickerman, 1986.

Taxonomy: The extent of hybridization between the

ALBATROSSES — FAMILY DIOMEDEIDAE

Laysan Albatross *Phoebastria immutabilis*

The Laysan is the most numerous of the three species of albatross breeding in the North Pacific (almost entirely on the northwestern Hawaiian Islands). But the bulk of the population forages in the northwest quadrant of the Pacific Ocean, making the species rare off California. In 1986 the Laysan Albatross established a new breeding colony just 210 miles south of San Diego on Guadalupe Island (Dunlap 1988). But the only certain records for San Diego County are of two birds found dead on beaches.

Migration: Linda Belluomini found a Laysan Albatross dead and partly decomposed on the beach just north of the Santa Margarita River mouth (G4) 31 March 1983 (SDNHM 42196). Charles Herzfeld found another at Torrey Pines City Beach (O7) 8 March 2000 (SDNHM 50396). The report of a Laysan Albatross found dead at the south end of Blair Valley (L24) 28 May 1982 is plausible, as there are eight well-supported records elsewhere in the Colorado Desert May–July, presumably of birds that wandered north out of the Gulf of California (Patten et al. 2003). But no remains of the albatross in Blair Valley were preserved (AB 36:893, 1982).

Photo by Philip Unitt

Conservation: Although the Laysan Albatross expanded its breeding range in the late 20th century by colonizing several islands in the eastern Pacific (Pitman 1988), its recent population trend has been downward. It faces two serious threats: death from swallowing the baited hooks trailed by longline fishing boats and death from swallowing bits of floating plastic trash, accumulating in massive quantities in the North Pacific gyres.

Black-footed Albatross *Phoebastria nigripes*

The Black-footed was the only albatross regular on the ocean off San Diego during the 20th century. It was once fairly common during late spring and summer, but its numbers off southern California have decreased greatly. An unsustainably high rate of mortality due to incidental kill by the longline fishery now threatens the entire species.

Migration: Off southern California, the Black-footed Albatross is most frequent in May and June, concentrating along the Santa Rosa–Cortés Ridge (Briggs et al. 1987). It is rare closer to shore than San Clemente Island, though it has been seen as near the mainland as 1 mile off Mission Beach 16 May 1981 (G. McCaskie) and 3 miles off San Diego 20 May 1989 (J. O'Brien, AB 43:536, 1989). The only specimen preserved from shore was found dead on the beach at Carlsbad (I6) 27 May 1981 (SDNHM 41400).

Conservation: From the maximum of 112 birds 25 miles west of Point Loma 5 August 1958 (AFN 12:436, 1958), the number of Black-footed Albatrosses seen off San Diego County has declined steadily. In the 1970s three to six could be expected on a spring or summer day

Photo by Richard E. Webster

spent on a boat well offshore (Unitt 1984). Since then the species has become rare, in parallel with the decline of the ocean productivity off southern California during the warm-water years of the 1980s and 1990s. Across the North Pacific Ocean, the number of Black-footed Albatrosses killed by swallowing the baited hooks drawn behind longline fishing boats is greater than what the species' reproductive rate can sustain. As a result, the International Union for the Conservation of Nature has designated the species as threatened.

Short-tailed Albatross *Phoebastria albatrus*

During the 19th century, before it was reduced to the verge of extinction by plume hunters at its nesting colonies in the western Pacific, the Short-tailed Albatross was common on the ocean off southern California year round. Gradual recovery began in the second half of the 20th century, and sporadic sightings off California—one far off San Diego—have increased in tandem. But the species remains of one of the world's most endangered birds.

Migration: Anthony (1924) wrote, "a quarter of a century ago … ten miles from land they [both the Short-tailed and Black-footed Albatrosses] were almost certain to be found, and in the waters nearer land they were by no means uncommon… So far as my experience goes, there was no particular time of year when either species was more abundant." Cooper (1868) reported collecting three immatures

inside San Diego Bay. The most recent specimen was taken off San Diego 9 January 1896 (SDNHM 68).

Conservation: From 1933 to 1950 the Short-tailed Albatross hovered on the brink of extinction. Protection and rehabilitation of its primary nesting site, the Japanese island of Torishima, has allowed the population to grow, reaching approximately 1500 birds in 2001 (www.fakr. noaa.gov/infobulletins/2001_infobulletins/albatrossbreeding.html). From 1898 to 1977 there were no well-supported records for California, but 11 accumulated from 1977 through 2002. The sightings closest to San Diego are of an immature 90 miles west of San Diego 28 August 1977 (Luther 1980) and another near Santa Barbara Island 19 February–22 March 2002 (Cole and McCaskie 2004). Although the population trend is now positive the species still faces threats: drowning of birds taking baited fish hooks from longline fishing boats and swallowing of floating plastic trash, blocking the birds' digestive tracts.

PETRELS AND SHEARWATERS — FAMILY PROCELLARIIDAE

Northern Fulmar *Fulmarus glacialis*

The Northern Fulmar is primarily a winter visitor to the ocean off San Diego County. Its distribution varies greatly from year to year, the birds dispersing far offshore when the ocean is warmer, concentrating nearer the coast when the ocean is cold (Briggs et al. 1987). Under the latter conditions the fulmar can sometimes be seen from shore when the wind is from the west. On at least two occasions, perhaps because of a scarcity of prey, large numbers of fulmars have washed up dead on the county's beaches.

Photo by Kenneth W. Fink

Winter: As for other pelagic birds, La Jolla (P7) is the spot in San Diego County where the Northern Fulmar is best seen from shore. Counts there range up to 260 in 2 hours on 21 October 2003 (S. Walens). Counts on the ocean near shore range up to 205 on the San Diego Christmas bird count 21 December 1963. During die-offs, dead fulmars are found scattered on beaches the length of San Diego County. The most severe die-offs, affecting hundreds if not thousands of birds, were in March 1976 and the winter of 2003–04.

Migration: Briggs et al. (1987) reported the fulmar arriving in southern California in October, departing largely in March and April. Data specific to San Diego County reflect the same schedule. After incursions stragglers remain later, rarely clear through the summer, with individuals off San Diego 12 September 1982 (B. Barrett, AB 37:223, 1983) and 5 September 1987 (J. L. Dunn, AB 42:134, 1988).

Taxonomy: Fulmars of the North Pacific Ocean are *F. g. rodgersii* Cassin, 1862.

Cook's Petrel *Pterodroma cookii*

Petrels of the genus *Pterodroma* typically remain over deep water, off the continental shelf, at least near California. Only one has been reported closer to the coast of San Diego County than San Clemente Island.

Migration: One Cook's Petrel was 16 miles west of La Jolla 13 June 1997 (M. Force, FN 51:1052, 1997). Other sightings of this species near the latitude of San Diego are at least 100 miles offshore.

Pink-footed Shearwater *Puffinus creatopus*

The Pink-footed Shearwater nests on Chilean islands in the southeast Pacific and winters (in the northern summer) in the northeast Pacific. Though its numbers have declined, it is still fairly common off San Diego County. The Pink-footed has been affected less dramatically than the Sooty Shearwater by the decline in ocean productivity off California of the 1980s and 1990s.

Migration: Briggs et al. (1987) found the number of Pink-footed Shearwaters off southern California to increase sharply from March to May, then decrease sharply from September to November. In some years there are two peaks, in May and August or September. Though usually uncommon within 5 miles of shore, the Pink-footed Shearwater can be seen regularly from La Jolla (P7) in August and September if the wind is favorable (S. Walens).

Winter: From December to February the Pink-footed Shearwater is uncommon to rare. A count of three off San Diego 21 January 1984 was high for this season (G. McCaskie, AB 38:357, 1984). Probably because of winter storms driving the birds inshore, sightings from land are more frequent in winter than in summer. An example

Photo by Brian L. Sullivan

is one from Torrey Pines State Reserve (N7) 4 February 1999 (D. K. Adams).

Conservation: In the 1960s and 1970s the Pink-footed Shearwater was common to abundant off San Diego, with up to 6000 on 9 September 1972 (G. McCaskie). By the beginning of the 21st century the species could be rated only as fairly common. In its breeding range, consisting of only three islands, however, the Pink-footed also faces threats: introduced predators, degradation of habitat, and collecting of chicks for human food.

Flesh-footed Shearwater *Puffinus carneipes*

The Flesh-footed Shearwater ranges mainly through the Indian and western Pacific oceans and is rare off California, especially so toward the south. There are only 12 records for the waters off San Diego County.

Migration: As a migrant from the southern hemisphere, the Flesh-footed occurs off California mainly in the northern spring, summer, and fall. Dates for San Diego County extend from 9 April (1996, La Jolla, P7, S. Walens, NASFN 50:332, 1996) to 9 September (1972, two or three off San Diego, AB 27:119, 1973), except for one seen from La Jolla 13 February 2001 (B. L. Sullivan, NAB 55:227, 2001). The

Photo by Brian L. Sullivan

two sightings at La Jolla are the only ones from shore and the only ones for the county since 1981. Of note were two

seen just south of the border near Los Coronados Islands 31 March 1996 (K. and C. Radamaker, NASFN 50:332, 1996).

Buller's or New Zealand Shearwater *Puffinus bulleri*

Buller's Shearwater nests on islands around New Zealand and migrates to the North Pacific, where it is sometimes abundant in fall along the coast of northern California. On the ocean off San Diego County, however, it is rare, with only about 16 records closer than San Clemente Island.

Migration: All but two of San Diego County's records of Buller's Shearwater range from 23 July (1981, eight 60 miles off San Diego, D. W. Povey) to 26 November (1994, one from shore at La Jolla, P7, S. Walens, G. L. Rogers, NASFN 49:100, 1995). The count of eight on 23 July 1981 is the maximum yet reported. Other than the one seen at La Jolla, the only fall record from shore is of one found dead along the Silver Strand (T9) 2 October 2002 (S. M. Wolf, SDNHM 50666).

Winter: Two winter records of Buller's Shearwater for

Photo by Richard E. Webster

San Diego County lie outside the species' usual seasonal pattern along the Pacific coast of North America. One was found dead on Black's Beach (O7) 19 February 1976 (SDNHM 39756), and another was seen from shore at La Jolla 21 January 1995 (A. DeBolt, P. A. Ginsburg, NASFN 49:195, 1995).

Sooty Shearwater *Puffinus griseus*

Few changes in bird distribution have been as sudden and dramatic as the Sooty Shearwater's desertion of the ocean off southern California. Before the 1980s, this visitor from the southern hemisphere was the most abundant seabird on the ocean off San Diego in summer. After El Niño hit in 1982–83 and the ocean remained at an elevated temperature for the next 20 years, the shearwater's numbers dropped by 90% (Veit et al. 1996). A comparison confined to the ocean near San Diego County's coast would likely show a decline even steeper.

Migration: The Sooty Shearwater begins arriving in April, peaks in May (Briggs et al. 1987), remains (or remained) common through September, and then decreases in number through December. In the 1960s and 1970s, on day-long boat trips out of San Diego, counts in the hundreds were routine. Estimates ran as high as 5000 on 9 September 1972 and 14 May 1977 (G. McCaskie) and 10,000 on 22 June 1970 (AFN 24:715, 1970). By the 1990s, typical daily counts were under 10. A feeding flock of about 200 off Point Loma (S7) 3 August 1998 was exceptional (P. A. Ginsburg). Sightings from shore, especially at La Jolla (P7), were more regular when the species was common. Guy McCaskie noted one following a fishing boat into San Diego Bay 5 May 1963. Sick or starving

birds are picked up regularly on the county's beaches.

Winter: From December to March the Sooty Shearwater is rare—currently much scarcer than the Short-tailed Shearwater. Before 1982, winter counts ranged up to 20 off San Diego 18 January 1969 (AFN 23:519, 1969). Since 1987, the highest winter count has been of three between San Diego and Los Coronados Islands 6 January 1995 (G. McCaskie).

Conservation: The decline of the Sooty Shearwater followed quickly on the heels of the decline in ocean productivity off southern California that began in the late 1970s: a decrease in zooplankton of 80% from 1951 to 1993 (Roemich and McGowan 1995, McGowan et al. 1998). The shearwater's declines were especially steep in years of El Niño, and from 1990 on there was no recovery even when the oceanographic pendulum swung the opposite direction (Oedekoven et al. 2001). Evidently much of the population has shifted farther north, into the north-central Pacific (Spear and Ainley 1999), but the species' total numbers may be declining as well (Oedekoven et al. 2001). The Sooty Shearwater offers the most striking example of how suddenly and profoundly a bird's distribution can be affected by climate change. It stands as a warning of how quickly anthropogenic global warming could render many places unsuitable for even their most abundant wildlife.

Short-tailed Shearwater *Puffinus tenuirostris*

Unlike other seabirds that breed in the southern hemisphere and migrate to the North Pacific, the Short-tailed Shearwater occurs off California mainly in the northern winter. Off San Diego County it

is generally uncommon to rare, though influxes of larger numbers are known in at least two winters. Like the Black-vented Shearwater, the Short-tailed prefers waters rather close to shore; it is seen typically within 5 miles of the coast.

Winter: A winter day's trip by boat into the Short-tailed Shearwater's preferred zone often yields one or two individuals. Seven off Oceanside (H5) 24 December 1988 (D. W. Povey, AB 43:365, 1989) and 10 off La Jolla (P7) 1 January 1999 (G. McCaskie, NAB 53:208, 1999) were high numbers for most years. Irruptions took place, however, in 1941–42 and 1983–84. In the former winter, Kenyon (1942, 1943) saw at least 120 one quarter mile off La Jolla 16 December 1941 and collected 18 specimens, both at sea and as beached casualties. In the latter winter, McCaskie saw 75 off San Diego 21 January 1984 (AB 38:357, 1984) and one was picked up dead on shore at Imperial Beach (V10) 1 December 1983 (SDNHM 43349). Because of the species' typically inshore distribution, it has been seen from shore on numerous occasions, with up to six at La Jolla 9 December 2001 (S. Walens).

Migration: Dates for the Short-tailed Shearwater in San Diego County extend from 19 October (1983, two off San Diego, D. W. Povey, AB 38:246, 1984) to 28 April and 2

Photo by Richard E. Webster

May (1997, individuals found sick or dead on the beach at Coronado, T9, B. Foster, E. Copper, FN 51:927, 1997; specimens not saved).

Manx Shearwater *Puffinus puffinus*

The Manx Shearwater, a close relative of the Black-vented Shearwater, nests on islands in the North Atlantic and winters along the coast of southern South America. Apparently some birds have rounded Cape Horn and migrated to the North Pacific, accounting for over 75 well-supported sightings off California through 2002. These records are all

since 1993, suggesting a shift in the species' distribution—possibly a still-undiscovered colonization of the Pacific Ocean—as well as birders' becoming aware of the species and its identification criteria.

Migration: The first Manx Shearwater conclusively identified near San Diego County was 16 miles off Oceanside 28 April 2004 (T. McGrath).

Black-vented Shearwater *Puffinus opisthomelas*

The ocean along San Diego County's coast is central to the nonbreeding range of the Black-vented Shearwater. At times, much of the population concentrates there, feeding on squid and fish. The Black-vented Shearwater nests in spring on islands around Baja California, principally Natividad, then migrates north, occurring off southern California primarily in fall and winter.

Winter: The Black-vented is less pelagic than most other shearwaters, concentrating within 15 miles of the coast. Briggs et al. (1987), however, recorded it out to the Santa Rosa–Cortés Ridge, 100 miles offshore. In the mid to late 1970s, they found the species most consistently in a strip from San Diego north about 75 km—essentially, the San Diego County coastline—and their highest densities, up to 80 birds per square kilometer, off Oceanside. When sardines or squid are concentrated, however, the numbers of Black-vented Shearwaters can be far higher, for example, 10,000 off San Diego 19 October 1983 (D. W. Povey, AB 38:246, 1984). Often the birds can be seen (with aid of a scope) in large numbers from shore. Our largest such count during the atlas period was of 3850 off Torrey Pines State Reserve (N7) 23 December 2001 (S. Walens). All these counts, however, were eclipsed on 23 and 24 January 2004. On the morning of the 24th, about 85,000 were off La Jolla (N7; S. Walens) while 30,000–50,000,

Photo by Brian L. Sullivan

possibly part of the same flock, were off Cardiff (L7; P. A. Ginsburg). The spectacle was broadcast on television news. These flocks must have constituted a substantial fraction of the world's Black-vented Shearwaters, given that the population breeding in 1997 on Natividad Island was about 77,000 pairs, and that island supports 95% of the species' entire population (Keitt et al. 2003). An abundance of juvenile sardines, observed by local bait seiners, probably attracted the shearwaters that day (S. E. Smith, National Marine Fisheries Service).

Migration: In general, the Black-vented Shearwater is most abundant off southern California from September through December (Briggs et al. 1987). Its movements vary, however, from year to year. Especially in years of El Niño, when the nesting of many seabirds around Baja California fails because of a shortage of food, Black-vented may arrive early, as in late July 1983, when hundreds were visible from La Jolla (G. McCaskie, AB 37:1026, 1983), and 7–9 July 1992, when 500 were in the same area (P. A. Ginsburg, AB 46:1177, 1992). Briggs et al. (1987) saw no Black-vented Shearwaters off southern California in April, but, on occasion, the species occurs in numbers in San Diego County even then, with up to 500 at La Jolla 7 April 2001 (S. Walens).

Conservation: Because the Black-vented Shearwater is so concentrated in both its nesting colony and pelagic range, it is especially vulnerable to disasters like oil spills that

could kill most of the population quickly. Inclusion of Natividad Island in the Vizcaíno Biosphere Reserve and the recent eradication of cats, goats, and sheep from the island were major steps toward safeguarding the species. But many threats remain, such as the establishment of a human settlement on the island, the driving of vehicles through the colony, and the constant danger that other mammals could escape and establish themselves. Because the colony has been censused adequately only once, the population trend is still unknown (Keitt et al. 2003).

Veit et al. (1996) found the Black-vented Shearwater's numbers off southern California increasing in response to ocean warming, so the recent high numbers suggest continuation of a trend.

STORM-PETRELS — FAMILY OCEANITIDAE OR HYDROBATIDAE

Wilson's Storm-Petrel *Oceanites oceanicus*

Breeding in the Antarctic and subantarctic, Wilson's Storm-Petrel migrates in large numbers to the North Atlantic but in only small numbers to the North Pacific. In California, it is seen annually in Monterey Bay and over Cordell Bank near Point Reyes but rarely elsewhere. There are just five sightings within 45 miles of San Diego County's coast.

Migration: San Diego County's records of Wilson's Storm-Petrel are all for August and September: 25 miles west-northwest of Point Loma 31 August 1935 (Miller 1936, UCLA 2222), 6 miles west of Point Loma 3 September

1980 (D. W. Povey, Roberson 1993), 25 miles west of Point Loma 28 August 1988 (G. McCaskie, Pyle and McCaskie 1992), 30 miles west of Point Loma 10 September 1988 (same individual as last?, W. Russell, Patten and Erickson 1994), and 45 miles off San Diego 8 September 1996 (G. McCaskie, NASFN 51:119, 1997).

Taxonomy: Wilson's Storm-Petrel is commonly divided into two subspecies, longer-winged *O. o. exasperatus* Mathews, 1912, nesting around Antarctica, and nominate *O. o. oceanicus* (Kuhl, 1820), nesting on subantarctic islands. The single specimen from San Diego County (UCLA 2222) needs to be reexamined for determination of its subspecies.

Fork-tailed Storm-Petrel *Oceanodroma furcata*

The Fork-tailed is the most boreal storm-petrel in the North Pacific, most abundant in Alaska and breeding south only to Humboldt County, California. The 13 records from San Diego County are the southernmost well-supported occurrences along the Pacific coast, though the species has been recorded in Hawaii as well.

Winter: The Fork-tailed Storm-Petrel is sporadic at the southern tip of its range, with occurrences clumped in small irruptions. In 1990, one was picked up on the beach at La Jolla (P7) 14 February 1990 (SDNHM 46392) and two were seen from shore there 19 February (G. McCaskie, AB 44:327, 1990). The only other December–February record is of one found dead at Ocean Beach (R7) 23 December 1918 (Stephens 1919b, SDNHM 2031).

Migration: Most records of the Fork-tailed Storm-Petrel for San Diego County are for spring rather than winter.

The total spread of dates is from 9 September (1990, one photographed off San Diego, J. O'Brien, AB 45:150, 1991) to 9 June (1939, one found exhausted on the beach at Cardiff, L7, Huey 1939, SDNHM 18075). Other records more recent than the five listed by Unitt (1984) are of up to seven seen from shore at La Jolla 13–23 April 1995 (S. Walens, NASFN 49:308, 1995) and birds found dead and partly decomposed by Brian Foster at the mouth of Aliso Creek, Camp Pendleton (F4), 1 May 1999 (SDNHM 50279) and 4 April 2001 (SDNHM 50867) and on the Silver Strand, Coronado (T9), 19 May 1997 (SDNHM 49806) and 7 May 1999 (SDNHM 50278).

Taxonomy: The Fork-tailed Storm-Petrel is generally divided into two subspecies: paler, more northern nominate *O. f. furcata* (Gmelin, 1789) and darker, more southern *O. f. plumbea* (Peale, 1848), including the specimens from San Diego County. Boersma and Silva (2001) suggested that the validity of the distinction needs reevaluation.

Leach's Storm-Petrel *Oceanodroma leucorhoa*

Of the storm-petrels of the North Pacific Ocean, Leach's has the widest range, in both dispersion of breeding colonies and dispersion of nonbreeding birds at sea—Leach's occurs even in the most remote

parts of the North Pacific, in areas where there are few if any other birds. Off San Diego County, Leach's occurs farther offshore than the other species and is rarely seen by day within 25 miles of land. Yet Los Coronados Islands, within sight of San Diego, are the site of a colony, a population showing the full spectrum of the species' variation from white rumped to dark rumped.

Migration: Leach's Storm-Petrel occurs off southern California year round but is common only from June to October, during the species' breeding season. From December to May numbers are low (Briggs et al. 1987). Leach's is less gregarious at sea than the Black or Least Storm-Petrels, so the maximum counts per day are less (up to 400 near San Clemente Island 1 September 1958, AFN 13:62, 1959), though Briggs et al. (1987) observed in August 1977 a density of 2.6 birds per square kilometer.

Four Leach's Storm-Petrels found in San Diego Bay have been brought to wildlife rehabilitators but died and are preserved as specimens. Their dates range from 23 July to 1 October, the time when young are fledging from the colony on Los Coronados Islands. Possibly the birds were disoriented by the lights of Tijuana and San Diego and flew toward shore, or, at night, they crashed onto boats that later came back to port at San Diego.

One picked up in El Cajon (Q13) 19 September 1988 was fatally disoriented (AB 43:538, 1989, SDNHM 45435).

Winter: One seen from shore at La Jolla (P7) 14 December 1995 (S. Walens, G. McCaskie, NASFN 50:220, 1996) provided the only specific winter record of Leach's Storm-Petrel near the coast of San Diego County.

Taxonomy: The classification of Leach's Storm-Petrel into subspecies is unsatisfactory. The highly variable population on Los Coronados Islands could be considered intergrades between the white-rumped *O. l. leucorhoa* (Vieillot, 1818) and the dark-rumped *O. l. chapmani* Berlepsch, 1906. Bourne and Jehl (1982) and Power and Ainley (1986) placed it with *chapmani*. Few white-rumped specimens collected away from nesting colonies can be identified as the larger *O. l. leucorhoa* versus the smaller *O. l. socorroensis* Townsend, 1890. The measurements tabulated by Huntington et al. (1996) suggest the degree of overlap in size may be too much for long-recognized distinction between these two subspecies to be maintained.

Ashy Storm-Petrel *Oceanodroma homochroa*

The Ashy Storm-Petrel is almost endemic to California. The small, possibly ephemeral colony on Los Coronados Islands is the only one south of the Mexican border. San Diego County is thus marginal to the Ashy Storm-Petrel's range, and the species appears rare in the county's offshore waters—though the difficulty in identifying it in the field undoubtedly means some are overlooked.

Migration: The Ashy Storm-Petrel is not strongly migratory; it remains year round in the California Current. On the ocean near the coast of San Diego County the species is rare, usually seen singly if at all. A count of 40 off San Diego 4 December 1966 (G. McCaskie) remains the highest. The Ashy Storm-Petrel is most frequent in fall and winter, with dates ranging from 25 July (1964, G. McCaskie) to 19 May (1973, AB 37:819, 1973; 1979, AB 33:805, 1979).

Surprisingly, the Ashy Storm-Petrel has been picked up within San Diego Bay or on land within the city of San Diego on several occasions, all between 6 September (found on the grounds of the San Diego Zoo, R9, SDNHM 30301) and 22 November (1981, found in an airplane hangar at Lindbergh Field, S9, SDNHM 41597).

Unitt (1984) listed four such records; more recent were one in National City (T10) 30 September 1995 (SDNHM 49486), one found in the trolley yard in downtown San Diego (S9) 25 September 2000 (SDNHM 50480), and one caught by a cat along Illinois Street near El Cajon Boulevard in the North Park area of San Diego (R10) 10 September 2002 (SDNHM 50664). The last was over 6 miles inland from the beach at Coronado. The coinciding of these onshore records in the fall with those of the Black and Leach's Storm-Petrels suggests that in all three species young fledging at night from the colony on Los Coronados Island became disoriented by city lights. Yet the population of the Ashy on Los Coronados is thought to be very small, much smaller than that of the other two species. Jehl (in Jehl and Everett 1985) suggested only two or three pairs, though Everett and Anderson (1991) thought it could be greater.

Conservation: The total population of the Ashy is much less than that of the other North Pacific storm-petrels, probably under 10,000. Increasing populations of Western Gulls nesting at the same sites, especially Southeast Farallon Island, could threaten it (Ainley 1995). On Los Coronados Islands the main threat has been the release of cats and rats. Much of the Ashy Storm-Petrel's population congregates in fall on Monterey Bay, another bottleneck of vulnerability.

Black Storm-Petrel *Oceanodroma melania*

The Black is the most numerous of the storm-petrels occurring on the ocean off San Diego County and nests on Los Coronados Islands. It is primarily a summer visitor, regular just two or three miles off shore but rarely seen from land. On several occasions disoriented young Black Storm-Petrels have been picked up inland in metropolitan San Diego.

Migration: The Black Storm-Petrel is seen off San Diego County mainly from April to November, corresponding to the time at which the birds are at the colony on Los Coronados Islands. At times, however, many more birds are seen off San Diego (up to 2000 on 17 September 1970, AB 32:107, 1971; 1300 on 13 September 1992, AB 47:148, 1993) than can be accounted for by the local population (estimated at 100 pairs on Middle Rock of Los Coronados Islands 1989–90, Everett 1991). The Black Storm-Petrel's migration reflects that of many seabirds nesting primarily around Baja California, with movement north in summer after breeding, then movement south in winter (Everett and Ainley 2001). Briggs et al. (1987) found the species reaching its peak numbers off southern California in August and September, within 50 km of the mainland coast.

Perhaps because it largely vacates the ocean off San Diego during the season of winter storms, the Black Storm-Petrel is rarely seen from shore. It has been noted, however, from San Onofre (C1; one on 21 June 1997, L. Ellis), La Jolla (P7; e.g., one 19–23 April 1995 (S. Walens, NASFN 49:308, 1995), and Point Loma (S7; one on 24 November 1983 (R. E. Webster, AB 38:246, 1984). One sighting has been reported from south San Diego Bay (U10), 15 September 2000 (J. L. Coatsworth, NAB 55:102, 2001).

Black Storm-Petrels have been picked up within urban areas and brought to wildlife rehabilitators from the intersection of 30th Street and El Cajon Boulevard (R10) 10 September 2002 (SDNHM 50687), the 32nd Street Naval Station (S10) 21 September 2001 (SDNHM 50614), Balboa Park (R9) 22 September 2000 (SDNHM 50481), near 19th and Market streets in downtown San Diego (S9) 22 October 1998 (SDNHM 50173), and along Woodside Avenue, Lakeside (P13), 11 November 2000 (SDNHM 50497). At about 18 miles from the coast, the last locality is the farthest inland. The convergence of all these dates in the fall suggests that the birds became disoriented as they fledged from Los Coronados Islands, an idea reinforced by the downy feather tips still adhering to the bellies of the specimens from Balboa Park and the 32nd Street Naval Station.

Winter: The only specific reports of the Black Storm-Petrel from or near San Diego County December–March are of one on the San Diego Christmas bird count 2 January 1961, one on the Rancho Santa Fe Christmas bird count 16 December 1984, four on the latter count 28 December 1996, five off San Diego 18 January 1969 (AFN 23:519, 1969), and five off San Diego 21 January

Photo by Mary Beth Stowe

1984 (G. McCaskie, AB 38:357, 1984). Briggs et al. (1987) reported the Black Storm-Petrel off southern California in all months but identified only a few in winter. Because of the difficulty in distinguishing all-dark storm-petrels in the field, unseasonal sightings, including those listed here, must be regarded with caution.

Conservation: Though still abundant, the Black Storm-Petrel is vulnerable because the overwhelming majority of the population nests in a small area, the three San Benito Islands off the Pacific coast of central Baja California. On all its nesting islands, including Los Coronados, the primary threat to the Black Storm-Petrel has been the introduction of mammals: cats, rats, dogs, and pigs. Though some of these predators have been eradicated from some islands, thanks mainly to the efforts of Island Conservation in cooperation with Mexico's Instituto Nacional de Ecología, preventing reintroduction requires constant vigilance. Through the 1980s, the numbers of Black Storm-Petrels seen near Los Coronados Islands decreased (Everett and Anderson 1991), but the numbers off southern California in general spike upward when the ocean warms during El Niño, as in 1992 (Ainley et al. 1995).

Least Storm-Petrel *Oceanodroma microsoma*

The Least Storm-Petrel nests on islands around Baja California and disperses north irregularly in late summer and fall across the international border. In some years it is seen on the ocean off San Diego County in flocks of hundreds; in others it is rare or absent.

Migration: Dates for the Least Storm-Petrel more or less near San Diego County range from 19 July (1927, one collected "a short distance north of the Mexican boundary," Willett 1933) to 1 November (1977 one 9 miles off San Diego, D. W. Povey) and 10 November 1990 (1990, 41 at the Tanner Bank about 100 miles off San Diego, J.

L. Dunn, AB 45:150, 1991). Two unseasonal records fall outside this interval: 35 off San Diego 2 June 1984 (G. McCaskie, AB 38:1061, 1984) and three seen from shore at La Jolla 19 April 1995 (S. Walens, NASFN 49:308, 1995). Exceptionally high estimates off San Diego are of 3000 on 17 September 1970 (AB 25:107, 1971), 3200 on 8 September 1979 (AB 34:200, 1980), and 3500 on 13 September 1992 (J. L. Dunn, AB 47:148, 1993).

The Least Storm-Petrel has been found once inside San Diego Bay, a bird picked up at Fisherman's Landing (S8) 11 August 1996 (SDNHM 50231). Possibly it had come aboard a boat offshore, got trapped, then was tossed overboard when the crew was cleaning the boat.

TROPICBIRDS — FAMILY PHAETHONTIDAE

Red-billed Tropicbird *Phaethon aethereus*

The Red-billed Tropicbird reaches the northern limit of its usual oceanic range at the latitude of San Diego. In late summer and early fall it is regular but rare. Though it has been seen as close as five miles from the coast, the only records from land are of dead birds washed ashore.

Migration: Away from the islands where it nests, the Red-billed Tropicbird is highly pelagic. On a trip west from San Diego, often a boat must pass the south end of San Clemente Island 60 miles west of San Diego before the first tropicbird appears. The sightings nearest land are from 5 miles west of Point Loma (Sefton 1938, Abbott 1941). On shore, dead birds have been found at

Coronado (T9) 21 September 1983 (SDNHM 42568), at Imperial Beach (V10) 4 August 1984 (SDNHM 47804), and at San Onofre (C1) 7 October 2001 (SDNHM 50607). Most records are for September; dates extend from 5 May (1987, near Tanner Bank about 100 miles west of Point Loma, R. R. Veit, AB 41:487, 1987) and 10 May (1969, 10 miles west of Imperial Beach, AFN 23:625, 1969) to 7 October.

Conservation: Sightings of several individuals per day, as on some trips between San Diego and San Clemente Island from the 1960s to 1982, have not been repeated since. The maximum count is still nine on 27 July 1968 (AFN 22:647, 1968).

Taxonomy: The subspecies of Red-billed Tropicbird in the eastern Pacific Ocean is *P. a. mesonauta* Peters, 1930.

BOOBIES — FAMILY SULIDAE

Masked Booby *Sula dactylatra*

Three species of boobies once absent along the coast of southern California became rare visitors there during the last two decades of the 20th century. Increasing ocean temperatures then favored tropical ocean birds wandering north. A Masked Booby on the coast of San Diego County in winter 2001–2002 remained 12 days, to be seen and photographed by crowds of birders.

Winter: A subadult Masked Booby rested with pelicans and cormorants on the rocks at La Jolla Cove (P7) 30 December 2001–10 January 2002 (M. Burcham, Garrett and Wilson 2003). The bird then evidently moved north to Corona del Mar, Orange County, where it was caught on 12 January 2002 (Cole and McCaskie 2004). The nearest pelagic record is of one 22 miles southwest of the south end of San Clemente Island 10 January 1977, the first record for California waters (Lewis and Tyler 1978). A Masked Booby reported from San Elijo Lagoon (L7) 14 November 1987 was not accepted by the California Bird Records Committee because of uncertainty over whether the bird was actually a Red-footed Booby (Patten and Erickson 1994).

Photo by Anthony Mercieca

Taxonomy: The bill color of the bird at La Jolla was close enough to that of an adult to identify it as a Masked Booby rather than the more orange-billed Nazca Booby (*S. granti*), confirmed to be a species distinct from the Masked by Pitman and Jehl (1998). No specimen of the Masked Booby has been collected in California. *Sula d. californica* Rothschild, 1915, breeds in the eastern tropical Pacific; *S. d. personata* Gould, 1846, breeds in the central Pacific.

Blue-footed Booby *Sula nebouxii*

Unlike the eastern Pacific Ocean's other boobies, the Blue-footed does not stray far from land, and it does not frequent the west coast of Baja California. Most or all of its sporadic incursions across the international border come by way of the Gulf of California, making the Salton Sea the species' primary location in the United States. Of the seven records for San Diego County, none is more recent than 1980.

Migration: Representing dispersal north after breeding, all but one of the San Diego County records of the

Blue-footed Booby fall between 4 August and 4 October: at sea off San Diego 4 October 1964 (AFN 19:78, 1965), Ocotillo Wells (I28/I29) 4 August 1968 (SDNHM 36707), bridge of Interstate 15 over Lake Hodges (K11) 8 September 1969 (SDNHM 37566), off Imperial Beach (V10) 6 September 1971 (AB 36:119, 1972), Lake San Marcos (I8/J8) late August–14 December 1972, when found dead (AB 27:120, 1973), and Camp Denver Fox 3.1 miles northwest of Lake Henshaw (F16) 18 August 1977 (AB 32:256, 1978; photo SDNHM). The exception is of one seen 2 miles off Camp Pendleton 16 March 1980 (Roberson 1993). The California Bird Records

Committee did not accept the identification of one off Point Loma 26 August 1977, though this report, like most of the others, came during irruptions of the Blue-footed Booby to the Salton Sea (Roberson 1993).

Taxonomy: Nominate *S. n. nebouxii* Milne-Edwards, 1882, occupies the species' entire range except for the Galapagos Islands.

Brown Booby *Sula leucogaster*

Of the boobies (and other tropical ocean birds) whose occurrences in California accelerated with the ocean warming of the late 20th century, none accelerated more than the Brown Booby. There was only one record along the California coast before 1983; since then, over 40 records have accumulated. In northwestern Baja California, the Brown Booby has been seen repeatedly on Todos Santos Islands off Ensenada, with a male carrying sticks and displaying in 2000 (Palacios and Mellink 2000), and on Los Coronados Islands off Tijuana, with up to six individuals in 1999 and 2002 and two pairs apparently nesting in the latter year (NAB 56:489, 2002).

Photo by Anthony Mercieca

Migration: In San Diego County, the Brown Booby is known from eight records, five accepted by the California Bird Records Committee. An adult male injured by a fish hook was picked up at Imperial Beach (V10) 2 April 1990 (SDNHM 46566). An immature was on the ocean 2 miles southeast of the entrance to San Diego Bay 14 December 1991 (D. W. Povey; Patten et al. 1995b). An immature at Point Loma (S7) 27–29 September 1997 was captured for rehabilitation (M. F. Platter-Rieger; Rogers and Jaramillo 2002). Adults were 10 miles southwest of Point Loma 11 September 1999 (M. B. Mulrooney; Rogers and Jaramillo 2002) and at Point Loma 8 April 2001 (R. E. Webster; Cole and McCaskie 2004). A Brown Booby at Shelter Island (R8) 17 November 1997 was afflicted with bumblefoot, leading the records committee to question whether the bird had

been kept in captivity for an extended period (Erickson and Hamilton 2001). Reports of an adult male at La Jolla (P7) 4 February 1998 and presumably the same bird at Point Loma three days later have not been assessed by the committee (P. Lonsdale, R. B. Riggan; FN 52:256, 1998).

Taxonomy: It is fortunate that the specimen from Imperial Beach is an adult male, because geographic variation in the Brown Booby is expressed in adult males only. It is *S. l. brewsteri* Goss, 1888, breeding on islands in the Gulf of California and farther south along the west coast of Mexico. In *brewsteri* males have the head whitish but not as pale as in *S. l. nesiotes* Heller and Snodgrass, 1901, of Clipperton Atoll.

Red-footed Booby *Sula sula*

First identified in California in 1975, the Red-footed Booby was known in the state from 14 well-supported records by 2002. Like those of the Masked and Brown Boobies, occurrences of the Red-footed accelerated with ocean warming. San Diego County has two records.

Migration: An immature was videotaped at La Jolla (P7) 24 May 1996 (P. Lonsdale; McCaskie and San Miguel 1999). Another caught on a fish hook at Scripps Institution of Oceanography (O7) 20 July 2002 was

captured for rehabilitation (Cole and McCaskie 2004). The report of one within 1 mile of shore off La Jolla 13 August 1993 (AB 48:151, 1994) was not accepted by the California Bird Records Committee (Erickson and Terrill 1996). A booby at San Elijo Lagoon 14 November 1987 was reported as a Masked but the observer's description suggests it was a Red-footed.

Taxonomy: The subspecies of Red-footed Booby reaching California is uncertain; *S. s. websteri* Rothschild, 1898, breeds in the eastern tropical Pacific; *S. s. rubripes* Gould, 1838, breeds in the central Pacific.

Pelicans — Family Pelecanidae

American White Pelican *Pelecanus erythrorhynchos*

Adapted to an environment of ever-changing water levels, shifting opportunistically from site to site, the White Pelican varies greatly in the numbers wintering in San Diego County. The birds use both shallow coastal wetlands and inland lakes. For decades a major fraction of the population has wintered on the Salton Sea, but with that lake's fish population collapsing, a major redistribution seems inevitable. It may account for the upsurge in the number of White Pelicans in San Diego at the beginning of the 21st century.

Winter: Over the final quarter of the 20th century, the White Pelican had no consistent site in San Diego County. From 1997 to 2002, along the coast, we found it most regularly at Buena Vista Lagoon (H5/H6; up to 21 in the east basin 23 January 2000, L. E. Taylor). Another frequent site, as recorded by both Stadtlander and Konecny (1994) and atlas observers, is the southernmost basin of San Diego Bay, between Highway 75 and 7th Street (V10). Being gregarious and foraging in teams, the White Pelican may show up in flocks even where it is infrequent, as at Famosa Slough (R8; 40 on 29 January 2002, M. Sadowski) and the Tijuana River mouth (V10; 48 on 12 February 2002, R. T. Patton).

During the atlas period the more heavily used lakes inland were O'Neill (E6; up to 90 on 16 December 2001, P. A. Ginsburg), Henshaw (G17; up to 75 on 8 December 2000, G. C. Hazard), Wohlford (H12; up to 250 on 19 January 2002, J. C. Worley), and Hodges (K10; up to 93 on 23 December 2001, R. L. Barber). Curiously, our second largest flock, of 100, was soaring far from water,

Photo by Anthony Mercieca

high over Coyote Mountain (D25), 16 December 2001 (P. R. Pryde). A flock of 48 was over Borrego Springs (F24) 2 January 1993 (M. Guest). These records suggest the birds shift to some extent between the Salton Sea and San Diego County's coastal slope.

Numbers of White Pelicans reaching San Diego County annually have varied from practically none in the early 1980s up to about 400 in 1988–89 and 1989–90, down to about 20 in 1997–98, and back up to over 300 in 2002–03.

Migration: The schedule of the White Pelican's movements is as irregular as the species' locations. The earliest fall date is 2 September (1968, one at Buena Vista Lagoon, A. Fries), and large flocks have been reported as early as 15 September (1962, 75 heading east over Culp Valley, I122, ABDSP file) and 20 September (1993, 70 over Warner Valley, G18, R. T. Patton). Some 187 in the San Diego Bay salt works 20 October 1993 were fall migrants, as fewer than 10 remained by January (Stadtlander and Konecny 1994).

Spring departure begins in February, but a few individuals remain until May, fewer still through summer. In 1988, summering White Pelicans occurred widely along San Diego County's coast (Macdonald et al. 1990). From 1997 to 2001 records after mid May were of two at Batiquitos Lagoon 28 May 2000 (J. Ciarletta), one there 1 August 1997 (C. C. Gorman), and eight at Buena Vista Lagoon 21 July 2001 (J. Smith). There has been no suggestion of White Pelican nesting in San Diego County

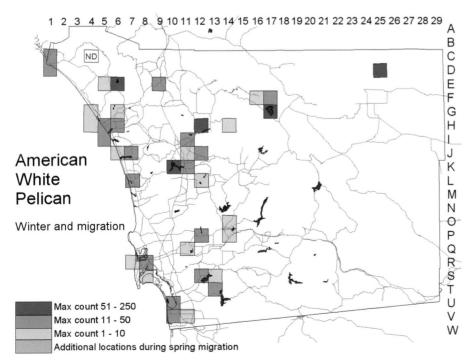

American
White
Pelican

Winter and migration

Max count 51 - 250
Max count 11 - 50
Max count 1 - 10
Additional locations during spring migration

since Willett (1933) wrote "J. B. Dixon (MS) finds it occurring frequently at Lake Henshaw and believes that it would nest there if not persecuted by fishermen. He has found several eggs dropped by the birds along the shores of the lake."

Conservation: By the 1980s the White Pelican's total population had increased to about 100,000 breeding birds from about 40,000 in 1964 (Sidle et al. 1985). But the degradation of the Salton Sea raises the question of whether these numbers can be sustained. If the over 10,000 pelicans wintering on the Salton Sea are forced to abandon that area some may shift to nearby alternative habitat in San Diego County, but most have no place to go. The process may have begun already; numbers in San Diego County increased continuously through the five years of the atlas period.

Brown Pelican *Pelecanus occidentalis*

The failure of Brown Pelican nesting in southern California in the late 1960s and early 1970s, and its link to DDT, was a key case alerting the world to the unintended ill effects of persistent pesticides. Happily, once the release of DDT in the United States was banned, the pelicans recovered quickly. By the 1990s Brown Pelican was again common along San Diego County's coast, numbers peaking in late summer and early fall. Nevertheless, the population remains fragile, and in California the Brown Pelican is still formally listed as an endangered species. The nesting colony nearest San Diego County is on Los Coronados Islands off Tijuana.

Winter: The Brown Pelican is common all along San Diego County's coast, as well as over the nearby ocean. The largest numbers are where secure roost sites, on coastal bluffs or man-made structures, lie near good fishing, as at Torrey Pines State Reserve (N7; up to 218 on 26 December 1999, B. C. Moore), La Jolla (P7; 150 on 26 December 1998, L. and M. Polinsky), Point Loma (S7; 156 on 18 December 1999, J. C. Worley), and North Island (S8; 302 on 18 December 1999, R. T. Patton). In San

Photo by Anthony Mercieca

Diego Bay the pelican is more numerous north and west of the bridge than to the south of it, though many roost on the dikes of the salt works at the south end.

Brown Pelicans enter all lagoons open to the tide but, except at one site, are only casual on fresh water. The exception is Sweetwater Reservoir (S12/S13), where the species has become regular in summer and fall, with up to 45 on 18 September 1996. Most records here fall between 21 May (1996) and 9 December (1998), but five are scattered through the winter and early spring, including single birds 28 February 1997 and 13 February 1998 (P. Famolaro). Other inland winter records are of one in San Pasqual Valley (J12) 30 December 2000 (K. L. Weaver) and one at Lake Wohlford (H12) 16 February 2002 (J. Ciarletta).

Migration: The low point of the Brown Pelican's year in San Diego County is from March to May, when the breeding birds are clustered at their colonies on offshore islands. Nevertheless,

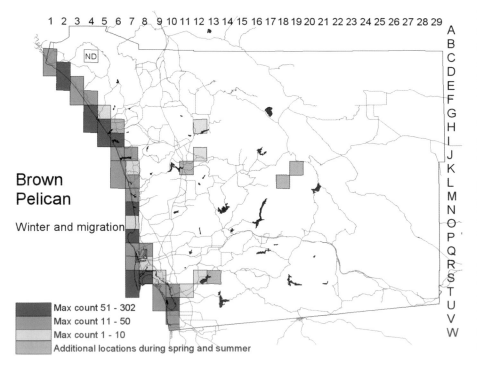

Brown Pelican

Winter and migration

Max count 51 - 302
Max count 11 - 50
Max count 1 - 10
Additional locations during spring and summer

nonbreeders are still common in spring at the species' favored spots. Weekly surveys of north San Diego Bay in this 3-month interval returned an average of 46 (Mock et al. 1994). Numbers increase sharply through the summer as the birds return from their nesting colonies and migrate northward from Baja California. They peak from August to October (Mock et al. 1994, Stadtlander and Konecny 1994, Manning 1995), then decrease through the late fall and winter. Mock et al. (1994) found that adults have a bimodal peak, the first in July, the second in October and November. Subadults peak in August and September, juveniles in September. Migration is earlier if nesting fails, as when the fish supply is reduced by El Niño.

Peter Famolaro found Brown Pelicans unexpectedly regular on Sweetwater Reservoir, recording them in four of five years of the atlas period. They arrived as early as 6 May in 1998 (two birds) and peaked at 17 on 10 August 1998. Elsewhere inland the Brown Pelican is rare but, besides the two winter records cited above, there are at least 19 from 14 April (2001, one at the east end of Lake Hodges, K11, E. C. Hall) and 5 May (2001, one possibly injured immature at Camp Marston, K19, S. E. Smith) to 23 September (1976, one over the Borrego Valley, ABDSP database). Many of these birds likely came in from the southeast, from the Gulf of California, as the species now migrates regularly from the gulf to the Salton Sea. Such an origin is especially clear in the case of a flock of 22 flying north over June Wash, Anza–Borrego Desert (M27), 15 May 1982 (ABDSP database).

Breeding distribution: On 17 and 18 May 1998, one bird carried a stick and a pair copulated on the cliffs at La Jolla (C. Oliver photos). But there is no further evidence of nesting in San Diego County. Perhaps it was behavior like this that prompted Sams and Stott (1959) to write "breeds … sometimes on secluded mainland cliffs (La Jolla)." The colony on Middle Island of Los Coronados had 285 active nests in 1988 (Everett and Anderson 1991).

Conservation: As a result of the contamination of the ocean off southern California with DDT, the regional population of the Brown Pelican declined until the mid 1970s (Anderson and Anderson 1976). After use of this pesticide in the United States was banned the population began to recover. In San Diego County, the increase was especially noticeable in the late 1980s. Since then the number of pairs nesting on the Channel Islands has been more or less stable at 4000–6000, with dips in years of El Niño (Shields 2002). From 1968 to 1974 the San Diego Christmas bird count averaged 125 Brown Pelicans, but from 1995 to 2002 it averaged 708.

In spite of the recent positive trend, the Brown Pelican still faces threats. Injuries from fish hooks and fishing line are common, and in San Diego County pelicans have even been found mutilated, their bills half sawed off. Because of the birds' sensitivity when nesting, colonies must be kept safe from human disturbance and release of predators. Even fishing boats approaching the nesting colonies on Los Coronados Islands reduced the birds' nest success (Anderson 1988). If climate change leads to an increased frequency of El Niño, the Brown Pelican as well as many other water birds may find the food supply insufficient to sustain them.

Taxonomy: The California Brown Pelican, *P. o. californicus* Ridgway, 1884, is the subspecies found on the west coast of North America.

CORMORANTS — FAMILY PHALACROCORACIDAE

Brandt's Cormorant *Phalacrocorax penicillatus*

Brandt's Cormorant is a strictly maritime bird, common on the ocean and San Diego Bay but not entering Mission Bay or the coastal lagoons. It can be seen far offshore—having colonies on all the Channel Islands and Los Coronados Islands—but is much more numerous within sight of land. The birds must come to coastal rocks or bluffs daily to roost and dry their plumage. Brandt's Cormorant occurs in San Diego County most abundantly as a winter visitor, but some remain year round, and a few nest on cliff ledges at La Jolla.

Breeding distribution: Brandt's Cormorants have nested at least sporadically at La Jolla (P7), on cliffs at La Jolla Caves, since before 1933, when Michael (1935a) called the colony "long established." A thorough survey of the colony requires that it be inspected from the water or from the air; not all nests are visible to an observer standing on the ground at the best vantage points near La Jolla Cove. In an aerial survey on 19 May 1997, McChesney et

Photo by Anthony Mercieca

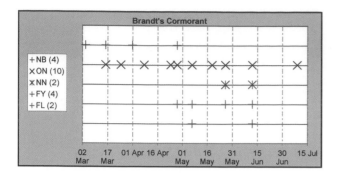

al. (1998) photographed nine active nests. In 1999 and 2000, viewing the colony from shore, L. and M. Polinsky counted at least six active nests each year. In 2001, they counted at least five active nests on 28 April; on 9 July, a survey of the caves by kayak revealed 20 nests, though only two of these were still active. In 2002 there were at least two nests active by 24 February (K. L. Weaver); in 2003, there were three nests with chicks on 29 June (M. Sadowski). Many more birds remain around the colony than actually nest; counts at La Jolla in late spring and summer range up to 100 on 7 May 2000 (L. Polinsky).

Most Brandt's Cormorants nest on offshore islands, with some on Los Coronados Islands just south of the border (Jehl 1977). The small colony at La Jolla is the only one on the mainland of southern California south of Santa Barbara County (McChesney et al. 1998). See Williams (1942) for two photographs of the colony taken in 1938.

In 1993, 1994, and 1995, a pair attempted to nest on the degaussing pier in the navy's submarine base on the east side of Point Loma (S7). In 1993, the eggs hatched, but the nesting was interrupted when a minesweeper was degaussed and the disturbance kept the adults from coming to feed their chicks. The chicks were then taken into captivity and raised successfully, learning to dive and fish

in a swimming pool and released back at the submarine base after fledging (M. F. Platter-Rieger, M. A. Faulkner). No chicks hatched from the attempts in 1994 and 1995.

From about 1985 to 1990 M. F. Platter-Rieger noted up to 25 Brandt's Cormorants on nests on the west side of Point Loma, just north of the sewage-treatment plant. Since the early 1990s, however, she has seen no activity at this location, and McChesney et al. (1998) noted only roosting birds there in 1997. Both visibility and access at this site controlled by the navy are difficult, so the cormorant's use of it is unclear.

Nonbreeding birds are seen through the summer along the San Diego County coast from La Jolla south (10 at Point Loma, S7, 17 June 1997, V. P. Johnson; up to 47 in north San Diego Bay 6 June 1995, K. L. Preston).

Nesting: At La Jolla, Brandt's Cormorants nest on ledges on cliffs or in caves. They have been seen carrying both sticks and kelp as nest material. Nesting on man-made structures, as at Point Loma, is rare in this species (McChesney et al. 1998).

Brandt's Cormorant nesting at La Jolla is notably unsynchronized. Michael (1935a) reported some birds beginning nest building on 21 December, others as late as 12 April. From 1997 to 2001 our dates for occupied nests ranged from 24 February (2002) to 9 July (2001). In 1980, three young fledged from two nests on 10 September (W. T. Everett), suggesting egg laying as late as early June.

Migration: Brandt's Cormorant shifts north then south of its nesting colonies after the breeding season. In southern California it is much more numerous in winter than in summer (Briggs et al. 1987). In north San Diego Bay surveys from 1993 to 1995 (Mock et al. 1994, unpubl. data) found that numbers peaked in February and reached their nadir in July. In central San Diego Bay surveys from 1993 to 1994 found Brandt's Cormorant from December to March only (Manning 1995). Even at Torrey Pines State Reserve, less than 5 miles from the colony at La Jolla, the species is recorded in spring no later than 4 May.

Winter: At this season Brandt's Cormorant occurs all along the coast of San Diego County. In the county's northern half, where there are fewer roost sites, it is less common. The maximum on any Oceanside Christmas bird count is 71 on 29 December 1996, but an exceptional 700 were off Agua Hedionda Lagoon (I6) 10 January 1999 (P. A. Ginsburg). In southern San Diego County numbers are highest at Torrey Pines State Reserve (N7/O7; 520 on 2 January 1998, S. E. Smith), La Jolla (300 on 28 January 2000, L. Polinsky), Point Loma

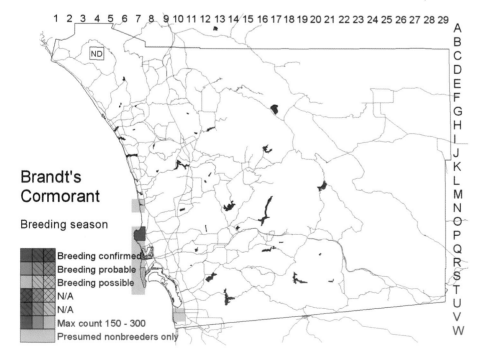

Brandt's Cormorant

Breeding season

Breeding confirmed
Breeding probable
Breeding possible
N/A
N/A
Max count 150 - 300
Presumed nonbreeders only

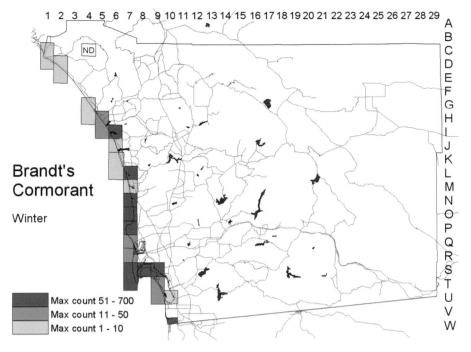

1 2 3 4 5 6 7 8 9 10 11 12 13 14 15 16 17 18 19 20 21 22 23 24 25 26 27 28 29

A B C D E F G H I J K L M N O P Q R S T U V W

Brandt's Cormorant

Winter

Max count 51 - 700
Max count 11 - 50
Max count 1 - 10

(Wallace and Wallace 1998). Michael (1935a) mentioned boys flushing cormorants from their nests at La Jolla by dropping objects on them from the tops of the cliffs. The greatest variations in the birds' numbers and nesting success result from the effect of El Niño on the abundance of fish. When El Niño arrives, the ocean warms, and the food supply is depressed, Brandt's Cormorants raise fewer young or forgo nesting entirely (Boekelheide et al. 1990).

The colony at La Jolla has not been studied consistently enough for its variations to be understood. It was active at least in 1933–34 (Michael 1935a), 1938 (Williams 1942), and 1980 (W. T. Everett) but vacant in June 1991 (McChesney et al.

(200 on 27 February 2001, V. P. Johnson), and on north San Diego Bay (S8; 343 on 22 February 1993, Mock et al. 1994; 400 on 10 February 2002, K. L. Weaver). Although Brandt's Cormorant is second only to Heermann's Gull as the most abundant bird on north San Diego Bay and variably common on central San Diego Bay (up to 174 on 16 February 1993, Mock et al. 1994), it is rare to absent from south San Diego Bay south of National City (Macdonald et al. 1990, Manning 1995). Flocks can be seen commuting between Los Coronados Islands and Point Loma.

Conservation: Brandt's Cormorants suffer from contamination with pesticides washed into the ocean, from oil spills, and from human disturbance of nesting colonies

1998). On 4 May 1995, K. B. Clark noted one active nest and another bird carrying nest material. Surveys for this atlas give the most continuous record of the colony to date and show it has been occupied annually at least since 1997. In 1997, McChesney et al. (1998) noted an increase in Brandt's Cormorants nesting throughout southern California (primarily on the Channel Islands) from previous surveys; a dearth of suitable nest sites may be the factor constraining the breeding population.

Taxonomy: No subspecies. On the basis of skeletal differences, Siegel-Causey (1988) recommended that the genus *Phalacrocorax*, currently encompassing all cormorants, be broken up, Brandt's going into *Compsohaliaeus*.

Double-crested Cormorant *Phalacrocorax auritus*

The Double-crested is our most versatile cormorant, occurring commonly as a nonbreeding visitor on water both fresh and salt. It nests near San Diego County on the Channel and Los Coronados islands and at the Salton Sea; two colonies within the county have formed only since 1988. The Double-crested Cormorant has had a difficult and contentious relationship with humanity, exploiting reservoirs and aquaculture but suffering from disturbance, pesticide contamination, and direct control as a pest. At the beginning of the 21st century, the cormorants were winning, increasing in numbers and establishing new colonies.

Breeding distribution: Double-crested Cormorants nested in two colonies during the atlas period, in the salt works at the south end of San Diego Bay (U10) and at the upper end of Sweetwater Reservoir (S13). The colony in the salt works formed in 1988, when the birds began nest-

Photo by Anthony Mercieca

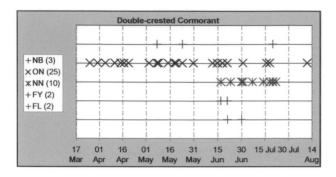

ing on a mobile dredge. Since 1997, maximum numbers of nests have been 51 on 1 June 1997 (M. R. Smith) and 71 on 30 June 1999 (R. T. Patton). The dredge has remained the focus of the colony, but in some years, such as 1993 (Stadtlander 1993), 1994 (Terp and Pavelka 1999), 1999, and 2001 (R. T. Patton), some birds nest on the ground on the dikes of the salt works. Nineteen pairs nested on the ground in 1993 (Stadtlander 1993). One such nest on 18 July 2001 accounts for the cormorant appearing as a nesting bird in atlas square V10 as well as U10—the salt works straddle both squares.

At Sweetwater Reservoir, the colony first formed in 1996, the birds building in a single tree. By 8 May 1998 they had spread to nine trees with a total of 28 nests in which adults were incubating or brooding. On 24 May 2001, the colony numbered 17 occupied nests in two trees (P. Famolaro).

Nonbreeding birds are locally common at other localities through the summer: 18 at Lake Henshaw (G17) 18 June 2000 (P. Unitt), 30 at San Elijo Lagoon (L7) 12 July 1998 (B. C. Moore), 18 at San Vicente Reservoir (N13) 20 May 2001 (R. and S. L. Breisch), 34 in north San Diego Bay (S8) 26 May 2000 (R. T. Patton), 26 at Barrett Lake (S19) 4 June 2000 (R. and S. L. Breisch), and 20 at Lower Otay Lake (U13) 8 May 1999 (P. Unitt). Summering Double-

crested Cormorants are widely scattered on inland lakes, as high as Cuyamaca Lake (M20; one on 25 June 1998, A. P. and T. E. Keenan) and as far east as Tule Lake (T27; up to two on 6 June 2001, J. K. Wilson).

Nesting: The Double-crested Cormorant builds a bulky nest of sticks and debris, placing it usually in a tree surrounded by water or on the ground in a site isolated from predators. On the dredge in the salt works, some nests are well supported on sheets of metal but others are balanced precariously across two cables; some of the latter blew down in 2001. Some Double-crested Cormorant nests, however, persist for years, the pair refurbishing them annually.

Because Double-crested Cormorant nests are typically difficult to inspect closely—and vulnerable to disturbance—there are few data on their nesting schedule in San Diego County. Reports of nestlings are concentrated from late June to late July, suggesting that egg laying ranges from about mid April to mid June. In the early 20th century eggs were collected at Lake Henshaw (G17) on 15 and 30 May. Reports of occupied nests, however, range from 31 March to 11 August. In 1998, nesting at the salt works began by 3 April and continued through late July (Terp and Pavelka 1999).

Migration: The Double-crested Cormorant is far more abundant in San Diego County in fall and winter than in spring and summer. Surveys of San Diego Bay (Mock et al. 1994, Stadtlander and Konecny 1994, Manning 1995) and San Elijo Lagoon (King et al. 1987) found cormorant numbers peaking variously from September to February and reaching their lows in June and July. In the salt works Stadtlander and Konecny (1994) recorded their maximum of 1012 on 17 November 1993.

In the Anza–Borrego Desert, the approximately 15 records range from 29 October (1991; two at the Roadrunner Club, F24, A. G. Morley) to 9 May (2001; one at Borrego Springs, G24, P. D. Ache). All are from artificial ponds in the Borrego Valley except for a sighting of two flying over Hawk Canyon (H27) 10 April 1988 (P. D. Jorgensen).

An unusual record of migrants on the coastal slope was of 44 in flight near Dulzura (T16) 21 April 2001 (S. Yamagata, T. Stands).

Winter: The Double-crested Cormorant is not only more numerous in the winter but more widespread. From 1997 to 2002 it was recorded in 47 atlas squares in winter but not the breeding season versus 16 for the converse. It occurs all along the coast, with up to 626 at Point Loma (S7) 16

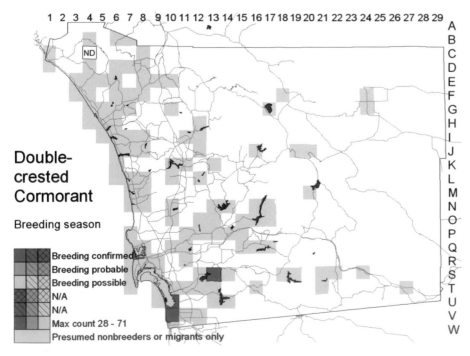

Double-crested Cormorant

Breeding season

Breeding confirmed
Breeding probable
Breeding possible
N/A
N/A
Max count 28 - 71
Presumed nonbreeders or migrants only

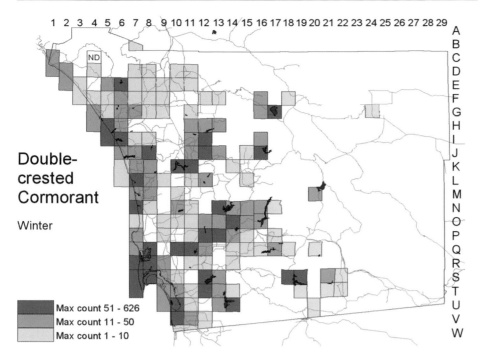

Double-crested Cormorant

Winter

▓	Max count 51 - 626
▒	Max count 11 - 50
░	Max count 1 - 10

and 1960s, which led to nesting failure (Gress et al. 1973). In the last quarter of the century, however, the population over much of North America increased rapidly (Hatch and Weseloh 1999). The increase included California, aided by adaptation to artificial nest sites (Carter et al. 1995). In San Diego County the Double-crested Cormorant has benefited from the building of reservoirs and the reservoirs being stocked with fish. Results of the Oceanside and Rancho Santa Fe Christmas bird counts show no great change, but the San Diego count averaged 296 Double-crested Cormorants per year from 1965 to 1974, 735 from 1997 to 2001. During its first ten years, 1986–94, the Escondido count averaged 100, but during the atlas period the figure rose to 263.

December 2000 (M. W. Klein), 300 in Mission Bay (Q8) 18 December 1998 (J. C. Worley), and 300 at the San Diego River flood-control channel (R8) 28 February 1999 (B. C. Moore). It is no less common on inland lakes, with up to 218 on Lake San Marcos (J8) 27 December 1997 (J. O. Zimmer), 250 on Lake Hodges (K10) 6 December 1999 (R. L. Barber), and 300 at the Wild Animal Park (J12) 8 January 2000 (D. and D. Bylin). Wintering Double-crested Cormorants occur as high as 3900 feet at Corte Madera Lake (Q20; up to seven on 20 February 1999, G. L. Rogers) and 4600 feet at Cuyamaca Lake (up to 33 on 14 December 1999, A. P. and T. E. Keenan). In Borrego Springs (G24) we had only two records of single individuals during the atlas period (P. D. Ache), but an exceptional 59 were at the Roadrunner Club 10 January 1993 (A. G. Morley).

Conservation: The Double-crested Cormorant's numbers decreased because of persecution early in the 20th century, then because of pesticide contamination in the 1950s

The cormorant's career of decline and recovery is also reflected in its status as a breeding bird in San Diego County. Shortly after Lake Henshaw was created, cormorants colonized, nesting "plentifully" at least in 1928 and 1932 (J. B. Dixon in Willett 1933; two egg sets collected in each year, WFVZ). The colony was evidently soon eliminated, however; fishermen often see cormorants as competitors. For many years the Double-crested Cormorant occurred in San Diego County as a nonbreeding visitor only. The colony at the salt works began with one or two pairs in 1988 (E. Copper), increasing to 14 nests the following year (Macdonald et al. 1990). The addition of the Sweetwater Reservoir colony in 1996 will probably not be the last.

Taxonomy: *Phalacrocorax a. albociliatus* Ridgway, 1884, with the crests of breeding adults partly white, is the subspecies of the Double-crested Cormorant in and near California.

Pelagic Cormorant *Phalacrocorax pelagicus*

The Pelagic is the least numerous and least widespread of San Diego County's three cormorants, easily overlooked among the Brandt's Cormorants that are always more abundant in its habitat. The Pelagic Cormorant has a close association with rocky shorelines, as it roosts on exposed rocks and forages primarily over submerged rocks. In San Diego County it is primarily a winter visitor, though occasional birds occur in summer and suggest the possibility of nesting at La Jolla or Point Loma.

Winter: In San Diego County, the Pelagic Cormorant occurs primarily along the coast from Torrey Pines State Reserve (N7) south to Point Loma (S7). It is generally

Photo by Anthony Mercieca

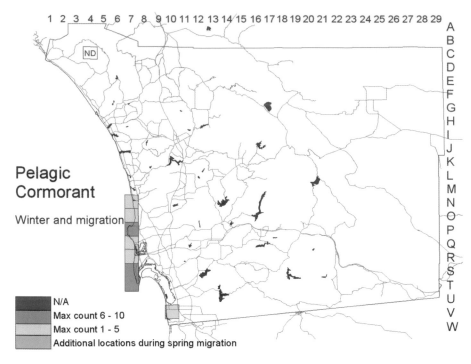

Pelagic
Cormorant

Winter and migration

N/A
Max count 6 - 10
Max count 1 - 5
Additional locations during spring migration

1997 to 2001 our only record later than 1 April was of one at Torrey Pines State Reserve (N7) 3 June 2001 (P. A. Ginsburg). During their surveys of north San Diego Bay in 1993, Mock et al. (1994) recorded the species in every month of the year except November, but only a single individual in June and July.

Breeding distribution: The Pelagic Cormorant is not confirmed to nest in San Diego County, but nesting is possible. From about 1985 to 1990 M. F. Platter-Rieger noted some Pelagic Cormorants with apparently nesting Brandt's Cormorants on the steep slopes of Point Loma north of the sewage-treatment plant. On 29 June 2003, M. Sadowski noted five to nine coming and going from the cliffs at La Jolla Caves. On 6 July, he surveyed the cliffs from a kayak and counted six Pelagic Cormorants, but they were not associated with any nests.

San Diego County lies near the southern tip of the Pelagic Cormorant's breeding range. Los Coronados Islands were the southernmost known breeding locality until 2000, when Palacios and Mellink (2000) reported two pairs nesting on Isla Todos Santos off Ensenada.

Conservation: No trend in Pelagic Cormorant numbers in or near San Diego County is clear, but at the Farallon Islands off San Francisco the population varies greatly and fails to breed when El Niño suppresses the supply of fish (Ainley et al. 1994). Increases in ocean temperature that reduce the food supply and have already affected some other birds could result in the Pelagic Cormorant's range retracting north, out of San Diego County.

Taxonomy: Pelagic Cormorants south of southern British Columbia have long been recognized as the subspecies *P. p. resplendens* Audubon, 1838, smaller than the nominate subspecies occurring farther north. The measurements tabulated by Hobson (1997), however, show great overlap, too much for the subspecies to be recognized on the basis of any single measurement.

uncommon; from 1997 to 2002 our highest counts were of 10 at La Jolla (P7) 4 January 1998 (B. C. Moore) and eight at Point Loma 11 February 19999 (C. Rideout). On the San Diego Christmas bird count, where the species is normally found only at Point Loma, totals during the atlas period ranged only from five to nine, but occasional years see larger influxes, yielding counts as high as 120 on 18 December 1982 and 127 on 19 December 1987.

No Pelagic Cormorants were reported from northern San Diego County during the atlas period, but a few occur occasionally at the entrance to the Oceanside harbor (H5). The species was noted on 10 of 27 Oceanside Christmas bird counts 1976–2001 with a maximum of five on 24 December 1994 but none since. Inside San Diego Bay the Pelagic Cormorant is uncommon in the north bay, north of the bridge. Mock et al. (1994) called it fairly common to common there, but in weekly surveys through 1993 their only count of more than seven was of 12 on 7 December. Similar surveys of central San Diego Bay in 1994 yielded only one Pelagic Cormorant (Preston and Mock 1995). There are no records from the south bay or Mission Bay.

Migration: The Pelagic Cormorant occurs in San Diego County principally from October through March. From

---

ANHINGAS AND DARTERS — FAMILY ANHINGIDAE

Anhinga *Anhinga anhinga*

Along the Pacific coast, the Anhinga is resident north to central Sonora, and vagrants farther north are few. In California only four records are supported well enough to have been accepted by the California Bird Records Committee. Just one of these is from San Diego County.

Winter: San Diego County's single known Anhinga, a female, remained continuously at Sweetwater Reservoir from 4 February 1977 at least to 20 January 1979 (W. T. Everett; Bevier 1990).

FRIGATEBIRDS — FAMILY FREGATIDAE

Magnificent Frigatebird *Fregata magnificens*

After fledging, a few immature Magnificent Frigatebirds sail north from their colonies in western Mexico, crossing the international border and reaching southern California as rare visitors in summer. Formerly, several were reported in San Diego County annually, but through the last two decades of the 20th century this frequency decreased, until by the beginning of the new millennium the county was averaging only about one per year.

Migration: Magnificent Frigatebirds have been seen all along San Diego County's coast and quite far out to sea. The atlas period had one in 1997, three in 1998, none in 1999 or 2000, and three in 2001. Late June to mid September is the species' normal season. One at Mariner's Point, Mission Bay (R7), 5 June 1998 (S. M. Wolf) and one off La Jolla (P7) 15 June 1996 (P. A. Ginsburg, NASFN 50:996, 1996) were exceptionally early; one along the Silver Strand (T9) 1 October 1977 (AB 32:256, 1978) was exceptionally late. An immature photographed on the ocean off San Diego 23 April 1989 (B. Archer, AB 43:536, 1989) was unseasonal.

There are six inland records, the most recent of one at Lake Henshaw 8 August 1983 (R. Higson, AB 38:246, 1984). The only frigatebird known from the Anza–Borrego Desert was over the Borrego Springs elementary school (G25) 25 June 1965 (ABDSP file). Unitt (1984) listed other inland records, most or all of which were of birds that reached the county by way of the Gulf of California or Salton Sea.

Winter: The three winter records are of one at National

Photo by Anthony Mercieca

City (T10) 5 January 1992 (G. McCaskie, AB 46:314, 1992), one at Cardiff (L7) 1 March 2001 (R. Trissel, NAB 55:227, 2001), and one photographed at La Jolla (P7) 4 January 2002 (A. Mercieca, NAB 56:223, 2002).

Conservation: The number of frigatebirds reported in San Diego County peaked in 1979, when five were in the Tijuana River valley 20 July and five were at Lake Cuyamaca (M20) 2 August (AB 33:896, 1979, 34:200, 1980). Since then it has declined steadily. At 20,000 pairs in the 1980s, the colony on Isla Santa Margarita, Baja California Sur, is one of the species' largest (Diamond and Schreiber 2002). But the concentration of the population on the Pacific side of Baja California into a single colony makes the birds vulnerable. Diamond and Schreiber (2002) attributed the frigatebird's decline rangewide largely to disturbance at nesting colonies. They noted the frigatebird's dependence on dolphins and tuna, themselves threatened, to drive small fish to the ocean surface where frigatebirds can seize them.

HERONS AND BITTERNS — FAMILY ARDEIDAE

American Bittern *Botaurus lentiginosus*

A secretive bird of marshes, the American Bittern has long been considered primarily a winter visitor to San Diego County. In this role it is now rare and decreasing. In the breeding season the American Bittern is also rare, with the first suggestion of actual nesting only in 1983. Yet from 1997 to 2001 we found possibly breeding bitterns at eight sites, almost as many as where we found the species wintering—an unexpected twist. A family at the mouth of Las Flores Creek in 1998 provided us with the first evidence of successful fledging of American Bitterns in San Diego County, the southern tip of the species' breeding range along the Pacific coast.

Breeding distribution: In the marsh at the mouth of Las Flores Creek (E3), American Bitterns were regular in 1998 and 1999, with two calling males 15 May 1999 and one calling male, an apparent adult female, and a fledgling 6 June 1998 (R. and S. L. Breisch). The other sites where

Photo by Anthony Mercieca

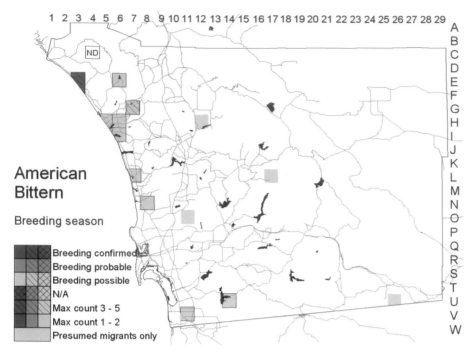

American
Bitterrn

Breeding season

Breeding confirmed
Breeding probable
Breeding possible
N/A
Max count 3 - 5
Max count 1 - 2
Presumed migrants only

One at O'Neill Lake (E6) 19 April 1999 was in suitable habitat but not relocated in spite of thorough coverage so was most likely a late migrant (P. A. Ginsburg). Unexpected were two American Bitterns away from extensive marshes in midsummer: one in Woods Valley (H12) 19 June 1998 (W. E. Haas) and one along the San Diego River near Boulder Creek (L17) 28 June 1997 (R. C. Sanger).

Nesting: American Bittern nests are usually built over water within dense marshes, making them difficult to find. The only nesting confirmation in San Diego County before that at Las Flores Creek was a sighting of one carrying nest material at Border Field State Park (W10) 26 June 1983 (J. Oldenettel).

the species possibly bred during the atlas period were Guajome Lake (G7; up to five on 8 May 2001, C. Andregg), Buena Vista Lagoon (one west of Interstate 5, H5, 18 July 1998, K. Messer, and 29 May 2001, R. Gransbury; two east of the freeway, H6, 11 August 1998, J. Ginger), the mouth of Agua Hedionda Creek (I6; one on 22 April 1998, W. E. Haas), San Elijo Lagoon (L7; four records of single birds, one as late as 1 June 1998, A. Mauro), lower Los Peñasquitos Canyon (N8; one on 7 May 2000, P. A. Ginsburg), and the Dairy Mart pond, Tijuana River valley (V11; up to two on 28 May 2001, G. McCaskie). The species had summered at least irregularly at Guajome Lake, San Elijo Lagoon, and the Tijuana River valley since the 1980s.

Migration: At O'Neill Lake, which P. A. Ginsburg covered intensively year round, he found the American Bittern in the spring as late as 19 April (1999) and in fall as early as 27 August (1997 and 1998). Outside the coastal lowland, records of spring migrants are of one at Jacumba (U28) 10 April 1976 (G. McCaskie), two at Lake Domingo (U26) 17 April 1998 (F. L. Unmack), one at Lower Willows, Coyote Creek (D23), 25 April 1981 (A. G. Morley), and one in the unsuitable habitat of Tamarisk Grove Campground (I24) 25 April 1982 (D. K. Adams). Records of fall migrants are of one found dead along Henderson Canyon Road, Borrego Valley (E24) 29 September 2002 (P. D. Jorgensen, SDNHM 50681) and one at Little Pass, between Earthquake and Blair valleys (K24), 3 October 1975 (ABDSP database).

Winter: During the atlas period we noted the American Bittern in winter 22 times at 11 sites, all but one in the coastal lowland and most in the valleys of the lower Santa Margarita and San Luis Rey rivers. Our only sightings of more than a single individual were of two at O'Neill Lake 13 December 1999 (P. A. Ginsburg) and two in the Tijuana River estuary (V10) 24 January 1998 (B. C. Moore). The salt marsh in the Tijuana estuary was our only winter site

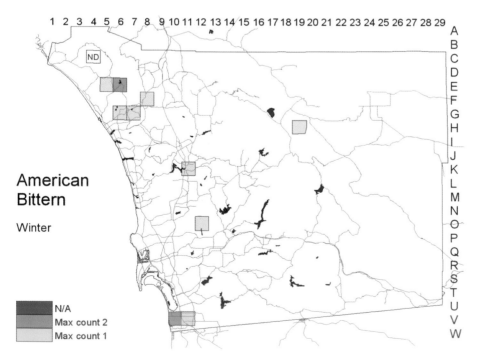

American
Bitterrn

Winter

N/A
Max count 2
Max count 1

for the species that was not freshwater marsh.

The American Bittern has been noted twice on Lake Henshaw Christmas bird counts, apparently the only winter records for the species at higher elevations in San Diego County: one at Lake Henshaw (G17) 19 December 1983 (D. K. Adams et al.) and one in Matagual Valley (I19) 18 December 2000 (G. Morse).

Conservation: Both atlas results and Christmas bird counts reveal a downward trend in the number of American Bitterns wintering in San Diego County. In the 1970s, counts at the Santa Margarita River mouth, Batiquitos Lagoon, and San Elijo Lagoon ranged up to

four or five per day (Unitt 1984, King et al. 1987), but these numbers could not be equaled from 1997 to 2002 despite greater effort. The annual average on San Diego Christmas bird counts from 1975 to 1984 was 1.6 but dropped to 0.7 from 1992 to 2001. On the Oceanside count, the annual average over the same periods dropped from 3.1 to 0.9. Presumably the change in San Diego County reflects the decline across the species' range, due to the elimination and degradation of wetlands (Gibbs et al. 1992). Stephens (1919a) called the American Bittern "rather common"; Sams and Stott (1959) wrote that it was easily found at Mission Bay before most of the marsh there was destroyed in the 1950s.

Least Bittern *Ixobrychus exilis*

An uncommon to rare and localized resident of marshes of cattail and tule, the Least Bittern is one of the more difficult species for the San Diego County birder to see. It is somewhat more numerous—or maybe just more conspicuous—in summer. Nevertheless, atlas observers found it to be regular in winter, a status it did not have—or was unknown—25 years earlier. Another perspective on the Least Bittern in San Diego County comes from wildlife rehabilitators. Each year, in late summer and fall, they receive several dispersing juvenile Least Bitterns that met a mishap in urban areas unsuitable for them.

Photo by Dave Furseth

Breeding distribution: Habitat for the Least Bittern lies largely in the coastal lowland, at brackish lagoons and lakes, ponds, and streams inland. Our most frequent sites for the species during the atlas period were O'Neill Lake, Camp Pendleton (E6; up to four on 21 and 29 July 1998, P. A. Ginsburg), the San Diego River between Santee and

Lakeside (P13; up to three on 26 April 1997, D. C. Seals), and Lake Murray (Q11; up to three on 22 August 1998, S. R. Helm). All sites where we recorded the species in spring and summer represent likely breeding sites, but the only locations where we actually confirmed breeding 1997–2001 were O'Neill Lake (fledgling 21 July 1998, P. A. Ginsburg), the east basin of Buena Vista Lagoon (H6; adult feeding young 18 July 1999, L. E. Taylor), Discovery Lake, San Marcos (J9; fledgling 17 May 1998, J. O. Zimmer), the borrow pit in the Sweetwater River at Dehesa (Q15; fledging 14 June 2001, H. L. Young), and the San Diego River in Mission Valley near Mission Center Road (R9; four fledglings with adult 3 May 1997, J. K. Wilson). Least Bitterns are known to nest also at San Elijo Lagoon (King et al. 1987). It is likely that only the species' secretive habits accounted for our missing it at some sites where it had been seen repeatedly before the atlas period, especially Guajome Lake (G7) and the upper end of Batiquitos Lagoon (J7).

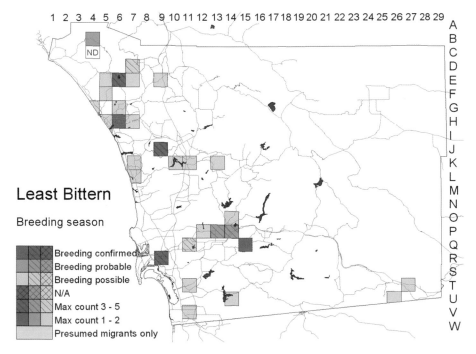

Least Bittern

Breeding season

- Breeding confirmed
- Breeding probable
- Breeding possible
- N/A
- Max count 3 - 5
- Max count 1 - 2
- Presumed migrants only

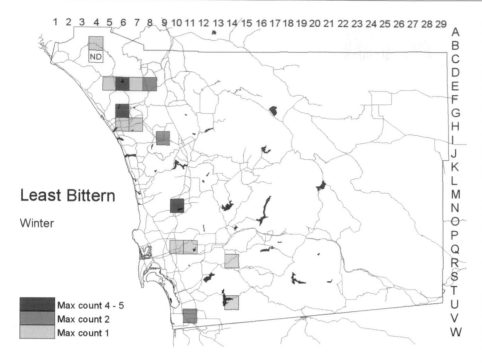

Least Bittern

Winter

Max count 4 - 5
Max count 2
Max count 1

from eggs laid in early July (P. Unitt).

Migration: With the increase in winter records of the Least Bittern, the species no longer follows a clearly defined seasonal schedule. Nevertheless, juveniles found away from marshes in developed areas demonstrate at least short-distance dispersal. Their dates range from 25 June (1991, near Chollas Reservoir, R11, SDNHM 47680) to 30 September (1998, Paradise Hills, T11, SDNHM 50223).

Winter: We noted the Least Bittern in winter on 44 occasions at about 16 sites from 1997 to 2002. Our largest winter numbers were five at O'Neill Lake 4 December 1999 (P. A. Ginsburg), four at Windmill Lake (G6) 26 December 1998 (P. Unitt), and four at Miramar Lake (N10) 29 January 1998 (M. B. Stowe). Most of the winter records are from sites where the species was regular during the breeding season. All are in the coastal lowland, and most are in northwestern San Diego County where freshwater marshes are more frequent.

The Least Bittern also occurs rarely on the Campo Plateau. Sams and Stott (1959) reported it at Campo Lake (U22). We found it twice at Lake Domingo (U26; one on 24 June 1999 and 21 April 2000) and three times at Tule Lake (T27), the best habitat for it in this region (one on 20 April and 3 July 2000; two, including an independent juvenile, 6 June 2001, J. K. Wilson, F. L. Unmack).

Nesting: The Least Bittern hides its nest effectively, screening it with a canopy of surrounding vegetation as well as building within the marsh itself. It is no surprise that atlas observers found no nests. Dates of eight egg sets collected 1901–37 range from 20 May to 8 July, but our earliest date of fledglings during the atlas period, 3 May, implies egg laying as early as about 1 April. A family of three fledglings with adults along the San Diego River in Mission Valley 16 August 1990 must have hatched

Conservation: Numbers of the Least Bittern are generally thought to have declined in parallel with the elimination of freshwater marshes. The species is so difficult to monitor, however, that real evidence for a decline is lacking at least in San Diego County. Its history in Mission Valley shows it retains the ability to recolonize regenerated habitat. In 1988, all vegetation along the San Diego River between Highway 163 and Stadium Way was removed, and the river banks were recontoured, as part of the "First San Diego River Improvement Project." The bitterns recolonized and nested successfully in 1990, the first year in which stands of cattails had regrown to full size.

Before 1981, there were only eight San Diego County records for December and January (Unitt 1984). It is unclear whether the apparent increase in winter is real or whether it is an artifact of birders covering the wintering sites more consistently and being more aware of the species' calls.

Taxonomy: All Least Bitterns in North America are nominate *I. e. exilis* (Gmelin, 1789); the supposed western subspecies *I. e. hesperis* Dickey and van Rossem, 1924, is invalid (Dickerman 1973).

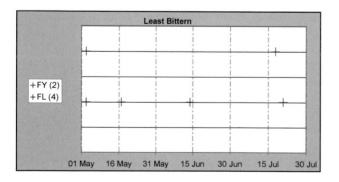

Great Blue Heron *Ardea herodias*

The Great Blue Heron is one of San Diego County's most familiar water birds, occurring year round at wetlands of all kinds. It uses dry land, too, commonly foraging away from water for gophers and rats. Some Great Blue Herons nest as isolated pairs, but

most are colonial, nesting high in tall trees. A majority of the county's approximately 250–300 nesting pairs are concentrated in the six largest colonies. The Great Blue Heron has taken readily to artificial nesting habitat like eucalyptus groves; it feeds largely on prey introduced by man. Yet, unlike those of the

Great and Snowy Egrets, the population of the Great Blue Heron has not exploded.

Breeding distribution: The Great Blue Heron nested at 30 recorded sites in San Diego County from 1997 to 2001. Thirteen of these had only isolated pairs, but 17 had from two to 54 nests (Table 6). Most of the colonies are in the coastal lowland, but a few are at higher elevations. The highest is at 4650 feet elevation in Rattlesnake Valley (N22) in the Laguna Mountains.

Also, two or three pairs have built nests but apparently not fledged any young at Santee Lakes (P12), as in 2002 (M. B. Mulrooney).

Breeding Great Blue Herons apparently forage within 5 miles or so of their colonies; for example, the birds nesting at the Rancho Santa Fe colony appear to forage primarily at San Elijo Lagoon. Away from known or probable nest sites, the Great Blue Heron occurs widely but uncommonly through the breeding season, with up to five at, for example, Cuyamaca Lake (M20) 25 June 1998 (A. P. and T. E. Keenan), Barrett Lake (S18) 18 June 2000 (R. and S. L. Breisch), and Lake Morena (S21) 7 July 2001 (R. and S. L. Breisch).

Nesting: In San Diego County, most Great Blue Herons build stick nests in trees, often adding to them year after year. At O'Neill Lake, Batiquitos Lagoon, Rancho

Photo by Anthony Mercieca

Santa Fe, and Lindo Lake they nest in eucalyptus trees, whereas at Carlsbad, Mission Bay, and Coronado they nest in planted pines. At North Island and Point Loma they nest in both. At the San Dieguito River mouth, Los Peñasquitos Lagoon (N7), and Sea World the herons nest in native or planted Torrey Pines, and at Pine Valley (P21) and Rattlesnake Valley they nest in tall Jeffrey pines. An isolated nest at the mouth of Couser Canyon (E10) was in a palm. In 1998 the colony at Lake Henshaw was in cottonwoods. Occasionally the herons use artificial structures; those reported during the atlas period were around San Diego Bay, on a crane in National City and on the catwalk of a power plant in Chula Vista. At least in 1994 the herons built 13 nests on abandoned platforms and barges off National City (T10; Manning 1995); we did not survey this site 1997–2001. Past nest sites included sycamores and a scrub oak among sandstone cliffs (WFVZ).

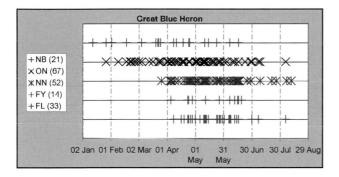

Table 6   Nesting Colonies of the Great Blue Heron in San Diego County, 1997–2001

Colony	Square	Maximum Count of Active Nests	Year of Maximum	Observer
O'Neill Lake	E6	25	2000	P. A. Ginsburg
West Fork Conservation Camp	E17	6+	2001	E. C. Hall, C. R. Mahrdt, J. O. Zimmer
Lake Henshaw	G17	4	1998	P. Unitt
Highland Dr. at Oak Ave., Carlsbad	I6	14	1999	P. A. Ginsburg
Batiquitos Lagoon	J7	3	2000	J. Ciarletta
Wild Animal Park	J12	"large"	1997	D. C. Seals
Escondido Creek at La Bajada, Rancho Santa Fe	L8	30	2000	A. Mauro
San Dieguito River mouth	M7	2	2001	D. R. Grine
Lucky 5 Ranch, Rattlesnake Valley	N22	2	1998, 1999	P. D. Jorgensen
El Capitan Reservoir	O16	1a	1999, 2001	S. Kingswood
Lindo Lake	P14	5	2001	C. G. Edwards
Sea World	R8	52	1997	Black et al. (1997)
Point Loma	S7	54	1999	M. F. Platter-Rieger
North Island Naval Air Station	S8	22	1999	P. McDonald
Spreckels Park, Coronado	S9	13	1998	Y. Ikegaya
Glorietta Blvd. at Miguel Ave., Coronado	S9	9	1997	P. Unitt
Hitachi crane, National City	T10	8b	2000	R. T. Patton

[a]One nest of the Great Blue with more of the Great and Snowy Egrets.
[b]Eight individuals; number of nests not specified.

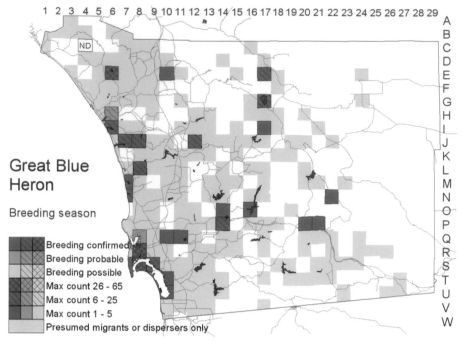

Great Blue Heron

Breeding season

Breeding confirmed
Breeding probable
Breeding possible
Max count 26 - 65
Max count 6 - 25
Max count 1 - 5
Presumed migrants or dispersers only

Unitt), suggesting laying as late as early June. At Point Loma some nests still had large young in mid September. Several Point Loma nests hatched and fledged two successive broods within the same year; it is unknown if the second brood was raised by the same parents (M. F. Platter-Rieger).

Migration: The Great Blue Heron is nonmigratory in southern California, but juveniles sometimes disperse long distances; an extreme example is of one tagged as a nestling in Orange County found the following winter at Elko, Nevada (K. Keane and P. H. Bloom). Surveys around San Diego Bay revealed somewhat higher numbers in fall, probably cor-

The Great Blue Heron's exact nesting schedule is difficult to follow because its nests are in the treetops where their contents are not obvious until the chicks are calling. The herons begin defending nest sites at the end of November (Black et al. 1997) and building or refurbishing their nests in early to mid January. They begin laying in early to mid January as well, as implied by hatching in mid February and fledglings by 4 April 1997 at Sea World (Black et al. 1997). Late February through March appears to be the time of peak laying. Herons nesting in established colonies may nest earlier than those in new colonies or those in isolated pairs. A nest at a new colony overlooking the San Dieguito River estuary still had young, nearly full grown, on 11 August 2001 (P.

responding with the dispersal of juveniles (Macdonald et al. 1990, Stadtlander and Konecny 1994). Surveys at San Elijo Lagoon found somewhat lower numbers in spring, probably corresponding with adults spending more time at nesting colonies (King et al. 1987).

In the Anza–Borrego Desert, where it is a rare nonbreeding visitor, the Great Blue Heron occurs mainly in fall and winter; the only records from late April through June are of one at Scissors Crossing (J22) 14 May 1998 (E. C. Hall), one at Borrego Springs (G24) 14 May 2000 (P. D. Ache), one in the north Borrego Valley (E24) 8–11 June 2001 (P. D. Jorgensen), and one along Coyote Creek (D24) 26 June 1988 (A. G. Morley).

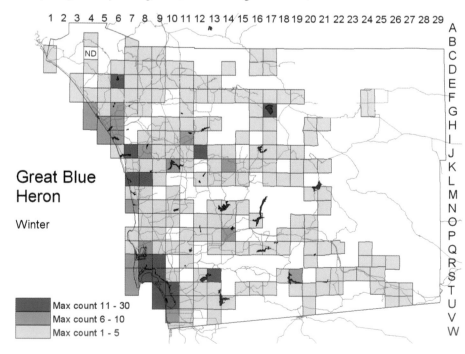

Great Blue Heron

Winter

Max count 11 - 30
Max count 6 - 10
Max count 1 - 5

Winter: Atlas results suggest that the number of Great Blue Herons in San Diego County does not vary much with the seasons. Our highest winter counts in single atlas squares 1997–2002 were of 27 around north San Diego Bay 18 December 1999 (D. W. Povey, M. B. Mulrooney), 27 at the Wild Animal Park 3 January 1998 (K. L. Weaver), and 30 at Lake Henshaw 3 December 2000 (L. J. Hargrove). Thus many birds remain near the nesting colonies through the winter. Great Blue Herons range in winter as high as 4500–4600 feet elevation, in Lower Doane Valley (D14; one 31 December 1999–7 January 2000, P. D. Jorgensen), at Cuyamaca Lake (many observations, with up to five on 17 January 2000, G. Chaniot), and in Thing Valley

(Q24; three records, J. R. Barth, P. Unitt). Wintering Great Blue Herons are irregular in the Borrego Valley, with five individuals seen during the atlas period and records on five of 18 Anza–Borrego Christmas bird counts 1984–2001, maximum three on 30 December 1990.

Conservation: In San Diego County the Great Blue Heron has become thoroughly integrated into the domesticated environment. Many colonies are directly over places heavily trafficked by people, the nesting birds being indifferent to human activity below. A study of the food of nestlings at the Point Loma colony in 1995 revealed the birds were fed largely on northern anchovy, crawfish, rats, domestic goldfish, and bullfrogs—hardly any of their diet consisted of items available before the founding of San Diego in 1769.

In spite of being something of an urban adapter, and establishing colonies at sites unsuitable before trees were planted there, the Great Blue Heron has increased in numbers only modestly. On the San Diego Christmas bird count, from 1953 to 1972, it averaged 61 (0.35 per party-hour); from 1997 to 2002, it averaged 113 (0.51 per party-hour). A factor likely keeping the population in check in San Diego County is the high rate of steatitis, an often fatal disease in which the birds are afflicted with large deposits of necrotic fat. Its cause is unknown, and its rate among other herons is much lower.

Taxonomy: The Great Blue Heron has been oversplit into many subspecies, primarily by Oberholser (1912). With most of these synonymized, the birds of southern California are best called *A. h. wardi* Ridgway, 1882 (Hancock and Kushlan 1984, R. W. Dickerman pers. comm.).

Great Egret *Ardea alba*

Decimated in southern California at the beginning of the 20th century, the Great Egret has enjoyed a recovery that is still continuing. In San Diego County it was long a nonbreeding visitor only, mainly in fall and winter, and it is still most numerous in that role. The first known nesting was in 1988, and more colonies formed soon thereafter, until by the arrival of the 21st century the county's breeding population numbered about 75 pairs, most at the Wild Animal Park and Rancho Santa Fe. But the establishment of new colonies, often mixed with those of other herons, continued past the end of the atlas period in 2002.

Breeding distribution: The primary Great Egret colony in San Diego County, founded in 1989, is in the Wild Animal Park (J12), in the multispecies colony of herons and egrets in the Heart of Africa exhibit. Counts here range up to 100 birds on 15 June 1998 (D. and D. Bylin) and 40 nests on 9 May 1999 (K. L. Weaver). The colony in Rancho Santa Fe (L8), in eucalyptus trees within a private estate along Escondido Creek near La Bajada, is second in size. In 1998, the first year in which the egret nested there in numbers, there were 25 to 30 nests, with a similar number of Great Blue Heron nests (A. Mauro).

The other colonies established themselves after the atlas period began in 1997. At El Capitan Reservoir (O16), nesting began in 2000 with a single pair with nestlings 21 June (D. C. Seals). The next year, on 9 July, one eucalyptus tree overlooking the lake contained three nests of the Great Egret, two of the Snowy, and one of the Great Blue Heron (J. R. Barth, R. T. Patton, P. Unitt). At Lindo Lake, Lakeside (P14), Great Egret nesting also began in 2000, with one carrying nest material 18 May (M. B. Stowe). On 9 July 2001, there were five nests of the Great Egret, among more of the Great Blue Heron, Snowy Egret, and Black-crowned Night-Heron (J. R. Barth, R. T. Patton, P. Unitt). On 11 August 2001, on the south side of the San Dieguito River estuary (M7), one nest of the

Photo by Anthony Mercieca

Great Egret, near two of the Great Blue Heron, had two nearly full-grown nestlings (P. Unitt). In the Great Blue Heron colony at the Point Loma navy research laboratory (S7), one pair of the Great Egret nested in 2000 but failed. In 2002, however, two pairs nested at this site, one successfully, and in 2003 three pairs nested, all successfully (M. F. Platter-Rieger).

Yet another new colony formed in 2000 was at the east end of Lake Wohlford (H12), with six birds on 28 May (P. Hernandez, S. Christiansen, E. C. Hall). On 20 May 2001, the colony appeared to be growing rapidly, with 35 individuals in courtship displays and nest building and incubation apparently begun in one nest. Less than seven weeks later, however, on 7 July, the colony had been deserted and not a single egret remained in the area (P. Unitt).

The establishment of new colonies continued after the atlas period with three nests of the Great Egret on the north side of Batiquitos Lagoon (J7) in 2003 (R. Ebersol).

Away from breeding colonies, the Great Egret is wide-

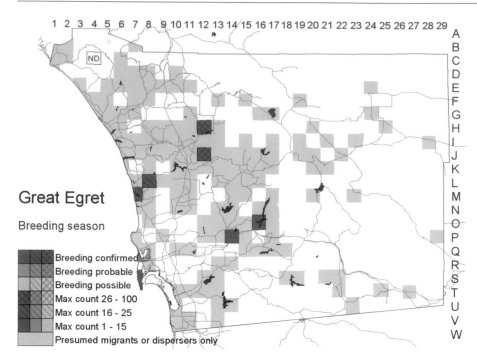

Great Egret

Breeding season

Breeding confirmed
Breeding probable
Breeding possible
Max count 26 - 100
Max count 16 - 25
Max count 1 - 15
Presumed migrants or dispersers only

Nesting: Like the Great Blue Heron, the Great Egret builds a platform of sticks high in trees. In the mixed colony at Rancho Santa Fe, the Great Blue's nests were higher, above the egrets'. At most sites in San Diego County, the nests are in eucalyptus, but at the San Dieguito River mouth and Point Loma the birds were in Torrey pines; at Lake Wohlford they were in coast live oaks.

The schedule of Great Egret nesting in San Diego County is variable. In 1998, egg laying in the Rancho Santa Fe colony had apparently begun by late February; a search underneath the colony on 5 March yielded some broken eggs fallen to the ground (A. Mauro). By 11 May some young from this colony

spread at both coastal and inland wetlands. Some of the larger concentrations, up to 75 at Lake Hodges 14 June 1999 (R. L. Barber) and 61 at San Elijo Lagoon 10 July 1999 (P. A. Ginsburg), were probably of birds commuting from or recently fledged from nearby colonies. But others, such as 16 at O'Neill Lake (E6) 9 June 1998 (P. A. Ginsburg), 33 at Batiquitos Lagoon 3 April 1998 (F. Hall, C. C. Gorman), and 18 at Los Peñasquitos Lagoon (N7) 3 April 1999 (K. Estey) were not—though they suggest sites for future colonies. In the mountains the Great Egret is rare during the breeding season, with reports of no more than two (at Wynola, J19, 17 April–2 July 1999, S. E. Smith; near Julian, K20, 10 June 1998, E. C. Hall).

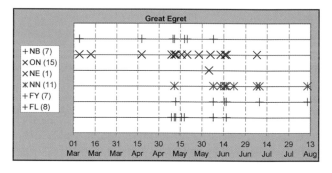

had already fledged while others were still downy. At Point Loma the young hatched in May and June (M. F. Platter-Rieger). The large nestlings at the San Dieguito River mouth 11 August 2001 must have hatched from eggs laid in early June.

Migration: Although the Great Egret has colonized San Diego County as a nesting species, its primary role is still that of a nonbreeding visitor. Censuses around San Diego Bay show the egret's numbers peaking from November to February and reaching their nadir in June, with gradual changes in between. Around north San Diego Bay, Mock et al. (1994) had their high count of 88 on 9 November 1994; in the salt works, Stadtlander and Konecny (1994) had their high count of 83 on 17 November 1993. Postbreeding dispersal to

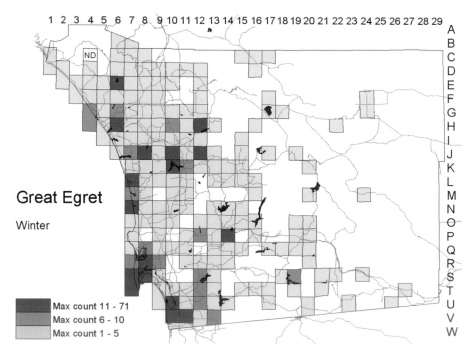

Great Egret

Winter

Max count 11 - 71
Max count 6 - 10
Max count 1 - 5

higher elevations is underway by August, with up to ten at Cuyamaca Lake (M20) 10 August 1998 (J. R. Barth).

In and near the Anza–Borrego Desert, the Great Egret occurs primarily as a rare migrant, recorded in fall as early as 21 July (1994, three at the Roadrunner Club, Borrego Springs, F24, M. L. Gabel), in spring as late as 6 May (1999, one at Banner, K21, P. K. Nelson). Generally the species is seen singly; exceptional concentrations are of ten at the Borrego Springs sewage pond (H25) 10 October 1992 (A. G. Morley) and seven in the north Borrego Valley (E24) 6 May 2000 (P. D. Ache). Most desert records are from the Borrego Valley, but a few are from scattered localities far from suitable habitat, such as Ocotillo Wells (I28; two on 1 April 2000, R. Miller) and Canyon sin Nombre (P29; one on 29 April 2000, F. A. Belinsky, M. G. Mathos).

Winter: In the coastal lowland, wintering Great Egrets are widespread and locally common. Many of the birds in the Wild Animal Park remain through the winter, with up to 71 on 30 December 2000 (K. L. Weaver). Farther inland, the Great Egret is uncommon and scattered, with up to five in Ramona (K15) 30 December 2000 (D. and C. Batzler) and seven at Barrett Lake (S19) 5 February 2000 (R. and S. L. Breisch). Even as high as Cuyamaca Lake the Great Egret is fairly regular in winter, with up to two on 18 February 1999 (A. P. and T. E. Keenan).

In the Anza–Borrego Desert in winter the Great Egret is rare, with just four records of single birds from 1997 to 2002. It has been recorded on just three of 18 Anza–Borrego Christmas bird counts 1984–2001, though the count on 20 December 1987 yielded eight.

Conservation: The Great Egret was decimated in southern California around 1900, when the birds were killed for their plumes, in fashion for decorating ladies' hats. Once this trade was suppressed, recovery began. In the winter of 1912–13, Grey (1913b) reported up to 20 at the south end of San Diego Bay 25 December; previously, he had seen no more than four. By 1936, a large roost had formed at Point Loma, with a maximum of "well over 150" on 25 February (Sefton 1936). The population began another upsurge in the late 1970s. King et al. (1987) noted an increase at San Elijo Lagoon from 1973 to 1983. From 1960 to 1977 the San Diego Christmas bird count averaged 26.5 Great Egrets; from 1997 to 2001 it averaged 106.4.

Nesting began in 1988 with a pair at the Dairy Mart pond in the Tijuana River valley (V11; G. McCaskie, AB 42:1339, 1988). This site soon became unsuitable, but the first nesting at the Wild Animal Park took place the following year (J. Oldenettel, AB 43:1367, 1989), and by 1991 the colony had grown to 30 pairs (J. O'Brien, AB 45:1160, 1991).

Herons and humanity have an uneasy relationship. People now admire the Great Egret's beauty without having to wear it themselves. But heron colonies are messy affairs, unwelcome when they form over public parks like Lindo Lake. The egrets prefer to nest near water where they can feed, so they are likely to choose sites frequented by people where they are hard to ignore and vulnerable to disturbance.

Taxonomy: Great Egrets in the New World are *A. a. egretta* Gmelin, 1789, differing from the subspecies in the Old World by their almost wholly yellow bills.

Snowy Egret *Egretta thula*

One of California's most elegant birds, the Snowy Egret frequents both coastal and inland wetlands. Since the 1930s, when it recovered from persecution for its plumes, it has been common in fall and winter. Since 1979, it has also established an increasing number of breeding colonies. Yet, in contrast to the Great Egret, the increase in Snowy Egret colonies has not been accompanied by a clear increase in the Snowy's numbers. Though dependent on wetlands for foraging, the Snowy Egret takes advantage of humanity, from nesting in landscaping to following on the heels of clam diggers at the San Diego River mouth, snapping up any organisms they suck out of the mud.

Breeding distribution: The first recorded Snowy Egret colonies in San Diego County were established at Buena Vista Lagoon in 1979 (J. P. Rieger, AB 33:896, 1979) and in the Tijuana River valley in 1980 (AB 34:929, 1980). By 1997 these were no longer active, but during the atlas period we confirmed nesting at eight other sites. Because Snowy Egrets often hide their nests in denser vegetation than do the Great Egret and Great Blue Heron, assessing the size of a Snowy Egret colony is more difficult than for the larger herons.

Photo by Anthony Mercieca

Two of the largest colonies lie near San Diego and Mission bays. The colony on the grounds of Sea World, behind the Forbidden Reef exhibit (R8), was founded in 1991 and contained 42 nests and fledged 44 young in 1997 (Black et al. 1997). The colony within North Island Naval Air Station (S8) contained 37 nests and fledged

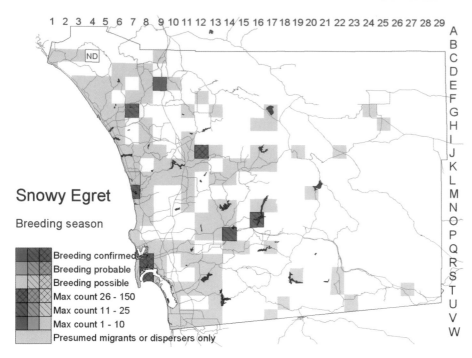

Snowy Egret

Breeding season

Breeding confirmed
Breeding probable
Breeding possible
Max count 26 - 150
Max count 11 - 25
Max count 1 - 10
Presumed migrants or dispersers only

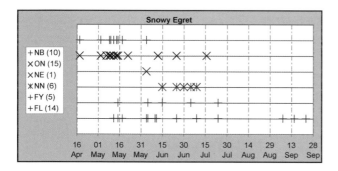

Snowy Egret

+NB (10)
×ON (15)
×NE (1)
×NN (6)
+FY (5)
+FL (14)

16   01   16   31   15   30   15   30   14   29   13   28
Apr   May   May   May   Jun   Jun   Jul   Jul   Aug   Aug   Sep   Sep

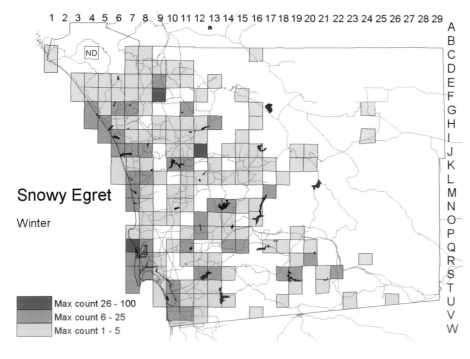

Snowy Egret

Winter

Max count 26 - 100
Max count 6 - 25
Max count 1 - 5

15 young in 1999 (McDonald et al. 2000). Another large colony is in the mixed heronry at the Wild Animal Park in the Heart of Africa exhibit (J12). Our maximum count of individuals here was 150 on 15 June 1998 (D. and D. Bylin); there were at least 14 active nests on 9 May 1999 (K. L. Weaver). The colony in Solana Beach (M7) at the corner of Plaza Street and Sierra Avenue had 10–20 nests in 1997 and was still active in 2001 (A. Mauro).

Other colonies are small or new. In the San Luis Rey River valley just east of Interstate 15, at least one pair nested in 2000 and 2001 at a pond formed when a new housing development blocked the drainage of Keys Canyon (E9; C. and D. Wysong, J. E. Pike). At Guajome Lake (G7), at least eight pairs nested in 2001 (K. L. Weaver). At El Capitan Reservoir (O16) Snowy Egrets founded a new colony in 2001, two pairs nesting in one eucalyptus tree with three pairs of the Great Egret and one of the Great Blue Heron (J. R. Barth). Snowy Egrets helped found the mixed heronry at Lindo Lake (P14) in 2000 (M. B. Stowe); they had about five active nests there on 9 July 2001 (P. Unitt). In 2002 Snowy Egrets joined the Great Blue Herons on the north side of Batiquitos Lagoon (J7); in 2003 there were about five nests of the Snowy (R. Ebersol). At the mouth of the San Luis Rey River—in trees over the parking lot of a Jolly Roger restaurant (H5)—were 48 nests of the Snowy Egret, plus four of the Great Blue Heron and two of the Black-crowned Night-Heron, on 3 July 2003 (K. L. Weaver). Information from nonbirders in the area, including one of the restaurant's managers, suggests that this colony, although probably not new, increased greatly in 2002 and 2003 (J. Determan).

Even during the breeding season Snowy Egrets are widespread in the coastal lowland away from nesting colonies. Some high counts exemplifying this are of 60 at Lake Hodges (K10) 16 June 1999 (R. L. Barber), 29 at Batiquitos Lagoon 1 May 1998 (F. Hall), and 25 at the upper end of Sweetwater Reservoir (S13) 23 March 2001 (P. Famolaro). In the foothills the Snowy Egret is uncommon and scattered in the breeding season, with counts of up to five only, as at Sutherland Lake (J16) 25 June 2000 (J. R.

Barth). In the mountains the Snowy Egret is rare, reported during the atlas period only from Wynola (J19; up to two on 17 April 1999, S. E. Smith) and Cuyamaca Lake (M20; one on 25 June 1998, A. P. and T. E. Keenan).

Nesting: Even though San Diego County colonies are few, they encompass a surprising variety of nest sites. At Solana Beach, where the egrets nest in company with Black-crowned Night-Herons only, the nests are in a dense-foliaged fig tree. At North Island, also shared with the night-heron, the nests are in eucalyptus and pines as well as figs. The mixed heronries at Lindo Lake and El Capitan Reservoir are in eucalyptus trees. At Sea World, where the only species nesting in close association with the Snowy Egret is the Little Blue Heron, most of the nests are in thick bamboo, a few in figs. At Guajome Lake and Keys Canyon, where the egrets' companions are White-faced Ibises, the birds nest on islands of matted cattails.

The schedule of Snowy Egret nesting in San Diego has been monitored most closely at Sea World (Black et al. 1997). In 1997, incubation had apparently begun in some nests by 21 March, and most young fledged between 22 May and 21 June, corresponding to laying from late March to late April. But eight nests were still active on 20 August, suggesting egg laying as late as the end of June.

Migration: Although the Snowy Egret occurs in San Diego County year round, its numbers vary with the seasons. Surveys of San Elijo Lagoon (King et al. 1987) and north San Diego Bay (Mock et al. 1994) found it most numerous in fall; those of south San Diego Bay (Macdonald et al. 1990, Stadtlander and Konecny 1994) found it most numerous in winter. Generally it is least numerous in summer.

In the Anza–Borrego Desert the Snowy Egret is a rare migrant, recorded mainly at artificial ponds, only a few times at natural oases, from 22 September (1999, four at the Borrego Springs sewage pond, H25, A. G. Morley) to 27 May (1990, one along Vallecito Creek, M24, Massey and Evans 1994). The only desert records of more than five individuals were of 11 in Borrego Springs (G24) 3 April 1999 and 19 there, in a pond filled by a flash flood, 24 August 2003 (P. D. Ache).

Winter: In winter, the Snowy Egret is more widespread than in spring or summer, visiting small ponds as well as larger lakes throughout the coastal lowland. The Wild Animal Park remains a major center for the species, with winter counts as high as 100 on 30 December 1999 (D. and D. Bylin). Along the coast, notable late fall or winter concentrations have been of up to 152 around north San Diego Bay 11 November 1994 (Mock et al. 1994), 91 at the outflow channel for the power plant in Chula Vista 7 February 1989 (Macdonald et al. 1990), and 115 in the salt works 17 November 1993 (Stadtlander and Konecny 1994).

Even in the foothills and mountains the Snowy Egret is more of a winter visitor. Our winter counts in this region ranged up to eight, at Barrett Lake 2 February 2001 (R. and S. L. Breisch) and at Corte Madera Lake (R20) 20 February 1999 (L. and M. Polinsky). Winter records range as high as 4000–4200 feet elevation near Julian (J20, one on 2 December 1999, M. B. Stowe; K20, one on 1 December 1997, E. C. Hall). There are only five winter records from the Anza–Borrego Desert, two during the atlas period, of one in Borrego Springs (G24) 9 February 1998 (P. D. Ache) and one at Tamarisk Grove (I24) 31 January 1999 (R. Thériault).

Conservation: Though "plentiful at all seasons" along the coast of southern California in the 1860s (Cooper 1870), the Snowy Egret was the species most gravely affected by hunting for hat plumes. It went unrecorded in San Diego County from 1890 to 1922. Recovery took place largely from 1929 to 1939. The egret's colonization of San Diego County beginning in 1979 suggests that another population expansion is underway, in parallel with the Great Egret's. Yet Christmas bird counts suggest another story, that the number of Snowy Egrets, at least in winter, peaked in the 1970s and 1980s and may have declined since the early 1990s. The factors governing Snowy Egret numbers in San Diego County, and the degree to which the birds move in and out of the county, are unknown.

Taxonomy: Snowy Egrets in San Diego County, like those elsewhere in the western United States, are closer in size to those of the eastern half of the country, smaller and thinner billed than those of Baja California, and so best called *E. t. candidissima* (Gmelin, 1789) (Rea 1983).

Little Blue Heron *Egretta caerulea*

The Little Blue Heron is a rather recent arrival in San Diego County, since the 1980s a rare but permanent resident of the coastal wetlands. It forages in shallow water and nests in colonies of its close relative, the Snowy Egret. Indeed, the egret's colonizing the county may have been a necessary precursor to the Little Blue Heron's colonizing. San Diego now represents the northwestern corner of the Little Blue Heron's usual range.

Breeding distribution: From 1997 to 2001 the Little Blue Heron was confirmed nesting only in the Snowy Egret colony at Sea World (R8), where one pair fledged one young

Photo by Anthony Mercieca

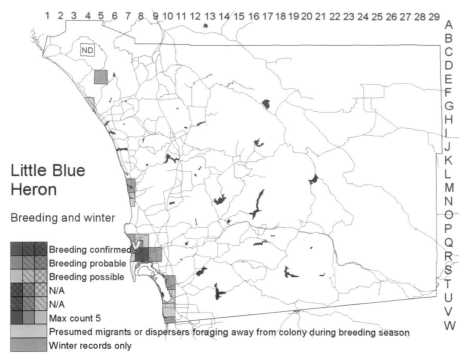

Little Blue Heron

Breeding and winter

- Breeding confirmed
- Breeding probable
- Breeding possible
- N/A
- N/A
- Max count 5
- Presumed migrants or dispersers foraging away from colony during breeding season
- Winter records only

World is in a thick stand of tall bamboo (Black et al. 1997). The mixed heronry at North Island is spread among eucalyptus, pine, and fig trees. Information on the Little Blue Heron's nesting schedule in San Diego County is still rudimentary. In 1994, one nest at Sea World was occupied by 8 April; in 1997, the nest was occupied by 6 May and the young fledged between 21 June and 12 July. In the former colony in the Tijuana River valley, fledging was in July.

Winter: The Little Blue Heron's distribution and abundance in San Diego County in winter are much the same as at other seasons. An exceptional winter concentration, the largest yet reported, was of 14 in the San Diego River flood-control channel 23 December 1997 (C. G. Edwards). Winter records from northern San Diego County were of two at Los Peñasquitos Lagoon 5 December 1999 (D. K. Adams), one at the San Dieguito River estuary 11 December 1999 (D. R. Grine), and one immature 5.8 miles inland at a sewage pond in the Santa Margarita River valley, Camp Pendleton (E5), 25 December 1999 (B. E. Bell).

Conservation: The Little Blue Heron was first recorded in San Diego County on 14 November 1967 (AFN 22:89, 1968) and remained a rare visitor until 1980. From then through 1993, one or two pairs nested in the multispecies heronry at the Dairy Mart pond, Tijuana River valley (V11). That colony disappeared, but the herons began nesting at Sea World in 1992. Since the mid 1980s the population of Little Blue Herons in the San Diego area seems to have been more or less stable at approximately 10–12 individuals. The close association in nesting between the Little Blue Heron and Snowy Egret suggests that the career of the former will follow in the steps of the latter.

in 1997 (Black et al. 1997). In 1993 and 1994, however, three and four pairs of the Little Blue nested there, respectively. Also, at least one pair evidently nested in the heronry within North Island Naval Air Station (S8) in 1996, as a recently fledged juvenile was picked up moribund beneath the colony 20 August (SDNHM 49605). Surveys there in 1999 did not reveal the species (McDonald et al. 2000)

Foraging Little Blue Herons are seen along the shores of Mission Bay, in the San Diego River flood-control channel (up to five on 29 July 2000, M. Billings), at Famosa Slough, in south San Diego Bay, and in the Tijuana River estuary. They have been seen repeatedly at Los Peñasquitos Lagoon (N7) but are rare farther north. The species has been recorded at most of the coastal lagoons between Del Mar and Oceanside, but during the atlas period the only summer records north of Los Peñasquitos Lagoon were of one at the Santa Margarita River mouth (G4) 15 June 1997 (B. Peterson) and 3–5 July 1999 (P. A. Ginsburg).

Nesting: The Snowy Egret/Little Blue Heron colony at Sea

Tricolored Heron *Egretta tricolor*

Like the Reddish Egret, the Tricolored or Louisiana Heron is a rare visitor from the south that reaches the northern tip of its normal range at San Diego. The Tricolored is most often seen foraging like other herons in the channels through the Tijuana River estuary or in shallow water around south San Diego Bay. Unlike many other herons, which are on the increase, the Tricolored has been decreasing in frequency since the mid 1980s, though one shows up in most winters.

Winter: The Tijuana River estuary (V10/W10) was our only site for more than a single Tricolored Heron

Photo by Anthony Mercieca

1997–2002, with two (one adult, one immature) there 5 December 1999 (B. C. Moore). There were also repeated

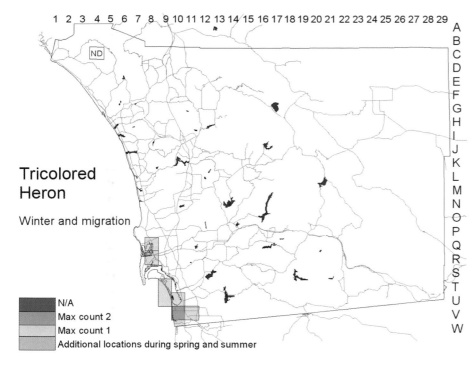

Tricolored Heron

Winter and migration

▮	N/A
▮	Max count 2
▮	Max count 1
▮	Additional locations during spring and summer

observations around south San Diego Bay (T9/U10), with birds presumably moving between there and the Tijuana estuary. During the atlas period, a Tricolored Heron also showed up twice in the San Diego River flood-control channel (R8; 9 June–3 July 1999; 6 November–9 December 1999, T. Hartnett, J. R. Sams, NAB 54:104, 220, 2000), once at Kendall–Frost Marsh, Mission Bay (Q8; 29 December 1998, J. C. Worley).

Migration: The Tricolored Heron has been seen in San Diego County in every month of the year, but is least frequent in summer. Immatures may arrive in fall as early as 23 September (1978, AB 33:213, 1979). Usually the birds disappear by 1 May, but some have remained through the summer, as in 1984 (AB 38:958, 1061, 1984). About a dozen have apparently arrived in summer.

Though largely coastal, Tricolored Herons have been found three times at fresh water in the Tijuana River valley (Unitt 1984) and once at Lake Henshaw (G17; 18 October 1983, R. Higson, AB 38:246, 1984). Because the species is also a rare visitor to the Salton Sea, this bird

may have moved into San Diego County from the east.

Conservation: Laurence M. Huey (1915) found the Tricolored Heron in San Diego County (and California) for the first time at the south end of San Diego Bay 17 January 1914 (SDNHM 30889). For the next 40 years, while observers were few, the species was seen irregularly. But from the mid 1950s through the mid 1980s, with an increase of birders, the heron proved regular along San Diego's coast in small numbers. During this interval, it occurred occasionally in the lagoons of northern San Diego County, with up to six at San Elijo Lagoon (L7) 1 November–27 December 1963 (McCaskie 1964). Since 1980, however, the only Tricolored Herons in coastal north county have been one at Los Peñasquitos Lagoon (N7) 8 January 1984 (D. B. King, AB 38:357, 1984) and one there 1 May 1988 (B. C. Moore, AB 42:481, 1988). In the San Diego area the numbers peaked in 1979–80 with five (AB 34:306, 1980). The winter of 1984–85 was the last with as many as three (AB 39:209, 1985). Nevertheless, at least one showed up each subsequent year through 2001 except the winter 1996–97.

Dredging and filling of the bays, siltation of the lagoons, and development of the shoreline have eliminated much Tricolored Heron habitat. The species was regular at Mission Bay before that area was developed (Sams and Stott 1959). Nevertheless, the increase of some other herons suggests that other factors are likely contributing to the Tricolored Heron's decrease, perhaps a diminution of the source population in Baja California.

Taxonomy: Tricolored Herons throughout North America are *E. t. ruficollis* Gosse, 1847, as *E. t. occidentalis* (Huey, 1927), described from Baja California, is generally considered a synonym.

Reddish Egret *Egretta rufescens*

San Diego County marks the northern limit of the Reddish Egret's usual range along the Pacific coast. Though the species does not (yet) nest here, two or three occur in the county's coastal wetlands each year as nonbreeding visitors. Though rare, the Reddish Egret calls attention to itself by its animated behavior, dashing about erratically in shallow water with wings spread, ready to nab any small fish its gyrations may startle.

Winter: The Reddish Egret has been seen in most of San Diego County's coastal wetlands but is considerably

more frequent in the San Diego area than in the north county lagoons. Over the final quarter of the 20th century an average of between two and three reached San Diego County each year. The exact number is often impossible to determine, as the birds move up and down the coast. The Reddish Egret is usually seen singly (though often near other foraging herons); during the atlas period two were noted at the south end of San Diego Bay (V10) 14 May 2000 (Y. Ikegaya; NAB 54:326, 2000) and in the San Diego River flood-control channel (R7/R8) 26 December 2001–7 February 2002 (M. Billings, NAB 56:223, 2002).

Sites along the coast of northern San Diego County where the Reddish Egret has been found are Los

Peñasquitos Lagoon (N7; two from 6 to 12 September 1968, AFN 23:107, 1969; one from 9 to 23 January 2000, D. K. Adams), the San Dieguito River estuary (M7; 8–24 October 1990, G. Deeks, Heindel and Garrett 1995; 16–19 October 1991, J. O'Brien, Patten et al. 1995b; 25 September 1999–30 January 2000, B. Foster, R. T. Patton, NAB 54:104, 220, 2000), San Elijo Lagoon (29 September 1968 and 13 December 1969, King et al. 1987; 19 May 1991, R. T. Patton, Heindel and Garrett 1995; 11–24 September 2000, D. Trissel, McKee and Erickson 2002), Batiquitos Lagoon (11–18 September 1962, King et al. 1987; 6 September–12 December 2001, G. C. Hazard, M. Baumgartel, NAB 56:223, 2002), and the Santa Margarita River estuary (17 April–3 May 1981, L. Salata, Langham 1991; 25 August 2001, B. Foster).

Migration: The Reddish Egret has been seen in San Diego County in every month of the year, but its frequency peaks in October and November with the dispersal of immatures. Yet the largest number recorded, seven at the south end of San Diego Bay, was seen on 6 May 1990 (G. McCaskie; Patten and Erickson 1994). The Reddish Egret is least frequent in June and July, with only about five records for each of those months.

Though the Reddish Egret has wandered on several occasions from the Gulf of California to the Salton Sea (Patten et al. 2003), in coastal southern California it sticks to the coastal wetlands almost exclusively. Except for four birds that moved a short distance inland in the Tijuana River valley, the only well-supported inland record for San Diego County is of an immature found in a weakened condition at a backyard goldfish pond along Tobiasson Road in Poway (M11) 6 September 2002 (SDNHM 50658).

Conservation: The numbers of the Reddish Egret reaching San Diego County appear to be on a gradual increase.

Photo by Kenneth Z. Kurland

From the time of the first report in 1931 (Huey 1931b) through the early 1970s the species was casual, but since 1980 not a year has passed without at least one. The increase is paralleled by a northward extension of the species' breeding range in Baja California. In 1999 two pairs colonized Islas Todos Santos off Ensenada (Palacios and Mellink 2000). Some day the Reddish Egret may join some of the mixed-species heronries around San Diego.

Taxonomy: Reddish Egrets in California have been ascribed to the west Mexican subspecies _E. r. dickeyi_ (van Rossem, 1926), adults of which are said to have a head and neck darker than in the nominate eastern subspecies. Both specimens from San Diego County (the one from Poway and one from the Tijuana River estuary 23 October 1963, SDNHM 30757, McCaskie 1964) are immatures, however, so cannot be identified.

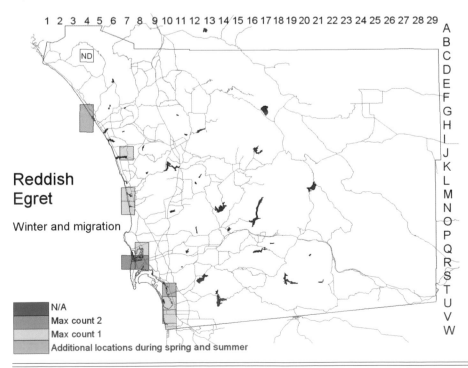

Cattle Egret *Bubulcus ibis*

The Cattle Egret has enjoyed the most explosive natural range expansion of any bird in recorded history. In 25 years it went from being a new arrival to the most abundant bird in southeastern California's Imperial Valley. In San Diego County, however, it has seen a reversal as well as an advance. Since the species first nested in 1979, colonies have formed and vanished in quick succession; from 1997 through 2001 the only important one was that at the Wild Animal Park. After a peak in the 1980s the population has been on the decline; the conversion of pastures and dairies to urban sprawl spells no good for this bird whose lifestyle is linked to livestock.

Breeding distribution: The Cattle Egret colony at the Wild Animal Park (J12) is part of the mixed-species heronry in the Heart of Africa exhibit—a site eminently suitable for this species of African origin. Maximum numbers reported here in the breeding season during the atlas period were 100 individuals on 15 June 1998 (D. and D. Bylin) and 43 nests on 9 May 1999 (K. L. Weaver).

In 2001, one or two pairs nested in the multispecies heronry at Lindo Lake, Lakeside (P14). One pair was feeding nestlings on 12 May (C. G. Edwards), but by 9 July no Cattle Egrets were in the colony.

Cattle Egrets from the Wild Animal Park colony evidently forage west to Escondido (J10; over 100 on 14 May 1997, O. Carter) and southeast to the Santa Maria Valley surrounding Ramona (L14; up to 88 on 28 March 1999, F. Sproul; K15, up to 300 on 4 April 1998, P. Unitt). The Ramona region currently offers the most foraging habitat for the Cattle Egret in San Diego County. Cattails in the pond on the north side of Highway 78 just west of Magnolia Avenue (K15) are a frequent Cattle Egret roost.

Photo by Anthony Mercieca

Beyond a 15-mile radius of the Wild Animal Park, the Cattle Egret is uncommon and irregular, especially during the breeding season. It is still rather frequent in the San Luis Rey River valley between Oceanside and Interstate 15 (up to 18 in northeast Oceanside, F7, 26 April 1997, A. Peterson). In southern San Diego County the largest flocks during the breeding season from 1997 to 2001 were of 12 at the upper end of El Capitan Reservoir (N17) 9 July 1999 (D. C. Seals) and 25 on Otay Mesa (V13) 10 May 1998 (P. Unitt). In the eastern half of the county the Cattle Egret is rare at this season; the only sighting of more than two birds was of 10 at Crestwood Ranch (R24) 20 May 2000 (J. S. Larson).

Nesting: The Cattle Egret builds a rough stick nest similar to that of other herons. Within a colony the nests may be packed so closely the incubating birds are within pecking distance of each other. The schedule of Cattle Egret nesting in San Diego County is not well defined and probably variable, at least when new colonies are forming. At the Wild Animal Park the birds have been seen apparently incubating by 18 April and to have young in the nest at least as late as 15 June (D. and D. Bylin). In the enormous heronries of the Imperial Valley, some young are still in nests as late as early September.

Migration: The Cattle Egret follows no well-defined migration in southern California, though it obviously disperses long distances. A bird color-marked at a nesting colony near the Salton Sea was seen near the Otay dump (U12) 15 November 1975 (AB 30:125, 1976).

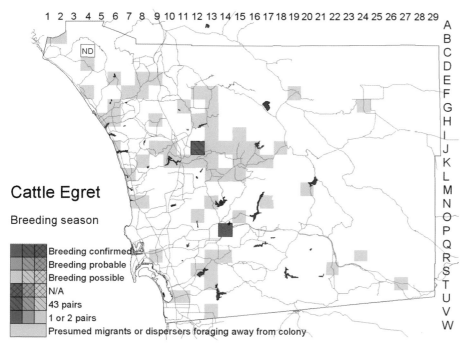

Cattle Egret

Breeding season

Breeding confirmed
Breeding probable
Breeding possible
N/A
43 pairs
1 or 2 pairs
Presumed migrants or dispersers foraging away from colony

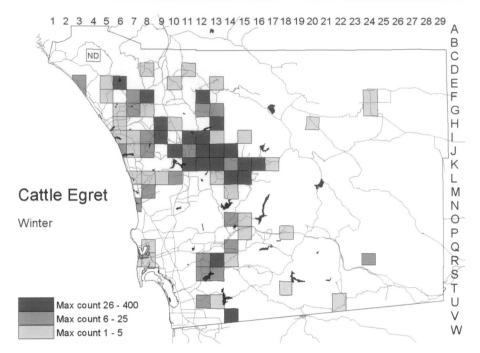

Cattle Egret

Winter

Max count 26 - 400
Max count 6 - 25
Max count 1 - 5

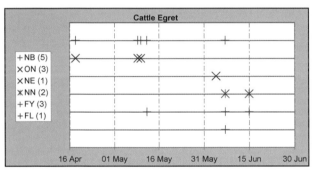

In eastern San Diego County the Cattle Egret is as rare in winter as in the breeding season, and again Crestwood Ranch was the only site of more than three, with 10 on 7 February 2000 (J. S. Larson). In the Borrego Valley we made only three sightings of one or two Cattle Egrets during the atlas period, all seasons combined, but earlier records there ran as high as 18 on 12 December 1990 (A. G. Morley).

Conservation: The first Cattle Egrets found in San Diego County, among the earliest for California, were in the Tijuana River valley 7 March 1964 (McCaskie 1965, SDNHM 35075). The species increased gradually as a nonbreeding visitor until fall 1977, when there was a large influx. Nesting began at Buena Vista Lagoon in 1979 (AB 33:896, 1979), at the Dairy Mart Pond in the Tijuana River valley in 1980 (AB 34:929, 1980), and at Guajome Lake in 1983 (AB 37:1026, 1983). All these colonies proved ephemeral, however. The population peaked in the 1980s, then declined as abruptly as it increased. Totals on San Diego Christmas bird counts, mainly from the Tijuana River valley, increased from an average of 5.3 from 1966 to 1976 to a peak of 3512 in 1985, then decreased to six in 1995. Since then that count has had none. During the five-year atlas period we had not a single Cattle Egret in the Tijuana River valley—where 15 years earlier there were thousands. On the Oceanside count the total peaked at 1087 in 1979, and a decrease was noticeable even from 1997 to 2001. Even on the Escondido count, whose circle encompasses most of the county's current Cattle Egret habitat, the number peaked at 875 in January 1997; during the atlas period a decline was almost continuous.

Why should the Cattle Egret have failed to maintain its abundance in San Diego County, as it has just to the east in the Imperial Valley? The most obvious contributing factor is the relative dearth of foraging habitat—and the decline in this habitat as agriculture gives way to urban development. The explosive increase of the late 1970s was due to immigration, and the sources of these immigrants may have stabilized.

Taxonomy: The nominate subspecies of the Cattle Egret, *B. i. ibis* (Linnaeus, 1758), crossing the Atlantic Ocean from Africa, is the one that colonized the New World, beginning on the Atlantic coast of South America.

Winter: In winter the Cattle Egret remains concentrated at the Wild Animal Park (up to 389 on 30 December 2000, K. L. Weaver), elsewhere in the San Pasqual Valley (up to 400 near Fenton Ranch, K13, 3 January 1998, M. Forman), and near Ramona (K15; up to 350 on 31 December 1998, M. and B. McIntosh), Escondido, San Marcos, and Valley Center—places all still within 15 miles of the Wild Animal Park. A secondary area of winter concentration during the atlas period was along the Sweetwater River from Sweetwater Reservoir (S12) to the Singing Hills golf course, especially in the Jamacha area (R13; up to 200 on 2 January 2000, M. and D. Hastings).

Numbers in northwestern San Diego County are somewhat higher in winter than during the breeding season, with up to 40 on lawns near O'Neill Lake (E6) 10 January 2001 (P. A. Ginsburg) and 40 at Bonsall (F8) 27 February 2001 (M. Freda). Cattle Egrets show up occasionally in coastal wetlands in winter, with up to 10 north of Batiquitos Lagoon (J6) 30 December 1997 (M. Baumgartel) and six at Los Peñasquitos Lagoon (N7) 3 January 1998 (K. Estey).

Green Heron *Butorides virescens*

Unlike most herons, which forage in the open in marshes and along shorelines, the Green Heron prefers to fish in ponds and channels bordered or shaded by trees. It is thus as much a bird of riparian woodland as one of marshes. And unlike many other herons it is not colonial, at least in San Diego County, so it appears uncommon. But because it takes advantage of many small wetlands little used by the other species, its population in the county may be just as large.

Breeding distribution: In San Diego County the Green Heron is most widespread in the northern part of the coastal lowland, where strips of riparian woodland and small ponds are most frequent. In the southern part of the county the distribution clearly traces the major rivers and lakes. Thirty at Lake Hodges (K10) 14 June 1999 (R. L. Barber) and 16 at Lower Otay Lake (U14) 4 July 1999 (S. Buchanan) were exceptionally high counts; otherwise, we noted no more than eight per day per atlas square. Small numbers use the scattered wet areas of southeastern San Diego County (family with three fledglings 19 June 1999 at Twin Lakes or Picnic Lake near Potrero, U20, R. and S. L. Breisch) and in the Julian area (up to two at Wynola, J19, 12 March 1999, S. E. Smith). The highest elevation at

Photo by Anthony Mercieca

which we found the Green Heron during the atlas period was 4600 feet in Lost Valley (D20; one on 2 June and 1 July 1999, J. M. and B. Hargrove, W. E. Haas).

Draining the east slope of the mountains, Coyote, San Felipe, and Banner creeks also likely support nesting Green Herons, at least occasionally. Though no nests have yet been found in the Anza–Borrego Desert, the birds are regular along Coyote Creek at Lower Willows (D23) in spring, with a maximum count of five on 25 April 1998 (B. Peterson) and sightings as late as 4 July (1999, B. Getty, K. Wilson).

Nesting: Egg collectors who described the sites of Green Heron nests in San Diego County all reported them in willows. A nest at Barrett Lake (S19) 18 June 2000 (R. and S. L. Breisch) was also in a willow. But the Green Heron may nest in cattails as well: one carrying a twig near Potrero 26 June 1999 took it into a stand of cattails (R. and S. L. Breisch).

The Green Heron has a long breeding season and may raise two broods per year. A fledgling near Valley Center (F12) 18 April 2001 (E. C. Hall) suggests laying as early as the second week of March; a nest at the upper end of Sweetwater Reservoir (S13) still had eggs on 14 July 1998 (P. Famolaro).

Migration: The Green Heron is somewhat less numerous in winter than in summer but does not follow a well-marked schedule of migration. In the Anza–Borrego Desert, away from possible breeding sites, it is reported most frequently in April and May, but these are also peak months for birders in the area. Most desert records are from oases or artificial ponds, but a few are far from water, such as one in a rocky cove on the east side of Blair Dry Lake (L24) 11 April 1999 (R. Thériault).

Winter: The Green Heron's winter distribution in San Diego

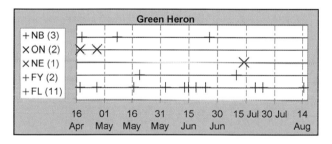

Green Heron

	16	01	16	31	15	30	15 Jul	30 Jul	14
	Apr	May	May	May	Jun	Jun			Aug

+ NB (3)
× ON (2)
× NE (1)
+ FY (2)
+ FL (11)

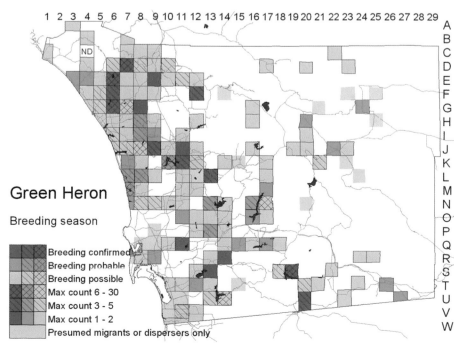

Green Heron

Breeding season

Breeding confirmed
Breeding probable
Breeding possible
Max count 6 - 30
Max count 3 - 5
Max count 1 - 2
Presumed migrants or dispersers only

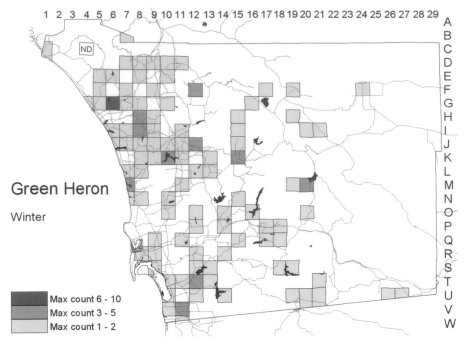

Green Heron

Winter

Legend	
■	Max count 6 - 10
▣	Max count 3 - 5
▢	Max count 1 - 2

(F24) 12 January 1998 and 19 December 1999 (M. L. Gabel, P. K. Nelson). The Green Heron has been noted on four of 18 Anza–Borrego Christmas bird counts 1984–2001, with no more than three birds per count.

Conservation: Early in the 20th century, the Green Heron occurred in San Diego County as a migrant and summer resident only. It was first noted in winter at Lindo Lake (P14) on 1 January 1928 (Huey 1928b) and was as numerous in winter as today by the 1950s. Both the breeding and winter ranges have long been spreading north along the Pacific coast (Davis and Kushlan 1994).

It is unclear how much the Green Heron has suffered from the loss of riparian woodland and freshwater marshes versus how much it has benefited from the importation of water. Results of Christmas bird counts suggest that since 1985 its numbers may be declining gradually.

County is similar to its breeding distribution but somewhat more patchy. The only site where we noted more than four individuals per day at this season was around Whelan Lake (G6), with up to ten on 14 December 2000 (P. A. Ginsburg). In the foothills and mountains wintering Green Herons are scarce, with seldom more than a single bird seen at a time and a maximum of three at Cuyamaca Lake (M20) 4 December 1998 (A. P. and T. E. Keenan). Our only winter records in the desert during the atlas period were of single birds in Borrego Springs

Taxonomy: Green Herons in California are *B. v. anthonyi* (Mearns, 1895), whose adults have the neck rufous, not deep maroon as in *B. v. frazari* (Brewster, 1888) of southern Baja California.

Black-crowned Night-Heron *Nycticorax nycticorax*

The Black-crowned Night-Heron spends much of the day resting quietly in marshes or trees, then at dusk flies off to forage, broadcasting a startlingly loud "quock!" In San Diego County it is locally common year round, both along the coast and at lakes and marshes inland. From 1997 to 2001 there were seven substantial colonies in the county, most mixed with other species of herons. Isolated pairs or small colonies also contribute to the population, to an unknown degree.

Breeding distribution: Like the Great Blue, the Black-crowned Night-Heron nests mainly in colonies, often in mixed heronries. Seven sites appear to account for most of San Diego County's population. At the Wild Animal Park (J12), in the multispecies heronry in the Heart of Africa exhibit, counts of the birds (fledglings included) ranged up to 150 on 15 June 1998 (D. and D. Bylin); our best count of nests was at least 20 on 8 May 1999 (K. L. Weaver). At Sierra Avenue and Plaza Street in Solana Beach (M7), Black-crowned Night-Herons nest in company with Snowy Egrets. There were 10 to 20 nests of the former in a fig tree in 1997, and by 2001 they had spread to some nearby eucalyptus trees (A. Mauro). Pine trees at

Photo by Anthony Mercieca

Scripps Institution of Oceanography (O7) were a colony site for many years, until some heavy construction at the campus in 2002. At least three, possibly seven, nests were active on 4 June 1998 (S. E. Smith). In 1999, Black-crowned Night-Herons founded the mixed heronry at Lindo Lake (P14; M. B. Stowe). By 9 July 2001, there were at least 10 nests of the night-heron, among lesser numbers of the Great Blue Heron, Snowy Egret, and Great Egret. The Point Loma submarine base (S7) hosts the county's longest-known Black-crowned Night-Heron colony, known since the 1970s and reaching a peak size of about 500 nests in 1980. Fledglings at this site suffered high mortality from steatitis, and the colony declined to 103 nests in 1995, 21 in 1996. From 1999 to 2001 the colony consisted of only 15 nests, all in fig trees (M. F. Platter-Rieger). The largest colony during the atlas period was that at North Island Naval Air Station (S8), shared with Snowy Egrets. In 1999, when McDonald et al. (2000) surveyed the colony regularly, the number of adults peaked at 140 and the number of nests peaked at 115 on 21 May. That year, 164 nests fledged a total of 166 young. A third colony near San Diego

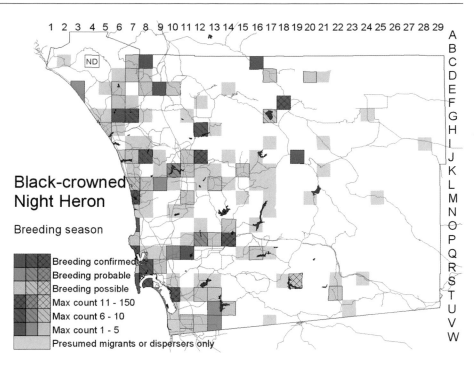

Bay is that at the 32nd Street Naval Station (T10); it contained about 30 nests in 1997 (M. F. Platter-Rieger).

Kenneth L. Weaver found an apparently isolated pair nesting in a willow along the Santa Margarita River near Fallbrook (C8) 1 May 1999, another in a cottonwood along Temecula Creek near Oak Grove (C16) 16 June 2001. On several other occasions we recorded single adults carrying prey or single families of fledglings begging from their parents, far from known colonies. These sites are scattered through the coastal lowland, inland to Swan Lake (F18) near Warner Springs (13, including a fledgling, 24 June 2000, C. G. Edwards) and Wynola (J19; fledgling on 19 June and 2 July 1999, S. E. Smith). The literature on the Black-crowned Night-Heron speaks only of colonies, yet these observations suggest that in San Diego County isolated pairs are not rare.

Apparently nonbreeding birds are widespread through the spring and summer all along the coast and at many lakes and ponds inland, as high as Cuyamaca Lake (one on 21 May and 5 June 1998 and 5 June 1999, A. P. and T. E. Keenan). Concentrations during the breeding season away from colonies range up to 20 at the east end of Lake Hodges (K11) 18 May 1997 (E. C. Hall) and 30 at Los Peñasquitos Lagoon (N7) 1 April 2000 (K. Estey), but these could be of birds commuting 5 miles or less from nests.

Nesting: Black-crowned Night-Herons build a stick platform in trees, similar to those of other herons of similar size. At some colonies the nests are in open-foliaged eucalyptus or palm trees, but more often the birds select sites that offer more concealment, especially dense-foliaged

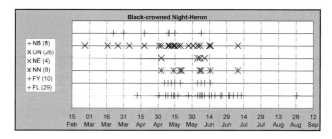

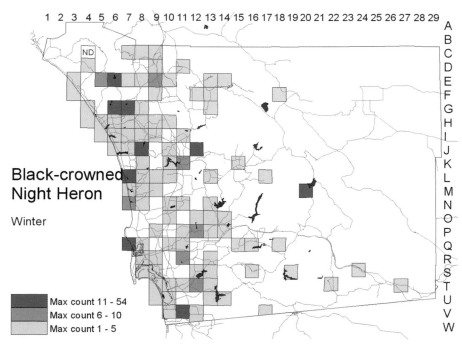

fig trees, used at Solana Beach, Point Loma, North Island, and 32nd Street.

In San Diego County the Black-crowned Night-Heron begins nesting in February. Our earliest date for birds apparently incubating was 26 February; young already out of the nest at Solana Beach 12 April 1997 (L. Ellis) suggest laying in the third week of February. Early March to early May appears to be the main period of nest initiation.

Migration: On the coastal slope of San Diego County numbers of Black-crowned Night-Herons show no consistent pattern of variation through the year. In the Anza–Borrego Desert the Black-crowned Night-Heron is a rare visitor, recorded in ones or twos, mainly in spring and summer. During the atlas period it was noted seven times in this area, from 30 March (1999, one at Desert Ironwoods Motel, I28, L. J. Hargrove) to 20 October (1999, one at Ocotillo Wells, I29, P. D. Jorgensen).

Winter: The Black-crowned Night-Heron's status in San Diego County in winter is similar to that in the breeding season: locally common and widespread in the coastal lowland, scarce and scattered farther inland. The largest winter concentrations have been reported from Whelan Lake (G6; up to 40 on 26 December 1998, D. K. Adams), the Wild Animal Park (up to 54 on 2 January 1999, K. L. Weaver), and the Dairy Mart pond, Tijuana River valley (V11; up to 40 on 18 December 1999, G. McCaskie). Though we found the night-heron wintering at few sites above 2000 elevation, it is regular in winter at Cuyamaca Lake, with up to 13 on 14 December 1999 (A. P. and T. E. Keenan), and there is a winter sighting at Doane Pond, Palomar Mountain (E14; one on 27 January 1995, M. B. Stowe).

The only winter records for the Anza–Borrego Desert

are of one near the Borrego Springs airport (F25) 21 December 1983, two at Santa Catarina Spring (D23) 24 December 1988 (ABDSP database), and one on the Anza–Borrego Christmas bird count 19 December 1993.

Conservation: There is little evidence for changes in the Black-crowned Night-Heron's abundance in San Diego County, though the results of the Rancho Santa Fe Christmas bird count show a downward trend. The decline of the Point Loma colony has been compensated for by the increase of the North Island colony, at least in part. All the major colonies are in planted trees in areas heavily used by people. Although the night-herons are surprisingly indifferent to people, especially while they are foraging at night, the converse is not always true. In 1992, a homeowner in Solana Beach, annoyed with a Black-crowned Night-Heron colony on his property, hired a tree-trimmer to chop down the tree where the birds were nesting—although he had already contacted the California Department of Fish and Game and had been instructed to remove the tree only after the herons were finished nesting. A neighbor filmed the nests, eggs, and chicks crashing to the ground, and the four surviving chicks were rescued from a dumpster the next morning—two were rehabilitated successfully. The film (broadcast on television) and testimony of neighbors supported a lawsuit by the California Department of Fish and Game, and the homeowner and tree-trimmer ultimately paid a fine.

Taxonomy: The North American subspecies of the Black-crowned Night-Heron is *N. n. hoactli* (Gmelin, 1789), with whiter underparts than that of South America and less white over the eye than in that of the Old World.

Yellow-crowned Night-Heron *Nyctanassa violacea*

Of the herons that reach San Diego County by dispersing north from Mexico, the Yellow-crowned Night-Heron is by far the scarcest. As few as nine individuals have been recorded, though the species has been seen many times more than this low number implies. One bird associated with the Black-crowned Night-Heron colony at the Scripps Institution of Oceanography for 20 years and probably accounted for all sightings in the county during the atlas period.

Breeding distribution: Even though only one Yellow-crowned Night-Heron joined the colony of the Black-crowned at Scripps (O7), it may have attempted nesting at least in 1989. That year, it "built a nest and stood by its mate sitting on the nest, but the eggs evidently did not hatch" (J. O'Brien, AB 43:1367, 1989). It was seen first at San Elijo Lagoon 25 October 1981 and intermittently into 1983 (T. Meyer; Binford 1985); it was presumed to be the same individual that appeared at Scripps annually from 1983 to 2001. Construction on the campus then disrupted the colony, but it may have relocated nearby, to the La Jolla Beach and Tennis Club (P7), where a Yellow-crowned

Photo by Anthony Mercieca

appeared 6 December 2001 (C. Nyhan, NAB 56:223, 2002). The same bird was probably responsible for sightings at Los Peñasquitos Lagoon (N7) 20 November 1999 (K. Messer, NAB 54:104, 2000), La Jolla Valley (L10) (T. Johnson; AB 52:531, 1998), along Rose Creek near Mission Bay (Q8) 22 June 1998 (B. O'Leary), and Famosa Slough (R8) 17–19 May 2001 (V. P. Johnson, NAB 55:355, 2001).

Migration: San Diego County's other records of the Yellow-crowned Night-Heron are scattered through the year. The first two were in fall at the Tijuana River estuary (V10) 3 November 1962 and 22–25 October 1963

(McCaskie 1964). Two in the Tijuana River near Dairy Mart Road (V11) arrived in summer or fall and remained through winter: an adult 30 September 1990–7 January 1991, returning 13 October 1991–31 March 1992, and joined by a subadult 16 June 1991–13 February 1992 (G. McCaskie; Heindel and Garrett 1995, Patten et al. 1995b). Spring and summer records are of adults at Sea World (R8) 3 April 1979, the Tijuana River estuary 15 April–2 May 1979 (same bird?), the south end of San Diego Bay (V10) 18–26 July 1980 (Binford 1983), and the Santa Margarita River mouth (G4) 9 May 1984 (L. R. Hays, Roberson 1986), and a subadult at San Elijo Lagoon

11 June–24 September 2002 (B. Chaddock, NAB 56:486, 2002, 57:117, 2003).

The California Bird Records Committee questioned the identification of an immature at San Elijo Lagoon 1–11 November 1963 (McCaskie 1964, Roberson 1993).

Taxonomy: The one specimen from San Diego County, from the Tijuana River estuary 25 October 1963 (SDNHM 30758) is the large-billed subspecies *N. v. bancrofti* Huey, 1927, from the Pacific coast of Mexico, rather than the smaller-billed nominate subspecies from the southeastern United States (McCaskie and Banks 1966, Unitt 1984).

IBISES AND SPOONBILLS — FAMILY PLATALEIDAE OR THRESKIORNITHIDAE

White Ibis *Eudocimus albus*

Although the White Ibis is a fairly common resident of mangroves and mudflats in the southern half of Baja California, it hardly ever wanders north, unlike the herons with a similar range. In Alta California there are only two well-supported records, one from San Diego County.

Migration: San Diego County's single White Ibis, an immature, was found roosting with egrets at the Sefton estate on Point Loma (S7) 15 November 1935 and was collected five days later (Huey 1936, SDNHM 17099).

Photo by Anthony Mercieca

White-faced Ibis *Plegadis chihi*

The White-faced Ibis nests in freshwater marshes and forages in shallow water and wet grass. After a decline through the middle of the 20th century, its population resurged and shifted west, leading to an increase in San Diego County. Currently dozens remain through the breeding season, with at least two nesting colonies, and hundreds winter, largely in the county's northwestern quadrant. But these gains are threatened by development of the flood-plains in which the ibises forage.

Breeding distribution: Two colonies of the White-faced Ibis were known to be active in San Diego County from 1997 to 2001. Kenneth L. Weaver observed the colony at Guajome Lake (G7) in 2001; his maximum count was 34 birds on 25 June. On 5 July he noted one large nestling being fed and two other juveniles. A complete census of the colony, however, requires a boat and cannot be done from the lake's shore. In 1995, T. A. Scott and P.-Y. Lee surveyed the lake more intensively, using a boat, and concluded that at least six and possibly as many as eight pairs nested that year. A new colony formed in 2000 in a pond in the San Luis Rey River valley at the mouth of

Photo by Jack C. Daynes

Keys Canyon, just east of Interstate 15 (E9). At this site D. and C. Wysong noted one carrying nest material into a marsh 5 May and adults feeding nestlings in two nests 5 June. In 2001 the colony evidently grew, with 15 juveniles seen there 10 June (J. E. Pike).

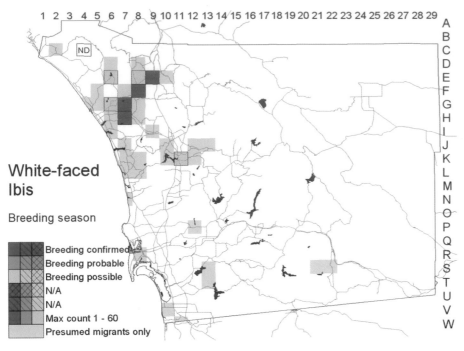

White-faced
Ibis

Breeding season

Breeding confirmed
Breeding probable
Breeding possible
N/A
N/A
Max count 1 - 60
Presumed migrants only

June 1997 (E. C. Hall), and 55 at Los Peñasquitos Lagoon (N7) 5 April 1998 (D. K. Adams). In southern San Diego County we encountered only a few scattered individuals through the breeding season, except for 25 at the upper end of Sweetwater Reservoir (S13) 4 June 2001 (P. Famolaro) and 15 flying north over the naval radio station at the south end of the Silver Strand (V10) 3 May 2001 (S. Yamagata).

Nesting: At some places White-faced Ibises nest in trees, in shrubs, or on the ground on islands. But at both colonies in San Diego County they nest in marshes of tule and cattail. The nest is supported on leaves that have been bent over to make a

Also, the ibises may have attempted nesting at Calaveras Lake (H8) in 2001, where one was carrying twigs 3 April (L. M. Holt), but no further activity was reported from this site. Undiscovered colonies may exist elsewhere, especially within private ranches in the San Luis Rey River valley around Bonsall (F8), between the two known colonies. Jane Evans noted a fledgling there 25 May 2000.

During the breeding season, the birds range at least for foraging throughout the lower Santa Margarita and San Luis Rey river valleys, to the coastal lagoons of northern San Diego County, and up Escondido Creek and the San Dieguito River to the San Pasqual Valley. High counts are of up to 60 near O'Neill Lake (E6) 19 July 1999 (P. A. Ginsburg), 52 near the east end of Lake Hodges (K11) 9

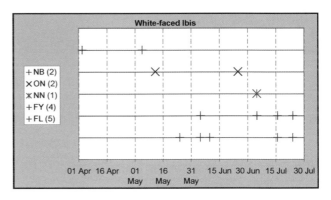

crude platform. In 1995 two nests at Guajome Lake were over water, three were over mud (T. A. Scott, P.-Y. Lee).

Observations during the atlas period of fledglings from late May to late July suggest that in San Diego County White-faced Ibises lay eggs from the last week of March to mid May. In 1995 T. A. Scott and P.-Y. Lee inferred that laying at Guajome peaked in the first two weeks of May and continued to the end of May.

Migration: Thousands of White-faced Ibises breeding in the Great Basin migrate to the Imperial Valley (Patten et al. 2003). In spite of the species' abundance there the only records from the Anza–Borrego Desert are of one at Carrizo Marsh (O29) 17 May 1991 (K. Dice) and one at the Borrego Springs sewage ponds (H25) 6

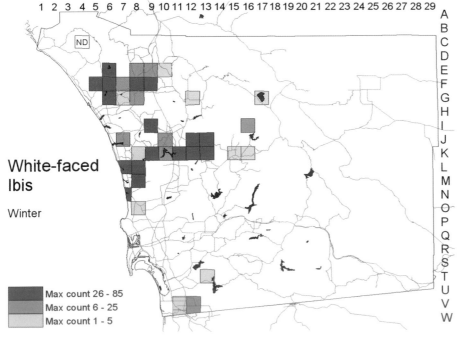

White-faced
Ibis

Winter

Max count 26 - 85
Max count 6 - 25
Max count 1 - 5

November 1995 (R. Thériault). Postbreeding dispersal or fall migration begins by late July (one at Lake Morena, S21, 28 July 2001, R. Breisch) and is substantial by late August (29 at Santee, P12, 26 August 1999, P. Willman).

Winter: The San Pasqual Valley (K11/K12/K13/J12/J13) is the primary center for wintering White-faced Ibises in San Diego County. We had many counts of 50 or more individuals in this area, with a high of 274 in the Wild Animal Park (J12) 29 December 2001 (K. L. Weaver). The lower Santa Margarita and San Luis Rey river valleys remain important as well, with up to 85 in a flooded field adjacent to the Camp Pendleton supply depot (F5) 28 December 1998 (B. E. Bell) and 70 at Bonsall 9 February 2001 (P. A. Ginsburg). At the coastal lagoons the ibises are irregular but occasionally numerous, with up to 40 at San Elijo Lagoon 7 December 1997 (A. Mauro) and 70 at Los Peñasquitos Lagoon (N7) 7 February 1999 (D. K. Adams).

White-faced Ibises are occasional in winter at Ramona (K15; up to two on 2 January 1999, D. and C. Batzler) and at the Dairy Mart pond in the Tijuana River valley (V11; maximum 1997–2002 only three on 20 December 1997, G. McCaskie). Elsewhere in the county they are rare; the only counts of more than four were of 24 on Otay Mesa (V12) 23 February 1998 (P. Walsh) and a flock of eight flying up the unsuitable habitat of Black Canyon (I16) 15 January 2002 (O. Carter, J. Decanio, M. Baumgartel). One at Lake Henshaw (G17) 29 December 1997 (J. O. Zimmer) was the only ibis ever recorded on the Lake Henshaw Christmas bird count, instituted in 1980–81.

Conservation: The White-faced Ibis has seen both ups and downs, its population and distribution affected by the management of wetlands, changes in agriculture, and climate cycles of wet and dry. In San Diego County, it nested at Guajome Lake at least in 1901, when Sharp (1907) reported "a colony of about a dozen birds," but no other nestings or colonies were reported from then until 1979. Then J. P. Rieger discovered two nests and estimated six breeding pairs at Buena Vista Lagoon (H5/H6;

AB 33:896, 1979), but that colony proved ephemeral. The ibises recolonized Guajome Lake by April 1986, when E. Copper noted 20 pairs building nests. Nesting has probably been annual there since, with six pairs in 1990 and six to eight in 1995 (T. A. Scott, P.-Y. Lee).

Changes in the species' winter distribution have been even more dramatic. On the San Diego Christmas bird count the ibis was recorded only twice before 1978, but then it became regular in the Tijuana River valley. The count peaked at 100 on 15 December 1984 but then declined as quickly as it increased. The pattern on the Oceanside count is similar but less extreme, with a peak of 184 on 21 December 1991 and decline since. On the Escondido count, by contrast, the ibis was recorded in only two of the count's first six years, 1985–90, but then it became regular and increased rapidly, peaking at 507 on 29 December 2001. Possibly the birds are shifting from the San Luis Rey River valley to the San Pasqual Valley, as is almost certainly the case with the Canada Goose, which winters in the same habitats where the ibis feeds.

After a decline earlier in the 20th century, numbers of the White-faced Ibis have increased greatly throughout the United States since the 1970s (Shuford et al. 1996). Maintenance of these enhanced numbers, however, depends on an adequate supply of water to marshes where the ibises nest and sufficient habitat in which the birds can forage. In San Diego County, loss of the latter is likely the primary threat. Much of the ibises' core foraging habitat, agricultural land and pastures along the San Luis Rey River, has already been consumed by the expanding city of Oceanside. What remains in the Bonsall area is in private ownership and in the path of further development. Ironically, the digging of a borrow pit to provide fill dirt for a housing development at the mouth of Keys Canyon created the site for the colony there. Changes in land-use policies in the Santa Margarita River valley (within Camp Pendleton) and in the San Pasqual Valley (zoned largely for agriculture) could deprive the ibis of the damp pastures and floodplains where it feeds.

Roseate Spoonbill *Platalea ajaja*

The Roseate Spoonbill has always been a sporadic vagrant to California. In 1973 and 1977, small irruptions reached the state, mainly the Salton Sea. The incursion of the latter year was responsible for the single sighting of the species in San Diego County. Since 1983, only two have been found in California, raising concern that the source population on the coast of western mainland Mexico has been depleted.

Migration: San Diego County's record of the Roseate Spoonbill is of three seen at the Santa Margarita River mouth (G4) 24 June 1977 (P. D. Jorgensen). These were presumably the same individuals that appeared 35 miles to the northwest at the San Joaquin Marsh in Irvine, Orange County, two days later and remained to 4 October (AB 31:1169, 1977; 32:256, 1978).

Photo by Kenneth Z. Kurland

STORKS — FAMILY CICONIIDAE

Wood Stork *Mycteria americana*

Once a common, if irregular, postbreeding visitor to San Diego County's coast, since the 1950s the Wood Stork has become ever scarcer. Nesting attempts by two pairs from 1987 to 1991 had no success. From 1990 to 2003 only one immature Wood Stork arrived in San Diego County. In 1986 a pair adopted the Wild Animal Park at San Pasqual as its permanent home, and one of these birds lived through 2003 as California's only resident Wood Stork.

Migration: In the first half of the 20th century, Wood Storks were recorded all along San Diego County's coast and on ponds and lakes in the coastal lowland. Sightings at lakes Cuyamaca (M20) and Henshaw (G17) demonstrate that the birds arrived overland from the head of the Gulf of California, as they do at the Salton Sea (Abbott 1935, AB 40:158, 1986). The maximum numbers known are 500 at Agua Hedionda Lagoon (I6) 1–14 August 1938 (Abbott 1938) and 300 at Buena Vista Lagoon (H5/H6) July–August 1953 (Rechnitzer 1954). Dates range primarily from "late May" (1930, 14 in Mission Valley, R8/R9, Abbott 1931) to 9 November (1981, near Oceanside, H5, T. Meixner, AB 36:217, 1982). Records at other times of year are of birds that failed to depart after the customary season.

An immature at Los Peñasquitos Lagoon (N7) 8 July–15 September 2000 (C. DeWitt, J. O. Zimmer, NAB 54:422, 2000, 55:102, 2001) was the first Wood Stork to arrive in San Diego County for at least 10 years.

Winter: A few Wood Storks have straggled through the winter in the coastal lowland. Up to two seen around northwestern San Diego County 1980–87 may have been the same pair that ultimately settled among the captive wading birds and mixed heron colony in the Heart of Africa exhibit at the Wild Animal Park (J12). They were seen here on six of seven Escondido Christmas bird counts January 1987–January 1994. Subsequently only a single bird remained, surviving through 2003.

Breeding distribution: When the Wood Stork was com-

Photo by Anthony Mercieca

mon, there was no suggestion of its breeding in California, so attempts at two sites in the late 1980s and early 1990s were unexpected. At the Dairy Mart pond in the Tijuana River valley (V11), 5 April–3 May 1987, a pair built a nest but fledged no young (B. and I. Mazin, AB 41:487, 1987). Similarly, the pair at the Wild Animal Park nested at least in 1989 and 1991, but no young were ever seen (N. Christianson, D. Rimlinger, AB 43:536, 1367, 1989; 45:1160, 1991).

Conservation: At the Salton Sea, the Wood Stork's decline has been reflected just as dramatically, if more recently, as in San Diego County (Patten et al. 2003). Bones of four Wood Storks excavated from the trash pit of the stagecoach station at Carrizo Marsh in the Anza–Borrego Desert (O29), dating from 1857 to 1861, demonstrate that the species was once even more widespread than attested by the written record (S. Arter). The stork is now rare in Sonora as well, where a former probable nesting site has been abandoned (Russell and Monson 1998). The Wood Stork has been listed as an endangered species in the United States since 1984, on the basis of a population decline and nesting failures in the Southeast.

NEW WORLD VULTURES — FAMILY VULTURIDAE OR CATHARTIDAE

Turkey Vulture *Cathartes aura*

Soaring on raised wings, rocking from side to side, the Turkey Vulture is a familiar sight. Yet it is also an enigma—its nests are so difficult to find that its breeding distribution is still known only roughly. Assembling in communal roosts instead of at nest sites, a substantial fraction of the population apparently does not breed, perhaps because the birds take several years to mature. The usual nest is in a crevice among granite boulders, with which San Diego County's mountains are well supplied. Both the breeding and winter distributions have retract-

Photo by Anthony Mercieca

ed from heavily developed areas, virtually eliminating the species along the coast.

Breeding distribution: In spite of our effort toward this atlas, the Turkey Vulture's breeding distribution in San Diego County remains poorly known. The birds carry no nest material, feed their young largely by regurgitation, visit their nests infrequently, and nest largely in rugged rocky hills, making them one of the most difficult species to confirm nesting. In the areas mapped for possible breeding there are possible nest sites and observations after 15 April, by which date almost all migrants have continued north. Nevertheless, in many of these areas the species may not actually nest.

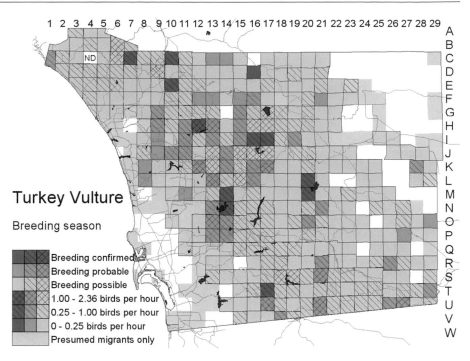

By far the most thorough study of Turkey Vulture nesting in San Diego County is by Manning (1997a, b), who searched for nests in the county's northwestern quadrant, from the Santa Margarita River to Lake Hodges, from 1993 to 1996. In this region, he found 19 nest sites distributed among six areas: eight sites in Rainbow Valley (C9), one along the Santa Margarita River (D6), one in the Merriam Mountains (G9), seven in the south fork of Moosa Canyon (G10), one in San Marcos Canyon (J8), and one in San Elijo Canyon (J9). From 1997 to 2001 we continued to see the vultures in all these areas and located two apparent nest sites near them: birds entering caves in steep rocky hills along Sandia Creek (C7) 11 April 1998 and at the northeast end of Rainbow Valley (C10) 16 and 21 May 2001 (K. L. Weaver).

Elsewhere in San Diego County the only definite nests reported were from Boulder Oaks Ranch (M14), the northeast corner of San Vicente Reservoir (N14), Black Canyon (I16, D. Bittner), and near Pringle Canyon (T17), where a Border Patrol agent told D. C. Seals of finding a Turkey Vulture chick when he followed the scent of a suspected decaying human body. Some areas of concentration with likely nest sites are around Starvation Mountain (K12; up to 25 on 10 May 1997, E. C. Hall), the south end of Pamo Valley (J15; up to 25 on 24 May 1998, L. E. Taylor), and Barrett Lake (S18/

S19; up to 22 on 28 May 1998, J. Hannan). Over most of San Diego County the vulture appears to be uncommon and rather uniformly distributed through the foothills and mountains.

Whether the Turkey Vulture nests in the mountains of the Anza–Borrego Desert is still unclear. There are no confirmations of nesting, yet small numbers have been seen repeatedly during the breeding season in the Vallecito Mountains and the southern part of the park (up to nine in Indian Valley, O27, 15–16 May 1999, P. R. Pryde). In the canyon of Alma Wash near Starfish Cove (K28), L. J. Hargrove noted apparent family groups (juvenile included) of three or four on 4 May 1999 and 20–21 May 2000. An exceptional concentration of 55 drawn to a

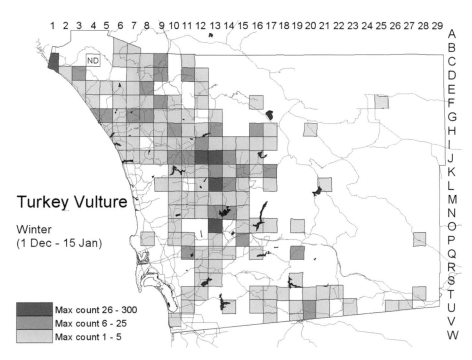

dead coyote along Highway S2 in Vallecito Valley (M24) 30 April 1999 (D. C. Seals) seems about two weeks late for a flock of migrants.

Nesting: In San Diego County, as elsewhere in western North America (Kirk and Mossman 1998), the Turkey Vulture usually nests in caves or crevices on steep rocky slopes. Of 16 nest sites studied by Manning (1997b), 14 were in crevices among granite boulders; the mean slope at these sites was 44°. All nests were on the ground in some kind of dark recess. Semicolonial nesting in areas with multiple suitable sites is implied by up to five pairs active within a radius of one-quarter mile. Yet these areas had up to eight sites among which the birds shifted (Manning 1997a).

On the basis of observed hatching dates ranging from 8 April to no later than 1 June, Manning (1997a) estimated that the Turkey Vultures he observed laid eggs from 28 February to at least 23 April. This range corresponds well with that of 61 egg sets collected 1894–1939, 2 March–12 May.

Migration: Over most of western North America Turkey Vultures are highly migratory, following well-defined routes. Birds commuting between the Pacific Northwest and Mexico pass through southern California. In fall their primary path, leading from Weldon on the Kern River to Victorville on the Mojave River and on to the Colorado River, bypasses San Diego County. In spring, however, the Borrego Valley is a stopover site for modest numbers, with a maximum of 85 at Borrego Springs (F24) 22 February 2000 (P. D. Jorgensen). The birds migrate throughout San Diego County, occasionally even along the coast (up to 50 at Los Peñasquitos Lagoon, N7, 28 March 1999, B. C. Moore). Records from the Anza–Borrego Desert suggest that the Turkey Vulture's spring migration begins in late January, rarely as early as mid January (six at Ocotillo Wells, I28, 12 January 1985, R. Thériault; 25 in the Borrego Valley 13 January 1973, A. G. Morley) and continues to mid April (10 at Borrego Springs 15 April 2001, P. D. Ache).

Winter: Because of the Turkey Vulture's early migration schedule, the map of its winter distribution shows locations for December and the first half of January only. During this interval the Turkey Vulture is less widespread and generally less numerous than in spring migration or the breeding season. Most of the birds concentrate at a few regular roost sites. By far the largest of these is in eucalyptus trees at the Wild Animal Park (J12). Fifty to 100 are typical here (K. L. Weaver), and the highest estimate is of 300 on 6 January 1999 (D. and D. Bylin). The next largest is in the Eucalyptus Hills area of Lakeside, at Valle Vista and Serena roads (O13), with up to 28 on 31 December 1998 and 50 on 2 March 1998 (D. C. Seals). Other sites of winter concentrations are at San Onofre State Beach (C1; up to 30 on 29 December 1997, L. Ellis), the Santa Margarita River mouth (G5; up to 20 on 27 December 1997, E. J. McNeil, T. A. Burr), and near Mt. Woodson (L13; up to 35 on 3 January 1998, P. M. von

Hendy). David Bittner reports 30–40 wintering annually in the Santa Maria Valley (K13/K14/L14) and 15–20 roosting year round in the Santa Teresa Valley (K16).

In winter, vultures remain around some low-elevation nesting habitat like Rainbow Valley (up to 19 on 3 January 2000, K. L. Weaver). But few occur at this season above 2500 feet elevation. Our only winter record at a high elevation during the atlas period was of three in the basin of Cuyamaca Lake (L21) 11 December 2000 (L. and M. Polinsky). In the Anza–Borrego Desert in winter the Turkey Vulture is essentially absent. In 19 years of Christmas bird counts, 1984–2002, it was recorded just once, in count week only. Records as early as 9 January (2000; one near Sweeney Pass, P28, J. R. Barth) could represent early migrants.

Conservation: Egg collections in the early 20th century attest to the Turkey Vulture's former regular nesting along the coast of northern San Diego County, in cavities in the bluffs overlooking the valleys and lagoons. None have nested there since the 1970s (W. T. Everett in Unitt 1984, Manning 1997a, b). Human disturbance, loss of foraging habitat to urbanization, and pesticide contamination probably all contributed to the species' decrease and range retraction. Urbanization and disturbance continue to threaten the birds; for example, urban sprawl has overrun the area around the nest site in San Marcos Canyon. The almost complete lack of Turkey Vultures at any season from metropolitan San Diego shows that intensive development eliminates them. Though the ruggedness of the habitat insulates the nests from disturbance to some extent, it attracts rock climbers, which Manning (1997b) often saw within 10 meters of nests. The Rainbow colony is threatened by the proposed installation of a power-transmission line (J. A. Manning pers. comm.).

Nevertheless, in the latter part of the 20th century the general trend for the species across its range was apparently of increase (Kirk and Mossman 1998). San Diego County Christmas bird counts show no clear trend since the 1970s, but the concentration of birds around roost sites, which can shift, makes broad-scale changes difficult to track.

Taxonomy: The two subspecies of the Turkey Vulture in western North America differ in size. *Cathartes a. meridionalis* Swann, 1921, is larger and breeds at least from southern California north to British Columbia; nominate *C. a. aura* (Linnaeus, 1758) is smaller and breeds from the lower Colorado River valley east through the desert Southwest and south through Mexico. Rea (1983) found wing-bone measurements to identify the subspecies better than external measurements. The lengths of the humeri (147–156 mm) and ulnae (178 and 187 mm) of all six San Diego County specimens are greater than Rea's ranges for *aura*; four are within the range of *meridionalis*, while two are intermediate. All three July–August specimens are *meridionalis*; the other specimens are from October, November, and February.

California Condor *Gymnogyps californianus*

California Condors could be seen regularly in San Diego County in the 1800s and nested in the rugged foothills and mountains. By the 1880s the population was in collapse, and the condor was extirpated from the county about 1910. By 1987 the species' extinction was imminent, when the last three wild birds were taken into captivity. Techniques for breeding and raising condors in captivity, pioneered at the San Diego Wild Animal Park, allowed releases of captive-bred birds to begin in 1992. By 2003, the releases nearest San Diego County were in Ventura County to the northwest and the Sierra San Pedro Mártir to the south.

Breeding distribution: The California Condor was "fairly common" in San Diego County until the 1880s (Stephens 1919a, Scott 1936) and survived along the San Luis Rey River until about 1910 (J. B. Dixon in Willett 1933). Definitely reported nest sites were "in the mountains near Warner's Ranch" (Heermann 1859), along Boulder Creek in the Cuyamaca Mountains (M18/M19; Gedney 1900), Palomar Mountain (Willett 1933), 1.5 miles north of De Luz (B6; WFVZ), and near the Escondido Canal intake from the San Luis Rey River (F14; L. F. Kiff). The birds ranged toward the coast at least as far as Poway (M11;

Photo by Anthony Mercieca

Emerson 1887). The latest sighting reported to be in San Diego County, of two "a few miles north of Palomar Mountain" on 3 August 1933 (Meadows 1933), was more likely in Riverside County.

Conservation: The most important of the many factors killing condors and causing the species' near extinction was poisoning by lead, ingested when the birds fed on animals that had been shot (Snyder and Schmitt 2002). For history of the condor's controversial decline and tentative restoration, see Koford (1953), Wilbur (1978), Snyder and Snyder (2000), and Snyder and Schmitt (2002).

HAWKS, KITES, AND EAGLES — FAMILY ACCIPITRIDAE

Osprey *Pandion haliaetus*

Through the middle of the 20th century the Osprey suffered the ill effects of pesticide poisoning, contracted through the contamination of its staple food, fish. After being released of much of this burden in the 1970s, the Osprey population resurged. In San Diego County this resurgence is conspicuous: once rare, the Osprey has become regular year round in small numbers both along the coast and on inland lakes. Several pairs have begun nesting.

Breeding distribution: The Osprey's recolonization of San Diego County as a breeding species coincided with the beginning of field work for this atlas in 1997. Each year from then through 2002 a pair nested in the northeast corner of North Island Naval Air Station (S9). They fledged young in 1998 and 2000 and probably other years as well (G. Perkins et al.). Another pair began nesting at Scripps Ranch High School (N10) in 1998 and continued annually, with success from 1999 at least through 2002 (G. Steinbach et al.). The birds made uncertain or aborted attempts to nest near Torrey Pines State Reserve (N7) or UCSD (O7) in 1998 (carrying sticks or seaweed, M. C. Jorgensen, S. E. Smith), at Lake Murray (Q11) in 1997 and 2002 (carrying sticks to platform, N. Osborn, P. Famolaro), on the mast of a boat in Mission Bay (R7) 2001–03 (all attempts unsuccessful, D. Bittner), and near Pepper Park, National City (T10), in 1998 (R. T. Patton).

Photo by Anthony Mercieca

With the conclusion of the atlas study in 2002 came a spurt of new Osprey nests: at Mesa College (Q9), San Diego State University (Q11), on some quarry equipment along Mission Gorge Road (Q11), and along the Tijuana River in Marron Valley (V16). Some of these were only tentative attempts, but the nests in Marron Valley and at Mesa College were successful (J. A. Martin, J. Hannan).

Nesting: Ospreys build huge stick nests, often augmenting and reusing them year after year. Their trend toward nesting on man-made structures is well illustrated in San Diego County: the most frequent nest site here is racks

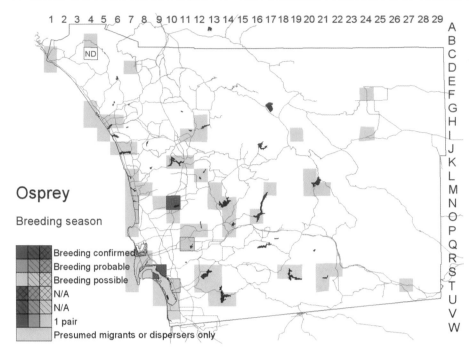

Osprey

Breeding season

Breeding confirmed
Breeding probable
Breeding possible
N/A
N/A
1 pair
Presumed migrants or dispersers only

over the top of Otay Mountain, and over 10 miles from Presa Rodriguez on the outskirts of Tijuana.

The schedule of Osprey nesting is tricky to ascertain because the nests are high, so the young are not visible until well grown, and the male feeds the female throughout incubation as well as the young after they hatch. At Scripps Ranch High School, incubation had apparently begun by 8 February 2000; a chick was visible in this nest by 4 April (G. Grantham). At North Island, the first of three young fledged in 2000 on 18 June, suggesting laying about 11 March (G. Perkins).

Migration: The Osprey is still more numerous in San Diego County during migration and winter than in the breeding season. In regular surveys of north and central San Diego Bay 1993–95 Mock et al. (1994) and Preston and Mock (1995) found the Osprey most frequently in September and October, with a maximum of six per day. From 1997 to 2001 numbers in fall ranged up to nine at San Elijo Lagoon (L7) 7 October 1999 (P. A. Ginsburg).

of floodlights for ball fields, used at Scripps Ranch High School, Mesa College, and North Island. The only nest site in a tree was the one in Marron Valley, in a eucalyptus. The nests at North Island and Scripps Ranch High School were used repeatedly, though the birds also built some new nests, some unused (typical for the species), accounting for nesting "confirmations" in adjacent atlas squares S8 and O10 (on a cell-phone tower at Alliant International University, D. Bainbridge). Osprey nests are generally near water; the one at Scripps Ranch High School was 0.5 mile from Lake Miramar. But the one at Mesa College was 2.3 miles from Mission Bay, and the one in Marron Valley was 8 miles from Lower Otay Lake,

Nonbreeding Ospreys are widely scattered over San Diego County through the spring and early summer, mainly along the coast (up to seven in the San Diego River flood-control channel, R8, 2 April 2000, Y. Ikegaya) and in the coastal lowland. Single individuals have been seen repeatedly at this season farther inland around lakes Cuyamaca, Barrett, and Morena and even at Tule Lake (T27; one on 6 and 27 June 2001, J. K. Wilson).

In the Anza–Borrego Desert the Osprey is a rare migrant, recorded on 1 and 25 October in fall and about nine times from 16 February to 12 April in spring (ABDSP database).

Winter: In winter the Osprey occurs more widely than in the breeding season. During the atlas period we noted it wintering at almost every coastal wetland and at most inland lakes. Sites getting the heaviest Osprey use in winter were Batiquitos Lagoon (J6/J7; up to 11 on 28 December 1999, R. and A. Campbell) and south San Diego Bay (U10/V10; up to six

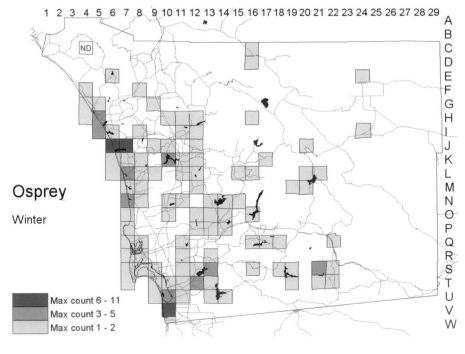

Osprey

Winter

Max count 6 - 11
Max count 3 - 5
Max count 1 - 2

on 3 December 1999, B. C. Moore). Especially favored lakes are Hodges, (K10; two counts of up to three, R. L. Barber), Sweetwater (S12/S13; up to five on 2 December 1998, P. Famolaro), and Morena (S21/T21; three counts of up to three, S. E. Smith). The Wildlife Research Institute (2004) found 21 individuals wintering in the southwestern quadrant of San Diego County in 2002. Perhaps because the Bald Eagle is so regular there, the Osprey is rare at Lake Henshaw, recorded on only one of 22 Lake Henshaw Christmas bird counts 1981–2002.

Conservation: The Osprey's resurgence gained traction in the late 1980s and continued through the end of the century. By 2001 it was more abundant in San Diego County than at any time in recorded history. From 1953 to 1972 the San Diego Christmas bird count averaged 0.4 per year; from 1997 to 2002 it averaged 23.5. The trend on Oceanside, Rancho Santa Fe, and Escondido counts is similar though less dramatic. On monthly counts of San Elijo Lagoon 1973–83, King et al. (1987) found the Osprey only occasionally and almost always singly. Before 1997 the only reported nesting attempts were on a boat in San Diego Bay, probably in the early 1860s (Cooper

1870), and on a beacon in the bay in 1912 (eggs collected 21 April, WFVZ 71019).

Reduced shooting and, especially, the banning of nondegradable organochlorine pesticides are the factors allowing the Osprey's increase. In San Diego County, the building of dams and the stocking of reservoirs with fish created much new Osprey habitat. Acclimatizing to human activity around nests and adopting man-made structures as nest sites allowed the Osprey to recolonize. But the uses for which these structures were designed may be incompatible with Osprey nesting, possibly leading to a new generation of conflict.

Taxonomy: Ospreys throughout North America have long been ascribed to *P. h. carolinensis* (Gmelin, 1788). On the basis of field observations, Blanco and Rodriguez (1999) reported Ospreys from Baja California Sur to have nearly white underwing coverts as in *P. h. ridgwayi* Maynard, 1887, of the West Indies. But a one-year-old male and two one-year-old females in the San Diego Natural History Museum from San Ignacio and Scammon's lagoons, Baja California, have the same amount of dark barring on the under primary coverts as specimens from farther north.

White-tailed Kite *Elanus leucurus*

The White-tailed Kite is not only one of southern California's most elegant birds of prey, it is one of the most interesting, because of its communal roosting, history of steep rises and falls in population, and concentration on a single species of prey, the California vole or meadow mouse. Though the kite is found in San Diego County year round, its numbers vary with those of the vole and the shifting of communal roosts. Unfortunately, urbanization of the grasslands in which kites forage threatens the recovery the species enjoyed from the late 1930s to the 1970s.

Breeding distribution: The White-tailed Kite is widespread over the coastal slope of San Diego County, preferring riparian woodland, oak groves, or sycamore groves adjacent to grassland. Regions of concentration are in the northwest from Camp Pendleton to Carlsbad and Vista, in the central region from Los Peñasquitos Canyon through Miramar to Poway, and in the south from the Tijuana River valley to Otay Mesa and Otay lakes. In the foothills the species is less common than in the coastal lowland but still fairly widespread—substantially more widespread than reported previously (Unitt 1984). It is absent from most of the higher mountains but occurs uncommonly up to about 4200 feet elevation in the Julian area with up to six, including a pair at a nest, at Wynola (J19) 22 May 1999 (S. E. Smith). It has been seen repeatedly at 4600–4700 feet elevation around Lake Cuyamaca (M20), where most birds are probably postbreeding dispersers (up to three on 6 August 1999, A. P. and T. E. Keenan).

The kite's range spills over the east side of the mountains possibly in McCain Valley (S27; juvenile 14 May

Photo by Anthony Mercieca

1999, M. Sadowski), certainly in San Felipe Valley, where there are many reports, including a pair with a probable nest in the upper valley (H20) 1 May 1998 (A. P. and T. E. Keenan) and a pair in courtship display near Scissors Crossing (J22) 13 April 1998 (E. C. Hall). Note that these suggestions of breeding were in the wet El Niño spring of 1998; monitoring at Scissors Crossing in two dry to average years, 2002 and 2003, yielded only occasional postbreeding visitors (J. R. Barth). The Anza–Borrego Desert State Park database has several records of the White-tailed Kite through the spring and summer, mostly of single individuals with no suggestion of breeding, but three were at Middle Willows (C22) 7 May 1972.

Nesting: White-tailed Kites build their nest in the crowns of trees, especially the coast live oak, or on clumps of mistletoe, both of which screen the nest well. They use nonnative trees freely, especially orange trees, as citrus orchards often offer good foraging (Dixon et al. 1957). Occasionally they use large shrubs such as scrub oak or toyon.

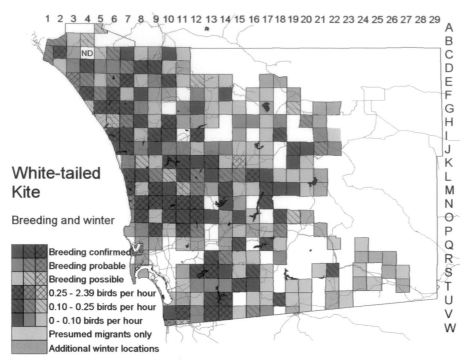

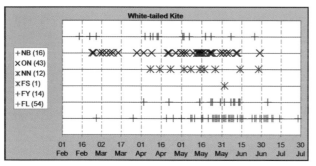

White-tailed Kite

Breeding and winter

Breeding confirmed
Breeding probable
Breeding possible
0.25 - 2.39 birds per hour
0.10 - 0.25 birds per hour
0 - 0.10 birds per hour
Presumed migrants only
Additional winter locations

Research Institute (2004) found the kite to constitute essentially the same percentage of the raptor fauna of southwestern San Diego County in winter as in summer. Atlas observers did find the species a bit more frequently in marginal areas like Warner Valley, Ranchita (G21/G22), Lake Cuyamaca, and McCain Valley in winter than in summer. Also in winter a few birds entered the developed areas of the city of San Diego, where kites are lacking during the breeding season.

The most notable aspect of the kite's nonbreeding biology is its communal roosting. From 1997 to 2002, flocks were reported from near the upper end of Agua Hedionda Lagoon (I6; up to 21 from 1 to 9 December 1998, L. E. Taylor, P. A. Ginsburg) and at the mouth of Spring Canyon, Mission Trails Regional Park (P11; up to 50 from 3 December 1998 to 7 February 1999, D. Mooney). In the latter case the flock was observed through the middle of the day. Another notable diurnal concentration was 113 (mostly juveniles) scattered over eastern Otay Mesa (V14) 31 July 1999 (S. D. Cameron).

Conservation: In the 19th century the White-tailed Kite was probably uncommon in San Diego County; A. M. Ingersoll told Willett (1912) that "from 1887 to 1892 he saw White-tailed Kites frequently in the vicinity of San Diego and knew of two pairs nesting in that region." From 1892 to 1920, however, the species went unrecorded and was probably extirpated. One pair nested 5 miles east of Del Mar (M8) in 1920, and one bird was shot at the Tijuana River mouth (V10) on 15 January 1930 (Huey 1931b). Dixon et al. (1957) saw no kites in northern San Diego County from 1900 to 1935, but then they colonized and increased, becoming common by 1956. San Diego Christmas bird counts show an upsurge in 1965, though this was due in part to the count circle's being shifted to include the Tijuana River valley. The population probably peaked in the 1970s and early 1980s. Long-term trends are difficult to track because the kites' numbers vary with rain and rodent numbers and the shifting of roost sites. Nevertheless, results of the Oceanside Christmas bird count may be a gauge; its circle once consisted largely of prime kite habitat. From 1976 to 1983 this count averaged 72; from 1997 to 2002 it averaged 30.

Shooting was likely responsible for the kite's first decrease. Agriculture may have been a boon to the species, as it nests and feeds commonly in orchards. But with citrus growing no longer profitable in San Diego County many groves have been developed into housing tracts. Most grassland has also already been lost. Poisoning of rodents may be affecting the kite by depressing its food

Dixon et al. (1957) reported eggs from 6 February to 10 July, with 10-day-old young in one nest 22 February, suggesting laying about 12 January. Our observations from 1997 to 2002 imply laying from late January to May, except that a brood of newly fledged young in lower Los Peñasquitos Canyon (N8) 27 February 1999 (B. C. Moore) must have hatched from a clutch laid around 1 January. From 1997 to 2001, all our early nestings of the kite were in 1999, following the wet spring of 1998, when rodent numbers were still high. Late nestings were in both 1998 and 1999. Our number of nesting confirmations per year similarly shows the effect of variation in rainfall and presumably in prey: 15 in 1997, 41 in 1998, 72 in 1999, 7 in 2000, and 11 in 2001.

Migration: The White-tailed Kite is nonmigratory but nomadic and dispersive. Dixon et al. (1957) reported a bird banded as a nestling in San Diego County recovered about 100 miles north two years later. The birds invaded San Clemente Island in 1984, one year after El Niño rains (Scott 1994). Records for the Anza–Borrego Desert in the state park database are scattered rather evenly through the year.

Winter: The White-tailed Kite's winter distribution differs little from the breeding distribution. The Wildlife

supply. The disappearance of kites from the long-developed areas of the city of San Diego is obvious from the map and suggests a scenario for the rapidly urbanizing areas of northern San Diego County. Another possible negative factor is the proliferation of crows and ravens; Dixon et al. (1957) reported crows robbing kites of their prey repeatedly; D. Bittner has observed ravens doing the same.

Taxonomy: The subspecies of White-tailed Kite in North America is *E. l. majusculus* Bangs and Penard, 1920, larger than the nominate subspecies of South America. The White-tailed Kite has sometimes been considered conspecific with the Black-shouldered Kite (*E. caeruleus*) of the Old World; at these times the name Black-shouldered Kite has been applied to the birds in the New World as well.

Mississippi Kite *Ictinia mississippiensis*

The Mississippi Kite breeds mainly in the southern Great Plains and southeastern United States; it is only a vagrant to California, where there are 29 well-supported records through 2000. A population increase and westward range expansion in the 1970s led to the prediction that the kite would colonize southern California (Parker and Ogden 1979), but all that followed was a spike in its frequency here in the early 1980s. This spike accounts for all records for San Diego County.

Migration: The California Bird Records Committee has accepted three identifications of the Mississippi Kite in San Diego County, of one seen in the Tijuana River valley (V11) 18 July 1982 (G. McCaskie, Morlan 1985), one photographed at Pio Pico Campground (T15) 12 June–30 July 1983 (D. W. Povey, Morlan 1985), and one seen at Point Loma (S7) 21 September 1985 (G. McCaskie, Bevier 1990). The committee considered to be a fourth record also in the early 1980s to be inadequately supported.

Photo by Anthony Mercieca

Bald Eagle *Haliaeetus leucocephalus*

In San Diego County the Bald Eagle is a rare but annual winter visitor to lakes in the foothills and mountains, especially Lake Henshaw. From 1997 to 2002 the number reaching the county varied from about 8 to 15 each year. A few individuals have remained into summer, and in 2001 an unmated bird was carrying sticks, suggesting the Bald Eagle could colonize San Diego County as a breeding species. Reintroduction programs, the banning of eagle shooting, and especially the ban on DDT have resulted in vigorous growth of the Bald Eagle population nationwide since the late 1970s.

Photo by Anthony Mercieca

Winter: Because its primary prey is fish, the Bald Eagle occurs mainly at lakes. At Lake Henshaw (G17), the species' favored site in San Diego County, at least two wintered each year from 1997 to 2002, and the maximum count was eight on 26 January 1999 (P. D. Jorgensen). The highest ever was 16 from 13 December 1972 to 28 January 1973 (AB 27:663, 1973). Cuyamaca (M20), Corte Madera (Q20/R20), and Morena (T21/S21/S22) are also fairly consistent sites. Atlas observers noted only one or two at a time away from Lake Henshaw but encountered the species at least occasionally at almost all lakes in the foothills

and mountains, even some rather small ones, as in Thing Valley (Q24; one on 7 January 2001, J. R. Barth).

On lakes in the coastal lowland the Bald Eagle is infrequent, with only two noted during the atlas period (O'Neill Lake, E6, 1 December 2000–14 January 2001, P. A. Ginsburg; Sweetwater Reservoir, S12, 30 December 2000, C. H. Reiser). It is even less frequent in coastal wetlands; 10 years of monthly surveys of San Elijo Lagoon (L7) yielded only one (King et al. 1987). From 1980 to 2002, the San Diego and Rancho Santa Fe Christmas bird

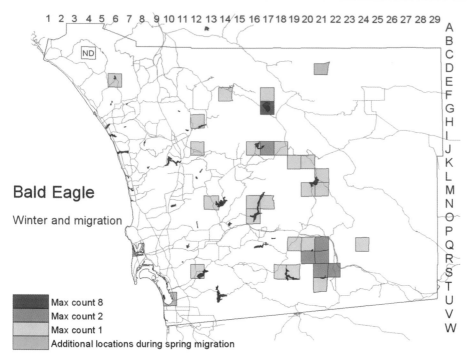

Bald Eagle

Winter and migration

- Max count 8
- Max count 2
- Max count 1
- Additional locations during spring migration

mit of Hot Springs Mountain (E20) 15 June (G. L. Rogers, NASFN 50:996, 1996). In 2000 an adult was at Lake Henshaw 18 June (P. Unitt) and another was at Lake Cuyamaca 20–23 June (D. Bittner, NAB 54:423, 2000). Then on 21 March 2001 an adult was carrying sticks to a sycamore tree at Lake Henshaw (W. E. Haas). Evidently lacking a mate, this bird got no farther with its attempt to nest and did not remain through the summer. But the episode suggests that the Bald Eagle could soon colonize San Diego County as a breeding species. Its nearest current nest site is at Lake Hemet, Riverside County, where two young fledged in 2003 (D. Bittner).

Nesting: Bald Eagles build an enormous stick nest, usually in a tall tree. They also nest on cliffs where trees are few or none; the nest on Little Tecate Peak was on a "pinnacle of rock."

counts recorded the Bald Eagle only once, the Oceanside count not at all. In the Anza–Borrego Desert the only records are of one over Whale Peak (L25) 18 February 1983 (A. G. Morley) and one over Indianhead (F23) 14 January 1997 (D. Waber).

Migration: Bald Eagles begin arriving in San Diego County in October, recorded as early as the 3rd (1978, Sweetwater Reservoir, D. Thompson) and the 4th (1982, Lake Henshaw, R. Higson, AB 37:223, 1983). Most depart in March; the latest date recorded for a migrant is 4 May (1984, immature at Lake Henshaw, R. Higson, AB 38:960, 1984). An immature at the Sweetwater River mouth on San Diego Bay (U10) 16 and 25 April 1998 (B. C. Moore) and an adult in Lost Valley (D21) 28 April 2000 (W. E. Haas) were unusual for both date and location.

The Bald Eagle has been reintroduced to the Channel Islands, and a tagged subadult released at Santa Catalina Island showed up at Lake Morena 24 July 2001 (R. Roedell).

Breeding distribution: The only known nesting of the Bald Eagle in San Diego County was in 1936, when A. O. Treganza collected an egg from Little Tecate Peak (V17) 8 March (WFVZ 55005). No summering birds were reported until 1988, when one was near Julian 18 May (J. Smith, AB 42:481, 1988) and 1996, when one was near the sum-

Conservation: The Bald Eagle suffered greatly from shooting and from poisoning by DDT and lead. It was among the first species formally listed as endangered by the federal government in 1967. With these adverse factors largely controlled, however, since 1980 the population has climbed steeply (Buehler 2000). In San Diego County, which is peripheral to the species' range, the most noticeable change is the occurrences in summer. Lake Henshaw Christmas bird counts, begun in January 1981, show no strong trend. But a change may be more likely detected in the number of lakes with Bald Eagles than in the number on a single lake.

Taxonomy: The Bald Eagle is usually divided into a larger northern subspecies, *H. l. alascanus* Townsend, 1897, and a smaller southern one, *H. l. leucocephalus* (Linnaeus, 1766). Birds nesting in San Diego County would be the smaller subspecies, but winter visitors are more likely the northern one, and measurements of the single specimen, from Lake Cuyamaca 20 December 1922 (MVZ 144728), identify it as *alascanus* (Unitt 1984). A Bald Eagle fitted with a radio transmitter and wintering at Lake Henshaw in 1999 and 2000 had migrated from Great Slave Lake, northern Canada (D. Bittner, B. J. Walton).

Northern Harrier *Circus cyaneus*

Long known in America as the Marsh Hawk, the Northern Harrier is as much a bird of grassland as of marshes. In San Diego County it is found year round but is more numerous and widespread as a winter visitor than as a breeding bird. The Northern Harrier's status as a breeding species in San Diego County is threatened by habitat loss and fragmen-

tation, to which grassland birds that nest on the ground are especially susceptible. The local breeding population undoubtedly varies much with rainfall and the abundance of prey but is between about 25 and 75 pairs.

Breeding distribution: In San Diego County breeding Northern Harriers are scattered, as patches of suitable habitat are separated by stretches of chaparral or urban development. Camp Pendleton, with its extensive grass-lands, functions as a refuge for the harrier; from 1997 to 2001 we noted possibly breeding birds in 17 of the 28 atlas squares fully or partly within the base. Originally, this grassland spread over much of northwestern San Diego County. Harriers nested in remaining undeveloped areas in Carlsbad (I7) at least until 2000 (fledglings on 15 June, D. B. Mayer) and at Guajome Lake (G7) at least until 2001 (female carrying a twig 25 June, K. L. Weaver). In central San Diego County the most important area for breeding harriers is Los Peñasquitos Canyon (N8/N9); five pairs nested there 1998–99 (J. Hannan), but none remained by 2001–02 (Wildlife Research Institute 2004). The Tijuana River estuary and valley evidently have the largest concentration of nesting harriers in San Diego County, with up to 13 pairs in the Border Field State Park (W10) alone in 2002 (Wildlife Research Institute 2004). Despite sprawling scattered industrial development, per-haps four to six pairs still nest on Otay Mesa. In south-western San Diego County, north to the San Dieguito River and east to San Pasqual, Alpine, and Dulzura, the Wildlife Research Institute reported 11 pairs in 2001, 24 in 2002. The harrier's numbers vary greatly with rainfall.

In the foothills and mountains harriers are few and scattered through the breeding season, and we did not

Photo by Anthony Mercieca

confirm nesting there. On the east slope of the mountains the harrier is apparently irregular in San Felipe Valley, where we noted it repeatedly in the springs of 1998 (after El Niño rains) and 1999, including a male in display flight at Sentenac Ciénaga (J23) 11 March 1999 (R. Thériault). But after four years of drought, in 2002 and 2003, the harrier was absent there. Similarly, an apparent pair in the Jacumba Valley (U28) 28 February 1999 (F. L. Unmack) was our only suggestion of breeding in southeastern San Diego County. The only late spring or summer record from the Anza–Borrego Desert is of a single bird at Lower Willows (D23) 4 July 1994 (M.Getty).

Nesting: The Northern Harrier nests on the ground, with the nest concealed within a marsh or other dense vegeta-tion. Our relatively few observations of nesting activity imply the birds lay eggs at least from 1 April to 1 May, an interval little different from the 5 April–11 May docu-mented by 12 egg sets collected 1918–44.

Migration: Winter visitors occur mainly from September to March. Except for the one July record, the harrier has been noted in the Anza–Borrego Desert from 6 September (1999, one at the Ram's Hill sewage ponds, H25, P. D. Jorgensen) to 1 May (2001, one at the north end of Clark Valley, C25, H. E. Stone).

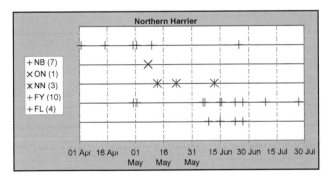

Winter: Though the Northern Harrier is considerably more numerous in San Diego County in winter than in spring or sum-mer, it is still generally uncom-mon. We found no commu-nal roosts. Our highest counts were of nine in Los Peñasquitos Canyon (N8) 1 February 1998 (D. K. Adams), eight in Sycamore Canyon (O12) 8 December 1998 (W. E. Haas), and eight at Border Field State Park (W10) 19 December 1998 (K. Aldern). Wintering birds are strongly

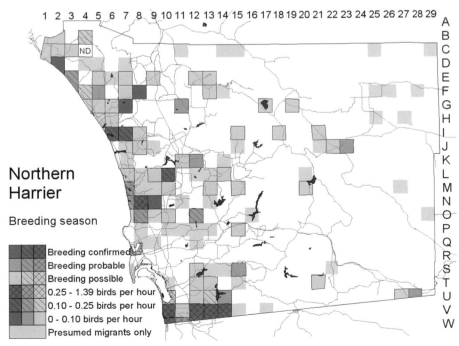

Northern Harrier

Breeding season

- Breeding confirmed
- Breeding probable
- Breeding possible
- 0.25 - 1.39 birds per hour
- 0.10 - 0.25 birds per hour
- 0 - 0.10 birds per hour
- Presumed migrants only

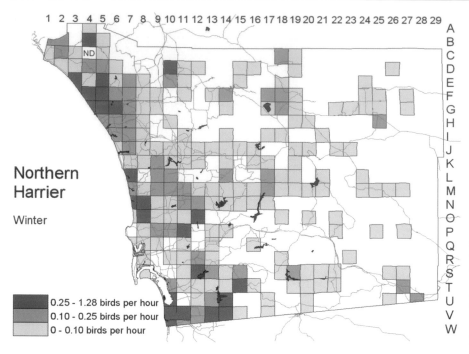

Northern Harrier

Winter

- ■ 0.25 - 1.28 birds per hour
- ▨ 0.10 - 0.25 birds per hour
- □ 0 - 0.10 birds per hour

drought-plagued 2001–02 was barely a third that in 1998–99, the year following El Niño rains.

Conservation: Early in the 20th century, the Northern Harrier was a common breeding resident (Willett 1912, Stephens 1919a). With urbanization, especially of floodplains, the harrier lost most of its habitat and became rare as a breeding species. Loss of foraging habitat and disturbance of nest sites are both likely factors. Unfortunately, data to quantify the change do not exist. Christmas bird counts suggest that the numbers of wintering birds remained more stable through the final third of the 20th century.

The Northern Harrier exemplifies the conundrum of rare wildlife with conflicting needs being squeezed together into small remnants of habitat. In the Tijuana River estuary, some harriers learned to specialize on the Clapper Rail as prey (P. D. Jorgensen); some prey on Least Terns (R. T. Patton). The Wildlife Research Institute (2004) reported that the most frequent issue confronting nesting harriers is disturbance from people walking near nests, dogs allowed to run free, and off-road vehicles.

concentrated in the coastal lowland, especially in the same regions with breeding birds. At higher elevations we found no more than three harriers per atlas square per day, even in extensive grasslands such as those near Lake Henshaw and Lake Cuyamaca. In the Anza–Borrego Desert wintering harriers are scarcer still, with only a few sightings of as many as two individuals at a time. The average on Anza–Borrego Christmas bird counts is 2.4.

Wintering as well as breeding birds vary in number with rainfall, which controls the abundance of the harrier's prey. The number atlas observers reported in

Taxonomy: The Northern Harrier comprises an Old World and a New World subspecies; *C. c. hudsonius* (Linnaeus, 1766) inhabits the latter.

Sharp-shinned Hawk *Accipiter striatus*

The Sharp-shinned Hawk is a widespread but uncommon winter visitor to San Diego County. It is found in a wide variety of habitats, though more frequently in areas with trees or tall shrubs than in those without them. Because the Sharp-shinned Hawk feeds predominantly on small birds, any place that concentrates flocks of House Finches, House Sparrows, White-crowned Sparrows, or juncos is likely to attract the hawk.

Winter: The Sharp-shinned Hawk is rather uniformly distributed over the coastal slope of San Diego County. On the scale of the atlas grid there is no clear region of concentration. In the Anza–Borrego Desert the species is sparser than on the coastal side, found mainly at oases, in developed areas, and in mesquite thickets. In winter 2002 the Wildlife Research Institute recorded the Sharp-shinned Hawk at only two of its 45 study sites in southwestern San Diego County.

Photo by Anthony Mercieca

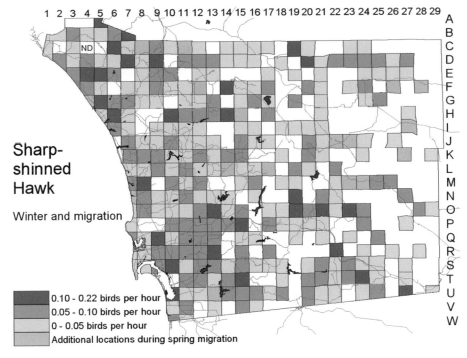

Sharp-shinned Hawk

Winter and migration

■	0.10 - 0.22 birds per hour
▓	0.05 - 0.10 birds per hour
□	0 - 0.05 birds per hour
▒	Additional locations during spring migration

a migrant is 28 April (1982; one at Point Loma, R. E. Webster, AB 36: 893, 1982).

Breeding distribution: The Sharp-shinned Hawk has been confirmed nesting in the San Bernardino Mountains and seen repeatedly in summer in the San Jacinto Mountains, but in San Diego County evidence for its breeding is slight. J. B. Dixon (in Willett 1933) reported seeing the species "in the Cuyamacas and other mountains in San Diego County in summer. In one instance, the actions of the birds indicated a nest nearby." No more specific information is available. Through the latter half of the 20th century the only records of possibly breeding or summering Sharp-shinned Hawks were an apparent pair in Banner Canyon (J20) 29 April 1978 (J. L. Dunn, AB 32:1208, 1978) and a single bird on Palomar Mountain (D14) 14 July 1982 (R. Higson, AB 36:1016, 1982).

Conservation: In contrast to the crash (due to slaughter of migrants) and recovery in the eastern United States, changes in the Sharp-shinned Hawk's numbers in California have been modest. Christmas bird counts in San Diego County suggest no long-term change. The birds use urban habitats as freely as natural ones. During the atlas period our highest daily count (of four) was in a heavily developed area, East San Diego (R10; 20 December 1997, J. A. Dietrick), as was our highest number per hour, in southeast San Diego (S10).

Taxonomy: *Accipiter s. velox* is the subspecies of the Sharp-shinned Hawk widespread across North America and the only one recorded in California.

Likewise, there is no great variation in the Sharp-shinned Hawk's abundance from year to year. From 1997 to 2002 the number of Sharp-shinned Hawks atlas observers reported per hour varied by no more than 23% from the mean for the five-year period.

Migration: In fall, the Sharp-shinned Hawk returns to San Diego County usually in the middle of September and is most numerous as a fall migrant in late September and early October, when up to 15 in a day have been seen migrating down Point Loma. In spring, it begins migrating out in March, and after the first week of April it is rare. From 1997 to 2001 our dates for the species ranged from 12 September (1997, one at Lake Hodges, K10, R. L. Barber) to 26 April (three records). Specimens range from 15 September (1889, Ballena, K17, SDNHM 325) to 6 April (1930, Point Loma, SDNHM 12716). The latest reliable date ever reported for

---

Cooper's Hawk *Accipiter cooperii*

Long a bird of oak groves and mature riparian woodland, Cooper's Hawk adapted abruptly to city living in the last two decades of the 20th century. The species is now at least as numerous in urban eucalyptus trees as in natural habitats. The breeding population increased to the point where the local birds probably outnumber winter visitors. Though Cooper's Hawk is still listed as a "covered species" under San Diego's multiple-species conservation plan, the idea that natural habitats and Cooper's Hawks are conserved together is now laughably obsolete.

Breeding distribution: Breeding Cooper's Hawks are widespread over San Diego County's coastal slope wherever there are stands of trees. They are most numerous in lowland and foothill canyons and in the urban areas

Photo by Jack C. Daynes

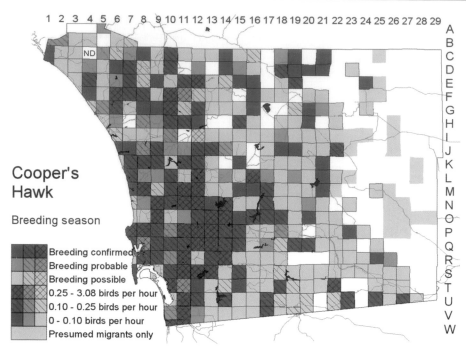

Cooper's
Hawk

Breeding season

Breeding confirmed
Breeding probable
Breeding possible
0.25 - 3.08 birds per hour
0.10 - 0.25 birds per hour
0 - 0.10 birds per hour
Presumed migrants only

ing range corresponds closely to the eastern limit of the oaks but goes down the east slope of the mountains in Alder Canyon (C21; used nest on 20 June 2001, P. D. Jorgensen) and San Felipe Valley (nests with nestlings near Scissors Crossing, J22, 28 June 2000 and 28 June 2001, M. C. and P. D. Jorgensen). Cooper's Hawks are seen rarely through the breeding season in the Anza–Borrego Desert, mainly but not exclusively in the Borrego Valley. Most of these are nonbreeding; our only nest of Cooper's Hawk in the Anza–Borrego Desert had nestlings in the north Borrego Valley (E24) 31 May 2001 (J. Fitch). In 1997 a pair may have nested at Vallecito (M25); two birds were both carrying prey 29 April (M. C. Jorgensen).

of the city of San Diego. We found up to four pairs per atlas square, and densities higher than this are likely. Asay (1987) reported distances between nests as low as 1.0 km in oak woodland in Riverside and San Diego counties. David Bittner, J. L. Lincer, and J. M. Wells found a similar density in riparian woodland of the Tijuana River valley in 2002 (Wildlife Research Institute 2004).

Cooper's Hawk is sparser in the mountains than at lower elevations. On Hot Springs Mountain (E20/E21) it has been seen only as a postbreeding visitor (juvenile 17 August 1996, K. L. Weaver, J. Dillane), but it has been found nesting as high as 5900 feet elevation in the Laguna Mountains (P23; occupied nest on 1 July 1999, E. C. Hall, J. O. Zimmer). The eastern margin of the species' breed-

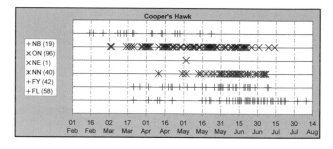

Nesting: Cooper's Hawks nest high in trees but beneath the canopy. Sometimes they nest in riparian willows, but oaks are the species' traditional nest site in California (Asay 1987). In San Diego County the hawks still use oaks commonly, but atlas observers described more than twice as many nests in eucalyptus trees as in oaks. Other reported nest sites were also in planted trees: pine, redwood, and avocado.

Most of our nesting confirmations of the Cooper's Hawk 1997–2001 corresponded to egg laying from late March to mid June, much like the 31 March–21 June interval of 32 egg sets collected 1897–1953. However, atlas observers also noted about 15 instances of earlier nesting, enough to suggest that a broader breeding season is part of the species' recent adaptations. An adult feeding a full-grown juvenile already out of the nest at Kimball Park, National City

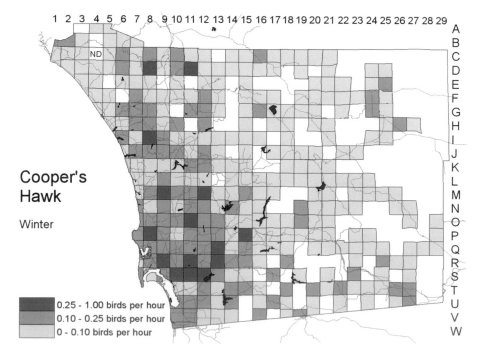

Cooper's
Hawk

Winter

0.25 - 1.00 birds per hour
0.10 - 0.25 birds per hour
0 - 0.10 birds per hour

(T10), 3 April 1999 (P. Unitt) suggests laying as early as the end of January.

Migration: Winter visitors occur in San Diego County mainly from September to March, but with the increase of Cooper's Hawk as a breeding bird the arrival and departure of migrants is seldom obvious. Occasionally, in late September and October, small numbers can be seen migrating south over Point Loma and through the Cuyamaca Mountains (D. Bittner).

Winter: Cooper's Hawk is just as widespread over the coastal slope in winter as in the breeding season but more strongly concentrated at low elevations and in developed areas. One of the atlas squares where we found the species most frequently in winter, for example, was Q13 in El Cajon, which has no significant natural habitat. Our maximum per square per day was nine in Imperial Beach and the Tijuana River valley (V10) 19 December 1998 and 18 December 1999 (P. K. Nelson, W. E. Haas, et al.).

In the Anza–Borrego Desert Cooper's Hawk is rare except at oases and in developed areas. But in Borrego Springs the birds are just as numerous as on the coastal slope. The Anza–Borrego Christmas bird count 19 December 1999 yielded the maximum of seven in one single atlas square (F24; P. K. Nelson et al.) and 16 in the count circle as a whole.

Conservation: In 1978 the California Department of Fish and Game listed Cooper's Hawk as a species of special concern (Remsen 1978), on the basis of population declines probably due to shooting, destruction of riparian woodland, and pesticide contamination. As the principal "chicken hawk," Cooper's Hawk attracted the wrath of man; even Stephens (1919a) wrote "it deserves no mercy." One specimen from San Diego tested in 1968

was highly contaminated with DDT (Risebrough et al. 1968), although such contamination was not widespread (Snyder et al. 1973).

In the 1980s, however, Cooper's Hawks began adapting to the urban environment, nesting in eucalyptus trees in Balboa Park (R9) and later elsewhere throughout the city. In the 1990s this adaptation accelerated and the birds' numbers increased conspicuously. By the time the atlas period began in 1997, Cooper's Hawks had colonized many small parks and schoolyards in inner-city San Diego: Roosevelt Junior High School (R9), the Educational Cultural Center (S10), Emerald Hills Park (S11), Kimball Park in National City, and Eucalyptus Park in Chula Vista (T10). At the same time reports of nests in suburban and rural areas proliferated. Numbers on San Diego Christmas bird counts increased from an average of 11 from 1961 to 1985 to 30 from 1997 to 2002.

Why did Cooper's Hawk adapt so suddenly? A shift in society's attitudes toward birds of prey coincided with the maturation of urban trees over many square miles of formerly treeless scrub. Collisions with windows are now the most serious source of mortality the hawk faces at the hand of man. Once enough Cooper's Hawks learned that people rarely pose a threat any longer, the barrier to their occupying a habitat to which they were preadapted fell. Though hawks in secluded areas defend their nests against people aggressively, in settled areas they usually ignore people even directly below the nest. The open "woodland" of a eucalyptus-planted park, school campus, or neighborhood may be even more attractive habitat for the hawks than a natural oak grove if the numbers of prey like Domestic Pigeons, Mourning Doves, Western Scrub-Jays, and California Ground Squirrels are inflated by a steady supply of lunch scraps or bird feeders.

Northern Goshawk *Accipiter gentilis*

The Northern Goshawk is extremely rare in southern California, with only sporadic nesting in the high mountain forests. Surprisingly, one of the old nesting records is from San Diego County. Otherwise, only three winter vagrants are known in the county.

Winter: One was collected at Lower Otay Lake (U13) 9 November 1916 (Stephens 1919b, SDNHM 11577), one was collected at Mesa Grande (H17) 5 January 1928 (Abbott 1928b, SDNHM 11756), and one was seen at Palomar Mountain (D15) 22 March 1984 (R. Higson, AB 38:960, 1984). The winter of 1916–17 was an invasion year for goshawks throughout California and Arizona.

Breeding distribution: Kiff and Paulson (1997) reported a set of goshawk eggs, preserved at the Slater Museum of Natural History, University of Puget Sound, collected by E. E. Sechrist at 5000 feet elevation in the Cuyamaca Mountains 7 May 1937. On the data card accompanying the eggs Sechrist noted that he saw two young at the same location in June of the following year. There have been

Photo by Anthony Mercieca

no subsequent reports from the area, and the next nearest known goshawk nests have been at Mount Pinos and Mount Abel in northern Ventura County, though there have been summer sightings in the intervening ranges (Kiff and Paulson 1997).

Taxonomy: The specimens from San Diego County are the relatively pale *A. g. atricapillus* (Wilson, 1812), widespread across North America and the only subspecies of the Northern Goshawk known from California.

Harris' Hawk *Parabuteo unicinctus*

Through recorded history, Harris' Hawk has been irregular in southeastern California, the northwestern corner of its range. It died out in the mid 1960s, and efforts to reintroduce it failed, as almost no native riparian woodland is left along the lower Colorado River. Then, in 1994, an incursion, apparently from Baja California, brought nearly 50 individuals north of the border, many of them to San Diego County. Over the next few years the numbers in the county dropped to about five, but one pair in McCain Valley nested repeatedly, achieving success in 2000, 2001, and 2002—the first known successful nesting of wild Harris' Hawks in California for over 40 years. By 2003, however, the birds had disappeared.

Breeding distribution: The irruption of 1994 brought nine Harris' Hawks to McCain Valley (S26) just north of Boulevard. Some arrived even earlier, according to local resident Randy West. In December 1994 another local resident, Leslie Mauris, showed me a photo of six huddled together on a phone line and a nest the birds had built earlier that year. Over the next few years four of the birds were killed in various mishaps—three electrocuted on one pole in 1996—but one pair attempted to nest annually, with no success until 2000, when it fledged three young from a nest about 2 miles from that of 1994.

Photo by Anthony Mercieca

The nest was successful again in 2001 and 2002, but one bird was found dead and mummified 11 September 2001 (R. West; SDNHM 50578). While nesting, the birds in McCain Valley moved little; we had only one sighting during the breeding season in an adjacent atlas square, of two near the fire station in Boulevard (T26) 11 May 2000 (F. L. Unmack).

In the Borrego Valley three Harris' Hawks arrived 15 April 1994 and increased to eight by 13 September (J. Ruddley, R. Thériault). Two were carrying sticks in the valley's mesquite bosque (G25) 8 May 1994, and a pair was copulating in a trailer park in Borrego Springs (G24) 1 March 1995 (P. D. Jorgensen). No further nesting activity was seen, however, and the last report of all eight birds was near Borrego Palm Canyon campground (F23) 12 March 1997 (B. Zuehl). From 1998 on there were no more than two, and by the end of the atlas period in February 2002 only one remained.

Nesting: The nests in McCain Valley in 1994 and 2000 were in the crowns of coast live oaks. Harris' Hawk's breeding season is notably flexible; if prey is abundant, the birds nest earlier and lay repeated clutches (Bednarz

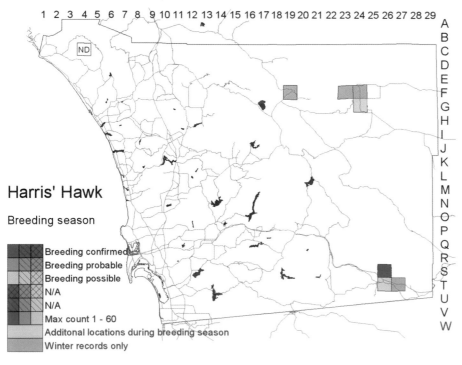

Harris' Hawk

Breeding season

- Breeding confirmed
- Breeding probable
- Breeding possible
- N/A
- N/A
- Max count 1 - 60
- Additonal locations during breeding season
- Winter records only

1995). In 2000, the clutch must have been laid in late April, as at least one chick hatched by 1 June and the brood began fledging on 1 July, though the young were still jumping in and out of the nest on 12 July (R. West, P. Unitt). In 2001, three young were still in the nest on 23 July. Late nesting that year may have been due to ravens preying on an earlier clutch (R. West).

Migration: Patten and Erickson (2000) proposed that the history of Harris' Hawk in southern California is a cycle of colonizations and extirpations, of fluctuations at the margins of the species' range. In San Diego County the only records before 1950 are of one collected in Mission Valley 7 November 1912 (Grey 1913a; SDNHM 1842) and one seen near Oceanside 1–6 November 1942 (Kent 1944). From the 1960s until the incursion of 1994, scattered sightings of Harris' Hawks were assumed to be of escapees from falconers, with whom the species is popular.

Besides the concentrations in Borrego and McCain valleys, the irruption of 1994–96 brought one bird to Santee (P13) 26 November 1994–29 October 1996 (D. C. Seals, R. Saldino, NASFN 50:114, 222, 1996; 51:120, 1997; McKee and Erickson 2002), one to Carrizo Creek (Q27/R27) 6–10 July 1995 (P. D. Jorgensen, C. Hayes), one to Tamarisk Grove (I24) 3 December 1995 (R. Thériault), one to the Sweetwater River above Sweetwater Reservoir (S13) 31 March 1996 (P. Unitt, Rogers and Jaramillo 2002), one to Kit Carson Park, Escondido (K11), 3 April 1996 (M. B. Stowe, NASFN 50:332, 1996), and one to Butterfield Ranch (M23) 8 September 1996 (E. Craven, NASFN 51:120, 1997). An adult near Jamacha Junction (R13) 24 April 2001 (M. A. Patten, NAB 55:356, 2001) may have been one of these birds still lingering.

Winter: Sightings of single Harris' Hawks in Coachwhip Canyon (F28) 4 October 1998 (R. Thériault), at Seventeen Palms (F29) 13 January 1999 (J. Meier), and at Warner Springs (F19) 17 December 2001 (N. Osborn, B. Siegel) suggest the birds at Borrego Springs moved up to 15 miles both east and west of their center. In McCain Valley in winter we saw up to four on 17 February 2001 but found none farther than 3 miles from the nest site, as near the corner of McCain Valley Road and old Highway 80 (T27) 29 January 2001 (F. L. Unmack).

Conservation: The Harris' Hawks in McCain Valley have suffered shooting and electrocution by utility wires, the latter a common problem for the species (Bednarz 1995, D. Bittner). Randy West, who lives in McCain Valley, is a licensed falconer who keeps two Harris' Hawks of Texas origin. The wild Harris' Hawks regularly visited his captive birds. West's birds may be responsible for the persistence and nesting of the wild individuals in a raptorial version of the "Wild Animal Park effect." That is, just as the wading birds kept in captivity at the Wild Animal Park and Sea World have served as nuclei for colonies of wild colonial wading birds, West's Harris' Hawks may have been the nucleus for the "colony" near Boulevard. A third bird emerged as a nest "helper" when the chicks hatched in 2002. The Harris' Hawk's highly social habits, entailing cooperative breeding, mark it as a candidate for the "Wild Animal Park effect."

Taxonomy: All North American Harris' Hawks are best called *P. u. harrisi* (Audubon, 1837); *P. u. superior* van Rossem, 1942, described from Imperial County, is not differentiated adequately by size or color (Bednarz 1995).

Red-shouldered Hawk *Buteo lineatus*

Once an uncommon resident of lowland riparian woodland, the Red-shouldered Hawk has more than compensated for the loss of much of its primitive habitat. Over the 20th century it spread into oak woodland at all elevations. It began nesting in eucalyptus trees as soon as they were introduced and adopted rural ranches as a new habitat. Through the last quarter of the century it became more and more of an urban bird, adding palms to its repertoire of nest sites.

Breeding distribution: The Red-shouldered Hawk is widespread over San Diego County's coastal slope, lacking only from areas like Otay Mountain devoid of tall trees. The inland valleys of northern San Diego County are home to the most concentrated population; the patchwork of riparian woodland, scattered rural residences, orchards, and eucalyptus groves that typifies this area makes ideal Red-shouldered Hawk habitat. Bloom et al. (1993) found that on average 39% of the home ranges of 17 Red-shouldered Hawks in Camp Pendleton and Orange County consisted of oak or riparian woodland.

Photo by Anthony Mercieca

But up to 25% of the home ranges consisted of water, asphalt, or buildings. Bloom et al. found the average home range of seven paired males to be 1.21 to 1.70 km², according to the method of calculation. In parts of

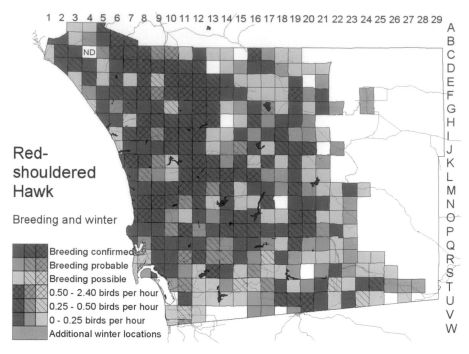

Red-shouldered Hawk

Breeding and winter

Breeding confirmed
Breeding probable
Breeding possible
0.50 - 2.40 birds per hour
0.25 - 0.50 birds per hour
0 - 0.25 birds per hour
Additional winter locations

frequently reuse their nests in successive years and take over old nests of other hawks. We noted two instances of the Red-shouldered Hawk adopting old raven nests, including one on the bridge of old Highway 395 over Los Peñasquitos Creek, adjacent to the heavily trafficked Interstate 15 bridge (N10), using it in both 2000 and 2001 (K. J. Winter).

Our observations from 1997 to 2001 implied Red-shouldered Hawks laying eggs from early March to late April, an interval similar to that of egg sets collected 1890–1952, 28 February–13 May. Sharp (1906b) reported a nest with two small chicks near Escondido 4 July 1906. Dixon (1928) reported the hawk to begin nesting earlier after wet winters, as do many San Diego County birds.

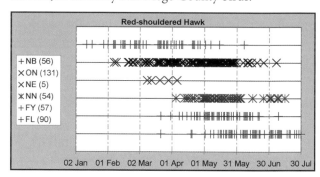

northwestern San Diego County the territories of this size may be packed together with no breaks. Our daily counts per atlas square in this region ranged up to 20 in northwest Escondido (I10) 16 May 1998 (E. C. Hall). Five pairs nest within the town of Ramona (Wildlife Research Institute 2004). In 1998 two pairs nested within 40 acres at Fallbrook (D8; E. Ashton).

In other parts of the county the hawk's population is sparser, though the species is still fairly common in many places. We recorded it repeatedly up to about 5000 feet elevation, finding it regularly in the wetter Palomar and Cuyamaca mountains but rarely in the drier Hot Springs and Laguna mountains. The hawk's preference for moister habitats reflects its diet, dominated by reptiles and amphibians found in these habitats (J. L. Lincer).

The eastern edge of the Red-shouldered Hawk's range corresponds closely with the eastern edge of oak woodland, but a few birds extend down San Felipe Creek to Scissors Crossing (J22; repeated sightings, including a probable nest and recently fledged juvenile on 14 and 20 May 1998, E. C. Hall; two juveniles 2 July 2002, J. R. Barth). Also, since at least 1993, a pair has nested in the cottonwoods planted at Butterfield Ranch (M23; Massey 1998). The nest was still occupied 21 March 2001 (P. K. Nelson). A juvenile in nearby Vallecito Valley (M24) 27 April 2001 (P. K. Nelson) most likely originated from this pair.

Nesting: The Red-shouldered Hawk builds a stick nest high in trees; sycamores and coast live oaks were the typical primitive sites. Soon after eucalyptus trees were introduced, Sharp (1906b) reported the hawk adopting them, and atlas observers described nests in eucalyptus as often as in all other sites combined. Another common novel site is the fan palm, reported eight times. In palms the nest is placed either in the middle of the crown or straddled across leaf bases under the crown. Red-shouldered Hawks

winters, as do many San Diego County birds.

Migration: The Red-shouldered Hawk is largely nonmigratory in California, but a few individuals move into the Anza–Borrego Desert, beginning in July: one at Middle Willows, Coyote Creek (C22) 5 July 1997, one (the same?) at Lower Willows (D23) the next day (ABDSP database), one injured juvenile at the Roadrunner Club, Borrego Springs (F24) 9 July 1996 (P. D. Jorgensen), and one juvenile at Tamarisk Grove Campground (I24) 9–10 July 1996 (R. Thériault). Most desert records are October–December, but there are two as late as April at orchards and nurseries in the Borrego Valley (F25), which the species could colonize: two on 8 April 2001, one on 28 April 1999 (P. D. Ache).

Winter: The Red-shouldered Hawk's pattern of abundance in winter is the same as during the breeding season; established pairs remain in their territories year round. Escondido Christmas bird counts have recorded up to 90, on 4 January 1997. The species is rare but fairly regular in winter in the developed areas of the Borrego Valley. It has been recorded on 14 of 19 Anza–Borrego Christmas bird counts 1984–2002, with a maximum of three but usually just one.

Conservation: Both Sharp (1906b) and Dixon (1928) considered the Red-shouldered Hawk "fairly common" in the inland valleys of northern San Diego County. Dixon reported 23 nesting locations within a radius of 30 miles of Escondido, an area encompassing most of the hawk's range within the county, and considered the Red-shouldered the most restricted in habitat of the area's raptors. Sharp, however, had already commented on its "great fondness" for eucalyptus groves, and the proliferation of these more than compensated for the loss of much of the hawk's original habitat of riparian woodland. The 23 nesting locations reported by Dixon might be equaled within a radius of 5 miles of Escondido today.

Both Sharp and Dixon were explicit on the species' upper limit in elevation, Sharp putting it at 1350 feet, Dixon at 1200 feet. Sharp's nest at Ramona was at the highest elevation recorded by any egg collector 1890–1952. By the 1970s, however, the birds had spread to higher elevations, taking advantage of oak woodland as freely as riparian (Unitt 1984). From 1999 to 2002 four pairs maintained territories in about one square mile between Highway 78 and Deer Lake Park Road, near Julian (K20), at elevation 4000–4400 feet (D. Bittner).

Sams and Stott (1959) reported the Red-shouldered Hawk as "less common than formerly," but the species' adaptation to urban life had already begun by then, as they wrote that it "also nests in eucalyptus trees in Balboa Park." In the core range of the Red-shouldered Hawk there does not seem to have been any change in the species' numbers through the final quarter of the 20th century, but in metropolitan San Diego those numbers increased greatly. From 1954 to 1973 the San Diego Christmas bird count averaged 3.1 Red-shouldered Hawks; from 1997 to 2002 it averaged 25.7. When expressed on the basis of birds per party-hour the factor of increase was 6.8. In spite of occasional collisions with windows and a susceptibility to eye injuries from the sharp-tipped seeds of exotic grasses (McCrary and Bloom 1984), the Red-shouldered Hawk has become one of San Diego County's most successful urban adapters.

Taxonomy: The California subspecies of the Red-shouldered Hawk, the Red-bellied Hawk, *B. l. elegans* Cassin, 1856, differs grossly from the subspecies of the eastern United States. Among other differences, its breast is solid rufous, and the more posterior underparts, including the thighs and undertail coverts, are heavily barred with deep rufous.

Broad-winged Hawk *Buteo platypterus*

The Broad-winged Hawk is common in the eastern United States but a rare visitor to California, mainly in fall migration. Records from San Diego County are mostly from Point Loma. The species' frequency has declined since the 1980s, becoming less than one per year by the turn of the century.

Migration: In a faint echo of the raptor migration at the Marin Headlands on the north side of the Golden Gate, Point Loma (S7) guides and accumulates migrating birds of prey, which are reluctant to cross over water. Thus it is the logical site for species like the Broad-winged Hawk moving south along the coast. In San Diego County records away from Point Loma are few and largely near the coast, such as one at La Jolla (O7) 6 October 1999 (S. E. Smith, NAB 54:104, 2000). Farthest inland was one at Palomar Mountain (D15) 31 October 1983 (R. Higson, AB 38:246, 1984). Records are concentrated in the first two weeks of October; fall migrants extend in date from 18 September 1991 (Point Loma, D. and M. Hastings, AB 46:148, 1992) to at least 17 November (1999, Point Loma, J. R. Sams, NAB 54:104, 2000). Some records in December may have been of late fall migrants as well.

The three spring records are all inland: Palomar Mountain 2 April 1969 (AFN 23:625, 1969), Pine Valley Creek 2 miles north of Noble Canyon (O21) 26 April 1995 (K. F. Campbell), and Scissors Crossing (J22) 20 April 2003 (J. R. Barth).

Winter: Of San Diego County's eight December–March records of the Broad-winged Hawk, only one is since 1981, at Point Loma 28–29 December 1991 (R. E. Webster, AB 46:314, 1992). Unitt (1984) listed earlier records. McCaskie (1968a) collected the only specimen, the first Broad-winged Hawk reported from California, in the

Photo by Anthony Mercieca

Tijuana River valley 11 December 1966 (SDNHM 36086).

Conservation: The Broad-winged Hawk was more frequent in San Diego County in the late 1970s and 1980s: the seven reported in 1977 and 1980 have not been equaled since. In the 1980s, Guy McCaskie (pers. comm.) expected to see a Broad-winged if he watched migrating hawks at Cabrillo National Monument between 11:00 AM and 1:00 PM during the species' peak season. But his similar effort there at the beginning of the 21st century returned an average of less than one individual per year.

Taxonomy: Broad-winged Hawks in North America are all nominate *B. p. platypterus* (Vieillot, 1823); other subspecies are confined to the West Indies.

Swainson's Hawk *Buteo swainsoni*

Swainson's Hawk performs one of the most spectacular of all bird migrations: on its voyages between western North America and Argentina, almost the entire population gathers into huge flocks as it funnels through Central America. Unfortunately, the hawk has been afflicted by contraction of its breeding range in North America and mass death by poisoning with pesticides in South America. Although a fairly common breeding bird in San Diego County early in the 20th century, Swainson's Hawk no longer nests anywhere in southern California and has been designated threatened by the California Department of Fish and Game. Over most of San Diego County, Swainson's Hawk is now a rare migrant, but the Borrego Valley is an important staging site in spring.

Breeding distribution: Sharp (1902) considered Swainson's the commonest nesting hawk in the valleys of San Diego County's coastal lowland. The birds nested at the edges of riparian woodland and foraged in nearby grassland. Only one specimen, from Campo (U23) 15 July 1877 (SDNHM 337), suggests breeding above 1000 feet elevation.

The first summer sighting of Swainson's Hawk in San Diego County since 1933 was one of the least expected discoveries generated by the atlas study. Eight molting subadults were in Warner Valley just north of Lake Henshaw (F17) 17 June 2000 (K. J. Winter, S. E. Smith), and these had increased to 25 one week later, 24–25 June (G. Rebstock, J. R. Barth, J. E. Pike, NAB 54:423, 2000). The birds were drawn to the vast swarms of grasshoppers then overrunning the valley. There was no previous record of Swainson's Hawks in flocks in southern California in summer.

Nesting: In San Diego County, Swainson's Hawks built their nests at heights of 35 to 75 feet in cottonwoods or sycamores (Sharp 1902). These two trees account for all but one of the 33 egg sets collected from San Diego County 1900–33. They attest to the hawk's attachment in southern California to riparian woodland, an attachment maintained by the remnant population in the Central Valley (Schlorff and Bloom 1983). The egg sets range in date from 12 April to 16 May; Sharp (1907) reported eggs near Escondido as late as 1 June.

Migration: Spring dates for Swainson's Hawk in San Diego County range from 31 January (1999, one at Lakeside, P14, M. B. Stowe, NAB 53:208, 1999) and 15 February (1996, one near Leucadia, K6, K. and C. Radamaker, NASFN 50:222, 1996) to 15 May (1977, one in the Borrego Valley, E. Copper) and 28 May (1999, one at Lake Cuyamaca, M20, A. P. and T. E. Keenan), with most from mid March to late April. Over most of the county the birds are seen singly, sometimes in small flocks. The Borrego Valley is on a migration corridor, the birds stopping to roost in strips of tamarisk trees and at nurseries (F25). In 2003 and especially 2004, Hal Cohen and Paul Jorgensen

Photo by Anthony Mercieca

organized daily (2004) or nearly daily (2003) monitoring. The watch yielded 2055 Swainson's Hawks between 27 February and 26 April in 2003 and 5210 between 22 February and 24 April in 2004. In 2004 the largest single concentration was of 1000–1500 arriving on the evening of 25 March. The birds feed on flying ants or dragonflies and on the caterpillars of the white-lined sphinx moth. When thermal air currents arise in mid morning, most of the hawks head northwest through Coyote Creek canyon. A few follow other routes such as San Felipe Valley, exemplified most notably by 74 near Scissors Crossing (J22) 18 March 1999 (ABDSP database).

In fall Swainson's Hawk is less frequent than in spring, but the birds still make some use of the route across the Anza–Borrego Desert. This was illustrated most dramatically on 20 October 1999, when a flock of at least 140 roosted at Ocotillo Wells (I29; P. D. Jorgensen), perhaps the same as 130 that arrived 35 miles to the southeast near El Centro, Imperial Co., four days later (K. Z. Kurland; NAB 54:104, 2000). The only other flocks reported in San Diego County in fall were 50–60 at Warner Springs (F19) 29 October 1988 (D. MacKenzie, AB 43:167, 1989) and 78 at Borrego Springs 21 October 2001 (P. D. Jorgensen). Fall dates range from 9 September (1975, Point Loma, S7, AB 30:126, 1976) to 1 November (1986, Wilderness Gardens, D13, C. G. Edwards, AB 41:143, 1987).

Winter: For many years, Swainson's Hawk was accidental in the United States in winter (Browning 1974). Since 1990, small numbers have begun wintering in the Sacramento–San Joaquin delta (Herzog 1996), and a few wintering birds have been noted elsewhere in California. In San Diego County the only winter records are of one at Whelan Lake (G6) 27 December 1986–8 March 1987 (G. McCaskie, AB 41:328, 1987), one in the Tijuana River valley 2 December 1995 (P. A. Ginsburg, NASFN 50:114, 1996), and one in Murphy Canyon (Q10) 19 December 2000 (M. A. Patten, NAB 55:227, 2001). The last two may have been delayed fall migrants.

Conservation: Swainson's Hawk was in decline by the 1930s, when E. E. Sechrist reported to Willett (1933) that it was "now scarce near San Diego." The last eggs collected in the county are dated 1933 as well. The factors extirpating Swainson's Hawk as a breeding bird from southern California are unclear, but shooting, elimination of riparian woodland, urban development, rodenticides, and other pesticides may all have contributed. Urbanization and changes in crops threaten the remaining population in the Central Valley, estimated at about 430 pairs in 1988 (California Department of Fish and Game 1993). Given that this is the only population remaining west of the Sierra Nevada, the numbers seen in the Anza–Borrego Desert suggest that most or all of California's Swainson's Hawks migrate across San Diego County.

After a low point from the mid 1960s to mid 1980s, numbers of Swainson's Hawk migrating through southern California have increased somewhat (Patten et al. 2003). An increase seems counterintuitive, given recent huge mortality in Argentina (Woodbridge et al. 1995). It may be related to a northward shift of the winter range to Mexico and Central America enabled by deforestation. Such a shift could account for more frequent wintering and arrival in February, another recent change. Sharp (1902) specified that Swainson's Hawk arrived in San Diego County 10–20 March.

Zone-tailed Hawk *Buteo albonotatus*

San Diego County lies at the northwest corner of the Zone-tailed Hawk's primarily Mexican range. At the beginning of the 21st century four or five were being seen in the county each year. A pair on Hot Springs Mountain from 1986 to 1992 was one of only two pairs ever known to have nested in California. Though sightings of the Zone-tailed Hawk are more frequent in winter than in summer, continued scattered individuals in San Diego County's mountains suggest that further nestings are likely. An apparent mimic of the Turkey Vulture, the Zone-tailed Hawk associates regularly with vulture roosts.

Photo by Anthony Mercieca

Winter: At least 30 Zone-tailed Hawks have been noted in San Diego County in fall and winter, mainly in the inland valleys of the coastal lowland. Several birds have apparently returned in successive years to the same area. During the atlas period one or two wintered regularly at the Wild Animal Park (J12), evidently attracted by the Turkey Vulture roost, and at nearby Oak Hill Cemetery,

Escondido (I12), where the gardener put out the gophers he trapped for the hawks. Other areas where Zone-tailed Hawks have wintered repeatedly are the San Luis Rey River valley from Oceanside to Vista and Bonsall (G6/G7/G8/F8; 1979–97) and Santee Lakes (O12/P12; 1991–96). Only five or six have been seen in winter at elevations above 2000 feet, but one was near the summit of Palomar Mountain (D15) 26 February–7 March 1983 (R. Higson, Roberson 1993).

Migration: All but one of the low-elevation sightings of the Zone-tailed Hawk fall within the interval 19 August (2001, Wild Animal Park, M. Billings) to 16 April (1998, same location, Rottenborn and Morlan 2000). The exception was a bird that wintered repeatedly, seen also 9–27 June 1984 at the Bonsall bridge over the San Luis Rey River (F8; C. Wilson, Roberson 1993).

The summering birds on Hot Springs Mountain (E20) were reported from 5 May (1991) to 10 August (1986).

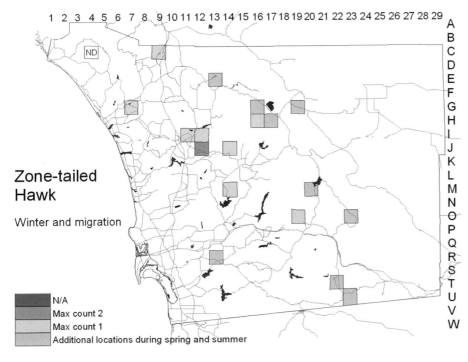

Zone-tailed Hawk

Winter and migration

■ N/A
■ Max count 2
□ Max count 1
□ Additional locations during spring and summer

Breeding distribution: A pair of Zone-tailed Hawks nested in a steep west-draining canyon of Hot Springs Mountain in 1986, 1987, and 1988, fledging one young at least in 1986 (R. Higson; AB 40:1255, 1986; 41:143, 1987; Langham 1991). The pair was seen annually through 1992, with only a single individual noted in 1993 and none subsequently. The only other nestings known in California, all unsuccessful, were by a single pair on the north slope of the Santa Rosa Mountains of Riverside County 1979–81 (Weathers 1983), about 8 miles north of San Diego County.

Other spring and summer sightings in San Diego County are from Nate Harrison Grade, southwest slope of Palomar Mountain (E13), 17 April 1999 (C. Sankpill), near Angel Mountain (G16) March 1999 (D. Bittner) and 31 May 1999 (W. E. Haas), 1.5 miles east-southeast of Angel Mountain (H17) 13 June 1998 (P. Unitt, Erickson and Hamilton 2001), near Warner's Ranch (G19) 24 June 2000 (E. C. Hall, NAB 54:423, 2000), at Mount Laguna (O23) 22 July 2000 (D. W. Aguillard, NAB 54:423, 2000),

1.25 miles northwest of Cameron Corners (T22) 7 May 2000 (R. and S. L. Breisch), and one at Campo (U23) 27 May 2001 (D. S. and A. W. Hester, NAB 55:356, 2001).

Nesting: Both California nests of the Zone-tailed Hawk have been in tall conifers on steep slopes: in a sugar pine in the Santa Rosa Mountains (Weathers 1983), in a conifer of unrecorded species on Hot Springs Mountain. In 1986 the young fledged in July.

Conservation: From 1862 to 1972 only six Zone-tailed Hawks were reported from San Diego County. Since 1973 the hawk has become ever more frequent, prompting the California Bird Records Committee to drop the species from its review list in 1998. The nestings in southern California are part of the evidence for a slight northward spread of the species' range (Johnson 1994). But urbanization and desiccation of riparian woodland have eliminated the species from other former habitat in Arizona and Texas (Johnson et al. 2000).

Red-tailed Hawk *Buteo jamaicensis*

The Red-tailed Hawk is not only San Diego County's most widespread bird of prey, it is one of the most widespread of all the county's birds. During the atlas study we found it in 472 of 478 covered atlas squares. It favors grassland with scattered trees that serve as lookout perches and nest sites but uses all of the county's terrestrial habitats to some extent. It tolerates considerable urbanization. From the hawk's point of view the additional nest sites afforded by eucalyptus trees and towers for electric lines have offset the reduction of foraging grounds.

Breeding distribution: Though the Red-tailed Hawk nests in all regions of San Diego County, the breeding population is concentrated in areas of extensive grassland like Camp Pendleton, Warner Valley, and the Santa Maria Valley around Ramona. Atlas observers noted up to three active nests per square, as along 1 mile of the San Diego River above El Capitan Reservoir (M17) in March and April 1999 (R. C. Sanger) and along 3 miles of Dulzura Creek northwest of Dulzura (T16) on 23 February 1998 (D. W. Povey). The Wildlife Research Institute (2004) reported 26 pairs in and around the roughly 5000 acres of grassland in Santa Maria Valley, a density of over three pairs per square mile. The total county population may be on the order of 1000 pairs.

In the Anza–Borrego Desert the Red-tailed Hawk is considerably sparser than on the coastal slope, but we found active nests in some of the most remote and dry desert wildernesses, as in Wonderstone Wash (D29) 29 March 2001 (R. Thériault) and in the north fork of Fish Creek Wash (L28) 13 April 1999 and 6 May 2001 (L. J. Hargrove, D. C. Seals). The Anza–Borrego Desert probably supports around 25 to 30 pairs after wet years, fewer after dry ones.

Photo by Anthony Mercieca

Nesting: The Red-tailed Hawk tends to build its nest in more exposed situations than other local hawks, though it participates with other hawks, the Common Raven, and the Great Horned Owl in the musical-chair reuse of each other's nests. Of 55 nests that atlas observers described, 10 were in sycamores, 4 were in coast live oaks, 19 were in eucalyptus, and 3 were in other species of trees. Seven, mainly in the Anza–Borrego Desert, were on bluffs or cliffs. Ten were on power-line towers, one was on a wooden telephone pole, and one was on a platform for floodlights for the ball field at Mount Carmel High School (M10).

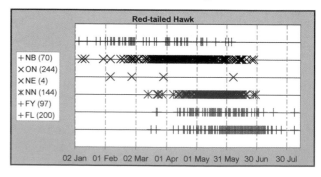

Red-tailed Hawks may begin refurbishing their nests in December and lay eggs mainly from late February to mid April. The earliest date among 160 egg sets collected 1890–1964 is 22 February. From 1997 to 2001, and especially in 1998 and 1999, however, about 20 observations suggested laying from early January to mid February. The date of our latest nest with nestlings, 29 June 1998, suggests laying about 30 April. Sharp (1907) reported eggs at Escondido as late as 4 May, and J. B. Dixon collected a set there as late as 3 June in 1926, following a wet winter (WFVZ 10082). The Red-tailed Hawk's breeding season tends to begin earlier and last longer after wet winters, like 1997–98,

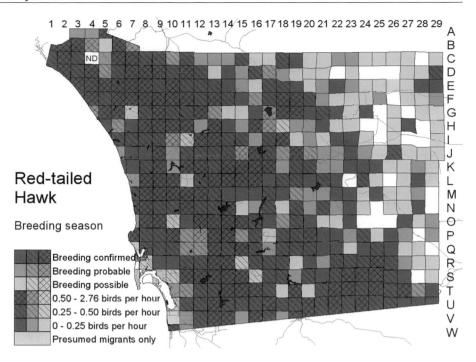

Red-tailed Hawk

Breeding season

- Breeding confirmed
- Breeding probable
- Breeding possible
- 0.50 - 2.76 birds per hour
- 0.25 - 0.50 birds per hour
- 0 - 0.25 birds per hour
- Presumed migrants only

and the following year, when the abundance of prey is still high.

Migration: On the basis of monthly censuses 1973–83 at San Elijo Lagoon (L7), King et al. (1987) found numbers of Red-tailed Hawks to be at their low from May to September, at their high (about 3 times larger) from December to February.

Winter: The Red-tailed Hawk is only slightly more common as a winter visitor than as a breeding species; from December to February counts per day per atlas square ranged up to 23 (between Santee and Lakeside, P13, 8 January 2000, D. C. Seals) but from March to July the maximum was only to 13. In winter it spreads to areas where it does not nest such as the Silver Strand (T9; up to six on 16 December 2000, P. R. Pryde). It is most numerous in the coastal lowland and scarcest in the Anza–Borrego Desert. We missed it in winter in only 15 atlas squares: one completely urbanized (Ocean Beach, R7), 14 in the desert.

Conservation: The Red-tailed Hawk uses any open area for foraging, however disturbed, giving the species great flexibility. Even though it has little use for heavily developed areas, it takes advantage of even small scraps of undeveloped habitat. It acclimatizes to human activity near nests, allowing it to breed in places like Switzer Canyon at the east edge of Balboa Park

(R10). From at least 1997 to 2000 a pair nested in this canyon surrounded by urbanization on three sides for nearly a century (J. M. Wells, J. A. Dietrick). The majority of the hawk's nests are now in eucalyptus trees and on power towers and other man-made structures, suggesting that the supply of nest sites limited the population, at least in the coastal lowland, before people introduced these features into the environment. Even with explosive growth of the human population, the Red-tailed Hawk population is still remarkably stable.

Taxonomy: Red-tailed Hawks breeding in San Diego County, and nearly all winter visitors, are the widespread subspecies of western North America, *B. j. calurus* Cassin,

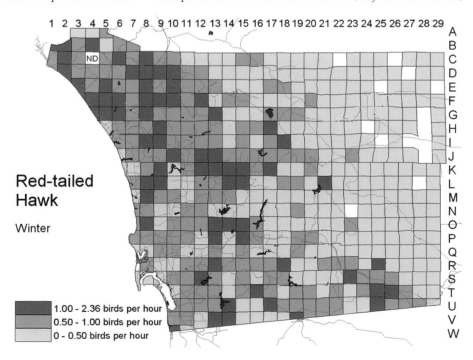

Red-tailed Hawk

Winter

- 1.00 - 2.36 birds per hour
- 0.50 - 1.00 birds per hour
- 0 - 0.50 birds per hour

1856. In *calurus* the light-morph adult has rufous-barred thighs and a rather distinct band of streaking on the lower breast and upper belly. Two specimens match the whiter subspecies *B. c. fuertesi* Sutton and van Tyne, 1935, and so are apparently dispersers from northern mainland Mexico or the southern Great Plains. One of these was at Ocean Beach (R7) 24 January 1921 (SDNHM 2235),

the other in Pringle Canyon (T16) 10 February 1935 (SDNHM 17074). There is one sight record of Harlan's Hawk, *B. c. harlani* (Audubon, 1830), the melanistic subspecies with a mottled grayish tail that breeds mainly in Alaska and winters mainly in the southern Great Plains: near Lower Otay Lake (U13/U14) 14 January 1992 (J. C. Lovio, AB 46:315, 1992).

Ferruginous Hawk *Buteo regalis*

Open plains are home to the Ferruginous Hawk, an uncommon winter visitor to San Diego County. About 100 individuals reach the county annually. Conservation of the county's most extensive grasslands is essential to maintenance of these numbers.

Winter: The Ferruginous Hawk's patchy distribution in San Diego County corresponds largely to the larger tracts of grassland, especially those more than 12 miles inland. Our highest counts 1997–2002 were from such areas: nine in the east arm of Warner Valley (G19) 15 March 1998 (P. D. Jorgensen), eight in the upper basin of Lake Cuyamaca (L21) 25 December 2001 (L. and M. Polinsky), and eight just southwest of Ramona (L14) 17 January 1999 (F. Sproul). The largest numbers of Ferruginous Hawks in San Diego County have been found on Lake Henshaw Christmas bird counts, with up to 34 on 19 December 1988. The years of high counts correspond with discoveries of Ferruginous Hawks roosting communally in trees and on telephone poles at Warner Springs (F19), up to 13 in a cluster (King et al. 1988).

Within 12 miles of the coast our only count of more than two individuals was of four in the Fallbrook Naval Weapons Station (D7) 28 February 2002 (K. L. Weaver). The maximum recorded on any of San Diego County's three coastal Christmas bird counts is four as well.

Photo by Anthony Mercieca

The Ferruginous Hawk also occurs fairly regularly in the Borrego Valley, where our highest counts per atlas square per day were of two individuals. The species was recorded on 15 of 19 Anza–Borrego Christmas bird counts 1984–2002, with an average of 1.5. One or two individuals are seen regularly in Earthquake Valley (J23/K23) but the species is rare in other desert valleys like Clark, Culp, Blair, and Vallecito.

Migration: The Ferruginous Hawk occurs in San Diego County mainly from October to March; extreme dates are 14 September (1962, San Diego area, AFN 17:68, 1963) and 17 September (year not specified, Lake Cuyamaca, J. G. Peterson in Grinnell and Miller 1944) in fall and 21 April (year not specified, Lake Cuyamaca, J. G. Peterson in Grinnell and Miller 1944) and 25 April (1997, between Carlsbad and San Marcos, J8, J. O. Zimmer) in spring.

Conservation: The Ferruginous Hawk has lost some habitat to urbanization, as at Rancho Otay (U12/U13). Conservation of the threatened Ramona grasslands in Santa Maria Valley is

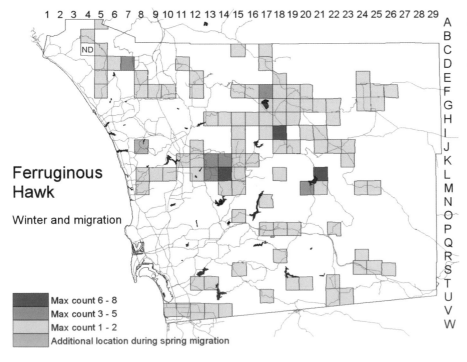

Ferruginous Hawk

Winter and migration

■ Max count 6 - 8
■ Max count 3 - 5
▨ Max count 1 - 2
□ Additional location during spring migration

critical to sustaining the hawk's numbers in San Diego County. Overgrazing could also degrade the Ferruginous Hawk's foraging habitat by reducing the supply of prey. Indiscriminate use of rodenticides could reduce the hawk's food supply as well. It appears from Lake Henshaw

Christmas bird count results that the numbers in Warner Valley were greater from 1983 to 1989 (average 28) than from 1997 to 2002 (average 8). Bad weather and no searches for communal roosts during the more recent interval, however, may account for some of the difference.

Rough-legged Hawk *Buteo lagopus*

Breeding on arctic tundra, the Rough-legged Hawk reaches the southern edge of its winter range in San Diego County. The only well-supported record for Baja California is of one soaring over the border fence in the Tijuana River valley (Erickson et al. 2001). The Rough-legged seeks the same open grasslands as the Ferruginous Hawk. Though the Rough-legged's abundance in California as a whole varies in a cycle of 3 to 5 years (Garrison 1993), the cycle is ill marked in San Diego County, where the average since the mid 1990s has been less than one per year.

Winter: Records of the Rough-legged Hawk are widely scattered over San Diego County's coastal slope as well as the Borrego and San Felipe valleys on the desert side. They are concentrated, however, in Warner Valley. This region, the county's largest block of grassland, is the only site of reports of more than two individuals: three on 21 March 1976 (AB 30:765, 1976) and five on the Lake Henshaw Christmas bird count 23 December 1985, with three remaining to 1 February 1986. But the three seen during the atlas period 1997–2002 were from other locations: Dameron Valley (C15) 6 February 1999 (K. L. Weaver), San Dieguito Valley (M8) 27 February 1999 (R. T. Patton), and Galleta Meadows (E23) 18 January 2001 (P. D. Jorgensen).

Ascertaining the Rough-legged Hawk's status in San Diego County has been bedeviled by misidentification since Huey (1924) misreported two specimens of the Ferruginous as the Rough-legged. The species' occurrence in the county is confirmed by photos of a bird at Lake Cuyamaca (M20) 2 December 1994 (M.B. Stowe).

Migration: Dates for the Rough-legged Hawk in San Diego County extend from 8 October (1985, one at Lake Henshaw, R. Higson) to 27 March (1982, one at Lake

Photo by Jack C. Daynes

Henshaw, R. E. Webster, AB 36: 894, 1982) and 28 March (1976, two at Lake Henshaw, AB 30:765, 1976). One at Point Loma (S7) 20 November 1984 was likely the same as one at Silver Strand State Beach (T9) four days later and a migrant heading south (D. M. Parker, E. Copper, AB 40:158, 1986). Garrison and Bloom (1993) found that of five Rough-legged Hawks banded in the breeding range and recovered in California, four originated in Alaska, one in arctic Canada.

Conservation: From the early 1990s through 2002 the Rough-legged Hawk was less frequent in San Diego County than in the 1970s and 1980s. Climatic warming could allow the winter range to shift northward so that the hawk no longer reaches its current southern limits.

Taxonomy: The single New World subspecies of the circumpolar Rough-legged Hawk is *B. l. sanctijohannis* (Gmelin, 1788).

Golden Eagle *Aquila chrysaetos*

As a top predator, the Golden Eagle has the largest territory and the lowest population density of any San Diego County bird. Pairs remain in their territories year round, though the young disperse widely. Most pairs nest on cliff ledges, the rest in trees on steep slopes, hunting in nearby grassland, sage scrub, or broken chaparral. San Diego County's Golden Eagle population has dropped from an estimated 108 pairs at the beginning of the 20th century to about 53 pairs at the century's end, mainly as a result of urban development of foraging habitat. Many of the territories persisting at the beginning

Photo by Anthony Mercieca

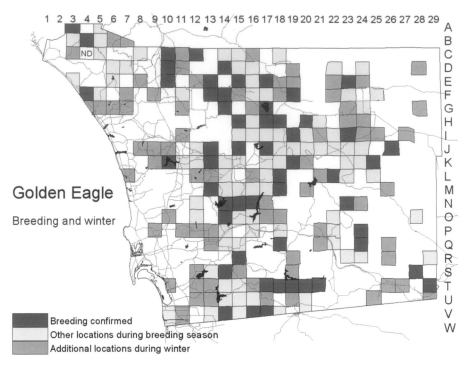

Golden Eagle

Breeding and winter

Breeding confirmed
Other locations during breeding season
Additional locations during winter

checked some inaccessible nest sites via helicopter. This account is based largely on data kindly provided by Bittner.

From 1997 to 2001, about 50–55 pairs nested in the county. Fewer than 20 pairs fledged young each year, averaging 1.5 young per successful nest. Only four of these territories lie west of Interstate 15: three in Camp Pendleton, one around Lake Hodges (K10). Most of the remaining pairs nest within a band 20 to 25 miles wide through the foothills. In southern San Diego County, San Miguel Mountain (S13/S14) and Otay Mountain (U15/V14/V15) mark the western limit of the current breeding range.

In and along the edges of the Anza–Borrego Desert there are 10 known nest sites or clusters of nest sites, though some of these went unused during the entire atlas study, even following the wet winter of 1997–98. Only seven of these territories were active during the atlas period 1997–2001, and at most three were active in any given year. In some nests (D27, L28) new material was added but no eggs were laid; these squares are shown as occupied only before 1997. Since 1998, drought has suppressed numbers of the eagle's principal prey in the Anza–Borrego Desert, the black-tailed jackrabbit. Only two young eagles fledged in the Anza–Borrego Desert in 2003 (D. Bittner).

The Golden Eagle is absent from some surprisingly large yet little disturbed areas of San Diego County, such as Cuyamaca Mountains and the Campo Plateau between Lake Morena and Jacumba.

The map of the species' breeding distribution somewhat overrepresents its abundance. A few pairs straddle two atlas squares. Nesting in three squares (F19, M13, R15) has ceased since 1997.

of the 21st century lie near the edge of the urban growth front, a shadow over the future of the capstone of San Diego County's ecosystem.

Breeding distribution: The Golden Eagle's distribution in San Diego County is known better through history than that of any other bird, thanks to study by generations of San Diegans: James B. Dixon, John Colton, John Oakley, Thomas A. Scott, David Bittner, and their collaborators through the Wildlife Research Institute. Since 1988, Bittner and Oakley have organized a team of observers to monitor the county's nesting eagles annually and have

Nesting: Scott (1985) found about 80% of San Diego County's Golden Eagle nests built on cliff ledges, 20% in trees, usually on steep slopes. A pair typically rotates among several nest sites, including both cliff and tree nests. Many of the cliff sites have been in regular use since the early 20th century and undoubtedly long before that. Though

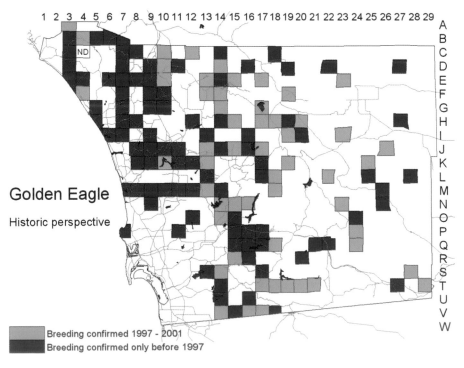

Golden Eagle

Historic perspective

Breeding confirmed 1997 - 2001
Breeding confirmed only before 1997

the giant stick nests are reused for years, the birds refurbish them annually. In San Diego County, fallen yucca leaves, with their tough fibers, are a common ingredient in the nest's lining (Dixon 1937, D. Bittner).

The Golden Eagle's schedule of nesting in San Diego County is also supported by abundant data. Nest building begins with the first heavy rain of fall (Dixon 1937). Copulation begins as early as 5 January (D. Bittner). Dates of 407 egg sets collected or observed from 1891 to 1957 range from 2 February to 26 April, except for one on 7 May and another on 16 June. The mean date is 4 March, standard deviation 17 days. Eggs laid after the first week of March, however, are probably replacement clutches (Dixon 1937). During his recent surveys, Bittner has found most eggs laid in mid February, most chicks hatching in late March or early April, and most young fledging in June. Occasionally, however, he encounters nestlings on dates suggesting they hatched from eggs laid in mid January (e.g., chicks five weeks old on 15 April 2004).

Migration: Once a Golden Eagle acquires a mate and a territory, it remains with them year round, except for occasional swapping (Kochert et al. 2002). Young birds, however, may disperse considerable distances: birds banded in San Diego County have been recovered in Ojai, Ventura County, in Apple Valley, San Bernardino County, in Utah, in the Grand Canyon, Arizona, and near Guadalajara in central Mexico (T. A. Scott, D. Bittner).

Winter: In spite of the mobility of immatures and nonterritorial adults, the nonbreeding distribution of the Golden Eagle in San Diego County does not differ greatly from the breeding distribution. In southern San Diego County a few birds often spread west to the Otay and Tijuana River valleys, accounting for the near regularity of the eagle on the San Diego Christmas bird count (noted on 16 of 20 counts 1983–2002). One on the fill north of the Sweetwater River mouth, National City (T10), 15 December 2001 (S. M. Wolf) was our only sighting during the atlas period of a Golden Eagle that must have flown several miles over developed areas. The count circles other than San Diego include at least one nesting territory. Our maximum winter count per atlas square per day was three, all within a few miles of nest sites.

Conservation: Following studies by Dixon (1937) and Scott (1985), David Bittner and John Oakley (pers. comm.) estimate the Golden Eagle population of San Diego County in 1900 at 108 pairs. It remained near 100 pairs until the rapid growth of the county's human popu-

lation following World War II. In the 1970s, following the building of the interstate highways and the spread of avocado and citrus orchards along Interstate 15, the decline became precipitous. By 2004, the population had dropped to about 53 pairs, with some uncertainty because of a few territories straddling the county line and long vacancy of some territories in the Anza–Borrego Desert. Since 1988, the surveys organized by the Wildlife Research Institute have located about 15 previously unknown pairs in remote parts of the county, accounting for the variation from the estimate of 40–50 pairs reported by Unitt (1984) on the basis of studies by T. A. Scott (pers. comm.).

The eagles abandoned four territories just within the five-year atlas period, and the Wildlife Research Institute estimates that nine more are in imminent danger of abandonment. Without better planning for habitat conservation, the institute estimates the county's eagle population could be halved again by 2030.

The most important factor in this decrease has been urban sprawl covering former foraging habitat. From 1900 to 1936, when eagle territories still filled northwestern San Diego County, Dixon (1937) found the territories of 27 pairs in that region to range from 19 to 48 square miles and average 36 square miles. Thus the area needed to support the species is considerably greater than for any other San Diego County bird. The viability of territories that become isolated from the main block of the species' range is also questionable. Of the 27 territories mapped by Dixon (1937), only nine were occupied at the beginning of the 21st century.

Other factors affecting the eagle are human disturbance, especially rock climbing on nesting cliffs, but also shooting (both recreational and for military training on Camp Pendleton), and agriculture (avocado orchards planted near nest sites). Electrocution on power lines is now the biggest source of mortality: 37 of 55 dead eagles picked up in and near San Diego County 1988–2003 and reported to Bittner had been electrocuted. The Golden Eagle was less subject to poisoning by insecticides like DDT than other birds of prey but has suffered poisoning by scavenging prey killed by rodenticides. Three of the 55 dead birds recovered had been killed through such secondary poisoning. Ever more prolonged droughts could depress the population further, a factor Hoffman and Smith (2003) suggested as affecting raptors throughout the western United States.

Taxonomy: *Aquila c. canadensis* (Linnaeus, 1758) is the only subspecies of the Golden Eagle in North America.

FALCONS — FAMILY FALCONIDAE

American Kestrel *Falco sparverius*

Ideal habitat for the American Kestrel is a grove of tall sycamore or oak trees, which offer cavities for nests, adjacent to grassland or open ground, where the birds can forage. In the Anza–Borrego Desert a few kestrels nest in niches in eroded bluffs. The kestrel has also become a fairly successful urban adapter by nesting among the leaf bases of palms. It is a year-round resident in San Diego County but more numerous in winter, with the arrival of migrants from the north.

Breeding distribution: The American Kestrel is widespread in San Diego County but most numerous in valley floors and broad canyons on the coastal slope. Our counts during the breeding season ranged up to 13 (including fledglings) near Rincon (F13) 12 June 1999 (S. L. Breisch, J. M. Hargrove), but generally the kestrel must be rated uncommon as a breeding bird in San Diego County, as only slightly over 1% of our daily totals in spring or summer were of over six individuals. In regions of extensive unbroken chaparral and at higher elevations the kestrel is sparse or lacking. Nevertheless, it nests at least as high as 4500 feet on Palomar Mountain (D14; active nest on 24 June 1997, P. D. Jorgensen) and in the Laguna Mountains (N22; fledgling on 7 July 2001, G. L. Rogers), probably as high as 5500 feet around Laguna Meadow (O23; pair and probable nest 21 June 1997, A. E. Klovstad, C. L. Mann). The kestrel is absent from much of the Anza–Borrego Desert but breeds in small numbers at oases like Lower Willows (D23), Butterfield Ranch (M23), and Vallecito (M25), in developed areas, and in the Borrego and Carrizo badlands.

Photo by Anthony Mercieca

Nesting: Over most of the kestrel's range it nests in tree cavities, either excavated by woodpeckers or resulting from decay. Such sites are common in San Diego County as well. But where fan palms or the Canary Island date palm have been planted, kestrels nest in the crevices

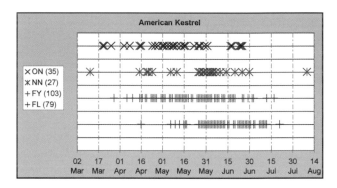

among the leaf bases or under the skirts of dead leaves. Atlas observers described nests in palms more frequently than any other type of site. Other man-made sites we observed were the hollow arms of power poles, the aircraft-warning spheres hung on power lines, an abandoned building, and the eaves of the headquarters building for the Ocotillo Wells state off-road vehicle area (I28; nestlings on 24 April 1997, J. Rudley). Kestrels commonly use nest boxes if good hunting habitat is nearby (J. L. Lincer). We did not see the actual nests, but evidently the kestrel also uses crevices in bluffs in desert badlands. Such sites were especially likely near

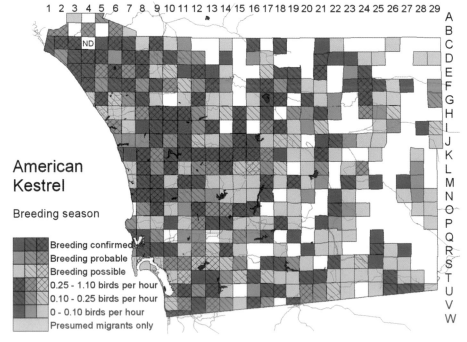

American Kestrel

Breeding season

- Breeding confirmed
- Breeding probable
- Breeding possible
- 0.25 - 1.10 birds per hour
- 0.10 - 0.25 birds per hour
- 0 - 0.10 birds per hour
- Presumed migrants only

Font's Point (F27; male carry-ing prey toward cliffs 1 May 1999, G. Rebstock, K. Forney) and between June Wash and Arroyo Tapiado (M27; male carrying lizard 26 April 2000, R. Thériault). One egg set col-lected at La Jolla (P7) in 1935 was from a hole in a sandstone bluff, and another from an unspecified location was from a granite cliff.

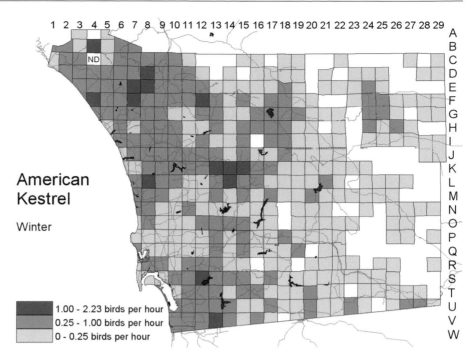

American Kestrel

Winter

1.00 - 2.23 birds per hour
0.25 - 1.00 birds per hour
0 - 0.25 birds per hour

Dates of kestrel eggs collect-ed in San Diego County 1894–1952 range from 21 March to 30 May, and the great majority of our observations 1997–2001 conform with this interval. A few, however, are earlier. Fledged young northwest of Santa Ysabel (I18) 16 April 2000 (S. E. Smith) imply egg laying as early as mid February; a nest with four nestlings in Los Peñasquitos Canyon (N8) 11 March 2000 (L. D. and R. Johnson) implies egg laying as early as late January or early February. Another nest with nestlings just a short distance up the same canyon (N9) 9 August 1999 (A. G. and D. Stanton) implies laying as late as mid June. This pattern prevails among many raptors (Wildlife Research Institute 2004).

Migration: Though there is a winter influx of kestrels into San Diego County, the only concentration of migrants noted is of 17 in Blair Valley and 5 in nearby Little Blair Valley (L24) 9 April 1999 (R. Thériault).

Winter: The kestrel is even more widespread in winter (recorded in 396 atlas squares) than in the breeding season (recorded in 366 atlas squares). The pattern of winter distribution is similar, but the birds are even more concentrated in grassland. Our highest rate of encounter with the species was in the Santa Maria Valley on the northwest side of Ramona (K14). The factor affecting the variation in the number of kestrels from winter to winter is most likely the supply of prey as determined by rainfall. We found the species at the same relatively high rate in the wet winter of 1997–98 as well as the following year. Then in dry 2000–01 and 2001–02 the rate dropped to

54–62% what it had been at the beginning of the five-year atlas period.

Conservation: Christmas bird counts and historical literature from San Diego County suggest the kestrel population has been fairly stable through time, though the Breeding Bird Survey suggests a trend of decline over California as a whole (Sauer et al. 2003). The species has gained foraging habitat through the clearing of chaparral but lost it through the paving and landscaping of open ground. The changes humanity has made to the environ-ment have meant a net increase in nest sites, which can be limiting to a secondary cavity user like the kestrel that is large in comparison to most of the primary cavity excava-tors, the woodpeckers.

Taxonomy: Almost all specimens of the American Kestrel from San Diego County, including 16 recent specimens of the local breeding population taken for predator control at Least Tern colonies, are the relatively large *F. s. sparverius* Linnaeus, 1758, widespread across North America. Just one specimen from San Diego 6 November 1921 (SDNHM 2288) is small enough to represent a wanderer of the smaller *F. s. peninsularis* Mearns, 1892 (Unitt 1984).

Merlin *Falco columbarius*

The Merlin is a rare winter visitor to San Diego County, seen most often in grassland, though it occurs occasionally in any habitat except dense woodland. Because it feeds largely on small birds, the Merlin may be attracted to any place where small birds flock, including mudflats and cattle pens. In the 1990s the number of Merlins wintering in San Diego County increased noticeably.

Winter: Wintering Merlins occur in all regions of San Diego County, though they are more frequent in the coastal lowland and less frequent in the Anza–Borrego Desert. The variation in their abundance from year to year is only moderate: the number per observer-hour each winter from 1997 to 2002 varied by up to 25% from the mean for the whole five years. Normally the species is seen singly; our maximum count per atlas square per day was three, southwest of Ramona (L14) 17 January 1999 (F. Sproul) and in the north Borrego Valley (E24)

20 December 1998 (P. R. Pryde). On San Diego County Christmas bird counts the maximum is nine on the San Diego count 19 December 1998, though some of these counts still occasionally miss the species. As an order-of-magnitude estimate of the number of Merlins wintering in the county annually I suggest 100 (more pass through in migration).

Migration: The Merlin occurs in San Diego County mainly from October to March. Extreme dates are 23 August (1980, Tijuana River valley, AB 35:226, 1981) and 26 April (1998; San Elijo Lagoon, L7, C. G. Edwards; Otay Mesa, V14, S. D. Cameron; 2001, Point Loma, S7, P. A. Ginsburg).

From mid September to late October a few Merlins can be seen moving south along Point Loma every year. Unlike the hawks of the genus *Buteo*, Merlins do not hesitate when they reach the tip of the point, instead speeding south over the ocean, even when fog prevents them from seeing North Island (G. McCaskie).

Conservation: Early in the 20th century the Merlin was "common" according to Willett (1912), and "rather common" according to Stephens (1919a). By the 1960s, however, it was rare, probably because of the same effects of DDT contamination that affected the larger birds of prey (Lincer 1975). From 1961 to 1980 San Diego Christmas bird counts averaged only 0.55 per year. A trend toward recovery did not become clear until the 1990s. From 1997 to 2002 the average on the San Diego Christmas bird count was 6.3. Similarly, the Escondido count went from an average of 1.3 from 1986 to 1994 to an average of 3.3 from 1997 to 2002.

Taxonomy: All three North American subspecies of the Merlin are known from San Diego County. By far the most frequent is the medium-dark *F. c. columbarius*

Photo by Anthony Mercieca

Linnaeus, 1758, which breeds almost across the continent in boreal forests. All data above apply to it.

The Prairie or Richardson's Merlin, *F. c. richardsoni* Ridgway, 1871, breeds on the northern Great Plains and is strikingly paler than nominate *columbarius*. It is casual as far west as San Diego County, with two sight records (Sweetwater Reservoir, S12, 5 February 1977, J. L. Dunn; Tijuana River valley, V10, 5 November 1977, P. Unitt) and five specimens: San Diego 10 January 1900 (Huey 1926b, SDNHM 360), Witch Creek (J18) 9 February 1904 (FMNH 1904), "about the end of September" 1915 (Grey 1925, SDNHM, mounted), Mission Valley (R9/Q10) 9 April 1925 (Bishop 1905, FMNH 157064), and Eichenlaub Ranch near Barrett Lake (S18) 23 September 2001 (SDNHM 50625).

Perhaps as a result of general population increase, the Black Merlin of the Pacific Northwest, *F. c. suckleyi* Ridgway, 1873, has begun appearing in San Diego County. The first was one at Lake Henshaw (G17) 6 October 1982 (R. E. Webster, AB 37:224, 1983); subsequent sightings have been at Whelan Lake (G6) 22 December 1987 (G. McCaskie, AB 42:321, 1988), Tijuana River valley (V11) 18 October 1991 and 13 December 1999 (G. McCaskie, AB 46:148, 1992, NAB 54:221, 2000), O'Neill Lake (E6) 20 February 2000 (L. J. Hargrove, P. Unitt), and probably in Moosa Canyon (F9) 3 December 1998 ("extremely dark," E. C. Hall). There is also one specimen, from the North Park area of San Diego (R9) 9 March 1997 (SDNHM 49941).

Merlin

Winter and migration

■ 0.10 - 0.15 birds per hour
■ 0.05 - 0.10 birds per hour
□ 0 - 0.05 birds per hour
▨ Additional locations during spring migration

Peregrine Falcon *Falco peregrinus*

The Peregrine Falcon was decimated in the 1950s and 1960s by DDT poisoning, which prevents birds from depositing adequate calcium in their eggshells. San Diego County's small population of about 12 breeding pairs of Peregrines was extirpated. Then, with the ban on DDT in 1972 and an ambitious reintroduction program, the falcon recovered, enabling two of its three North American subspecies to be removed from the federal endangered-species list by 1999. By 2004, five pairs had recolonized San Diego County, nesting at both artificial and natural sites (Wildlife Research Institute 2004). Since the 1980s the number of winter visitors has increased as well, with about 15 to 35 being seen in the county annually by the beginning of the 21st century.

Photo by Anthony Mercieca

Breeding distribution: The reestablishment of the Peregrine Falcon in San Diego began with a captive-bred female, released at Point Loma (S7) in 1986, that mated with a wild male and began nesting annually at the San Diego end of the San Diego Bay bridge (S9) in 1989 (Pavelka 1990). She died at the age of at least 17 in 2000. Another pair nested on a crane along the waterfront of National City (T10) at least from 1995 to 1997 (A. Mercieca). Yet another pair colonized the cliff at the tip of Point Loma, nesting repeatedly, including at least 1997 and 1999; one of the birds from National City shifted to Point Loma in 1997 (A. Mercieca). A fourth pair nested in Ysidora Gorge along the lower Santa Margarita River (G5) in 2000, reoccupying a site used regularly before 1950 (S. Buck). In 2003, a pair nested on a ledge of the U. S. Grant hotel in downtown San Diego (S9; M. Sadowski).

Other nest sites are so far unconfirmed but possible. At Torrey Pines State Reserve (N7/O7), an apparent pair

was calling to each other, one bird in display flight, 23 March 1998 (B. C. Moore), two were regular through the winter of 2000–01 (K. Estey), and one was harassing ravens repeatedly in February 2002 (S. E. Smith). In lower Tecolote Canyon (Q8) 16 April 1998 an apparent pair was in courtship flight, then flew off together toward Mission Bay (E. C. Hall). From 22 to 26 April 1998 an apparent pair along the Chula Vista bayfront (U10) was carrying Mourning Doves toward the salt works (B. C. Moore). An apparent pair was at the California Center for the Arts, Escondido (J12), 19 February 1999 but did not remain later in the breeding season (C. Rideout). Two birds were together around the courthouse in El Cajon (Q13) 5 December 1997–19 January 1998 (A. Mercieca), but only a single individual remained into the spring, staying at least until 30 March 2001 (K. Neal). A pair, including a bird escaped from a falconer, was back at this site in spring 2004 (D. Bittner).

Nesting: The Peregrine Falcon's traditional nest site is on a cliff ledge, sometimes in an old nest of another bird of prey or a raven, more often in just a scrape in debris (White et al. 2002). With recolonization and adaptation to urban living, the falcons have adopted man-made structures like buildings, cranes, and bridges. The nest on the Coronado bridge in 1989 was on a ledge 12 to 14 inches wide, in a scrape in about 1 inch of pigeon feces and dust (Pavelka 1990). Sites recorded with collected eggs in San Diego County include cliffs of granite, clay, and eroded earth overlooking the ocean, as well as old nests of the Golden Eagle and Common Raven. A pair commonly rotates among nest sites on a single cliff, and some sites, including those in San Diego County, have been used for generations.

Dates of San Diego County egg sets, collected 1894–1950 or reported in the literature, range

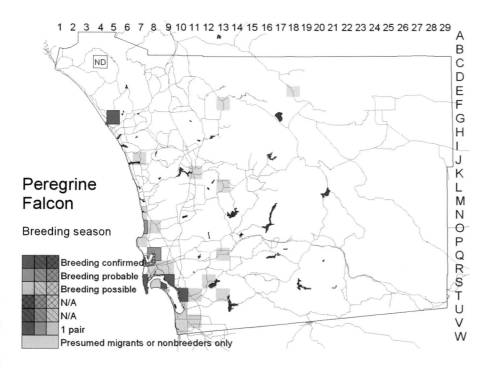

Peregrine Falcon

Breeding season

	Breeding confirmed
	Breeding probable
	Breeding possible
	N/A
	N/A
	1 pair
	Presumed migrants or nonbreeders only

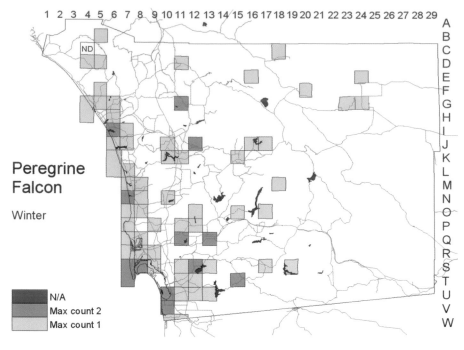

Peregrine
Falcon

Winter

N/A
Max count 2
Max count 1

Conservation: In the early 20th century the Peregrine nested regularly in San Onofre Canyon (C3), at Las Flores (E3), in Ysidora Gorge, near Pala (D10), in Bandy Canyon (K13), at Torrey Pines, and at Point Loma. John Oakley estimates about 12 historic Peregrine territories in San Diego County. No nesting was reported between 1950 and 1989, corresponding to the widespread use of DDT beginning in the 1940s (Fyfe et al. 1987). By 1960 the falcon was nearly if not completely extirpated as a breeding bird from Santa Barbara to San Diego, including the Channel Islands (Walton et al. 1988). From 1956 to 1980 the San Diego Christmas bird count averaged just 0.4 per year. In 10 years of monthly counts at San Elijo Lagoon 1973–83 King et al. (1987) saw only two. An increase in wintering Peregrines became noticeable in the mid 1980s, and by 1997–2002 the average on the San Diego Christmas bird count was 6.3. The Wildlife Research Institute (2004) estimated 20 wintering in the southwestern quadrant of San Diego County in 2002.

The effort to restore the Peregrine Falcon through reintroduction included San Diego County, with 12 birds released at Point Loma 1982–88 (Pavelka 1990). Only the one nesting on the bridge, however, originated from these releases. With most or all of the historic sites still intact, and many new possible sites on man-made structures, San Diego County's Peregrine population could easily grow beyond its historic level. Though there is less habitat for shorebirds than formerly, the introduction of the Domestic Pigeon and the continued abundance of the Mourning Dove, staples of the falcon's diet, assure its food supply. A return to a small, stable population is likely unless new environmental poisons or other challenges intervene.

Taxonomy: The resident subspecies of the Peregrine Falcon in California, and most migrants, are the widespread medium-dark *F. p. anatum* Bonaparte, 1838. The very dark and, in immatures, heavily streaked subspecies of the Pacific Northwest, *F. p. pealei* Ridgway, 1873, migrates in some numbers to northern California (Anderson et al. 1988, Earnheart-Gold and Pyle 2001). Two have been reported from San Diego County, a specimen from San Diego Bay 31 March 1908 (Swarth 1933, CAS 11694) and the bird banded in British Columbia reported by Anderson et al. (1988). The pale *F. p. tundrius* White, 1968, likely occurs rarely, though there is yet no specimen or conclusive report from San Diego County. It nests in the tundra and migrates far to the south. White (1968) reported one specimen from Los Angeles County, and Earnheart-Gold and Pyle (2001) reported 10 sightings from Southeast Farallon Island.

from 8 March to 25 May. The current population begins nesting somewhat earlier. In 1997 the clutch at Point Loma hatched around 3 April, in 1999 around 6 April (A. Mercieca), corresponding to egg laying in the last week of February. Similarly, Pavelka (1990) estimated the young on the Coronado bridge to be one and a half to two weeks old on 18 April 1989, corresponding to egg laying around 1 March. These young fledged from 14 to 20 May.

Migration: On the basis of recoveries of banded birds, Anderson et al. (1988) demonstrated substantial migration of Peregrines along the Pacific coast. They reported an immature banded as a nestling near Aristazabal Island, British Columbia, found stunned on a hotel balcony in San Diego seven months later. With the species' recolonization, its migration schedule in San Diego County is less clear. Nevertheless, the Peregrine still occurs here mainly as a winter visitor, being most frequent from October to February. There are still few sightings away from known or possible nest sites during the breeding season from March through June.

Winter: Wintering Peregrines are most numerous along the coast, where prey like shorebirds and ducks concentrate. San Diego Bay serves as a nucleus for the wintering birds as well as the breeding population. San Diego Christmas bird counts have returned up to 11, on 16 December 2000; no other San Diego County count has had more than three. The species is usually seen singly; from 1997 to 2002 our maximum count per atlas square per day was two.

Away from the coast, the Peregrine Falcon is seen most often around lakes, such as Sweetwater Reservoir (Wildlife Research Institute 2004), but occasionally far from water. During the atlas period we did not encounter the species in the higher mountains, on the Campo Plateau of southeastern San Diego County, or anywhere in the Anza–Borrego Desert except the Borrego Valley.

Prairie Falcon *Falco mexicanus*

The Prairie Falcon is one of San Diego County's scarcest breeding birds, with a population of 20 to 30 pairs. The birds nest on ledges on cliffs or bluffs and forage in open desert or grassland. They are somewhat more numerous in winter, enough so to be considered merely uncommon at that season in San Diego County's largest grassland, Warner Valley. In spite of nesting birds' sensitivity to human disturbance the San Diego County population seems stable.

Breeding distribution: The Prairie Falcon has an inland distribution; all known or likely current nest sites are at least 23 miles from the coast. Five to ten pairs are in rugged areas of the coastal slope, down to an elevation of about 1000 feet. Six to ten pairs are on the steep east slope of the county's mountains, and about seven pairs are in rocky hills or badlands within the Anza–Borrego Desert. Most nest sites are near grassland or desert plains where the birds forage, but some on cliffs on the coastal slope are surrounded by chaparral, sage scrub, and oak woodland for up to 2 miles in all directions. Clearly, the birds often range farther than this from their nests. In Idaho, Marzluff et al. (1997) found that Prairie Falcons commonly foraged over 4 miles from their nests and sometimes as far as 24 miles. Such long commutes are likely in areas like the badlands of the Anza–Borrego Desert where the density of prey is low, especially in dry years.

Nesting: Prairie Falcons build no nest, typically laying their eggs directly on ledges, sometimes in caves. Both rocky cliffs and eroded earthen bluffs in desert badlands offer nest sites. Sometimes the birds reuse the stick nests of hawks or ravens; R. Thériault noted one such nest in the Anza–Borrego Desert 29 March 2001, and the only

Photo by Anthony Mercieca

egg set collected in the county was from an old raven nest. Of seven nests checked by D. Bittner in the Anza–Borrego Desert in 2004, three were in rock cavities, two were in old raven nests, and two were in old eagle nests.

Data on the Prairie Falcon's nesting schedule in San Diego County are still minimal. The one egg set was collected 4 April 1926 (WFVZ 63160). A fledgling in the Anza–Borrego Desert 24 April (R. Thériault) suggests egg laying as early as mid February, while large chicks

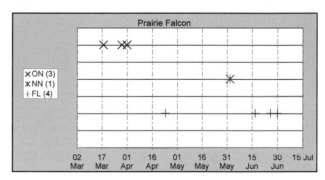

still in a nest on the coastal slope 2 June (P. P. Beck) suggest egg laying as late as late April or early May.

Migration: The Prairie Falcon moves more in response to changes in the availability of prey than in a conventional migration. In summer, the falcons vacate deserts where rodents estivate (Steenhof 1998), so this pattern could be expected in the Anza–Borrego Desert. The state park database has only two records for August (two in Hawk Canyon, H27, 12 August 1991, J. Zemon; one at View of Badlands, N27, 16 August 1991, R. Thériault) and none for September. Along the coast, the Prairie Falcon occurs mainly from September to February, though it shows up

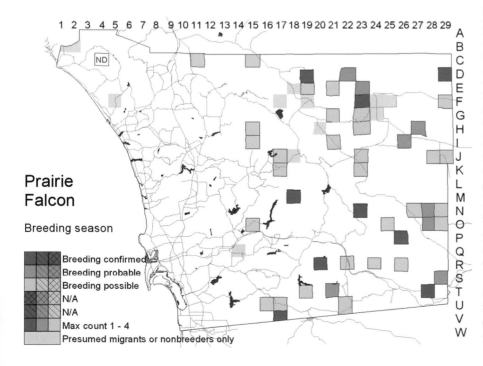

Prairie Falcon

Breeding season

- Breeding confirmed
- Breeding probable
- Breeding possible
- N/A
- N/A
- Max count 1 - 4
- Presumed migrants or nonbreeders only

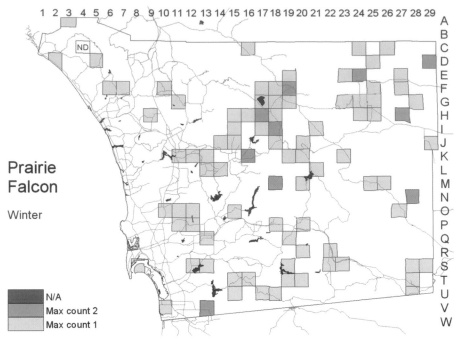

Prairie Falcon

Winter

- N/A
- Max count 2
- Max count 1

Conservation: The Prairie Falcon did not undergo the same DDT-induced population crash as some other birds of prey, and its numbers in California as a whole remained approximately stable through the 1970s (Boyce et al. 1986). The numbers we observed in San Diego County 1997–2001 are about the same as those reported from San Diego County in the 1970s as well (Unitt 1984). Evidently the breeding population here was always small. Records before 1997 list several sites where we did not see the falcon during the atlas period, but most of these are not far from current sites, which could be alternates. At least one former nest site on the fringe of the city of San Diego has apparently been abandoned, however: Fortuna Mountain (P11), active at least in 1980 (Calif. Dept. Fish and Game data).

exceptionally at other times (e.g., one in Cristianitos Canyon, B2, 17 May 1998, L. Allen).

Winter: In winter the Prairie Falcon is encountered more often than in the breeding season, especially in the Borrego Valley and in the larger grasslands of the coastal slope: Warner, Santa Ysabel, and Santa Maria valleys and Otay Mesa. From 1997 to 2002, however, we never noted more than two per atlas square per day. The maximum reported on any of San Diego County's six Christmas bird counts was 10 on the Lake Henshaw count 19 December 1988; the Lake Henshaw count is the only one of the six in the county that has yielded more than five. Though more frequent along the coast in winter than in spring or summer, the Prairie Falcon tends to keep inland in winter as well; the Tijuana River valley is the only coastal location where the species occurs in winter with any regularity.

The greatest threat to the Prairie Falcon currently is probably human disturbance near nest sites. Although in other parts of its range the falcon nests occasionally where there is some level of human activity, in San Diego County it may find it difficult to habituate to the intermittent disturbance of people hiking, driving vehicles, and especially climbing rocks near nest sites on weekends and holidays. Boyce et al. (1986) found that fledging success in areas of the Mojave Desert with heavy recreational use was less than in more secluded areas. Other threats are loss of grassland on the coastal slope to urbanization and a trend toward a drier climate, which could leave parts of the Anza–Borrego Desert with so little prey that the falcons can no longer nest successfully.

RAILS, GALLINULES, AND COOTS — FAMILY RALLIDAE

Yellow Rail *Coturnicops noveboracensis*

The Yellow Rail lives in dense marshes of grass. It is extremely secretive and one of the most difficult North American birds for the human observer to see. It has also declined greatly, at least in its frequency as a winter visitor to California. From southern California there are only three recent records, one for San Diego County, all of birds lost in unsuitable urban habitat.

Winter: The single record for San Diego County is of one found alive on a city street in a recently developed area of north Santee (O12) before dawn on 16 December 1998. The bird was exhausted or sick; though it was brought to rehabilitators at Project Wildlife it died later that day

Photo by Jim Melli

and is now preserved as SDNHM 50186. The only other two Yellow Rails known from southern California since 1917 resulted from similar episodes in Santa Barbara and in Manhattan Beach near Los Angeles (Rottenborn and Morlan 2000, Erickson and Hamilton 2001).

Black Rail *Laterallus jamaicensis*

One of the earliest casualties of the decimation and degradation of San Diego County's wetlands was the Black Rail, now extirpated. The California Department of Fish and Game has listed it as threatened statewide; small numbers persist only in the San Francisco Bay area, at Bodega, Tomales, and Morro bays, in the Imperial Valley, and along the lower Colorado River. The Black Rail was last known to nest in San Diego County in 1954; since then, only a dwindling number of vagrants has reached San Diego County, the last in 1983.

Breeding distribution: Early in the 20th century, the Black Rail occurred widely if possibly irregularly in San Diego County's coastal wetlands. It was known best from the tidal marshes of San Diego Bay, especially the estuary of the Sweetwater River (T10/U10), where Ingersoll (1909) estimated 30 pairs in 1908. "During some seasons, [E. E. Sechrist] estimated breeding populations of 25 to 30 pairs, [but] during other seasons he was unable to locate the species at all" (Willett 1933). The Black Rail was probably resident also at Mission Bay, where one was collected 22 June 1908, and in the Tijuana River estuary, where one was collected in November 1908 (Stephens 1909). In northern San Diego County, nesting was documented only at Los Peñasquitos Lagoon (N7; 28 May 1952, eggs collected, WFVZ 17222), but Stephens reported a specimen also from Encinitas 8 December 1886 (SDNHM 148), which was probably shot at nearby San Elijo or Batiquitos lagoons.

In 1974, Paul Jorgensen discovered Black Rails at Carrizo Marsh (O29) in the Anza–Borrego Desert, with six to ten on 18 and 19 May and 8 June 1974 (AB 28:949, 1974). Four were detected 27 June 1976 (AB 30:1003, 1976), but the following September flooding from tropical storm Kathleen destroyed the marsh, and saltcedar dominated its recovery. Despite many searches, no Black Rails have been found there since 1976.

Nesting: San Diego Bay was the first known and long the only proven site of Black Rail nesting in the western United States. The birds built their nests in marshes of pickleweed, either on the ground underneath the pickleweed (and thus subject to flooding by high tides) or elevated within the pickleweed, though still screened under its canopy. See Huey (1916) for a photo of a nest and an account of his hunt for the birds and their nests. Egg dates (39) ranged from 12 March to 9 June.

Photo by Anthony Mercieca

Migration: Although the California subspecies of the Black Rail is nonmigratory, the birds do disperse across unsuitable habitat. Early records of such dispersers are of one killed by flying against the lighthouse on Point Loma 4 August 1876 (Grinnell et al. 1918) and another picked up under the towers of the former Chollas Heights Naval Radio Station (R11) 30 August 1929 (Gander 1930; SDNHM 12710).

Winter: Since 1970, the only reports of the Black Rail in San Diego have been of vagrants in the nonbreeding season: one at San Elijo Lagoon (L7) 28 October 1973 (A. Fries), another there 21 February 1983 (L. R. Santaella, AB 27:338, 1983), and one heard at a pond in San Felipe Valley near Paroli Spring (I21) 19 December 1983 (P. Unitt).

Conservation: Factors contributing to the Black Rail's extirpation from San Diego County include the destruction of most salt marsh and probably water pollution and an increase in predators. For refuge during high tides, Black Rails need a buffer of upland habitat, now practically eliminated around San Diego County's salt marshes. Around San Francisco and Tomales bays, where such a buffer is reduced, at high tide the rails become prey to Great Blue Herons, Great Egrets, Northern Harriers, Short-eared Owls, and gulls (Evens and Page 1986). The remaining population in southeastern California depends largely on seeps from irrigation canals, so efforts to improve the efficiency of water distribution by lining canals and pumping leaked water back into them reduces or eliminates Black Rail habitat (Evens et al. 1991).

Taxonomy: The California Black Rail, *L. j. coturniculus* (Ridgway, 1874), has a thinner bill, darker underparts, and more extensive chestnut on the nape than the subspecies of the eastern United States.

Clapper Rail *Rallus longirostris*

Recognized as endangered since the inception of the formal lists in 1970, the Light-footed Clapper Rail numbers only about 100 pairs in San Diego County. Once common in southern California's coastal salt marshes, especially where cordgrass dominates, the rail was decimated as these marshes were filled and degraded. The Tijuana River estuary is an especially critical site; only Newport Bay in Orange County supports more Light-footed Clapper Rails. In spite of its precariously low numbers and continuing habitat degradation, the Clapper Rail retains some flexibility: it recovered from a population crash in the 1980s, and a few individuals have colonized some new brackish or freshwater sites.

Breeding distribution: Richard Zembal has led spring censuses of the Light-footed Clapper Rail throughout its U.S. range annually since 1980, mapping calling birds to maximize precision (Zembal and Massey 1981). His effort has yielded an almost exhaustive inventory of the subspecies' population and history of its fluctuations (Figure 12). In San Diego County, the sites where Zembal has found the

Photo by Anthony Mercieca

rail, from north to south, are as follows. Data are from his surveys (Zembal and Hoffman 2002b) except as noted.

Cockleburr Canyon mouth (G4): one pair in 1982, none since.

Santa Margarita River estuary (G4): one or two pairs 1982–88, unpaired individuals in 1993 and 1997, two individuals on 16 April 1999 (P. A. Ginsburg), one pair in 2002.

San Luis Rey River mouth (H5): unpaired individual in 1990, one pair in 1992, none since.

Guajome Lake (G7): one pair in 1983, two in 1984, one individual on 25 June 2001 (K. L. Weaver).

Buena Vista Lagoon (H5/H6): One individual in 1990, two pairs in 1991, and present continuously since, with up to seven pairs in 1997.

Agua Hedionda Lagoon (I6): Up to seven pairs 1980–85, then absent until 1997; up to two pairs 1997–2002.

Batiquitos Lagoon (J7): Unmated individuals 1990–91, then present continuously 1993–2002, with up to three pairs in 1999, 2001, and 2002.

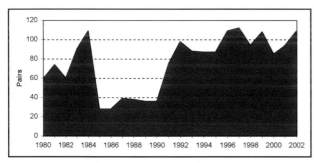

FIGURE 12. San Diego County Clapper Rail census, 1980–2002.

San Elijo Lagoon (L7): Sporadic before 1981 (King et al. 1987), then present almost continuously since, with up to eight pairs in 1997 but only one pair in 2000 and 2001.

San Dieguito River estuary (M7): Unmated individuals in 2000 and 2001.

Los Peñasquitos Lagoon (N7): One pair in 1988, sporadic unmated individuals 1989–93, one or two pairs 1994–2002.

Kendall–Frost Marsh, Mission Bay (Q8): Regular site, maximum 24 pairs in 1984, as few as one pair in 1996—trend is decreasing.

San Diego River flood-control channel (R8): Absent in only two years 1981–2002, maximum six pairs in 2002.

Famosa Slough (R8): Two pairs in 1995 only.

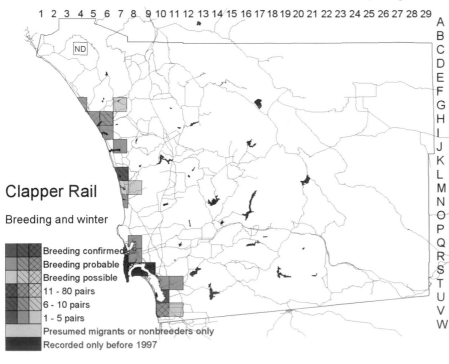

Clapper Rail

Breeding and winter

- Breeding confirmed
- Breeding probable
- Breeding possible
- 11 - 80 pairs
- 6 - 10 pairs
- 1 - 5 pairs
- Presumed migrants or nonbreeders only
- Recorded only before 1997

Paradise Creek marsh, National City (T10): Up to three pairs 1980–84, one in 1992, one in 1995, two in 1996, but only sporadic visitors since (one on 19 August 2000, T. A. Godshalk).

Sweetwater River estuary, including E and F Street marshes (U10): Regular site, maximum 17 pairs in 1984, minimum 2 in 1990.

J Street marsh (U10): One pair in 1981 and 2000 only.

Otay River mouth (along edge of salt works; U10): Up to five pairs 1980–86; up to three pairs 1995–2002, but only one pair 1999–2002.

South Bay Marine Biology Study Area (U10): Up to five pairs 1980–93; subsequently only one pair in 1997 and 1998.

Tijuana River estuary (V10): Up to 41 pairs 1980–84, crash to zero in 1985, gradual recovery beginning in 1986, reaching a maximum of 80 pairs in 1999.

Dairy Mart ponds, Tijuana River valley (V11): One pair 1988 and 1993, unmated individuals 1989–92, one bird 28 May 2001 (G. McCaskie).

Three additional freshwater sites not covered by Zembal have also come to light. The most significant is that in the Sweetwater River at Interstate 805 (T11), where the birds have been present at least since 1997, with up to six individuals 27 March 1998 (P. Famolaro). In San Dieguito Valley, along San Dieguito Road at the northeast corner of the Fairbanks Ranch Country Club (M8), the Clapper Rail has been found regularly since 1998; records from the breeding season are of one on 16 May 1999 (P. Unitt) and one on 1 April 2001 (M. and B. McIntosh). Finally, one was calling along the Otay River between Beyer Boulevard and Beyer Way (V11) 25 April 1999 (P. Unitt).

Nesting: Described in detail by Massey et al. (1984). Clapper Rails prefer to nest in tidal marshes where cordgrass dominates, building their nests largely of the hollow cordgrass stems and weaving the nest around upright cordgrass stems. Thus the nest can float with the changing tides while remaining attached in place. The nest is typically equipped with a ramp leading to the ground and a canopy of live cordgrass woven over the nest, screening it. If insufficient cordgrass is available, the birds will build under pickleweed or a tumbleweed blown into the marsh. Nests in freshwater marshes lack a canopy. Birds obliged to nest outside of low marshes, away from cordgrass, suffer more predation.

April and May represent the peak of the Light-footed Clapper Rail's nesting season, but eggs have been collected as early as 6 March (WFVZ), and active nests with eggs have been seen as late as 15 July, meaning laying no earlier than late June (P. D. Jorgensen).

Migration: The Light-footed Clapper Rail is nonmigratory, and the site tenacity of adults is high. But young birds disperse from their natal marshes, as attested by rare sightings in unsuitable habitat, recolonization of some sites following extirpation, and the rail banded in September 1982 at Newport Bay observed the following September at Seal Beach, Orange County, 13.5 miles away (Zembal et al. 1985).

Winter: There is no evidence for the Clapper Rail's range or numbers in San Diego County being any different in winter than in summer. We found the species occasionally at some of the same freshwater localities in winter as in summer: San Dieguito Valley (up to two on 28 February 2000, R. T. Patton), Sweetwater River near Interstate 805 (up to two on 19 December 1998, L. J. Hargrove), and the Dairy Mart ponds (one on 15 December 2001, G. McCaskie).

Conservation: The elimination of 90–95% of southern California's coastal wetlands was the primary factor reducing the Clapper Rail to an endangered species. Currently, deliberate destruction has been halted, but serious habitat degradation continues. Siltation of lagoons and estuaries accelerated greatly with the development of their watersheds, leading to conversion of low marsh with cordgrass ideal for the rails into high marsh of marginal use to them. The fills supporting the railroad and freeway crossing the lagoons of northern San Diego County constrict tidal flushing, compounding the problem of siltation. Restoration of tidal flow at San Elijo and Batiquitos lagoons has enhanced these sites from the rail's perspective. But at Los Peñasquitos Lagoon, home to over 100 Clapper Rails in 1968, much former marsh is now upland. In the Tijuana estuary, debris as well as massive quantities of silt washes in from the Mexican side of the border. Closure of the estuary's mouth led to the marsh's flooding and the population crash of 1985; recovery after reopening of the estuary took six years.

The limited extent of marsh dominated by cordgrass appears to be the primary current factor preventing the population's recovery. Although the numbers in the Tijuana estuary have increased, those at Kendall–Frost and the Sweetwater estuary have decreased, leading to greater dependence on the Tijuana estuary. In spite of this estuary's protection as a national wildlife refuge, problems there persist, including high levels of predation (Northern Harriers specializing on Clapper Rails) and human disturbance (from both illegal immigrants and the Border Patrol) as well as siltation and pollution.

The species' colonization of new sites is a hopeful sign, but its biology suggests that freshwater sites are inferior to those in cordgrass-dominated salt marshes (Massey et al. 1984). Further study enabling comparison of the contributions of the freshwater and traditional saltmarsh sites is desirable.

Public acquisition of south San Diego Bay as the San Diego National Wildlife Refuge opens the possibility for restoration of some former salt marsh, a possibility that must be balanced against the needs of the many birds that take advantage of the salt works that replaced the marsh.

Yet another concern with the Clapper Rail is low genetic diversity and a low rate of genetic interchange among isolated populations. This concern is being addressed in part through captive breeding and transplanting young raised in captivity to sites away from the origin of their parents. The Chula Vista Nature Center and Sea World hatched and raised the Clapper Rail in captivity for the first time in 2001.

Taxonomy: The Light-footed Clapper Rail, *R. l. levipes* Bangs, 1899, is the subspecies resident from Santa Barbara

County south probably at least to Estero de Punta Banda, Baja California. It differs from Clapper Rails farther north, north of Point Conception, mainly by its brighter orangish

breast; it differs from those farther south, in central and southern Baja California, by its paler back.

Virginia Rail *Rallus limicola*

Being a secretive marsh bird, the Virginia Rail is difficult to observe and census accurately. It is noticed mainly by its peculiar series of grunts. Though generally uncommon, it is a widespread resident in freshwater and brackish marshes, even rather small ones, in all parts of San Diego County. The resident population is augmented in winter by migrants, which occasionally visit salt marshes as well.

Breeding distribution: Though the Virginia Rail's distribution in an arid region like San Diego County is naturally very patchy, we found the species to be surprisingly widespread. It occurs in most if not all of the coastal wetlands of northern San Diego County, with up to eight at the mouth of Las Pulgas Creek (E3) 29 May 1999 (R. and S. L. Breisch) and six at the upper end of Agua Hedionda Lagoon (I6) 25 April 1999 (P. A. Ginsburg). It is perhaps more numerous at some of the lakes and ponds in the coastal lowland, with up to 10 at O'Neill Lake (E6) 10 July 2001 and nine in the San Luis Rey River valley just north of Bonsall (F8) 6 July 2000 (P. A. Ginsburg). An effort focused on this species—surveys using taped recordings—could yield even higher numbers in good habitat (18 in San Pasqual Valley, J12, 26 July 1980, K. L. Weaver).

A region where the Virginia Rail was poorly known before the atlas study but proved relatively common was the Campo Plateau. Among the more notable sites for the species here are Boundary and Carrizo creeks from Jacumba north to Dubber Spur (five in square U28 on 22 April 1999 and five in T28 on 30 April 1999, with only

Photo by Anthony Mercieca

a fraction of the habitat sampled, F. L. Unmack), Lake Domingo (U26; four on 20 April 1999, possibly gathering nest material 17 April 1998, F. L. Unmack), Tule Lake (T27; two on 1 April 1999, J. K. Wilson), La Posta Creek (two in square R24 on 12 July 2000, J. Larson; three in S23 on 20 June 1999, L. J. Hargrove), and Campo Creek in the Campo Indian Reservation (T24; two on 3 May 1998 and 5 May 2001, P. Unitt).

In the northern Anza–Borrego Desert the Virginia Rail is resident along Coyote Creek at Middle Willows (C22; up to four on 28 May 1999, P. D. Jorgensen) and Lower Willows (D23; up to six on 1 April 2001, R. and S. L. Breisch; chicks on 25 July 1995, P. D. Jorgensen in Massey 1998) and along San Felipe Creek from above Scissors Crossing (J22; up to two on 21 July 2002, J. R. Barth) and Sentenac Ciénaga (J23; at least eight on 3 May 1978, P. D. Jorgensen, but no more than one during the breeding season 1997–2002). At Carrizo Marsh (O29) the Virginia Rail is irregular or a recent extirpation, found regularly until 1994 but not 1997–2001 (P. D. and M. C. Jorgensen). At other desert sites it is more likely a winter visitor only.

Nesting: The Virginia Rail proved to be one of the most difficult species for us to confirm breeding. All our confirmations were of chicks accompanying their parents, at the mouth of Las Pulgas Creek 29 May 1999 (R. and S. L. Breisch), at San Elijo Lagoon (L7) 10 May 1998 (G. Rebstock), and in Carmel Creek at El Camino Real (N8) 26 June and 12 July 2001 (S. Scatolini). The nests are well hidden in flooded marshes, touching the

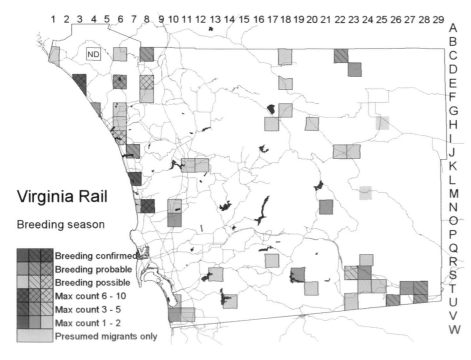

Virginia Rail

Breeding season

- Breeding confirmed
- Breeding probable
- Breeding possible
- Max count 6 - 10
- Max count 3 - 5
- Max count 1 - 2
- Presumed migrants only

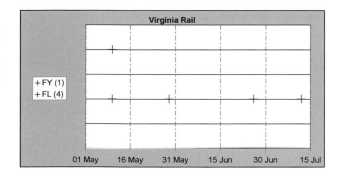

feet at Cuyamaca Lake (M20; one on 4 December 1998, A. P. and T. E. Keenan). In addition to the sites in the Anza–Borrego Desert where it summers, the Virginia Rail winters occasionally at sewage ponds in the Borrego Valley (up to two on 26 October 1992, A. G. Morley) and along Vallecito Creek between Mason and Vallecito valleys (M23/M24; up to three on 22 January 1999, P. K. Nelson). From 1985 to 1992, Massey and Evans (1994) recorded the Virginia Rail at the latter site from September to May only.

Conservation: As a marsh species, the Virginia Rail is subject to the many habitat disruptions affecting wetland

water or elevated only slightly above it (Conway 1995). Egg sets collected in San Diego County number only five, 9 April–20 May. The chicks in late July at Lower Willows suggest laying as late as early to mid June.

Migration: The timing of Virginia Rail migrations is still poorly known because the birds are difficult to census accurately and few sites have been surveyed consistently through the year. Data from the Anza–Borrego Desert suggest that migrants arrive in numbers by 16 September (1978, 25 near Scissors Crossing, P. D. Jorgensen) and are still moving on 8 April (1998, four at the Borrego Springs sewage ponds, H25, H. L. Young, M. B. Mosher).

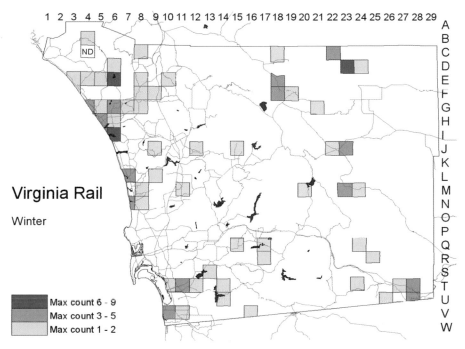

Virginia Rail

Winter

Max count 6 - 9
Max count 3 - 5
Max count 1 - 2

Winter: In winter the Virginia Rail is somewhat more widespread than in the breeding season and invades tidal salt marshes in small numbers (two at Kendall–Frost Marsh, Q8, 2 January 1987, P. Unitt; two in the Tijuana estuary, V10, 20 December 1997, W. Mittendorff). Numbers reported by atlas participants in winter were no greater than in summer, but monthly surveys of San Elijo Lagoon revealed a distinct peak from October to January, with a maximum count of 17 on 4 November 1973 (King et al. 1987). The Virginia Rail is recorded in winter exceptionally as high as 4600

birds. But because of the lack of surveys focused on it, data that could define a trend are insufficient. The elimination of natural marshes may be partly offset by artificial ponds and reservoirs. Carrizo Marsh has been badly degraded by the invasion of saltcedar, likely accounting for the rail's apparent disappearance there.

Taxonomy: Nominate *R. l. limicola* Vieillot, 1819, is the only subspecies of the Virginia Rail in North America; others occur in South America.

Sora *Porzana carolina*

The Sora is the most migratory member of the rail family in southern California, now occurring as a winter visitor almost exclusively. Soras usually remain hidden in marshes, noticed only by sound. Though generally uncommon, they are widespread, visiting even small isolated marshes scattered in the mountains and desert. Formerly, San Diego County represented the southern tip of the Sora's breeding range, and rare stragglers still occur in summer, but there has been no confirmation of nesting here for 50 years.

Photo by Anthony Mercieca

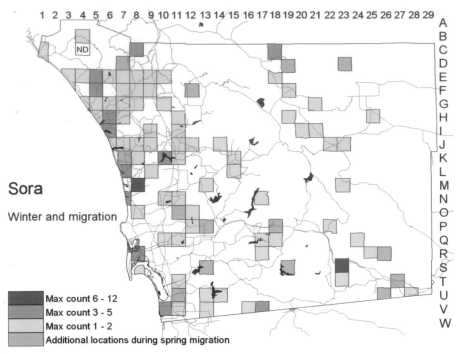

Sora
Winter and migration

Max count 6 - 12
Max count 3 - 5
Max count 1 - 2
Additional locations during spring migration

1951 (SDNHM 31214) and one found dead in the driveway of a house near the Borrego Sink (G25) 15 August 1994 (ABDSP database) were away from possible breeding habitat.

Possibly because of increased calling in spring, King et al. (1987) noted numbers of Soras at San Elijo Lagoon more than twice as large in March and April than from September to January. Concentrations of spring migrants have been noted occasionally at oases in the Anza–Borrego Desert, up to at least eight at Sentenac Ciénaga 3 May 1978 and at least six at Carrizo Marsh (O29) the following day (P. D. Jorgensen).

Migrants occasionally strike power lines or other obstacles while flying through urban areas. These casualties occur during the winter as well as during spring and fall migration, suggesting the birds cross unsuitable habitat at night regardless of season (e.g., one at Coronado, S9, 17 January 1982, SDNHM 42219).

Winter: The Sora's distribution in San Diego County is concentrated in the northwest, where the coastal lagoons and ponds in the low-lying valleys offer more habitat than in the rest of the county. Most of the larger numbers were reported from this area, such as five in the Santa Margarita River valley, Camp Pendleton (F5) 1 December 2001 (P. A. Ginsburg), five at the mouth of Agua Hedionda Creek (I6) 19 December 1999 (P. A. Ginsburg), seven in San Dieguito Valley (M8) 27 December 1998 (P. Unitt), and five at Los Peñasquitos Lagoon (N7) 1 March 1998 (D. K. Adams). The Sora is less frequent in salt marshes than in brackish or freshwater ones but uses them in small numbers (four at Kendall–Frost Marsh, Mission Bay, Q8, 2 January 1987, P. Unitt).

The Sora occurs at least sporadically at marshes throughout the county, at elevations as high as 4100 feet at Twin Lakes, Cooper Canyon (C18; up to three on 6 February 2000, M. and B. McIntosh), 4500 feet in Thing Valley (Q24; one on 25 December 2001, J. R. Barth), and 5000 feet in Crouch Valley, Laguna Mountains (P22; one on 31 December 1998, P. Unitt). Our largest count from 1997 to 2002 was from such an isolated location, 12 at a pond in La Posta Creek just north of Interstate 8 (S23) 9 December 1998 (L. J. Hargrove).

In the Anza–Borrego Desert the Sora is more frequent as a migrant but still occurs as a rare winter visitor at both sewage ponds (e.g., two at Ram's Hill, H25, 16 January 1999, P. D. Jorgensen) and natural oases (e.g., two at Sentenac Ciénaga, J23, 12 February 1999, R. Thériault).

Migration: Late August to early May is the Sora's usual season in San Diego County. From 1997 to 2001 our dates for the species ranged from 27 August (1997, one at O'Neill Lake, E6, P. A. Ginsburg) to 11 May (1999, two in McCain Valley, R26, L. J. Hargrove). Extreme dates are difficult to ascertain because of occasional summering birds, but one at Hillsdale near El Cajon (Q14) 7 August

Breeding distribution: The only specific published account of Sora breeding in San Diego County is Sharp's (1907) statement that "for several years a pair has nested in nearly the same locality on the river below Escondido. Each year the nest was discovered before the clutch of eggs was complete and on going back a few days later the nest was always empty." The San Bernardino County Museum has an egg set collected at National City (T10) 20 April 1935 and another from "San Diego County" without a more precise locality collected 4 May 1954. A. M. Ingersoll (in Willett 1912) believed Soras bred occasionally "in the vicinity of San Diego," and Stephens (1919a) wrote that the species was "occasional throughout the year."

More recent summer records are few, with no suggestion of breeding. For example, King et al. (1987) noted single individuals only three times in June or July on monthly censuses of San Elijo Lagoon, 1973–83. The only June or July record during the atlas period was of one in the San Luis Rey River just north of Indian Flats (D19) 2 June 2001 (L. J. Hargrove).

Conservation: Early in the 20th century, the Sora was common year round in coastal southern California (e.g., Willett 1912), though probably more so in the Los Angeles basin and Orange County's former Gospel Swamp than in San Diego County. Unfortunately, the breeding population was nearly eliminated by draining of marshes before it was well documented. Nevertheless, a few birds continue to breed at a few sites in Orange County (Hamilton and Willick 1996), so breeding in San Diego County remains possible.

The trend in the winter population is less clear but it too may be downward. For example, from 1976 to 1986, the Oceanside Christmas bird count, whose circle constitutes the core of the Sora's range in San Diego County, averaged 17, but from 1997 to 2001 it averaged only six. The reduction of natural marshes in floodplains has likely

been compensated partly, from the Sora's point of view, by the installation of many ponds that are quickly colonized by aquatic plants.

Purple Gallinule *Porphyrio martinicus*

The Purple Gallinule is widespread in the American tropics, but in the United States it breeds only in the Southeast. On the Pacific coast it is resident north only to the Mexican state of Nayarit. Thus California is far out of its normal range, and there are only three records for the state, one for San Diego County.

Migration: On 1 October 1961, San Diego County's single and California's first Purple Gallinule, a juvenile, struck a wire in a residential area of Point Loma (S7), where Fay Dalton picked it up. It died the next day and is now SDNHM 30289 (Huey 1962).

Common Gallinule or Moorhen
Gallinula chloropus

The Common Gallinule (moorhen in British English) is an uncommon to fairly common resident of freshwater marshes in the coastal lowland. It favors areas with about an equal mix of emergent vegetation and open water. It frequents coastal wetlands if they are only slightly brackish but avoids salt water. It is nonmigratory in California but disperses occasionally; the atlas revealed the species to be a rare winter visitor outside its breeding range, at elevations up to 3500 feet.

Photo by Anthony Mercieca

Breeding distribution: In San Diego County, the Common Gallinule is strongly concentrated in the northwest, in the valleys of the Santa Margarita and San Luis Rey rivers and in the coastal lagoons. In the north county's coastal wetlands, numbers are highest in lagoons lacking tidal influence, especially at the mouth of San Mateo Creek (C1; up to seven on 5 July 1997, P. D. Jorgensen) and in Buena Vista Lagoon (seven in the west basin, H5, 10 August 1999, M. Freda; 15 in the east basin, H6, 25 July

1999, L. E. Taylor, including young all these dates). At a few places a short distance inland the gallinule is fairly common, with up to 10 on O'Neill Lake (F6) 29 July and 21 August 1997 (P. A. Ginsburg), 12 on sewage ponds in the Santa Margarita River valley, Camp Pendleton (F5), 26 June 1999 (R. E. Fischer), and 13 at La Costa Country Club (J7) 10 May 2000 (C. C. Gorman).

Farther south, where ponds are fewer, the gallinule is scarcer and more scattered. Our only count during the breeding season of more that four individuals in central or southern San Diego County was of six along the Sweetwater River between Bonita and Sweetwater Dam (T12) 19 July 2001 (T. W. Dorman). Our only sites for the gallinule east of the coastal lowland were at 3300 feet at Sunshine Summit (D17; two at artificial ponds landscaping a mobile-home park, 3 June 2001, P. K. Nelson) and at 4100 feet at Twin Lakes, Cooper Canyon (C18; five, including young, 15 June 2000, M. and B. McIntosh).

Nesting: Common Gallinules nest within a marsh, often on flattened cattails. The nests are

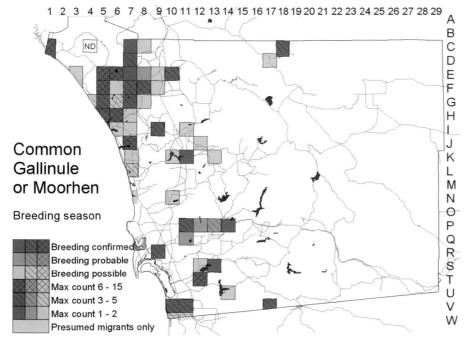

Common Gallinule or Moorhen

Breeding season

- Breeding confirmed
- Breeding probable
- Breeding possible
- Max count 6 - 15
- Max count 3 - 5
- Max count 1 - 2
- Presumed migrants only

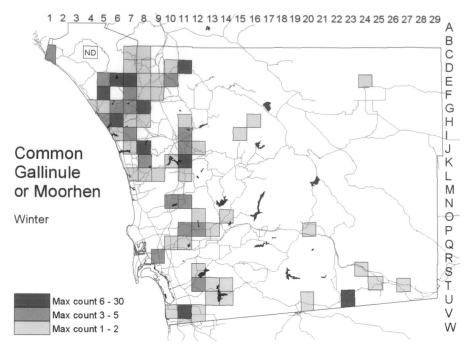

Common Gallinule or Moorhen

Winter

Max count 6 - 30
Max count 3 - 5
Max count 1 - 2

Winter: The gallinule is slightly more widespread in winter than spring and summer, reported in 27 atlas squares in winter but not the breeding season, versus 11 for the reverse. Unusually large numbers have been seen occasionally at O'Neill Lake (up to 30 on 13 December 1999, P. A. Ginsburg). Occasionally numbers at some other spots were notably higher than in the breeding season (up to 10 at the Dairy Mart pond, Tijuana River valley, V11, 18 December 1999, G. McCaskie). At sites where we missed the species in the breeding season, eight at Wilderness Gardens (D11) 7 December 1997 (M. B. Mosher) and eight on San Marcos Creek near Rancho Santa Fe Road (J8) 23 December 2000 (E. C. Hall) were our only counts of more than four. The gallinule could be an irregular resident at all these additional sites in the coastal lowland, however.

usually screened from view, so atlas observers reported only one (along the San Diego River in Mission Valley, R9, 1 May 1997, H. L. Young). Almost all of our confirmations of gallinule breeding were of young accompanying their parents; the precocial chicks leave the nest soon after hatching. Our dates for chicks ranged from 29 April to 16 August, implying egg laying from early April to early July.

Before our atlas study, there were no winter records of the gallinule in San Diego County outside the coastal lowland, so it was a surprise that we accumulated ten from 1997 through 2002. Five of these were from the southeastern part of the county from Potrero (U20) to Tule Lake (T27), all of single birds except for seven at Campo (U23) 3 February 1999 (D. C. Seals). Other sites were Pamo Valley (I15, two records, O. Carter), near Mesa Grande (H16; one on 15 December 1999, E. C. Hall), and near Descanso (P20; one on 15 February 2002, J. K. Wilson). The only record for the Anza–Borrego Desert is of one on a farm pond at the north end of the Borrego Valley (E24) 20 December 1998 (P. R. Pryde).

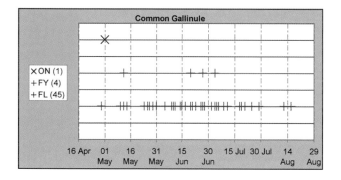

Conservation: The gallinule has never been very common in San Diego County; in spite of many disruptions to the county's wetlands, there is no clear trend in the species' numbers here. Most of the sites that it occupies now are not natural.

Migration: The Common Gallinule is a nonmigratory species in California but occasionally disperses outside its usual range. Records of birds crossing atypical habitat are of one found dead near the Palomar Observatory (D15) 31 October 1983 (R. Higson, AB 38:246, 1984) and one found injured on Main Street in Otay (V11) 2 December 2002 (SDNHM 50753).

Taxonomy: *Gallinula c. cachinnans* Bangs, 1915, is the only subspecies of the Common Gallinule in North America. Many others occur in other parts of the species' vast range.

American Coot *Fulica americana*

The American Coot is one of America's most successful water birds, common in San Diego County as a breeding species and abundant as a winter visitor. An ability to graze on lawns preadapted the coot to urbanization, to some extent. Nesting birds need marshes around fresh or brackish water, but winter

visitors spread to salt water and ponds with little surrounding vegetation.

Breeding distribution: The coot breeds throughout San Diego County's coastal slope wherever there are freshwater marshes and ponds. Breeding birds are most numerous around lakes in the coastal lowland (up to 200 at Lake Hodges, K10, 14 June 1999, R. L. Barber; 100 at O'Neill

Lake, E6, 19 April 1999 and 30 July 2001, P. A. Ginsburg) and at Buena Vista Lagoon (up to 318 in the west basin, H5, 10 August 1999, M. Freda). The lack of tidal influence and abundant cattail surrounding Buena Vista make it the best coot habitat among the county's coastal wetlands. Nevertheless, the coot still breeds to some extent in brackish lagoons, as attested by two chicks on the north shore of Batiquitos Lagoon (J7) 4 May 2001, after the restoration of tidal flushing there (C. C. Gorman).

If it contains water, even San Diego County's highest lake, Big Laguna at 5400 feet (O23), supports breeding coots (up to 65 on 7 July 2001, J. R. Barth). In the Anza–Borrego Desert, coots remain into spring only sporadically at ponds in the Borrego Valley. During the atlas period such records were of single individuals only, with only two later than 17 April (E24 and G24; 4 and 6 May 2000, P. D. Ache). The coot has been confirmed nesting in the Anza–Borrego Desert just once, on 19 May 1974, when a newly hatched chick was seen with its parents at Oso Ranch in the north Borrego Valley (E24; ABDSP database).

Nesting: The American Coot nests over water in matted vegetation. Though the nest is often hidden within a marsh, the coot nests closer to edges than other California

Photo by Anthony Mercieca

species of the family Rallidae, so atlas observers saw many more coot nests than they did of the other species. Chicks, however, accounted for most of our confirmations of coot breeding. Coots evidently begin nesting in the third week of March, as we noted chicks as early as 14 April; they leave the nest just a day or two after hatching. An occupied nest as late as 24 July translates to egg laying no earlier than 1 July. We observed young being fed by their parents as late as 2 September.

Migration: Coots begin moving into habitat where they do not breed as early as 11 August (1993, 16 in the south San Diego Bay salt works, V10, Stadtlander and Konecny 1994) but arrive gradually, perhaps not reaching full abundance until late October or early November (432 at Batiquitos Lagoon, J6/J7, 27 October 1997, Merkel and Associates 1998; 460 at San Elijo Lagoon, L7, 26 October 1992, P. Unitt). King et al. (1987) found that numbers at San Elijo Lagoon peaked from November to January. One coot at the Borrego Springs Country Club (G24) 5 September 1998 (P. D. Jorgensen) provided the species' earliest fall record for the Anza–Borrego Desert.

In spring, wintering coots remain common until early April (667 at Batiquitos Lagoon 3 April 1997; 402 there the following day, Merkel and Associates 1998) but depart soon after that. Almost all are gone after the third week of April. Migrants have been noted in the Anza–Borrego Desert from 21 March (2001, two in Vallecito Valley, M24, P. K. Nelson) to 17 April (1999, one at the Borrego sewage ponds, H25, H. L. Young, M. B. Mosher).

A small number of nonbreeders remains on salt water through the summer (three sightings of single individuals on central San Diego Bay 9 May–27 June 1994, Preston and Mock 1995; three at Shelter Island, S8, 5 July 1998, P. Unitt).

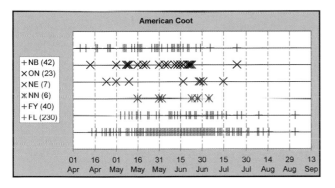

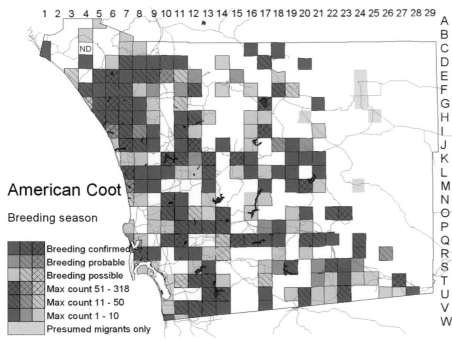

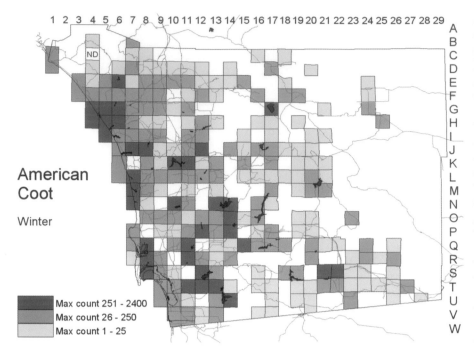

American
Coot

Winter

Max count 251 - 2400
Max count 26 - 250
Max count 1 - 25

ators). The landscaped shores of Mission Bay are especially attractive, accounting for our highest winter numbers (up to 2400 in the northeast quadrant of the bay, Q8, 21 December 1998, J. C. Worley). On sheltered salt water where lawns are not close by, the coot occurs in much smaller numbers. Around south San Diego Bay outside the salt works, Macdonald et al. (1990) had no daily count greater than 50. Within the salt works, Stadtlander and Konecny (1994) had no more than 10 wintering coots per weekly survey 1993–94, but from 1997 to 2001 Christmas bird counts in this area yielded up to 131 on 18 December 1999 (D. C. Seals et al.).

Winter: Huge numbers of coots migrate into San Diego County for the winter. Even at the species' prime breeding sites, numbers are far higher in winter (up to 2100 in the west basin of Buena Vista Lagoon 26 December 1998, M. B. Stowe; 2000 at O'Neill Lake 1 and 4 December 2000, P. A. Ginsburg). The coot is no more restricted elevationally in winter than in summer, with up to 150 at Big Laguna Lake 18 January 1998, P. Unitt).

In the Anza–Borrego Desert wintering coots are restricted to ponds in the Borrego Valley, where they are irregularly common (highest count 70 in the Ram's Hill development 20 December 1998, R. Halford).

A habitat that coots exploit in winter but not summer is lawns (which they graze like cattle) near water (in which they take refuge from disturbance and pred-

Conservation: Data to suggest a trend in numbers of coots breeding in San Diego County are insufficient. But as a winter visitor the species has likely increased, since it takes such advantage of reservoirs, ponds, cemeteries, and the county's many and proliferating golf courses. Among San Diego County's Christmas bird counts, results from Escondido and Anza–Borrego suggest an increase. The Anza–Borrego count averaged 5.6 coots from 1985 to 1996, 59.2 from 1997 to 2001. In some places in California, coots have been considered a nuisance and subjected to pest control (Brisbin and Mowbray 2002).

Taxonomy: Nominate *F. a. americana* Gmelin, 1789, is the subspecies of American Coot that covers the North American continent.

CRANES — FAMILY GRUIDAE

Sandhill Crane *Grus canadensis*

At the turn of the 20th century, Sandhill Cranes migrated over southern California in numbers, stopping at least occasionally, perhaps more often in the Los Angeles basin than in San Diego County. A century later, such flocks are ancient history, and the cranes winter at only three sites in the region: the Carrizo Plain, the Imperial Valley, and the Palo Verde Valley along the Colorado River. Since 1920 there have been only three specific records for San Diego County.

Migration: Of the three recent records of wild Sandhill Cranes in San Diego County, one was of a fall migrant flying over south San Diego Bay along the Silver Strand (T9) 4 December 1999 (D. M. Parker, NAB 54:104, 2000), the other two were of spring migrants, in the east basin

Photo by Anthony Mercieca

of San Elijo Lagoon (L7) 26 April 1998 (M. Baumgartel) and in the San Luis Rey River valley near Bonsall (E8) 28 February 2000 (P. A. Ginsburg, NAB 54:221, 2000). The only other report since the early 20th century was of seven at Cuyamaca Lake 24–30 September 1977 (AB 32:357, 1978).

In one of the more bizarre episodes in the history of San Diego County birds, a tame Sandhill Crane fitted with a radio transmitter showed up on the lawn of an apartment complex near the corner of Telegraph Canyon and Otay Lakes roads (U12) 23–26 November 1998. It had been raised in captivity and released in northeastern Arizona as part of an experimental reintroduction program.

Conservation: Unfortunately, the early naturalists in southern California left us only meager information on the Sandhill Crane. Emerson (1887) saw large flocks flying over Volcan Mountain 16 and 20 March 1884. Grinnell et al. (1918) reported that at Campo "many flocks have been seen passing high overhead in a southeasterly direction which would have led them to the head of the Gulf of California, where the species is known to winter abundantly. In early spring flocks have been noted traversing the same course in reverse direction." Stephens (1919a) wrote, "the cranes migrate in considerable flocks in fall and spring, often without stopping in the county. Occasional in winter on grass and grain fields." The species was decimated by hunting and habitat changes, extensive grasslands and grain fields now being things of the past. The desiccation of the Colorado delta following the river's damming eliminated the crane's primary winter habitat in the region.

The number of Sandhill Cranes wintering in the Imperial Valley began increasing in the 1990s (Patten et al. 2003). The increase may account for the occurrences in San Diego County in 1999 and 2000 and may foreshadow more frequent occurrences in the 21st century, though the species' future in southern California is at the mercy of agricultural water and land-use policies.

Taxonomy: No specimen was ever collected in San Diego County, so the subspecies occurring here is (are?) not known. In the Imperial Valley the Lesser Sandhill Crane, *G. c. canadensis* (Linnaeus, 1758), predominates, but the Greater, *G. c. tabida* (Peters, 1925), has also been seen and collected there.

PLOVERS — FAMILY CHARADRIIDAE

Black-bellied Plover *Pluvialis squatarola*

The Black-bellied Plover is one of San Diego County's more numerous wintering shorebirds with about 1500 to 3000 annually. The species prefers tidal mudflats but uses a variety of habitats including brackish lagoons, sandy beaches, and rocky shorelines. Away from the coast the Black-bellied Plover is now rare, as the agricultural fields it formerly frequented inland are almost gone.

Winter: Because it uses sandy beaches, the Black-bellied Plover is found all along San Diego County's coast. Its numbers are by far the greatest, however, on the mudflats around south San Diego Bay. On their weekly counts in and near the salt works (U10/V10), 1993–94, Stadtlander and Konecny (1994) found an average of about 500–600 in December and January and a maximum of 1155 on 1 December 1993. In the same area, the San Diego Christmas bird count 15 December 2001 yielded 1418 (D. C. Seals et al.). Numbers can be large elsewhere on San Diego Bay (312 at the D St. fill, T10, 18 February 2000, R. T. Patton), in northeastern Mission Bay (Q8; up to 526 on 18 December 1998, J. C. Worley), and in the Tijuana River estuary (V10; 150 on 19 December 1998, A. DeBolt). Because the Black-bellied Plover forages individually rather than in flocks, such large numbers are seen generally when the birds congregate on dry ground to loaf and wait out the high tide.

In northern San Diego County wintering Black-bellied Plovers are less common. The Oceanside Christmas bird count averages 100, the Rancho Santa Fe count 43. Counts of 85 at San Onofre State Beach (C1) 28 January 2001 (R. Breisch), 200 at the Santa Margarita River mouth

Photo by Anthony Mercieca

(G4) 25 January 1998 (B. C. Moore), and 80 in the east basin of Batiquitos Lagoon (J7) 26 December 1998 (R. and A. Campbell) were exceptionally high for this area. Away from coastal wetlands the Black-bellied Plover is generally uncommon. A high count for a bluff-backed beach is 37 at San Elijo State Beach (L7) 8 February 2004 (E. Garnica); for rocky shoreline, 27 at Point Loma 16 December 2000 (M. W. Klein).

From 1997 to 2002 we found wintering Black-bellied Plovers inland only at the east end of Lake Hodges (K11; two on 13 December 1999, B. C. Moore; one still present 26 December, E. C. Hall) and along the San Dieguito River in San Dieguito Valley (M8; up to 40 on 10 January 1998, R. T. Patton) and Osuna Valley (L8; up to 15 on 27 December 1998, A. Mauro). One at Lake Henshaw (G17) 16 December 2002 (P. Unitt) is the only one recorded on a Lake Henshaw Christmas bird count.

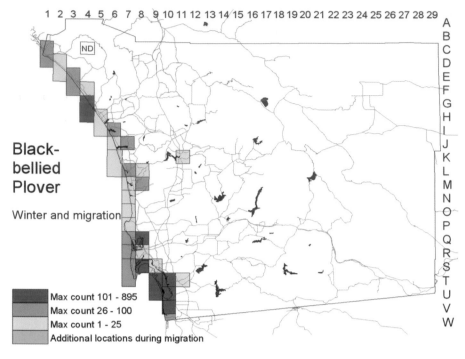

Black-bellied Plover

Winter and migration

- Max count 101 - 895
- Max count 26 - 100
- Max count 1 - 25
- Additional locations during migration

coast (up to eight at Batiquitos Lagoon 4 June 1999, B. C. Moore). Migrants begin returning in July and finish leaving in May. There is no clear peak of migration in spring but there is in fall, with the arrival of juveniles in August and September.

Well inland, migrating Black-bellied Plovers are rare. Besides a few scattered individuals at lakes Hodges and Henshaw, 184 fall migrants were at Lake Henshaw 31 July 1981, and 30 spring migrants flew over Palomar Mountain (D15) 16 April 1982 (R. Higson, AB 36: 894, 1982).

Conservation: Development of Mission and San Diego bays eliminated a large fraction of the tidal mudflats where Black-bellied Plovers feed, but there are no adequate data suggesting any change in the species' status along the coast. Inland, however, urban development supplanting agriculture has eliminated most of the fields the plovers formerly used; far fewer occur inland now than in the 1960s and 1970s.

Taxonomy: The subspecies maintained by Engelmoer and Roselaar (1998) are differentiated insufficiently for taxonomic recognition (Patten et al. 2003).

Migration: As for all shorebirds, understanding Black-bellied Plover migration requires that the plumage types be recorded separately, as nonbreeding birds summer commonly around south San Diego Bay (55 on 24 June 1988, Macdonald et al. 1990) and in the Tijuana River estuary (30 on 6 June 1998, B. C. Moore). Two hundred around south San Diego Bay 1 June 1987 (R. E. Webster, AB 41:1487, 1987) were an unusually large number for summering birds. A few summer elsewhere along the

American Golden-Plover *Pluvialis dominica*

The American Golden-Plover occurs—or occurred—in San Diego County as a rare fall migrant. Its primary site was the Tijuana River valley, where the extensive irrigated pastures that once attracted the birds no longer exist.

Migration: The American Golden-Plover has been seen in San Diego County mainly from mid September to late October. The maximum number recorded was 15 in the Tijuana River valley 8 October 1966 (G. McCaskie). These could have included Pacific Golden-Plovers as well; at that time criteria for distinguishing the golden-plovers in the field were not well understood. The only specimen of the American was collected in the Tijuana River valley 18 October 1972 (SDNHM 38234). Extreme dates are 26 July (1980, AB 34:930, 1980) and 23 November (1992, E. R. Lichtwardt, AB 47:149, 1992). With a couple of sod farms being the only agricultural fields remaining in the Tijuana River valley, the American Golden-Plover has

Photo by Anthony Mercieca

become less than annual. One was there 30 September–23 October 2003 (G. McCaskie). Of the spring records of golden-plovers in San Diego County, none is certainly of the American.

Pacific Golden-Plover *Pluvialis fulva*

Many migrating Pacific Golden-Plovers cross the North Pacific Ocean, but only a few follow the west coast of North America. Only since the 1990s have criteria for distinguishing them in the field from the American Golden-Plover become widely known, and specimens in California are few (none from San Diego County). Thus the status of the Pacific Golden-Plover could use further clarification, but apparently one to three reach the county's coastal wetlands each year, in both migration and winter. Of this pair of species, only the Pacific has been confirmed wintering on North America's Pacific coast.

Photo by Anthony Mercieca

Winter: In San Diego County, the Pacific Golden-Plover has been found wintering in the San Dieguito River estuary (M7; 3 January–9 February 2002, N. Ferguson, NAB 56:223, 2002), Mission Bay (Q8; 10 December 2000, E. Wallace), at the San Diego River mouth (R7; one or two annually 1962–74, G. McCaskie), San Diego Bay at Coronado (S9; 12 January 1908, Torrey 1909), in the Tijuana River valley (up to six in the 1960s, AFN 21:458, 1967; 23:521, 1969), and, most frequently, in the Tijuana estuary (V10). From 1999 to 2002, one individual apparently returned to that site annually, and up to three were there 30–31 January 1999 (J. L. Coatsworth, NAB 53:208, 1999).

Migration: Because of the difficulty in distinguishing the Pacific Golden-Plover from the American, especially when the birds are in molt between their breeding and winter plumages, the migration schedules of both species are uncertain. The Pacific has been reported at least from 1 August (1995, San Elijo Lagoon, P. A. Ginsburg, NASFN 50:114, 1996) to 11 May (1997, south San Diego Bay, D. M. Parker, FN 51:927, 1997; 2000, Tijuana River mouth, R. T. Patton, NAB 54:221, 327, 2000). A golden plover in the Tijuana estuary 27 June 1998 (C. G. Edwards) was most likely the Pacific wintering regularly there, returned early. The identification of one at the San Diego River mouth 4–8 June 1983 is uncertain (D. B. King, AB 37:912, 1983). A spring migrant at Point Loma 10 May 1985 was at an atypical site (R. E. Webster, AB 39:350, 1985).

Taxonomy: The Pacific and American Golden-Plovers were considered subspecies until Connors et al. (1993) confirmed assortative breeding where both occur in western Alaska.

Snowy Plover *Charadrius alexandrinus*

Nesting on beaches, dunes, and salt flats, the Snowy Plover is among San Diego County's scarcest and most threatened breeding birds. In 1993 the U.S. Fish and Wildlife Service listed it as threatened along the entire Pacific coast. Thorough surveys from 1995 to 1998 put the county's breeding population between 240 and 325 individuals, most concentrated in two areas, Camp Pendleton and the Silver Strand (Powell et al. 2002). Surveys from 1978 to 1998 suggest the decline of this once common bird has continued. When not breeding the Snowy Plover is more widespread along the county's coast but it is not much more numerous, in spite of considerable migration. Human disturbance of the remaining habitat and a high level of predation mean that intensive management is needed to sustain the population.

Breeding distribution: Powell et al. (2002) surveyed San Diego County's coastline intensively from 1994 to 1998 and provided an exhaustive view of the Snowy Plover's distribution. Their detailed table enumerated nests rather than birds per site; because of multiple clutches per year, this figure is greater than the number of nesting pairs by 35%. Tracking of banded birds showed that, within a

Photo by Anthony Mercieca

single breeding season, some individuals shift from site to site, although most remain at one site.

These variables considered, about half the population breeds in Camp Pendleton, with six to eight nests per year at the mouths of Aliso and French creeks (F4) and 67 to 88 at the Santa Margarita River mouth (G4). The high count of individual plovers was 120 at the latter site 11 June 1997 (B. L. Peterson). At Batiquitos Lagoon (J6/J7), the plovers nest at both the east and west ends on sandy fills installed to provide nesting habitat for the Least Tern,

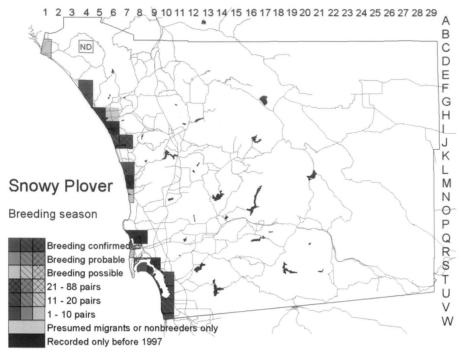

Snowy Plover

Breeding season

Breeding confirmed
Breeding probable
Breeding possible
21 - 88 pairs
11 - 20 pairs
1 - 10 pairs
Presumed migrants or nonbreeders only
Recorded only before 1997

habit of leaving the chicks with the male while they start a new nest with another male (Page et al. 1995).

Migration: The Snowy Plover is highly mobile: even during the breeding season banded birds have moved as far as 500 miles along the California coast between successive broods (Stenzel et al. 1994). A few birds are seen at places where they do not nest even near the peak of egg laying (up to four at Los Peñasquitos Lagoon, N7, 27 April 1999, M. B. Stowe). Migrants away from nesting sites become more numerous by August (15 at San Onofre State Beach, C1, 6 August 1999, P. A. Ginsburg). Snowy Plovers banded as far north as Santa Cruz County have been seen wintering in San Diego; birds banded in San Diego County have been seen north to San Luis Obispo County, west to San Clemente Island, and south to Scammon's Lagoon in Baja California (Powell et al. 2002). Each year, however, 15–27% of plovers banded by Powell et al. wintered near their nesting sites.

Inland in San Diego County, the Snowy Plover is rare, recorded only at lakes Henshaw (G17; one on 5 November 1978, AB 33:213, 1979) and Hodges (K10/K11; noted once in spring, 11 May 1985, and sporadically in fall from 7 July [2 in 1982] to 2 October [1 in 1982] K. L. Weaver). Exchange of birds between the coast and inland sites is regular, however (Page et al. 1995).

Winter: Snowy Plovers winter widely along San Diego County's coast, using not only their nesting sites but also several beaches and estuaries where they do not nest. During the atlas period our winter counts ranged up to 90 at the Tijuana River mouth 15 December 2001 (R. B. Riggan), 70 along the Silver Strand 19 December 1998 (N. Osborn), 90 at North Island 11 January 2002 (R. T. Patton), 52 in northeastern Mission Bay (Q8) 7 December 1998 (J. C. Worley), and 34 at San Onofre State Beach 28 January 2001 (J. M. and B. Hargrove). Powell et al. (2002) reported up to 177 at the Sweetwater River

as part of a lagoon-enhancement project. The number of nests at Batiquitos Lagoon 1995–98 varied from 15 to 40. At San Elijo Lagoon (L7), as a result of variable water levels, the plover nests only intermittently, with five nests in 1994, none for the next four years, and one in 1999 (R. T. Patton). Mariner's Point in Mission Bay (R7) hosted one unsuccessful pair in 1995 and none since.

The Silver Strand (T9) is the plover's other main breeding site in San Diego County, with 17 to 38 nests in the Naval Amphibious Base (both bay and ocean shores) and 4 to 10 at Silver Strand State Beach. Zero to two nests per year were found at the Naval Radio Station at the south end of the strand (U10/V10). Four Snowy Plovers at North Island (S8) 26 May 2000 included a fledgling (R. T. Patton). Within San Diego Bay, Powell et al. (2002) found 2 to 13 nests per year at the D Street fill in the Sweetwater River estuary (T10) and zero to four at the salt works (U10/V10). One pair nested at the D Street fill in 1999, another at the Chula Vista Wildlife Reserve in 1998 (R. T. Patton). Around the Tijuana River mouth (V10/W10) the plovers nest on both the north and south sides, with 11 to 17 nests 1995–98 (Powell et al. 2002) and 12 in 2001 (R. T. Patton).

In 2002 and 2003 the county's population was slightly less than the 240–325 found 1995–98, with 102 estimated pairs (323 nests) in 2002 and 233 individuals (but only 67 nests) in 2003 (R. T. Patton).

Nesting: The Snowy Plover nests in a shallow scrape in sand or dried mud, variably lined with pebbles, bits of shell, or bits of vegetation. Powell et al. (2002) charted the species' breeding season on the basis of 801 nests. Their earliest nest was 10 March; egg laying peaked in late May and ended in late July. Hatching begins in the latter half of April, peaks in the latter half of June, and ends in the latter half of August. Even successful females may lay up to three clutches in a breeding season, helped along by their

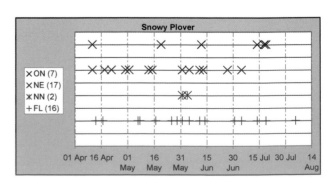

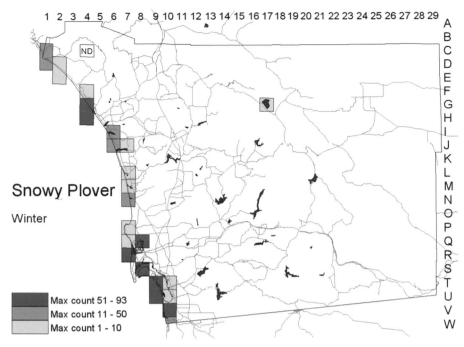

1 2 3 4 5 6 7 8 9 10 11 12 13 14 15 16 17 18 19 20 21 22 23 24 25 26 27 28 29

A B C D E F G H I J K L M N O P Q R S T U V W

Snowy Plover

Winter

Max count 51 - 93
Max count 11 - 50
Max count 1 - 10

more intensive and covered areas missed by the earlier ones. The plovers have abandoned Agua Hedionda Lagoon (I6), site of 27 pairs in 1978, and become sporadic at San Elijo Lagoon, site of 12 pairs in 1978. The birds have concentrated at the Santa Margarita River mouth and the Naval Amphibious Base, perhaps because predators are controlled at these places, under a program designed to protect nesting Least Terns. Although the endangered birds nesting on these military lands are monitored and managed intensively, changes in military policy toward endangered species—already announced—could change the plover's status quickly. The effort to restore Batiquitos Lagoon, by establishing tidal flow and providing nesting habitat, attracted plovers (Powell et al. 2002), though their nesting success there was low (Powell and Collier 2000).

mouth but on occasion found zero birds at almost every site—flocks sometimes forage on one beach, then rest on another (B. L. Peterson). Powell et al. (2002) estimated the county's winter population at 227–367 individuals. A cooperative census the length of San Diego County's coast 10–13 January 2001 yielded 390; another 8–11 January 2003 yielded 547. The most significant increases were in the north county, where projects to replenish beach sand have augmented the plover's habitat (R. T. Patton).

The single winter record inland is of one at Lake Henshaw 21 December 1998 (S. J. Montgomery).

Conservation: Stephens (1919a) called the Snowy Plover "abundant" in San Diego County. In 1978, Page and Stenzel (1981) censused 257 individuals in the county; in 1989, Page et al. (1991), repeating the survey, censused only 149. The higher numbers found by Powell et al. (2002) are not comparable with the results of the earlier surveys because the more recent study was much

At many sites, disturbance and nest predation are constant problems. The plover's productivity in San Diego County is less than in coastal northern California (Powell et al. 2002). The trend has been for the species to disappear from sites accessible to the public, like Agua Hedionda Lagoon and the Tijuana River estuary. Development surrounding almost all sites concentrates predators there, leading to further conflicts. The plover's only defenses are camouflage and renesting after losing a clutch. All ground-nesting birds retreat from urbanization, and in San Diego County none has retreated more than the Snowy Plover.

Taxonomy: The subspecies of the Snowy Plover in North America is *C. a. nivosus* (Cassin, 1858).

Wilson's Plover *Charadrius wilsonia*

Wilson's Plover is locally common in Baja California Sur but only a rare vagrant along the Pacific coast north of the international border. Of nine well-supported records from California, four are from San Diego County, in April, May, and June. All these Wilson's Plovers were on sandy beaches.

Migration: Ingersoll (1895) found California's first Wilson's Plover at Pacific Beach (Q7) 24 June 1894, collecting it 29 June (MVZ 31920). One at the Tijuana River mouth (V10) 9 April 1991 (D. Parker-Chapman) and one at Delta Beach, Silver Strand (T9), 27 April–1 May 1998 (E. Copper) were both photographed (Heindel and Garrett 1995, Erickson and Hamilton 2001). The California Bird Records Committee also accepted a sight record from North Island Naval Air Station (S8) 5 May 2000 (R. T.

Photo by Anthony Mercieca

Patton, McKee and Erickson 2002). A few other published sightings lack details, though the one by Ingersoll (1918)

at Imperial Beach (V10) 11 May 1918 was likely valid.

Intensive monitoring of Least Terns and Snowy Plovers along San Diego County's beaches accounts for the apparently increased frequency of Wilson's Plover here.

Taxonomy: California's specimen of Wilson's Plover is *C. w. beldingi* (Ridgway, 1919), resident along the Pacific coast from Baja California south to Peru.

Semipalmated Plover *Charadrius semipalmatus*

The Semipalmated Plover prefers coastal mudflats, as might be predicted from its mud-colored upperparts. Small numbers also visit sandy beaches and inland lakeshores. Like other shorebirds that breed in the far north, it spends most of its life in its winter range: the last northbound migrants and the first southbound migrants almost meet each other in June. Small numbers of nonbreeders remain year round. The Semipalmated is especially common in fall migration but common in winter as well—the number wintering in San Diego County is about 750 to 1000.

Photo by Anthony Mercieca

Winter: Wintering Semipalmated Plovers are well distributed along San Diego County's coast, as a result of the birds' using beaches as well as mudflats. In spite of the lack of extensive mudflats in this heavily developed part of Mission Bay, El Carmel Point (Q7) emerged as a hot spot for the species, with up to 250 on 12 February 2000 (L. Polinsky) and 400–500 on 24 October 1998 (J. L. Coatsworth). Elsewhere wintering Semipalmated Plovers are often common at north county lagoons (up to 77 at San Elijo Lagoon, L7, 23 December 2001, E. Garnica; 75 at Agua Hedionda Lagoon, I6, 12 February 2000, J. Ciarletta), in the San Diego River flood-control channel (R8; 30 on 5 January 1998, M. B. Stowe), around San Diego Bay (maximum 321 in the salt works, U10/V10, 26 January 1994, Stadtlander and Konecny 1994), and in the Tijuana River estuary (V10; 75 on 15 December

2001, R. B. Riggan). Our maximum numbers on sandy beaches were 23 at Encinitas (K6) 10 December 2000 (E. Garnica) and 21 at Torrey Pines (O7) 11 February 2000 (D. G. Seay).

Inland the Semipalmated Plover is uncommon in migration and generally rare in winter, when it has been found only in the coastal lowland. From 1997 to 2002 our sites for the species inland in winter were O'Neill Lake (E6; up to five on 14 December 1997, B. C. Moore), Lake Hodges (K10/K11; up to 30 on 22 December 2000, R. L. Barber), and Sweetwater Reservoir (S12/S13; up to two on 20 December 1997 and 18 December 1999, P. Famolaro).

Migration: Adult Semipalmated Plovers begin returning in late June or early July; from 1997 to 2001 our earliest was one at the Santa Margarita River mouth (G4) 3 July 1999 (P. A. Ginsburg). Fall migration peaks in September and October with the arrival of juveniles. There is no clear peak of spring migrants, but the species occurs rarely at inland sites where it does not winter in both spring and fall migration (Unitt 1984). Our only record for southeastern San Diego County was of one at the upper end of Lake Morena (S22) 13 August 2000 (R. and S. L. Breisch). In the Anza–Borrego Desert all records are for spring: one at Middle Willows (C22) 3 May 1975 (G. Salzberger), two there 29 April 1997 (P. D. Jorgensen), six at Borrego Springs (G24) 25 April 1998, two there 15 April 2000 (P. D. Ache), and one at the Borrego sewage ponds (H25) 29 April 1990 (A. G. Morley).

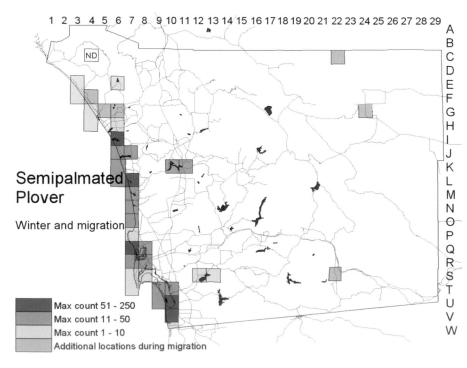

Semipalmated Plover

Winter and migration

Max count 51 - 250
Max count 11 - 50
Max count 1 - 10
Additional locations during migration

Though a few migrants may still be moving north in early June, most Semipalmated Plovers seen then are probably staying for the summer. Maximum numbers are 16 at Batiquitos Lagoon (J7) 7 June 1998 (C. C. Gorman), 45 around south San Diego Bay 1 June 1987 (R. E. Webster, AB 41:1487, 1987), at least 40 there 12 June 1989 (Macdonald et al. 1990), and 20 in the Tijuana River estuary 6 June 1998 (B. C. Moore).

Conservation: Although the mudflats around San Diego Bay are much reduced from their primitive extent, results of San Diego Christmas bird counts 1953–2002 suggest a possible modest trend toward increase over the latter half of the 20th century. From 1953 to 1977 the count averaged 0.22 Semipalmated Plovers per party-hour, whereas from 1978 to 2002 it averaged 0.39.

Killdeer *Charadrius vociferus*

Being adapted to use disturbed bare ground and a minimum of water enabled the Killdeer to become San Diego County's most widespread shorebird. It is common from coastal wetlands and bayfills to agricultural fields, lakeshores, golf courses, ball fields, sand mines, graded clearings, cobbly washes with intermittent pools, and even some oases in the Anza–Borrego Desert. Despite the Killdeer's predilection for bare dry dirt, its distribution suggests it needs water to drink, at least during the breeding season. One of the few shorebirds that breeds in San Diego County, Killdeer appears more abundant in winter, perhaps just a result of the local population clumping into loose flocks.

Breeding distribution: In San Diego County the Killdeer is most widespread in the coastal lowland, at coastal wetlands (up to 31 at Los Peñasquitos Lagoon, N7, 2 April 2000, D. K. Adams) and in inland valleys (up to 89 along the San Diego River between Santee and Lakeside, P13, 23 April 1998, W. E. Haas). At higher elevations, more rugged topography and less imported water mean the species' distribution is patchier, but it is just as common where habitat is available (38 on the north side of Lake Morena, S21, 7 July 2001, R. and S. L. Breisch; 50 at Tule Lake, T27,

Photo by Anthony Mercieca

27 June 2001, J. K. Wilson). If the habitat is suitable, the Killdeer is not constrained in San Diego County by elevation, as it breeds up to 5400 feet at Big Laguna Lake (O23; 10, including young, 9–10 June 2001, C. G. Edwards).

In the Anza–Borrego Desert, the Killdeer breeds widely in the irrigated parts of the Borrego Valley (up to 16 at golf-course ponds in Borrego Springs, G24, 25 April 1998, P. D. Ache). Along Coyote Creek the Killdeer breeds regularly at both Lower Willows (D23; up to four on 19 May 2001, M. L. Gabel) and Middle Willows (C22; up to seven, including young, on 6 May 2001, P. D. Jorgensen). Near the junction of San Felipe Creek and Grapevine Canyon (I23), where the species was absent from 1997 to 2001, it bred in 1982, with nests on 7 and 25 April (P. D. Jorgensen, ABDSP database). Clearing in 2002 of the saltcedar clogging Sentenac Ciénaga (J23) allowed a pair to colonize in 2003 (J. R. Barth); our only Killdeer in this area from 1997 to 2002 was a single individual at nearby Scissors Crossing (J22) 25 May 1998 (E. C. Hall). In the southern section of the desert the Killdeer's only site is Carrizo Marsh (O29; up to four, including a pair in distraction display, on 25 April 2001, M. C. Jorgensen).

Nesting: The Killdeer nests in a scrape on the ground, lining it with shells, pebbles, or debris. It compensates for the nest's being

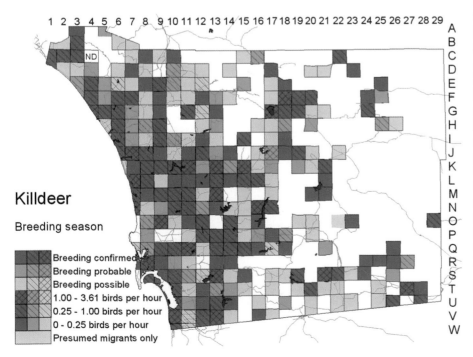

1 2 3 4 5 6 7 8 9 10 11 12 13 14 15 16 17 18 19 20 21 22 23 24 25 26 27 28 29

A B C D E F G H I J K L M N O P Q R S T U V W

ND

Killdeer

Breeding season

- Breeding confirmed
- Breeding probable
- Breeding possible
- 1.00 - 3.61 birds per hour
- 0.25 - 1.00 birds per hour
- 0 - 0.25 birds per hour
- Presumed migrants only

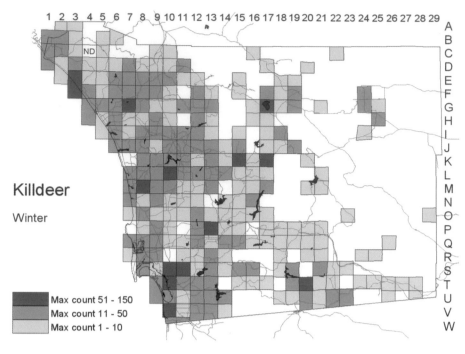

Killdeer

Winter

Max count 51 - 150
Max count 11 - 50
Max count 1 - 10

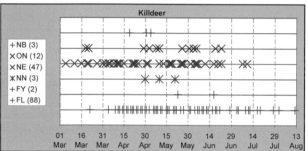

School (R14) 22 March 2001 suggests egg laying as early as the last week of February (S. Brad).

Migration: There is little evidence in San Diego County for Killdeers migrating through areas where they neither nest nor winter. Possible migrants through the Anza–Borrego Desert are one in Culp Valley (G23/H23) 18 March 1992 (M. L. Gabel) and up to two near Tamarisk Grove (I24) 19–21 April 1985 (N. Foley).

Winter: The Killdeer's distribution in San Diego County in winter differs little from that in the breeding season, but the birds are seen often in flocks rather than in pairs. Most are still in the coastal lowland, but our largest flock, of 150 on 25 January 1998, was at about 2400 feet elevation in Long Potrero (T20; D. C. Seals). In spite of the freezing temperatures, the Killdeer is fairly regular in winter at Big Laguna Lake (up to six on 23 February 2002, K. J. Winter). The species' desert locations are the same as in the breeding season except for Tamarisk Grove, site of three on 2 December 1998 (P. K. Nelson).

Conservation: The Killdeer benefits from many human modifications of the San Diego County environment such as importation of water, maintenance of lawns, and bulldozing of brush. But a countryside dominated by agriculture and pastures is far more favorable to the Killdeer than one dominated by pavement, buildings, and manicured landscaping. Presumably as a result of more intensive urbanization, the number of Killdeers per party-hour on San Diego Christmas bird counts declined from 2.05 from 1953 to 1977 to 1.23 from 1978 to 2002.

Taxonomy: Killdeers throughout North America are nominate *C. v. vociferus* Linnaeus, 1758.

so exposed by distracting predators—and birders—with loud calls and conspicuous displays of feigned broken wings. It also nests regularly on flat gravel rooftops, obliging the chicks to leap to the ground. Our records of nests with eggs extend from 5 March (1998, Rancho Santa Fe, L8, A. Mauro) to 10 July (2001, two nests, D Street fill in Sweetwater River estuary, T10, R. T. Patton), an interval considerably wider than the 18 March–10 June known from egg sets collected 1901–64. A chick at Valhalla High

Mountain Plover *Charadrius montanus*

The Mountain Plover is one of North America's most seriously threatened birds. The U.S. Fish and Wildlife Service proposed that it be listed as an endangered species in 1999, then canceled the proposal in 2003. The primary factor decimating the plover is apparently habitat change in its breeding range on the Great Plains and intermountain plateaus: conversion of short-grass prairie to cropland and pastures of taller grass and elimination of the prairie dogs that once kept the prairie partly open (Leachman and Osmundson 1990, Knopf 1996). But in its winter range in southern California the plover

Photo by Kenneth Z. Kurland

has also lost much of its habitat, of open plains and plowed fields of bare dirt. The Mountain Plover's former regular wintering in San Diego County came to an end in 1991. Only a single migrant has been reported since then.

Winter: Though Stephens (1919a) called the Mountain Plover "rather common" in San Diego County, specific locations recorded for the species are rather few: Stuart Mesa (G4; eight on 22 December 1979, E. Copper), San Luis Rey (G6; 6 March 1960, A. M. Rea), Warner Valley along Highway 79 near Highway S2 (G18; up to 50 on 18 and 29 December 1981, C. G. Edwards), Ocotillo Wells (I28/I29; three on 18 March 1978, AB 32:1055, 1978), Lake Cuyamaca (L21; one on 9 November 1980, D. M. Parker), the airfield in what is currently known as Marine Corps Air Station Miramar (O9/O10; two collected of 75 seen 18 November 1939, SDNHM 18089–90, Abbott 1940; two seen 17 November 1956, AFN 11:61, 1957), Pacific Beach (Q7, on large lawn, no date, Sams and Stott 1959), Otay Mesa (V12/V13; up to 250 on 12 December 1971, G. McCaskie), Coronado Heights at the south end of the Silver Strand (U10/V10; five collected of 25 seen 1 January 1938, SDNHM 17677–81, Abbott 1940), and the Tijuana River valley (regular 1962–91 with up to 201 on 18 December 1976, AB 31:882, 1972). In the last area the birds used both agricultural fields and the short grass around the airstrip at Ream Field (Imperial Beach Naval Air Station or Outlying Field; V10).

Migration: October to February was the Mountain Plover's main season in San Diego County, with extreme dates in fall of 20 September (1972, 15 in the Tijuana River valley, G. McCaskie), in spring of 18 March (at Ocotillo Wells) and 3 April (1884, flocks seen—but no specimen collected—in Santa Ysabel Valley, I18/J18, Emerson 1887). The only report since 1991 is of a migrant at Stuart Mesa (G4) 19 October 1999 (P. A. Ginsburg, NAB 54:105, 2000).

Conservation: Abbott (1940) implied the Mountain Plover was already in decline by the late 1930s. On San Diego Christmas bird counts, the species was found in the Tijuana River valley almost annually from 1966, when the count circle was shifted to include the area, until 1979, when the count yielded 108. During the 1980s the numbers were much smaller, and the last report from the area was of five from 19 October through November 1991 (G. McCaskie, AB 46:149, 1992).

OYSTERCATCHERS — FAMILY HAEMATOPODIDAE

American Oystercatcher *Haematopus palliatus*

The American Oystercatcher ranges widely, if not continuously, along the Pacific coast of the Americas from Chile north to Mexico. The normal distribution falls barely short of the United States: up to four individuals are seen regularly on Los Coronados Islands off Tijuana, though they are not confirmed to breed there. In southern California the species is rare, most frequent on the Channel Islands.

Migration: There are only two records of apparently pure American Oystercatchers in San Diego County. Cooper (1868) collected one at San Diego 16 May 1862 (MVZ 4488). Over a century passed until the next, seen at Point Loma 20–21 April 1978 (Luther et al. 1983). Another oystercatcher photographed at Point Loma 11 March–7 May 1992 was a hybrid between the American and the Black (Erickson and Terrill 1996).

Photo by Kenneth W. Fink

Taxonomy: The subspecies of the American Oystercatcher reaching southern California is *H. p. frazari* Brewster, 1888, darker on the back and with less white than the nominate subspecies of the Atlantic coast. In the northern half of Baja California the American Oystercatcher hybridizes frequently with the Black Oystercatcher (Jehl 1985).

Black Oystercatcher *Haematopus bachmani*

Though a fairly common resident on Los Coronados Islands, the Black Oystercatcher is just a rare visitor on the nearby coast of San Diego County, seen at all seasons. The oystercatcher frequents natural rocky shorelines, occasionally jetties of riprap. In 2003 a pair was courting on Zuñiga Jetty at the mouth of San Diego Bay—they may have nested and fledged one young.

Winter: Point Loma (S7) and La Jolla (P7) are the primary sites for the Black Oystercatcher in San Diego County.

Photo by Anthony Mercieca

From 1997 to 2002 (all seasons combined) we recorded two sightings at Point Loma, three at La Jolla, plus one from the north end of Sunset Cliffs Natural Park (R7; 24 April 2000, V. P. Johnson). All sightings during the atlas period were of one or two individuals, but up to five were at Point Loma 20 March–2 May 1992 (M. and B. McIntosh, AB 46:480, 1992). Three were at Imperial Beach (V10) 24 September 1980 (AB 35:226, 1981), and one was there 1 May and 13 June 1982 (D. M. Parker, E. A. Cardiff, AB 36: 894, 1016, 1982). The only record for northern San Diego County is of one on the breakwater for the Oceanside harbor (H5) 7 February 1987 (J. O'Brien, AB 41:328, 1987).

Migration: Records of the Black Oystercatcher in San Diego County form no clear seasonal pattern.

Breeding distribution: On 16 May 2003, Robert T. Patton found a pair in courtship display and apparently prospecting for nest sites on Zuñiga Jetty (S8). The birds were seen regularly through 13 June, then disappeared (during incubation?) until 9 July. On 23 July, the last date the oystercatchers were seen at this site in 2003, there were three birds, suggesting a possible juvenile (D. M. Parker, M. Sadowski, L. Norton).

Conservation: Before 1972 the only specific record of the Black Oystercatcher in San Diego County was of the single specimen, collected at Coronado (T9) 2 June 1915 (SDNHM 20645). Since 1977 the species has occurred nearly annually. The possible colonization in 2003 may be part of a continuing trend to slow increase.

STILTS AND AVOCETS — FAMILY RECURVIROSTRIDAE

Black-necked Stilt *Himantopus mexicanus*

The comical Black-necked Stilt is a common year-round resident of shallow lagoons and ponds along San Diego County's coast. It avoids tidal mudflats but uses some inland lakes and ponds—especially sewage ponds. The salt works of south San Diego Bay are by far the stilt's primary site in San Diego County, hosting a third to a half of the approximately 1000 stilts wintering in the county. The stilt apparently colonized the county as a breeding species in the 1930s and 1940s; by the beginning of the 21st century it was about as abundant in summer as at other seasons.

Photo by Anthony Mercieca

Breeding distribution: The ponds of the south San Diego Bay salt works (U10/V10) offer the stilt ideal foraging habitat, while the dikes offer ideal nest sites. On their weekly surveys of the salt works through spring and summer 1993, Stadtlander and Konecny (1994) found close to 200 stilts, and in summer 1997 Michael R. Smith estimated 100 nests. In the Tijuana River estuary (V10), the stilts prefer the old sewage ponds and gravel pits, now reintegrated into the estuary (up to 70 on 21 March 1999, C. G. Edwards). Mission Bay attracts few stilts, with no suggestion of breeding, but the San Diego River flood-control channel and Famosa Slough (R8) are regular breeding sites (up to 25 on 8 April 2000, Y. Ikegaya). In northern San Diego County the stilt occurs at all coastal wetlands, with nesting confirmed for most of them. In this region the most important sites are the east basin of Batiquitos Lagoon (J7; up to 140 on 3 April 1998, F. Hall) and San Elijo Lagoon (L7; average 100 on June–September monthly surveys 1973–83, King et al. 1987).

Breeding stilts are also fairly widespread inland, though generally uncommon. There they occur mainly in the coastal lowland and especially in the valleys

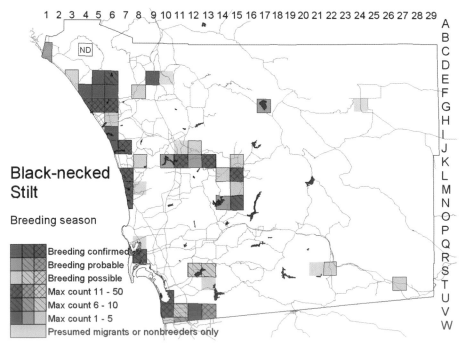

Black-necked Stilt

Breeding season

- Breeding confirmed
- Breeding probable
- Breeding possible
- Max count 11 - 50
- Max count 6 - 10
- Max count 1 - 5
- Presumed migrants or nonbreeders only

of the lower Santa Margarita and San Luis Rey rivers, where there are many ponds. Fifty on a pond at Siempre Viva and La Media roads, Otay Mesa (V13), 12 June 2001 (P. Unitt) and 24 (including juveniles) at ponds at the west end of Santa Maria Valley (K13) 14 July 2000 (P. M. von Hendy) are high inland counts for the breeding season. At 1300–1400 feet elevation, the most inland sites at which we confirmed stilt breeding were Santa Maria Valley, sewage ponds at the base of Spangler Peak in San Vicente Valley (L15; 12 on 6 June 2000, A. Mauro), and Barona Valley (N15; six, including young, on 16 July 2001, J. Smith). But the species may breed also at Lake Henshaw (G17; up to four on 18 June 2000, P. Unitt), the upper end of Lake Morena (S22; up to 12 on 2 July 2000, R. and S. L. Breisch), and Tule Lake (T27; up to four on 6 June 2001, J. K. Wilson).

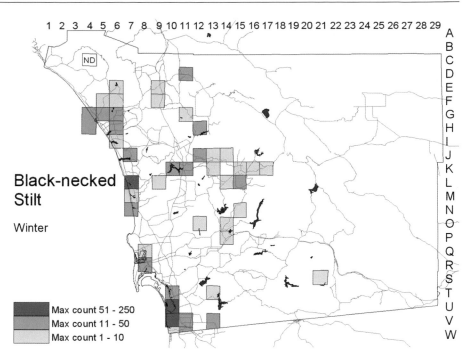

Black-necked Stilt

Winter

Max count 51 - 250
Max count 11 - 50
Max count 1 - 10

Nesting: The Black-necked Stilt nests on the ground, sometimes amid low vegetation, sometimes in the open, as on the dikes of sewage ponds or the salt works. If there is loose debris around the nest, the birds gather it around the eggs. The adults call constantly and feign injury and incubation as an intruder approaches the nest, driving birders as well as predators to distraction. Our dates for nests with eggs or incubating adults ranged from 15 April to 18 July.

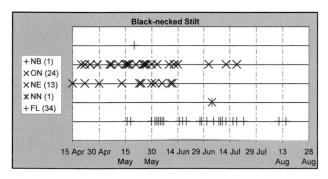

Migration: Information on stilt movements in San Diego County is contradictory, perhaps because of changes in habitat use by season and the irregularity of water levels attractive to the birds. Unitt (1984) reported the species most abundant in fall migration, peaking in August. At Lake Hodges K. L. Weaver noted a maximum of 30 on 3 August 1985. At San Elijo Lagoon, King et al. (1987) found the stilt most common from June to September, least common from November to March. In the salt works, Stadtlander and Konecny (1994) found the numbers maintained from February to August 1993 increasing to a higher level from September 1993 to February 1994.

At ponds in the Borrego Valley the stilt is a rare migrant, recorded from 28 March (P. D. Ache) to 12 May in spring, from 31 July to 22 September in fall (ABDSP database). Numbers there are usually small; the maximum is of 25 at the Borrego sewage ponds (H25) 25–26 April 1987 (A. G. Morley).

Winter: The stilt's distribution in winter is quite similar to that during the breeding season. In the salt works, Stadtlander and Konecny (1994) found up to 685 on 9 February 1994; during the atlas period, our maximum there was 253 on 19 December 1998 (D. C. Seals et al.). Along the north San Diego County's coast, where the stilt becomes less abundant in winter, our high counts were of 40 in the Santa Margarita River estuary (G4) 10 December 1999 (P. A. Ginsburg), 39 at sewage ponds near there (G5) 6 December 1998 (R. E. Fischer), and 80 at San Elijo Lagoon 22 December 2000 (G. C. Hazard). Numbers inland ranged up to 30 at Whelan Lake (G6) 23 December 2000 (D. K. Adams) and 41 at Siempre Viva and La Media roads 29 December 2000 (P. Unitt).

From 1997 to 2002 our winter records farthest inland were of one in Ballena Valley (K17) 15 January 1999 (D. C. Seals) and three on the north side of Lake Morena (S21) 24 February 2002 (R. and S. L. Breisch). The species has been found once on a Lake Henshaw Christmas bird count, with two on 19 December 1994, and once on an Anza–Borrego Christmas bird count, with one on 31 December 1988.

Conservation: The Black-necked Stilt was first found nesting in San Diego County in 1931 (Willett 1933); previously it was known as a migrant only (Stephens 1919a). Creation of the salt works undoubtedly increased the stilt's numbers greatly, and the installation of sewage ponds and reservoirs added new sites. Kenneth L. Weaver suspected nesting inland at Lake Hodges since the late 1970s and first confirmed it there and in the San Pasqual Valley (J12) in 1982. Over the final quarter of the 20ᵗʰ century, however, the stilt's numbers seem to have held steady.

Taxonomy: The classification of the world's stilts has varied, but the current practice (A. O. U. 1998) is to group the subspecies of the New World, including that of Hawaii, under *Himantopus mexicanus* (Müller, 1776). The nominate subspecies occurs throughout North America.

American Avocet *Recurvirostra americana*

The American Avocet's primitive habitat is shifting shallow wetlands, which it sweeps for aquatic invertebrates. In spite of the loss of much of this habitat, the avocet remains locally common in San Diego County by taking advantage of salt ponds, sewage ponds, and partially blocked lagoons. Once considered just a migrant in San Diego County, the avocet now occurs year round. Though it nests on the ground, the avocet often enjoys success, with the help of its screaming and strafing of any approaching predator.

Photo by Anthony Mercieca

Breeding distribution: From 1997 to 2001, Batiquitos Lagoon was the center of avocet abundance in San Diego County, with up to 184 adults in the east basin (J7) 3 April 1998 (F. Hall) and 36 nests within one Least Tern colony in 2001 (S. M. Wolf). The species occurred in all the other wetlands of coastal northern San Diego County, however, from Aliso Creek (F4) to Los Peñasquitos Lagoon (N7), with nesting confirmed at almost all of these. Also, small numbers nest at several sites up to 8 miles inland in the valleys of the Santa Margarita and San Luis Rey rivers. Along the county's south coast known nesting sites are Famosa Slough (R8; nest 25 April–7 May 1997, J. A. and B. J. Peugh), the south San Diego Bay salt works (U10/ V10; 40 nests estimated in 1997, M. R. Smith), Camp Surf along the beach just north of Imperial Beach (V10; nest 22 April 2001, T. Stands, S. Yamagata), the Tijuana River estuary (V10/W10; five nests 22 April 1997, B. L. Peterson), and inland in the Tijuana River valley (W11;

pair in distraction display 19 June 1999, P. Unitt).

We also found avocets nesting at several scattered sites well inland. The largest numbers of birds were at Lake Henshaw (G17; up to 30, some in distraction display, 18 June 2000, P. Unitt), the east end of Lake Hodges (K11; up to 40, including young, 9 June 1997, E. C. Hall), and the pond at Siempre Viva and La Media roads, Otay Mesa (V13; up to 20, including young, 12 June 2001, P. Unitt). Some other sites, such as a sewage pond near the Barona Casino (N14), had just an isolated pair (nest 29 June 1997, P. R. Pryde). All of these sites are on the coastal slope except for one on the Campo Plateau at Tule Lake (T27; six on 21 June 2000, J. K. Wilson).

Nesting: Sometimes avocets nest in shallow depressions with no nesting material whatsoever. The birds apparently nesting on extensive flats devoid of vegetation on the north side of Lake Henshaw were in such a situation. Often, however, as in marshes of pickleweed, they build a substantial platform of debris. Our dates for avocet nests ranged from 20 April to 29 June, with one already with four eggs in the salt works 1 April 1997 (M. R. Smith).

Migration: The seasonal pattern of avocet abundance in San Diego County varies from site to site with variations in water levels, which may mask the evidence of large-scale migrations. On the basis of monthly counts at San Elijo Lagoon (L7) 1973–83, King et al. (1987) found the avocet's average abundance peaking in March and April, relative-

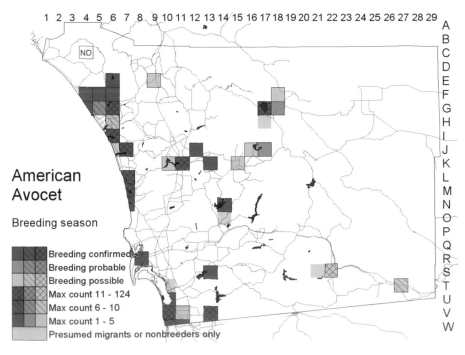

1 2 3 4 5 6 7 8 9 10 11 12 13 14 15 16 17 18 19 20 21 22 23 24 25 26 27 28 29

ND

A B C D E F G H I J K L M N O P Q R S T U V W

American Avocet

Breeding season

Breeding confirmed
Breeding probable
Breeding possible
Max count 11 - 124
Max count 6 - 10
Max count 1 - 5
Presumed migrants or nonbreeders only

ly low from August to January. Yet their maximum count was in December. On the basis of weekly counts in the salt works February 1993–February 1994, Stadtlander and Konecny (1994) found avocet abundance peaking in winter, with a maximum count of 467 in January, then falling to an average of about 25 from May to August. In the Anza–Borrego Desert, where the avocet is a rare visitor, records range from 11 September (1982, 12 at Middle Willows, C22) to 12 May (1974, three at Bow Willow Ranger Station, P28, ABDSP database). None was found there during the atlas period. Indeed, from 1997 to 2002, atlas observers saw almost no avocets far from sites of likely breeding.

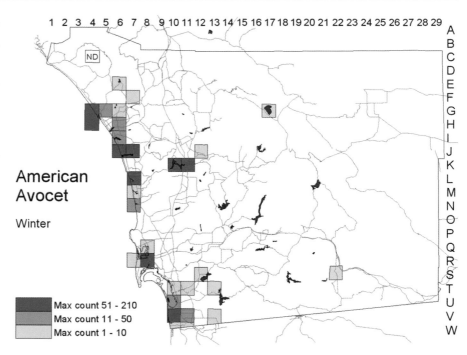

American Avocet

Winter

Max count 51 - 210
Max count 11 - 50
Max count 1 - 10

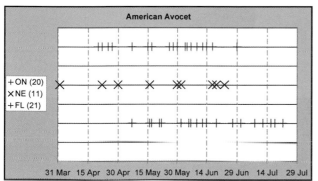

American Avocet

+ON (20)
×NE (11)
+FL (21)

31 Mar   15 Apr   30 Apr   15 May   30 May   14 Jun   29 Jun   14 Jul   29 Jul

Winter: In winter the avocet is concentrated at the same coastal wetlands where it nests. During the atlas period the primary sites were Batiquitos Lagoon (up to 210 on 2 January 1998, C. C. Gorman), San Elijo Lagoon (up to 600 on 23 February 1997, A. Mauro), and the old sewage ponds and gravel pits now reintegrated into the Tijuana estuary (up to 197 on 18 December 1999, R. B. Riggan). Inland, the major site by far is Lake Hodges, with up to

70 on 9 December 1997 (E. C. Hall). We did not find the avocet in winter at several inland sites where we found it during the breeding season. Our only winter records outside the coastal lowland were from the upper end of Lake Morena (S22; one on 5 December 1999, R. and S. L. Breisch) and Lake Henshaw (noted on 5 of 22 Lake Henshaw Christmas bird counts 1981–2002, with up to six on 19 December 1994 but no more than two 1997–2002). The Anza–Borrego count has recorded the avocet only once, a flock of 19 on 17 December 1995.

Conservation: The American Avocet has lost considerable habitat throughout its range, including southern California. But the establishment of the salt works, reservoirs, and sewage ponds created new habitat in San Diego County, probably increasing what was available under primitive conditions. The avocet's colonizing the county as a breeding species evidently began in the 1950s (Sams and Stott 1959). By the 1970s the birds were not yet nesting regularly in the salt works (Unitt 1984). Their nesting inland in the county was first confirmed in 1982 with five pairs at Lake Hodges 19 June (K. L. Weaver).

SANDPIPERS AND SNIPES — FAMILY SCOLOPACIDAE

Greater Yellowlegs *Tringa melanoleuca*

The Greater Yellowlegs is one of San Diego County's most widespread shorebirds, found at reservoirs and small ponds inland as well as along the coast. It seldom gathers in flocks, however. It is common as a fall migrant, generally uncommon as a winter visitor and spring migrant, and rare as a nonbreeding summer visitor—during an interval barely four weeks long from late May to mid June.

Winter: The Greater Yellowlegs is widespread in San Diego County's coastal wetlands, especially those with extensive

Photo by Anthony Mercieca

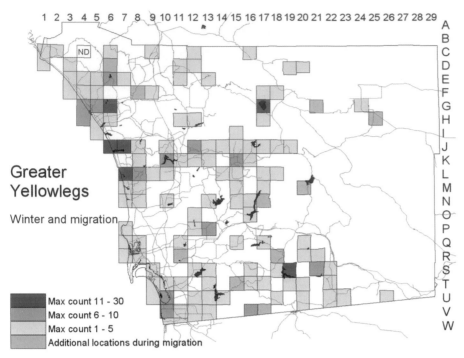

Greater Yellowlegs

Winter and migration

Max count 11 - 30
Max count 6 - 10
Max count 1 - 5
Additional locations during migration

Migration: The Greater Yellowlegs is one of the earliest migrants to return in "fall," even before the summer solstice. Our earliest apparent migrants 1997–2001 were seven at the upper end of Sweetwater Reservoir (S13) 17 June 1999 (P. Famolaro) and one at Chollas Reservoir 18 June 1998 (P. Unitt). Fall migrants are regular by the first week of July and peak in September, according to weekly censuses in the salt works 1993–94, where Stadtlander and Konecny (1994) recorded a high 46 on 15 September 1993. At San Elijo Lagoon, King et al. (1987) recorded the peak monthly average of 15 in August and September.

In spring, migration takes place from March to mid May. Its amplitude at that season is less than in fall, though a concentration of 45 was at Bonsall (F8) 3 April 1998 (L. Gammie). Our latest spring migrants were one at the upper end of Lake Sutherland (J17) 17 May 2000 (J. O. Zimmer) and four at the upper end of Lake Hodges (K11) 18 May 1997 (E. C. Hall). In the Borrego Valley the Greater Yellowlegs is more frequent in migration than in winter, though still rare, from 25 September (1999, one at Borrego Springs Country Club, G24, P. D. Jorgensen) to 3 May (1997, one at the Borrego Springs sewage ponds, H25, H. L. Young, M. B. Mosher).

During the atlas period, we had 12 reports of single Greater Yellowlegs between 21 May and 12 June, evidently summering. Most of these were coastal but one was at O'Neill Lake (G6) 12 June 2001 (P. A. Ginsburg), another at the east end of Lake Hodges 3 June 1997 (E. C. Hall). Much larger numbers of summering birds occur occasionally on south San Diego Bay, however: up to 40 in June 1987, 62 on 15 June 1991 (R. E. Webster, AB 41:1487, 1987; 45:1161, 1991), and 26 on 12 June 1989 (Macdonald et al. 1990).

tidal mudflats. Numbers along the coast range up to 30 in the east basin of Batiquitos Lagoon (J7) 15 February 1998 (R. Campbell), 18 at San Elijo Lagoon (L7) 23 December 2001 (E. Garnica), 25 in and near the south San Diego Bay salt works (U10/V10) in December 1993 (Stadtlander and Konecny 1994), and 10 in the Tijuana River estuary (V10) 24 January 1998 (B. C. Moore). On the basis of monthly counts 1973–83, the November–April average at San Elijo Lagoon was 4.3 (King et al. 1987); on the basis of weekly counts 1993–94, the December–February monthly averages in and near the salt works were 7 to 17.

The Greater Yellowlegs can be just as numerous inland, even far inland, as along the coast. From 1997 to 2002, our inland counts in winter ranged up to 20 at Whelan Lake (G6) 21 January 1998 (D. Rorick), 10 in San Pasqual Valley (J12) 26 February 1999 (D. and D. Bylin), 20 at Lake Henshaw (G17) 29 December 1997 (J. O. Zimmer), and 13 at Barrett Reservoir (S19) 2 February 2001 (R. and S. L. Breisch). The Escondido Christmas bird count averages 4.8, the Lake Henshaw count 4.4. Winter records range in elevation up to about 4000 feet, exceptionally to about 4600 feet in Lost Valley (D20; one on 21 January 2000, J. M. and B. Hargrove). In the Anza–Borrego Desert there are four winter records of single birds on ponds in the Borrego Valley, just one during the atlas period, in Borrego Springs (G24) 9 February 1998 (P. D. Ache).

Conservation: With its less social habits and more diverse habitats, the Greater Yellowlegs has sustained its numbers better than have some other large shorebirds. Over the second half of the 20th century there was no trend in the species' numbers in San Diego County. Loss of tidal mudflats and seasonal wetlands in floodplains may have been offset by importation of water and creation of ponds and reservoirs.

Lesser Yellowlegs *Tringa flavipes*

The Lesser Yellowlegs is much less conspicuous and usually less numerous than its larger relative, the Greater Yellowlegs. In San Diego County, the Lesser is fairly common in migration but rare in winter; California is the northern limit of the species' winter range. For habitat, the Lesser Yellowlegs prefers salt marshes, brackish coastal lagoons, and shallow freshwater ponds. It is much less frequent inland than the Greater.

Migration: The Lesser Yellowlegs is most numerous in San Diego County as a fall migrant. It arrives rarely as early as 29 June (1977, one at the San Dieguito River mouth, M7, P. Unitt), regularly in early July. Numbers peak in August and September, then drop in October.

Spring migration begins in late February, as indicated by two in southwest Escondido (J10) 19 February 1998 (O. Carter) and six at the Santa Margarita River mouth (G4) 25 February 2000 (P. A. Ginsburg). Most spring migrants pass through in March and April; from 1997 to 2001 our latest date was 25 April (2001; one at Daley Ranch, H11, A. Mauro). On their monthly surveys of San Elijo Lagoon (L7) 1973–83, King et al. (1987) found the Lesser Yellowlegs twice in May, the latest one on 4 May 1975. The only records of oversummering Lesser Yellowlegs are of one near Imperial Beach (V10) 17 June 1987 (R. E. Webster, AB 41:1487, 1987) and two at San Elijo Lagoon 1 June 2000 (A. Mauro).

The lagoons of northern San Diego County are the species' favored sites. At San Elijo Lagoon, King et al.

Photo by Anthony Mercieca

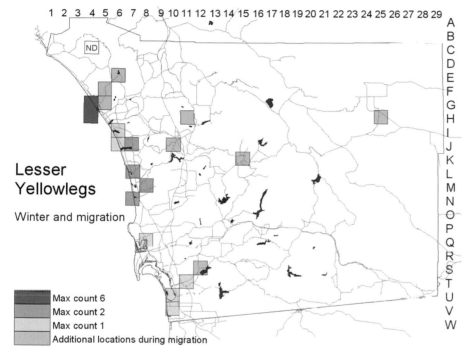

Lesser Yellowlegs

Winter and migration

Max count 6
Max count 2
Max count 1
Additional locations during migration

(1987) found an average of 10 in August and September and an average of 7.5 in March and April. Their fall maximum was 44 on 12 September 1976; their spring maximum was 37 on 1 April 1979. Along the coast of southern San Diego County the Lesser Yellowlegs is uncommon; in surveys of south San Diego Bay and the salt works, neither Macdonald et al. (1990) nor Stadtlander and Konecny (1994) found more than six per day.

Inland the Lesser Yellowlegs is scarcer still and found mainly in floodplains and at reservoirs near the coast. Eight in Ysidora Basin (F5) 12 April 1998 (R. E. Fischer) was our largest count during the atlas period. On the coastal slope our most inland site for the Lesser Yellowlegs was Ramona (K15), with three on 19 March 1999 and one on 20 April 1998 (M. and B. McIntosh). At the east end of Lake Hodges (K11), K. L. Weaver noted up to six on 6 August 1981. There are three records from the Borrego Valley, of one at the Roadrunner Club (F24) 17 April 1991

(A. G. Morley), one at the Ram's Hill ponds (H25) 24 April 1994, and one at the Borrego sewage ponds (H25) 21 March 1999 (P. D. Jorgensen).

Winter: From December through mid February atlas observers reported no more than two Lesser Yellowlegs per atlas square per day. Macdonald et al. (1990) reported up to four around south San Diego Bay 6 February 1989. Totals on San Diego Christmas bird counts range up to nine, though they average 2.1. The Rancho Santa Fe count averages 1.8, the Oceanside count 0.7. Thus, contrary to what I reported previously (Unitt 1984), the Lesser Yellowlegs now winters in the north county lagoons just as often as around San Diego Bay. During the atlas period, 18 of 24 winter reports were in the north county. The only inland area where we found the species 1997–2002 was San Dieguito Valley (M8), with three sightings of single individuals. There are just two other inland winter records, of one in San Pasqual Valley (J12) 4 January 1997 (P. Unitt) and one on the Anza–Borrego Christmas bird count 30 December 1990.

Conservation: The winter range of the Lesser Yellowlegs may have spread north into California in the 20th century, though this inconspicuous species could have been overlooked. Grinnell and Miller (1944) listed only three winter records for California, and the one from San Diego County (Michael 1935b) was more likely of misidentified Greater Yellowlegs. Nevertheless, in San Diego County wetlands attractive to the Lesser Yellowlegs have been much reduced, especially freshwater wetlands in floodplains near the coast.

Spotted Redshank *Tringa erythropus*

The Spotted Redshank is a shorebird of the Old World, seldom seen in North America. Of the five records for California, one is from San Diego County.

Migration: San Diego County's Spotted Redshank was photographed in percolation basins just west of O'Neill Lake, Camp Pendleton (E6), 19–23 May 1989 (E. Dore, AB 43:396, 538, Pyle and McCaskie 1992).

Photo by Anthony Mercieca

Solitary Sandpiper *Tringa solitaria*

The Solitary Sandpiper is a sandpiper of fresh or brackish water only, found mainly on ponds, lakeshores, and sluggish streams, especially where these are overhung by vegetation. In San Diego County it is principally a fall migrant, uncommon to rare. There are just a few records for winter and spring.

Migration: Because of its preference for fresh water, the Solitary Sandpiper occurs widely over San Diego County's coastal slope. Most records, though, are from the coastal lowland, where the suitable habitat is concentrated. The Tijuana River valley yields the largest numbers, up to 10 on 4 September 1998 (P. A. Ginsburg). The species has been found up to Lake Henshaw (G17; up to three on 12 August 1985, R. Higson) and Lake Cuyamaca (M20; one on 12 August 1986, D. B. King). The only fall record for the Anza–Borrego Desert is of one in the Borrego Valley (F24/G24) 26 September 1991 (M. L. Gabel).

Photo by Anthony Mercieca

The Solitary Sandpiper passes through San Diego County mainly in August and September. Extreme dates are 14 July (2000, one in Santa Maria Valley west of Ramona, K13, P. M. von Hendy) and 18 October (1975, one at Otay Mesa, V13, AB 30:126, 1976), except for a late straggler at Upper Otay Lake (T13) 20 November 1999 (P. Unitt, NAB 54:105, 2000).

Three spring sightings during the atlas period were unexpected. Two Solitary Sandpipers were in the estuary of Aliso Creek (F4) 31 March 2001 (B. Anderson, K. Estey, J. M. Roberts), one was at a vernal pool in the Santa Maria Valley west of Ramona (K13) 24 April 1999 (F. Sproul), and one was along San Ysidro Creek at the Pacific Crest Trail (G20) 27 April 1999 (L. J. Hargrove). In the Borrego Valley, one was at the Ram's Hill sewage pond (H25) 4–10 April 1994 (ABDSP database). The three earlier spring records for San Diego County, listed by Unitt (1984), fall within the range of dates of the more recent ones.

Winter: The winter records of the Solitary Sandpiper in San Diego County probably represent only two individuals. One was in the Tijuana River valley 28 February–13 April 1988 (F. Dexter, AB 42:321, 481, 1988). Another apparently returned repeatedly to Santee Lakes (O12/P12), being reported 6 March 1990 (C. G. Edwards, AB 44:329, 1990), 21–23 March 1992 (AB 46:480, 1992), and 8–14 February 1995 (NASFN 49:197, 1995).

Conservation: Like other shorebirds preferring fresh water, the Solitary Sandpiper has lost much habitat with the decline of agriculture and the spread of cities. Muddy ponds seldom fit in a landscape being managed ever more intensively.

Taxonomy: All specimens of the Solitary Sandpiper collected in California, including the one from San Diego County (southeast San Diego, S10, 1 September 1931, SDNHM 15606), are of the western subspecies *T. s. cinnamomea* (Brewster, 1890). It has the spots on the upperparts deeper buff than in the more eastern nominate subspecies, which should occur occasionally as a vagrant but has yet to be recorded in California.

Willet *Catoptrophorus semipalmatus*

The Willet is one of the more abundant shorebirds along San Diego County's coast, especially around south San Diego Bay and in the Tijuana River estuary, where it can be seen in flocks of hundreds, often with Marbled Godwits. The population wintering in the county as a whole is about 2500 to 3000, and even larger numbers occur in fall migration. Dozens of nonbreeding birds remain through the summer. Tidal mudflats and salt marshes are the Willet's primary habitats, though the species is fairly common on beaches, lagoons, and rocky shores as well.

Photo by Anthony Mercieca

Winter: From 1997 to 2002, our numbers of the Willet in the Tijuana River estuary (V10) ranged up to 700 on 3 December 1999 (B. C. Moore); in south San Diego Bay at Chula Vista (U10) they ranged up to 630 on 16 December 2000. In weekly surveys in and near the salt works 1993–94, Stadtlander and Konecny (1994) found numbers from December to February averaging around 600 to 750. Numbers elsewhere around San Diego are also substantial, with up to 200 in the Paradise Creek marsh, National City (T10), 6 March 2000 (T. A. Godshalk), 138 around North Island (S8) 18 December 1999 (R. T. Patton), and 150 in northeastern Mission Bay (Q8) 29 December 1998 (J. C. Worley).

In northern San Diego County the Willet is much less abundant, as shown by the averages of 93 for the Oceanside Christmas bird count 1976–2002 and 74 for the Rancho Santa Fe count 1980–2003 versus 1219 for the San Diego count 1953–2002. The species' primary sites in the north county during the atlas period were the east basin of Batiquitos Lagoon (J7; up to 139 on 27 December 1997, F. Hall) and Los Peñasquitos Lagoon (N7; up to 80 on 5 December 1999, D. K. Adams).

Inland, the Willet is rare. In winter, it is known inland only in the coastal lowland. Our nine winter records from fresh water during the atlas period ranged in number up to five at the Dairy Mart pond, Tijuana River valley (V11) 20 December 1997 (G. McCaskie) and extended inland as far as San Pasqual Valley (J12; one on 2 January 1999, M. Cassidy, the only Willet found on an Escondido Christmas bird count), the upper end of Lake Hodges (K11; one on 13 December 1999, B. C. Moore), and Lower Otay Lake (U13; one on 14 February 1999, J. R. Barth).

Migration: For many shorebirds the interval between spring and fall migration is brief, but for the Willet it is one of the briefest, perhaps only two weeks. Along the coast, because of the prevalence of summering birds, the arrival and departure of migrants is obscured. Nevertheless, migrants may arrive as early as 19 June. Even three at Barrett Lake (S19) 10 June 2001 (R. and S. L. Breisch) must have been early fall migrants. By 1 July migrants are returning in large numbers. A female Willet nesting at Lakeview, southeastern Oregon, was banded and radiotagged 31 May 1999, suffered predation of her clutch of eggs between 11 and 14 June, departed on 23 June, and was seen at Mission Bay 8 July (J. Plissner, L. D. Johnson). Monthly surveys of San Elijo Lagoon (L7) 1973–83 found Willet numbers peaking in August and September (King et al. 1987), whereas weekly surveys of the San Diego Bay salt works 1993–94 found them peaking in October and November, with a maximum of 1385 on 3 November 1993 (Stadtlander and Konecny 1994).

In spring, in contrast to fall, there is no distinct peak of migration. Occasional migrants may still be moving as late as 29 May (Unitt 1984), but the surveys of San Elijo Lagoon and the salt works found Willet numbers

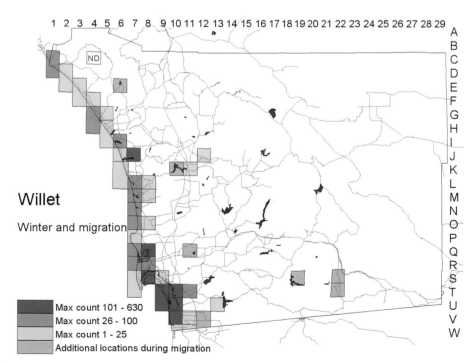

Willet

Winter and migration

- ■ Max count 101 - 630
- ■ Max count 26 - 100
- ▨ Max count 1 - 25
- ▧ Additional locations during migration

to be at their lows for the year in May as in early June.

Migrating Willets have been recorded a few times in the foothills and desert as well as nearer the coast. Richard and Susan Breisch noted Willets twice at the east end of Lake Morena (S22/T22), 12 July and 2 August 1997, while the Anza–Borrego Desert State Park database has records from the Borrego Palm Canyon campground (F23) 25 April 1985, the Roadrunner Club, Borrego Springs (F24), 28 March 1994, and from a gravel pit along Highway S2 near the Imperial County line (Q29), miles from any water, 19 August 1975.

Conservation: The development of Mission and San Diego bays eliminated much prime Willet habitat. Christmas bird count results, however, show no trend in the species' numbers over the final quarter of the 20th century.

Taxonomy: The Willet consists of two well-marked subspecies. The larger and, in breeding plumage, less heavily marked *C. s. inornatus* (Brewster, 1887), breeding in the intermountain region and northern Great Plains, is the subspecies wintering in California.

Wandering Tattler *Heteroscelus incanus*

Of San Diego County's shorebirds, the Wandering Tattler is the most restricted to rocky shorelines, though the rocks may be breakwaters of riprap as well as natural formations. The tattler is an uncommon migrant and winter visitor to San Diego County, occurring mainly from August to April.

Winter: San Diego County's two principal areas of natural rocky shoreline, La Jolla and Point Loma, are the tattler's principal sites. At La Jolla (P7), our counts from 1997 to 2002 ranged up to six on 24 February 2002 (K. L.Weaver). Around La Jolla, the tattlers are found regularly from Torrey Pines State Reserve (N7) to Pacific Beach (Q7). At Point Loma (S7), our counts during the atlas period ranged up to only five on 20 December 1997 (M. W. Klein), but totals on San Diego Christmas bird counts range up to 25 on 20 December 1980, and much of the tattler habitat on Point Loma is outside the count circle. Small numbers of tattlers are regular on Zuñiga Jetty at the mouth of San Diego Bay (S8; up to four on 16 December 2000, seven on 18 December 1976, D. W.

Photo by Anthony Mercieca

Povey), occasional on the breakwaters at the mouth of Mission Bay (R7; up to two on 26 February 2000, V. P. Johnson).

In northern San Diego County the Wandering Tattler is regular only on the breakwaters for the Oceanside harbor (G4/H5). From 1997 to 2002 our maximum counts here were of only two individuals; totals on Oceanside Christmas bird counts average 1.9 and range up to five on 22 December 1979. One tattler was at the mouth of Agua Hedionda Lagoon (I6) 26 December 1998 (C. Sankpill); another was at the mouth of San Elijo Lagoon (L7) 30 December 1998 (R. T. Patton).

Within Mission and San Diego bays the Wandering Tattler is rare. During the atlas periods the only records were both from Mission Bay (Q8), of single birds 13 December 1998 (J. C. Worley) and 1 January 2002 (G. C. Hazard). Neither Macdonald et al. (1990) nor Stadtlander and Konecny (1994) found the tattler on their regular surveys in south San Diego Bay.

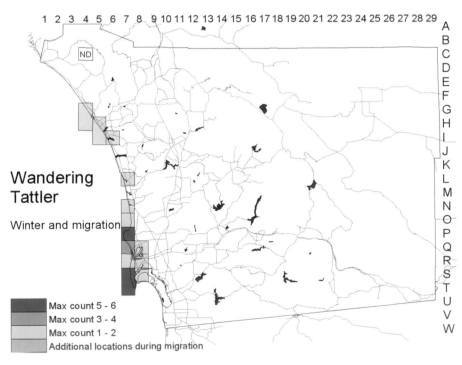

Wandering Tattler

Winter and migration

Max count 5 - 6
Max count 3 - 4
Max count 1 - 2
Additional locations during migration

Migration: Dates for the tattler in San Diego County range from 12 July (1999, one on the breakwater for the harbor at Camp Pendleton's Camp Del Mar, G4, P. A. Ginsburg) to 22 May (1971, one at Shelter Island, S8, A. Fries). Though most immature Wandering Tattlers remain through the summer in their winter range (Gill et al. 2002), the only records of oversummering birds in San Diego County remain the three listed by Unitt (1984).

Conservation: The installation of breakwaters gave the Wandering Tattler a little additional habitat in San Diego County.

Spotted Sandpiper *Actitis macularius*

After the Greater Yellowlegs, the Spotted Sandpiper is the most widespread sandpiper in San Diego County, found widely inland as well as along the coast. It is not gregarious, however, so it is generally uncommon in winter, fairly common in migration. It is seldom found on tidal mudflats, preferring instead lakeshores, freshwater ponds, brackish lagoons, rocky ocean shores, and sandy beaches. The Spotted is the only sandpiper that nests in San Diego County, albeit in small numbers. The county's breeding records are the southernmost for the species.

Photo by Anthony Mercieca

Winter: Because of its diverse habitats, the Spotted Sandpiper is widespread on San Diego County's coast, though its density in winter is low. In San Diego Bay, the Spotted Sandpiper is more numerous on the sandy and riprap-lined shores of the north bay (up to seven on the waterfront of downtown San Diego, S9, 20 December 1998, Y. Ikegaya) than on the mudflats of the south bay [no more than four per day reported by atlas observers, Macdonald et al. (1990), or Stadtlander and Konecny (1994)].

Wintering Spotted Sandpipers are more numerous inland than along the coast. The largest numbers, up to 21 on 26 December 1999, have been found at Lake Hodges (K10; R. L. Barber). Other sites of notable concentrations from 1997 to 2002 were Lake Henshaw (G17;

up to eight on 21 December 1998, S. J. Montgomery), along San Marcos Creek near Questhaven Road (J8; up to 10 on 23 December 2000, J. O. Zimmer), and Sweetwater Reservoir (S12; up to nine on 19 December 1998, P. Famolaro). The Spotted Sandpiper is regular at Lake Morena (T21/S21/S22), with up to four on 24 February 2002 (R. and S. L. Breisch), but at 3000 feet this is the highest elevation where we found the species in winter.

The Spotted Sandpiper is a rare winter visitor to ponds in the Borrego Valley with one or two recorded on 11 of 19 Anza–Borrego Christmas bird counts 1984–2002. During the atlas period our only winter record from this area was of one in the north Borrego Valley (E24) 19 December 1999 (P. R. Pryde).

Migration: The Spotted Sandpiper's migration schedule cannot be established precisely because of the small number of summering birds. Nevertheless, fall migrants arrive in July, exceptionally as early as 30 June (1978, one at the San Diego River mouth, R7, C. G. Edwards). Their peak is in September or October, with up to 17 at San Elijo Lagoon 10 September 1978 (King et al. 1987) and 17 at Batiquitos Lagoon (J6/J7) 27–28 October 1997 (Merkel and Associates 1997). Four fall records for the Anza–Borrego Desert include four birds at an ephemeral pond in Mortero Wash Narrows (R29) 22 August 1991 (M. C. Jorgensen).

Spring migration takes place mainly from mid April to mid May. Spring migrants are widespread, occurring occasionally

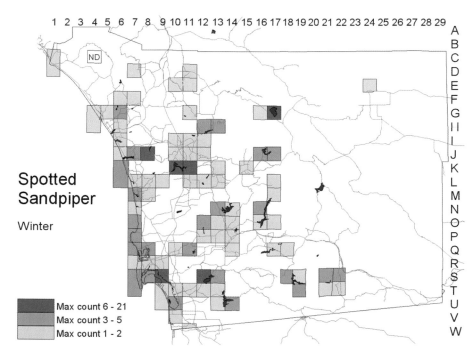

Spotted Sandpiper

Winter

- Max count 6 - 21
- Max count 3 - 5
- Max count 1 - 2

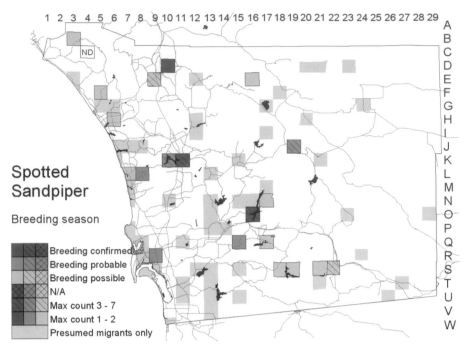

Spotted
Sandpiper

Breeding season

Breeding confirmed
Breeding probable
Breeding possible
N/A
Max count 3 - 7
Max count 1 - 2
Presumed migrants only

ing listed above, these included Wynola (J19; agitated pair 15 May 1999, S. E. Smith), the borrow pit in the Sweetwater River bed at Dehesa (Q15; pair 6 May and 1 June 1999, W. E. Haas), San Diego River in Mission Valley just east of Highway 163 (R9; pair 15 May 1997, J. K. Wilson; up to four on 10 and 15 May 1991, P. Unitt), and the upper end of Lake Morena (S22; up to three on 30 May 1999, R. and S. L. Breisch).

Nesting: The Spotted Sandpiper nests in a scrape on the ground, screened by low vegetation and lined with nearby grass (Oring et al. 1997). The limited data from San Diego County indicate the species lays here from at least mid May to late June. The

as high as 5400 feet at Big Laguna Lake (O23; two on 10 May 1997, M. R. Smith) and at isolated desert oases like Carrizo Marsh (O29; one on 27 April 2000 and 11 May 2001 (M. C. and P. D. Jorgensen). Ten at Sweetwater Reservoir 23 April 1998 (P. Famolaro) was our largest spring concentration during the atlas period. Spring dates for the Anza–Borrego Desert, where summering is implausible, run as late as 22 May 2001 (one in Borrego Springs, G24, P. D. Ache).

Breeding distribution: Confirmed nesting sites for the Spotted Sandpiper in San Diego County are at a borrow pit in the San Luis Rey River between the aqueduct and Gomez Creek (D10; chick with adult 22 June–4 July 2000, C. M. Manning), the upper end of Lake Hodges (K11; pair with young 26–30 July 1981 and 16–25 July 1982, G. McCaskie, K. L. Weaver, AB 36:1016, 1982; nest with eggs 3 June 1997, E. C. Hall), San Elijo Lagoon (L7; three pairs and two young 6 June 1982, D. M. Parker, AB 36:1016, 1982; three pairs nesting in summer 1983 D. King, AB 37:1027, 1983; nest with eggs 14 July 1986, S. and J. Gallagher, AB 40:1255, 1986), and the south end of El Capitan Reservoir (O16; pair with chicks 9 July 2001, R. T. Patton, J. R. Barth, P. Unitt). Also, in the Tijuana River valley, a pair "appeared to be defending a territory" 9 June 1984 (J. Oldenettel, AB 38:1062, 1984).

One surprise of field work for this atlas was the number of locations for possibly breeding Spotted Sandpipers: at least 18. In addition to the sites of confirmed nest-

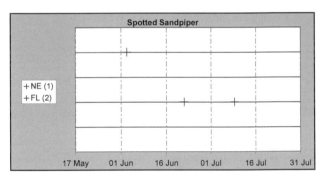

Spotted Sandpiper's habit of polyandrous mating, well studied in Minnesota, may be less prevalent in an area like San Diego County, marginal to the species' range, where the nesting population is sparse.

Conservation: The Spotted Sandpiper's breeding in San Diego County is recent, reported first in 1981. The creation of reservoirs and ponds (including the borrow pits left by sand mining in riverbeds) probably allowed the sandpiper to extend its breeding range south to San Diego County. Nevertheless, a few possible breeding sites are along undammed wilderness creeks, especially San Mateo Creek (B3; one on 27 May 2001, P. Unitt) and the west fork of the San Luis Rey River in Barker Valley (E16; one on 30 May 1999, R. Bergstrom). The same reservoirs and ponds allow the Spotted Sandpiper to winter more widely inland than under primitive conditions.

Upland Sandpiper *Bartramia longicauda*

Unlike other sandpipers, the Upland Sandpiper avoids water; rather than probing mud, it plucks insects from grass. It breeds largely in central North America and reaches California only as a vagrant. There is only one record for San Diego County.

Migration: The single Upland Sandpiper known from San Diego County was photographed on the sod farm at the east end of the Tijuana River valley (W11) 19–23 October 1999 (G. McCaskie, NAB 54:104, 105, 2000, Rogers and Jaramillo 2002). The 10 other fall records for California are all for August and September.

Photo by Jack W. Schlotte

Whimbrel *Numenius phaeopus*

The Whimbrel can be seen along San Diego County's coastline year round but is by far most common in fall migration, July through September. The number remaining through the winter is on the order of 100 to 200. The Whimbrel prefers tidal mudflats but also uses salt marshes, sandy beaches, and rocky shorelines. More than 5 miles inland the species is rare and seen only during migration.

Winter: Wintering Whimbrels are generally uncommon in San Diego County, though widespread along the coast. Kjelmyr et al. (1991) estimated the number wintering as high as 10–100 only in the Tijuana River estuary (V10/W10); at other sites they estimated fewer than 10. On counts of south San Diego Bay in November 1988 and February 1989 Macdonald et al. (1990) found no more than four, whereas monthly averages of weekly counts of the salt works (U10/V10) 1993–94 were never more than 10 (Stadtlander and Konecny 1994). Nevertheless, larger concentrations are occasional: 50 along the Silver Strand

Photo by Anthony Mercieca

(T9) 30 January 2000 (Y. Ikegaya), 31 in the salt works 15 December 1993 (Stadtlander and Konecny 1994), and 30 in the Tijuana River estuary (V10) 20 December 1997 (W. Mittendorff). From 1953 to 2002 the San Diego Christmas bird count averaged 21, with a range from 3 to 85.

In the north county wintering Whimbrels are even less numerous. The Rancho Santa Fe and Oceanside Christmas bird counts both average seven to eight. Monthly surveys of San Elijo Lagoon (L7) 1973–83 yielded a November–January average of only 0.3 (King et al. 1987). With the restoration of tidal flow to Batiquitos Lagoon (J6/J7) the Whimbrel has become more frequent there with up to 20 on 9 February 1998 (B. C. Moore).

The Whimbrel's only regular winter site inland is the San Dieguito Valley (M8), with up to 20 on 22 December 2000 (P. Unitt). One flying over eastern Carlsbad (J8) 7 December 1999 (J. O. Zimmer) was exceptional.

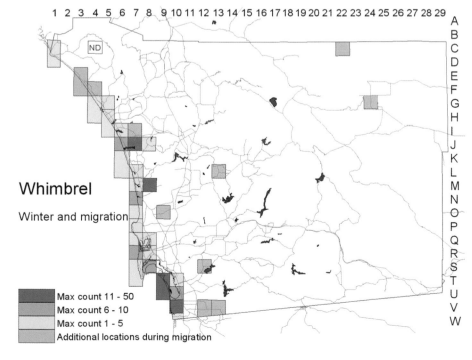

Whimbrel

Winter and migration

Max count 11 - 50
Max count 6 - 10
Max count 1 - 5
Additional locations during migration

Migration: On their journey south, Whimbrels arrive in San Diego County in the first week of July and build to a peak in late July and early August. Concentrations of over 50 are unusual, though the Whimbrel is most common as a fall migrant. King et al. (1987) reported a maximum at San Elijo Lagoon of 230 on 6 August 1978; Macdonald et al. (1990) found up to 151 around south San Diego Bay 27 August 1988. In spring, the main migration route passes east of San Diego County, through the Salton Sea, so not much of a peak is evident at that season.

Migrating Whimbrels are rarely seen inland. In fall, all records are still in the coastal lowland, e. g., three at Sweetwater Reservoir (S12) 27 July 2001 (P. Famolaro). In spring, there are records for the coastal lowland, inland as far as the southwest corner of Santa Maria Valley (L13; one on 14 April 2001, K. J. Winter), plus five for the Anza–Borrego Desert, undoubtedly of birds straying west of the main migration corridor through the Salton Sea: two at Middle Willows, Coyote Creek (C22), 29 April 1997 (P. D. Jorgensen), one at Borrego Springs (G24) 25 April 1998 (P. D. Ache), one at Culp Valley (G23/H23) 30 April 1983 (ABDSP database) and 7 May 1995 (M. L. Gabel), and one at Carrizo Marsh (O29) 13 April 1994 (P. D. and M. C. Jorgensen). In spring, inland records range in date from 29 March (2000, one at Sweetwater Reservoir, P. Famolaro) to 7 May and in number up to six on Otay Mesa (V13) 29 April 2000 (N. Perretta).

Small numbers of nonbreeding Whimbrels summer regularly along San Diego County's coast, with up to five at Batiquitos Lagoon 7 June 1998 (C. C. Gorman), eight around south San Diego Bay 24 June 1988 (Macdonald et al. 1990), 10 in the salt works in June 1994 (Stadlander and Konecny 1994), and 10 in the Tijuana River estuary 27 June 1998 (C. G. Edwards).

Conservation: The Whimbrel suffered considerably less than two of North America's other curlews, the Long-billed and Eskimo, during the era when the birds were hunted commercially. Over the last half of the 20th century there has been little change in the Whimbrel's abundance in San Diego County, though habitat has been reduced, especially inland. The Whimbrel's winter range may have extended north to include southern California in the early 20th century; winter records were almost unknown before about 1920 (Grinnell et al. 1918, Stephens 1919a, Willett 1933).

Taxonomy: All of North America's brown-rumped Whimbrels are best called *N. p. hudsonicus* Latham, 1790, the Hudsonian Curlew (Patten et al. 2003). Five vagrants of the partially white-rumped *N. p. variegatus* (Scopoli, 1786), breeding in east Asia, have been seen in the western conterminous United States, the southernmost at China Lake, Kern County, California (Heindel 1999). The Hudsonian Curlew was long considered a species distinct from the Whimbrel of the Old World and may be so again.

Long-billed Curlew *Numenius americanus*

North America's largest shorebird, the Long-billed Curlew, has two main habitats in San Diego County: tidal mudflats and open grassland. It is primarily a migrant and winter visitor, but small numbers remain along the coast through June, the brief interval between spring and fall migration. The curlew's population has been reduced greatly, first by uncontrolled hunting, then by loss of habitat in both the breeding and winter ranges, until its total numbers at the beginning of the 21st century were estimated at about 20,000.

Winter: The most consistent sites for wintering Long-billed Curlews in San Diego County are south San Diego Bay and the Tijuana River estuary. From 1997 to 2002 our counts in these areas ranged up to 54 along the Chula Vista bayfront (U10) 15 December 2001 (C. H. Reiser) and 26 in the Tijuana estuary (V10) 18 December 1999 (A. DeBolt). A count of 127 along the north edge of the salt works 10 December 1988 (Macdonald et al. 1990) was exceptional; weekly surveys of the salt works 1993–94 yielded no more than 21 December–February and no more than 23 at any season. Kjelmyr et al. (1991) rated the winter abundance of the curlew at Mission Bay and the San Diego River flood-control channel (R8) at 10–100, but during the atlas period our maximum counts in this area ranged up to only 10, as in the flood-control channel 28 December 1999 (S. D. Cameron).

Photo by Anthony Mercieca

In northern San Diego County the Long-billed Curlew is generally scarce; in most years a dozen individuals or fewer are scattered among the various lagoons. The opening of Batiquitos Lagoon (J7) to the tide led to a spike in curlew numbers there, with up to 40 on 26 December 1998 (R. Stone). At other north county sites our counts during the atlas period ranged up to 12 at Agua Hedionda Lagoon (I6) 28 December 1999 (R. Gransbury) and seven at Los Peñasquitos Lagoon (N7) 26 December 1999 (B. C. Moore). A total of 93 on the Rancho Santa Fe Christmas bird count 20 December 1992 was exceptional.

San Diego County's only remaining upland habitat the curlew uses with any regularity is on Otay Mesa (V13/

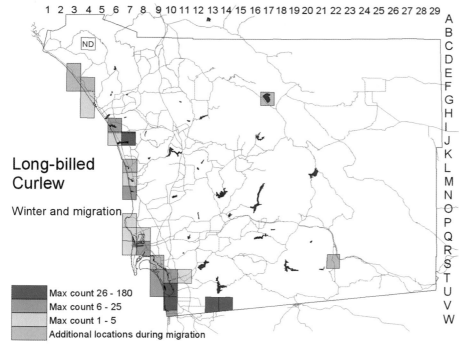

Long-billed Curlew

Winter and migration

- Max count 26 - 180
- Max count 6 - 25
- Max count 1 - 5
- Additional locations during migration

There is no clear peak of migration in spring. Three records inland are of spring migrants, of one at Lake Henshaw 12 May 2001, three at the upper end of Lake Morena (S22) 16 May 1998 (R. and S. L. Breisch), and one at De Anza Country Club, Borrego Springs (F24), 22 May 1967 (ABDSP database).

The number of Long-billed Curlews failing to migrate and remaining to summer is small. During the atlas period we noted up to three at Los Peñasquitos Lagoon 5 June 1999 (K. Estey), four at the Sweetwater River mouth (U10) 10–14 June 1998 (B. C. Moore), and seven in the Tijuana estuary 27 June 1998 (C. G. Edwards). The largest number of summering curlews recorded is 24 around south San Diego Bay 24 June 1988 (Macdonald et al. 1990).

Conservation: Hunting for the market took its toll on the Long-billed Curlew in the late 19th and early 20th centuries; Stephens (1919a) called the species "formerly abundant." Development of San Diego and Mission bays and urbanization of grasslands near the coast has eliminated most of the curlew's habitat in San Diego County. San Diego Christmas bird counts, however, suggest that the number wintering in the remaining habitat on San Diego Bay has remained fairly static since the 1950s.

Taxonomy: The Long-billed Curlew has been divided into two subspecies on the basis of bill length. The difference is apparently insufficient for a taxonomic distinction, though a definitive analysis remains to be published.

V14). We found the species here in three of the five winters of the atlas period, in both natural grassland and fallow agricultural fields. Numbers ranged up to 180 one mile east of the Otay Mesa border crossing (V14) 22 December 1998 (M. Fugagli) and 86 one mile west of the crossing (V13) 25 December 2001 (P. Unitt). Two of 18 Escondido Christmas bird counts 1986–2002 yielded three near Fenton Ranch, San Pasqual Valley (K13), 2 January 1987 (C. G. Edwards) and one there 29 December 1990 (M. B. Stowe).

Migration: Fall migrant Long-billed Curlews begin arriving in July, if not late June, and their numbers peak in August and September. Seven fall migrants were inland at Lake Henshaw (G17) 5 September 1978 (B. Cord); one was at Lake Hodges (K11) 15 August 1982 (K. L. Weaver).

Bar-tailed Godwit *Limosa lapponica*

The Bar-tailed Godwit is primarily a species of the Old World. Though it breeds on the coasts of western Alaska, its migration crosses mainly the western half of the Pacific Ocean. In California it is casual, recorded 28 times through 2002, mainly in the northern half of the state. In San Diego County there are only two well-supported records.

Migration: San Diego County's first Bar-tailed Godwit was on the beach at the Hotel del Coronado (T9) 4–27 November 1981, where it foraged with turnstones in the kelp washed ashore (B. Shear; Binford 1985). The second was in the flood-control channel at the mouth of the San Diego River (R7) 4–5 September 2000 (J. A. Martin; McKee and Erickson 2002); both identifications were supported with photographs.

Photo by Anthony Mercieca

Taxonomy: Even in the lack of specimens the birds in San Diego County were identifiable as the east Siberian and Alaskan subspecies *L. l. baueri* Naumann, 1836, by their mostly brown axillars and barred lower backs.

Marbled Godwit *Limosa fedoa*

The Marbled Godwit is one of the dominant shore-birds along San Diego County's coast, especially around San Diego and Mission bays and in the Tijuana River estuary. In terms of biomass, in winter the Marbled Godwit is probably the dominant shorebird. Though the species is principally a winter visitor, with usually around 2500 to 3000 annually, several hundred remain through the summer.

Photo by Anthony Mercieca

Winter: As a winter visitor to San Diego County, the Marbled Godwit is almost exclusively coastal. Tidal mud-flats and salt marshes are its primary habitats, though smaller numbers are regular on sandy beaches, in brack-ish lagoons, and on rocky ocean shores. Weekly surveys of the salt works 1993–1994 found an average of about 800 to 1000 in fall and winter and a maximum of 1300 on 26 January 1994 (Stadtlander and Konecny 1994). Quarterly surveys of other parts of south San Diego Bay 1988–89 found a maximum of 526 on 29 November 1988 (Macdonald et al. 1990). An estimate of 5000 along the Chula Vista bayfront (U10) 16 December 2000 (B. C. Moore) is exceptional; a tenth of this is more typical for the area. Other areas important to the species are the Tijuana River estuary (V10; up to 500 on 3 December 1999 and 24 January 1998, B. C. Moore), North Island (S8; up to 471 on 19 December 1998, R. T. Patton), and northeastern Mission Bay (Q8; up to 340 on 29 December 1998, J. C. Worley).

In northern San Diego County's lagoons the godwit is less numerous and less consistent. Winter counts as high as 124 at Batiquitos Lagoon (J7) 27 December 1997 (F. Hall) and 70 at Los Peñasquitos Lagoon (N7) 5 December 1999 (D. K. Adams) are unusual. The Oceanside Christmas bird count averaged 79 from 1976

to 2002; the Rancho Santa Fe count averaged 43 from 1980 to 2003.

On inland ponds and lakes wintering godwits are now rare. From 1997 to 2002 we recorded them only nine times, and the only counts of over 10 were of 20 at O'Neill Lake (E6) 14 December 1997 (B. C. Moore) and 15 in Otay Valley (V11) 19 December 1998 (P. Unitt). Two at the east end of Lake Hodges (K11) 9 December 1997 (E. C. Hall) were unusually far inland.

Migration: The Marbled Godwit's migration in San Diego County is partially masked by the abundance of nonbreeding summering birds, probably immature. Monthly averages of weekly counts in the salt works 1993–94 show a fairly smooth change from a maximum of about 900 in November to a minimum of about 300 in June. At San Elijo Lagoon, in contrast, on the basis of monthly counts 1973–83, King et al. (1987) found godwit numbers to reach their annual low from November to January. The subtlety of difference between the species' plumages means that differences in the migration of adults and immatures are poorly known. Nevertheless, adults whose attempt to breed failed probably begin arriving in late June, while immatures are still arriving in December (Gratto-Trevor 2000).

Inland, fall migrants are more frequent than winter visitors, though still uncommon. In the early 1980s at Lake Hodges, K. L. Weaver recorded the species 15 August–5 October with a maximum of 15 on 29 September 1985. A unique spring record there is of two on 7 June 1987 (K. L. Weaver). The surveys of San Elijo Lagoon and the salt works suggest a minor peak of spring migrants in March or April. Most godwits probably commute between California and the Great Plains with only one stop along the way, at Great Salt Lake, Utah (Shuford et al. 2002).

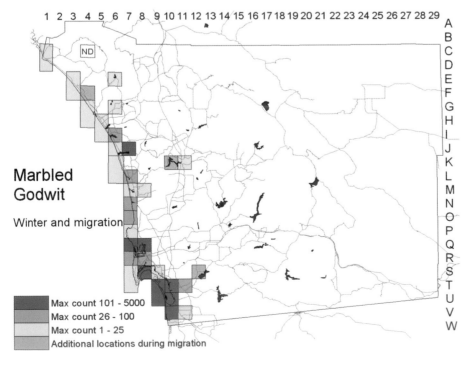

**Marbled
Godwit**

Winter and migration

■ Max count 101 - 5000
■ Max count 26 - 100
□ Max count 1 - 25
□ Additional locations during migration

Conservation: In spite of market hunting in the late 19th and early 20th centuries, loss of much breeding habitat on the Great Plains, and loss of much winter habitat in California, evidence for change in the Marbled Godwit's numbers in San Diego County is slight. Torrey (1913) wrote that on San Diego Bay "I have seen godwits and willets together lining the grassy edge of the flats for a long distance, and so densely massed that I mistook them at first for a border of some kind of herbage. Thousands there must have been; and when they rose at my approach, they made something like a cloud." San Diego Christmas bird counts since 1954, however, show no clear trend. One more recent change is a decrease in the godwit's occurrence inland, as seasonal wetlands in floodplains have been lost to development.

Taxonomy: All specimens of the Marbled Godwit from San Diego County in the San Diego Natural History Museum are nominate *L. f. fedoa* (Linnaeus, 1758), breeding on the northern Great Plains. The shorter-winged *L. f. beringiae* Kessel and Gibson, 1989, breeds on the Alaska Peninsula and has been reported in winter no farther south than San Francisco Bay.

Ruddy Turnstone *Arenaria interpres*

Turnstones got their name from their habit of foraging by flipping pebbles, looking for invertebrates hiding beneath them. In San Diego County, however, it is in sea lettuce on the mudflats around San Diego Bay or in kelp washed up on beaches that the Ruddy Turnstone is most likely to be seen rummaging. Breeding in the arctic, the Ruddy Turnstone is a locally common migrant and winter visitor along San Diego County's coast. Small numbers of nonbreeding birds remain through the summer.

Winter: The Ruddy Turnstone occurs along most of San Diego County's coast but is concentrated on the mudflats around San Diego Bay (70 on 15 December 2001, M. Bache). Rocky shorelines are also one of the Ruddy Turnstone's regular habitats (25 at La Jolla, P7, L. and M. Polinsky). The Ruddy Turnstone is far less numerous in northern San Diego County: though the San Diego Christmas bird count averages 86 (1954–2002), the Oceanside count averages 5.2 (1976–2002), the Rancho Santa Fe count 4.4 (1980–2003). From 1997 to 2002 our

Photo by Jack C. Daynes

highest winter counts in northern San Diego County were of 13 on the jetty at Camp Del Mar (G4) on 20 January and 14 February 2000 (P. A. Ginsburg).

Migration: Fall migrants begin arriving in July but are not clustered in a distinct seasonal peak. In spring, by contrast, there is a distinct peak in April. In and near the San Diego Bay salt works (U10/V10), on weekly surveys 1993–94, Stadtlander and Konecny (1994) had their highest count of 50 on 14 April 1993. Ruddy Turnstones heading north clear out in early May; late records of migrants are of one at La Jolla 7 May 2000 (L. Polinsky) and three in definitive alternate plumage at the south end of San Diego Bay 9 May 1978 (P. Unitt).

Modest numbers of nonbreeding Ruddy Turnstones summer in San Diego County, mainly on San Diego Bay. Macdonald et al. (1990) tallied 28 on 24 June 1988, whereas Stadtlander and Konecny (1994) charted up to 21 in June 1993. The largest number of summering birds reported there is 100 in 1987 (R. E. Webster, AB 41:1487, 1987). In northern San Diego County summering turnstones are rare.

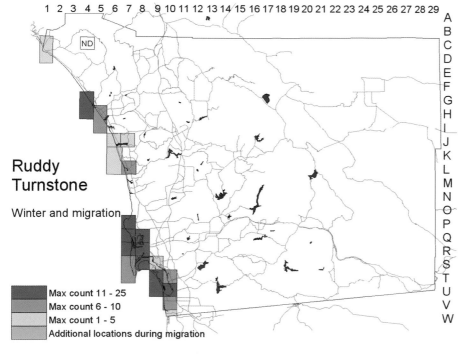

Ruddy Turnstone

Winter and migration

- Max count 11 - 25
- Max count 6 - 10
- Max count 1 - 5
- Additional locations during migration

On the basis of monthly counts 1973–83, King et al. (1987) recorded an average of 0.4 from May to August. During the atlas period our only summering turnstones in the north county were four on the jetty at Camp Del Mar 3 July 1999 (P. A. Ginsburg).

The only inland records are from Lake Hodges (K10/K11), of one 26 September 1982 (K. L. Weaver, AB 37:224, 1983) and one 14 August 1987 (G. McCaskie, AB 42:135, 1988).

Conservation: San Diego Christmas bird counts show

no trend in Ruddy Turnstone numbers, but counts of migrants as high as 500 in the early 1960s have not been repeated since. Like many shorebirds, the Ruddy Turnstone lost much habitat with the development of San Diego and Mission bays. The cleaning of kelp and other debris from beaches also deprives the turnstone of opportunity to forage.

Taxonomy: Nominate *A. i. interpres* (Linnaeus, 1758) is the subspecies of Ruddy Turnstone migrating along the Pacific coast of North America.

Black Turnstone *Arenaria melanocephala*

Rocky shorelines are the Black Turnstone's principal habitat, where it is more common than the Ruddy Turnstone. It is less numerous but still fairly common on tidal mudflats and beaches. The Black Turnstone occurs in San Diego County as a migrant, winter visitor, and rare nonbreeding summer visitor.

Winter: In San Diego County the Black Turnstone is strictly coastal, concentrating in the two regions of rocky shore, La Jolla (O7/P7/Q7; up to 25 on 20 January 2000, L. Polinsky) and Point Loma (S7; up to 44 on 16 December 2000, M. W. Klein). At times, the Black Turnstone is common also in Mission Bay (R8, 50 on 24 December 1997, P. Unitt; Q8, 30 on 4 and 20 January 1998, B. C. Moore). In San Diego Bay it occurs on both breakwaters (S8; 24 on 16 December 2000, D. W. Povey) and mudflats (T9; 25 on 19 December 1998, N. Osborn).

In the north county the Black Turnstone is uncommon to rare, restricted largely to the breakwaters at the mouths of lagoons and the Oceanside harbor. From 1997 to 2002 our highest count in this region was of six at San Elijo Lagoon (L7) 22 December 2000 (G. C. Hazard). The

Photo by Anthony Mercieca

Rancho Santa Fe Christmas bird count averages 3.5, the Oceanside count only 0.8.

Migration: Black Turnstones begin arriving in mid July and depart largely by early May, though a few stragglers have been seen until early June (Unitt 1984). No distinct peaks of migration have been reported, but a count of 79 in the San Diego Bay salt works (U10/V10) 3 November 1993 was exceptionally high (Stadtlander and Konecny 1994).

Summering nonbreeders do not remain on rocky shorelines but they do in small numbers on San Diego Bay. Macdonald et al. (1990) reported two on 24 June 1988; Stadtlander and Konecny (1994) had up to 10 in June 1994. During the atlas period our only records of probably summering Black Turnstones were of one at North Island (S8) 27 May 2000 (R. T. Patton) and five on the jetty and Camp Del Mar (G4) 3 July 1999 (P. A. Ginsburg), though these could have been a late spring migrant and early fall migrants, respectively.

Conservation: The Black Turnstone's minor gain of habitat in the form of breakwaters and riprap is overshadowed by the loss of mudflats around Mission and San Diego bays.

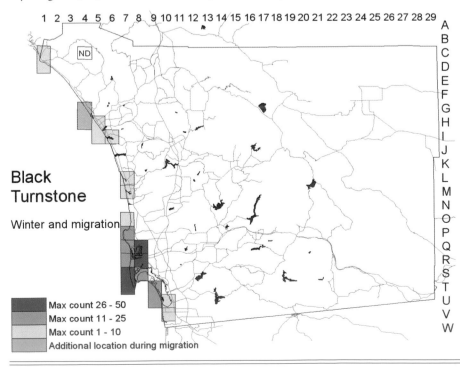

Black Turnstone

Winter and migration

- Max count 26 - 50
- Max count 11 - 25
- Max count 1 - 10
- Additional location during migration

Surfbird *Aphriza virgata*

The Surfbird is one of the characteristic birds of rocky shorelines, taking advantage of jetties and breakwaters at least as much as natural rock formations. Occasionally it visits sandy beaches, mainly during migration. In San Diego County, it is a locally common migrant and winter visitor, most abundant during spring migration.

Photo by Anthony Mercieca

Winter: Primitively, the rocky shores of La Jolla (P7) and Point Loma (S7) were the Surfbird's main habitat in San Diego County. From 1997 to 2001, our winter numbers in these habitats were up to eight at La Jolla 15 December 1999 (L. Polinsky) and seven at Point Loma 20 December 1997 (M. W. Klein). We found even greater numbers, however, on breakwaters of riprap: 45 at the entrance to Mission Bay (R7) 1 January 1999 (P. Unitt), 19 on Zuñiga Jetty at the entrance to San Diego Bay (S8) 15 December 2001 (D. W. Povey). Unexpected were 21 feeding with turnstones on mudflats at the southeast corner of Mission Bay (R8) 24 December 1997 (P. Unitt). The jetties for the harbors at Camp Del Mar (G4) and Oceanside (H5) give the Surfbird its only winter habitat in northern San Diego

Migration: During the atlas period our dates for the Surfbird ranged from 31 July (2001; two at Camp Del Mar, P. A. Ginsburg) to 28 April (2001; 15 at La Jolla, L. and M. Polinsky), the expected spread. No peak of fall migrants is known, but the Surfbird is considerably more numerous as a spring migrant than in winter, beginning in late March (100 at La Jolla 25 March 2000, L. and M. Polinsky). Our highest count was of 130 at La Jolla 15 April 1999 (J. R. Barth). Spring migrants show up occasionally at sites where the species does not winter, as did eight on the jetty at Camp Surf near Imperial Beach (V10) 24 March 2001 (T. Stands) and six on the beach at Encinitas (K6) 15 April 2001 (E. Garnica).

Though the Surfbird migrates overland from the Gulf of California to the Pacific coast, this migration apparently takes place largely over northern Baja California. There are no inland records for San Diego County, and the Surfbird is rare at the Salton Sea (Patten et al. 2003).

There are six records of summering Surfbirds in San Diego County, of one near Imperial Beach (V10) 26 June–16 July 1983 (R. E. Webster, AB 37:1027, 1983), one on San Diego Bay 12 June 1985 (R. E. Webster, AB 39:962, 1985), and three on south San Diego Bay 24 June–3 July 1988 (J. O'Brien, AB 42:1340, 1988), plus three listed by Unitt (1984).

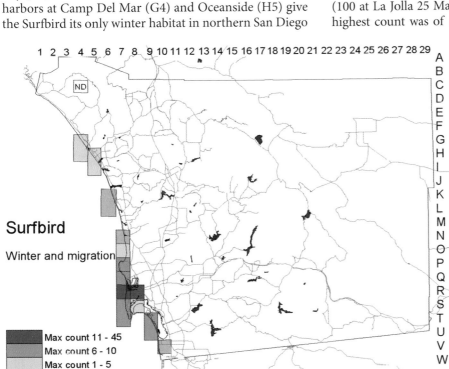

Surfbird

Winter and migration

- ▨ Max count 11 - 45
- ▨ Max count 6 - 10
- ▨ Max count 1 - 5
- ▨ Additional locations during migration

County. Our maximum here during the atlas period was five at Camp Del Mar 20 January 2000 (P. A. Ginsburg). On Oceanside Christmas bird counts 1976–2002, where the count of Surfbirds on the jetties is exhaustive, the average is 0.9 and the maximum is six on 21 December 2002. Wintering Surfbirds are irregular on the beach at Coronado (T9) with up to nine on 16 December 2000 (N. Osborn).

Conservation: The installation of breakwaters gave the Surfbird additional habitat in San Diego County. The species' frequency on the Oceanside Christmas bird count is on the increase, perhaps the result of invertebrates colonizing the breakwaters.

Red Knot *Calidris canutus*

In California, the Red Knot has a remarkably circumscribed distribution: it winters in numbers at only a few sites, the tidal mudflats of San Diego and Mission bays prominent among them. The total wintering in San Diego County is about 400 to 700, perhaps less in some years. During migration the knot is more widespread and abundant than in winter, occurring at times in flocks of hundreds on San Diego Bay and in flocks of dozens elsewhere along the coast.

Photo by Anthony Mercieca

Winter: The Red Knot's preference for tidal mudflats in winter is even stricter than that of the Short-billed Dowitcher. As a result, knots concentrate around San Diego Bay. The mudflats at and near the Sweetwater River mouth (T10/U10) are an especially favored site (up to 258 on 18 February 2000, R. T. Patton; 225 on 13 February 1989, Macdonald et al. 1990). The species occurs around the bay, however, often in association with large flocks of Short-billed Dowitchers. It is regular also in the Tijuana River estuary (V10; 73 on 19 December 1998, R. B. Riggan), in the San Diego River flood-control channel (R8; 30 on 7 December 1997, B. C. Moore), and in Mission Bay (Q8; 120 on 21 December 1998, J. C. Worley).

The estimate of 400–700 for the county's winter knot population comes from a convergence of atlas results, focused studies of San Diego Bay (Macdonald et al. 1990, Stadtlander and Konecny 1994), and Christmas bird counts. The maximum on any San Diego Christmas bird count was 935 on 17 December 1977. Kjelmyr et al. (1991) estimated the numbering of wintering knots at 100–1000 at both San Diego and Mission bays.

In northern San Diego County, however, wintering knots are very rare. We had no records from 1997 to 2002. Five on 4 January 2003 were the first ever on a Rancho

Santa Fe Christmas bird count. The Oceanside count has recorded the knot on only three of 28 counts 1976–2002, with two individuals on each occasion. In 10 years of monthly counts at San Elijo Lagoon 1973–83, King et al. (1987) found no knots from November to April.

Migration: From 1997 to 2001 our dates for migrating knots ran from 12 July (1999, two at the Santa Margarita River mouth, G4) to 21 May (2001, five at the same locality, P. A. Ginsburg). Earlier records extend from 5 July to 21 May (Unitt 1984). At San Elijo Lagoon, King et al. (1987) found the knot to be most frequent in September (average 7.4), whereas in and near the south San Diego Bay salt works, Stadtlander and Konecny (1994) found the fall peak in October, with a high count of 706. The latter study also recorded a strong spring peak in April and May, with maximum counts between 400 and 425 in both months. Along the Chula Vista bayfront, Macdonald et al. (1990) recorded numbers higher than in winter during both spring and fall migration, with a maximum of 425 on 14 April 1989. A single knot at Lake Hodges (K11) 7 September 1979 (AB 34:201, 1980) is still the only one reported inland.

Knots in nonbreeding plumage summer regularly on San Diego Bay, in numbers of up to 125 on 15 June 1978 (P. Unitt), at least 100 through summer 1987 (G. McCaskie, AB 41:1487, 1987), and 65 at the Sweetwater River mouth 24 June 1988 (Macdonald et al. 1990).

Conservation: Because much of the Red Knot's population stages in migration at just a few sites, it is of more conservation concern than many shorebirds (Harrington 2001). Though the numbers of knots in San Diego County are lower than those of many other shorebirds, the importance of San Diego in a statewide context

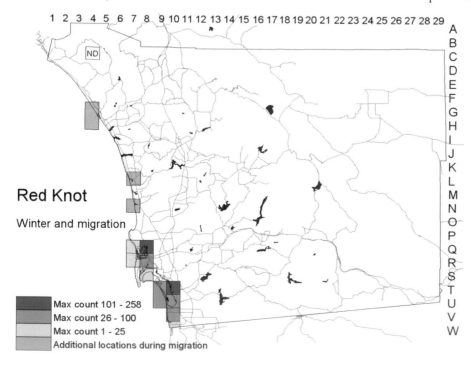

Red Knot

Winter and migration

Max count 101 - 258
Max count 26 - 100
Max count 1 - 25
Additional locations during migration

looms comparatively large. San Francisco Bay is the only wetland in California besides San Diego and Mission bays where Kjelmyr et al. (1991) estimated a wintering population as high as 100–1000. Development of San Diego and Mission bays, however, has already eliminated a large fraction of the bays' original tidelands.

Taxonomy: Most of the Red Knots occurring in California are apparently *C. c. roselaari* Tomkovich, 1990, which breeds on Wrangel Island in the Siberian Arctic and in northwestern Alaska (Patten et al. 2003).

Sanderling *Calidris alba*

Everyone who goes to a beach in San Diego County is familiar with the Sanderling, scurrying back and forth on the beach with each advance and retreat of a wave. It winters commonly on beaches, less so within the lagoons and bays and on rocky shores. In migration the number of Sanderlings using these other habitats increases.

Winter: The Sanderling is common all along San Diego County's coast, with up to 200 between the mouths of Horno and Las Pulgas canyons (E3) 16 February 1998 (R. and S. L. Breisch), 359 at Cardiff State Beach and San Elijo Lagoon (L7) 23 December 2001 (E. Garnica), and 302 at North Island (S8) 24 February 2000 (R. T. Patton). Away from the beaches, the Sanderling is less abundant. For example, our highest count in the east basin of Batiquitos Lagoon (J7) was eight on 5 December 1997 (C. C. Gorman). Inside Mission Bay (Q8), our counts ranged up to 40 on 5 February 1999 (E. Wallace); inside San Diego Bay, up to 27 at Coronado (S9) 20 December 1997 (R. T. Patton). In south San Diego Bay, Macdonald et al. (1990) found up to 35 on the mudflat adjacent to the D Street fill (T10) 22 November 1988. On weekly surveys in and near the salt works December 1993–February 1994, Stadtlander and Konecny (1994) recorded up to about 25.

Migration: In San Diego County, Sanderlings begin arriving in numbers in late July. Most depart in mid May,

Photo by Anthony Mercieca

with a few migrants still moving through late May. Inside northern San Diego County's lagoons, the Sanderling is most abundant in fall migration. At San Elijo Lagoon King et al. (1987) found the peak to be in September, with a maximum of 590 on 7 September 1980. In and near the salt works, however, Stadtlander and Konecny (1994) found the fall peak in October. In 1978 I noted the peak of spring migration in early May (Unitt 1984), but in the salt works in 1993 Stadtlander and Konecny (1994) found a sharp peak in March, with up to 267 on 7 March.

Substantial numbers of Sanderlings in nonbreeding plumage remain through the summer on sandy beaches (50 at Pacific Beach, Q7, 15 June 1998, E. Wallace).

San Diego County's five inland records of the Sanderling are all of fall migrants, at Lake Hodges (K10/K11; 17 August 1979, AB 34:201, 1980; 18 September 1982, R. E. Webster, AB 37:224, 1983) and Lake Henshaw (G17; 4 October 1982 and 7 October 1983, R. Higson, AB 37:224, 1983; 38:246, 1984; 26 July 1998, R. A. Hamilton, FN 52:503, 1998).

Conservation: Because most Sanderlings are dispersed along beaches rather than clumped into wetlands, they seem less vulnerable to habitat loss than most other shorebirds. Nevertheless, the habitat may be degraded from the Sanderling's point of view when kelp is cleaned off the beaches.

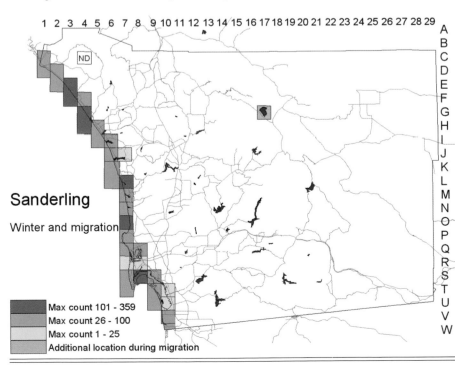

Sanderling

Winter and migration

Max count 101 - 359
Max count 26 - 100
Max count 1 - 25
Additional location during migration

Semipalmated Sandpiper *Calidris pusilla*

The Semipalmated and Western Sandpipers are very similar and have often been confused. Detection of the Semipalmated as a rare but regular fall migrant in coastal southern California began only when the identification criteria were well publicized in the late 1970s. In San Diego County, the Semipalmated Sandpiper has been seen mainly in wetlands of fresh or brackish water; it avoids the tidal mudflats of San Diego and Mission bays.

Migration: Since 1978, when it was first identified here, the Semipalmated Sandpiper has been found nearly annually in San Diego County, with up to six in the Tijuana River valley 10 August 1980 (AB 35:226, 1981) and three at Batiquitos Lagoon (J7) 15 August 1987 (J. O'Brien). The atlas period from 1997 to 2001 seems to have been typical, yielding four sightings, all of single birds at San Elijo Lagoon (L7): 26 August 1999 (P. A. Ginsburg), 10 August 2000 (G. McCaskie), 21 August 2000 (J. C. Worley), and 22 September 2001 (G. McCaskie). Published dates range

Photo by Richard E. Webster

from 28 July (1991, Batiquitos Lagoon, G. McCaskie, AB 45:1161, 1991) to 24 September (1983, Tijuana River valley, R. E. Webster, AB 38:246, 1984). All records so far have been of juveniles, all within 5 miles of the coast, except for one at the upper end of Lake Hodges (K11) 29 August 1981 (K. L. Weaver).

Western Sandpiper *Calidris mauri*

The Western Sandpiper is by far the most abundant shorebird along San Diego County's coast. The number wintering in the county is roughly 10,000 to 15,000, and even larger numbers pass through in migration. Tidal mudflats are the sandpiper's preferred habitat, used by flocks of thousands. The species is also common in brackish lagoons, uncommon on beaches and rocky shores, and variably common on lakeshores. Though there are several sites of greater importance to the Western Sandpiper than San Diego County's coastal wetlands, San Diego and Mission bays rank among the top dozen sites for the species in California.

Winter: The Western Sandpiper's primary wintering sites around San Diego are northeastern Mission Bay (Q8; 5000 on 21 December 1998, J. C. Worley), south San Diego Bay (U10/V10; 7885 on 1 December 1993, Stadtlander and Konecny 1994), and the Tijuana River estuary (V10/W10; 1200 on 16 December 2000, S. Walens). In the north county the principal sites are the Santa Margarita River estuary (G4; 300 on 25 February 2000, P. A. Ginsburg), Agua Hedionda Lagoon (I6; 300 on 22 January 2000, P. A. Ginsburg), Batiquitos Lagoon (530 in the west half, J6, 15 January 1999, M. Baumgartel; 1000 in the east basin, J7, 5 January and 9 February 1998, B. C. Moore), and San Elijo Lagoon (L7; 456 on 22 December 2000, G. C. Hazard). The Western Sandpiper occurs at all coastal wetlands except Buena Vista Lagoon (H5/H6), where there are no longer suitable mudflats. It even occurs regularly in small numbers on rocky shorelines, with up to 12 at Point Loma (S7) 19 December 1998 (M. W. Klein) and six at La Jolla (P7) 28 December 1998 (L. and M. Polinsky).

Inland, wintering Western Sandpipers are much out-

Photo by Anthony Mercieca

numbered by Least Sandpipers. Large numbers of the Western are known only at Lake Hodges (K10/K11; up to 50 on 9 December 1997, E. C. Hall) and Sweetwater Reservoir (S12/S13; up to 150 on 16 December 2000, P. Famolaro). Smaller numbers are regular in the lower San Luis Rey River valley, with up to 22 at Whelan Lake (G6) on 17 December 1997 (D. Rorick). Elsewhere inland, from 1997 to 2002, we found no more than 10 wintering Western Sandpipers. The only sites above 1500 feet elevation where we encountered wintering Western Sandpipers were the upper end of Lake Morena (S22; two on 5 December 1999, R. and S. L. Breisch) and Lake Henshaw (G17), where the species is regular in small numbers, up to six on 18 December 2000 (J. Coker). Reports of larger numbers on Lake Henshaw Christmas bird counts in 1982 and 1999 are probably based on misidentified Least Sandpipers. In the Anza–Borrego Desert two or three were found at the Borrego sewage ponds (H25) on Christmas bird counts in 1987 and 1989; one was at Borrego Springs (G24) 27 February 2001 (P. D. Ache).

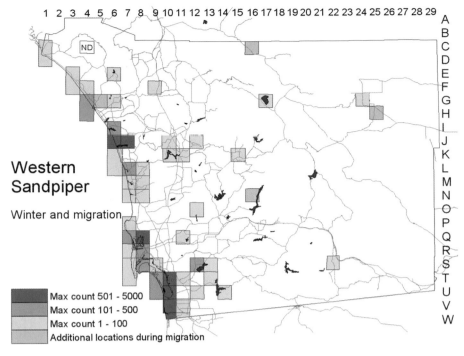

Western
Sandpiper

Winter and migration

■ Max count 501 - 5000
▨ Max count 101 - 500
▢ Max count 1 - 100
▨ Additional locations during migration

Migration: Western Sandpipers begin arriving in late June, becoming common by the beginning of July. A count of 474 on south San Diego Bay, mainly between the salt works and Chula Vista Wildlife Reserve (U10), 24 June 1988 is unusually high for so early in migration (Macdonald et al. 1990). Early arrivals are adults; juveniles begin arriving at the end of July. Both King et al. (1987) at San Elijo Lagoon and Stadtlander and Konecny (1994) in the salt works found the Western Sandpiper's fall migration peaking in October.

The species' spring migration through San Diego County takes place mainly in March and April. On their weekly surveys of the salt works 1993–94, Stadtlander and Konecny (1994) recorded their maximum of 8010 on 3 March 1993. A peak in early or mid April is probably more typical. By the second week of May, most migrants have continued north. Our latest date for the Western

Sandpiper during the atlas period was 9 May; Stadtlander and Konecny (1994) did not record the species at all in May or June. Nevertheless, birds in breeding plumage, presumably still heading north, have been seen as late as 5 June (Unitt 1984).

Inland, the Western Sandpiper is more widespread and numerous in both spring and fall migration than in winter (up to 80 at Lake Hodges 27 April 1997, E. C. Hall; 800 there 24 August 1985, K. L. Weaver). In the Anza–Borrego Desert the Western Sandpiper occurs as a rare spring migrant, mainly at artificial ponds, from 21 March (1999, four at the Borrego sewage ponds) to 8 May (1994, one at the same site, P. D. Jorgensen). Desert records are of 10 or fewer, except for 70 along Coyote Creek (D23/D24) 17 April 1991 (A. G. Morley).

Summering Western Sandpipers in nonbreeding plumage are generally rare and confined to tidal mudflats. Numbers as high as 46 on south San Diego Bay 17 June 1987 (R. E. Webster, AB 41:1487, 1987) and 50 in the Tijuana River estuary 6 June 1998 (B. C. Moore) are exceptional. At San Elijo Lagoon, King et al. (1987) noted only two Western Sandpipers in June in 10 years of surveys 1973–83; one was there 13 June 1998 (B. C. Moore).

Conservation: Though abundant, the Western Sandpiper is vulnerable because of its concentrating in migration at a few staging sites, such as San Francisco Bay and the Copper River delta, Alaska (Wilson 1994). The relative importance of San Diego County to the species may have been greater before so much of the mudflats of San Diego and Mission bays were filled for development.

Least Sandpiper *Calidris minutilla*

San Diego County's smallest sandpiper is also one of its most widespread, being common at wetlands inland as well as those along the coast. Though often found near or in mixed flocks with the other common small sandpiper, the Western, the Least differs slightly in its microhabitat. The Least Sandpiper prefers higher, drier mudflats, wading less in water and soft mud than does the Western Sandpiper. In San Diego County the Least is a migrant and winter visitor occurring mainly from early July to early May.

Winter: Along San Diego County's coast, the Least is generally outnumbered by the Western Sandpiper, especially on the tidal mudflats of San Diego and Mission bays so favored by the Western. Nevertheless, the Least

Photo by Anthony Mercieca

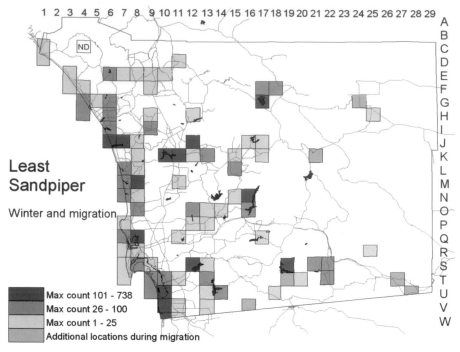

**Least
Sandpiper**

Winter and migration

- Max count 101 - 738
- Max count 26 - 100
- Max count 1 - 25
- Additional locations during migration

Manzanita Indian Reservation (R25) 22 January 2000 (J. K. Wilson).

In the Anza–Borrego Desert wintering Least Sandpipers are rare, reported only from sewage ponds in the Borrego Valley (H25). From 1997 to 2002 our only record was of up to four from 23 to 30 January 2000 (P. D. Jorgensen). On Anza–Borrego Christmas bird counts 1984–2002 the species has been found in 7 of 19 years, with six or fewer except for 28 on 24 December 1989.

Migration: In San Diego County, fall migration of the Least Sandpiper begins in early July, exceptionally in late June. The numbers build to a peak in October that is not much higher than the level maintained through the winter.

may winter in large numbers; counts as high as 600 in the east basin of Batiquitos Lagoon (J7) 2 January 1998 (C. C. Gorman), 500 along the Chula Vista bayshore (U10) 16 December 2000 (B. C. Moore), and 738 in the Tijuana River estuary (V10) 19 December 1998 (R. B. Riggan) are exceptional. On weekly counts in and near the salt works 1993–94, Stadtlander and Konecny (1994) found numbers from December to February varying from almost none to about 220. In February 1989, Macdonald et al. (1990) found about 275 in south San Diego Bay outside the salt works. On the basis of monthly surveys of San Elijo Lagoon (L7) 1973–83, King et al. (1987) recorded an August–February average of 65.

Inland the Least Sandpiper winters on both small temporary ponds and the shores of larger reservoirs. Sites of especially large numbers inland are Lake Henshaw (G17; 270 on 21 December 1998, S. J. Montgomery), Lake Hodges (K10; 208 on 22 December 2000, R. L. Barber), El Capitan Reservoir (N16; 185 on 2 January 2002, J. R. Barth), and Sweetwater Reservoir (S12; 250 on 20 December 1997, P. Famolaro). The natural seasonal wetlands most frequented by the Least Sandpiper are in the San Pasqual Valley (J12; 125 on 3 January 1998, P. Unitt) and San Dieguito Valley (M8; 125 on 28 February 1999, R. T. Patton). The sandpiper's use of these wetlands is subject to variation in rainfall, as suggested by the wide variation in the species' numbers on Escondido Christmas bird counts, from 129 in the wet winter of 1997–98 to zero on 4 of 18 counts 1986–2002. The Least Sandpiper winters regularly up to 3000 feet elevation around the upper margins of Lake Morena (S21/S22/T22; up to 80 on 23 January 2000, S. E. Smith), but our only winter record at a higher elevation was of one about 4000 feet in the

In spring, migrants appear occasionally on creeks where they do not winter, e.g., five in Marron Valley (V16) 7 April 1999 (D. C. Seals), 12 along Banner Creek (K21) 22 April 1999 (P. K. Nelson), and three at Lower Willows, Coyote Creek (D23), 15 April 1987 (A. G. Morley). The last provided the only desert record away from artificial ponds, where spring counts range up to 40 at Borrego Springs (G24) 25 April 1998 (P. D. Ache). Stadtlander and Konecny (1994) encountered a pulse of spring migrants in the salt works on 21 April 1993, yielding their maximum count of 375. In spite of a peak of spring migration in mid to late April, the numbers of Least Sandpipers drop abruptly in early May. Stadtlander and Konecny (1994) did not encounter the species in May or June. From 1997 to 2001 our dates for migrants ranged from 3 July to 3 May; previously I reported 28 June–8 May (Unitt 1984).

Summering Least Sandpipers average fewer than one per year and are known only from the coast. In 10 years of surveys of San Elijo Lagoon King et al. (1987) found just one, and the only record published in *American Birds* and its successors since 1981 is of one near Imperial Beach (V10) 8 June 1987 (R. E. Webster, AB 41:1487, 1987). The only one reported during the atlas period was at Los Peñasquitos Lagoon (N7) 4 June 2000 (K. Estey).

Conservation: Human modification of the environment has both created and destroyed habitat for the Least Sandpiper, as for many water birds. Reservoirs offer new habitat, but most of the tidelands and nearly all of the seasonal wetlands in floodplains have been lost. San Diego County's Christmas bird counts imply considerable chaotic variation in the Least Sandpiper's numbers and local distribution from year to year but no clear trend.

Baird's Sandpiper *Calidris bairdii*

Breeding in the Arctic and wintering in South America, Baird's Sandpiper migrates principally along the east flank of the Rocky Mountains. As a result it is rare in San Diego County; almost all occurring here are juveniles in fall migration. Baird's Sandpiper prefers fresh or brackish water; it is not expected on tidal mudflats.

Migration: Baird's Sandpiper is seen most regularly at northern San Diego County's coastal lagoons and in the Tijuana River valley. High counts for these areas are four at the Santa Margarita River mouth (G4) 25 August 1998 (P. A. Ginsburg) and six at the sod farm in the Tijuana River valley (W11) 13 September 2001 (B. Foster). Though reports inland are fewer, the largest concentrations of Baird's Sandpipers recorded in San Diego County have been at Lake Henshaw (G17): by far the largest was of 92 on 2 September 1985 (R. Higson, AB 40:158, 1986). In the early 1980s, K. L. Weaver found Baird's Sandpiper almost annually at the east end of Lake Hodges (K11) with up to four on 22 September 1985. Regular surveys of inland reservoirs in fall (not part of the atlas study) might reveal Baird's Sandpiper to be more frequent there than along the coast.

The earliest fall record of Baird's Sandpiper in San Diego County is the only record of an adult, at Batiquitos

Photo by Jack C. Daynes

Lagoon (J7) 11–14 July 1982 (G. McCaskie, AB 36:1016, 1982). Juveniles begin to appear shortly after this date, however, their frequency peaking in late August and early September. The latest apparently valid date is 29 October (1964, one in the Tijuana River valley, AFN 19:79, 1965).

Conservation: Over the last quarter of the 20th century, muddy ponds, irrigated pastures, and temporary wetlands in coastal San Diego County have been reduced, eliminating many sites where Baird's Sandpiper formerly occurred.

Pectoral Sandpiper *Calidris melanotos*

Every fall a few Pectoral Sandpipers visit San Diego County's coastal marshes, where they keep to well-vegetated areas and avoid open mudflats. The largest numbers, however, are seen at fresh water, in wet pastures or on lakeshores. Nearly all Pectoral Sandpipers seen in San Diego County are juveniles.

Migration: The Pectoral Sandpiper has been found at most of San Diego County's coastal wetlands. Since the 1990s it has generally been seen singly (or in flocks with other shorebirds), though larger numbers occurred in the past, up to 20 at San Elijo Lagoon (L7) 11 October 1963 and 10 October 1965 (G. McCaskie). The former flooded pastures in the Tijuana River valley were a draw to Pectoral Sandpipers, yielding up to 40 on 22 September 1984 (G. McCaskie, AB 39:102, 1985). Farther inland, the species has been reported less frequently, but Lake Henshaw (G17) has had numbers as large as 36 on 17 September 1977 (P. Unitt) and 23 on 20 September 1984 (R. Higson, AB 39:102, 1985). Covering the upper end of Lake Hodges (K11) regularly through the early 1980s, K. L. Weaver found the Pectoral Sandpiper only in 1982 with a maximum of eight on 26 September. The only fall record for the Anza–Borrego Desert is of one at the Borrego sewage ponds (H25) 9–15 October 1990 (A. G. Morley).

Adult Pectoral Sandpipers have been seen in San Diego County at San Elijo Lagoon 29 June 1977 (E. Copper, AB 31:1190, 1977) and at Los Peñasquitos Lagoon (N7) 23 July 2000 (S. E. Smith, NAB 54:423, 2000), providing the

Photo by Brian L. Sullivan

earliest fall records. But not until late August, with the arrival of juveniles, is the species expected. It is most frequent in September and October. The latest reliable date is 18 November (1983, one photographed at Lake Henshaw, R. Higson, AB 38:246, 1984); 25 November seems too late for the five reported on that date at Mission Bay in 1955 (AFN 10:57, 1956).

In spring, the Pectoral Sandpiper reaches California only casually, and there are just two spring records for San Diego County, of one bird at the Borrego sewage ponds 15 April 1991 (A. G. Morley) and another at Lindo Lake, Lakeside (O14), 10–11 May 2000 (N. Osborn, NAB 54:327, 2000).

Conservation: The decrease in Pectoral Sandpiper numbers in San Diego County since the early 1980s is likely due to local habitat changes. The elimination of pastures and the reduction of irrigation in the Tijuana River valley have decreased that area's attractiveness to fresh-water shorebirds.

Sharp-tailed Sandpiper *Calidris acuminata*

Though it is known to breed only in Siberia and to winter only in Australasia, the Sharp-tailed Sandpiper is a regular fall vagrant along the Pacific coast of North America. But its frequency on this continent decreases from north to south, and there are only three records for San Diego County.

Migration: Anthony (1922) collected a juvenile, California's second Sharp-tailed Sandpiper, at Mission Bay (Q8/R8) 16 September 1921 (SDNHM 2255; specimen label says 15 September). Another juvenile at Border Field State Park (W10) 27 October–2 December was photographed (E. Copper, AB 32:258, 1978). A Sharp-tailed Sandpiper at Batiquitos Lagoon (J7) 24–25 July 1988 stands as virtually the only adult recorded along the Pacific coast (J. Oldenettel, G. McCaskie, AB 42:1340, 1988).

Dunlin *Calidris alpina*

Though sometimes seen in large flocks on San Diego and Mission bays and in the Tijuana River estuary, the Dunlin is outnumbered there by the Western Sandpiper, Short-billed Dowitcher, Marbled Godwit, and Willet. The shifting of flocks and annual irregularity make the Dunlin's abundance difficult to assess, but the number wintering in San Diego County at the beginning of the 21st century was about 750 to 1000. The Dunlin's arrival in fall, beginning in September, is later than that of other shorebirds because, unlike the others, virtually the entire North American population remains in Alaska and northern Canada to molt before heading south.

Photo by Anthony Mercieca

Winter: The Dunlin's primary habitats in San Diego County are the tidal mudflats of San Diego and Mission bays, the San Diego River flood-control channel, and the Tijuana River estuary. From 1997 to 2002 our largest concentration was of 300 on the mudflat at the west end of the D Street fill in the Sweetwater River estuary (T10) 18 December 1999 (P. Unitt). Macdonald et al. (1990) found this site and the northern margin of the south San Diego Bay salt works (U10; 160 on 10 December 1988) to be the foci for Dunlins on San Diego Bay. Stadtlander and Konecny (1994), on their weekly surveys in and near the salt works 1993–1994, found huge variation in the number of wintering Dunlins, from almost none on one survey in February 1993 to about 950 on 26 January 1994. The numbers on San Diego Christmas bird counts have also fluctuated wildly, from a high of 4146 on 26 December 1970 to a low of 7 on 19 December 1998. Whether these differences are due to actual variation or to flocks simply being missed because of incomplete coverage of the bayfront is unclear.

Away from San Diego Bay, our numbers of wintering Dunlins during the atlas period ranged up to 50 in the Tijuana

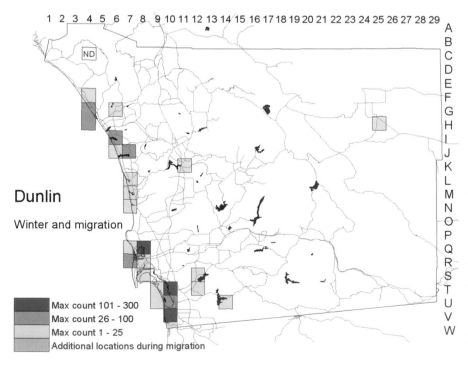

Dunlin

Winter and migration

- Max count 101 - 300
- Max count 26 - 100
- Max count 1 - 25
- Additional locations during migration

River estuary (V10) 16 December 2000 (A. DeBolt), 133 in northeast Mission Bay (Q8) 21 December 1998 (J. C. Worley), 100 at Agua Hedionda Lagoon (I6) 26 December 1998 (P. Unitt), and 50 at the Santa Margarita River mouth (G4) 27–29 January 1999 (P. A. Ginsburg). In the north county the Dunlin's numbers are at least as variable as in the San Diego area. Both the Oceanside and Rancho Santa Fe Christmas bird counts occasionally miss the species. On the basis of monthly surveys 1973–83, King et al. (1987) reported an October–April average at San Elijo Lagoon of 13.

On fresh water, wintering Dunlins are rare. From 1997 to 2002 our only sightings of more than single individuals were of ten and five at Sweetwater Reservoir (S12) on 20 December 1997 and 18 December 1999, respectively (P. Famolaro), and eight flying up the Sweetwater River near Bonita (T12) 16 December 2000 (G. C. Hazard). Eighteen years of Escondido Christmas bird counts have yielded only a single Dunlin, 29 December 1990. The species has turned up on 3 of 22 Lake Henshaw counts; the only record of more than a single individual was of eight on 3 January 1981. The only record for the Anza–Borrego Desert is of one at the Borrego sewage ponds (H25) 19 December 1999 (H. L. Young, M. B. Mosher).

Migration: Dunlins, already in winter plumage, begin arriving in numbers in late September. Previously I reported the species' span of dates in San Diego County as 13 September–22 May (Unitt 1984), and in their surveys of San Diego Bay Macdonald et al. (1990) did not extend this span. At San Elijo Lagoon, King et al. (1987) had an earliest date of 4 September 1977. A molting adult—not juvenile as originally published—at Batiquitos Lagoon (J6/J7) 2 September 1993 (P. A. Ginsburg) was unusual enough to merit notice in *American Birds* (48:152, 1994). Stadtlander and Konecny (1994), however, reported arrival in August and plotted counts during that month ranging as high as about 50, suggesting misidentification. Fall migration peaks in October and November, and during these months the Dunlin is fairly common inland (Unitt 1984).

Spring migration takes place largely in March and April, with few birds left by 1 May. Stadtlander and Konecny (1994) reported none in May. During the atlas period our latest Dunlin was one at Batiquitos Lagoon 4 May 2001 (C. C. Gorman).

There are just four records of the Dunlin summering in San Diego County: one from the San Diego River mouth 9 July 1982 and three from San Diego Bay, 15 June 1976, 6–18 July 1982, and (up to five individuals) 9–22 June 1984 (AB 30:1003, 1976; 36:1016, 1982; 36:1016, 1982; 38:1062, 1984).

Conservation: Because of great annual variation, it is difficult to say whether the changes in Dunlin numbers on San Diego Christmas bird counts constitute a trend. But figures of over 1000 were frequent in the late 1960s and 1970s, whereas from 1981 to 2002 the count did not yield more than 500. Like other shorebirds, the Dunlin lost much habitat with the development of the bays.

Taxonomy: Dunlins migrating along the coast of California, including all specimens from San Diego County, are *C. a. pacifica* (Coues, 1861), distinguished by its relatively long bill and gray streaks on its flanks (Browning 1977, Unitt 1984).

Curlew Sandpiper *Calidris ferruginea*

The Curlew Sandpiper reaches the west coast of North America as a vagrant from Asia. The 26 records for California through 2000 encompass fall, winter, and spring. But the three for San Diego County are all of adults early in fall migration.

Migration: One was photographed at San Elijo Lagoon (L7) 4 July 1981 (Binford 1985), another was seen there 9 August 2001 (A. Mauro, M. B. Mulrooney, D. V. Blue; Garrett and Wilson 2003), and another was seen at the Santa Margarita River mouth (G4) 10 July 1996 (C. G. Edwards, McCaskie and San Miguel 1999).

Stilt Sandpiper *Calidris himantopus*

The Stilt Sandpiper migrates largely via central North America in spring, the Atlantic coast in fall, and is rare along the Pacific coast, occurring mainly in fall. In San Diego County, on average, one or two sightings are reported per year. The Salton Sea represents the northern tip of the Stilt Sandpiper's normal winter range, but there is only one winter record for San Diego County. The Stilt Sandpiper typically associates with dowitchers in shallow brackish or fresh water.

Photo by Kenneth Z. Kurland

Migration: Though the Stilt Sandpiper has been reported from many of San Diego County's coastal wetlands, the locations where it is most frequent are Batiquitos Lagoon (J6/J7), San Elijo Lagoon (L7), and the Tijuana River valley. The sites farthest inland are Lake Hodges (K10/K11; up to two on 15 September 1985, K. L. Weaver) and Lower Otay Lake (U13/U14; 22 August 1974, AB 29:121, 1975). From 1997 to 2001 records were of one at the Santa Margarita River mouth (G4) 21–25 August 1998 (P. A. Ginsburg), one (the same?) at sewage ponds just inland of there (G5) 30 August 1998 (R. E. Fischer), two at San Elijo Lagoon 22 July 1998 (R. T. Patton), four there 30 September 2000 (E. C. Hall, NAB 55:103, 2001), and one at the northeast corner of Mission Bay (Q8) 31 October 2001 (J. C. Worley). The highest count ever was of up to six at San Elijo Lagoon 21 September–9 October

1992 (P. A. Ginsburg, AB 47:149, 1993). Stilt Sandpiper occurrences range from 22 July (1998, San Elijo Lagoon, R. T. Patton), to 20 November (1987, Chula Vista, C. G. Edwards, AB 42:135, 1988) and peak in September.

Winter: The one Stilt Sandpiper recorded in San Diego County in winter was at San Elijo Lagoon 21–22 February 1982 (T. Meyer, AB 36:331, 1982).

Buff-breasted Sandpiper *Tryngites subruficollis*

The Buff-breasted Sandpiper is one of those shore-birds that breeds largely in arctic Canada and migrates largely down the middle of the continent. It is rare on either coast; almost all seen in California are juveniles in fall migration. Nineteen Buff-breasted Sandpipers have been seen in San Diego County, on grass or dry mud. This rather short-billed species does not probe wet mud.

Migration: Of San Diego County's 19 Buff-breasted Sandpipers, all have been in the Tijuana River valley except one at the upper end of Buena Vista Lagoon (H6; on land subsequently developed into a shopping center) 16 September 1967 (AFN 22:90.1968), one at Batiquitos Lagoon (J7) 8 September 1991 (Patten et al. 1995b), two at the upper end of Lake Hodges (K11) 2–3 September 1978 (Binford 1983), and one at North Island Naval Air Station (S8) 19 October 2001 (R. T. Patton). Dates range from 26 August (1991, Patten et al. 1995b) to 25 October (1990,

Photo by Anthony Mercieca

Heindel and Garrett 1995), except for a late straggler 4–7 December 1993 (P. Chad, NASFN 48:248, 1994). All of San Diego County's Buff-breasted Sandpipers have been juveniles, except for an adult 26 August–7 September 1991.

Ruff *Philomachus pugnax*

Though primarily a species of the Old World, the Ruff is a regular rare migrant and winter visitor to North America. About 30 have been found in San Diego County, from 1962 through 2002. In this region, tidal mudflats, brackish lagoons, pastures, and fields of sod have all been habitat to the Ruff.

Winter: Only four individual Ruffs are known to have wintered in San Diego County, but one of these returned to the shore of San Diego Bay at Chula Vista (U10) for eight consecutive years, 1984–1991. The other winter records are from the Tijuana River valley 2 November 1968–6 April 1969 (AFN 23:108, 521, 1969) and 16–31 December 1989 (J. Oldenettel, AB 44:329, 1990), and from the south San Diego Bay salt works and nearby beach of the naval radio-receiving facility (U10/V10) 25 October 2002–30 March 2003 (D. M. Parker, G. McCaskie, NAB 57:257, 2003). One at Batiquitos Lagoon (J7) 31 March 1990 (D. R. Willick, AB 44:496, 1990) and California's first Ruff, in the San Diego River flood-control channel (R8) 30 March 1962 (McCaskie 1963, SDNHM 30290), may have been winter visitors or spring migrants.

Photo by Anthony Mercieca

Migration: It is as a fall migrant that the Ruff is most frequent in San Diego County. All records are coastal except for one from Lake Henshaw (G17) 4–6 October 1982 (R. Higson, AB 37:224, 1983). The earliest fall record is from the Tijuana River valley 26 June 1983 (G. McCaskie, AB 37:1027, 1983). The bird wintering at Chula Vista was found as early as 15 July in 1984 and 19 July in 1989 (AB 39:103, 1985; 43:1368, 1989).

Short-billed Dowitcher *Limnodromus griseus*

The Short-billed Dowitcher is a major constituent of the shorebird flocks on the tidal flats around San Diego. The winter population is around 2000, and even larger numbers are seen in migration. Migrants use freshwater ponds, lakeshores, and brackish lagoons as well as tidal mudflats, but wintering birds are rare in northern San Diego County's lagoons and absent from fresh water, making the two dowitchers' winter distributions somewhat complementary. The difficulty in distinguishing the two species in the field, however, still clouds our understanding of their relative status.

Photo by Anthony Mercieca

Winter: The mudflats of south San Diego Bay are the Short-billed Dowitcher's center in San Diego County. Macdonald et al. (1990) counted up to 431 along the Chula Vista bayfront (T10/U10) 29 November 1988, while Stadtlander and Konecny (1994), on weekly surveys in and near the salt works (U10/V10), recorded a December–February maximum of about 700 and averages of 200 to 450. Large numbers also winter in the Tijuana River estuary (V10), with up to 670 on 19 December 1998 (R. B. Riggan), and northeastern Mission Bay (Q8), with up to 300 on 18 December 1998 (J. C. Worley).

At northern San Diego County's lagoons the Short-billed Dowitcher is rare in winter. Some may be overlooked, but the Long-billed Dowitcher outnumbers it greatly. On the basis of monthly counts 1973–83, King et al. (1987) reported an average of 3.7 from November to April at San Elijo Lagoon (L7). Numbers as high as 25 (possibly including some Long-billed) at Agua Hedionda Lagoon (16) 24 January 1999 (P. A. Ginsburg), 24 at Batiquitos Lagoon (J6/J7) 7 January 1997 (Merkel and Associates 1997), and 13 at Los Peñasquitos Lagoon (N7) 7 January

2001 (D. K. Adams) were unusually large for winter in this area. Agua Hedionda is more attractive than the other lagoons because, being dredged, it resembles the bays. The deepening and opening of Batiquitos Lagoon in the mid 1990s converted that previously unsuitable site into possible winter habitat for the Short-billed Dowitcher.

Migration: Adult Short-billed Dowitchers begin arriving in the last week of June and are common by the first week of July. Juveniles beginning arriving in late July. Macdonald et al. (1990) recorded a fall peak of 1194 around south San Diego Bay on 27 August 1988, while Stadtlander and Konecny (1994) found dowitchers' peak abundance at the salt works in October, with up to 1156 on 27 October 1993. The latter study found the peak of spring migrants to be smaller (maximum about 470 in April 1993), but Macdonald et al. (1990) counted 3376, most along the Chula Vista bayfront, on 10 April 1989. Nearly all Short-billed Dowitchers depart by early May. Some nonbreeding birds remain through the summer, mainly on south San Diego Bay (250 through June 1987, AB 41:1487, 1987; 84 on 24 June 1988, Macdonald et al. 1990), at the Tijuana River estuary, and irregularly in the north county. The only records of summering Short-billed Dowitchers in the north county 1997–2001 were of four at the Santa Margarita River mouth (G4) 15 June 1997 (B. L. Peterson) and two at the San Dieguito River mouth (M7) 5 June 2000 (D. R. Grine).

In contrast to winter, during migration the Short-billed Dowitcher is common at the north county lagoons and regular at freshwater ponds in the coastal lowland. King et al. (1987) reported an average of 18 at San Elijo Lagoon in September and October; Merkel and Associates (1997) reported 126 at Batiquitos

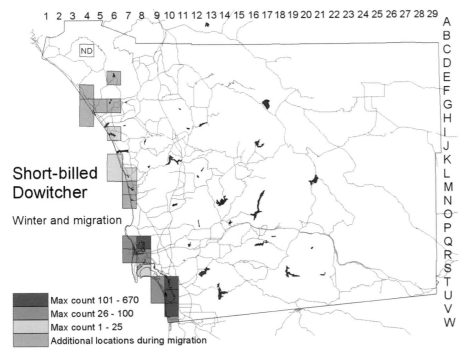

Short-billed Dowitcher

Winter and migration

- ■ Max count 101 - 670
- ▨ Max count 26 - 100
- ▧ Max count 1 - 25
- □ Additional locations during migration

Lagoon 3 April 1997. The only record for the Anza–Borrego Desert is of one at the Borrego sewage ponds (H25) 30 September 1992 (A. G. Morley).

Conservation: Kjelmyr et al. (1991) listed San Diego Bay as one of six coastal estuaries in California with 1000 or more wintering dowitchers. Before so much of the tidal mudflats of Mission and San Diego bays were filled, the area's importance to the Short-billed Dowitcher was probably even greater.

Taxonomy: *Limnodromus g. caurinus* Pitelka, 1950, which breeds in southern Alaska, is the subspecies wintering commonly along the California coast. On the basis of its smaller size, a juvenile from Whelan Lake (G6) 24 September 1961 (A. M. Rea, SDNHM 3098) is *L. g. hendersoni* Rowan, 1932, breeding in central Canada. In breeding plumage *hendersoni* has more rufous and less spotting on the underparts, but in juvenile plumage it differs only in size.

Long-billed Dowitcher *Limnodromus scolopaceus*

The Long-billed Dowitcher is one of the more common shorebirds in San Diego County on fresh water, surpassed inland only by the Least Sandpiper and Killdeer. It is even more common in coastal estuaries, but it is scarce on the tidal mudflats of San Diego and Mission bays sought by the Short-billed Dowitcher. The Long-billed arrives later in the fall than the Short-billed, and, unlike the Short-billed, rarely remains as a nonbreeding visitor through the summer.

Winter: The Long-billed Dowitcher occurs in equal abundance both along the coast and inland. Along the coast, the main sites are the San Diego River flood-control channel and Famosa Slough (R8), with up to 185 at the latter 6 January 2000 (J. A. Peugh), and the north county lagoons, with up to 310 at Batiquitos (J7) 2 January 1998 (C. C. Gorman) and 297 at San Elijo (L7) 23 December 2001 (E. Garnica). The Long-billed Dowitcher frequents the channels within the marshes in the estuaries of the Tijuana and Sweetwater rivers but avoids the open tide flats of San Diego Bay preferred by the Short-billed Dowitcher. Nevertheless, the two species have ample opportunity to mix.

Photo by Brian L. Sullivan

Inland, the Long-billed Dowitcher occurs both around reservoirs and in shallow ponds or wetlands wet only during winter rains. Large concentrations in the former habitat are 309 at Lake Hodges (K10) 22 December 2000 (R. L. Barber) and 160 on the north side of Lake Morena (S21) 23 January 2000 (S. E. Smith). Large concentrations in the latter habitat are 100 at the Dairy Mart pond, Tijuana River valley (V11) 16 December 2000 (G. McCaskie) and 36 in San Dieguito Valley (M8) 28 February 1999 (R. T. Patton). Lake Morena, at 3000 feet elevation, was the highest site where we noted wintering dowitchers. One at Borrego Springs (G24) 23 February 1998 (P. D. Ache) was most likely an early spring migrant.

Migration: A few migrant Long-billed Dowitchers may arrive by late June, but the bulk of adults begins arriving in late July, that of juveniles, in late August. Thus the fall migration of the Long-billed is later than that of the Short-billed. Spring migration extends from late February, as suggested by the record from Borrego Springs, to early or mid May. Our latest spring date from 1997 to 2001 was 11 May (1999, three at Buena Vista Lagoon, H6,

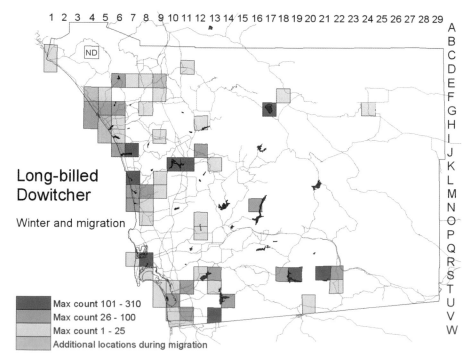

Long-billed Dowitcher

Winter and migration

■ Max count 101 - 310
■ Max count 26 - 100
□ Max count 1 - 25
▨ Additional locations during migration

M. Freda; nine at San Elijo Lagoon, M. B. Stowe). Unlike the Short-billed, the Long-billed has no strong peaks of migration in San Diego County.

The Long-billed is far less frequent than the Short-billed as a nonbreeding visitor through the summer. Nevertheless, there are a few records: one on south San Diego Bay and one at the Tijuana River mouth 9 June 1984 (R. E. Webster, G. McCaskie, AB 38:1062, 1984), two at the Sweetwater River mouth (U10) 24 June 1988 (Macdonald et al. 1990), one at Batiquitos Lagoon 5–7

June 1998 (F. Hall, C. C. Gorman). From their monthly surveys of San Elijo Lagoon 1973–83, King et al. (1987) reported an average in June and July of 1.2.

Conservation: The Long-billed Dowitcher has taken advantage of new habitat created with reservoirs, but it has suffered loss of considerable habitat because of channelizing of rivers, development of floodplains, and elimination of seasonal wetlands.

Wilson's Snipe *Gallinago delicata*

Unlike many members of the sandpiper family, snipes avoid the seashore, seeking fresh or brackish water with low vegetation and soft mud. Development of the coastal lowland has eliminated most of the seasonal wetlands ideal for snipes, and the species is on the decline in that area. Wilson's Snipe is basically a winter visitor to San Diego County, but it has probably nested less than 20 miles north of the county line in the Garner Valley of Riverside County and 50 miles south of the border at Ojos Negros (Huey 1928a). Thus the few summer sightings in southeastern San Diego County suggest the species could nest there irregularly.

Photo by Anthony Mercieca

Winter: Wilson's Snipe is widespread in San Diego County, but its habitat is naturally patchy in this arid region. Where the rivers have not been channelized, the floodplains of the coastal lowland offer some of the most extensive habitat. Even there the species is generally uncommon, though concentrations in this zone range up to 25 in San Dieguito Valley (M8) 27 December 1998 (P. Unitt). Low-lying places in San Diego County's largest grassland, Warner Valley, are also a center for

the snipe and had the largest number noted 1997–2002: 31 in the east arm of the valley along Buena Vista and San Ysidro creeks (G19) 10 December 2000 (R. and S. L. Breisch). Coastal wetlands attract fewer snipes than those inland, but Los Peñasquitos Lagoon (N7) has the species regularly, with up to 15 on 3 February 2002 and 20 on 3 March 2002 (S. E. Smith, D. K. Adams). If montane wetlands remain free of ice and snow the snipe may winter on them, with up to six at Lake Cuyamaca (M20) 7 January 2001 (R. B. Riggan) and four at Big Laguna Lake (O23) 18 January 1998 (P. Unitt). In the Anza–Borrego Desert the snipe occurs at both artificial and natural oases. It winters regularly at Lower Willows along Coyote Creek (D23), where A. G. Morley has noted up to five per day (Massey 1998).

The numbers and distribution of the snipe in San Diego County may be expected to vary with the severity of the winter farther north and rainfall locally. Nevertheless, the number we recorded per hour varied little through the atlas period and was only 8% lower in the very dry winter of 2001–02 than in the wet 1997–98.

Migration: The snipe occurs in San Diego County primarily from early September to early April.

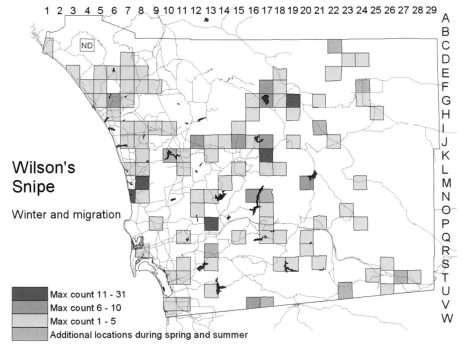

Wilson's Snipe

Winter and migration

- ■ Max count 11 - 31
- ▨ Max count 6 - 10
- ▢ Max count 1 - 5
- ▨ Additional locations during spring and summer

Dates range from 16 August (1964, one at San Diego) and 20 August (1983, one in the Tijuana River valley, G. McCaskie, AB 37:1027, 1983) to at least 6 May (2001, one at Los Peñasquitos Lagoon, D. R. Grine). One along Buena Vista Creek in Warner Valley (G18) 12 May 2001 (T. Stands, S. Yamagata) could have been summering.

Breeding distribution: Though the snipe is not known to breed in San Diego County, field work for this atlas yielded an unexpected number of sightings in summer. The only previous summer record was of one at Boulevard (T26) 6 July 1993 (P. Unitt, AB 47:1150, 1993). The most intriguing reports are from Tule Lake (T27), where J. K. Wilson noted the species repeatedly, with up to three on 21 June and 3 July 2000. On the latter date, two birds remained together at length, suggesting a pair. Sites of other summer records, all of single birds, are O'Neill Lake (E6; 2 July 1999, P. A. Ginsburg), Lake Henshaw (G17; 26 July 1998, R. A. Hamilton, FN 52:503, 1998), the upper end of El Capitan Reservoir (N17; 9 July 1999, D. C. Seals), Pine Valley (P21; 5 June 2001, M. B. Mulrooney),

and the south side of Corte Madera Lake (R20; 20 June 1998, P. Unitt, FN 52:503, 1998). Corte Madera and Tule lakes are the most likely nesting sites.

Conservation: Snipe numbers on the San Diego, Rancho Santa Fe, Oceanside, and Escondido Christmas counts all show a trend of decrease. The San Diego count averaged 46 from 1962 to 1981 but only 2.4 from 1997 to 2001. Development of floodplains and channelizing of streams eliminate snipe habitat. Though the upper ends of reservoirs are some of the county's main snipe sites, the filling of the reservoirs covered former habitat.

The recent upsurge in summer records probably reflects only attention paid during the atlas period to areas previously poorly known. Overgrazing, pumping of ground water, and a trend toward a drier climate are bad signs for wetland birds like the snipe.

Taxonomy: With its Eurasian and South American relatives ranked again as full species (Banks et al. 2002), Wilson's Snipe of North America is left as a monotypic species.

Wilson's Phalarope *Phalaropus tricolor*

Most of the world's Wilson's Phalarope population stages at a few saline lakes in western North America before migrating to the altiplano of the Andes (Jehl 1988). San Diego County is thus off the species' main migration route, but the birds are locally common from mid June through September on brackish lagoons, inland lakes, and above all the salt works at the south end of San Diego Bay. Yet otherwise they avoid San Diego and Mission bays almost totally. Spring migrants are uncommon. Occasional wintering in the salt works ceased in the mid 1980s.

Photo by Anthony Mercieca

Migration: Wilson's Phalarope is noted for its early fall migration, begun by adult females, which can depart the breeding range as soon as they lay their eggs, leaving the tasks of incubation and brood rearing to the males. Arrival in the third week of June is typical; even 15 in breeding plumage at Batiquitos Lagoon (J6/J7) 9 June 1979 (E. Copper) were likely early "fall" migrants. In the salt works, on the basis of weekly surveys through 1993, Stadtlander and Konecny (1994) found a sharp peak in July, with a high count of 370. At San Elijo Lagoon (L7), however, on the basis of monthly surveys 1973–83, King et al. (1987) found a peak in August, with a high count of 360 on 5 August 1979. The differences may be related to different habitat use by adults, which arrive earlier, and juveniles, which arrive later. Inland, Wilson's Phalarope is uncommon in fall, frequenting small lakes or mudflats at the upper ends of large reservoirs. From 1997 to 2002 our maximum inland counts were of six at Tule Lake (T27) 21 June 2000 (J. K. Wilson), 12 at O'Neill Lake (E6) 28 June 2000 (P. A. Ginsburg), and 11 at the upper end of Lake Morena (S22) 2 July 2000 (R. and S. L. Breisch). The

only fall record from the Anza–Borrego Desert is of one at a gravel pit along Highway S2 near the Imperial County line (Q29) 19 August 1975 (M. Getty).

In spring the species' numbers are far smaller. Although Guy McCaskie noted up to 300 in the salt works 5 May 1962, on their weekly counts in spring 1993 Stadtlander and Konecny (1994) observed an average of fewer than 10 Wilson's Phalaropes, in April only. Away from the salt works, during the atlas period, our only spring record of more than a single bird was of 20 at Agua Hedionda Lagoon (I6) 30 April 2000 (J. Ciarletta). In spring Wilson's Phalarope is rare inland, recorded just at Ramona (K15; one on 30 April 2003, M. B. Stowe) and at the Borrego sewage ponds (H25; three from 15 to 25 April 1987 and on 29 April 1990, A. G. Morley). The interval 21 March–22 May reported for spring migration by Unitt (1984) still stands. Records of apparently summering birds are of seven in the salt works 27 May 1979 (M. U. Evans) and single individuals at San Elijo Lagoon 2 June 1974 and 7 June 1981 (King et al. 1987).

Winter: From at least 1960 to 1985 small numbers of Wilson's Phalaropes wintered occasionally in the salt works; the species was recorded on 8 of 24 San Diego Christmas bird counts 1960–83. The high count was of eight from 19 January to 1 March 1963 (AFN 17:358, 1963), and the most recent winter record was of two from 14 to 23 February 1985 (G. McCaskie, AB 39:210, 1985).

Conservation: Whatever change to the salt works terminated phalaropes' wintering there, it affected the Red-necked and Wilson's simultaneously. At the beginning of the 21st century, Wilson's Phalarope seems less numerous as a migrant than in the 1960s and 1970s. Part of the change may be due to local habitat changes, as few muddy ponds remain in the coastal lowland. The restoration of tidal flow at Batiquitos and San Elijo lagoons rendered these sites less attractive to Wilson's Phalaropes.

Red-necked or Northern Phalarope
Phalaropus lobatus

The Red-necked Phalarope is an abundant migrant in the south San Diego Bay salt works, a common migrant on the ocean offshore, and common in fall on northern San Diego County's lagoons. At other times and places it is uncommon to rare. The Red-necked Phalarope's formerly regular wintering in the salt works, like that of Wilson's Phalarope, ceased in the mid 1980s.

Migration: The salt works are by far the Red-necked Phalarope's principal site in San Diego County. In their weekly surveys of the salt works 1993–94, Stadtlander and Konecny (1994) found numbers peaking at about 12,000 on 18 August 1993. Even their minimum August count reached 4300. In their monthly surveys of San Elijo Lagoon (L7) 1973–83, King et al. (1987) found an average of 250 in September and October and a maximum of 1400 on 4 September 1977. Only during fall migration is the Red-necked Phalarope regular on inland lakes, with up to seven at Lake Hodges (K11) 18 September 1982 (K. L. Weaver) and 10 at Lake Henshaw (G17) 17 September 1978 (P. Unitt). The species occurs in fall primarily from mid July (exceptionally 24 June, 1988, two at the northeast corner of the salt works, Macdonald et al. 1990) to October. The single Red-necked Phalarope reported during the winter atlas season, in the San Diego River flood-control channel (R8) 7 December 1997 (B. C. Moore), was evidently a late fall straggler.

In spring the Red-necked Phalarope is much less common. In May 1993, Stadtlander and Konecny (1994) found an average of about 700 and maximum of about 1500 in the salt works. Though spring migrants are often common on the ocean as well, away from the salt works they are rare even at other coastal wetlands. From 1997 to 2001 there was no spring report of more than eight, and at San Elijo Lagoon King et al. (1987) recorded a May aver-

Photo by Anthony Mercieca

age of only 0.4. Our only Red-necked Phalarope inland during the atlas period, at the Borrego sewage ponds (H25) 3 May 1997 (H. L. Young, M. B. Mosher), was one of just three recorded in the Anza–Borrego Desert, the others being at the same locality 14 April 1992 and at Lower Willows (D23) 7 May 1988 (A. G. Morley). Spring dates range from 5 April (1998, eight at Los Peñasquitos Lagoon, N7, D. K. Adams) and 7 April (1998, one at La Jolla Shores, P7, SDNHM 50293) to 23 May (1926, two off Point Loma, S7, SDNHM 10794–5).

Winter: From at least 1953 to 1985 the Red-necked Phalarope wintered fairly regularly in the salt works. It was recorded on 21 of the 31 San Diego Christmas bird counts 1953–83 with up 230 on 23 December 1967. Since 1985, however, wintering Red-necked Phalaropes have been found there only once, with six on 16 December 1995.

Conservation: The building of the salt works created hypersaline ponds with abundant brine shrimp, ideal staging stops for the Red-necked and Wilson's Phalaropes. But why the Red-necked Phalarope's wintering on the salt works came to an abrupt end is unknown.

Red Phalarope *Phalaropus fulicarius*

The Red Phalarope is the most pelagic of the three phalaropes, rarely found on land except when driven onshore by storms. The Red Phalarope's abundance is notably irregular: usually the species is rare, but large flocks are occasional. Such concentrations may appear abruptly at any time in fall, winter, or spring.

Migration: In San Diego County the Red Phalarope occurs mainly from October to early May, but dates range from 23 July (1935, "abundant offshore," Miller 1936) to 29 May (1964, one on San Diego Bay, G. McCaskie). There are only a few inland records, of scattered single individuals, except on 11 November 1982, when 60 were on Lake Henshaw (G17; G. McCaskie) and over 100 were on Lake Hodges (K10/K11; K. L. Weaver, AB

37:224, 1983). The only Red Phalarope reported from the Anza–Borrego Desert was near Borrego Springs 7 March 1992 (K. Ellsworth, AB 46:480, 1992).

Winter: The Red Phalarope is just as frequent along San Diego County's coast in winter as during migration. From 1997 to 2002 the only significant influx was in early January 2001. At least 5000 were on the ocean within 5 miles of La Jolla (P7) 1 January 2001 (S. Walens, NAB 55:228, 2001), and 80 were visible from Torrey Pines State Reserve (N7) 7 January 2001 (D. K. Adams). The species' irregularity is exemplified by the results of San Diego Christmas bird counts. The Red Phalarope was noted on 30 of 50 counts 1953–2002 with a median of 2, a mean of 95, and a maximum of 2032, the last on 21 December 1963.

Photo by Anthony Mercieca

GULLS AND TERNS — FAMILY LARIDAE

South Polar Skua *Stercorarius maccormicki*

Of the ocean birds that migrate from the southern hemisphere to the North Pacific for the austral winter, the South Polar Skua comes the farthest, for it nests around the coasts of Antarctica. Off San Diego County it is a rare migrant, recorded in both spring and fall.

Migration: The South Polar Skua has been recorded off San Diego most frequently in spring, from 5 May (1987, one at Tanner Bank 100 miles off shore, R. R. Veit, AB 41:488, 1987) to 4 June (1983, R. E. Webster, AB 37:1027, 1983). In most cases just a single individual was seen in a full day's boat trip, but four were counted 20 May 1978 (AB 32:1055, 1978). Fall records extend from 12 August (1961, AFN 15:493, 1961) to 14 October (1971, Cortez Bank, Jehl 1973), except for the one from shore, the only specimen,

Photo by Joseph R. Jehl, Jr.

picked up at Silver Strand State Beach (T9) 23 November 1975 (AB 31:376, 1977, CSULB 4785). The only fall record of more than one individual was of two off San Diego 7 September 1991 (G. McCaskie, AB 46:149, 1992).

Pomarine Jaeger *Stercorarius pomarinus*

The Pomarine Jaeger is primarily a migrant over the ocean off San Diego County and the commonest jaeger here in both spring and fall. It is regular if uncommon in winter as well. Occasional Pomarine Jaegers remain through the summer. The species is rarely seen on shore; perhaps any that alight on beaches are in poor health.

Winter: Most Pomarine Jaegers winter in the tropics; California is at the northern edge of the species' normal winter range. Of San Diego County's Christmas bird counts, the San Diego and Oceanside counts regularly deploy a boat on the ocean, thanks to the consistent dedication of David W. Povey. The San Diego count has recorded the Pomarine Jaeger in 15 of 34 years, 1969–2002, with a maximum of three individuals. The Oceanside count has recorded it in 17 of 28 years, 1976–2002, with a maximum of four, except for 25 on 28 December 1980. The birds can occasionally be seen from shore; our maximum 1997–2002 was of four from Torrey Pines State Reserve (N7) 22 December 2000 (S. Walens).

Photo by Kenneth W. Fink

Migration: The Pomarine Jaeger is most numerous in fall migration (up to 140 between San Diego and San Clemente Island 11 September 1971, G. McCaskie), and common also in spring migration. It is seldom seen in June or July, but eight were off San Diego 17 June 1982 (D. W. Povey, AB 36:1016, 1982). One was in the south San Diego Bay salt works (U10) 9 June 1999 (found dead 13 June, SDNHM 50438); another was there 23 June 1999 (R. T. Patton).

Parasitic Jaeger *Stercorarius parasiticus*

A migrant and winter visitor along San Diego County's coastline, the Parasitic is less numerous here than the Pomarine but seen uncommonly, from shore as well as at sea. The Parasitic Jaeger enters San Diego Bay rarely. There are two summer records.

Winter: The Parasitic Jaeger, like other ocean birds, is most likely to be seen from shore, especially at La Jolla (P7), during the strong northwest winds that follow the passage of a cold front. Maximum daily counts from shore are of 18 at La Jolla 13 February 2001 (B. L. Sullivan) and 17 at Oceanside (H5) 26 December 1998 (S. Walens). The San Diego Christmas bird count has recorded the Parasitic Jaeger on 25 of 34 counts 1969–2002, with a maximum of eight on 20 December 1986. The Oceanside count has recorded it on 19 of 28 counts 1976–2002, with a maximum of 19 on 26 December 1998 (including 18 from shore). There were no reports within San Diego Bay during the atlas period, but weekly surveys of the bay 1993–94 yielded four sightings totaling five individuals (Mock et al. 1994).

Photo by Kenneth W. Fink

Migration: The Parasitic Jaeger's seasonal distribution in San Diego County remains that reported by Unitt (1984): 27 August–23 May, except for sightings of one at the Santa Margarita River mouth (G4) 12 June–10 July 1971 (AB 35:906, 1971) and of two 1 mile off La Jolla 14 June 1978 (AB 32:1208, 1978).

Long-tailed Jaeger *Stercorarius longicaudus*

The smallest of the jaegers is also the scarcest in San Diego County, where it occurs as a rare fall migrant. It typically remains far out to sea, and there are only two reports from shore. The only jaeger identified inland in San Diego County, however, was a Long-tailed grounded by Tropical Storm Doreen in 1977.

Migration: Off San Diego, the Long-tailed Jaeger is usually seen singly, if at all. The largest concentration reported near San Diego was nine that were 20 miles east of Cortez Bank (and thus about 90 miles west of San Diego) 13 October 1971 (Jehl 1973). Onshore, H. W. Marsden collected an immature at Pacific Beach 19 September 1904 (Bishop 1905, FMNH 135805).

All three jaegers undertake extensive overland migrations but seldom stop en route. The only inland record for San Diego County remains the adult found exhausted at Pala (D11) after Tropical Storm Doreen 18 August 1977 (SDNHM 40390). An unidentified jaeger, however, was at Lake Hodges (K10) 9 September 1982 (D. Hayward, AB 37:224, 1983).

Photo by Richard E. Webster

The seasonal spread of fall records remains the 18 August–18 October reported by Unitt (1984). In spring, one was at the south end of San Diego Bay 11 May 1962 (G. McCaskie, AFN 16:447, 1962), one was off San Clemente Island 1 May 1987 (R. R. Veit, AB 41:488, 1987), and one was at Cortez Bank 22 April 2000 (T. McGrath, NAB 54:327, 2000).

Laughing Gull *Larus atricilla*

Though a common postbreeding visitor and even a sporadic breeding species at the Salton Sea, the Laughing Gull is only a rare vagrant to the Pacific coast of California. In contrast to its status as an almost exclusively summer visitor just to the east, in San Diego County the Laughing Gull has no strong seasonal pattern; the approximately 30 records are scattered throughout the year.

Winter: The atlas study from 1997 to 2002 was a slow period for the Laughing Gull in San Diego County,

Photo by Anthony Mercieca

yielding just one record, of two first-winter birds at Buena Vista Lagoon (H6) 16 January–28 March 1998 (T. Hathaway, FN 52:257, 1998). The winter of 2002–03, however, was unusual in having three. Winter records of the Laughing Gull in San Diego County are coastal or up to 13 miles inland, as far as Santee Lakes (P12; 17 January–12 February 1993, C. G. Edwards, AB 47:301, 1993) and Lake Murray (Q11; 8–29 December 2002, M. Sadowski, NAB 57:257, 2003).

Migration: There were no summer records of the Laughing Gull in San Diego County before 1983 (Unitt 1984). Since then five have accumulated, including one of an immature at Lake Henshaw (G17) 30 September 1983 (R. Higson, AB 38:247, 1984), which presumably arrived over the mountains from the southeast. Two adults were together at San Diego 4 June 1983 (D. M. Parker, AB 37:913, 1983).

Franklin's Gull *Larus pipixcan*

On its commute between a breeding range in the intermountain basins and the Great Plains and a winter range off the Pacific coast of Central and South America, Franklin's Gull passes largely to the east of San Diego County. The species is a rare migrant here, with a few immature stragglers recorded in winter.

Migration: In spring, Franklin's Gull has been recorded in San Diego County only about 12 times, on dates from 11 April (1971, Oceanside, H5, AB 25:801, 1971) to 29 June (1998, Santee Lakes, P12, M. B. Mulrooney). The latter was unusual in also being the only inland record in spring or early summer. The only other observations during the atlas period were of one in the south San Diego Bay salt works (U10) 19 May 1999 (R. T. Patton) and three at the mouth of Las Flores Creek (E3) 30 May 1998 (R. and S. L. Breisch), the latter being the only spring sighting of more than a single bird.

In fall Franklin's Gull is more frequent than in spring, though its frequency has decreased since the 1970s. Fall records extend from 6 September (1963, one at the Santa Margarita River mouth, G4, McCaskie and Cardiff 1965), exceptionally 29 July (1951, same locality, AFN 5:308, 1951), to 8 December (1966, Lake Henshaw, G17, C. G. Edwards, NASFN 51:802, 1997). Fall records are mainly

Photo by Anthony Mercieca

coastal but include at least two from Lake Henshaw and one from Lake Hodges (K10; G. McCaskie).

Winter: Franklin's Gull has been noted in San Diego County seven times in winter. Unitt (1984) listed four records, including the only one inland, at Lake Hodges 10 November 1979–5 January 1980 (AB 34:306, 1980). Subsequently one was at the San Diego River mouth (R7) 29 December 1987–20 January 1988 (E. Lodge, AB 42:321, 1988), one was at Chula Vista (U10) 16 January–11 February 1990 (E. R. Lichtwardt, AB 44:329, 1990), and one was at Coronado (S9/T9) 18 February 1997 (E. Copper, NASFN 51:802, 1997).

Little Gull *Larus minutus*

From the first sighting near the north end of the Salton Sea in 1968, the Little Gull has become ever more frequent in California, as this originally Old World species colonizes North America from the northeast. Of the 79 well-supported records for California through 2002, however, only two are from San Diego County.

Winter: An immature at the Oceanside harbor (H5) 27 December 1981 became entangled in fishing line and was taken to Sea World, where it died 27 March 1982 (SDNHM 41883). Another was seen at La Jolla (P7) 18 November 1994 (S. Walens, G. McCaskie, NASFN 49:101, 1995; Howell and Pyle 1997).

Photo by Kenneth W. Fink

Bonaparte's Gull *Larus philadelphia*

The only small gull regular in San Diego County, Bonaparte's Gull is most abundant on the ocean, where, in winter, it can often be seen in flocks of hundreds a short distance offshore. Along the coast, it is much less numerous, though still often common in San Diego Bay or the north county lagoons. Inland, Bonaparte's Gull is quite irregular, both from lake to lake and from year to year. Even along the coast Bonaparte's Gull appears to be becoming patchier in its distribution, perhaps as a symptom of the faltering productivity of the ocean off southern California.

Photo by Anthony Mercieca

Winter: Offshore, the flocks of Bonaparte's Gulls undoubtedly shift widely with the shifting of fish and plankton. Onshore, however, the species has a few favored concentration points, especially the sewage ponds near the Santa Margarita River along Stuart Mesa Road (G5; up to 70 on 6 December 1998, R. E. Fischer), Buena Vista Lagoon (H5; 150 on 7 February 1999, J. Determan), Los Peñasquitos Lagoon (N7; 100 on 3 January 1999, D. K. Adams), and the San Diego River mouth (R7; 200 on 22 February 2000, V. P. Johnson). Bonaparte's Gull is scarce in Mission Bay but fairly common in San Diego Bay. On weekly surveys of central and south San Diego Bay 1993–94, Manning (1995) noted a maximum of 138; on weekly surveys in and near the salt works through the same period, Stadtlander and Konecny (1994) noted a maximum of 108, though usually numbers were much lower.

Atlas observers also found Bonaparte's Gulls on several inland lakes, especially Henshaw (G17; up to 185 on 7 February 1999, W. E. Haas), Sutherland (J16; 100 on 22 February 2000, M. B. Stowe), and Hodges (K10/K11;

100 on 14 December 1997, B. Schram). At other lakes our counts were of 15 or fewer. Inland, however, the species' occurrence is quite irregular, as exemplified by the history of Lake Henshaw Christmas bird counts: Bonaparte's Gull has been recorded on 17 of 22 counts 1981–2002, with a median of 25, a mean of 59, and a maximum of 418 on 23 December 1996.

The only winter records from the Anza–Borrego Desert are of birds lost far from water, along the Montezuma Grade of Highway S22 (G23) 2 January 1993 (E. Post) and at Vallecito (M25) 12 December 2001 (S. Martin).

Migration: Bonaparte's Gull does not arrive in any significant numbers until November. On their weekly surveys of north San Diego Bay 1993 94, Mock et al. (1994), recorded an earliest date of 19 October, the earliest among any of the regular surveys of San Diego Bay. One fall migrant has been noted in the Anza–Borrego Desert, on a golf-course pond at the Roadrunner Club (F24) 29 October–6 November 1991 (A. G. Morley).

In spring migration Bonaparte's Gulls make use of the migration corridor over San Diego County's relatively low mountains, following the same route as the Brant, Surf Scoter, and Common Loon. During the atlas period our most striking example of this was 300 at Lake Cuyamaca (M20) 2 April 2001 (P. D. Jorgensen). Spring counts at Lake Henshaw range as high as 490 on 31 March 1979 (R. Higson, AB 33:806, 1979). Another notable sighting was of eight flying west down Hauser Canyon (T21) 25 April 1998 (R. and S. L. Breisch). Dates for such migrants range from 27 March

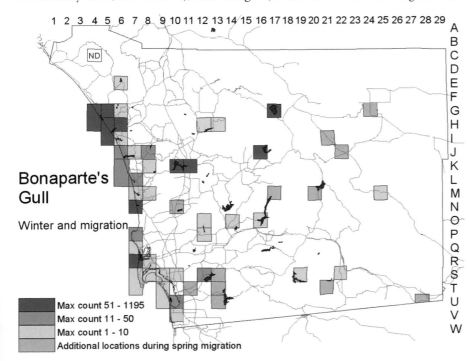

Bonaparte's Gull

Winter and migration

- Max count 51 - 1195
- Max count 11 - 50
- Max count 1 - 10
- Additional locations during spring migration

(one at the Borrego sewage ponds, H25, A. G. Morley) to perhaps 5 June (1998, nine at Lake Cuyamaca, A. P. and T. E. Keenan). When spring migration ends is difficult to say because of occasional summering birds in nonbreeding plumage (Unitt 1984). We recorded no clearly summering Bonaparte's Gulls 1997–2001; one at San Elijo Lagoon (L7) as late as 13 June 1998 (B. C. Moore) was still in breeding plumage.

Conservation: Numbers of Bonaparte's Gulls on San Diego County's three coastal Christmas bird counts fell noticeably in the 1990s. The San Diego count, with a 50-year average of 734, reached its all-time lows of four in 1999, one in 2000, and three in 2002. The Rancho Santa Fe count averaged 317 from 1980 to 1990 but 64 from 1991 to 2003. The Oceanside count hit its post-1976 lows of three in 2000 and 53 in 2002, even though it hit its high of 1400 in 2001. Similarly, the Escondido count found Bonaparte's Gull regularly at Lake Wohlford (H12) 1987–93 but only sporadically since. Such irregularity characterizes birds that feed on scarce, clumped resources.

Heermann's Gull *Larus heermanni*

This most distinctive and attractive of North America's gulls is common along San Diego County's coast. Seasonally, the abundance of Heermann's Gull varies in tandem with that of the Brown Pelican, which the gull follows, stealing its fish. That is, the gull's numbers are lowest in spring, increase in summer as the birds return from their nesting colonies in the Gulf of California, then decrease again through the winter. Most Heermann's Gulls probably circumnavigate the peninsula, but a few cross overland, as there are scattered records from San Diego County's inland lakes.

Photo by Anthony Mercieca

Winter: Heermann's Gull occurs the length of San Diego County's coast and well out to sea. Areas of concentration are Torrey Pines State Reserve (N7; up to 560 on 23 December 2001, S. Walens), north San Diego Bay (444 on 14 December 1993, Mock et al. 1994), and the bight from Point Loma to Imperial Beach (535 on 15 December 2001, D. W. Povey). Few Heermann's Gulls, however, enter northern San Diego County's lagoons (maximum 10 in the east basin of Batiquitos Lagoon, J7, 22 December 2001, R. and A. Campbell) or even the inner reaches of Mission Bay (Q8; maximum 13 on 26 January 1999, J. C. Worley). Despite its abundance in north San Diego Bay, Heermann's Gull is uncommon in the south bay. On their regular surveys there, neither Macdonald et al. (1990) nor Stadtlander and Konecny (1994) found more than nine per day.

The only winter record inland is of one at Lake Henshaw (G17) 18 January 1980 (AB 34:306, 1980).

Migration: Numbers of Heermann's Gulls begin increasing in June, to reach a peak in September and October. On the basis of weekly counts of San Diego Bay, Mock et al. (1994) recorded their daily maximum of 1033 on 8 September 1993. On surveys of central San Diego Bay, both Mock et al. (1994) and Manning (1995) found numbers greatest in October. After this, Heermann's Gull decreases in abundance, to reach its nadir from March to May. Even during this interval, however, nonbreeding immatures are fairly common (up to 119 in north San Diego Bay 19 April 1995, P. J. Mock; 30 at La Jolla, P7, 1 April 2001, L. and M. Polinsky).

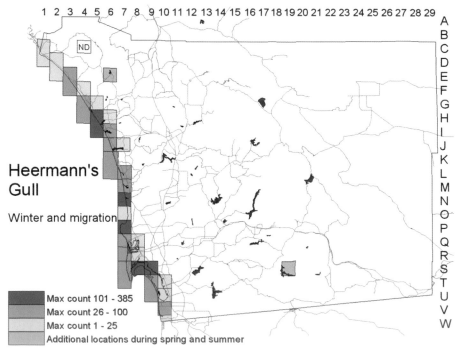

Heermann's Gull

Winter and migration

■ Max count 101 - 385
■ Max count 26 - 100
■ Max count 1 - 25
■ Additional locations during spring and summer

Most of San Diego County's inland Heermann's Gulls, like those at the Salton Sea, occurred at the time of postbreeding dispersal and likely arrived overland from the southeast. Up to two were at Lake Henshaw 5–7 July 1985, four were there 6 July 1986 (R. Higson, AB 39:962, 1985, 40:1255, 1986), and one was there 24 June 1989 (G. McCaskie, AB 43:1368, 1989). One was flying northwest over Scissors Crossing (J22) 7 July 2002 (J. R. Barth, not 3 July as in NAB 56:486, 2002), two were on Barrett Lake (S19) 21 June 1997 (J. Hannan), and one was at Jacumba (U28) 14 July 1968 (AFN 22:649, 1968). Also at this season but closer to the coast, so possibly originating from that direction, were one at O'Neill Lake (E6) 19 June 1998 (P. A. Ginsburg) and one on Otay Mesa (V13) 16–17 October 1979 (E. Copper).

Conservation: Heermann's Gull nests in just a few colonies around Baja California, and at least 90% of the population nests in a single massive colony on 150-acre Isla Rasa in the Gulf of California, making it vulnerable to catastrophes. Fortunately, Isla Rasa has been a wildlife refuge since 1964, putting an end to egging and enabling the eradication of rats. Careful management has allowed the population to increase from 55,000 pairs in 1975 to 150,000–200,000 pairs by the end of the 20th century (E. Velarde). A corresponding increase in numbers in San Diego County, however, is not evident. In Christmas bird counts, annual variability overwhelms any trend.

Belcher's or Band-tailed Gull *Larus belcheri*

With little doubt the least expected vagrant reaching San Diego County during the five-year atlas period from 1997 to 2001 was the Band-tailed or Belcher's Gull, normally confined to the coasts of Peru and Chile washed by the Humboldt Current. Vagrants have occurred north to Panama, exceptionally to Florida, but the bird amply photographed at the Tijuana River mouth represents the only well-supported record for California.

Winter: San Diego County's single Band-tailed Gull remained more or less continuously at the Tijuana River mouth (V10) from 3 August 1997 to 2 January 1998 (D. G. Shaw; Rottenborn and Morlan 2000). Perhaps its occurrence so far from its normal range was related to El Niño, that climatic variation striking in 1997–98 and

Photo by Anthony Mercieca

felt most strongly in the gull's range on the west coast of South America.

Black-tailed Gull *Larus crassirostris*

Proper interpretation of occurrences of rare birds requires context, and in the case of very rare birds accumulating that context may take decades. This is the story of San Diego County's—and California's—only Black-tailed Gull. Collected in 1954, this Asian bird was long dismissed as so unlikely to reach San Diego unaided that it was presumed to have been brought across the Pacific on a ship. More recently, additional individuals have shown up elsewhere in North America, suggesting that the Black-tailed Gull occasionally does reach this continent as a vagrant on its own (Lethaby and Bangma 1998).

Migration: Monroe (1955) collected California's only Black-tailed Gull at the former Naval Training Center on north San Diego Bay (S8) 28 November 1954, after finding it two days earlier (UMMZ 136176). The next nearest record is of one photographed at El Golfo de Santa Clara, Sonora, 7 June 1997 (Garrett and Molina 1998). Heindel and Patten (1996) outlined the basis for the California Bird Records Committee's reversing course and adding the Black-tailed Gull to the state's bird list.

Photo by Brian L. Sullivan

Mew Gull *Larus canus*

San Diego County lies near the southern limit of the Mew Gull's winter range, so the species occurs here as an uncommon winter visitor. It is almost exclusively coastal in this area, being rare just a few miles inland. For no clear reason, in San Diego County Mew Gulls are clumped in just two areas.

Winter: From 1997 to 2002, Mew Gulls concentrated in San Diego County at just two sites. One is the basin and breakwater at Camp Del Mar, within Camp Pendleton (G4), where counts averaged 20–25 and reached a maximum of 69 on 10 January 2001 (P. A. Ginsburg). Often some of these birds use the nearby sewage ponds at Stuart Mesa Road and Vandegrift Boulevard (G5), where counts ranged up to 14 on 26 December 1998 (T. A. Burr). The other site is the beach at North Island Naval Air Station (S8), where counts in the 20s are usual and 100 on 5 January 1998 (B. C. Moore) was exceptional. Sometimes the birds flock near the Hotel del Coronado (T9), but we did not record any such concentration there during the atlas period.

Elsewhere along San Diego County's coast the Mew Gull is widely scattered but uncommon. During the atlas period we had no count away from the two main sites greater than five at Encinitas (K6) 29 December 1998 (S. Schultz). The only inland locations where we recorded Mew Gulls 1997–2002 were Lake San Marcos (J8), with up to two on 27 December 1997 and 2 February 1999 (J. O. Zimmer), and Kit Carson Park, Escondido (K11), with

Photo by Anthony Mercieca

a first-year bird found after a storm 4 February 1998 (E. C. Hall). Previous inland records are all within 7 miles of the coast (Unitt 1984).

Migration: The Mew Gull occurs primarily from late November to late March, though it does not reach peak numbers until early January (Devillers et al. 1971). Extreme dates are 15 October (1955, one at Oceanside, H5, AFN 10:57, 1956) and 4 May (1962, one at the San Diego River mouth, R7, G. McCaskie). There are also two summer records, of one collected on Mission Bay (Q8) 31 July 1922 (SDNHM 2351) and one seen on San Diego Bay at Chula Vista (U10) 6–30 July 1977 (AB 31:1190, 1977).

Conservation: The sites where Mew Gulls flock shift over time. In the 1970s the San Luis Rey River mouth (H5), San Diego River mouth (R7), and Tijuana River mouth (V10) were the main sites (Devillers et al. 1971, Unitt 1984), but by the beginning of the 21st century the gulls were not using these regularly. Nevertheless, the numbers reaching the county have changed little in 30 years: Devillers et al. (1971) wrote "the total population probably does not exceed 100 birds." Christmas bird counts suggest considerable annual variation; the San Diego count has ranged from highs of 227 in 1982 and 183 in 1983 (El Niño?) to lows of one in 1973 and 1995.

Taxonomy: Only the New World subspecies of the Mew Gull, *L. c. brachyrhynchus* Richardson, 1831, has been found in California.

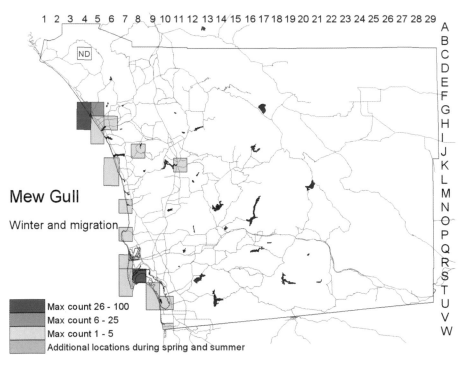

Mew Gull

Winter and migration

Max count 26 - 100
Max count 6 - 25
Max count 1 - 5
Additional locations during spring and summer

Ring-billed Gull *Larus delawarensis*

The Ring-billed is San Diego County's most wide-spread gull, the common gull scavenging in parking lots as well as on lakes, estuaries, and beaches. The ocean is the one aquatic habitat the species typically avoids—the Ring-billed is not a "sea" gull. Though the Ring-billed Gull is primarily a winter visitor to San Diego County, substantial numbers of non-breeders remain through the summer, far more than those of the other migratory gulls.

Winter: The Ring-billed Gull is common near water throughout San Diego County's coastal lowland. Its abundance is greatest along the coast: up to 500 at the mouth of Las Pulgas Creek (E3) 24 December 1999 (R. and S. L. Breisch) and 700 at Mission Bay (Q8) 26 January 1999 (J. C. Worley). But numbers inland can be high as well, with up to 328 at the Wild Animal Park (J12) 29 December 2001 (K. L. Weaver) and 815 at Santee Lakes (P12) 13 February 1999 (I. S. Quon). Between 1500 and 3100 feet elevation the gull's numbers are variable but sometimes high, with up to 325 at Lake Henshaw (G17) 7 February 1999 (W. E. Haas), 200 at Lake Sutherland (J16) 19 January 2000 (E. C. Hall), and 200 in Santa Teresa Valley (K16) 14 January 1999 (G. L. Rogers). Figures on Lake Henshaw Christmas bird counts range from 2 to 329 with a mean of 57 and a median of 19. We found no wintering Ring-billed Gulls at elevations higher than 3100 feet at Morena Village (T22; 35 on 19 December 1999, R. and S. L. Breisch). In the Borrego Valley the Ring-billed Gull is rare. Thirty-four at Club Circle (G24) 20 December 1998 (P. D. Ache), were the only ones found in 19 years of Anza–Borrego Christmas bird counts, and three in Borrego Springs (F24) 12 December 2001 (P. D. Jorgensen) were the only others seen there in winter during the atlas period.

Photo by Anthony Mercieca

Migration: Ring-billed Gull migration has not been well studied in San Diego County. At the Salton Sea, juveniles begin arriving by 16 July (Patten et al. 2003), and the species' numbers in San Diego begin increasing in this month. In their weekly surveys of the San Diego Bay salt works 1993–94, Stadtlander and Konecny (1994) found the gull's numbers spiking sharply in November and dropping to summer lows in April. Dates for the Anza–Borrego Desert range from 1 November (1988, three at the Borrego sewage ponds, H25, A. G. Morley) to 9 May (2001, five at Club Circle, G24, P. D. Ache), except for a sick bird at Bow Willow (P27) 8 June 1973 (ABDSP file) and an anomalous four at Agua Caliente Springs (M26) 4 June 1998 (E. C. Hall).

By mid May the Ring-billed Gull is generally uncommon. Our highest summer counts were of 31 at the mouth of Las Pulgas Creek 17 May 1998 (R. and S. L. Breisch), 30 at Agua Hedionda Lagoon (I6) 20 June 1999 (J. Ciarletta), and 40 at La Jolla (P7) 27 May 1999 (L. Polinsky). Almost all summering Ring-billed Gulls are along or near the coast; the only lakes well inland where we noted them 19 May–15 July were Henshaw (eight on 18 June 2000, P. Unitt), San Vicente (N13; one on 16 June 2000, R. and S. L. Breisch), and Morena (S21/S22; up to three on 1 July 2000, R. and S. L. Breisch).

Conservation: With its food supply hugely augmented by human waste, the Ring-billed Gull enjoyed an increase in number and spread of its breeding range through the 20th century (Ryder 1993). But numbers in San Diego County have declined since the 1960s, as suggested by results of San Diego Christmas bird counts: Ring-billed Gulls averaged 5400 from 1963 to 1970 but only 1131 from 1997 to 2002. Changes in agriculture, more packaging of waste, the reduction in the number of landfills, and the assiduous exclusion of gulls from landfills that remain likely contributed to this decrease.

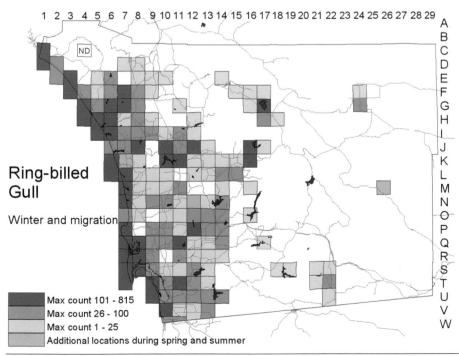

Ring-billed
Gull

Winter and migration

■ Max count 101 - 815
■ Max count 26 - 100
▨ Max count 1 - 25
▦ Additional locations during spring and summer

California Gull *Larus californicus*

Though the California Gull, like the Ring-billed, arrives in southern California from the interior of North America, in San Diego County the California Gull is much more concentrated along the coast. Hundreds, sometimes thousands, can be seen on the ocean within a few miles of the coast. On beaches loafing California Gulls commonly flock with other species of gulls. A few nonbreeding California Gulls—far fewer than Ring-billed Gulls—remain in San Diego County through the summer.

Winter: The large numbers of California Gulls seen foraging at sea are likely the same birds seen resting on beaches: up to 700 at Oceanside (H5) 26 December 1998, 1430 at Torrey Pines State Reserve (N7) 23 December 2001 (S. Walens), and an exceptional 3600 in the San Diego River flood-control channel (R8) 2 February 2001 (J. C. Worley). The species' abundance drops off rapidly with distance inland. From 1997 to 2001, the only place more than 5 miles from the coast where we found more than 50 was Sweetwater Reservoir (S12), where large numbers are regular, with up to 200 on 16 December 2000 (P. Famolaro). But the species is fairly common on lakes throughout the coastal lowland. Above an elevation of 1500 feet, we found wintering California Gulls at just two lakes. At Henshaw (G17), our highest count during the atlas period was 40 on 12 December 2000 (J. R. Barth), but Lake Henshaw Christmas bird counts have found up to 161 (23 December 1996), noting the species on 16 of 22 counts 1981–2002. At Morena (S21), S. E. Smith found a single individual in January of three successive years. In the Anza–Borrego Desert, the only records from December to February are of one at Club Circle, Borrego Springs (G24) 21 February 1999 (P. D.

Photo by Anthony Mercieca

Ache) and three at Ram's Hill (H25) 16 December 1998 (R. Halford).

Migration: No study has addressed variation in California Gull numbers in San Diego County by the birds' ages, and without such study, knowledge of the species' migration schedule will remain inadequate. At the Salton Sea, Patten et al. (2003) reported juveniles returning as early as 3 July and the numbers of the California Gull in general increasing steadily from July through October. On the basis of weekly counts at the south San Diego Bay salt works 1993–94, however, Stadtlander and Konecny (1994) found California Gull numbers remaining at their low summer level until November. They found another peak in April and a maximum of 500 on 21 April 1993. At Lake Hodges (K10/K11) a peak count of 200 on 24 April 1982 (K. L. Weaver) probably reflects spring migration. Numbers decrease through May, with migrants remaining possibly as late as 21 May (2001; 15 at the Santa Margarita River mouth, G4, P. A. Ginsburg). The few records for the Anza–Borrego Desert range from 10 October (1990, five at the Borrego sewage ponds, H25) to 27 March (1990, two at the same site, A. G. Morley).

In San Diego County, summering California Gulls are uncommon to rare. From 1997 to 2001, all our records between 21 May and 10 July were of seven or fewer individuals, except for 20 at Lake Henshaw 18 June 2000 (P. Unitt). All summer records were coastal except for this and one at El Capitan Reservoir (O16) 18 June 1998 (S. Kingswood).

Conservation: With colonization of the San Francisco Bay area and the Salton Sea, the California Gull's breeding range has been expanding to the west and south (Molina 2000, Shuford

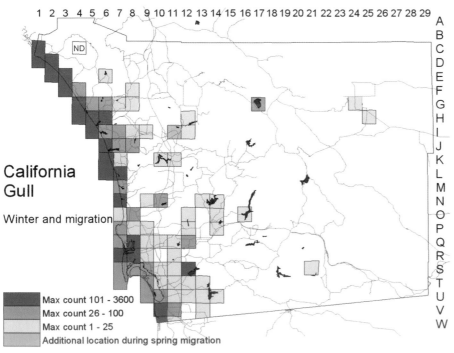

California
Gull

Winter and migration

- Max count 101 - 3600
- Max count 26 - 100
- Max count 1 - 25
- Additional location during spring migration

and Ryan 2000). The total population increased considerably through at least the second half of the 20th century (Conover 1983, Shuford and Ryan 2000). No trend in numbers wintering in San Diego County is obvious; the shifting of flocks makes monitoring in winter difficult. California Gulls formerly concentrated in huge numbers at garbage dumps (6500 at the Otay dump, U12, 16 December 1978, G. McCaskie). But since the early 1990s they have been excluded from the county's landfills.

Taxonomy: Of the California Gull's two subspecies, the predominant one in San Diego County is nominate *L. c. californicus* Lawrence, 1854, which nests in the southwestern part of the species' breeding range. Of eight San Diego County specimens of adults or three-year-old birds, seven are *californicus*, with a value for darkness of the back, as measured by a Minolta CR300 electronic colorimeter, of $L = 45.2$ to 49.4 (compare values in table 12 of Patten et al. 2003). One of these, picked up at San Elijo Lagoon (L7) 5 January 1975, had been banded in a nesting colony in Weld County, Colorado.

One specimen from San Diego County, however, is *L. c. albertaensis* Jehl, 1987, distinguished by its paler back and larger bill and breeding in Canada and the Dakotas. A female collected at the Otay dump 8 January 1975, it has an exposed culmen of 46.4 mm, bill depth at gonys of 15.5 mm, and a value for L on the back of 51.6 (higher values correspond to paler colors).

Herring Gull *Larus argentatus*

Of all of San Diego County's gulls, the Herring has been affected the most by the exclusion of gulls from the county's landfills. Formerly an abundant winter visitor at the dumps, the Herring Gull is now uncommon to at best fairly common anywhere in San Diego County. In habitat it has the versatility of a wide-ranging scavenger, using ocean, beaches, coastal wetlands, and inland ponds and lakes.

Winter: Though widespread, the Herring Gull is more frequent along the coast than inland. Usually it constitutes a small minority of mixed flocks dominated by the Western, California, and Ring-billed Gulls. Concentrations as large as 100 at Point Loma (S7) 18 December 1999 (M. W. Klein), 55 at a pond on Otay Mesa (V13) 10 February 2001 (P. Unitt), and 136 at Border Field State Park (W10) 18 December 1999 (S. Walens) are now exceptional. In the north county our largest numbers 1997–2002 were 27 at Oceanside (H5) 27 December 1997 (D. Rorick) and 14

Photo by Anthony Mercieca

at the Santa Margarita River mouth (G4) 29 December 1999 (P. A. Ginsburg). During the atlas period wintering Herring Gulls were all in the coastal lowland, as far inland as Lake Wohlford (I12, one on 23 February 2002, P. Unitt) and El Capitan Reservoir (O16; one on 3 January 1998, S. Kingswood). The Herring Gull has also been noted at Lake Henshaw (G17) on two of 22 Christmas bird counts there 1981–2002, with a maximum of four on 21 December 1987.

Migration: The Herring Gull occurs primarily late October to early April, with extreme dates of 23 September and 17 May (Unitt 1984). Unusual records of migrants are of one at Lake Cuyamaca (M20) 25 April 1978 (AB 22:1055, 1978), and the only one for the Anza–Borrego Desert, an adult at the Borrego Country Club (G24) 3 April–9 May 1999 (P. D. Ache). Summer stragglers were one near Imperial Beach (V10) 22 June 1980 (AB 34:930, 1980) and up to five in the San Diego Bay salt works (U10/V10) through summer 1993 (Stadtlander and Konecny 1994).

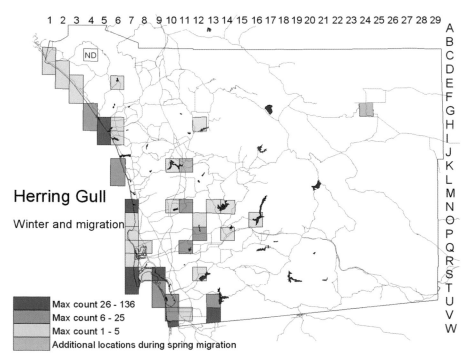

Herring Gull

Winter and migration

- ⬛ Max count 26 - 136
- ◩ Max count 6 - 25
- ◻ Max count 1 - 5
- ◻ Additional locations during spring migration

Conservation: Stephens (1919a) called the Herring Gull "rather common"; Sams and Stott (1959) called it "fairly common." An increase likely corresponded with the rapid increase of the county's human population and the establishment of garbage dumps. The number tallied on San Diego County Christmas bird counts peaked at 7323 on 2 January 1966. Since 1985, however, the count has not returned more than 350, and it reached its all-time low of 18 on 16 December 2000. The decrease may not be restricted just to dumps: from 1973 to 1983 King et al.

(1987) found an average of 1.3 Herring Gulls per monthly census at San Elijo Lagoon (L7), December–April. From 1997 to 2002 not one Herring Gull was reported from this site.

Taxonomy: The only subspecies of Herring Gull nesting in North America is the pale-backed *L. a. smithsonianus* Coues, 1862, and only this subspecies has been recorded with certainty in California.

Thayer's Gull *Larus thayeri*

Thayer's Gull nests in the Canadian Arctic and winters mainly along the Pacific coast north of San Diego. In San Diego County it is annual but rare—now far less numerous than before the exclusion of gulls from landfills.

Winter: Currently, Thayer's Gull is almost exclusively coastal in San Diego County, and considerably more frequent in the southern half of the county than in the north. From 1997 to 2002 we had only two reports of as many as three individuals, at Los Peñasquitos Lagoon (N7) 26 December 1999 (B. C. Moore) and at Border Field State Park (W10) 18 December 1999 (S. Walens). Though the species was formerly regular at landfills in the coastal lowland, the only inland sightings during the atlas period were of single birds at Lindo Lake (O14/P14) 20–25 January 2002 (R. T. Patton, M. B. Stowe), Santee Lakes (P12) 21 February 1998 (J. L. Coatsworth), Lower Otay Lake (U13/U14) 20 January and 13 December 2001 (S. Buchanan, P. Unitt), and the Dairy Mart pond, Tijuana River valley (V11), 16 December 2000 (G. McCaskie).

Photo by Richard E. Webster

Migration: Thayer's Gulls arrive in late October or early November; their numbers increase during November and December, peak in January and February, and decline during March (Devillers et al. 1971). The extreme dates listed by Unitt (1984), 17 October and 10 April, apparently still stand.

Conservation: The estimate reported by Devillers et al. (1971), of 100 to 150 wintering in the San Diego area, is obsolete. The driving of gulls from the county's garbage dumps decimated Thayer's. The closing of a former favored site, a pig farm near the Otay dump, did not help either.

Taxonomy: Thayer's Gull is evidently conspecific with the Iceland Gull (Snell 2002). Under the broader species concept, the name for Thayer's Gull depends on the disposition of the name applied to the intermediate populations: *kumlieni* Brewster, 1883, antedates *thayeri* Brooks, 1915.

Thayer's Gull

Winter and migration

Max count 3
Max count 2
Max count 1
Additional locations during spring and summer

Iceland Gull *Larus glaucoides*

Identification of the Iceland Gull far from its normal range in the North Atlantic is fraught with uncertainty, because of extensive intergradation with Thayer's Gull. Indeed, evidence suggests these two are at best subspecies (Snell 2002). The California Bird Records Committee has accepted just two identifications of the Iceland Gull from California, one from San Diego County.

Winter: San Diego County's sole Iceland Gull was a first-winter bird photographed at the Otay dump (U12) 17–25 January 1986 (D. Delaney, Erickson and Hamilton 2001).

Taxonomy: See Snell (2002) for an analysis of variation in the Iceland and Thayer's Gulls. With its primaries almost uniformly white, the bird at the Otay dump resembled nominate *L. g. glaucoides* Meyer, 1822, which breeds mainly in Greenland, more than *L. g. kumlieni* Brewster, 1883, the intermediate between *glaucoides* and *thayeri* that breeds in the southeastern Canadian Arctic.

Lesser Black-backed Gull *Larus fuscus*

Through the 20th century, the Lesser Black-backed Gull enjoyed a great expansion of its European breeding range, from the 1930s bringing an increasing number of vagrants to North America. By 1978 the first of these crossed the continent to reach California, and in 1996 the species reached another milestone, the southwesternmost county in the continental United States.

Winter: San Diego County's first and so far only Lesser Black-backed Gull was an adult photographed on the beach at the mouth of the San Luis Rey River, Oceanside (H5), 22 February–2 March 1996 (P. A. Ginsburg, NASFN 50:222, 1996; McCaskie and San Miguel 1999). With the species' continuing range expansion (Post and Lewis 1995), more occurrences are to be expected.

Taxonomy: Lesser Black-backed Gulls reaching California, like almost all others in North America, are *L. f. graellsii* Brehm, 1857, whose breeding range centers on the British

Photo by Jack W. Schlotte

Isles but has spread northwest to Iceland and Greenland. It is distinguished by its back being paler than that of other subspecies of the Lesser Black-backed, a shade close to that of subspecies *wymani* of the Western Gull.

Yellow-footed Gull *Larus livens*

Replacing the Western Gull in the Gulf of California, the Yellow-footed Gull is regular and increasing at the Salton Sea but just a rare vagrant to the Pacific coast. Though at the Salton Sea the Yellow-footed Gull is primarily a postbreeding summer visitor, the seven records for San Diego County form no distinct seasonal pattern.

Migration: In San Diego County, the Yellow-footed Gull has been noted at La Jolla (P7; one on 21 May 1985, J. Nysteun, AB 39:350, 1985), Mission Bay (Q8; one on 23 June 1966, SDNHM 36001), the Otay dump (U12; one on 19 January 1979, AB 33:314, 1979; two photographed 13–28 February 1981, AB 35:336, 1981; one 25–26 February 1984, G. McCaskie, AB 38:357, 1984), and the Tijuana River mouth (V10; one on 7 December 1978, AB 33:314, 1979; one on 24 August 1992, D. W. Aguillard, AB 47:149, 1992). All birds were adults, but juveniles have

Photo by Richard E. Webster

been found on the Pacific coast of Baja California north at least to Guerrero Negro so could be expected in San Diego County.

Western Gull *Larus occidentalis*

Of the gulls so ubiquitous along San Diego County's coast, it is the rowdy Western Gull that often dominates in both numbers and size. The Western is the only gull that nests in the county; the number of breeding pairs is modest but growing. A large colony is within sight of San Diego, however, on Los Coronados Islands off Tijuana. Typically coastal, the Western Gull seldom penetrates more than 15 miles inland in southern San Diego County, more than 5 miles in the north county.

Breeding distribution: The first site where the Western Gull was reported nesting in San Diego County was the cliffs at La Jolla, in 1935 (Miller 1936, Unitt 1984). Some birds continue to nest on these cliffs (at least two pairs in 1999), but many more have begun using the tops of nearby buildings (at least seven on 12 June 1999, L. and M. Polinsky). Other described sites are on artificial structures scattered around Mission and north San Diego bays, including the tram station at Sea World (R8), towers in the channel leading from San Diego Bay to the Marine Corps Recruit Depot (R8), and the roof of the Kona Kai Hotel, Shelter Island (S8). At North Island Naval Air Station (S8), the birds continue to nest on the cement pilings in San Diego Bay they have used since the 1970s; on 27 May 2000 one pair was nesting along one of the runways. It is also likely that a few Western Gulls nest on San Onofre Bluff, near which pairs were seen copulating 30 May 1998 (E3; R. and S. L. Breisch) and 15 May 2001 (D2; P. D. Jorgensen).

Away from nesting sites the Western Gull is still common in the middle of the breeding season, with up to 100 at Encinitas (K6) 27 April and 22 May 1997 (J. M. Dart) and 85 at Los Peñasquitos Lagoon (N7) 7 June 1999 (D. K. Adams). Inland numbers in the breeding season range

Photo by Jack C. Daynes

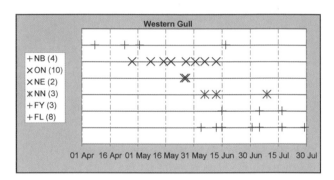

up to 50 at Chollas Reservoir (R11) 15 April 1998 (P. Unitt) and 50 at Sweetwater Reservoir (S12) 8–9 June 1998 (P. Famolaro).

Nesting: Cliff ledges and predator-free islands were the Western Gull's primitive nesting sites. Increasingly, the gulls are now augmenting these with man-made structures, on which they build a rough nest of debris. Before the atlas study, few data were available on the species' nesting season in San Diego County. Our observations suggest the Western Gull lays mainly in April in May, with young fledging mainly in June and July.

Migration: At San Elijo Lagoon, King et al. (1987) found the Western Gull to be most numerous from June to August, least numerous in April and May. At the south San Diego Bay salt works, however, Stadtlander and Konecny (1994) found it most numerous in September and October, least numerous in June. Variation in the number of Western Gulls in San Diego County is more related to the birds' concentration in breeding colonies than to long-distance migration. Regular commuting between Los Coronados Islands and the mainland is attested by

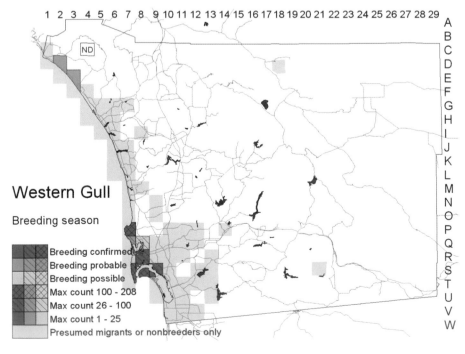

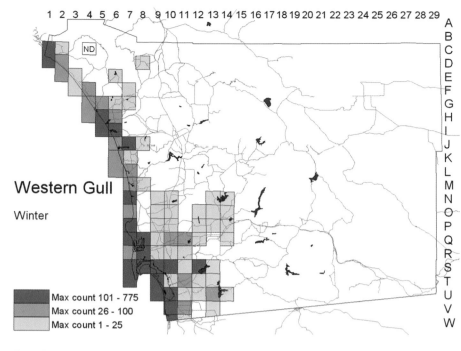

Western Gull

Winter

Max count 101 - 775
Max count 26 - 100
Max count 1 - 25

tribution in San Diego County is that the birds disperse inland farther and in greater numbers through metropolitan San Diego than in the north county. Now, with extensive urbanization and many ponds and reservoirs in the north county, the difference between these two areas lacks a clear explanation. Lakes Hodges and Lower Otay are the same distance inland, yet the Western Gull is absent from Hodges (K10) but regular at Lower Otay (U13), where counts ranged up to 35 (6 January 2001, P. Unitt). It is especially common at Sweetwater Reservoir, with up to 200 on 15 December 2001 (P. Famolaro). Winter records extend up to 19 miles inland at San Vicente Reservoir (N14; one on 21 January 2001, N. Osborn).

the chicken bones littering the gull colonies on the islands.

During the atlas period, we twice noted Western Gulls much farther inland than they had been recorded in San Diego County previously. One in second-year plumage was at Lake Morena (S21) 7 June 1997 (S. E. Smith); one was flying over Previtt Canyon (D18) 3 August 2001 (M. B. Stowe). With the Western Gull becoming increasingly frequent at the Salton Sea (Patten et al. 2003), more sightings well inland in San Diego County are to be expected.

Winter: Even if the Western Gull is most numerous in summer or fall, it is still abundant in winter. From 1997 to 2002 our winter counts ranged up to 482 at Oceanside (H5) 28 December 1999 (S. Walens), 775 at Torrey Pines State Reserve (N7) 26 December 1999 (B. C. Moore), and 1212 on the ocean from the mouth of San Diego Bay to Imperial Beach 18 December 1999 (D. W. Povey). One curious feature of the Western Gull's dis-

Conservation: The Western Gull's colonization of San Diego County may be part of a trend of population increase in southern California as a whole. The banning of DDT and reduced contamination of the ocean off southern California favors the gull, while reduced upwelling and lowered productivity of the same waters disfavor it (Pierotti and Annett 1995).

Taxonomy: The subspecies of Western Gull resident in southern California is *L. o. wymani* Dickey and van Rossem, 1925. The paler-backed nominate subspecies, *L. o. occidentalis* Audubon, 1839, breeds in northern California, Oregon, and Washington and reaches San Diego County as a rare winter visitor (Devillers et al. 1971). Two juveniles banded in June on the Farallon Islands off San Francisco were recovered at San Diego the following October.

Glaucous-winged Gull *Larus glaucescens*

A winter visitor from the north, the Glaucous-winged Gull is uncommon in San Diego County, usually seen on beaches and bays in mixed flocks of the more common gulls. With gulls now driven from the county's landfills, there is no longer any place where the species can be seen consistently.

Winter: The Glaucous-winged Gull ranges all along San Diego County's coast with no consistent site of concentration. Any large mixed flock of gulls is likely to yield one or two. From 1997 to 2002 our highest count was of nine at Oceanside (H5) 28 December 1999 (S. Walens). When gulls were allowed to scavenge at garbage dumps these were the Glaucous-winged's primary haunts. During the atlas period, however, we found few away from the coast.

Photo by Anthony Mercieca

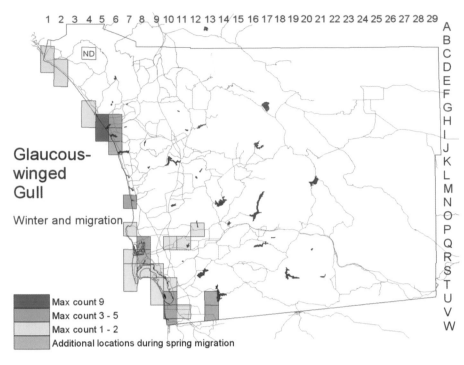

Glaucous-winged Gull

Winter and migration

Max count 9
Max count 3 - 5
Max count 1 - 2
Additional locations during spring migration

San Diego River mouth (R7) 31 May 2001 (N. Perretta) and one at the south end of the Silver Strand (U10) 27 June 1998 (C. G. Edwards). Unitt (1984) listed six previous summer records.

Conservation: The breeding population of the Glaucous-winged Gull has increased through the 20th century (Verbeek 1993), and winter visitors inland are becoming ever more frequent (Binford and Johnson 1995). But the numbers seen in San Diego County have declined since the 1970s. The San Diego Christmas bird count recorded its maximum of 270 in 1968; since 1988 the count has not yielded more than seven. Devillers et al. (1971) estimated that numbers in the San Diego area varied from 100 to 300

The site farthest inland was 12.5 miles from Mission Bay at Santee Lakes (P12; one on 7 January 1999, J. L. Coatsworth; one on 7 December 1999, M. B. Mulrooney); the only other inland sites were Lower Otay Lake (U13; up to four on 13 December 2001) and the pond at Siempre Viva and La Media roads, Otay Mesa (V13; up to five on 10 February 2001, P. Unitt).

Migration: Glaucous-winged Gulls typically begin arriving in early November, peak in late January and February, and depart through March and April. One at La Jolla (P7) 4 October 2001 (S. Walens) was exceptionally early. Any left after mid May are probably not migrating and may be in poor health, failing to molt on schedule. During the atlas period we noted two such stragglers, one at the

annually, but from 1997 to 2002 they were probably no more than 50. The exclusion of gulls from garbage dumps and changes in agriculture near the coast are presumably responsible for the decrease.

Taxonomy: The Glaucous-winged Gull has always been regarded as a distinct species, but it hybridizes with the Western Gull over a long strip of coastline in Washington and Oregon, and assortative mating is weak (Hoffman et al. 1978, Bell 1996, 1997, Good et al. 2000). A second-winter bird collected at the former Balboa Park dump (R8) 23 December 1969 (SDNHM 37626) appears to be a hybrid between the Glaucous-winged and the northern subspecies of the Western Gull, *L. o. occidentalis*.

Glaucous Gull *Larus hyperboreus*

The Glaucous Gull is the northernmost of the large gulls and only a rare winter visitor as far south as San Diego County. It is reported here at a rate of about one per year.

Winter: Most records of the Glaucous Gull in San Diego County are coastal, ranging from a few miles offshore to 9 miles inland at Miramar Lake (N10; 25 January 1992, T. L. Williams, AB 46:315, 1992). The Otay dump (U12) is the site with the most records, but gulls are now excluded there. The species is typically found with other gulls, but only twice have as many as two Glaucous Gulls been found together in San Diego County—at the Otay dump. During the atlas period from 1997 to 2002 six were noted, at Oceanside (H5) 4 May 1997 (R. T. Patton, FN 51:928, 1997), Quivira Basin, Mission Bay (R7), 4 February 2002 (D. K. Adams, NAB 56:224, 2002), San Diego Bay near Seaport Village (S9) 19 December 1998 (R. and S. L. Breisch, NAB 53:209, 1999), and Imperial Beach (V10)

Photo by Richard E. Webster

13–15 March 1998 (P. A. Ginsburg, FN 52:257, 1998), 4 March 2000 (T. R. Clawson, NAB 54:221, 2000), and 4–11 March 2001 (H. L. Young, NAB 55:228, 2001).

Migration: Occurrences of the Glaucous Gull in San Diego County are concentrated late in the winter, from late January to mid March. Extreme dates are 22 November (1988, off San Diego, D. W. Povey, AB 43:168, 1989) and 31 March (1968, Otay dump, AFN 22:478, 1968), except for three stragglers in May: 4 May 1997 (cited above), 5 May 1994 (Cardiff, L7, M. B. Stowe, NASFN 48:341, 1994), and 20 May 1973 (Point Loma, S7, AFN 27:820, 1973).

Taxonomy: The only specimen for San Diego County, from a former dump on the Silver Strand (T9) 22 January 1966 (SDNHM 36019), is *L. h. barrovianus* Ridgway, 1886. Banks (1986a) identified all Glaucous Gulls from the Pacific coast of North America as this relatively dark, small-billed subspecies.

Sabine's Gull *Xema sabini*

Sabine's Gull crosses North America on its long migration between the Arctic and the Southern Hemisphere, but it seldom stops inland. Off San Diego County, it is uncommon to fairly common on the ocean out of sight of land and is rarely seen from shore.

Migration: In spring, Sabine's Gull is recorded in San Diego County from 23 April to 3 June, with up to 35 between San Diego and San Clemente Island 8 May 1976 (AB 30:891, 1976). The only records onshore in spring are of one on San Diego Bay 23 April 1908 (CAS 11542), one at Silver Strand State Beach (T9) 29 May 1962 (AFN 16:447, 1962), and one at Del Mar (M7) 2 June 1983 (D. Delaney, AB 37:1027, 1983).

In fall, Sabine's Gull occurs mainly from 11 July to October, with up to 100 between San Diego and San Clemente Island 4 September 1965 and 3 September 1967 (G. McCaskie, AFN 22:90, 1968). Exceptionally late were one off San Diego 22 November 1969 (J. L. Dunn) and one at La Jolla (P7) 6 December 1999 (G. McCaskie,

Photo by Richard E. Webster

NAB 53:209, 1999). Though still rare, the species is seen from shore more frequently in fall than in spring. San Diego County's two inland records are in fall, of a juvenile "about 32 miles east of the Pacific" 10 October 1920 (Lee 1921) and one at Lake Morena (T21) 2 October 1988 (B. McCausland, AB 43:168, 1989).

Black-legged Kittiwake *Rissa tridactyla*

This primarily pelagic gull is a highly irregular winter visitor to San Diego County. In some years there are none; in most, there are few; occasionally, the species is abundant. It is best looked for during the strong northwest winds following winter storms, when the birds are driven to shore and may rest on the beach.

Winter: Because of the orientation of the coastline, La Jolla (P7) is the site where the kittiwake is most easily seen in San Diego County, as for other pelagic birds. During the only major invasion that hit shore during the atlas period, February–April 2001, seawatching at La Jolla yielded up to 142 in 3.5 hours on 13 February 2001 (B. L. Sullivan, NAB 55:228, 2001). On 11 February 1999 at least 60 were 30–40 miles west San Diego (P. Lonsdale, NAB 53:209, 1999), but none were seen from shore that winter. The largest known invasion was in 1975–76, when up to 350 were on the ocean within 5 miles of shore between San Diego and Del Mar 28 March 1976 (P. Unitt). There are three inland records, of single birds at Lake Henshaw (G17) 15 January 1981 (R. Higson, AB 35:336, 1981), Lake Murray (Q11) 3 February 1976 (SDNHM 39849), and the east end of Sweetwater Reservoir (S13) 21 April 1995 (SDNHM 49172).

Photo by Kenneth W. Fink

Migration: The earliest date known for the Black-legged Kittiwake is 16 November (1962, one on San Diego Bay, AFN 17:69, 1963), but not until late December or January does it become abundant. In spring, most depart in April and early May; in 2001, the latest bird was at La Jolla 21 April (M. Wilson). After some invasions kittiwakes stay into summer. In 1976, 60 remained at La Jolla on 17 May (J. L. Dunn), six were still there 11 July (G. McCaskie), and one was at the Oceanside harbor (H5) 8 October (A. Fries).

Taxonomy: *Rissa t. pollicaris* Ridgway, 1884, is the subspecies of Black-legged Kittiwake in the Pacific Ocean.

Gull-billed Tern *Sterna nilotica*

San Diego County's first Gull-billed Tern showed up in south San Diego Bay in 1985, and the species began nesting in the salt works two years later. It has nested there annually ever since, the population growing to 32–37 pairs by 2003. The Gull-billed Tern's only other site in the western United States is the Salton Sea, from 1992 to 2001 home to 72–155 pairs (Molina 2004). Only seven colonies are known in western Mexico (Palacios and Mellink 2003). Thus, even though the San Diego population is small, it has an important role in the species' conservation in western North America.

Breeding distribution: The south San Diego Bay salt works (U10/V10) are the Gull-billed Tern's only nesting site in San Diego County. From three pairs in 1987, the population grew to 27–30 pairs in 1991 and 1992 (Terp and Pavelka 1999, E. Copper, AB 45:1162, 1991, 46:1178, 1992). From 1993 to 1998 it stabilized around 8 to 12 pairs, then increased to 11–20 in 1999, 20–27 in 2000, 30 in 2001, 32–36 in 2002, and 32–37 in 2003. The number of young fledged reached 31–41 in 2003 (R. T. Patton).

For foraging, the birds range from the salt works throughout south San Diego Bay, along the beach at Imperial Beach (V10; 5–12 seen daily through spring 2001, T. Stands), and to the Tijuana River estuary (two or three at Border Field State Park, W10, 19 July 2001, R. T. Patton). In 2002, studying the foraging behavior of the Gull-billed Tern, K. C. Molina noted 77% of foraging over beach strand and the tidal zone of the estuary, 23% over dunes and upland scrub. During weekly surveys of north San Diego Bay through 1993, Mock et al. (1994) encountered the Gull-billed Tern only once, two on 11 May. One flying over the intersection of Palomar Street

Photo by Jack C. Daynes

and Broadway in Chula Vista (U11) 11 July 2001 was 0.8 mile inland (R. T. Patton).

Nesting: Like the other terns, the Gull-billed nests on the bare dirt atop the dikes of the salt works. Unlike the larger terns and skimmers, the Gull-billed lines the rim of its nest scrape with materials at hand—pebbles, bits of veg-

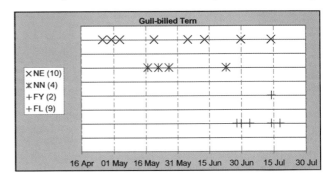

etation, shells, and other debris (Parnell et al. 1995). Egg dates range from 19 April to 24 July, suggesting laying of replacement clutches until 1 July. From 1999 to 2003, dates of first hatching varied from 17 to 27 May, and dates of first fledging varied from 19 June to 4 July (R. T. Patton).

In 2002 the Gull-billed Terns nesting in the salt works fed their young primarily on small invertebrates (43% of all deliveries observed) and fish (25%) (Molina and Marschalek 2003).

Migration: Dates for the Gull-billed Tern in San Diego County extend from 1 March (1993, Stadtlander and Konecny 1994)

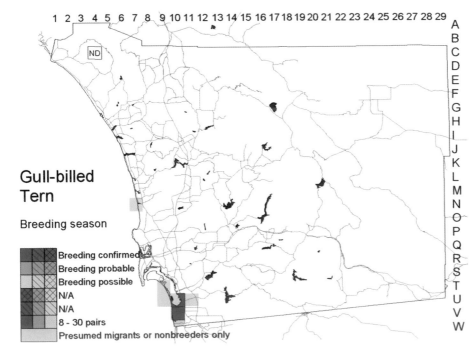

and 10 March (1995, G. McCaskie, NASFN 49:308, 1995) to 19 September (2002, R. T. Patton). The first sighting more than a few minutes' flight away from the salt works was of one at Los Peñasquitos Lagoon (N7) 14 April 2001 (K. Estey). Sightings elsewhere along the coast increased 2002–04 with up to six at the Santa Margarita River mouth (G4) 13 July 2003 (C. M. Manning, D. M. Parker). Nearly 10 miles inland were 10–15 at the north end of Lower Otay Lake (T13/U13) 24 April 2003 (A. Grassi) and single individuals there 26 April 2003 (R. T. Patton) and 14 June 2003 (A. Grassi).

Conservation: The survey of Mexican colonies by Palacios and Mellink (2003) yielded only 376 pairs, so the population of the entire subspecies *vanrossemi* of the Gull-billed Tern is less than 600 pairs (K. C. Molina). The California population is under 200 pairs, and the future of the colony at the Salton Sea is murky, given the decreasing water levels and wholesale environmental change in the offing there. Thus the colony at San Diego Bay represents a critical hedge against the species' extirpation from California. The California Department of Fish and Game has recognized the precarious position of the Gull-billed Tern by designating it a species of special concern—the position is more precarious than that of some species listed as endangered.

Ironically, around San Diego Bay the Gull-billed Tern preys regularly on the chicks of two endangered birds, the Snowy Plover and Least Tern. As a result, several Gull-billed Terns were killed as part of the predator control undertaken to sustain these smaller species (SDNHM 48544–5, 48943, 49343–4). Though the predation continues, after considerable debate among biologists and wildlife-management agencies, in 1999 the Gull-billed Tern was excused from the control program—at least temporarily. One proposal is that the eggs of the Gull-billed be removed, possibly for incubation and release of the young at the Salton Sea or Gulf of California. The conundrum is a prime example of the conflicts that arise when wildlife is confined to ever dwindling habitat, requiring ever more intensive management.

Taxonomy: On the basis of specimens from the Salton Sea, Bancroft (1929) described the Gull-billed Terns of the Pacific side of North America as *S. n. vanrossemi*. His measurements show their bills as substantially larger than those of the east coast, *S. n. aranea* Wilson, 1814, with no overlap in length or depth at angle of gonys. But the measurements tabulated by Parnell et al. (1995) show great overlap and suggest the difference may be inadequate for recognition of subspecies.

Caspian Tern *Sterna caspia*

The salt works of South San Diego Bay have been the site of a major colony of the Caspian Tern since at least the 1940s. For foraging the birds range widely along San Diego County's coast and on its inland lakes. The species is primarily a summer visitor, being common from April to September, generally uncommon from October to March. Over much of North America the Caspian Tern population is on the increase—the lack of suitable sites elsewhere is probably the reason why the salt works remain the site of the county's only viable colony.

Breeding distribution: Caspian Terns had begun nesting in the salt works by 1941, when E. E. Sechrist collected a set of eggs on 23 April and recorded a "colony of 78 pair" (WFVZ 28472). Over the next 40 years, the colony increased, reaching an estimated 412 pairs in 1981 (F. C. Schaffner). Subsequently, the population has hovered around 200 to 300 pairs, with up to 320 in 1994, at least 198 in 1998 (Terp and Pavelka 1999), at least 261 in 1999, and at least 249 in 2003 (R. T. Patton). In 1998, most of the nests were in a single cluster in the north half of the salt works (U10); in other years, they have been more dispersed.

The only nesting known in San Diego County outside the salt works took place in 1998, when six pairs attempted nesting at Zuñiga Point at the mouth of San Diego Bay (S8). All the nests suffered predation, however; only one chick hatched (R. T. Patton, B. Foster).

Even during the breeding season the Caspian Tern occurs fairly commonly outside the salt works all along

Photo by Anthony Mercieca

San Diego County's coast (up to 30 at the Santa Margarita River mouth, G4, 21 May 2001, P. A. Ginsburg; 45 at Los Peñasquitos Lagoon, N7, 3 May 1998, K. Estey; 46 around North Island, S8, 26 May 2000, R. T. Patton). Inland, summering Caspian Terns are generally uncommon. Twenty at Barrett Lake (S19) 29 April 2001 (R. and S. L. Breisch) were exceptional; otherwise our highest inland count before postbreeding dispersal was of eight at Lake Hodges (K10) 26 April 1999 (R. L. Barber). Nonbreeding Caspian Terns visit lakes as high as Cuyamaca (M20), where our counts ranged up to four on 5 June 1998 and 5 June 1999 (A. P. and T. E. Keenan).

Nesting: In the salt works, Caspian Terns nest in scrapes in the dirt on top of the dikes. The Elegant and Royal Terns cluster around the Caspians, taking advantage of the larger species' aggressive defense of the colony. Cuthbert and Wires (1999) reported that egg laying at San Diego Bay begins in the first week of April, but in 1997, the first eggs were found 15 April (M. R. Smith), in 1998 on 28 April (Terp and Pavelka 1999), in 1999 on 12 May, and in 2003 on 23 April (R. T. Patton). In 1998, most females laid in the first three weeks of May, but some laid as late as 24 July and hatched as late as about 15 August. Late clutches are presumably replacements for ones lost to predators or accidents; the Caspian Tern raises only one brood per year.

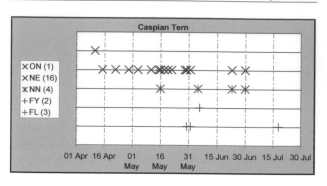

Migration: In their 10 years of monthly censuses at San Elijo Lagoon (L7), King et al. (1987) observed peaks in Caspian Tern numbers in April and July–August.

The latter months correspond to postbreeding dispersal from the salt works; the shrill call of young still begging from their parents can be heard widely both along the coast and at inland lakes at this season. During the atlas period counts away from the colony ranged up to 200 in northeastern Mission Bay (Q8) 27 June 1998 (E. Wallace). Inland, they ranged up to 14 at San Vicente Reservoir (N13) 27 July 1997 (C. G. Edwards) and at Sweetwater Reservoir (S12) 7 August 1998 (P. Famolaro), though counts before the atlas period were of up to 100 at Lake Hodges 24 April 1982 and 47 there 23 July 1982 (K. L. Weaver). Throughout the county, numbers drop sharply in October, then begin increasing again in March. There is still only one record for the Anza–Borrego Desert, of six flying over Borrego Springs (G24) 2 April 1977 (G. McCaskie).

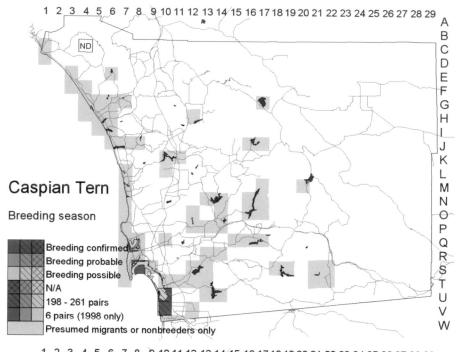

Caspian Terns banded at San Diego Bay have been recovered as far south as Chiapas in southernmost Mexico and as far north as Montana and Gray's Harbor, Washington (Gill and Mewaldt 1983). These authors noted that the San Diego Bay colony enjoyed good success but remained stable at around 400 pairs, so they concluded that it has been a source population for the species' colonization elsewhere along the Pacific coast.

Winter: From December through February atlas observers reported only four sightings of more than 12 Caspian Terns, and the highest winter count, of 34 along the Silver Strand (T9) 27 February 2000 (Y. Ikegaya), may have been of early spring

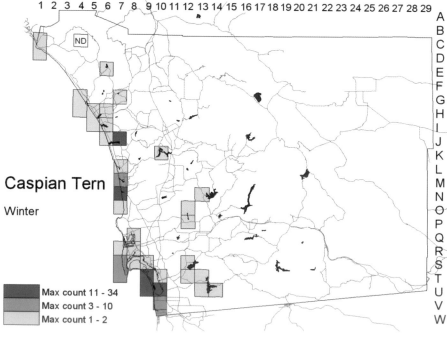

migrants. Other high recent winter counts are of 28 at Batiquitos Lagoon (J7) 26 December 1998 (R. Stone) and 21 on the Silver Strand 24 January 2000 (J. L. Coatsworth). Inland, our Caspian Tern sightings were of one or two individuals only, and confined to the coastal lowland, east to Lake Hodges (one on 27 December 1998, R. L. Barber), San Vicente Reservoir (one on 4 January 2002, N. Osborn), and Lower Otay Lake (U14; one on 4 December 1999, S. Buchanan).

Conservation: The Caspian Tern's colonization of San Diego Bay was part of a range expansion covering the entire Pacific coast of North America (Gill and Mewaldt 1983). Until 1932, there was only one record for San Diego County, in December (Saunders 1896). Not only at the salt works but elsewhere along the Pacific coast the expansion has been facilitated by the birds' nesting in man-made habitats, especially salt works. In spite of the positive trend regionally, the trend locally is flat. In spite of the Caspian Tern's defending its nest so aggressively, the colony is vulnerable to disturbance.

The Caspian Tern's abundance in winter appears to have declined somewhat since the early 1970s. Since 1972, San Diego County's Christmas bird counts have not returned more than 30; before that year, the San Diego count yielded up to 77 (in 1967).

Royal Tern *Sterna maxima*

The Royal Tern is found along San Diego County's coast year round, commonly in fall and winter, fairly commonly in spring and summer. It forages mainly on the ocean near shore, then loafs in flocks on beaches and in estuaries. A few pairs nest with other terns. Irregular from 1959 from 1998, nesting of the Royal Tern in the salt works of south San Diego Bay became annual at the beginning of the 21st century, with up to 35 pairs. In the first third of the 20th century, the Royal was the county's commonest large tern; today, it is vastly outnumbered by the Caspian and Elegant. In the middle of the 20th century, numbers of the Royal apparently decreased in tandem with those of the Pacific sardine.

Breeding distribution: Gallup and Bailey (1960) reported the first nesting of the Royal Tern in California in the salt works in 1959, the year the Elegant Tern first colonized there. Schaffner (1985) located the egg they collected in the Western Foundation of Vertebrate Zoology and

Photo by Jack C. Daynes

confirmed the identification. In 1960, over 30 nests were reported in late May (AFN 14:447, 1960); there is a possibility these were misidentified Elegant Terns. The next known nestings were in 1980, when a pair laid an egg subsequently broken by a Ruddy Turnstone, and 1982, when two pairs fledged one chick each (Schaffner 1985). In 1984, one or two pairs nested; in 1985, one pair had a large chick 12–15 June (R. E. Webster, AB 38:1062, 1984; 39:962, 1985). In 1997, at least one, possibly as many as four pairs nested (M. R. Smith, E. Copper, FN 51:1054, 1997). In 1999, R. T. Patton noted 35 nests on 27 May; in 2003, about 27 nests on 7 May.

Even during the breeding season the Royal Tern is widespread along San Diego County's coast. Spring flocks are usually rather small, of 15 or fewer birds, but range up to 34 at North Island (S8) 26 May 2000 (R. T. Patton).

Nesting: In the salt works, Royal Terns nest in close association with Caspian and Elegant Terns. The two smaller species rely on the aggressive Caspian for defense

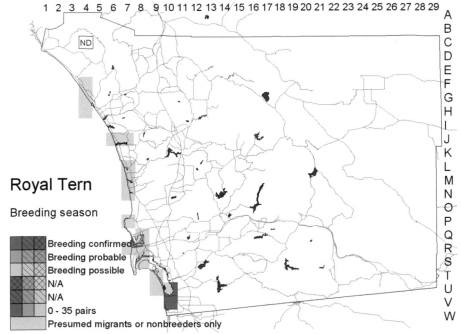

1 2 3 4 5 6 7 8 9 10 11 12 13 14 15 16 17 18 19 20 21 22 23 24 25 26 27 28 29

A B C D E F G H I J K L M N O P Q R S T U V W

Royal Tern

Breeding season

- Breeding confirmed
- Breeding probable
- Breeding possible
- N/A
- N/A
- 0 - 35 pairs
- Presumed migrants or nonbreeders only

ND

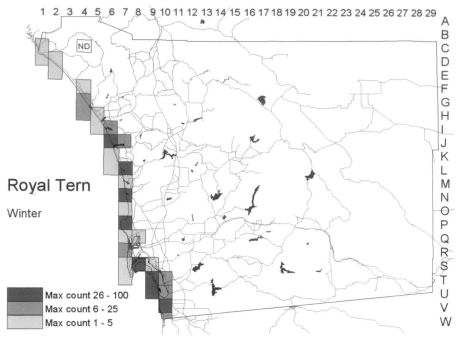

February 1993–February 1994, Stadtlander and Konecny (1994) found no more than seven in winter but up to 36 in September. Evidently local movement can obscure larger-scale migration. There are no records inland.

Winter: In winter the Royal Tern is widespread along San Diego County's coast, but resting flocks aggregate at a few regular sites, especially beaches at estuary mouths (up to 35 at San Elijo Lagoon, L7, 22 December 2000, G. C. Hazard; 100 at Los Peñasquitos Lagoon, N7, 2 December 2000, K. Estey) and around San Diego Bay (up to 60 on the Silver Strand, T9, 19 December 1998, N. Osborn). Foraging birds are often common on the ocean at La Jolla (P7; up to 40 on 28 January 2000, L. Polinsky).

of the colony (Schaffner 1985). The Royal's nesting is thus synchronized with that of the other species. In 1982, the birds laid on or just before 8 May and the chicks hatched between 8 and 15 June (Schaffner 1985). In 1999, adults were incubating from 12 May to 30 June; in 2003, from 29 April to 4 June (R. T. Patton).

Migration: The Royal Tern is generally regarded as primarily a postbreeding and winter visitor to southern California. During the atlas periods our highest counts were in December. During their monthly counts at San Elijo Lagoon (L7) 1973–83, however, King et al. (1987) found numbers highest in spring (April–May) and fall (September–October), lowest in December and January. During their weekly counts in and near the salt works

Conservation: In spite of the Royal Tern's decrease earlier in the 20th century, the species' colonization of San Diego Bay represents a northward extension of the breeding range. This extension continued beyond San Diego as the Royal began nesting with the tern colonies at Bolsa Chica, Orange County, in 1988 and the Los Angeles harbor in 1998 (K. C. Molina unpubl. data). The Royal Tern's nesting biology is harnessed behind that of the other large terns; all the species depend on the same man-made colony sites and have the same need for security from disturbance and predators.

Taxonomy: Royal Terns on both coasts of North America are nominate *S. m. maxima* Boddaert, 1783.

Elegant Tern *Sterna elegans*

At the beginning of the 21st century, the world's 50,000–60,000 Elegant Terns were nesting in only five known colonies. Isla Rasa in the Gulf of California is the most important of these, but the salt works of south San Diego Bay are important too. With variation in the abundance of anchovies (the tern's principal prey) and the birds' shifting among colonies, the number of nests in the salt works has varied from none in 1990 to an unprecedented 10,300 in 2003. After nesting, many of the birds nesting on Isla Rasa migrate to southern California, making the Elegant Tern an abundant visitor to San Diego County's coast in late summer and early fall.

Breeding distribution: Gallup and Bailey (1960) discovered the Elegant Tern nesting in the salt works in May 1959, with 31 pairs. The colony grew fairly steadily until the early 1980s, reaching at least 861 in 1981 (Schaffner 1986). Until this time, San Diego Bay was the species'

Photo by Jack C. Daynes

only nesting site in the United States. With the establishment of colonies at Bolsa Chica, Orange County, in 1987 (Collins et al. 1991) and the Los Angeles harbor in 1998, the number nesting in San Diego Bay became irregular. The number of pairs nesting was 1870 in 1995 then dropped to only two in 1997 and about 100 in 1998

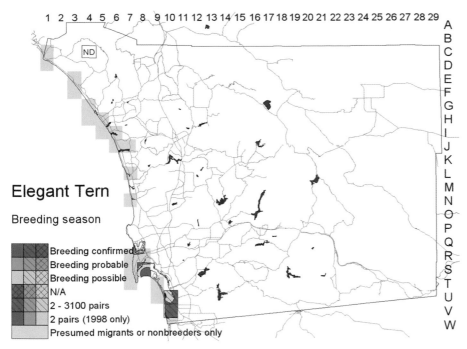

Elegant Tern

Breeding season

- Breeding confirmed
- Breeding probable
- Breeding possible
- N/A
- 2 - 3100 pairs
- 2 pairs (1998 only)
- Presumed migrants or nonbreeders only

1980 and 1981, the terns laid from 4 April to 6 June (Schaffner 1982). In 1999 and 2003 they were later, with first nests found 5 May and 29 April, respectively (R. T. Patton). After hatching, the young cluster into crèches. After fledging, they follow their parents far from the colony and are seen being fed all along San Diego County's coast.

Migration: Elegant Terns begin returning to San Diego typically in the second week of March, exceptionally as early as 3 March, as in 1968 (AFN 22:478, 1968) and 1982 (AB 36:893, 1982). Postbreeding dispersal from Mexico may begin as early as late May, depending on the success of the colony at Isla Rasa (Burness et al. 1999). Numbers peak from July to September, then drop through October and November. At the peak, flocks from 500 to 2000 are routine. During the atlas period our highest estimate was of 3500 at San Elijo Lagoon 8 August 1998 (B. C. Moore).

The only records even a short distance inland are from the San Diego River in Mission Valley (R9), from which one was picked up sick or injured and brought to rehabilitators 19 October 1990 (SDNHM 47145) and where I saw one on 3 May 1992.

Winter: A few stragglers sometimes remain as late as the third week of December, accounting for the Elegant Tern being recorded occasionally on San Diego Christmas bird counts. Records from the 1950s and 1960s into early January could represent misidentified Royal Terns, but experienced observers reported single individuals at North Island (S8) 6 January 2000 (R. T. Patton) and on south San Diego Bay 5 January 2003 (D. M. Parker, NAB 47:257, 2003). The only Elegant Tern that clearly wintered in San Diego County was at North Island (S8) 20 January–8 February 2002 (R. E. Webster, R. T. Patton, NAB 56:224, 2002).

Conservation: Before 1926, when Abbott (1927e) saw flocks off La Jolla, the Elegant Tern was known in San Diego County from just one specimen (FMNH 137053; Bishop 1905). By the early 1950s, it had become regular and common as a postbreeding visitor (Monroe 1956). Though the long-term trend in the tern's numbers in California has been up, the species faces many threats, acknowledged in its listing as a species of special concern by the California Department of Fish and Game. An intensely gregarious species nesting at so few sites is inevitably vulnerable. Several colonies in the Gulf of California were eliminated in the early 20th century, and that at Isla Rasa was reduced by commercial egging. In the salt works, disturbance and predation by dogs have been the principal threats, and

(Terp and Pavelka 1998)—perhaps as a result of El Niño reducing the fish supply, perhaps as a result of predation and disturbance. In 1999, with the onset of La Niña and improved management of predators—or just shifting of the population back from Bolsa Chica—the colony shot up to 3100 nests on 27 May. On 3 May 2000 there were 81 active nests with eggs. The count of 10,300 nests 28 May–4 June 2003 was over three times that in any previous year (R. T. Patton).

The only site outside the salt works where the Elegant Tern has attempted to nest in San Diego County is Zuñiga Point at the mouth of San Diego Bay (S8). In 1998, two pairs had laid eggs there by 22 May, but both nests were depredated and abandoned by 5 June (R. T. Patton).

Even during the middle of the breeding season the Elegant Tern is seen all along San Diego County's coast, sometimes in large numbers: up to 800 at the Santa Margarita River mouth (G4) 5 June 1998 (B. L. Peterson) and 2000 at San Elijo Lagoon (L7) 13 June 1998 (B. C. Moore).

Nesting: Within the salt works, the Elegant Terns nest in a few tight clusters, in association with Caspian Terns, on the bare dirt on top of the dikes. The exact sites shift from year to year. Within each subcolony, egg laying is usually synchronous, after the Caspians begin (Kirven 1969). In

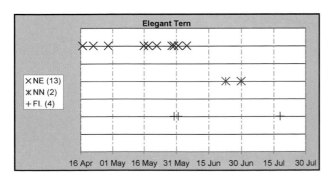

Elegant Tern

× NE (13)
× NN (2)
+ Fl (4)

16 Apr   01 May   16 May   31 May   15 Jun   30 Jun   15 Jul   30 Jul

policing is essential to ensure that any intruders, including people, are excluded. The salt works were included in the San Diego National Wildlife Refuge in 1999, but continuing management will be necessary to maintain the dikes and protect the terns. The failure of the nesting attempt at Zuñiga Point suggests that the Elegant Tern would estab-

lish new colonies if there were suitable sites but none are available. Elegant Tern numbers and nesting success in San Diego Bay are linked to the abundance of the northern anchovy offshore, suggesting the tern could be affected by overfishing or changing oceanographic conditions that affect the anchovy (Schaffner 1986).

Sandwich Tern *Sterna sandvicensis*

The Sandwich Tern breeds only on Atlantic coasts but winters in part on the Pacific coast of southern Mexico and Central America. In 1980 one joined the Elegant Terns moving along the Pacific coast and arrived in the Elegant Tern colony in south San Diego Bay. Presumably the same individual accounted for sporadic sightings of the Sandwich Tern at San Diego through 1987. The only other Sandwich Tern known from California (perhaps still the same individual) hybridized with Elegant Terns in the colony at Bolsa Chica, Orange County, from 1993 to 1995 (Collins 1997).

Breeding distribution: The Sandwich Tern in the south San Diego Bay salt works (U10/V10) 11–20 May 1980 unsuccessfully courted Elegant Terns in the colony there (Schaffner 1981). It was seen and photographed again around San Diego Bay and the San Diego River mouth

Photo by Anthony Mercieca

(R7/R8) 15 May–13 June 1982, 12–14 June 1985, and 18 April–16 May 1987 (Morlan 1985, Bevier 1990, Langham 1991).

Taxonomy: *Sterna s. acuflavida* Cabot, 1847, is the subspecies of Sandwich Tern in the New World.

Common Tern *Sterna hirundo*

As far as San Diego County is concerned, "common" is now a misnomer for the Common Tern, now far outnumbered at any season by the similar Forster's Tern. Abundant as a fall migrant as recently as the 1970s, the Common Tern is now uncommon. Former regular summering and irregular wintering appear to have ceased.

Migration: In San Diego County, the Common Tern migrates primarily offshore, but the birds pause to rest on beaches and in coastal wetlands. Fall migrants begin arriving by 12 July (1999, four at the Santa Margarita River mouth, G4, P. A. Ginsburg), peak in late August, then dwindle away through November. In spring, arrival is normally in mid April, but two at the San Diego River mouth (R7) 21 March 1991 were most likely early spring migrants, as none had been in the area earlier in the winter (G. McCaskie, AB 45:496, 1991). Some may still be moving north in early June.

Though the Common Tern was long common at the Salton Sea (Patten et al. 2003), the only inland records in San Diego County have been from Lake Hodges (K10) in fall 1979 (two on 5 August, G. McCaskie; one on 2 September, D. M. Parker) and at Bonita (T11) 2 May 1931 (SDNHM 14529).

In the 1960s and 70s, 30–60 immature Common Terns typically summered on the Silver Strand (T9), with a maximum of 150 on 23 June 1967 (AFN 21:605, 1967). But the only recent report of a clearly summering bird

Photo by Jack C. Daynes

was of one at the south end of San Diego Bay (V10) 25 June 2002 (M. Sadowski).

Winter: Formerly, a few Common Terns wintered on San Diego Bay or at the San Diego River mouth. Numbers as high as 51 on the San Diego Christmas bird count 21 December 1968 may have included some misidentified Forster's Terns, but up to 15 were at Shelter Island (S8) 18–31 January 1975 (J. L. Dunn, AB 29:742, 1975). By 1980 only one or two were being found annually; after 1990 no more were reported.

Conservation: The atlas study was not designed to sample migrating water birds, so the numbers of Common Terns occurring currently in San Diego County are unclear. But even though the Common can be overlooked easily among the abundant Forster's Terns the complete lack of Common Terns recorded by the various systematic studies of birds on San Diego Bay from the late 1980s to mid 1990s suggests a significant change. Former numbers of Common Terns in fall ranged up to 1000 migrating south off La Jolla (P7) 17 August 1977 (J. L. Dunn) and 750 at the Santa Margarita River mouth 22 August 1978 (P. Unitt). But no such flocks of this size have been encountered recently; from 1997 through 2003 the only large concentrations reported were of 200 at the San Diego River mouth 5 September 2002 and 123 on the Silver Strand 15 August 2003 (M. Sadowski).

The decrease of Common Terns migrating through San Diego County may be due to problems in the breeding range, in the winter range, or both. Of the adverse factors identified by Nisbet (2002), the Common Tern's high susceptibility to environmental contaminants and displacement of nesting colonies by burgeoning populations of gulls seem most likely to be affecting the birds breeding in central North America, the source for migrants reaching California.

Taxonomy: The only subspecies of the Common Tern collected in California is the red-billed *S. h. hirundo* Linnaeus, 1758, the subspecies breeding in North America.

Arctic Tern *Sterna paradisaea*

The Arctic Tern is famed for its migration that takes the birds from a breeding range in the Arctic to a winter range in the Antarctic. Modest numbers pass over the ocean off San Diego County. Only a few times have Arctic Terns—perhaps all injured or oiled—been seen on the county's shores.

Migration: The Arctic Tern is most numerous in fall, with up to 350 between San Diego and San Clemente Island 11 September 1976 (G. McCaskie). Fall records extend from 27 July (1968, one collected of seven seen 80 miles west of San Diego, SDNHM 36752) to 25 October (1959, 30 near San Clemente Island, AFN 14:173, 1960), except for a straggler at the 43-fathom bank 36 miles off San Diego 10 December 1977 (J. L. Dunn).

The species is less numerous in spring, with a maximum of 15 off San Diego 16 May 1981 (E. Copper). Spring records extend from 1 May (1987, four off San Clemente Island, R. R. Veit, AB 41:488, 1987) to 7 June (1978, one off San Diego, AB 32:1209, 1978).

Arctic Terns seen on shore at the San Diego River mouth (R7) 6 October 1991 (G. McCaskie, AB 46:149,

Photo by Anthony Mercieca

1992) and at the Santa Margarita River mouth (G4) 4 June 2000 (D. M. Parker, NAB 54:423, 2000) were both stained with oil.

Conservation: As with most other ocean birds, numbers of Arctic Terns off San Diego County have decreased since the early 1980s.

Forster's Tern *Sterna forsteri*

Forster's is the most widespread tern in San Diego County, most abundant in the coastal lagoons and bays but found regularly on inland lakes as well. Though migratory, it is common in the county year round. Hundreds of pairs nest annually in the salt works, site of the oldest and largest Forster's Tern colony in southern California. Since 1990, the birds have attempted to establish new colonies elsewhere along the county's coast, though these are still small and often unsuccessful.

Breeding distribution: First observed in 1962 (Gallup 1963), the Forster's Tern colony on the dikes of the salt works (U10/V10) has fluctuated between 100 and 600 pairs since 1963. Because of renesting and the nests' dispersion throughout the salt works the population is difficult to census accurately, but some recent figures are 548 nests in 1991, at least 510 in 1993, at least 345 in 1994,

Photo by Anthony Mercieca

520 in 1997, at least 225 in 1998 (Terp and Pavelka 1999), 126 in 1999, and at least 203 in 2003 (R. T. Patton). The Chula Vista Wildlife Reserve, a similar artificial site on

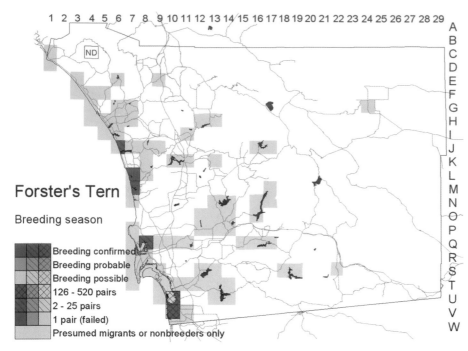

Forster's Tern
Breeding season

Breeding confirmed
Breeding probable
Breeding possible
126 - 520 pairs
2 - 25 pairs
1 pair (failed)
Presumed migrants or nonbreeders only

(M7) 5 June 2001 (D. R. Grine) were aborted. In 2001 the terns colonized Kendall–Frost Marsh, Mission Bay (Q8). On 10 July, scanning from Crown Point Drive, R. T. Patton noted one chick, two young fledglings, and 17 adults, including three incubating and six feeding chicks hidden in the marsh. Some nests were lost to tidal flooding. Nesting at Kendall–Frost continued through 2003; abandoned chicks were picked up there 7 and 15 June (SDNHM 50786, 50867).

During the breeding season, nonbreeding Forster's Terns are common away from the colonies at both coastal wetlands (50 at San Elijo Lagoon 2 May 1999, B. C. Moore; 40 at Famosa Slough, R8, 2 July 1998, A. E. Klovstad) and lakes in the coastal lowland (50 at Sweetwater Reservoir, S12, 4 May 1998, P. Famolaro; 45 at Lower Otay Lake, U14, 29 May 2001, N. Osborn). Even on foothill reservoirs the tern is fairly common at times, with up to 22 at Barrett Lake (S19) 4 June 2000 (R. and S. L. Breisch) and 20 at the upper end of Loveland Reservoir (Q17) 20 May 1998 (P. Famolaro). If there were suitable secure islands in these reservoirs the birds would likely nest there; they engaged in courtship feeding at Barrett Lake 23 May 1999 and 4 June 2000 (J. Hannan, R. and S. L. Breisch) and at the upper end of El Capitan Reservoir (N16) 29 June 2001 (J. R. Barth).

the north side of the salt works (U10), had 173 nests in 2001 (R. T. Patton). Within the salt works, the Forster's nests are less clumped than those of the larger terns; in 1998 the perimeter road was the section used most heavily (Terp and Pavelka 1999).

At the west end of Batiquitos Lagoon (J6) Forster's Terns began nesting in 1990 (mummified chick picked up 3 August, SDNHM 46863) and were still doing so at least in 1997, 1998 (M. Baumgartel), and 2002 (R. T. Patton). The number that nest is apparently small, though the birds are common in the area (122 in the lagoon's east basin, J7, 1 May 1998, F. Hall; 247 throughout the lagoon 10 July 1997, Merkel and Associates 1997). Attempts by single pairs at San Elijo Lagoon (L7) 5 June 2000 (A. Mauro) and at the San Dieguito River estuary

Nesting: In the salt works, Forster's Terns tend to nest on the shoulders of the dikes, often in vegetation such as pickleweed and crystalline iceplant rather than on bare dirt on top of the dikes like the larger terns. The birds lay eggs from late April to late June, occasionally to early August. A fledgling at Batiquitos Lagoon 12 June 1997 must have hatched from an egg laid no later than 23 April (M. Baumgartel). Some eggs were still being incubated in the salt works as late as 18 July in 2001 and 2 September in 2003 (R. T. Patton).

Migration: Seasonal variation in Forster's Tern abundance in San Diego County is not well marked. In the salt works, on the basis of weekly surveys February 1993–February 1994, Stadtlander and Konecny (1994) noted two seasonal peaks, in May and

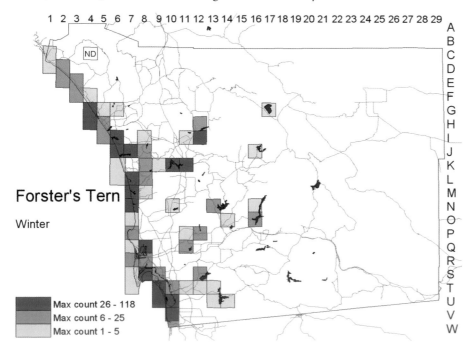

Forster's Tern
Winter

Max count 26 - 118
Max count 6 - 25
Max count 1 - 5

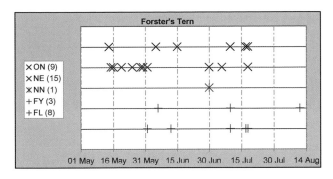

Forster's Tern

×ON (9)
×NE (15)
×NN (1)
+FY (3)
+FL (8)

01 May 16 May 31 May 15 Jun 30 Jun 15 Jul 30 Jul 14 Aug

November, and a maximum of 368 on 3 November. In central and southern San Diego Bay, on the basis of weekly surveys April 1993–April 1994, Manning (1995) noted larger numbers October–March than during the breeding season. At San Elijo Lagoon, however, on the basis of monthly surveys 1973–83, King et al. (1987), reported the largest numbers from July through September. At Lake Hodges (K10/K11) K. L. Weaver noted a peak in spring of 100 on 24 April 1982, a peak in late summer of 90, including many juveniles, on 13 August 1983. A Forster's Tern at Borrego Springs (G24) 30 March 1998 (P. D. Jorgensen) is the only one recorded in the Anza–Borrego Desert.

Winter: In winter Forster's Tern concentrates more along the coast, especially in San Diego Bay. Counts there range

up to 263 in the central bay 14 December 1994 (Mock et al. 1994). Winter numbers at other coastal sites range up to 75 at the Santa Margarita River mouth (G4) 27 January 1999 (P. A. Ginsburg) and 74 at San Elijo Lagoon 26 December 1999 (R. T. Patton). Inland, wintering Forster's Terns are sometimes common on Lake Hodges (K10; up to 75 on 22 December 2000, R. L. Barber) but generally uncommon elsewhere in the coastal lowland (up to 27 at Lake Wohlford, I12, 4 January 2001, J. O. Zimmer; 20 at San Vicente Reservoir, N13, 28 January 2002, N. Osborn). Above 1500 feet elevation, the only lakes where we found Forster's Tern in winter were Sutherland (J16; one on 22 February 2000, M. B. Stowe) and Henshaw (G17; three on 2 December 2001, C. G. Edwards; noted on 7 of 22 Christmas bird counts 1981–2002, maximum count seven).

Conservation: Between the salt works and the reservoirs inland, Forster's Terns exploit habitats not available in San Diego County until the 20th century. The attempts to colonize new sites suggest the population is vigorous. The dearth of suitable nesting sites secure from predators and disturbance, however, probably limits the population. Even within the salt works the intrusion of terrestrial predators is a constant problem for all the water birds nesting there.

Least Tern *Sterna antillarum*

The beaches that are now the summer playground of millions of southern Californians were once the home of the Least Tern. With disturbance and development of its habitat, this once common bird became rare and was among the first species listed as endangered in 1970 by both the California Department of Fish and Game and U.S. Fish and Wildlife Service. Intensive study, monitoring, and management have allowed San Diego County's Least Tern population to increase from about 500 pairs in the late 1970s to about 2100–2800 pairs 1997–2002 and nearly 4000 pairs in 2003. The tern's future, however, is now in the hands of man: special protection of colony sites and control of weeds and predators are inescapable if a ground-nesting bird like the Least Tern is to survive in its now urbanized environment.

Breeding distribution: The Least Tern's nesting sites in San Diego County in the late 20th and early 21st centuries are listed in Table 7, on the basis of data provided by Robert T. Patton and recorded by him, Elizabeth Copper, Brian Foster, and Shauna Wolf.

The colonies at Aliso Creek, the Santa Margarita River mouth, Naval Amphibious Base, and Tijuana River mouth are also notable because they are the county's only sites where the tern still nests on dunes and flats more or less in their natural condition. At Batiquitos Lagoon, the terns nest on several artificial sand flats installed for them at the time the lagoon was dredged and reopened to

Photo by Anthony Mercieca

the tide, as part of an attempt at restoration of this badly silted lagoon in the mid 1990s. Around Mission and San Diego bays, most of the tern's nesting sites are fills, islands, or dikes built of dredge spoil, sometimes covered with sand.

Least Terns have a high level of fidelity to colonies where they have established themselves as adults, less so to their natal colonies (Atwood and Massey 1988). But high levels of disturbance and a high rate of nest failure mean that shifting among colonies is frequent. Site fidelity may be lower in San Diego County than in Los Angeles and Orange counties (area of Atwood and Massey's study) because in San Diego there are more colonies with less distance between them. The terns sometimes take advantage of new sites (whether they were designed for the birds or not) as soon as they are created. For example, during the building of Seaport Village in downtown San Diego in 1977, 17 pairs nested on new bayfill there, and

Table 7   Estimated Minimum Number of Nesting Pairs of the Least Tern in San Diego County, 1997–2003

Site	Square	1997	1998	1999	2000	2001	2002	2003
Aliso Creek mouth	F4	17	33	53	36	37	39	87
Santa Margarita River mouth	G4	808	727	619	993	953	545	1091
Batiquitos Lagoon (west half)	J6	142	93	126	110	113	147	398
Batiquitos Lagoon (east half)	J7	129	86	28	26	62	72	176
San Elijo Lagoon	L7	9	1	8	15	8	1	0
Mission Bay: FAA Island	Q8	20	31	66	173	184	192	216
Mission Bay: north Fiesta Island	Q8	76	21	0	15	53	60	60
Mission Bay: Mariner's Point	R7	268	528	562	282	227	220	250
Mission Bay: South Shores	R8	0	9	0	0	0	0	0
Naval Training Center	R8	0	0	0	0	2	0	0
North Island Naval Air Station	S8	22	59	75	128	105	71	165
Lindbergh Field	S9	102	17	20	25	35	48	46
Naval Amphibious Base	T9	410	495	570	541	664	534	954
D Street Fill	T10	38	5	30	28	30	23	79
Chula Vista Wildlife Reserve	U10	0	2	2	0	0	3	25
Salt works	U10/V10	36	39	15	35	35	26	39
Tijuana River mouth	V10/W10	211	81	87	178	252	146	358
Total		2288	2227	2261	2585	2760	2127	3944

the first year after the installation of the Chula Vista Wildlife Reserve in 1980, 55 pairs nested there. The trend over time, however, with development of the coastline almost complete, has been for the tern's distribution to become more stable from year to year.

Least Terns forage in the bays and estuaries near their colonies, on the ocean near shore, and at inland lakes in the coastal lowland. No nesting was reported inland during the atlas period 1997–2001, but in earlier years the birds established small, ephemeral colonies up to 4 miles from the coast. For example, in 1981, nine pairs nested in Encinitas (K7) in a then-vacant lot 2 miles from the beach and 2 miles from San Elijo Lagoon. O'Neill Lake, Camp Pendleton (E6), is the terns' most heavily used inland foraging site, with up to 40 there 26 July 1999 (P. A. Ginsburg). More birds go inland after the young fledge in late July and August and the birds are no longer tied to their nests. But even in the middle of the breeding season some birds forage inland, with up to 15 at O'Neill Lake 15 June 1998 (P. A. Ginsburg) and 10 at San Dieguito Reservoir (K8) 14 June 1998 (J. Determan). The most inland sites are Depot Lake in the Fallbrook Naval Weapons Station (D6; one on 16 May 2002, J. R. Barth), Lake Hodges (K10; two on 14 June 1999, R. L. Barber), and a pond in the San Luis Rey River valley at the mouth of Keys Creek just east of Interstate 15 (E9; two engaging in courtship feeding 10 June 2001, J. E. Pike). At 15.8 miles from the beach the last locality is the farthest inland. Apparently Least Terns move inland much more in the northern than the southern half of San Diego County. South of the San Dieguito River we had no records during the atlas period, though in past years Least Terns have been seen in Mission Valley (R9), along the Sweetwater River at Bonita (T10/T11), and at the Dairy Mart pond in the Tijuana River valley (V11).

Nesting: The Least Tern's nest is a simple scrape in the sand or dirt, usually lined with a few broken bits of shell or debris. At Lindbergh Field and North Island, the birds nest in cracks in the pavement, other gravelly areas, or the small depressions for electric lights to guide airplanes at night, in spite of the heavy traffic of aircraft around them. Within a colony, nests may be within a few feet of each other, as on the FAA Island when large numbers of terns use that site, or well separated, as in most colonies—a strategy for making the nests difficult for predators to discover.

In southern California, the Least Tern lays its eggs generally

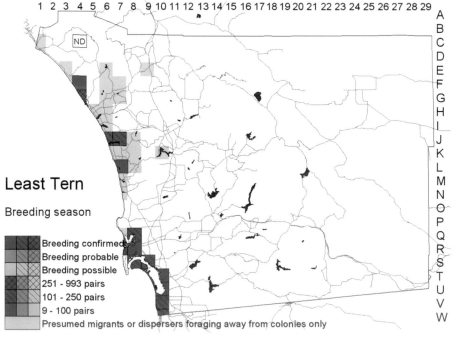

1 2 3 4 5 6 7 8 9 10 11 12 13 14 15 16 17 18 19 20 21 22 23 24 25 26 27 28 29

A B C D E F G H I J K L M N O P Q R S T U V W

ND

Least Tern

Breeding season

Breeding confirmed
Breeding probable
Breeding possible
251 - 993 pairs
101 - 250 pairs
9 - 100 pairs
Presumed migrants or dispersers foraging away from colonies only

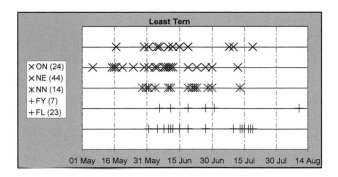

from mid May to early July. A second "wave" of laying by two-year-olds and birds that lost their first clutches follows the first by about four to five weeks (Massey and Atwood 1981). At the Santa Margarita River mouth in 1997, the terns began laying 6 May (exceptionally early), began hatching 29 May, and finished hatching 13 July (B. Foster). At the salt works in 1998, they laid from at least 15 May to 30 June and hatched from 12 June to 21 July (Terp and Pavelka 1999). The terns may lay as late July, but these eggs are abandoned by mid August. Eggs being incubated up to 8 August can still hatch into chicks that fledge (E. Copper).

Migration: Least Terns typically begin arriving in San Diego in mid April. During the atlas period the earliest report was 13 April (Batiquitos Lagoon, M. Baumgartel), but in 1995 it was 4 April (two on San Diego Bay, B. Foster, NASFN 49:308, 1995), and in 1994 it was 30 March, the earliest ever (E. Copper, NASFN 48:341, 1994). Postbreeding dispersal begins immediately after the chicks start fledging in June. By the first week of July, flocks can be seen away from colonies (52 birds at San Onofre State Beach, C1, 6 July 1997, P. D. Jorgensen), but many remain in San Diego County through August. Most Least Terns leave the county in early September, and by mid September the species is rare. There are two records of stragglers as late as October: of one near Imperial Beach (V10) 9 October 1993 (G. McCaskie, AB 48:152, 1994) and one at the San Diego River mouth (R7) 27–28 October 1981 (C. G. Edwards, E. Copper, AB 36:218, 1982).

Birds banded as chicks in San Diego County have been seen in nesting colonies as far north as Alameda County, the northern limit of the Least Tern's range in California. Least Terns banded in southern California, including San Diego County, have been seen in winter along the Pacific coast of Guatemala, of Chiapas, southern Mexico, and of Colima, western Mexico (Massey 1981).

Conservation: The Least Tern's increase over the final quarter of the 20th century is a success, but there is no room for complacency. The forces that made the tern an endangered species are as strong as ever and would overwhelm it without intensive management. A basic problem is that the colony sites are now fixed: with the rest of the San Diego County coastline developed, no alternative sites are available if a site is overgrown with vegetation and so becomes unsuitable or when predators learn the location of a colony and return repeatedly. Accelerated silting in of lagoons, the result of the vegetation being

stripped from watersheds during development, has eliminated some former nesting sites, as at Los Peñasquitos Lagoon (N7). The tern's strategy of shifting colony sites as conditions demand is no longer possible.

Many techniques have been used to encourage and protect the terns. Teams of volunteers organized by the San Diego Audubon Society and U.S. Fish and Wildlife Service have controlled invasive vegetation that would otherwise overrun sites such as Mariner's Point, Fiesta Island, the FAA island, and the Tijuana River mouth. Papier-mâché models of Least Terns have been set out as decoys to draw the birds to nest at sites where they can best be protected. Sites that lack adequate protection for chicks have been supplied with pieces of Spanish roof tiles, under which the chicks can take refuge. Some sites have been fenced and posted—fencing must be of sturdy chain link to be really effective, though this sometimes provides perches from which predators can survey the colony. Predators have been controlled through both trapping and shooting. The list of predators attacking the Least Tern in San Diego County is long and varied, including the Western Gull, American Kestrel, Common Raven, California ground squirrel, coyote, opossum, rat, ant, and domestic dog and cat. Even species as apparently innocuous as the Western Meadowlark and Domestic Pigeon have destroyed Least Tern eggs (E. Copper). In one week in 1999, a single coyote destroyed or caused the abandonment of about 340 of the 790 nests at the Santa Margarita River mouth, site of California's largest Least Tern colony (B. Foster). Unfortunately, several known predators are themselves rare, declining, or endangered species, including the Peregrine Falcon, Northern Harrier, Burrowing Owl, Loggerhead Shrike, and Gull-billed Tern, making predator control for the sake of the Least Tern a balancing act.

Adequate funding and coordinated management for activities this intensive is a constant challenge. Sites must be cleared before the birds arrive—not after. Vehicles, horses, and pedestrians must be kept out of colonies before they crush eggs and chicks. Control appropriate for one predator is inappropriate for another, and which predator will strike which colony next is difficult to predict.

Oceanographic variations may also affect the Least Tern's food supply and nesting success. From 1993 to 1997, San Diego County colonies produced an average of 1200 fledglings per year, but in 1999 the figure was only around 100. That year, newly hatched chicks were smaller than normal by roughly 25%, and many died within just a couple of days of hatching. The nest-abandonment rate was also higher than normal, so many of the eggs laid never had a chance to hatch. An ocean cooler than usual, as a result of La Niña, apparently delayed the breeding of the small fish on which the terns feed (B. Foster). Conversely, the increased ocean temperature and reduced fish abundance associated with El Niño also have a negative effect: Atwood and Massey (1988) suggested that the dip in California's Least Tern population in 1984 was due to high mortality in the winter range during El Niño. The population did not recover to its 1983 level until 1988 (Massey et al. 1992).

Taxonomy: The type locality for the California Least Tern, *S. a. browni* Mearns, 1916, is in San Diego County, on the beach at the international border. The validity of this subspecies has often been questioned, but Johnson et al. (1998) investigated the Least Tern's variation in color and upheld the distinction of *browni* from subspecies *athalassos* of the Mississippi basin and *antillarum* of the Atlantic coast on the basis of a combination of color differences. The trend of these is that *browni* differs from these two in its paler nape but duller back and darker (though still whitish) breast. Johnson et al. did not compare *browni* with two subspecies in Mexico, but the more northern of these, *S. a. mexicana* van Rossem and Hachisuka, 1937, was described as still darker than *browni*, the difference evident in the field.

Sooty Tern *Sterna fuscata*

Among the tropical ocean birds that began to appear in southern California in the 1990s was the Sooty Tern. The four reports for San Diego County include two pairs in tern colonies. But the nesting attempt that got as far as incubation of an egg ended in failure when both adults were killed by a Peregrine Falcon.

Breeding distribution: Brian Foster and Patricia A. Campbell found a Sooty Tern at the Santa Margarita River mouth (G4) 6 July 1996 and photographed a copulating pair there the following day (McCaskie and San Miguel 1999). Later that summer, probably the same birds accounted for reports of one at San Elijo Lagoon (L7) 28 July and two in the south San Diego Bay salt works (U10) 23 August 1996 (N. Shany, J. Konecny, NASFN 50:997, 1996).

The following year, in 1997, a pair nested in the salt works. Smith (1999) noted the first adult 15 April, saw the pair together 30 May, and found the egg 3 June. But on 6 June one adult, and on 10 June the other adult, were dead and partially dismembered, indicating predation by a Peregrine Falcon, which had been seen in the area. The egg and remains of both adults are preserved (SDNHM 49807, 49966).

Migration: The California Bird Records Committee accepted the identification of an immature Sooty Tern, California's first of this species, at the San Diego River

Photo by Brian Foster

mouth (R7) 27 September 1982 (R. E. Webster, Morlan 1985). Another Sooty Tern was reported on the ocean off Coronado (T9) 2 September 1998 (B. Foster, FN 52:126, 1998).

Conservation: The appearance of the Sooty Tern and other warm-water birds in southern California presumably reflects the increase in ocean temperatures. The Sooty Tern nests normally on predator-free oceanic islands; the pair at the salt works did not engage in the mobbing defense typical of the other terns nesting there (Smith 1999).

Taxonomy: The gray lower belly and crissum of the birds at the salt works are typical of the subspecies of Sooty Tern in the Pacific Ocean (Smith 1999). *Sterna f. crissalis* (Lawrence, 1871) was described from Socorro Island in the Revillagigedo archipelago, one of the nesting sites nearest San Diego.

Black Tern *Chlidonias niger*

The Black Tern nests in inland marshes (no closer to San Diego County than California's Central Valley), then heads to a pelagic winter range off southern Mexico, Central America, and South America. Much of the population migrates by way of the Salton Sea, and few Black Terns now reach the coast of southern California. The species' population decline is reflected in greatly reduced numbers seen in San Diego County.

Migration: The Black Tern occurs in San Diego County primarily as a fall migrant, though by the beginning of the 21st century it was averaging only about two birds reported per year. In 1999 and 2001 it was missed completely. It is most frequent from late July to mid September but also occurs occasionally in spring and early summer. Extreme dates are 26 April (1991, San Diego, J. Brisson, AB 45:496,

Photo by Anthony Mercieca

1991) and 21 November (1958, Sweetwater Reservoir, S12, AFN 13:66, 1959), the six winter records excluded. The maximum number seen together recently is three, at San Elijo Lagoon (L7) 13 June 1998 (B. C. Moore) and the San Diego River flood-control channel (R8) 11 May 2002

(M. B. Mulrooney). Black Terns generally occur along the coast or at ponds and lakes in the coastal lowland, inland to Lake Hodges (K10). Exceptions are two at the Borrego Springs sewage ponds (H25) 12 May 1990 (A. G. Morley) and a remarkable 41 at Lake Henshaw (G17) 10 August 1984 (R. Higson, AB 39:103, 1985).

Winter: Unitt (1984) summarized the six winter records, all coastal, and none more recent than 1977.

Conservation: No numerical data on the Black Tern's former status are available, but Willett (1933) considered the species a "common migrant" in coastal southern California, and Stephens (1919a) considered it "rather common" in San Diego County. Even in the 1970s it was seen much more frequently than at the turn of the millennium, with up to 13 in the Tijuana River valley 17 August 1977 (J. L. Dunn). Even though Black Terns take advantage of agriculture, making rice fields their principal nesting habitat in northern California (Shuford et al. 2001), their population as a whole has decreased seriously, possibly because of pesticide contamination, degradation of wetlands, and overfishing in the winter range (Dunn and Agro 1995).

Taxonomy: *Chlidonias n. surinamensis* is the subspecies of the Black Tern in the New World.

Black Skimmer *Rynchops niger*

Through the final third of the 20th century, this avian oddity expanded its range greatly, moving northwest from the coast of mainland Mexico and colonizing California. The salt works of south San Diego Bay have become a major colony with hundreds of pairs. The skimmer resides in San Diego County year round, but most of the birds shift between the salt works in summer and Mission Bay in winter. Elsewhere along the county's coast the skimmer is much less abundant, but a small colony has established itself at Batiquitos Lagoon.

Photo by Anthony Mercieca

Breeding distribution: Within the salt works (U10/V10), the skimmers nest on several dikes spread throughout the system; the locations vary year to year and shift through the course of each season. The number of distinct nest clusters or subcolonies has ranged from 7 in 2002 to 13 in 1998 (R. T. Patton, Terp and Pavelka 1999). During the atlas period the total number of nesting pairs varied from about 485 in 1997 to at least 280 in 1998 (Terp and Pavelka 1999) to about 200 in 1999 to 187–216 in 2000 to 268–280 in 2001. In 2002 and 2003 it went back up to 331 (R. T. Patton).

In the west basin of Batiquitos Lagoon (J6), 14 pairs of skimmers colonized in 1995 on dredge spoil installed as nesting habitat for the Least Tern and Snowy Plover in 1994. Ten pairs nested there in 1996 (Whelchel et al. 1996). Subsequently, the birds shifted to an island in the east basin (J7), where they nested at least in 1997, 1998, and 2001–03. In the last three years the number of pairs increased from 8 to 10 to at least 26, fledging 19, 5, and 15–19 young, respectively (S. M. Wolf).

Nesting: Black Skimmers nest in a scrape on bare ground, using no nest material. In the salt works, they nest either near the large terns or in separate clusters of their own, the nests spaced a few feet apart. The birds may begin selecting their nest sites and scraping as early as 5 May (1999). From 1997 to 2003, egg laying began between 16 May and 2 June (R. T. Patton, Terp

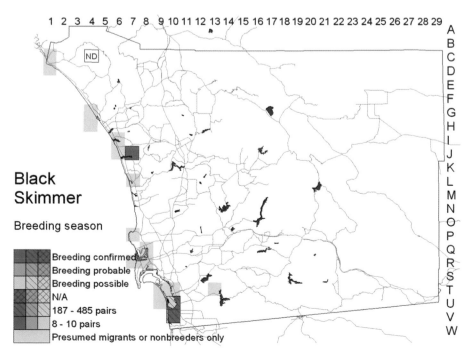

Black Skimmer

Breeding season

- Breeding confirmed
- Breeding probable
- Breeding possible
- N/A
- 187 - 485 pairs
- 8 - 10 pairs
- Presumed migrants or nonbreeders only

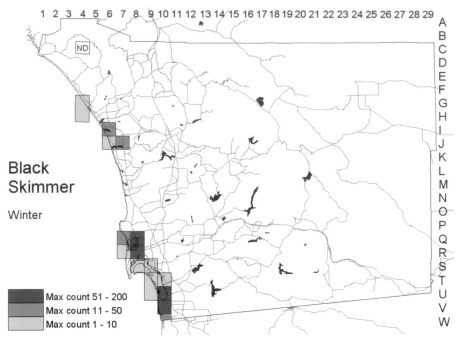

Black
Skimmer

Winter

■ Max count 51 - 200
▨ Max count 11 - 50
░ Max count 1 - 10

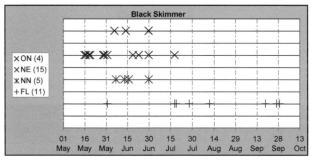

Beach (C1) 1 July 1999 (P. D. Jorgensen) and at the San Diego River mouth (R7) 28 June 1999 (F. Shaw). Through July skimmers are seen increasingly at other coastal wetlands and occasionally flying past places where they neither rest nor feed (two at La Jolla, P7, 17 July 1999, E. Wallace). The wintering flock at Crown Point, Mission Bay (Q8), peaks in fall and early winter (up to 140 on surveys 1992–95, Gazzaniga 1996; up to 278 on 18 December 2002, K. C. Molina), but it may remain large until late April (90 on 15 April 1999, E. Wallace)

Only one skimmer has been reported inland in San Diego County, at Upper Otay Lake (T13) 19 July 2000 (T. W. Dorman). Because of population exchange across the mountains and sightings at Lake Elsinore and Mystic Lake in western Riverside County (Garrett and Dunn 1981), such a record is not too surprising.

Winter: Mission Bay is the skimmer's primary winter site in San Diego County; the birds concentrate on the east side of Crown Point. Counts there during the atlas period ranged up to 130 on 13 February 2000 (B. Hendricks). But the birds move around the area; our highest winter count was of 200 in the San Diego River flood-control channel and at Fiesta Island (R8) 28 February 1999 (B. C. Moore). The number remaining in south San Diego Bay is variable, sometimes large (up to 70 on 19 December 1998, D. C. Seals), sometimes small or zero. Other sites where skimmers often winter in some numbers are Agua Hedionda Lagoon (I6; up to 35 on 9 February 2001, P. A. Ginsburg), Batiquitos Lagoon (up to 16 on 4 December 1998, C. C. Gorman), and the Tijuana River estuary (V10/W10; up to 50 on 19 December 1998, S. Walens). Winter sightings elsewhere along the coast were of six or fewer.

Conservation: The skimmer's range expansion has been facilitated by its use of artificial habitats like the salt works. The species was first seen in the county 18–19 September 1971 (AB 26:121, 1972) and first nested at the salt works (a single pair) in 1976 (AB 30:1004, 1976). For the next 20 years the population increased fairly steadily; the 485 pairs estimated in 1997 is the highest figure yet. Subsequently the population seems to have stabilized at around 300 to 400 pairs (K. C. Molina unpubl. data).

Even though its numbers have increased, the skimmer is vulnerable to several threats. The heavily urbanized coast of southern California offers few secure nesting sites to colonial water birds that nest on the ground. The concentration of the population at just three or four locations means that a disruption of one site has a large effect on the entire population. In the first years of the 21st

and Pavelka 1999). In 1998, the great majority of the birds laid between 10 and 20 June. Some nesting, however, presumably laying of replacement clutches by birds losing first clutches, continued to late August in 1998 (Terp and Pavelka 1999) and 22 August in 2001 (R. T. Patton). From 1999 to 2003, incubation continued through 22 August to 18 September. Chicks began hatching from 7 to 18 June, and nonflying young were observed as late as 4 September to 7 October. Newly hatched chicks were found as late as 11 September. The first flying fledglings were observed each season between 18 and 28 July, and some remained through 19 September to 7 October.

The year the skimmers first colonized Batiquitos Lagoon they nested late, laying from 30 July to 21 August and fledging from 25 September to 17 October (Whelchel et al. 1996). From 2001 to 2003 their egg dates ranged from 23 May to 2 August with latest fledging in 9 September (S. M. Wolf).

Migration: Recoveries of banded birds show that the skimmers move among the colonies on the coast of southern California, at the Salton Sea, and at the head of the Gulf of California (Collins and Garrett 1996). In San Diego County the birds are most concentrated at the nesting colonies from late May through the first week of July. During that interval atlas observers saw no more than four at other locations, as at San Onofre State

century, skimmer nesting at the Salton Sea began to fail as the sea could no longer sustain fish (K. C. Molina, NAB 56:486, 2002; 57:545, 2003). The incorporation of the San Diego Bay salt works into the San Diego National Wildlife Refuge was an important step, facilitating monitoring and management of a site critical to many nesting water birds, but threats remain. The site must be policed with vigilance; disturbance by people, dogs, and predators getting onto the dikes is a continuing problem. Disturbance at a critical time could eliminate an entire year's production of young.

Taxonomy: Black Skimmers on both the Pacific and Atlantic coasts of North America are nominate *R. n. niger* Linnaeus, 1758. It is distinguished from other subspecies in South America by having the tail white except for the central black pair of rectrices.

Auks, Murres, and Puffins — Family Alcidae

Common Murre *Uria aalge*

The Common Murre is an irregular winter visitor to the ocean off San Diego County, which represents the southern extreme of the species' range—there are only a few records for northernmost Baja California. Because of its high sensitivity to changing oceanographic conditions like El Niño and ocean warming, the murre experiences wide swings in food availability and nesting success. These ever-changing factors affect how many birds end up in marginal habitat like the coast of San Diego County.

Photo by Richard E. Webster

Winter: The Common Murre is usually uncommon off San Diego County and seldom seen from shore except at La Jolla (P7) during northwest winds. Some years bring larger influxes, however, like 1958 (140 on the San Diego Christmas bird count 21 December), 1976 (72 offshore between Point Loma and Imperial Beach 18 December, D. W. Povey), 1982 (60 off San Diego 9 January, G. McCaskie, AB 36:331, 1982), and 2002 (34 at La Jolla 18 December, B. L. Sullivan).

Migration: The Common Murre's appearance and departure in San Diego County vary much from year to year as well. Eleven at La Jolla 10 October 2000 (P. A. Ginsburg, NAB 55:103, 2001) were exceptionally early. Few remain after early May, but after the influx of 1976–77, stragglers were noted as late as 6 July (one off Pacific Beach, Q7, D. W. Povey), after that of 2002–03, to 29 June (one at La Jolla, M. Sadowski). One in molt but with the primaries almost completely worn off, found at La Jolla 26 September 1998 (SDNHM 50139), had undoubtedly summered locally.

Conservation: In their turn, commercial egg collecting, oil spills, and gill netting have all taken their toll on the Common Murre in California (Ainley et al. 2002). The birds' sensitivity to the variations of ocean temperature and fish abundance seen through the 20th century suggests that large-scale ocean warming would have a devastating effect. Even so, it is curious that the Common Murre was not known from San Diego County before 1942, when a specimen was collected at Cardiff (L7) 4 February (SDNHM 18950).

Taxonomy: The California Common Murre, *U. a. californica* (Bryant, 1861), inhabits the Pacific coast from California to British Columbia.

Pigeon Guillemot *Cepphus columba*

Though it breeds as close as the Channel Islands, the Pigeon Guillemot is only a rare vagrant to San Diego County. After fledging, most young birds migrate north, away from San Diego.

Migration: The first Pigeon Guillemots reported from San Diego County were two 50 miles off San Diego 1 September 1976 (R. L. Pitman, AB 31:223, 1977). From 1992 to 1996 the species was seen sporadically in spring at La Jolla (P7): one 14–17 May 1992 (D. W. Povey, AB 46:481, 1992); two 12–14 June 1992 (T. Clawson, AB 46:1178, 1992); one 19 April–13 May 1994 (S. Walens, NASFN 48:341, 1994); one 7 April–16 May 1995 (S. Walens, NASFN 49:309, 1995); one 15 April 1996 (S. Walens, NASFN 50:333,

Photo by Kenneth W. Fink

1996). Juveniles were found dead on the beach at the Santa Margarita River mouth (G4) 25 June 2000 (B. Foster, SDNHM 50448) and within the Naval Amphibious Base on the Silver Strand (T9) 29 August 2003 (M. Sadowski, SDNHM 50801).

Taxonomy: The California subspecies of the Pigeon Guillemot, *C. c. eureka* Storer, 1950, differs from other subspecies in its longer bill.

Marbled Murrelet *Brachyramphus marmoratus*

The Marbled Murrelet is famed for its nesting habits unique for a seabird: it lays its egg on a bed of moss or debris in large trees in the rain forests of the Pacific Northwest. It is not highly migratory, however, so it is only a rare vagrant to southern California. There are only three records from San Diego County.

Winter: One was photographed in the Mission Bay entrance channel (R7) 29 November 1979 and seen again 3 December. Two at the Imperial Beach pier (V10) 15 December 1979 were photographed the following day (AB

34:307, 1980). One was on the ocean just beyond the breakers at Coronado (T9) 15 December 2001 (D. W. Povey).

Conservation: The Marbled Murrelet's dependence on old-growth forests prized for logging has put it in the center of political and economic controversy. The murrelet is listed as threatened by the U.S. Fish and Wildlife Service and endangered by the California Department of Fish and Game.

Taxonomy: With the recognition as a distinct species of the Marbled Murrelet's Asian counterpart, the Longbilled Murrelet (*B. perdix*), the Marbled Murrelet is left monotypic.

Kittlitz's Murrelet *Brachyramphus brevirostris*

In the New World, Kittlitz's Murrelet is almost confined to Alaska. The single record for San Diego County is the only one south of northwestern Washington.

Migration: A juvenile "alive but in weakened condition" was picked up on the beach north of La Jolla (O7) 16 August 1969 (Devillers 1972, SDNHM 37215). The bird's being so far out its normal range no more than six weeks after fledging has raised the question whether its occurrence in San Diego was assisted by man. The specimen shows no sign of having been in captivity, however, and its wing feathers are fully grown.

Xantus' Murrelet *Synthliboramphus hypoleucus*

Xantus' Murrelet breeds currently only on the Channel Islands of southern California and Los Coronados Islands, Guadalupe Island, and San Benito Islands of Baja California. The total population is small, perhaps only 7000 birds, apportioned among two subspecies. Thus, even though the ocean off San Diego County is central to the species' range, Xantus' Murrelet is uncommon there. Only rarely is it seen from land.

Winter: Xantus' Murrelets, like other seabirds, are occasionally driven close to shore at La Jolla (P7) by strong winds. Two were there 15 December 1999 (L. Polinsky); one was there 13 February 2001 (B. L. Sullivan).

Migration: Xantus' Murrelet is most numerous off San Diego County during the species' breeding season from March to July. Counts have ranged up to 30 between San Diego and Los Coronados Islands 17 March 1974 (G. McCaskie), but in recent years only one or two, if any, are typically seen in a day offshore. After breeding, some of the population migrates north, out of southern California. But the species occurs off San Diego year round.

Breeding distribution: Los Coronados Islands are home to about 750 Xantus' Murrelets and therefore about 20%

Photo by Richard E. Webster

of the total population of subspecies *scrippsi* (Drost and Lewis 1995).

Conservation: Cats and rats introduced on the murrelet's nesting islands are the greatest threat to the species; they have extirpated several former colonies (Everett and Anderson 1991).

Taxonomy: *Synthliboramphus h. scrippsi* (Green and Arnold, 1939) nests through most of the species' range and is the subspecies occurring most frequently off San Diego. It has the line between black and white on the face cutting nearly straight from the base of the bill back past the eye. Nominate *S. h. hypoleucus* (Xantus, 1860), however, occurs rarely in summer and fall, recorded from

3 July (1992, far off San Diego, P. Pyle, AB 46:1179, 1992) to 4 December (1996, two collected 43 miles west of Point Loma 4 December 1966 (SBCM 3887–8). Other specimens are one picked up alive at Imperial Beach (V10) 27 July 1993 (SDNHM 48493) and another at Mission Beach

(R7) 29 July 1990 (SDNHM 46957). The latter is a recent fledgling with some down persisting on the head and neck. Nominate *hypoleucus* is distinguished by the white on the face extending up through the lores and curling over the top of the eye (Jehl and Bond 1975).

Craveri's Murrelet *Synthliboramphus craveri*

Many of Baja California's seabirds disperse north after breeding. Some, like the Brown Pelican, Elegant Tern, and Heermann's Gull, become abundant along San Diego County's coast. Craveri's Murrelet, however, is rare, recorded only in late summer and early fall.

Migration: Craveri's Murrelet has been noted off San Diego County from 11 July (1972, two off San Diego, AB 26:906, 1972) to 13 October (1971, two seen 12 miles off San Diego, Jehl 1973). The only report from shore is of one in the surf at Border Field State Park (W10) 11 August 1981 (R. E. Webster). Laurence M. Huey collected two 10 miles west of Point Loma 28 August 1925 (SDNHM 9938–9). One found alive on a boat in San Diego Bay 23 September 2003 (SDNHM 50824) could have come aboard far offshore, as murrelets confused by the lights often fly onto ships at night.

Conservation: Whether because of the decreased productivity of the ocean off southern California or because

Photo by Joseph R. Jehl, Jr.

of problems on the nesting islands, numbers of Craveri's Murrelets off San Diego County appear to have decreased since the 1980s. The maximum seen off San Diego per day was 30 on 9 September 1972, but since 1980 the only report of more than four was of 12 off San Diego 10 September 1983 (G. McCaskie, AB 38:247, 1984).

Ancient Murrelet *Synthliboramphus antiquus*

San Diego County is about the southern limit of the Ancient Murrelet's usual winter range; there are only a few records from Baja California. Increased attention to La Jolla as a site for seabird watching has revealed the murrelet to be regular if uncommon. It remains within a few miles of the coast and does not spread over the open ocean. An incursion in December 1995 brought vastly greater numbers than recorded before or since.

Winter: La Jolla (P7) is the site where the Ancient Murrelet is seen most frequently in San Diego County. From 1997 to 2002 the highest counts there were of at least 20 flying south from 25 to 30 November 2001 (P. A. Ginsburg, G. McCaskie, S. Walens, NAB 56:106, 2002) and 10 on 21 December 2001 (J. C. Worley). The species is seen occasionally from shore elsewhere, as in the Oceanside harbor (H5; one on 22 December 1979, D. W. Povey), at Sea Cliff Park, Encinitas (K6; two flying south 11 December 2002, G. C. Hazard), and Coronado (T9; one on 24 November 1997, B. Foster, FN 52:126, 1998). There are a few records from the entrances to Mission (R7) and San Diego bays (S8; one on 26 November 1986, M. and D. Hastings, AB 41:145, 1987).

The influx of 1995, which affected the species' entire North American winter range, yielded a count of 487

Photo by Joseph R. Jehl, Jr.

migrating south past La Jolla in 11.5 hours of watching from 14 to 18 December (S. Walens, NASFN 50:224, 1996).

Migration: The Ancient Murrelet occurs in San Diego County mainly from November to March but has been found as early as 1 August (1999, found ashore at Ocean Beach, R7, SDNHM 50312) and 28 August (1928, off Point Loma, S7, SDNHM 12163). Many of the murrelets seen at La Jolla in December are still migrating south. The latest date is 25 April (1904, picked up oiled at Pacific Beach, Q7, Bishop 1905). Most Ancient Murrelets reaching San Diego County are immature; of eight county specimens in the San Diego Natural History Museum, seven are immature, including the two collected in August.

266

Auks, Murres, and Puffins — Family Alcidae

Cassin's Auklet *Ptychoramphus aleuticus*

Once the most frequently seen alcid on the ocean off San Diego, Cassin's Auklet has been surpassed by the Rhinoceros Auklet. Cassin's Auklet is among the seabirds most adversely affected by the decline in the biological productivity of the California Current through the late 20th century. The status of the colony at Los Coronados Islands near San Diego is tenuous: Jehl (1977) reported it extirpated, but Everett and Anderson (1991) found some active nests in 1989.

Photo by Kenneth W. Fink

Winter: Cassin's Auklet usually stays at least 5 miles from the coast of San Diego County but is seen occasionally from shore during strong winds. For example, two were at Torrey Pines State Reserve (N7) 7 December 1997 (D. K. Adams), and two were at La Jolla (P7) 7 April 2001 (S. Walens).

Migration: Data specific to San Diego County are insufficient to define Cassin's Auklet's seasonal variation. Briggs et al. (1987) found California's Cassin Auklet population concentrating around major nesting colonies in the breeding season, then shifting in large part off the continental shelf in the nonbreeding season, when the state receives a large influx of winter visitors.

Conservation: As a species feeding on plankton, Cassin's Auklet is sensitive to variation in ocean productivity. Presumably as a result of the increase in ocean temperature and decrease in productivity since the 1970s, the population in California has declined considerably, by over 56% at the primary colony on Southeast Farallon Island off San Francisco (Pyle 2001). By the 1990s numbers seen on boat trips out of San Diego were consistently under those of the 1960s and 1970s (maximum 250 on 21 November 1970, AB 25:109, 1971).

Taxonomy: San Diego County lies within the range of the larger of the two subspecies of Cassin's Auklet, nominate *P. a. aleuticus* (Pallas, 1811).

Parakeet Auklet *Aethia psittacula*

The Parakeet Auklet nests largely in Alaska; southern California is remote from its normal range. The single record for San Diego County is the southernmost along the coast of North America and the only one along the mainland coast south of Point Conception. The few other records from near the latitude of San Diego are from San Nicolas Island or still farther offshore.

Photo by Kenneth W. Fink

Winter: Kenyon (1937) found three birds dead on the beach north of La Jolla (O7/P7) 28 January 1937. Two of these were "badly mutilated," but he preserved the third (USNM 529104).

Rhinoceros Auklet *Cerorhinca monocerata*

In contrast to California's other alcids, whose numbers have declined, the Rhinoceros Auklet has increased and spread, at least as a breeding species. On the ocean off San Diego County, however, the Rhinoceros Auklet is primarily a winter visitor. The decrease of other alcids has left the Rhinoceros Auklet as the most frequently seen of its family off San Diego, where it is an uncommon to fairly common winter visitor.

Photo by Anthony Mercieca

Winter: Off southern California, Rhinoceros Auklets constitute up to 30% of the wintering seabirds, but most remain seaward of the continental shelf (Briggs et al. 1987). They are regular if uncommon, however, within a few miles of land, and seen occasionally from shore during strong winds. Seventeen in La Jolla Cove (P7) 11 January 2003 (S. Walens) were exceptional. Consistent coverage by D. W. Povey of the ocean near Oceanside and San Diego during Christmas bird counts since the mid 1970s has yielded a maximum of eight on the Oceanside count, 22 December 1990.

Migration: On southern California's continental shelf and slope, Briggs et al. (1987) found the Rhinoceros Auklet arriving in October or November, peaking from January to March, and departing in April and May. Stragglers remain rarely through the summer, such as one off San Diego 28 July 1982 (D. W. Povey, AB 36:1016, 1982), one in La Jolla Cove 28 August 2002 (M. Billings),

and birds washed ashore at Ocean Beach (R7) 4 July 1970 (SDNHM 37588) and at Torrey Pines State Reserve (N7) 29 July 1973 (SDNHM 38514).

Conservation: The Rhinoceros Auklet was extirpated as a breeding species from California about 1865 (Grinnell and Miller 1944). Since the 1970s, it has recolonized several sites (McChesney et al. 1995), but the number reaching San Diego County as winter visitors has changed little with these variations. Most Rhinoceros Auklets reaching San Diego County probably come from far to the north.

Horned Puffin *Fratercula corniculata*

The Horned Puffin nests principally in Alaska and winters far out to sea. There are still only five records for San Diego County, none more recent than 1976.

Migration: In the second half of the 20th century, the Horned Puffin occurred along the west coast of the contiguous United States mainly in spring, with an unusual influx in 1975 and 1976 (Hoffman et al. 1975, Briggs et al. 1987). Records for the coast of San Diego County are of dead birds washed up 3 miles north of La Jolla (O7) 25 February 1933 (Huey 1933, SDNHM 16183), near La Jolla 28 September 1974 (SDNHM 38925), and at Del Mar (M7) 12 May 1976 (AB 30:891, 1976). Also, one was seen 19 miles southeast of San Clemente Island 1 June 1971 (AB 35:801, 1971), and seven were seen (one photographed) within 10 miles southeast of the south end of San Clemente Island 10 May 1975 (AB 29:909, 1975).

Photo by Kenneth W. Fink

Tufted Puffin *Fratercula cirrhata*

Once nesting commonly on the Channel Islands, the Tufted Puffin was extirpated there in the early 1900s. Even though it has recolonized Prince Islet off San Miguel Island, it remains rare in southern California: Briggs et al. (1987) estimated one bird per 10 square kilometers far offshore. Two dead Tufted Puffins have washed ashore in San Diego County; otherwise, the nearest record is from the vicinity of San Clemente Island.

Migration: Tufted Puffins were picked up at Ocean Beach (R7) 10 September 1972 (SDNHM 38221) and 0.5 mile northwest of the Santa Margarita River mouth (G5) 12 July 2003 (N. Basinski, SDNHM 50799). The pelagic record nearest San Diego is of one seen near the south end of San Clemente Island 1 June 1971 (AB 25:801, 1971).

Photo by Anthony Mercieca

PIGEONS AND DOVES — FAMILY COLUMBIDAE

Domestic Pigeon, Rock Dove, or Rock Pigeon
Columba livia

Native to rocky cliffs in the Old World, the Rock Dove has been domesticated for millennia. Domestic Pigeons were brought to North America by the earliest French and English settlers (Schorger 1952) and spread in tandem with western civilization. Historical data on their establishment in southern California are practically nonexistent, but the pigeons have been abundant here for decades. In San Diego County they nest on buildings almost exclusively; in natural habitats only occasional wanderers are seen flying overhead.

Breeding distribution: The Domestic Pigeon is common in heavily urbanized areas. Our counts for this atlas do not represent its true abundance, as even in cities observers focused their time far more on parks and remnant native habitats than around the buildings where pigeons congregate. In the breeding season our highest count was at Encinitas (K6), where the birds use supports for the railroad bridge (154 on 22 April 2001, J. Ciarletta). In San Diego's back country Domestic Pigeons are common around farm buildings in some places (up to 55 in Ballena Valley, K17, O. Carter), absent in others. In the higher mountains they are rare but nest possibly at Julian (J20; up to three on 26 June 2001, O. Carter) and definitely near Mount Laguna (P23; pair building a nest 5 July 2000, E. C. Hall). In the Anza–Borrego Desert, Domestic Pigeons are resident in small numbers in the communities of Borrego Springs (up to 20 in square F25 on 31 March 1998 and 28 April 1999, P. D. Ache) and Ocotillo Wells (up to three, plus a nest with eggs, in square I29 on 8 May 2001, J. R.

Photo by Anthony Mercieca

Barth). A single bird was in the community of Canebrake (N27) 29 April 2000 (R. and S. L. Breisch).

Nesting: In San Diego County the Domestic Pigeon nests on buildings and bridges almost exclusively. The only other nest site atlas observers described was inside a railroad tunnel, where R. Breisch and J. Determan found an abandoned egg 2 December 2001. Most nesting in San Diego County appears to take place from March to July, though this season may represent more the season when

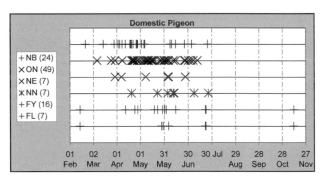

atlas observers were looking for it. Some nesting takes place almost if not completely year round, as attested by adults feeding fledglings in Santee (P12) 14 February 1998 (C. G. Edwards) and in an underground parking garage in the Hillcrest area of San Diego (R9) 12 November 2001 (P. Unitt), meaning egg laying in late December and late September, respectively. Even as far north as Alberta some pigeons nest in midwinter (McGillivray 1988).

Migration: The Domestic Pigeon is nonmigratory but seen occasionally in transit, flying over native habitats, as in El Capitan Open Space Preserve (N15) 8 April 2001 (P. Unitt). A few such records could represent birds

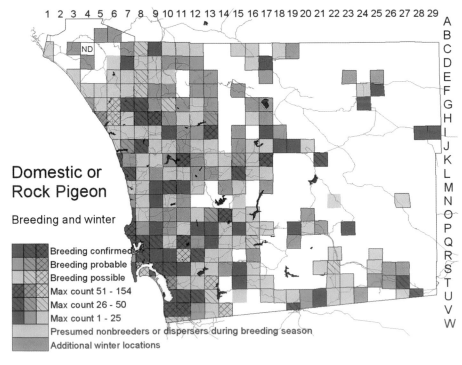

Domestic or Rock Pigeon

Breeding and winter

- Breeding confirmed
- Breeding probable
- Breeding possible
- Max count 51 - 154
- Max count 26 - 50
- Max count 1 - 25
- Presumed nonbreeders or dispersers during breeding season
- Additional winter locations

using nearby natural cliffs (four near Garnet Mountain, N22, 24 May 1997, G. L. Rogers; one near the summit of Otay Mountain, U15, 1 April 2001, P. Unitt).

Winter: In winter Domestic Pigeons gather into larger flocks than in spring and summer, up to 620 in Escondido (J10) 22 December 2000 (W. E. Haas). The Domestic Pigeon has a slightly wider distribution in winter: we recorded it in 42 atlas squares in winter but not the breeding season versus 24 for the converse. We noted the species only a few times flying over more or less wilderness areas, for example, six near Margarita Peak (B5) 31 January 1998 (W. E. Haas), one at 4200 feet elevation in Henderson Canyon (E23) 26 February 2002

(R. Thériault), and ten near Garnet Mountain (N22) 10 December 1997 (G. L. Rogers).

Conservation: Urban development, of course, creates new habitat for Domestic Pigeons, but newer buildings are designed to discourage them, and some older ones have been retrofitted with porcupine wire to the same end. Even though the birds feed heavily on waste food left by people, farmland may on the whole offer better foraging than cities, so urbanization of former farmland may not benefit the birds. Except possibly at Borrego Springs, Christmas bird counts show no clear trend in Domestic Pigeon numbers in San Diego County since the species was included in the counts beginning in 1973.

Band-tailed Pigeon *Patagioenas fasciata*

California's only native large pigeon can be seen year round in San Diego's mountains, sometimes in large flocks, sometimes as only scattered individuals. Elderberries and acorns are its staple foods, so the Band-tailed Pigeon frequents woodland with abundant oaks. Though it inhabits all the mountains where the black and canyon live oaks are common, its distribution is oddly patchy in foothill woodland dominated by the coast live oak. Both migratory and nomadic, the Band-tailed Pigeon may be common in some areas in some years and absent in others; it shows up occasionally in all regions of the county as a vagrant.

Photo by Anthony Mercieca

Breeding distribution: As its name in Spanish suggests, Palomar Mountain is the center of Band-tailed Pigeon abundance in San Diego County (*paloma* = pigeon or dove). The pigeons move up and down the mountain, descending to the base in summer to feed on elderber-

ries in dry scrub. Eleanor Beemer noted this movement at Pauma Valley in the 1930s, and it continues today. Some of our larger summer counts, including the largest, were in elderberries around the base of Palomar: 35 near Rincon (F13) 7 July 2000 (M. B. Mosher); 110 in Dameron Valley (C16) 23 June 2001 (K. L. Weaver). Most of the birds nest in the forested area high on the mountain, but some nest around the base, as shown by a fledgling in Pauma Valley (E12) 19 May 2001 (E. C. Hall) and an occupied nest near the West Fork Conservation Camp (E17) 12 May 2001 (J. O. Zimmer).

Band-tailed Pigeons occur throughout the county's other mountains as well, with up to 40 on the south slope of Hot Springs Mountain (F20) 13 May 2001 (M. and B. McIntosh), 35 in Sherilton Valley, Cuyamaca Mountains (N19), 12 June 2001 (G. Wynn, P. D. Jorgensen), and 50 near the head of La Posta Creek, Laguna Mountains (P23), 3 June 1999 (E. C. Hall, J. O. Zimmer).

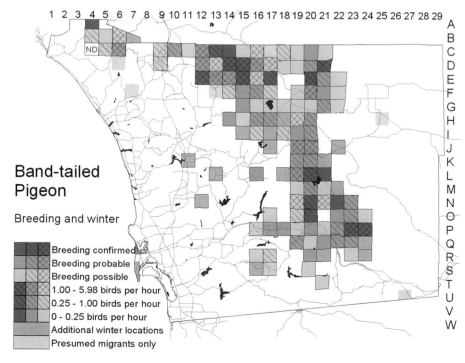

Band-tailed Pigeon

Breeding and winter

- Breeding confirmed
- Breeding probable
- Breeding possible
- 1.00 - 5.98 birds per hour
- 0.25 - 1.00 birds per hour
- 0 - 0.25 birds per hour
- Additional winter locations
- Presumed migrants only

At lower elevations, in northwestern San Diego County Band-tailed Pigeons appear to be regular in small numbers around Rainbow (C10; up to 12 on 21 April 1999, D. C. Seals) and in much larger numbers in the Santa Margarita Mountains (up to 95 around De Luz, B6, 22 April 2000, K. L. Weaver). They spread over other areas of northwestern San Diego County irregularly. For example, K. L. Weaver found them irregularly common to absent during breeding-bird censuses along the Santa Margarita River east of Sandia Canyon (C8) from 1989 to 1994; in spite of thorough coverage he never recorded them there from 1997 to 2002. The Band-tailed Pigeon's nesting in the Santa Margarita Mountains is confirmed by a fledgling in Cold Spring Canyon (A4) 17 June 2001 (J. M. and B. Hargrove).

In the foothills of central San Diego County there is considerable oak woodland that seems attractive to Band-tailed Pigeons, yet our only spring sighting in this area was of one pair in San Vicente Valley (L16) 27 April 2000 (J. D. Barr). Then in the southern third of the county the pigeon recurs in this habitat, occurring in small numbers at elevations as low as 1400 feet in Peutz Valley north of Alpine (P16; up to two on 11 July 1999, P. Unitt). We found the species consistently in an enclave slightly isolated from the rest of the range from Lawson Creek south to Lyons Peak (R16/R17/S17), with up to nine in Lawson Valley (R17) 29 March 1999 (J. R. Barth). This population may be of long standing, as A. O. Treganza collected a Band-tailed Pigeon egg from Lyons Peak 12 March 1929 (WFVZ 28947)—the southernmost confirmed nesting ever of subspecies *P. f. monilis*. From 1997 to 2002 the southernmost likely site of Band-tailed Pigeon nesting was near Morena Butte (T21), where R. and S. L. Breisch noted three juveniles 5 July 1997. One 0.8 mile southeast of Music Mountain (U27) in April 1997 sang regularly for four to five weeks but never attracted a mate and was in marginal habitat (F. L. Unmack), as was another nearby in Jewell Valley (U26) 6 July 1993 (P. Unitt).

Nesting: Band-tailed Pigeon nests are difficult to find; over five years we noted only eight. The nest is placed on a tree branch, often quite high in the tree. Conifers may offer better nest sites than do oaks, accounting for the pigeon's occurring principally in mixed coniferous/oak woodland. But the birds nest in oaks as well: see Abbott (1927b) for a photograph of a nest of in a black oak at Mesa Grande (H17). The Band-tailed Pigeon usually lays only one egg per clutch but makes up for this low number with a long breeding season. Sharp (1919) and Abbott (1927b) reported several fall nests of the Band-tailed Pigeon in San Diego County, and fall nesting is common elsewhere too (Keppie and Braun 2000), probably stimulated by the ripening of acorns. The nesting activity we

observed during the atlas period all falls well within the interval of 6 March–14 October based on collected eggs and literature reports.

Migration: In the northern part of its range the Band-tailed Pigeon is highly migratory. Some of these migrants reach San Diego County; pigeons banded in northern California have been recovered here (Keppie and Braun 2000). Occasional vagrants reach the coast at almost any season, most often in late spring and fall, less often in summer, and least often in late winter. Our only spring migrant toward the coast during the atlas period was one about 0.5 mile southwest of Morro Hill (F7) 27 April 1997 (A. Peterson), but there are over a dozen reports from Point Loma (S7) at various seasons, with up to 25 during May 1981 (G. McCaskie).

In the Anza–Borrego Desert there are eight records, two in April, one each in May and June, and two each in August and November. Most are of single individuals, but up to three were in Indian Gorge (P27) 20 November 1988 (ABDSP database). The only one in the desert during the atlas period was in the developed area of Ram's Hill, Borrego Springs (H25), 20 April 2000 (R. Halford).

Winter: In spite of the Band-tailed Pigeon's nomadism, the distribution we observed in winter was closely similar to that in spring and summer. Our maximum numbers in winter were somewhat larger, up to 175 coming to bait set out for turkeys in Green Valley, Cuyamaca Rancho State Park (N21), 25 February 1998 (P. D. Jorgensen). At low elevations in northwestern San Diego the pigeons occurred in almost exactly the same areas in winter as in summer, with an exceptional high count of 92 near Ross Lake (B7) 2 January 2002 (K. L. Weaver). The situation with the isolated population in the Lyons Peak region was parallel, with a maximum count of 11 between Lyons and Lee valleys (S16) 17 January 2000 (J. R. Barth).

From 1997 to 2002 we had four winter records of vagrants well outside the known breeding range, with five at the Vineyard golf course (K11) 1 December 1998 (E. C. Hall). Right along the coast the Band-tailed Pigeon is generally less frequent in winter than at other seasons, but the winter of 1989–90 broke this pattern. That year the species was reported widely, with up to 170, by far the largest flock of coastal vagrants reported, in Los Peñasquitos Canyon (N8) 18 January 1990 (B. Zepf, AB 44:329, 1990).

Conservation: Over California as a whole, the Band-tailed Pigeon was decimated by overhunting early in the 20th century (Grinnell 1913). In San Diego County the reduction may have been milder, as local naturalists were largely silent on this topic. Subsequent protection led to at least a partial recovery. Current trends are unclear because of the species' inherent irregularity and the difficulty of devising survey methods applicable over diverse habitats (Keppie and Braun 2000). The pigeon's biology entails relying on one food that is abundant at one season, then shifting to another food abundant at another season. If one link in this seasonal chain is broken, the pigeons could suffer even though the other links remain intact.

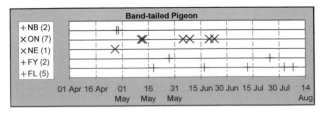

For example, if development around the base of Palomar Mountain removes a substantial fraction of the elderberry trees, the carrying capacity of the entire Palomar range could be affected.

Taxonomy: Band-tailed Pigeons along the Pacific coast are *P. f. monilis* (Vigors, 1839), darker than the other subspecies in the United States and Mexico. It breeds from the Pacific Northwest south to San Diego County, apparently reaching northern Baja California as a nonbreeding visitor only.

Eurasian Collared Dove *Streptopelia decaocto*

Introduced from the Old World to the Bahamas, the Collared Dove spread to Florida then across the entire width of North America in less than 20 years (Romagosa and McEneaney 1999). There have also been independent releases in the United States, establishing local populations, such as one in southern California in Ventura County in the early 1990s (Cole and McCaskie 2004). Sightings in San Diego County are likely the results of birds arriving from the east, as the number in Calipatria, Imperial County, had built to over 50 by 2003.

Photo by Kenneth Z. Kurland

Migration: The first Collared Dove in San Diego County was one at Marina View Park, Chula Vista (U10), 29 May 2002 (G. McCaskie). Subsequently, up to two were at the Roadrunner Club, Borrego Springs (F24), from 12 April 2003 onward (M. B. Mulrooney), and one was in the Mission Hills area of San Diego (R8/R9) 28 September 2003 (D. Dobson). Colonization is inevitable; the Collared Dove is an urban bird.

Spotted Dove *Streptopelia chinensis*

When a plant or animal is released in a place where it is not native, often it dies out quickly because the new environment does not meet its needs. Sometimes, in the lack of its usual predators or other mechanisms of population control, it proliferates, becoming a pest or upsetting an ecological balance. And there are paths between these extremes, as exemplified by the Spotted Dove. Introduced from Asia to Los Angeles about 1915, the Spotted Dove multiplied and spread, arrived in San Diego County by 1950, and established itself here as an uncommon and local resident. But in the 1980s and 1990s it decreased, and with the turn of the century it died out completely.

Photo by Anthony Mercieca

Breeding distribution: From 1997 to 2001, in spring and summer, we found the Spotted Doves at only two sites in San Diego County. Though Encanto (S11) and Spring Valley (R12/S12) were long the center for the species in metropolitan San Diego, our only sighting in this area was of a single bird singing in Encanto 21 June 1997 (P. Unitt). In the north county, the only area where the Spotted Dove persisted into the atlas period was Rainbow (C9), where our single record during the breeding season was of two on 19 April 1999 (D. C. Seals).

Nesting: The Spotted Dove's nesting habits are similar to those of other doves, with a flimsy nest and some breeding year round (Garrett and Walker 2001). Nesting in San Diego County was never well described.

Winter: We noted the Spotted Dove at Rainbow in winter as well as in spring with three on 28 January 1999 (D. C. Seals) and one on 18 February 2000 (K. L. Weaver). Our two other sightings in fall and winter, of one at Imperial Beach (V10) 2 November 1998 (P. Unitt) and one at O'Neill Lake (E6) 18 December 1998 (P. A. Ginsburg), represented wandering individuals rather than resident populations.

Conservation: The Spotted Dove was first reported in San Diego County on the Oceanside Christmas bird count 30 December 1950, when four were noted. The species first appeared on the San Diego count 26 December 1954. Sams and Stott (1959) reported it from Spring Valley, the Oceanside area, and Balboa Park, "among other

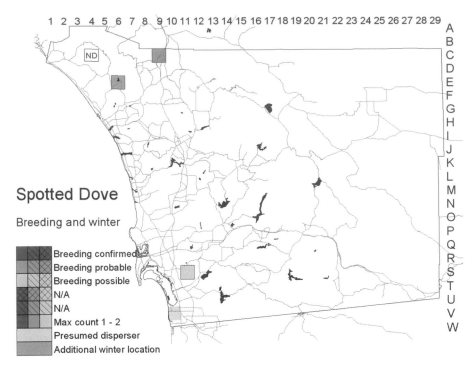

Spotted Dove

Breeding and winter

- Breeding confirmed
- Breeding probable
- Breeding possible
- N/A
- N/A
- Max count 1 - 2
- Presumed disperser
- Additional winter location

residents of Spring Valley called the San Diego Natural History Museum to inquire about the birds' disappearance. The last record on any Christmas bird count was of two on the San Diego count 16 December 1995. It seems certain that the five-year atlas period, 1997–2002, saw the extirpation of the county's resident population; if any more are seen, they are likely to be rare dispersers only.

The Spotted Dove's reversal of fortune is not confined to San Diego County but has been noted widely in southern California (McClure 1992, Garrett and Walker 2001). The reasons for the decline are unclear. Garrett and Walker (2001) suggested predation by the increasing population of American Crows and increased density of urban development as contributing factors. The areas the doves colonized in San Diego County longest were of relatively low-density development or dominated by agriculture, but the birds have disappeared whether the land use has changed or not. The story of the Spotted Dove in California parallels that of some other birds like the Varied Tit (*Parus varius*) in Hawaii or the Crested Mynah (*Acridotheres cristatellus*) on Vancouver Island, introduced populations that thrived for decades but ultimately failed.

Taxonomy: Nominate *S. c. chinensis* was the subspecies of the Spotted Dove introduced to southern California.

places." In San Diego County the Spotted Dove was always uncommon and local, never approaching the abundance it reached in metropolitan Los Angeles. All five county specimens in the San Diego Natural History Museum are from East San Diego or Spring Valley. Outside the coastal lowland the only reports are three from Borrego Springs (F24/G24), the last of six on 22 October 1996 (E. Jorgensen), and of one on the Lake Henshaw Christmas bird count 16 December 1991. Numbers on the San Diego Christmas bird count peaked at 9 on 29 December 1957; numbers on the Oceanside count peaked at 27 on 31 December 1977. By 1980, however, the species was declining. Marjorie and Don Hastings last noted it at their home in Spring Valley (R12) in 1989, and about that time other

White-winged Dove *Zenaida asiatica*

The White-winged Dove is a characteristic bird of the desert Southwest, at the edge of its range in eastern San Diego County. In the Anza–Borrego Desert it is common at oases and human settlements. Its numbers are on the increase, as part of a pattern that reaches from California to Florida. Formerly a summer visitor only to California, the dove is losing its habit of migration, establishing itself year round first in San Diego County and increasingly elsewhere in the Colorado Desert.

Breeding distribution: The White-winged Dove is found in all the developed areas of the Anza–Borrego Desert and at almost all of the oases, extending up canyons on the mountains' east slope occasionally as far west as Banner (K21; six on 17 May 1999, P. K. Nelson). The largest numbers are at the oases of the southern half of the desert, with up to 150 at Vallecito County Park (M25) 16

Photo by Anthony Mercieca

May 2001 and 120 at Carrizo Marsh (O29) 11 May 2001 (M. C. Jorgensen). The grapefruit orchards at the north end of the Borrego Valley (E24) are the area of the next largest concentrations, with up to 50 on 11 June 2001 (P. D. Jorgensen).

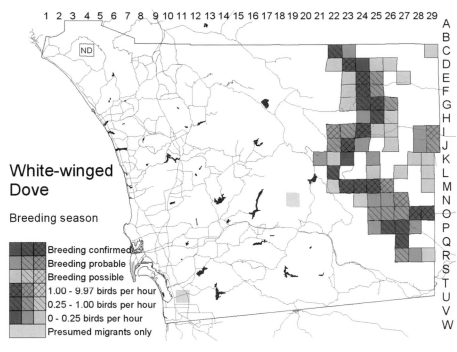

White-winged
Dove

Breeding season

Breeding confirmed
Breeding probable
Breeding possible
1.00 - 9.97 birds per hour
0.25 - 1.00 birds per hour
0 - 0.25 birds per hour
Presumed migrants only

were willow (twice), mesquite, palo verde, and California fan palm. The birds may nest colonially or as scattered pairs.

The White-winged Dove is noted for its midsummer nesting even in the hottest climate, as along the lower Colorado River (Rosenberg et al. 1991). In the Anza–Borrego Desert, where many White-winged Doves stay through the winter, the birds can start earlier, as they do in urban settings in Texas (Hayslette and Hayslette 1999). Our observations from 1997 to 2001 indicate that in San Diego County the doves lay from the beginning of April to early June. A notable exception was in the wet winter of 1998, when one was building a nest at Tamarisk Grove (I24) 27 January (P. K. Nelson)

In Arizona, White-winged Doves feed heavily on the nectar and fruit of the saguaro and may be able to meet their need for water from these sources. In the Anza–Borrego Desert, where there are no native saguaros, the doves probably must drink free water daily. The distance to which they will commute to water is not known precisely but may be at least 2 miles, about the distance to water from a nest along Carrizo Wash (O28) 31 May 2001 (P. D. Jorgensen). On rare occasions it may be farther, as suggested by one singing in Fish Creek Wash (M29) 1 May 2001 (J. R. Barth).

Nesting: The White-winged builds a typical dove nest, a flimsy platform of sticks, usually on a large branch or in the fork of a trunk. Nest sites atlas observers described

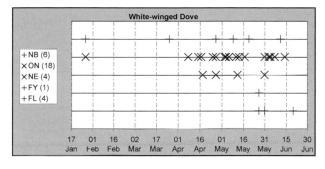

Migration: In the Salton Sink, where at the beginning of the new millennium it was just starting to winter regularly, the White-winged Dove arrives mainly in April and departs mainly in August (Patten et al. 2003). Evidently some in the Anza–Borrego Desert still follow this schedule because the species is more widespread there in summer than in winter. Small numbers of stray migrants reach the coastal slope regularly in fall, less frequently in spring. At least 40 such migrants have been reported in spring, most frequently from Point Loma (S7), on dates ranging from 30 April (Point Loma, R. E. Webster, AB 36: 894, 1982) to 6 June (1966, Tijuana River valley, AFN 20:600, 1966). During the atlas period, at least one was at Point Loma 12–23 May 2001 (D. K. Adams) and one was at Chula Vista (U11) 4 May 2001 (A. Mercieca). Coastal migrants are considerably more frequent

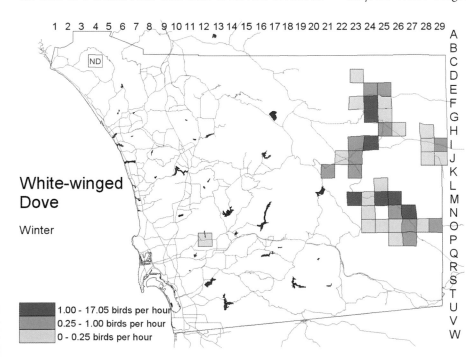

White-winged
Dove

Winter

1.00 - 17.05 birds per hour
0.25 - 1.00 birds per hour
0 - 0.25 birds per hour

in fall than in spring, occurring annually with as many as 22 in 1982 (AB 37:224, 1983). A few are seen as they cross the mountains, such as one in Sherilton Valley (N19) 23 August–4 September 1999 (G. and R. Wynn) and one flying west over the Laguna Summit along Interstate 8 (Q22) 16 August 1986 (P. Unitt). Late August to mid September is the peak period for coastal White-winged Doves, but the species has been noted in the Tijuana River valley 3 July 1995 (B. Foster, NASFN 49:982, 1995) and at Point Loma 12 July 1985 (R. E. Webster), and occasional stragglers occur through the fall.

Winter: The White-winged Dove is more concentrated in the major oases and developed areas in winter than in summer. At some places the doves are as abundant in winter as in summer. But at others they are absent in winter. At Angelina Spring (I22), for example, where P. K. Nelson found the birds regularly in the breeding season, with up to 20 per day, he found none in winter. White-winged Doves are especially numerous at Agua Caliente Springs (M26), with up to 150 on 26 February 2000 (E. C. Hall); many winter also in Borrego Springs (up to 141 throughout the valley 19 December 1999, Christmas bird count)

Winter visitors to the coastal lowland are rare, now averaging fewer than one per year. From 1997 to 2002 there was only one, at Santee (P12) 7 January 2001 (S. D. Cameron).

Conservation: The White-winged Dove spread north and west into southeastern California as the Colorado River and Imperial valleys were converted to agriculture in the early 20th century (Rosenberg et al. 1991, Patten et al. 2003). It was first reported from the Anza–Borrego Desert at Yaqui Well (I24) in July 1946 (Krutzsch and Dixon 1947), and it was first reported wintering in 1956, with one at Agua Caliente Springs 4 January (AFN 10:282, 1956). By 1984 the largest number reported at any season was only 20 and the species was still uncommon (Unitt 1984). Numbers on the Anza–Borrego Christmas bird count increased abruptly beginning in 1991. During its first seven years, 1984–90, the count averaged 2.6; from 1997 to 2001 it averaged 87. Although the creation of new habitat in the form of farms and cities is probably responsible for the White-winged Dove's northward spread, the colonists use natural habitat as well as artificial, as can be seen at the Anza–Borrego Desert's oases.

Curiously, the number wintering in the San Diego area has peaked and declined. From 1965 to 1971 the White-winged Dove was found almost annually on the San Diego Christmas bird count with an average of 1.7. Yet none has been found on any Christmas count on the coastal slope since 1992. Perhaps the change is the result of the population in the Anza–Borrego Desert becoming more sedentary.

Taxonomy: Only the large, pale subspecies *Z. a mearnsi* Ridgway, 1915, occurs in California.

Mourning Dove *Zenaida macroura*

One of our most familiar birds, the Mourning Dove is common over most of San Diego County year round. The doves benefited from the arrival of western civilization; they are now more abundant in agricultural areas and suburbs than in native woodland or scrub. But they are found in all of the county's habitats from the coastal strand to open montane coniferous woodland to the desert floor.

Breeding distribution: The Mourning Dove is tied with the House Finch for the title of San Diego County's most widespread bird. Both species were missed in just two covered atlas squares; we failed to find the Mourning Dove only in two of the least-vegetated parts of the Anza–Borrego Desert. The dove is most abundant in the coastal lowland, especially in urban and agricultural areas, in Warner Valley (G19; up to 300 on 25 June 2000, P. Unitt), and at oases and in developed areas of the Anza–Borrego Desert (up to 250 in the orchard-planted region of the Borrego Valley, E24, 8 June 2001, P. D. Jorgensen). It is least abundant in the coniferous woodland of San Diego County's higher mountains and in the drier regions of the Anza–Borrego Desert. The Mourning Dove needs to drink regularly, but evidently almost all of the Anza–Borrego Desert is within the distance the birds can commute to water daily. A nest with nestlings along Fish Creek Wash (L27) 13 April 2000, for example, was miles from the nearest known spring (M. B. Mulrooney).

Photo by Anthony Mercieca

Nesting: Mourning Doves nest in situations as diverse as their habitats, but most nests are in trees or large shrubs. Because the nest is so flimsy the birds often build it on the thicker branches. This preference for firm supports also leads the doves to use man-made sites like building eaves, bridge girders, and hanging flower baskets. Nests on the ground are fairly common, too, accounting for about 18% of all Mourning Dove nests atlas observers described (ground nests may have been commented on disproportionately often). Some ground nests were somewhat protected by being built under cacti or thistles, but others did not have even this defense.

One key to the Mourning Dove's success is that in spite of laying only two eggs per clutch, it has a short nest-

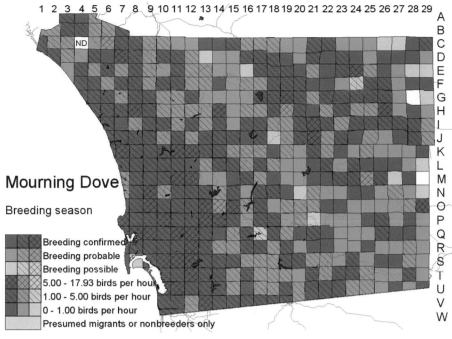

Mourning Dove

Breeding season

- Breeding confirmed
- Breeding probable
- Breeding possible
- 5.00 - 17.93 birds per hour
- 1.00 - 5.00 birds per hour
- 0 - 1.00 birds per hour
- Presumed migrants or nonbreeders only

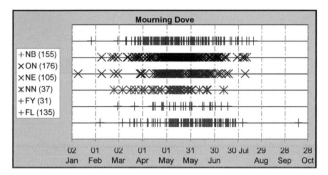

Mourning Dove

+NB (155)
×ON (176)
×NE (105)
✳NN (37)
+FY (31)
+FL (135)

02 Jan 01 Feb 02 Mar 01 Apr 01 May 31 May 30 Jun 30 Jul 29 Aug 28 Sep 28 Oct

ing cycle, long nesting season, and nests repeatedly in a single year. Most nesting takes place from March to July, but activity outside this interval is not rare. In residential

areas of San Diego, we noted a nest with eggs as early as 10 January 1998 and a recent fledgling on 7 February 2001, implying egg laying in early January. In late summer and fall, we noted nest building as late as 19 August 2000 and a fledgling as late as 16 October 1999, implying egg laying in early September. Sharp (1907) found eggs at Escondido as late as 2 September. In natural habitats the dove's season is less extended, but in the wet spring of 1998 the birds began nesting in the Anza–Borrego Desert in the last week of February, when the earliest desert report was of an occupied nest near the Borrego Air Ranch (H26) 22 February (M. L. Gabel).

Migration: The Mourning Dove is highly migratory; the large flocks seen in winter may consist largely of winter visitors from the north. A few may be seen out of sight of land on almost every pelagic trip off San Diego in May and September. Birds banded at San Diego 3 January 1929 and 11 March 1929 were recovered at Boise, Idaho, 7 September 1929 and at Reno, Nevada, 10 September 1929, respectively (Lincoln 1936).

Winter: In the coastal lowland and inland valleys, the Mourning Dove is even more abundant in winter than in spring and early summer. Wintering birds often gather into large flocks, up to 600 along Dulzura Creek (T15) 5 February 1999 (D. W. Povey). At higher elevations, however, the dove is less common. In extensive chaparral, montane woodland, and sparse desert scrub the dove is rare to absent in winter, even where it is fairly common in spring and summer.

Conservation: Though the Mourning Dove's population in the western United States has declined since the 1960s (Dolton 1993), in San Diego County the trend is likely flat to positive. With their buildings and trees, developed areas offer more nest sites than the natural scrub and chaparral they replace. The importation of water favors a bird that must drink. San Diego County Christmas bird counts show no clear trend.

Taxonomy: The pale *Z. m. marginella* Woodhouse, 1852, is the only subspecies of the Mourning Dove occurring in California.

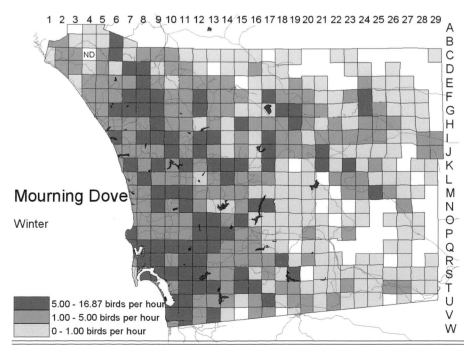

Mourning Dove

Winter

- 5.00 - 16.87 birds per hour
- 1.00 - 5.00 birds per hour
- 0 - 1.00 birds per hour

Inca Dove *Columbina inca*

The history of the Inca Dove has been one of slow, steady spread to the northwest. The dove reached Tucson by 1872, Yuma by 1942, and the Imperial Valley by 1984. In San Diego County only a few pioneers have been noted yet, but colonization of the Anza–Borrego Desert at least is only a matter of time. In California, the Inca Dove is a commensal of man, living only in towns or rural ranchyards.

Migration: The Inca Dove is still known in San Diego from about eight records. The reason for the "about" is that some individuals may have been escapees from captivity rather than pioneers of the wild population. This was evidently the case with the single specimen from San Diego County, a bird wearing an unmarked anodized aluminum band, found dead in East San Diego (R10) 13 March 1994 (SDNHM 48791). The first individual seen in the county, in the Tijuana River valley 9 September–30 November 1974 (AB 29:122, 1975), preceded the range's growth front so much that Garrett and Dunn (1981) raised the possibility of the bird's being an escapee. A natural origin seems almost certain for the records for the Anza–Borrego Desert, of one in Borrego Springs (G24) 16 February–April 1992 (A. G. Morley, AB 46:315,

Photo by Anthony Mercieca

481, 1992), another nearby 22 December 1996 (P. D. Ache, NASFN 51:802, 1997), one at Butterfield Ranch (M23) 18 February–24 April 2000 (M. B. Mulrooney, NAB 54:221, 327, 2000), and two at the Roadrunner Club, Borrego Springs (F24), 20 June 2000 (M. L. Gabel). Records from the coastal slope are of one photographed in Spring Valley (R12) 3 February–12 May 1997 (M. and D. Hastings), one singing and photographed in the Hillcrest area of San Diego (R9) 1–9 June 2001 (J. W. Schlotte, P. Unitt, NAB 55:483, 2001), and one in Encinitas (K7) 22 July 2001 (L. E. and C. Taylor, NAB 55:483, 2001).

Common Ground-Dove *Columbina passerina*

In spite of urban sprawl, agriculture remains important in San Diego County. Orchards, nurseries, and rural ranchettes are the Common Ground-Dove's principal habitat here. Indeed, agriculture is doubtless responsible for the dove's colonization of San Diego County, which began in the 1950s. Currently, the ground-dove is common and increasing in the Anza–Borrego Desert, mainly in the Borrego Valley, and uncommon and more or less static on the coastal slope, mainly in the inland valleys of the north county.

Breeding distribution: In San Diego County, the Common Ground-Dove is most widespread in the region of northwestern San Diego County dominated by avocado and citrus orchards. In this region it uses riparian woodland as well as artificial habitats. During spring and summer we encountered up to 10 per day in this area, as along the San Luis Rey River between Rice Canyon and Pala (D10) 10 June 2000 (K. Aldern, M. Bache) and at Valley Center (G11) in April 1997 (V. Dineen). One was at Buena Vista Lagoon (H6) 26 May 1997 (D. Rorick), but otherwise records at this season are at least 7 miles inland and below 1500 feet elevation. In southwestern San Diego County the only site where the ground-dove is currently resident year round is Rios Canyon just east of Lakeside (P15), an area of avocado orchards (nine on 11 May 2001, C. G. Edwards).

In the Anza–Borrego Desert, the ground-dove is concentrated in the Borrego Valley, in both the area of grapefruit orchards in the north end of the valley (E24; up

Photo by Anthony Mercieca

to 20 on 18 April 1998, P. K. Nelson) and in the residential areas of Borrego Springs (G24; up to 15 on 30 April 1997, P. D. Ache). It is evidently a permanent resident also in the mesquite thicket at Vallecito (M25), with up to five on 12 May 1999 (M. C. Jorgensen). Elsewhere in the Anza–Borrego Desert the ground-dove is irregular and not confirmed breeding, though this is possible, as the birds have been heard singing and seen in pairs, as at Yaqui Well and Tamarisk Grove (I24) 21 May 1998 (P. K. Nelson).

Nesting: Like other doves, the Common Ground-Dove builds only a minimal platform of twigs. Nest sites atlas observers described were in a palo verde, a tamarisk, a California fan palm, on an eave of a house, and inside a greenhouse. In the last, the eggs hatched on 25 July 1999, in spite of daily high temperatures in the shade at the nest ranging from 115 to 130° F, 10–20 degrees hotter than outside the greenhouse (P. D. Jorgensen).

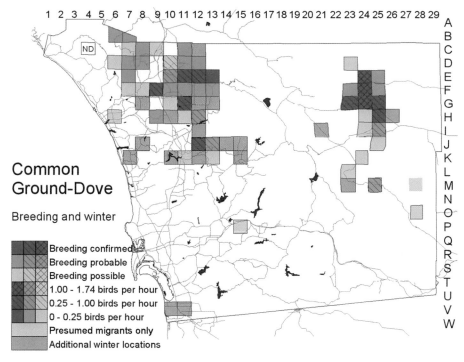

Common Ground-Dove

Breeding and winter

- Breeding confirmed
- Breeding probable
- Breeding possible
- 1.00 - 1.74 birds per hour
- 0.25 - 1.00 birds per hour
- 0 - 0.25 birds per hour
- Presumed migrants only
- Additional winter locations

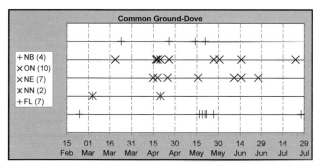

over seeds from old gourds in a gourd farm. Other counts on the coastal slope are of 12 or fewer.

The ground-dove is nonmigratory but disperses somewhat when not breeding, accounting for records a short distance from sites of residency, such as one near San Marcos Creek and Questhaven Road (J8) 2 December 1998 (J. O. Zimmer), one at Ramona (K15) 30 December 2000 (D. and C. Batzler), and two in San Felipe Valley (I21) 27 December 1999 (W. E. Haas). The ground-dove was seen repeatedly in winter in Pamo Valley (J15), with up to seven on 2 January 1999 (I. S. Quon); it is probably resident here and just missed during the breeding season. The small population in Rios Canyon (P15) was found in winter as well as spring, with six on 28 January 2001 (C. G. Edwards).

Though formerly breeding fairly commonly in the Tijuana River valley (V10/V11), currently the ground-dove reaches that area only irregularly in fall and winter, presumably by dispersing north across the international border. The maximum reported there in winter during the atlas period was only four on 20 December 1997 (G. L. Rogers).

The Common Ground-Dove has an unusually long breeding season, nesting repeatedly even if successful. Most nesting in San Diego County takes place from March through June, but a nest with nestlings in Borrego Springs (G24) 4 March 1997 (R. Thériault) and a fledgling on Hellhole Bajada (G23) 24 February 1999 (M. L. Gabel) translate to egg laying in mid February and late January, respectively. Even in the Anza–Borrego Desert the doves lay as late as the first half of July, as shown by a juvenile that fledged in Borrego Springs 27 July 1999 (R. Thériault) and the eggs that hatched in the greenhouse 25 July 1999. Morley (1959) reported ground-doves nesting in the Tijuana River valley as late as 2 October 1958, with one nest with eggs and another with young on that date.

Winter: The Common Ground-Dove gathers into small flocks when not breeding, probably accounting for reported numbers in winter being greater than those in spring and summer. The Anza–Borrego Christmas bird count has yielded up to 339 in the Borrego Valley on 16 December 2001, and the highest count in a single atlas square was 76 in Borrego Springs (F24) 19 December 1999 (P. K. Nelson et al.). On the coastal slope, the highest winter count by far was of 36 at De Luz (B6) 31 January 1998 (K. L. Weaver), where the birds were feeding on left-

Conservation: Before 1957, the Common Ground-Dove was known in San Diego County only from five specimens, collected at San Pasqual "about 1900" (Willett 1912), 3 miles north of Escondido 29 June 1915 (Dixon 1916), in Mission Valley 10 November 1915 (Grey 1916, SDNHM 1887), at Lakeside 21 December 1923 (SDNHM 2846), and at Santee 28 February 1939 (SDNHM 18051). In 1957 the birds were discovered in the Tijuana River valley and confirmed nesting there the following year (Morley 1959, Sams 1959). The ground-dove apparently colonized northwestern San Diego County beginning in 1962; this was the first year it was recorded on the Oceanside Christmas bird count and noted at Pauma Valley by Eleanor Beemer, who observed birds there since the mid 1930s. In the Anza–Borrego Desert the first observation was in 1964 and the first recorded nest in 1972 (ABDSP database). Numbers in the Borrego Valley have increased steadily since—from 1984 to 1988 the average on the Anza–Borrego Christmas bird count was 60, whereas from 1997 to 2001 it was 217.

In the Tijuana River valley, however, the breeding population died out in 1984 after having persisted continuously since 1957. Presumably this change was the result of the steady encroachment of urbanization on both sides of the border, leaving the valley as a shrinking enclave of open space. Even though the ground-dove is a bird of modified habitats in southern California, it requires extensive open ground for foraging. It does not tolerate high-intensity development in which the earth is scraped, paved, and landscaped. The scenario in the Tijuana River valley warns that the ground-dove could be eliminated from northwestern San Diego County too, as agriculture gives way to urban sprawl. Conservation of riparian woodland benefits the ground-dove, too. Along the Santa Margarita River north of Fallbrook, the ground-

dove population crashed in 1993, when floods washed away mature trees (K. L. Weaver).

Taxonomy: Common Ground-Doves in southern California are *C. p. pallescens* (Baird, 1860), as its name states a subspecies paler than others occurring farther east and south.

Ruddy Ground-Dove *Columbina talpacoti*

The Ruddy Ground-Dove is following in the footsteps of its relatives the Common Ground-Dove and Inca Dove, spreading north out of Mexico to colonize the southwestern United States. Since the first in 1984, the California Bird Records Committee has archived close to 100 occurrences in the state, with up to ten individuals at a time in Death Valley, a site of probable nesting. The species was confirmed nesting for the first time in California in the Imperial Valley in 2003 (McCaskie 2003). In San Diego County there are six accepted records.

Migration: Five of the San Diego County Ruddy Ground-Dove reports accepted by the California Bird Records Committee are from the Tijuana River valley in fall: one from 12 to 20 October 1988, up to two from 14 to 31 October 1989 (G. McCaskie, K. A. Radamaker; Patten and Erickson 1994), one on 8 September 1990 (G. McCaskie, Heindel and Garrett 1995), one on 23 October 1992 (Heindel and Patten 1996), and one on 18 October 1997 (G. McCaskie, T. R. Clawson, Rottenborn and Morlan 2000). The only spring record is of one photographed at

Photo by Anthony Mercieca

Santee (P12) 16 May 1999 (M. B. Mulrooney, Rogers and Jaramillo 2002). A few other reports were rejected or not submitted.

As with almost every bird originating from mainland Mexico, there is a possibility that some of these Ruddy Ground-Doves were escapees from captivity. But the species' surge north and west—even across the Gulf of California—is so well established that some of the San Diego County records must be part of this pattern.

PARROTS — FAMILY PSITTACIDAE

Red-crowned Parrot *Amazona viridigenalis*

The Red-crowned is by far the most numerous parrot naturalized in California and the only one considered thoroughly established by the California Bird Records Committee. The population in the Los Angeles region is well over 1500 (K. L. Garrett and K. T. Mabb); that in San Diego County, at least several hundred. The species has a rather small natural range confined to northeastern Mexico, where its numbers have been seriously depleted by both deforestation and trapping for the cage-bird trade.

Breeding distribution: The Red-crowned Parrot has two centers in San Diego County, Ocean Beach/Point Loma and El Cajon. The Point Loma population is the larger, with up to about 360 roosting together near Point Loma High School (R8) 31 January 1998 (J. A. Martin). The birds have been nesting in this area at least since 1997 (injured fledgling picked up in Ocean Beach, R7, 3 July, B. Kenk). In El Cajon (Q13), the parrots concentrate between First Street on the west, Second Street

Photo by Kenneth W. Fink

on the east, Broadway on the north, and Interstate 8 on the south. Our highest count there was 80, including fledglings being fed by adults, 17 September 1997 (D. C. Seals). From these centers the parrots scatter widely over San Diego and probably nest in other places, such as La

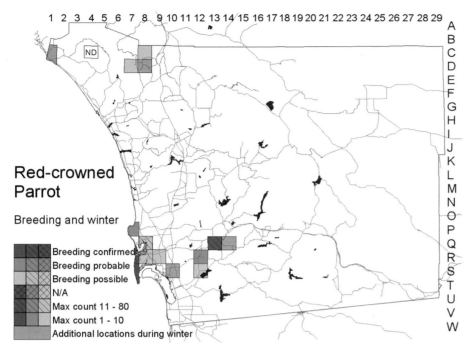

Red-crowned Parrot

Breeding and winter

- Breeding confirmed
- Breeding probable
- Breeding possible
- N/A
- Max count 11 - 80
- Max count 1 - 10
- Additional locations during winter

few. Young fallen prematurely out of nests have been found in April and on 25 June; fledglings still dependent on their parents have been seen from 3 July to 17 September.

Migration: Since 1998 J. A. Martin has found the Red-crowned Parrot conspicuous in Ocean Beach from early March to about late August and only sporadic from August to February. In winter perhaps the entire Ocean Beach population clumps into a single flock, as suggested by the numbers at Point Loma High School 31 January 1998. Around El Cajon the birds move considerably as well, taking advantage of the pecan and walnut trees planted commonly in that area (D. C. Seals).

Jolla (P7; copulation noted 17 April 1999; six, including a juvenile, on 11 July 1999, M. G. Mathos). Our only sightings outside of metropolitan San Diego were one of two birds at San Onofre (C1; M. Lesinsky) and three of single birds around Fallbrook (C8/D7/D8; K. L. Weaver, M. Freda). As yet the Red-crowned Parrot is breeding only in densely developed residential areas and not invading rural areas or orchards. Apparently the Red-crowned Parrot's establishment in San Diego was independent of that in Los Angeles, and population exchange between the two cities is little or none. The Los Angeles population extends southeast to Tustin in central Orange County.

Nesting: In its native range, the Red-crowned Parrot nests in cavities in a variety of trees, the cavities being the result of natural decomposition or woodpecker excavation (Enkerlin-Hoeflich and Hogan 1997). In the San Gabriel Valley of Los Angeles County, the birds nest mainly in silver maple trees; pruning of the trees exposes heartwood that rots out and leaves a cavity (Mabb 1997). Data from San Diego County are few but suggest that palms are the principal nest site here (probable nest in a palm in Ocean Beach, V. P. Johnson; apparent nest holes in the sawed-off leaf bases of Canary Island date palms, J. A. Martin; nestling found under a palm at Point Loma, J. Colclough).

Data on the species' nesting schedule are likewise

Winter: In contrast to the situation at Ocean Beach, at El Cajon the Red-crowned Parrot remains in winter in the same numbers as in spring and summer, with up to 60 on 12 February 2001 (J. R. Barth).

Conservation: The cage-bird trade has been the principal factor driving down the numbers of the Red-crowned Parrot in its natural range. Poachers taking parrot chicks often cut down nest trees, and most of the range has been converted to cattle pasture (Enkerlin-Hoeflich and Hogan 1997). The decrease in Mexico combined with establishment and increase in southern California means that the latter area may now account for a significant fraction of the species' entire population. The Los Angeles population is reproducing vigorously (K. T. Mabb), but whether the San Diego population is self sustaining is uncertain. How much input continues as a result of escape and release from pet owners and smugglers is unknown.

Taxonomy: The Red-crowned Parrot is closely related to the Lilac-crowned Parrot, the counterpart of the Red-crowned in western Mexico. A few instances of probable hybridization are known in Los Angeles County (Mabb 1997). In San Diego County an apparent hybrid was picked up, injured by gunshot, in Ocean Beach 22 May 1999 (B. Kenk).

CUCKOOS — FAMILY CUCULIDAE

Yellow-billed Cuckoo *Coccyzus americanus*

In western North America, the Yellow-billed Cuckoo lives only in extensive stands of mature riparian woodland. On a statewide basis, the cuckoo is now the bird closest to extirpation from California, reflecting the decimation of its habitat. The California Department of Fish and Game has

listed it as endangered. In San Diego County the Yellow-billed Cuckoo is now only a rare and sporadic summer visitor, not known to have nested for decades.

Breeding distribution: Since 1980, the Yellow-billed Cuckoo has been encountered in San Diego County nine times, always in or near significant stands of riparian willows and cottonwoods. Along the Santa Margarita River, at the upper end of Ysidora Basin (F5), there was one 4–5 July 1984 (L. Salata, AB 38:1062, 1984) and another 7–11 July 2000 (D. Kisner, J. M. Wells). One was at Guajome Lake (G7) 11–12 June 1992 (F. R. Tainter, AB 46:1179, 1992). At the uppermost end of the basin of Lake Hodges (K11), up to three individuals were seen 14–22 July 1992 (J. Smith, AB 46:1179, 1992) and a single bird was seen 1–4 June 1997 (E. C. Hall, FN 51:1054, 1997). In the Tijuana River valley one was seen 18 August 1985 (J. Oldenettel, AB 40:159, 1986) and another, in Smuggler's Gulch (W10), 28 June 2001 (P. Howard, NAB 55:483, 2001). On the desert slope of the mountains, along San Felipe Creek 1 mile west-northwest of Scissors Crossing (J22), one was seen and heard 6–12 July 2001 (T. Gallion, P. D. Jorgensen, NAB 55:483, 2001) and again 12 July 2002 (P. D. Jorgensen, NAB 56:486, 2002)

Nesting: Using primarily willow twigs in southern California, the Yellow-billed Cuckoo builds a rather coarse nest, placing it in the outer branches of willow trees (Jay 1911, which see for photos of nests). The only dates of nesting reported from San Diego County are of a female with a brood patch collected at Escondido 30 June 1915 (Dixon 1916) and egg sets collected at Escondido 2 July 1932 and 3 July 1915 (Willett 1933).

Migration: Of all summer visitors to California, the Yellow-billed Cuckoo is the latest to arrive, seldom seen before the first of June. Before the population collapse, the cuckoos sometimes occurred earlier; at Pauma Valley (E12) E. Beemer noted one 4 May 1948, and in Los Angeles County Jay (1911) reported seeing one 5 May 1907 and finding newly hatched young 10 May 1901. But otherwise dates for the cuckoo in San Diego County range only from 1 June to 23 August (1969, one at Batiquitos Lagoon, J7, AFN 24:100a, 1970). There are only three or four records of migrants away from riparian woodland.

Conservation: The Yellow-billed Cuckoo was never common in San Diego County but was confirmed nesting at Escondido in 1915 and 1932 and at Bonita in 1932 (Dixon 1916, Willett 1933). Before 1980 it was reported also from possible breeding habitat at Pauma Valley, the San Luis Rey River near Bonsall (E. Beemer), 3 miles north of Vista (C. S. Wilson, AB 32:1209, 1978), Poway (Belding 1890), Sorrento Valley (Sams and Stott 1959), and the Tijuana River valley (von Bloeker 1931).

Photo by Anthony Mercieca

The collapse of Yellow-billed Cuckoo's population throughout the western United States was due primarily to the wholesale destruction of riparian woodland, which now covers only a few percent of its original extent. Spraying of pesticides in the 1950s was likely responsible for decimating the cuckoos in the remaining tracts of their habitat in coastal southern California (Gaines and Laymon 1984). Along the Colorado River, a possible source for repopulation of coastal southern California has been nearly eliminated. Most of the once vast forest of native willows and cottonwoods there was chopped down and bulldozed, then replaced with the exotic saltcedar, a process greatly accelerated by floods in the mid 1980s (Laymon and Halterman 1987, Rosenberg et al. 1991). Factors operating over a regional scale are driving the cuckoo to extirpation; it has declined even where habitat is stable or increasing. The cuckoo requires the largest stands of riparian woodland of any of California's riparian birds; in the Sacramento Valley, Gaines (1974) reported it absent from tracts covering less than 3 hectares, and far larger tracts may be necessary to sustain a viable population.

Taxonomy: The Yellow-billed Cuckoos of western North America are significantly larger than those of the East, but there appears to be too much overlap in measurements for the populations to be recognized as subspecies (Patten et al. 2003). In any case, the taxonomic question does not vitiate the urgency of conservation measures to save the Yellow-billed Cuckoo over a huge fraction of its natural range.

Greater Roadrunner *Geococcyx californianus*

An emblem of the deserts of America's Southwest, the Greater Roadrunner is an uncommon resident of San Diego County's Anza–Borrego Desert. It also occurs in sage scrub and open chaparral on the coastal slope but is retreating in the face of urban sprawl. As a large bird requiring a large territory, with a low capability for dispersal, the roadrunner copes poorly with habitat loss and fragmentation. It is disappearing rapidly from canyons surrounded by developed areas.

Breeding distribution: Roadrunners range through most of San Diego County in low density. On the coastal slope, they are most numerous in sage scrub with little development or scattered rural homes and agriculture only. Some higher counts are of four, including three calling males, in Las Pulgas Canyon (E4) 26 May 2001 (P. A. Ginsburg), five, all singing males, southeast of Fallbrook (D9) 19 May 1999 (E. C. Hall), and five in the eastern undeveloped part of the Wild Animal Park (J13) 3 June 1999 (D. and D. Bylin). The roadrunner also occurs in broken chaparral up to about 4000 feet elevation (pair in Scove Canyon, P22, 18 June 1997, P. Unitt).

In the better-vegetated parts of the Anza–Borrego Desert the roadrunner's numbers are similar to those in coastal sage scrub (up to five calling males in the Box Canyon area, L23, 26 April 1999, R. Lantz). In the badlands and sparsely vegetated sandy areas near the Imperial County line the roadrunner is scarce—in 10 atlas squares we noted used nests or tracks in the sand but never saw the birds themselves. In some areas, such as the Santa Rosa Mountains, Borrego Mountain, Ocotillo Badlands, and Split Mountain, our not finding even these traces may reflect the roadrunner's absence.

Nesting: The roadrunner's nest is a shallow dish about one foot across, built of coarse sticks. In the Anza–Borrego Desert the nests are built in various trees or shrubs; observers reported ocotillo, mesquite, palo verde, desert apricot, and the skirt of a fan palm as sites. On the coastal slope thickets of prickly pear, where we noted three nests, may be preferred for their ability to deter predators. But we also noted nests in some nonnative plants: tamarisk, Peruvian pepper, and eucalyptus.

In the wet spring of 1998 we noted nest building by roadrunners as early as 9 February and adults carrying food items as early as 20 March (near the Borrego Air Ranch, H26, M. L. Gabel). Sharp (1907) collected roadrunner eggs at Escondido as early as 14 February, and K.

Photo by Anthony Mercieca

L. Weaver found a nest with three eggs near Lake Hodges as early as 13 February in 1982. But both egg collections and our observations from 1997 to 2001 point to March through early June being the season for the roadrunner's egg laying in dry to average years.

Winter: Mated pairs of adult roadrunners maintain their territories year round, and the degree to which the young disperse is unknown (Hughes 1996). The winter distribution we observed did not differ appreciably from the breeding distribution, though we noted roadrunners twice in winter at elevations higher than we found them in the breeding season, with one about 4000 feet near Julian (K20) 1 December 1997 (E. C. Hall) and one at 4700 feet at Stonewall Mine (M20) 4 January 2000 (S. Jorgensen). Our highest winter count in a single atlas square was of nine in south Borrego Springs (G24) 19 December 1999 (P. D. Ache et al.).

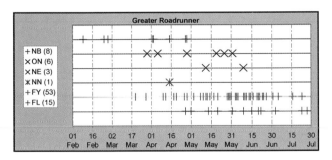

Conservation: The roadrunner adapts to low-intensity rural development that leaves much open ground. It appears to be more numerous in the town of Borrego Springs than in the surrounding undisturbed desert. But the style of urban development characteristic of coastal southern California, where the ground surface is covered completely with buildings, landscaping, and pavement, eliminates the roadrunner. The roadrunner's very name harks back to the days of the horse and buggy, when the birds could be seen commonly along San Diego's unpaved streets (Belding 1890, Stephens 1919a). Today, speeding traffic kills roadrunners regularly. The species' decline in metropolitan San Diego is evident from results of San Diego

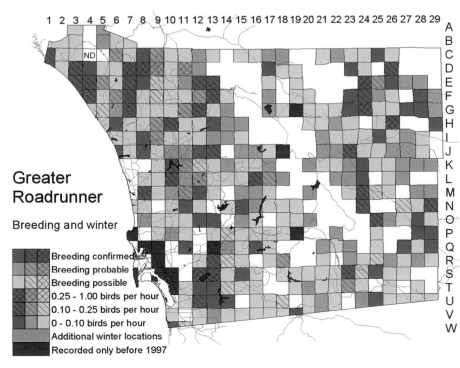

Greater
Roadrunner

Breeding and winter

Breeding confirmed
Breeding probable
Breeding possible
0.25 - 1.00 birds per hour
0.10 - 0.25 birds per hour
0 - 0.10 birds per hour
Additional winter locations
Recorded only before 1997

Christmas bird counts: from 1963 to 1972 the count's average was 8.2 roadrunners; from 1997 to 2001 it was only 1.8. At San Elijo Lagoon (L7) the roadrunner was in decline from 1973 to 1983 (King et al. 1987) and extirpated by 1997.

Soulé et al. (1988) and Crooks et al. (2001) identified the roadrunner as the most sensitive to habitat fragmentation among the eight scrub species they addressed. On the basis of surveys in 1997, Crooks et al. (2001) reported the roadrunner from only one (Sandmark Canyon, Q9) of 34 canyons isolated by urbanization in metropolitan San Diego. They projected that the roadrunner has a 95%

possibility of persisting for 100 years only in fragments of 157 hectares or larger. Even this, however, likely underestimates the roadrunner's sensitivity. Atlas observers did not report the species from any long-isolated canyon, only from recently isolated ones like Rice Canyon, Chula Vista (U11; most recent report, juvenile 24 July 2000, T. W. Dorman). The long-isolated native scrub of Point Loma (S7) and Tecolote Canyon (Q8/Q9) has been covered exhaustively, so the roadrunner's extirpation from those sites is certain—and suggests that isolated habitat of even 400 hectares is insufficient to sustain the birds indefinitely.

BARN OWLS — FAMILY TYTONIDAE

Barn Owl *Tyto alba*

An uncommon permanent resident through much of San Diego County, the Barn Owl is the county's most urban owl. It nests in buildings and among the bases of palm leaves more often than in cavities in native trees or on natural cliff ledges. Also, the owls readily use nest boxes designed for them. An increasing number of San Diegans are turning to the Barn Owl as an agent of natural rodent control, encouraging the owls by hanging these boxes in trees.

Breeding distribution: The Barn Owl is widespread on the coastal slope of San Diego County at low to moderate elevations, occurring in riparian and oak woodland as well as in any open area where trees, buildings, or other man-made structures offer secure sites for roosting and nesting. Its numbers are greatest in the inland valleys, with up to 12 in Poway (M12) 10 June and 15 July 1998 (P. von Hendy), and 10 at Wilderness Gardens (D11) 5 April 1997 (V. Dineen). The availability of suitable nest sites probably governs the species' numbers more than

Photo by Anthony Mercieca

the nature of the surrounding habitat, provided that there is ample open ground over which the owls can hunt.

In the higher mountains the Barn Owl is rare but recorded as high as around 5000 feet elevation near the upper end of the middle fork of Borrego Palm Canyon (E21; one on 18 June 1999, K. L. Weaver, C. R. Mahrdt) and about 4650 feet near Camp Hual-Cu-Cuish, Cuyamaca Mountains (M20; one on 2 July 2000, R. E. Webster). It is confirmed breeding as high as 3900 feet at Oakzanita Springs Campground (O20; fledgling on 2 September 1998 at nest site used regularly in previous years, D. W. Povey).

In the Anza–Borrego Desert the Barn Owl is uncommon, found mainly in the developed or agricultural areas of the Borrego Valley and at campgrounds elsewhere in the desert. It has been confirmed nesting only in the Borrego Valley and at Tamarisk Grove (I24; fledgling on 8 May 1988, A. G. Morley). It has never been found in the badlands, even though the deeply eroded can-

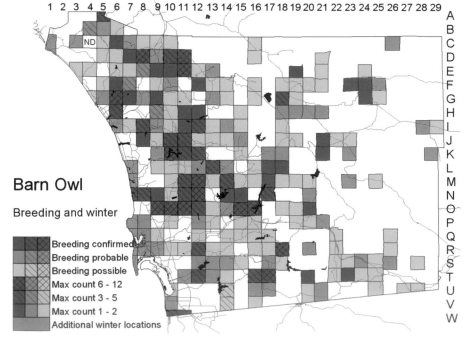

Barn Owl

Breeding and winter

- Breeding confirmed
- Breeding probable
- Breeding possible
- Max count 6 - 12
- Max count 3 - 5
- Max count 1 - 2
- Additional winter locations

yons in them offer many suitable nest sites similar to those the owls exploit on the coastal slope. In spite of being so partial to planted palms on the coastal slope, and even in Borrego Springs, the Barn Owl makes almost no use of native groves of the California fan palm in the Anza–Borrego Desert (only record is of three at Southwest Grove, Mountain Palm Springs, P27, 8 July 1993, P. D. Jorgensen). Perhaps there is too little prey in native desert habitats to support breeding Barn Owls, at least in dry to average years (1992–93 was unusually wet).

Nesting: Primitively, Barn Owls nested in San Diego County in tree cavities and crevices in sandstone bluffs; they still nest in these sites where available. Atlas observers reported three nests in large cavities in coast live oaks, one in a cottonwood. Road cuts now offer sites similar to those of natural bluffs, and in the exposed dirt the owls may dig their own burrows (Martin 1973). With palms so widely planted in San Diego County, both the skirts of fan palms and the crevices among the leaf bases of Canary Island date palms attract many Barn Owls. The bases of sawed-off palm leaves often break off in clumps, leaving sheltered niches in which the owls can nest. The species' habit of nesting in buildings, of course, is responsible for its name; any structure that offers a solid support below and shelter above will do. Besides barns, aircraft hangars at the Miramar Air Station (O9/O10), the Mission San Luis Rey (G6), and an air conditioner in a building at Fallbrook High School still under construction (D8) were reported as nest sites during the atlas period. The nest site atlas observers reported most frequently were nest boxes set out for the owls—the boxes have become popular as the Barn Owl's role as means of natural gopher control is more widely understood. They are now available commercially or can be built simply as a box with an opening at least 6 inches across, mounted on a post or hung in a tree.

The Barn Owl's breeding season is governed more by food supply than by the calendar. Following the wet winter of 1997–98, Barn Owls nested far later than in other years, with four fledglings on 14 August near the mouth of Beeler Canyon, Poway (N11; K. J. Winter), one on 2 September at Oakzanita Springs Campground (O20; D. W. Povey), and two on 10 November, one at the De Anza golf course, Borrego Springs (F24; R. Thériault), the

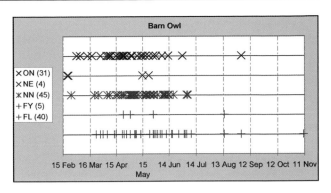

other at the Club Circle golf course, Borrego Springs (G24; B. Zuehl). In the other years of the study our observations imply the owls laid eggs from late December to late April. The Barn Owl is thus, along with Anna's Hummingbird, one of San Diego County's earliest nesting birds.

Winter: The Barn Owl is nonmigratory, and its breeding season extends over much of the winter. So the species' winter and breeding distributions are essentially the same; almost all variations are most likely due to chance. Winter counts ranged as high as 12 in Miramar Air Station (O11) 24 February 1999—already at nests with nestlings on this date (W. E. Haas). We did note the species twice in winter in the Anza–Borrego Desert far from likely breeding sites: one in an isolated tamarisk tree 3 miles north of Clark Dry Lake (C26) 29 December 2001 and another in the Elephant Tree Area (K29) 24 November 2000 (L. J. Hargrove).

Conservation: There is no good numerical basis for assessing trend in Barn Owl numbers in San Diego County, but the species has likely benefited from the clearing of scrub and erecting of structures that accompany low-intensity development. Though the species lives in cities, urbanization probably disfavors it; housing tracts offer few nest sites, and traffic takes a heavy toll on the Barn Owl.

Taxonomy: Over its cosmopolitan range the Barn Owl breaks into many subspecies, but only *T. a. pratincola* (Bonaparte, 1838) occurs on the mainland of North America.

TYPICAL OWLS — FAMILY STRIGIDAE

Flammulated Owl *Otus flammeolus*

The Flammulated Owl is widespread through the montane pine forests of the western United States but is only a rare and sporadic visitor to San Diego County's mountains. A few individuals have been seen and heard calling territorially, but there is no evidence any were mated and breeding, though some could have been. The Flammulated is only a summer visitor to California; it migrates to southern Mexico and Central America for the winter. There are three records in San Diego County of migrants near the coast.

Photo by Anthony Mercieca

Breeding distribution: Though the Flammulated Owl has never been found breeding in San Diego County, most records are from coniferous woodland in summer, where breeding is possible. In its core range, the Flammulated Owl inhabits open forests of ponderosa pine, habitat like that preferred by the Pygmy Nuthatch. In San Diego County, therefore, one might expect the species in the Laguna Mountains, dominated by the similar Jeffrey pine. However, the records are from Palomar, Hot Springs, and Cuyamaca mountains, though sometimes from open pine woodland. The Flammulated Owl has been found five times on Palomar Mountain, with two on 13 and 16 June 1971 (AB 25:907, 1971), two on 29 April 1972 (Winter 1974), one near the observatory (D15) 24 May–3 June 1981 (R. Higson), three along East Grade Road near Dyche Valley (F16) 14 May 1988 (K. L. Weaver, E. Littlefield), and another heard at 5100 feet elevation along Observatory Trail (D15) 19 July 2000 (K. L. Weaver). On Hot Springs Mountain, two were heard, one of which was seen, at 6000 feet elevation 1.8 miles

southeast of the summit (E21) 8 June 1985 (P. Unitt et al., AB 39:962, 1985), one was reported in June 1987 (J. O'Brien, AB 41:1488, 1987), and one was heard at 6200 feet elevation 0.25 mile east-southeast of the summit (E20) 2–3 June and 17 June 2000 (K. L. Weaver, C. R. Mahrdt). In the Cuyamaca Mountains the only report is of one within Cuyamaca Rancho State Park 27 April 1972 (Winter 1974).

Migration: Though the Flammulated Owl is highly migratory, it is rarely seen in migration. In San Diego County, one was captured on a ship in San Diego Bay 10 October 1962 (Banks 1964); unfortunately, the specimen is no longer extant. A specimen (SDNHM 41184) from "San Diego area" bears the information "died 21 Oct. 1971" and "found locally, fallen out of tree, injured leg; brought in to S. D. Zoo by Cal. Fish and Game." One was at photographed at Cabrillo National Monument, Point Loma (S7), 30–31 May 1991 (R. E. Webster, AB 45:496, 1991).

Western Screech-Owl *Megascops kennicottii*

The Western Screech-Owl is seldom seen without a special search, but it is a fairly common permanent resident in San Diego County's oak and coniferous woodlands. Its ideal habitat is a grove of mature coast live oaks with an ample supply of rotted-out cavities. The screech-owl is active only at night so is normally found by call, a series of 7 to 15 soft hoots that accelerates over about 2 seconds.

Breeding distribution: Because of spotty nocturnal effort, our results for the Western Screech-Owl are less complete than for those of most birds. But they show that the owl's distribution follows the pattern set by other birds of oak woodland. That is, the species ranges from the mountains

Photo by Anthony Mercieca

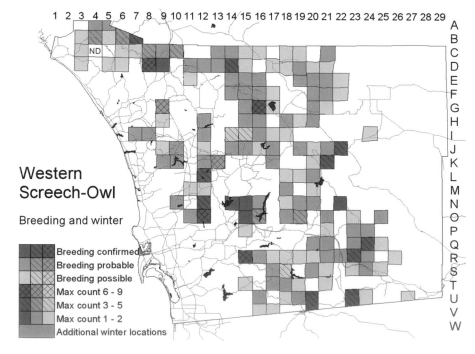

Western Screech-Owl

Breeding and winter

- Breeding confirmed
- Breeding probable
- Breeding possible
- Max count 6 - 9
- Max count 3 - 5
- Max count 1 - 2
- Additional winter locations

west toward the coast but does not touch the coast, approaching it toward the north and retreating inland ever farther toward the south. In Camp Pendleton we found the screech-owl about 3 miles from the coast along the south fork of San Onofre Creek (D3; one on 25 June 1999, D. C. Seals), whereas along the Mexican border our most coastal locality was 20 miles inland in Marron Valley (V16; one on 31 May 2000, D. C. Seals). Numbers are greatest in foothill canyons, with up to nine per night along the San Luis Rey River near the Forest Service picnic area (G16) 3 July 1999, in Bandy Canyon (K13) 6 May 2001, and in Sloan Canyon (R15) 5 May 1999 (all W. E. Haas). In conifer-dominated woodland in the higher mountains the screech-owl is widespread but less common.

On the east slope of the mountains the Western Screech-Owl extends beyond the oaks along Banner and San Felipe creeks as far as the riparian woodland at Scissors Crossing (J22; two adults with fledglings 4–5 July 2001, T. Gallion). At lower elevations in the Anza–Borrego Desert it is rare, probably irregular, and has never been confirmed breeding. There are few nest sites, though the birds might use the skirts of California fan palms (G. L. Rogers in Cannings and Angell 2001). From 1997 to 2001 our only record in this region was of one calling territorially at Yaqui Well (I24) 18 March 1998 (P. K. Nelson), and the only previous records in the breeding season are of five (one family?) in Hellhole Canyon (G23) 9 June 1973 (M. C. Jorgensen), one at Palm Spring (N27) 2 April 1978 (P. Unitt), and one at Lower Willows (D23) 30 April 1995 (L. Clark, C. Sankpill).

Nesting: The Western Screech-Owl nests in tree cavities, either the result of decay or excavated by the Northern Flicker—San Diego County's only woodpecker whose caliber equals the screech-owl's. The nests are difficult to locate; only two certain nests in natural sites came to light during the atlas study, both in coast live oaks. The owls also take readily to nest boxes designed to their needs. Almost all our confirmations of screech-owl breeding were sightings of fledglings. Dates of these ranged from 15 April (1999 at Banner, K21, P. K. Nelson) to 15 July (1999, Palomar Mountain State Park, D14, P. D. Jorgensen), translating to egg laying from mid February to about early May. The breeding season we observed from 1997 to 2001 was thus somewhat earlier than that reported previously, on the basis of egg sets collected from 1897 to 1939, which extend from 11 March to 31 May (Sharp 1907, Unitt 1984).

Migration: The Western Screech-Owl is nonmigratory, but the young disperse short distances. Such dispersal may be responsible for about 12 records for the Anza–Borrego Desert extending from 12 August (1992, one along Pinyon Mountain Road, K24/K25, R. Thériault) to 12 February (1990, one in Cougar Canyon, D23, D. Minock, ABSDP database).

Winter: The differences between the distribution we recorded in winter and that in spring and summer are probably due to sampling error only. Because males call most actively in winter, as they advertise their territories in preparation for breeding, the screech-owl is noted in largest numbers at this season, up to 16 near De Luz (B6) 25 January 1998 and 11 in Corte Madera Valley (R21) 20 February 1999 (both W. E. Haas).

Conservation: No changes in the Western Screech-Owl's abundance in San Diego County have been reported; if any, they have been slight. Egg sets collected in 1916 and 1923, respectively, in Rose Canyon (P8) and Oceanside (H5), outside the range where we found the species 1997–2002, suggest retreat from urbanization. Like other nocturnal birds, screech-owls are especially susceptible to being struck by moving vehicles. Human population growth brings increased road traffic to the foothills where screech-owls are concentrated, but the owls still survive in good numbers in the canyon of the upper San Luis Rey River along Highway 76, where traffic is heavy and growing. Extended droughts disfavor the screech-owl, like most other birds; Hardy et al. (1999) reported a 70% decline in southwestern Arizona over three years of drought.

Taxonomy: Marshall (1967) reported Western Screech-Owls from San Diego County to be closest to the finely barred subspecies of northern Baja California, *M. k. cardonensis* (Huey, 1926a). But the barring on the underparts on all 12 skins of adults in the San Diego Natural History Museum is coarser than in *cardonensis*, matching instead *M. k. bendirei* (Brewster, 1882), which ranges throughout cismontane Alta California.

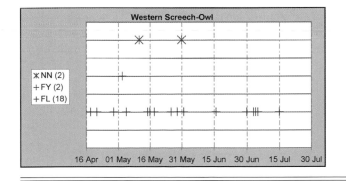

Great Horned Owl *Bubo virginianus*

The Great Horned Owl is San Diego County's most widespread owl, a year-round resident in all parts of the county. It lives in all types of woodland and in any open scrub growing over rugged topography. It nests wherever there are old hawk or raven nests, be these in trees, on cliff ledges, or on buildings. In spite of being such a large bird, naturally living in well-dispersed territories, the Great Horned Owl appears to be maintaining its numbers and distribution in the face of urbanization.

Breeding distribution: Great Horned Owls are found nearly throughout San Diego County, from the coast to

Photo by Anthony Mercieca

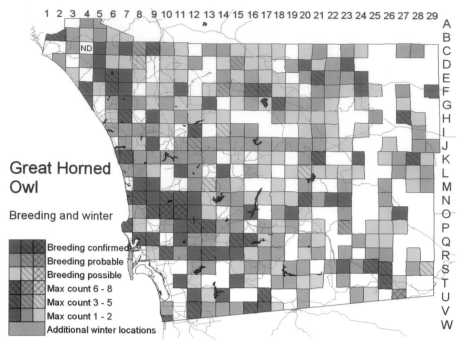

Great Horned Owl

Breeding and winter

- Breeding confirmed
- Breeding probable
- Breeding possible
- Max count 6 - 8
- Max count 3 - 5
- Max count 1 - 2
- Additional winter locations

Horned Owl also lays its eggs on ledges of cliffs or buildings where there is no preexisting nest; one nest that fledged two young in Poway (M11) in 1998 was on the second-story window ledge of a medical center, situated so a person could see it only by standing on the desk of a psychiatrist's office (E. J. McNeil).

Great Horned Owls often begin nesting as early as late January, occasionally even earlier. Our earliest occupied nest was 28 January; nestlings on Air Station Miramar on 24 February 1999 (W. E. Haas) must have hatched from eggs laid no later than the third week of January, and a fledgling in Lopez Canyon (N8) 8 March 1999 (B. C. Moore) implies a nest initiated in late December. The latest pairs lay in early April, and many young fledge during that month. The nesting activity we observed from 1997 to 2001 was thus consistent with the 28 January–13 April spread of 67 egg sets collected in San Diego County 1890–1943, and a female collected 6 January 1963 with a fully developed egg in her oviduct (A. M. Rea).

near the summit of Hot Springs Mountain (E20; pair 19 May 2001, K. L. Weaver, C. R. Mahrdt) to the floor of the Anza–Borrego Desert. A birder traveling on foot seldom encounters more than one pair or family per day, so the species is best termed uncommon, though it is relatively numerous for a large bird of prey. Regions where the Great Horned Owl appears especially plentiful are Los Peñasquitos Canyon Preserve (two active nests in square N8 on 19 April 1997, L. Ellis) and Miramar Air Station (eight in square O10 and another eight in O11 on 24 February 1999 (W. E. Haas). In the Anza–Borrego Desert the species is sparser than on the coastal slope but still confirmed nesting in the Borrego Valley, in badlands, and on steep rocky slopes.

Nesting: The Great Horned Owl does not build its own nest but typically takes over old nests of other large birds. Starting to nest in midwinter, the owl gets a head start over other species that might want to reuse these nests. Rarely does the Great Horned Owl make any effort to refurbish its nest, and we noted this behavior just once, at the north end of Blair Valley (K24) 22 March 2001, where the owls were adding to a nest they had used the previous year (R. Thériault). Known builders of nests we observed Great Horned Owls using were the Common Raven and Red-tailed and Red-shouldered Hawks. The Great

Winter: The Great Horned Owl is nonmigratory in southern California, and its breeding season overlaps much of the winter defined by our survey protocol. The species is probably resident in all the atlas squares where we noted it in winter but not spring or summer, the difference being due to variations of our nocturnal effort rather than to movements of the owls themselves. Also, the birds call most consistently early in their breeding season, which means mid to late winter. Sites of notable concentrations recorded in winter were Pamo Valley (J15; up to eight on 3 January 1998, W. E. Haas) and Boden Canyon (J14; up to six on 2 January 1999, C. R. Mahrdt, R. L. Barber).

Conservation: There is no evidence for change in the Great Horned Owl's abundance through San Diego County history. The species fares surprisingly well in cities, though it is less common there than in rural or natural areas. Buildings offer new nest sites, and some of the other birds that supply the owls with nests are thriving in the urban environment. Great Horned Owls, like other nocturnal birds, are more subject than diurnal species to being killed by moving cars, so increasing traffic threatens them. Offsetting this factor is society's improved attitude toward birds of prey in general, so shooting of the owls is less frequent than in the past.

Taxonomy: San Diego County lies in the zone of intergradation between *B. v. pacificus* Cassin, 1854, and *B. v. pallescens* Stone, 1897. A few specimens are the darker *pacificus*, buffer and more heavily barred, especially on

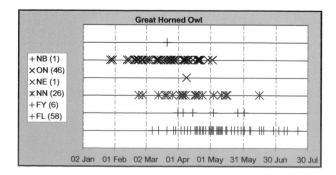

Great Horned Owl

+NB (1)
×ON (46)
×NE (1)
×NN (26)
+FY (6)
+FL (58)

02 Jan   01 Feb   02 Mar   01 Apr   01 May   31 May   30 Jun   30 Jul

the feet. Others, even near the coast, are as pale (gray and white) and lightly barred as any *pallescens*. Most are intermediate between the two. The one specimen from

the desert slope (San Felipe Valley, 22 December 1993, SDNHM 48720) is *pallescens*. For more details, see Rea (1983) and Unitt (1984).

Burrowing Owl *Athene cunicularia*

No bird in San Diego County is more endearing than the Burrowing Owl. And no bird is in more imminent danger of being extirpated from the county. Living mainly in grassland and open scrub, the Burrowing Owl was once common here but is now reduced to a few scattered sites, some threatened by development. If the population crash continues at its current rate the Burrowing Owl will be the next species extirpated from coastal southern California. Intensive management such as provision of artificial burrows, habitat modification, and reintroduction of captive-bred birds may already be the owl's only hope.

Photo by Anthony Mercieca

Breeding distribution: Breeding Burrowing Owls remain tenuously in only five areas of San Diego County. Perhaps the most viable site is North Island Naval Air Station (S8). Though there is no thorough census, there are several pairs scattered over various parts of the station, including the golf course, around runways, and near Zuñiga Jetty. The maximum single-day count there was of seven on 26 May 2000 (R. T. Patton). At the Imperial Beach Naval Auxiliary Landing Field (Ream Field; V10), two pairs nested in 1999 (C. Winchell), and one pair fledged four young in 2001 (L. and M. Polinsky). The largest numbers occur probably on Otay Mesa. Again, there is no complete census; the maximum count, of 11 in square V14 and two in V13 on 15 April 2000 (S. D. Cameron, P. Unitt), did not include the site of four nests in V13 monitored in 1998 (and possibly eliminated by 2000). Two pairs of Burrowing Owls are on or near navy property

not accessible to the public at the northwest corner of Brown Field (V12; J. L. Lincer). The greatest concentration on Otay Mesa is at the mesa's extreme east end, at the southwest base of Otay Mountain, where the scrub is kept very open by frequent fires, started by children in Tijuana tossing burning objects over the international fence to taunt the Border Patrol.

A few Burrowing Owls may persist in Warner Valley. From 1997 to 2001, however, our only record during the breeding season was of one pair carrying food items to a burrow just northwest of the intersection of highways 79 and S2 (G18) 12 May 2001 (G. L. Rogers). In the Borrego Valley, two pairs nested northeast of the intersection of Palm Canyon Drive and Borrego Valley Road (F25) in 1998 (M. C. and P. D. Jorgensen), up to five were at burrows along Coyote Creek Wash (F25) 1–27 March 1999 (P. D. Ache), and a pair was at a burrow near the Borrego Air Ranch (H26) 26 March–27 April 1998 (M. L. Gabel). In the last two cases, the burrows were dug out by dogs or coyotes before any young fledged. Two individuals along Highway 78 between Ocotillo Wells and the Imperial County line (I29) 15 June 1999 (A. Lotz) may have dispersed from the Imperial Valley.

Nesting: Burrowing Owls take over the burrows of mammals, especially those of the California Ground Squirrel. In the Imperial Valley, and probably in the Borrego Valley, the Round-tailed Ground Squirrel provides the owls' burrows (Patten et al. 2003). The owls maintain the burrows after appropriating them; if the owls are permanent residents (probably many

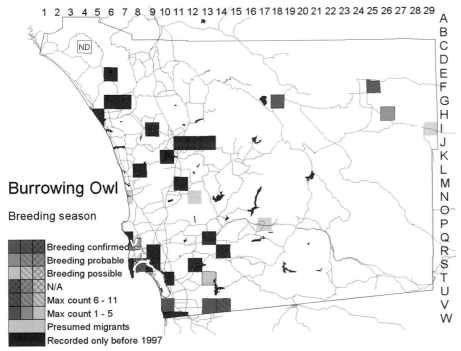

Burrowing Owl

Breeding season

Breeding confirmed
Breeding probable
Breeding possible
N/A
Max count 6 - 11
Max count 1 - 5
Presumed migrants
Recorded only before 1997

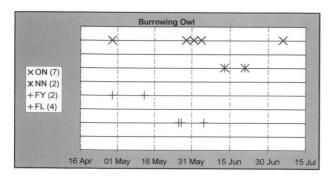

places where it breeds (up to seven at North Island 22 February 2000, R. T. Patton) and occasionally at other places (up to four at the Chula Vista Nature Center, U10, 20–24 January 1998 (B. C. Moore). We noted the Burrowing Owl wintering in 20 atlas squares where it evidently no longer breeds. At some of these sites, such as the east end of Lake Hodges (K11; six winter sightings of single birds), the owls had bred fairly recently and the habitat was little changed, though ground squirrels were in short supply (J. L. Lincer). Another area where Burrowing Owls still winter fairly regularly is along the flood-control channel at the San Diego River mouth and the southeast corner of Mission Bay (R8; up to three on 27 February 2002, L. Hughes).

of those breeding in San Diego County) they use their burrow year round. Burrowing Owls also use culverts and artificial burrows designed for them (Collins and Landry 1977).

Because of the species' rarity its breeding schedule is not well represented by our atlas data. Sharp (1907) found eggs at Escondido from 23 March to 16 June. On the basis of an incubation period of 29 days and a nestling period of 44 days fledglings at North Island 27 May 1998 (T. Plunkett) hatched from eggs laid as early as 17 March.

Migration: The Burrowing Owl is migratory over much of its range and far from sedentary even in southern California. In the Imperial Valley it is considerably more numerous in summer than in winter, but in San Diego County, with the breeding population almost gone, it is more frequent in winter. Young still in juvenile plumage can disperse soon after fledging, as suggested by one at Los Peñasquitos Lagoon (N7) 6 August 2000 (P. A. Ginsburg). Observers covered this area regularly, not finding the species there earlier in the year. In the northeastern corner of the Miramar Air Station (N12), Burrowing Owls occurred regularly on ridge tops through the winter of 1996–97, with the last individuals being three on 18 March (W. E. Haas).

Winter: In winter the Burrowing Owl is seen both at the

Conservation: The Burrowing Owl's population collapse is well documented. Stephens (1919a) called the species a "common resident in open ground from the seashore to the higher foothills." Collections and observations in the early 20th century attest to the owls' nesting at numerous locations such as Pauma Valley, Escondido, San Pasqual Valley, Poway, Rancho Santa Fe, Point Loma, and La Presa, where they do not remain today, although at some of these suitable habitat remains. As late as the 1970s and 1980s the birds remained in the lower San Luis Rey valley, at San Marcos, near Palomar Airport, Mission Bay, Sweetwater Reservoir, Lower Otay Lake, and the Tijuana River valley (Unitt 1984, J. L. Lincer), all locations where they are now gone. The Burrowing Owl was last recorded on both the Oceanside and Escondido Christmas bird counts, where it was formerly regular, in 1993. We evidently witnessed the extirpation of the Burrowing Owl from the region east of Chula Vista during the atlas period: the last individual observed during the breeding season was one near Upper Otay Lake (T13) 29 April 1998 (J. F. Walters). Burrowing Owls were resident on the nearby campus of Southwestern College in the early 1970s (J. W. Schlotte), but the region has now been blanketed by urban sprawl. Yet even the county's most extensive grasslands, the Warner and Santa Maria (Ramona) valleys, now support few or no breeding Burrowing Owls.

Abbott (1930) provided the most interesting perspective on the history of the Burrowing Owl in San Diego: In 1921, "on El Cajon Boulevard, which was a well-traveled thoroughfare even in those days, Burrowing Owls could often be seen perched on the side-walk curb. They lived in the culvert drains under the intersecting streets. The paving of this boulevard has driven these birds away…, yet in spite of San Diego's present 150,000 population Burrowing Owls still subsist wherever there is any

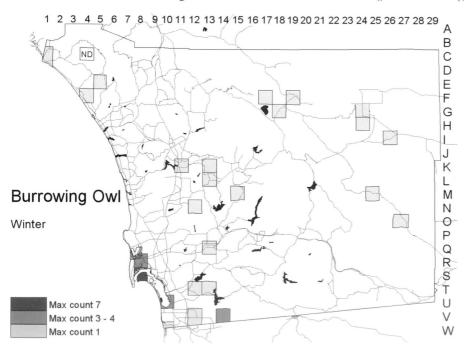

Burrowing Owl

Winter

Max count 7
Max count 3 - 4
Max count 1

extent of vacant land. . . . On Reynard Way, which is a short-cut between downtown and the Mission Hills residential district, these owls are common, because many of the sloping lots on each side have not yet been built upon. Even in broad daylight a 'ground owl' may often be seen standing upon some advertising sign, apparently unconcerned at the passing stream of automobiles. On the other hand, I have more than once seen the flattened body of one of these owls on the cement roadway. . . . Whereas such observations seem common-place and trivial, it may not be amiss to place them on record. At the speed with which some western cities are growing, remnants of primitive conditions are bound to disappear completely before long."

Thus we can infer that the Burrowing Owl suffers from the factors that afflict other grassland birds: not only direct loss of habitat but high sensitivity to habitat fragmentation, proliferation of terrestrial predators, and high mortality from collisions with cars. The Burrowing Owl provides a clear warning that conservation of habitat that seems sufficient to conserve dozens or hundreds of pairs can be insufficient to counteract bad population dynamics over a large region. All remaining Burrowing Owl sites in coastal San Diego County are on either military land or private property largely or entirely already approved for development. Reintroduction may be necessary to establish the species on suitable public property, such as lands owned by the California Department of Fish and Game in Rancho Jamul or San Felipe Valley, or those owned by the city of San Diego in Pamo Valley, Marron Valley, Spring Canyon, or around Otay Lakes (J. L. Lincer). The Chula Vista Nature Center has raised the species successfully in captivity, and the Wildlife Research Institute has begun efforts at captive breeding as well.

The Burrowing Owl is on the decline over most of North America, suffering considerable contraction of its range. Yet in spite of much research on the species (Lincer and Steenhof 1997), the importance of the contributing factors remains unclear (Holroyd et al. 2001). In various parts of the range, low productivity, high mortality, adverse effects of pesticides, decreased food supply, and reduction of the mammals that supply the owl with burrows have all been documented (Haug et al. 1993, Wellicome and Holroyd 2001).

Taxonomy: All Burrowing Owls in western North America are *A. c. hypugaea* (Bonaparte, 1825).

Spotted Owl *Strix occidentalis*

William E. Haas

In San Diego County the Spotted Owl lives year round in shady woodlands of oaks and conifers on steep to moderate slopes. Ideal habitat is a stand of mature oaks with a closed canopy, a source of permanent water, and an ample supply of rotted-out cavities, abandoned raptor nests, or debris platforms. An abundance of the owl's favored prey, the big-eared or dusky-footed woodrat, enhances the habitat as well. Although the Spotted Owl uses a wide range of forest types, in San Diego County it is limited by the paucity of forest: probably only 25–50 pairs currently reside here.

Breeding distribution: In San Diego County the Spotted Owl typically breeds at elevations above 2500 feet and is most frequent between 4000 and 6000 feet, where oak woodlands and dusky-footed woodrats are common. Recent known nest sites range from about 5800 feet elevation in the Laguna Mountains down to 2100 feet in Black Canyon (I16; nest in 1994, Cleveland National Forest data). They may be on moderate slopes or in steep ravines within conifer-dominated woodlands (e.g., in upper Agua Tibia Canyon, C13, Cleveland National Forest data). A nest near Espinosa Creek (R20) 24 May 1999 (W. E. Haas) is the southernmost known for the California subspecies of the Spotted Owl; the Spotted Owl's occurrence in Baja California is based on only three sight records from the Sierra San Pedro Mártir.

On the basis of a survey in 1988, Gutiérrez and Pritchard (1990), estimated a population for all of Palomar

Photo by Anthony Mercieca

Mountain to be 21 individuals, distributed among 13 locations.

Albert M. Ingersoll collected a set of two Spotted Owl eggs from a cliff ledge "near Oceanside" (= Ysidora Gorge, G5, along the Santa Margarita River?) 24 March 1894, and B. P. Cole collected another from a hole in a sycamore in San Onofre Canyon (C3/C4) 20 March 1908 (Willett 1912, WFVZ 21133, 69985). One recent sighting suggests a few Spotted Owls could persist in the Santa Margarita Mountains: one at 2350 feet elevation 1.3 miles south of Margarita Peak along a tributary to San Onofre Creek (C5) 14 August 1997 (J. M. Wells).

Nesting: In San Diego County, the Spotted Owl nests in abandoned raptor nests, in tree cavities, atop accumula-

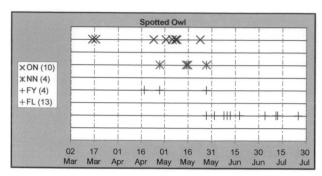

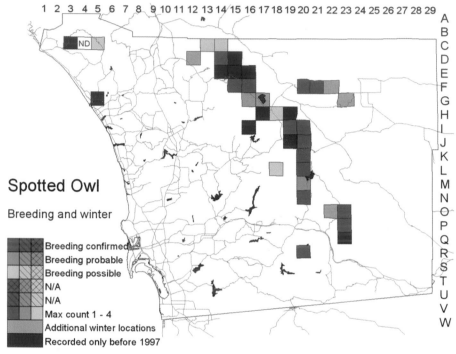

Spotted Owl

Breeding and winter

- Breeding confirmed
- Breeding probable
- Breeding possible
- N/A
- N/A
- Max count 1 - 4
- Additional winter locations
- Recorded only before 1997

Diego County. Occurrences at lower elevations outside of the breeding season are few, just a couple of reports by Eleanor Beemer in the mid 20th century (Unitt 1984). Young Spotted Owls may disperse short distances from their natal territories, but climate-driven altitudinal migration as reported from the Sierra Nevada (Verner et al. 1992) is probably unnecessary in San Diego County, where there is no evidence for it. A report of one at the San Diego Sports Arena (R8) 19 November 1973 (Gould 1977) seems unlikely and lacks supporting details.

Winter: Winter records for the Spotted Owl are similar in location to those for the breeding season, as expected for a nonmigratory species. One at 2200 feet elevation in Agua Tibia Canyon (D12) 20 February 2002 (K. L. Weaver) was calling territorially. Some records from the upper San Luis Rey River valley (F15/F16), including one of a juvenile, may have been the result of displacement from breeding sites at higher elevations nearby that were burned in the fire of November 1999 (W. E. Haas).

Conservation: Data adequate to demonstrate a trend in the Spotted Owl population are not available for San Diego County, but elsewhere in southern California it is declining (LaHaye et al. 1994). Gutiérrez and Pritchard (1990) found the species' density on Palomar Mountain in 1988 to be unusually high and suggested that a wildfire the previous year was responsible for driving birds away from former territories and concentrating them in the remaining habitat. Because of its low numbers and need for woodlands with a closed canopy, the Spotted Owl may be especially susceptible to habitat loss to fires. Many of the owl's known sites burned between 1999 and 2003. High fidelity of adults to their territories, low survivorship of young, and lack of knowledge about dispersal of juveniles (see Gutiérrez et al. 1995) mean that the owl's reoccupation of burned habitat is uncertain, even if the trees recover adequately.

Although the Spotted Owl is found in areas of relative isolation, the burgeoning of San Diego County's human population into rural areas may affect this rare species. Many of the observations during the atlas period were on public lands, suggesting inherent protection. However, the health of the forests is related to availability of ground water during the dry season and extended droughts. Demands for ground water to provide for the needs of the human population expansion into the back country, in addition to drawdown of the water table for bottled drinking water, may lead to the extirpation of this

tions of debris trapped in the crotches of large oaks, and probably in broken tree trunks, if sufficiently high above the ground. Large trees (tall, and of large diameter) and a closed canopy are characteristic of all nest sites in San Diego County. At breeding sites throughout the species' range, high canopy closure is common (Gutiérrez et al. 1992), and the presence of large trees is critical (Gutiérrez et al. 1995). Historically, however, Spotted Owls also nested on cliffs (Bent 1938, Gutierrez et al. 1995), as attested by the eggs collected near Oceanside.

The Spotted Owl frequently begins broadcasting its advertisement calls in December, when pair bonds are strengthened prior to the breeding season. It evidently lays eggs from mid March to April, though actual egg data from San Diego County are confined to the two collected sets mentioned above. Our dates for occupied nests range from 16 March to 24 May; our dates of fledglings range from 28 May to 25 July. At one nest in Cuyamaca Rancho State Park (N20) followed by Betty Siegel in 1999, the chicks were still all downy 16 May, then fledged with only the heads still downy 25 July. These records are within the Spotted Owl's normal distribution of breeding activities rangewide (Gutiérrez et al. 1995).

Migration: The Spotted Owl is nonmigratory in San

species from all but the most remote natural areas. The owl's ability to tolerate nearby development may be low; all currently known nest sites are secluded from human dwellings.

Taxonomy: The California Spotted Owl, *S. o. occidentalis* (Xantus, 1859) is the subspecies of Spotted Owl in San Diego County, as elsewhere in southern California. It is intermediate between the darker, more finely spotted Northern Spotted Owl, *S. o. caurina* (Merriam, 1898), of the Pacific Northwest and the paler, more coarsely spotted Mexican Spotted Owl, *S. o. lucida* (Nelson, 1903), of the southern Rocky Mountains. The subspecies differ in mitochondrial DNA sequences as well as in plumage (Gutiérrez et al. 1995).

Long-eared Owl *Asio otus*

William E. Haas

There is no sound in San Diego County's woodlands more haunting than the caterwauling of the Long-eared Owl during the breeding season—a usually two-noted lingering moan given by the female when a trespasser approaches her active nest. In San Diego County the Long-eared Owl is a rare resident in shady oak woodlands and broad riparian forests. Ideal habitat includes a closed canopy, nearby open habitats for foraging, and a good supply of abandoned raptor and corvid nests or debris platforms for nesting. Another enhancement is an abundance of prey—the California vole, the big-eared or dusky-footed woodrat, or, in the desert, spiny pocket mice. Although widespread in San Diego County the Long-eared Owl is limited by the paucity of forest, reduction of adjacent grasslands, and human disturbance. Recent study suggests 50–200 pairs currently nesting within the county, far more than previously suspected. Atlas observers found nonbreeding birds surprisingly widespread in the Anza–Borrego Desert.

Breeding distribution: The Long-eared Owl occurs in all parts of San Diego County. Its breeding distribution sug

Photo by Anthony Mercieca

gests that away from the coast it favors oak woodlands. Near the coast, riparian forest is its habitat of choice, though few remain in the latter habitat. Few colonies remain of the often colonial species; perhaps the largest is that of five to eight pairs in Sycamore Canyon (N12/O12) 1997–2002 (W. E. Haas). Nests have been found most frequently in the foothills and inland valleys, but they range as near the coast as Guajome Lake (G7; two fledglings 13 April 1999, S. Grain) and the Tijuana River Valley near the west end of Sunset Road (V10; three active nests 22 April 2000, W. E. Haas). The Long-eared Owl probably persists at some of the sites in Camp Pendleton where Bloom (1994) reported it 1974–92, here all mapped in red. Atlas observers did not cover Camp Pendleton at night. The highest elevations at which we found the Long-eared Owl nesting were 4286 feet in Johnson Canyon (D19; two calling males 14 March 1998, W. E. Haas) and 4320 feet at the more eastern of Twin Lakes (C19; adult with fledgling 2 June 2001, P. D. Jorgensen).

During the atlas period 1997–2002 we did not confirm Long-eared Owl breeding in the Anza–Borrego Desert, perhaps

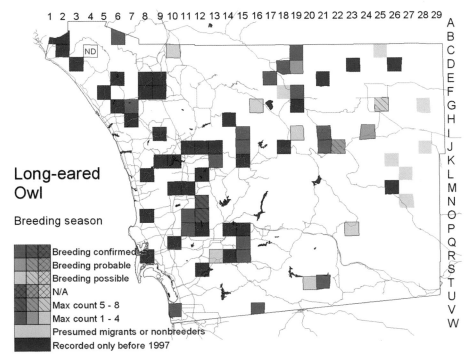

Long-eared
Owl

Breeding season

Breeding confirmed
Breeding probable
Breeding possible
N/A
Max count 5 - 8
Max count 1 - 4
Presumed migrants or nonbreeders
Recorded only before 1997

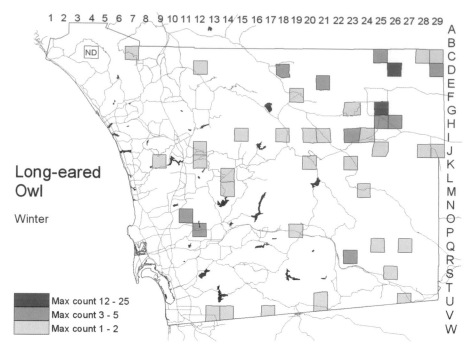

Long-eared Owl

Winter

Max count 12 - 25
Max count 3 - 5
Max count 1 - 2

eucalyptus and one was in an orange tree. At Tamarisk Grove the birds nested in the athel tamarisks. Nests may be a variety of heights, from the ground (rarely) to 40 feet up in trees. Higher nests are probably unsuitable because they lack sufficient cover or leave the young vulnerable to the wind; nests of the Long-eared Owl are rarely if ever improved, so the eggs and young typically develop in a shallow depression or on a platform of sticks or debris rather than in a more protected cuplike nest (Marks et al. 1994). The increase in San Diego County of the American Crow, Cooper's Hawk, and Red-shouldered Hawk has augmented the supply of nest sites; the owl uses all of these, as well as old nests of the Red-tailed Hawk and, formerly, Swainson's Hawk (Bloom 1994, W. E. Haas).

because of the drought conditions prevailing over most of this interval. Previously, however, breeding was known at Tamarisk Grove (I24; nested frequently at least 1964–95, ABDSP database, Massey 1998) and Clark Dry Lake (D26; nested 1993–95, M. L. Gabel in Massey 1998). In 1998 a pair remained at Tamarisk Grove as late as 5 April but failed to nest (P. K. Nelson, P. D. Jorgensen). In 1999, three remained in the mesquite bosque of the Borrego Sink as late as 15 April; in 1993, six were there 8 May (R. Thériault).

Unexpected were four scattered sightings of single Long-eared Owls in sparsely vegetated desert 1–13 April 2000 (R. and S. L. Breisch, J. R. Barth, M. B. Mulrooney). These are mapped as presumed nonbreeding, though the birds might nest in crevices in eroded badlands, as does the Great Horned Owl. Also mapped as presumed nonbreeding are two additional sites of Long-eared Owl pellets found in late April and May (D. C. Seals).

Nesting: In San Diego County, the Long-eared Owl nests typically in abandoned raptor nests in willows and oaks and atop woodrat nests and accumulations of debris trapped in the crotches of large oaks. Of 69 egg sets collected 1889–1961 and summarized by Bloom (1994), 57 were in oak, willow, or cottonwood, but four were in

Strengthening the pair bond before the breeding season, the male Long-eared Owl frequently begins broadcasting its advertisement calls in December or January—in San Diego County earlier than recorded farther north, as in Idaho and Montana (Marks et al. 1994). Egg-laying occurs from February to May. Dates of 66 egg sets collected 1889–1961 range from 7 February to 4 May; Sharp (1907) reported eggs on 10 May. Our dates for occupied nests range from 24 February (1998) to 26 May (also 1998—the breeding season was most extended in the wettest year of the atlas period). Our dates of fledglings range from 28 April to 10 June. These records are within the Long-eared Owl's normal breeding season in North America (Marks et al. 1994).

Migration: In San Diego County, the Long-eared Owl is at least partially migratory. Some pairs remain year round near nest sites; others move short distances. For example, owls banded in Bandy Canyon (K13) 16 May 2001 were found in winter in the nearby San Pasqual Valley (J12/K12), and some from the oaks of Sycamore Canyon were found in winter in the riparian forest near Kumeyaay Lake (P11; W. E. Haas). Young may migrate much greater distances: a bird banded in Escondido 22 April 1934 was found at Corbeil, Ontario, Canada, 9 October of the same year (Lincoln 1936a). At many breeding sites Long-eared Owls cannot be found once fledglings become independent. This may be the result of migration and dispersal but also because the birds go nearly silent once the breeding season has ended. The migration schedule, if any, is obscured by the several sightings of apparently nonbreeding birds through the breeding season.

Winter: Winter records for the Long-eared Owl range from single individuals to relatively large communal roosts. Roost sites and the number of owls using them

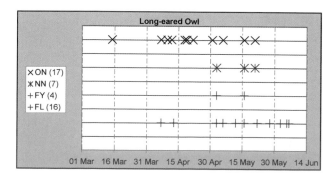

Long-eared Owl

×ON (17)
✳NN (7)
+FY (4)
+FL (16)

01 Mar 16 Mar 31 Mar 15 Apr 30 Apr 15 May 30 May 14 Jun

change from year to year. Communal roosting is common in this nomadic species; in Europe but not in North America it has been linked to fluctuations in the abundance of prey (Hagen 1965, Korpimäki and Nordahl 1991). Long-eared Owls roosted in Sycamore Canyon continuously from November 1997 through the following breeding season, corresponding to heavy rain and a population explosion of the California vole, which far outweighed all other prey items taken by the owls during that period.

Communal winter roosts are known mainly from the Anza–Borrego Desert, especially in rows of athel tamarisk near Clark Dry Lake (D26; 12 on 3 January 2002, S. Bell) and the Borrego Sink (G25; 25 on 8 February 1999, R. Thériault; 30 on 22 December 1991, G. L. Rogers). In natural desert habitats aggregations are smaller, up to five in Wonderstone Wash (D29) 10 January 2002 (P. D. Jorgensen), three in an isolated palo verde at the north end of Clark Valley (C25) 1 December 2001 (H. E. Stone). On the coastal slope a former roost in Rancho Otay (U12) had up to 12 on 15 December 1979 (B. Cord). But in this area wintering Long-eared Owls are more frequently solitary, roosting in a wide assortment of tree species including willows, oaks, eucalyptus, and tamarisk.

Conservation: The Long-eared Owl has experienced a steep decline in southern California during the 20th century, usually attributed to the loss of riparian and grassland habitats (Marti and Marks 1989, Bloom 1994). Historically, the Long-eared Owl was common in riparian forests along the coast (Cooper 1870, Sharp 1907). By 1944 their declining numbers had been noted, "in the main probably as a result of clearing of bottomlands" (Grinnell and Miller 1944). Garrett and Dunn (1981) considered the species "rare coastally, and virtually eliminated there as a breeder." In 20 years of monitoring birds of prey in Camp Pendleton, Bloom (1994) located only seven territories, three of which had been abandoned by the early 1990s. It should be noted that Bloom's data on

the Long-eared Owl were incidental to his other work with raptors; he undertook no focused surveys for the species in San Diego County.

Although the original data presented here suggest that the Long-eared Owl has made a comeback of sorts since the early 1990s, none of the recent records even faintly echoes the size of historic breeding colonies. Most breeding locations are sites of single pairs only, rarely clusters of three to eight territories. The Long-eared Owl's ability to tolerate nearby development and other types of disturbance is low—all currently known nest sites are secluded from human dwellings. Bloom (1994) suggested that this species rarely tolerates disturbance within one kilometer of a breeding territory. Most of our records during the atlas period support this hypothesis. Where the hypothesis did not hold true, a mitigating factor could be found; for example, the nest in Mission Trails Regional Park (P11) was isolated from nearby development by a steep canyon—and abandoned after 1998.

Continued loss of and encroachment near riparian woodlands will surely reverse what gains the species has made during the past decade. Conversely, maintenance and enhancement of existing riparian corridors and oak groves and preservation or restoration of adjacent lands to grassland will be needed to provide breeding habitat sufficient to ensure a reasonably stable breeding population within the county. Bloom (1994) emphasized that in ever decreasing patches of natural habitat the Long-eared Owl loses out in competition for territories and nesting sites with other large birds, suffering predation by hawks, crows, and ravens.

Taxonomy: In North America, the Long-eared Owl has been divided into two subspecies, *A. o. wilsonianus* (Lesson, 1830) in the east and the paler *A. o. tuftsi* Godfrey, 1947, in the west. Kenneth C. Parkes (in Rea 1983) and Marks et al. (1994), however, questioned the validity of this distinction, which seems unlikely in view of the species' highly nomadic tendencies.

Short-eared Owl *Asio flammeus*

Most owls live in woodland and forest, but the Short-eared Owl lives in marshes and grassland. It is principally a winter visitor to San Diego County, regular in small numbers around south San Diego Bay and in the Tijuana River estuary but seldom seen elsewhere. The Short-eared Owl is rare and declining in California, recognized as a species of special concern by the California Department of Fish and Game. Thus the finding in 1998 and 2000 of at least three individuals from mid April to mid July, including an apparent pair, was most unexpected.

Winter: In San Diego County, the Short-eared Owl occurs regularly in small numbers only around south San Diego Bay and in the Tijuana River estuary. From 1997 to 2002, the highest counts here were of at least two between the Chula Vista Nature Center and the salt works (U10) 18 December 1999 (B. C. Moore et al.) and two in the

Photo by Anthony Mercieca

Tijuana estuary (V10) the same day (R. B. Riggan). The Short-eared Owl has also been seen with some frequency at Fiesta Island, Mission Bay (Q8/R8), with up to six on

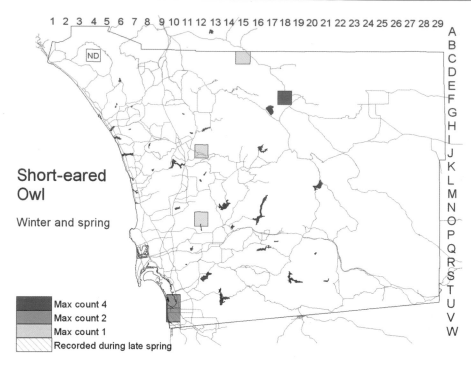

Short-eared Owl

Winter and spring

- ▨ Max count 4
- ▨ Max count 2
- ▨ Max count 1
- ▨ Recorded during late spring

report of E. E. Sechrist collecting two sets of eggs at National City (T10) 10 April 1906. J. B. Dixon (in Willett 1933) observed the species in summer at San Diego Bay and the Santa Margarita River mouth (G4). Alice Fries noted one at the latter locality 23 May and 12 June 1972. By the time the atlas study began, the species was long inferred as absent from coastal southern California in summer (e.g., Garrett and Dunn 1981, Small 1994). Therefore its showing up at the Tijuana River estuary in 1998 was a great surprise. Brian Bonesteel trapped and photographed one in the Least Tern nesting colony there (W10) 28 May, then photographed two on the fence separating the refuge from the Imperial Beach naval auxiliary landing field (Ream Field; V10) 16 June. In 2000, R. T. Patton and S. M. Wolf noted one at the Chula Vista Wildlife Reserve in south San Diego Bay on 12 and 19 April. Thus it is possible that the occasional pair of Short-eared Owls still attempts to nest in San Diego County.

30 January 1976 (J. L. Dunn) and one found dead 18 December 1996 (SDNHM 49048).

At least three are known from the San Pasqual Valley, with one seen near the east end of Lake Hodges (K11) 16 November 1985 (K. L. Weaver), one found long dead there in spring 1997 (SDNHM 50409), and one seen near Ysabel Creek Road (J12) 1 December 1998 (W. E. Haas) and 2 January 1999 (C. G. Edwards). The few other records are scattered over the coastal wetlands like San Elijo Lagoon and grasslands in the coastal lowland like Lopez Canyon and Otay Ranch (the latter now developed). During the atlas period there were three winter records away from the San Pasqual Valley, San Diego Bay, and the Tijuana estuary, of one in Dameron Valley (C15) 3 February 2001 (K. L. Weaver), four near Swan Lake between Lake Henshaw and Warner Springs (F18) 10 December 2000 (J. R. Barth, M. G. Mathos), and one in Sycamore Canyon (O12) 27 February 1998 (G. L. Rogers).

In the Anza–Borrego Desert the only identifications of the Short-eared Owl probably correct are of one in Clark Valley (D25) 15 October 1977 and one in Collins Valley (D23) 21 December 1983 (A. G. Morley).

Migration: Dates for the Short-eared Owl away from coastal wetlands in San Diego County range from 30 September (1980, one at Point Loma, S7, AB 35:226, 1981) to 11 April (1975, one in the Santa Margarita River valley at Basilone Road, E6, A. Fries).

Breeding distribution: The only record of the Short-eared Owl's breeding in San Diego County is Willett's (1933)

Nesting: Short-eared Owls nest on the ground among marsh vegetation or grasses. No details on the nests in San Diego County beyond that mentioned above are available.

Conservation: Stephens (1919a) called the Short-eared Owl "rather rare" in San Diego County, but Willett (1933) said it was "common" in coastal southern California in general. Grinnell and Miller (1944) called attention to a decrease, attributing it to shooting by duck hunters. In San Diego County, there seems to have been a decrease since the 1960s; the San Diego Christmas bird count averaged 4.7 per year from 1966 to 1972 but only 0.85 from 1989 to 2001. A factor contributing to the decline is undoubtedly the loss and degradation of coastal wetlands and native grasslands, both of which now cover only a small fraction of their original extent. Increased predation and human disturbance threaten all ground-nesting birds along the coast, including high-level predators like the Short-eared Owl.

Taxonomy: As a species breeding on four continents and numerous islands the Short-eared Owl not surprisingly consists of several subspecies. But only nominate *A. f. flammeus* (Pontoppidan, 1763) occurs on the mainland of North America.

Northern Saw-whet Owl *Aegolius acadicus*

In San Diego County the Northern Saw-whet Owl occurs in coniferous woodland almost exclusively, spilling over into pure oak woodland around Palomar Mountain. A year-round resident, it is largely nocturnal and difficult to see, generally detected only by its monotonous hooting. One surprise coming from the atlas study was that the owl often calls in the evening before sunset and rarely even at midday. Until 1994, when the species was first reported in Baja California, San Diego County was thought to represent the southern tip of its range along the Pacific coast.

Photo by Anthony Mercieca

Breeding distribution: The Saw-whet Owl is found in all of San Diego County's mountains with coniferous woodland but is more common on Palomar and Hot Springs mountains than farther south. Indeed, in the coniferous forest on these mountains, it is the most numerous owl. Nightly counts within a single atlas square in the breeding season range up to six calling territorially near the Palomar Observatory (D15) 13 May 1999 (K. L. Weaver) and eight near the summit of Hot Springs Mountain (E20) 18 May 2001 (K. L. Weaver, C. R. Mahrdt). The owl is particularly widespread on Palomar Mountain, extending into oak woodland with few or no conifers, on the north slope down to at least 3400 feet elevation in Cutca Valley (C14; up to four on 24 June 2000, J. M. and B. Hargrove), on the south slope down to about 3200 feet along South Grade Road (F14; one on 20 March 1999, K. L. Weaver, R. Wissa) and to 2550 feet along the San Luis Rey River near Wigham Creek (F16; male calling sporadically but apparently unmated, W. E. Haas).

Elsewhere the Saw-whet Owl is uncommon but occurs on Bucksnort Mountain (C20; one on 26 June 1999, L. J. Hargrove), in the Cuyamaca Mountains (one at Pine

Hills Fire Station, L19, 22 May 1999, R. Breisch et al.; one on North Peak, L20, 31 March 2001, G. L. Rogers), and in the Laguna Mountains (up to two near Morris Ranch, P23, 27 March 2001, E. C. Hall, J. O. Zimmer). The species is undoubtedly resident as well on Volcan Mountain (H20/I20), where we found it in winter but missed it in the breeding season.

Nesting: Very little information is available on Saw-whet Owl nesting in San Diego County. From 1997 to 2001, our only breeding confirmations were of a family of two adults and two fledglings near the summit of Hot Springs Mountain 15 August 2000 (W. E. Haas) and a fledgling just south of Filaree Flat, Laguna Mountains (N22), 7 July 2001 (G. L. Rogers). The only previous records are of young seen in Cuyamaca Rancho State Park 4 July 1939 (Grinnell and Miller 1944), on Middle Peak, Cuyamaca Mountains (M20), 19 July 1987 (R. E. Webster, AB 41:1488, 1987), and on Hot Springs Mountain 21 June 1986 (C. G. Edwards, AB 40:1256, 1986). The species nests in tree cavities and uses nest boxes; one calling from a nest box along the San Luis Rey River at Wigham Creek was apparently advertising an available nest site (W. E. Haas).

Winter: San Diego County's Saw-whet Owls are sedentary; the sites where we noted the species in winter but not spring or summer do not represent any dispersal. Late February, the time of many of our winter records, begins the season of the species' peak in calling. Winter counts range up to 10 near the summit of Hot Springs Mountain 15–16 February 2002, when the birds called most of the night (K. L. Weaver, C. R. Mahrdt). Numbers on Volcan Mountain in winter, where we missed the species during the breeding season, ranged up to three on 17 December 2001 (R. T. Patton).

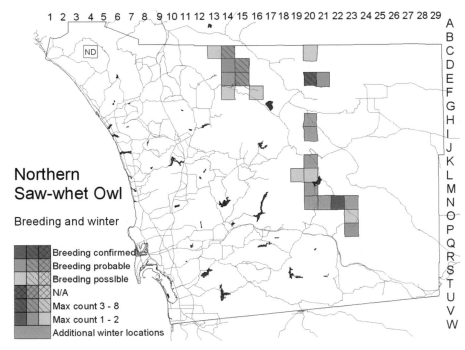

Northern Saw-whet Owl

Breeding and winter

- Breeding confirmed
- Breeding probable
- Breeding possible
- N/A
- Max count 3 - 8
- Max count 1 - 2
- Additional winter locations

Migration: The Saw-whet Owl is partly migratory in the northern part of its range and a casual winter visitor to the deserts of southeastern California. There are no records of migrants, however, from San Diego County.

Conservation: During the atlas period we found the Saw-whet Owl more often than expected on the basis of the meager previously published records, but this apparent increase probably reflects only better nocturnal coverage of the spe-

cies' habitat. Roger Higson observed the species regularly around the Palomar Observatory through the early 1980s.

Taxonomy: The Northern Saw-whet Owl consists of two subspecies, the dark *A. a. brooksi* (Fleming, 1916), endemic to the Queen Charlotte Islands, and *A. a. acadicus* (Gmelin, 1789), extending over the remainder of the species' transcontinental range.

NIGHTJARS — FAMILY CAPRIMULGIDAE

Lesser Nighthawk *Chordeiles acutipennis*

The Lesser Nighthawk is San Diego County's most easily seen nightjar, often flying at sunset and sometimes active at midday. Nesting on bare ground, it inhabits sparsely vegetated areas: open desert scrub or sage scrub, broken chaparral (as among vernal pools or along ridge tops), and even disturbed areas if these are not thickly grown to weeds. Mainly a summer visitor, it is generally uncommon and patchily distributed even in the Anza–Borrego Desert, its stronghold within the county. In the coastal lowland it has been greatly reduced by urbanization.

Breeding distribution: The Lesser Nighthawk is most numerous in the Anza–Borrego Desert, but even there we found it to be quite local. It is frequent in the Borrego Valley, though the largest concentration there, of 100 on 27 April 2000 (G24; P. D. Ache) may have included migrants. Another large concentration was of 48 at the northeastern corner of San Diego County (C29) 1 August 1998 (R. Theriault). The birds had roosted by day in the undisturbed desert within Anza–Borrego Desert State Park then at dusk flew toward the Salton Sea and irrigated

Photo by Anthony Mercieca

agriculture of the Coachella Valley where flying insects abound. Generally, however, daily counts numbered 10 or fewer. The nighthawk tends to be more frequent in flatter desert and absent from rocky or rugged regions, but there are exceptions, such as the nine on the northeast slope of the Santa Rosa Mountains (C28) 3 May 2000 (R. Thériault). Probably the abundance of flying insects is more important than the nature of the terrain.

In the coastal lowland the Lesser Nighthawk is now found mainly in Marine Corps Air Station Miramar and nearby areas remaining undeveloped north into eastern Poway. This region still has the dry cobbly washes and mesa tops studded with vernal pools that constitute ideal Lesser Nighthawk habitat. Numbers in this area still range as high as 12 in Goodan Ranch County Park (N12) 28 April and 3 May 1998 (W. E. Haas). Elsewhere in the coastal lowland, the Lesser Nighthawk is rare, especially in northwestern San Diego County, and found mainly in scattered sage scrub. A few still nest near developed areas, as on Mira Mesa at the edge of Los Peñasquitos Canyon (N9; adult with fledgling 13 June 1998, A. G. and D. Stanton), in Sandmark Canyon, Serra Mesa (Q10; nest in spring 2001, M. A. Patten), and in the Lynwood Hills area of Chula Vista (T11; adults with fledgling 24 July 2001, T. W. Dorman)

At higher elevations the Lesser Nighthawk is lacking over most of San Diego County but scattered over the Campo

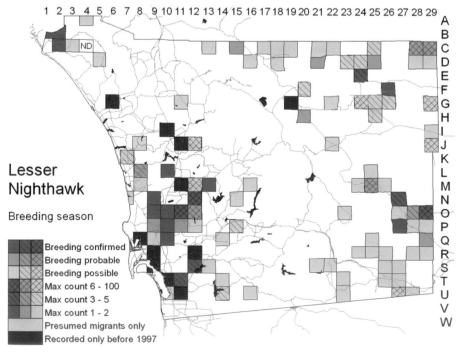

Lesser Nighthawk

Breeding season

- Breeding confirmed
- Breeding probable
- Breeding possible
- Max count 6 - 100
- Max count 3 - 5
- Max count 1 - 2
- Presumed migrants only
- Recorded only before 1997

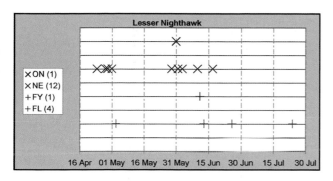

Plateau (up to six just east of Old George Mountain, U27, 7 May 1997, F. L. Unmack). It also occurs sparsely in central northern San Diego County, even up to 5800 feet on the south slope of Hot Springs Mountain (F20; four on 14 July 2000, K. L. Weaver) and 4600 feet elevation in Lost Valley (D21; two on 26 June 1999, L. J. Hargrove; male with moderately enlarged testes collected 24 June 1998, SDNHM 50059). The only other record from a high elevation is of one at 5500 feet in the Laguna Mountains (O23) 9 or 10 June 2001 (C. G. Edwards).

Nesting: The Lesser Nighthawk lays its eggs on the bare ground, perhaps in a slight scrape, often in full sun. One nest in Murphy Canyon (P10) 3 June 1998 was in sand and gravel remaining on the foundation of a demolished building (G. L. Rogers). Our egg dates ranged from 24 April to 17 June, practically the same interval attested by early egg collections. Chicks at Goodan Ranch County Park (N12) 3 May 1998, however, must have hatched from eggs laid no later than 14 April (W. E. Haas). There is no evidence for the species' nesting earlier in the desert than on the coastal slope.

Migration: The Lesser Nighthawk arrives consistently in late March. From 1997 to 2001 our earliest spring dates ranged from 20 March to 1 April, except for one at 2000 feet elevation on the east slope of Otay Mountain 8 March 2001 (K. J. Winter), possibly a bird that had wintered. In the past, flocks of postbreeding birds had been seen in the coastal lowland, up to 40 in the Tijuana River valley 20 September 1977 (J. L. Dunn), but there are no recent reports of such numbers. The species decreases in abundance in October and is only rarely reported in November.

Winter: The Lesser Nighthawk is very rare in winter, with all 14 records being from the coastal lowland, mainly in southern San Diego County. The only winter occurrence during the atlas period was of two at Poway (M12) 11 February 1998 (P. von Hendy). This is also the northernmost winter record for the county. All winter records are of single birds except this and another of two at Lower Otay Lake (U13/U14) 5 January 1991 (K. A. Radamaker, AB 45:321, 1991).

Conservation: The historical record is meager, but clearly the Lesser Nighthawk is much scarcer than formerly. Emerson (1887), misidentifying it as the Common Nighthawk, reported it as "common" at Poway. Stephens (1919a) considered it a "rather common summer resident of the coast region and foothills." Egg collections attest to former nesting at Escondido, La Mesa, and National City. Nesting on the ground, the Lesser Nighthawk is highly susceptible to disturbance and predation. Most of the flat mesas and floodplains that constitute the best Lesser Nighthawk habitat have already been developed. Lovio (1996) identified the Lesser Nighthawk, along with the Sage Sparrow, as the species most sensitive to habitat fragmentation on the east edge of metropolitan San Diego. He found it remaining only in blocks of appropriate habitat greater than 100 hectares. Air Station Miramar is currently serving as a refuge for the species, but shifting military priorities could change this. The Lesser Nighthawk is under less pressure in the Anza–Borrego Desert, though off-road vehicles could pose a threat. Wildlife rehabilitators have encountered at least two instances of Lesser Nighthawks nesting in San Diego County on flat gravel-topped roofs, as the Common Nighthawk does commonly in parts of its range. But in the Lesser such a habit must be rare, because over most of the developed areas of San Diego County the Lesser Nighthawk is never seen.

Taxonomy: *Chordeiles a. texensis* Lawrence, 1858, is the only subspecies of Lesser Nighthawk occurring in California.

Common Nighthawk *Chordeiles minor*

In spite of its name, the Common Nighthawk is extremely rare in San Diego County. Though it breeds as close as the San Bernardino Mountains, its migration swings to the east, and the species is seldom seen at low elevations anywhere in southern California. The Common Nighthawk resembles the Lesser closely and is best distinguished by its loud call, like an alarm buzzer.

Migration: There are four records of the Common Nighthawk in San Diego County, of one heard at Cabrillo National Monument, Point Loma, 5 June 1975 (J. L. Dunn), one seen in the Tijuana River valley 25 September 1976 (AB 31:233, 1977), one seen and heard at Escondido

Photo by Anthony Mercieca

11 July 1981 (K. L. Weaver), and one seen and heard at El Cajon 6 July 1988 (G. and R. Levin, AB 42:1341, 1988).

Common Poorwill *Phalaenoptilus nuttallii*

The Common Poorwill rests quietly on the ground during the day, hidden under chaparral or camouflaged on rocky desert slopes. After dark it forages for flying insects and advertises its territory with its eponymous trisyllabic call, "poor-will," or, more accurately, "poor Philip." The poorwill is fairly common at least locally but seldom found except by voice. Thus apparent variations in its abundance could be due more to weather conditions that affect the birds' calling—and human listeners' ability to hear—than to variations in the birds' numbers by habitat.

Breeding distribution: The poorwill is perhaps the bird most poorly sampled by our atlas protocol. Because we had no standards for nocturnal coverage, some atlas squares were covered at night much better than others, and the poorwill was undoubtedly missed in dozens of squares where it occurs. Nevertheless, the species is widespread in San Diego County, though lacking from developed and forested areas. It may avoid the coast, or the dearth of coastal records during the breeding season may be a by-product of urbanization. In the Anza–Borrego Desert the poorwill inhabits rocky hills, alluvial slopes, and badlands but probably not flat valley floors. The few records from flat sandy areas (latest, one near Peg Leg Road in the Borrego Valley, F25, 7 May 1998, P. D. Ache) may be of migrants, not locally breeding birds. On the coastal slope the largest numbers are in areas of extensive chaparral, as in Goodan Ranch County Park (N12; 16 on 28 April and 3 May 1998, W. E. Haas) and along Kitchen Creek Road (R23; 12 on 13 April 1997, L. J. Hargrove). The Campo Plateau offers much habitat for poorwills, and some high counts came from this area (eight 1.5 miles east of Lake Domingo, U27, 2 May 2000, F. L. Unmack), but our noc-

Photo by Anthony Mercieca

turnal coverage of this region was light. The site nearest the coast was 1.5 miles inland in Leucadia (K7; two on 29 April 1998, B. Bothner), but we seldom noted the species less than 10 miles inland. The poorwill is not confined by elevation and is confirmed breeding up to 5000 feet elevation in the Laguna Mountains (N22; eggshells found 14 July 2001, G. L. Rogers).

Nesting: The poorwill lays its eggs on the bare ground with the benefit of no nest whatsoever. Even if the species were diurnal its nesting would be difficult to track, as it carries no nest material and feeds its young by regurgita-

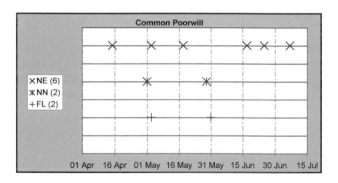

tion. As a result, we confirmed breeding only a few times, finding just five nests with eggs (15 April–25 June), two broods of young chicks three or four days old (about 1 May 2001, Mission Trails Regional Park, P11, D. C. Bostock; 29 May 1999, near Jamacha, R14, W. E. Haas), and fledglings twice, plus the broken eggshells in the Laguna Mountains.

Migration: Specimens of the inland subspecies on the coastal slope attest to the poorwill's migrating through San Diego County in both spring and fall (see Taxonomy). Furthermore, the poorwill has been found repeatedly if rarely in both spring and fall in areas and habitats where it does

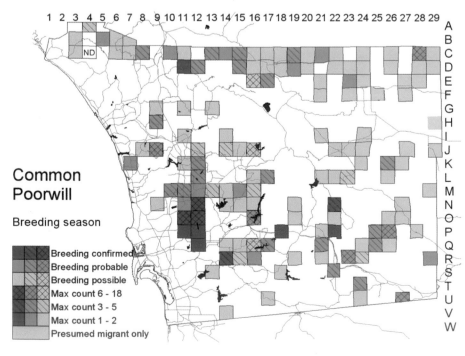

Common Poorwill

Breeding season

- Breeding confirmed
- Breeding probable
- Breeding possible
- Max count 6 - 18
- Max count 3 - 5
- Max count 1 - 2
- Presumed migrant only

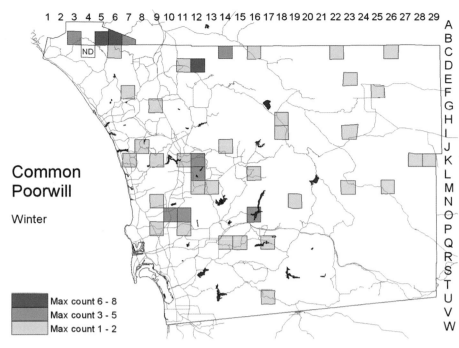

Common Poorwill

Winter

Max count 6 - 8
Max count 3 - 5
Max count 1 - 2

the Otay–Sweetwater unit of San Diego National Wildlife Refuge. Poorwills often use the openings in chaparral provided by roads as launch pads for their nocturnal foraging. As a result, they are particularly susceptible to being killed by moving cars; the San Diego Natural History Museum has received many specimens as a result. As the human population of San Diego County's back country increases, so does the number of roads and traffic on them, increasing the toll on the poorwill.

Taxonomy: San Diego County is an area of contact and intergradation between the dark brownish subspecies *P. n. californicus* Ridgway, 1887, and the pale nominate *P. n. nuttallii* (Audubon, 1844), in which the pale areas on the upperparts are silvery-gray, making the black spots and triangles stand out in bolder contrast. Subspecies *californicus* matches leaf litter; *nuttallii* matches granite. A small minority of the 45 specimens from the coastal slope of San Diego County are as dark as *californicus* from northern California, such as a male from Dulzura (T16) 15 May 1917 (SDNHM 31432) and a female that had recently ovulated from Lakeside (P14) 23 July 1992 (SDNHM 48121). Most, however, are slightly paler, intermediate toward *nuttallii*, including the one winter specimen, from Mission Trails Park (P11) 31 December 1991 (SDNHM 47868), and two specimens from slightly east of the mountain crest, from San Felipe Valley near Paroli Spring (I21) 10 October 1983 (SDNHM 42604) and Boulevard (T26) 12 September 1981 (SDNHM 41585).

not breed, especially at Point Loma. The local population may be largely resident, the birds going torpid rather than migrating when the supply of night-flying insects is low.

Winter: One surprising result of the atlas study was the number of poorwills found in winter and how that number was related to rainfall. Before 1984 there was only one record of the poorwill in San Diego County in December or January; from 1997 to 2002 we noted it 35 times in those two months. The detections of the poorwill in winter (February included) were concentrated strongly in the wet year 1997–98, which yielded 32 reports totaling 59 individuals. The next winter the figures dropped to 17 reports totaling 29 individuals, and in the drought-plagued final three winters of the study they stabilized at 6 to 9 reports and 11 to 18 individuals per year. Though the nights during El Niño were often cool and wet, the rain clearly stimulated the birds to call and feed. The largest numbers found per night were greatest at this time (up to six near De Luz, B6, 25 January 1998, and eight in the Santa Margarita Mountains, B5, 31 January 1998, W. E. Haas). The winter report from the highest elevation, about 3200 feet in Sherilton Valley (N19; one on 18 January 1998, G. and R. Wynn), was also during the wet year.

Though we found poorwills in winter in a few places where we did not find them in the breeding season, these were all most likely locations where the species is resident.

Conservation: No adequate data exist from which trends in poorwill numbers in San Diego County can be judged. Nevertheless, as a bird that roosts and nests on the ground, the poorwill is ill adapted to the habitat loss, human disturbance, and cats that accompany urbanization. It appears absent from urban canyons, though still inhabiting areas on the urban fringe such as Marine Corps Air Station Miramar, Mission Trails Regional Park, and

Fourteen specimens from the coastal slope are typical of *nuttallii* or closest to it. Some of these are probably migrants from the north or northeast; *nuttallii* definitely migrates through southeastern California (Rea 1983, Patten et al. 2003). But some of the specimens of *nuttallii* from the coastal slope represent the breeding population, especially one from Mission Valley 19 May 1922 (SDNHM 31460) and one still in molt from Pamo Valley 8 miles north of Ramona (I15) 10 August 1992 (SDNHM 48118). The situation of the poorwill thus resembles that of the Great Horned Owl, in which the population of San Diego County's coastal slope is heterogeneous, covering all variations between the coastal and desert subspecies.

Of the ten specimens of the poorwill from the lower elevations of the Anza–Borrego Desert most are typical of *nuttallii*. These very likely represent the local breeding population; some of those collected in April had moderately enlarged gonads, though none was in full breeding condition. The breeding range of *nuttallii* thus extends south of that mapped by Grinnell and Miller (1944). One specimen from 0.25 mile west of San Felipe Narrows (I25) 6

May 1966 (SDNHM 36000) is closer to *californicus*, resembling most specimens from the coastal slope. Two specimens from the Anza–Borrego Desert (SDNHM 17937, 40974) have the black spots on the upperparts more or less reduced and are thus somewhat intermediate toward *P. n.*

hueyi Dickey, 1928. Their color, though, is still the silver gray of *nuttallii*; true *hueyi*, pinkish and finely patterned, appears narrowly restricted to the lower Colorado River valley, being unrecorded even in the Salton Sink.

Whip-poor-will *Caprimulgus vociferus*

The Whip-poor-will has colonized some of southern California's higher mountain ranges, though its breeding there remains unconfirmed. But it is still a casual vagrant to San Diego County, where there are only three records.

Migration: One was captured and released at Point Loma 14 November 1970 (Craig 1971). Another was seen roosting daily in Coronado from late December 1971 to 25 March 1972 (AB 26:655, 1972). One was heard calling near Julian 8 July 1971 (AB 25:907, 1971).

Taxonomy: Two subspecies of the Whip-poor-will occur in the United States, nominate *C. v. vociferus* Wilson, 1812, in the East and *C. v. arizonae* (Brewster, 1881) in the mountains of Arizona. The two are well differentiated by voice and in juvenile plumage (Ridgway 1914) but weakly differ-

Photo by Anthony Mercieca

entiated in adult plumage (Hubbard and Crossin 1974). The bird near Julian was undoubtedly *arizonae* because summering Whip-poor-wills elsewhere in southern California sing the song of this subspecies. Craig (1971) reported the bird at Point Loma as *vociferus* on the basis of its short wings and entirely black rictal bristles, but Hubbard and Crossin (1974) questioned this identification.

Swifts — Family Apodidae

Black Swift *Cypseloides niger*

Nesting only around waterfalls and sea cliffs, the Black Swift is one of southern California's rarest breeding birds. Only six sites are known (Foerster and Collins 1990), none in San Diego County. Here the Black Swift occurs as a rare migrant, mainly in spring, flocking with other swifts and swallows.

Migration: Only a few Black Swifts are found in San Diego County each year, and some years pass with none at all. The atlas period from 1997 to 2001 was typical with zero to six noted each year and no more than three per day. There are three records, however, of large flocks, of 300 at Carlsbad (probably Buena Vista Lagoon) 29 May 1948 (AFN 2:189, 1948), up to 40 at Buena Vista Lagoon (H5/H6) 21–24 May 1980 (AB 34:816, 1980), and up to 200 at Point Loma (S7) 27–28 May 1987 (M. Rosenquist, R. E. Webster, AB 41:488, 1987). Records of the Black Swift are concentrated in two regions of San Diego County: a narrow strip along the coast and Palomar Mountain. The concentration along the coast is due to the overcast that commonly blankets the coast in spring and keeps the swifts flying low, as well as to the coastal lagoons (two at Buena Vista Lagoon, 23 May 1999, L. E. Taylor). Black Swifts, like other swifts and swallows, are drawn to forage over water. The accumulation of records

from the Palomar Observatory (D15) is due to Roger Higson's observations there from 1980 to 1985. But Black Swifts may also be attracted to mountain tops, as suggested by three at the summit of Hot Springs Mountain (E20) 8 June 2001 (K. L. Weaver).

In spring, the Black Swift occurs principally in May. The only April records are of two along the Santa Margarita River at De Luz Road (C7) 24 April 1999 (K. L. Weaver) and one along Miramar Road 0.5 mile east of Interstate 805 (O8) 30 April 1999 (W. E. Haas). The only records for June are that for Hot Springs Mountain and the only specimen for San Diego County, found dead under a telephone wire 4 miles north of Escondido 5 June 1921 (MVZ 41912; Dixon 1921).

The Black Swift is even less frequent in San Diego County in fall than in spring. From 1997 to 2001 there were seven records in spring, only one in fall. Of at least 16 fall records total, all are from Palomar Mountain or Point Loma except for two at Lake Henshaw (G17) 7 October 1984 (R. Higson, AB 39:103, 1985) and one at Escondido (I10) 24 October 1963 (AFN 18:74, 1964). Fall records extend from 23 August (1985, one at Point Loma, R. E. Webster, AB 40:159, 1986) to 24 October (1963, at Escondido, and 1983, two at Palomar Mountain, R. Higson, AB 38:247, 1984). The largest flock yet noted in fall was of 12 at Palomar Mountain 14 October 1981 (R. Higson, AB 36:218, 1982).

Chimney Swift *Chaetura pelagica*

The Chimney Swift breeds largely in the eastern half of the United States. Since the 1980s, however, small numbers have been showing up regularly at a few spots in California, especially Los Angeles, where the birds are suspected to breed. The Chimney Swift is now known to be more likely in southern California in midsummer than Vaux's Swift. Nevertheless, this range expansion has hardly touched San Diego County, where there are only 11 records.

Migration: San Diego County's Chimney Swifts have all been near the coast, on dates ranging from 21 May to 22 August—thus overlapping minimally with the migration of Vaux's Swift. Records more recent than the four listed by Unitt (1984) are of six to eight in downtown San Diego (S9) 11 July 1982 (E. Copper, AB 36:1017, 1982), one near Del Mar (M7) 7–12 June 1983 (D. Delancy, AB 37:913, 1983), two at the northeast corner of Balboa Park (R10) 16 June 1989 (P. Unitt, AB 43:1368, 1989), three near Santee (P12) 22 June 1990 (R. E. Webster, AB

Photo by Alden Johnson

44:1188, 1990), three at Chula Vista (U10) 21 July 1990 (E. Copper, AB 44:1188, 1990), two at San Elijo Lagoon (L7) 21 May 1991 (R. E. Webster, AB 45:496, 1991), and two in Mission Valley 6.5 miles inland (R9) 29–30 June 1994 (P. Unitt, NASFN 48:989, 1994). The only specimen is still the one from San Elijo Lagoon 12 July 1968 (Devillers 1970b, SDNHM 36690).

Vaux's Swift *Chaetura vauxi*

California's smallest swift is largely a migrant through San Diego County, occasionally common. It winters regularly, though, around Oceanside, its only area of regular wintering north of central Mexico. Migrating flocks sometimes roost in large numbers in chimneys and other man-made structures, where they are at risk of being burned or cooked, as well as of blundering into living rooms. Concentrated roosts represent a bottleneck of vulnerability for a species already of conservation concern because of

its reliance for breeding on old-growth forests in the Pacific Northwest.

Migration: In spring, Vaux's Swifts are seen mainly in the coastal lowland and Anza–Borrego Desert, with very few observations between; the birds evidently fly over San Diego County's mountains quickly. During the atlas period, our high counts were of 160 at Torrey Pines State Reserve (N7) 1 May 1999 (K. Estey), 150 near Dehesa (Q15) 22 April 1999 (A. Young), and 145 near the east end of Agua Hedionda Lagoon 4 May 1996 (W. E. Haas).

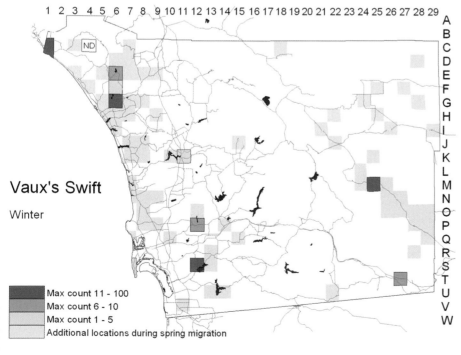

Vaux's Swift

Winter

- Max count 11 - 100
- Max count 6 - 10
- Max count 1 - 5
- Additional locations during spring migration

These figures were eclipsed in 2002 with the discovery of a roost in an old brick chimney at 8th Avenue and Broadway in downtown San Diego (S9). From 4 to 7 May at least 1000 individuals were around downtown San Diego, many entering this chimney (K. B. Clark). In 2003 several hundred used the roost at least from 25 April to 6 May (M. Sadowski). Vaux's Swifts are much less common in the desert than along the coast; maximum counts are of 30 in Vallecito Valley (M24) 6 May 1998 (R. Thériault) and 50 at the Ram's Hill sewage ponds (H25) 8 May 1994 (P. D. Jorgensen).

The species' spring migration peaks in the last week of April and first week of May. From 1997 to 2001, first spring dates ranged from 5 to 11 April and last spring dates ranged from 1 May (1997) and 10 May to 26 May, except for one in lower Los Peñasquitos Canyon (N8) 6 June 1999 (M. Baumgartel). Extreme dates in previous years are 4 April (1981, San Diego, AB 35:862, 1981) and 2 June (1984, Point Loma, S7, D. M. Parker, AB 38:961, 1984).

In fall, Vaux's Swift is generally seen in numbers smaller than in spring, though the difference may be due to the difference in weather at the two seasons. In cloudy or stormy weather the birds fly low and are more conspicuous than in the clear weather that commonly prevails uninterrupted through September and October. In fall 2002, Vaux's Swifts roosted in the same chimney at 8th and Broadway as in the spring; they were seen 4 September–21 October, practically the same interval defined by all previous fall records combined, with a daily maximum of 70 individuals (M. Sadowski).

Winter: The subspecies of Vaux's Swift breeding in western North America winters primarily in southern Mexico and Central America, being only casual at this season over most of California. Yet it is annual in winter in San Diego County, in the valleys of the lower Santa Margarita and San Luis Rey rivers. It has been recorded on 15 of 34 Oceanside Christmas bird counts, 1968–2001, with a maximum of 208 on 22 December 1979. From 1997 to 2002 we found it at Whelan Lake (G6), Windmill Lake (G6), or O'Neill Lake (E6) every winter, with as few as four in 1999–2000 but up to 40 at Whelan Lake 14 December 2000 (P. A. Ginsburg) and 15 at Windmill Lake 23 December 2000 (P. Unitt). Away from this center Vaux's Swift is far less frequent, recorded on only two Rancho Santa Fe Christmas bird counts, 1981–2001 (one or two individuals), and two San Diego counts, 1953–2001 (maximum 10 on 15 December 1990). Other winter records in the coastal lowland are from near San Onofre (C1; one on 7 February 1996, L. R. Hays, NASFN 50:224, 1996; at least 100 on 24 February 1999, D. W. Aguillard, NAB 53:209, 1999), Batiquitos Lagoon (J6/J7; one on 21 December 1987, D. R. Willick, AB 42:321, 1988), Escondido (I10; one on 22 January 1980, AB 34:307,

1980), the east end of Lake Hodges (K11; one on 14 December 1997, B. K. Schram, FN 52:258, 1998), San Elijo Lagoon (L7; one on 6 and 22 March 1964, AFN 18:388, 1964), Old Mission Dam (P11; five on 15 January 1980, AB 34:307, 1980), Santee Lakes (P12; nine on 15 January 2001, E. Wallace), Point Loma (S7; one on 6 January 2001, J. C. Worley), Sweetwater Reservoir (S12; 50 on 16 and 17 January 2001, G. Chaniot, NAB 56:224, 2002), and the Tijuana River valley (one on 8 December 1990, G. McCaskie, AB 45:321, 1991). Most unexpected were two small flocks on the east side of the mountains in 2000–01, of about 20 near Vallecito Stage Station (M25) 2 December 2000 (P. K. Nelson) and six at Tule Lake (T27) 16 February 2001 (F. L. Unmack).

Conservation: The northern subspecies of Vaux's Swift has suffered population declines as a result of logging of its breeding range, where it depends on large old trees and holes excavated by Pileated Woodpeckers (Bull and Cooper 1991, Bull and Hohmann 1993, Sterling and Paton 1996). The California Department of Fish and Game considers Vaux's Swift a species of special concern. Of relevance in southern California is migrants concentrating in communal roosts in artificial structures, where large numbers may be trapped or killed. Originally hollow trees served as roosts, but now buildings attract the swifts' attention. A flock at Point Loma died when it attempted to roost in a boiler for heating a building (M. F. Platter-Rieger). Sometimes, especially in stormy or drizzly weather, flocks of Vaux's Swifts attempting to roost in chimneys come down into houses, bringing bedlam to the terrorized residents and death to most of the swifts (e.g., Huey 1960). Large roosts may contain a significant fraction of the entire population; one in downtown Los Angeles is used by up to 10,000 birds (K. L. Garrett, K. C. Molina).

Taxonomy: Only the pale nominate subspecies of Vaux's Swift, *C. v. vauxi* (Townsend 1839), is known from California.

White-throated Swift *Aeronautes saxatalis*

Cruising the skies by day for flying insects, the White-throated Swift touches ground only where it can cling to vertical surfaces. Cliffs, sea bluffs, and desert badlands offer the swift crevices for both roosting and nesting. In addition to these traditional habitats, the White-throated Swift now also takes advantage of crevices and holes in buildings and bridges. The White-throated is the only swift that breeds in San Diego County; it is locally common year round.

Breeding distribution: The White-throated Swift occurs widely through San Diego County during the breeding season, but actual nesting is constrained by the need for suitable sites. The distance the birds range from nest sites to forage is not known but probably is at least 10 miles

Photo by Anthony Mercieca

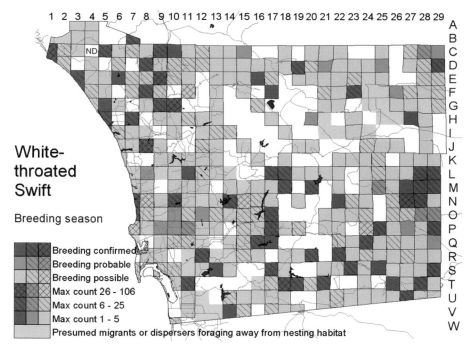

White-
throated
Swift

Breeding season

Breeding confirmed
Breeding probable
Breeding possible
Max count 26 - 106
Max count 6 - 25
Max count 1 - 5
Presumed migrants or dispersers foraging away from nesting habitat

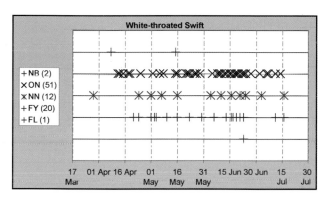

White-throated Swift

+NB (2)
×ON (51)
×NN (12)
+FY (20)
+FL (1)

17 Mar   01 Apr 16 Apr   01 May   16 May   31 May   15 Jun 30 Jun   15 Jul   30 Jul

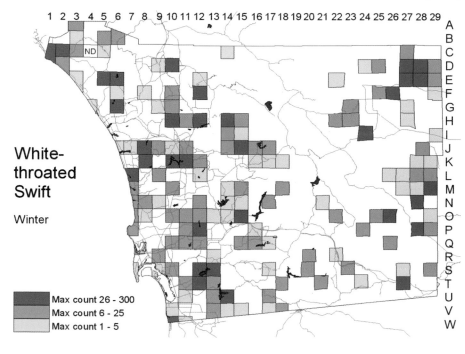

White-
throated
Swift

Winter

Max count 26 - 300
Max count 6 - 25
Max count 1 - 5

(Ryan and Collins 2000). In the Anza–Borrego Desert White-throated Swifts inhabit the badlands, where deep crevices have been eroded into steep banks. The Carrizo Badlands constitute the single largest block of atlas squares in which we confirmed White-throated Swift nesting, and counts here range up to 30 near Palm Spring (N27) 24–27 April 1998 (D. C. Seals). In San Diego County's rugged mountains there are many cliffs and boulder outcrops offering nest sites. Undoubtedly we missed many of these sites because of difficult access, but the birds take advantage of them throughout the county, nearly to the summit of Cuyamaca Peak (M20; four on 14 July 2001, entering crevices in the west-facing cliffs just below the summit, J. R. Barth). Along the coast, sea cliffs, especially the bluffs between La Jolla and Los Peñasquitos Lagoon, provide another major habitat for the White-throated Swift. This was our most regular site for large numbers of swifts, up to 106 in Torrey Pines State Reserve (N7) 4 March 2000 (K. Estey).

Nesting: Hidden in crevices in cliffs, White-throated Swift nests are almost impossible for a person standing safely on the ground to see. Atlas observers had to rely on seeing the swifts entering crevices repeatedly and hearing the young calling from within them to identify nest sites. The White-throated Swift has also taken to nesting in man-made structures; the artificial sites we noted most frequently were the drain holes under box-frame bridges, the same sites so favored by the Northern Rough-winged Swallow. Other nests are in crevices in tall buildings, such as expansion joints in the hospital in Camp Pendleton (E6; P. A. Ginsburg).

White-throated Swifts appear to begin nesting appreciably earlier in the Anza–Borrego Desert than on the coastal slope. Several reports of nests in April, and one of a nest with nestlings in Cañon sin Nombre (P29) 29 March 1999 (D. C. Seals), suggest the birds begin laying in this area in the first week of March. Desert nesting may extend into summer as well, with a nest with nestlings in Sandstone Canyon (M27) 21 June 2001 (R. Thériault) and occupied nests about 2200 feet elevation in Borrego Palm Canyon (F23) 2–5 July 1999 (L. J. Hargrove). On the coastal slope our earliest nests were in the Interstate 805 bridge over the Sweetwater River (T11) 18 April 1999 (W. E. Haas), latest (with nestlings) in a bridge over the San Luis Rey River, Oceanside (G5), 16 July 2000 (R. E. Fischer).

Winter: The White-throated Swift is migratory over much of its range, but in San Diego County there is no clear variation in its abundance by season. It is seen at many of the same sites year round. Winter estimates during the atlas period range up to 300 at Sweetwater Reservoir 16 December 2000 (P. Famolaro). Weather conditions affect its visibility greatly: swifts are best seen on overcast days, when they must forage below the clouds. On warm clear days the birds may forage so high they are out of sight; when the weather is cold or stormy they remain in their roosts all day, revealing themselves only with occasional calls. They may also go torpid (Bartholomew et al. 1957).

The White-throated Swift is seen far less frequently in the mountains in winter than in summer, but we still noted the species three times in the Cuyamaca and Laguna mountains above 4000 feet elevation, with up to 20 at 5100–5600 feet elevation along upper La Posta Creek (P24) 19 December 2001 (E. C. Hall, J. O. Zimmer). The swift appears to be regular through the winter at elevations up to 5800 feet in the Santa Rosa Mountains (C27), with up to 15 on 21 January 2000 (P. Unitt).

Conservation: No trends in the abundance of the White-throated Swift in San Diego County are clear. Variation in numbers seen on systematic counts due to variation in weather is enormous, overwhelming variation due to other sources. Man-made structures, especially freeway bridges, have given the species many new nesting sites. Some natural sites have been converted to rock quarries, but the swift has recolonized some abandoned quarries. Urbanization is likely bad for the swift's food supply, however, extensively paved areas generating fewer aerial insects than natural habitats.

Taxonomy: According to Behle (1973), all White-throated Swifts in the western United States and northern Mexico constitute one subspecies, the nominate *A. s. saxatalis* (Woodhouse, 1853).

HUMMINGBIRDS — FAMILY TROCHILIDAE

Broad-billed Hummingbird *Cynanthus latirostris*

Largely a Mexican species, the Broad-billed Hummingbird breeds no closer to California than southeastern Arizona. Yet it has crossed the Colorado River as a vagrant to California over 75 times, yielding 16 more or less well-supported records for San Diego County, all in fall and winter.

Migration: Eight of San Diego County's Broad-billed Hummingbirds have occurred in fall between 9 September and 9 November. Of these, one was at Point Loma (S7) 22 October 2001 (R. E. Webster, Garrett and Wilson 2003), and seven were in the Tijuana River valley (two on 9 November 1963, single birds 14 October 1962, 20–23 September 1977, 8–9 October 1981, 9–11 September 1983, and 5–8 October 1997).

Evidence for all but those in 1963 has been submitted to and accepted by the California Bird Records Committee. The committee rejected a spring report published in *American Birds* (Patten et al. 1995b).

Winter: The county's nine winter records of the Broad-billed Hummingbird, from 10 November to mid March, are more widely scattered. Seven are from the coastal lowland, from San Diego mid November 1961–mid March 1962 (Dunn 1988), from Spring Valley (R12) 8–10 March 1979 (M. Thornburgh, AB 33:314, 1979), from Balboa Park (R9) 28 November 1979–29 February 1980 and returning in at least four of the five subsequent winters (Bevier 1990), from Rancho Santa Fe (L8) 18 December 1982–15 January 1983 (L. R. Santaella, AB 27:339, 1983),

Photo by Anthony Mercieca

from Coronado (S9) 11 January–28 February 1986 (R. E. Webster, Bevier 1990), from San Elijo Lagoon (L7) 5–10 January 1998 (M. B. Stowe, R. T. Patton, Erickson and Hamilton 2001), and from Upper Otay Lake (U13) 12 December 1999–10 March 2000 (G. Morse, D. Griffin, McKee and Erickson 2002). Two records are from Agua Caliente Springs (M26) in the Anza–Borrego Desert, 16 January–10 February 1977 (G. McCaskie, Luther 1980) and 15–21 March 1982 (D. Dewey, AB 36:894, 1982).

Taxonomy: No specimen is preserved from San Diego County (or anywhere in California), but the birds at Balboa Park and Upper Otay Lake were photographed. Presumably the subspecies reaching us is *C. l. magicus* (Mulsant and Verreaux, 1872).

Xantus' Hummingbird *Hylocharis xantusii*

The exquisite Xantus' Hummingbird is endemic to Baja California, resident from Cabo San Lucas north to the Sierra San Francisco, still over 350 miles south of the international border. Nevertheless, there are three records of vagrants farther north, one from British Columbia (Toochin 1998), one of a female that, despite the lack of a male, built a nest in Ventura County (Hainebach 1992), and one rather shaky report of a male from the Anza–Borrego Desert.

Winter: Richard Klauke of Alberta reported a male at Yaqui Well (I24) 27 December 1986. Although the record has been accepted by the California Bird Records Committee (Pyle and McCaskie 1992, McKee and Erickson 2002), the bird was seen by only a single observer who did not take notes at the time of the observation.

Violet-crowned Hummingbird *Amazilia violiceps*

The breeding range of the Violet-crowned Hummingbird barely extends across the Mexican border into extreme southeastern Arizona, and the species is one of the rarest vagrants to California, with only five records through 2002. One of these is for San Diego County, of a bird that remained for an entire month, to be seen and enjoyed by over 500 spectators.

Migration: The single record of the Violet-crowned Hummingbird in San Diego County is of one that stayed around the home of Frank and Betty Scheible in Carlsbad east of La Costa (J9) from 3 November to 3 December 1996 (C. L. Mann, A. E. Klovstad; McCaskie and San Miguel 1999). Abundant flowers of the Cape honeysuckle sustained the bird. The Scheibles graciously opened their home to the crowds of eager birders from throughout California who arrived to see this cooperative visitor.

Photo by Anthony Mercieca

Taxonomy: Though there are no specimens of the Violet-crowned Hummingbird from California, photographs strongly suggest the greenish-tailed northern subspecies *A. v. ellioti* (Berlepsch, 1889).

Magnificent or Rivoli's Hummingbird *Eugenes fulgens*

This large hummingbird breeds in high mountains north to central Arizona and is partially migratory. But until 2003 the only reports from California were inadequate for giving the species a place on the state bird list. Then, within months of each other, two appeared, both well photographed: the second in Eureka, the first in San Diego.

Migration: California's first well-documented Magnificent Hummingbird was an immature male at Kate Sessions Park (Q8) 11 October 2–29 November 2003 (N. Shrout).

Photo by Matt Sadowski

Black-chinned Hummingbird *Archilochus alexandri*

Unlike Costa's and Anna's Hummingbirds, the Black-chinned has a rather conventional biology, occurring in San Diego County as a fairly common migrant and summer resident, in the latter role mainly in riparian and oak woodland. Like other hummingbirds the Black-chinned feeds on nectar, but its special relationship to a plant is not for food but for nesting material. Fuzz from the leaves of the western sycamore is typically the basis of the Black-chinned Hummingbird's nest, and the abundance of the hummingbird seems to parallel that of the sycamore.

Breeding distribution: The Black-chinned Hummingbird is fairly widespread over San Diego County's coastal slope but strongly concentrated in the county's northwest corner. In this region it can be quite common, with daily counts as high as 33 along the Santa Margarita River north of Fallbrook (C8) 24 May 2001 (K. L. Weaver). Weaver's breeding-bird censuses of an 11.7-hectare plot of riparian woodland in this area revealed four to nine females each year from 1989 to 1994 (average 0.5 per hectare). In coast live oak woodland the density is even higher; a census of this habitat in the Santa Margarita Ecological Reserve (C9) in 1989 yielded 1.8 per hectare (Weaver 1990). Farther south and east the species becomes more localized to the larger riparian strips in the coastal lowland and groves of oak woodland in the foothills. Few Black-chinned Hummingbirds occur above 3500 feet elevation, and the species is largely if not completely absent as a breeding bird from the Campo Plateau east of Pine Valley and Campo. Yet it breeds rarely even as high as 5500 feet on the north slope of Hot Springs Mountain (E21; active nest 19 June 1999, K. L. Weaver, C. R. Mahrdt). The apparent breeding range barely spills over onto the desert slope at San Ignacio at the head of the middle fork of Borrego Palm Canyon (E21; one on 18 June 1999, K. L. Weaver, C. R. Mahrdt) and in upper San Felipe Valley (two at the south base of Cerro de la Hechicera, H20, 23 May 1999, A. P. and T. E. Keenan; one near Paroli Spring, I21, 26 April 1999, J. O. Zimmer).

Nesting: To build their nests, female Black-chinned Hummingbirds gather plant down and mat it together with spider webs. The fuzz from the blades and petioles of sycamore leaves is the dominant material in San Diego County, giving the nest the golden-buff color of that fuzz. The amount of lichen and other flaky material used to decorate the nest is variable but is often little or none, making the nest look like a smooth orange sponge. But the birds use the fluff from willow and cottonwood trees as well, sometimes to the exclusion of sycamore fuzz, so

Photo by Anthony Mercieca

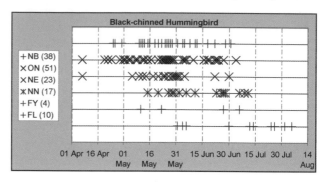

we noted some grayish-white nests too. Not surprisingly, we noted many nests in sycamore trees but even more in coast live oaks.

Our observations from 1997 to 2001 corresponded to egg laying from late April to the beginning of July, the same interval documented by 96 egg sets collected in San Diego County from 1895 to 1942.

Migration: The Black-chinned Hummingbird's spring migration takes place largely in April. From 1997 to 2001, the earliest date reported ranged from 15 March (2001, two at Whelan Lake, G6, J. Smith) to 2 April. The Black-chinned Hummingbird is a rare migrant through the Anza–Borrego Desert, recorded as late as 12 May (1997, three at Agua Caliente Springs, M26, E. C. Hall) and 21 May (1995, one at Lower Willows, D23, L. Clark, C. Sankpill). At the latter location, a riparian oasis, the species could nest irregularly.

Fall migration begins by 11 July with reports from nonbreeding localities on that date from Bucksnort Mountain (C20) in 1999 (P. Flanagan) and Cuyamaca Rancho State Park (N20) in 1998 (B. Siegel). Fall migration peaks in late August and early September. Adult males depart in August,

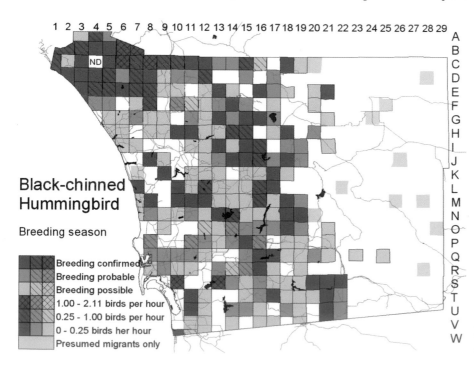

Black-chinned Hummingbird

Breeding season

- Breeding confirmed
- Breeding probable
- Breeding possible
- 1.00 - 2.11 birds per hour
- 0.25 - 1.00 birds per hour
- 0 - 0.25 birds her hour
- Presumed migrants only

weeks before the last females or immatures are seen (and heard) in early October. The latest recorded dates are 10 October (1981, Tijuana River valley, E. Copper, AB 36:218, 1982) and 12 October (1980, one at Point Loma, AB 35:227, 1981).

Winter: The Black-chinned Hummingbird is casual in California in winter, not yet confirmed with a specimen. Most reports are likely misidentifications. The best-supported records are of birds, none adult males, identified by call by observers aware of the species' rarity at this season. In San Diego County such records are of one at La Jolla 13 January 1990 (J. O'Brien, AB 44:330, 1990), two at Point Loma 28 December 1986 (J. Oldenettel, AB 41:330, 1987), and six in Balboa Park, although four of these are likely of a single individual that returned annually to the

same canyon from 1979 to 1982 (AB 27:339, 1983). All wintering birds were in ornamental trees including flowering eucalyptus.

Conservation: In contrast to Anna's and Costa's, the Black-chinned Hummingbird has undergone no obvious changes in its distribution or abundance in San Diego County. Breeding birds have moved into developed areas built over former sage scrub on only a small scale, where sycamores or cottonwoods have been used in landscaping, as in Greenwood Cemetery, San Diego (S10) or Hilltop Park, Chula Vista (U11). Where native trees have been retained amid low-intensity development, the Black-chinned Hummingbird remains, though it may be outcompeted by Anna's Hummingbird around feeders, as is Costa's (Stiles 1973).

Anna's Hummingbird *Calypte anna*

Few birds have taken to man-made surroundings more thoroughly than Anna's Hummingbird. In its range, Anna's is by far the most abundant hummingbird in gardens and at feeders while still remaining common in native sage scrub, chaparral, and riparian and oak woodland. Where feeders and ornamental plants fuel it year round, Anna's Hummingbird is a permanent resident; in natural habitats, many birds depart for the fall. During winter they return, and some begin nesting as early as December, earlier than any other San Diego County bird.

Breeding distribution: Anna's Hummingbirds breed widely over San Diego County, lacking only in the more sparsely vegetated parts of the Anza–Borrego Desert. But they are most abundant in the coastal lowland and lower foothills. High counts come from both heavily urbanized areas (41 in Pacific Beach, Q7, 1 June 1997,

Photo by Anthony Mercieca

J. C. Worley) and native habitats (40 in Boden Canyon, I14, 24 April 2000, R. L. Barber). It is likely that many of the Anna's Hummingbirds seen in the mountains in summer are postbreeding dispersers from lower elevations. Nevertheless, some do nest in montane forest, as illustrated by a female building a nest about 4200 feet elevation at Heise County Park (K20) 19 May 1998 (E. C. Hall) and by fledglings at about 4500 feet elevation in Lower Doane Valley (D14) 12 July 1998 (J. O. Zimmer) and about 4000 feet on Volcan Mountain (J20) 24 June 2001 (A. P. and T. E. Keenan).

In the Anza–Borrego Desert Anna's Hummingbird is locally common in developed areas, with up to 17 in the north Borrego Valley (E24) 12 March 2000 (P. D. Ache). We confirmed the species' nesting in all desert atlas squares with substantial agricultural or residential development, as well as in many canyons draining the desert slope of the mountains. In other parts

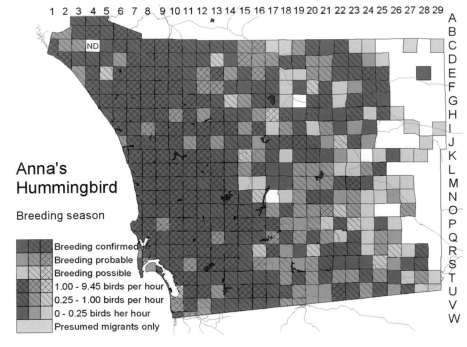

Anna's Hummingbird

Breeding season

- Breeding confirmed
- Breeding probable
- Breeding possible
- 1.00 - 9.45 birds per hour
- 0.25 - 1.00 birds per hour
- 0 - 0.25 birds her hour
- Presumed migrants only

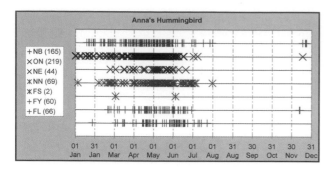

of the desert Anna's Hummingbird is rare and much outnumbered by Costa's. Nevertheless, occasional birds nest in the desert far from oases: we found nests with nestlings in Smoke Tree Wash (E28) 25 April 1997 (P. D. Jorgensen), in upper Pinyon Canyon (K26) 9 May 2000 (E. Jorgensen), and in Smuggler Canyon (L25) 15 February 1999 (R. Thériault).

Nesting: Anna's Hummingbirds build their nests mainly of plant fluff bound together with spider web. The action of the female in collecting spider webs, grabbing a strand, backing up by about a foot, moving in to grab another strand, and repeating the cycle several times, is so characteristic that it proved an easy way to find nests. The nest is typically decorated or camouflaged with flakes of lichen and dead leaves, sometimes of paint (Maender et al. 1996). The sites in which the birds build are so diverse that a pattern is difficult to discern. They make little effort to conceal the nest, usually protecting it only by placing it on slender twigs that terrestrial predators cannot negotiate.

If trees are in a female's territory, she appears to prefer them over shrubs as nest sites, but in treeless habitats the birds nest in many other plants, including small shrubs. Eleven of 12 nests found by M. A. Patten and colleagues in sage scrub around San Diego in 2001 and 2002 were in

laurel sumac. In urban areas man-made artifacts are common nest sites. Perhaps the most extreme site described by atlas observers was a nest with nestlings in full sun atop a chain-link fence (M. and B. McIntosh).

Our observations from 1997 to 2001 show that mid February to early June is the season when most Anna's Hummingbirds nest in San Diego County. Nevertheless, a minority of the birds in the coastal lowland start earlier, some as early as the third week of December. Our earliest observation of nest building was at Guajome Lake (G7) 18 December 1998 (P. A. Ginsburg), and a nest with nestlings at Del Mar (M7) 5 January 1998 (L. Ellis) implies egg laying no later than 20 December. A nest with one egg and one recently hatched chick at Old Mission Dam (P11) 31 December 1974 (J. L. Dunn) must have been started about 15 December, and a recent fledgling being fed by its mother in the Tijuana River valley (V11) 13 December 1998 (G. McCaskie) must have come from an egg laid about 7 November. Our observations of eggs, nestlings, and fledglings suggest that egg laying ends rather abruptly in late June, yet on six occasions we noted nest building from 30 June to 1 August; perhaps these late attempts are aborted.

Migration: Our field schedule for this atlas, with an off season from August to November, was not well situated to detect seasonal changes in Anna's Hummingbird's distribution or abundance. The species is scarce in natural habitats during the fall dry season, and migration between California and Arizona is confirmed on the basis of one band recovery (Russell 1996). Yet there are records from late summer through fall from oases and irrigated areas in the Anza–Borrego Desert, up to 10 at the Roadrunner Club, Borrego Springs (F24), 10 October 1992 (A. G. Morley). In San Diego County's mountains Anna's Hummingbird increases noticeably from December to January (see under Winter). In urban areas the species is common year round, though individuals may move.

Winter: From December through February Anna's Hummingbird is about as widespread in San Diego County as in spring and summer but even more concentrated in the coastal lowland. We found it somewhat more widespread in the Anza–Borrego Desert in winter but sparse or lacking at the higher elevations. In 28 squares encompassing the county's higher mountain ranges, we noted Anna's Hummingbird only seven times in December (maximum two individuals per day) versus 27 times in January (maximum 12 per day on 31 January) and 32 times in February (maximum 25 per day). Three Anna's

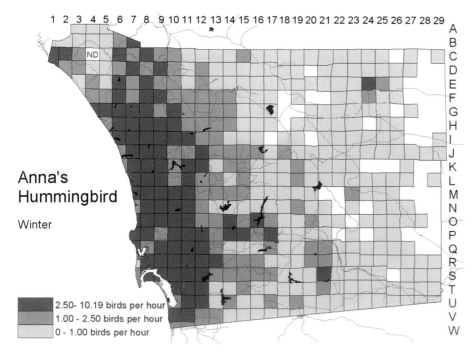

Anna's
Hummingbird

Winter

2.50- 10.19 birds per hour
1.00 - 2.50 birds per hour
0 - 1.00 birds per hour

Hummingbirds had returned to the summit of the county's highest peak, Hot Springs Mountain (E20), by 13 February 1999, when there was still much snow and no plants in bloom (K. L. Weaver).

Conservation: The proliferation of exotic nectar-bearing plants like eucalyptus, tree tobacco, and Cape honeysuckle, not to mention thousands of hummingbird feeders, has allowed the population of Anna's Hummingbird to increase enormously and extend its range (Zimmerman 1973). Sharp (1907) and Dixon (1912) considered the Black-chinned and Costa's Hummingbirds more numerous than Anna's at Escondido; now Anna's surpasses them

not only in man-made habitats but in many natural ones as well. The increase continued into the 21st century. The San Diego Christmas bird count, for example, averaged 324 Anna's Hummingbirds from 1966 through 1975 but 875 from 1997 through 2001, though the number of party-hours per count was 222–223 for both intervals. All other counts in the county also show increases, except for Lake Henshaw, where there is great annual variability. Bolger et al. (1997) found Anna's Hummingbird to be more common along the interface between urban development and native scrub in metropolitan San Diego than in native habitat away from development.

Costa's Hummingbird *Calypte costae*

Some birds' lifestyle is to find a territory that can support them reliably and defend that territory as long as they can. Other species—like Costa's Hummingbird—find abundant but ephemeral resources, exploit them while they last, then move on. Where flowers bloom in abundance, Costa's Hummingbirds gather in numbers, then disappear as the flush fades. The birds capitalize on the desert's bloom in late winter and spring, that of sage scrub and chaparral in spring and summer, especially where wildflowers proliferate following a fire.

Photo by Anthony Mercieca

Breeding distribution: Costa's Hummingbirds breed over most of San Diego County though not at the same time in all regions. They occur throughout the Anza–Borrego Desert, where they are common in spring (up to 50 near Whitaker Horse Camp, D23, 12 April 1999, P. Unitt). Their abundance varies with rainfall and the abundance of flowers that follows. Our count per hour in eastern San Diego County varied from 0.96 in the wet 1998 to 0.38 in the dry 2000. In the desert, alluvial slopes, with their rich

flora, offer the best habitat to Costa's Hummingbird, while valley floors dominated by halophytes offer little. As a food source the chuparosa, with its longer flowering season, is the most important shrub to Costa's Hummingbird in the Anza–Borrego Desert (Stiles 1973). Ocotillo, desert lavender, desert thorn, and desert "willow" are also important, and the birds feed on many other plants as well.

On the coastal slope Costa's Hummingbird is also widespread, more abundant in the inland valleys and foothills than in the higher mountains or along the coast (up to 60 near Tule Springs, N18, 2 July 2001, J. R. Barth, E. C. Hall, A. P. and T. E. Keenan). In mature sage scrub and chaparral Costa's Hummingbird is fairly common, especially where white sage and Cleveland sage are common. Cox (1981) suggested that Cleveland sage is specialized for pollination by Costa's Hummingbird.

A study comparing recently burned and mature chaparral near Pine Valley revealed that Costa's Hummingbirds move into recovering burned chaparral in large numbers when the habitat is still dominated by herbs and subshrubs, especially woolly bluecurls, vinegar weed, showy

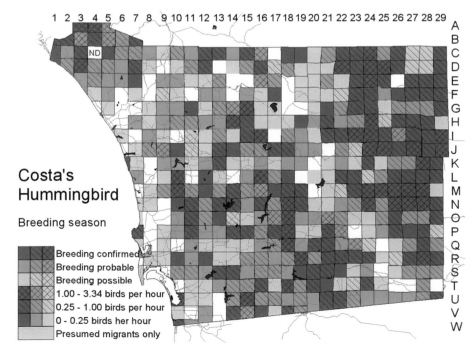

Costa's Hummingbird

Breeding season

- Breeding confirmed
- Breeding probable
- Breeding possible
- 1.00 - 3.34 birds per hour
- 0.25 - 1.00 birds per hour
- 0 - 0.25 birds her hour
- Presumed migrants only

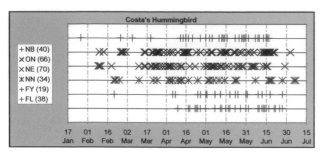

penstemon, sticky nama, and the slope semaphore or wide-throated yellow monkeyflower. Following heavy rain in the winter of 1992–93, these plants bloomed so profusely on recently burned slopes that the hillsides they covered looked purple from distances over a half a mile. Costa's Hummingbird was the most abundant bird in these areas, yet in the following years, as chaparral shrubs recovered, the fire-following plants dwindled and the number of Costa's Hummingbirds fell in tandem. In spite of the brevity of this irruption, the influx sufficed to make Costa's Hummingbird the sixth most common bird in the recently burned areas according to point counts from 1993 to 1997 (Cleveland National Forest data).

Nesting: Female Costa's Hummingbirds build a typical tiny hummingbird nest, well decorated with flaky material, making no effort to conceal it. Even on the floor of the Anza–Borrego Desert nests are often placed in full sun. The diversity of nest sites atlas observers described is too great to list, but in chaparral the birds often use the dead flowering stalks of the chaparral yucca. After they have burst open and dried, the yucca's fruits make an ideal tripod for supporting the nest. We also found, however, numerous nests in trees, including coast live and Engelmann oaks, cottonwood, and sycamore, habitats where the Black-chinned and Anna's Hummingbirds occur alongside Costa's.

Costa's Hummingbird's breeding seasons in the desert and chaparral differ yet overlap. In the Anza–Borrego Desert the species lays primarily from February through April. Even earlier nesting is possible, perhaps when the birds are stimulated by early rains, as attested by a nest with eggs at Truckhaven Rocks (F28) 9 November 1986 (P. D. Jorgensen) and a nest with nestlings in the Borrego Valley 3 February 1962 (Bakus 1962). Our latest desert nest, in Borrego Springs (G24), had eggs on 18 May 1999 (P. D. Ache).

On the coastal slope, Costa's Hummingbirds lay mainly from mid April to mid June. The activity we observed in this area from 1997 to 2001 agrees closely with the interval of 13 April–13 June attested by 26 egg sets collected from 1895 to 1952, except for two exceptionally early records: an occupied nest in Spring Valley (R12) 1 December 1999 (M. and D. Hastings; not shown on chart) and a nest at the Chula Vista Nature Center (U10) in which the eggs hatched 22–23 February 2001 (B. C. Moore).

Migration: The movements of Costa's Hummingbird are complex and unconventional, as outlined by Baltosser (1989). In the Anza–Borrego Desert the species arrives in numbers by December, remains common through May, and departs largely in June. On the coastal slope the bulk of the population arrives in April and remains into July. The species is seen rarely at oases in the Anza–Borrego Desert through the fall. Its status in native habitats on the coastal slope at that season is still unclear, but the birds are seen in urban gardens in fall, perhaps more often than at other times of the year.

Winter: Because most Costa's Hummingbirds return to the Anza–Borrego Desert before 1 December, the distribution we recorded there during winter was similar to that in spring. The main exception was at the higher elevations of the Santa Rosa and Vallecito mountains, where the species was lacking before March. The Anza–Borrego Christmas bird count commonly yields the highest return of Costa's Hummingbird of any such count in the United States, up to 157 on 19 December 1999. During the atlas period the species' numbers in desert in winter varied with rainfall in the same way as in the breeding season; the birds responded immediately by arriving in larger numbers in the wet winter of 1997–98.

On the coastal slope, wintering Costa's Hummingbirds are uncommon and local, rarely occurring above an elevation of 1500 feet. Many of the birds wintering in the coastal lowland are in flowering ornamental vegetation, but some frequent sites of native semidesert scrub. Most records from sites at higher

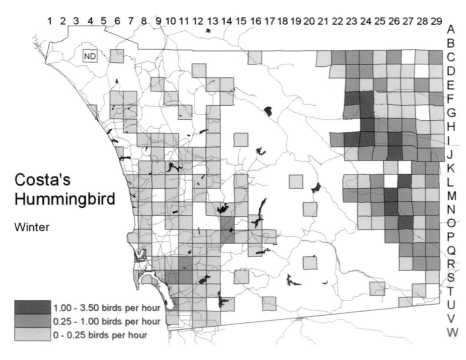

Costa's
Hummingbird

Winter

1.00 - 3.50 birds per hour
0.25 - 1.00 birds per hour
0 - 0.25 birds per hour

elevations, such as Dameron Valley (C16; one on 12 December 1998, K. L. Weaver) and Pamo Valley (I15; up to three on 30 December 2000, M. Dudley), are from such habitat, shared with occasional visitors of other species more typical of desert like Scott's Oriole and Brewer's Sparrow. Following the call of two Costa's Hummingbirds at the south base of Spangler Peak (L15) 17 December 1998 led me to a patch of chuparosa, scarce on the coastal slope. The garden in the San Diego Wild Animal Park featuring the plants of Baja California is the most consistent site for Costa's Hummingbird on the Escondido Christmas bird count.

Conservation: Any long-term trends in Costa's Hummingbird numbers are difficult to discern because of the species' inherent irregularity. Like other hummingbirds, Costa's readily exploits feeders and ornamental plants. The tree tobacco, an exotic plant that proliferates in disturbed open areas, has become an important food source for Costa's and other hummingbirds and has even allowed Costa's to extend its range (Baltosser 1989). All the early writers found Costa's Hummingbird on San

Diego County's coastal slope only in spring and summer. On the San Diego Christmas bird count, it was first noted in 1956; since 1980 the count has yielded an average of 20. Urban areas may be a refuge for the species in fall, allowing some to dispense with the need to migrate south or east to regions of summer rain. Nevertheless, urbanization is not an unmitigated boon to Costa's Hummingbird. Anna's Hummingbird appears far better adapted to the relatively static environment of urban gardens. Anna's has increased greatly, and that larger species dominates and displaces Costa's at food sources (Stiles 1973). On the basis of surveys from 11 April to 1 June 1993, Bolger et al. (1997) reported Costa's Hummingbird to be sensitive to habitat fragmentation around metropolitan San Diego. This finding may be due at least in part, however, to a natural preference for sunnier climate; atlas results show the species tends to avoid the coastal strip, commonly blanketed with low clouds in late spring and early summer. The points in fragmented habitat surveyed by Bolger et al. tended to be closer to the coast than those in unfragmented habitat.

Calliope Hummingbird *Stellula calliope*

North America's smallest bird breeds in western coniferous forests and winters in central Mexico. At the latitude of San Diego County, its usual nesting habitat lies at an elevation higher than the tops the county's highest mountains. Thus it occurs in San Diego County mainly as a rare spring migrant. A few birds have occurred in summer on Palomar and Hot Springs mountains and even engaged in courtship displays, but the species' nesting in the county has not yet been confirmed.

Migration: The Calliope Hummingbird is seen in San Diego County mainly in April, occasionally as early as the last week of March. Exceptionally early records are of one in Presidio Park (R8) 5 March 1976 (AB 30:892, 1976) and one that struck a window in downtown San Diego (S9) 18 February 2000 (L. van Epps, NAB 54:221, 2000, SDNHM 50375). During the atlas period our latest was one at Point Loma (S7) 16 May 2001 (G. C. Hazard); in previous years the species was reported as late as 24 May (1982, one in the Tijuana River valley, T. Meixner, AB 36: 894, 1982) and 25 May (1985, one at Point Loma, C. G. Edwards).

Numbers of Calliope Hummingbirds passing through San Diego County vary somewhat from year to year. Usually the species is rare and seen singly, but Point Loma has been the site of concentrations as large as 15 on 30 April 1989 (J. Oldenettel, AB 43:537, 1989). In the exceptionally dry spring of 2002 Calliope Hummingbirds, like some other migrants, concentrated in irrigated ornamental plantings in San Diego and were reported continuously from 9 March to 20 May with up to 12 per day (R. E. Webster, NAB 56:357, 2002). The species is encountered most frequently along the coast, especially at Point Loma,

Photo by Anthony Mercieca

but occurrences are scattered over the coastal slope. In the Anza–Borrego Desert the only records are of one along Coyote Creek 26 March 1979 (B. Cord), one in nearby Box Canyon (C23) 19 April 2000 (M. B. Mulrooney), one at the Borrego sewage ponds (H25) 20 April 2002 (G. C. Hazard), two at Yaqui Well (I24) 26 April 1984 (A. Baker), and two at nearby Tamarisk Grove 18 April 2002 (R. Thériault).

The only fall record is of a single bird in the Tijuana River valley 26 September 1981 (E. Copper). The Calliope Hummingbird migrates in a loop heading north along the Pacific coast, south along the Rocky Mountains (Phillips 1975), so the species is not expected in San Diego County in fall. The route by which the bulk of the population crosses from mainland Mexico to the Pacific coast of the United States is not well known but probably largely north of San Diego County.

Breeding distribution: Before we initiated field work for this atlas, the only summer records of the Calliope Hummingbird in San Diego County were of a male displaying to a female on Hot Springs Mountain (E21) 24 June 1980 (Unitt 1981) and a male near the Palomar

Observatory (D15) throughout July 1983 (R. Higson, AB 37:1028, 1983). Thus the number of possibly breeding Calliope Hummingbirds we noted from 1997 to 2001 was a surprise. On Hot Springs Mountain, at 5040 feet elevation near San Ignacio (E21), K. L. Weaver and C. R. Mahrdt noted one 18 May 2001. Near the north base of the mountain, at 4850 feet elevation 3.1 miles north-northwest of the summit (D20), J. M. and B. Hargrove observed a male displaying to a female 10 May 1999. Around High Point, Palomar Mountain (D15), at patches of scarlet bugler and scarlet larkspur, Weaver noted one 13–14 May 1999, two males and one female 20 May 2000, and one male and two females 12 July 2000. Completely unexpected was his discovery of a male and female in a small glade at 1900 feet elevation in Marion Canyon on the southwest slope of Palomar Mountain (D12) 18 June 2001. Nesting of the Calliope Hummingbird may be possible even in this area; it has been reported exceptionally from foothill oak woodland at 420 feet elevation in Placer County (Williams 2001).

Rufous Hummingbird *Selasphorus rufus*

The Rufous, the world's northernmost hummingbird, commutes annually between the Pacific Northwest and Mexico. It passes through San Diego County in both directions, taking advantage of the bloom of desert flowers like ocotillo in spring, of mountain flowers like the scarlet bugler in late summer, and of exotic plants like eucalyptus and tree tobacco at both seasons. Hummingbirds of the genus *Selasphorus* also occur as rare winter visitors, though hardly any of these are adult males. Distinguishing the Rufous and Allen's Hummingbirds in other plumages usually requires careful study of birds in hand.

Migration: The migrations of the Rufous Hummingbird are early, though not quite so early as those of Allen's Hummingbird. Spring migration begins in February (one at Quail Botanical Gardens, K7, 1 February 1999, R. Campbell; two at La Jolla, P7, 5 February 2000, L. and M. Polinsky), exceptionally late January (one male in Borrego Springs, G24, 23 January 1993, A. G. Morley; one at Valley Center, G11, 27 January 1974, AB 28:693, 1974). Migration peaks in late March and early April. Even then the species is usually uncommon, though large concentrations can be seen occasionally around flowering trees or shrubs. Our largest numbers during the atlas period—up to 40 at Yaqui Flat (I23) 7 April 1998 (P. K. Nelson)—were along the east base of the mountains, a line of concentration for migrants crossing from the desert to the coast. Rufous Hummingbird numbers in the desert, however, are irregular, perhaps varying with weather conditions. The species can be seen more consistently in spring in the coastal lowland. Most birds have continued north by the end of April, though stragglers have been seen as late as 12 May (1976, one male at Point Loma, S7, J. L. Dunn) and 16 May (1999, two at La Jolla, P7, L. and M. Polinsky). Spring specimens range in date between 1 March (1963, San Luis Rey, G6, SDNHM 3195; 1990, El Cajon, Q13, SDNHM 46608) and 30 April (1990, Point Loma, SDNHM 46887).

Though the bulk of the population makes a loop route, returning south along the Rocky Mountains after heading north along the Pacific coast (Phillips 1975), many Rufous Hummingbirds also go south through southern California. Because few of the birds at this season are adult males, especially after early July, the ratio between the Rufous and Allen's is uncertain. In the SDNHM collection, there are six specimens of fall migrant Rufous

from San Diego County, five of Allen's. Specimen dates of the Rufous range from 19 July (1934, Balboa Park, SDNHM 16536) to October (no exact date, 1968, Point Loma, SDNHM 37615). Sight records are as early as 22 June (1970, one banded at Point Loma, AFN 24:717, 1970) and 23 June (2000, one near Cutca Valley, C14, J. M. and B. Hargrove). After peaking from July to early August, numbers of *Selasphorus* hummingbirds dwindle, with the latest seen typically in early October. Fall migrants concentrate at patches of native wildflowers in the mountains (up to 30, including seven male Rufous, near the Palomar Observatory, D15, 12 July 2000, K. L. Weaver) and at exotic flowering plants in the coastal lowland (up to 65 at Quail Botanical Garden, K7, 7 July 1997, C. C. Gorman). There are a few fall records of *Selasphorus* hummingbirds in the Anza–Borrego Desert, the maximum being up to six coming to feeders near the Borrego Palm Canyon campground (F23) 26 July–6 August 1989 (L. L. Jee).

Winter: A few *Selasphorus* hummingbirds winter in San Diego County annually, in exotic flowering vegetation, especially eucalyptus. During the atlas period the number reported per winter varied from ten in 1998–99 to just one in 2000–01. Most wintering *Selasphorus* hummingbirds are in parks, cemeteries, and well-landscaped residential areas in the coastal lowland, with up to three in La Jolla 3 January 1999 (L. and M. Polinsky) and eight on the San Diego Christmas bird count 20 December 1975. A few wintering birds have been adult male Rufous, and an immature male from Carlsbad (I6) 14 January 1994 (SDNHM 48887) is a Rufous.

More surprising are three winter records from the Anza–Borrego Desert. One, of a male Rufous in Borrego Springs (F24) 19 December 1999 (M. L. Gabel), was from an ornamental planting, but two have been from natural canyons, Glorieta Canyon (H24) 29 December 1985 (L. Grismer, M. Galvan) and Hellhole Canyon (G23) 1 January 1999 (A. G. and D. Stanton).

Conservation: The introduction of diverse exotic flowering plants has augmented the food supply for migrating hummingbirds and has allowed a few of the Rufous to cut short their long migration and winter in southern California. The county's first winter record of any *Selasphorus* hummingbird was on the San Diego Christmas bird count 2 January 1961.

Allen's Hummingbird *Selasphorus sasin*

Breeding only in a slender strip along the coast of California and southern Oregon, Allen's Hummingbird has a remarkably limited distribution. A migratory subspecies breeding south to Ventura County passes through San Diego County on its way to and from a winter range centered on the mountains around Mexico City. Preadapted to suburbia, a nonmigratory subspecies resident on the Channel Islands spread to metropolitan Los Angeles and southward through Orange County. It has now reached San Diego County, where it was found nesting for the first time at San Onofre in 2001.

Photo by Anthony Mercieca

Migration: Allen's Hummingbird is famous for its migrations being shifted early in the year; the earliest arriving Allen's Hummingbirds are the first of any land bird in both spring and fall. "Spring" migration takes place largely before the equinox marks the beginning of spring; "fall" migration begins before the summer solstice and concludes by the beginning of September. As a spring migrant Allen's Hummingbird is uncommon in San Diego County; from 1997 to 2001 there was no report of more than two per day. A concentration as large as the 200 noted by G. McCaskie in the Tijuana River valley 15 February 1964 has never been approached since. At this season the species occurs mainly in the coastal lowland, rarely in the Anza–Borrego Desert (only two reports 1997–2001), and rarely as high in the mountains as 4000 feet elevation (one in Corte Madera Valley, R20, 21 February 1999, D. Herron). Specimens range in date from 18 February (1940, La Jolla, P7, SDNHM 18095) to 31 March (1961, Alpine, P17, SDNHM 30263), with one mist-netted and measured 10 April (1971, Point Loma, S7, G. McCaskie). The early specimen date is not representative, however, because the species begins arriving in its breeding range in late January. Sight records for San Diego County range from 16 January (1988, near San Diego, J. Oldenettel, AB 42:322, 1988) to 22 April (1997, one at the upper end of Sweetwater Reservoir, S13, P. Famolaro). An unidentified *Selasphorus* hummingbird north of Lake Morena (S21) 10 January 1998 (S. E. Smith) was most likely an early Allen's. Two reports in May could be of misidentified Rufous Hummingbirds or pioneers of the nonmigratory subspecies.

Allen's Hummingbird is probably more numerous in San Diego County in summer as a southbound migrant than in late winter as it heads north. But in summer adult males make up a smaller proportion of the population. Because only adult males are identifiable in the field, high counts are concentrated during the last week of June and first week of July (at least 10 in Barker Valley, E16, 25–29 June 1997, D. Rawlins), the time when most adult males pass through. Specimens of southbound migrants range from 30 June (1997, Mission Hills area of San Diego, R9, SDNHM 50045) to 1 September (1996, La Jolla, SDNHM 49586). Sight records range from 3 June (2000, Horno Area, Camp Pendleton, D3, R. Breisch; 1997, probable Allen's along upper Pine Valley Creek, O21, R. A. Hamilton) and 4 June (1970, two banded at Point Loma, AFN 24:717, 1970) to 10 September (1998, Point Loma, P. A. Ginsburg). At this season Allen's Hummingbirds are scattered over the coastal slope but there are no reports from the Anza–Borrego Desert.

Winter: *Selasphorus* hummingbirds are rare winter visitors in coastal San Diego County, and some percentage of these are Allen's. There are at least ten sight records of apparent adult males, all within 3 miles of the coast, from late November to early January, such as one that remained at Del Mar (N7) from fall migration to 26 December 1999 (B. C. Moore) and one at Point Loma 6 January 2002 (R. E. Webster, NAB 56:224, 2002). More important, there are two specimens, from Coronado (S9) 29 November 1968 (SDNHM 37875) and La Jolla 22 December 1999 (SDNHM 50350), plus one mist-netted at Point Loma 1 January 1968 (AFN 22:479, 1968).

Breeding distribution: Allen's Hummingbird was confirmed nesting in San Diego County for the first time in 2001, when John and Beverly Hargrove noted three, including a displaying male and a female gathering nest material, at San Onofre State Beach (C1) 20 January 2001. In the same area, a territorial male had edged a few feet across the line from Orange County 18 May 1998, when P. A. Ginsburg observed one defending a clump of bottlebrush.

Further knowledge of Allen's Hummingbird's colonization of San Diego County should be based on actual breeding behavior and observations in late May, during the brief window between the departure of the last Rufous Hummingbirds and the arrival of the first migratory Allen's.

Nesting: Nesting in January, as seen at San Onofre, is expected for Allen's Hummingbird in southern California. On the Palos Verdes Peninsula, Los Angeles County, Wells and Baptista (1979) reported females attending nests or fledglings in all months of the year except September and October.

Conservation: On the California mainland, the Channel Islands subspecies of Allen's Hummingbird was discovered nesting on the Palos Verdes Peninsula in 1966 and was common there by the following year (Wells and Baptista 1979). From there the birds began spreading into the Los Angeles basin, reaching Orange County by 1980, when they were first found nesting at Newport Beach and Costa Mesa. By 1997 they had spread south along the coast to Laguna Beach, less than 15 miles northwest of the San Diego county line (Gallagher 1997). They use ornamental vegetation as least as much as native willow

trees, so further spread south along San Diego County's coast seems assured.

The primitive migration route for Allen's Hummingbird was north at low elevations along the coast, then south at high elevations through the mountains, a strategy geared to the availability of flowers in each zone (Phillips 1975). With the proliferation of exotic plants that flower over intervals different from those of native species, this constraint is relaxed. The spread of the tree tobacco in particular appears to be allowing southbound Allen's Hummingbirds to migrate at low as well as at high elevations.

Taxonomy: The two subspecies of Allen's Hummingbird differ in size, especially bill length. The migratory nominate *S. s. sasin* (Lesson, 1829) is smaller that the nonmigratory *S. s. sedentarius* Grinnell, 1929. See Stiles (1972) for a key; identifying the bird's age and sex is a necessary precursor to identifying the subspecies, as it is for distinguishing the Rufous and Allen's as species.

All specimens from San Diego County are *sasin* except for one collected at Point Loma 25 April 1971 (SDNHM 37764). Note that the date of this early pioneer of *sedentarius* falls outside the normal migration schedule of *sasin*.

Kingfishers — Family Alcedinidae

Belted Kingfisher *Ceryle alcyon*

Forty million years ago, before the advent of the songbirds, members of the order Coraciiformes were the dominant small land birds in North America. Today, over most of the continent, only one is left: the Belted Kingfisher. Fishing by plunging into the water head first, Belted Kingfishers exploit any water, fresh or salt, clear enough that they can see fish in it. The kingfisher occurs in San Diego County largely as an uncommon winter visitor. Breeding birds are rare, and the county lies at the southern tip of the species' breeding range.

Winter: Nonbreeding Belted Kingfishers are widespread over the coastal slope of San Diego County wherever there is water. The largest numbers are in the coastal lagoons (up to eight at Batiquitos Lagoon, J7, 26 December 1998, R. Stone), in south San Diego Bay (up to four at Chula Vista, U10, 18 December 1999, E. J. McNeil), and at reservoirs (up to seven at Lake Hodges, K10, 27 December 1998, R. L. Barber). But the birds also search out small ponds and creeks, making their distribution at the scale of an atlas square look almost uniform over much of the coastal lowland. The birds are seen occasionally flying long distances over dry country. In the more rugged foothills and mountains they are sparser but occur even high in the mountains, up to 4600–4700 feet elevation at Doane Pond, Palomar Mountain (E14; one on 27 February 2000, P. Unitt), and Lake Cuyamaca (M20; four sightings of single birds, A. P. and T. E. Keenan). In the Anza–Borrego Desert wintering kingfishers are rare and

Photo by Anthony Mercieca

restricted to man-made ponds in the Borrego Valley (F24/G24/H25). During the atlas period single birds were reported from this area 16 times, though some may have been repeated sightings of the same individual.

Migration: The Belted Kingfisher's migrations through San Diego County are not well defined because the species occurs year round. In the Anza–Borrego Desert, we encountered only one spring migrant away from wintering habitat during the atlas period, at Agua Caliente Springs (M26) 13 April 1998 (E. C. Hall). But 15 earlier records in the state park database range from 15 March (1981, one at Lower Willows, D23, A. G. Morley) to 15 May [1972 and 1976, single birds at Lower (D23) and Middle (C22) willows and in Cougar Canyon (D22), M. Getty, R. T. Patton]. Fall arrival is even less clear, as short-distance dispersal of birds breeding in southern California may begin much earlier than arrival of migrants from farther north. By the second week of July, however, kingfishers are showing up in many places where they were absent in May and June.

Breeding distribution: Before field work for this atlas began in 1997, very few Belted Kingfisher nests had been found in San Diego County, though scattered summering birds in northern San Diego County suggested some were being overlooked. In addition to the two older nesting records (Carpenter 1917; E. E. Sechrist in Willett 1933), a pair fledged young 2.1 miles north of Bonsall (E8) 25–29 May 1987 (J. C. and F. Aldrich).

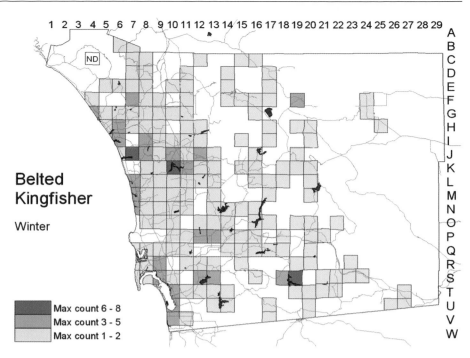

From 1997 to 2001, we confirmed nesting eight times. A sighting of one carrying food to young at the east end of Lake Hodges (K11) 24 April 1998 (E. C. Hall) was perhaps one of a pair with two fledglings at Bernardo Bay, Lake Hodges (K10), 26 June 1998 (M. and B. McIntosh). An agitated pair in the gorge of the upper San Diego River, elevation 1500 feet (K18), 9 July 2000 was near a hole in a bank with fresh scrape marks and fish bones below it (L. J. Hargrove, R. C. Sanger). The male of a pair at Ramona Dam (L12) spent much time inside a burrow, probably still digging, on 23 March 1998. On 5 April, only the male was visible outside the burrow; the female was presumably inside incubating (M. and B. McIntosh). Along Chicarita Creek 0.4 mile south of Carmel Mountain Community Park (M10) a pair was attending a nest burrow with nestlings 30 May–22 June 1998 (K. J. Winter). In a bank on the southwest side of Los Peñasquitos Lagoon (N7), a pair was at a nest hole 4 May 1997 (A. DeBolt); one was seen feeding young in the same area 3 May 1998 (D. K. Adams). One was carrying a crayfish to a hole in a bank of the huge borrow pit in the Sweetwater River near Dehesa (Q15) 1 June 1999 (W. E. Haas). At the upper end of Sweetwater Reservoir (S13), a nest found occupied 18 April 1997 had nestlings on 23 May 1997; the birds probably nested there again in 1998 (P. Famolaro). The last site is the southernmost nesting locality known for the Belted Kingfisher in western North America.

It is likely that the species nests irregularly at other places in San Diego County as well. Sites where it was suspected of nesting or noted repeatedly in late May and June are the Santa Margarita River north of Fallbrook (C8) and near its mouth (G4/G5), near the confluence of the San Luis Rey River and Couser Canyon (E10), 1.5 miles northeast of Weaver Mountain (E11), in Moosa Canyon near the Castle Creek golf course (G10), along Escondido Creek in Olivenhain (K8), San Pasqual Valley (K12), the San Dieguito River estuary (M7), El Capitan Reservoir (O16), Loveland Reservoir (Q17), Barrett Lake (S19), and Hauser Canyon (T20). Some birds seen through the breeding season, however, are undoubtedly unmated nonbreeders. The single record from the east slope of the mountains during the breeding season is of one at Banner (K21) 3 June 1999 (P. K. Nelson).

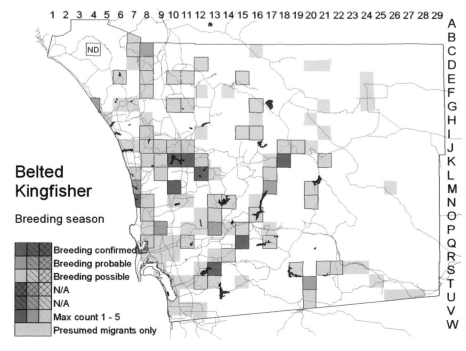

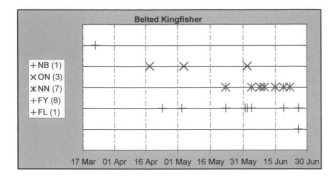

Nesting: The Belted Kingfisher typically digs a burrow in a bank for its nest, and all sites described in San Diego County have been in such burrows. The burrow is often but not necessarily over or near water in which the birds can feed. The kingfisher's nest site is thus similar to that of the Northern Rough-winged Swallow; the pair nesting at Ramona Dam in 1997 had to defend its burrow against swallows attempting to take it over.

With data on Belted Kingfisher nesting in San Diego County so meager, the species' breeding season here remains uncertain. Observations during the atlas period

suggest egg laying at least from early April to early May. Carpenter's (1917) nest with young "fully feathered" on 6 May 1916 must have been started in mid March.

Conservation: The Belted Kingfisher presumably benefited from the importation of water and the installation of many ponds and reservoirs, then stocked with exotic fish. The introduction of the crayfish also gave the kingfisher another important food. The species' absence from undeveloped areas of Camp Pendleton contrasts strikingly with its wide distribution over most of the coastal slope. Nevertheless, San Diego County Christmas bird counts show no trend in kingfisher numbers. Channelizing of streams and stabilization of banks eliminates kingfisher nesting habitat, though this has not resulted in the species' breeding range retracting north, as it has for the Bank Swallow.

Taxonomy: The degree of overlap between the larger western and smaller eastern populations of the Belted Kingfisher is greater than the level appropriate for the populations to be recognized as subspecies (Rand and Traylor 1950, Phillips 1962).

WOODPECKERS — FAMILY PICIDAE

Lewis' Woodpecker *Melanerpes lewis*

Lewis' Woodpecker is an uncommon winter visitor to San Diego County. It occurs mainly in the mountains and foothills, seeking large trees at the edges of meadows or scattered in grassland. Its distribution is patchy, the birds often recurring year after year at favored spots while ignoring other habitat that looks similar. On the other hand, the numbers wintering in San Diego County vary greatly from year to year, and in irruption years occasional birds reach the coast or the desert floor.

Winter: Oak savanna and mountain meadows constitute the main habitats for Lewis' Woodpecker in San Diego County. The species occurs mainly above 1000 feet elevation, rarely within 20 miles of the coast. From 1997 through 2002, our highest counts were of eight at San Ignacio, Los Coyotes Indian Reservation (E21), 19 December 1999 (M. C. Jorgensen), seven at Lake Cuyamaca (M20) 11 February 1999 (D. Aklufi), and eight in upper McCain Valley (R26) 23 January 2000 (J. R. Barth). In irruption years, however, numbers can be much larger. Totals on the Lake Henshaw Christmas bird count vary from zero in 1991 and 1992 to 45 on 29 December 1981. On the Escondido count, Lewis' Woodpecker has been recorded on only three of 17 counts from 1986 to 2001, yet the count on 30 December 1989 yielded 36. The largest number ever reported in San Diego County was at least 60 on Palomar Mountain (D15) 26 October 1982 (R. Higson, AB 37:225, 1983).

During the atlas period our winter record nearest the coast was of one about 9 miles inland at Case

Photo by Anthony Mercieca

Spring, Camp Pendleton (B4), 17 December 2000 (P. A. Ginsburg). Most of the few sightings along the coast are during migration periods. Lewis' Woodpeckers, single individuals in all cases, have been found just twice on the Oceanside Christmas bird count (1 January 1979, 21 December 2002), once on the Rancho Santa Fe count (16 December 1984), and once on the San Diego count (16 December 1989). The only records from the Anza–Borrego Desert are of one at Peña Spring and in Culp Valley (G23/H23) 26 September and 6 November 1991 (M. L. Gabel) and of up to three at Club Circle, Borrego Springs (G24), 31 October 1989–17 April 1990 (A. G. Morley et al.).

Migration: The arrival and departure of Lewis' Woodpecker in San Diego County vary greatly from year to year. Fall arrival is generally in late September or early October; 15 September (1950, one at Palomar

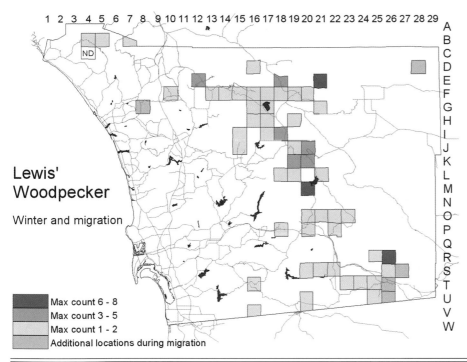

Lewis'
Woodpecker

Winter and migration

- Max count 6 - 8
- Max count 3 - 5
- Max count 1 - 2
- Additional locations during migration

Mountain, E. Beemer) is the earliest recorded date. In 1998 the latest report was on 8 February, but in 1999 it was 24 April, in 2000 it was 1 June, and in 2001 it was 6 May. The occurrence on 1 June 2000 was the latest ever for San Diego County; on that date a Lewis' Woodpecker got trapped and died in the shed for donations to the Salvation Army in Descanso (P20; G. Wynn, SDNHM 50439).

Acorn Woodpecker *Melanerpes formicivorus*

The Acorn Woodpecker is famed for its unique habit of storing acorns in granary trees, which the birds may riddle with thousands of holes. It will also store acorns in utility poles, the walls of wooden buildings, and boulders composed of soft granite. Its communal breeding and social life have attracted intensive study, leading to new perspectives on animal behavior. With acorns so important in its diet, the woodpecker is intimately linked with oak woodland. In San Diego County it is common year round wherever there are extensive groves of oaks.

Breeding distribution: The Acorn Woodpecker's distribution in San Diego is essentially the same as that as oak woodland. The habitat can be groves of the coast live oak only, riparian woodland containing some oaks, or montane forest in which the black, canyon live, and coast live oaks are mixed with conifers. The latter may be superior habitat, as pine trees, with their softer bark, make better granary trees than oaks, in which the woodpeckers typically drill granaries in dead snags only. Also, the tannin content of canyon live oak acorns is less than that of coast live oak acorns, making the former a superior food (Koenig and Heck 1988, Koenig 1991). Our highest estimates of Acorn Woodpecker numbers were all from mixed montane forest, up to 100 as in Palomar Mountain State Park (E14) 17 May 1997 (K. Messer, R. Turner), in Cuyamaca Rancho State Park (N20) 17 July 2000 (B. Siegel), and around Mount Laguna (O23) 6 June 1998 (A. E. Klovstad, C. L. Mann). With decreasing elevation, the Acorn Woodpecker becomes less common and more localized, in tandem with oaks. The range approaches within 3 miles of the coast along San Onofre Creek (D2; up to four on 31 March 2001, R. E. Fischer), then con-

Photo by Anthony Mercieca

tracts inland toward the south. Outlying locations toward the south are Los Peñasquitos Canyon (up to 22 in square N9 on 15 June 1997, L. D. and R. Johnson; up to 6 in square N8 on 2 May 1999, P. A. Ginsburg), San Clemente Canyon (P8; up to three on 27 April 1999, M. B. Stowe), and Tecolote Canyon (Q8/Q9; up to four on 8 August 1998, E. Wallace).

A unique outlying colony of the Acorn Woodpecker is in Quail Botanical Gardens, Encinitas (K7), a completely man-made woodland outside the species' natural range. Counts here during the breeding season averaged 13 birds (R. and A. Campbell). At Quail Gardens, the tree supplying the woodpecker's acorns is an Old World species, the cork oak.

The eastern edge of the Acorn Woodpecker's range tracks the eastern edge of the range of the coast live oak almost exactly, though the birds are lacking from small

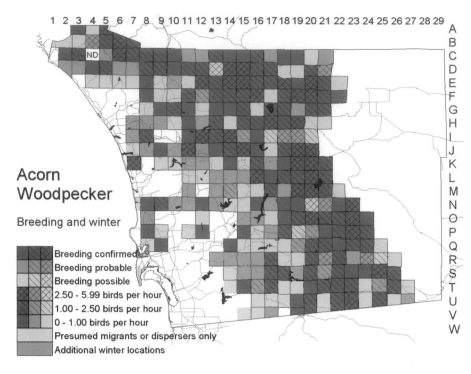

Acorn
Woodpecker

Breeding and winter

- Breeding confirmed
- Breeding probable
- Breeding possible
- 2.50 - 5.99 birds per hour
- 1.00 - 2.50 birds per hour
- 0 - 1.00 birds per hour
- Presumed migrants or dispersers only
- Additional winter locations

Migration: The Acorn Woodpecker is nonmigratory, rarely appearing outside its breeding range. There is little if any seasonal pattern to these wanderers, which crop up in the middle of the breeding season as often as in fall and winter. Most records of them are within 5 miles of sites where the species is resident. But there are at least 15 records from Point Loma, most of single individuals, though five were there 15 September–15 October 1987 (R. E. Webster, AB 42:136, 1988). Only one Acorn Woodpecker has been noted on the coastal slope as far from the breeding range as the Tijuana River valley, on 10 September 1972 (AB 27:122, 1973).

Similarly, a few Acorn Woodpeckers have been noted on the east slope of San Diego County's mountains, east of the oaks. On or near the desert floor there are only three records, of one at Lower Willows (D23) 26 June 1988 (A. G. Morley), one near Barrel Spring in the Ocotillo Wells off-road vehicle area (H29) 10 June 1987 (A. G. Morley), and one at the former Fish Creek Ranger Station (L29) 15 May 1973 (ABDSP database).

Winter: The Acorn Woodpecker's distribution and abundance in winter do not differ materially from those in the breeding season. Our highest winter count was of 175 in Pine Hills (K19) 6 February 1999 (S. E. Smith, D. W. Au).

Conservation: There is no evidence for any change in the Acorn Woodpecker's status in San Diego County through recorded history. The species tolerates low-intensity development of its habitat provided oaks are left undisturbed. Whether such development is compatible with the long-term regeneration of oak woodland, however, is another question. The woodpeckers sometimes take over wooden buildings as granary sites, much to the consternation of the building's human owners. The population at Quail Gardens appears to represent the only instance of Acorn Woodpeckers colonizing an artificial habitat in San Diego County. The birds there rely, however, on dead branches and trees that will have to be removed. The natural processes of tree death and decay that provide the Acorn Woodpecker with nest sites may be incompatible with the intensive management a botanical garden requires. The drought of 1999–2004 left many oaks in San Diego County stressed or dead, suggesting that climate change leading to a drier climate could affect the Acorn Woodpecker adversely.

isolated groves. The easternmost point in San Diego County where the species is resident is at the south end of McCain Valley Road, at the junction with old Highway 80 (west edge of T27; up to three on 3 July 2000, J. K. Wilson).

Nesting: In California, most Acorn Woodpeckers live in groups, in which both sexes share mates and a single nest cavity. Koenig and Mumme (1987) studied the woodpecker's unusual sex life extensively, putting it in its ecological context. The species' nest holes, though, are typical of the woodpecker family, bored on the underside of slightly angled trunks or branches. Atlas observers noted nests in power poles and snags of pine and white alder, as well as in coast live, black, and Engelmann oak. In Quail Gardens, K. L. Weaver found nests in a dead palm and a dead pine.

Our observations show that in San Diego County the Acorn Woodpecker usually begins egg laying in early April and continues through mid June. A few suggest laying in late March; a record of fledglings at Live Oak Park (D8) 23 April 1998 (M. Freda) implies laying by 12 March, earlier than the earliest date of 17 May for the well-studied Hastings Reservation, Monterey County (Koenig et al. 1995).

Taxonomy: Acorn Woodpeckers resident in San Diego County and elsewhere in California are *M. f. bairdi* Ridgway, 1881, larger and heavier billed than the subspecies east of the Colorado River.

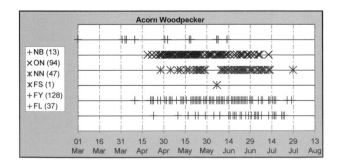

Gila Woodpecker *Melanerpes uropygialis*

The Gila Woodpecker reaches the northwestern tip of its range in the Imperial Valley. In San Diego County there were only unsubstantiated reports until 2003–04, when one spent the winter in Borrego Springs. Although the Gila Woodpecker is common in the towns of Brawley and El Centro, the dying off of cottonwood trees in the Imperial Valley disfavors the woodpecker from spreading.

Winter: San Diego County's first well-supported Gila Woodpecker appeared in a residential area of Borrego Springs (G24) 25 September 2003–1 March 2004 (P. D. Jorgensen), to be observed and photographed by many. The report of one near Jacumba (U28) 17 October 1952 (Gardner 1959) was based on a recollection several years old, and the report of one at Tamarisk Grove 18 January 1986 (Massey 1998) was not substantiated.

Williamson's Sapsucker *Sphyrapicus thyroideus*

Though resident in the higher elevations of the San Jacinto Mountains just 15 miles to the north of the county line, and in the Sierra San Pedro Mártir to the south, in San Diego County Williamson's Sapsucker is a rare winter visitor only. On average, about one individual is found per year, usually in montane coniferous forest.

Winter: During the atlas period, only four Williamson's Sapsuckers were found in San Diego County, one near Wynola (J19) 29 December 1997 (J. Alpert), one at Observatory Campground, Palomar Mountain (E14), 24 February 1999 (G. L. Rogers), one along the Azalea Glen Trail, Cuyamaca Rancho State Park (M20), 23 September 2001 (S. Buchanan), and one at 4472 feet elevation in upper Sheep Canyon (C21) 10 February 2002 (L. J. Hargrove, J. Determan). Earlier records are from similar conifer-dominated habitat on Palomar Mountain, at Julian, and in the Cuyamaca and Laguna mountains. The species is usually seen singly, occasionally in twos.

Only seven Williamson's Sapsuckers have been recorded in San Diego County at elevations below 3500 feet, one at Bonita (T11) 16 December 1968–March 1969 (AFN 23:522, 1969), one near Lakeside (P14) 25 November 1972–1 February 1973 (AB 27:122, 664, 1973), one in La Jolla (P8) 22 November 1989–16 February 1990 (J. Moore, AB 44:162, 330, 1990), and four on Point Loma, 11 October, 15–17 October, and 20–22 October 1987 (AB

Photo by Anthony Mercieca

42:136, 1988), and 2 December 1996–3 January 1997 (V. P. Johnson, NASFN 51:802, 1997). Most of these occurrences at low elevations coincide with irruptions of other montane birds.

Migration: San Diego County records of Williamson's Sapsucker range in date from 23 September (cited above) and 27 September (1980, Palomar Mountain, AB 35:227, 1981) to 10 April (1979, same locality, AB 33:806, 1979).

Taxonomy: Two subspecies of Williamson's Sapsucker were long recognized on the basis of a difference in bill size, but they overlap too much for the distinction to be maintained (Browning and Cross 1999, Patten et al. 2003).

Yellow-bellied Sapsucker *Sphyrapicus varius*

With improved information on the species' identification, birders are finding the Yellow-bellied Sapsucker to be an annual though rare winter visitor to southern California. At least 25 have been found in San Diego County. Most are immature birds retaining the largely brown mottled head of juvenile plumage.

Winter: Records of the Yellow-bellied Sapsucker are scattered throughout San Diego County, on the coastal slope from Fallbrook (D8) in the north (one from 1 December 1984 to 17 February 1985, R. Higson, AB 39:210, 1985) to Imperial Beach (V10) in the south (one on 18 February 2001, G. McCaskie). But at least ten are from that mecca for sapsuckers, the Santa Ysabel Mission (I18). Only two

Photo by Anthony Mercieca

have been identified in the Anza–Borrego Desert, both at man-made oases: the Roadrunner Club, Borrego Springs (F24), 6 November 1999, and Casa del Zorro (H25) 4 November 2001 (P. D. Jorgensen).

The historical record for this species is still short, but numbers reaching San Diego County may vary appreciably from year to year. During the five-year atlas period, there were none in 1997–98, six in 1998–99, and one each in the three following years.

Migration: Dates of Yellow-bellied Sapsuckers in San Diego County range from 19 October (1985, one at the Santa Ysabel Mission, C. G. Edwards, AB 40:159, 1986) to 3 March (1998, one in the Tierrasanta area of San Diego, P10, D. K. Adams, FN 52:258, 1998).

Conservation: An apparent increase in Yellow-bellied Sapsuckers wintering in southern California could be a result not only of improved identification criteria but of the breeding range spreading west, into Alaska (Erwin et al. 2004).

Red-naped Sapsucker *Sphyrapicus nuchalis*

Coming from a breeding range in the Great Basin and Rocky Mountain region, the Red-naped Sapsucker reaches San Diego County as an uncommon winter visitor. It occurs most often in oak woodland but shows up occasionally throughout the county. There is no difference in habitat and behavior between the Red-naped and Red-breasted Sapsuckers here, and the former is only slightly less numerous than the latter. In the lack of previous summer records from southern California, one of the greatest surprises of the atlas field work was three summer observations of the Red-naped Sapsucker from Palomar Mountain, including one of hybridization with the Red-breasted.

Photo by Anthony Mercieca

Winter: Though the ranges of the Red-naped and Red-breasted Sapsuckers, winter as well as breeding, are largely complementary, in San Diego County both are found in similar numbers in similar areas. The county lies at the northwestern corner of the Red-naped's main winter range. In the five winters from 1997 to 2002 we recorded the Red-breasted 165 times (183 individuals); we recorded the Red-naped 149 times (180 individuals). Like the Red-breasted, the Red-naped is most frequent in the mountains and wooded canyons in the foothills, as well as in the coastal lowland of northern San Diego County. Our highest daily counts were of four around Sunshine Summit (D17) 23 January 1999 (J. K. Wilson) and four around Santa Ysabel (J18) 14 December 1997 (S. E. Smith). In the south coastal area the species is rare.

With only three, our records of the Red-naped in the Anza–Borrego Desert during the atlas period were even fewer than those of the Red-breasted Sapsucker. Earlier records (Massey 1998, ABDSP database), like these three, are largely from developed areas and oases like Lower Willows.

Migration: The Red-naped Sapsucker occurs in San Diego County mainly from October through March. One in the Borrego Palm Canyon campground (F23) 18 September 1992

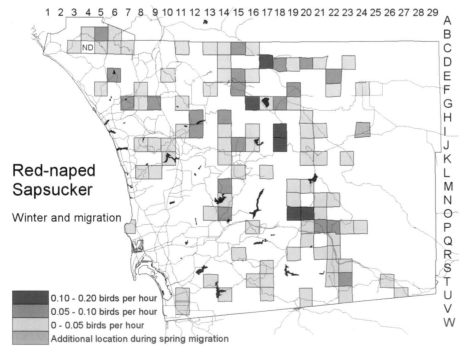

Red-naped Sapsucker

Winter and migration

- 0.10 – 0.20 birds per hour
- 0.05 – 0.10 birds per hour
- 0 – 0.05 birds per hour
- Additional location during spring migration

(R. Thériault) was early; one at Banner (K19) 18 April 1999 (P. K. Nelson) and one near Jewell Valley (U27) 25 April 1999 (F. L. Unmack) were unusually late.

Breeding distribution: Completely unexpected were three records of the Red-naped Sapsucker from Palomar Mountain in summer. The first was of one paired with a Red-breasted Sapsucker and accompanied by a fledgling just east of Doane Pond (E14) 19 July 1998 (D. S. Cooper). Another, or perhaps the same individual, was in the same area 17 July 1999 (J. R. Barth). Yet another was about 3.4 miles to the southeast in Bull Pasture (E15) 18 June 1999 (C. R. Mahrdt, E. C. Hall). All the birds were observed carefully by participants aware that the species was unexpected for the season. There are no previous records of the Red-naped Sapsucker summering, much less hybridizing with the Red-breasted Sapsucker, in southern California. The mountains of southern Nevada are the nearest point of the species' traditional breeding range.

Conservation: Numbers of the Red-naped Sapsucker on San Diego Christmas bird counts show a pattern of decrease similar to that of the Red-breasted. The average per count of the Red-naped was 1.4 from 1975 (the first year figures for the two species were consistently listed separately) to 1988 but 0.8 from 1989 to 2001. On counts elsewhere in San Diego County the trend is slight or none. Thus it seems that in spite of the sapsuckers' feeding on exotic trees, especially the Peruvian pepper, increasing urbanization discourages them.

Taxonomy: The Red-naped, Red-breasted, and Yellow-bellied Sapsuckers were long classified as a single species. Various sources of evidence, however, suggest that they have crossed the threshold of speciation, though the Red-naped hybridizes with both other species along much of the line where their breeding ranges abut (Johnson and Zink 1983, Johnson and Johnson 1985, Cicero and Johnson 1995).

Red-breasted Sapsucker *Sphyrapicus ruber*

The Red-breasted Sapsucker occurs in San Diego County in two roles. As a winter visitor it is widespread but uncommon, found mainly in oak and coniferous woodland, as well as in nonnative trees, especially pepper and eucalyptus. In these trees the sapsuckers drill rows of holes, tapping the sap. The scars on the trees last for decades, long after the birds have gone. As a breeding species the Red-breasted Sapsucker is rare and confined to coniferous forest. Curiously, the species is spreading as a breeding bird at the same time the number of winter visitors is shrinking.

Breeding distribution: Breeding Red-breasted Sapsuckers are best known in San Diego County from Palomar

Photo by Anthony Mercieca

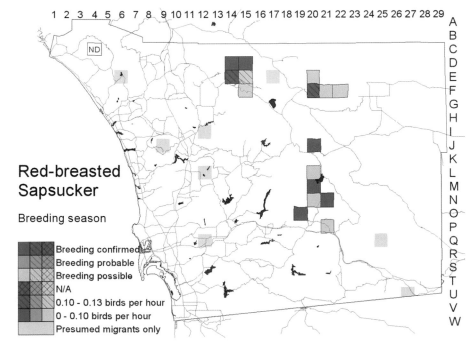

Red-breasted Sapsucker

Breeding season

Breeding confirmed
Breeding probable
Breeding possible
N/A
0.10 - 0.13 birds per hour
0 - 0.10 birds per hour
Presumed migrants only

Mountain. During the atlas period they were widely distributed on Palomar at elevations from 4600 to 6000 feet with at least 10 pairs. We recorded them on Hot Springs Mountain on eight occasions, with up to four at 5800 to 6000 feet elevation along the road leading north from San Ysidro (F20) 25 May 2001 (M. and B. McIntosh).

The Red-breasted Sapsucker was found for the first time on Volcan Mountain in 2001 with single birds around the south base of the mountain (J20) 7 June (M. B. Stowe) and 15 June (E. C. Hall, J. O. Zimmer).

With 11 reports during the atlas period in the Cuyamaca Mountains, we found the Red-

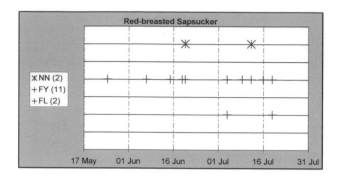

at Point Loma (S7) 5 May 1982 (R. E. Webster, AB 36:894, 1982), one was at Cottonwood Campground (Q25) 6 May 2001 (A. P. and T. E. Keenan), and one was near Deadman Hole (E17) 19 May 2001 (J. D. Barr). The last two were at elevations of 3100 to 4300 feet in oak woodland and may have been pioneers scouting for breeding territories.

Winter: As a winter visitor the Red-breasted Sapsucker is widely but thinly distributed over the county's coastal slope from sea level to 6000 feet in the mountains. Its numbers in the coastal lowland decrease from north to south. Though the birds feed on a variety of native trees, they are more frequent around some exotic ones, especially the Peruvian pepper. The abundance of pepper trees in the landscaping of the campgrounds at O'Neill Lake and Guajome Lake (G7) accounts for the sapsucker's being recorded more frequently at these sites than at any others. Our highest daily count in one atlas square in winter, of four on 1 December 1998, was at O'Neill Lake (P. A. Ginsburg).

In the Anza–Borrego Desert the Red-breasted Sapsucker is rare, recorded mainly from exotic planted trees in the Borrego Valley or the cottonwoods planted at Butterfield Ranch (M23). From 1997 to 2002 we noted single individuals in the desert on only six occasions, and only one of these was in native vegetation, the mesquites at Vallecito County Park (14 January 2000, M. C. Jorgensen).

Conservation: Despite its frequent use of ornamental trees, the Red-breasted Sapsucker may be on the decrease as a winter visitor to San Diego County. Numbers on the San Diego Christmas bird count averaged 3.9 per year from 1975 to 1988 but 0.8 per year from 1989 to 2001 and only 0.4 per year from 1997 to 2001. Before 1975 the numbers of the Red-breasted and Red-naped on the count were usually combined and reported as Yellow-bellied. But the average per count of the combined species from 1954 to 1974 was 6.5, so the trend may go back even fur-

breasted Sapsucker more frequently than expected in that range. All observations were of just one or two birds, except for a family group of four along the Sweetwater River at Hulburd Grove (O19) 4 July 2000 (J. R. Barth). At 3400 feet, this site represents the lowest elevation at which the Red-breasted Sapsucker has been known to breed in San Diego County and the southernmost point of recorded breeding in the species' entire range. One at Pine Valley (P21) 19 May 2001 (M. B. Mulrooney) was even farther south, also at an unexpectedly low elevation (3680 feet), and also at the lower limit of the pines.

Nesting: Little is yet known of Red-breasted Sapsucker nesting in San Diego County. The two nest sites described by atlas observers were in a black oak and in an ornamental deciduous tree on the grounds of the Palomar Observatory. Our observations of breeding activity imply the birds lay at least from mid May to early June; 13 egg sets from throughout California range from 12 May to 21 June (Bent 1939).

Migration: The Red-breasted Sapsucker occurs as a winter visitor to San Diego County mainly from October through March. Dates of such migrants range from 19 September (1994, one at O'Neill Lake, E6, P. A. Ginsburg) to 29 March, except for three stragglers in May. One was

ther. Old sap wells on eucalyptus trees throughout metropolitan San Diego remain as mute testimony to the former widespread occurrence of sapsuckers in an area where we noted only four individual Red-breasteds over the five-year atlas period. Figures from the county's Christmas bird counts other than San Diego, however, do not show so clear a trend. The species' winter range could be retracting northward as the trend toward warmer winters compels less migration.

On the other hand, as a breeding bird the Red-breasted Sapsucker is spreading. Early naturalists did not report it in the county in summer; the first record at this season was from Palomar Mountain in 1957 (A. G. Morley

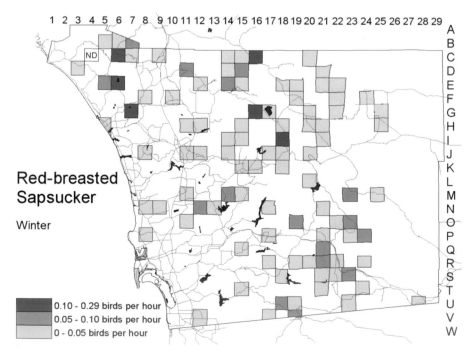

Red-breasted
Sapsucker

Winter

0.10 - 0.29 birds per hour
0.05 - 0.10 birds per hour
0 - 0.05 birds per hour

in Devillers 1970a). By 1981 there were at least five pairs on Palomar (R. Higson in Unitt 1984). On Hot Springs Mountain I found one on 8 June 1985 but none over three visits in 1980 (Unitt 1981). The first breeding-season reports from the Cuyamaca Mountains were in 1974 (Unitt 1984) and 1983 (C. G. Edwards, AB 37:1028, 1983). It is in these last two areas where the species' establishment and increase since 1980 have been most noticeable.

Taxonomy: The Red-breasted Sapsucker consists of two subspecies, *S. r. ruber* (Gmelin, 1788), breeding in the Pacific Northwest, and *S. r. daggetti* Grinnell, 1901, breeding mainly in California. *S. r. daggetti* accounts for almost all the winter visitors as well as the breeding popu-lation. The one specimen of *ruber*, from 5 miles northeast of Lakeside (N14) 9 November 1957 (SDNHM 30061), is the southernmost of this largely nonmigratory subspe-cies. *Sphyrapicus r. ruber* differs from *daggetti* mainly in its brighter red head (in fresh plumage scarlet rather than crimson), less extensive white head stripe, and smaller yellow-tinged spots on the back.

The Red-breasted, Red-naped, and Yellow-bellied Sapsuckers are closely related, apparently barely over the threshold as species. The Red-breasted and Red-naped hybridize to some extent, chiefly along the eastern flank of the Sierra Nevada, and hybrids have been collected as winter visitors in San Diego County (Devillers 1970a).

Ladder-backed Woodpecker *Picoides scalaris*

The Ladder-backed Woodpecker is characteristic of desert slopes, the hills and alluvial fans well vegetat-ed with large shrubs like the desert apricot, Mojave yucca, and above all the desert agave. In this habitat the Ladder-backed is an uncommon permanent res-ident. On the desert floor it is rare, even where there are trees like mesquite and desert ironwood large enough to offer nest sites. Field work for this atlas revealed two areas of semidesert scrub inhabited by Ladder-backed Woodpeckers on the county's coastal slope, in Dameron and Oak Grove valleys along the Riverside County line, and in Miller Valley on the Campo Plateau.

Breeding distribution: The factor accounting for the Ladder-backed Woodpecker's distribution in San Diego County is the availability of agaves and yuccas. On desert slopes where these plants are common, the woodpecker is uncommon. Our maximum daily count in one atlas

Photo by Anthony Mercieca

square during the breeding season was eight on the east side of Earthquake Valley (K24) 19 May 2000 (L. J. Hargrove). Rarely, however, did we find more than four. The species ranges as high as 5800 feet elevation in the Santa Rosa Mountains (C27; one bird and one nest hole 4 May 2000, P. Unitt). On the desert floor, or in washes through the badlands, the Ladder-backed Woodpecker is scarce; we found no more than one individual per day in such habitats. Along Fish Creek Wash near the Elephant Knees (M29), we found an old nest hole but never found any birds. Along the western margin of its range, the Ladder-backed Woodpecker drops out as desert-edge scrub merges into chaparral, extending west to Alder Canyon (C21; one on 3 May 2000, G. Rebstock), San Felipe Valley (I21; up to three, including adults feeding young,

Ladder-backed Woodpecker

Breeding and winter

Breeding confirmed
Breeding probable
Breeding possible
0.25 - 0.57 birds per hour
0.10 - 0.25 birds per hour
0 - 0.10 birds per hour
Presumed migrants or dispersers only
Additional winter locations

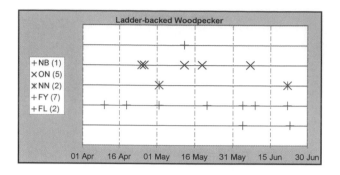

on 9 June 2000, J. O. Zimmer), and near Bankhead Springs (T27; two on 23 April 2000, P. Unitt).

In addition, the Ladder-backed Woodpecker occurs in two areas of the coastal slope. From the Aguanga region of Riverside County, it extends into north-central San Diego County into Dameron Valley (C15, up to two males 19 April 1997; C16, up to six, including fledglings, 23 June 2001) and even to the north base of Palomar Mountain near High Point Road (C15, two on 14 June 1997, K. L. Weaver).

In Miller Valley (S24) we found the species in 1998, 1999, and 2000, with up to four, including a pair at a nest, 22 June 2000 (L. J. Hargrove). Though on the coastal slope, both Dameron and Miller valleys have many elements of desert biota, such as the cane or snake cholla and white-tailed antelope squirrel.

Nesting: By far the most frequent site for Ladder-backed Woodpecker nests in San Diego County is the flowering stalk of the desert agave. The soft tissue of the stalk is easy for the birds to excavate, while the rosette of spine-tipped leaves below offers protection from predators. As atlas observers learned of this preference, they found holes in agaves more often than they found the birds themselves. The woodpeckers also excavate in the other large monocots growing in their habitat, the Mojave yucca and Parry's nolina. They use true wood, even if dead, only occasionally. We also noted holes in a mesquite snag, a telephone pole, and a railroad trestle. Massey (1998) reported a nest in a gate post. The one nest found in Miller Valley was in a large willow snag.

If the still unknown incubation and nestling periods for the Ladder-backed Woodpecker are the same as the 14 and 15 days, respectively, reported for Nuttall's (themselves based on minimal data, Lowther 2000a), atlas observations suggest that the Ladder-backed lays at least from late March to late May. Only one egg set was ever collected in San Diego County (6 April). Bent's (1939) range of 11 April–9 May for all of California was based on only seven records.

Migration: The Ladder-backed Woodpecker is nonmigratory, undertaking short-distance dispersal only. The only well-supported record far from the species' breeding range is still of one female in the Tijuana River valley

(W11) 9 October 1974 (J. L. Dunn, P. Unitt, AB 29:122, 1975). Other reports, such as that of one in Vista 22 July 1982 (AB 36:1017, 1982), were almost certainly based on misidentified juvenile Nuttall's Woodpeckers, which then gave observers the erroneous impression that the Ladder-backed was resident in the area.

Winter: In winter, the Ladder-backed Woodpecker is seen in its breeding range in much the same numbers as in the breeding season. Our highest daily count in winter was of nine in Box Canyon (L23) 10 January 1998 (S. D. Cameron, S. M. Wolf). Nevertheless, the species does spread to a modest extent in winter; at that season we noted it in 34 squares where we did not find it during the breeding season. These records included four from Oak Grove Valley on the coastal slope, three on the south-facing slopes north of the valley (C17) where the species is probably resident, plus one on the south side of the village of Oak Grove (D16; 26 January 2002, R. C. Sanger, K. S. Williams) where it is a visitor only. On the Campo Plateau, we found the species repeatedly in Miller Valley and also on nine occasions at other scattered locations, west to La Posta Valley (S23; one on 14 February 1999, L. J. Hargrove) and Campo Creek 4.1 miles east-northeast of Cameron Corners (U24; one on 5 January 2001, J. R. Barth).

Conservation: No trends in Ladder-backed Woodpecker numbers in San Diego County are known, though quantitative data from its range are minimal. Most of the species' habitat is protected within the Anza–Borrego Desert, but development threatens the outlying population in Dameron Valley. A trend toward a drier climate could constrict the woodpecker's range in the Anza–Borrego Desert but enable it to spread west into new areas. This may be happening already to the north of San Diego County in the San Bernardino Valley (E. A. Cardiff pers. comm.). In May 2000 a pair apparently nested along the Santa Ana River near Mentone, about 18 miles northwest of the traditional edge of the species' range in San Gorgonio Pass at Banning (D. R. Willick, NAB 54:423, 2000).

Taxonomy: Ladder-backed Woodpeckers throughout southeastern California are *P. s. cactophilus* Oberholser, 1911, with pale buffy-gray underparts, not distinctly brown as farther south in Baja California.

Hybridization between the Ladder-backed and Nuttall's Woodpeckers is frequent in Baja California (Short 1971), and regular at some places in Alta California such as Warner Pass and Morongo Valley, but rare in San Diego County. The species are segregated by habitat in their narrow zone of overlap, the Ladder-backed in desert-edge scrub on slopes, Nuttall's in riparian trees in canyon bottoms. Lori J. Hargrove suspected that a Ladder-backed in Borrego Palm Canyon (F23) 5 July 2001 was paired with a Nuttall's; G. L. Rogers reported one near Warner Springs (F19) 17 December 2001, well outside the Ladder-back's breeding range, as a possible hybrid.

Nuttall's Woodpecker *Picoides nuttallii*

Nuttall's is San Diego County's most widespread woodpecker, a common permanent resident in riparian, oak, and coniferous woodland. And it is spreading farther, colonizing formerly treeless scrub now replaced by urban landscaping. For reasons still not clear, numbers of Nuttall's Woodpeckers began increasing throughout San Diego County in the late 1980s, and that increase continued through the five-year atlas period.

Breeding distribution: Nuttall's Woodpecker inhabits almost the entire coastal slope of San Diego County. The population is most concentrated in inland canyons and foothills where the coast live oak is most numerous. The species breeds at all elevations within the county, nearly to the summit of Hot Springs Mountain (E20; up to six, including adults feeding young, 9 June 2001, K. L. Weaver). Otay Mesa, Otay Mountain, and Tecate Peak, along the Mexican border, now form the only extensive area on the coastal slope where Nuttall's Woodpecker is absent as a breeding bird.

On the desert slope of the mountains, for the most part, the east edge of Nuttall's Woodpecker range tracks the east edge of the oaks. The birds extend a short distance down slope in canyons with willows. Along Coyote Creek they occur in the breeding season only at Middle Willows on the Riverside County line (C22; three sightings of single birds in April and May, P. D. Jorgensen). They occur also in Borrego Palm Canyon and along San Felipe Creek downstream to the head of Sentenac Canyon (J23; nest with nestlings 2 May 1998, R. Thériault). In southern San Diego County Nuttall's Woodpecker ranges beyond the oaks to Jacumba (U28) and the mesquite-dominated thicket along Carrizo Creek 2 miles north of

Photo by Jack C. Daynes

Jacumba near Arsenic Springs (T28; one on 30 April and 24 June 1999, J. K. Wilson).

Nesting: Nuttall's Woodpeckers excavate their nest cavities in dead branches or snags of various trees, preferring the underside of a slanting trunk, a site that enhances protection from predators. Native trees were the most frequently described sites, with willow, sycamore, and oak

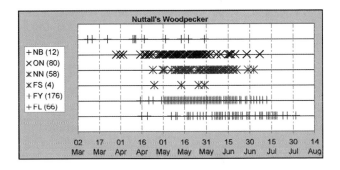

(both coast live and black) being mentioned six to eight times each, elderberry once. Nonnative vegetation in which atlas observers described Nuttall's Woodpecker nests included elm (one nest), eucalyptus (two), and, most interestingly, the flowering stalks of the non-native Americana agave (three).

The schedule of nesting activity we observed from 1997 to 2001 was consistent with a range of California egg dates of 25 March–18 June (Bent 1939, Sharp 1907). Two early reports of fledglings however, suggest occasional laying as early as mid March (earliest at Oak Hill Cemetery, I12, 16 April 2001, J. O. Zimmer).

Migration: Nuttall's Woodpecker is nonmigratory, dispersing little

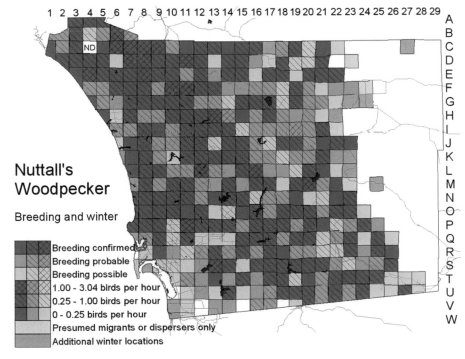

Nuttall's Woodpecker

Breeding and winter

- Breeding confirmed
- Breeding probable
- Breeding possible
- 1.00 - 3.04 birds per hour
- 0.25 - 1.00 birds per hour
- 0 - 0.25 birds per hour
- Presumed migrants or dispersers only
- Additional winter locations

outside its breeding range, normally for short distances only. Dates for such dispersers in the Anza–Borrego Desert range from 10 August (2000, one at Lower Willows along Coyote Creek, D23, P. D. Jorgensen) to 20 February (1978, one at the same location, B. Cord).

Winter: We noted Nuttall's Woodpecker in winter in 17 atlas squares where it probably does not breed. Almost all of these, however, were adjacent to squares where it probably does. Farthest afield were one in upper Barton Canyon, Santa Rosa Mountains (C27), 9 January 2002 (P. Unitt), three on the floor of the Borrego Valley in Borrego Springs (F24/G24; two on 19 December 1999, P. K. Nelson, P. D. Ache; one on 16 December 2001, R. Thériault), and two at Vallecito County Park (M25; 2 December 2000, P. Unitt; 25 February 2001, J. R. Barth).

Conservation: Before the mid 1980s Nuttall's Woodpecker was confined in San Diego County to native woodlands almost exclusively. Even in well-wooded Balboa Park it was a only rare winter visitor. Since then, however, it has spread widely into cities, taking advantage of woodpecker-friendly trees like liquidambar, birch, white alder, and even agaves. The average on San Diego Christmas bird counts has increased tenfold from 2.9 from 1953 to 1988 to 29.6 from 1997 to 2001 (maximum 48 in 2001).

The maturation of large numbers of urban trees is an attractive hypothesis that may help explain Nuttall's Woodpecker increase and spread. Nevertheless, some other forces still to be identified must be operating as well. Numbers on the Oceanside, Rancho Santa Fe, Escondido, and Lake Henshaw Christmas bird counts have all increased as well, if not so dramatically as at San Diego. On the Escondido count, for example, well within the woodpecker's traditional range, the average per count increased by a factor of 2.6 from 1985–89 to 1997–2001. Even when corrected by number of party-hours the factor of increase was 2.3. The Breeding Bird Survey (Sauer et al. 2003) has not revealed any such increase covering the species' range in general.

Whatever the reason for Nuttall's Woodpecker increase, it opens an opportunity for increases in other small birds that nest in its used holes, such as the House Wren, Western Bluebird, and White-breasted Nuthatch.

Downy Woodpecker *Picoides pubescens*

Among San Diego County's more interesting bird stories is that of the Downy Woodpecker. There were a few records, including breeding, before the early 1970s, but by that time the woodpecker was essentially a lost species. In the late 1970s it was found locally in northwestern San Diego County, then in the 1980s it spread abruptly throughout the coastal lowland. Currently it is an uncommon but widespread resident of riparian woodland and gradually spreading inland to ever higher elevations.

Breeding distribution: The Downy Woodpecker's center of distribution remains the riparian woodlands of northwestern San Diego County, where daily counts in one atlas square are as high as six (along the San Luis Rey River near Gird Road, E8, 21 and 26 March, 26 April, and 9 July 1999, P. A. Ginsburg). In this region the birds have moved beyond the main rivers to colonize many subsidiary creeks with willow thickets. In the southern half of the county the Downy Woodpecker still occurs mainly along the principal watercourses: Los Peñasquitos Canyon, the San Diego River, the Sweetwater River, the Otay River, and the Tijuana River. The most inland sites where the species is known during the breeding season are Temecula Creek near Oak Grove (C16; up to four on 20 June 1998, K. L. Weaver), the San Luis Rey River near Puerta La Cruz (E18; two on 18 June 2000, J. K. Wilson, P. K. Nelson), Warner Springs (F19; one on 3 May 1999, C. G. Edwards), the San Luis Rey River near the Forest Service picnic ground (G16; up to two, a pair, on 3 July 1999, W. E. Haas), Witch Creek (J18; female with two fledglings 12 July 1999, S. E. Smith), Hatfield Creek 3.2 miles east of Ramona (K16; pair at nest 11 June 2000, L. J. Hargrove), Sweetwater River above Loveland Reservoir

Photo by Jack C. Daynes

(Q17; one on 21 May 1999, P. Famolaro), and Marron Valley (V17; four on 12 June 2000, P. P. Beck).

The records along the Mexican border, in Marron Valley and the Tijuana River valley (W11; up to three, including a fledgling, 19 June 1999, P. Unitt) are notable because the Downy Woodpecker is not known to breed in Mexico. By 2001 there were only four well supported records from Baja California, all from November through February (Erickson et al. 2001; M. A. Patten).

Nesting: In San Diego County, the Downy Woodpecker nests typically in willow snags. Dates of breeding activity observed suggest egg laying from mid April to mid June; Bent (1939) gave 7 April–9 June as the range for 82 California egg sets.

Migration: The Downy Woodpecker is nonmigratory, but there must be considerable dispersal for the species to have spread so rapidly. Some, perhaps most, of this is done by the young soon after fledging. A juvenile found dead in the Fletcher Hills area of El Cajon (Q12) 14 June

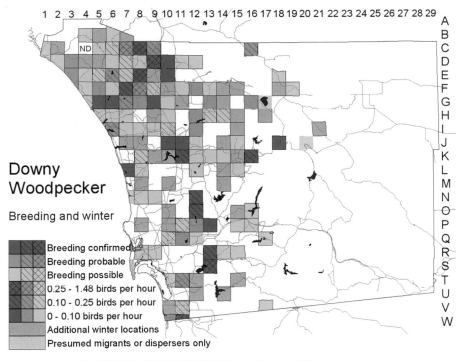

Downy
Woodpecker

Breeding and winter

Breeding confirmed
Breeding probable
Breeding possible
0.25 - 1.48 birds per hour
0.10 - 0.25 birds per hour
0 - 0.10 birds per hour
Additional winter locations
Presumed migrants or dispersers only

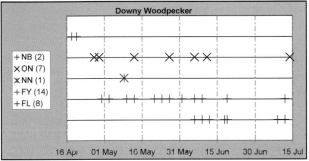

1998 (C. Tratnyek, SDNHM 50417) was crossing unsuitable habitat. Other records of apparent dispersers or pioneers away from breeding sites are of single birds at Point Loma (S7) 12 April 1986 (R. E. Webster, AB 40:524, 1986) and 22 May 2001 (P. A. Ginsburg), one in the Hillcrest area of San Diego (R9) 25 July 2001 (P. Unitt), one at Lake Henshaw (G17) 17 July 1998 (C. G. Edwards), and one near Julian (J20) 17 August 2000 (M. B. Stowe). At 4000 feet, the last, and one at 4650 feet at Lake Cuyamaca (M20) 11 March 1988 (C. G. Edwards), were at the highest elevations where the Downy Woodpecker has yet been recorded in San Diego County.

Winter: Our winter observations of the Downy Woodpecker included several in marginal or atypical habitat, suggesting further pioneering. Such birds included individuals at 2650–3350 feet elevation along the San Luis Rey River between Lake Henshaw and Puerta La Cruz (F18) 10 December 2000 (J. R. Barth, M. Mathos), at Mesa Grande (H17) 17 December 2001 (K. L. Weaver, J. McColm), and, most notably, one a short distance onto the desert slope in San Felipe Valley (I21) 3 December 2000 (W. E. Haas).

Conservation: In the first half of the 20th century the Downy Woodpecker was rare in San Diego County but

recorded at Bonsall, the head of Lake Hodges (eggs collected, WFVZ), San Pasqual ("rather rare," eggs collected, Sharp 1907), 2–3 miles northeast of Old Mission Dam, and 2 miles northeast of Lakeside (Short 1971). Then the species evidently declined almost to extirpation: in the 1950s and 1960s there were only two records. In the 1970s it was absent from the San Pasqual and Old Mission Dam areas but present in small numbers along and near the Santa Margarita and lower San Luis Rey rivers (Unitt 1984). From 1981 on the Downy Woodpecker could be found consistently along the San Diego River. It was first noted in the Tijuana River valley 25 September 1983 (C. G. Edwards, AB 38:247, 1984), and by 1990 it was resident there. Since then the Downy Woodpecker has been filling in by colonizing smaller patches of riparian woodland and spreading inland. It was found on only one San Diego Christmas bird count before 1986, but since then it has been found annually, the numbers increasing gradually, reaching 10 on 15 December 2001.

The Downy Woodpecker's reversal of fortune in San Diego County seems counterintuitive for a species dependent on riparian woodland, so much of which has been degraded and removed. A possible factor is the damming of most rivers and creeks, stabilizing the riparian environment in a way it never experienced previously. Under natural conditions winter floods knock over trees and perhaps prevent many from growing to maturity and developing enough dead snags for nest sites. Now such flooding has been greatly reduced, allowing more trees to live to maturity and senility. Changing land use has allowed riparian woodland to regenerate in some areas, such as the Tijuana River valley, where it was absent in the 1960s.

Some other subtle factors may be at work, too. The Downy Woodpecker may be benefiting from whatever causes are enabling the Nuttall's Woodpecker to spread also. The southward spread of the Downy Woodpecker parallels that of some other species of similar habitats, especially the Western Flycatcher and Orange-crowned Warbler.

Taxonomy: Downy Woodpeckers in San Diego County, as in most of cismontane California, are *P. p. turati* (Malherbe, 1860), small with the underparts lightly tinged smoke-gray. In the field, the difference from white is difficult to appreciate in spring and summer when the birds are in worn plumage and more or less stained from months of contact with trees, but it can be seen in a good view in fall and winter when the birds are clean and fresh.

Hybrids between the Downy and Nuttall's Woodpeckers continue to turn up occasionally, as 2.3 miles northeast of Bonsall (E8) 7 May 1984 (SDNHM 43956, Unitt 1986) and in the Tijuana River valley 25 February 1984 (G. McCaskie, AB 38:358, 1984) and 5 December 2000 (P. Unitt).

Hairy Woodpecker *Picoides villosus*

The Hairy Woodpecker's sharp call, like a rubber squeeze-toy, is a characteristic sound of coniferous forests in San Diego County's mountains. The species is an uncommon year-round resident in this habitat. Only a few individuals spill over into nearby oak-dominated woodland with few or no conifers. Winter vagrants far from the breeding range are very rare. But the Hairy Woodpecker also occurs irregularly at low elevations in the breeding season, mainly in the county's northwestern corner.

Breeding distribution: During the breeding season, atlas results show a close correspondence between the Hairy Woodpecker and San Diego County's coniferous forests. The highest counts per day are of only six, as on Hot Springs Mountain (E20) 27 June 2001 (K. L. Weaver, C. R. Mahrdt) and in the Cuyamaca Mountains (M20), on Middle Peak 11 June 2000 (R. E. Webster) and on Cuyamaca Peak 13 July 2000 (J. R. Barth). In the southern half of the county the Hairy Woodpecker breeds down to about 3800 feet elevation, but around Palomar Mountain it breeds locally even lower, down to 2470 feet along the San Luis Rey River (F16; pair nesting June–July 2000 and 2001, W. E. Haas) and about 1600 feet in Marion Canyon (D12; one agitated 18 June 2001, K. L. Weaver). Some outlying locations for the species are Bucksnort Mountain (C20; up to two on 24 June 2000, L. J. Hargrove) and Corte Madera Mountain (R20; one on 20 June 1998, P. Unitt).

Photo by Anthony Mercieca

The Hairy Woodpecker occurs in the breeding season rarely and irregularly in lowland riparian and oak woodland in northwestern San Diego County. Otherwise, the species' lowland distribution extends south to the Santa Ana River valley in northwestern Riverside County (Garrett and Dunn 1981, Gallagher 1997). On 28 June 1998, an adult was feeding a fledgling along the Santa Margarita River near Rifle Range Road (F5; R. E. Fischer)—the southernmost confirmation of the Hairy Woodpecker nesting at low elevation along the Pacific coast. At Los Jilgueros Preserve, Fallbrook (D7), there was a single individual on 21 January and 7 May 1998 (E. Ashton). In 1983, Scott (1984) found two territories and one nest in riparian woodland along the Santa Margarita River at De Luz Creek (D6); in 1989 Weaver (1990) found one territory in coast live oak woodland in the Santa Margarita Ecological Reserve (C9). At a mere 850–900 feet, though only about 6 miles west of the species' normal habitat, was a single Hairy Woodpecker along the San Diego River between Cedar and Boulder creeks (M17) 21 March and 6 June 1998 (R. C. Sanger).

Nesting: The Hairy Woodpecker excavates a typical woodpecker hole in a tree, commonly a dead snag, but atlas observers found few nests in San Diego County. One nest on Hot Springs Mountain was about 25 feet above the ground. The nest along the San Luis Rey River was

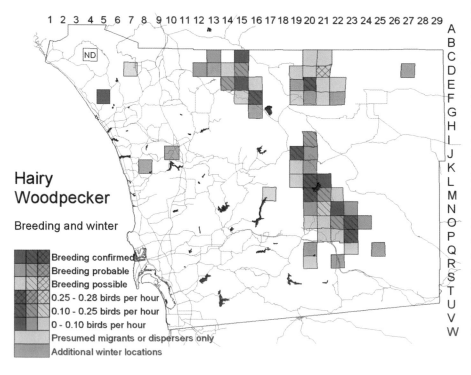

Hairy Woodpecker

Breeding and winter

- Breeding confirmed
- Breeding probable
- Breeding possible
- 0.25 - 0.28 birds per hour
- 0.10 - 0.25 birds per hour
- 0 - 0.10 birds per hour
- Presumed migrants or dispersers only
- Additional winter locations

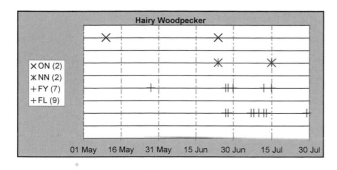

Hairy Woodpecker

X ON (2)
✕ NN (2)
+ FY (7)
+ FL (9)

01 May 16 May 31 May 15 Jun 30 Jun 15 Jul 30 Jul

in a sycamore, an atypical site for the species in southern California. Our rather meager records of breeding activity range from an occupied nest on 10 May to young fledging in the third week of July and fledglings out of the nest on 29 July. These dates suggest egg laying at least from mid May to early June, well within the range of 23 March–21 June given for 43 California egg sets by Bent (1939).

Migration: The few records of Hairy Woodpeckers outside their breeding range in San Diego County are scattered from 27 August (1988, one in the Tijuana River valley, B. E. Daniels, AB 43:169, 1989) to 26 February (1980, one at Old Mission Dam, P11, C. G. Edwards).

Winter: The Hairy Woodpecker remains in its breeding range year round. Our highest daily count in winter was of four around Mount Laguna (O23) 21 January 2002 (E. C. Hall, J. O. Zimmer). The species has been noted outside its known breeding range in San Diego County on about 25 occasions. During the atlas period the one farthest from the usual range was at Olivenhain (K8) 28 December 1997 (L. R. Santaella), but earlier records extend as far as Otay Valley (V11; one from 15 December

1979 to 26 January 1980, AB 34:307, 1980; one on 15 December 1990, P. Unitt) and the Tijuana River valley (cited above). There are only two records from the Anza–Borrego Desert, of one in pines planted on a golf course in Borrego Springs (F24) 21 December 1991 (M. L. Gabel) and one in pinyons between 4800 and 5000 feet in the Santa Rosa Mountains 1.6 miles east-southeast of Villager Peak (D27) 9 January 2002 (L. J. Hargrove). The latter had probably dispersed along the ridge from more heavily wooded areas of the Santa Rosa Mountains in Riverside County, where the species is resident.

Conservation: Data sufficient to demonstrate any trend in the Hairy Woodpecker's status in San Diego County do not exist. Anecdotal observations suggest no significant change. On 26 May 1976 A. Fries noted two at Mesa Grande (H17), an area of oak woodland where we found none during the atlas period; the species could be irregular in this area.

Taxonomy: The Hairy Woodpeckers resident in San Diego County are *P. v. hyloscopus* (Cabanis and Heine, 1863), in which the whitish underparts are lightly tinged buffygray. Long-distance vagrancy of Hairy Woodpeckers is unknown in California, yet the one specimen from outside the breeding range in San Diego County, from Cottonwood Campground (Q25) 19 January 1985 (SDNHM 43460), has conspicuously whiter underparts than any specimen of *hyloscopus*. It matches specimens of *P. v. orius* (Oberholser, 1911), which breeds from south-central British Columbia south to Arizona, including the Sierra Nevada and mountains of the Great Basin, if *P. v. leucothorectis* (Oberholser, 1911) is considered a synonym of *orius* (Phillips et al. 1964, Short 1982).

White-headed Woodpecker *Picoides albolarvatus*

In San Diego County, which represents the southern tip of its range, the White-headed Woodpecker is uncommon to rare, breeding only in coniferous forest near the mountain tops. Even here it occupies only a fraction of the habitat, occurring mainly where the sugar pine is an important constituent of the forest. Only twice have vagrants been recorded in San Diego County away from the mountains.

Breeding distribution: The White-headed Woodpecker is most numerous on Hot Springs Mountain; in places there it can be the most conspicuous woodpecker (up to eight, representing probably five pairs, east of the summit, E21, 19 June 1999, K. L. Weaver, C. R. Mahrdt). On the south side of the mountain it is found only above 5800 feet elevation, but on the north side it extends down to the mountain's base, occurring at 4600 feet in Lost Valley (D20/D21; up to three on 28 April 2000, W. E. Haas). On Palomar Mountain, the White-headed Woodpecker occurs mainly around the observatory (D15; up to three, including a pair, on 18 April 1998, K. L. Weaver). In Palomar Mountain State Park (D14) only a single individual was noted during the breeding season from 1997

Photo by Anthony Mercieca

to 2001, on 2 June 1998 (P. D. Jorgensen). On Volcan Mountain (I20), the species is rare, occurring above 5300 feet elevation (five, including a family group, 16 July 2001, J. R. Barth). In the Cuyamaca Mountains, the White-headed Woodpecker is uncommon above 5300 feet elevation on North Peak (L20), Middle Peak (M20; maximum daily count three on 2 July 2000, R. E. Webster), and Cuyamaca Peak (M20/N20). In the Laguna Mountains,

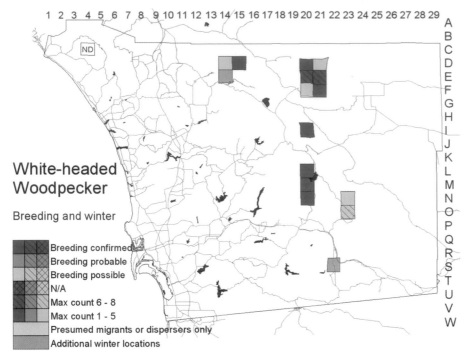

White-headed Woodpecker

Breeding and winter

Breeding confirmed
Breeding probable
Breeding possible
N/A
Max count 6 - 8
Max count 1 - 5
Presumed migrants or dispersers only
Additional winter locations

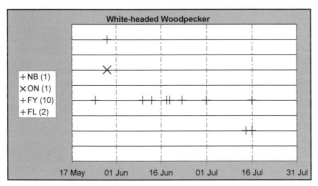

Winter: The White-headed Woodpecker is essentially sedentary, seen in winter in the same places in much the same numbers as during the breeding season. During the atlas period our highest winter count was of five on Hot Springs Mountain (E21) 11 December 1999 (K. L. Weaver, C. R. Mahrdt). The addition of atlas square E14 as a winter location resulted from one bird seen at Observatory Campground, just 1.2 miles southwest of the Palomar Observatory, 24 February 1999 (G. L. Rogers). The only winter record from the Laguna Mountains during the atlas period was of one at the north end of Big Laguna Lake (O23) 6 December 1999 (D. S. Cooper).

Of California's high-mountain birds, the White-headed Woodpecker is one of the least inclined to vagrancy. San Diego County's only winter records more than about 2 miles from breeding localities are of one at Ramona (K15) 20 November 1955 (AFN 10:58, 1956) and one male in planted pines at the Cottonwood Fire Station, at 3080 feet elevation northeast of Lake Morena (S22), 27 February 2000 (R. Breisch). The last made the species' southernmost record ever. The winter of 1955–56 was an invasion year for several species of mountain birds, but that of 1999–2000 was not.

Conservation: San Diego County's small population of the White-headed Woodpecker may be decreasing slowly. My count of 13 on Hot Springs Mountain 23–24 June 1980 (Unitt 1981) was not equaled from 1997 to 2002. During the atlas period the species was reported less frequently and from fewer locations on Palomar Mountain than before 1980. We did not find it at William Heise County Park (K20), where it occurred in the 1970s (Unitt 1984). The woodpecker's habitat in San Diego County covers under 4 square miles on Hot Springs Mountain, less in the other ranges. Thus it is vulnerable to factors like extended droughts, forest fires, and irruptions of bark beetles killing pine trees. Logging, silviculture, and fire suppression are thought responsible for the White-headed Woodpecker's decline in Washington, Oregon, and Idaho (Garrett et al. 1996).

Taxonomy: White-headed Woodpeckers in San Diego County belong to the large-billed subspecies *P. a. gravirostris* Grinnell, 1902.

the White-headed Woodpecker is rare and confined to the vicinity of Al Bahr Shrine Camp (O23); the highest number reported there, seven on 9 and 10 June 2001, was spread over two days so may have entailed some double counting (C. G. Edwards). One on 4 June 2001 along the trail to Garnet Peak about 1.4 miles north-northwest of Al Bahr Shrine Camp (N23; K. J. Winter) was the most distant from that site.

Nesting: Like other woodpeckers, the White-headed excavates its own nest hole, usually in a dead snag. A pair on Hot Springs Mountain (F21) was excavating a nest cavity 29 May 1999 (J. M. and B. Hargrove). Atlas observers noted the birds carrying food items from 25 May to 16 July. These dates suggest egg laying at least from mid May to early June, well within the range of 24 April–16 June for 53 California egg sets given by Bent (1939).

Northern Flicker *Colaptes auratus*

San Diego County's largest woodpecker is a fairly common resident in coniferous forest, oak woodland and sycamore groves. Though it nests in tree cavities like other woodpeckers, it feeds largely on the ground, specializing on ants. The local population is much augmented in winter by migrants from the north, which occur in the same habitats as the residents, as well as invading grassland, desert, and developed areas where breeding flickers are few or none.

Breeding distribution: The pattern of flicker abundance in San Diego County resembles that of many other oak woodland birds: the birds are most numerous in the mountains and foothills, and they extend toward the coast more commonly in the north than in the south. In the core range, daily counts in the breeding season range up to 15 at Mount Laguna (O23) 24 July 1998 (E. C. Hall), 15 at Wynola (J19) 22 May 1999 (S. E. Smith), and 17 at De Luz (B6) 20 June 2000 (K. L. Weaver). An area outside the core where flickers are especially common, with its abundant oaks and sycamores, is Los Peñasquitos Canyon (N8/N9), with up to 18 on 1 April 2001 (N8; B. Siegel). In south-coastal San Diego County breeding flickers are uncommon to rare, with no count of over three per day from mid April through August. On the east slope of the mountains, the edge of the flicker's range follows the edge of the oaks closely, though the birds occur also in riparian woodland at Scissors Crossing (J22; courting pair 13 April 1998, E. C. Hall), in planted cottonwoods at Butterfield Ranch (M23; occupied nest hole 17 April 1999, P. K. Nelson; pair with fledgling 18 June 1999, H. and. K. Williams), and along Carrizo Creek north of Jacumba (T28; one on 3 May 1998 and 11 May 2001, F. L. Unmack).

Photo by Anthony Mercieca

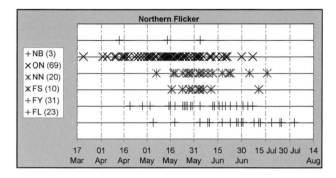

Nesting: Flickers excavate their nest holes typically in dead trees or dead snags of living trees but sometimes in live trunks or branches. The most frequent nest site described by atlas observers was coast live oak; willows, cottonwoods, and sycamores were also mentioned. A flicker in Johnson Canyon on the north slope of Otay Mesa (V13) 1 April 2000 was attending a hole in a dead eucalyptus (P. Unitt); no suitable native trees were in the area. Another nest was in a telephone pole along the Santa Margarita River at De Luz Road (C7) 11 April 1998 (K. L. Weaver).

The nesting schedule we observed from 1997 to 2001 was largely consistent with the 9 April–20 June range of 33 egg sets collected in San Diego County 1894–1945. A fledgling near Dyche Valley (F15) 5 May 1997 (M. Dougan) suggests egg laying about 1 April.

Migration: Migrant flickers occur in San Diego County mainly from October through March. Specimens attest to dates from 2 October to 2 April (see under Taxonomy). The earliest date of a sight report away from a breeding locality is 15 September (1973, one in Tubb Canyon, H23; one at Borrego Palm Canyon campground, F23), except for one at Tamarisk Grove (I24) 20 August 1984 (B.

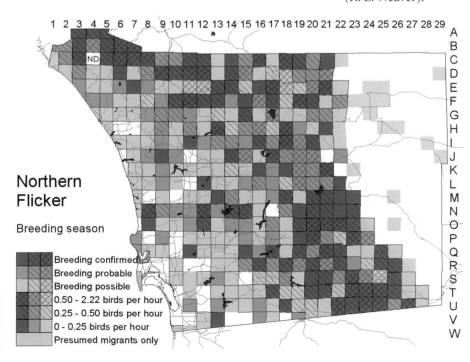

Northern Flicker

Breeding season

- Breeding confirmed
- Breeding probable
- Breeding possible
- 0.50 - 2.22 birds per hour
- 0.25 - 0.50 birds per hour
- 0 - 0.25 birds per hour
- Presumed migrants only

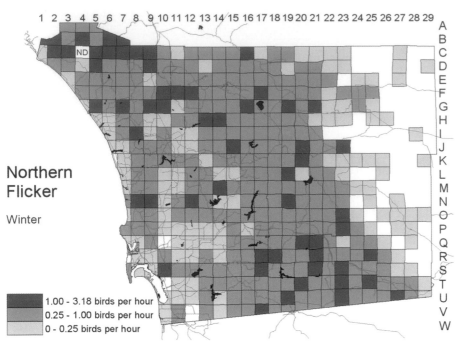

Northern Flicker

Winter

■ 1.00 - 3.18 birds per hour
▨ 0.25 - 1.00 birds per hour
▨ 0 - 0.25 birds per hour

colonize the Tijuana River valley, where it was not known in the breeding season before 2000 (one in Goat Canyon, W10, 13 and 23 May 2000, W. E. Haas). The number of flickers using these novel habitats, however, is very small. On the negative side, the proliferation of the European Starling has been blamed for a decline of flickers over much of North America. Cities offer little opportunity for foraging to a bird like the flicker that feeds primarily in the dirt. From 1997 to 2001, the number of flickers on the San Diego and Oceanside Christmas bird counts was barely over half what it was from the mid 1960s through 1970s, probably as a result of the urbanization of the count circles.

Knaak, ABDSP database). Probably sightings before the last week of September represent short-distance dispersal of the local population, not the arrival of migrants from farther north. In spring, records after the first week of April are few. The only reports later than 24 April are of one at Angelina Spring (I22) 2 May 1997 (P. K. Nelson) and one at Agua Caliente Springs (M26) 4 June 1998 (E. C. Hall).

Winter: In winter, the flicker is more common than in the breeding season, with daily counts up to 30 near the Pine Hills Fire Station (L19) 6 February 1999 and 35 in the Wooded Hill/Morris Ranch area of the Laguna Mountains (P23) 19 February 1999 (E. C. Hall). Winter visitors spread over the whole coastal slope, including areas where the species does not breed (up to nine in the southeast quadrant of the Tijuana River valley, W11, 5 December 2000, P. Unitt). Wintering flickers also reach the Anza–Borrego Desert, occurring mainly at oases and around the trees planted in Borrego Springs (F24; up to 17 on 20 December 1998, R. Thériault et al.).

Conservation: The Northern Flicker both benefits and suffers from man-made changes in the environment. The planting of trees in what was once treeless scrub has enabled the species to colonize areas like Point Loma and Chula Vista, where it was doubtless absent as a breeding bird before urbanization. The regeneration of riparian woodland may be allowing the flicker to

Taxonomy: The subspecies of flicker resident in San Diego County is *C. a. collaris* Vigors, 1829, a Red-shafted Flicker with the nape and crown the same dark brown color as the back. It breeds along the Pacific coast from northern California to northern Baja California. In winter *collaris* is outnumbered by *C. a. canescens* Brodkorb, 1935, which is often paler on the back than *collaris* and has the nape and crown grayer. It breeds inland from the Sierra Nevada to the Rocky Mountains and occurs in San Diego County as a winter visitor at least from 2 October (1981, Clairemont area of San Diego, P8, SDNHM 41613) to 2 April (1988, Chula Vista, U11, SDNHM 47783).

The Yellow-shafted Flicker is a rare winter visitor to San Diego County. Three were reported during the atlas period (one along the Sweetwater River near Highway 94, R13, 3 January 2000, M. and D. Hastings; one in Mission Gorge, P11, 8 January 2000, D. Kisner; one in Thing Valley, Q24, 25 December 2001, J. R. Barth), and other flickers with some but possibly not all of the characters of the Yellow-shafted were also noted. One specimen (Point Loma, S7, 15 February 1954, SDNHM 30001) shows all the features of a Yellow-shafted; it is of the large northern subspecies *C. a. luteus* Ridgway, 1911. Several specimens of *canescens* have just one feature of the Yellow-shafted, either yellowish shafts or red in the nape. Sight records of Yellow-shafted Flickers extend from 4 October (1973, Point Loma, G. McCaskie) to 4 April (1978, Point Loma, AB 32:1056, 1978).

TYRANT FLYCATCHERS — FAMILY TYRANNIDAE

Olive-sided Flycatcher *Contopus cooperi*

Quick, THREE beers! Delivered from the tops of tall Jeffrey pines or big-cone Douglas firs, the far-carrying song of the Olive-sided Flycatcher is unforgettable. The bird is only an uncommon summer visitor in the coniferous woodland of San Diego County's mountains, but it is easily located. It occurs widely though still uncommonly at lower elevations during migration (mainly May and September). Even in migration it has the same habit, seeking out the tops of the highest trees for its lookout perch. The promise of the Olive-sided Flycatcher's incipient adaptation to lowland eucalyptus groves is offset by serious population decline over parts of its range—the bird is considered a species of special concern by the California Department of Fish and Game.

Breeding distribution: The Olive-sided Flycatcher occurs in all of San Diego County's mountains supporting extensive stands of conifers: Palomar, Hot Springs, Volcan, Cuyamaca, and Laguna. Even isolated Bucksnort Mountain (C20) has a few (up to six, including four singing males, on 24 June 2000 (L. J. Hargrove). In most of these ranges the species occurs primarily at elevations over 4500 feet, rarely down to 3500 feet. On the steep southwest face of Palomar Mountain, though, where the big-cone Douglas fir descends into the deep canyons of Marion, Agua Tibia, and Pauma creeks, the Olive-sided Flycatcher follows it, down to 1500 feet in Marion Canyon (D12; one singing male on 17 July 2001, K. L. Weaver).

The Olive-sided Flycatcher's population density is naturally low. The entire county population is probably only a few hundred birds. Seldom does one encounter

Photo by Jack C. Daynes

more than two or three singing males in a day. The highest counts are ten along upper La Posta Creek, Cuyapaipe Indian Reservation (P24), 28 June 1999 (D. C. Seals), eight in the Agua Tibia Wilderness (C13) 18 May 2001 (K. J. Winter), and eight along upper Nate Harrison Grade (E13) 16 May 1999 (C. Sankpill).

The Olive-sided Flycatcher is known to have bred once in San Diego County along the coast. From 2 May through 5 July 1982, a pair nested in a cypress tree at San Elijo Lagoon (L7) and fledged one young (King et al. 1987). Recalling this event were single singing birds at an elevation of only about 600 feet in eucalyptus trees around Alliant International University (O10) 24 June 1998 (G. L. Rogers) and 19 and 23 June 2001 (G. Grantham). Eucalyptus groves, with bare snags frequently emerging above their crowns, mimic the open woodland of tall conifers sought by the Olive-sided Flycatcher, especially when the trees have been partially defoliated by lerp psyllids. A single silent individual about 3200 feet elevation between Lake Morena and Hauser Canyon (T21) 5 July 1997 (R. and S. L. Breisch) was also outside the usual range, though there are a few tall pines in the area.

Nesting: The Olive-sided Flycatcher builds its shallow cup nest in the clusters of needles toward the outer ends of conifer

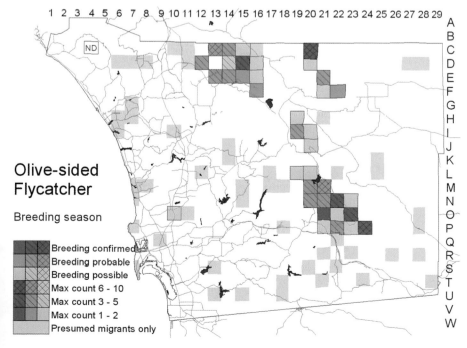

Olive-sided Flycatcher

Breeding season

- Breeding confirmed
- Breeding probable
- Breeding possible
- Max count 6 - 10
- Max count 3 - 5
- Max count 1 - 2
- Presumed migrants only

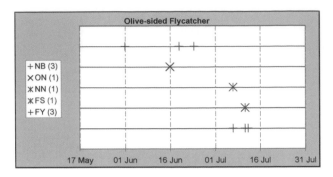

branches, at the middle levels of tall trees. Atlas observers estimated the heights of the two nests at 25 and 40 feet. The dates of breeding confirmations we recorded are consistent with the 5 June–4 July spread of three collected egg sets. Spending fewer than four months in their breeding range, even, as in San Diego County, near that range's southern tip, Olive-sided Flycatchers have time to raise only a single brood per season (Altman and Sallabanks 2000).

Migration: The earliest six spring dates recorded 1997–2001, 15–23 April, are all at or near sites where the Olive-sided Flycatcher nests. Thus, as in so many other species, the locally breeding population evidently arrives before migrants headed farther north. The Olive-sided Flycatcher is not regular at low elevations until the last week of April, though some sightings there are earlier, as early as 6 April (Unitt 1984). Migrants peak in early May, then decrease through the third week of June. The latest spring migrant was one in Tecolote Canyon (Q9) on 15 June 2000 (T. Plunkett), unless it too was summering.

In fall, migrants are encountered even less frequently than in spring, although a maximum of six was noted at Point Loma (S7) 8 September 1998 (P. A. Ginsburg). Almost all reports are from September; dates range from 29 August (2000, one at Point Loma, J. C. Worley) to 25 October (1972, one in the Tijuana River valley, G. McCaskie).

Winter: Accidental, with one good sight record, of one at Vista (H8) 8 January 1983 (R. E. Webster, AB 27:339, 1983).

Conservation: Several independent sources of evidence point to a significant decline in the Olive-sided Flycatcher's

population over much of its range (Altman and Sallabanks 2000). But in San Diego County, even though there is no quantitative study, no decline is obvious. Our atlas results show the species still present throughout its historic range in numbers no lower than reported in the past. Local increases in logged areas, in the context of broader-scale decline, led Altman and Sallabanks (2000) to hypothesize that logged forests are an "ecological trap," for the Olive-sided Flycatcher. Despite the lack of obvious change in San Diego County, the Olive-sided Flycatcher's breeding range here is so limited and the numbers are so small that forest fire, prolonged drought, or runaway infestation of bark beetles could destroy enough old trees that the flycatcher population could fall below a sustainable threshold. Warming of the climate could lead to conifers—and the many organisms dependent on them—being unable to recover from such calamities.

The species' disappearance, between 1938 and 1986, from a seemingly unchanged tract of giant sequoia forest in the Sierra Nevada led Marshall (1988) to postulate that the decline was due to habitat loss in the winter range. The Olive-sided Flycatcher winters in mature forest at middle altitudes, the most threatened zone, in a range centering on the seriously deforested Andes of Colombia (Altman and Sallabanks 2000).

Taxonomy: Todd (1963) supported the division of the Olive-sided Flycatcher into two subspecies on the basis of size: larger *C. c. majorinus* (Bangs and Penard, 1921), breeding in the mountains of southern California and northern Baja California, and smaller nominate *C. c. cooperi* (Nuttall, 1832), breeding in boreal forests elsewhere in North America. Among specimens in the San Diego Natural History Museum, one male from Mount Pinos, Ventura County, one male from the Sierra Juárez, and two males from the Sierra San Pedro Mártir are indeed large (wings 112.5–114.5 mm). Three breeding females from San Diego County are also large (wings 104.5–106.0 mm). But one male from San Diego County, from Julian (K20) 15 June 1915 (SDNHM 31919) is smaller, in line with *cooperi* (wing 109.5 mm). So the validity of the distinction between the two subspecies could still use further testing. Three of four specimens of migrants from San Diego County are relatively small, matching *cooperi*.

Greater Pewee or Coues' Flycatcher
Contopus pertinax

In summer and migration, the Western Wood-Pewee and Olive-sided Flycatcher are the only medium to large olive-gray flycatchers expected in San Diego County. Yet in winter, though any flycatcher meeting this description is rare, the most likely such species is the Eastern Phoebe, and the second most likely is the Greater Pewee. Breeding in mountain forests north to central Arizona, Greater Pewees show up in southern California only occasionally. But those that do often remain the entire winter,

establishing territories in groves of planted conifers or eucalyptus trees.

Winter: Though perhaps as few as ten individual Greater Pewees have been noted in San Diego County, the records form a tight pattern: birds overwintering in tall trees in urban parks. Some individuals have evidently returned to the same spot in successive years, especially one that spent at least five consecutive winters on the grounds of the San Diego Zoo in Balboa Park (R8). Such returnees accounted for the Greater Pewee being recorded in San Diego County every winter from 1984 to 1995. The only record since then, of one in Bonsall (F8) 2 December 2000 (P. A. Ginsburg), differed from those earlier in its slightly more inland location. Previous records were from Buddy Todd Park in Oceanside (H6), Presidio (R8) and Balboa parks and the Maple St. canyon in San Diego (R9), and the Tijuana River valley. The records extend from 18 October (1990, San Diego Zoo, B. and I. Mazin, AB 45:152, 1991) to 14 April (1985, Presidio Park, Dunn 1988), except for the single record of a non

wintering bird, one photographed on Point Loma (S7) 6–7 October 1984 (R. E. Webster, Dunn 1988). Two records as early as 19 September were not considered or were rejected by the California Bird Records Committee (McCaskie and San Miguel 1999). The Greater Pewee was first recorded in California in 1952 (Cardiff and Cardiff 1953), in San Diego County in 1974. The planting and maturation of tall conifers and eucalyptus trees must have been a prerequisite for the bird's establishing its pattern of winter occurrence here.

Western Wood-Pewee *Contopus sordidulus*

The Western Wood-Pewee's monotonous drawled song, "rrreea-ear" or "dear me," lulls the ear on hot summer days in San Diego County's foothills and mountains. The species is common in coniferous and oak woodland, especially at openings and edges. As a breeding bird it is uncommon in riparian woodland of the inland valleys but as a migrant it occurs in trees throughout the county. Strictly a summer visitor to California, the Western Wood-Pewee is unknown here from November through March.

Breeding distribution: The Western Wood-Pewee has a breeding distribution typical of that of several species of oak woodland. It approaches the coast in Camp Pendleton, along San Onofre Creek (D2), then swings inland, keeping at least 8 to 10 miles from the coast through most of the county; along the Mexican border it breeds no farther west than Marron Valley (V16/17). Along the crest of the mountains the pewee's distribution tracks the eastern edge of the oaks almost precisely. The one outlying site of nesting on the desert slope is along San Felipe Creek near Scissors Crossing (J22), where perhaps there is no more than one pair (fledgling on 18 June 2001, P. D. Jorgensen).

Photo by Anthony Mercieca

Western Wood-Pewees are most numerous in open pine–oak woodland in the mountains: highest counts are 35 in the Edwards Ranch on the west flank of Volcan Mountain (I19) on 21 July 2001 (D. W. Au, S. E. Smith) and 30 around Johnson and Boulder creeks on the west flank of the Cuyamaca Mountains (M19) on 22 May 1999 (K. J. Winter, S. McKelvey). Below 3000 feet elevation, as woodland becomes more confined in canyons, the pewee population becomes sparser and patchier. At low elevations, the greatest concentration is in the De Luz area of northwestern San Diego, with up to 15, including 12 singing males, around Sandia Canyon (C7) 18 July 1998 (K. L. Weaver).

Nesting: Western Wood-Pewee nests are rather easy to find, placed on horizontal or slanting branches of large trees, usually at a fork, sometimes saddled atop a branch wide enough to support the nest completely. The degree of openness of the surrounding vegetation appears to be more important to the suitability of a nest site than the exact type of woodland or tree. The nests are rather shaded but readily open to long foraging flights and view of possible predators. Atlas observers reported nests in sycamore, coast live oak, black oak (in one case burned), willow, Jeffrey pine, and incense cedar.

The Western Wood-Pewee is one of San Diego County's later

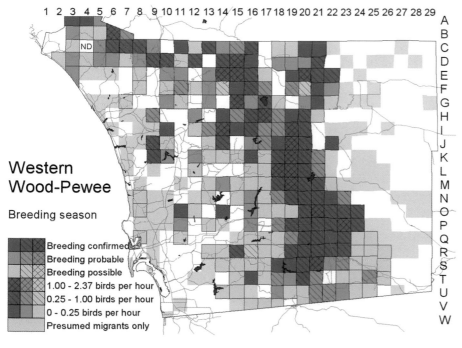

Western Wood-Pewee

Breeding season

- Breeding confirmed
- Breeding probable
- Breeding possible
- 1.00 - 2.37 birds per hour
- 0.25 - 1.00 birds per hour
- 0 - 0.25 birds per hour
- Presumed migrants only

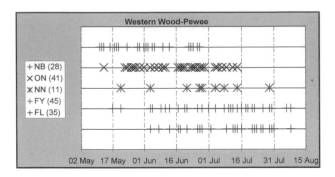

nesting species, with nesting activity seen commonly through the end of July. Several records, though, suggest the birds can lay as early as the first few days of May, earlier than the 19 May–7 July spread of 25 collected egg sets and the 10 May reported by Sharp (1907) at Escondido. For example, Karen Messer and Robert Turner noted a pewee carrying insects at Palomar Mountain State Park (E14) 17 May 1997, and Lori Hargrove noted one feeding fledglings near Shingle Spring (D21) 4 June 2001.

Migration: As a migrant the Western Wood-Pewee occurs throughout San Diego County, though it attempts to overfly treeless desert and heavily developed areas. Spring arrival of the Western Wood-Pewee is usually about 20 April, rarely as early as 10 April (1999, one along the Santa Margarita near the Riverside County line, C8, K. J. Burns). A bird banded by A. M. Craig at Point Loma (S7) 4 April 1969 (AFN 23:624, 1969) was exceptional. Even at the peak of spring migration in early to mid May migrants are less concentrated than the breeding population in prime habitat, with a maximum of 12 around Scissors Crossing (J22) 14 May 1998 (E. C. Hall). Spring migration continues commonly through the first week of June, occasionally as late as 13 June (1999, one at Oceanside, H5, J. Determan) and 17 June (2002, one at Point Loma, S7, J. C. Worley). Atlas observers noted two midsummer stragglers well outside the breeding range

along the coast, one at Los Peñasquitos Lagoon (N7) 4 July 1999 (C. Sankpill), the other near Villa La Jolla Park (P8) 11 July 1998 (M. B. Mosher). Fall migration takes place largely in August and September, adults preceding juveniles. One at Upper Otay Lake (T13) on 27 July 2001 (T. W. Dorman) was exceptionally early. By mid October pewees are very rare, and the latest dates are 21 October (2003, Rancho Santa Fe, L8, SDNHM 50837), 22–24 October (1988, one at Point Loma, G. McCaskie, AB 43:169, 1989) and 30 October (1971, one in the Tijuana River valley, G. McCaskie).

Winter: Unrecorded, and hardly expected even as an accidental, given that the northern limit of the species' winter range is Costa Rica.

Conservation: Results of the Breeding Bird Survey suggest the Western Wood-Pewee is declining over a significant portion of its range, including California (Sauer et al. 2003). But no decrease is obvious in San Diego County, and most of the species' breeding habitat is not heavily disturbed. Even campgrounds and moderate cattle grazing seem unlikely to affect a bird whose stratum of activity is in the middle level of trees and descends to the ground only to pick up nest material. Loss of winter habitat—mature montane tropical forest (Bemis and Rising 1999)—may be a greater issue for the Western Wood-Pewee than changes within the breeding range.

Taxonomy: The birds nesting in San Diego County, as well as most migrants, are the comparatively pale *C. s. veliei* Coues, 1866. A darker subspecies, *C. s. saturatus* Bishop, 1900, breeds in the Pacific Northwest and migrates through San Diego County to some extent. A nonbreeding specimen from the San Diego River at Cedar Creek (M17) 20 April 1985 (SDNHM 43845) and a juvenile from Pine Valley Creek at Horsethief Canyon (R19) 2 October 1992 (SDNHM 48173) are at the dark extreme for the species and thus apparently *saturatus*.

Yellow-bellied Flycatcher *Empidonax flaviventris*

During its breeding season, the Yellow-bellied Flycatcher ranges widely across the boreal forest of Canada, having a distribution similar to many warblers that reach California as vagrants annually. The flycatcher's apparent rarity in California (only 15 well-supported records through 2003) is due in part to the difficulty of distinguishing it from the common Western Flycatcher. In the juvenile Yellow-bellied, however, the wingbars are yellowish white; in the juvenile Western they are ocher.

Migration: San Diego County's first Yellow-bellied Flycatcher was in Fort Rosecrans National Cemetery, Point Loma (S7) 28 September–1 October 2003 (M. Sadowski, M. Billings, G. McCaskie, E. Copper, et al.). The bird responded in kind to playing of taped recordings of the Yellow-bellied Flycatcher's characteristic "pyoowip" call. The identification is supported by excellent photographs.

Photo by Matt Sadowski

Willow Flycatcher *Empidonax traillii*

William E. Haas and Philip Unitt

The southwestern subspecies *E. t. extimus* of the Willow Flycatcher is one of southern California's rarest birds, listed as endangered and restricted to a few colonies in riparian woodland. In San Diego County the population numbers fewer than 90 pairs, out of fewer than 200 statewide. During migration, the darker northwestern subspecies *E. t. brewsteri*, which breeds from the Sierra Nevada north through the Pacific Northwest, also occurs in San Diego County. Subspecies *extimus* is seen only at its breeding sites.

Breeding distribution: As a breeding species, the Willow Flycatcher is now restricted in San Diego County to two modest colonies and a few additional scattered pairs. The largest colony, with between 45 and 50 territorial males from 1993 through 2001, is along 4.6 miles of the upper San Luis Rey River between East Grade Road (just below Lake Henshaw) and the La Jolla Indian Reservation (F16, G16). The other is along the Santa Margarita River in Camp Pendleton. From 1999 to 2001, the birds maintained 18 or 19 territories, most along 3 miles of the river from the base airfield to Ysidora Basin (F5, G5) (Kus 2000, Kus et al. 2003a). Near O'Neill Lake (E6), where there were three territorial males, at least two paired, in 1998 (P. A. Ginsburg).

Four small new colonies have recently formed. After apparent absence from the lower San Luis Rey River in the late 1970s and 1980s, a few Willow Flycatchers repopulated the lower San Luis Rey River by 1999, with four pairs near Whelan Lake (G6) in 2001, four territorial males (two paired) north of Guajome Lake (G7) in 2001, two at Couser Canyon (E10) 1999–2001, and one or two

Photo by Anthony Mercieca

at Pala (D10/D11) in 2000 and 2001 (Kus et al. 2003a). About 3 miles from the San Luis Rey River, in a boggy glade along Agua Tibia Creek (D12), elevation 2200 feet, K. L. Weaver noted a pair, one carrying away craneflies, 17 July 2001. Another small colony was discovered in 1992 along the San Dieguito River between Lake Hodges and Tim's Canyon (K11/K12/J12/J14—in 1997 one pair in each); it has since varied between two and four pairs (Kus and Beck 1998, Kus et al. 2003a). Two territories were located along the San Diego River at the upper end (at low water) of El Capitan Reservoir (N17) in 2001 (Kus et al. 2003b). On the east slope of the mountains, a small colony has formed in San Felipe Valley near Paroli Spring (I22), from 1996 to 2001 fluctuating between two and five pairs (W. E. Haas). In 2002, two pairs nested downstream, 1 to 2 miles west of Scissors Crossing (J22) (W. E. Haas).

Elsewhere, there are only scattered pairs or unmated summering individuals. In Macario Canyon just southeast of Agua Hedionda Lagoon (I6) a pair maintained a territory in 1999 but apparently did not nest (W. E. Haas). Along Agua Caliente Creek near Warner Springs (F19) two males maintained territories in 2000 but never attracted mates (W. E. Haas). One along Cedar Creek near William Heise County Park (L20) 16 July 2000 was followed by a pair at a nest there on 10 July 2001 (J. R. Barth). One singing at the upper end of Sweetwater Reservoir (S13) 29 May–2 July 1997 was followed by a pair that nested there unsuccessfully from 29

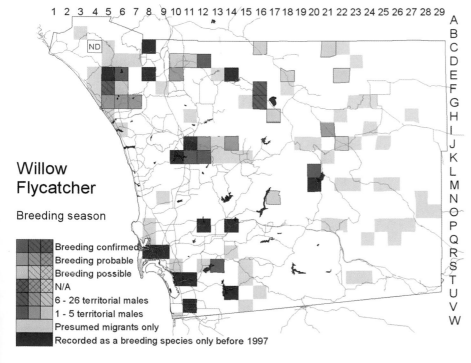

Willow Flycatcher

Breeding season

- Breeding confirmed
- Breeding probable
- Breeding possible
- N/A
- 6 - 26 territorial males
- 1 - 5 territorial males
- Presumed migrants only
- Recorded as a breeding species only before 1997

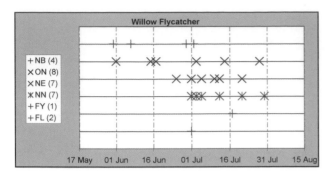

synchrony, with older, experienced birds building the earliest nests. Earliest documented fledging date from the upper San Luis Rey River is 24 June 1995. The latest nest initiation date recorded is 16 July (1999), though later nests have been reported elsewhere (M. K. Sogge pers. comm.). Though laying of a second clutch following the fledging of a first brood is extremely rare among the more northern subspecies of the Willow Flycatcher, it is only uncommon on the upper San Luis Rey River. On 21 June 2000 a freak storm, dumping one inch of hail in less than one hour, ruined 19 of 31 active nests. Within 10 days all birds renested, including one female that built her new nest directly above the destroyed first nest.

Migration: The local population of subspecies *extimus* usually arrives in early May. From 1997 to 2001 the earliest recorded date was 1 May 2001, along the upper San Luis Rey River (W. E. Haas), and no earlier date is known. Subspecies *brewsteri* arrives later, typically in mid May. Our earliest date away from a nesting site 1997–2001 was 11 May (1999, three in Macario Canyon, I6, W. E. Haas; 2001, two at Carrizo Marsh, O29, M. C. Jorgensen); the only earlier such date published is 8 May (1988, Point Loma, S7, R. E. Webster, AB 42:482, 1988). The migration of *brewsteri* peaks in early June (e.g., 25 at Fort Rosecrans Cemetery, S7, 8 June 2002, P. Unitt), then falls off quickly, though occasional migrants are seen at least as late as 20 June (1998, 3 miles southeast of El Cajon, R14, N. Perretta).

Most territories of *extimus* remain occupied through early August; Haas' latest date for an adult (female) along the upper San Luis Rey River is 3 September (1999). Juveniles depart somewhat later; at the upper San Luis Rey the latest date for a known (banded) juvenile from the colony is 11 September (1998). Fall migration of adults of *brewsteri* begins in the third week of July and presumably accounts for the two "pairs" reported from nonbreeding habitat on Middle Peak (M20) 19 July 1987 (R. E. Webster, AB 41:1488, 1987). These adults' migration takes place primarily in August but largely bypasses San Diego County, as the birds swing east, avoiding Baja California and a crossing of the Gulf of California. Juveniles of *brewsteri* are more numerous, though still uncommon, in the county, and occur primarily in September. By mid October they are rare; the latest dates recorded are 26 October–3 November (1981, three at Point Loma, R. E. Webster, AB 36:218, 1982).

Winter: Unrecorded. There are fewer than 10 apparently valid sight records of the Willow Flycatcher elsewhere in southern California (no specimens). Central Sinaloa, in western Mexico, is the northern extreme of the normal winter range.

Conservation: Early in the 20th century, the Willow Flycatcher was locally common in San Diego County (Sharp 1907, Willett 1912, Stephens 1919a; 35 egg sets in WFVZ). Like that of so many riparian songbirds, the population collapsed in the mid 20th century, as the effects of cowbird parasitism and clearing of riparian woodland compounded each other. The riparian forest along the upper San Luis Rey River was not spared, being cleared by

May to 29 July 1998; one male maintained a territory in 1999 but did not return in 2000 or 2001 (P. Famolaro). Some of the following, though in suitable nesting habitat, could have been migrant *brewsteri*: one singing male along Temecula Creek northwest of Oak Grove (C16) 20 June 1998 (K. L. Weaver)—confirmed pair a short distance downstream in Riverside County in 1997 (Kus and Beck 1998); one individual along the San Luis Rey River near Puerta La Cruz (E18) 18 June 2000 (P. K. Nelson); two along Highway 76 at Kumpohui Creek (H17) 13 June 1998 (P. Unitt); on the desert slope, silent individuals in Alder Canyon (C21) 20 June 2001 (P. D. Jorgensen) and at the head of Middle Fork Borrego Palm Canyon near San Ignacio (E22) 16 June 1999 (P. Unitt).

Nesting: The Willow Flycatcher attaches the sides of its open-cup nest to slender stems and twigs, which may be vertical, horizontal, or slanting. The nest may be in an upright crotch or without support from below. Willow Flycatcher nests, remarkably similar to those of the Lesser Goldfinch, differ notably in virtually always having loosely attached nest material hanging below the cup and the adults' not letting the nestlings' fecal matter decorate the nest's edge. From one to four eggs are laid, with smaller numbers more common late in the season and in second and third nests. Nests are often over water or in the outer branches of a tree. In historic egg collections from southern California, 86% of nests were in willows, 4% in stinging nettle, and 10% in other plants (Unitt 1987). Along the upper San Luis Rey River, however, the Army Corps of Engineers removed willows in the 1950s, and coast live oaks press closely against the streamside ash and alder trees in the narrow canyon. Here, of 292 nests studied between 1995 and 2001, 71% were placed in oak trees, another 8% in multi-substrate association with live oak, most commonly incorporating California blackberry (W. E. Haas). The nest height there may vary from 14 inches to 62 feet. Along the lower Santa Margarita, heavily invaded by exotic plants, the birds nevertheless often nest in those exotics; of 25 nests in 2001, 11 were in poison hemlock and 3 were in giant reed (B. E. Kus pers. comm.).

Female Willow Flycatchers begin building their nests usually within one week of pairing, 10–14 days after spring arrival. Construction takes three to eight days (average 4.2 days along the upper San Luis Rey River). Eggs may be laid as early as mid May, but typically first nests are initiated between 25 May and 20 June, often in

the Army Corps of Engineers in the 1950s. It is probable that a remnant population of Willow Flycatchers persisted below Henshaw Dam and fortuitously began to nest in an alternative substrate, the coast live oak. In the late 20th century, clearing of riparian woodland was regulated, and the woodland regenerated itself in some areas. Following the formal listing of the Least Bell's Vireo as an endangered species in 1986, cowbirds were trapped widely, reducing parasitism pressure on all hosts. Yet, unlike the vireo, Blue-gray Gnatcatcher, and Yellow Warbler, the Willow Flycatcher has failed to respond in proportion. With no cowbird trapping nearby at the time, though, from the mid 1980s to the mid 1990s the upper San Luis Rey River colony evidently increased, to the point where it is now the largest colony of *extimus* in California, eclipsing that on the South Fork Kern River. Along the Santa Margarita River in Camp Pendleton, the number of territories increased from five in 1981 to 17 in 1986 (L. Salata in Unitt 1987), but the figures for 1986 through 2001 are virtually static. The incipient new colonies along the lower San Luis Rey River, in San Pasqual Valley, in San Felipe Valley and above El Capitan Reservoir are promising. Notably, the last two are in woodland that has grown only since the 1980s. But against these gains must be balanced the species' disappearance from several sites listed by Unitt (1987): Santa Margarita River north of Fallbrook, south end of Lake Cuyamaca, east end of Lower Otay Lake, and the Tijuana River valley. All of these were well surveyed between 1997 and 2001. The decline seems to have been arrested, and recovery has begun, but only slowly. In 2001, the known San Diego County population was 88 territorial males (Kus et al. 2003a).

Clearly, low rates of cowbird parasitism are a necessary but not sufficient condition for the Willow Flycatcher's recovery. Displacement of woodland by the exotic giant reed has become serious in many floodplains, especially that of the lower Santa Margarita River. In the Fallbrook area, clearing of steep chaparral-covered slopes for avocado orchards led to excessive runoff and catastrophic flooding during heavy rain in 1993, scouring the river channel. The vegetation recovered subsequently, but several years of below-average rainfall left the river frequently dry, and so unattractive to the flycatchers. Along the upper San Luis Rey River, the flow depends on the Vista Irrigation District's (VID) use of the river as a conduit for sending groundwater pumped from the basin of Lake Henshaw to the city of Escondido. Flow through the summer is maintained to support recreation in the La Jolla Indian Reservation, the result of a lawsuit among the La Jolla band of Luiseño Indians, the VID, and the

federal government. Though cattle were removed from the Forest Service and VID lands within the colony in the early 1990s, it is still common for cattle to wander out of nearby pastures and into the Willow Flycatcher habitat.

In the upper San Luis Rey colony, human recreation, including picnicking, floating downriver in tire tubes, hunting, and fishing, is on the increase (through the summer the river is stocked at the Forest Service day use area with nonnative trout). The spring hunting season for the recently introduced "Wild" Turkey overlaps the flycatchers' arrival, and hunters typically use the Forest Service's land to reach private property (W. E. Haas). Open fires, though prohibited, are common. Willow Flycatchers in this area are especially susceptible to fire because they depend on the coast live oak trees that are more prone to burn than more typically riparian trees. The colony barely missed huge fires just to the north in 1999 and to the west in 2003.

Because of the Willow Flycatcher's semicolonial habits—the clumping of territories near each other—restoration efforts should be focused near existing colonies. Lamberson et al. (2000) suggested that an important factor in the recovery of the Southwestern Willow Flycatcher is the need for adequate habitat within 15 km of existing population centers. Restoration attempts should recognize that low cowbird-parasitism rates, multilayered riparian woodland, and surface water are all important to the success of any attempt to bring back one of southern California's most endangered birds.

Taxonomy: The locally breeding subspecies is the pale *E. t. extimus* Phillips, 1948, while the birds passing through in migration are the darker *E. t. brewsteri* Oberholser, 1918 (Unitt 1987). The color of the crown, back, and neck are the best characters, though a difference is often evident on the underparts, too. In good light, the contrasting gray neck of *extimus*, differing clearly from the darker, more uniform olive neck and back color typical of *brewsteri*, is visible in the field. In the spring, when the birds are in fresh plumage, the pale olive edges on the crown feathers of *extimus* contrast with the dark centers, giving the crown a dappled appearance not obvious on the uniformly dark crown of *brewsteri*. The pale edges wear off over the summer, though, and even in fresh plumage reliable identification of the subspecies requires quantification of the color or comparison with museum specimens. The song of *extimus* is slower than that of other subspecies of the Willow Flycatcher (Sedgwick 2001), and this slow song is well attested by Haas' recordings from the colony along the upper San Luis Rey River.

Least Flycatcher *Empidonax minimus*

A rare fall vagrant and casual winter visitor from northeastern North America, the Least Flycatcher resembles other species of *Empidonax* closely, being most distinctive in its bill, as short as a Hammond's but wider and entirely pale. Its identification requires thorough familiarity with the range of variation in

all the more frequent species of the genus.

Migration: The Least Flycatcher occurs in California primarily as a vagrant in fall. In San Diego County, at least 26 have been recorded, all but four in fall between 10 September (1980, Tijuana River valley, AB 35:227, 1981; 1985, Point Loma, R. E. Webster, AB 40:159, 1986) and 21 October (1979, Point Loma, AB 34:202, 1980). All of these were along the coast from Point Loma to the Tijuana River valley. There is still only one specimen, from Point Loma 16 September 1967 (A. M. Craig, SDNHM 35354).

Winter: Four records: San Diego, 14–18 December 1993 (R. E. Webster, NASFN 48:248, 1994); San Dieguito River estuary (M8), 16 December 1994 (P. Unitt, AB 49:821, 1995); La Jolla, 1–3 December 1996 (K. and C. Radamaker, NASFN 51:802, 1997); Dairy Mart Pond, Tijuana River valley (V11) 28 January 1998, 26 December 1998–23 January 1999, 17 November 1999–3 February 2000, and 9 December 2001, presumably the same individual returning in successive years, despite the hiatus in 2000–2001 (G. McCaskie). The recency of the winter records suggests a trend toward increase in this species, whose main winter range extends as far north in western Mexico as Sinaloa.

Photo by Anthony Mercieca

Hammond's Flycatcher *Empidonax hammondii*

An uncommon migrant in spring and fall, Hammond's Flycatcher is not a familiar bird in San Diego County. But, in April and early May, after the Western Flycatcher, it is the next most likely *Empidonax* to be encountered here. In migration it has no special habitat preferences, other than trees or shrubs—it is as likely to be seen in sparsely vegetated desert washes as in oak or riparian woodland. The few winter records are all from parks and gardens near the coast, except for one from the Anza–Borrego Desert.

Migration: In spring, Hammond's Flycatcher is more frequent in the eastern half of San Diego County than near the coast, as one might expect in a species that typically avoids Baja California, keeping to the east side of the Gulf of California on its way north from wintering in the mountains of mainland Mexico. It arrives usually in early April, rarely as early as 20 March (1994, Agua Caliente County Park, M26, Massey 1998). Most are seen from mid April to early May, but the highest one-day count 1997–2001 was of only five, in the Inner Pasture (N25) 2 May 2001 (A. P. and T. E. Keenan). By the last week of May Hammond's Flycatcher is rare; the latest spring record is of one in Hauser Canyon (T21) 5 June 1997 (J. M. Wells, J. Turnbull).

In fall, Hammond's Flycatcher is probably most frequent in the mountains, though most records are along the coast, where birders concentrate. It overflies the desert almost entirely at that season. Fall records extend from 1 September (1986, 0.3 mile west of High Point, Palomar Mountain, D15, SDNHM 44416) to 5 November (1984, Point Loma, S7, R. E. Webster, AB 39:103, 1985), exceptionally to 16–17 November (1974, Old Mission Dam, P11, G. McCaskie, SDNHM 40738).

Photo by Anthony Mercieca

Winter: The only winter record 1997–2002 was of one in the Golden Hill section of Balboa Park (S9) 16 December 2001–1 March 2002 (M. B. Mulrooney, P. Unitt), returning 2 November 2002–18 January 2003 and 15 November 2003–24 January 2004 (G. Hollenbeck). There are only three previous winter records of Hammond's Flycatcher in San Diego County: October 1991–24 January 1992, Point Loma (R. E. Webster, AB 46:315, 1992), 1 December 1992–24 January 1993, Point Loma (R. E. Webster, AB 47:301, 1993), and 6 December 1992–20 January 1993, Yaqui Well (I24; A. G. Morley, AB 47:301, 1993). Note the coincidence of the previous records with El Niño. A supposed migrant at San Diego 10 March 1983 (another El Niño!) (AB 37:911, 1983) is so early that it may more likely have been wintering, paralleled by a specimen still in molt from Thermal in the Coachella Valley of Riverside County 19 March 1921 (Patten et al. 2003). The species undergoes its spring molt in its winter range (Johnson 1970).

Gray Flycatcher *Empidonax wrightii*

Though a rare migrant and winter visitor in San Diego County, the Gray Flycatcher can be found—after a wet year—by the birder willing to invest time in the mesquite bosques and palo verde-lined washes of the Anza–Borrego Desert. In the inland valleys of the coastal lowland it was once fairly common but is now only occasional.

Winter: The Gray Flycatcher's main winter range lies in Mexico—the bird is common in the thorny scrub covering the southern half of Baja California and decreases toward the north. So San Diego County lies near the northwestern extremity of its winter range. The Gray Flycatcher is most frequent in the Anza–Borrego Desert, but that frequency is governed by rainfall. Ten of 11 desert winter records 1997–2002 were in the two years following the wet El Niño year of 1998; there were none at all in the extremely dry two final winters of the atlas period. Most of the desert winter records are from the floors of the Clark, Borrego, and Carrizo valleys, in or near mesquite thickets or developed areas. There are three records also from the riparian corridor of San Felipe Valley: one on 16 December 1998 (I21; J. O. Zimmer), up to two on 23 February 1999 (J22: E. C. Hall).

On the coastal side, the seemingly random scatter of winter records of the Gray Flycatcher (14 from 1997 to 2002) conceals a preference for open riparian scrub in inland valleys. Pockets of semidesert scrub on south-facing slopes at some locations, especially those of repeated occurrences such as the east end of Lake Hodges (K11), and Proctor Valley (T13/14), suggest wintering Gray Flycatchers seek warm, dry microclimates, in spite of being more frequent in wet years. The burned scrub with prickly pear thickets remaining as the most prominent vegetation, habitat of two in Jardine Canyon (C3) 15

Photo by Anthony Mercieca

February 1999 (P. Unitt), also evoked an image of desert. But other records from parks, cemeteries, and disturbed areas imply the Gray Flycatcher's winter habitat needs are not overly specialized. One bird returned to Whelan Lake (G6) for seven consecutive winters, 1980–86 (AB 41:330, 1987).

Most winter records are from low elevations (under 1000 feet), but a few are higher, exceptionally up to 3100 feet at Warner Springs (F19; one on 9 December 2001, C. G. Edwards).

Migration: Despite wintering commonly in Baja California, the Gray Flycatcher is rare as a migrant in San Diego County. It is a bit more widespread in that role than in winter, especially in the Anza–Borrego Desert in spring. Almost all spring migrants are seen in April and the first week of May. Aside from birds known to have wintered, the earliest was one near the Borrego Air Ranch (H26) 20 March 1998 (M. L. Gabel); late were two near Yaqui Well (I24) 13 May 1998 and 23 May 1997 (P. K. Nelson). Normally only one or two individuals can be seen in a day; eight in San Felipe Valley (I21) 24 April 1999 during a spectacular fallout of migrants made by far the highest one-day count (W. E. Haas). Along the coast, three at Point Loma (S7) 15 April 2001 (J. C. Worley) and nine there between 6 and 30 April 1983 (AB 37:913, 1983) are maximal.

In fall, records extend from 24 August to 18 November (1984, three at Point Loma, R. E. Webster, G. McCaskie, AB 39:103, 1985).

Conservation: The Gray Flycatcher was "fairly common" or "rather common" as a winter visitor in coastal southern California early in the 20th century (Grinnell 1915, Stephens 1919a, Willett 1933). Yet no one since at least 1950 would use such a term for it. Why would

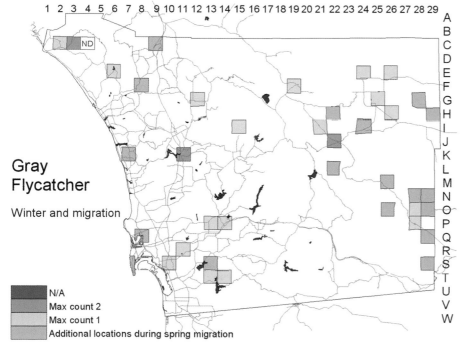

Gray Flycatcher

Winter and migration

N/A
Max count 2
Max count 1
Additional locations during spring migration

a bird's winter range retract south at a time when winter low temperatures are on the rise? Most of the floodplains and semidesert scrub making up the Gray Flycatcher's typical winter habitat have been developed, but the species' scarcity in the remaining habitat, and its use of disturbed areas, leave the explanation of habitat loss unsatisfying. No further change in the Gray Flycatcher's winter status has been evident for decades. The trend of numbers in the

breeding range is, if anything, positive, and since 1970 the species has colonized new areas north, west, and, south of its historic range in the Great Basin and intermountain plateau region (Sterling 1999). Its spread along the north slope of the Transverse Ranges, and a summer record even for the Santa Rosa Mountains of Riverside County (Garrett and Dunn 1981), suggest the possibility of the Gray Flycatcher's breeding some day in San Diego County.

Dusky Flycatcher *Empidonax oberholseri*

One of America's most obscure birds, the Dusky Flycatcher is a summer visitor to San Diego County only in coniferous woodland on the tops of the highest mountains. It is uncommon in the Cuyamaca Mountains, rare and irregular on Hot Springs, Volcan, Laguna, and probably the Santa Rosa mountains. Though it nests widely in the mountains of western North America to the north of San Diego, its rarity as a migrant at lower elevations implies that its migration route to its winter range in mainland Mexico lies well to the east of us.

Breeding distribution: The lower end of the elevation zone occupied by the Dusky Flycatcher barely grazes the tops of San Diego County's highest mountains. The species is normally found only above 5200 feet elevation, in conifer-dominated woodland. The vegetation zone is that where the white fir grows, though the flycatcher has no special attachment to any particular species of plant. Most records and the highest numbers are from Cuyamaca and Middle peaks (M20) in the Cuyamaca Mountains. The maximum daily count is 12, including nine singing males, on Middle Peak 11 June 2000 (R. E. Webster). Elsewhere the Dusky Flycatcher is rare, with records 1997–2001 also from Hot Springs Mountain (E20/E21; 19 June 1999

Photo by Anthony Mercieca

and 19 May 2001, K. L. Weaver, C. R. Mahrdt) and from Morris Ranch Road (P23; 30 July 1999, K. Smeltzer) and the head of La Posta Creek in the Laguna Mountains (P23; 23 June 2000, E. C. Hall, J. O. Zimmer)—single individuals only in each case. Previous records from the Laguna Mountains were from nearby Agua Dulce Creek and the unusually low elevation (4150 feet) of Cibbets Flat (Q23) (feeding fledgling cowbird on 4 July 1978, AB 32:1209, 1978). Before the atlas period the Dusky Flycatcher was noted on Volcan Mountain (I20), with one on 25 May 1993 (R. T. Patton) and two on 31 May 1993 (P. Unitt), as well as on Hot Springs Mountain (Unitt 1981) and Cuyamaca Peak. Also, the species may be a rare summer resident in the sparse stands of pinyons along the ridgeline of the Santa Rosa Mts., with two at 5700 feet elevation barely inside San Diego County 0.6 mile south of Rabbit Peak (C27) 2 May 2000 (P. Unitt) and one probable Dusky Flycatcher at 5400 feet near the

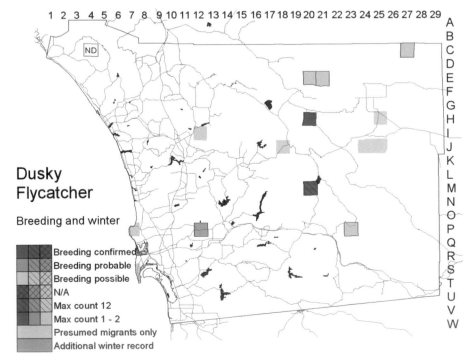

Dusky Flycatcher

Breeding and winter

- Breeding confirmed
- Breeding probable
- Breeding possible
- N/A
- Max count 12
- Max count 1 - 2
- Presumed migrants only
- Additional winter record

summit of Villager Peak (C27) 5 June 2001 (R. Thériault). The Dusky Flycatcher breeds commonly in the Riverside County portion of the Santa Rosa Mountains (Weathers 1983). The single San Diego County record of breeding Dusky Flycatchers away from these principal mountains is of a pair, the female building a nest, in a north-facing canyon at 3800–4000 feet elevation about 0.75 mile southeast of Barrel Spring at the north end of the San Felipe Hills (H20; A. P. and T. E. Keenan).

San Diego County lies near the southern tip of the Dusky Flycatcher's breeding range; the small population discovered by Erickson and Wurster (1998) in the Sierra San Pedro Mártir is the only one known farther south.

Nesting: The Dusky Flycatcher's cup nest is typically attached by its sides to vertical twigs, either upright or hanging. Knowledge of the species' nesting in San Diego County, though, is minimal. Besides the record from near Barrel Spring, the only breeding confirmations 1997–2001 were of one nest building in tall *Ceanothus* or *Cercocarpus* at the south side of Cherry Flat near the summit of Cuyamaca Peak on 23 May 1998 (G. L. Rogers) and of one feeding young one quarter mile from the summit of Cuyamaca Peak 6 August 1999 (A. P. and T. E. Keenan). Earlier records are of an occupied nest in a sugar pine on the north slope of Middle Peak 25 June 1988 (P. Unitt) and a nest with young near Agua Dulce Creek (O23) 13 July 1974 (AB 28:950, 1974).

Migration: Because of the difficulty in identifying silent Dusky Flycatchers in the field, information on the species' migration is scanty and uncertain. Nevertheless, the Dusky Flycatcher is very rare in both spring and fall. It is very rare also in the Salton Sink (Patten et al. 2003)

and essentially absent as a migrant in Baja California (Erickson et al. 2001), so its migration route evidently swings far to the east before it reaches the latitude of San Diego County. Eight published spring records from Point Loma extend from 21 April to 9 May (AB). Fall dates extend from 11 September to 12 October (Unitt 1984).

Winter: Brennan Mulrooney studied one along the San Diego River in Santee (P12) 17 December 1999 (NAB 54:221, 2000). He noted a medium-long narrow bill with a largely dark mandible, thin even eye-ring, tail flicked up repeatedly, and a "whit" call, features that in combination appear to eliminate all similar species. This is the first winter record for San Diego County and one of very few for southern California.

Conservation: Though Stephens (1919a) said "breeds in small numbers in the higher mountains" (at a time before the Dusky and Gray Flycatchers were adequately distinguished), he collected none. No details of Dusky Flycatcher nesting were reported in San Diego County's mountains until 1974. The species has remained rare except in the Cuyamaca Mountains, where it has increased and can be found regularly in small numbers. The species as a whole is maintaining itself or increasing (Sedgwick 1993). Johnson (1974) attributed an increase from the 1930s to the 1970s in the mountains of southern Nevada to a shift toward a cooler, wetter climate. The birds' habitat in San Diego County is little disturbed, but climatic warming and drying could dislodge the Dusky Flycatcher from its toehold on the mountain tops. Annual rainfall and summer temperature data from Cuyamaca 1948 to 2002 reveal no long-term trend.

Western or Pacific-slope Flycatcher
Empidonax difficilis

Few birds' invasions of San Diego County have been as aggressive yet as little noticed as that of the Western Flycatcher. Hardly known as a breeding species here in the early 20th century, the Western Flycatcher is now a fairly common summer resident in native oak and riparian woodland from the coast to the mountains, as well as in groves of eucalyptus trees. Range expansion and ability to adapt to urbanization give it a double boost. In addition, the Western Flycatcher is common in migration throughout the county and rare in winter in the coastal lowland.

Breeding distribution: Breeding Western Flycatchers occur almost throughout the coastal slope of San Diego County in riparian and oak woodlands. Only a few areas (Warner Valley, Otay Mesa, Otay Mountain) are so lacking in these habitats that they yield holes in the distribution as seen at the scale of our atlas grid. The breeding distribution extends south practically to the Mexican border in the Tijuana River valley (W10, nest building on 23 May 2000, W. E. Haas; feeding fledglings on 2 July 2001,

Photo by Jack C. Daynes

M. B. Mulrooney; W11, occupied nest on 19 June 1999, P. Unitt). It extends down the desert slope along San Felipe Creek as far as Sentenac Ciénaga (J23; one on 8 July 2000, R. Thériault; juvenile on 6 July 2002, J. R. Barth) but does

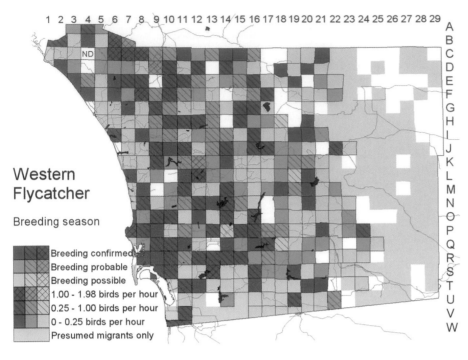

Western Flycatcher

Breeding season

- Breeding confirmed
- Breeding probable
- Breeding possible
- 1.00 - 1.98 birds per hour
- 0.25 - 1.00 birds per hour
- 0 - 0.25 birds per hour
- Presumed migrants only

and 16 March 1998 (M. and B. McIntosh).

Nesting: However closely the Western resembles other small flycatchers, its choice of nest site is distinctive. The nest is a cup, but it is placed atop a solid support, with a solid surface behind it, and preferably above it, too. Broken-off snags and knotholes in trees are the Western Flycatcher's typical nest sites in San Diego County. The widespread planting of eucalyptus trees, though, gave the birds a new opportunity. Slabs of bark hanging half attached to the eucalyptus offer ideal supports and shelters for Western Flycatcher nests and allow the birds to occupy eucalyptus groves lacking any other vegetation. Man-made sites our observers

not quite reach the Tecate Divide east of Campo along the border. In addition, Western Flycatchers breed, still uncommonly and patchily, in parks, eucalyptus groves, and residential areas.

The greatest concentrations, as one might expect in a species expanding its range south, are still in northwestern San Diego County, especially along the Santa Margarita River near Fallbrook (C7, 25 males on 13 June 1998; C8, 27 males on 24 May 2001, K. L. Weaver). Other notable counts were of 25 along the west fork of the San Luis Rey River below Barker Valley (E16) 23 June 2000 (J. M. Wells, J. Turnbull, P. Unitt), 20 in the Agua Tibia Wilderness (C13) 18 May 2001 (K. J. Winter), and 18–20 in Blue Sky Canyon Ecological Reserve (L12) 6 June 1997

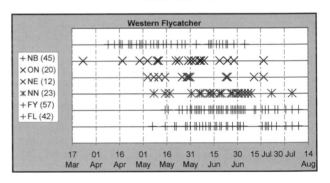

described were atop a pipe bracketed to the underside of a bridge, a ledge over a patio, and on the support structures below wooden decks. Another interesting site was in an old Cliff Swallow nest under a bridge.

Because past data on the Western Flycatcher's nesting in San Diego County are minimal, our atlas results establish the first baseline for understanding the species' nesting schedule here. Two reports of fledglings on 7 May imply that at low elevations the birds lay as early as the first week of April, earlier than farther north (cf. Lowther 2000). An occupied nest in Stelzer County Park (O14) on 24 March 1998 (M. Farley, M. B. Mulrooney) may still have been under construction. A nest with nestlings in Palomar Mountain State Park (D14) on 4 August (2000, P. D.

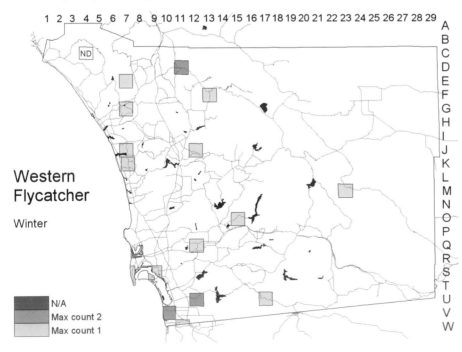

Western Flycatcher

Winter

- N/A
- Max count 2
- Max count 1

Jorgensen) implies that in the mountains they lay at least as late as the first week of July. Early spring arrival gives the Western Flycatcher, unlike its close relatives, ample time to raise two broods in San Diego County.

Migration: Western Flycatchers typically begin arriving in San Diego County in the third week of March and quickly reach full abundance. One along the Sweetwater River at Highway 94 (R13) 3 March 1999 (J. R. Barth) was exceptionally early, beating the previous early record of 9 March 1983 (AB 37:911, 1983) by six days. The highest counts of migrants are from along the east base of the mountains: Agua Caliente County Park (M26), 70 on 11 May 1998; Scissors Crossing (J22), 60 on 14 May 1998 (both E. C. Hall). The species' spring migration period is notably long, regularly extending through the first week of June. The latest atlas record from a nonbreeding locality (6 June 2001, one in Carrizo Valley, O28, P. D. Jorgensen) is typical; stragglers can be expected later, even to 23 June (Unitt 1984).

Fall migrants begin returning in mid August, peak in September, and trail off through October and November. The latest specimen of an adult is dated 16 September; all seen later in the fall are juveniles.

Winter: At this season the Western Flycatcher is rare but occurs annually. Eight, nearly half of the 19 reported 1997–2002, were in a single winter, the wet El Niño year of 1997–1998. Almost all winter records are from low elevations on the coastal slope, from riparian woodland or ornamental vegetation in parks. As many of the winter records are from inland valleys as from the coastal strip, east (during El Niño) to near Dulzura (U17), with one on 24 January 1998 (W. Pray, O. Carter, C. R. Mahrdt). One at Butterfield Ranch (M23) 22 January 1999 (P. K Nelson) made the first winter record for the Anza–Borrego Desert. The following year saw the first two winter records of the Western Flycatcher for the Imperial Valley (Patten et al. 2003).

Conservation: At the turn of the 20th century, the Western Flycatcher probably bred in San Diego County, as in northern Baja California still, at the highest elevations only. Though Willett (1912) called the species common in southern California generally, the only report in the early literature of breeding Western Flycatchers likely identified correctly in San Diego County is that by Anthony (1895), who called them "rather common" between 4000 and 6000 feet elevation on Cuyamaca Peak in late June 1895. Frank Stephens collected four specimens (MVZ) at Julian and Volcan Mt. from 31 July to 6 August 1908. F. E. Blaisdell (in Belding 1890) called the

Western Flycatcher "a summer resident" at Poway but misidentified enough other birds to cast doubt on this one. In the early 1900s the southern limit of the species' lowland breeding distribution was apparently north of San Diego County.

Egg collections, dating primarily from 1890 to 1940, contain only a single set from San Diego County, collected by Griffing Bancroft at an unspecified location in 1926 (WFVZ 75013). Thus it appears that the invasion of breeding Western Flycatchers gained momentum only after 1940 and was largely overlooked because the species has always been common in migration. By the late 1970s the breeding population was still uncommon and scattered (Unitt 1984). Our atlas data confirm that the spread has continued and suggest that low-elevation nesting in northwestern Baja California is now likely.

What factors prompted the Western Flycatcher's invasion? The planting of eucalyptus trees, the erecting of structures that offer nest sites, and the maturation of riparian woodland in floodplains where scouring by floods is now rare must all have contributed. Yet much of the spread has happened in canyons little touched by these forces. The species is only lightly parasitized by cowbirds, perhaps because its nests are usually hidden from above. No clear increase of the breeding population has been reported in California north of San Diego County, but at its northern end the Western Flycatcher's range has also expanded, in this case to the east (Lowther 2000).

Taxonomy: The comparatively bright yellow subspecies *E. d. difficilis* (Baird, 1858) ranges along the Pacific coast from southeastern Alaska south at least to San Diego County. The slightly larger and drabber *E. d. insulicola* Oberholser, 1897, is a summer visitor only to the Channel Islands but has not been identified conclusively in migration on the California mainland. The drab yellow-deficient subspecies *E. d. cineritius* Brewster, 1888, breeds in Baja California and ranged at least formerly north to the Sierra Juárez (Laguna Hanson, 24 July 1924, SDNHM 31899). Anthony (1895) reported his late June specimens from Cuyamaca Peak (M20) as *cineritius*. But six more recent (1984–1993) San Diego County breeding specimens are all typical of nominate *difficilis*. The southward expansion of *difficilis* has probably already swamped any former population of *cineritius*.

The split of the Western Flycatcher into two species seems premature in the lack of adequate study in most of the area of possible sympatry in southeastern British Columbia, northeastern Washington, eastern Oregon, and northwestern Montana.

Black Phoebe *Sayornis nigricans*

Few birds were as preadapted to urbanization as the Black Phoebe. A lawn, pond, or horse corral serves for foraging habitat, a building or bridge for a nest site, and a mud puddle for nest material. The Black Phoebe is a common year-round resident where

these elements are common. Rural ranchettes, urban parks, and reservoirs offer ideal habitat, but some birds use the expanses of single-family houses. The Black Phoebe is uncommon in wild areas where it has to content itself with its original habitat, canyons with intermittent pools and overhanging rocks.

Breeding distribution: At the scale of our atlas grid, the Black Phoebe is almost uniformly distributed over San Diego County's coastal slope. The high rate of nesting confirmation reflects the ease with which its nests can be found. Despite the birds' requiring mud for their nests, even ephemeral puddles suffice, allowing at least sporadic breeding in such largely waterless areas as the Jamul Mountains (T14) and Otay Mountain (V15). Buildings, bridges, and culverts now offer abundant nest sites anywhere on the coastal plain that once lacked them, and in the foothills Black Phoebes still use the rocky canyons that must have been their primitive habitat. Twenty-five to 35 in a day may be seen in the coastal regions where the population is densest, but the numbers are much lower at the higher elevations; for example, none of our observers reported more than a single family of Black Phoebes per day in the Palomar and Laguna mountains. The Black Phoebe is scarce along the east face of the mountains but nests locally along the few perennial creeks, as in Borrego Palm Canyon (F23; fledging on 4 May 1997, P. Famolaro) and Bow Willow Canyon (P26; used nest and adults feeding fledglings on 19 May 2001, L. J. Hargrove). On the floor of the Anza–Borrego Desert, breeding Black Phoebes are confined to developed oases and uncommon even there, with no reports of more than four individuals in a day.

Nesting: An open half-bowl built of pellets of mud, plastered to a solid surface, sheltered from above, the Black Phoebe's nest is distinctive; only the Barn Swallow's resembles it. The phoebe's habit of building under bridges and the eaves of buildings is so well known that frequently our observers did not describe the situation of the nests they located; they simply confirmed breeding by checking out the nearest such structure when they found the birds. Nevertheless, 32 nests were described as on buildings (ranging from occupied apartment and office buildings

Photo by Anthony Mercieca

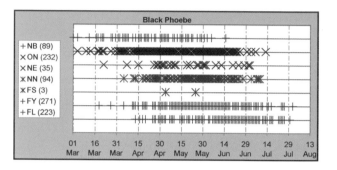

to abandoned shacks), 10 under bridges, six on drainage structures (including two below ground level in storm drains), one in a railroad tunnel, one on an old farm wagon, and nine on natural rock overhangs along creeks. The durability of the nests, in their protected locations, means they persist from year to year and allows the birds to refurbish them, reinforcing the rims with new mud or stacking a new nest atop an old one. The nests' durability also led to our observers' reporting many old nests, up to 16 in a day southeast of Mesa Grande (I17) 15 June 2000 (D. C. Seals). Still, nests poorly supported from below can collapse, destroying a clutch, as F. L. Unmack noted near Bankhead Springs (U27) 20 April 1997.

Unlike our more migratory flycatchers, the Black Phoebe regularly raises two broods per year (Wolf 1997). Thus it has a long breeding season, beginning in early March (nest building as early as 1 March, nest occupied as early as 4 March, and young being fed as early as 19 March) and running through July (nest with eggs as late as 2 July, young being fed as late as 1 August). The season is therefore somewhat more extended at both ends than attested by the egg-date span of 17 March–16 June from collections and Sharp (1907).

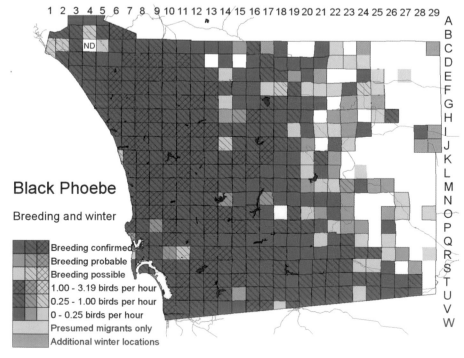

Black Phoebe

Breeding and winter

- Breeding confirmed
- Breeding probable
- Breeding possible
- 1.00 - 3.19 birds per hour
- 0.25 - 1.00 birds per hour
- 0 - 0.25 birds per hour
- Presumed migrants only
- Additional winter locations

Migration: There is no clear evidence of Black Phoebe migration in San Diego County.

Winter: In spite of a diet consisting almost exclusively of insects, the Black Phoebe appears practically sedentary in San Diego County, remaining in winter even at the higher elevations—up to 5400 feet at Big Laguna Lake (O23; up to two on 18 January 1998, P. Unitt). There may be some influx from farther north in winter, as there is around the Salton Sea (Patten et al. 2003), or the local population may disperse only short distances, concentrating around water and insects. The only area of San Diego County where numbers are clearly higher in winter is the Borrego Valley, where daily counts range up to 36 in north Borrego Springs (F24) on 19 December 1999 (P. K. Nelson). On the coastal side, the highest count per day in winter is 64 around Lake Hodges (K10) 27 December 1998 (R. L. Barber).

Conservation: Importation of vast quantities of water, and the building of vast numbers of structures ideal for nest sites, have turned much of San Diego County into

Black Phoebe paradise. Though the species has long been common, its numbers along the coast continue to increase, as suggested by results of the Oceanside, Rancho Santa Fe, and San Diego Christmas bird counts. San Diego count results imply that Black Phoebe numbers in that circle roughly tripled from the 1950s and 1960s to 1997–2001. Little or no change is evident farther inland, from the Escondido, Lake Henshaw, and Anza–Borrego circles, though the terms of these counts are shorter. Thus we may infer that the increase is a response to development creating more habitat, rather than a response to climate warming or other factors. The Black Phoebe's wintering in the Anza–Borrego Desert is undoubtedly a by-product of irrigation and development, and its continuing increase as a breeding species in the Salton Sea region (Patten et al. 2003) suggests that an increase in the Borrego Valley can be expected.

Taxonomy: Only the subspecies *S. n. semiatra* (Vigors, 1839), distinguished by its extensively white belly and undertail coverts, occurs in or near California.

Eastern Phoebe *Sayornis phoebe*

None of the olive-drab flycatchers is common in winter, and the most frequent at that season is actually a vagrant from eastern North America, the Eastern Phoebe. It occurs at a rate of about one bird per year, and it usually visits ponds or irrigated areas, the same habitats as the Black Phoebe's.

Migration and winter: The difference between these two roles is blurred with the Eastern Phoebe, as the records (at least 46 total) are concentrated in November and December. Close to half are clearly of birds wintering. The records extend from 27 September (1983, Lake Henshaw, G17, R. Higson, AB 38:247, 1984) and 8–12

Photo by Dave Furseth

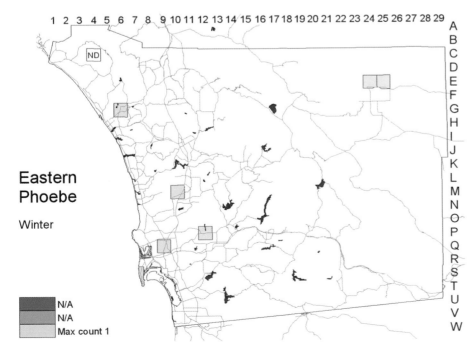

Eastern Phoebe

Winter

■ N/A
■ N/A
□ Max count 1

October (1992, near Imperial Beach, V10, J. O. Zimmer, AB 47:150, 1993) to 12 March (1994, near San Diego, C. G. Edwards, NASFN 48:248, 1994). Two later records (1–2 April 1997, Point Loma, S7, R. E. Webster, FN 51:928, 1997; 18 April 1989, Agua Caliente Springs, M26, D. and M. Hastings, AB 43:537, 1989) appear to be of spring migrants.

Most Eastern Phoebes in San Diego County have been found in the coastal lowland, but five are from elevations up to 3200 feet at Lake Henshaw, Mesa Grande (H17; Unitt 1984), and Lake Morena (T21; 24 February 1994, R. Gardner, NASFN 48:248, 1994). There are also four records from the Borrego Valley: 10 November 1992–22 February 1993 (A. G. Morley, AB 47:150, 301, 1993), 13 December 1994 (K. Burton, NASFN 49:199, 1995), 20 December 1998 (E24, P. R. Pryde, NAB 53:209, 1999), and 17 December 2000 (E25, L. J. Hargrove, P. Unitt).

Say's Phoebe *Sayornis saya*

Expanses of bare earth, often disturbed, or areas of sparse grass or weeds, with only scattered shrubs, Say's Phoebe's habitat hardly meets most people's expectations for "habitat." Yet this bird specializes in such places, scanning the ground for insects that can be hover-gleaned, as well as foraging for aerial insects in typical flycatcher fashion. Say's Phoebe is primarily a winter visitor to San Diego County, uncommon to fairly common. But it is also widespread as an uncommon breeding species in the Anza–Borrego Desert, on the Campo Plateau, and, increasingly, in the inland valleys of the coastal slope.

Breeding distribution: The Say's Phoebe's distribution is complex and dynamic. The species is widespread in the Anza–Borrego Desert, where most atlas squares contain some of the canyons, bluffs, or buildings offering the shaded niches it needs for nesting. Over most of the desert, breeding Say's Phoebes are uncommon and scattered, but, as around Canebrake (N27) 30 April 2000 (R. and S. L. Breisch), counts per day range up to 14, where scattered houses or eroded gorges winding through badlands offer more nest sites. The desert distribution extends up to Scissors Crossing (J22) and over the divide to Ranchita (G21/G22) and Warner Valley. A pair nesting in a drain pipe at 4900 feet elevation on the east side of Hot Springs Mountain (E21) 19 June 1999 (K. L. Weaver) was the highest known in San Diego County. Yet Say's Phoebe appears absent from the higher elevations of the Santa Rosa and Vallecito mountains, enclosed within the

Photo by Anthony Mercieca

Anza–Borrego Desert. A few Say's Phoebes also extend up onto the Campo plateau. Though we did not confirm breeding in this area, we recorded the species through the spring and early summer and noted a few pairs.

In the coastal half of the county, Say's Phoebe has become widespread in the inland valleys. The numbers are still small, with rarely more than a single family encountered in a day. The maximum count per day in this region during the breeding season is six, as at Lake Hodges (K10) 23 June 1998 (R. L. Barber). A few pairs are nesting practically along the coast, illustrated most notably by a fledgling 0.5 mile from the beach near San Onofre (C1) 2 June 2000 (C. Reynolds), another at La Costa (J7) 24 June 1998 (M. Baumgartel), two in Gonzalez Canyon (M8) 17 June 2001 (S. E. Smith), and one picked up injured at Mar Vista High School in Imperial Beach (V10) 26 June 1998 (SDNHM 50127). A nest on a building at the naval radio station at the south end of the Silver Strand (U10/V10) in 2003 and 3 March 2004 was only 1000 feet from the beach (D. M. Parker). Some interchange between the coastal and desert populations is likely, with pairs nesting as far inland as Santa Ysabel (J18; under the porch of Don's Market, both 1998 and 1999, J. R. Barth, S. E. Smith) and Tecate (V19; pair

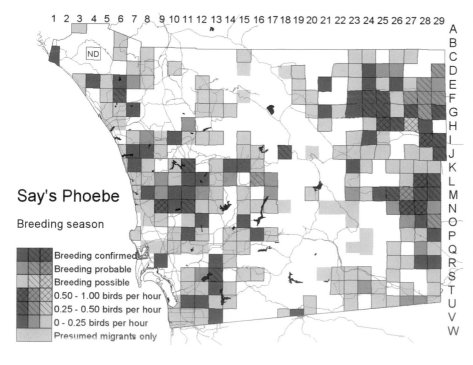

Say's Phoebe

Breeding season

- Breeding confirmed
- Breeding probable
- Breeding possible
- 0.50 - 1.00 birds per hour
- 0.25 - 0.50 birds per hour
- 0 - 0.25 birds per hour
- Presumed migrants only

feeding young 10 June 2000, M. and B. McIntosh).

Complicating the distribution are scattered individuals, including independent juveniles, seen in the foothills and mountains at times when Say's Phoebes could be nesting. Nevertheless, only one of these falls between 8 April and 6 June, one at Cuyamaca Lake (M20) 28 May 1999 (A. P. and T. E. Keenan). Only this record is mapped as in suitable habitat; the birds seen from June onward may be postbreeding dispersers from the desert.

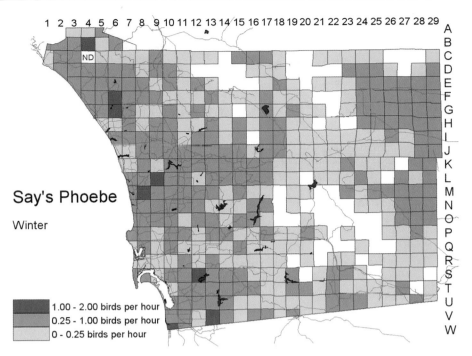

Say's Phoebe

Winter

1.00 - 2.00 birds per hour
0.25 - 1.00 birds per hour
0 - 0.25 birds per hour

Nesting: Say's Phoebes rely heavily on man-made structures for nest sites, and all nests reported from the coastal slope were in such situations. We noted four nests on sheltered ledges inside crevasses eroded into desert badlands, but the 14 other nests whose placement our observers described were on such things as houses, outbuildings, carports, restrooms, a metal stairway, a bridge over Poway Creek, and the Anza–Borrego Desert State Park headquarters office.

Our observations of Say's Phoebe nesting imply that the species usually begins laying in the third week of March, with little difference between the coastal slope and the desert. A nest begun in Mira Mesa (N9) 3 March 2000 took two weeks to complete (S. L. Breisch). An exceptionally early nest with two eggs at the Anza–Borrego Desert State Park headquarters 7 February 2000 was abandoned shortly thereafter; the pair renested at a more usual time (P. D. Jorgensen). In the wet spring of 1998, though, the birds nested early, with adults carrying insects to young apparently still in the nest as early as 6 March in north Borrego Springs (F24; P. D. Jorgensen), implying laying no later than 18–20 February. Our five earliest records of Say's Phoebe feeding young, in fact, are from 1998. Second or replacement clutches may be laid as late as mid June, as demonstrated by an ill-fated pair at Mira Mesa, which still had young in an replacement nest 16 July 1999, fledging by 21 July (S. L. Breisch).

Migration: Say's Phoebes wintering in San Diego County depart primarily in March and arrive in September. But

exact dates of migrants can no longer be picked out because of the local breeding population is increasing, apparently shifts over short distances, and the locally breeding subspecies, at least along the coast, is the same as that farther north. Some desert breeders vacate their range from June through August (Rea 1983, Patten et al. 2003) and may disperse west into the foothills and mountains of San Diego County, as implied by scattered summer observations.

Winter: Say's Phoebe is widespread in San Diego County as a winter visitor, but it is scarce above 4000 feet elevation and lacking from unbroken forest, chaparral, or urban development, though it uses small areas of open ground within these habitats. Thus the distribution is patchier than evident on the scale of our atlas grid. The species is most numerous in the inland valleys of the coastal lowland, with up to 35 in a day around Sweetwater Reservoir (S12) 20 December 1997 (P. Famolaro), and on the floor of the Borrego Valley, with up to 35 in north Borrego Springs 20 December 1998 (R. Thériault). Over most of the county, though, the species has to be rated as uncommon, with five or fewer individuals detected per day.

Conservation: No change in the Say's Phoebe's status in the Anza–Borrego Desert is known, but on the coastal slope the species decreased, then increased, for reasons still obscure. Until 1939, nesting of Say's Phoebes was noted occasionally, with records for Escondido, 3 to 6 miles east of Encinitas, Sorrento, San Diego, and Chula Vista. Then 40 years followed in which the species was known in the coastal lowland as a winter visitor only. Following a report from the Tijuana River valley 9 June 1979 (AB 33:898, 1979), scattered observations cropped up in the inland valleys in the 1980s, and their rate accelerated in the 1990s. Nesting Say's Phoebes in this area were a novelty to our atlas observers, many of whom commented on them with surprise. Why should Say's Phoebe

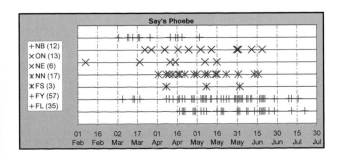

have disappeared, and why should it have returned? The disappearance coincided with a period in which much former Say's Phoebe habitat was converted, with irrigation and landscaping, into Black Phoebe habitat. Though much suitable habitat remained, from Pauma Valley to Ramona to Jamul, perhaps the small population dropped below a sustainable threshold. The accelerating return suggests that Say's Phoebe is adapting anew, perhaps aided by a long-term trend toward a warmer, drier climate. Clearing of scrub and erection of buildings create new Say's Phoebe habitat, but landscaping and paving remove it. The bird's need for open ground for foraging suggests its potential as an urban adapter is limited. But further increase is likely with further adaptation to low-density suburban development. Urban nesting of Say's Phoebes may expose the birds to unaccustomed threats: one pair that nested repeatedly atop a bell at a Mira Mesa school (N9) suffered losses to both clean-up by maintenance workers and predation by European Starlings (S. L. Breisch).

Taxonomy: Winter visitors are the dark *S. s. saya* (Bonaparte, 1825), widespread in western North America north of San Diego. The coastal population, judged from the quite dark juvenile specimen from Imperial Beach, is this subspecies too. This identification also implies that the recent increase in breeding Say's Phoebes on the coastal slope is the result of colonization from the north. Breeding Say's Phoebes in eastern San Diego County are more likely *S. s. quiescens* Grinnell, 1926, paler than nominate *saya*, especially on the crown, which is practically the same color as the back. The only specimen so far from the Anza–Borrego Desert is *quiescens*, though it was collected in winter, in Mason Valley (M23) 15 January 1925 (SDNHM 2915). Two juveniles from Laguna Hanson in the Sierra Juárez are *quiescens*, as are several specimens from the Colorado Desert (Rea 1983, Patten et al. 2003).

Vermilion Flycatcher *Pyrocephalus rubinus*

Spectacular, tame, and easy to see, habitually perching on the lowest branches of isolated trees, the Vermilion Flycatcher is a birder's favorite. One would think such a species a perfect poster child for promoting conservation of its desert riparian habitat. Yet its decline in its historic California range continues unabated. The Vermilion Flycatcher was always rare in San Diego County, but since the mid 1980s it has become even more so. It survives precariously in five areas and seldom pioneers far from these.

Photo by Anthony Mercieca

Breeding distribution: Here at the northwestern corner of its usual breeding distribution along the Pacific coast, the Vermilion Flycatcher is rare and scattered in San Diego County. Its characteristic habitat of open riparian woodland and mesquite bosques on desert floodplains is barely represented in San Diego County, though the birds and their habitat occur in the drainage basin of the Tijuana River at Valle de las Palmas in northwestern Baja California. The most regular site for the species in San Diego County is the private Butterfield Ranch campground in Mason Valley (M23), with up to four individuals, as on 16 April 1999 (M. B. Stowe) and 21 March 2001 (P. K. Nelson). The Vermilion Flycatcher was first reported from this site in summer 1984 (C. G. Edwards; AB 38:1062, 1984) and has remained more or less continuously ever since. The "population" in this region extends also to adjacent Vallecito Valley (M24), with one pair, the female building a nest, at a private ranch house 21 March 2001 (P. K. Nelson). The Vermilion Flycatcher is irregular in the Borrego Valley. At De Anza Country Club (F24), one pair nested in March 1993 (Massey 1998); one was at a nest with eggs 2 May 1997, and a single individual was noted 5 April and 27 May 2001 (M. L. Gabel). A pair was at Whitaker Horse Camp (D24) 13–14 May 2001 (R. and

S. L. Breisch), the male in courtship display, but the birds did not remain to nest.

One surprise of our atlas effort was the occurrence of the Vermilion Flycatcher in Warner Valley. One pair nested north of Lake Henshaw (F17) 27 May–11 July 1997 (P. P. Beck), another near the old Warner Ranch house (G19) 17–25 June 2000 (J. D. Barr, E. C. Hall, M. U. Evans). Another pair was at Lake Henshaw (G17) 12 May 2001 (R. and S. L. Breisch); single males were west of Warner Springs (F18) 28 May 1997 (P. P. Beck). Elsewhere in eastern San Diego County, single males were at an old corral near Sentenac Ciénaga (J23) 14 June 1998 (R. Thériault), in McCain Valley (S26) 19 April 1999 (G. L. Rogers), and at Cameron Corners (U23) 1 April 2001 (L. and A. Johnson, *fide* D. S. and A. W. Hester).

Nearer the coast, the Vermilion Flycatcher appears regular at only two sites. At Bonsall (F8), there was one 9 July 1997 (L. Gammie) and an adult with two fledglings 25 May 2000 (J. Evans). Along the Sweetwater River, a singing male was at the Singing Hills golf course (Q14) 30 April 2000 (J., E., and K. Berndes) and a pair was a short distance downstream at the Rancho San Diego golf course in Jamacha Valley (R14) 11 April 1999

(N. Perretta, P. Nance), with a single male noted there 19 July 1999 (D. Stokes). The Vermilion Flycatcher has been reported from this area sporadically for years. Not far away was one at the end of Eula Lane 3.6 miles east-northeast of downtown El Cajon (Q14) 1 May 1999 (J., E., and K. Berndes). The only other report of a possibly breeding Vermilion Flycatcher 1997–2001 was at the Eagle Crest golf course, east Escondido (J12), 31 May 1998 (C. Rideout).

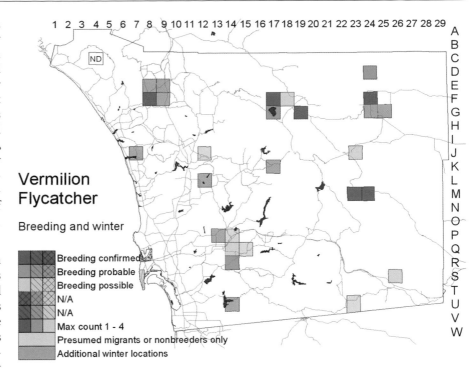

Vermilion
Flycatcher

Breeding and winter

Breeding confirmed
Breeding probable
Breeding possible
N/A
N/A
Max count 1 - 4
Presumed migrants or nonbreeders only
Additional winter locations

Nesting: The Vermilion Flycatcher typically places its shallow nest in a horizontal fork in the middle level of trees (Wolf and Jones 2000). Because the fork selected is free of leaves and the habitat itself is semiopen, the nests are not difficult

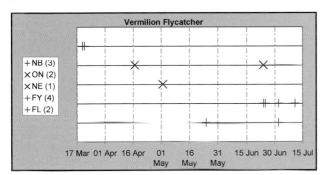

to find—possibly making the Vermilion Flycatcher especially vulnerable to predators and cowbirds. Because of the species' rarity in San Diego County, our records, encompassing only eight pairs, do not define its breeding season well. But the spread of dates, ranging from nest building on 20 March to fledglings on 11 July, implies the Vermilion Flycatcher may raise two broods, as elsewhere in the southwestern United States (Wolf and Jones 2000).

Migration: The Vermilion Flycatcher no longer has a clear-cut migration in California; the former pattern of largely summer residency has now changed to irregular dispersal. The only record of a spring migrant 1997–2001, of a female at Point Loma (S7) 22 May 1999 (P. A. Ginsburg), was exceptionally late. Previous records from nonbreeding localities run no later than 28 April (1990, San Diego River mouth, R7, R. E. Webster, AB 44:497, 1990). The Vermilion Flycatcher is most widespread during fall dispersal, beginning by 16 September (1983, Tijuana River valley, E. Copper, AB 38:247, 1984) and extending through October.

Winter: At this season, the Vermilion Flycatcher is little more widespread than during spring and summer. Most

records 1997–2002 were at or near locations where it was noted also during the breeding season: Bonsall, Lake Henshaw, Borrego Valley, San Pasqual Valley, Butterfield Ranch, Lakeside, Singing Hills. Only a few records were more than 7 miles from breeding-season locations: one at La Costa (J7) 13 December 1997 (M. Baumgartel), one on the east edge of Poway (L12) 1 February 2001 (K. J. Winter), and one in Ballena Valley (K17) 25 February 2000 (D. C. Seals) and 16 February 2001 (O. Carter). Winter numbers were also similar to those during the breeding season, with a maximum of five in the San Luis Rey River valley 1–2 miles northeast of Bonsall (E8) 14 December 1999 (P. A. Ginsburg).

Conservation: Though the Vermilion Flycatcher has colonized several new locations in the Mojave Desert, its career through the history of California as a whole has been one of calamitous decline. This decline is reflected in San Diego County as well, however marginal the region is to the flycatcher's main range. Results of Christmas bird counts reflect the decline most clearly. From 1960 through 1974 the Vermilion Flycatcher was annual on the San Diego count, with a maximum of eight in 1968. From 1975 through 1986, it occurred in only five of 12 years, with no more than one individual. Since 1986 the species has gone unrecorded. Likewise, on the Oceanside count, the Vermilion Flycatcher was noted in 10 of the 18 years from 1970 to 1987, with a maximum of three on 22 December 1979, but not since 1987. The areas around Bonsall where the species occurs are largely outside the count circle and within private ranches. Nesting of Vermilion Flycatchers at Santee in 1958, Balboa Park from 1958 to 1960 (Crouch 1959), Bonita in 1968 (G. McCaskie), and Jacumba in 1986 (AB 40:1256, 1986) proved ephemeral.

Degradation of riparian woodland is probably the factor affecting the Vermilion Flycatcher most strongly.

Because San Diego County is marginal to the flycatcher's range, it may be even more susceptible to environmental change here than closer to the core. Population collapse in the Coachella, Imperial, and Colorado River valleys decimated a source of immigrants. The Vermilion Flycatcher occurs most often now in parks, campgrounds, and golf courses, which have proliferated with development. Yet the flycatcher's continuing decline suggests that these habitats are poor substitutes for natural riparian woodland. Recent riparian restoration, along with flood control, favors dense woodland in narrow strips, rather than broad open woodland more suitable to the Vermilion Flycatcher. Meanwhile, pumping of groundwater desiccates the remaining habitat.

Taxonomy: However brilliant the male Vermilion Flycatcher appears to those of us who are familiar only with *P. r. flammeus* van Rossem 1934, this subspecies, the only one in California, is actually paler, less intensely colored than others farther south.

Dusky-capped or Olivaceous Flycatcher
Myiarchus tuberculifer

The Dusky-capped Flycatcher reaches California as a rare winter visitor from the southeast. San Diego County accounts for so small a fraction of the state's 64 records (through 2002) that we may infer that the trajectory of most vagrants passes to the north of us. In the United States, the "Dusky-capped" Flycatcher has no dusky cap; it must be distinguished from the similar Ash-throated by its smaller size, flatter and proportionately longer bill, less rufous in the wings and tail, and, most characteristically, by its soft mournful whistle, "peeeur."

Winter: Four records, of one photographed at La Jolla (P7) 8 March 1985 (L. Bevier et al., AB 39:211, 1985, Dunn 1988), one on the grounds of the San Diego Zoo (R9) 16 February–7 April 1988 (B. and I. Mazin, AB 42:322, 1988, Pyle and McCaskie 1992), one at Point Loma (S7) 12 April–1 May 1997 (P. A. Ginsburg, FN 51:928, 1997, Rottenborn and Morlan 2000), and one at Greenwood Cemetery (S10) 15 December 2001–22 February 2002 (J. O. Zimmer et al.). Though the date of at least the Point Loma record suggests a spring migrant, the species' pattern of winter occurrence in California is so well established that it seems certain that all San Diego County Dusky-capped Flycatchers arrived at that season but may not have been discovered until late in their stay.

Photo by Anthony Mercieca

Taxonomy: The one California specimen, from Death Valley, has been identified as *M. t. olivascens* Ridgway, 1884, the subspecies ranging north to the northern limit of the species' breeding range, in the mountains of southern Arizona (Suffel 1970). *Myiarchus t. olivascens* has less rufous edging on its remiges and rectrices than other Middle American subspecies. Like some other west Mexican subspecies of *M. tuberculifer*, it has a crown no darker than the back.

Ash-throated Flycatcher *Myiarchus cinerascens*

Common in summer, rare in winter, the Ash-throated Flycatcher breeds from the inland valleys to the mountains to the Anza–Borrego Desert in any habitat where it can find a suitable nest cavity. The members of the genus *Myiarchus* are the only North American flycatchers that nest in enclosed spaces like old woodpecker holes, other tree hollows, pipes, or bird houses. Despite the scarcity of suitable cavities, and the birds' willingness to use man-made nest sites, nesting Ash-throated Flycatchers remain largely outside the urban fringe. In the coastal strip the species is seen primarily in migration.

Breeding distribution: The Ash-throated Flycatcher is one of San Diego County's most widespread breeding

Photo by Jack C. Daynes

birds. It is most common in the mountains or foothill canyons where there is extensive woodland. Exceptionally high counts during the breeding season are of 40 around Case Spring, Camp Pendleton (B4), on 25 July 1998 (P. A. Ginsburg), 50 in Matagual Valley (I19) 18 June 2000 (S. E. Smith), and 35 in the Edwards Ranch northeast of Santa Ysabel (I19) on 9 June 2001 (D. W. Au, S. E. Smith). It is only along the coast and in the Anza–Borrego Desert where we see significant gaps in the Ash-throated Flycatcher's range. The Ash-throated resembles the Western Kingbird in avoiding the coastal strip as a breeding species, though it can be common just a short distance inland (e.g., 13 in Los Peñasquitos Canyon, N8, 7 June 1998, P. A. Ginsburg). In the Anza–Borrego Desert, because it depends for nest cavities largely on the Ladder-backed Woodpecker, it is rare or lacking where the woodpecker is rare or lacking, especially in the Borrego Badlands and Ocotillo Wells regions.

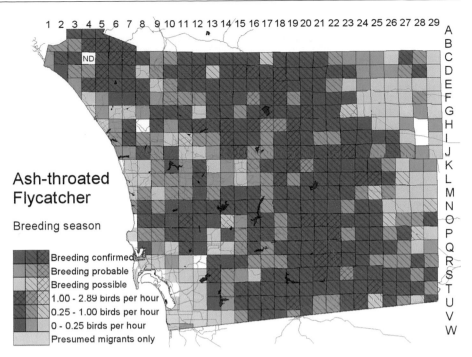

Ash-throated
Flycatcher

Breeding season

Breeding confirmed
Breeding probable
Breeding possible
1.00 - 2.89 birds per hour
0.25 - 1.00 birds per hour
0 - 0.25 birds per hour
Presumed migrants only

Nesting: Like most other cavity-nesting birds the Ash-throated Flycatcher is flexible and resourceful. Old woodpecker holes in trees are the most frequent site, but the cavity may be natural. Atlas observers described four nests in oaks (coast live, black, and Engelmann), three in sycamores, two in yuccas, one in cottonwood, and one in the split trunk of a desert willow. Nests in artificial sites included nine in nest boxes, five in metal or plastic pipes, one in a woodpecker hole in a fence post, one in a mailbox, and one in the tailpipe of wrecked vehicle used for target practice. Possible but unconfirmed sites in the Anza–Borrego Desert include cavities in rocks or bluffs and rodent burrows in sandy hummocks.

Bent (1942) reported 79 California egg sets ranging in date from 12 April to 5 July. In San Diego County, however, we found the Ash-throated Flycatcher nesting somewhat earlier, in several cases beginning around 1 April. Nest building was reported as early as 4 April (1997, in Earthquake Valley, K23, G. Sanders), occupied nest cavities as early as 6 April (2000, at Wilderness Gardens County Park, D11, V.

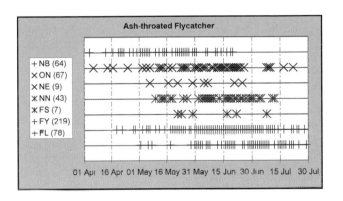

Ash-throated Flycatcher

+ NB (64)
× ON (67)
× NE (9)
× NN (43)
× FS (7)
+ FY (219)
+ FL (78)

01 Apr 16 Apr 01 May 16 May 31 May 15 Jun 30 Jun 15 Jul 30 Jul

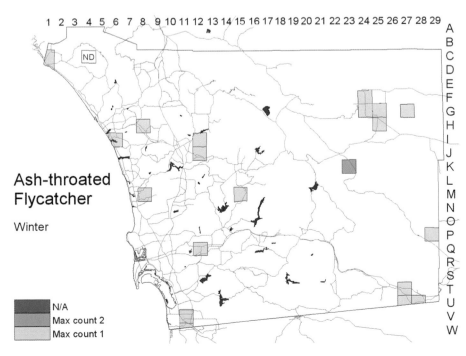

Ash-throated
Flycatcher

Winter

N/A
Max count 2
Max count 1

Dineen). Reports of adults feeding young as early as 19 April (1998, near Sunset Mountain, J26, F. L. Unmack, R. Orr) and fledglings as early as 2 May (2001, Inner Pasture, N25, A. P. and T. E. Keenan) also point to egg laying around 1 April. Many of these records, though, are from the Anza–Borrego Desert, poorly sampled by early egg collections. From Baja California, over much of which the Ash-throated Flycatcher is a year-round resident, Bent (1942) reported egg dates as early as 13 March. Most Ash-throated Flycatcher nesting in San Diego County, though, takes place later in the summer. An occupied nest in the Agua Tibia Wilderness (C13) on 22 July (2000, J. M. Wells) suggests the birds could be laying even later than Bent's spread implies.

Migration: Ash-throated Flycatchers begin arriving in the latter half of March; 17 March (1998, one near Angelina Spring, I22, P. K. Nelson) is the earliest date. As in many other species, these early arrivals (concentrated in the Anza–Borrego Desert) are likely of the local breeding population, with migrants headed farther north coming later, not in numbers until the second week of April. Peak migration is in late April, as implied by the 75 grounded in strong wind at Vallecito (M25) 29 April 1997 (M. C. Jorgensen). By the third week of May almost all migrants have continued north; 21 May (1999, one near the Santa Margarita River mouth, G4, P. A. Ginsburg) was the latest we recorded from 1997 to 2001. Even later stragglers have been recorded to 6 June (1974, two at Point Loma, S7, J. L. Dunn). Fall migration begins by 26 July (2001, one in Chula Vista, U11, T. W. Dorman) and trails off through October.

Winter: The Ash-throated Flycatcher is rare in winter but occurs annually, with 20 records 1997–2002. Of these, nine were at low elevations along the coast or in the inland valleys, one was around 1350 feet elevation in Barona Valley (M15; one on 28 December 2000, J. Smith), four were around 2800 to 3500 feet elevation in the Jacumba area (F. L. Unmack), one was around 2350 feet elevation in Earthquake Valley (K23; two on 12 February 2000, P. Flanagan, the only winter record of more than one individual), and five were on the floor of the Anza–Borrego Desert. Previous winter records, at least 30, are all from the coastal lowland or desert floor. San Diego County lies just to the northwest of the Ash-throated Flycatcher's main winter range; wintering birds are quite a bit more numerous in eastern Imperial County and at the east base of the Sierra San Pedro Mártir in northern Baja California.

Conservation: Although the Ash-throated Flycatcher readily uses man-made structures for nesting, it is not an urban adapter. It is absent from the developed areas of the city of San Diego and very rare in the urban canyons, with scant evidence of breeding ("distraction display" in Tecolote Canyon, Q8, 10 June 1999, J. C. Worley). Other heavily developed areas likewise have few or no breeding Ash-throated Flycatchers. But because of the species' "anticoastal" distribution urbanization has likely had only a minor effect on the Ash-throated Flycatcher population. The species is most concentrated in areas where development pressure so far is light or none. Smooth-sided vertical plastic pipes, into which the birds can descend but not escape, are a hazard to this species (P. D. Jorgensen).

Taxonomy: The resident Baja California population of the Ash-throated Flycatcher, though averaging smaller than the migratory birds farther north, overlaps with the latter too much for two subspecies to be recognized. *Myiarchus cinerascens* is thus best considered monotypic (Patten et al. 2003).

Great Crested Flycatcher *Myiarchus crinitus*

The only representative of the genus *Myiarchus* in eastern North America and a rare fall vagrant to California, the Great Crested closely resembles the Brown-crested and Ash-throated Flycatchers. Fortunately, the birds reaching California are fresh-plumaged immatures that show the species' characters well—a darker throat and breast and broad, crisp white edge on the innermost tertial that expands in width from tip to base.

Migration: All five San Diego County records of the Great Crested Flycatcher are from Point Loma in fall. By date, these are 19 September 1975 (G. McCaskie, AB 30:128, 1976), 20 September 1983 (R. E. Webster et al., Roberson 1986), 25 September 1987 (G. McCaskie, Pyle and McCaskie 1992), 6 October 1978 (E. Copper, P. Unitt, AB 33:216, 1979; Binford 1983), and 10–13 October 2001 (R. E. Webster, NAB 56:107, 2002). The record for 20 October 1974 was rejected by the California Bird Records Committee.

Photo by Anthony Mercieca

Brown-crested or Wied's Crested Flycatcher
Myiarchus tyrannulus

The Brown-crested Flycatcher presents the same paradox as the Summer Tanager: a species expanding its range while its habitat has been decimated. First found on the Colorado River in 1921, occurring in numbers there by 1930, and first found west of the Colorado, at Morongo Valley, in 1963, the flycatcher is clearly spreading northwest, out of its stronghold in the riparian woodland and saguaros of southern Arizona. Yet in California it depends for nest sites on large riparian trees, largely eliminated with the taming of the Colorado River. The Brown-crested Flycatcher arrived in San Diego County as a new breeding species in 2000.

Photo by Anthony Mercieca

Breeding distribution: Mary Beth Stowe's discovery of a family of Brown-crested Flycatchers at the Roadrunner Club in Borrego Springs (F24) 26 August–18 September 2000 was among the more sensational events of the atlas project's five years. The two adults fed three fledglings high in eucalyptus trees at a pond in this community of mobile homes within a golf course. Photographed, seen, and heard by many, these birds represented the first well-supported identification of the Brown-crested Flycatcher in San Diego County as well as the first breeding. The pair returned the following year, first found 16 May 2001 (P. D. Jorgensen, NAB 55:356, 2001). Nesting was not confirmed that year, but the last report, on 17 August 2001, may have been of a juvenile (*fide* P. D. Jorgensen).

At least one, probably two, Brown-crested Flycatchers were calling in riparian woodland near the confluence of San Felipe and Banner creeks (J22) 13 July 2001 (M. B. Mulrooney, P. Unitt). Two pairs summered there in 2002, and at least one of these nested in a cavity in a cottonwood (nestlings 7 July). A pair summered there again in 2003 (J. R. Barth, P. D. Jorgensen). Another pair colonized Lower Willows along Coyote Creek (D23) in 2002, attending a nest hole 9 July (J. R. Barth).

Nesting: Like the other species of *Myiarchus*, the Brown-crested Flycatcher is a cavity nester, in Arizona relying mainly on old holes of the Gila Woodpecker and flicker for nest sites. As no large woodpeckers nest at Borrego Springs, the flycatchers at the Roadrunner Club probably used an artificial site, possibly the space behind a loose slab of eucalyptus bark.

The incubation and nestling periods of the Brown-crested Flycatcher are still unknown, so it is difficult to estimate when the pair at Borrego Springs may have nested. But the family was discovered so late in the year that the birds must have laid at the very end of the species' breeding season; Bent (1942) reported a latest egg date from Arizona of 17 July. Perhaps these pioneers wandered southeastern California for much of the summer before finding each other, and a suitable nest site, at Borrego Springs.

Migration: The Brown-crested Flycatcher is a summer visitor to the southwestern United States, rarely arriving before the first week of May, and with an earliest California date of 24 April (Garrett and Dunn 1981). Fall departure is usually in August, rarely as late as early September, making the late date of the birds at Borrego Springs in 2000 noteworthy, and reinforcing the idea that as pioneers they were delayed beyond the species' usual schedule. During regular monitoring of San Felipe Creek 2002–03, the earliest date on which J. R. Barth noted the species was 19 May 2002.

Two sightings have been reported from Point Loma (S7), 9 June 1991 (R. E. Webster, AB 45:497, 1991) and 13 October 2001 (R. E. Webster, D. M. Parker, NAB 56:107, 2002). Only the latter is well supported (G. McCaskie pers. comm).

Winter: Unrecorded. But two winter records for Orange County suggest that the Brown-crested Flycatcher could start a pattern of winter occurrence resembling that of other flycatchers from southern Arizona and western Mexico—the Dusky-capped Flycatcher, Tropical Kingbird, and Greater Pewee.

Conservation: The Brown-crested Flycatcher's push west was likely inhibited by the decimation of riparian forest along the Colorado shortly after its arrival, then the lack of woodpeckers large enough to excavate cavities large enough for this biggest species of *Myiarchus*. Thus west of the Colorado the Brown-crested Flycatcher may depend largely on man-made cavities. Its spread into natural habitats is contingent on the maintenance of mature desert riparian woodland, easily degraded by the proliferation of saltcedar.

Taxonomy: Specimens from the Colorado River south through western Mexico are the large *M. t. magister* Ridgway, 1884; presumably Brown-crested Flycatchers farther west are the same.

Sulphur-bellied Flycatcher
Myiodynastes luteiventris

Though more strongly migratory than some other subtropical flycatchers that reach California as vagrants, the Sulphur-bellied is one of the rarest. With its heavy dark streaks and bright rufous tail, it is also one of the more distinctive.

Migration: Of California's 14 records of the Sulphur-bellied Flycatcher, two are from San Diego County. Both are from Point Loma in fall, 7 October 1979 (C. Carpenter, G. McCaskie et al., AB 34:202, 1980; Binford 1983) and 16–20 September 1983 (R. E. Webster et al., photographed, AB 38:247, 1984, Roberson 1986).

Photo by Brian L. Sullivan

Tropical Kingbird *Tyrannus melancholicus*

Among the vagrant flycatchers that originate from southern Arizona and western Mexico, the Tropical Kingbird is the most frequent. In San Diego County it is rare but annual in fall, very rare in winter. The yellow-suffused breast and longer, heavier bill are better features for distinguishing the Tropical from the Western and Cassin's Kingbirds than the notched tail. With the extremely similar Couch's Kingbird (*T. couchii*) now demonstrated, on the basis of tape recordings of the diagnostic call, to have reached Orange County (Rottenborn and Morlan 2000), noting the high-pitched twittering call of the Tropical becomes all the more important to its identification in California.

Photo by Anthony Mercieca

Migration: The Tropical Kingbird reaches California primarily in the fall. A few individuals are found every year, along or near the coast. The earliest known date in San Diego County is 12 September (1962, one at Coronado, T9, McCaskie and Banks 1964). The species is most numerous from late September through mid October. The maximum for a single day is seven in the Tijuana River valley 8 October 1966 (AFN 21:78, 1967). The species' frequency declines gradually through November, so there is no division between fall and winter records. One photographed at Border Field State Park (W10), 26–28 April 2001 (M. B. Mulrooney, NAB 55:357, 2001) provided a unique spring record.

Winter: There are at least 11 winter records, all within 11 miles of the coast. Four were between 1997 and 2002: one at Bonsall (F8) 9 February 2001 (P. A. Ginsburg), one at Rohr Park (T12) 1 December 2001–14 January 2002 (C. G. Edwards et al.), two in Imperial Beach (V10) 20 December 1997–24 January 1998 (C. G. Edwards et al.), and one at the Dairy Mart pond in the Tijuana River valley (V11) 13 December 1998–5 February 1999 (G. McCaskie, NAB 53:209, 1999). The latest winter record is of one at Coronado Cays on the Silver Strand (T9) on 2 March 1974 (AB 28:693, 1974).

Cassin's Kingbird *Tyrannus vociferans*

"ChiBEER!" The loud call of Cassin's Kingbird is becoming ever more familiar as this noisy bird's population increases. Once localized to sycamore groves in the coastal lowland, Cassin's Kingbird has capitalized on the proliferation of eucalyptus and other exotic tall trees, which offer it nest sites and perches as it sits on the lookout for flying insects—and flying predators. The clearing of chaparral and

sage scrub and their replacement with suburbs and rural ranches has allowed Cassin's Kingbird to expand its range and become a common year-round resident.

Breeding distribution: Cassin's Kingbird is widespread over the coastal slope of San Diego County wherever large trees are scattered on open ground. It occurs up to about 3000 feet elevation, rarely as high as about 3800 feet, as along Los Coyotes Road (F20; pair on 17 April 1999, K. L. Weaver, C. R. Mahrdt). On the east slope of the mountains, the species nests at only one site, Jacumba (U28; six on 9 April 1998, C. G. Edwards; pair nest building on 1 May 2001, F. L. Unmack).

Cassin's Kingbird is most numerous in the inland valleys, where it lives in the same habitat as the Western Kingbird. But Cassin's is fairly common along the coastal strip, as a breeding species far more common there than the Western. Thus in San Diego County the two breeding kingbirds reverse the pattern over most of their ranges, where Cassin's is the species breeding at higher elevations (Tweit and Tweit 2000). Some areas where Cassin's Kingbirds were reported in exceptionally high numbers were Lake Hodges (K10; 40, including several fledglings, 9 July 1998, R. L. Barber), Los Peñasquitos Canyon (N8; 28 on 5 July 1998, D. K. Adams), and Valley Center (G12; 21 on 6 June 1998, A. G. and D. Stanton). Along the coast, daily counts range up to 12, as at Batiquitos Lagoon (J7) 8 July 1998 (C. C. Gorman). At the upper limit of their elevational range, the birds are rare. For example, in Dameron Valley (C15) K. L. Weaver had only one record, of three on 14 June 1997; around Lake Morena (T21) R. and S. L. Breisch had no more than one pair, on 5 July 1997.

Nesting: Cassin's Kingbirds place their nests in the forks of large branches in the upper levels of tall trees. Of the 13 nests whose locations our observers described, eight were in eucalyptus trees, three in sycamores, one in a pine, and one in an unidentified conifer, at heights estimated up to 70 feet. The nests may be in rather open situations, allowing them to be seen from the ground, even when in the canopy. Cassin's Kingbird relies on aggressive nest defense rather than nest concealment, as reflected in the 61 times our observers specified "distraction display" for such defense, against crows, ravens, Western Scrub-Jays, and Red-tailed and Cooper's Hawks. Nevertheless,

Photo by Anthony Mercieca

they noted also success against the kingbirds by all these predators except the Red-tailed.

Because Cassin's Kingbirds nest high in trees, determining their nesting schedule is not easy. An earliest occupied nest on 2 April, earliest nest with nestlings on 23 April, and earliest fledglings on 2 May suggest the birds begin laying in the first few days of April, agreeing with Cooper's (1870) finding them "breeding at San Diego as early as March 28th." Nest building at Oak Hill Cemetery (I12) as early as 1 March 1999 (C. Rideout) and

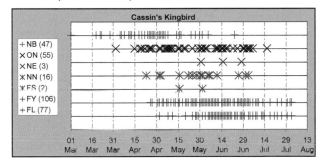

a male with greatly enlarged testes from Santee (P12) 14 March 2001 (SDNHM 50529) suggest that some Cassin's Kingbirds begin even earlier. With adults feeding fledglings as late as 2 August 2001 in Gold Gulch, Balboa Park (S9) and 18 August 1978 near the Santa Margarita River mouth (G4; P. Unitt), it seems likely that some Cassin's Kingbirds are double-brooded in San Diego County, in contrast to other parts of the range where the species begins nesting much later (cf. Tweit and Tweit 2000).

Migration: With Cassin's Kingbirds increasing in San Diego County in both the breeding season and winter, the passage of migrants becomes less and less noticeable. Nevertheless,

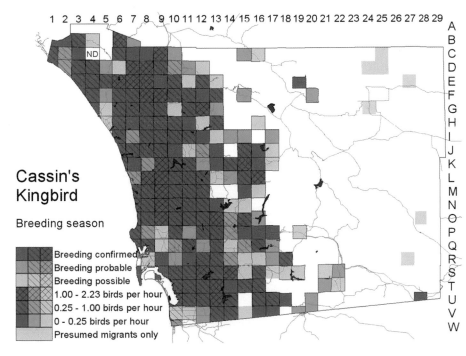

Cassin's Kingbird

Breeding season

- Breeding confirmed
- Breeding probable
- Breeding possible
- 1.00 - 2.23 birds per hour
- 0.25 - 1.00 birds per hour
- 0 - 0.25 birds per hour
- Presumed migrants only

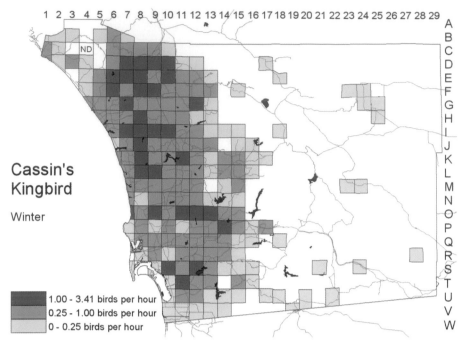

Cassin's
Kingbird

Winter

■ 1.00 - 3.41 birds per hour
▨ 0.25 - 1.00 birds per hour
☐ 0 - 0.25 birds per hour

M. and B. McIntosh). There are now 12 winter reports from the Anza–Borrego Desert, where the species was first noted at this season only on 17 December 1995 (Christmas bird count). Most of these records are from the Borrego Valley, but there are single reports each from Butterfield Ranch (M23, one on 26 February 2000, E. C. Hall), Vallecito Valley (M24, two on 21 January 2001, B. Siegel), and Carrizo Palms (R28, one on 6 January 2000, J. O. Zimmer).

Conservation: Cassin's Kingbird is on the increase in San Diego County, both in winter and as a breeding species. Stephens (1919a) called it "rather rare." Most other early writers called it "uncommon," and that term still applied in the 1970s (Unitt 1984). Christmas bird count results suggest that a gradual increase began accelerating in the mid 1980s. Our atlas results revealed the species in both greater numbers and ranging to higher elevations than reported previously. The next step may be colonization of the Anza–Borrego Desert. The species was unknown there even as a vagrant before 1985, but one or two individuals were noted in the Borrego Valley on Christmas bird counts each year 1998–2001. Cassin's Kingbird is also becoming more of an urban bird, infiltrating residential areas as trees mature.

our highest counts from 1997 through 2001, of 60 southwest of Fallbrook (E7) 28 March 2001 (P. A. Ginsburg) and 41 at Lower Otay Lake (U13) 23 March 2001 (T. Stands), suggest concentrations of migrants at a season suggested by past records. Eight reports from the Anza–Borrego Desert, outside the breeding distribution, extend from 15 April (2001, one in south Borrego Springs, G24, L. Polinsky) to 7 May (2001, two in Box Canyon north of Coyote Creek, C25, D. C. Seals); four other sightings reported by Massey (1998) range as early as 22 March (1993, Yaqui Well/Tamarisk Grove, I24) and so include more of the March migration evident on the coastal side. Some of these desert records are from wilderness areas remote from trees but others are from developed areas that the species could colonize.

Winter: Neither the distribution nor abundance of Cassin's Kingbird in winter differs appreciably from that during the breeding season. The species is most concentrated in winter in the inland valleys of northwestern San Diego County. Daily counts there range up to 44 in Fallbrook (D8) 24 February 2001 (M. Freda), 36 in Rancho Santa Fe (L8) 28 December 1997 (A. Mauro), and 36 east of Lake Hodges (K11) 15 January 1998 (E. C. Hall). Winter records range in elevation as high as 3500 feet feet in Miller Valley (S24, one on 21 Feb 1998,

Why should Cassin's Kingbirds be increasing? A trend toward warmer temperatures, especially of winter lows, may help them. The planting of ornamental and shade trees, especially eucalyptus, gives them nest sites in many areas that once had none. Development, especially low-density suburban development that leaves large cleared areas around scattered houses, shaded by a tree or two, has created much new Cassin's Kingbird habitat. Urban parks, schoolyards, and ranchettes have become more important to Cassin's Kingbird than the sycamore groves that constituted its primitive habitat.

Taxonomy: Binford (1989) synonymized the only subspecies of *Tyrannus vociferans*, leaving Cassin's Kingbird monotypic.

Thick-billed Kingbird *Tyrannus crassirostris*

The fall-and-winter pattern of the extremely rare Thick-billed Kingbird, another species from southern Arizona and western Mexico, is a faint echo of that of the Tropical. A dark crown and the heavy bill most obviously distinguish the Thick-billed from the other kingbirds.

Migration and winter: The Thick-billed Kingbird is known in San Diego County from five records, of 15 total

Photo by Jay M. Sheppard

for California. One was seen in the Tijuana River valley 19 October 1965 (McCaskie et al. 1967a), two were seen at Point Loma (S7) 3 December 1966 (AFN 21:78, 1967) and 18–23 October 1967 (AFN 22:90, 1968), one was photographed at Bonita (T11) 26–27 December 1966 (AFN 21:459, 1967), and one was seen at Rickey Lake (T13) 3 November 1993 (E. R. Lichtwardt, Erickson and Terrill 1996).

Western Kingbird *Tyrannus verticalis*

The Western Kingbird is a common migrant throughout San Diego County and a common summer visitor in the inland valleys. Like Cassin's it nests in tall trees next to grassland and clearings. The Western also takes advantage of man-made structures, especially utility poles. Despite its abundance in spring and summer, it is extremely rare in winter, less frequent even than the Tropical Kingbird at that season.

Breeding distribution: The Western Kingbird breeds widely on the coastal slope of San Diego County where tall trees or telephone poles for nest sites are near open grassland, pastures, or clearings for foraging. Thus its habitat is the same as the Cassin's Kingbird's, but the Western's distribution is centered at higher elevations. The Western is most common between 1500 and 4000 feet elevation, in broad valleys. Areas of concentration are in Warner Valley (up to 55 at Lake Henshaw, G17, 17 July 1998, C. G. Edwards), Santa Ysabel Valley (up to 25 north of Santa Ysabel, I18, 20 May 2000, S. E. Smith), Santa Maria Valley (up to 36 northeast of Ramona, K15, 18 June 1999, M. and B. McIntosh), and Campo Valley (U23, up to 30 on 20 April 1997, D. S. and A. W. Hester). The Western Kingbird shares the inland valleys at lower elevations with Cassin's but drops out along the coast. Within 5 miles of the coast we confirmed nesting only a few times, e.g, in the Wire Mountain area of Camp Pendleton (G5; pair nest building 20 June 1999, R. E. Fischer) and on the campus of the Educational Cultural Complex in

Photo by Anthony Mercieca

southeast San Diego (S10; active nest 11 May 1997, P. Unitt). At the higher elevations the Western Kingbird is fairly common around Lake Cuyamaca (M20) but absent from Palomar Mountain and scarce on Hot Springs (E21; pair on 18 June 1999, K. L. Weaver) and Laguna (O23; one from 6 to 14 June 1999, C. G. Edwards). On the east slope of the mountains, the Western Kingbird breeds down to Earthquake Valley (K23), but on the floor of the Anza–Borrego Desert it is uncommon as a breeding species (maximum eight in the northern Borrego Valley, E24, 8 June 2001, P. D. Jorgensen) and apparently confined to developed oases: the Borrego Valley, Ocotillo Wells (I28, I29, J29), Butterfield Ranch in Mason Valley (M23), and Vallecito Stage Station (M25).

Nesting: The Western Kingbird usually builds its nest in the upper levels of open-foliaged trees. Atlas observers reported six nests in sycamores, five in eucalyptus, four in oaks (both coast live and Engelmann), and one each in a palm, poplar, pine, avocado, and desert ironwood. The nests are typically on the larger branches, so they have a solid support from below. The nest at Ocotillo Wells in an ironwood was atop an old House Sparrow nest. Another very common site is the bracket holding an electrical transformer to a utility pole; the five nests specifically described in such stations are certainly an underestimate.

Western Kingbird

Breeding season

- Breeding confirmed
- Breeding probable
- Breeding possible
- 1.00 - 2.54 birds per hour
- 0.25 - 1.00 birds per hour
- 0 - 0.25 birds per hour
- Presumed migrants only

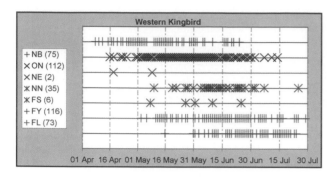

Though the Western Kingbird begins arriving in early March, it does not begin nest building until the second week of April or laying until the third week of April. The schedule we observed is consistent with the 17 April–9 July spread of 106 California egg dates given by Bent (1942), though the fledglings at Vallecito 16 May 2001 (M. C. Jorgensen) may have hatched from eggs laid a day or two before 17 April.

Migration: After the hummingbirds and the swallows, the Western Kingbird is one of our earliest spring migrants, and one of the most punctual. From 1997 to 2001, the earliest spring report varied only from 11 to 14 March. The earliest date ever reported is 6 March (1982, Anza–Borrego Desert State Park, AB 36:893, 1982). The Western Kingbird migrates by day, often in flocks, and most of the population breeds north of San Diego County, so migrants are often conspicuous. A concentration of 150 atop Spooner Mesa (W10) 15 May 1999

(P. Unitt) was extraordinary. Numbers drop rapidly in mid May; late dates of birds away from breeding habitat are 27 May (1999, one in La Jolla, P7, L. Polinsky) and 3 June (2001, one in extensive treeless chaparral 3.1 miles east-northeast of Sunshine Summit, D18, P. Unitt). In fall, migrants are seen from 12 July (2000, one on Palomar Mountain, D15, K. L. Weaver) through late September or early October, exceptionally to 3 November (1963, one in the Tijuana River valley, G. McCaskie).

Winter: Only four well-supported records ever, of single individuals at Oceanside (H5) 28 January 1962 (G. McCaskie), Lake Hodges (K10) 5 December 1995 (photographed; M. B. Stowe, G. L. Rogers, NASFN 49:199, 1995), near San Elijo Lagoon (L7) 26 December 1999 (R. T. Patton), and in Greenwood Cemetery (S10) 16 December 2001–7 February 2002 (G. McCaskie et al.). Other winter reports, some in Christmas bird counts, more likely represent misidentified Cassin's or Tropical Kingbirds.

Conservation: The advent of eucalyptus trees and utility poles gave the Western Kingbird many new nest sites, but in San Diego County these factors did not lead clearly to population increase and range expansion, as tree planting has in the Great Plains (Gamble and Bergin 1996) or utility poles have in the Imperial Valley. The Western has always been considered common here. Its habitat was converted entirely to cattle grazing, but this evidently does not affect a bird that comes to the ground only to gather nest material.

Eastern Kingbird *Tyrannus tyrannus*

With its simple but bold pattern of blackish upperparts, whitish underparts, and white-tipped tail, the Eastern differs conspicuously from the other kingbirds. It is a casual fall vagrant to San Diego County, with one record in late spring. Its frequency here appears to be on the decline.

Migration: The Eastern Kingbird is known in San Diego County from 19 records, all but one in fall from 15 July (1972, one in the Tijuana River valley, AB 26:907, 1972) to 17 October (1978, one at Vallecito, M25, AB 33:216, 1979). All fall records are along the coast except for the one from Vallecito and another from Kit Carson Park (K11) 22 September 1979 (AB 34:202, 1980). Only three records are since 1981, from San Elijo Lagoon (L7) 28 September–1 October 1986 (C. G. Edwards, AB 41:145, 1987) and 12 September 1988 (R. T. Patton, AB 43:169, 1989), and the single late spring record, from the Sweetwater River 0.7 mile below Highway 94 (S13) 15

Photo by Anthony Mercieca

June 1991 (P. Unitt, AB 45:1162, 1991). There is still only one specimen, from San Elijo Lagoon 28 September 1963 (SDNHM 30767, McCaskie et al. 1967a).

Scissor-tailed Flycatcher *Tyrannus forficatus*

Most vagrant Scissor-tailed Flycatchers reaching California are immatures, lacking the adults' long tail streamers. Nevertheless, with its delicate pink wing linings, the Scissor-tailed is one of the most distinctive and attractive of its family. Though as

few as 20 individuals have been seen in San Diego County, the records encompass every month of the year except July.

Migration: The Scissor-tailed Flycatcher is most frequent in fall, with 13 records extending from 17 August (1986, Tijuana River valley, adult, G. McCaskie, Bevier 1990) to 24 November (1933, one at La Jolla, P7, Grinnell and Miller 1944). The single specimen was collected at San Elijo Lagoon (L7) 22 November 1963 (SDNHM 30769, McCaskie et al. 1967a).

There are three records for late spring and summer, of one photographed at San Diego 13–17 June 1986 (M. and J. Fader, Bevier 1990), one at Lake Cuyamaca (M20) 25–29 June 1991 (D. D. Gemmill, Heindel and Garrett 1995), and one at Point Loma (S7) 27–31 May 1995 (J. C. Worley, P. Unitt, Garrett and Singer 1998).

Winter: Records at this season number four. One was in the Tijuana River valley 22 February–3 April 1965 (McCaskie et al. 1967a). One at San Dieguito County Park (L8) 4 December 1992 was presumed to be the same as one at San Elijo Lagoon (L7) 27–28 March 1993 (P. A. Ginsburg, B. C. Moore, Heindel and Patten 1996, Erickson

Photo by Anthony Mercieca

and Terrill 1996). One was at Lake Hodges (K10) 4–17 January 1994 (S. B. Grain, Howell and Pyle 1997). Another at Lake Hodges 23 December 1998 (R. T. Patton) was likely the same as one at the east end of the same valley (K12) 2 January 1999 (C. G. Edwards).

SHRIKES — FAMILY LANIIDAE

Loggerhead Shrike *Lanius ludovicianus*

The Loggerhead Shrike is famed as the "butcher bird," preying on large arthropods or small vertebrates, then skewering them on thorns, stiff twigs, or barbed wire for butchering or storage. In San Diego County the shrike is an uncommon year-round resident in grassland, open sage scrub and chaparral, and desert scrub. Its numbers are on the decline over most of North America. Until the 1980s this trend did not affect coastal San Diego County greatly, but in the 1990s it accelerated alarmingly.

Breeding distribution: In San Diego County, the Loggerhead Shrike is most numerous in the Anza–Borrego Desert, where it is widespread on both the desert floor and in desert-edge scrub on the east slopes of the mountains. It is absent, however, from the pinyon woodlands in the higher elevations of the Santa Rosa and Vallecito mountains. It prefers washes with scattered trees or shrubs, or valley floors with scattered thickets of mesquite or saltbush. The shrike's habitat requirements include plants that can protect and conceal a nest and much open ground for foraging. Even in good habitat the species occurs in low density; high counts in one atlas square per day are of 10 in the Elephant Tree area (K29) 18 April 1999 (M. D. Hoefer), 10 in Chuckwalla Wash (J24) 18 April 1998 (S. D. Cameron, S. M. Wolf), and 14 in the Borrego Valley (F25) 7 May 1998 (P. D. Ache). Elevationally, the shrike ranges in the breeding season up to about 4000 feet, as near Ranchita (G22) and Live Oak Springs (S25).

In northern and central San Diego County forest and thick chaparral break the shrike's distribution, but in the south it extends over the Tecate Divide onto the Campo Plateau and almost continuously along the Mexican border to the coast. The best remaining site for the shrike on

Photo by Anthony Mercieca

the coastal slope is Otay Mesa, mainly the less developed eastern end at the base of Otay Mountain (V14), where daily counts ranged as high as nine on 16 May 1999 (S. D. Cameron). The shrike's distribution farther north on the coastal slope is much fragmented. Even in Camp Pendleton and Marine Corps Air Station Miramar we found no breeding shrikes in some atlas squares having suitable habitat and lacking urban development.

Nesting: The ideal nest site for a Loggerhead Shrike is a dense-foliaged thorny shrub or small tree, one that can offer protection as well as concealment from predators. In the Anza–Borrego Desert, thorny plants described as nest sites encompassed mesquite (7 nests), desert lavender (4), palo verde (3), and catclaw (1), plus clumps of mistletoe in mesquite or catclaw (2). But some nests were in plants that lack spines, such as jojoba (2), and juniper (1). On the coastal slope thorny shrubs are less prevalent, and we found nests in an elderberry, an olive tree, and unidentified ornamental shrubs, though two were in redberry, and one was in an orange tree, one was in a California desert thorn, and one was in a saltbush, all more or less

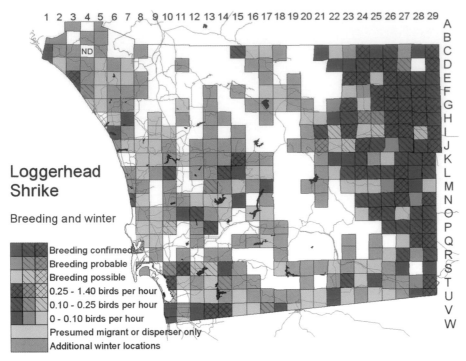

Loggerhead Shrike

Breeding and winter

- Breeding confirmed
- Breeding probable
- Breeding possible
- 0.25 - 1.40 birds per hour
- 0.10 - 0.25 birds per hour
- 0 - 0.10 birds per hour
- Presumed migrant or disperser only
- Additional winter locations

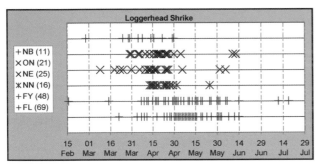

San Clemente Island, as part of the recovery program there, was later found dead along the Silver Strand (T9; Patten and Campbell 2000).

Winter: We found the species in 93 more atlas squares in winter than in spring and summer. Postbreeding dispersal takes a few birds to even higher elevations than they reach in the breeding season, up to 4600 feet in the basin of Lake Cuyamaca (L21; up to two on 29 February 2000, J. K. Wilson). The species' numbers in winter, however, are much the same as in the breeding season (maximum in one atlas square 14 on Otay Mesa, V13, 1 February 1998, P. Unitt; other counts of nine or fewer). On the coastal slope, areas of extensive grassland, even if now dominated by European annuals (Camp Pendleton, Warner Valley, Santa Maria Valley, Otay Mesa, Marron Valley), show clearly as important shrike habitat.

Conservation: The Loggerhead Shrike retreats from urbanization and is now failing to sustain its numbers even in undeveloped areas on the coastal slope. The decimation is documented by Christmas bird counts: on the San Diego count, for example, the average from 1966 through 1975 was 106 shrikes per count, but from 1997 through 2001 it was only 11. On the Oceanside count, the average from 1976 through 1985 was 81.5, but from 1997 through 2001 it was only 6. Even within the five-year atlas period the decrease was noticeable, with lower numbers 1999–2001 than in 1997 and 1998. In southeast San Diego, the last pair in atlas square S10, with a territory between Greenwood Cemetery and the Educational Cultural Complex in 1997, was eliminated when a Home Depot store with its accompanying vast parking lot were built on the site. At San Elijo Lagoon (L7), King et al. (1987) found the shrike a fairly common resident and yearly breeder from 1974 through 1983, with no trend. By 1997, however, it was a rare winter visitor only (A. Mauro et al.). In the Anza–Borrego Desert the shrike may be stable; since 1984 Christmas bird counts show no trend. But atlas observers found the species scarce or absent during the breeding season from the main developed areas of Borrego Springs (F24/G24).

The suddenness with which the shrike's decline hit San Diego County raises questions about the factors affecting it and the scales on which these factors operate. The species' decline in undeveloped areas suggests that it is susceptible to the ill effects of habitat fragmentation, as are many other grassland birds. Occupying a rather high position on the food chain, it occurs naturally in low density, heightening this sensitivity. Intensive work with the

spiny. Along the coast these last two shrubs offer the shrike its best nesting habitat.

Toilet paper figures prominently in the lining of many Loggerhead Shrike nests; even in the most remote wildernesses of the Anza–Borrego Desert shrikes are able to find it.

We found that shrikes began nesting considerably earlier in the one wet year of the atlas period, 1998, than in the other four. This is shown best in the data for fledglings, our most frequent means of confirmation of shrike nesting. In 1998, we observed fledglings regularly beginning in early April, with one family near the West Butte of Borrego Mountain (H27) as early as 22 March (M. L. Gabel), corresponding to egg laying in mid February. A pair of shrikes feeding a fledgling near Halfhill Dry Lake (J29) on 16 and 18 February (L. J. Hargrove) implies egg laying even in mid January. In the other four years we saw no shrike fledglings earlier than 23 April, corresponding to egg laying in mid March. Bent's (1950) range of 126 California egg dates is 24 February–1 July.

Migration: The Loggerhead Shrike does not appear to engage in long-distance migration in southern California, but the birds disperse considerably in their nonbreeding season. One raised in captivity and then released on

shrikes on San Clemente Island since the early 1990s has shown how difficult reversing a decline in this species can be. The Loggerhead Shrike could easily be extirpated from coastal southern California early in the 21st century.

Taxonomy: Rea (in Phillips 1986) identified the Loggerhead Shrikes breeding in coastal San Diego County as the dark-backed *L. l. grinnelli* Oberholser, 1919, and this is amply supported by specimens in SDNHM. The San Diego sample averages even darker than a sample from the range of *grinnelli* as originally delimited in northern Baja California. As measured by a Minolta CR300 electronic colorimeter, 15 fresh-plumaged specimens from coastal San Diego County, collected from late September to early March, have values of L for the back of 32.5–37.1, mean 34.9, against 34.9–37.7, mean 36.0, for seven from the core range of *grinnelli*. Higher values of L represent paler colors, lower values darker ones. Whether *grinnelli* can be adequately diagnosed from *L. l. gambeli* Ridgway, 1887 (or *L. l. mexicanus* Brehm, 1854) needs further testing; the range in L of ten specimens from northern California and Oregon is 36.3–40.0, overlapping somewhat with *grinnelli*. A discriminant function designed to distinguish the Channel Islands subspecies of the shrike did not yield good separation between *grinnelli* and *gambeli* (Patten and Campbell 2000).

Only two specimens have been collected on the desert side of the mountains in San Diego County. One from La Puerta (= Mason) Valley (M23) 7 December 1912 (SDNHM 1849) is paler than *grinnelli* and typical of *gambeli* (L = 37.7), whereas the other, from "San Felipe Cañon" 22 March 1895 (SDNHM 1290) is on the dark side even for *grinnelli* (L = 33.0). There is one specimen from San Diego County matching the pale desert subspecies *L. l. sonoriensis* Miller, 1930, which is a synonym of *L. l. excubitorides* Swainson, 1832, according to Phillips (1986). It is SDNHM 1287, collected at Santa Ysabel (J18) 5 March 1890. It has the long white supercilium typical of this subspecies, and the value of L for its back is 40.3; 32 specimens from the Colorado River east to New Mexico average 40.4 in this variable. The validity and ranges of all mainland subspecies of the Loggerhead Shrike need further quantification and testing; those proposed by Miller (1930) appear to be too finely split.

VIREOS — FAMILY VIREONIDAE

White-eyed Vireo *Vireo griseus*

The White-eyed Vireo breeds in the southeastern United States and northeastern Mexico and is only a rare vagrant to California. Like some other birds whose ranges center on the Southeast, it irrupted in 1992: that one year accounted for 12 of the 44 records for California and two of the five for San Diego County.

Migration: Three quarters of California's White-eyed Vireos have occurred in May and June, but in San Diego only the first record, of one at Point Loma (S7) 7 June 1982 (R. E. Webster, Morlan 1985), fits into this category. Two records, both also from Point Loma, are for fall: one 16–30 October 1988 (J. O'Brien, Pyle and McCaskie 1992), the other 25 October 1992 (P. A. Ginsburg; Heindel and Patten 1996). Most interesting, two records are of singing males remaining for several days in July, in population centers for Bell's Vireo in riparian woodland: one along the Santa Margarita River near De Luz Creek

Photo by Anthony Mercieca

(D6) 12–17 July 1992 (P. A. Ginsburg, Heindel and Patten 1996), the other along the Sweetwater River between Sweetwater Reservoir and Highway 94 (S13) 5–15 July 2000 (P. Famolaro, McKee and Erickson 2002).

Bell's Vireo *Vireo bellii*

Early in the 20th century, California's subspecies of Bell's Vireo was abundant. Then clearing of its riparian woodland habitat and parasitism by the invading Brown-headed Cowbird decimated it. By the early 1980s the population in the United States was down to about 300 pairs—about half in San Diego County. As a result, the California Department of Fish and Game listed the subspecies, the Least Bell's Vireo, as endangered in 1984, and the U.S. Fish and Wildlife Service followed suit in 1986. Listing

Photo by Anthony Mercieca

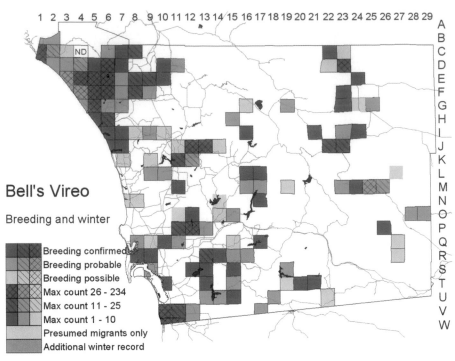

Bell's Vireo

Breeding and winter

- Breeding confirmed
- Breeding probable
- Breeding possible
- Max count 26 - 234
- Max count 11 - 25
- Max count 1 - 10
- Presumed migrants only
- Additional winter record

Santee (Q10/Q11/P11/P12; 55 territorial males in 1997, Kus and Beck 1998), the Sweetwater River from Sweetwater Reservoir to the Rancho San Diego/Cottonwood golf course (S13/R13/R14; 102 territorial males in 2001, P. Famolaro), Jamul and Dulzura creeks (U14/U15/T15; 24 territorial males in 1996, USFWS 1998), Otay River (V11/V12; about 19 territorial males in 1997, Kus and Beck 1998, C. W. Bouscaren), and the Tijuana River valley (V10/V11/W10/W11; 134 territorial males in 1997, Wells and Turnbull 1998). Spread away from the major centers has been less extensive in central and southern San Diego County than in the northwest, though it is still noticeable, with up to three territorial males in La Jolla Valley (L10) 7 May 2000

opened the door to protection of the vireo's habitat and widespread trapping of cowbirds, leading to a remarkable recovery: an increase by a factor of six in just 15 years (Kus 2002). Nevertheless, many threats remain; weaning the vireo from cowbird trapping in perpetuity will be a delicate experiment.

Breeding distribution: Riparian woodland supporting the Least Bell's Vireo typically has both a dense canopy, where the birds forage, and a dense understory, where they nest. The population is concentrated in the coastal lowland, especially along the Santa Margarita River, other creeks in Camp Pendleton, along the San Luis Rey River upstream to Pala (D11), and along Windmill and Pilgrim creeks, tributaries of the San Luis Rey. This area accounted for about 74% of the 1423 territorial males known in the county in 1996—and about 59% of California's total population, demonstrating that it is the core habitat for the entire subspecies (USFWS 1998). By 1998, the population in Camp Pendleton alone had increased to 1010 territorial males, though it dropped to 783 in 2000 (J. and J. Griffith, data courtesy of Camp Pendleton), and the birds spread along small side creeks as well as all the major ones. In the late 1990s, the vireos continued to recolonize sites in northwestern San Diego County where they had not been recorded up until 1996 (USFWS 1998), sometimes in fair numbers, as along Buena Vista Creek (H6; 15 territorial males in 1997, Kus and Beck 1998), Agua Hedionda Creek (I6; seven on 25 April 1999, P. A. Ginsburg), and in a side canyon north of San Marcos Creek at La Costa (J7; seven on 24 June 1998, M. Baumgartel).

Elsewhere in the coastal lowland, the major sites are the San Dieguito River from Lake Hodges east to San Pasqual (K11/K12/J12/J13; 104 territorial males in 1997, Kus and Beck 1998), the San Diego River from Interstate 805 to

(K. J. Winter) and three in Sycamore Canyon (O12) 3 May 1998 (I. S. Quon).

In San Diego County's foothills, Bell's Vireo is scattered in small numbers at only a few sites, principally the San Diego River above El Capitan Reservoir (L17/M17; five territorial males in 1997, Kus and Beck 1998; N17; four, including a fledgling, 20 June 2000, D. C. Seals), Cottonwood Creek in Hauser Canyon (T20/T21; up to 11 territorial males and eight nesting pairs in 1998, J. M. Wells), and Cottonwood and Tecate creeks in Marron Valley (V17; eight on 12 June 2000, P. P. Beck). At most other foothill sites the species is irregular. For example, it was absent 1997–2002 from a section of Pine Valley Creek (R19) where six to eight territorial males persisted from the late 1980s to 1994 (Winter and McKelvey 1999, Kus et al. 2003b). Along Santa Ysabel Creek at Black Canyon (I16) Bell's Vireos occurred regularly from the early 1990s to 1998 (pair at nest 22 May, K. J. Winter) but were absent in 2002 (Kus et al. 2003b). From 1997 to 2003, during his intensive study of the Willow Flycatchers nesting along the San Luis Rey River below Lake Henshaw, W. E. Haas encountered only a single Bell's Vireo, 31 May 1999. Two observations during the atlas period 1997–2001 well away from previously reported sites were along Boulder Creek at Boulder Creek Road (M19; one singing male and one juvenile 29 June 1997. C. Jones) and along Buena Vista and San Ysidro creeks 2.1–2.4 miles east of Warner Ranch (G19; two singing males 25 June 2000, P. Unitt). At 3800 feet, one in Noble Canyon (O22) 10 and 26 July 2002 was at the highest elevation yet reported for Bell's Vireo in San Diego County (Kus et al. 2003b); the species was absent at that site during repeated surveys 1992–99.

Oases in the Anza–Borrego Desert also contribute significantly to the population. The vireos there use thickets of mesquite as well as woodland dominated by willows.

In this region the important sites are along Coyote Creek, at both Middle Willows (C22; up to five territorial males 28 May 1998, P. D. Jorgensen) and Lower Willows (D23; 18 territorial males or pairs in 2000, Wells and Kus 2001; 31 in 2002, J. R. Barth), Borrego Palm Canyon (F23; up to seven territorial males 5–8 July 2001, L. J. Hargrove), along San Felipe Creek near Paroli Spring (I21; up to six singing males 16 June 2000, J. O. Zimmer), near Scissors Crossing (J22; about 17 territorial males or pairs in 2002, 20 in 2003, J. R. Barth), and in Sentenac Ciénaga and Canyon (J23; up to 17 territorial males 9 May 2001, R. Thériault; I23; up to five on 23 April 1997, P. K. Nelson), and along Vallecito Creek, near Campbell Grade (M23/ M24; up to 17 territorial males 6 May 1998, R. Thériault) and near Vallecito Stage Station (M24/M25; counts of territorial males varying from 19 in 2002 to in 33 in 1996, M. C. Jorgensen, P. D. Jorgensen; Wells and Kus 2001).

Several smaller oases also support a few Bell's Vireos. Some of these were previously known: Sheep and Indian canyons (D22), Hellhole Canyon (G23), Yaqui Well (I24), Agua Caliente Springs (M26), and Carrizo Wash and Marsh (O28/O29). Our numbers at Agua Caliente were notably higher than previously reported, up to six territorial males 6 June 1998 (E. C. Hall). Other sites came to light as a result of field work for this atlas and may represent newly established territories: the Borrego Valley's mesquite bosque (G25), with one territorial male 27 April and 4 June 1998 and an apparent family group of four on 11 June 1998 (R. Thériault), Bow Willow Canyon (P26), with up to four territorial males 12 May 2000 and 19 May 2001, Jacumba Jim Canyon, elevation 1350 feet (Q27), with one on 13 May 2000, and Carrizo Canyon, elevation 1110 feet (R27), with one on 23 April 2000 (L. J. Hargrove). An unexpected site for nesting Bell's Vireos in the Borrego Valley was Ellis Farms, a commercial nursery (E24); three there 11 June 2001 included a singing male and a fledgling (P. D. Jorgensen).

Although Bell's Vireo is a characteristically riparian species, it uses upland scrub adjacent to riparian woodland regularly, foraging at distances up to 200 feet from the riparian edge and even nesting in the nonriparian habitat (Kus and Miner 1989). The use of such marginal habitats increases when, after an unusually wet winter, nearby riparian woodland is flooded and the upland habitat becomes unusually lush. In the wet El Niño year 1998, 8 of 31 territories along Pilgrim Creek (F6) were at the base of slopes in mustard that had grown to a height of 10 feet (B. E. Kus). That year, near Sweetwater Reservoir (S12), one pair nested in sage scrub 1 mile from riparian woodland and three others nested in a field dominated by mustard and exotic trees (P. Famolaro). The vireos persisted in these nonriparian territories near Sweetwater Reservoir for some years but eventually abandoned them.

Nesting: Many studies have addressed the Least Bell's Vireo's nesting (e.g., Franzreb 1987, Greaves 1987, Kus 1999, 2002). Typically, the birds nest at openings and edges where there is dense vegetation near the ground, placing the nest, on average, about 1 meter off the ground in a fork of slender twigs. On the coastal slope, willows

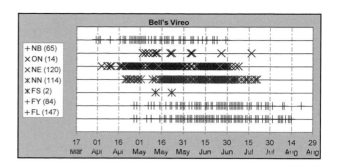

and mulefat predominate as nest sites (USFWS 1998); in the Anza–Borrego Desert, willows and mesquite predominate (Wells and Kus 2001). Even where cowbirds have been trapped almost to elimination, Bell's Vireos lose many nests to predation; of 25 nests videotaped by Peterson (2002, Peterson et al. 2004), 12 suffered predation, eight to scrub-jays and three to nonnative scavengers, two to Virginia opossums and one to Argentine ants. Along the Sweetwater River P. Famolaro has repeatedly observed nests destroyed by Argentine ants.

In San Diego County, Bell's Vireo's nesting season generally lasts from April to July, with egg laying from about 1 April to late June, rarely mid July. Around Sweetwater Reservoir, P. Famolaro has noted nests with eggs from 4 April to 8 July, nests with nestlings from 21 April to 21 July. On the basis of 34 nests followed in the Anza–Borrego Desert in 2000, Wells and Kus (2001) estimated egg laying to have taken place from 14 April to 16 June, peaking in late April. Our dates for fledglings ranged from 27 April to 21 August.

Migration: The Least Bell's Vireo usually arrives in San Diego County in the third week of March. During the atlas period our first dates varied from 13 March (1997) and 14 March (1998) to 29 March (2000) and 31 March (2001); arrival was notably late in the two latter years. Fall departure generally takes place from mid August to late September; stragglers in breeding habitat as late as October are rare. At the upper end of Sweetwater Reservoir, surveyed regularly, the latest date on record is 16 September 1998 (P. Famolaro).

Many Least Bell's Vireos have been banded, and these studies show the birds are highly site tenacious, usually returning in successive years to the same drainage basin, males nearly always to the same territory. Males generally maintain the same territory through a season; females sometimes move from male to male with successive nest attempts (Greaves 1987). But longer-distance dispersal is known on the basis of birds banded in San Diego County observed in Santa Barbara and Ventura counties and vice versa (Greaves and Labinger 1997, USFWS 1998). Among the more notable examples are of an adult female banded on the Santa Clara River that later nested along the Sweetwater River (P. Famolaro) and a young banded along the Santa Margarita River in summer 1987 that was seen in Carpenteria, Santa Barbara County, 24 August–1 September that same year (AB 42:138, 1988).

Sightings of migrant Bell's Vireos away from breeding habitat are rare, suggesting that most birds fly nonstop between nesting sites in southern California and their next stop in Mexico. In spring such migrants are most likely in the Anza–Borrego Desert, where records during the atlas period were of one in Borrego Springs (G24) 24 and 29 April 2000 (R. Thériault) and one in Fish Creek Wash (L27) 13 April 2000 (M. B. Mulrooney). Fall migrants have been noted at Point Loma (S7) 10 October 1988 (R. E. Webster, AB 43:169, 1989) and 16 October 1993 (G. McCaskie, AB 48:153, 1994).

Winter: Bell's Vireo essentially vacates the United States for the winter, but 13 winter occurrences are known for San Diego County. Eleven of these are near the coast. Unitt (1984) listed the first five; subsequently, winter records have been published from Carlsbad (I6) 2 February 1982 (E. Copper, AB 36:332, 1982), Coronado (S9) 19 January–3 March 1985 (D. R. Willick, AB 39:211, 1985) and 15 December 2001 (R. E. Webster, NAB 56:224, 2002), and the Tijuana River valley 27 January 1982 (C. G. Edwards, AB 36:332, 1982), 2 December 1990–5 January 1991, and 15 December 1990 (R. E. Webster, G. McCaskie, AB 45:322, 1991). Two winter records are from the Anza–Borrego Desert, of one at Yaqui Well (I24) 20 January 1984 (B. Wagner, AB 38:358, 1984) and one in the mesquite bosque 3.3 miles southeast of Borrego Springs 24 January 1984 (SDNHM 42925).

Conservation: Though Stephens (1919a) called the Least Bell's Vireo "common" in San Diego County, surveys of the best remaining habitat from 1978 to 1981 (Goldwasser et al. 1980, L. R. Salata) revealed only 61 territorial males. More thorough surveys in 1985 raised this to 223—76% of the population in the entire state (Franzreb 1987). Once the subspecies was listed as endangered by the California Department of Fish and Game in 1984 and the U.S. Fish and Wildlife Service in 1986, the regulatory mechanism allowing the species' recovery was in place. The vireo's subsequent history must be regarded as one of the greatest successes for the Endangered Species Act anywhere in the United States.

Arresting and reversing the loss of riparian woodland was critical to arresting and reversing the vireo's decline. Once the vireo was formally designated as endangered, section 404 of the Clean Water Act of 1977 obliged the U.S. Army Corps of Engineers and U.S. Fish and Wildlife Service to confer on any proposal to disrupt wetlands— and therefore Least Bell's Vireo habitat. As a result, the pace of the vireo's habitat loss, through the installation of reservoirs and the building of roads, housing, golf courses, and other commercial developments, slowed considerably. Designation in 1994 of about half of the habitat occupied by the vireo as "critical" under the Endangered Species Act helped as well. Once disturbance of many stands of riparian woodland was minimized, the vireo's habitat was able to spread through natural regeneration. Though noticeable at many places in San Diego County, this spread was most striking in the Tijuana River valley, where riparian woodland increased from almost none in the 1970s to extensive by the late 1990s and vireos increased from one territory in 1980 to 134 by 1997.

Bell's Vireos recolonize and nest successfully in adequately restored riparian woodland, more rapidly if the restored habitat is adjacent to mature habitat. They nested in restored habitat the first year in Mission Trails Regional Park, where previously occupied habitat was adjacent (Kus 1998), but took eight years to colonize revegetated shores of the San Diego River in Mission Valley, at a site surrounded by commercial development (P. Unitt).

Brood-parasitism by the Brown-headed Cowbird has also been critical to the vireo's decline. Soon after the cowbird invaded coastal southern California in the early 1900s, the vireo became a primary host (Hanna 1928). In the early 1980s, parasitism rates in San Diego County varied from 47% to 80%; few if any vireos fledge from parasitized nests (USFWS 1998). Even pairs that desert parasitized nests suffer significantly reduced success, as their subsequent nests are parasitized disproportionately often (Kus 1999, 2002).

Once trapping of cowbirds was instituted widely in the late 1980s, the rate of parasitism dropped, to 1% or less in intensively trapped Camp Pendleton (USFWS 1998). Kus (1999, 2002) noted an inverse association between the intensity of trapping and parasitism rate along the San Luis Rey River. It appears that cowbird trapping is most effective where many traps can be deployed and the cowbird population depressed over a wide region. The critical role of trapping in enabling the vireo's recovery is especially clear in Anza–Borrego Desert State Park, where the habitat has changed little while the vireo population has rebounded. In the Cleveland National Forest, however, where the vireos are scattered and rugged topography makes the traps difficult to deploy and monitor, trapping proved ineffective, parasitism rates remained high, and the vireo deserted two sites in the 1990s (Winter and McKelvey 1999).

Cowbird trapping, however successful, is a finger-in-the-dike approach to managing an endangered species. Ideally, habitat should be managed so as to be less attractive to cowbirds and the parasitism rate kept down to a level where the vireo (and other parasitism-sensitive species) can maintain themselves. Ideally, exposure to some level of parasitism would allow the vireo to persist while compelling it to evolve better defenses, if only an increased rate of deserting parasitized nests (Kus 2002). The cycle of flooding and regeneration has been broken by the dams built on most of San Diego County's rivers, allowing some riparian woodland to become senescent. Invasion of exotic plants, especially saltcedar and giant reed, threatens native riparian woodland. Some of the vireo's primary nest predators, especially the Western Scrub-Jay, are on the increase. In spite of the short-term success in recovering the Least Bell's Vireo, balancing conflicts until the vireo becomes self sustaining is a long-term challenge.

Taxonomy: The Least, *V. b. pusillus* Coues, 1866, is the drabbest of the four subspecies of Bell's Vireo; it has only a hint of olive color on the rump in fresh plumage, and that fades to gray by the time the birds return to their breeding range in spring. Identified by Phillips (1991), the January specimen from the Borrego Valley is *V. b. arizonae* Ridgway, 1903; it has the lower back and rump distinctly olive and the flanks vaguely yellowish. A Bell's Vireo at Point Loma 10 October 1988 was "felt to be of the nominate race" (R. E. Webster, AB 43:169–170, 1989). This subspecies, breeding in the Mississippi basin and the green extreme of the species, is likely in California as a rare vagrant but has not been confirmed with a specimen or photograph.

Gray Vireo *Vireo vicinior*

The Gray Vireo is the rarest breeding bird of San Diego County's chaparral. Its preferred habitat is on south-facing slopes, where the chaparral is dry but dense, mainly between 3000 and 5000 feet elevation. The reason for the Gray Vireo's rarity is unclear, but susceptibility to cowbird parasitism may confine it to large tracts of chaparral remote from open areas where cowbirds forage. The California Department of Fish and Game has recognized the Gray Vireo as a highest-priority species of special concern. Field work for this atlas led to the discovery of Gray Vireos wintering in the Anza–Borrego Desert, in California's single largest stand of the elephant tree.

Photo by Anthony Mercieca

Breeding distribution: The Gray Vireo is concentrated in two regions of San Diego County. The more northern lies in a region of chaparral dominated by chamise and redshank north of Warner Springs and largely east of Highway 79. The largest numbers have been seen along Lost Valley Road south of Indian Flats Campground and along the Pacific Crest Trail east of this road (E19; up to eight, including seven singing males, 27 June 2001, K. L. Weaver). A few birds are scattered west to Aguanga Ridge east of High Point, Palomar Mountain (D15; three singing males 14 May 1999, K. L. Weaver) and east to the south fork of Alder Canyon (C20; four singing males 3 June 2001, L. J. Hargrove).

The southern population is centered in chaparral dominated by chamise and cupleaf ceanothus south of the Laguna Mountains and north of Interstate 8. Here maximum counts from 1997 to 2001 were near Buckman Springs, on slopes both east and west of Cottonwood Valley (R22; 12, including 11 singing males, 15 May 1999, L. J. Hargrove), along the Pacific Crest Trail just south and east of Yellow Rose Spring (R23; 10 on 17 May 1998, L. J. Hargrove), and on the ridge 1.0–1.4 miles northeast of Buckman Springs (Q22; nine singing males 25 April 1999 and 11, including eight singing males, 10 June 1999, J. K. Wilson). Outward from this hub, the population becomes quickly more scattered but extends northwest to near Tule Springs (N18; four, three singing males and one juvenile, 2 July 2001, J. R. Barth et al.), west to 2.1 miles west of Corte Madera Mountain (R19; two singing males 8 June 2001, L. J. Hargrove), south to 4.7 miles east of Cameron Corners (U24; pair on 20 May 2000, A. Mauro, P. K. Nelson), and east to Sacotone Spring (S27; one singing male 17 May 2001, J. O. Zimmer, E. C. Hall). The population in San Diego County does not appear continuous with that in the Sierra Juárez south of the international border.

Between the two main populations we recorded the Gray Vireo on only five occasions in four atlas squares, with never more than two territorial males, on or near the east slope of the mountains in chamise-dominated chaparral. At one of these locations, however, the Pacific Crest Trail south of Barrel Spring (G20/H20), A. G. Morley had counted eight on 10 June 1987.

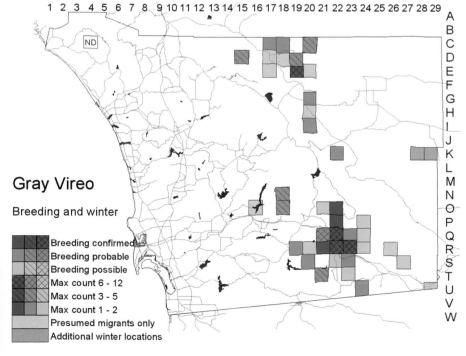

Gray Vireo

Breeding and winter

- Breeding confirmed
- Breeding probable
- Breeding possible
- Max count 6 - 12
- Max count 3 - 5
- Max count 1 - 2
- Presumed migrants only
- Additional winter locations

Outliers in the south were one singing male 0.4 mile west of El Capitan Dam (O16) 21 April 1998 (K. J. Winter) and another in juniper woodland along the Imperial County line 4.4 miles east of Jacumba (U29) 27 April 1999 (J. K. Wilson). The latter was the only record during the atlas period from juniper woodland away from chaparral, though six were reported from such habitat 1972–84 (Anza–Borrego Desert State Park records). At another outlying site, 2500 feet elevation on the southwest slope of Potrero Peak (U19), there was a singing male 2 June 1992 (P. Unitt) but none could be found 1997–2001. At such locations away from the main population centers the Gray Vireo appears to be irregular. The bird near El Capitan Dam was at the unusually low elevation of 640 feet. Otherwise the sites range in elevation from 2100–2300 feet along Goudie Road (O18) to 5400 feet east of La Posta Creek in the Cuyapaipe Indian Reservation (P24; one singing male 11 May 2001, D. C. Seals).

Although vast tracts of seemingly suitable and uniform chaparral remain, the Gray Vireo's distribution is distinctly clumped in only a small fraction of this habitat, even within the two main zones of concentration. For example, five singing males along Goudie Road 6 June 1999 (L. J. Hargrove) were isolated by at least 8 miles from their nearest known neighbors to the south and east in the direction of the population center. Much of the Gray Vireo's range consists of rugged hills, covered with impenetrable chaparral, in which unknown numbers may remain out of earshot. But enough roads and trails crossing the habitat have now been surveyed to demonstrate the species' rarity and pattern of dispersion. The county's population is probably in the low hundreds—small, but still larger than any known elsewhere in California.

Nesting: The Gray Vireo builds its nest in the upper levels of the shrubs that constitute its habitat. Nests described by atlas observers were 3 to 5 feet off the ground in chamise, scrub oak, cupleaf ceanothus, and mountain mahogany. Because of these shrubs' intricately branched structure, the Gray Vireo's nest may be more extensively supported from the sides than the typical vireo nest hanging from a horizontal fork. Data on the nesting schedule of the Gray Vireo are still meager; no collected eggs are known from San Diego County. Atlas participants' observations suggest the species lays from late April to mid June.

Migration: The Gray Vireo arrives in San Diego County regularly in late March, rarely as early as 14 March (2001, one on the Pacific Crest Trail near Kitchen Creek Road,

R23, L. J. Hargrove). It remains at least as late as 19 August (2001, five, three still singing, at the same locality, L. J. Hargrove) but may be difficult to find after the birds stop singing and the chaparral is hot and still. In the San Jacinto Mountains, the Gray Vireo is known as late as 27 August (Grinnell and Swarth 1913), in Joshua Tree National Park, as late as 10 September (Miller and Stebbins 1964). There are five published records of migrants from the Anza–Borrego Desert (AFN 13:456, 1959; AB 42:482, 1988; Massey 1998), plus records of two at Bonita (T11) 1 May 1962 (AFN 16:448, 1962) and one at Palomar Mountain (D15) 19 September 1981 (AB 36:219, 1982). The Gray Vireo is seen in California as a migrant away from breeding habitat so rarely, however, that most individuals evidently commute between the breeding and winter ranges in a single nonstop flight. Some of the reports of migrant Gray Vireos may represent misidentified Bell's or Plumbeous Vireos.

Winter: Wintering of the Gray Vireo in the elephant trees of the Anza–Borrego Desert was one of the most notable discoveries emerging from field work for this atlas. Previously the species was not known to winter in California. Because the fruit of the elephant tree is a principal food of Gray Vireos wintering in Sonora (Bates 1992), we organized an expedition 4–5 December 1999 to search California's largest stand of this plant, along Alma Wash west to Starfish Cove (K28/K29), for Gray Vireos. The expedition revealed a minimum of five individuals, all near fruiting elephant trees (Unitt 2000). On subsequent visits to this area, Lori Hargrove has found the Gray Vireo as early as 21 October but no more than a single bird per day and none in 2000–01. The quantity of elephant tree fruit varies and, apparently, the number of wintering Gray Vireos with it.

Conservation: A century ago, the Gray Vireo may have been more widespread and numerous than currently. Stephens (1878) reported the species "not uncommon" around Campo (U23) and reported or collected it at Julian (K20) and Oak Grove (C16) as well. After 1908, however, the species lapsed into obscurity, going unreported until Michael U. Evans rediscovered the county's southern population in 1978. The population may have declined even since then, since the numbers along Kitchen Creek Road (Q23/R23) and La Posta Truck Trail (Q24/R24) 1997–2001 were less than in the late 1970s.

Cowbird parasitism has been inferred as the likely cause of the Gray Vireo's rarity in southern California (Remsen 1978), though the species has always been sparse; Grinnell and Swarth (1913) estimated 16 pairs per square mile in the San Jacinto Mountains. Friedmann (1963) considered the Gray Vireo a frequent victim of the Brown-headed Cowbird. The degree to which cowbirds are currently affecting the Gray Vireo is not known but needs study before any management to benefit the vireo is undertaken.

Because the Gray Vireo is so localized, it is susceptible to fire. Much of the area now occupied by San Diego County's southern population was burned in the Laguna

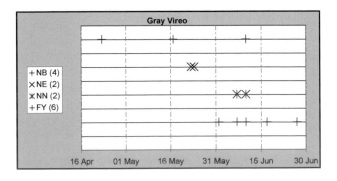

fire of October 1970. The Gray Vireo is likely disfavored both by frequent fire that keeps chaparral low and open and by fire suppression that leads to fuel buildup and catastrophic large-scale fires. The species' ecology with respect to postfire succession needs study too.

Yellow-throated Vireo *Vireo flavifrons*

The Yellow-throated Vireo is a rare vagrant from the eastern United States, more frequent in California in spring than in fall. San Diego County seems to have got less than its fair share; though there have been at least 90 well-supported records in California, 1963–2003, only six are from San Diego County.

Migration: Two of San Diego County's Yellow-throated Vireos have occurred in fall, both in Fort Rosecrans National Cemetery, Point Loma (S7): one photographed 13–20 November 1985 (M. and D. Hastings, Bevier 1990), another 19 October 2002 (P. A. Ginsburg, Cole and McCaskie 2004). One in spring was also at Point Loma, 17 May 1992 (G. L. Rogers, Heindel and Patten 1996). One was singing from willows and coast live oaks along old Highway 80 in Pine Valley (P21) 11–16 June 2001 (M. B. Mulrooney; Garrett and Wilson 2003), and another was along the San Diego River just below Old Mission Dam (P11) 20–21 June 2001 (T. Pepper, G. McCaskie).

Photo by Anthony Mercieca

Winter: One in Greenwood Cemetery (S10) 11 December 2003–7 January 2004 (J. O. Zimmer) was only the third Yellow-throated Vireo reported wintering in California.

Plumbeous Vireo *Vireo plumbeus*

In sharp contrast to most vireos, whose ranges have shrunk, the Plumbeous Vireo has spread. It was first noted in southern California in 1962, small numbers colonizing the east slope of the Sierra Nevada, San Gabriel Mountains, and San Bernardino Mountains, and becoming a regular and widespread if still rare migrant and winter visitor.

Migration: In San Diego County, the Plumbeous Vireo has been recorded from 16 September (1973, one in the Tijuana River valley, G. McCaskie) to 10 May (1981, one on Palomar Mountain, D15, R. Higson). From 1997 to 2001, 12 spring migrants were reported, between 26 March (2000, one at Yaqui Well, I24, E. Moree) and 24 April (2001, one at Point Loma, S7, J. C. Worley; one in Wonderstone Canyon, D29, R. Thériault). Spring migrant Plumbeous Vireos are scattered throughout San Diego County; the 12 during the atlas period were evenly split between the coastal lowland and the Anza–Borrego Desert. All records were of single individuals except for two in oak woodland in Poway 1.9 miles southwest of Starvation Mountain (K12) 16 April 1998 (E. C. Hall).

A unique summer record is of one at Banner (K21) 26 June 1994 (P. D. Jorgensen). A few Plumbeous Vireos have colonized the San Bernardino Mountains, a considerable jump in the breeding range, but the breeding habitat is pine woodland, not the riparian woodland found at Banner.

The first specimen of the Plumbeous Vireo for San Diego County was an immature found dead at Mission Santa Ysabel (I18) 1 November 2002 (A. Mercieca, SDNHM 50893).

Photo by Anthony Mercieca

Winter: The Plumbeous Vireo is a regular winter visitor in the coastal lowland, mainly in riparian woodland, occasionally in urban trees. From 1997 to 2002, between 17 and 26 individuals were reported, depending on how many birds seen in the same area in successive winters were returnees. All records were of single individuals except for three at the Dairy Mart pond in the Tijuana River valley (V11) 19 December 1998 (G. McCaskie). The only wintering Plumbeous Vireos outside the coastal lowland during the atlas period were from planted pines in Borrego Springs (F24), 1 November–20 December 1998 (P. D. Jorgensen, R. Thériault) and 17 December 2000 (N. Osborn). Two earlier winter desert records are of one at Butterfield Ranch (M23) 8 February 1987 (D. B. King, AB 41:331, 1987) and one at Yaqui Well 11 February 1989 (D. and M. Hastings, AB 43:367, 1989). The species is now annual in winter in the Salton Sink (Patten et al. 2003).

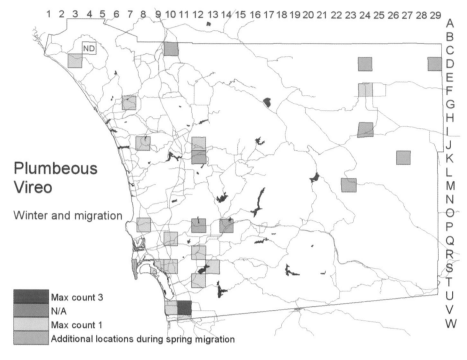

Plumbeous Vireo

Winter and migration

Max count 3
N/A
Max count 1
Additional locations during spring migration

more striking shift in the species' distribution in migration
and winter. In San Diego County
the Plumbeous Vireo was first
noted 16 November 1969, with
one in the Tijuana River valley (G. McCaskie). Soon after
that occurrences became annual.
Numbers seen on San Diego
County Christmas bird counts,
however, have remained stable
at about two per year since the
mid 1980s.

Taxonomy: Plumbeous Vireos in
the United States are all nominate
V. p. plumbeus Coues, 1866—if
the species is indeed polytypic.
The genetic studies supporting
the split of the Solitary Vireo
into the Plumbeous, Cassin's,
and Blue-headed were confined
to the United States (Johnson
1995), and the "Plumbeous

Conservation: The breeding range of the Plumbeous
Vireo is spreading gradually north and west (Johnson
1994), and this change has been accompanied by an even
Vireos" resident in southeastern Mexico and Central
America look more like Cassin's (Phillips 1991).

Cassin's Vireo *Vireo cassinii*

William E. Haas

Rare in San Diego County as a breeding bird,
Cassin's Vireo is best found by visiting oak and
coniferous woodlands above 4000 feet elevation
from late May to mid July. It is seen throughout
the county in migration, though uncommonly. It is
a regular winter visitor to riparian woodland and
ornamental trees near the coast but rare in that role
as well. Though Cassin's Vireo was never abundant,
parasitism by cowbirds is likely responsible for the
vireo's population decline and current rarity.

Breeding distribution: Currently, Cassin's Vireos summer in San Diego County only in montane mixed oak and
conifer woodland above 4000 feet elevation. On Palomar
Mountain, our 15 records during the atlas period were
all of single individuals except for one nesting pair near
Doane Pond (E15) 12 June 1999 and two nesting pairs
at the lower end of Jeff Valley (F16) 30 May 1999 (W. E.
Haas). Around Hot Springs Mountain, our only record
during the atlas period was of a nesting pair at the north
base in a small pocket of incense cedars in Lost Valley
(D20) 10 June 2000 (W. E. Haas), though previously the
species occurred near the summit (E20/E21; five, including a nesting pair, 8 June 1985, P. Unitt). Similarly, on
Volcan Mountain (I20) and around Julian (K20) during
the atlas period we had only three observations of single
individuals, though numbers not long before were higher;
for example, five on Volcan 30–31 May 1993 (P. Unitt). In

Photo by Jack C. Daynes

the Cuyamaca Mountains we had 13 sightings at various
sites, the best of which was Middle Peak (M20), with up
to four, including three singing males, 11 June 2000 (R. E.
Webster) and nesting of two pairs confirmed 3 June 1998,
18 June 2000, and 9 June 2001 (W. E. Haas). In the Laguna
Mountains the 11 observations were concentrated around
Wooded Hill and the heads of Agua Dulce and La Posta
creeks (P23), with up to five on 3 June 1999 (E. C. Hall,
J. O. Zimmer). The only sighting in the breeding season
away from these areas was of one about 3500 feet elevation 2.6 miles southeast of Mesa Grande (I17) 15 June
2000 (D. C. Seals).

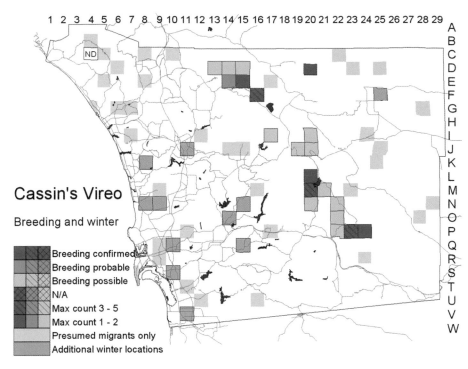

Cassin's Vireo

Breeding and winter

Breeding confirmed
Breeding probable
Breeding possible
N/A
Max count 3 - 5
Max count 1 - 2
Presumed migrants only
Additional winter locations

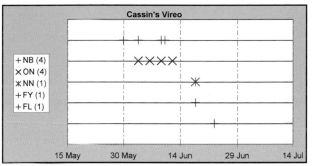

to 20 May. Our earliest migrants were single birds at Bonsall (E8) 21 March 1999 and Carlsbad (I7) 23 March 1999 (P. A. Ginsburg); latest were along Vallecito Creek near Campbell Grade (M23) 20 May 1999 (R. Thériault) and at Crestwood Ranch (R24) 24 May 1999 (D. C. Seals). The extreme early date of 14 March 1970 still stands (AFN 24:643, 1970). Early arrivals are probably of migrants headed farther north; birds breeding in San Diego County's mountains arrive later. A survey of Jeff Valley 15–16 May 1999 revealed no Cassin's Vireos (W. E. Haas).

In fall, Cassin's Vireo migration, extending from early September to November, is even less noticeable than in spring; most birds probably keep to the mountains.

Winter: The usual winter habitat for Cassin's Vireo is riparian woodland in the coastal lowland, as at Kit Carson Park (J11; one on 12 December 1998, W. Pray), lower Los Peñasquitos Canyon (N8; one on 1 March 1998, D. K. Adams), and the species' most consistent site, around the Dairy Mart pond in the Tijuana River valley (V11; up to two on 26 December 1998, G. McCaskie). Cassin's Vireo also winters in ornamental trees, as at Greenwood Cemetery (S10; 12–21 January 2002, G. McCaskie), rarely in coast live oaks, as Steltzer County Park (O14; 8 January 2002, M. B. Stowe). The two winter records for the Anza–Borrego Desert are of one at Agua Caliente Springs (M26) 10 February 1977 (J. L. Dunn) and one at Ellis Farms, Borrego Valley (F25), 15 February 2002 (P. D. Ache).

Through the atlas period 1997–2002, the number of wintering Cassin's Vireos found annually ranged from one to five. Four on the Oceanside count 22 December 1979 is the record for a San Diego County Christmas bird count.

Conservation: Cassin's Vireo was more widespread and common in the past than now. Egg collections up to 1933 attest to its nesting at somewhat lower elevations than currently, at Witch Creek (J18), Descanso (P19), Campo (U23), and even Lake Hodges (K11). Cooper (1874) called Cassin's Vireo "not rare" in the Cuyamaca Mountains and, just as the cowbird was beginning its population explosion, Stephens (1919a) called it a "rather common summer resident of timbered cañons in the mountains." Presumably brood-parasitism by the Brown-headed Cowbird is the factor most responsible for the change; cowbirds parasitize Cassin's Vireo more heavily than expected from its abundance (Goguen and Curson 2002). Yet in spite of widespread cowbird trapping in San

Nesting: Like many vireos, the male Cassin's is not hesitant to sing at or near the nest, which is typically suspended by its rims from a forked twig of a small forest tree or bush. Nests are rarely placed at heights of more than 20 feet; most are built between 3 and 7 feet of the ground. Of six San Diego County nests, one nest was in a tangle of snowberry, honeysuckle, and an unidentified oak (Palomar State Park), two were in coast live oaks (Jeff Valley), and three were in incense cedars (two on Middle Peak, one in Lost Valley). Although Cassin's Vireo nests are typically shaded in dense foliage (Harrison 1978), as were those in incense cedars, one in Jeff Valley was in a sparsely foliaged oak directly over a major footpath.

Our few observations of Cassin's Vireo nesting 1997–2001 suggest laying of a single clutch from late May to mid June: four records of nest building 30 May–10 June, five of occupied nests 3–12 June, one of a nest with nestlings (Middle Peak 18 June 2000, W. E. Haas), and one of fledglings (Laguna Mountains 18 June 2000, E. C. Hall, J. O. Zimmer). These sightings all fit within historical data on Cassin's Vireo nesting in San Diego County, 40 egg sets collected 15 May–28 June 1895–1933.

Migration: Spring migration of Cassin's Vireo through San Diego County is spread rather evenly from 10 April

Diego County since the late 1980s, Cassin's Vireo, unlike Bell's, has yet to show any evidence of recovery. From the viewpoint of San Diego County, the trend toward increase reported for the species as a whole (Sauer et al. 2003) looks unlikely; in all of the species' local roles the trends look flat to negative.

Taxonomy: With the split of the Solitary Vireo into the Blue-headed, Plumbeous, and Cassin's, the last consists of only two subspecies, nominate *V. c. cassinii* Xantus, 1858, being the only one in the United States.

Blue-headed Vireo *Vireo solitarius*

The Blue-headed Vireo breeds east of the Rocky Mountains and reaches California primarily as a fall vagrant. Its reclassification as a species distinct from the Cassin's and Plumbeous Vireos has attracted birders' attention to it, but it is at least as rare here as birds with a similar breeding range, such as the Philadelphia Vireo.

Migration: Of San Diego County's 13 records of the Blue-headed Vireo, 12 are for fall, from 15 September (1991, Point Loma, S. Mlodinow, AB 46:151, 1991) to 10 November (Point Loma, AB 35:227, 1980). All fall records are from Point Loma except for three from the Tijuana River valley in the 1970s.

Winter: The single winter record is of one in San Diego 16 January–22 March 1987 (J. L. Dunn, AB 41:331, 1987). The Blue-headed Vireo winters at the latitude of San Diego in the southeastern United States, so further winter records here should be expected.

Photo by Anthony Mercieca

Taxonomy: *Vireo s. solitarius* (Wilson, 1810), smaller and greener backed than the Appalachian *V. s. alticola*, is undoubtedly the subspecies reaching California; the only specimen (San Nicolas Island, SDNHM 38562) is this. But the Blue-headed Vireo has not yet been collected or even photographed in San Diego County.

Hutton's Vireo *Vireo huttoni*

A fairly common resident of San Diego County's oak woodland, Hutton's Vireo is the only nonmigratory member of its family in California. Its mindlessly monotonous song can be heard nearly year round. Beginning breeding early in the spring, before the Brown-headed Cowbird, Hutton's Vireo was able to withstand this parasite's invasion, which decimated San Diego County's other breeding vireos. Hutton's Vireo has even been able to spread into riparian woodland with few or no oaks and to colonize recently regenerated habitat.

Breeding distribution: As a characteristic bird of oak woodland, Hutton's Vireo has a distribution largely following that of the coast live oak. It is most common in oak-dominated woodlands in the foothills, with daily counts of up to 15 in Boden Canyon (I14) 6 June 2000 (R. L. Barber), near Warner Springs (F19) 14 May 1999 (C. G. Edwards), and near Campo (U24) 9 May 1998 (C. R. Mahrdt). But it can be common too in riparian woodland in which oaks are a minority of the trees (16 along the Santa Margarita River north of Fallbrook, C8, 24 May 2001, K. L. Weaver). Furthermore, the vireo approaches the coast more closely in many places, following strips of riparian woodland with few or no oaks, though it is uncommon in such woodland. A few Hutton's Vireos inhabit Balboa Park (R9), with records including an adult building a nest 2 August 1977 (D. Herron),

Photo by Anthony Mercieca

one feeding a fledgling at the west end of the Cabrillo Bridge 7 June 2000 (P. A. Ginsburg), a fledgling collected 4 August 1991 (SDNHM 47660), and an adult collected 7 August 1928 (SDNHM 12160). Hutton's Vireo now occurs even in southwesternmost San Diego County, along the Sweetwater River in Bonita (T11; e.g., pair with fledglings 22 May 1997, P. Famolaro) and in the Tijuana River valley (e.g., two singing males along the river east of Hollister St., W11, 19 June and 13 July 1999, P. Unitt).

Hutton's Vireo can be common in lower montane forest mixed with conifers (13 near Pine Hills Fire Station, L19, 24 May 1988, P. Unitt), but it is uncommon between 4500 and 5500 feet elevation and absent from the summits of the county's highest mountains. The eastern limit of the range largely coincides with the eastern limit of coast live oaks, but Hutton's Vireo also extends in oakless riparian woodland down San Felipe Valley as far as Scissors Crossing (four, including a pair building a nest, near Paroli Spring, I21, 27 July 2000, J. O. Zimmer; up to three singing males west of Scissors Crossing, J22, 6 May 2002, J. R. Barth).

Nesting: Hutton's Vireo builds a conventional vireo nest, attached to twigs by its rim and suspended from a fork. Three nests described by atlas observers were in the crowns of coast live oaks, as is typical for the species, but one was only 2 feet off the ground in a snowberry, exceptionally low. One of the oak nests was being built directly over busy Highland Valley Road (K13).

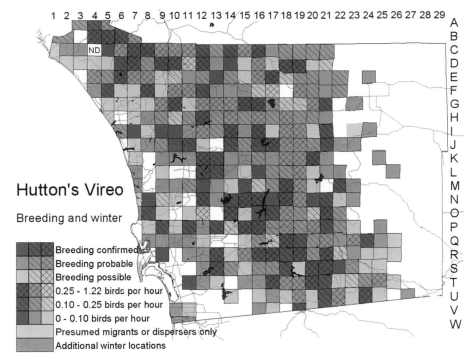

Hutton's Vireo

Breeding and winter

- Breeding confirmed
- Breeding probable
- Breeding possible
- 0.25 - 1.22 birds per hour
- 0.10 - 0.25 birds per hour
- 0 - 0.10 birds per hour
- Presumed migrants or dispersers only
- Additional winter locations

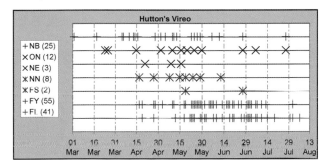

Hutton's Vireo

+NB (25)	
×ON (12)	
×NE (3)	
×NN (8)	
×FS (2)	
+FY (55)	
+FL (41)	

01 Mar 16 Mar 31 Mar 15 Apr 30 Apr 15 May 30 May 14 Jun 29 Jun 14 Jul 29 Jul 13 Aug

Late March to early July is the main season of Hutton's Vireo nesting in San Diego County, but occasional birds start earlier, as illustrated by a pair building a nest near Old Mission Dam (P11) 2 March 1998 (K. J. Burns) and an active nest perhaps still under construction along the Sweetwater River near Highway 94 (R13) 12 March 1999 (J. R. Barth). Eggs have been collected elsewhere in California as early as 10 February, and nest building has been reported from San Diego County as early as the first week of February (Davis 1995). The nests under construction in San Felipe Valley 27 July 2000 and in Balboa Park 2 August 1977 were remarkably late. We saw no suggestion that birds laying after the first week of July actually fledged young.

Migration: Hutton's Vireo is largely resident, but a few birds disperse out of their breeding habitat. The species is occasional on Point Loma (S7); records include one seen 16 October 2000 (V. P. Johnson) and specimens collected 7 January 1932 (SDNHM 15659) and 21 September 1987 (SDNHM 44823). The latter was a vagrant from northern California (see Taxonomy). The only record of a possible migrant in the Anza–Borrego Desert during the atlas

period was of one near the mouth of Sentenac Canyon (I23) 17 April 1998 (P. K. Nelson), only 2 or 3 miles from the nearest point where the species is resident along San Felipe Creek. But there are earlier spring records, from Borrego Springs (G24) and Tamarisk Grove (I24), both 5 May 1991 (A. G. Morley), and one fall record, from Lower Willows (D23) 16 October 1994 (L. Clark, K. Smeltzer).

Winter: We saw only slight spread of Hutton's Vireo away from breeding localities in winter. Most records of winter visitors at nonbreeding locations were of just a single individual. Numbers in the Tijuana River valley, though, were distinctly higher in winter than in summer, with up to seven in the northwest quadrant of the valley (V10) 16 December 2000 (W. E. Haas) and five in the southwest quadrant (W10) 15 December 2001 (G. L. Rogers). In the Anza–Borrego Desert Hutton's Vireo is rare, and most records are from the desert's edge. The only winter records from the desert floor are of one in north Borrego Valley (E24) 21 December 1997 (P. R. Pryde) and two at Tamarisk Grove and Yaqui Well 16 January 2000 (P. E. Lehman), with one still there 20 February (R. Thériault). Also of note are two in pinyon–juniper woodland in the Vallecito Mountains, one in Pinyon Mountain Valley (K25) 11 February 2000, the other on the east slope of Whale Peak (L26) 3 February 2000 (J. R. Barth).

Conservation: Unlike San Diego County's other breeding vireos, Hutton's did not suffer any great population decline after the invasion of the Brown-headed Cowbird. Though Hutton's is a suitable and frequent host of the cowbird (we noted six instances of successful parasitism during observations for this atlas), some aspects of its biology buffer it from cowbird parasitism. Probably most important is that Hutton's Vireo, as a resident species, often begins nesting well before breeding cowbirds arrive and start to lay, generally in late April. Furthermore,

Hutton's Vireo's prime oak woodland habitat has been far less disturbed than the riparian woodlands favored by Bell's Vireo. Hutton's Vireo has, if anything, increased over San Diego County's recorded history. Stephens (1919a) called the species only an "infrequent winter resident and occasional in summer." Most of the species' colonization of coastal riparian woodland outside the oak zone appears to have taken place since the early 1980s (cf. Unitt 1984). Such is certainly the case in the recently regenerated riparian woodland of the Tijuana River valley. This is the habitat largely responsible for increased numbers of Hutton's Vireos on San Diego Christmas bird counts. From 1999 to 2001 the numbers ranged from 11 to 17; on no count before 1999 did the total exceed five.

Taxonomy: Bishop (1905) reported the Hutton's Vireos of southern California to be darker and grayer than those of the central California coast, describing them as *V. h. oberholseri* and selecting a San Diego County specimen from Witch Creek (J18) as the type. Rea (in Phillips 1991) supported the recognition of *oberholseri*, though others had synonymized it with nominate *huttoni*. The specimen from Point Loma 21 September 1987 is conspicuously yellower than the local population and evidently a vagrant of *V. h. parkesi* Rea, 1991, which breeds along the coast of northern California from Humboldt to Marin County.

Warbling Vireo *Vireo gilvus*

The Warbling Vireo is a common migrant through San Diego County but rare as a breeding bird and very rare as a winter visitor. Migrants stop in any tree, but breeding birds seek mature riparian and oak woodland. Of any California bird, the Warbling Vireo is perhaps the most susceptible to cowbird parasitism. Cowbird trapping intended to benefit Bell's Vireo is likely responsible for bringing the Warbling Vireo back—just barely—from the brink of extirpation as a breeding species in San Diego County. Atlas participants observed only two Warbling Vireo nests, but female cowbirds were scrutinizing or entering both of them while the vireos were building them and birders were watching them.

Breeding distribution: In San Diego County the breeding population of Warbling Vireos is now concentrated in the riparian woodlands in the county's northwest, especially in the area of De Luz and Fallbrook. The largest number of breeding birds found, nine singing males 20 June 2000, was along De Luz and Cottonwood creeks north of the De Luz school (B6; K. L. Weaver). The Santa Margarita River near Fallbrook also supports several Warbling Vireo territories, with four singing males west of Sandia Creek Road (C7) 25 April 1998 and six east of that road (C8) 24 May 2001 (K. L. Weaver). Elsewhere in northwestern San Diego County, however, breeding Warbling Vireos are still uncommon to rare. At low elevations in southern San Diego County, the only area where the Warbling Vireo seems likely to breed is the Sweetwater River, with a singing male and a pair near the upper end of Sweetwater Reservoir (S13) 24 May 2000 (P. Famolaro) and one near Highway 94 (R13) 24 June 1998 (M. and D. Hastings).

A few breeding Warbling Vireos are also scattered through the county's mountains. High numbers in this area are of six (all singing males) around Palomar Mountain (E15) 18 June 1999 (C. R. Mahrdt, E. C. Hall), nine (including three singing males and a courting pair) at Wynola (J19) 22 May 1999 (S. E. Smith), and four (including a pair) near Wooded Hill, Laguna Mountains

Photo by Anthony Mercieca

(P23) 3 June 1999 (E. C. Hall, J. O. Zimmer). There is one summer record of the Warbling Vireo from riparian woodland at the desert's edge: two, including a singing male, along San Felipe Creek 1.2 miles west northwest of Scissors Crossing (J22) 13 July 2001 (P. Unitt et al.). The species' use of this site is evidently irregular; thorough surveys of the Scissors Crossing area in 2002 did not reveal any summering Warbling Vireos.

Determining the Warbling Vireo's precise breeding distribution, however, is difficult. Spring migrants are still moving through late in the spring (see Migration), long after the local population has begun nesting. Ideally, any assessment of whether Warbling Vireos are territorial or paired would be followed up with observations after the last of the migrants are gone. This was not possible in every instance; a few squares where the species is shown as possibly breeding are based on observations of apparently territorial singing males during the spring migration period only. Nevertheless, none of these locations lies more than 8 miles from locations where the species occurred in midsummer.

Nesting: We confirmed nesting of the Warbling Vireo only five times from 1997 to 2001, on the basis of an adult feeding a fledgling near De Luz (B6) 22 July 2000 (K. L. Weaver), a fledgling along the Santa Margarita River northwest of Fallbrook (C7) 4 July 1998 (K. L. Weaver), a pair adding to a nearly completed nest at 1900 feet elevation in Castro Canyon (C12) 13 May 2000 (J. Determan, P. Unitt), a singing male with a fledgling at 4550 feet elevation 1 mile north of San Ignacio on the northeast flank of Hot Springs Mountain (E22) 21 June 2001 (J. R. Barth), and a bird building a nearly completed nest (that later failed) at Cibbets Flat (Q23) 29 May 1999 (A. Lazere, J. R. Barth). The nests in Castro Canyon and at Cibbets Flat were both in the outer canopy of coast live oaks. These sites are typical for the species, which commonly builds its nests in the middle to upper levels of tall trees. Dates of eight egg sets collected in San Diego County 1900–21 range from 13 May to 16 June, and none of the recent observations augments this interval.

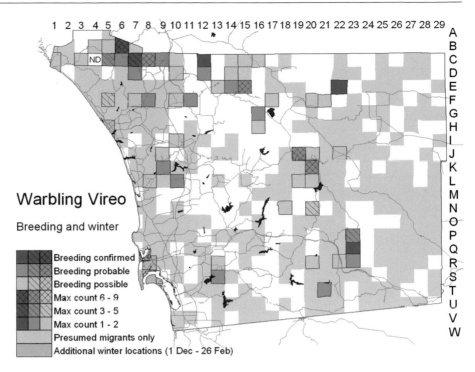

Warbling Vireo

Breeding and winter

Breeding confirmed
Breeding probable
Breeding possible
Max count 6 - 9
Max count 3 - 5
Max count 1 - 2
Presumed migrants only
Additional winter locations (1 Dec - 26 Feb)

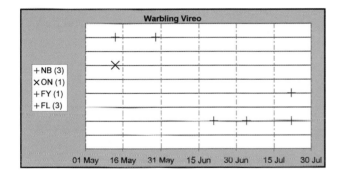

Warbling Vireo

+NB (3)
XON (1)
+FY (1)
+FL (3)

01 May   16 May   31 May   15 Jun   30 Jun   15 Jul   30 Jul

Migration: In spring migration, the Warbling Vireo occurs throughout San Diego County, but, as with many other species, the largest numbers are seen along the east base of the mountains (25 at Vallecito, M25, 29 April 1997, M. C. Jorgensen; 23 at Agua Caliente Springs, M26, 12 May 1997, E. C. Hall). It begins arriving by late March, but occasional birds show up earlier. From 1997 to 2001, the first spring report varied from 27 February to 29 March. Occurrences before 15 March, though, are rare, with only six reported during the atlas period. The two sightings that coincided on 27 February 1999, of two in upper San Felipe Valley (H20; A. P. and T. E. Keenan) and one at Yaqui Well (I24; P. D. Jorgensen), are the earliest recorded in San Diego County. Spring migration peaks in late April and early May. The Warbling Vireo is not only an early migrant but a late one, seen regularly into the first week of June. The latest apparent migrant reported 1997–2001 was one in Tecolote Canyon (Q9) 15 June 2000 (T. Plunkett); previous records extend to 22 June (1977, Point Loma, S7, P. Unitt).

Fall migration extends from August through October at least, peaking in September. Nearly all Warbling Vireos passing through San Diego County in September and October are immatures.

Winter: The Warbling Vireo is rare in winter, occurring in urban trees in a narrow strip along the coast. Four were noted during the atlas period, at Buena Vista Lagoon (H5) 22 December 2001 (J. Determan, NAB 56:224, 2002), at the Marine Corps Recruit Depot (R8) 15 December 1998 (P. A. Ginsburg, NAB 53:210, 1999), at North Island Naval Air Station (S8) 20 December 1997 (R. T. Patton), and at Coronado (S9) 16 December 2000 (E. Copper). Most of the approximately 20 winter records of the Warbling Vireo are from metropolitan San Diego; only three are from the north county. Most are for December, in part an artifact of the scheduling of Christmas bird counts, but suggesting that most of these stragglers do not remain or survive the entire winter. There are only two records from San Diego after 10 January, of one that remained to 24 January 1984 (P. E. Lehman, AB 38:358, 1984) and another 11 February 1985 (R. E. Webster, AB 39:211, 1985).

Conservation: Early in the 20th century, the Warbling Vireo was considerably more common in San Diego County. Sharp (1907) said that, as a breeding bird, it was "not uncommon around upper end of Escondido Valley." Stephens (1919a) called it a "common summer resident" in San Diego County's mountains. Willett (1912) wrote that it was a "common summer resident, locally" on the coastal slope of southern California generally. Sites of eggs collected 1900–20 included Descanso (P19), Lakeside (O14), El Monte (O15), and Dulzura (T16), where the species is now absent. However tenuous these data may be, they suggest that the Warbling Vireo had declined precipitously by the late 1970s, when the breeding population was on the verge of extirpation from San Diego County (Unitt 1984). Parasitism by the Brown-headed Cowbird is almost certainly the major factor responsible for this decrease. The vireo's decline followed the cowbird's invasion about 1915. The success of parasitized nests is low to none (Rothstein et al. 1980). And, in the Sierra Nevada, vireo and cowbird abundances are related inversely (Verner and Ritter 1983). Low success of even unparasitized nests may make the Warbling Vireo unusually susceptible to the cowbird (Ward and Smith 2000). Evidence is mounting that the decline is spreading from San Diego County north into the core of the range of subspecies *swainsonii* (Gardali and Jaramillo 2001).

A minor rebound in the number of breeding Warbling Vireos in northwestern San Diego County, at least, has followed the widespread trapping of cowbirds since the mid 1980s. But the rebound is far less than that of the Blue-gray Gnatcatcher or Bell's Vireo.

Taxonomy: Only the Pacific coast subspecies of the Warbling Vireo, *V. g. swainsonii* Baird, 1858, has been collected in California. Differences between *swainsonii* and nominate *gilvus* in molt schedule (Voelker and Rohwer 1998) and response to cowbird parasitism (Sealy et al. 2000) imply that the distinction between the eastern and western Warbling Vireos is more profound than the minor differences in size, plumage color, and bill shape suggest.

Philadelphia Vireo *Vireo philadelphicus*

Breeding in the boreal forest east of the Rocky Mountains, wintering mainly in southeastern Mexico and Central America, the Philadelphia Vireo is a vagrant to California. All but two of San Diego County's 20 records are from a seven-week period in the fall.

Migration: Fall records of the Philadelphia Vireo in San Diego extend from 19 September (1975, Point Loma, S7; 1976, Tijuana River valley) to 10 November (1999, Lindo Lake, Lakeside, O14, G. McCaskie, NAB 54:105, 2000). The last record, of a bird found first on 3 November, is the only one away from Point Loma and the Tijuana River valley. Two specimens have been collected, California's first Philadelphia Vireo, in the Tijuana River valley 9 October 1965 (SDNHM 35511, McCaskie 1968b), and another at Point Loma 9 November 1969 (SDNHM 37390).

The single spring record for San Diego County is of one at Point Loma 29–31 May 1982 (N. B. Broadbrooks, Morlan 1985).

Photo by Anthony Mercieca

Winter: San Diego County's one winter record of the Philadelphia Vireo, of one in Coronado (S9) 15–16 December 2001, was only the fourth for California (R. E. Webster, NAB 56:224, 2002). Even in mid December, though, it may have been a late fall vagrant.

Red-eyed Vireo *Vireo olivaceus*

The Red-eyed Vireo is one of the most abundant birds in the unbroken forests of eastern North America and breeds west to Washington and Oregon. But it migrates mainly east of the Rocky Mountains and is only a rare vagrant to California. In fall, occurrences in San Diego County average about 0.75 per year. There are also four spring records.

Migration: There are at least 30 fall records of the Red-eyed Vireo in San Diego County, most from Point Loma (S7), some from the Tijuana River valley, one from Otay Mesa (V13), and one from the home of L. M. Huey in the Logan Heights neighborhood of San Diego (S10), where he collected California's first on 6 October 1914 (Huey 1915, SDNHM 33177). Their dates extend from 9 September (1970, Tijuana River valley, AB 25:110, 1971) to 3 November (1974, same locality, AB 29:123, 1975). The largest number reported in a single year was four in 1989 (AB 44:164, 1990).

The spring reports are of single birds at Kit Carson Park (K11) 17 May 1980 (K. L. Weaver, AB 34:921, 1980), Point Loma 28 May 1995 (R. E. Webster, NASFN 49:310,

Photo by Anthony Mercieca

1995), the Tijuana River valley 5 June 1979 (AB 33:806, 1979), and Coronado (S9) 14 June 1993 (E. Copper, AB 47:454, 1993).

Taxonomy: The North American population of the Red-eyed Vireo is generally considered a single subspecies, *V. o. olivaceus* (Linnaeus, 1766).

Yellow-green Vireo *Vireo flavoviridis*

Though the Yellow-green Vireo breeds almost entirely in Middle America, barely crossing the border along the Rio Grande in southernmost Texas, it is highly migratory, wintering in Amazonian Peru and Bolivia. In California it is a rare but now annual fall vagrant, mainly along the coast.

Migration: Sixteen Yellow-green Vireos have been accepted from San Diego County by the California Bird Records Committee, on dates ranging from 6 September (1996, Point Loma, D. W. Aguillard, McCaskie and San Miguel 1999) to 25 October (1976, Tijuana River valley, Luther et al. 1979). A few other reports have been rejected or not submitted. All accepted records are from Point Loma or the Tijuana River valley except for the two specimens, both found dead or injured in residential areas of San Diego: one on 7 October 1967 (SDNHM 36247), the other 16 September 1996 (SDNHM 50241).

Taxonomy: The relatively dull northwesternmost sub-

Photo by Peter LaTourrette

species of the Yellow-green Vireo, *V. f. hypoleucus* van Rossem and Hachisuka, 1937, breeding in Sonora and Sinaloa, seems the most likely one to reach California. A. R. Phillips identified the 1967 specimen as this. But the 1996 specimen has the yellow on the underparts conspicuously darker and should be compared with the yellower *V. f. flavoviridis* (Cassin, 1851).

CROWS AND JAYS — FAMILY CORVIDAE

Steller's Jay *Cyanocitta stelleri*

The bird most linked in San Diegans' minds with coniferous woodland in the county's mountains is Steller's Jay. Around campgrounds and picnic areas the jays are common and unavoidable; for generations the birds have learned to demand handouts from people. But in more remote areas the jays are less common and less obtrusive. One of the surprises generated by the atlas field work was how widespread Steller's Jay proved to be in oak woodland with no conifers, especially in southeastern San Diego County.

Breeding distribution: The higher mountains—Palomar, Hot Springs, Volcan, Cuyamaca, and Laguna—are the core of Steller's Jay's range in San Diego County. The species is most abundant on Palomar (up to 60 around Jeff Valley, E15, 28 May 1999, E. C. Hall, C. R. Mahrdt) but common in all the other ranges too. On Palomar's southwest slope, Steller's Jay is resident down to about 2300 feet elevation, even to about 1800 feet in deep canyons with big-cone Douglas firs (e.g., two in Agua Tibia Canyon, D12, 17 July 2001, K. L. Weaver). A local resident reported a Steller's Jay trapped in a greenhouse at 1600 feet elevation along Magee Road (C11) in late May 1998 (*fide* J. M. and B. Hargrove). The population on Palomar is linked broadly with that in central San Diego County through oak woodland in the Mesa Grande area (up to 15 in the Edwards Ranch northwest of Santa Ysabel, I18, D. W. Au). Steller's Jay appears absent from the stand of conifers on Bucksnort Mountain (C20), but we did find an isolated population at Adobe Springs in Chihuahua Valley (C18; six on 2 May 1999, A. Mauro).

In the southern half of San Diego County, Steller's Jay

Photo by Anthony Mercieca

inhabits oak woodland up to 8 miles away from coniferous woodland. Points defining the southern limits of the species' breeding range are Wilson Creek just west of Barrett Lake (S18; up to 10 on 25 May 2001; R. and S. L. Breisch); Morena Village (T22; pair nest building on 1 April 2000; R. and S. L. Breisch), and McCain Valley (S26; up to 18, plus an occupied nest, on 20 May 2000, J. K. Wilson). Steller's Jays are apparently irregular in Hauser Canyon (T20), with a single observation of two on 15 May 1997 (J. M. Wells). The birds' extensive use of oak woodland habitat in southeastern San Diego County is a paradox because the area is the southern tip of the range of subspecies *C. s. frontalis*. Steller's Jays are absent from Baja California, their range terminating just 7 miles short of the international border.

Nesting: Steller's Jay nests are typically well concealed in trees with dense foliage. The birds take advantage, however, of man-made structures that offer sheltered sites. Observers noted two nests under eaves of houses, one atop a sheltered bulletin board at the Doane Valley

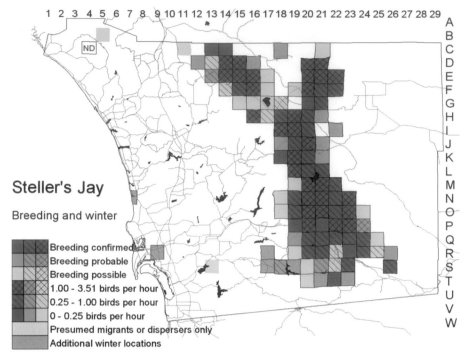

Steller's Jay

Breeding and winter

- ☒ Breeding confirmed
- ☒ Breeding probable
- ☒ Breeding possible
- 1.00 - 3.51 birds per hour
- 0.25 - 1.00 birds per hour
- 0 - 0.25 birds per hour
- Presumed migrants or dispersers only
- Additional winter locations

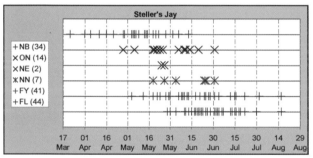

C. Hall, J. O. Zimmer), and 13 June (1984, one at 800 feet elevation along the San Diego River, M17, P. Unitt, AB 38:1062, 1984). The Santa Margarita Mountains offer much oak woodland, but the species is absent from the contiguous Santa Ana Mountains in Orange County, so evidently the bird at Sky Ranch was a vagrant. On the desert slope, Steller's Jays have been noted east of their breeding range six times between 17 August (1986, two in Borrego Palm Canyon, F23, and two at Tamarisk Grove, I24, R. Thériault) and 26 April (1996, one in Borrego Palm Canyon campground, F23, M. C. Jorgensen).

Winter: Steller's Jay is largely sedentary, so the winter and breeding distributions follow the same pattern. Most of the few additional localities where we found the species in winter could be sites where it is resident in very small numbers. The most notable of these were about 2200 feet elevation on the south side of Hidden Glen (R17; one on 22 January 2001, J. R. Barth) and about 2300 feet elevation in Lyons Valley (S17; one on 24 January 1998, S. M. Wolf). Some but not all of the low-elevation occurrences of Steller's Jay are during invasion years for other montane birds. The two during the atlas period, of one in the Mission Hills neighborhood of San Diego (R9) 16 December 2000 (J. K. Wilson) and one in Torrey Pines State Reserve (N7) 22 December 2000 (S. Walens) coincided with irruptions of Mountain Bluebirds, Cassin's Finches, and a flock of Pinyon Jays. The one winter record during the atlas period on the desert slope, however, of one at Angelina Spring (I22) 2 December 1998 (P. K. Nelson), was in a year with no such invasions.

campground (E14), and one on a cow skull nailed to the side of a building.

Our observations in San Diego County imply that Steller's Jays lay eggs at least from mid April to mid June, probably to late June, with three records of birds carrying nest material as late as 13 June. The species' nesting season is thus the same as that reported by Bent (1946), who gave a range of 12 April–24 June for California egg dates.

Migration: In parts of its range, Steller's Jay engages in altitudinal movements or irregular irruptions, but these events rarely touch San Diego County. On the coastal slope more than 5 miles west of its breeding range, the species has been recorded only 10 times from 4 October (1978, one at Point Loma, S7, AB 33:216, 1979) to 27 April (1998, one along the Sweetwater River above Sweetwater Reservoir, S13, P. Famolaro), 24 May (2001, one at Sky Ranch, Santa Margarita Mountains, B5, E.

Conservation: Steller's Jays capitalize on the supplemental food and nesting sites that accompany the campgrounds and rural homes in their breeding range. But there seem to have been no changes in the species' numbers over time; Lake Henshaw Christmas bird count results since 1981 show no real trend.

Taxonomy: The Steller's Jays resident in southern California are *C. s. frontalis*, which lacks any white marks around the eye and is paler than other subspecies found farther north along the Pacific coast.

Western Scrub-Jay *Aphelocoma californica*

A year-round resident, the Western Scrub-Jay is well known to San Diegans, conspicuous in most urban areas and dominating bird feeders. Nevertheless, it remains most abundant in native chaparral and oak

woodland, where it feeds heavily on acorns. Scrub oaks as well as tree oaks support the jay. In fall and early winter, when the oaks are bearing, the jays can be seen shuttling between oak groves and chaparral, carrying acorns to be cached and eaten later.

Breeding distribution: The Western Scrub-Jay is common over most of San Diego County's coastal slope, with regions of greatest abundance in the northwest from the north side of the Santa Margarita Mountains east to Rainbow, in the north-central area from the north slope of Palomar Mountain east to Chihuahua Valley and Warner Springs, and in the southeast on the Campo Plateau. Surveys near Pine Valley revealed it as one of the most common birds of mature chaparral, exceeded significantly only by the Spotted Towhee and Wrentit and on a par with the Mountain Quail and Bewick's Wren (Cleveland National Forest data). Daily counts in the breeding season run as high as 50, as around Sunshine Summit (D17) 1 May 1999 (A. Mauro) and in Tecolote Canyon (Q9) 10 May 2001 (T. Plunkett). Field work for the atlas disclosed two areas on the coastal slope where scrub-jays are rare to absent: the lowest 5 or 6 miles of the Santa Margarita and San Luis Rey River valleys and from the Tijuana River valley east to Otay Mesa and Lower Otay Lake (U13/V13), a region of riparian woodland, sage scrub, and grassland but little chaparral.

In the Anza–Borrego Desert, the eastern margin of the scrub-jay's range largely follows the edge of scrub that retains components of chaparral; very likely the availability of acorns of the desert scrub oak is the species' limiting factor here. The jay occurs in small numbers at the higher elevations of the Santa Rosa and Vallecito mountains, where the desert scrub oak is an important component of the vegetation. But it also ranges in small numbers down Coyote Creek to the riparian oasis of Lower Willows (D23; up to two on 10 May 1997 and 25 April 1998, B. L. Peterson), where oaks are absent.

Nesting: Western Scrub-Jays build a bowl of coarse twigs, usually concealing it in dense-foliaged trees or shrubs. We found one nest, however, on the support for a satel-

Photo by Anthony Mercieca

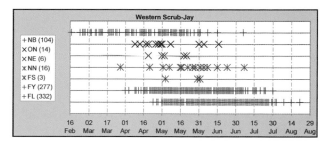

lite dish in a rural yard. Our observations from 1997 through 2001 imply egg laying from mid March to about 1 June—the same interval attested by 51 egg sets collected from 1894 to 1956 (WFVZ).

Winter: In California the Western Scrub-Jay is essentially sedentary, mated pairs maintaining their territories year round unless the supply of acorns fails. In San Diego County the jay's pattern of abundance in winter is very similar to that in the breeding season, with hardly any dispersal into the areas on the coastal slope where it is absent in the breeding season. Nevertheless, it is sometimes seen in winter in numbers considerably greater than in the breeding season, possibly because of nonterritorial birds concentrating where the feeding is good. Such concentrations were noted especially on the Campo Plateau, with up to 150 north of Lake Morena (S21) 16 February 1998 (S. E. Smith), 125 west of Campo (U22) 31 January 2000 (E. C. Hall, C. R. Mahrdt), and 235 around Campo (U23) 14 January 2001 (D. S. and A. W. Hester, M. and B. McIntosh).

Only rarely do scrub-jays venture even a short distance outside their breeding range along the edge of the Anza–Borrego Desert. There are three records for the floor of the Borrego Valley: one in Borrego Springs

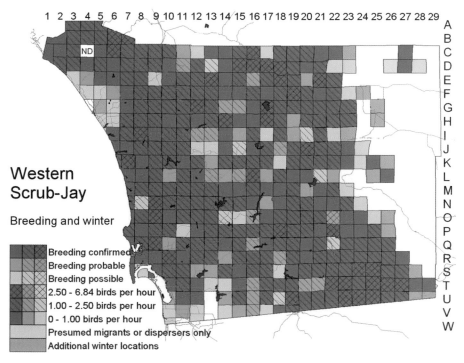

Western Scrub-Jay

Breeding and winter

- Breeding confirmed
- Breeding probable
- Breeding possible
- 2.50 - 6.84 birds per hour
- 1.00 - 2.50 birds per hour
- 0 - 1.00 birds per hour
- Presumed migrants or dispersers only
- Additional winter locations

(F24) 20 December 1998 (R. Thériault), one in the mesquite bosque of the Borrego Sink (G25) 17 December 2000 (B. Siegel), and one at Casa del Zorro (H25) 19 December 1999 (L. D. and R. Johnson). Also on the desert floor were two on the north side of Clark Dry Lake (D26) 11 March 2000 (P. K. Nelson).

Conservation: The Western Scrub-Jay is a familiar component of San Diego County's urban avifauna. In residential areas, bird feeders probably help compensate for the lack of oak trees as a food source. Urbanization has enabled the jays to spread into former sage scrub that was once unsuitable. In the San Diego Christmas bird count circle, most of which was marginal scrub-jay habitat before urbanization, count results show a definite upward trend in the species' numbers. The number of scrub-jays per party-hour on the count 1997–2002 was larger by a factor of 1.93 than the 20-year average 1962–81. An increase and spread of the scrub-jay is relevant to conservation of other birds because the jay is a major predator of eggs and nestlings; Peterson (2002, Peterson et al. 2003) found the scrub-jay to be the principal predator on Bell's Vireo nests along the San Luis Rey River. Nevertheless, the scrub-jay remains considerably more abundant in its native habitats. Bolger et al. (1997) found it to be among the birds insensitive to habitat fragmentation, neither attracted nor repelled by the urban edge.

Taxonomy: The local subspecies of the Western Scrub-Jay, *A. c. obscura*, is a classic exemplar of a bird whose range and characters define the San Diegan District of the California Floristic Province. *Aphelocoma c. obscura* is the dark extreme of the species—as long as the Santa Cruz Island Scrub-Jay (*A. insularis*) is excluded.

Pinyon Jay *Gymnorhinus cyanocephalus*

Although Pinyon Jays are common in Garner Valley of the San Jacinto Mountains only 10 miles north of the county line, and are common in the Sierra Juárez an equally short distance south of the border, they occur in San Diego County only as rare vagrants at long intervals. The stands of pinyons in the Santa Rosa and Vallecito mountains are evidently too small to support a resident population.

Winter: Of the montane birds prone to sporadic irruptions, the Pinyon Jay is one of the least frequent in San Diego County, recorded in only 10 seasons since 1877. In 1973 only a single individual was noted, but on other occasions the birds have been in flocks. Sometimes multiple flocks occur in a single year, as in 1987, when 25 were in Cuyamaca Rancho State Park (M20) 19 September (S. Mlodinow, AB 42:137, 1988) and 10 were on Volcan Mountain (J20) 28 October (P. Unitt). Some of the early records that lack good detail may also represent large flocks, but the largest with estimates of their size are of about 75 near San Onofre (C1) in March 1915 (year implied; W. M. Pierce in Willett 1933), up to 200 in the Laguna Mountains (O23) 6–12 January 1990 (D. and M. Hastings et al., AB 44:330, 1990), and the single record during the atlas period, of up to 55 at Stonewall Mine, Cuyamaca Mountains (M20), 28 December 2000–2 May 2001 (K. Satterfield, NAB 55:357, 2001). Most Pinyon Jays in San Diego County have been in the mountains or foothills; only those at San Onofre reached the coast. On the desert side, F. Stephens collected two at Vallecito (M25) 27 November 1891 (SDNHM 757–8), and L. M. Huey collected two 3 miles east of Jacumba (U29) 11 March 1945 (SDNHM 19150–1).

Photo by Anthony Mercieca

Migration: As expected with such an irregular species, records of the Pinyon Jay are scattered seasonally. The extreme dates are 19 September and 2 May, both records cited above. In general, Pinyon Jay irruptions start in late August or early September and continue through early January (Balda 2002).

Conservation: Pinyon Jays appear no more frequent than they did a century ago, despite the far greater number of observers, suggesting they may actually be on the decrease. The long-term trend toward a drier climate, since the end of the Pleistocene, disfavors trees like pinyons that grow in arid regions and could be a bad sign for birds like the jay that depend on them.

Clark's Nutcracker *Nucifraga columbiana*

A bird of subalpine forests, Clark's Nutcracker lives in an elevation zone too high for San Diego County's mountains. Yet it is a permanent resident in the San Jacinto Mountains (it is seen easily at the top of the Palm Springs Aerial Tramway) and sporadic in the Sierra San Pedro Mártir. It reaches San Diego County only as a vagrant, principally to the mountains, and principally during broaderscale irruptions that often coincide with those of the Pinyon Jay. Both species rely for food primarily on pine seeds, and both are forced out of their normal habitats if the trees fail to bear.

Winter: Clark's Nutcracker invasions of San Diego County's mountains are rare: just eight winters (1877, 1920, 1935, 1955, 1972, 1973, 1996–97, and 2000–01) account for almost all of the records. Sometimes the irruptions bring scattered individuals, sometimes flocks. The most notable were on 21 February 1877 ("a fair-sized flock" at Mount Laguna, O23, F. Stephens in Willett 1912, SDNHM 755), in spring 1920 (see under Migration), and in fall 1935 (flocks of 50 to 60 in the Volcan and Cuyamaca mountains; anonymous 1935; two specimens from Volcan Mountain, I20, 28 September 1935, SDNHM 17095–6). The winter preceding the five-year atlas period brought six to Cuyamaca Rancho State Park (M20) 7 November 1996 (J. Katetzky) and three to Buddy Todd Park, Oceanside (H6), 29 December 1996–1 January 1997 (D. and C. Wysong, NASFN 51:800, 1997). In 2000–01, 15 were on Cuyamaca Peak (M20) 16 October (P. D. Jorgensen), with two seen as late as 15 April (R. Wheeler), two were in Pine Valley (P21) 17 October (M. Heilbron), and five were on Volcan Mountain (I20) 18 December 2000 (R. T. Patton).

Though occurring mainly in the mountains, Clark's Nutcrackers have been noted seven times in the coastal lowland (at Oceanside in 1996–97; earlier records listed by Unitt 1984). The only nutcrackers recorded in the Anza–Borrego Desert are still the five during the irruptions of 1955 and 1972 (Unitt 1984).

Migration: Records of Clark's Nutcracker in San Diego County form an interesting seasonal pattern. Most are for fall and winter, on dates ranging from 11 August (1972, one at Palomar Mountain, AB 26:907, 1972) to 21 February (1877, the flock at Mount Laguna), except for the two at Cuyamaca Peak 15 April 2001. Eight records, though, are

Photo by Anthony Mercieca

from late May and June: "flocks ranging from a few birds to 15 or 20 in the flock" in the Laguna Mountains 31 May–1 June 1920 (Fortiner 1920), one on Palomar Mountain 24 June 1967 (A. G. Morley, AFN 21:605, 1967), one along Agua Dulce Creek, Laguna Mountains (O23), 25 May 1974 (P. Unitt, AB 28:853, 1974), one along High Point Truck Trail, north slope of Palomar Mountain (C15), 31 May 1997 (K. L. Weaver), one near Filaree Flat, Laguna Mountains (N22), the same day (G. L. Rogers, FN 51:926, 1997), one near Laguna Campground (O23) 8 June 1997 (C. G. Edwards, FN 51:1054, 1997), four flying north in Lark Canyon (S26) 9 June 2001 (P. Unitt), and one at the southwest base of Volcan Mountain (J20) 15 June 2001 (E. C. Hall, J. O. Zimmer). Evidently some nutcrackers leaving their breeding range in fall have still not made it back by the middle of the following breeding season.

American Crow *Corvus brachyrhynchos*

No change among San Diego birds has been more striking than the proliferation of the American Crow. Until the mid 1980s the species ranged no farther south along the coast than Carlsbad, no nearer the coast in metropolitan San Diego than El Cajon. Then it surged south and west, spreading over the coastal lowland. By the new millennium it was abundant in many areas where it was absent only 15 years earlier. Primitively the crow occurred in oak and riparian woodland near grassland; now orchards, eucalyptus groves, and cities support large numbers.

Breeding distribution: The American Crow now occurs almost throughout the coastal slope of San Diego County, most abundantly in the inland valleys of the county's northern half. Concentrations during the breeding season are as large as 200 at Lake Hodges (K10) 9 March 1999 (R. L. Barber), and 220 northeast of Ramona (K15) 26 April 1999 (M. and. B. McIntosh). The crow is abundant locally south to the Mexican border (up to 138 at Potrero, U20,

Photo by Anthony Mercieca

26 June 1999, R. and S. L. Breisch). The eastern margin of the range follows that of oak woodland closely, except that the species occurs uncommonly in San Felipe Valley down to Scissors Crossing (J22; up to nine on 3 June 2002, J. R. Barth; fledgling on 13 July 2001, P. Unitt). The crow is uncommon and local in montane coniferous forest and absent from sage scrub and chaparral. Its breeding

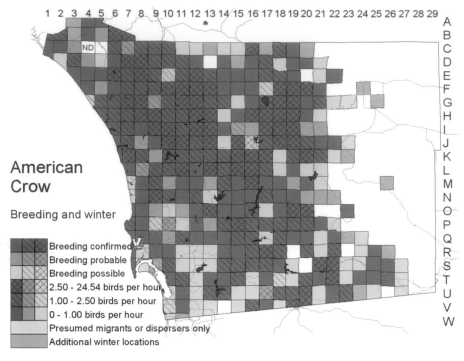

American Crow

Breeding and winter

Breeding confirmed
Breeding probable
Breeding possible
2.50 - 24.54 birds per hour
1.00 - 2.50 birds per hour
0 - 1.00 birds per hour
Presumed migrants or dispersers only
Additional winter locations

of these in San Diego County is at the east end of Lake Hodges (K11), where counts range up to 1800 on 1 December 1998 (E. C. Hall). Wintering crows are already abundant in areas the species has only recently colonized, especially Bonita and eastern National City (T11), with up to 800 on 16 December 2000 (G. C. Hazard) and possibly 4000 on 15 December 2001 (D. W. Aguillard).

The American Crow is a rare winter visitor to the Anza–Borrego Desert east of its breeding range with at least 15 records, eight during the atlas period. Some of these are of small flocks, of up to six in Earthquake Valley (K23) 17 February 2001 (A. P. and T. E. Keenan) and five in Borrego Springs (F24) 17 December 2000 (J. York).

range has now extended south along the coast to Point Loma (S7; birds seen carrying nest material repeatedly in 1997, J. C. Worley) and Otay Valley (V11; fledgling on 26 June 1999, P. Unitt), probably to the Tijuana River valley (V10/W10; up to 30 on 18 June 1997, C. G. Edwards).

Nesting: American Crows nest in the crowns of trees with dense foliage. In San Diego County, coast live oaks are the traditional nest site; now the birds also make much use of palms, pines, Italian cypress, and especially eucalyptus. In groves of such trees, crows nest colonially, as they do elsewhere in California (Verbeek and Caffrey 2002).

Thirty-five egg sets collected in San Diego County from 1888 to 1962 range in date from 24 March to 18 May, and 112 from throughout California range from 21 March to 12 June. But, on the basis of an incubation period of 18 days, our observations from 1997 to 2001 suggest egg laying from the second week of March to mid May, with records of nest building as early as 12 February, nestlings being fed as early as 30 March, and fledglings as early as 25 April. In Los Angeles, Verbeek and Caffrey (2002) reported egg laying beginning 17 March.

Winter: In San Diego County the American Crow is nonmigratory, and its distribution in winter is similar to that in spring and summer. But in winter the birds gather into even larger flocks and roosts. Probably the largest

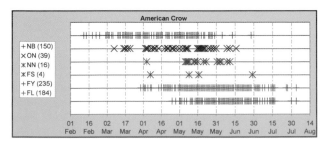

Conservation: The crow's primitive distribution paralleled that of other oak woodland birds whose range retracts inland from north to south, though it was always common in riparian woodland without oaks in northwestern San Diego County. In many of the areas where it occurred historically the population increased: from 1975 to 1979 the Oceanside Christmas bird count averaged 253 crows; from 1997 to 2001 it averaged 1031. From 1985 to 1989 the Escondido count averaged 571; from 1997 to 2001 it averaged 2161. On the San Diego count before 1984 the crow was irregular, occurring only at the eastern margin of the circle; it was regular in small to moderate numbers from 1985 through 1995 and then increased rapidly. Yet there has been no significant change in the Lake Henshaw circle where, in contrast to the other circles, there has been little development.

The crow adapted quickly to urbanization in its original range. The mysteries in San Diego County are why the crow took so long to take advantage of new suitable habitat, why the expansion took place at the moment in history when it did, and why the increase was so explosive when it arrived.

Many San Diegans express concern for the survival of other birds in the face of proliferation of a predator on eggs and nestlings. But the effects of the crow's population explosion remain unknown. On the other hand, the American Crow is particularly susceptible to West Nile virus, which appeared in New York City in 1999 and is spreading rapidly across North America; crows have already been decimated in parts of the eastern United States.

Taxonomy: The crow inhabiting southern California is *C. b. hesperis* Ridgway, 1887, the smallest subspecies of the American Crow—if the Northwestern Crow (*C. caurinus*) is in fact a distinct species.

Common Raven *Corvus corax*

The world's largest passerine, the Common Raven is a common permanent resident of San Diego County. It occurs in all habitats, from beaches to mountaintops to desert floor. The change in the raven is less dramatic than that of the American Crow, but the raven too is on the increase, aided by increases in man-made food sources like refuse and road kills and man-made nest sites like buildings, bridges, and power-line towers.

Breeding distribution: After the House Finch, the Common Raven is the most widespread breeding bird in San Diego County. Field work for this atlas identified it as possibly breeding in 475 of 478 covered squares, and as confirmed breeding in 359. Ravens breed as dispersed pairs, but flocks may be seen through the breeding season. Such flocks presumably consist of immature birds; ravens do not breed until they are at least two years old (A. M. Rea). Sites of frequent large concentrations are Warner Valley (up to 175 east of Lake Henshaw, G18, 12 May 2001, T. Stands), Torrey Pines State Reserve (N7; up to 62 on 3 April 1998, K. Estey), and from Potrero to Canyon City (U20/U21; up to 180 near Canyon City 21 June 1999, D. C. Seals). In some cases, including the last, the reason for the concentration was a communal roost. The Common Raven tends to be less numerous in the Anza–Borrego Desert than on the coastal slope, but flocks can be seen through the breeding season there too, with up to 25 east of Peg Leg Road (F26) 1 May 2001 (B. Siegel) and 39 at a communal roost in palo verde trees near the northeast corner of the county (C29) 8 July 1999 (R. Thériault).

Nesting: Ledges and crevices in cliffs are the raven's most common traditional nest site. Atlas observers described

Photo by Anthony Mercieca

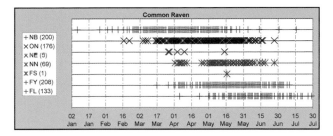

several on cliffs of both rock and eroded earth. Large trees are also frequent nest sites; atlas observers reported raven nests in coast live oaks, palms, eucalyptus, athel tamarisks, and one in a mesquite. Many ravens now nest on man-made structures, especially bridge abutments and the towers supporting electrical lines. Following major electricity-supply lines, such as the one crossing much of southern San Diego County, often leads to an alternating succession of raven and Red-tailed Hawk nests. Ravens nest in San Diego's most distinctive landmark, the California Tower in Balboa Park (R9; J. K. Wilson).

Our observations reveal that in San Diego County Common Ravens lay mainly from early March to at least early May, with some in the Anza–Borrego Desert and along the Mexican border beginning in mid February (as implied by young already fledged at Tecate, V19, on 6 April 2000, M. and B. McIntosh). Bent (1946) listed California egg dates from only 2 March to 19 May, but Boarman and Heinrich (1999) reported laying as early as mid February. The wide spread of dates of ravens carrying nest material suggests that some birds start their nests weeks before egg laying and maintain them as long as they are occupied.

Winter: The Common Raven's pattern of distribution in San Diego County in winter is much the same as that in the breeding

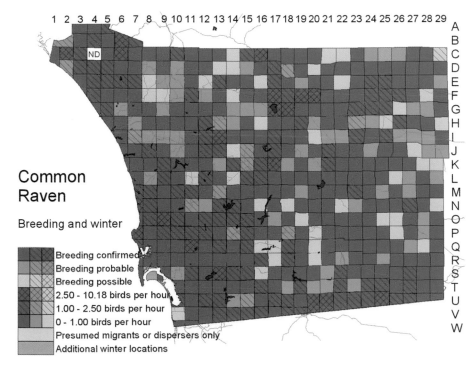

Common Raven

Breeding and winter

- Breeding confirmed
- Breeding probable
- Breeding possible
- 2.50 - 10.18 birds per hour
- 1.00 - 2.50 birds per hour
- 0 - 1.00 birds per hour
- Presumed migrants or dispersers only
- Additional winter locations

season, with concentrations in the same areas. The highest numbers reported in winter were, with one exception, little greater than the maxima in the breeding season: 228 in Borrego Springs (F24) 20 December 1998 (R. Thériault et al.), 229 at Oak Grove (C16) 12 December 1998 (K. L. Weaver), and 395 east of Lake Hodges (K11) 2 January 2000 (C. G. Edwards). We found the Common Raven even more widely in the winter than in the breeding season, picking it up regularly in the three squares where we missed it then (up to 10 along the Silver Strand, T9, 28 February 1998, J. L. Coatsworth).

Conservation: The Common Raven is on the increase over much of its range, including California (Sauer et al. 2003). The increase includes San Diego County, though perhaps not uniformly. Christmas bird count results suggest roughly a doubling of the population from the early 1980s to the new millennium in the Anza–Borrego, Escondido, Rancho Santa Fe, and San Diego circles but no significant change in the Oceanside or Lake Henshaw

circles. Factors favoring ravens include road building and increased traffic, which lead to more carrion that ravens scavenge. Man-made structures offer many new nest sites. In Idaho, Common Ravens prefer electrical-line towers over natural sites (Steenhof et al. 1993). The distribution of these towers may account in part for the pattern of raven abundance in San Diego County.

The increase of ravens can have a negative effect on other birds. The Common Raven is a major predator of Least Tern colonies in San Diego County, leading to efforts at control and experiments in aversive conditioning.

Taxonomy: The Common Ravens of San Diego County, like those elsewhere in both Alta and Baja California, are of the small subspecies *C. c. clarionensis* Rothschild and Hartert, 1902 (Rea 1983, Rea in Phillips 1986). A genetic study revealed a high degree of differentiation between it and others in both mitochondrial DNA and nuclear microsatellites (Omland et al. 2000).

LARKS — FAMILY ALAUDIDAE

Horned Lark *Eremophila alpestris*

The coastal strand, arid grasslands, and sandy desert floors are home to the Horned Lark in San Diego County year round. The birds seek open ground, walking in search of seeds and insects. Plowed fields, bayfill, and land graded in preparation for building attract them—disturbance only enhances a habitat from the Horned Lark's point of view. But typically such disturbances precede landscaping and paving, which exclude the larks permanently. As a result, the Horned Lark is in retreat, to the extent that the coastal subspecies *E. a. actia* is now regarded as a bird of special concern by the California Department of Fish and Game.

Breeding distribution: The Horned Lark's patchy distribution in San Diego County reflects the fragmentation of its habitat. One of these habitats is the coastal strand, including salt flats around lagoons and fills in Mission and San Diego bays. Thus the larks share nesting sites—and threats—with the Least Tern and Snowy Plover. They are generally uncommon in this habitat, though counts range up to 30 around the southeast corner of Mission Bay (R8) 18 May 1998 (B. C. Moore) and 29 at Las Flores Creek mouth (E3) 14 March 1999 (R. and S. L. Breisch). The coastal mesas and inland valleys were once the center of Horned Lark abundance in San Diego County. Sometimes the birds are in areas that are sparsely vegetated naturally, but usually they are where some disturbance has thinned the vegetation or created openings. Grazing, the maintenance of firebreaks, and grading preceding development are common factors. The firebreaks tracing the ridgelines of Air Station Miramar are now a population center for the Horned Lark in the coastal lowland (40 in square O12 and 35 in N12 on 3 May 1998, I. S. Quon,

Photo by Anthony Mercieca

W. E. Haas). Grading can lead to large but temporary concentrations (50 along the north edge of Mira Mesa, N9, 6 May 1999, A. G. and D. Stanton).

Currently, Warner Valley is the Horned Lark's primary population center in San Diego County (175 around Lake Henshaw, G17, 18 June 2000, P. Unitt; 165 around Swan Lake, F18, 24 June 2000, C. G. Edwards). Substantial numbers also inhabit the upper basin of Lake Cuyamaca (M21; 20 on 16 June 1998, P. D. Jorgensen) and Santa Maria Valley (K14; 20 on 25 June 2000, G. and A. Kroon). Better access allowing more thorough surveys might reveal the population in the Santa Maria Valley (Ramona grasslands) to rival that of Warner Valley. Over large areas of central San Diego County unbroken chaparral and rugged topography exclude Horned Larks.

Yet another region that supports the Horned Lark is the Anza–Borrego Desert. Here the birds occur largely in dry lake beds and on sandy valley floors, occasionally in broad sandy washes. Numbers vary with rainfall. During the five-year atlas period the Horned Lark's numbers in the Anza–Borrego Desert were low in 1997, peaked in 1999, one year after El Niño rains, then declined sharply as drought set in. High counts for the desert during the breeding season were 52 in Blair Valley (L24) 3 April 1998 (R. Thériault), 70 near Font's Point (F27) 10 April 1999 (G. Rebstock, K. Forney), and 85 east of Peg Leg Road (F26) 31 March 1999 (D. C. Seals).

Nesting: Horned Larks nest on the ground, digging or selecting a small hollow so the nest is sunken slightly below ground level. Often a small plant, clump of grass, or rock shelters the nest on one side. The nesting season recorded by atlas observers was slightly broader than the 5 April–20 June attested by 35 collected egg sets from San Diego County but little different from the 20 March–23

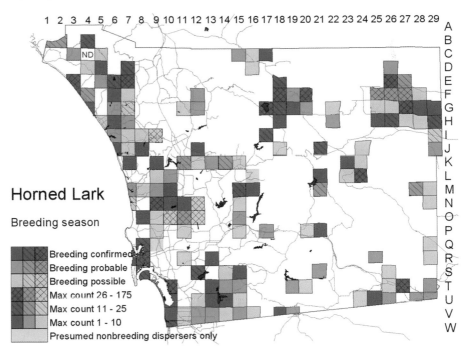

Horned Lark

Breeding season

- Breeding confirmed
- Breeding probable
- Breeding possible
- Max count 26 - 175
- Max count 11 - 25
- Max count 1 - 10
- Presumed nonbreeding dispersers only

June attested by 106 from all of California (Bent 1942). Rainfall stimulates the birds to nest; all the early activity we observed, implying laying in late March or the first week of April, followed the wet winter of 1997–98. An exceptionally late nest, its eggs laid no earlier than the last day or two of June, had three chicks on 19 July 2001 (south side of Tijuana River estuary, W10, R. T. Patton).

Migration: The Horned Lark appears to be largely nonmigratory in San Diego County, but during the nonbreeding season the birds gather into flocks. These flocks may remain together as late as 9 March (1999, 120 on the D Street fill in San Diego Bay, T10, R. T. Patton). Later, the flocks break up into pairs and the males establish territories. Specimens suggest some degree of population interchange between the desert and coastal slope (see Taxonomy).

Winter: The small differences between the breeding and winter distribution of the Horned Lark in San Diego County suggest only short-distance dispersal away from breeding sites. In winter, however, because of its flocking, the species appears appreciably more abundant. As in the breeding season, the largest numbers occur in Warner Valley, San Diego County's largest grassland (up to 800 around Lake Henshaw 29 December 1997, J. O. Zimmer). Sites of other large flocks included the upper basin of Lake Cuyamaca (L21; 300 on 27 January 2000, J. K. Wilson), Blair Valley (L24;

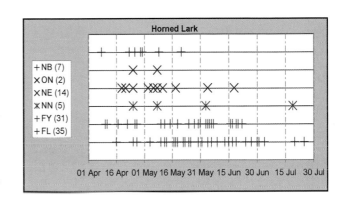

Horned Lark

+ NB (7)
× ON (2)
× NE (14)
✳ NN (5)
+ FY (31)
+ FL (35)

01 Apr 16 Apr 01 May 16 May 31 May 15 Jun 30 Jun 15 Jul 30 Jul

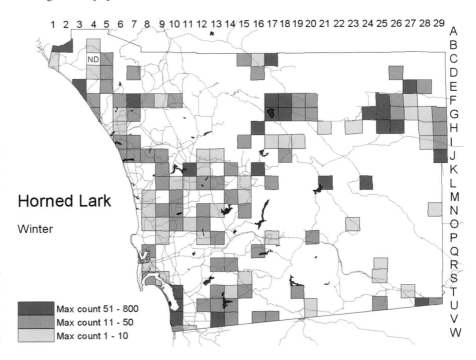

Horned Lark

Winter

- Max count 51 - 800
- Max count 11 - 50
- Max count 1 - 10

550 on 5 December 1998, R. Thériault), and Little Clark Dry Lake (E27; 370 on 7 December 2000, R. Thériault). Paralleling the pattern in the breeding season, winter numbers in the Anza–Borrego Desert peaked one year after the wet winter, in 1998–99. I noted Horned Larks twice in winter at Big Laguna Lake (O23), elevation 5400 feet (3 on 18 January 1998, 10 on 24 December 2001), where we did not find them during the breeding season.

Conservation: Nearly a century ago, C. S. Sharp (1907) called the Horned Lark the commonest bird at Escondido. Today, it persists only on that city's outskirts. Because the gentle topography the Horned Lark inhabits is easy to build on, cities have already spread over much of the terrain the bird once occupied in coastal southern California. The Horned Lark is subject to the increased risk of predation run by all ground-nesting birds as they are restricted to ever smaller patches of habitat. San Diego County atlas results suggest the Horned Lark is sensitive to habitat fragmentation, even though it retains the capability to colonize new sites. Previous studies of the effects of habitat fragmentation in San Diego, focusing on birds of sage scrub, have neglected grassland and open-country species, even though these species' sensitivity to fragmentation appears even greater. If judged simply by the number of atlas squares in metropolitan San Diego from which the species is lacking, the Horned Lark's sensitivity to fragmentation is similar to that of the Greater Roadrunner and Western Meadowlark and higher than that of the Rufous-crowned Sparrow.

Taxonomy: *Eremophila a. actia* (Oberholser, 1902) occupies the coastal slope of San Diego County, extending east to Montezuma Valley (Ranchita), Mason Valley, and Jacumba, the last being the subspecies' type locality. *E. a. actia* has the back streaked with dark on a medium warm brown background, an essentially unstreaked breast, and a cinnamon nape in the male. A few specimens from the coastal strip look like intergrades with *insularis* (Townsend, 1890) of the Channel Islands, which is distinguished by its darker upperparts and dusky streaking on the underparts.

Of six specimens picked up (poisoned by pesticide?) in the Tijuana River valley 15 October 1978, four appear intermediate between *actia* and *insularis*, and one is typical of *insularis* (SDNHM 41285). Behle (1942) reported four August specimens from Imperial Beach (V10) and one from San Diego as *insularis* also. Presumably the frequent fog and overcast along the coast are responsible for dark variants being selected for in this area.

Eremophila a. leucansiptila (Oberholser, 1902) has the back feathers edged with pinkish-buff, paler than in *actia*. In the male, the nape is tinted with a delicate vinaceous color. This subspecies inhabits the Colorado Desert and extends west to the lower elevations of the Anza–Borrego Desert, as attested by a specimen from "below Borrego Springs" 29 April 1896 (SDNHM 670). Occasionally it wanders into the range of *actia* and the two may interbreed, as Behle (1942) reported at Pamo Valley (H15/I15). Behle (1942), also reported two specimens of *leucansiptila* collected at Jacumba (U28) 17 March 1921, and Frank Stephens collected two there 10 January 1918 (SDNHM 2021, 2022). Apparently, however, the biogeographically simple distributions of the two subspecies are now being disrupted. Twenty-six specimens from the Imperial Valley collected since 1985 are highly variable, but most are darker than specimens from the same area taken early in the 20th century (Patten et al. 2003). Presumably irrigation and cultivation darkened the valley's general background color to the point where the paleness of *leucansiptila* was no longer adaptive. With the Anza–Borrego Desert intervening between the range of *actia* and the Imperial Valley, and birds shifting between cultivated areas and natural desert, a similar change could be affecting eastern San Diego County.

A few San Diego County specimens match *E. a. ammophila* (Oberholser, 1902), intermediate between *actia* and *leucansiptila*. Some of these may be migrants from the Mojave Desert, the breeding range of *ammophila*, but more likely they are variants of *actia* or intergrades *actia* × *leucansiptila*. The validity of the distinction between *actia* and *ammophila* needs to be reevaluated.

Swallows — Family Hirundinidae

Purple Martin *Progne subis*

A rare and declining summer visitor now restricted almost entirely to the mountains, in California the Purple Martin struggles for survival. Its preferred nest site is specialized: holes in prominent isolated dead trees. It is loosely colonial, several pairs sometimes nesting in a single cavity-ridden snag, but in the Southwest it has failed to make the shift to the multicompartment birdhouses that now are its mainstay in the eastern U.S. In our area the European Starling, a more aggressive secondary-cavity nester, has now taken over most of the martin's nest sites. Even as a migrant the Purple Martin is now very rare here.

Photo by Anthony Mercieca

Breeding distribution: The Purple Martin now nests only on and around San Diego County's higher mountain ranges, and the birds are few and scattered. On Palomar, they occur not only at the higher elevations but at a few places around the base as well: along Magee Rd. (C11; up to six, with one or two pairs nesting annually in holes in a power pole, J. M. and B. Hargrove), Cutca Trail in Long Canyon (C14/15; one on 16 May 1999; J. M. and B. Hargrove), and near Rincon Junction (F13; four, including at least one pair, 12 June 1999, E. Wallace). Purple Martins are also widely but thinly distributed through the Volcan, Cuyamaca, and Laguna mountains. In this area, they may nest downslope as far as Santa

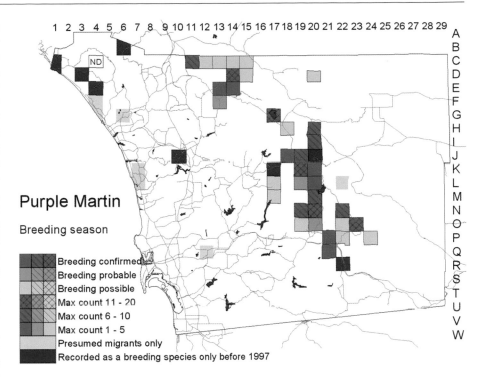

Purple Martin

Breeding season

- Breeding confirmed
- Breeding probable
- Breeding possible
- Max count 11 - 20
- Max count 6 - 10
- Max count 1 - 5
- Presumed migrants only
- Recorded as a breeding species only before 1997

Ysabel (J18; five, including fledgling, 17 July 2001, J. R. Barth), possibly down into the gorge of the San Diego River above El Capitan Reservoir (L17, two on 14 June 1997; M17, one the same day, R. C. Sanger). The only site south of Interstate 8 is in Rancho Corte Madera near Long Valley Peak (Q21; four, including at least one occupied nest, 20 June 1998, M. U. Evans). Around Hot Springs Mountain, the county's highest peak, the only record is of a single female circulating among snags at the Lost Valley Boy Scout camp (D20) 25 June 1998 (P. Unitt). At least in 1998, there must have been a colony near Lake Henshaw (G17); the site was not located, but up to 20 birds, including adults feeding fledglings, were there from 17 to 19 July (C. G. Edwards, K. L. Weaver).

Colony sites shift with the availability of suitable snags and, undoubtedly, the intensity of competition for them with other hole-nesting birds. Over the years, Cuyamaca Peak has been the most consistent site. From 1997 to 2001, numbers here ranged up to 20 on 18 April 1998 (N20; possibly including some migrants on this date, E. Siegel), 10 (including fledglings) 14 July 2001 (M20; J. R. Barth), and 8 on 14 June 2000 (M20; P. D. Jorgensen). The only other areas with likely more than two pairs were near Lake Henshaw, Pine Hills (K19; 18 on 26 June 2001, M.

B. Stowe), Mt. Laguna (O23; up to 16 on 13 and 14 June 1999, C. G. Edwards), and Volcan Mt. (H20/I20; up to eight, including apparent juveniles, 16 July 2000, A. P. and T. E. Keenan). The total San Diego County population during the atlas period was probably about 100 pairs.

Nesting: The Purple Martin is a secondary-cavity nester, in southern California usually selecting tall isolated trees, dead or partly dead, for its nest hole. The trees are typically on the upper third of a slope, in open woodland of under 20% canopy cover (Williams 2002). The cavities may be natural, the result of decay following a fire or lightning strike, or excavated by woodpeckers. The only artificial sites reported by our atlas observers were those along Magee Rd. and in a telephone pole in Sherilton Valley (N19; G. and R. Wynn). Only once has use of a birdhouse been reported in San Diego County, by three or four pairs at Palomar Mt. in June 1985 (J. Robinson, AB 39:963, 1985).

Observations in the mountains of nest building (the birds carry material into their cavities) on 22 April and feeding young on 28 May suggest the martin may lay there as early as the first half of May. At low elevations nesting starts even earlier, though by 2000 there may have been only a single pair left to exemplify this. In 1905 and 1906, respectively, at San Onofre (C1) Dixon (1906) found a nearly completed nest in a sycamore on 27 March and the birds selecting nest sites on 31 March. Our latest record of young in the nest, on 28 July, agrees with eggs laid in mid June; collected egg sets (WFVZ) are dated 3, 18, and 22 June.

Migration: Currently, the Purple Martin usually returns to southern California in April. From then through mid May migrants are rarely seen far from nesting sites. The earliest date recorded by our atlas observers, 22 March 1998 (one along Magee Rd., J. M. and B. Hargrove),

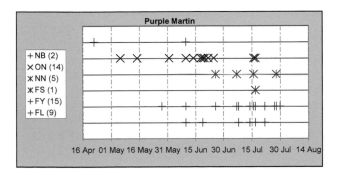

Purple Martin

+NB (2)
×ON (14)
*NN (5)
*FS (1)
+FY (15)
+FL (9)

16 Apr 01 May 16 May 31 May 15 Jun 30 Jun 15 Jul 30 Jul 14 Aug

matched the earliest reported previously (Unitt 1984) and, notably, was from the lowest elevation where the birds are currently known to nest. The latest in spring the Purple Martin was noted away from nesting habitat from 1997 to 2002 was 25 May (2000, one in Oriflamme Canyon, L22, J. R. Barth), but past records of stragglers extend to 6 June. Locally breeding birds may remain to 15 August (1999, seven in Sherilton Valley, G. and R. Wynn). Fall migrants from the north pass through mainly in September, and there is still only one record for October.

Conservation: The Purple Martin has long been in decline in southern California (Garrett and Dunn 1981). Our atlas effort revealed several new sites for one or two pairs but no large colonies. The martin's decrease on Palomar Mountain is particularly alarming. As recently as 1983 Roger Higson reported 45 pairs nesting there (AB 37:1028, 1983), with a colony in a snag just north of the observatory. That site is now deserted, and the largest one-day count on Palomar 1997–2001 was of a single family. In 2002, though, larger numbers returned to Lower French Valley (D14), where Paul Jorgensen saw 20 on 31 May, entering at least four cavities in three tall Jeffrey pines, and local resident Tony Jaramillo reported 60. The former low-elevation population in northwestern San Diego County, never large, known mainly from Dixon (1906) and Alice Fries' observations from 1967 to 1978, was last reported in the latter year.

The central factor in the Purple Martin's decline is generally acknowledged to be competition for nest sites with the European Starling. Williams (2002) reviewed the species' California distribution and found that it survives only where starlings are rare or absent. Willett (1933) reported the birds' beginning to nest in crevices in buildings in the Los Angeles basin, but this adaptation failed to reach San Diego before the starlings arrived in the early 1960s, and now has disappeared throughout southern California. Unfortunately, the martins' predilection for nest trees with some open country surrounding them usually means the trees are in the middle of good foraging habitat for the ground-feeding starling. Any effort to encourage the martin to recover will have to entail aggressive starling control, accompanied by habitat enhancement that builds on what little remains. The species' social system implies that its apparent coloniality is a by-product of the scarcity of suitable nest sites, not of innate gregariousness (Brown 1997). Therefore, the population could be rebuilt through the production of isolated pairs; the loss of larger colonies is not the irreversible calamity it would be with more social birds like the Tricolored Blackbird and Least Tern. The martins' beginning to use nest boxes in the Pacific Northwest (Brown 1997) implies that enhancement in southern California could begin with the providing of nest boxes in or near existing nest trees, followed by monitoring and elimination of any starlings. Such boxes need not be the elaborate apartment houses now traditional in the eastern U.S., just a few simple wooden boxes installed in trees or snags that meet the martins' criteria and as remote as possible from foraging starlings. Williams' (2002) study in the Tehachapi Mountains suggests this distance should be at least 1 km from residential development, which favors starlings. Unfortunately, these criteria mean rugged terrain where the installation and monitoring of the boxes will be difficult.

Taxonomy: In their medium size and dusky-throated females, the Purple Martins of southern California are consistent enough with *P. s. subis* (Linnaeus, 1758) of the eastern U.S. to be called the same subspecies (Grinnell 1928a, Unitt 1984).

Tree Swallow *Tachycineta bicolor*

The Tree Swallow is primarily a migrant through San Diego County, seen by the hundreds especially in early spring. In winter it is our most common swallow but still localized and only irregularly numerous then. San Diego County lies at the southern tip of the Tree Swallow's breeding range. Until 1980 it was rare here as a breeding species but since then it has increased, colonizing holes in snags around lakes and in riparian woodland.

Breeding distribution: As might be expected at the edge of a range, as a breeding bird in San Diego County the Tree Swallow is only locally common. It is most widespread in the lower valleys of the Santa Margarita and San Luis Rey rivers in northwestern San Diego County, more local farther south and east. Many nesting sites are at or near lakes, and most of the remainder are in riparian woodland. Breeding Tree Swallows are rare in the mountains, where we have only five records, none of more than two individuals. Nesting is confirmed south to the east end of Lower Otay Lake (U14), with a pair occupying a nest hole 20 May 2001 (O. Osborn), and likely in

Photo by Anthony Mercieca

Marron Valley (V17), with two on 16 May and 12 June 2000 (P. Beck). Thus, even though the Tree Swallow is still unknown as a breeding species in Mexico, its spreading there now seems likely.

The species is not colonial, but the population is nevertheless clumped. The largest concentrations of breeding birds reported 1997–2001 were at Barrett Lake (S19, up to 60 on 18 June 2000, R. and S. L. Breisch), Sutherland

Reservoir (J16, up to 40 on 26 May and 22 June 1998, B. Travis), Lower Otay Lake (U14, up to 30 on 4 July 1999, S. Buchanan), Guajome Lake (G7, up to 30 on 11 May 1999, S. Grain), and Santee Lakes (P12, up to 28 on 5 May 1997, E. Post).

Nesting: Tree Swallows nest in tree cavities, usually old woodpecker holes. Drowned trees in reservoirs are especially attractive, though the birds nest also in snags at the edge of small openings in the middle of riparian woodland. At Whalen (G6) and Guajome lakes Tree Swallows used cavities in the flowering stalk of agaves (J. Smith, S. Grain). At Wynola (J19) one used a nest box (A. Mercieca), a common site elsewhere in the Tree Swallow's range.

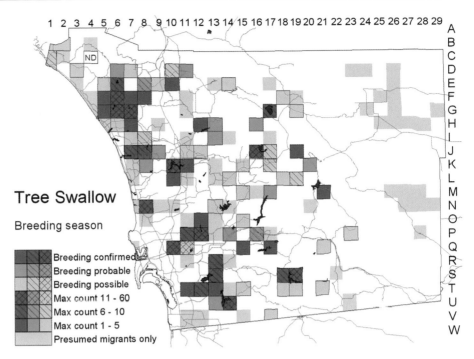

Tree Swallow
Breeding season

Because of the dearth of collected eggs of the Tree Swallow, our atlas data add considerably to knowledge of the species' nesting in San Diego County. Tree Swallows claim nest holes as soon as they return in the spring, leading to reports of "occupied nests" as early as 14 February, before actual nesting begins. Fledglings as early as 29 April (2001, Barrett Lake, S18, R. and S. L. Breisch) imply that the adults may lay as early as late March, much earlier than the 18–28 May of three egg sets collected in the early 20th century. Similarly, fledglings along the lower San Luis Rey River (G5) 1 August 1999 (R. E. Fischer) must have come from eggs laid in late June and imply that Tree Swallows could easily raise two successive broods in San Diego County. Over most of the species' range, second broods are rare (Robertson et al. 1992).

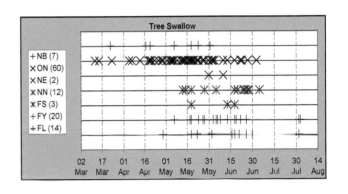

Migration: Spring return of the Tree Swallow is usually in the first week of February, occasionally the last week of January (one flying northwest at Ocotillo Wells, I28, 25 January 2001, J. R. Barth). Thus the Tree Swallow is one of our earliest spring migrants. The birds quickly become common, reaching peak abundance in March. By the end of April they are rare away from breeding locations, and two northeast of Borrego Springs (F25) 7 May 1998 (P. D. Ache) were the latest that were clearly migrants. A few birds in unsuitable habitat on the coastal slope through May and June may have been

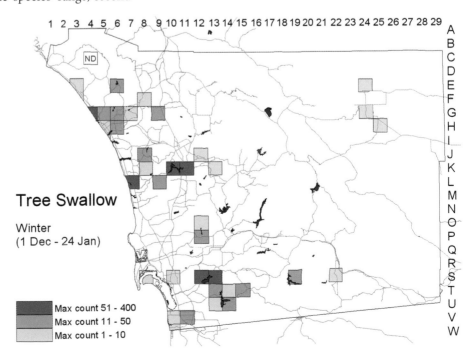

Tree Swallow
Winter
(1 Dec - 24 Jan)

Max count 51 - 400
Max count 11 - 50
Max count 1 - 10

unable to find nest sites. One at Agua Caliente County Park (M26) 4 June 1998 (E. C. Hall) made the only such record for the Anza–Borrego Desert.

Fall migration begins by 13 July (1999, one in the Tijuana R. valley, W11, P. Unitt), possibly as early as 3 July (1999, 30 at Turner Lake—a nesting location?—G11, S. L. and S. J. Farrow), but is often not noticeable until August. In fall, migrating Tree Swallows are less numerous than in spring, and the main migration route at that season is apparently more across the Salton Sea than along the coast (cf. Patten et al. 2003).

Winter: The Tree is by far the most numerous swallow in southern California in winter, but its distribution then is still quite patchy. The birds occur usually around lakes, lagoons, and ponds at low elevations. In San Diego County, winter records are concentrated in the lower Santa Margarita and San Luis Rey valleys, along Escondido Creek from San Elijo Lagoon to Lake Hodges, Sweetwater Reservoir, at Santee Lakes, Lower Otay Lake, and the Tijuana River valley, especially in the first three areas: up to 100 at the Santa Margarita River mouth (G4) 22 January 1999 and 15 January 2001 (P. A. Ginsburg), 177 at Lake Hodges (K10) 23 December 2001 (R. L. Barber), 500 at Sweetwater Reservoir (S12/13) 22 December 1998 (P. Famolaro). Nevertheless, the Tree Swallow is irregular

even at these spots of concentration. Above 1000 feet elevation, atlas observers encountered the species only twice, at Barrett Lake (S19; 50 on 26 December 1999, R. and S. L. Breisch) and at the upper end of Lake Morena (S22; five on 20 December 1998; R. and S. L. Breisch). Over 21 years of Lake Henshaw Christmas bird counts, the Tree Swallow was recorded only twice, with no more than three individuals. In the Borrego Valley the Tree Swallow is rare. Two of the four records between 1997 and 2002 were on 23 January so possibly of very early spring migrants; the others are of one on 19 December 1999 (E24, P. R. Pryde) and three on 16 January 2000 (G24, P. D. Jorgensen). There is only one earlier record of a single Tree Swallow on an Anza–Borrego Christmas bird count.

Conservation: As a breeding species, the Tree Swallow increased dramatically in San Diego County over the last two decades of the 20th century. Before 1980, it bred here only "very rarely and sporadically" (Unitt 1984). Because many of the new sites are around reservoirs, it seems reasonable to infer that the building of these reservoirs, which drowned trees, allowed the Tree Swallow to spread its breeding range south. Yet there must be other factors too—most of the reservoirs were there decades before the spread began.

Violet-green Swallow *Tachycineta thalassina*

The Violet-green is the characteristic, common swallow of San Diego County's mountains, easily seen cruising over meadows and nesting in cavities in nearby oaks or conifers. It has converged on the White-throated Swift's ecology by nesting also in rock crevices in cliffs. It is common as a spring migrant throughout the county, and as a fall migrant in the mountains. In winter the Violet-green Swallow is irregular, usually rare, and strangely localized in northern coastal San Diego County.

Breeding distribution: The Violet-green Swallow is common and widespread in woodland in the mountains. It has the honor of being the bird nesting at the highest altitude in San Diego County—on 8 June 2001 in a cavity in the fire-lookout tower atop the summit of Hot Springs Mountain, at 6533 feet the county's highest peak (E20; K. L. Weaver). Numbers in the mountains range up to 200 in a day, as near Stonewall Mine (M20) 26 May 1998, when the birds were discouraged from foraging on a cold foggy morning (B. C. Moore). In the foothills, outside the zone of coniferous and oak woodlands, the Violet-green Swallow is uncommon and local. Our atlas effort revealed several scattered outlying populations toward the coast: San Onofre Mt. area (D2, E3, E4), San Marcos and Merriam Mts. (G8, G9), hills south of San Marcos (J8, I9, J9), Mission Gorge (P11, Q11), Otay Mt. (U15, V14, V15), and Tecate Mt. (V17, V18). On Otay and Tecate mountains numbers as large as 30 in a day have been reported (V15, 25 May 1999, D. Seals; V17, 28

Photo by Anthony Mercieca

May 2001, A. P. and T. E. Keenan). At the more northern outlying sites the count per day is seldom more than two, maximum only six. In the Anza–Borrego Desert, the Violet-green Swallow summers along the ridge of the Santa Rosa Mts. (C27, D27, D28), with up to 20 around benchmark Rosa (D28) 2 May 2000 (L. J. Hargrove). Though at 3000–4000 feet the elevation zone is occupied by Violet-green Swallows elsewhere, in southeastern San Diego County east of Cottonwood Valley (R22) and Lake Morena (T21) there is only one record in the breeding season, of a single individual at Tule Lake (T27) 3 July 2000 (J. K. Wilson).

Nesting: Abandoned woodpecker holes and natural cavities in trees are the Violet-green Swallow's most common nest site, especially in semiopen woodland. Because of the difficulty of approaching them closely, nests in cliff crevices are probably far more common than the three our observers noted. Most of the nests at lower elevations are probably in cliffs, undoubtedly so in places like Otay and Tecate mountains that lack large trees and woodpeckers. Cliffs offer more sites in the Santa Rosa Mts. than do the small, sparse pinyons.

Atlas data suggest the Violet-green Swallow often lays its clutch earlier than the 28 May–22 June range of the seven egg sets collected 1915–31. A pair evidently feeding young 12 April 1997 suggests eggs laid as early as late March, though this was at the comparatively low elevation of Fernbrook (M14; J. Savary). Many reports from higher elevations imply that laying is regular by mid to late April. Adults removing a fecal sac from a nest hole 29 July 2000 (O23; J. R. Barth) and a fledgling 5 August 2000 (C8; K. L. Weaver) imply laying as late as about 1 July.

Migration: In spring, Violet-green Swallows arrive in early February, always by 5–10 February, occasionally by 1 February (1998, two at Lake Morena, T21, R. and S. L. Breisch). Two in south Ramona (L14) 23 January 2000 (G. Moreland), farther inland than other winter records, may have been exceptionally early migrants. Spring migration peaks in March and continues to mid May, rarely as late as 24 May (1999, four near Yaqui Well, I24, P. Nelson). King et al. (1987) reported two early June sightings at San Elijo Lagoon (L7).

In fall, migration begins by 19 July (1999, one at O'Neill Lake, E6, P. A. Ginsburg), peaks in August and September, and trails off through October to early November. Fall migration is mainly through the mountains and seldom conspicuous unless unseasonal stormy weather compels the birds to fly low.

Winter: At this season, the Violet-green Swallow is still regular only in the lower San Luis Rey River valley, around Whelan and Windmill Lakes (G6), as I reported in 1984. The maximum reported from 1997 through 2002, 20 on 20 January 2000 (J. Smith), is less than the high counts in some past years (maximum on Oceanside Christmas bird count 60 on 31 December 1977). A new wintering site, though, may be emerging at San Elijo Lagoon, with records in three of the five years of the atlas period and up to 20 birds 28 December 2000 (A. Mauro). King et al. (1987) found no wintering Violet-greens at

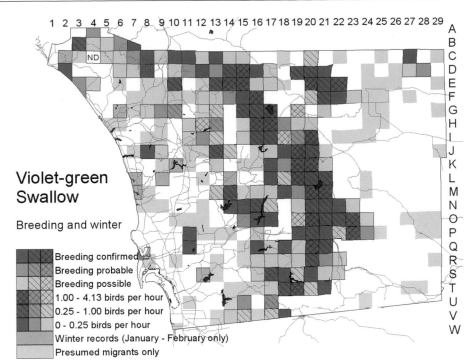

Violet-green Swallow

Breeding and winter

Breeding confirmed
Breeding probable
Breeding possible
1.00 - 4.13 birds per hour
0.25 - 1.00 birds per hour
0 - 0.25 birds per hour
Winter records (January - February only)
Presumed migrants only

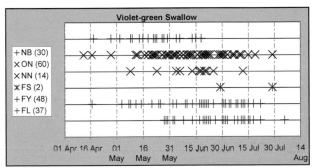

the lagoon from 1973 through 1983, but the species has been noted on 15 of 21 Rancho Santa Fe Christmas bird counts, 1980–2001. There were only single atlas records at other winter locations, but at Sweetwater Reservoir (S12) P. Famolaro noted 25 individuals 13 December 1999.

Conservation: The Violet-green is our only swallow not obviously affected by environmental change. Its core habitat of montane woodland is little disturbed. The birds' use of nest boxes and exotic trees is known but still rare. Evidently the Violet-green can use cavities too small to accommodate starlings. The breeding distribution we recorded from 1997 through 2001 is considerably more extensive than that previously described, but the difference may be due only to more thorough exploration of regions once poorly known.

Taxonomy: Phillips (1986) found too much overlap in both size and color to uphold a distinction between *T. t. thalassina* (Swainson, 1827), of the mountains of mainland Mexico, and *T. t. lepida* Mearns, 1894 (type locality Laguna Mountains), from farther north. Eliminating *lepida* leaves the smaller Baja California form *brachyptera* Brewster, 1902, as the only other subspecies of the Violet-green Swallow.

Northern Rough-winged Swallow
Stelgidopteryx serripennis

As the fan palm to the Hooded Oriole, so the box-frame bridge to the Northern Rough-winged Swallow—an accoutrement of southern California civilization opens a door of opportunity to a bird preadapted to capitalize on it. Armed only with the flexibility it shares with many species programmed to nest in cavities, the Rough-winged Swallow has maintained its status as a common summer resident. It is even more common in migration but rare in winter.

Breeding distribution: The Northern Rough-winged Swallow is widespread in San Diego County's coastal lowland, becoming scarcer and patchier at higher elevations. It is absent as a breeding bird from Point Loma and Coronado. A few pairs nest as high in the mountains as about 4000 feet, as at Pine Hills (K19; nest building 5 May 2001, S. E. Smith) and near Green Valley Falls Campground (N20; nest building 23 May 1999, B. Siegel). In the Anza–Borrego Desert, the Rough-winged is widespread as a migrant but rare as a breeding species. Occasional pairs evidently nest in the eroded bluffs of the Borrego and Carrizo badlands: one pair at Font's Point (F27) 27–28 May 2000 (G. Rebstock), another pair copulating in Arroyo Seco del Diablo (O28) 8 May 1999 (R. and S. L. Breisch). The species is regular in small numbers around Carrizo Marsh (O29), with up to 15 on 6 May 1998 (P. D. Jorgensen). Though the Rough-wing nests commonly in the Imperial Valley, and man-made structures are now its primary nest sites on the coastal slope, the only place in the Anza–Borrego Desert where the birds have been seen near buildings in the breeding season is around the Casa del Zorro (H25; two on 23 May 1998, H. L. Young).

Photo by Anthony Mercieca

The Rough-winged Swallow is not colonial, so large numbers are usually of migrants rather than of breeding birds. But if suitable nest sites are clumped—as with several drain holes under a single bridge—multiple pairs often nest in amity. From 1997 to 2001, the largest numbers were reported consistently from lower Los Peñasquitos Canyon (N8), up to 150 on 2 May 1999 (P. A. Ginsburg). Such large concentrations during the breeding season may be of birds unable to find suitable nest sites—the availability of sites may limit the population (DeJong 1996).

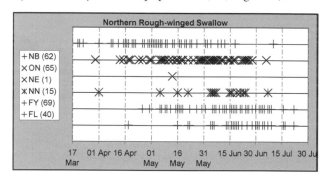

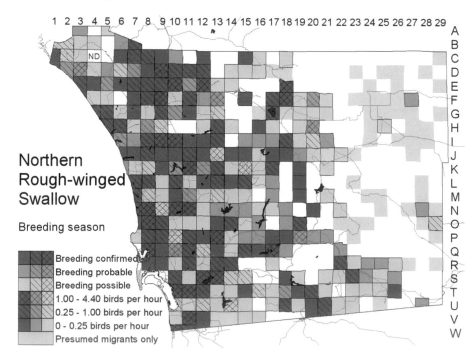

Northern Rough-winged Swallow

Breeding season

- Breeding confirmed
- Breeding probable
- Breeding possible
- 1.00 - 4.40 birds per hour
- 0.25 - 1.00 birds per hour
- 0 - 0.25 birds per hour
- Presumed migrants only

Nesting: Burrows in banks and bluffs were the Rough-winged Swallow's primitive nest site. The literature is inconsistent on the question of whether the birds dig the burrows themselves, as does the Bank Swallow. None of our atlas observers reported the species excavating. Clearly, the birds spare themselves the work of digging whenever possible, preferring existing burrows or artificial structures that mimic them. Of the 32 nest sites our observers described, seven were in banks, bluffs, or cliffs, three were in road cuts, three were in buildings, one was in a pipe in a water tank, and 18 were in drain holes under bridges. I investigated one reachable nest hole in the

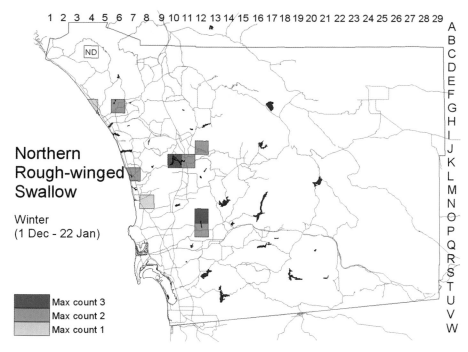

Northern Rough-winged Swallow

Winter
(1 Dec – 22 Jan)

Max count 3
Max count 2
Max count 1

Canyon (F23) between 2 and 5 July 1998 (L. J. Hargrove) and one at Big Laguna Lake (O23) 7 July 2001 (J. R. Barth) were remote from nesting locations. Numbers of fall migrants build to August then decline through September, until by mid October the species is very rare.

Winter: In December and early January the Rough-winged Swallow is rare but annual around lagoons, lakes, and ponds in the coastal lowland, with one to four records each year 1997–2002. The highest winter counts during the atlas period were of three individuals (Lake Hodges, K10, 22 December 2000, R. L Barber; upper Santee Lakes, O12, 5 January 2001, I. S. Quon). The only earlier records of larger numbers are of nine near Oceanside 16 December 1983 (R. E. Webster, AB 38:358, 1984) and at least six at Santee Lakes in winter 1992–93 (C. G. Edwards, AB 47:301, 1993).

Hollister St. bridge over the 1993 channel of the Tijuana River (W11) and found that the nest was right at the lip of the hole—therefore far closer to the entrance than the mean 82.4 cm Hill (1988) reported for 44 nests in pipes.

Our observations imply that egg laying by Rough-winged Swallows is concentrated from mid April to early June, encompassing the range 1–23 May of eight egg sets collected 1911–39. Reports of a nest with nestlings at Fallbrook (D8) 1 April 1998 (M. Freda) and fledglings along the Sweetwater River at Interstate 805 (T11) 18 April 1999 (W. E. Haas) suggest that a few birds lay as early as mid March. Rough-winged Swallows raise only one brood per year (DeJong 1996).

Migration: The Northern Rough-winged Swallow is one of southern California's earliest spring migrants. Even those seen in late December and early January may be returnees, as records in late October and November are so few. From 1997 to 2002 the earliest clear spring migrants were 12 north of Lake Morena (S21) 23 January 1999 (S. E. Smith). Scattered individuals at low elevations in late January and early February could have been wintering. The birds arrive by mid February every year, and by the last week of February they are common. Records from the Anza–Borrego Desert imply that spring migration continues regularly through the first week of May, possibly as late as 15 May (1999, two northwest of Clark Dry Lake, D25, K. J. Winter). Like that of spring migrants, the return of fall migrants is also early, in early July. Three in Borrego Palm

Conservation: Much of the Northern Rough-winged Swallow's original nesting habitat has been eliminated with the conversion of wild meandering streams, with their eroding banks, into channels lined with riprap and concrete. But the species' adaptability to man-made nest sites has probably more than compensated. Quarries, road cuts, and borrow pits are substitute habitat. The birds are opportunistic, quickly investigating new excavations—as I saw out the windows of the San Diego Natural History Museum when the pit dug for the building's expansion stood idle for weeks. Above all, the building of bridges composed of box-frame girders of concrete, with their drain holes beneath, has created thousands of new nest sites. Though European Starlings also use these holes, apparently they do not prefer them, perhaps because of their vertical orientation, and leave many to the more agile Rough-winged. In winter the Rough-winged appears to be increasing gradually: eight records before 1982 (Unitt 1984) versus 12 from 1997 to 2002.

Taxonomy: The paler, more southern subspecies *S. s. psammochroa* breeds locally, while the darker, more northern *S. s. serripennis* passes through in migration (specimen collected 3 miles west of Santee, P11, 1 May 1921, SDNHM 32101).

Bank Swallow *Riparia riparia*

The Bank Swallow has long been extirpated from the site of its single known colony in San Diego County, and now it is rare even as a migrant. Its specialized nesting habits confine it to vertical sandy riverbanks, cut by erosion, or, as in San Diego County,

bluffs overlooking the beach. The birds dig their own burrows, forming colonies. Unfortunately, in its dependence on a naturally unstable and shifting habitat, the Bank Swallow is losing out to the work of flood-control engineers and society's demand for a static, tamed environment.

Breeding distribution: Long ago, the Bank Swallow nested in coastal bluffs at Las Flores (E3), then the southernmost nesting colony known in North America. Nelson K. Carpenter collected 11 egg sets there on 13 May 1917, eight on 2 May 1919 (WFVZ). Another set taken "north of Oceanside" on 9 May 1925 (SBCM) is the last record of the colony.

Nesting: Carpenter (1918) described the colony at Las Flores as consisting of hundreds of tunnels (many abandoned) in a bed of sandstone sandwiched between layers of cobbles and clay. The bluff in which they were dug rose 25 to 100 feet above the narrow beach.

Migration: Even as a fall migrant the Bank Swallow is now very rare in San Diego County. In spring, when the species is still less frequent than in fall, we had only two records from 1997 through 2002, of one with other migrating swallows at a pond on Otay Mesa (V13) on 15 April 2000 (P. Unitt, S. D. Cameron), the other of one at sewage ponds near the Santa Margarita River mouth (G5) on 14 April 2002 (P. A. Ginsburg).

Winter: The Bank Swallow is casual at this season, with only three records, of one in the Otay River valley (V11) 21–22 December 1968 (AFN 23:522:1969), one at Old Mission Dam (P11) 26 January 1976 (AB 30:768, 1976), and up to four near Oceanside (H5) 27 December 1986–8 February 1987 (AB 41:331, 1987).

Conservation: With the wholesale channelizing of California's rivers, eliminating most of the eroding banks

Photo by Anthony Mercieca

the Bank Swallow needs for colony sites, the population collapsed and the range retracted north. Even colonies in unaltered habitat, like the coastal bluffs at Las Flores, were abandoned. The last reported nesting anywhere in southern California was in 1976 (Garrett and Dunn 1981). The decline continues with elimination of habitat for thousands along the Sacramento River (Garrison et al. 1987, Small 1994). The decline of the breeding population is reflected in the dwindling numbers seen of migrants, once "rather common" (Stephens 1919a). Like so many colonial birds, the Bank Swallow is more vulnerable than species that breed as dispersed pairs.

Taxonomy: The only subspecies of the Bank Swallow in North America, as across northern Eurasia, is *R. r. riparia* (Linnaeus, 1758).

Cliff Swallow *Petrochelidon pyrrhonota*

Bottles made of mud pellets and stuck to bridges and buildings, Cliff Swallow nests are perhaps more easily found and identified than those of any San Diego County bird. Living overwhelmingly around these man-made environments, usually in colonies, Cliff Swallows are familiar to San Diegans—sometimes too familiar, when the colonies are over doors, walkways, and patios. The species is still a common summer resident, locally abundant around some lakes and lagoons, but creeping signs of decline suggest that the Cliff Swallow's bargain with humanity carries a price.

Breeding distribution: The Cliff Swallow is widespread though the coastal lowland, with colonies known from the great majority of atlas squares in the western half of the county. Along the coast, the only exception is Point Loma (S7), where the species is a rare migrant or non-breeding visitor only. The largest colonies are on bridges over the lagoons, such as Buena Vista (H6, 1100 on 11 May 1999, M. Freda), Agua Hedionda (I6, 425 on 11 May 1999, W. E. Haas), and San Dieguito (M7, 400 on 31 May 1998, D. R. Grine). Farther inland, the reservoirs are home to substantial colonies, but the swallows also nest on buildings far from lakes, sometimes in large numbers. The species becomes more scattered at higher elevations

Photo by Anthony Mercieca

and farther inland, but Cliff Swallow colonies trace the route of Interstate 8 as far east as Jacumba (U28). There are few colonies above 4000 feet elevation, but the highest site is at 6140 feet on the fire lookout tower atop High Point, Palomar Mt. (D15, up to nine on 1 July 1999, K. L. Weaver).

The Cliff Swallow's breeding range barely extends onto the desert slope at Tule Lake (T27) and where Carrizo Creek crosses under Interstate 8 (T28). In the Anza–Borrego Desert, the species is only a migrant or nonbreeding visitor, with one interesting exception. On 25 June 1998, on a rock overhang near a *tinaja* where big-

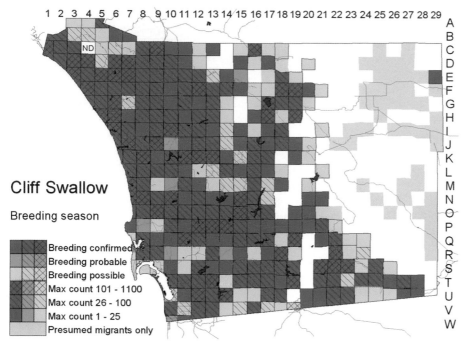

Cliff Swallow

Breeding season

- Breeding confirmed
- Breeding probable
- Breeding possible
- Max count 101 - 1100
- Max count 26 - 100
- Max count 1 - 25
- Presumed migrants only

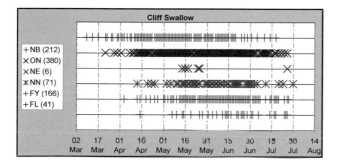

may investigate and enter old nests, accounting for a report of an occupied nest as early as 17 February (P. A. Ginsburg). Checking old nests for parasites helps the swallows decide whether to build a new nest or refurbish an old one (Brown and Brown 1995). Atlas data imply that Cliff Swallows lay as early as the first week of April; otherwise they are consistent with the 29 April–3 July range of 51 egg sets collected 1896–1935.

Migration: In spring, the Cliff Swallow typically arrives from mid February to early March— well before the birds' fabled return to San Juan Capistrano on St. Joseph's day, 19 March. The earliest arrival recorded 1997–2002, at Fallbrook (D7) 7 February 2001 (K. L.Weaver), differs little from the earliest arrivals recorded in the past, in the first week of February (Unitt 1984). Most Cliff Swallows pass through in March and April, with only a few stragglers noted far from breeding colonies by the first week of May. Three in the northeastern Borrego Valley (E25) 13 May 2000 (P. D. Ache) were apparently our latest spring migrants. Five at Ocotillo Wells (I29) 27 May 2000 (R. Miller) and one in Bow Willow Wash (O28) 7 June 2001 (P. D. Jorgensen) may have been ranging from colonies in the Imperial Valley, while one in San Felipe Valley (I21) 16 June 2000 (J. O. Zimmer) may have been ranging from those in the Lake Henshaw region.

After nesting, Cliff Swallows desert their colonies in August, but fall migrants show up in large numbers in mid July, sometimes in early July (86 at Sentenac Ciénaga, J23, 7 July 1999, R. Thériault). Their numbers drop rapidly in early September, and records from late September through October are few.

Winter: Only three records ever: San Diego Christmas bird count, six on 23 December 1967 (AFN 22:394, 1968), Otay (V11), one on 15 December 1973 (J. L. Dunn, AFN 28:536, 1974), and Oceanside, one on 23 December 1984 (G. McCaskie, AB 39:211, 1985).

Conservation: The Cliff Swallow presents a paradox: a species that relies for a nest site almost totally on man-made structures—yet shows signs of decline. At many colonies atlas observers reported that only a fraction of the nests were active, and other colonies were abandoned entirely. Results of the Breeding Bird Survey suggest a significant decline in southern California since 1982 (Brown and Brown 1995). At San Elijo Lagoon (L7), from 1973 to 1983, King et al. (1987) recorded an April–July average of 230 and a maximum of 620 on 3 June 1979. From 1997 to 2002, with 26 records, the maximum reported there was only 100, on 2 May 1999 (B. C. Moore). Similarly,

horn sheep come to drink in the north fork of Palm Wash (E29), Paul Jorgensen noted the remains of three old Cliff Swallow nests. The nests, in one of the most remote and arid parts of the Anza–Borrego Desert, could have been many years old—Mark Jorgensen had seen nests here in the 1970s. Though the Cliff Swallow began colonizing the Imperial Valley in 1977, and is now abundant there (Patten et al. 2003), it has not done so around Borrego Springs, even on buildings near golf-course ponds.

Nesting: The Cliff Swallow's retort-shaped nest, built from pellets of mud, is unique in North America. Though cliffs were the species' primitive nest site, the nests now are plastered typically under bridges, on concrete structures in reservoirs, and under the eaves of buildings—always where a vertical surface is sheltered from above. They often put the nests in corners and against neighboring nests, minimizing the amount of mud needed to enclose the nest. Our observers reported only a few colonies on natural cliffs or boulders, though another is on simulated rocks at the Wild Animal Park, San Pasqual (J12; K. L. Weaver).

Nest building begins usually in late March but began in mid March in the wet year 1998. The birds repair the nests whenever needed, accounting for nest building throughout the breeding season. Early in the season they

at Batiquitos Lagoon (J7), Mona Baumgartel's maximum monthly count decreased from 920 in 1994 to 32 in 2001.

The erection of thousands of bridges and millions of buildings has given Cliff Swallows countless new colony sites, and the importation of huge quantities of water has given them new sources of mud. But the paving over of so much of the coastal lowland, and the landscaping of so much of what has not been paved, must be more than compensating, by reducing the supply of both mud for nests and insects for food. Homeowners and building managers annoyed with the mess underneath a Cliff Swallow colony may knock or hose the nests down; atlas observers occasionally noted nests deliberately destroyed. A citation from the health department obliged the Cuyamaca school camp (N21) to destroy nests over the door to its cafeteria (P. D. Jorgensen). San Diego State University adopted a policy of "no swallows," so the former large colonies there are now history (P. R. Pryde). One of the most frequent public inquiries I get is how to prevent Cliff Swallows from nesting on buildings.

Few birds test the limit of human toleration of wildlife more than the Cliff Swallow, and the evidence is growing that intolerance is winning.

In the northeastern U.S., House Sparrows usurping nests are responsible for Cliff Swallows declining (Brown and Brown 1995), and this problem is likely a factor in San Diego too. The proliferation of ravens and crows may be a threat as well—observers at Barrett Reservoir (S19/T19) repeatedly reported ravens destroying Cliff Swallow nests and eating the young.

Taxonomy: The small subspecies *P. p. tachina* Oberholser, 1903, is the one nesting in San Diego County, as elsewhere in southern California. Though there are as yet no specimens, the larger, more northern nominate *pyrrhonota* may pass through in migration, as through the Salton Sink (Patten et al. 2003), or it may bypass San Diego County. At 104 mm, the wing chord of a juvenile fall migrant picked up near Lake Henshaw 21 September 2000 (W. E. Haas, SDNHM 50553) is equivocal (cf. Phillips 1986).

Barn Swallow *Hirundo rustica*

The Barn Swallow is one of the most widespread and familiar birds of North America, but San Diego County is peripheral to its breeding range. Here the species occurs mainly—though commonly—in migration. Along the Pacific coast, Los Coronados Islands off Tijuana are its southernmost nesting site. The small San Diego breeding population still clings to its ancestral nesting habitat in sea caves, though nesting on man-made structures, now the rule over most of the species' range, may be on the increase. In winter the Barn Swallow is rare but increasing.

Photo by Jack C. Daynes

Breeding distribution: Sea caves at La Jolla (P7) and Point Loma (S7) were the Barn Swallow's original breed-

ing habitat in San Diego County and still consistent sites for small numbers, such as six at La Jolla 27 May and 27 June 1999 (L. Polinsky) and eight at Point Loma 15 June 1998 (V. P. Johnson). As long ago as 1912, though, when a pair nested on the Hotel del Coronado (T9; WFVZ), Barn Swallows began taking to man-made structures over or near the water. From then through 1980 there was little evidence of population increase, but this trend may now be accelerating. Between 1997 and 2002 we recorded the species as at least possibly breeding, outside its migration seasons, in over two thirds of the atlas squares along the coast. There is some spread a short distance inland from Oceanside. Farther inland, as throughout the 20th century, we noted breeding Barn Swallows only sparingly: near Pala (D11),

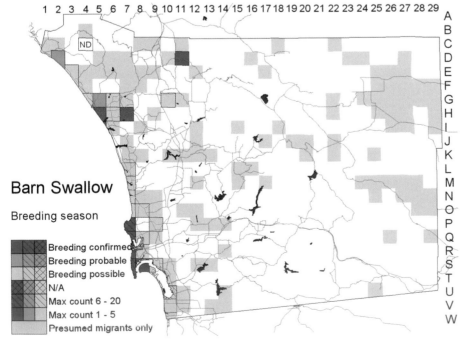

Barn Swallow

Breeding season

Breeding confirmed
Breeding probable
Breeding possible
N/A
Max count 6 - 20
Max count 1 - 5
Presumed migrants only

two at an active nest 18 May 2000 (V. Dineen), Hidden Meadows (G10), three on 26 May 2000 (J. O. Zimmer), and Kearny Mesa (P9), three on 25 June 1997 (K. Kenwood). There are also a few scattered records of single individuals in mid-summer, not coded for "suitable habitat," at Oak Grove (D16) 13 June 2001 (K. L. Weaver), San Pasqual Valley (K12) 27 May 1998 (E. C. Hall), Sweetwater Reservoir (S13) 23 June 1997 (P. Famolaro), and, most surprisingly, Borrego Sink (G25) 4 June 1998 (R. Thériault), although the species has bred in the nearby Salton Sink.

At most of the known or presumed nesting sites, Barn Swallows are few, sometimes only an isolated pair. The largest numbers during the breeding season are around the Chula Vista Nature Center in the Sweetwater River estuary (U10), with up to 20 between 10 and 14 June 1998 (B. C. Moore).

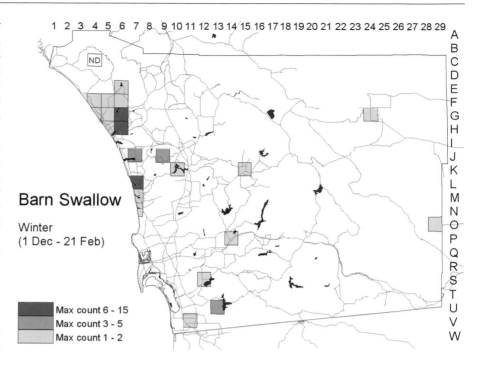

Barn Swallow

Winter
(1 Dec - 21 Feb)

Max count 6 - 15
Max count 3 - 5
Max count 1 - 2

Nesting: The Barn Swallow's nest is built of mud pellets, like the Cliff Swallow's, but when finished is only an open-topped bowl. Thus the nest of the Barn Swallow closely resembles that of the Black Phoebe and is built in similar situations, on a solid support and sheltered from above. Outside the sea caves, our observers noted nests under the eaves of nearby buildings (along Coast Walk in La Jolla) and underneath boat docks at the Catamaran Hotel and Mission Bay Yacht Club (Q7) and the San Diego Yacht Club (S8).

Our rather meager records of Barn Swallow breeding from 1997 to 2001 imply egg laying from about 1 May through mid June and thus fit within the spread of the equally meager previous records (eggs as early as 24 March, nestlings as late as 6 August).

Migration: In spring, Barn Swallows arrive typically in early March, occasionally late February. Four near Hills of the Moon Wash (G27) 22 February 2001 (D. Seals) and two in Borrego Springs (G24) 24 February 1998 (P. D. Ache) were clearly spring migrants. Perhaps because it is less gregarious, the Barn Swallow appears less numerous as a spring migrant than some of the other swallows;

the maximum reported 1997–2002 was 50 at O'Neill Lake (E6) 3 March 1999 (P. A. Ginsburg). The last of the spring migrants depart in the third week of May: 23 May 2000, three in the Tijuana River valley (W10; W. E. Haas); 23 May 2001, four near Tecolote Canyon (Q9; T. Plunkett).

Fall migrants begin returning in early July, giving the Barn Swallow a migration schedule like that of shorebirds nesting in the Arctic. Early fall dates are 2 July 1997 (Poway, M12, P. von Hendy) and 3 July 2000 (west base of Otay Mt., V14, S. D. Cameron). Fall migrants increase through July and August, peak in September, and remain common until the end of October, later than the other swallows except the Tree.

Winter: At this season the Barn Swallow is rare but annual and increasing, as throughout the Southwest. From 1982 to 1992 the total number of Barn Swallows reported on San Diego County Christmas bird counts was 13, whereas from 1992 to 2002 it was 81. Most winter records are along and near the coast from O'Neill Lake in the lower Santa Margarita River valley south to the San Dieguito River estuary, Del Mar (M7), and the largest winter counts are in this region: 12 at Whelan Lake (G6) 22 December 2001 (D. K. Adams, G. L. Rogers, and J. L. Coatsworth), eight at Buena Vista Lagoon (H6) the same day (J. C. Lovio), and 15 at San Elijo Lagoon (L7) 23 December 2001 (E. Garnica). Nevertheless, a few have shown up farther inland, as far as Ramona (K15, one on 2 January 2000, D. and C. Batzler), Lindo Lake (P14, one on 20 January 2002, M. Sadowski), and Lower Otay Lake (U13, three on 3 January 2001, V. Marquez). Most notable are the first winter records ever for the Anza–Borrego Desert, of two at Borrego Springs (G24) 25 December 2001 (P. D. Ache) and two at Carrizo Marsh (O29) 9 February 2001 (P. D. Jorgensen). The Barn Swallow has become a regular winter visitor in small numbers to the Salton Sink, though, just 25 to 30 miles farther east (Patten et al. 2003).

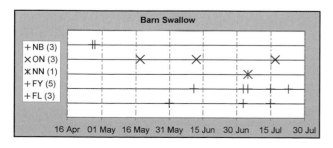

Barn Swallow

+ NB (3)
× ON (3)
✳ NN (1)
+ FY (5)
+ FL (3)

16 Apr 01 May 16 May 31 May 15 Jun 30 Jun 15 Jul 30 Jul

Conservation: With a trend of increase and adaptability to man-made structures as nest sites, the Barn Swallow appears unlikely to present a conservation problem. The natural nest sites are inaccessible. The species' recent colonization of the drainage culverts in the city of Riverside (Lee 1995) suggests that further spread is in store for San Diego County. The Barn Swallow's noncolonial habits suggest it is less likely to suffer to the same degree from the problems afflicting the Cliff Swallow. The Barn Swallow's increase in winter could be a symptom of climatic warming, which is seen primarily in an increase in winter low temperatures.

Nevertheless, trends can be reversed: the Barn Swallow's colonization of the Imperial Valley in the 1970s, by a few pairs, proved ephemeral (Patten et al. 2003).

Taxonomy: Some geographic variation is expected in a species like the Barn Swallow with a nearly world-wide distribution. But the subspecies *H. r. erythrogaster* Boddaert, 1783, distinguished (in adult plumage) by its deep rufous underparts and virtual lack of a dark breast band, is the only one nesting in North America.

TITMICE AND CHICKADEES — FAMILY PARIDAE

Mountain Chickadee *Poecile gambeli*

The Mountain Chickadee is one of the most abundant birds—perhaps the most abundant bird—in the conifers of San Diego County's mountains. The chickadee remains in the mountains in large numbers year round yet disperses regularly to low elevations as well, in numbers varying from year to year. Such visitors are most numerous in planted conifers in northwestern San Diego County, and a few observations in May and June suggest the Mountain Chickadee could be on the verge of colonizing this area as a breeding species.

Photo by Anthony Mercieca

Breeding distribution: The Mountain Chickadee occurs in all of San Diego County's main mountain ranges. The largest numbers live in mixed conifer/oak forests, whether these be dominated by Jeffrey pine or big-cone Douglas fir: up to 130 on the east side of Hot Springs Mountain (E21) 24 July 1999 (K. L. Weaver, C. R. Mahrdt), 100 on Volcan Mountain (I20) 28 June 2000 (A. P. and T. E. Keenan), and 120 on Middle Peak, Cuyamaca Mountains

(M20) 11 June and 2 July 2000 (R. E. Webster). Much smaller numbers extend into oak woodland with few or no conifers in a halo just one atlas square wide surrounding the conifer-dominated core. Small numbers of chickadees range also through the oak woodland of the Mesa Grande area (up to seven along Highway 76 near Lake Henshaw, G17, 17 July 1998, C. G. Edwards). In San Diego County, the breeding range of the Mountain Chickadee, and thus of the subspecies *P. g. baileyae*, extends south to Corte Madera Mountain (R20) except for a few birds isolated at Live Oak Springs (S25; pair feeding nestlings in a birdhouse 9 June 2001, R. and S. L. Breisch). A single singing male along Cottonwood Creek in Hauser Canyon (T20) 26 April 1997 (J. M. Wells, J. Turnbull) was not seen subsequently.

In the pinyons of the Santa Rosa Mountains, the Mountain Chickadee barely extends into San Diego County with one pair just within the county line at 5800 feet elevation 0.5 mile south of Rabbit Peak (C27) 2 May 2000 (P. Unitt).

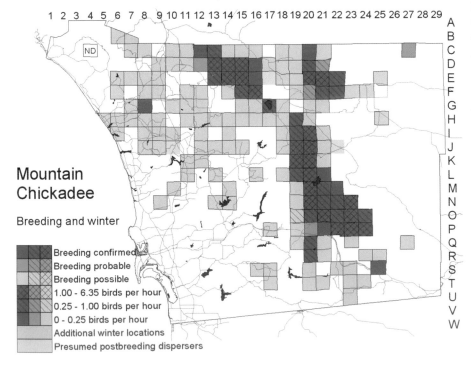

Mountain Chickadee

Breeding and winter

- Breeding confirmed
- Breeding probable
- Breeding possible
- 1.00 - 6.35 birds per hour
- 0.25 - 1.00 birds per hour
- 0 - 0.25 birds per hour
- Additional winter locations
- Presumed postbreeding dispersers

Over most of San Diego County the Mountain Chickadee breeds only above 3500 feet elevation, but around Palomar Mountain it descends to about 2700 feet, and even below 2000 feet in deep canyons such as Agua Tibia (D12; pair 17 July 2001, K. L. Weaver). There are also a few records, including one breeding confirmation, at low elevations in northwestern San Diego County. One bird was about 4 miles east-southeast of Fallbrook (D9) 7 June 2000 (E. C. Hall), one was 1.5 miles southwest of the Pauma Valley post office (F12) 23 June 2001 (J. Simmons), one was at Felicita Park, Escondido (J10), 22 May 2000 (D. Parker), and one was 2.75 miles north of the Vista post office (G8) 31 May 2001 (E. C. Hall, J. O. Zimmer). The last was seen carrying insects, the first evidence for the Mountain Chickadee breeding at low elevations in San Diego County. In spring 2002, a pair was exploring tree cavities at O'Neill Lake (E6), Camp Pendleton, elevation 105 feet, and on 12 May 2003 a pair was feeding nestlings there in a cavity in a Peruvian pepper tree (P. A. Ginsburg). Summer 2002 also yielded unspecific reports of nesting in eastern Escondido and Rancho Bernardo (L11; D. W. Aguillard).

Nesting: The Mountain Chickadee is a secondary cavity nester, occupying old woodpecker holes or natural hollows in trees. It patronizes birdhouses readily. Our observations 1997–2001 suggest that in San Diego County Mountain Chickadees start laying regularly in late April, occasionally by 15 April (adults gathering insects along Nate Harrison Grade, E13, 29 April 2000, C. Sankpill). Thus the Mountain Chickadee begins breeding earlier in San Diego County than reported elsewhere in the species' range (spread of California egg dates 4 May–11 July, Bent 1946). Because of the dearth of historical data from San Diego County (only three collected egg sets), it is unclear whether early nesting of the Mountain Chickadee in San Diego County is a recent change or simply a reflection of the county's position near the southern tip of the species' range.

Migration: Records of the Mountain Chickadee outside the breeding range extend from 16 August (1999, one 1.2 miles north-northeast of Morro Hill, E7, P. A. Ginsburg) to 5 April (1997, one at Wilderness Gardens, D11, V. Dineen). Because of the few breeding-season records for northwestern San Diego County, extreme dates from this area may overestimate the species' dispersal, but wanderers in the opposite direction are known as early as 2 September 1992 in Culp Valley (H22; M. L. Gabel)

and 8 September 2000 near Scissors Crossing (J22; three individuals, P. D. Jorgensen).

Winter: The Mountain Chickadee remains common through the winter in San Diego County's mountains, even at the highest elevations (82 around the summit of Hot Springs Mountain, E20, 16 February 2002, K. L. Weaver, C. R. Mahrdt). Nevertheless, it can be appreciably more numerous in the Mesa Grande area in winter than in the breeding season (H17; 18 on 27 December 1999, K. L. Weaver), and there is a significant movement each winter to low elevations in northwestern San Diego County. Generally the species is uncommon in the lowlands, but numbers 1997–2002 were as high as eight at Wilderness Gardens (D11) 20 December 1998 (V. Dineen), nine in Carlsbad 0.4 mile south of Carrillo Ranch Park (J8) 5 December 1998 (J. O. Zimmer), and 10 around Paradise Mountain (H13) 29 December 2001 (W. Pray). The greatest recorded incursion was in 1987–88. The Mountain Chickadee was recorded on 21 of 26 Oceanside Christmas bird counts 1976–2001, maximum 50 on 26 December 1987. It was recorded on 16 of 17 Escondido counts 1986–2001, maximum 79 on 2 January 1988. South of Escondido wintering Mountain Chickadees become rare; in the southwestern quadrant of the county they were noted during the atlas period no nearer the coast than Lee Valley (S16; two on 7 December 1998, P. Unitt). Rarely have they reached Point Loma (S7; male collected 25 September 1965, SDNHM 35520; six seen 7 September 1987, J. L. Dunn, AB 42:137, 1988). The species was recorded on four of 50 San Diego Christmas bird counts 1953–2002, maximum two on 19 December 1987.

In the Anza-Borrego Desert the Mountain Chickadee is a rare winter visitor, recorded mainly in planted trees in the Borrego Valley. The highest number reported is five in Borrego Palm Canyon (F23) 25 January 2001 (J. D. Barr). The only sighting away from the Borrego Valley is of two in Carrizo Canyon (Q27) 18 January 1998 (D. Julian). In the Santa Rosa Mountains the Mountain Chickadee has been seen in winter south to Villager Peak (C27; two on 10 January 2002, P. Unitt). Small numbers also disperse directly south of the breeding range, reaching practically to the Mexican border at Campo (U23; 11 on 14 January 2001; D. S. and A. W. Hester)—not surprising considering that four specimens of subspecies *baileyae*, breeding only north of the border, have been collected in northern Baja California (Panza and Parkes 1992).

Conservation: The Mountain Chickadee appears to be doing well in San Diego County. The recent summer records at low elevations may foreshadow a spread of the breeding range. Such a change may be a response to the use of conifers in landscaping or it may reflect more general—and more obscure—environmental changes. The Mountain Chickadee may follow in the steps of the Purple Finch, another mountain bird whose colonization of the lowland northwestern San Diego County is more advanced.

Taxonomy: All San Diego County specimens of the Mountain Chickadee, including the one from Point Loma

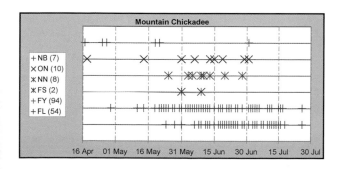

(examined by Panza and Parkes 1992), are *P. g. baileyae* (Grinnell, 1908). Those from the Laguna Mountains, however, are slightly darker on the back and thus intermediate

toward *P. g. atratus* (Grinnell and Swarth, 1926), the dark subspecies breeding in the sierras Juárez and San Pedro Mártir of northern Baja California (Patten et al. 2003).

Oak or Plain Titmouse *Baeolophus inornatus*

A plain gray bird ornamented only with a crest, the Oak Titmouse was long known as the Plain Titmouse, and as the San Diego Titmouse in the days when each subspecies was called by its own English name. It is indeed most common in oak woodland, though common also wherever there are trees in San Diego County's foothills and mountains. A year-round resident, the titmouse is familiar to many because of its tameness around campgrounds and picnic tables and because of its patronizing bird feeders and birdhouses. But in spite of this familiarity with humanity it has not spread into cities now landscaped into urban forest.

Breeding distribution: The Oak Titmouse's range is the prime exemplar of a pattern typical of birds of oak woodland. The distribution of species following this pattern covers most of the coastal slope but does not reach the coast itself. The range approaches the coast most closely in the north (within 3 miles along San Onofre Creek in the northeast corner of square D2), then retracts inland with increasing distance to the south. The Oak Titmouse thus extends west to Talega Canyon (B2; up to nine on 28 May 2001, P. Unitt) and San Onofre Creek (D2; six on 17 June 2001, R. E. Fischer) in Camp Pendleton. Along the Mexican border, however, the westernmost site for the titmouse is 20 miles inland at Marron Valley (V16; up to seven on 11 May 2000, B. E. Kus).

Titmice reach their maximum abundance around

Photo by Anthony Mercieca

3000–4000 feet elevation with up to 80 in Matagual Valley (H19) 18 June 2000 (S. E. Smith), 79 near Warner Springs (F19) 14 May 1999 (C. G. Edwards), and 75 around Descanso (P19) 28 April 2001 (M. and B. McIntosh). They occur in smaller numbers in conifer-dominated woodland up to the tops of San Diego County's highest peaks (up to 10 near the summit of Hot Springs Mountain, E20, 19 May 2001, K. L. Weaver, C. R. Mahrdt). Chaparral offers titmice foraging habitat, and they occupy it where there are only scattered oaks affording nest sites. They extend some distance down the desert slope as long as there are some components of chaparral, as in Culp Valley (H23; three on 16 June 1999, M. L. Gabel). The Oak Titmouse also occurs uncommonly in the pinyon–juniper woodland of the Santa Rosa Mountains (C27; up to four on 2 June 1999, P. D. Jorgensen) and the Vallecito Mountains (up to 10 on the north slope of Whale Peak, L25, 25 June 1998, R. Thériault). The desert scrub oak is an important component of this habitat, but old Ladder-backed Woodpecker holes in Mojave yucca or Parry's nolina are probably the essential feature allowing titmice to occupy these areas.

Nesting: The Oak Titmouse typically nests in cavities in trees, either natural hollows or old woodpecker holes. Coast live oak, Engelmann oak, and sycamore were the usual sites atlas observers reported in San Diego County. Nevertheless, the titmouse exemplifies the resourcefulness of most secondary cavity nesters in selecting a home. On the desert slope, we twice confirmed it using old holes of the

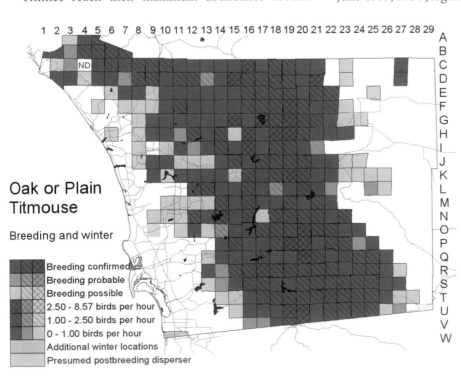

Oak or Plain Titmouse

Breeding and winter

- Breeding confirmed
- Breeding probable
- Breeding possible
- 2.50 - 8.57 birds per hour
- 1.00 - 2.50 birds per hour
- 0 - 1.00 birds per hour
- Additional winter locations
- Presumed postbreeding disperser

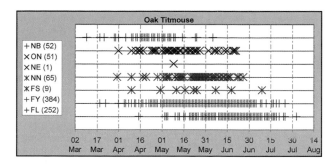

Ladder-backed Woodpecker in yuccas. Titmice nest commonly in man-made structures like birdhouses and metal fence posts. A crack in a building's stucco may create a nest cavity, as at Tierra del Sol (U25) 6 May 2001 (J. R. Barth). The most unusual titmouse nest noted was in an old Cliff Swallow nest on a house in Rancho Cuca (F14) 7 June 1998 (P. Unitt).

Cicero (2000) reported that eggs of the southern California subspecies of the Oak Titmouse had been collected from 19 March to 31 May, and our observations in San Diego County reflect this interval almost exactly. A nest with nestlings near Mocogo Ranch (U16) 31 March 2001 (P. Unitt) implies egg laying by 17 March, while an adult disposing of a nestling's fecal sac along Klondike Creek (M15) 9 July 2001 (P. K. Nelson) implies it as late as 8 June.

Winter: Wandering of the Oak Titmouse outside its breeding range in winter is rare. Nevertheless, the species has reached the Tijuana River valley (W10, one on 1 December 2001 and 6 January 2002, G. L. Rogers, M. Billings; W11, one on 8 December 2001, C. G. Edwards), in the longest possible dispersal within San Diego County toward the coast. In the Anza–Borrego Desert the titmouse is occasional at Lower Willows along Coyote Creek (D23; one on 21 February 2001 and 16

December 2001, M. L. Gabel, P. R. Pryde) and has been recorded a few times even on the floor of the Borrego Valley (G24, one on 17 December 2000, S. and J. Berg; E25, one on 21 January 2001, P. D. Ache). Massey (1998) noted one sighting in the valley's mesquite bosque (G25) and that the species was rare in fall and winter at Yaqui Well and Tamarisk Grove (I24). Multiple winter records from Earthquake Valley (J23/K23) suggest the disjunct population in the Vallecito Mountains is not isolated, with titmice dispersing across the gap in winter.

Conservation: On the basis of the Breeding Bird Survey (Sauer et al. 2003) the Oak Titmouse has been reported as in decline, but no decline is obvious in San Diego County. The species' range here has remained stable over the past century, in spite of many changes in the county's environment. Several other species that once shared the titmouse's pattern of distribution, primary and secondary cavity nesters as well as open-cup builders, have spread coastward by taking advantage of urban trees. But for unknown reasons the titmouse itself still remains static, though it thrives around rural homes, capitalizing on bird feeders and birdhouses.

Taxonomy: The subspecies *B. i. affabilis* Grinnell and Swarth, 1926, darker than other Oak Titmice and with a more deeply scoop-shaped mandible, has a range coextensive with the San Diegan District in southwestern California and northwestern Baja California. It was originally described as *B. i. murinus* by Ridgway (1904), and the substitution of *affabilis* was necessitated when the genus *Baeolophus* was lumped with *Parus*, in which the name *murinus* had already been used. When the genera were split again (AOU 1997) the name did not revert to Ridgway's original because of a provision in the latest version of the code of scientific nomenclature that conserves such changes if they happened before 1961.

VERDIN AND PENDULINE TITS — FAMILY REMIZIDAE

Verdin *Auriparus flaviceps*

Perhaps no bird is more characteristic of the Anza–Borrego Desert than the Verdin. Wherever thorny trees are common so is this little gray bird with a yellow head. It is a permanent resident, the birds maintaining their unique globular nests for roosting year round. The nests, placed conspicuously in the outer branches of spiny shrubs or trees, are sometimes more easily found than the birds themselves. If suitable nest sites are sparse, the Verdin is rare, and in desert scrub consisting of only creosote bushes or low halophytes it is absent.

Breeding distribution: The Verdin's breeding distribution in San Diego County is coextensive with the Anza–Borrego Desert. The birds occur on the desert slope wherever one finds the thorny shrubs in which they nest. The range extends west to Alder Canyon (C21; two juveniles 19–20 June 2001, P. D. Jorgensen), just north

Photo by Anthony Mercieca

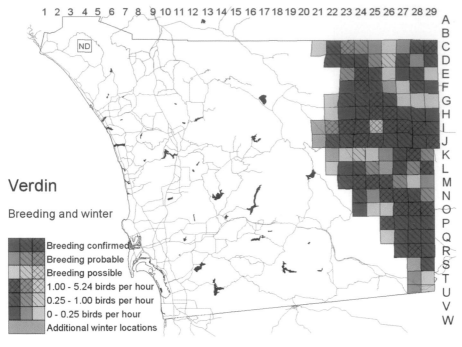

Verdin

Breeding and winter

Breeding confirmed
Breeding probable
Breeding possible
1.00 - 5.24 birds per hour
0.25 - 1.00 birds per hour
0 - 0.25 birds per hour
Additional winter locations

building the nest in spiny plants. The smoketree was the most frequent site of Verdin nests atlas observers reported; other sites noted were catclaw, desert ironwood, mesquite, desert lavender, desert apricot, and teddy bear cholla. In the Imperial Valley, where native desert shrubs are now rare, Verdins nest commonly in the exotic saltcedar, but in the Anza–Borrego Desert they preserve their primitive preference for spiny native species.

Verdins build and maintain nests for roosting year round, so the nests alone are no clue to the species' breeding cycle. The contents of the enclosed nests are secure from prying eyes, usually even from prying fingers, so typically one must wait until the young hatch and the par-

of La Ciénaga at the west end of Culp Valley (G22; one on 12 May 2001, P. D. Jorgensen; at 3400 feet the highest elevation where we noted the Verdin), the upper end of Vallecito Wash in Mason Valley (L22; one on 15 March 2001, R. Thériault), and Jacumba (U28; up to 10 on 20 March 1998, C. G. Edwards). The Verdin is most abundant in the gardens of Borrego Springs (F24; up to 65 on 20 March 2001, K. L. Weaver), in well-vegetated washes and on alluvial fans (up to 60 on Mescal Bajada, J25, 10 and 26 April 1998, M. and B. McIntosh), and at oases (up to 30 at Agua Caliente Springs, M26, 27 March 1997, E. C. Hall; 30 at Carrizo Palms, R28, 6 May 1998, J. O. Zimmer). It is lacking from the pinyon–juniper woodland of the higher elevations within the Anza–Borrego Desert and very sparse in badlands in which shrubs adequate to support a Verdin nest are few and far between. In such areas, the nests may be easier to find than the birds themselves. On the east slope of the Santa Rosa Mountains in square C27 Robert Thériault found two apparently active roosting nests between 2500 and 3100 feet elevation 9–10 January 2002 but never saw the birds themselves at any season. In four other atlas squares we found nests but saw the birds only in winter. In square M28 along Fish Creek Wash, in spite of 58.9 hours of effort, breeding season and winter combined, we found just one Verdin.

The Verdin appears to be less susceptible than many desert birds to the vagaries of the rains. As might be expected, the numbers counted per hour in the field were highest in the wet year 1998 and lowest after three years of drought in 2001, but the factor of difference was less than 2.

Nesting: The Verdin's nest is like nothing else: an ellipsoid bristling on the outside with spines, entered through a tiny hole on the bottom at one end. The birds make no effort to conceal their nests, relying for protection from predators on the nest's porcupinelike exterior and by

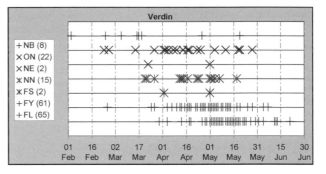

ents begin feeding them to confirm Verdin breeding. Such observations suggest that in San Diego County Verdins lay mainly from early March through early May. Unusually early laying, no later than 12 February, is implied by adults gathering insects near Borrego Air Ranch (H26) 26 February 1999 (M. L. Gabel).

Winter: The Verdin's pattern of distribution in winter is practically identical to that in the breeding season. The one area slightly outside the breeding range where the species was noted repeatedly during the winter was San Felipe Valley (I21/J21), though counts there never exceeded two individuals. The Verdin may be an irregular resident even here; on 6 May 1978 I noted one near Banner Queen Ranch (K21), where we did not find the species from 1997 to 2002.

From 1962 to 1975, a few Verdins occurred in fall and winter (12 September–14 February) in the Tijuana River valley. Single winter vagrants were reported also near Chula Vista (U10/U11) 22 January 1956 (AFN 10:284, 1956) and at San Elijo Lagoon (L7) 9 January–17 February 1975 (AB 29:743, 1975). There have been no coastal records since.

Conservation: In the Imperial Valley the Verdin has adapted to environmental change on a scale far beyond what it confronts in the Anza–Borrego Desert. In Borrego

Springs, native desert trees are commonly used in land-scaping, so the Verdin needs to make little adjustment to development there. Prolonged drought disfavors the Verdin like all other desert birds. By 2002, after three years of drought, many of the shrubs on which Verdins rely were dormant or dying. Occasional flash floods are needed to renew the stands of smoketrees in washes that constitute prime Verdin habitat.

The Verdin is resident in the drainage basin of the Tijuana River at least at Valle de las Palmas in Baja California (Unitt et al. 1995). Presumably this area was the origin of the birds formerly reaching the Tijuana River valley north of the international border, and presumably the growth of the city of Tijuana cut off former routes of dispersal. Further clearing of vegetation in northwestern Baja California may lead to the Verdin's range on the Pacific slope retracting south.

Taxonomy: All Verdins in California are *A. f. acaciarum* Grinnell, 1931. This subspecies is paler than most others and lacks any tinge of yellow on the breast, belly, or rump. Its usually four-noted song, "tew, tew, tew, tew," differs at least from that of the subspecies of central and southern Baja California.

BUSHTIT AND LONG-TAILED TITS — FAMILY AEGITHALIDAE

Bushtit *Psaltriparus minimus*

San Diego County's smallest songbird is also one of its most common. The Bushtit is a year-round resident, gathering into flocks of as many as 40 birds in late summer, fall, and winter. In spring, for nesting, the flocks break up into pairs, which sometimes have helpers. The Bushtit is one of southern California's most successful urban adapters, familiar because of its flocking habits, characteristic baglike nest, and indifference to people. Yet it remains common in native habitats too, in oak and riparian woodland, chaparral, and sage scrub.

Breeding distribution: The Bushtit is resident over San Diego County's entire coastal slope and down the east slope of the mountain to the desert edge. Numbers are greatest in the coastal lowland, where estimates for single days are as high as 260 at San Elijo Lagoon (L7) 11 May 1999 and 250 in Lakeside (P14) 20 May 1999 (M. B. Stowe). Even as high in the mountains as 4000–4500 feet

Photo by Anthony Mercieca

elevation, however, the Bushtit can be abundant in oak woodland (100 at Wynola, J19, 2 July 1999, S. E. Smith; 100 north of Julian, J20, 1 July 1999, M. B. Stowe). East down the desert slope the Bushtit becomes sparser as the chaparral gives way to open scrub, but it can be common at oases even at the base of the mountains. Points along the edge of the range are Lower Willows in Coyote Creek canyon (D23; up to 20 on 12 May 2001, B. L. Peterson), Yaqui Well (I24; family of five on 4 May 1998, P. K. Nelson), Agua Caliente Springs (M26; only one record, of one on 25 April 1998, M. U. Evans), and Dos Cabezas Spring (S29; pair nest building 18 April 1999, P. Unitt). Furthermore, the Bushtit occurs uncommonly in the pinyons and junipers of the Santa Rosa and Vallecito mountains. Counts in these areas are under

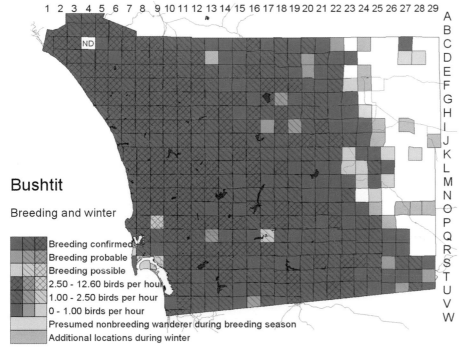

1 2 3 4 5 6 7 8 9 10 11 12 13 14 15 16 17 18 19 20 21 22 23 24 25 26 27 28 29

A B C D E F G H I J K L M N O P Q R S T U V W

Bushtit

Breeding and winter

Breeding confirmed
Breeding probable
Breeding possible
2.50 - 12.60 birds per hour
1.00 - 2.50 birds per hour
0 - 1.00 birds per hour
Presumed nonbreeding wanderer during breeding season
Additional locations during winter

ND

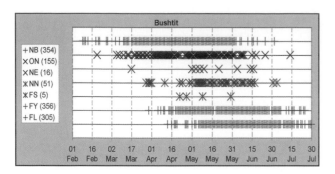

10, except for 36 near Whale Peak (L25) 18 June 2000 (R. Thériault). A single Bushtit in Alma Wash at the east base of the Vallecito Mountains (K28) 20 May 2000 (L. J. Hargrove) was an unusual outlier. Robert Thériault (in Massey 1998) reported the Bushtit as an occasional visitor in spring as well as winter to the mesquite bosque in the center of the Borrego Valley (G25), but even with thorough coverage he did not find it there at any season from 1997 to 2002.

Nesting: The Bushtit's nest is unique: a bag about 6 to 8 inches long, roofed over its top, and entered through a small hole at the side just under the roof. The nest is built of spider web and bits of plant material matted into the consistency of felt or dryer lint. Some nests hang free, so their bottom swings in the wind, but often the nest is well attached by its sides to multiple vertical twigs, either hanging down or growing up. Thus the outer canopy of a coast live oak, where the twigs hang down, is an especially favored site, and this tree was the most frequent site of Bushtit nests reported by atlas observers. The exotic Peruvian pepper tree, with many pendulous twigs, is also attractive. Bushes like the broom baccharis and coyote brush with many vertical twigs are frequent sites as well; they allow the Bushtit to occupy low scrub in which these are the only taller shrubs. Bushtits nest in a wide variety of other plants, however, both native and exotic, including the invasive saltcedar and pampas grass. In and at the edges of coastal sage scrub around San Diego, of 28 nests found in 2001 and 2002 by M. A. Patten and co-workers, 10 were in laurel sumac and 7 were in California

sagebrush. Nests whose heights atlas observers reported ranged from 3 to 45 feet above the ground. The nests are surprisingly durable; months after being built, even if they have been torn apart or have fallen to the ground, the fragments can be identified by their unique texture.

The Bushtit's nesting season begins early, with nest building noted in La Jolla (O7) as early as 9 February 1998 (S. E. Smith). Eggs have been collected in California as early as 26 February (Bent 1946), but our observations do not suggest any successful clutches in which incubation was begun before about 13 March. The breeding season continues through July, with a nest along the Sweetwater River (S13) still active 14 July 1997 (P. Famolaro) and fledglings in family groups to the end of the month.

Winter: The Bushtit is nonmigratory, but dispersal takes occasional individuals or flocks onto the desert floor, outside the species' breeding range. Such visitors are regular in the northern half of the Borrego Valley (E24/F24), with up to 75 at Borrego Springs (F24) 19 December 1999 (P. K. Nelson et al.). Four near Halfhill Dry Lake (J29) 10 January 2000 (L. J. Hargrove), 16 in Alma Wash at the east base of the Vallecito Mountains (K28) 4 December 1999 (P. Unitt et al.), and two at Carrizo Marsh (O29) 15 February 2001 (M. C. Jorgensen) had made it almost to the Imperial County line. Bushtits remain at the higher elevations year round, as illustrated by 36 on 13 February 1999 and 40 on 9 December 2000 near the summit of Hot Springs Mountain (E20), San Diego County's highest peak (K. L. Weaver, C. R. Mahrdt).

Conservation: The Bushtit is as much at home in urban shade trees as in native woodland or chaparral. Bolger et al. (1997) reported the Bushtit indifferent to fragmentation of native habitat by urban development. The birds move freely between natural and artificial environments.

Taxonomy: Bushtits from San Diego County are like those from northwestern Baja California in being darker on the crown, back, and flanks than those from the coast of central California. Thus they represent *P. m. melanurus* Grinnell and Swarth, 1926, extending that subspecies' range north of the international border (Rea in Phillips 1986; many SDNHM specimens).

NUTHATCHES — FAMILY SITTIDAE

Red-breasted Nuthatch *Sitta canadensis*

The Red-breasted Nuthatch is one of those mountain birds whose elevational range is barely touched by the tops of San Diego County's highest peaks. It is a rare resident in deep forest on the north slopes of the Palomar, Hot Springs, Volcan, and Cuyamaca mountains. The Red-breasted is by far the most dispersive of California's nuthatches, occurring widely outside its breeding range as an irregular winter visitor. These visitors seek conifers, being seen in other trees only if no conifers are near. Invasions may plant new isolated breeding populations at low elevations, such as the one on Point Loma.

Photo by Anthony Mercieca

Breeding distribution: From 1997 to 2002, we found the Red-breasted Nuthatch regularly and most numerously on Palomar Mountain. Its habitat there is forest dominated by the big-cone Douglas fir between 4500 and 5700 feet elevation, from Pauma Creek (D14) southeast to Dyche Valley (F15), mainly on the north-facing slopes of the southwestern of the mountain's two parallel ridges. In this area the species is uncommon, with maximum daily counts of five or fewer, except for 11 (including fledglings) along Highway S6 near Fry Creek 31 May 2000 (E15, E. C. Hall, C. R. Mahrdt). It is regular on Middle Peak and the northeast slope of Cuyamaca Peak (M20) above 5200 feet elevation. During the atlas period the high count in the Cuyamaca Mountains was nine on Middle Peak (M20) 19 May 1998 (R. E. Webster); previously, as many as 20 were noted in the same area 19 July 1987 (AB 41:1488, 1987). There is one report from North Peak (L20), of two about 5200 feet elevation on the northwest slope 14 July 2000 (J. R. Barth).

On Hot Springs Mountain the Red-breasted Nuthatch has been known since the peak's avifauna was first explored in 1980 (Unitt 1981), with a maximum of six 19 July 1986 (R. E. Webster, AB 40:1256, 1986). During the atlas period, however, K. L. Weaver and C. R. Mahrdt found it in the breeding season only twice, single individuals in square E20 on 9 June 2001 and in E21 on 19 June 1999. Atlas observers found it during the breeding season on Volcan Mountain for the first time, with two on Oak Ridge (I20) 22 July 1999 (L. J. Hargrove), a pair near Catfish Spring (I20) 16 June 2000 (A. P. and T. E. Keenan), and three at 5100 feet elevation 0.35 mile south of Simmons Flat (J20) 16 July 2001 (J. R. Barth).

On Point Loma (S7), mainly on and near the campus of Point Loma Nazarene University, the Red-breasted Nuthatch has been an uncommon resident since it colonized after the invasion of 1963. It may have died out in the mid 1990s, only to recolonize again after the invasion of 1996. Virginia P. Johnson netted a female with a brood patch on 10 March 1997.

Nesting: Like the other nuthatches, the Red-breasted nests in tree cavities. It may use a preexisting cavity or may excavate or enlarge its own. It is famous for smearing the nest entrance with pitch, deterring predators. Nesting in San Diego County, however, is still little known. One nest at Point Loma was in a hole in the sawed-off leaf base of a Canary Island date palm 2 June 1978 (Unitt 1984). Nesting confirmations in the mountains were of nest building on Cuyamaca Peak 23 May 1998 (G. L.

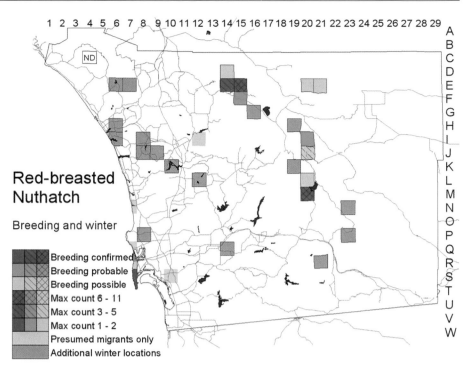

Red-breasted Nuthatch

Breeding and winter

■ Breeding confirmed
■ Breeding probable
□ Breeding possible
■ Max count 6 - 11
■ Max count 3 - 5
■ Max count 1 - 2
□ Presumed migrants only
■ Additional winter locations

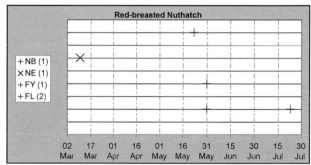

Rogers) and of fledglings on Palomar 31 May 2000 (E. C. Hall) and 23 July 2000 (J. R. Barth). Nesting in the coastal colony at Point Loma may begin considerably earlier, as implied by the female with a brood patch on 10 March.

Migration: Red-breasted Nuthatch incursions are notoriously irregular. In San Diego County the species has been recorded away from breeding locations from 27 August (1998, one at O'Neill Lake, E6, P. A. Ginsburg) to 4 May (1997, three in Greenwood Cemetery, S10, P. Unitt). The largest numbers are seen in October and November, some invasions petering out as the winter wears on. Red-breasted Nuthatches have occurred in all regions of San Diego County, but records for the Anza–Borrego Desert are few, with one in "San Felipe Canyon" 2 October 1908 (F. Stephens, MVZ 3880; Grinnell and Miller [1944] reported this specimen as from Vallecito Creek), one at Tamarisk Grove Campground (I24) 4 November 1973 (P. Unitt), one in planted pines in Borrego Springs (F24) 30–31 October 1996 (P. D. Jorgensen), one on Villager Peak (C27) 19 October 1998 (P. D. Jorgensen), and one in Nolina Wash, Pinyon Mountains (K25) 15 October 1999 (D. C. Seals, S. Peters).

Winter: The Red-breasted Nuthatch is one of the more frequent montane invaders, with a few recorded in San

Diego County in most winters, including every year from 1997 to 2002. But the larger incursions, during which the species would be rated as uncommon rather than rare, are sporadic. The falls and early winters of 1963, 1969, 1972, 1975, 1983, and 1996 saw the largest. San Diego County Christmas bird counts in December 1996 and January 1997 yielded a total of 26, more than in any previous year. Thus the five-year atlas period began with the winding down of a major invasion, accounting for several records of stragglers remaining into spring 1997. Numbers over the next five winters were small, with the maximum daily count of six near the San Luis Rey Picnic Area (G16) 22 January 2001 (W. E. Haas).

Conservation: The magnitude of Red-breasted Nuthatch invasions is controlled by factors outside San Diego County (Koenig 2001, Koenig and Knops 2001), but the planting of ornamental conifers has made conditions more amenable to the birds when they arrive. Certainly the species never would have colonized Point Loma if the area had not been heavily planted with pines. Its colonization of San Diego County's mountains, however, may also be fairly recent, as it was not reported there in the breeding season until 1970. And its population may be increasing gradually; numbers reported from Palomar Mountain 1997–2001 were greater than known there previously, though coverage was much more thorough. Nevertheless, the areas of forest suitable for breeding Red-breasted Nuthatches are so small that a fire could eliminate these isolated populations.

White-breasted Nuthatch *Sitta carolinensis*

The White-breasted Nuthatch is the most wide-spread of San Diego County's three nuthatches. It is a common year-round resident in mountain forests and a familiar patron of bird feeders near this habitat. It is uncommon in oak woodland in the foothills. At low elevations it is a rare and irregular wanderer, apparently most frequent when stressed in its normal range by drought.

Breeding distribution: The White-breasted Nuthatch is one of the common birds of the conifer-dominated woodlands of San Diego County's mountains. Daily counts range as high as 52 on Hot Springs Mountain (E21) 24 July 1999 (K. L. Weaver), 40 on North Peak, Cuyamaca Mountains (L20), 14 July 2000 (E. C. Hall), and 40 at Mount Laguna (O23) 9 June 2001 (C. G. Edwards). The species is locally common as well in oak woodland at

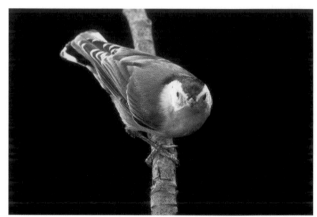

Photo by Anthony Mercieca

lower elevations (up to 15 in Camp Pendleton 1.5 miles south of Margarita Peak, C5, 25 May 1997, J. M. Wells, and in Boden Canyon, I14, 27 June 1997, R. L. Barber). The White-breasted Nuthatch's distribution in San Diego resembles that of other oak woodland birds like the Acorn Woodpecker and Oak Titmouse. The nuthatch, however, does not approach the coast as closely as those species; the western margin of its range is shifted a few miles to the east. If the nuthatch requires larger patches of woodland than the other species, then that requirement could account for the difference in distribution. In northwestern San Diego County, in Camp Pendleton, it ranges to about 8 miles from the coast, at about 600 feet elevation in Las Pulgas Canyon (D5; up to six on 28 May 2001, P. Unitt). Near the Mexican border, the site nearest the coast is Dulzura, 19 miles

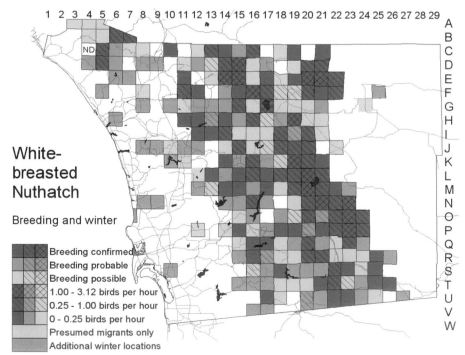

White-breasted Nuthatch

Breeding and winter

- Breeding confirmed
- Breeding probable
- Breeding possible
- 1.00 - 3.12 birds per hour
- 0.25 - 1.00 birds per hour
- 0 - 0.25 birds per hour
- Presumed migrants only
- Additional winter locations

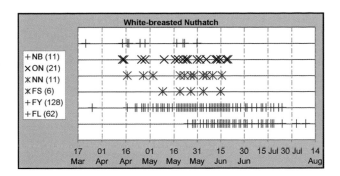

inland and about 1200 feet elevation (U17; up to four, including a male feeding a fledging, 19 June 1998, D. W. Povey). Single birds were at low elevations in isolated oak groves in Gopher Canyon (F8) 27 June 2000 (P. A. Ginsburg) and near the east end of Lake Hodges (K11) 9 June 1997 (E. C. Hall). One was in riparian woodland lacking oaks along the San Diego River in Santee (P12) 26 June 2001 (M. B. Mulrooney), but this may already have been a postbreeding disperser.

Along the eastern side of its range, however, the White-breasted Nuthatch follows the limits of the oaks almost exactly. It descends to about 4400 feet elevation in the middle fork of Borrego Palm Canyon (F22; up to 10 on 18 July 2001, J. R. Barth) and ranges east to Boulevard (T26) near the Mexican border (nest with nestlings on 20 May 1999, J. K. Wilson). The White-breasted Nuthatch may be a rare resident along San Felipe Creek or only a postbreeding visitor: one was near Paroli Spring (I21) 16 June 2000 (J. O. Zimmer), another near Scissors Crossing (J22) 13 July 2001 (P. Unitt). In 2002, when J. R. Barth monitored the Scissors Crossing area intensively, the first individual showed up 16 June and numbers reached their maximum of 10 on 14 July. High elevation is no limit to the White-breasted Nuthatch in San Diego County, as it breeds near the summit of Hot Springs Mountain (E20; up to 14 on 19 May 2001, K. L. Weaver, C. R. Mahrdt).

Nesting: The White-breasted Nuthatch is a secondary cavity nester, using natural holes in trees or those excavated by woodpeckers. Earlier literature summarized by Pravosudov and Grubb (1993) reported no nests lower than 13 feet, but all the nests whose heights atlas observers described were lower: about 8 feet (in a coast live oak east of Rainbow, C10, P. Unitt), 6 feet (in an ornamental broad-leafed tree at Cameron Corners, U23, M. McIntosh), 4 feet (in a coast live oak in along San Vicente Creek, L15, A. Mauro), and just 1 foot off the ground (southeast of Lake Cuyamaca, N21, P. D. Jorgensen). Our observations suggest that in San Diego County White-breasted Nuthatches lay at least from early April through mid May, well within the range of 21 March–9 June for 56 California egg dates given by Bent (1948).

Migration: The White-breasted Nuthatch does not engage in regular migration, but small numbers disperse occasionally outside the breeding range. This dispersal begins possibly as early as mid June, as suggested by the records from San Felipe Valley, certainly by mid July.

Most dispersers are seen on the coastal slope, but one was at Borrego Springs (G24) 31 July 1999 (M. C. Jorgensen), another at Tamarisk Grove (I24) 3 August–2 September 1990 (B. Knaak). White-breasted Nuthatches have been noted at least as late as 22 March at locations where they do not breed (1997, one at Blue Sky Ecological Reserve, L12, M. and B. McIntosh). The end of such dispersal is uncertain because scattered individuals occur through the breeding season at such locations on the margin of the breeding range.

Winter: In winter most White-breasted Nuthatches remain in their breeding range. The species is still most abundant at higher elevations; our maximum daily count was 50 around Mount Laguna (O23) 21 January 2002 (E. C. Hall, J. O. Zimmer). Winter visitors outside the breeding range decrease rapidly with distance from the edge of that range, suggesting they result largely from short-distance local dispersal, not long-distance migration. The only desert records are of one at Ellis Farms, Borrego Springs (F25), 17 December 2000 (L. J. Hargrove, P. Unitt) and two at Butterfield Ranch, Mason Valley (M23), 13 January 2000 (H. and K. Williams). The highest count outside the breeding range during the atlas period was of five at Lake Hodges (K10) 22 December 2000 (R. L. Barber et al.), but the few winter wanderers 1997–2002 were eclipsed the following fall and winter by the largest incursion ever recorded in San Diego County. For example, from 1953 to 2001 the White-breasted Nuthatch was noted on only 13 of 49 San Diego Christmas bird counts, maximum seven on 31 December 1961, whereas the count on 14 December 2002 yielded 20.

Conservation: No trend in White-breasted Nuthatch numbers in San Diego County is clear. The species depends on mature trees for foraging and nest sites, so it depends on the maintenance and regeneration of oak and coniferous woodland. The nuthatch may benefit from the spread of Nuttall's Woodpecker, a primary cavity excavator whose old holes the nuthatch uses. The two largest invasions outside the breeding range, in 1961 and 2002, followed the two driest years in San Diego County history, so some birds may have been driven out of their normal range by drought-induced lack of food.

Taxonomy: *Sitta c. aculeata* Cassin, 1857, is the subspecies of White-breasted Nuthatch resident in San Diego County and the only one collected here. It inhabits the Pacific coast region from Washington to northern Baja California and is characterized by a comparatively short bill and brown-tinged female. The subspecies breeding in the Great Basin/Rocky Mountain region, *S. c. nelsoni* Mearns, 1902, and *S. c. tenuissima* Grinnell, 1918, differ in call as well as bill length and plumage. A bird giving calls characteristic of these subspecies has been heard once at Point Loma (4 October–November 2000, R. E. Webster), as well as once in the Imperial Valley (Patten et al. 2003). Other White-breasted Nuthatches recorded in the latter area called like *aculeata*, as did the one in Borrego Springs 17 December 2000.

Pygmy Nuthatch *Sitta pygmaea*

The Pygmy Nuthatch is a bird of montane coniferous forests, where it prefers open stands of pines. As a result, it is most common in the Laguna Mountains, where such habitat is widespread, less common in the Cuyamaca, Volcan, and Hot Springs mountains, and rare and localized on Palomar Mountain. The Pygmy Nuthatch is highly social, flock members calling to each other constantly, roosting, and even breeding communally. Invasions of Pygmy Nuthatches out of their normal range are rare.

Breeding distribution: The Pygmy Nuthatch is one of the commonest birds in the Laguna Mountains, where daily counts run as high as 75 between Burnt Rancheria Campground and Horse Meadow (P23) 23 June 2000 (E. C. Hall, J. O. Zimmer). The large pines surrounding the meadows on the mountains' plateau offer ideal habitat. The Pygmy Nuthatch is also common in the Cuyamaca Mountains (up to 25 on Middle Peak, M20, 2 July 2000, R. E. Webster) and in the Volcan Mountains down to Julian (up to 20 north of Julian, J20, 17 August 2000, M. B. Stowe), but there is a short gap between these populations: during the breeding season we noted only a single individual on one occasion between Julian and William Heise County Park (K20). Another population is isolated on Hot Springs Mountain, where it is concentrated near the summit (E20; up to 14 on 17 June 2000, K. L. Weaver, C. R. Mahrdt). On Palomar Mountain, forested largely in big-cone Douglas fir rather than pine, the Pygmy Nuthatch has been found during the breeding season only in Lower Doane Valley (D14; seven on 17 July 1999, J. R. Barth; six, including a juvenile, on 4 August 2000, P. D. Jorgensen). Elevationally, the Pygmy Nuthatch ranges in San Diego County from about 4000 feet in Green

Photo by Anthony Mercieca

Valley, Cuyamaca Mountains (N20; three on 26 June 1999, B. Siegel) to 6533 feet at the summit of Hot Springs Mountain.

Nesting: The Pygmy Nuthatch nests in tree cavities, which it often excavates itself. Unmated males often serve their relatives as nest helpers (Kingery and Ghalambor 2001). In San Diego County the birds commonly nest in pine snags but also use big-cone Douglas fir or oak if these trees are mixed among the pines. Our observations from 1997 to 2001 indicate that Pygmy Nuthatches

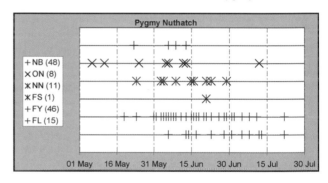

lay from about 4 May to about 5 June, slightly extending the 14 May–1 June range of seven egg sets collected in San Diego County 1920–35 but well within the 17 April–27 June range of 89 egg sets from throughout California (Bent 1948).

Migration: Dispersal of Pygmy Nuthatches outside their breeding range is very rare, concentrated into a few recorded invasions. None of these took place during the five-year atlas period. Large-scale irruptions are known only in 1966–67, 1972–73, and 1987–88. Wanderers have been recorded in San Diego County from 29 August (1987, 16 at Point Loma, S7, R. E. Webster, AB 42:137, 1988) to 30 May (1966, one at Point Loma, AFN

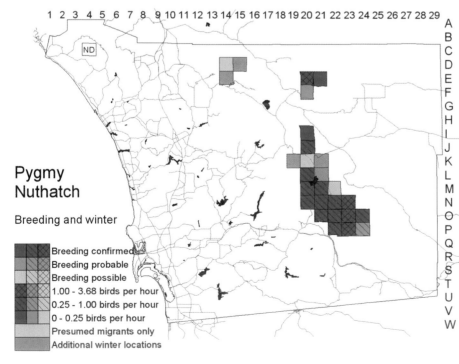

30:546, 1966). The pines planted on Point Loma have served as an attraction for dispersing Pygmy as well as Red-breasted Nuthatches.

Winter: The Pygmy Nuthatch, as a resident species, is seen in winter in much the same numbers as in summer (maximum daily count 100 around Laguna Meadow, O23, 21 January 2002, E. C. Hall, J. O. Zimmer). During exceptionally cold or stormy weather numbers seen may be depressed because the nuthatches may go a whole day without emerging from their roost holes (Kingery and Ghalambor 2001). Occasional birds are seen at sites, still in pine woods, where they are not known in the breeding season (up to six at Pine Hills, K19, 6 February 2002, M. B. Stowe). On Palomar Mountain, winter records are still largely from Lower Doane Valley, but the species has been noted also at nearby Doane Pond (E14; 24 December 2000, G. C. Hazard) and at the Palomar Observatory (D15; 13 on 28 December 2000, K. L. Weaver).

In invasion years Pygmy Nuthatches have dispersed over much of San Diego County's coastal slope but are unrecorded in the Anza–Borrego Desert. The most recent irruption was in 1987–88, which yielded 17 on the Oceanside Christmas bird count and four on the Rancho Santa Fe count—the only records of the Pygmy Nuthatch on either of these counts.

Conservation: Like other birds of coniferous forest, the Pygmy Nuthatch is threatened more by fire, prolonged drought, and climate change than by habitat loss to development. When stressed by drought, the pines on which the nuthatch depends are susceptible to attack by a bark beetle. Many pines died during the drought beginning in 1999. The effect of the death of these on birds is unknown, but the Pygmy Nuthatch, which forages in pines almost exclusively, is more likely to be affected than other species.

Taxonomy: The Pygmy Nuthatches resident in San Diego County are *S. p. leuconucha* Anthony, 1889, which occurs also in the sierras Juárez and San Pedro Mártir of Baja California. This subspecies has been defined primarily by its larger size, especially of the bill, although the measurements tabulated by Norris (1958) reveal that no single linear measurement suffices to distinguish *leuconucha* from *S. p. melanotis* van Rossem, 1929, which inhabits mountain forests over the rest of western the United States. Though *leuconucha* does average significantly larger, it fails the test for extent of overlap (Patten and Unitt 2002) on the basis of any single measurement. Nevertheless, colorimetry of a small sample of fresh-plumaged specimens suggests that the paler back and especially paler crown of *leuconucha* might, perhaps combined with measurements in a multivariate function, distinguish the subspecies adequately. On the crown, seven August–November specimens of *melanotis* from northeastern California, Oregon, Nebraska, Colorado, and Arizona read $L = 28.1–33.3$, whereas six September–December specimens of *leuconucha* from the Laguna Mountains and Sierra Juárez read $L = 33.3–36.2$

The one lowland specimen (Point Loma, 3 September 1985, SDNHM 35442) is *S. p. melanotis* on the basis of both its short bill (9.9 mm from nostril) and comparatively dark crown ($L = 32.9$). Thus it originated from north of San Diego County, a pattern likely typical of montane invaders.

CREEPERS — FAMILY CERTHIIDAE

Brown Creeper *Certhia americana*

A bird of deep forest like the Brown Creeper finds little habitat in a region as arid as San Diego County, but the county's higher mountains support a small population. Thick stands of big-cone Douglas fir and incense cedar on north-facing slopes and in deep canyons offer the best habitat. The local population is probably more or less resident, but a few winter visitors, perhaps from farther north, scatter to lower elevations.

Breeding distribution: Breeding Brown Creepers are confined to the coniferous forests of San Diego County's higher mountains, occurring above about 4200 feet elevation in all five ranges: Palomar, Hot Springs, Volcan, Cuyamaca, and Laguna. They are more numerous on Palomar (up to 20 around Fry Creek Campground, D14, 18 July 1998, D. S. Cooper) and in the Cuyamaca Mountains, especially on Middle Peak (M20; up to 12 on 11 June and 2 July 2000, R. E. Webster). The steep slopes of these more humid ranges support more of the big-cone Douglas fir and incense cedar that favor creepers.

Photo by Anthony Mercieca

Numbers in the dryer Laguna Mountains, dominated by open stands of pine, are considerably lower (maximum daily count three around Mount Laguna, O23, 29 July 2000 and 7 July 2001, J. R. Barth). The Laguna Mountains represent the southern tip of the Brown Creeper's range

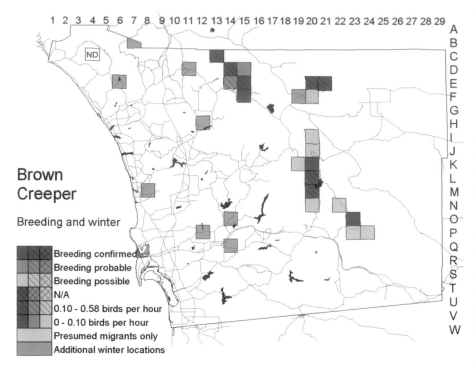

Brown
Creeper

Breeding and winter

Breeding confirmed
Breeding probable
Breeding possible
N/A
0.10 - 0.58 birds per hour
0 - 0.10 birds per hour
Presumed migrants only
Additional winter locations

Winter: In the creeper's breeding range, its numbers in winter seem little different from those in the breeding season (maximum count 9 in Palomar Mountain State Park, E14, 27 February 2000, P. Unitt). At that season creepers often associate with mixed flocks of other small arboreal birds. Away from coniferous woodland creepers are rare; we noted them at low elevations on only 13 occasions from 1997 to 2002. These records are scattered over the coastal slope south to Singing Hills golf course (Q14; one on 5 December 1999, N. Perretta), though in previous years the species had been recorded south occasionally to the Tijuana River valley (3 November 1963, G. McCaskie; 19 December 1987, P. Unitt). The Brown Creeper is recorded rarely

along the Pacific coast, as there is no resident population in Baja California.

Nesting: The Brown Creeper typically builds its nest behind a loose slab of bark. In San Diego County the incense cedar, with its shaggy reddish bark, is the tree offering the most nest sites. The two nests described by atlas observers, both on Hot Springs Mountain (E20/E21; K. L. Weaver, C. R. Mahrdt), were in incense cedars.

Our records of creepers' breeding activity imply incubation begun on dates ranging from mid April to late June. Thus the breeding season we observed was practically equivalent to the range of 33 California egg dates, 16 April–8 July, reported by Bent (1948).

Migration: Outside its breeding range, the Brown Creeper is a very rare migrant and winter visitor, visiting diverse trees. Dates of such dispersers range from 13 August (1970 and 1983, Point Loma, S7, AB 24:718, 1970 and 38:247, 1984) to 19 February (1978, Wilderness Gardens, D11, Unitt 1984), though there are only two records earlier than late September. The three records for the Anza–Borrego Desert range only from 19 October to 2 November (ABDSP database).

on Escondido, Oceanside, Rancho Santa Fe, and San Diego Christmas bird counts, in frequencies ranging from four times in 17 years for Escondido to three times in 50 years for San Diego. Its occurrences are not as irregular as those of many other montane birds, but there was a larger incursion in 1987–88, when these four counts yielded a total of six individuals; their annual average is only 0.13. San Diego County represents the southern tip of the creeper's winter range as well as its breeding range on the Pacific coast; only five sightings have been reported from northern Baja California (Erickson et al. 2001).

Conservation: With much of its habitat in state parks and the Cleveland National Forest, the Brown Creeper is under little threat of direct habitat loss in San Diego County. But as a less common coniferous forest species, clinging to the edge of its range, it is susceptible to climate change that could reduce or eliminate its habitat. Drought at the turn of the millennium has already stressed the trees on which the creeper depends. Fires sweeping the county's mountain ranges could eat away at the creeper's limited range.

Taxonomy: The subspecies of the Brown Creeper resident from San Diego County north to southern Oregon is *C. a. zelotes* Osgood, 1901, distinguished by its dark chestnut rump, whitish underparts, and whitish streaks on the upperparts. The white streaking of the upperparts is much reduced by plumage wear; the Brown Creeper is especially susceptible to wear because of its delicate plumage and constant contact with tree bark. It was the more extensive white streaking of fresh-plumaged birds that led me to misidentify a specimen of *zelotes* from the Laguna Mountains as a migrant of *C. a. montana* Ridgway, 1882, from the Rocky Mountain region (Unitt 1984). The color of the rump (paler tawny in *montana*, darker cinnamon

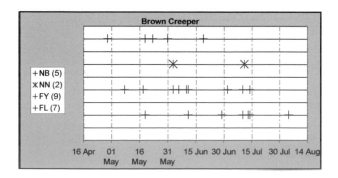

Brown Creeper

+NB (5)
✕NN (2)
+FY (9)
+FL (7)

16 Apr   01   16   31   15 Jun 30 Jun 15 Jul 30 Jul 14 Aug
         May   May   May

in *zelotes*) is less affected by wear and a better diagnostic character (Unitt and Rea 1997). Nevertheless, migrants of more distant subspecies are possible in San Diego County, as *montana* has been collected at Hinkley and Yermo in the Mojave Desert and *C. a. americana* Bonaparte, 1838, has been collected in the Imperial Valley and at Cambria, San Luis Obispo County. *C. a. zelotes* is likely at low elevations as well, having been collected at Riverside, Rialto, and Yucaipa. No lowland specimens have been collected in San Diego County (Unitt and Rea 1997).

WRENS — FAMILY TROGLODYTIDAE

Cactus Wren *Campylorhynchus brunneicapillus*

Few birds are as dependent on a specialized habitat as the San Diego Cactus Wren is on cactus thickets. The birds remain in their stands of cholla or prickly pear year round, maintaining their nests for roosting. San Diego County has two subspecies of the Cactus Wren, *C. b. anthonyi*, widespread and fairly common in and near the Anza–Borrego Desert, and the San Diego Cactus Wren, *C. b. sandiegensis*, localized and seriously threatened in the coastal lowland. The survival of the San Diego Cactus Wren is one of the county's greatest challenges in bird conservation. Development or fires threaten the wren's remaining habitat, and that habitat is so reduced and fragmented that its ability to support the birds over the long term may already be impaired.

Breeding distribution: In San Diego County, the San Diego Cactus Wren is concentrated in four regions: southern Camp Pendleton/Fallbrook Naval Weapons Station (about 70 pairs), Lake Hodges/San Pasqual (90 pairs), Lake Jennings (25 pairs), and Sweetwater/Otay (extending from Dictionary Hill on the north to Otay Mesa on the south, from Euclid Avenue on the west to Upper and Lower Otay lakes on the east; 80 pairs). Other San Diego County sites combined contribute probably fewer than

Photo by Anthony Mercieca

50 individuals. Population estimates, from Mock (1993), are based on data extending back to the 1980s and are not comparable with our atlas results, so trends in the short term are unclear. From 1997 to 2001, high counts in one day in one atlas square were of 30 in the Fallbrook Naval Weapons Station (E6) 8 April 2000 (W. E. Haas), 14 at Lake Hodges (K10) 13 August 1997 (R. L. Barber), 12 in the Wild Animal Park (J13) 3 June 1999 (D. and D. Bylin), 12 at Lake Jennings (O14) 19 June 1998 (M. B. Stowe), and 12 at Sweetwater Reservoir (S12) 9 June 1998 (P. Famolaro). Because these figures are not the results of surveys for the Cactus Wren specifically, they are not comparable with the larger numbers yielded by Weaver's earlier focused surveys: 20 at Lake Hodges 25 February 1989, 47 in the Wild Animal Park and at San Pasqual Battlefield in March 1990, and 33 at Lake Jennings 9 March 1990. Also, some sites on private property where Cactus Wrens were known before 1997 could not be surveyed for this atlas because of lack of access. This problem rather than habitat loss accounted for our missing the Cactus Wren near Ramona (K13/K14) and on Mother Miguel Mountain (T13), though urban sprawl is extending into the latter area.

Rea and Weaver (1990) listed 77 sites in San Diego County and mapped the species as extirpated in the 1980s at 26 of these. Subsequent records submitted to

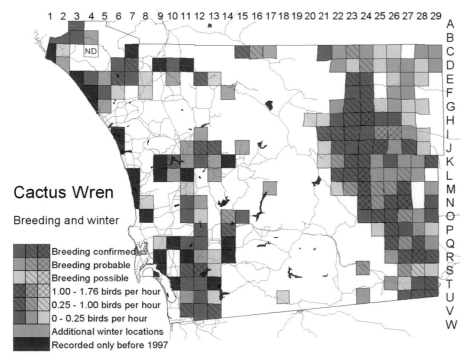

Cactus Wren

Breeding and winter

- Breeding confirmed
- Breeding probable
- Breeding possible
- 1.00 - 1.76 birds per hour
- 0.25 - 1.00 birds per hour
- 0 - 0.25 birds per hour
- Additional winter locations
- Recorded only before 1997

the California Natural Diversity Data Base and San Diego County's Multiple Species Conservation Plan added 16 sites, and field work for this atlas, 1997–2001, added about 18 further sites and relocated the species near six sites where Rea and Weaver (1990) thought it extirpated. The "population" at several of these sites, however, consists of as little as a single individual and therefore may be ephemeral or not viable. Very isolated sites, especially likely to fall into this category, are lower Los Peñasquitos Canyon (N8), very well covered, with only one record, of one singing male 7 June 1998 (P. A. Ginsburg), and Sandrock Canyon, Serra Mesa (Q9), with one singing male 2 May–15 June 2000 (J. A. Martin).

The cactus thickets on which the San Diego Cactus Wren depends are restricted to stands of open sage scrub at elevations below 1500 feet on south- and west-facing slopes, at the bases of hillsides within a quarter mile of river valleys. Along San Mateo Creek and the Otay River, they occur in broad dry washes. The wrens especially favor hillside gullies in which cacti can grow especially tall. The birds' territories range in size from 0.8 to 2 ha, averaging 1.3 ha, thus tending to be smaller than those of Cactus Wrens in Arizona (Rea and Weaver 1990).

In and near the Anza–Borrego Desert, subspecies *anthonyi* is most common on well-drained soil with abundant cacti (counts in the breeding season up to 31 on Mescal Bajada, J25, 12 June 1998, M. and B. McIntosh; 20 near Indian Hill, R28, 6 May 1998, J. O. Zimmer; 20 near Jacumba, U28, 20 March 1998, C. G. Edwards). It is fairly common in the town of Borrego Springs, where houses are scattered and native desert plants are used widely in landscaping (up to 12 on 15 March 1997, P. D. Ache). But it is lacking from valley floors, where cacti cannot grow in the alkaline soil, from badlands almost lacking in vegetation, and from the sandy region around Ocotillo Wells. Cactus Wrens extend well up the mountains' east slope, nearly to the head of San Felipe Valley (H20; two in April and May 2000, A. P. and T. E. Keenan) and Boulevard (T26; one on 31 May 1998 and 31 May 1999, D. S. and A. W. Hester). Their elevational range extends up to about 3900 feet (Rea and Weaver 1990). We discovered two sites a short distance onto the coastal slope in southeastern San Diego County, in semidesert scrub with considerable snake cholla: Miller Valley (S24; up to three on 9 May 2000) and 4 miles east of Cameron Corners (U24; two singing males 10 May 1999, L. J. Hargrove). Cactus Wrens, *anthonyi* on the basis of Weaver's observations and photographs, also occur on the coastal slope in Dameron and Oak Grove valleys (C15/C16/C17), in sage scrub dominated by flattop buckwheat and deerweed with abundant cacti and yuccas (up to seven, including fledglings, in Dameron Valley, C15, 7 June 1997, K. L. Weaver). Here, in a habitat shared with several other typically desert species, the wrens appear to nest exclusively in the cane (or valley) cholla.

Nesting: The Cactus Wren's nest, a hollow football-shaped structure with the entrance hole at one end, is unique. Subspecies *sandiegensis* builds in chollas or prickly pears almost exclusively; of 584 nests observed by Rea

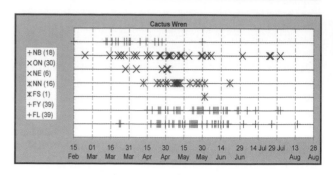

and Weaver (1990), only two, in yellow bush penstemons, were not in cacti. But the birds evidently do not discriminate among the coast cholla and either species of prickly pear (*Opuntia littoralis* or *O. oricola*). Rea and Weaver (1990) found the median height of 98 cacti in which the wrens were nesting to be 138 cm, range 74–226 cm. Cacti lower than this range do not offer suitable habitat, presumably because the nest is too accessible to predators.

Though also usually selecting cacti, subspecies *anthonyi* is slightly more flexible in choice of nest site. We noted four nests in Mojave yucca, one in a palo verde, one in a deformed ocotillo, and one apparently hidden in the skirt of a California fan palm, besides many in four species of cholla.

Because Cactus Wrens maintain nests for roosting year round, observations of nest building and occupied nests are not valid clues to the species' breeding schedule. Likewise, old nests do not confirm breeding. Nevertheless, because the species is almost completely sedentary, the difference between the distribution of nests and the distribution of breeding wrens is minor. The most conspicuous possible exception was at Barrett Junction (U18), where I found a nest but no Cactus Wrens 13 February 2000. Repeated checks of the site through the following spring never revealed any birds, only a gradually deteriorating nest.

Our observations from 1997 to 2001 suggest that mid March to early June is the main season for Cactus Wrens to lay in San Diego County. Forty-three collected egg sets from San Diego County (all but three of the San Diego Cactus Wren) range in date from 7 March to 10 July. Bent (1948) reported a California date as early as 2 March. Our only observations outside this window were in the wet spring of 1998, when fledglings in Culp Valley (G23/H23) 23 and 24 March implied laying as early as mid February (M. L. Gabel).

Migration: Dispersal of Cactus Wrens away from their breeding sites is minimal, but the rare instances of such dispersal may be vital to the species' viability. Guy McCaskie's two coastal records of vagrants well away from breeding habitat, from Point Loma 14 October 1967 and Mission Bay 14 February 1970, have not been replicated since. A juvenile found at the south base of Cowles Mountain (Q11) 23 June 2001 (SDNHM 50564) shows that juveniles may leave their natal territories soon after independence from their parents. The known nesting pairs nearest this site are about 1.9 miles to the southwest below Lake Murray and an equal distance to the northeast near Cowles Mountain's northeast base in southern Santee.

Winter: Winter numbers differ little from those in the breeding season. High winter counts of *sandiegensis* were of 23 in the Wild Animal Park (J13) 29 December 2001 (K. L. Weaver) and 21 at Lake Jennings (O14) 7 February 1998 (M. B. Stowe). High winter counts of *anthonyi* were of 22 in north Borrego Springs (F24) 19 December 1999 (P. K. Nelson et al.) and 20 in Box Canyon (L23) 10 January 1998 (S. D. Cameron). The only winter record more than 3 miles away from a known colony was from about 2800 feet elevation in Rancho Cuca (F14; one on 26 and 27 December 1999, S. and J. Berg). Seemingly isolated occurrences in Pamo Valley (J15; two on 2 January 2000, W. E. Haas), along Highland Valley Road about 5.5 west of Ramona (L13; one on 2 January 1999, J. McColm), and in the canyon of the San Diego River above El Capitan Reservoir between Boulder and Isham creeks (M17; one on 24 January 1998, R. C. Sanger) reflect sites possibly occupied only intermittently or sites previously known but missed during the breeding season because of access problems.

In the Anza–Borrego Desert we noted Cactus Wrens in winter in seven squares where we did not see them in the breeding season, suggesting occasional winter dispersal into marginal habitat. In two squares we saw nests but never the birds themselves at any season.

Conservation: Because of its restriction to stands of chollas and prickly pears, the San Diego Cactus Wren has always had a rather patchy range (Bancroft 1923). Nevertheless, it was formerly widespread at elevations below 1000 feet in coastal San Diego County, especially in the area now covered by the inner city of San Diego (Rea and Weaver 1990, specimens in San Diego Natural History Museum). Habitat destruction in the form of urban sprawl threatens the San Diego Cactus Wren gravely. W. L. Dawson recognized this as early as 1923, and since then the threat has only intensified. Cactus Wrens occurred formerly on the south-facing slopes just north of northern San Diego County's coastal lagoons but were eliminated from them during the 1980s. The pressure from urbanization is especially strong in the range of the Sweetwater/Otay population. The environmental impact statement for Highway 125 specifies elimination of 11 Cactus Wren territories (V. Marquez pers. comm.). Recent public acquisitions of significant tracts of coastal sage scrub for San Diego County's multiple-species conservation plan include few if any Cactus Wren sites, lying largely too far inland. With the population so reduced and fragmented, the long-term viability of what remains is an open question (Mock 1993).

Rea and Weaver (1990) also identified fire as a threat to the San Diego Cactus Wren, citing Benson (1969) in calling fire "the chief limiting factor in the distribution of cacti in southern California." The long time required for a burned cactus thicket to regrow to a height sufficient for nesting Cactus Wrens can result in the species' dying out in burned habitat. One year after the Laguna Canyon fire

in the San Joaquin Hills, Orange County, the population of Cactus Wrens was down 72% (Bontrager et al. 1995). The threat was dramatized in February 2002 when the Gavilan fire burned much of the Cactus Wren habitat in the Fallbrook Naval Weapons Station.

Habitat fragmentation may compound the negative effect of habitat destruction. Rea and Weaver (1990) noted that during the 1980s all 26 sites where they documented the bird's disappearance had supported fewer than five pairs and that at 18 of these sites the extent of the habitat still appeared sufficient to support at least one pair. If the habitat is adequate, however, rather isolated populations may persist. At Malcolm X Library in southeast San Diego (S11), in partly degraded sage scrub isolated for decades from the rest of the Sweetwater/Otay population, I found that about six pairs persisted from 1997 through 2001. At this site and on Dictionary Hill (R12/S12) Cactus Wrens make some use of spiny garden plants around houses adjacent to colonies in native cactus thickets, so the birds' ability to colonize appropriate landscaping should be explored further, as a means of extending—not replacing—populations in natural habitat.

Other recommendations listed by Rea and Weaver (1990) for conservation of the San Diego Cactus Wren apply now more than ever. The protection of all remaining sites is critical, even if they fall outside multiple-species conservation plans and in the path of proposed highways. Degraded and burned areas need restoration, through planting of cacti. The subspecies' precise numbers are not clear because of difficult access to many sites; some sites on private property could not be surveyed by atlas observers. A thorough census and continued regular monitoring of the population is essential.

The San Diego Cactus Wren has benefited to some extent from the formal listing of the California Gnatcatcher as threatened, since almost all of the wren's sites also support the gnatcatcher, but because of the wren's specializations listing remains important. The petition to list the San Diego Cactus Wren was denied only on the basis of unpublished letters disputing the subspecies' validity and the statement "no apparent morphological or other morphometric differences have been detected to date that distinguish coastal birds from other cactus wrens" (Beattie 1994), in disregard of the evidence of Rea and Weaver (1990).

Taxonomy: Rea and Weaver (1990) analyzed the subspecies of Cactus Wren in southern California thoroughly, detailing the seven characters in which *C. b. sandiegensis* Rea, 1986, differs from both *C. b. anthonyi* (Mearns, 1902), and *C. b. bryanti* (Anthony, 1894) of northern Baja California. *C. b. sandiegensis* differs from *anthonyi* primarily in its more extensively barred tail (especially on rectrices 4 and 5), larger spots on the belly, paler ochre background color on the belly, and less concentration of the breast spots into a dense patch. All known specimens of *sandiegensis* are distinguishable from *anthonyi* by at least one character, 87% by three or more characters. A genetic study (Eggert 1997) found evidence of population isolation at a level even finer than the subspecies evident on the basis of external characters. Rea and Weaver (1990) described a difference between the subspecies in song—slower, lower, and raspier in *sandiegensis*—that has yet to be studied in detail. On the basis of freshly col-

lected fresh-plumaged topotypes, Rea (1983) supported the distinction of *anthonyi* of the Sonoran Desert from *C. b. couesi* Sharpe, 1881, of the Chihuahuan Desert.

Rock Wren *Salpinctes obsoletus*

Like the Canyon Wren, the Rock Wren is a bird of rocky canyons and boulder-covered slopes. But the Rock Wren is more flexible, living also in badlands of eroded earth, the beds of partially filled reservoirs, and sparsely vegetated areas of little relief. It is more dispersive than the Canyon Wren, wintering regularly if uncommonly in small rock outcrops and expanses of disturbed bare dirt where it does not breed. From 1997 to 2002 we saw this more opportunistic lifestyle illustrated by striking fluctuations in numbers in the Anza–Borrego Desert. Rock Wrens increased sharply during the wet winter of 1997–98, remained common for one year, then decreased in the following dry years.

Breeding distribution: The Rock Wren is most widespread and numerous in the Anza–Borrego Desert, especially on rocky slopes. Daily counts in the breeding season ranged up to 50, including 30 singing males, around Indian Hill and Carrizo Palms (R28) 6 May 1998 (J. O. Zimmer), 40 on a bajada southwest of Halfhill Dry Lake (J29) 10 April 1998 (L. J. Hargrove), and 40 at Split Mountain (L29) 18 April 1998 (G. Rebstock, K. Forney). The convergence of these high counts in a single year is no coincidence but followed a winter of unusually plentiful rain. The number of Rock Wrens reported per hour in the eastern third of San Diego County was at least 50% greater in 1998 than it was in any other of the atlas period's five years. In 1998, Rock Wrens were common

Photo by Jack C. Daynes

also in the Borrego and Carrizo badlands (25 near Five Palms Spring, G29, 16 May 1998, G. Rebstock, K. Forney; 29 in Arroyo Seco del Diablo, N28, 16 May 1998, R. and S. L. Breisch). Even on the flat floor of the Borrego Valley (F24) Rock Wrens breed occasionally (four, adults feeding young, 27 May 2001, M. L. Gabel).

On the coastal slope Rock Wrens are more localized, but their numbers are more consistent from year to year. Here they are most numerous in the rocky foothills near the Mexican border, then decrease toward the northwest. The largest number reported from the coastal slope was 20 on the south side of Otay Mountain (V15) 25 May 1999 (D. C. Seals). In northwestern San Diego County the only sites of reports of more than three Rock Wrens in a day were on the southwest slope of Double Peak (J9; 12 on 14 March 1998, four on 15 May 1998, J. O. Zimmer) and near Willow Spring (A5) on the Riverside County line (six on 10 and 22 June 1999, K. J. Winter). We seldom found the Rock Wren above 4000 feet elevation, but the record at the highest elevation was of a nest with nestlings near the summit of Hot Springs Mountain (E20) 8 June 2001 (K. L. Weaver). The Rock Wren is rare along the coast, where the only records in the breeding season are of a singing male 1 mile inland from the Santa Margarita River mouth

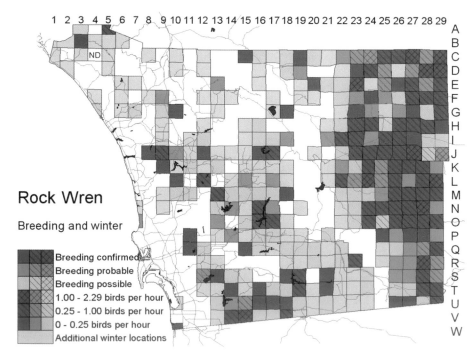

Rock Wren

Breeding and winter

- Breeding confirmed
- Breeding probable
- Breeding possible
- 1.00 - 2.29 birds per hour
- 0.25 - 1.00 birds per hour
- 0 - 0.25 birds per hour
- Additional winter locations

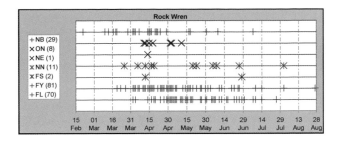

Rock Wren

+NB (29)	
×ON (8)	
×NE (1)	
×NN (11)	
×FS (2)	
+FY (81)	
+FL (70)	

15 Feb, 01 Mar, 16 Mar, 31 Mar, 15 Apr, 30 Apr, 15 May, 30 May, 14 Jun, 29 Jun, 14 Jul, 29 Jul, 13 Aug, 28 Aug

(G4) 16 April and 1 May 1999 (P. A. Ginsburg), a pair at Torrey Pines (O7) 22 April 1997 (D. G. Seay), and two pairs, each with one fledgling, in Goat Canyon (W10) 12 June 1999 (W. E. Haas).

Nesting: Rock Wrens usually nest in crevices among or under rocks, sometimes in rodent burrows in earthen banks. Several nests reported by atlas participants were furnished with the "porch" of small rock chips, unique to this species. Most nests were in rock piles, banks, or road cuts; one at Morena Dam (T21) 12 April 1997 was in a hole in the dam's concrete (R. and S. L. Breisch).

Our observations from 1997 to 2001 imply egg laying beginning in early March (fledglings in Blair Valley, L24, 2 April 1998, R. Thériault) and continuing through early June (adult disposing of nestling's fecal sac between San Dieguito Reservoir and Mount Israel, K9, 28 June 1998, L. E. Taylor), exceptionally to early July (nest with nestlings at upper end of El Capitan Reservoir, N16, 1 August 2000, J. R. Barth). The span falls well within the range 5 February–28 July given for 77 California egg sets by Bent (1948). The wide range suggests multiple broods when the food supply is favorable.

Migration: The Rock Wren shows up in only small numbers away from sites where it could breed, so its migration is inconspicuous. On Point Loma (S7), where it is unknown as a breeding bird, it is recorded from 16

September to 22 February (Unitt 1984). From 1997 to 2001, the latest record from an atlas square where the species was not found during the breeding season was of one at Torrey Pines State Reserve (N7) 3 March 1999 (K. Estey).

Winter: Any winter influx of Rock Wrens into San Diego County is only slight. Numbers in winter are not conspicuously higher than in the breeding season (maximum count 40 near Indian Hill 8 February 1998, J. O. Zimmer). The winter distribution follows a pattern similar to the breeding distribution. We found the species in winter in 99 atlas squares where we did not find it during the breeding season, however, so there is at least considerable dispersal of the local population. The species still occurs rarely at high elevations (one near the summit of Hot Springs Mountain 13 February 1999, K. L. Weaver; one at Mount Laguna, O23, 21 January 2002, E. C. Hall, J. O. Zimmer). It is appreciably more frequent in northwestern San Diego County in winter but still rather rare along the coast, with only 13 records 1997–2002, none of more than two birds.

The Rock Wren's fluctuations in abundance in the Anza–Borrego Desert in winter were similar to those in the breeding season. The number reported per hour in the last three winters of the project was only one third that in 1997–98.

Conservation: No changes through history in the Rock Wren's status in San Diego County are known. The Rock Wren benefits to a small degree from human modifications of the environment, using road cuts, riprap, quarries, and areas of disturbed bare dirt—more in winter than in the breeding season.

Taxonomy: Rock Wrens in San Diego County, as throughout the mainland of North America north of southern Mexico, are *S. o. obsoletus* (Say, 1823).

Canyon Wren *Catherpes mexicanus*

No bird sound evokes a feeling of wilderness more than the spiraling, echoing song of the Canyon Wren. Cliffs, talus slopes, desert gorges, rocky ravines, and boulder-studded chaparral are the Canyon Wren's habitat. A year-round resident, the Canyon Wren is uncommon, living in well-spaced territories.

Breeding distribution: The Canyon Wren's range is constrained by the birds' need for rugged topography. Such conditions are widespread in San Diego County's foothills, mountains, and desert, but even here the wren's distribution is quite patchy. San Diego County's mosaic of geology also affects the Canyon Wren: mountains formed of granite, such as Woodson or Corte Madera, offer far more exposed rock and so more Canyon Wren habitat than those formed of gabbro, such as Viejas or McGinty, which lack extensive rock outcrops and are more uniformly clothed in chaparral. The higher counts on the coastal slope are from granitic terrain like the San Diego River gorge near Dye Mountain (K18; nine on 9 July 2000,

Photo by Suzanne I. Bond

L. J. Hargrove), Lyons Peak (S17; seven on 11 July 1999, J. R. Barth), and the gorge of Cottonwood Creek below Barrett Dam (T18; seven on 8 June 2000, L. J. Hargrove). Nevertheless, the wrens still occur in fair numbers on some steep gabbro peaks like Otay Mountain (four on the north slope, U15, 31 May 2000, L. J. Hargrove).

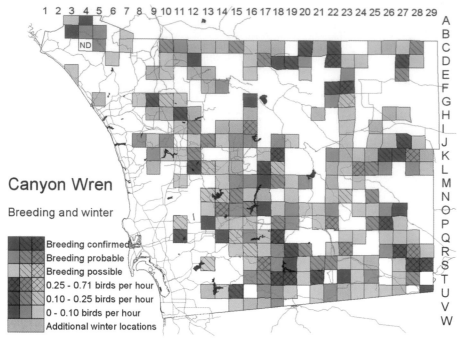

Canyon Wren

Breeding and winter

- Breeding confirmed
- Breeding probable
- Breeding possible
- 0.25 - 0.71 birds per hour
- 0.10 - 0.25 birds per hour
- 0 - 0.10 birds per hour
- Additional winter locations

Other than a single singing male near the mouth of Horno Canyon (E3) 30 May 1998 (R. and S. L. Breisch) we did not find the Canyon Wren during the breeding season within about 5 miles of the coast. The most coastal localities were in San Mateo Canyon (B3; two singing males 28 May 2000, P. Unitt), the canyon of San Marcos Creek (J8; pair 28 June 1997, J. O Zimmer), and Mission Gorge (Q11; up to six on 11 July 1999, N. Osborn). Elevation is not a concern to the Canyon Wren in San Diego County; the species occurs near the summits of both Hot Springs Mountain (E20; singing male 19 May 2001, K. L. Weaver, C. R. Mahrdt) and Cuyamaca Peak (M20; two singing males 23 May 1998, G. L. Rogers). Canyon Wrens reach their peak abundance in the steep canyons descending the east face of the mountains: the maximum count was 14, including eight singing males, in Borrego Palm Canyon (F23) 5–8 July 2001 (L. J. Hargrove). Farther out into the desert the birds are fewer but well distributed in suitable terrain, with up to seven along Alma Wash near Starfish Cove (K28) 24 March 2000 (L. J. Hargrove).

Nesting: The Canyon Wren typically nests in rock crevices, in caves, or on sheltered rock ledges. One nest near

Indian Flats (D19) 23 May 2001 was in a vertical crevice just below some White-throated Swift nests (J. R. Barth). The Canyon Wren takes advantage of man-made nest sites too. One nest near the rocky slopes of the south fork of Moosa Canyon (G9) 30 May 1998 was in an outdoor light on a patio (C. Cook); another at Lake Morena (T21) 31 May 1999 was inside an equipment shed (R. and S. L. Breisch).

Bent (1948) reported that 68 California egg sets ranged in date from 28 March to 11 July. The breeding season we observed in San Diego County 1997–2001 agrees with this almost exactly, except that a bird between Lake Poway and Mount Woodson (L12) carrying insects 4 April 1998 (M. and B. McIntosh) implies young hatched from eggs laid by about 19 March. Several species nested exceptionally early in the wet spring of 1998.

Winter: The Canyon Wren engages in only minor dispersal away from its breeding territories in winter. Furthermore, most locations where the species was seen in winter but not the breeding season may be suitable breeding habitat, perhaps occupied only intermittently. The only site where the species occurred in winter more than one atlas square away from where it was found in the breeding season was Ysidora Gorge (G5), along the Santa Margarita River in Camp Pendleton (one on 26 December 1998 and 23 December 2000, P. Unitt). There is little if any retreat from the higher elevations in winter. One individual was near the summit of Hot Springs Mountain 5 February 2000 (K. L. Weaver); others were around 5600 feet elevation near Garnet Mountain (N22) 19 and 26 February 2000 (G. L. Rogers).

Conservation: The Canyon Wren has become a village and even city bird in places in Mexico. At San Javier in Baja California Sur it enters the old stone mission and takes advantage of the church's acoustics to amplify its song. But in San Diego County it shows little sign of urban adaptation: the walls of packed adobe common in Mexico are a microhabitat no longer duplicated in the United States. Most Canyon Wren habitat is insulated from development by its very ruggedness. The only possible change in the species' distribution we detected was its absence 1997–2002 from the bluffs at Torrey Pines City Park (O7), where J. L. Dunn noted it occasionally from 1974 to 1976 (Unitt 1984).

Taxonomy: Canyon Wrens in San Diego County are *C. m. conspersus* Ridgway, 1873, which ranges from the Great Basin south to northwestern Mexico.

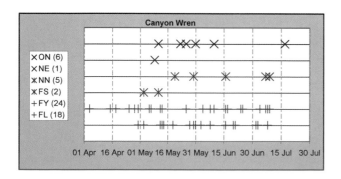

Bewick's Wren *Thryomanes bewickii*

Bewick's Wren is something of an enigma, a cavity nester that is common in chaparral and sage scrub, habitats with no trees offering cavities. The answer is the wren's flexible definition of a cavity: rocks, caves, holes in the ground, and the litter of humanity serve for nest sites just as well as holes in trees. Bewick's Wren thus can occupy any habitat with at least moderately dense shrubbery: sage scrub, the understory of oak, riparian, and pinyon–juniper woodland, desert-edge scrub, and desert washes, as well as chaparral, the habitat where it is most abundant. Though a year-round resident, Bewick's Wren spreads uncommonly in winter even into the sparsest desert scrub.

Breeding distribution: The Bewick's Wren is one of San Diego County's most widespread birds. In the breeding season it occurs over the entire coastal slope except the Coronado Peninsula, ranging as high as the summit of Hot Springs Mountain (E20; pair with fledglings 15 July 2000, K. L. Weaver, C. R. Mahrdt). Its abundance on the coastal side follows no strong pattern except that numbers are low in extensively urbanized or heavily forested areas. Numbers can be high in both the coastal lowland (e.g., 50 in Vista, H8, 16 May 1999, J. O. Zimmer) and in the mountains (e.g., 33 in Noble Canyon, O22, 22 April 1997, P. Unitt). Counts in the Pine Valley area (O21/O22/P21/P22) 1993–97 suggested that in mature chaparral the only species exceeding Bewick's Wren in abundance are the Wrentit, Spotted Towhee, and Black-chinned Sparrow (Cleveland National Forest data).

Field work for this atlas revealed Bewick's Wren to be considerably more widespread than expected on the desert slope. Even in the breeding season it is lacking only from the most sparsely vegetated valley floors and

Photo by Jack C. Daynes

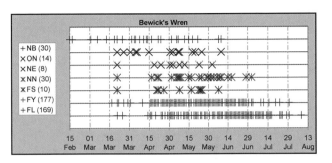

badlands. It is one of the more common birds on scrubby rocky slopes and among pinyons and junipers in desert mountains, with numbers up to 29 on the northwest slope of Whale Peak (L25) 25 June 1998 (R. Thériault). Bewick's Wren is rare in the town of Borrego Springs itself but resident in the thicket of mesquites on the Borrego Valley's floor (G25; up to eight on 8 April 1997; pair entering possible nest crevice in a mesquite 11 March 1997, R. Thériault).

Nesting: Bewick's nests in tree cavities like those used by the House Wren; atlas participants noted three nests in coast live oaks and one in a willow. Trees isolated or scattered in chaparral offer Bewick's Wrens nest sites in areas too sparsely wooded for House Wrens. But more often we found nests in man-made structures: in crevices of wooden buildings, in pipes, under roof tiles, and in birdhouses. Bewick's Wrens take advantage of discarded trash that offers cavities, and in treeless chaparral such trash may provide the best nest sites. We noted Bewick's Wren nests in a discarded hub of a truck wheel, in a cardboard beer carton, in a coffee can, and in an abandoned bullet-riddled car. One nest was reported from a yucca, and it is likely the wrens nest among the leaf bases of Mojave yuccas as

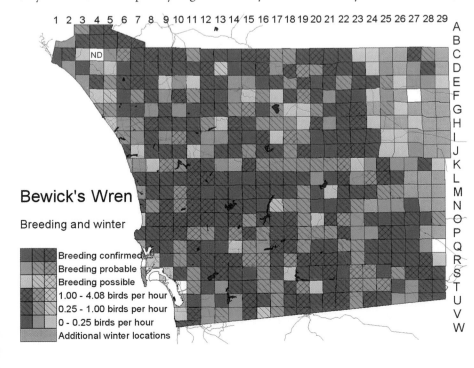

Bewick's Wren

Breeding and winter

- Breeding confirmed
- Breeding probable
- Breeding possible
- 1.00 - 4.08 birds per hour
- 0.25 - 1.00 birds per hour
- 0 - 0.25 birds per hour
- Additional winter locations

well as in woodpecker-excavated cavities in them. Caves, rock crevices, and brush piles have also been noted as nest sites for Bewick's Wren (Bent 1948).

Our observations from 1997 to 2001 suggest that Bewick's Wrens lay mainly from mid March to mid June, in agreement with 54 egg sets collected in San Diego County from 1887 to 1937. Occasional pairs may start earlier, building nests as early as 15 February (2001, Pauma Valley, E12, K. Fischer). Nest building may take over three weeks to complete, however (Kennedy and White 1997), so such dates may not be good guides to dates of egg laying. Reports of Bewick's Wrens "feeding young" as early as 18 March could refer to males feeding incubating females. But fledglings near Ross Lake (B7) 26 March 1999 (K. L. Weaver) must have come from a clutch in which incubation began about 24 February.

Migration: Because there are so few areas in San Diego County where Bewick's Wren is not resident, there is almost no information on its migration here. At places in the Anza–Borrego Desert where it is not suspected to breed, Bewick's Wren has been seen as late in spring as 26 March (1999, one in June Wash, M27, R. Thériault). Away from its few breeding locations in the Salton Sink Bewick's Wren has been recorded from 29 August to 17 April (Patten et al. 2003).

Winter: Bewick's Wren is even more widespread in San Diego County in winter than in the breeding season. Over most of the county winter numbers are very similar to those in the breeding season (maximum daily count 50, north of Morena Reservoir, S21, 16 February 1998, S. E. Smith, and along Espinosa Trail, R19, 23 February 1999, G. L. Rogers). The birds remain through the winter at least in small numbers at high elevations, being recorded from the summits of Hot Springs Mountain (E20) and Monument Peak in the Laguna Mountains (O23). Even there the impression of numbers lower than in the breeding season could be due simply to less calling and no singing in the winter. Though territorial pairs may be sedentary, there is appreciable movement, perhaps mainly by young birds. We noted Bewick's Wren in winter in almost every atlas square in the Anza–Borrego Desert where it was absent during the breeding season. Numbers of such dispersers into sparse desert scrub are usually small, but daily counts were sometimes as high as nine, along Fish Creek Wash (M27) 2 February 2000 (M. B. Mulrooney) and at Split Mountain (L29) 2 December 1999 (P. D. Jorgensen).

Conservation: Despite its heavy use of man-made artifacts as nest sites, Bewick's Wren is not an urban adapter. Apparently its need for extensive shrubbery for foraging, or a dependence on insects of native habitats for food, keeps it in territories with a component of native scrub. But it is relatively tolerant of this habitat being fragment-

ed. Bolger et al. (1997) and Crooks et al. (2001) identified Bewick's Wren as a species of low sensitivity to fragmentation, and this is corroborated by our atlas results. In central San Diego, Bewick's Wren is missing from only those squares that have been totally urbanized, lacking any significant native scrub. Of the eight chaparral birds analyzed by Crooks et al. (2001), the Bewick's Wren was the least sensitive, predicted to have a 95% chance of surviving for 100 years in fragments as small as 13 hectares.

In the eastern U.S., Bewick's Wren has experienced serious population decline and range contraction, attributed to the increase and spread of the House Wren, which competes for nest cavities and destroys the eggs of other birds (Newman 1961). Even though the House Wren is increasing in San Diego County, a concomitant decrease of Bewick's Wren seems unlikely here. The treeless chaparral in which Bewick's Wrens are so common is unsuitable for breeding House Wrens. Unless development of the entire coastal slope penetrates far deeper into foothill chaparral than it does now, into the Cleveland National Forest and other open-space reserves, it seems that large numbers of Bewick's Wrens will remain well isolated from both the inroads of the House Wren as well as from direct loss of habitat.

Taxonomy: Bewick's Wrens breeding in San Diego County are *T. b. charienturus* Oberholser, 1898, in which the upperparts are dark chocolate brown and the central rectrices are so dark as to mute the blackish bars. *T. b. correctus* Grinnell, 1928, is a synonym of *charienturus*, based on the comparison of newer unfoxed and older foxed specimens (Rea 1986). With a range encompassing southwestern Alta California and northwestern Baja California, this subspecies—darker than others in the western United States—is another taxon characterizing the San Diegan District of the California Floristic Province.

A few Bewick's Wrens from farther north reach San Diego County as winter visitors. At least one specimen is the paler *T. b. drymoecus* Oberholser, 1898, which breeds mainly inland from southern Oregon south to central California: La Mesa (R12) 1 November 1914 (SDNHM 32621). One specimen is the more rufous *T. b. spilurus* (Vigors, 1839), which breeds in the San Francisco Bay area: 3.3 miles southeast of Borrego Springs (G25) 24 January 1985 (SDNHM 42874). A small fraction of the Bewick's Wren population of the Anza–Borrego Desert is unusually pale and gray, resembling the pale gray subspecies *T. b. eremophilus* of the Great Basin and southern Rocky Mountains. Two specimens from Mason Valley (M23), collected 30 November 1913 (SDNHM 32620) and 9 September 1984 (SDNHM 43308) look like *eremophilus*, but the latter was still in molt so must be of the local population rather than a migrant.

House Wren *Troglodytes domesticus*

The House Wren breeds commonly in San Diego County's woodlands of oak, sycamore, and conifers, but here it is only beginning to take on the city-dwelling habits that justify its name over so much of the United States. Within its historic range, almost coextensive in San Diego County with that of the coast live oak, the wren has long patronized bird-houses as well as natural nest holes. But only since the 1990s has it spread into suburbs built over former sage scrub. It is on the increase as a winter visitor or year-round resident too, possibly in response to climatic warming.

Breeding distribution: The House Wren is widespread on San Diego County's coastal slope, most numerous in oak woodland and riparian woodland with large sycamores. It is common from low elevations (100 in Horno Canyon and along the south fork of San Onofre Creek, D3, 31 May 1998, K. Perry, D. Gould; 135 in Los Peñasquitos and Lopez canyons, N8, 11 April 1999, P. A. Ginsburg et al.) to the higher mountains (13 near the summit of Hot Springs Mountain, E20, 18 June 2000, K. L. Weaver, C. R. Mahrdt; 25 at Mount Laguna, O23, 13–14 June 1998, C. G. Edwards). The eastern edge of the House Wren's range follows the eastern edge of the coast live oak's range almost exactly. The exception is along San Felipe Creek, where the wren extends in riparian woodland east to Sentenac Ciénaga (J23; up to three, all singing males, 14 June 1998, R. Thériault). Also, there is one record of the House Wren nesting in the cottonwoods at Butterfield Ranch in Mason Valley (M23; two on 17 April 1999, P. K. Nelson).

In the city of San Diego the House Wren has begun colonizing eucalyptus groves and urban trees away from natural habitat, using birdhouses, man-made structures,

Photo by Anthony Mercieca

and possibly crevices behind loose strips of eucalyptus bark for nest sites. The spread is going from north to south. The largest concentration found in nonnative habitat is in Pottery Canyon, La Jolla (P7), with up to 11 on 27 May 1999 (L. and M. Polinsky). South of Mission Valley House Wrens are still uncommon through the breeding season but probably nesting at Point Loma College (S7; courting pair 10 May 1997, J. C. Worley) and confirmed nesting in the Tijuana River valley (W10; nest with nestlings 8 May 2001, T. Stands, S. Yamagata) and at the west edge of Otay Mesa (V12; male singing while female carried nest material into a horizontal pipe, 13 April 2001, P. Unitt).

Nesting: As a cavity nester, the House Wren takes advantage of a wide variety of nest sites. Most frequently, it uses old woodpecker holes and natural cavities in large trees, especially coast live oaks and western sycamores. Other trees in which atlas observers noted House Wren nests were cottonwood, willow, Engelmann oak, and black oak. The House Wren is also San Diego County's leading customer of birdhouses. Electrical boxes, open-ended pipes, and street lamps were other man-made nest sites reported repeatedly. We noted Cliff Swallow nests taken over by House Wrens on three occasions.

The House Wren offers one of the strongest examples of a breeding season shifting earlier in the year. Fifty-six egg sets collected in San Diego County from 1890 to 1942 range in date from 14 April to 13 June. The range for 119 sets collected throughout California reported by Bent (1948) is 11 April–26 June. Our observations from 1997 to 2001, however, show that House Wrens now begin laying regularly about

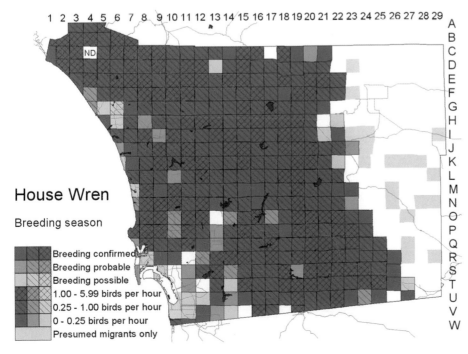

House Wren

Breeding season

- Breeding confirmed
- Breeding probable
- Breeding possible
- 1.00 - 5.99 birds per hour
- 0.25 - 1.00 birds per hour
- 0 - 0.25 birds per hour
- Presumed migrants only

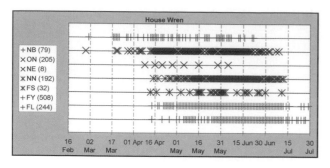

1 April. These observations include several of nests with nestlings, adults disposing of fecal sacs, and adults carrying insects as early as 13 April, as well as a nest with eggs in a box along the Sweetwater River near Highway 94 (R13) 9 April 1997 (A. Mercieca). Occasionally the birds may lay even as early as about 16 March, as implied by young already fledged at the upper end of Sweetwater Reservoir (S13) 14 April 1999 (P. Famolaro). The change has taken place only at the beginning of the season, as we observed nests with nestlings as late as 12 July, meaning egg laying as late as about 14 June.

Migration: Because the House Wren occurs in San Diego County year round, its migrations are difficult to define exactly. It is not clear whether the population turns over completely from summer to winter or whether some breeding birds remain as permanent residents. Spring migrants return to their breeding territories at low to moderate elevations in March; even as high as 4400 feet (Upper Green Valley, M21) the birds may be singing and paired as early as 21 March (1997, P. D. Jorgensen). In the Anza–Borrego Desert, away from sites where it winters, the House Wren is recorded as an uncommon migrant from 13 March (1999, two in Borrego Palm Canyon, F23, A. G. Morley) to 13 May (1995, one in Hellhole Canyon, G23, H. A. Wier). The 15 spring migrants reported by Massey at Agua Caliente Springs (M26) 4 April 1994 were

exceptional; from 1997 to 2001 we did not note any concentration in the Anza–Borrego Desert greater than four.

Postbreeding dispersal begins as early as 29 July (1992, one in Culp Valley, H23, M. L. Gabel), though fall migration is generally not obvious until late August.

Winter: Wintering House Wrens are most numerous in the coastal lowland, where daily counts can be as high as 22 along the Santa Margarita River north of Fallbrook (C8) 23 February 2002 (K. L. Weaver), 21 in San Pasqual Valley (K12) 29 December 2001 (C. G. Edwards), and 21 in lower Los Peñasquitos and Lopez canyons (N8) 2 December 2001 (D. K. Adams). With increasing elevation, the birds become scarcer, though as high as 4100 feet elevation we noted numbers up to six around Twin Lakes (C18) 24 January 1999 (P. Unitt). The highest winter House Wren locations were around 5300 feet in the Laguna Mountains (N22, 12 December 1998, G. L. Rogers; P23, 14 January and 21 December 1999, E. C. Hall, J. O. Zimmer) and at nearly 5500 feet at the Palomar Observatory (D15, one on 20 December 2001, K. L. Weaver).

On the east side of the mountains, wintering House Wrens are regular in San Felipe Valley (up to five near San Felipe, H20, 21 December 1998, I. S. Quon, and 27 February 1999, A. P. and T. E. Keenan). But at lower elevations in the Anza–Borrego Desert they are quite uncommon (no count of more than two per day) and restricted almost exclusively to oases and the irrigated floor of the Borrego Valley.

Conservation: The House Wren's primitive breeding distribution followed that of oak woodland closely, in a pattern much like that of the Oak Titmouse or Acorn Woodpecker. Since the 1970s, breeding House Wrens have become ever more widespread in the coastal strip from which they were once absent. It is unclear why a bird that occupies suburban backyards over much of North America should have been so slow to take advantage of the city of San Diego. The wren's spread has followed that of the Nuttall's Woodpecker, one of the primary excavators of cavities in which House Wrens nest.

The House Wren's range and numbers have increased considerably in winter as well. In spite of Emerson's (1887) report of one collected and another seen on Volcan Mountain (I20) on 24 and 28 January 1884, and another collected at Witch Creek (J18) 13 December 1904 (FMNH 144799), Willett (1912) and Stephens (1919a) said that only "a few" wintered in the coastal lowland and mentioned no wintering at higher elevations. The House Wren's status as a widespread if uncommon winter visitor in San Diego County's foot-

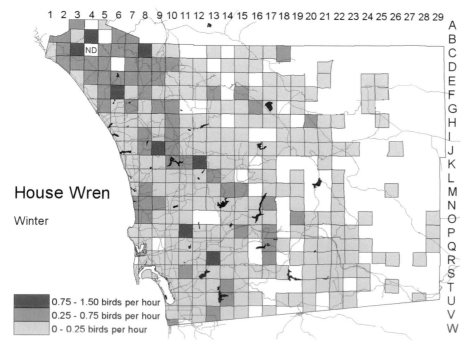

House Wren

Winter

0.75 - 1.50 birds per hour
0.25 - 0.75 birds per hour
0 - 0.25 birds per hour

hills and mountains emerged only as a result of the field work for this atlas. Numbers on San Diego Christmas bird counts have increased, the total per party-hour more than doubling from 0.052 from 1966 to 1975 to 0.132 from 1992 to 2001. The warming of winter low temperatures may be enabling more House Wrens to remain through that season. As a hypothesis for testing, I suggest that an increasing proportion of the breeding population is failing to migrate, and these now permanent residents are responsible for the breeding season shifting earlier in the year.

Taxonomy: Only the grayish western subspecies of the House Wren, *T. d. parkmanii* Audubon, 1839, is known from California. The name *T. aedon* (Vieillot, 1809) has been shown clearly to have been proposed after *T. domesticus* (Wilson, 1808) (Oberholser 1974, Rea 1983, Banks and Browning 1995). Continued use of *aedon* is based on tradition rather than conformity to the international code of zoological nomenclature.

Winter Wren *Troglodytes troglodytes*

The Winter Wren reaches the southern limit of its range in San Diego County, where it is a rare winter visitor. The wren's apparent rarity is exacerbated by the difficulty of finding it: the birds hide in dense woodland undergrowth, revealing themselves only with their double "chick" note. One summer occurrence of the Winter Wren on Palomar Mountain was far outside the species' breeding range and one of the least expected events brought to light by the field work for this atlas.

Photo by Alan M. Craig

Winter: Most of the published records of the Winter Wren for San Diego County are from well-birded sites around metropolitan San Diego, especially Point Loma (S7) and the Tijuana River valley. The more uniform coverage of the county directed toward this atlas, however, yielded Winter Wrens only in the foothill and mountain zones, likely reflecting the species' distribution more accurately. Three of the nine reported from 1997 to 2002 were around Palomar Mountain, and together with previous records for the area (e.g., Beemer 1949) suggest this is the most likely area for Winter Wrens in San Diego County. Nevertheless, at least 45 Winter Wrens have been

reported in the county, south to Smuggler's Gulch (W10), site of the southernmost record of the Winter Wren along the Pacific coast. In the Anza–Borrego Desert the Winter Wren has been reported only from Coyote Creek Canyon (D23; 7 December 1977 and 16 February 1978, AB 32:400, 1978) and Pinyon Mountain Road (K24; 26 November 1983, B. Massey).

Winter Wrens have been seen in San Diego County only singly, except for two in Marion Canyon (D12) 6 March 1949 (Beemer 1949). The number reported per winter during the atlas period varied from zero in 1997–98 to five in 1999–2000; the only earlier year with more was 1983–84, with six.

Migration: Dates for the Winter Wren in San Diego County range from 30 September (1981, Point Loma, R. E. Webster, AB 36:218, 1982) to 6 March (cited above), except for one at Warner Springs (F19) 3 May 1999 (C. G. Edwards) and the single summer record.

Breeding distribution: The sole summer record of the Winter Wren in San Diego County is the only one from anywhere in California south of Santa Barbara County and the Sierra Nevada. Clark R. Mahrdt and Edward C. Hall observed one

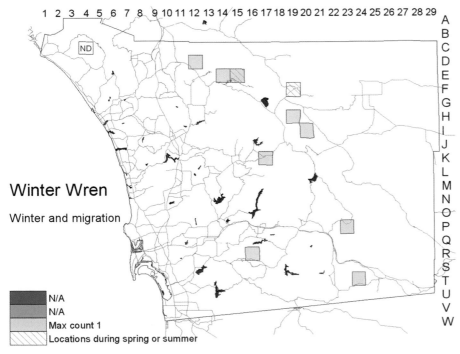

Winter Wren

Winter and migration

N/A
N/A
Max count 1
Locations during spring or summer

in Jeff Valley (E15), at 4900 feet elevation on Palomar Mountain, repeatedly from 28 May to 12 July 1999. It sang territorially, and on the final date was carrying twigs, but since only one bird was ever seen, presumably it was an unmated male. Hall tape-recorded the song and sent the recording to K. L. Garrett at the Los Angeles County Museum of Natural History; Garrett confirmed the song as typical of western Winter Wrens.

Taxonomy: The Winter Wren has yet to be collected in San Diego County, so the subspecies occurring here is (are?) uncertain. Both the dark rufous *T. t. pacificus*

Baird, 1864, and the less rufous *T. t. salebrosus* Burleigh, 1959, have been collected well to the south of their breeding ranges (Rea in Phillips 1986). One in the Tijuana River valley 3–15 December 1990 was "thought to be a bird from the eastern population (i.e, *T. t. hiemalis* Vieillot, 1819) on the basis of its call" (D. M. Parker, AB 45:322, 1991). Winter Wrens giving the call of *hiemalis* have been heard in Death Valley and the Imperial Valley (Patten et al. 2003) and probably photographed in southeastern Arizona (Monson and Phillips 1981), but the subspecies has yet to be collected in winter west of New Mexico.

Marsh Wren *Cistothorus palustris*

The Marsh Wren is well named, for it is rarely seen outside a marsh. It occurs in San Diego County in two roles. As a year-round resident it inhabits freshwater and brackish marshes mainly along and near the coast—home of subspecies *C. p. clarkae*, narrowly restricted to coastal southern California. As a winter visitor from farther north it is more widespread, invading salt marshes, wet grassy areas, and marshes too small to support a resident population. As a conservation issue the Marsh Wren is complex too: much of its primitive habitat has been destroyed, yet in San Diego County, over the second half of the 20th century, its breeding range spread considerably.

Breeding distribution: The core of the Marsh Wren's distribution in San Diego County is the "Mesopotamia" between the Santa Margarita and San Luis Rey rivers. The birds inhabit many lakes and ponds in these river valleys as well as marshes in the river channels themselves, upstream along the Santa Margarita to north of Fallbrook

Photo by Anthony Mercieca

(C8; pair with nestlings 24 July 2001, K. L. Weaver) and along the San Luis Rey to Couser Canyon (E10; two on 6 and 13 June 1998, K. Aldern, M. Bache). Numbers in this area are as high as 30 at Guajome Lake (G7) 31 May 1999 (D. and C. Wysong), 20 at Whelan Lake (G6) 19 April 2001 (J. Smith), and 15 at O'Neill Lake (E6) 5 June 1998 (P. A. Ginsburg). Marsh Wrens are also resident in the coastal wetlands, even small ones, from San Onofre (C1) to Los Peñasquitos Lagoon (N7). At the larger lagoons, numbers are as high as 50 at San Elijo (L7) 6 June 1999 (B. C. Moore) and 27 at Los Peñasquitos 2 May 1999 (D. K. Adams).

Elsewhere in the county breeding Marsh Wrens are quite localized. The largest colonies outside the core range are in La Jolla Valley (L10; up to 10 on 7 May 2000, K. J. Winter), along the Sweetwater River near Interstate 805 (T11; 28 on 18 April 1999, W. E. Haas), and at the Dairy Mart pond in the Tijuana River valley (V11; eight on 9 May 1999, P. Unitt). At other places numbers are small—no more than five reported in one atlas square per day. Outside the coastal lowland there are only a few breeding-season records,

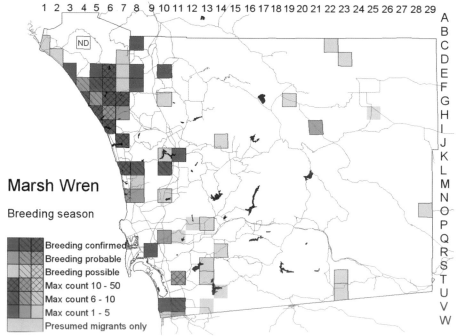

Marsh Wren

Breeding season

- Breeding confirmed
- Breeding probable
- Breeding possible
- Max count 10 - 50
- Max count 6 - 10
- Max count 1 - 5
- Presumed migrants only

and the species is apparently inconsistent at any site. On the coastal slope such reports are from near Warner's Ranch (G19; one on 17 June 2000, J. D. Barr) and a pond straddling the line between squares T23 and U23 1.25 miles northeast of Cameron Corners (one singing male 16 June 2001, L. J. Hargrove). On the county's desert slope, the Marsh Wren has never been confirmed breeding but has occurred during the breeding season along Coyote Creek at both Middle Willows (C22; two, including a singing male, 6 May 2001, P. D. Jorgensen) and Lower Willows (D23; one on 19 May 1999, B. L. Peterson; one on 21 May 2001, M. L. Gabel; three on 12 June 1994, Massey 1998), in San Felipe Valley near Paroli Spring (I21; two singing males 13 June 1999, J. O. Zimmer), at Carrizo Marsh (O29; one on 4 May 1978, P. D. Jorgensen; one on 17 April 1998, M. C. Jorgensen).

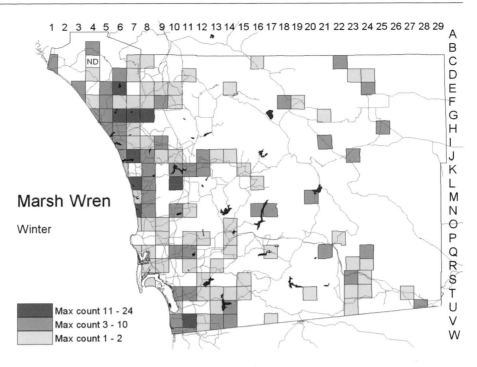

Marsh Wren

Winter

- Max count 11 - 24
- Max count 3 - 10
- Max count 1 - 2

Nesting: Using strips of marsh plants, Marsh Wrens build a characteristic globular nest with a side entrance, lashing it to several erect leaves, typically of cattail or tule, emerging from water. Placement over water rather than concealment helps protect the nest from predators. Males build several nests; for the eggs, females select one of the male's nests or build yet another of their own. The sedentary Marsh Wrens of western Washington use their nests for roosting through the winter (Verner 1965), and a report of an "occupied nest" at the Santa Margarita River mouth (G4) 12 February 1998 (B. L. Peterson) suggests that San Diego County's breeding Marsh Wrens, also sedentary, may do so as well.

Marsh Wrens enjoy a long breeding season in San Diego County. Two families of newly fledged young at Buena Vista Lagoon (H5) 15 April 2000 (J. Determan) must have hatched from eggs laid as early as 20 March; nestlings in the Santa Margarita River north of Fallbrook 24 July 2001 (K. L. Weaver) must have hatched from eggs laid as late as the first week of July. Thus the breeding

season we observed extends the 29 April–20 June range of 22 San Diego County egg sets preserved at WFVZ and even the 24 March–22 July range of 113 sets from throughout California reported by Bent (1948).

Migration: Occasional Marsh Wrens show up away from breeding localities as early as August (one in the Tijuana River valley—before the species colonized this area—14 August 1978, P. Unitt; one at the Borrego sewage ponds, H25, 23 August 1998, P. D. Jorgensen). Most likely these early birds are short-distance dispersers of the local population—possibly from the Salton Sea in the latter case. The main influx of long-distance migrants from east of the Sierra Nevada does not begin until the third week of September (Unitt et al. 1996). In spring, our latest record during the atlas period of a Marsh Wren away from any suspected breeding site was of two at the Borrego sewage ponds 4 April 1997 (H. L. Young, M. B. Mosher). But in previous years the Marsh Wren had been noted at San Diego as late as 25 April (1965, G. McCaskie), and this date agrees with migrants' schedule elsewhere in southern California and Baja California (Unitt et al. 1996). A climatic shift toward warmer winters could result in the migratory subspecies of the Marsh Wren departing earlier—and, because their migration is facultative, reaching southern California in smaller numbers.

Winter: San Diego County's local population of Marsh Wrens is greatly augmented in winter by migrants from the north and northeast. The migrants mix with the local subspecies *clarkae* but show up at many additional places. In the coastal lowland numbers in such places range up to 20 in Vista (G8) 23 December 2001 (M. Lesinsky), 10 at San Dieguito Reservoir (K8) 28 December 1997 (J. Determan), and 10 at the upper end of El Capitan Reservoir (N17) 6 February 2001 (D. C. Seals). Marsh Wrens occur uncommonly and locally at higher elevations

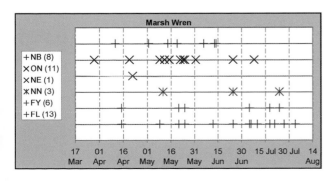

Marsh Wren

+NB (8)
×ON (11)
×NE (1)
×NN (3)
+FY (6)
+FL (13)

| 17 | 01 | 16 | 01 | 16 | 31 | 15 | 30 | 15 Jul | 30 Jul | 14 |
| Mar | Apr | Apr | May | May | May | Jun | Jun | | | Aug |

as well, where 10 at Swan Lake (F18) 18 December 2000 (G. L. Rogers) was a high count. No more than four were reported from any other foothill or mountain location, but these locations ranged in elevation as high as 4600 feet at Lake Cuyamaca (M20; up to three on 18 February 1999, A. P. and T. E. Keenan), 4650 feet at Doane Pond (E14; one on 24 December 2000, G. C. Hazard), and 5100 feet in Crouch Valley, Laguna Mountains (P22; two on 31 December 1998, P. Unitt). In the Anza–Borrego Desert the Marsh Wren is uncommon, very local, and irregular except possibly at Middle and Lower Willows in Coyote Creek Canyon. The highest desert counts 1997–2002 were of four at ponds in the northern Borrego Valley (E24) 19 December 1999 (P. R. Pryde) and 18 February 2001 (P. D. Ache).

Conservation: With the elimination of almost all coastal wetlands from Los Angeles and Orange counties, southern California's endemic subspecies of the Marsh Wren undoubtedly experienced a huge population decline. Presumably Orange County's vast "Gospel Swamp," whose birds were never adequately documented before the swamp was destroyed (Hamilton and Willick 1996), was once the center of this subspecies' population. *Cistothorus p. clarkae* is now recognized as a species of special concern by the California Department of Fish and Game. In San Diego County, however, until 1953 the only sites where Marsh Wrens were known to breed were Guajome Lake, the county's largest natural freshwater marsh (20 egg sets in WFVZ), and nearby San Luis Rey (G6; Sharp 1907). Even Sharp's "San Luis Rey" may have actually been Guajome Lake. Willett (1912) wrote that A.M. Ingersoll had noted the (presumed) local subspecies in "early spring" at Lindo Lake (O14/P14), but without a specimen or precise date we cannot be sure the birds were not migrants. Marsh Wrens apparently first colonized the San Pasqual Valley and Mission Valley in 1978, the Tijuana River valley in 1980 (Unitt 1984). Other likely nesting sites such as the Sweetwater River emerged only during the field work for this atlas.

Because of near total human control of water in coastal San Diego County, the Marsh Wren is at the mercy of wetland management. But it has apparently benefited more from the installation of ponds and reservoirs than

it has suffered from elimination of wetlands. In Mission Valley, where vegetation was removed along the San Diego River in 1988 and 1989, then allowed to regrow, Marsh Wrens recolonized in 1993. Increased siltation of the coastal lagoons, combined with reduced tidal flushing, converts saltwater habitat into freshwater habitat suitable for nesting Marsh Wrens, and this is probably the most important factor contributing to the birds' spread (Unitt et al. 1996).

A trend toward a dryer climate is a concern for a bird as dependent on wetlands as the Marsh Wren. The drying up in 2001 of the Dairy Mart ponds in the Tijuana River valley (V11) rendered unsuitable what had become one of the species' more important local sites.

Taxonomy: The subspecies of the Marsh Wren breeding in coastal San Diego County is *C. p. clarkae* Unitt, Messer, and Théry, 1996, distinguished from other subspecies by its small size, dark rufous rump and scapulars, and extensively black crown (brown usually reduced to a small patch on the forehead). Its known range is confined to the coastal strip from Los Angeles to San Diego, except for two singing males, presumably *clarkae*, at Lagunita El Ciprés near Ensenada, Baja California, 6 July 1999 (Erickson et al. 2001). The east end of Batiquitos Lagoon (J7) is the type locality. For many years, California's coastal Marsh Wrens were called *C. p. paludicola* Baird, 1864, but that subspecies, with an extensively brown back and crown, apparently ranges no farther south than Lincoln County, Oregon (Unitt et al. 1996). Summering birds in the Anza–Borrego Desert are most likely *C. p. aestuarinus* (Swarth, 1917), as this is the subspecies resident in the Imperial Valley (Unitt et al. 1996). It is somewhat larger and paler than *clarkae*, with more brown than black on the crown and more white streaking on the back. No specimens of *aestuarinus* have yet been collected in the county, however. Winter visitors are *C. p. pulverius* (Aldrich, 1946), from the western Great Basin and Columbia Basin, and *C. p. plesius* Oberholser, 1897, from the intermountain region east of *pulverius*. These partially migratory subspecies are longer-winged than the sedentary ones and, *pulverius* especially, have whiter underparts and paler tawny scapulars and rump.

DIPPERS — FAMILY CINCLIDAE

American Dipper *Cinclus mexicanus*

Cold, rushing streams of pure water in pristine wilderness—the American Dipper is an emblem of this fragile habitat. Arid San Diego County lies at the southern tip of the dipper's range along the Pacific coast. The species survives here along less than 3 miles of a single creek draining Palomar Mountain.

Breeding distribution: The American Dipper is resident at a single known site in San Diego County: Pauma Creek, on the steep southwest slope of Palomar Mountain (E13). Following reports of dippers along Pauma Creek by trout fishermen and Evan Jorgensen's sighting of an

Photo by Anthony Mercieca

agitated pair on 24 May 2001, we undertook a more intensive survey of the creek between 1800 and 2000 feet elevation two weeks later on 7 June. This search revealed no more than one adult seen at a time, sometimes carrying insects, plus a fledgling hiding under boulders and behind a small waterfall (C. Ferguson, K. J. Winter, R. Breisch, P. Unitt, NAB 55:483, 2001). Earlier records from Pauma Creek range from about 4500 feet elevation (one on 16 June 1971, AB 25:907, 1971) down to 1200 feet (one on 8 December 1946, E. Beemer).

Searches of sections of Marion and Agua Tibia creeks (D12) and the west fork of the San Luis Rey River from Barker Valley to the former West Fork Conservation Camp (E16) yielded no dippers. Though the dipper nested at 2600 feet elevation on the San Luis Rey River (G16) in 1933 (eggs collected 25 May, J. B. Dixon in Willett 1933; WFVZ 754), and was seen at the same site 11–23 June 1984 (R. Higson, AB 38:1063, 1984) and 22 May 1988 (M. and B. McIntosh, AB 42:482, 1988), W. E. Haas has surveyed the area intensively since 1995, finding no dippers. The location of the nests reported from "a falling stream of water in the Cleveland National Forest at about 3500 feet elevation" by Abbott (1927a) has been lost.

American Dippers may have been resident at least formerly in canyons draining east and northeast from Hot Springs Mountain. None of the records from this area are from the breeding season, but our coverage of this extremely rugged area in either the breeding season or winter was not exhaustive.

Nesting: Dippers nest close to streams, often directly over water or behind waterfalls, in sheltered crevices among rocks or tree roots or on banks. Nesting data from San Diego County are confined to the egg set collected 25 May 1933 and the nests found in August 1925 and on 20 June 1926 (Abbott 1927a). On the latter date the nest contained large nestlings, which fledged by 27 June. The species' breeding season varies from year to year with variation in local weather and stream conditions (Kingery 1996).

Migration: The American Dipper is largely nonmigratory, known to move long distances only in the northern part of its range.

Winter: A winter survey of Pauma Creek between 1800 and 2400 feet elevation on 18 January 2002 revealed three individuals (J. O. Zimmer, R. Breisch, et al.). The only winter records for San Diego County away from Pauma Creek are from canyons draining north and northeast from Hot Springs Mountain. From 1977 to 1990, the dipper was reported 10 times from this area, twice from Alder Canyon (C21), four times from Sheep Canyon (D21/D22), twice from Cougar Canyon (D22), and twice from Borrego Palm Canyon (F23), on dates from 23 November to 30 January (A. G. Morley et al., Anza–Borrego Desert State Park database).

Conservation: The lack of recent records from the San Luis Rey River or the canyons draining Hot Springs Mountain is not a good sign for the American Dipper's outlook in San Diego County. On the basis of the length of suitable habitat, the population along Pauma Creek is very small, perhaps only four or five pairs. Much of the creek is within the Cleveland National Forest, but it could be degraded by multiple factors. Drought or groundwater extraction upstream could reduce the stream flow below what can sustain dippers. Water pollution has affected dippers elsewhere. Though the deep canyon of Pauma Creek is little visited by people now, additional recreational use could disturb the dippers significantly, as well as contribute to pollution.

Taxonomy: No specimen from San Diego County has been collected, but all American Dippers resident north of the Mexican border are *C. m. unicolor* Bonaparte, 1827.

KINGLETS — FAMILY REGULIDAE

Golden-crowned Kinglet *Regulus satrapa*

At home in deep forests of redwood, fir, or spruce, the Golden-crowned Kinglet seems out of place in southern California. It is a rather recent arrival to San Diego, reaching the county as a winter visitor since 1954, as a summer resident since 1986. As a winter visitor it occurs annually, but numbers vary greatly from year to year. Generally it is rare and expected only in coniferous woods near the tops of the county's highest mountains. Occasional irruptions, though, bring small numbers down to the coast and south to the border.

Winter: In San Diego County, the Golden-crowned Kinglet occurs in mountain forests, especially where white fir and big-cone Douglas fir dominate. During the atlas period it was recorded in all five of San Diego

Photo by Scott Streit

County's main ranges bearing this habitat. Numbers were largest on Hot Springs Mountain, with up to 17 around the summit (E20) 9 December 2000 and 12 just to the

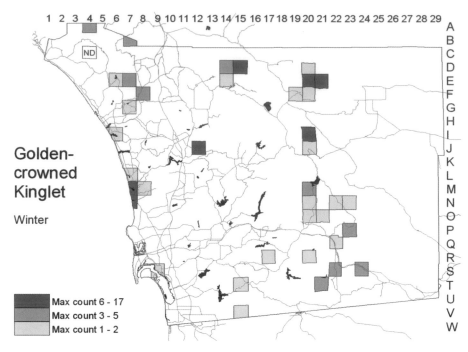

Golden-crowned Kinglet

Winter

Max count 6 - 17
Max count 3 - 5
Max count 1 - 2

Loma in October. The earliest date published is 25 September (1976, Point Loma, G. McCaskie). During the atlas period the only reports of winter visitors later than 20 February were of one at Golden Hill, Balboa Park (S9), 22 March 2000 (T. Vought) and one on West Mesa, Cuyamaca Mountains (N20) 27 March 1999 (B. Siegel). But after the invasion of 1976 one occurred at Point Loma as late as 14 April 1977 (AB 31:1048, 1977).

Breeding distribution: The Golden-crowned Kinglet was first found summering in San Diego County in 1986, when C. G. Edwards reported up to six on Hot Springs Mountain in June and July (AB 40:1256, 1986), and 1987, when R. E. Webster reported 25 on Middle Peak, Cuyamaca Mountains (M20), 19 July (AB 41:1488, 1987). Since that time the birds have been seen regularly in summer above 5200 feet elevation on both Cuyamaca and Middle peaks, though in smaller numbers. From 1997 to 2001, the maximum count during the breeding season was of four on Middle Peak 2 July 2000 (R. E. Webster). The colonization of Hot Springs Mountain, however, proved transitory. During the atlas period the Golden-crowned Kinglet was absent from this area in summer, in spite of its numbers there in winter. This pattern may suggest that San Diego County's population was established by a single invasion in the mid 1980s and has been dwindling away ever since. However, the Golden-crowned Kinglet was found summering for the first time on Palomar Mountain in 2000, with repeated reports from the steep north-facing canyon of Chimney Creek (E14) 21 May–15 July (G. Hazard, J. R. Barth). No more than a single individual was noted per day.

east of it (E21) 13 February 1999 (C. R. Mahrdt, K. L. Weaver). High counts on the other mountains were of six near the Palomar Observatory (D15) 28 December 2000 (K. L. Weaver), six on Volcan Mountain (I20) 18 December 2000 (R. T. Patton), five on Cuyamaca Peak (M20) 4 February 2001 (M. B. Mulrooney), and three near Wooded Hill, Laguna Mountains (P23), 14 January 1999 (E. C. Hall, J. O. Zimmer).

Away from the higher mountains, Golden-crowned Kinglets are rare and sporadic in oak and riparian woodland, Torrey pines, and planted conifers. One unusual habitat, more chaparral than woodland, was Tecate cypresses near the summit of Otay Mountain (V15), site of two on 1 January 2001 (J. R. Barth). High counts at low elevations were of five in Torrey Pines State Reserve 7 January 2001 (D. K. Adams et al.), six to eight in Torrey and Canary Island pines in an apartment complex near the intersection of Interstate 5 and Del Mar Heights Road (N7) 29 November 1998–16 February 1999 (S. E. Smith), and six in planted conifers in the Wild Animal Park, San Pasqual (J12), 30 December 2000 (K. L. Weaver). There are only two records for the Anza–Borrego Desert, of one in pines planted at the Ram's Hill golf course (H25) 8 November 1987 (P. R. Johnson) and another in Culp Valley (H23) 5 October 1996 (M. L. Gabel).

Golden-crowned Kinglet numbers in San Diego County are highly variable. During the five-year atlas period incursions and off years alternated. The total reported was 6 in 1997–98, 66 in 1998–99, 4 in 1999–2000, 84 in 2000–01, and 9 in 2001–02. The greatest invasion recorded was that of 1976, when the San Diego Christmas bird count alone, held 18 December, yielded 19, 18 of them at Point Loma (S7).

Migration: As an irregular invader, the Golden-crowned Kinglet follows no strict schedule. During invasion years small numbers are usually found in conifers at Point

Nesting: No nest of the Golden-crowned Kinglet has yet been found in San Diego County. The only evidence of the species' breeding is a probable fledgling on Middle Peak 11 June 2000 and a family group of one adult and two fledglings there 2 July 2000 (R. E. Webster). The birds generally build their nests high in conifers, screened by dense clusters of needles (Galati 1991).

Conservation: The Golden-crowned Kinglet's hold as a breeding species on San Diego County is tenuous. Repeated droughts in which conifers succumb to bark beetles erode a habitat already very limited here. Climatic warming bodes ill for this bird of boreal forests at the southern tip of its range. Though the species' migrating as far south as San Diego County is relatively new, the amplitude of the invasions seems to be on the decline. The Golden-crowned Kinglet was noted on 13 of 27 San Diego Christmas bird counts from 1966 to 1992 but none since. Nevertheless, the planting of conifers in the lowlands has created habitat for Golden-crowned Kinglets in an area that once had little to hold them.

Taxonomy: Phillips (1991) identified the one specimen, from Point Loma 1 November 1966 (SDNHM 38062) as the darker-backed *R. s. olivaceus* Baird, 1864, which breeds in the Pacific Northwest and migrates south to southern California. The specimen from Point Loma is the southernmost of the subspecies. The identification is corroborated by electronic colorimetry: the value of *L* (a

measure of darkness) on the back of the Point Loma specimen is 33.6; the range of variation in *olivaceus* is about 33.0–36.0, whereas in specimens of *R. s. apache* Jenks, 1935, from the east slope of the Cascade Range, Sierra Nevada, and high mountains of southern California it is about 35.5–37.5. The kinglets summering in San Diego County are presumably *apache*, however, and this subspecies likely contributes winter visitors as well.

Ruby-crowned Kinglet *Regulus calendula*

The Ruby-crowned Kinglet is a winter visitor, commonest in riparian and oak woodland. It uses a wide variety of other habitats too, from urban eucalyptus trees to pines and firs in the mountains to desert oases. The Ruby-crowned Kinglet is San Diego County's leading practitioner of hover gleaning: hovering momentarily at a leaf to glean minute insects. A northward contraction of the species' breeding range is not yet reflected in a decline in its winter numbers.

Photo by Anthony Mercieca

Winter: The Ruby-crowned Kinglet is one of San Diego County's most widespread winter visitors, recorded in 96% of all atlas squares covered. Only in the bleakest parts of the Anza–Borrego Desert, near the Imperial County line, is it likely to be missed. It is most abundant in northwestern San Diego County, where riparian woodland is most extensive. During the atlas period the highest counts were around Lake Hodges (K10), of up to 137 on 22 December 2000 (R. L. Barber et al.). Farther inland numbers can be quite high as well, up to 40 around Indian Flats (D19) 6 January 1999 (K. J. Burns) and 30 at the north end of Lake Morena (S21) 27 December 1998 (S. E. Smith). Even at elevations between 4000 and 6000

feet the Ruby-crowned Kinglet is common in winter, with counts up to 25 on West Mesa, Cuyamaca Mountains (N20), 9 January and 6 February 1999 (B. Siegel) and 23 near Filaree Flat, Laguna Mountains (N22) 9 January 1999 (G. L. Rogers). Around the summit of San Diego County's highest peak, Hot Springs Mountain (E20), C. R. Mahrdt and K. L. Weaver noted it repeatedly, with a maximum five on 9 December 2000. In the Anza–Borrego Desert the Ruby-crowned Kinglet occurs mainly at oases and in developed areas, where it is generally uncommon. In dry desert washes it is uncommon to rare, but desert numbers were considerably larger in the wet winter of 1997–1998 than in the subsequent four years of the atlas period. The number reported per hour in the desert that year was higher than in any of the other four by a factor of at least 2.8. The highest single-day counts in the Anza–Borrego Desert were of 25 at Agua Caliente Springs (M26) 1 December 1997 (E. C. Hall) and 20 near Sunset Mountain (J26) 11 January 1998 (J. Determan, A. Mauro).

Migration: In fall, the Ruby-crowned Kinglet arrives typically in the last week of September, exceptionally as early as 6 September (1973, one at Otay Mesa, V12, AB 28:106, 1974). In spring, most individuals depart

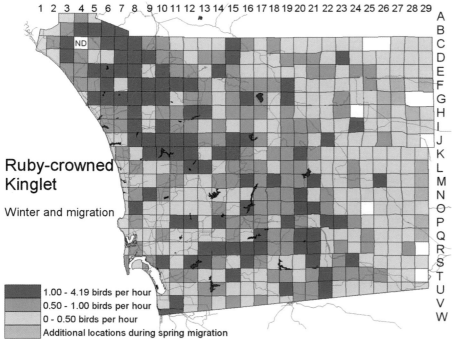

Ruby-crowned Kinglet

Winter and migration

- 1.00 - 4.19 birds per hour
- 0.50 - 1.00 birds per hour
- 0 - 0.50 birds per hour
- Additional locations during spring migration

by the end of April, and by the second week of May the species is rare. During the atlas' term the latest date for the Ruby-crowned Kinglet ranged from 3 to 24 May. The only records after 16 May were of one near the Santa Margarita River mouth (G4) 21 May 2001 (P. A. Ginsburg), one at Point Loma (S7) 22 May 1999 (P. A. Ginsburg), and one near Filaree Flat, Laguna Mountains (N22), 24 May 1997 (G. L. Rogers). The last record recalls that of a singing male along Agua Dulce Creek, Laguna Mountains, 30 May 1974 (AB 28:950, 1974).

Breeding distribution: W. O. Emerson (in Belding 1890) thought that the Ruby-crowned Kinglet "perhaps breeds in the firs on Volcan Mountain," and Stephens (1919a) reported it as a "rare summer resident of the highest mountains" in San Diego County. Neither reported specimens or definite observations to support these statements, however. The Ruby-crowned Kinglet formerly bred south to the San Jacinto Mountains (Grinnell and Swarth 1913). Now it may have retracted as a breeding

species north out of southern California entirely (Lentz 1993), though it may persist at the highest elevations of the San Bernardino Mountains.

Conservation: In spite of the apparent contraction of the breeding range, there is no clear trend in the number of Ruby-crowned Kinglets wintering in San Diego County. The birds use urban trees freely, helping to compensate for the loss of native riparian woodland.

Taxonomy: The widespread *R. c. calendula* (Linnaeus, 1766) is the predominant subspecies of Ruby-crowned Kinglet in San Diego County, as throughout southern California. However, the darker, buffier *R. c. grinnelli* Palmer, 1897, breeding in coastal southeastern Alaska and British Columbia, is known from one specimen collected at sea 10 miles west of Point Loma 25 September 1953 (SDNHM 29986). This is the southernmost record of *grinnelli*, which usually comes no farther south than northern California.

OLD WORLD WARBLERS AND GNATCATCHERS — FAMILY SYLVIIDAE

Blue-gray Gnatcatcher *Polioptila caerulea*

The Blue-gray Gnatcatcher uses a wide variety of habitats: oak woodland, riparian woodland and scrub, pinyon/juniper, desert washes, chaparral, and sage scrub. It is migratory, occurring mainly in the foothills in the breeding season and at low elevations in winter. In open groves of the Engelmann oak and stands of the Tecate cypress it can be fairly common, but over most of the county it is still uncommon or rare as a breeding bird. The Blue-gray Gnatcatcher is perhaps the greatest beneficiary of the cowbird trapping intended to benefit Bell's Vireo; it is now

Photo by Anthony Mercieca

far more numerous and widespread as a breeding species than known in the 1980s.

Breeding distribution: The Blue-gray Gnatcatcher's current distribution appears strangely patchy. The species is most numerous between 1000 and 4000 feet elevation but far from uniform even there. Zones of concentration lie around the base of Palomar Mountain (maximum count 20 in Agua Tibia Wilderness, C13, 18 May 2001, K. J. Winter), north and northwest of Hot Springs Mountain (C20/D19/D21), from Lusardi Canyon to Black Canyon west of Mesa Grande (G15/ I16), around Viejas and Poser mountains (O17/O18), south of Pine Valley (Q20/R20/R21),

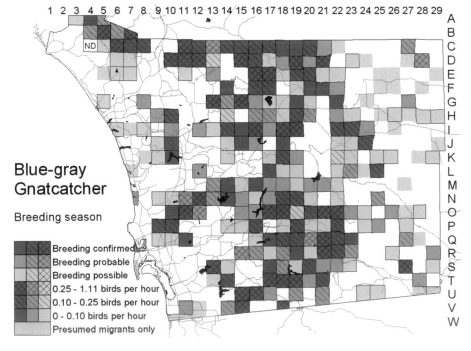

Blue-gray Gnatcatcher

Breeding season

- Breeding confirmed
- Breeding probable
- Breeding possible
- 0.25 - 1.11 birds per hour
- 0.10 - 0.25 birds per hour
- 0 - 0.10 birds per hour
- Presumed migrants only

from Mother Grundy Peak to McAlmond Canyon north of Barrett Junction (T17/T18/T19), and on Otay Mountain (U15/U16/V15). The Blue-gray Gnatcatcher ranges uncommonly as high as the tops of the county's highest peaks with four, including a pair building a nest, near the summit of Hot Springs Mountain (E20) 29 June 2001 (K. L. Weaver). One area of concentration, however, Miramar Air Station, especially east of Interstate 15 (N11/N12/O11/O12), lies largely at an elevation of 500–1000 feet (O11; 12 on 20 June 1999, G. L. Rogers). There are a few breeding-season records right along the coast (e.g., Torrey Pines State Reserve, N7, two on 11 July 1998, K. Estey; Tijuana River valley, W10, one on 13 and 23 May 2000, W. E. Haas), but breeding is confirmed no nearer the coast than about 5 miles inland in southwestern Miramar (P9; nest with eggs 8 May 1997, K. Kenwood).

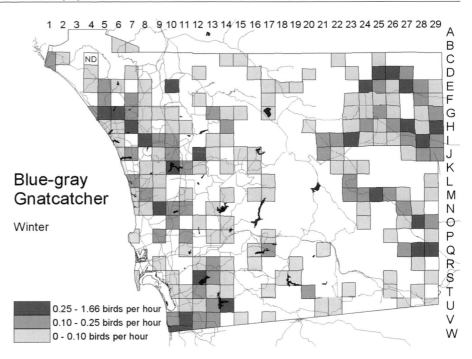

Blue-gray Gnatcatcher

Winter

- 0.25 - 1.66 birds per hour
- 0.10 - 0.25 birds per hour
- 0 - 0.10 birds per hour

In the Anza–Borrego Desert the Blue-gray Gnatcatcher occurs sparsely in the pinyons of the Santa Rosa and Vallecito mountains (up to five in the Santa Rosas near the Riverside County line, C27, 3 May 2000, P. Unitt). At lower elevations in the desert it is even scarcer, irregular at any given site, occurring mainly in junipers, at oases like Lower Willows (D23), or in well-vegetated washes (maximum six, one building a nest, in Mine Canyon, J24, 15 April 2001, L. and M. Polinsky). Occasional birds, singing territorially, are found in scattered clumps of mesquite even in the emptiest desert (e.g., two, one singing, 2.7 miles northeast of Ocotillo Wells, H29, 27 April 2001, J. R. Barth).

Nesting: The Blue-gray Gnatcatcher builds its nest in either trees or shrubs, high or low. Heights of nests atlas observers described ranged from 4 to 50 feet. The most frequently reported supporting plant was Engelmann oak with five nests; coast live oak was second with four nests. Other trees were sycamore, black oak, Coulter pine, pinyon, and Tecate cypress; shrubs were scrub oak, redshank, chamise, white sage, and laurel sumac. Blue-gray Gnatcatchers often build in quite exposed situations with

little or no foliage screening the nest. The Engelmann oak's open branches offer little concealment. Two nests were in dead oaks; one was in a leafless burned snag of a shrub. This failure to hide the nest may contribute to the Blue-gray Gnatcatcher's being so frequent a host of the Brown-headed Cowbird.

In San Diego County the Blue-gray Gnatcatcher lays mainly from mid April to early July. Nest building as early as 24 March (1998, near Angelina Spring, I22, P. K. Nelson) suggests laying earlier, though females may delay laying five to ten days after a nest has been completed (Ellison 1992). Adults gathering insects in Dameron Valley (C16) 4 April 1998 and near Wilderness Gardens (D12) 15 April 2000 (K. L. Weaver), however, confirm laying by about 22 March and 2 April, respectively, earlier than historically known for California. Bent's (1949) earliest egg date for the state was 5 April.

Migration: Determining the Blue-gray Gnatcatcher's migration schedule is difficult to do with precision because the species is so widespread in both summer and winter. On the basis of sightings in breeding habitat in winter, probably some fraction of the breeding population is nonmigratory. Most of the breeding birds, however, are migratory, beginning to arrive in mid March. Root (1969) observed arrival in Monterey County one year as early as 24 February. The species' movement appears to peak in the first week of April, and spring migrants are largely gone by the middle of April. Exceptionally late records of apparent migrants were of one in the Borrego Valley (F25) 25 April 1999 (P. D. Ache) and one at Point Loma (S7) 16 May 2001 (J. L. Coatsworth). Fall migrants begin returning regularly in the first week of September, rarely in late August (one at Point Loma 26 August 1999, D. K. Adams).

Winter: At this season the Blue-gray Gnatcatcher occurs most commonly in riparian scrub, especially in the

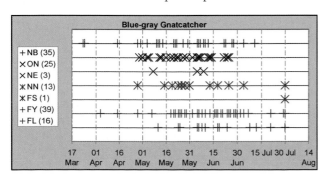

Tijuana River valley, where counts are as high as 20 near the Dairy Mart pond (V11) 16 December 2000 (G. McCaskie). Elsewhere in the coastal lowland the species is generally uncommon. The Blue-gray Gnatcatcher also winters widely if uncommonly in washes and on valley floors in the Anza–Borrego Desert; maximum counts there are of seven in the Borrego Valley's mesquite bosque (G25) 20 December 1998 (P. Unitt), near Barrel Spring (H29) 15 January 2002 (J. R. Barth), and in Box Canyon (L23) 10 January 1998 (S. D. Cameron). The Blue-gray Gnatcatcher even occurs rarely in winter in the same oak-wooded and chaparral-covered foothills where it breeds most commonly. Maximum counts in this habitat are of three along Bear Valley Road (Q21) 20 February 1999 and along the Espinosa Trail (R19) 18 February 2001 (A. P. and T. E. Keenan). Such winter records range in elevation as high as 4600 feet near Lost Valley (D20; two on 12 December 1998, J. M. and B. Hargrove).

Conservation: Willett (1912) and Stephens (1919a) called the Blue-gray Gnatcatcher "common" as a breeding bird; Sharp (1907) called it "not uncommon." The 37 egg sets collected in San Diego County 1890–1938 attest to the species' abundance in the early 20th century as well. By the 1970s, however, breeding Blue-gray Gnatcatchers had become rare, retracting out of the coastal lowland entirely (Unitt 1984). The decline coincided with the Brown-headed Cowbird's invasion of southern California. The Blue-gray Gnatcatcher is a frequent host (Friedmann et al. 1977). In the late 1980s and 1990s, however, the gnatcatchers resurged, and the coincidence of this recovery with the beginning of cowbird trapping suggests that the gnatcatcher benefited, perhaps even more so than Bell's

Vireo, whose sixfold increase over the same period is far better documented (Kus 2002). Yet this simple hypothesis raises further questions: the gnatcatcher's repopulation of lowland riparian woodland, where cowbird trapping has been most intensive, is quite modest. The increase is far more noticeable in chaparral and oak woodland away from the cowbird traps. Is the difference due to the gnatcatcher's habitat preferences? Has the reduction of cowbird numbers been widespread enough over San Diego County to have effects several miles from the traps? Data on both the Blue-gray Gnatcatcher's biology and trends in cowbird numbers are insufficient to answer these questions.

Wintering of the Blue-gray Gnatcatcher in San Diego County at elevations above 1500 feet was unknown before the 1980s. Might climatic warming, reflected mainly in an amelioration of winter low temperatures, be allowing the species to winter at higher elevations and obviating the need for some individuals to migrate? If some birds adopt sedentary habits, they may account for nesting earlier than historically known and help the species avoid cowbird parasitism. On the other hand, if more extended droughts accompany climatic warming, all insectivorous birds will suffer from a reduction in their food supply.

Taxonomy: Phillips (1991) reported too much overlap between *P. c. amoenissima* Grinnell, 1926 (widespread in the western United States), and *P. c. obscura* Ridgway, 1883 (of southern Baja California), for the former to be recognized. Tail length is reported to be the primary defining character, but an adequate quantitative comparison remains to be done.

California Gnatcatcher *Polioptila californica*

Patrick J. Mock

Within the United States, the California Gnatcatcher lives only in coastal southern California's sage scrub, a habitat threatened by the continuing spread of agriculture and suburbia. Even within the sage scrub the gnatcatcher is localized, preferring patches dominated by California sagebrush and flat-top buckwheat and avoiding those dominated by sage, laurel sumac, and lemonadeberry (Weaver 1998a). The east edge of its range appears constrained by winter cold rather than by vegetation type (Mock 1998). As an "umbrella" or flagship species for its habitat, the California Gnatcatcher has been the focus for regional habitat-conservation planning in San Diego County since before it was listed as a threatened species by the federal government in 1993 (Atwood 1993).

Breeding distribution: In spite of its habitat being much constricted by urbanization, the California Gnatcatcher still occurs widely in San Diego County's coastal lowland. It prefers open sage scrub with California sagebrush as

Photo by Anthony Mercieca

the dominant or co-dominant plant (habitat use summarized by Atwood and Bontrager 2001). In general it is more numerous near the sage scrub–grassland interface than where sage scrub grades into chaparral; it occupies dense sage scrub less frequently than more open sites. In the more open chaparral on the flat mesa of Miramar, however, many territories encompass both sage scrub and chamise (K. Fischer). Much of the gnatcatcher's range in the United States has been surveyed according to a standard protocol approved by the U.S. Fish and Wildlife Service. Elevation appears to limit the distribution in San Diego County, where over 90% of locations are below 1000 feet (Atwood and Bolsinger 1992, Mock 1993, 1998). The only sites above 2000 feet are on the east side of the San Diego River near Cedar and Boulder creeks (L17/L18), where the species has occurred up to 2400 feet. "Core" population areas supporting 30 or more pairs include Camp Pendleton/Fallbrook, Oceanside, north Carlsbad, southeast Carlsbad, southwest San Marcos, Rainbow/Pala, Olivenhain/Lake Hodges/San Pasqual, Poway, upper San Diego River/El Capitan Reservoir, Mission Trails Regional Park/ Miramar, Lakeside/Dehesa, Sweetwater River/Reservoir, Jamul Mountains, Otay Lakes/ Mesa, west Otay Mountain, and Tijuana River mouth (Mock

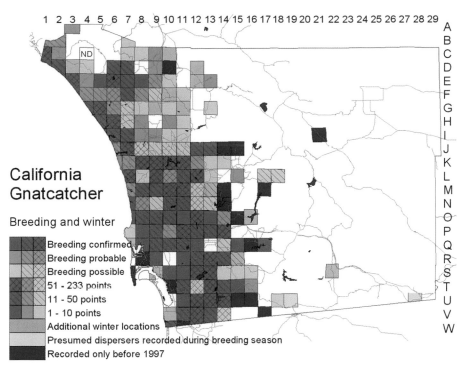

1993). Probably the single largest population concentration is around Lake Hodges (K10): the highest daily count reported by an atlas observer was 36 there on 21 March 1998 (R. L. Barber). The greatest number of gnatcatcher locations in the database for San Diego's Multiple Species Conservation Plan (MSCP), based largely on surveys 1987–95, is from the same area.

San Diego County's California Gnatcatcher population exceeds 2000 pairs, but fires in 1996 and 2003 temporarily reduced the carrying capacity of several of the habitat cores, Lake Hodges/Olivenhain, Mission Trails/Miramar, Jamul Mountains, and west Otay Mountain (Mock 1993, USFWS 1996, Bond and Bradley 2004). The size of a breeding pair's territory is highly variable but correlated with distance from the coast, ranging from less than 1 hectare along the coast to over 9 hectares farther inland (Mock and Bolger 1992, Braden 1992, Preston et al. 1998, Atwood et al. 1998). During the nonbreeding season, a pair's home range is about 80% larger than during the breeding season (Preston et al. 1998, Bontrager 1991).

The easternmost locations for the gnatcatcher in the breeding season are the base of Nate Harrison Grade, Pauma Valley (E13; one on 16 May 1999, C. Sankpill), 0.5 mile east of Saddleback along Cedar Creek (L18; male 28 August 2001, pair building a nest 20 March 2002, J. Turnbull), the upper end of Loveland Reservoir (Q17; pair and four nestlings banded 26 May 1997, P. Famolaro), and Grapevine Creek (U19; one on 13 June 1999, M. and B. McIntosh). The species is irregular at these marginal locations.

Completely unexpected was the sighting of a male California Gnatcatcher apparently paired with a female Blue-gray on Jacumba Peak (U28) 23 April 2000 (C. Jones, J. Radtke). The photos taken are not adequate to distinguish the bird from a Black-tailed Gnatcatcher, but the observers were experienced with the species and

heard the typical mewing calls. This record offers the only recent parallel to old specimens of the California Gnatcatcher from the desert slope at Palm Springs in Riverside County (Atwood 1988) and "San Felipe Canyon" (probably San Felipe Valley, I21) in San Diego County (13 February 1893, SDNHM 1678).

The map for the California Gnatcatcher expresses the species' abundance in terms of number of points by square in the MSCP and Camp Pendleton databases. These sources include many records before 1997, many from sites where the species has been eliminated subsequently. Conversely, a single pair or territory may be represented by more than one point. Therefore, as with most other species, this feature of the map should be taken as an indication of only relative, not absolute, abundance.

Nesting: The California Gnatcatcher's biology has been studied intensively; see the many papers in *Western Birds* volume 29, issue 4 (1998). The birds typically nest on slopes of a gradient less than 40%. The lower portions of gullies and drainages, when available within the territory, are frequently used as nest sites. Though nest success varies significantly by host shrub species, the birds are not selective, using shrubs in proportion to their availability, typically California sagebrush, flat-top buckwheat,

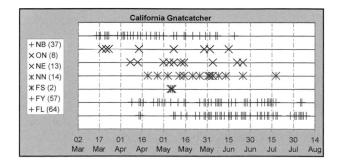

California sunflower, and broom baccharis (Mock and Bolger 1992, Grishaver et al. 1998). Many other less common sage scrub species are used less frequently. Grishaver et al. (1998) found the nest's average height from the ground to be 82 cm (range 30–292, *n* = 101), in shrubs of average height 135 cm (range 62–155, *n* = 103). The shrub cover around the nest is typically between 20% and 60%, with a gap between shrubs of 153 to 176 cm (Bontrager 1991, Mock and Bolger 1992, Grishaver et al. 1998). Site selection may influence risk of nest predation; nests within 70 cm of the ground are less successful than those placed higher (Sockman 1997).

Mid March to early July is the main season for California Gnatcatchers to lay in San Diego County. Frequent nest predation results in many replacement clutches during the nesting season. Roach (1989) found the California Gnatcatcher nesting as early as late February in San Diego County; Patten and Campbell (1994) reported two nests fledging young in Orange County as late as 12 and 25 August in 1991, implying laying as late as about 16 and 29 July. Patten and Campbell (1998) suggested that cowbird parasitism is responsible for a historical trend toward California Gnatcatchers nesting earlier in the year. Warming of the climate could contribute to this trend as well.

Migration: The California Gnatcatcher is nonmigratory. During postbreeding dispersal, in late summer and fall, juveniles typically move less than 3 km; their longest documented dispersal distance is 20 km (Hunsaker et al. 2000). Dispersing young cross riparian woodland, chaparral, and artificial landscapes, including major highways and residential development (Lovio 1996, Bailey and Mock 1998, Campbell et al. 1998, Galvin 1998, Haas and Campbell 2003). Nonbreeding California Gnatcatchers have been detected three times on Point Loma (S7; Bailey and Mock 1998). The many examples of occupied habitat patches isolated by extensive development also attest to such movement. First-year birds establish territories by October and remain on them through the winter (Mock and Bolger 1992, Preston et al. 1998). Extensive movements by adults are relatively rare (Bailey and Mock 1998); the longest documented dispersal distance by an adult is 10 km (Hunsaker et al. 2000).

Winter: The gnatcatcher's winter numbers and distribution differ little from those in the breeding season (maximum daily count 53 around the upper end of Lake Hodges, K11, 26 December 1999, E. C. Hall). The species is probably resident in low density in all atlas squares where we noted it in winter but not the breeding season, except for V10 on the floor of the Tijuana River valley (two on 16 December 2000, W. E. Haas). An exceptional winter sighting about 21 km from the nearest site where the species breeds was of one at the northeastern corner of Lake Morena (S22) 5 December 1999 (R. and S. L. Breisch).

Conservation: Historical data on the California Gnatcatcher's abundance are minimal; its listing as a threatened species is based on the high fraction of its habitat already lost to agriculture and urbanization and

the pressure to develop what remains. The primary strategy for its conservation is the establishment of a network of habitat reserves, encompassing enough of the remaining "core" regions to sustain a viable population, connected by habitat linkages. The strategy is being pursued through the state of California's Natural Communities Conservation Plans, entailing negotiation among many public agencies, landowners, and environmental organizations. Land for the reserves is being acquired through mitigation agreements for developments and public agencies' purchase of privately owned lands under a "willing seller only" policy. Although the design of the network is incomplete, as of early 2004 over 65% of the 172,000-acre reserve network in the area covered by the MSCP was in place. In the incorporated cities of the north county a 19,900-acre network has been proposed, and the participating cities need to develop their detailed plans for approval by the wildlife agencies. As of early 2004, the county of San Diego had initiated an amendment to the MSCP to cover the unincorporated areas of the north county not included in the original plan, but the area to be conserved in this region had not been formally proposed. San Diego County's major military installations (Camp Pendleton, Fallbrook Naval Weapons Station, Marine Corps Air Station Miramar) support important gnatcatcher populations and are mandated under the Sikes Act and Endangered Species Act to manage for this and other formally listed endangered species through "integrated natural resource management plans" that are updated every five years.

Though the California Gnatcatcher is eliminated by development of its habitat, it does not appear especially sensitive to fragmentation of that habitat at the landscape scale (Bailey and Mock 1998), in spite of the report to the contrary by Crooks et al. (2001). Data supporting this conclusion include the species' persistence in patches of sage scrub long isolated from extensive stands, as in Florida Canyon, Balboa Park (R9; pair with two fledglings 1 June 1998, J. K. Wilson) and Chollas Valley near Fairmount Avenue (S10; seven, including three pairs, 11 May 1997, P. Unitt).

Fire and the invasion of exotic vegetation, especially grasses and annual forbs, interact to threaten the gnatcatcher's habitat. In much of coastal southern California, where these exotic plants are well-established and where the irreversible conversion of shrublands to grasslands is likely, fire frequency and burn size should be kept low (Zedler et al. 1983). Where possible, flammable exotics should be removed or reduced. The wildfires of October 2003 affected 4% of known gnatcatcher occurrences, 16% of designated critical habitat, and 28% of the area the U.S. Fish and Wildlife Service's model for suitable habitat (Bond and Bradley 2004).

Disturbances that reduce sage scrub cover, such as frequent fire, mechanical disruption, livestock grazing, off-highway vehicles, and military training appear to reduce habitat suitability for the gnatcatcher (Bontrager et al. 1995, Mayer and Wirtz 1995, Beyers and Wirtz 1997, Wirtz et al. 1997, Atwood et al. 1998). Construction-monitoring studies suggest that California Gnatcatchers tolerate adjacent construction (Atwood and Bontrager 2001, URS Corp. 2004) and high noise levels (Famolaro and Newman 1998). Over 16% of the point locations recorded for the gnatcatcher in San Diego County are within 500 feet of major roads.

Predation is the most common cause of gnatcatcher nest failure. Information on whether predation rate is influenced by anthropogenic factors is lacking, but the species' nest success along habitat edges is no less than that within the interior of habitat blocks (Mock and Preston 1995, Atwood et al. 1998). Depending on the adjacent habitat's suitability to cowbirds, cowbird parasitism affects some populations of the California Gnatcatcher more than others (Braden et al. 1997, Grishaver et al. 1998, Atwood and Bontrager 2001). But the net demographic effect of nest parasitism may be small, parasitism just substituting for other forms of predation on gnatcatcher nests (Braden et al. 1997). The low rate of parasitism (3 of 134 nests)

observed around Rancho San Diego (R13) 1989–92 suggests that the gnatcatchers benefited from cowbird trapping along the nearby Sweetwater River (Grishaver et al. 1998).

Taxonomy: The subspecies of California Gnatcatcher in the United States is nominate *P. c. californica* Brewster, 1881, the dark extreme of the species. It ranges south along the coast to Ensenada, south of which it is replaced by *P. c. atwoodi*, in which the back and flanks of the female are paler brown (Mellink and Rea 1994), and by still paler subspecies from El Rosario south to Cabo San Lucas. Analysis of mitochondrial DNA shows little geographic structure of genetic variation in the California Gnatcatcher throughout its range (Zink et al. 2000), suggesting that the subspecies' characteristics are being maintained by natural selection for plumage suitable to their local habitat rather than by restricted gene flow.

Black-tailed Gnatcatcher *Polioptila melanura*

The Black-tailed Gnatcatcher is one of the Anza–Borrego Desert's characteristic birds, fairly common within the desert, essentially absent elsewhere. Like the better-studied California Gnatcatcher, the Black-tailed apparently remains in pairs year round. It is a permanent resident among spiny trees and shrubs like mesquite, smoketree, and palo verde, the preferred sites for nests. We found no current overlap between the California and Black-tailed Gnatcatchers in San Diego County, though there is one such site just north of the county line near Aguanga, and strays of both species have been seen near the Mexican border in the gap between their ranges.

Photo by Anthony Mercieca

Breeding distribution: The Black-tailed Gnatcatcher occurs almost throughout the Anza–Borrego Desert, being absent only from the higher mountains, stands of low halophytic scrub, and the most barren badlands. Within the desert it was missed during the breeding season in only five atlas squares: in the Santa Rosa Mountains (C27), from Peg Leg Road to Font's Point (F26/F27), and around Ocotillo Wells (I28/I29). Even in the latter area it should be expected occasionally in the scattered ironwood trees. The birds are most concentrated in mesquite thickets and in well-vegetated washes and bajadas. The largest numbers were reported from the west end of Clark Dry Lake northwest along Rockhouse Truck Trail (D25; 40 on 14 April 2000, K. J. Winter) and from Mescal Bajada (J25; 30 on 26 April and 12 June 1998, M.

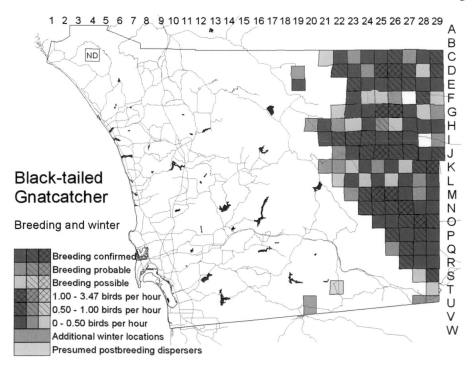

Black-tailed Gnatcatcher

Breeding and winter

- Breeding confirmed
- Breeding probable
- Breeding possible
- 1.00 - 3.47 birds per hour
- 0.50 - 1.00 birds per hour
- 0 - 0.50 birds per hour
- Additional winter locations
- Presumed postbreeding dispersers

and B. McIntosh). As spiny vegetation becomes sparser, so do the gnatcatchers. The species is confirmed breeding up to an elevation of about 3100 feet in Smuggler Canyon (L25, building nest 21 March 2000, R. Thériault) and recorded in the breeding season up to about 3400 feet at the western edge of Culp Valley (G22; one on 28 May 2001, P. D. Jorgensen). Points on the west edge of the range are Alder Canyon (C21; one on 3 May 2000, G. Rebstock), about 3200 feet elevation on the northeast side of San Felipe Valley (H21; seven on 22 May 2001, E. C. Hall, J. O. Zimmer), the northwest corner of Mason Valley (L22; two on 2 May 2001, R. Thériault), and near Jacumba (U28; up to four on 20 March 1998, C. G. Edwards).

The Black-tailed Gnatcatcher occurs on the coastal slope within 2 miles of the San Diego County line northeast of Aguanga in south-central Riverside County (Weaver 1998b). But, unlike the Ladder-backed Woodpecker and Black-throated Sparrow, it does not extend into the semi-desert scrub of nearby Dameron Valley (C15/C16). Two completely unexpected sightings, however, suggest that the Black-tailed Gnatcatcher may be a rare resident in the arid chaparral about 3800 feet elevation along Lost Valley (Indian Flats) Road north of Warner Springs. The first report was of a pair building a nest 28 April 1998 (E19; W. Pray, O. Carter). Then, on 6 June 2001, a short distance farther north in square D19, southeast of Pine Mountain, a pair appeared agitated, as if disturbed near a nest (K. J. Burns, E. Sgariglia). These observations are unprecedented, and the area was surveyed repeatedly on other occasions with no other observations. Yet rare occurrences in this area could connect the population seemingly isolated near Aguanga with the species' main range.

Another sighting on the coastal slope out of the known range was of two males, still with black caps and making short buzzy calls typical of the Black-tailed and dissimilar from the California, about 3200 feet elevation near Morena Village (T22) 1 July 2000 (R. and S. L. Breisch). Might the Black-tailed Gnatcatcher, like the Verdin whose habitat it shares, extend locally onto the coastal slope in northern Baja California, providing a source of dispersers across the border? (See also under Winter.)

Nesting: The Black-tailed Gnatcatcher has a strong preference for nesting in spiny shrubs or trees. Of the 17 nests whose placement atlas observers described, four were in smoketrees, four in palo verde, three in mesquite (two of these in or under clumps of mistletoe), two in desert thorn, two in desert lavender, one in desert apricot, and only one in a nonspiny plant, a California juniper. The

heights of the nests ranged from 3 to 12 feet but were mainly around 5 feet.

The Black-tailed Gnatcatcher begins nesting in March. Our earliest record of nest building was 6 March 1997 at Yaqui Well (I24; P. K. Nelson), of an occupied nest (incubation probably begun) was 17 March 2000 at the west end of Clark Dry Lake (D25; K. L. Weaver), and of a nest with eggs 19 March 1998 along Borrego Sink Wash (G26; P. D. Jorgensen). If the Black-tailed Gnatcatcher's incubation and nesting periods are the same average 14 and 13 days, respectively, as the California Gnatcatcher's (Grishaver et al. 1998), fledglings near Halfhill Dry Lake (J29) 10 April 1998 (L. J. Hargrove) hatched from eggs laid by 14 March. The close of the nesting season is more difficult to gauge and probably varies from year to year, variation in rainfall governing the abundance of insects and whether the birds can raise more than one brood. Our later observations of nesting activity, however, were not disproportionately concentrated in the wet year of 1998. Birds building nests in lower Carrizo Valley (O28) 31 May and 1 June 2001 (P. Famolaro, P. D. Jorgensen) suggest laying in early June.

Winter: The Black-tailed Gnatcatcher's dispersal in winter out of its breeding range is almost nil. In the Anza–Borrego Desert, we noted the species in seven squares with marginal habitat where we did not find it in the breeding season, though it could be a very sparse or irregular resident even in those. Winter records extend west to the edge of the range of the honey mesquite at Banner Queen Trading Post (K21), a well-covered site where the only sighting was of one on 2 December 1999 (P. K. Nelson). Two reports from chaparral in Potrero County Park (U20), of one on 25 January 1998 and two on 29 December 1999 (R. and S. L. Breisch), however, lie 23 miles west of the Black-tailed Gnatcatcher's nearest known locality of residence at Jacumba. The birds' calls were heard and the undersides of their tails were seen well. Like the July record from Morena Village, these observations could reflect an unknown extension of the range in Mexico.

Numbers of the Black-tailed Gnatcatcher varied less over the five years of the project than those of many other desert birds, but even this species was not immune to the cycle of wet and dry years. The count per hour in the drought-plagued final two winters of the project was 69% of that in the first three.

Conservation: The Black-tailed Gnatcatcher has always been considered common in the Anza–Borrego Desert, and most of its habitat is conserved in the state park. In spite of its nesting in a habitat unsuitable for cowbird foraging, the Black-tailed Gnatcatcher is subject to cowbird parasitism; we noted two instances of gnatcatchers feeding fledgling cowbirds as well as two instances of pairs mobbing cowbirds. Also, overpumping of groundwater could kill mesquites, eliminating one of the Black-tailed Gnatcatcher's primary habitats.

Taxonomy: All Black-tailed Gnatcatchers in California are *P. m. lucida* van Rossem, 1931. The Black-tailed

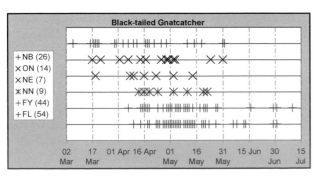

Gnatcatcher has had a tortured taxonomic history. Aside from being lumped with the California Gnatcatcher as a single species from 1926 to 1988, the Black-tailed was long known as the Plumbeous Gnatcatcher, *Polioptila plumbea* (Baird, 1854). When it was realized that the name *plumbea* had been applied earlier to the species now called the Tropical Gnatcatcher, the next oldest name, *Polioptila melanura* Lawrence, 1857, had to be substituted, and the common name Black-tailed Gnatcatcher, already in use for what we now call the California Gnatcatcher, was applied to the entire complex. When *P. melanura* and *P. californica* were shown to be distinct species (Atwood 1988), the English name Black-tailed went with the former, in agreement with the scientific name, which means black-tailed in Greek. This agreement between the scientific and common names, however, reverses traditional usage and contradicts the birds' actual characters—the Black-tailed Gnatcatcher has less black in the tail than the California Gnatcatcher.

THRUSHES — FAMILY TURDIDAE

Northern Wheatear *Oenanthe oenanthe*

The Northern Wheatear breeds widely in Alaska and northwestern Canada, but instead of migrating south it migrates far to the west, halfway around the world, to winter in sub-Saharan Africa. Along the Pacific coast of the lower 48 states it is only a casual vagrant, with 11 records for California and one for San Diego County.

Migration: The single Northern Wheatear known for San Diego County was in a patch of open sage scrub in the La Jolla Coast Preserve (O7) 18 October 2001 (D. W. Au, S. E. Smith; Garrett and Wilson 2003). This occurrence is the southernmost known for the Pacific coast of North America and one of only two for southern California.

Western Bluebird *Sialia mexicana*

The Western Bluebird is a common resident of San Diego County's foothills and mountains, especially where meadows lie among groves of oak or pine. In winter the birds gather into flocks and move in search of berries, especially mistletoe. Despite being a cavity nester that must compete with many other species for scarce holes in trees, the Western Bluebird shows signs of spreading out of its primitive range, colonizing urban areas with mature trees and wide lawns.

Breeding distribution: Montane coniferous and oak woodlands constitute the core of the Western Bluebird's range in San Diego County. In these habitats, daily counts late in the breeding season, when recently fledged young are common, range up to 60 in the Cuyamaca Mountains (N20) 16 July 2000 (B. Siegel), 90 on Hot Springs Mountain (E21) 14 July 2000 (K. L. Weaver, C. R. Mahrdt), and 100 in the Laguna Mountains (O23) 24 July 1998 (E. C. Hall, J. O. Zimmer). Toward the coast, the species becomes less abundant and more localized, but it is still common in many places, especially in northern San Diego County, with up to 20 in Valley Center (G11) 4 June 1997 (L. Seneca) and 20 in Horno Canyon, Camp Pendleton (D3) 25 June 1999 (D. C. Seals). The outline of the Western Bluebird's distribution is basically similar to that of other oak woodland birds like the Oak Titmouse and Acorn Woodpecker, but the atlas effort revealed a surprising number of Western Bluebird nestings in south-coastal San Diego County outside this historic range. These records ranged as near the coast as an apartment complex on the west side of the University of California campus (O7; nest in a Nuttall's Woodpecker

Photo by Anthony Mercieca

hole in a wooden lamp post 31 May 1999, young in a nest box 6 June 2001, D. G. Seay), the San Diego River next to the Fashion Valley shopping center (R9; fledging young in both 1997 and 1998 from woodpecker holes in cottonwoods, J. K. Wilson), and Glen Abbey Cemetery, Bonita (T11; feeding young 18 June 2001, T. W. Dorman).

The eastern edge of the Western Bluebird's range in San Diego County follows the eastern edge of oak woodland closely, with just a little extension into other trees infested with mistletoe, as in mesquites near Arsenic Spring (T28; two on 11 May 2001, F. L. Unmack). The species may summer irregularly in riparian woodland at Scissors Crossing (J22), where E. C. Hall noted two on 20 May 1998 and one on 21 June 1999 but J. R. Barth found none in 2002. Two nestings on the floor of the Anza–Borrego Desert were completely unexpected: one nest with two nestlings was in a dead planted tree at Canebrake (N27) 17 May 1998 (R. Thériault), and an adult female was tending three fledglings on the grounds of Borrego Springs

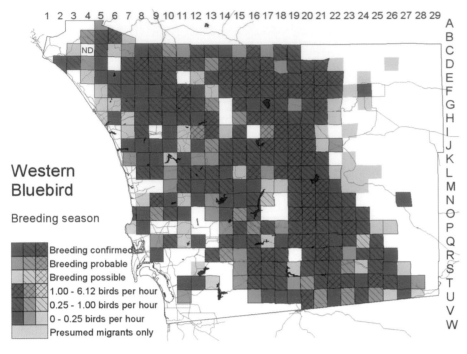

Western
Bluebird

Breeding season

Breeding confirmed
Breeding probable
Breeding possible
1.00 - 6.12 birds per hour
0.25 - 1.00 birds per hour
0 - 0.25 birds per hour
Presumed migrants only

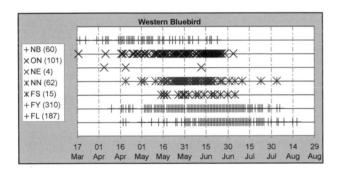

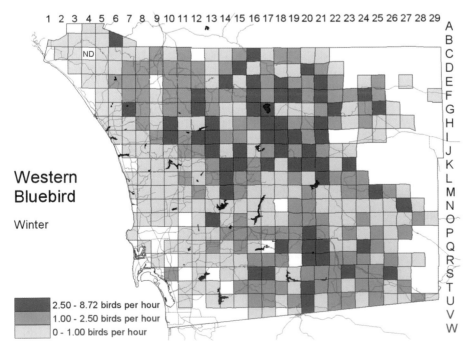

Western
Bluebird

Winter

2.50 - 8.72 birds per hour
1.00 - 2.50 birds per hour
0 - 1.00 birds per hour

High School (F24) 20 July 2000 (P. D. Jorgensen). Two in upper Indian Valley (P26) 9 May 1998 (P. R. Pryde) thus could have been nesting too. I know of no other instances of the Western Bluebird nesting in low desert anywhere in its range.

Nesting: The Western Bluebird is a secondary cavity nester, traditionally using holes in trees, usually excavated by woodpeckers. From 1997 to 2001 we noted nests in a wide variety of native trees as well as in eucalyptus trees and fan palms. The Western Bluebird is a leading patron of nest boxes. We also noted two nests in houses: under an eave or under roof tiles. One nest along Highway 80 between Boulevard and Bankhead Springs (T27) 3 May 1998 was in a splice sleeve on a large suspended telephone cable (F. L. Unmack). In its choice of nest site the Western Bluebird exemplifies the opportunism common to most secondary cavity nesters.

Our many observations of Western Bluebird nesting indicate that the species lays mainly from early April through the end of June, closely matching the range 4 April–29 June that Bent (1949) reported from California on the basis of 104 collected egg sets. Several observations, though, suggested that some birds started in late March; for example, a nest at Wilderness Gardens (D11) already had seven eggs on 5 April 1997 (V. Dineen), and fledglings at Bell Gardens, Valley Center (F12), 18 April 2001 (E. C. Hall, C. R. Mahrdt) must have hatched from eggs laid around 23 March.

Migration: The Western Bluebird occurs outside its breeding range in San Diego County mainly from October, exceptionally 23 September (1956, "flocks" at Blair Dry Lake, L24, ABDSP file), to early April. After 15 April migrants are normally rare, yet by far the largest concentration observed was on the latest recorded date, 24 April 1999. On that day, in San Felipe Valley (I21), a huge multispecies fallout of migrants included 370 Western Bluebirds (W. E. Haas).

Winter: Western Bluebirds remain throughout their breeding range in San Diego County year round, even at high elevations (up to 18 near the summit of Hot Springs Mountain, E20,

13 February 1999, K. L. Weaver, C. R. Mahrdt). But they also spread in fall and winter into the Anza–Borrego Desert. In this region, they seek developed and agricultural areas or fruiting fan palms and mistletoe, avoiding other habitats. The birds are usually in small flocks, occasionally in flocks of dozens. By far the highest daily count for a single atlas square in the Anza–Borrego Desert was of 604 in Borrego Springs (F24) 20 December 1998 (R. Thériault et al.).

The Western Bluebird spreads in winter in the coastal lowland as well, more numerously in the north county, less so to the south. It does not normally reach Point Loma or the Tijuana River valley; Greenwood and Mount Hope cemeteries in San Diego (S10; up to 22 on 18 December 1999 and 16 December 2000, C. Sankpill), Lower Otay Lake (U13; up to eight on 21 January 2001, T. Stands, S. Yamagata), and Marron Valley (V16; five on 1 December 2001, J. K. Wilson) marked the southwestern limits of its winter dispersal during the atlas period. The margin of the winter range in the coastal lowland parallels the margin of the breeding range, suggesting that these winter visitors are only short-distance dispersers.

Conservation: Over much of its range the Western Bluebird is in decline, apparently as a result of loss of nest cavities to logging and fire suppression, and from competition for cavities with European Starlings and House Sparrows (Guinan et al. 2000). In San Diego County, however, despite many competitors for nest sites, the Western Bluebird appears to be holding its own and actually extending its breeding range. In spite of a few nesting records from Rose Canyon and Balboa Park from 1915 to 1926 (Abbott 1927d), the species' breeding range stayed static for decades. So the nestings we observed in the city of San Diego from 1997 to 2001 were unexpected and appeared to represent new colonizations. The spread continued after the atlas period into 2002, with nesting that year in Presidio Park (R8) and Balboa Park near the Hall of Champions (S9; P.Unitt), adding two more squares beyond those in which the Western Bluebird had nested previously.

Why should the Western Bluebird in San Diego County be bucking the general trend? The planting of trees in what was once treeless scrub created new prospective habitat, and the spread of Nuttall's Woodpecker into urban areas as a breeding species has brought a primary cavity excavator into an area that once had none. The bluebird may be adapting to novel nest sites such as the crevices behind the leaf bases of certain species of palms, the most likely site for the birds that fledged young in Balboa Park. Installation of hundreds of nest boxes in Orange County in the late 1990s increased the population just to the north of San Diego County greatly (R. Purvis unpubl. data). As people notice bluebirds appearing, they may set up nest boxes appropriate for them, accelerating the increase. The small numbers of Western Bluebirds nesting in the heavily developed areas of San Diego County so far only hint at this species' becoming an urban adaptor. Yet another possibility is a general southward range expansion, paralleling that of the Orange-crowned Warbler and Western Flycatcher. Stephens (1919a) called the Western Bluebird a "common winter resident" but said that only "a few breed in the mountains."

Taxonomy: Western Bluebirds so far collected in San Diego County are the Pacific coast subspecies *S. m. occidentalis* Townsend, 1837. Even winter specimens from the Anza–Borrego Desert have the reduced chestnut on the back suggesting *occidentalis* rather than *S. m. bairdi* Ridgway, 1894, which breeds in the intermountain region and reaches southeastern California as a winter visitor.

Mountain Bluebird *Sialia currucoides*

In winter, the season when it reaches San Diego County, the Mountain Bluebird contradicts its name, seeking flat valley floors. Extensive grasslands, plowed fields, and dry lake beds are the species' principal habitats in San Diego County. The Mountain Bluebird is highly irregular in southern California, usually localized and uncommon. But in rare invasion years it is seen in flocks of hundreds, an amazing sight of glittering blue against the plain brown earth. Unfortunately, the Mountain Bluebird cannot withstand urbanization—winter visitors as well as breeding birds can lose habitat to development.

Winter: The Mountain Bluebird is quite localized in San Diego County, as tracts of grassland or bare dirt large enough to attract it are few and scattered. On the coastal slope, the bluebird's principal sites are Warner Valley, Santa Ysabel Valley, Santa Maria Valley (Ramona grasslands), Lake Cuyamaca, and an arc surrounding

Photo by Anthony Mercieca

Otay Mountain, from Otay Mesa north to Sweetwater Reservoir, east to Jamul and Dulzura, and south to Marron Valley. On the desert side of the mountains, the main sites are the Borrego Valley, San Felipe Valley, Earthquake Valley, and Blair Valley.

The species' numbers are so irregular, however, that the birds may be rare or absent even at favored sites in some years. The Mountain Bluebird's irregularity was

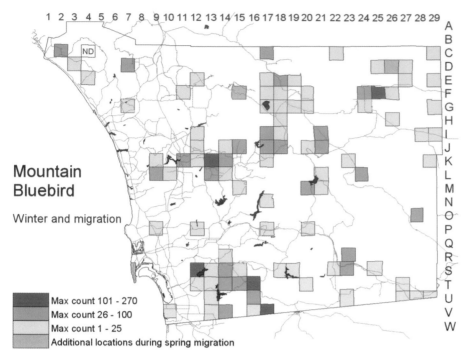

Mountain Bluebird

Winter and migration

■ Max count 101 - 270
▨ Max count 26 - 100
□ Max count 1 - 25
▨ Additional locations during spring migration

Las Pulgas Canyon (E4) 11 and 17 February (P. A. Ginsburg), and 70 about 3.5 miles inland near San Mateo Creek (C2) 19 February (J. R. Barth).

Migration: The Mountain Bluebird occurs in San Diego mainly from November to mid March. Early dates are 18 October 1998 (one in Blair Valley, L24, R. Thériault) and 25 October 1984 (one at Point Loma, S7, R. E. Webster, AB 39:104, 1985). Late dates are 2 April 2001 (six in Borrego Springs, F24, M. L. Gabel), 3 April 1998 (one in Blair Valley, R. Thériault), and 4 April (1884, one at San Diego, Belding 1890).

Conservation: One would hardly think that a bird that seeks areas with as little vegetation as possible could suffer habitat loss, but this is what has happened in San Diego County. In the 1960s and 1970s the Mountain Bluebird was found annually for the San Diego Christmas bird count in Rancho Otay (U12). Since then urban sprawl has spread past the eastern edge of the count circle and is eating away at much of the bluebird's traditional habitat from Otay Mesa north to San Miguel Mountain. Since 1980 the Mountain Bluebird has been found on only two San Diego counts. Elsewhere in the county, the Ramona grasslands are also prime Mountain Bluebird habitat threatened by urban encroachment. Keeping to grassland, sparse sage scrub, and agriculture, the bluebirds retreat from the urban growth front. The response of wintering birds to habitat fragmentation is poorly studied, but the Mountain Bluebird is a prime subject with which this topic could be addressed.

on full display during the five years of field work for this atlas. In 1998–99 and 2001–02, scarcely 30 individuals were reported each winter. In 2000–01, however, San Diego County received perhaps the greatest invasion of Mountain Bluebirds ever recorded. Daily counts in a single atlas square that winter ranged as high as 160 near Peg Leg Road in the Borrego Valley (F25) 17 December (L. J. Hargrove, P. Unitt), 200 along Rangeland Road, Ramona (K13), 16 January (L. and M. Polinsky), 150 at Sweetwater Reservoir (S12) 22 February (P. Famolaro), 240 between Dulzura and Sycamore Canyon (T16) 13 January (L. J. Hargrove), and 270 in Marron Valley (V17) the same day (E. C. Hall). That winter, Mountain Bluebirds ranged practically to the coast, where they are rare, with three at the Tijuana River estuary (V10) 29 January (T. Stands, S. Yamagata), seven at the mouth of

Townsend's Solitaire *Myadestes townsendi*

Townsend's Solitaire is a bird of coniferous forest at high elevations. Its breeding range extends south to the Santa Rosa Mountains—falling just a few miles short of San Diego County. The species thus reaches San Diego County principally as a rare migrant and winter visitor to the mountains, though there are also three summer records. Feeding on flying insects in summer, Townsend's Solitaire shifts to a diet largely of berries in winter.

Winter: In San Diego County, Townsend's Solitaire is most numerous in the higher mountains. Our highest counts were of six on Hot Springs Mountain (E20) 26 January 2002 (K. L. Weaver), seven on Volcan Mountain (I20) 17 December 2001 (R. T. Patton), and six on Cuyamaca Peak (M20) 17 January 2000 (E. Wallace). The solitaire's

Photo by Jack C. Daynes

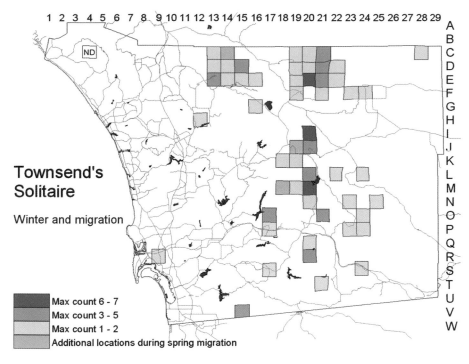

Townsend's
Solitaire

Winter and migration

■ Max count 6 - 7
░ Max count 3 - 5
▫ Max count 1 - 2
▨ Additional locations during spring migration

Migration: Townsend's Solitaire occurs primarily from mid October, exceptionally 29 September (1973, one at Point Loma, AB 28:109, 1974), to mid March, with a few remaining into April (latest 21 April 1999, one along Boulder Creek near Eagle Peak, M18, R. C. Sanger). Stragglers have been noted three times in May: one at Point Loma 8–9 May 1990 (B. and I. Mazin, AB 44:497, 1990), one in the Tijuana River valley 24 May 1963 (AFN 24:375, 1963), and two at Palomar Mountain (D15) lingering to 25 May 1983 (R. Higson, AB 37:913, 1983). Though still quite rare, Townsend's Solitaire is considerably more frequent along the coast (especially at Point Loma) as a migrant than as a winter visitor.

frequency decreases with decreasing elevation. In the coastal lowland, the only report from 1997 to 2002 was of one in Balboa Park (R9) 2 January 2001 (J. Roberts). Only one Townsend's Solitaire has been seen on any San Diego Christmas bird count, 1953–2002, and only one has been seen on any Oceanside count, 1976–2002. The species is more frequent in the Anza–Borrego Desert, though still rare, with nine records during the atlas period.

Like other frugivorous winter visitors, Townsend's Solitaire varies considerably in numbers from year to year. During the five-year atlas period, solitaires were scarce in 1997–98 (only six reported) and 1999–2000, more numerous in 1998–99, 2000–01 (53 reported), and 2001–02.

Breeding distribution: Townsend's Solitaire is another of those mountain birds whose elevational range in summer lies above the tops of San Diego County's highest mountains. It breeds south to the Santa Rosa Mountains of Riverside County, where it is rare (Weathers 1983). Nevertheless, there are three summer records from San Diego County, one from the Palomar Observatory (D15), of one bird 19 July 1980 (AB 34:931, 1980), and two from Middle Peak, Cuyamaca Mountains (M20), of one bird 19 July 1987 (R. E. Webster, AB 41:1488, 1987) and an apparent pair 19 June 1988 (P. Unitt).

Taxonomy: Townsend's Solitaires in San Diego County, like those elsewhere in the United States, are of the paler subspecies *M. t. townsendi* (Audubon, 1838).

Gray-cheeked Thrush *Catharus minimus*

Though it breeds far to the west of the longitude of California, even into northeastern Siberia, the Gray-cheeked Thrush passes far to the east of the state on its way to and from a winter range in South America. It is only a casual vagrant to California, largely in fall from mid September to late October. Thrushes of the genus *Catharus* are less susceptible to errors of navigation than most other long-distance migrants.

Migration: The three records of the Gray-cheeked Thrush in San Diego County are all from Point Loma (S7): 1 October 1986 (R. E. Webster, Langham 1991), 2–10 October 1987 (G. McCaskie, Roberson 1993), 10–11 September 1990 (V. P. Johnson, Heindel and Garrett 1995). Though none is supported by a specimen, the second and third birds were photographed, and the third was trapped and examined in hand.

Photo by Anthony Mercieca

Swainson's Thrush *Catharus ustulatus*

San Diego County straddles Swainson's Thrush's main migration route along the Pacific coast of North America, so the species passes through in large numbers, however inconspicuously. The average San Diegan is more likely to find the low-flying Swainson's Thrush dead—killed by a cat or having flown into a window—than to see the bird alive. The county lies at the southern tip of the species' breeding range, so Swainson's Thrush is rare here as a breeding bird, confined to a few stands of riparian woodland.

Photo by Anthony Mercieca

Breeding distribution: San Diego County's small breeding population of Swainson's Thrush centers on the lower Santa Margarita River in Camp Pendleton. From O'Neill Lake (E6) downstream to Stuart Mesa Road (G5), there may be as few as seven pairs. After spring migrants have departed, the highest counts in single atlas squares were of four birds near O'Neill Lake 2 July 1998, two, including a fledgling, near the base airfield (E5) 28 June and 22 July 2000 (P. A. Ginsburg), three, including a pair, between Rifle Range Road and the north end of Ysidora Basin (F5) on 28 June 1998, and two in Ysidora Gorge (G5) 19 June 1998 (R. E. Fischer). Breeding was confirmed along the Santa Margarita by a nest with nestlings near Rifle Range Road (F5) 28 June 2000 (J. M. Wells) and a fledgling being fed a short distance farther upstream, just north of the base airfield, 28 June–22 July 2000 (P. A. Ginsburg). Swainson's Thrush also breeds along the lower San Luis Rey River in Oceanside, with one near Lawrence Canyon (H5) 11 July 1999 (J. Determan) and up to four, including a nest, about 0.5 mile downstream of the Oceanside airport (G5) 2–14 June 2000 (J. M. Wells). It is likely that a few other Swainson's Thrushes breed elsewhere in northwestern San Diego County, along the Santa

Margarita and San Luis Rey rivers, San Mateo Creek, Las Pulgas Creek, and De Luz Creek, though the only other records during the atlas period after migration were of up to four singing males along San Mateo Creek, San Onofre State Beach (C1), 14 June–7 July 1997 (L. Ellis), three birds (two singing males) along Las Pulgas Creek (E4) 27 June 2001 (P. A. Ginsburg), and up to three birds (two singing males) along the San Luis Rey River near Gird Road, Bonsall (E8), as on 23 July 1999 and 27 June 2001 (P. A. Ginsburg). Records before 1997 attest to Swainson's Thrushes summering along the Santa Margarita River north of Fallbrook (C8).

Elsewhere in San Diego County there are only a few scattered records of Swainson's Thrushes summering. A single singing male was along Temecula Creek near Oak Grove (C16) 20 June 1998 (K. L. Weaver). A single singing male along the San Luis Rey River near Rincon (F13) 12 June 1999 (E. Wallace) could have been an exceptionally late migrant. A single bird was along Santa Maria Creek in Bandy Canyon (K13) 25 June 1999 (P. von Hendy, B. Hendricks). Two singing males about 3800 feet elevation in Juch Canyon along Wynola Road (J19) 12 July 1999 (S. E. Smith) furnished the only summer record for Swainson's Thrush in San Diego County's mountains. One singing male summered along the San Diego River near Santee Lakes (P12) in 1999 and 2001; on 4 July 2001 it was carrying berries from an ornamental tree into a dense riparian thicket, apparently feeding young (M. B. Mulrooney). Up to two singing males along the Tijuana River near Saturn Blvd. (W10) 30 June–2 July 2001 (M. B. Mulrooney) were the southernmost summering Swainson's Thrushes ever found; the previous southernmost record was based on an egg set collected at Bonita (T11) 10 June 1914 (WFVZ 65276).

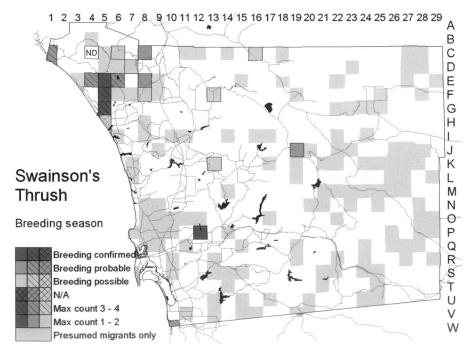

Swainson's Thrush

Breeding season

- Breeding confirmed
- Breeding probable
- Breeding possible
- N/A
- Max count 3 - 4
- Max count 1 - 2
- Presumed migrants only

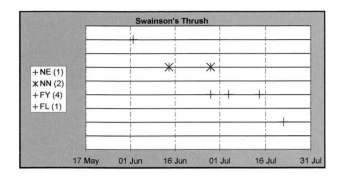

Nesting: In California, Swainson's Thrush typically nests at heights under 2 meters in riparian woodland with a rather closed canopy (T. Gardali unpubl. data). Little is known of the species' nesting in San Diego County, however. The nest found by J. M. Wells along the San Luis Rey River was about 2.25 meters up in a giant reed—an invasive pest plant that hardly constitutes a traditional nest site. This nest had four eggs on 2 June 2000 and nestlings about four days old on 14 June, suggesting the clutch had been completed around 30 May. The nest along the Santa Margarita River had nestlings about eight or nine days old on 28 June 2000, suggesting that clutch was completed around 8 June. The three egg sets collected in San Diego County 1914–20 are dated 31 May, 10 June, and 26 June.

Migration: In spring, Swainson's Thrush is a rather late migrant through San Diego County, with peak numbers in May. From 1997 through 2001, our dates for spring migrants ranged from 11 April (1998, one in Arroyo Seco del Diablo, N28, R. and S. L. Breisch) to 11 June (1999, one in Black Canyon, I16, K. J. Winter) and 12 June (1999, one in Oceanside, H5, J. Determan). Over the five years, the early dates ranged from 11 to 28 April, but the earliest date ever reported for the species is 1 April (1996, San Mateo Creek mouth, C1, L. J. Edson, NASFN 50:333, 1996), from a site where it is known to summer. Thus, as for many other species with a wide range on the Pacific coast, it appears that the local population arrives earlier than migrants headed farther north. Migrant Swainson's Thrushes are usually seen in small numbers, seldom more than six per day. The species' secretive habits mean that many birds are overlooked. But occasional larger concentrations are noted, up to 30 on 14 May 1998 at Scissors Crossing (J22; E. C. Hall), a riparian oasis along the primary corridor for migrants crossing from the desert to the coast. One found near Tecolote Canyon (Q9) 15 May 2002 (S. K. Niemann, SDNHM 50638) had been banded as a juvenile at the Wright Wildlife Refuge just north of Eureka, California, 17 August 2001 (T. L. George pers. comm.).

Fall migrants occur mainly from September to mid October; dates range from 26 August (1972, San Marcos,

I9, AMR 4094) to 8 November (1981, Point Loma, S7, J. L. Dunn, AB 36:218, 1982), exceptionally 1 December (1964, San Diego, SDNHM 35141).

Winter: A Swainson's Thrush in Coronado (S9) 15–16 December 1979 (G. McCaskie) had an injured wing, probably accounting for its remaining so late. All other winter reports from California presumably are of misidentified Hermit Thrushes; Swainson's has been collected in winter no nearer than Nayarit in western Mexico.

Conservation: As a species restricted for breeding to riparian woodland, Swainson's Thrush has suffered from the removal and degradation of most of this habitat in southern California. Stephens (1919a) called it a "rather common summer resident," but by the 1970s it was rare in this role. From 1997 to 2001 we did not find the species at several locations from which Unitt (1984) reported it in the 1970s. Perhaps the most serious current threat to Swainson's Thrush habitat in San Diego County is the proliferation of the giant reed, which was accelerated along the lower Santa Margarita River by the floods of 1993. Along the coast of northern California, Swainson's Thrush's reproductive success appears insufficient to sustain the population, for unknown reasons (T. Gardali unpubl. data). Loss of wintering habitat in southern Mexico and Central America may account for the species' disappearance from seemingly unaltered breeding habitat in the Sierra Nevada (Marshall 1988).

Taxonomy: Swainson's Thrushes occurring in San Diego County are Russet-backed Thrushes, the *ustulatus* subspecies group breeding along the Pacific coast from southeastern Alaska to San Diego County. Within this group, three subspecies have been described, the paler, grayer *C. u. oedicus* (Oberholser, 1899), breeding from southern California north to the inner Coast Ranges and Sierra Nevada of northern California, the darker, more rufous *C. u. ustulatus* (Nuttall, 1840), breeding from northwestern California north through the Pacific Northwest, and the very rufous *C. u. phillipsi* Ramos, 1991, breeding on the Queen Charlotte Islands of British Columbia. No specimens of San Diego County's breeding population have yet been collected. Among migrants, *ustulatus* is by far the most abundant. Of 44 spring specimens, collected from 29 April to 10 June, apparently only two are drab enough to qualify as *oedicus*: one from Borrego Springs (G24) 10 May 2000 (P. D. Jorgensen, SDNHM 50462) and one from Chula Vista (U11) 19 May 1990 (S. Kingswood, SDNHM 46849). Of 19 fall specimens, collected from 7 September to 1 December, only one, from San Diego 25 October 1981 (J. Shrawder, SDNHM 41615), even approaches *oedicus*. I have not seen specimens that would allow me to distinguish *phillipsi* from *ustulatus*, but the former may pass through San Diego County as well.

Hermit Thrush *Catharus guttatus*

In winter, the Hermit Thrush is common in chaparral and riparian or oak woodland, foraging quietly on the ground for insects or plucking berries from shrubs. Smaller numbers occur in sage scrub, desert-edge scrub, parks, and residential areas. The species is also taking on a new role, a few birds beginning to colonize shady forest in the county's mountains. Field work for this atlas yielded the first confirmations of Hermit Thrushes breeding in San Diego County.

Photo by Anthony Mercieca

Winter: Wintering Hermit Thrushes are widespread over San Diego County's coastal slope, most concentrated in and near the Santa Margarita Mountains in the county's northwest corner. But large numbers can be seen anywhere in dense chaparral, with up to 146 around Lake Hodges (K10) 27 December 1998 (R. L. Barber et al.) and 60 at Cabrillo National Monument and Fort Rosecrans Cemetery, Point Loma (S7), 15 December 2001 (J. C. Worley). The Hermit Thrush can be fairly common in winter even at high elevations (up to 12 near High Point, Palomar Mountain, D15, 21 December 1999, K. L. Weaver). In the Anza–Borrego Desert it is rare, occurring mainly at oases at the base of the mountains.

Numbers of Hermit Thrushes in San Diego County vary somewhat from year to year, though less so than those of other frugivorous winter visitors. At lower elevations, this variation was rather modest from 1997 to 2002, but in some previous years it was striking. Totals on Christmas bird counts (results of all six counts in the county combined) illustrate this: 651 in 1989–90 and 737 in 1990–91, versus 40 in 1991–92 and 38 in 1995–96. This variation could be due to annual variation in both the numbers reaching San Diego County and to variation in the birds' distribution within the county, according

to food availability and whether mountain chaparral is covered with snow. In the mountains, the Hermit Thrush was much more numerous in the winter of 1998–99, with little snow, than in the winter of 1997–98, with far more.

Migration: The Hermit Thrush occurs in San Diego primarily from late September through April. By mid May it is rare. During the atlas period 19 May (1999, one at Lake Domingo, U26, J. K. Wilson) was our latest date except for stragglers at Point Loma 22 May 1999 and 4 June 1998 (P. A. Ginsburg). An even later straggler was at the same location 6 June 1984 (R. E. Webster, AB 38:961, 1984).

Even without the specimens that would prove the birds are of different subspecies, the pattern of the Hermit Thrush's migrations assures us that the county's incipient breeding population is different from the wintering population. So far the breeding population has been recorded only from 15 May (1999, one on Cuyamaca Peak, M20, G. L. Rogers) to 19 July (1998, three or four singing along Chimney Creek, E14, Palomar Mountain, D. S. Cooper, FN 52:504, 1998), but further observations would likely extend this interval.

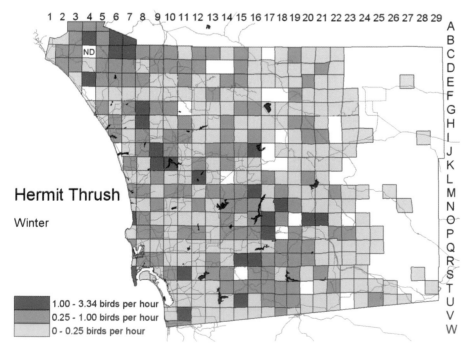

Hermit Thrush

Winter

- 1.00 - 3.34 birds per hour
- 0.25 - 1.00 birds per hour
- 0 - 0.25 birds per hour

Breeding distribution: Summering Hermit Thrushes are now known in San Diego County from the Palomar, Hot Springs, Volcan, and Cuyamaca mountains, though still in very small numbers. In all areas, they occur in deep forest on north-facing slopes. During the atlas period, they were found most frequently on Palomar Mountain (eight records), between 4400 and 5200 feet elevation from upper Pauma Creek (D14; up to two—a pair—on 15 July 1999, P. D. Jorgensen) southeast to Chimney Creek. On Volcan Mountain (I20), an adult and a fledgling were at 5000 feet elevation in a steep northeast-draining canyon 28 June 2000 (A. P. and T. E. Keenan)—at the same site as one or two singing males 31 May 1993 (P. Unitt, AB 47:1151, 1993). In the Cuyamaca Mountains, above 5200 feet elevation, summering Hermit Thrushes are known from both Cuyamaca Peak (M20; one on 23 May 1998 and 15 May 1999, G. L. Rogers) and Middle Peak (M20; two singing males 11 June 2000; adult feeding barely fledged young 2 July 2000, R. E. Webster). The first summer record of the Hermit Thrush in San Diego County was from Hot Springs Mountain (E21) 24 June 1980 (Unitt 1981), but there have been no subsequent reports from this site.

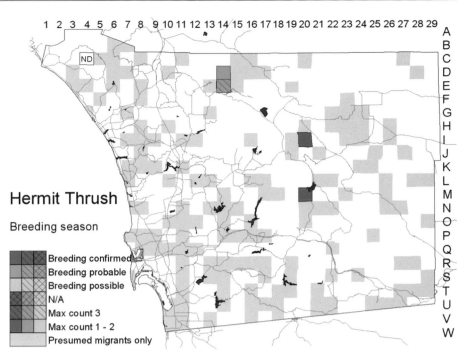

Hermit Thrush

Breeding season

- Breeding confirmed
- Breeding probable
- Breeding possible
- N/A
- Max count 3
- Max count 1 - 2
- Presumed migrants only

A Hermit Thrush was in pinyons at 5600 feet elevation on the north slope of Villager Peak, Santa Rosa Mountains (C27), 2 June 1999 (P. D. Jorgensen). The habitat is atypical for breeding Hermit Thrushes, and visits to the site in 2000 and 2001 did not reveal the species again, so most likely this bird was a wanderer.

Nesting: No nest of the Hermit Thrush has yet been found in San Diego County; the fledglings seen on Volcan Mountain and Middle Peak in 2000 constitute the only evidence for the species' breeding here. Elsewhere in the western United States, the species nests on the ground or up to moderate heights in small trees. The dates of the fledglings seen in San Diego County suggest egg laying in early June.

Conservation: San Diego County's remaining large tracts of chaparral are central to the winter range of at least one subspecies of Hermit Thrush, *C. g. guttatus*. Hermit Thrushes use modified habitats as well, orchards, parks, and gardens with adequate shrubbery. Because they are active mainly on and near the ground, however, when the light is dim, in these habitats they suffer considerable predation from domestic cats and mortality from striking wires and windows.

The traditional southern limit of the breeding range of the Hermit Thrush was the San Bernardino Mountains (e.g., Grinnell and Miller 1944). Thus the species' appearance in summer in San Diego County represents a southward range extension, more likely the result of natural range expansion than the birds being overlooked in the past.

Taxonomy: The Hermit Thrush shows great variation in its broad range, but in spite of the studies of Aldrich (1968) and Phillips (1991), the interpretation of this variation leaves much to be desired. At the San Diego Natural History Museum we have 122 skins of the species from San Diego County, in part because the birds so often fly into windows or otherwise come to grief in places where people

find them. But without a broad sample of specimens from the breeding range, categorizing the variation in the San Diego sample can be only rudimentary. Nevertheless, it is clear that the bulk of Hermit Thrushes wintering in San Diego are the subspecies *C. g. guttatus* (Pallas, 1811), with a medium brownish-gray back and breeding at least in south-coastal Alaska. A significant minority of the specimens (about 15) have darker upperparts, deeper gray flanks, larger blackish breast spots, and a deeper buff wash on the breast. These are apparently *C. g. vaccinius* (Cumming, 1933), breeding on and near Vancouver Island. San Diego County represents the southern limit of this subspecies' winter range (Phillips 1991). The Hermit Thrushes of southeastern Alaska, *C. g. nanus* (Audubon, 1839), also winter in San Diego County, in numbers smaller than those of *guttatus*. They are more rufous above than *guttatus* but not as dark as the species' dark extreme.

Between Vancouver Island and the Olympic Peninsula is an abrupt break. Along the Pacific coast from Washington to central California breeding Hermit Thrushes are paler and longer billed, though even smaller in other dimensions, than those farther north. This subspecies is *C. g. slevini* (Grinnell, 1901), which occurs in San Diego County primarily as an uncommon migrant. Its identity may be suspected even in the field on the basis of its pale grayish upperparts, small sparse breast spots, and pale flanks. One specimen has been collected in fall (Volcan Mt., 9 October 1993, SDNHM 48587), two in early spring (4 April 1877, Campo, U23, SDNHM 1701; 11 April 1984, La Posta Truck Trail, R24, SDNHM 42997). *C. g. slevini* winters mainly in the tropical dry forest of western Mexico, but San Diego County may be at the northern fringe of its normal winter range. Allan R. Phillips identified specimens from Balboa Park (R9) 15 December 1958 (SDNHM 30128) and Pacific Beach (P7) 18 February 1971 (SDNHM 37879) as *C. g. jewetti*

Phillips, 1962, which he split from *slevini* on the basis of browner birds from the Olympic Peninsula. Subsequently he recognized *jewetti* only inconsistently (Monson and Phillips 1981, Phillips 1991).

Finally, the birds summering in San Diego County's mountains must be *C. g. sequoiensis* (Belding 1889),

though no specimen has yet been collected. *C. g. sequoiensis* breeds from the Sierra Nevada south to the mountains of southern California and migrates to and from a winter range in the mountains of western Mexico with only rare stops in the Mojave Desert. It is pale like *slevini* but larger, with heavier breast spots.

Wood Thrush *Hylocichla mustelina*

This handsome bird breeding in the eastern United States is only a rare vagrant to California, with 16 well-supported records from 1967 through 2001. These are spread through fall, winter, and spring, though all from San Diego County are for late fall.

Migration: The California Bird Records Committee has accepted four records of the Wood Thrush from San Diego County: one collected in the Tijuana River valley (W10) 18 November 1967 (McCaskie 1971; SDNHM 36355), one seen at the same locality 25 October 1978, found killed by a cat the following day (not preserved; AB 33:216, 1979), one photographed at Point Loma (S7) 24 October–6 November 1981 (B. E. Daniels; Binford 1985), and one seen there 1–25 November 1982 (D. and N. Kelly; Morlan 1985). Details of another sighting at Point Loma 21 October 1990 (R. E. Webster, AB 45:152, 1991) were never submitted.

Photo by Anthony Mercieca

Rufous-backed Robin *Turdus rufopalliatus*

A species of western mainland Mexico, the Rufous-backed Robin has, since the 1960s, been dispersing annually in small numbers north to Arizona in fall and winter. Nine of these vagrants are known to have strayed west to southern California, one reaching San Diego County.

Winter: The single Rufous-backed Robin known for San Diego County was photographed on the lushly landscaped grounds of the Casa del Zorro, Borrego Springs (H25), 16 March–16 April 1996 (K. Ellsworth; McCaskie and San Miguel 1999). Though the bird occurred in early spring, its long stay suggested it was a winter visitor, presumably passing unnoticed until March. Other California records range from November to early April.

American Robin *Turdus migratorius*

A traditional harbinger of spring in northern North America, the American Robin is a traditional harbinger of winter in San Diego County. At that season it is an irregular visitor, common in some winters, scarce in others, as flocks roam in search of berry-bearing plants like toyon, wild grape, California coffeeberry, and many ornamentals. Since the 1940s, however, the American Robin has spread south as a breeding species, occupying mountain forests, orchards, urban parks, and college campuses year round.

Breeding distribution: The American Robin's patchy distribution in San Diego County is explained by its three habitats: montane forest, orchards, and parks and residential areas with shade trees and lawns. In San Diego County's mountains, the robin is fairly common among conifers (up to 12 at Palomar Mountain, E15, 18 June 1999, E. C. Hall, C. R. Mahrdt), locally so in higher-

Photo by Anthony Mercieca

elevation oak woodland with few or no conifers (up to 13 around Hulburd Grove, O19, C. Anderson). It inhabits all the wooded ranges, south to Corte Madera Valley (R20/R21; up to five on 20 June 1998, J. K. Wilson).

The importance of orchards as American Robin habitat in San Diego County became clear only as a result of the atlas field work. The region from De Luz and Bonsall east to Pauma Valley and Valley Center, extensively planted with avocado and citrus groves, emerges as one of the robin's major population centers. Some of our highest counts of breeding robins were around such orchards (up to 20, 1 mile northeast of Heriot Mountain, C12, 1 April 2000, J. Determan; 18 between Fallbrook and Monserate Mountain, D9, 19 May 1999, E. C. Hall).

In urban parks and residential areas breeding robins are still local. They are fairly common in a few places (up to 24 in southern Balboa Park, S9, 28 April 1997, Y. Ikegaya) but lacking from much seemingly suitable habitat. Berry Community Park, Nestor (V10; one on 18 July 1997, C. G. Edwards), and parks in Chula Vista (U11/U12) mark the southern limit of the robin's range along the coast of San Diego County—and thus on the Pacific coast of North America.

Outside these three main habitats, there are scattered records from rural areas with oak groves or lawns, southeast to Boulevard (T26; two including a singing male 6 June 2001, J. K. Wilson).

Nesting: The American Robin may nest high or low, in a wide variety of trees or shrubs. The nest is often well screened by foliage, but we also noted nests in more open trees like eucalyptus and Coulter pine. Because the American Robin is a recent colonist of San Diego County, no eggs have been collected here, and atlas data are the best information yet on the species' breeding schedule. They suggest the species lays mainly from April through June, in agreement with the 6 April–14 July range of 46 egg sets from elsewhere in California (Bent 1949). In the less constrained environment of orchards and lawns, however, a few birds start

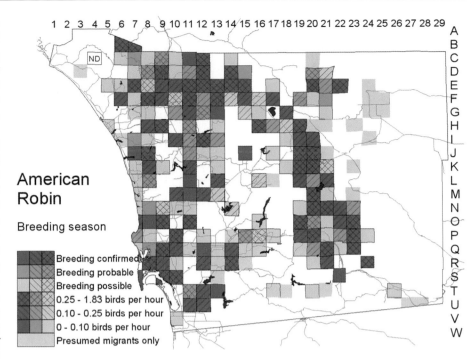

American
Robin

Breeding season

Breeding confirmed
Breeding probable
Breeding possible
0.25 - 1.83 birds per hour
0.10 - 0.25 birds per hour
0 - 0.10 birds per hour
Presumed migrants only

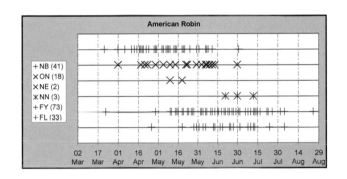

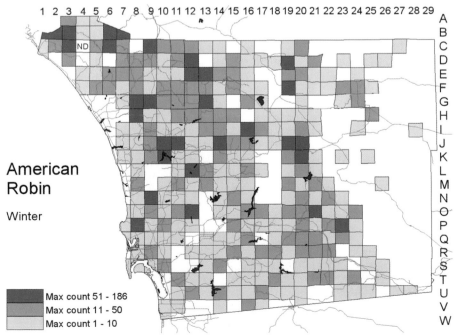

American
Robin

Winter

Max count 51 - 186
Max count 11 - 50
Max count 1 - 10

earlier, possibly in the second week of March, as shown by one carrying nest material at Point Loma (S7) 1 March 1997 (J. C. Worley), one carrying food to a nest at the Pala Mesa resort (D9) 23 March 1997 (M. San Miguel), and a fledgling along San Marcos Creek at Rancho Santa Fe Road 26 April 1997 (J. O. Zimmer). A robin carrying nest material in Presidio Park (R8) 1 July 1998 (C. L. Mann) and fledglings being fed in Coronado (S9) 4 August 1997 (M. Molloy), and at Granite Spring, Cuyamaca Mountains (N21), 25 August 1999 (P. D. Jorgensen) suggest egg laying as late as July.

Migration: American Robins do not follow a rigid schedule of migration, at least in southern California. Rather, they move nomadically through their nonbreeding season. From 1997 to 2002, dates of birds away from breeding habitat ranged from 10 October (1998, one at Borrego Springs, G24, P. D. Jorgensen) to 24 April (2000, one in San Felipe Valley at the east base of Volcan Mountain, J21, P. K. Nelson). A couple of reports later in April from sites where the species was missed later in the spring were from urban or agricultural areas that it could colonize. Even a single robin in Borrego Springs (G24) 14 May 1998 (P. D. Ache) could have been a prospective colonizer. The species has nested irregularly at Brawley in the Imperial Valley since 1992 (Patten et al. 2003), though Belding (1890) reported a late straggler at Campo 14 May 1884.

Winter: As a winter visitor the American Robin is widespread but very irregular, abundant in some years, scarce in others. Even within the county invasions take place at different times. During the five-year atlas period, robins were by far most numerous in eastern San Diego County

in 2000–01, whereas in coastal north county they were most numerous in 2001–02. High counts in a single day in one atlas square were 186 south of De Luz (C6) 6 January 2001 (K. L. Weaver) and 175 near Wooded Hill, Laguna Mountains (P23) 19 February 1999 (E. C. Hall, J. O. Zimmer). In the Anza–Borrego Desert the American Robin is confined largely to developed areas and mesquite thickets festooned with mistletoe.

Conservation: As a breeding bird the American Robin is a recent colonist of San Diego County, first reported breeding in the Cuyamaca Mountains by Grinnell and Miller (1944) and in the coastal lowland at Rancho Santa Fe (L8) in July 1951 by Mead (1952). Over the next 50 years, breeding robins spread widely. The distribution by the end of the millennium was much broader than known just 20 years earlier (Unitt 1984). The spread has continued past San Diego County with the species colonizing the sierras Juárez and San Pedro Mártir in Baja California in the 1990s (Erickson et al. 2001).

Lawns with earthworms, of course, offer the robin a suitable habitat lacking before urbanization, but the reason why the range expansion included natural montane forest as well is less clear. Possibly the urbanization of southern California allowed the entire region's population to increase to the point where the birds moved into all suitable habitats. But the southward spread of other montane birds suggests that other, more subtle factors could be playing a role with the robin as well.

Taxonomy: The only subspecies of the American Robin known from southern California is *T. m. propinquus* Ridgway, 1877, pale and usually lacking white corners to the tail.

Varied Thrush *Ixoreus naevius*

Finding a Varied Thrush in San Diego County is always a pleasant surprise, a reminder of the rainforests of the Pacific Northwest. This rare and irregular winter visitor occurs mainly in the oak and coniferous woodland in the foothills and mountains, though records are scattered almost throughout the county.

Winter: The Varied Thrush reaches San Diego County only irregularly, though its incursions often coincide with those of other irruptive winter visitors. In some years there are none, in others there are a few scattered individuals, and occasionally there are modest numbers. During the atlas period, the number of individuals noted per year was zero in 1997–98, six in 1998–99, 13 in 1999–2000, zero in 2000–01, and six in 2001–02. The best-documented incursions were in 1906–07, 1924–25, 1972–73, 1983–84 (highest totals on Christmas bird counts that year, with three on the San Diego count and 12 on the Lake Henshaw count), 1989–90, and 1996–97. The only records of more than a single bird in one atlas square per day from 1997 to 2002 were of four in Palomar Mountain State Park (D14) 26 February 1999 (P. D. Jorgensen), four

Photo by Dave Furseth

in the Cuyapaipe Indian Reservation (P24) 28 January 2000 (D. C. Seals), and two in the Manzanita Indian Reservation (R25) 22 January 2000 (J. K. Wilson). Past reports ran as high as 16 along Agua Dulce Creek, Laguna Mountains (P23), 17 January 1978 (C. G. Edwards).

The Varied Thrush may be most frequent on Palomar Mountain; seven of the 18 records during the atlas period were from this area. It is least frequent in the Anza–Borrego Desert, but even here there are about a dozen

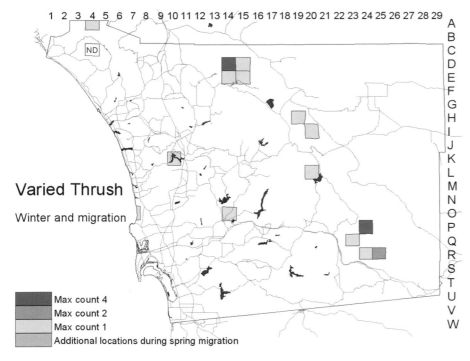

Varied Thrush

Winter and migration

- Max count 4
- Max count 2
- Max count 1
- Additional locations during spring migration

Webster, FN 51:928, 1054, 1997). As expected in an irruptive species, Varied Thrush migrations follow no well-defined schedule.

Taxonomy: The subspecies of the Varied Thrush differ in the color of the upperparts of the females, brown in the more coastal, more southern *I. n. naevius* (Gmelin, 1789), grayish with variable brown tips in the more inland, more northern *I. n. meruloides* (Swainson, 1832). Both subspecies occur in San Diego County, but *meruloides* is much the more frequent, at least among the more recent specimens. Of the 13 skins of female Varied Thrushes in SDNHM, two to five are *naevius*, the southernmost known of this subspecies (Unitt 1984). Complicating the identification is the foxing of specimens: with time, the gray feathers turn brownish, making *meruloides* look more like *naevius*.

Phillips (1991) split off the Varied Thrushes from the southern segment of the breeding range of *meruloides* as a new subspecies *godfreii*, intermediate between *meruloides* and *naevius*, but I have not seen specimens allowing me to evaluate this proposal.

records total, from oases and developed areas, south to Tamarisk Grove (I24).

Migration: Records of the Varied Thrush in San Diego County range mainly from mid October to March. After invasion years, stragglers have occurred at Point Loma (S7) as late as 13 May in 1984 (M. and B. McIntosh, AB 38:961, 1984) and 17 May and 6 June in 1997 (R. E.

BABBLERS AND WRENTIT — FAMILY TIMALIIDAE

Wrentit *Chamaea fasciata*

The Wrentit is one of the most abundant birds in San Diego County's most abundant habitat. It vies only with the Spotted Towhee for the title of most numerous bird in mature chaparral. The Wrentit also uses sage scrub and the understory of riparian and oak woodland—the fruit of the poison oak so prevalent in these woodlands is one of the Wrentit's staple winter foods. The Wrentit is famously sedentary, mated pairs remaining together for life in one small territory. Though they do not adapt to urban development, Wrentits remain in many undeveloped canyons within the city, clinging tenaciously to scraps of native scrub.

Breeding distribution: The Wrentit occurs throughout San Diego County's coastal slope and east down the desert slope as far as chaparral plants like the sugarbush and manzanita can grow. It is rather uniformly distributed in its habitats but may be somewhat more concentrated in northwestern San Diego County, where daily counts run as high as 75 along the Santa Margarita River north of Fallbrook (C8) 24 May 2001 (K. L. Weaver), 60 northwest of Morro Hill (E7) 26 July 1999 (P. A. Ginsburg), and 60

Photo by Anthony Mercieca

in the Santa Margarita Mountains near Cold Spring (A4) 24 June 2001 (J. R. Barth).

Points along the east edge of the species' range are Lower Willows (D23; up to nine on 20 June 1998, B. Peterson), Culp Valley (H23; up to five on 20 April 1998

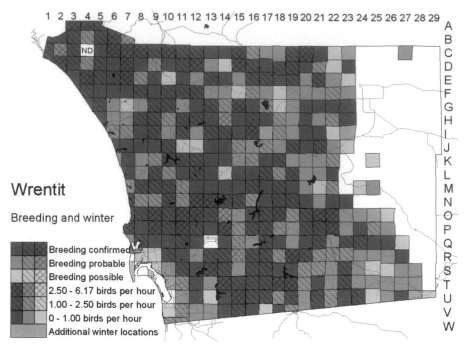

height from 20 to 150 cm off the ground, averaging 64 cm, and 55% of the height of the supporting plant. Those plants encompassed 15 species, most often California sagebrush (29 nests). Some other plants were large shrubs like the laurel sumac, yellow bush penstemon, broom baccharis, redberry, and chamise that could protect or conceal the nest. But many were in smaller, more delicate shrubs like the flat-top buckwheat, white sage, and San Diego sunflower. Three nests were even placed in plants with almost no ability to conceal them, one each in bedstraw, cobwebby thistle, and California bee plant.

Like many birds of the chaparral, the Wrentit typically begins laying in the third or fourth week of March, and this is what most atlas observers' records imply. M. A. Patten's egg dates in 2001 ranged from 29 March to 21 June. But the total spread of egg dates known from California is 1 March–2 July (Bent 1948), and a couple of reports from the Sweetwater River near Highway 94 (R13) imply laying around the first of March: a nest with large young 2 April 1997 (A. Mercieca) and a nest with eggs 8 March 1998, followed by fledglings 2 April (M. and D. Hastings). The large number of reports of fledglings being fed through July suggests that many Wrentits lay well into June, and young still being fed 23 August 2000 (Fallbrook Naval Weapons Station, D6, W. E. Haas) suggest that they lay rarely as late as early July.

Winter: The Wrentit does not spread in winter outside its breeding range. The four atlas squares along the desert edge where the species was recorded in winter but not in the breeding season are probably areas where it is resident in very low numbers. Wrentits remain through the winter even near the summit of Hot Springs Mountain (E20), where C. R. Mahrdt and K. L. Weaver noted them repeatedly, with a maximum of three on 16 February 2002. The only isolated locality where the species was encountered in winter was the north-facing slope of Pinyon Mountain Valley, with one at 4050 feet elevation 9 December 2001 (R. Thériault).

Conservation: The Wrentit is not an urban adapter, but in spite of its seemingly poor capability for dispersal, it is one of the scrubland birds least sensitive to habitat fragmentation. Our results imply that it takes nearly total elimination of sage scrub or chaparral from an atlas square to eradicate the Wrentit, and only five squares in metropolitan San Diego that presumably once had Wrentits have lost them. Studies addressing habitat fragmentation specifically (Bolger et al. 1997, Crooks et al. 2001) also identified the Wrentit as one of the less sensitive species. Unfortunately, current construction practices entail

and 16 June 1999, M. L. Gabel), Sentenac Ciénaga (J23; one on 16 July 2000, R. Thériault), the Tierra Blanca Mountains between Canebrake Wash and Indian Valley (O26; up to two on 7 April 2000, J. R. Barth), and the Imperial County line east of Jacumba (U29; one on 15 April 2001, P. Unitt). In the Anza–Borrego Desert, small numbers are isolated along Vallecito Creek, both near Vallecito Stage Station County Park (M25; two singing on 6 May 2001, one on 5 May 2002, J. R. Barth) and in the gorge between Mason and Vallecito valleys (one in the lower gorge, M24, 28 March 2001, P. K. Nelson; one pair resident there from 1985 to 1993, Massey and Evans 1994; specimen from the upper gorge, M23, 6 October 1984, SDNHM 43342). The Wrentit is rare in the pinyon–juniper zone of the Santa Rosa and Vallecito mountains with one breeding-season record in each range. A pair was at 4650 feet in upper Barton Canyon (C27) 17 June 2001 (R. Thériault), and a singing male was on the north-facing slope of Pinyon Mountain Valley (K25) 26 May 2000 (J. R. Barth).

Nesting: The Wrentit usually places its cup nest at a fork in the outer branches of a shrub, occasionally in a tree such as coast live oak. In and near Mission Trails Regional Park and the Otay–Sweetwater Unit of the San Diego National Wildlife Refuge, M. A. Patten monitored 76 Wrentit nests in sage scrub in 2001. The nests ranged in

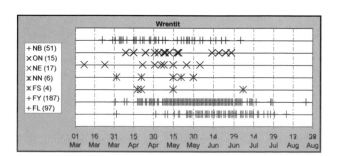

recontouring topography completely. Pockets of native scrub in canyons, as were left in San Diego County's older residential neighborhoods, are now being eliminated.

Taxonomy: San Diego County Wrentits represent the pale grayish subspecies, the Pallid Wrentit, *C. f. henshawi* Ridgway, 1882. Independent genetic techniques suggest that the Wrentit, long placed in a monotypic family, then

with the babblers (Timaliidae), is related most closely to the Old World genus *Sylvia* (Barhoum and Burns 2002). The Wrentit's similarity to the Dartford (*S. undata*) and Marmora's (*S. sarda*) Warblers of the Mediterranean maquis, once presumed to be the result of convergent evolution in similar habitats on opposite sides of the world, now appears to be the result of close relationship after all.

Mockingbirds and Thrashers — Family Mimidae

Gray Catbird *Dumetella carolinensis*

Though the Gray Catbird breeds west almost to the coast of British Columbia, it is only a rare vagrant to California—the bulk of the population migrates east of the Rocky Mountains. But the species is on the increase: of 107 reports accepted by the California Bird Records Committee 1884–1999, one third were in just the last four years of this interval. Similarly, of the 20 records of the Gray Catbird in San Diego County, 10 have come since initiation of the field work for this atlas in 1997.

Photo by Anthony Mercieca

Migration: Half of San Diego County's known catbirds have been fall migrants, occurring as early as 24 September (1976, one at Point Loma, S7, K. van Vuren, Luther et al. 1979). Besides eight fall records from Point Loma, there is one from the Tijuana River valley 7–8 November 1964 (the only specimen, SDNHM 35095), one from a boat 15 miles off Oceanside 26 October 1983 (M. W. Guest, Bevier 1990), and two from Paso Picacho Campground (M20) 29 October 1988 (D. W. Aguillard, Pyle and McCaskie 1992) and 17 November 2002 (T. McGrath, M. San Miguel, NAB 57:118, 2003). The four spring records are of single birds in San Clemente Canyon (P8), 27 April 1999 (M. B. Stowe, Rogers and Jaramillo 2002), at Southwest Grove, Mountain Palm Springs (P27), 31 May 2000 (D. G. Seay; NAB 54:327, 2000), and at Point Loma 28 May–2 June 2001 (R. E. Webster, M. U. Evans, NAB 55: 357, 583, 2001) and 27–28 May 2002 (R. E. Webster, NAB 56:358, 2002). One in riparian woodland along the Santa Margarita River near the Camp Pendleton airport (E5) 28 June 2000 (P. A. Ginsburg, NAB 54:424, 2000) may have been summering, and one in molt at

Cabrillo National Monument, Point Loma 11–17 July 1988 (B. and I. Mazin, Pyle and McCaskie 1992) certainly was.

Winter: Three wintering Gray Catbirds have been reported from San Diego County, from Balboa Park (R9) 16 December 1972 (P. Unitt) and from Point Loma 7 November 1983–13 March 1984 (V. P. Johnson, Roberson 1986) and 31 October 1999–21 January 2000 (D. Aklufi, NAB 54:222, 2000).

Conservation: The Gray Catbird's increase in California most likely reflects the westward expansion of the breeding range; the species exemplifies changes in migration route lagging behind changes in breeding distribution.

Taxonomy: The validity of the division of the Gray Catbird into eastern and western subspecies is dubious. The difference of a paler crissum in western catbirds, upheld by Phillips (1986), is not evident in specimens in the San Diego Natural History Museum.

Northern Mockingbird *Mimus polyglottos*

The Northern Mockingbird has become such a fixture in southern California's domesticated landscape that it now seems out of place in natural habitats. From inner-city neighborhoods to rural ranches it is common year round. Nevertheless, mockingbirds still occur also in desert washes and in open sage scrub with scattered large shrubs or cacti. Field work for this atlas revealed that in the Anza–Borrego Desert the mockingbird nests widely in wetter years, retreating to towns and oases in dry ones.

Breeding distribution: The mockingbird is widespread in San Diego County, but its breeding distribution is neatly divided into two blocks. It is common in agricultural and urbanized areas throughout the coastal lowland and lower foothills and lacking only from the north side of the Santa Margarita Mountains, where development so far is almost nil. It is generally absent from unbroken chaparral. Its upper elevational limit is about 4000 feet, where it is rare (one near Julian, J20, 24 June 2001, A. P. and T. E. Keenan; one in Pine Valley, P21, 29 June 1997, J. K. Wilson).

The mockingbird's primitive habitat along the coast was probably open sage scrub with scattered large shrubs and cactus thickets. The birds are still common in this now rare habitat wherever it remains, as in the San Diego Wild Animal Park (J12/J13) and along the western and northern slopes of Otay Mesa (V12/V13).

The mockingbird also occurs throughout the Anza–Borrego Desert, at least in wet years. It is common around houses and mesquite thickets, competing with the Phainopepla for mistletoe berries. From the desert, it ranges west in small numbers onto the coastal slope in Warner Valley and on the Campo Plateau. The narrow gap in the Mockingbird's range is due to the zone of thick chaparral as well as to the forests of the higher mountains.

The most interesting thing we observed about the mockingbird from 1997 to 2002 was its response to variation of rainfall in the Anza–Borrego Desert. In this area, away from the town of Borrego Springs, the number recorded per hour in the wet year 1998 was 67% higher than in the year with the next highest number, 2001. And the hourly count in 2001 was over twice that in 1997, 1999, or 2000. The jump from 1997 to 1998 was by a factor of over 8. The pattern parallels that of the Horned Lark and some wintering sparrows. It recalls the scenario observed by Gale Monson in southwestern Arizona in 1952 and 1958, when, after wet winters, "Mockingbirds, Western Meadowlarks, and other species appeared 'from nowhere' and nested abundantly" (Phillips et al. 1964).

Nesting: Mockingbirds build their nests in trees or shrubs with dense screening foliage or protective thorns. As expected of a bird so well adapted to the urban landscape, it uses ornamental plants freely. Garden plants with both dense foliage and thorns, such as pyracantha and bougainvillea, are particularly attractive nest sites. Prickly pear cacti are favored sites as well. In the desert,

Photo by Anthony Mercieca

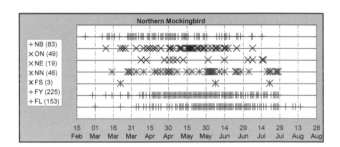

use of mesquite is common; mesquite often hosts mistletoe, which offers the mockingbird a staple food as well as an ideal nest site. In more sparsely vegetated desert, we noted nests in ocotillo, placed in the "cage" formed by the multiple spreading thorny branches at the plant's base.

The Northern Mockingbird enjoys an unusually long breeding season, commonly raising two broods per year, rarely three (Bent 1948). Observations of adults carrying food to a nest as early as 10 March imply egg laying by 26 February; we found nests with eggs as late as 16 July. Our earliest observations of nesting activity were from Borrego Springs, but some along the coast followed just a few days later. Interestingly, our latest records of eggs were also from Borrego Springs, in mid July when high temperatures were reaching 116° F. Collected egg sets extend the nesting season we observed even further; Bent (1948) reported California egg dates ranging from 16 February to 2 September.

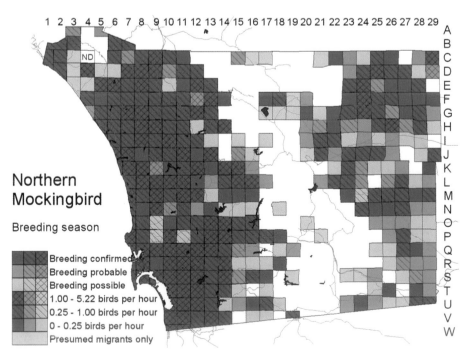

Northern Mockingbird

Breeding season

Breeding confirmed
Breeding probable
Breeding possible
1.00 - 5.22 birds per hour
0.25 - 1.00 birds per hour
0 - 0.25 birds per hour
Presumed migrants only

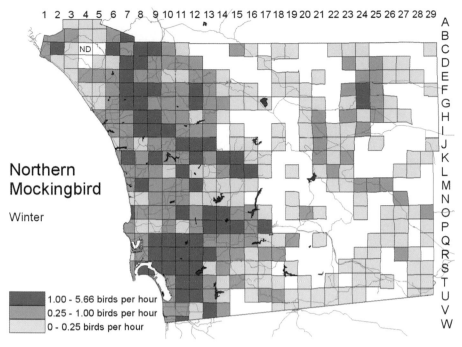

Northern Mockingbird

Winter

- 1.00 - 5.66 birds per hour
- 0.25 - 1.00 birds per hour
- 0 - 0.25 birds per hour

rarely but, surprisingly, more frequently and more widely than in summer. Winter numbers in these areas were generally small, three or fewer per day, but up to five were at Santa Ysabel (J18) 17 December 2001 and seven were in La Jolla Indian Reservation (F15) 21 January 2000 (W. E. Haas et al.). Winter records also are all from about 4000 feet elevation and lower, except for one about 4900 feet elevation near San Ignacio, Los Coyotes Indian Reservation (E21), 19 December 1998 (K. L. Weaver, C. R. Mahrdt).

Conservation: The mockingbird adapted to the urbanization of southern California as soon as it began. Grinnell (1911) noted the suitability of orange groves as nesting habitat and estimated that suburban development plus the planting of orange groves allowed the Mockingbird population of Los Angeles County to increase by a factor of five. More recent data, such as Christmas bird counts, show no consistent trend, though the species' numbers probably continue to increase in tandem with increase in the extent of development. Because of lack of early data, the mockingbird's history in the Anza–Borrego Desert is unclear; there has been no obvious change since the 1960s. The opportunistic breeding we observed suggests that the Mockingbird has always been an irregular species in this area. Yet the species was absent from the nearby Salton Sink at the beginning of the 20th century, colonizing only after the area was turned to farmland (Arnold 1935, 1980).

Migration: Though the mockingbird is a permanent resident in San Diego County, whether or not individual birds are sedentary probably varies by habitat. Birds living in urban areas may have no need to move. At my home in the Hillcrest area of San Diego (R9), one pair of mockingbirds maintained the same territory year round for four years; the female was recognizable as the same individual by an injury to one foot. The species' irregularity in the Anza–Borrego Desert, however, suggests that many mockingbirds move opportunistically as conditions demand.

Winter: The mockingbird's distribution in San Diego County in winter shows interesting differences from that in spring and summer. On the coastal side, the species is still widespread and clearly concentrated in the agricultural areas of the north county and the urbanized area of metropolitan San Diego. In the Anza–Borrego Desert, however, the mockingbird is much more restricted in winter than in spring to developed areas and oases. Even in the wet winter of 1997–98 we did not find it over much of the sparsely vegetated desert, so the winter distribution shows large gaps where the breeding distribution appears nearly continuous. In the upper foothills and lower mountains we found the Mockingbird in winter

Taxonomy: An eastern and a western subspecies of the Northern Mockingbird are commonly recognized, but Phillips et al. (1964) ascribed the color difference to soot and fading; the figures in Ridgway (1907) suggest the measurement differences are insufficient to diagnose the subspecies either. So all Northern Mockingbirds of mainland North America are best called *M. p. leucopterus* (Linnaeus, 1758).

Sage Thrasher *Oreoscoptes montanus*

The Sage Thrasher is a migrant and winter visitor in San Diego County, rare from September to mid January, uncommon from late January through March. It occurs mainly in and near the Anza–Borrego Desert, frequenting scrub like saltbush and mesquite, as well as stands of the big sagebrush at higher elevations that resemble its breeding habitat in the Great Basin. Near the coast the Sage Thrasher is rare—the sage scrub that it once visited more numerously now being largely converted to cities.

Photo by Anthony Mercieca

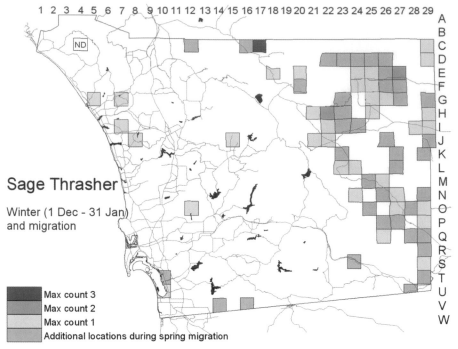

Sage Thrasher

Winter (1 Dec - 31 Jan)
and migration

- Max count 3
- Max count 2
- Max count 1
- Additional locations during spring migration

during the atlas field work in high, dry valleys in north-central San Diego County: three in Oak Grove Valley (C17) 23 January 1999, one at Puerta La Cruz (E18) 23 January 1999 (R. and S. L. Breisch), one about 3700 feet elevation along Agua Caliente Creek at the west base of Hot Springs Mountain (E20) 26 January 2002 (K. L. Weaver), and three in big sagebrush at Ranchita (H21/H22) 14–15 January 1999 (P. Unitt).

Lower on the coastal slope we encountered the Sage Thrasher only eight times from 1997 to 2002, generally in sage scrub or cactus thickets, as in Pamo Valley (J15; one on 2 and 30 January 2000, W. E. Haas, L. E. Taylor). The Sage Thrasher formerly occurred with some regularity in halophytic scrub along the coast, but our only sightings from this habitat, of which hardly any remains, were of one at the south end of Ysidora Basin (G5) 26 December 1998 (P. Unitt) and another at the south end of San Diego Bay (U10) 16 December 2000 (P. R. Pryde).

The abundance of the Sage Thrasher varied greatly over the atlas period. Figures for winter and the following spring combined, the number reported varied from 7 in 1997–98 to 90 in 1998–99 to 55 in 1999–2000 to 20 in 2000–01. Possibly the birds enjoyed an exceptionally productive breeding season following the wet winter of 1998, leading to a population spike, then the numbers declined steadily over the following dry years.

Migration: Sage Thrashers may arrive in San Diego County as early as 18 September (1974, one in the Tijuana River valley, G. McCaskie) but remain rare through mid January. By the end of January their numbers increase gradually, to reach a peak in late February and March. Patten et al. (2003) reported spring migration in the Salton Sink beginning as early as 17 January, but in San Diego County establishing an exact date for spring arrival is impossible. The highest count ever reported in the Anza–Borrego Desert, of 20 in Little Blair Valley (L24) 2 February 1991 (B. Cord), was presumably of migrants. The highest count during the atlas period was of seven east of the Borrego Sink (G26) 17 February 2000 (M. B. Mulrooney). The species is rare by early April, and the latest dates are 16 April (1999; one in the Borrego Valley east of Peg Leg Road, F26, M. B. Stowe; 1999, three near In-Ko-Pah, T29, D. C. Seals), 25 April (1999, four in the Borrego Valley, F25, P. D. Ache), "May" (1881, two specimens collected at San Diego, Belding 1890), and 4 June (1970, one at Agua Caliente Springs, M26, A. Fries, AFN 24:718, 1970). G. Holterhoff (in Belding 1890) reported the Sage Thrasher as "common" near National City in the summer of 1883 but apparently collected no specimen and the record has not been repeated since.

Winter: Because of the Sage Thrasher's migration schedule, the map shows only records for December and January in blue for winter. The species is widely but thinly scattered through the Anza–Borrego Desert, all records before February being of just one or two birds. A few apparently wintering Sage Thrashers turned up

Conservation: Though the Sage Thrasher was never common in coastal San Diego County, it was once considerably more frequent than it is now, though still irregular. Heermann (1859) "remarked it on several occasions in the environs of San Diego," and Baird (1858) listed two specimens collected there. Huey (1924) listed several specimens collected around San Diego; on 15 March 1923, 5 miles east of National City, "Sage Thrashers were abundant on the mesa, and a great many could have been collected" (four actually were: SDNHM 8545–48). Single birds were noted on five San Diego Christmas bird counts from 1966 to 1974 but on only one from 1975 through 2002. Apparently a bird whose winter habitat around San Diego is the same as that of the San Diego Cactus Wren and California Gnatcatcher declined with the loss of that habitat. The lack of early data from the Anza–Borrego Desert precludes assessment of any trend there.

Brown Thrasher *Toxostoma rufum*

The only thrasher breeding in the eastern United States is a rare vagrant to California. Though there are just 18 records for San Diego County, they are scattered through every month of the year. Nevertheless, the Brown Thrasher occurs primarily as a migrant and winter visitor between 20 September and 15 May, with only two known in summer.

Photo by Anthony Mercieca

Migration: There are six records of the Brown Thrasher in fall migration, four from Point Loma (S7), one from La Jolla (P7; 17 October 2001, F. A. Belinsky, NAB 56:107, 2002), and one from the Borrego Springs sewage pond (H25; 1 November 1992; A. G. Morley, AB 47:150, 1993). In spring, there are five records of birds not known to have wintered, two from Point Loma (5 April 1973, AB 27:821, 1973; 15 May 1979, AB 33:806, 1979), one from Pio Pico Campground (T15; 10 April 1981, D. W. Povey), one from Oceanside (H6; 24 April 1973, AB 27:821, 1973), and one from Borrego Springs (G24; 27 April 1998, P. D. Ache). One at Tamarisk Grove Campground (I24) 19–21 June 1988 (L. Walton, R. Thériault, AB 42:482, 1341, 1988) was also likely a late spring vagrant. However, one at Point Loma 24 July–10 September 2001 was in molt, as expected of the species in its summer breeding range (V. Conway, L. M. Dorman, NAB 55:483, 2001).

Winter: The Brown Thrasher has been recorded in San Diego County five times in winter; four of the birds were known to have remained at least 11 days, on dates ranging from 15 October to 3 May. Four of the records are from parks and gardens in San Diego (Unitt 1984); one is from chaparral on the south side of San Elijo Lagoon (L7) 13 January–24 February 1996 (P. A. Ginsburg, NASFN 50:224, 1996).

Taxonomy: No specimen of the Brown Thrasher has yet been collected in San Diego County, but only the expected paler western subspecies *T. r. longicauda* is known from elsewhere in California and Arizona.

Bendire's Thrasher *Toxostoma bendirei*

In California, Bendire's Thrasher is confined largely to the Mojave Desert. Even there it is so rare and irregular it is regarded as a species of special concern by the California Department of Fish and Game. San Diego County is off the species' normal migration route, so it occurs here less than annually, as a very rare migrant and winter visitor. Nevertheless, a single pair nested successfully near Ocotillo Wells in 1993.

Photo by Anthony Mercieca

Breeding distribution: I found the single known nest of Bendire's Thrasher in San Diego County 2.5 miles southwest of Ocotillo Wells (J28) on 26 April 1993. On that date the nest contained two chicks, one of which later fledged successfully (AB 47:1151, 1993). The winter of 1992–1993 was unusually wet; presumably the lush growth and better food supply of the following spring allowed the species to spread exceptionally far to the southwest of its normal range. On 19 May 1998—also following a wet winter—Lori Hargrove found a single Bendire's Thrasher in ornamental trees around a house 3 miles southeast of Ocotillo Wells (J29)—San Diego County's only other record of the species during the breeding season (FN 52:504, 1998).

Nesting: The nest near Ocotillo Wells was in a large, dense desert lavender, about 5 feet off the ground. It was thus typical for the species in height and selection of a rather spiny shrub as a site.

Migration: Of San Diego County's 28 records of Bendire's Thrasher, 13 are of fall migrants, on dates as early as 18 August (1991, Point Loma, S7, R. E. Webster, AB 46:151, 1991) and 27 August (1964, Solana Beach, L7, McCaskie et al. 1967b). Of the four spring records of birds not known to have wintered, two are from near the coast (one at Sweetwater County Park, T12, 6 March 1999, S. L. Breisch; one in the Tijuana River valley 4 April 1970, AFN 24:645, 1970), two from the Anza–Borrego Desert (two in Smoke

Tree Wash, E28, 9 March 1997, P. D. Jorgensen, NASFN 51:928, 1997; one at Palm Spring, N27, 19 March 1983, E. A. Cardiff, AB 37:913, 1983).

Winter: Winter records of Bendire's Thrasher in San Diego County are nine, four from the Tijuana River valley (Unitt 1984), one from Coronado (S9; 28 January–3 March 1985, J. L. Coatsworth, AB 39:211, 1985), one from Otay Mesa (V12; 16 February–16 March 1985, M. Orell, AB 39:211, 1985), one from Escondido (J11; 2–22 January 1994, J. L. Coatsworth, NASFN 48:249, 1994), one from San Felipe Valley 1.1 miles northwest of Paroli Spring (H21; 21 December 1998, P. Unitt, NAB 53:210, 1999), and one from Agua Caliente Springs (M26; 21 January 1999, E. C. Hall, NAB 53:210, 1999). Several of these records are

of birds remaining for extended periods, yielding a range of 8 November–16 March for known wintering Bendire's Thrashers.

Conservation: The reasons for Bendire's Thrasher's rarity in California are not clear, as much of its high-desert habitat is little disturbed. Nevertheless, habitat fragmentation and disturbance resulting from development, often spreading over large areas at low density, is a concern (J. Sterling unpubl. data). Sterling's survey in 2001 yielded only two or three Bendire's Thrashers in areas where England and Laudenslayer (1989) found 41 and 23 in 1986 and 1987, respectively. The difference may have been due to population cycles following rainfall variation, however, than to long-term decline.

Curve-billed Thrasher *Toxostoma curvirostre*

The Curve-billed Thrasher is common in southern Arizona but known in California from only 14 records from the Colorado River and Imperial Valley. When I saw one on Otay Mesa, I questioned whether it might be an escapee from captivity, as it was less than one half mile from the Mexican border. Nevertheless, the California Bird Records Committee accepted the bird as a natural vagrant, noting the lack of Curve-billed Thrashers reported in captivity by Hamilton (2001) and the species' history of vagrancy as far north as Canada (Cole and McCaskie 2004).

Migration: The Curve-billed Thrasher on Otay Mesa (V13) 28 April 2002 was singing and calling with the species' characteristic "whit-wheet!"

Photo by Anthony Mercieca

California Thrasher *Toxostoma redivivum*

A sickle-shaped bill, long tail, and creative song give the California Thrasher the character its plain brown plumage does not. A sedentary resident, the thrasher is one of the characteristic birds of chaparral, though it occurs in lower density in sage scrub, oak and riparian woodland, desert-edge scrub, and mesquite thickets as well. It is still common over much of San Diego County but does not adapt to urban development. Within the city of San Diego it survives in large canyons like Florida and Tecolote but disappears from small canyons surrounded by housing tracts.

Breeding distribution: The California Thrasher is widespread over the coastal slope of San Diego County, lacking only in heavily urbanized areas. It is common wherever there is extensive chaparral and considerably more common in dense chaparral than in coastal sage scrub or other habitats (Cody 1998). So it is no surprise that the greatest concentrations are where chaparral is most extensive: along the north side of the Santa Margarita

Photo by Anthony Mercieca

Mountains east to Fallbrook, along the north side of Palomar Mountain east to Bucksnort Mountain and Indian Flats, in central San Diego County from Miramar east to El Cajon Mountain and Alpine, and all across southern San Diego County from Otay Mountain to the Jacumba Mountains. The species ranges from sea level to the summit of Hot Springs Mountain (E20; up to three on 9 June 2001; K. L. Weaver).

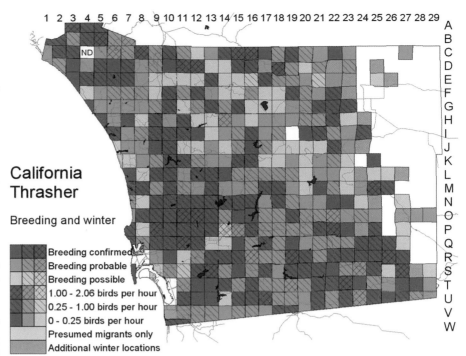

California
Thrasher

Breeding and winter

- ▨ Breeding confirmed
- ▨ Breeding probable
- ▨ Breeding possible
- ▨ 1.00 - 2.06 birds per hour
- ▨ 0.25 - 1.00 birds per hour
- ▨ 0 - 0.25 birds per hour
- ▨ Presumed migrants only
- ▨ Additional winter locations

The California Thrasher extends down the east slope of the mountains to their bases, being uncommon in open desert-edge scrub. Small numbers are isolated in the pinyon/juniper zone of the Vallecito Mountains (up to three in Pinyon Mountain Valley, K25, 26 May 2000, D. C. Seals). In the Santa Rosa Mountains the California Thrasher ranges barely into San Diego County on the south flank of Rabbit Peak (C27; two singing on 3 May 2000, P. Unitt). At low elevations in the northern Anza–Borrego Desert the species ranges east to Lower Willows (D23; up to five on 12 May 2001, B. Peterson) and Tamarisk Grove (I24; up to six on 17 March 1998, P. K. Nelson), except for irregular occurrences in the mesquite thicket at the west end of Clark Dry Lake [E25; seen repeatedly in 1993, M. L. Gabel in Massey (1998); one on 17 March 2000, K. L. Weaver]. In the southern Anza–Borrego Desert the California Thrasher occurs at all the oases along the bases of the mountains, being especially numerous in the extensive mesquites at Vallecito (M25, up to 12 on 27 April 1998, M. C. Jorgensen). Along Carrizo Creek it ranges east to Carrizo Marsh on the Imperial County line (O29; up to three, including an agitated pair, on 6 May 1998, P. D. Jorgensen).

Nesting: California Thrashers build a bulky cup nest of sticks, usually placing it in the upper half of a dense shrub where it is screened from above by foliage. Like most sedentary chaparral birds, the California Thrasher begins laying typically in the third week of March, but occasionally it begins earlier. Reports of feeding young as early as 18 March and fledglings as early as 28 March imply incubation begun about 1 March. California Thrasher eggs have been collected at San Diego as early as 9 February,

however, and at Pasadena, Los Angeles Co., as early as 15 December (Grinnell 1900, Bent 1948). November nests have been reported from Pasadena by Sargent (1940) and from Los Angeles by Davis (1952). In San Diego County a barely fledged young was picked up in Valley Center (G11) 16 October 1997 (SDNHM 49967). Michael A. Patten noted young one to two weeks out of the nest near Spring Valley (R13) 11 March 2002. Evidently a few California Thrashers will nest in fall or winter if stimulated by conditions such as early rain.

Winter: As expected for a sedentary species, the California Thrasher's pattern of abundance in winter is the same as in the breeding season. Our maximum daily count was 45 around Oriflamme Mountain (M22) 22 February 2000 (J. R. Barth).

The species' dispersal outside its breeding range is minimal. In winter, we noted it in the Anza–Borrego Desert in 12 atlas squares where we did not record it during the breeding season, but all these were adjacent to squares where we did find it in spring or summer. Winter records include two for the mesquite thicket at the west end of Clark Dry Lake (D25; up to two on 20 December 1998, E. Post).

Conservation: The California Thrasher is moderately sensitive to habitat fragmentation. Among San Diego's canyons isolated by urbanization, Crooks et al. (2001) found thrashers consistently in tracts of scrub of 30 or more hectares only; they found them inconsistently in fragments of 8 to 30 hectares and not in fragments smaller than 8 hectares. By 1997 they had disappeared from 4 of 11 canyons where they occurred in 1987 and colonized only one additional canyon (Crooks et al. 2001). On the scale of our atlas grid, however, the California Thrasher appears absent from only the most heavily urbanized areas.

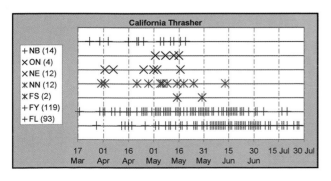

The California Thrasher prefers a habitat that is subject to fire, but it is among the slower species to recolonize recovering burned chaparral. Surveys near Pine Valley found the California Thrasher to be one of three chaparral birds still significantly less abundant in areas averaging 6 years since a fire than in areas averaging 30 years since a fire (Cleveland National Forest unpublished data).

Taxonomy: The California Thrasher has been divided into two or three subspecies, but the differences (in color) are slight. Whether they suffice to support a taxonomic distinction needs reevaluation on the basis of unfoxed, freshly molted specimens.

Crissal Thrasher *Toxostoma crissale*

Here at the western limit of its range, the Crissal Thrasher has one precarious toehold on San Diego County: the thicket or bosque of mesquite in the floor of the Borrego Valley. Though year-round residents, the birds are rare, shy, and difficult to see. The poor health of the bosque, likely the result of a water table lowered by groundwater pumping, bodes ill for the thrasher's long-term survival here. The Crissal Thrasher is scarce throughout its California range and is regarded as a species of special concern by the California Department of Fish and Game.

Breeding distribution: The Crissal Thrasher's habitat in San Diego County covers about 3 square miles, almost entirely within atlas square G25 between the Borrego Valley airport and Borrego Sink, east of Borrego Valley Road. The population's size is unknown but is unlikely to be more than 10 pairs. The highest daily counts during the breeding season consisted of just one family group of five, on 4 and 11 June 1998 (R. Thériault). The only sighting outside of square G25 was of two just to the east, on the northeast side of the Borrego Sink in G26 18 April 1998 (P. Unitt, F. L. Unmack).

Melvin L. Gabel (in Massey 1998) noted the Crissal Thrasher in the mesquite thicket at the west end of Clark

Dry Lake (D25/E25) on 4 June 1993 and 27 June 1994 but found the California Thrasher there more consistently. From 1997 to 2002 our only sighting here was of one in winter. Lying 7 miles north of the Borrego Valley mesquite bosque, this is the only place in California where both the California and Crissal Thrashers have occurred. Reports of the Crissal elsewhere in the Anza–Borrego Desert are based on misidentified California Thrashers.

Nesting: The Crissal Thrasher usually builds its nest in dense thorny shrubs, using mesquite primarily if it is available (Gilman 1909, 1915, Hanna 1933). The only information recorded on Crissal Thrasher nesting in San Diego County is Robert Thériault's observations in 1998: fledglings following or being fed by their parents on 4, 11, and 15 June. On the basis of an incubation period of 14 days and a nestling period of 11–16 days, these young hatched from eggs laid in early May. Most likely they were the result of a second or replacement clutch, as the mean date of eggs collected in the Coachella Valley, Riverside County, is 27 March (Cody 1999). Fifty-six egg sets from throughout California range from 10 February to 10 June (Bent 1948).

Winter: Winter records of the Crissal Thrasher are from the same area in the Borrego Valley as those in the breeding season, except for a few sightings near the Borrego Springs sewage ponds, on the south side of the Borrego Sink (H25; P. D. Jorgensen, Massey 1998), and one at the northwest corner of Clark Dry Lake (D25) 4 February 1999 (B. Scheible et al.). All winter sightings during the atlas period were of single individuals only. The species is found on most Borrego Springs Christmas bird counts, always as a result of a targeted search; the maximum recorded on the count was four on 28 December 1986.

Conservation: The Crissal Thrasher has been noted continuously in the Borrego Valley's mesquite bosque since Stott and Sams (1959) first reported four on 12 December 1958. Data are too skimpy to suggest any trend. But the long-term outlook is not good: the mesquite bosque suffers from a falling water table and illegal wood cutting (R.

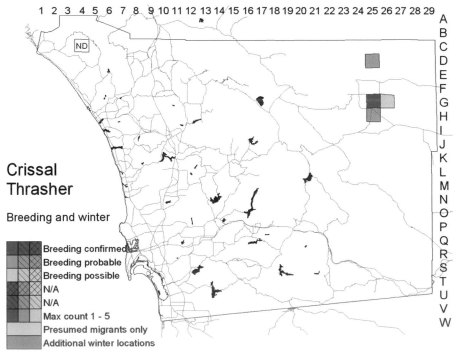

1 2 3 4 5 6 7 8 9 10 11 12 13 14 15 16 17 18 19 20 21 22 23 24 25 26 27 28 29

ND

Crissal Thrasher

Breeding and winter

- Breeding confirmed
- Breeding probable
- Breeding possible
- N/A
- N/A
- Max count 1 - 5
- Presumed migrants only
- Additional winter locations

Thériault in Massey 1998). The area is divided among multiple privately owned parcels, but public access is uncontrolled. Overpumping of groundwater, putting the water table out of reach of mesquite roots, is probably the most serious threat to this habitat, unique in San Diego County. Habitat loss to agriculture, urbanization, and the spread of saltcedar threaten the Crissal Thrasher throughout its California range (Laudenslayer et al. 1992, S. D. Fitton unpubl. data).

Taxonomy: The Crissal Thrashers of California belong to the pale subspecies *T. c. coloradense* van Rossem, 1946. The species has not yet been collected in San Diego County.

Le Conte's Thrasher *Toxostoma lecontei*

No North American bird is more adapted to extreme desert conditions than Le Conte's Thrasher. Year round it lives on the floor of the Anza–Borrego Desert, in washes and sandy areas with only scattered shrubs. Its population density is very low, so the county's total population may be no more than a few dozen pairs. Its need for sandy terrain makes it especially vulnerable to disturbance and habitat loss from off-road vehicles.

Breeding distribution: Le Conte's Thrasher occurs in two disjunct blocks of the Anza–Borrego Desert, corresponding to areas of sandy soil. The vegetation can be halophytic scrub dominated by saltbushes or open creosote bush scrub, as long as there are a few cacti or shrubs capable of protecting or concealing a nest. In the northern part of the desert, the thrasher ranges from Box Canyon (D23) and the north end of Clark Valley (C25) southeast to the Ocotillo Wells off-road vehicle area. A few range west along San Felipe Wash to Mescal Bajada (J25); at Yaqui Meadows (H24), south of Borrego Springs, P. K. Nelson noted one on 10 and 25 April 1999. The birds appear to be most numerous around Clark Dry Lake; our maximum daily count was of 11 birds and four nests on the north side of the lake bed (D26) 11 May 2000 (P. K. Nelson). Le Conte's Thrashers avoid any rugged or rocky terrain,

Photo by Jerry Oldenettel

the mesquite bosque, and the developed area around Borrego Springs, being absent even where houses are scattered sparsely. Several pairs persist, however, in the state off-road vehicle area (up to seven, in two family groups, northwest of Squaw Peak, H29, 13 May 2001, J. R. Barth).

The southern block lies south of the Vallecito Mountains and Split Mountain. In this region Le Conte's Thrasher ranges northwest from Dos Cabezas Spring (S29) and South Mesa (N29) to Vallecito (M25; one on 27 April and 24 May 1998, M. C. Jorgensen, C. G. Edwards) and The Potrero (N24; up to three on 7 February 2002, J. R. Barth). The highest count in this area is of six near Palm Spring (N27) 18 April 1999 (R. and S. L. Breisch).

Nesting: Le Conte's Thrashers commonly build their nests in the densest thorny shrub in their territory. The site maximizes protection from predators and often from the sun. Plants in which atlas observers described nests were in desert thorn (3), saltbush (2), pencil cholla, mesquite, ocotillo, smoketree, mistletoe, and athel tamarisk.

The species' nesting season probably varies with the vagaries of the rains, though our data are too skimpy to establish this clearly. Our observations establish egg laying at least from late February to about 1 May, much the same as the 22 February–25 April of

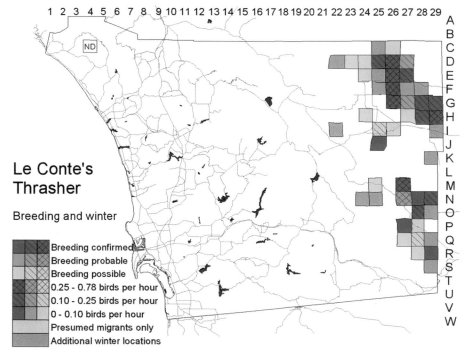

Le Conte's
Thrasher

Breeding and winter

Breeding confirmed
Breeding probable
Breeding possible
0.25 - 0.78 birds per hour
0.10 - 0.25 birds per hour
0 - 0.10 birds per hour
Presumed migrants only
Additional winter locations

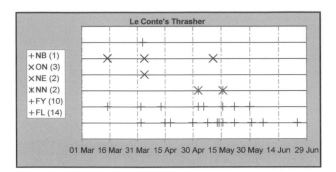

six San Diego County egg sets. At Palm Springs in the Coachella Valley, however, Le Conte's Thrasher eggs have been collected as early as 22 January (Sheppard 1996).

Winter: Le Conte's Thrasher is a permanent resident. The nine atlas squares in which we saw the species December–February but not March–July were most likely areas in which it occurs year round in low numbers. In Collins Valley (C22/D22) there are multiple breeding-season observations before 1997 (Anza–Borrego Desert State Park database). "Winter" records from Grapevine Canyon (I22; one on 24 February 2002, A. P. and T. E. Keenan) and Inner Pasture (N25; two on 18 February 2000, M. B. Mulrooney) represent, at 2200–2400 feet, the highest elevations at which we recorded Le Conte's Thrasher (late February already being within the species' breeding season).

Conservation: The range of Le Conte's Thrasher has retreated somewhat from Borrego Springs. From 1997 to 2002 we did not find the species in or near the town, including Borrego Palm Canyon (F23) and Hellhole Bajada (G23), where it was noted at least to 1973 (Anza–Borrego State Park database). Frank Stephens found it in the San Felipe Valley in late August 1911, from which there have been no subsequent records.

Urban development, conversion of desert to agriculture, fire, and livestock grazing have all contributed to the contraction of Le Conte's Thrasher's range and the reduction of its numbers in various parts of its range (Laudenslayer et al. 1992, Patten et al. 2003, S. D. Fitton unpubl. data). In San Diego County, the greatest threat to Le Conte's Thrasher is habitat degradation by off-road vehicles. The sandy terrain the thrasher requires attracts the drivers of these vehicles. In the state park, vehicles are confined to existing trails, but many of these follow washes, which the thrasher favors. In the Ocotillo Wells State Vehicular Recreation Area motorists have free range. In this extremely arid area, where shrubs grow very slowly, crushed plants do not have the opportunity to regenerate themselves. Much of the thrasher's best habitat in the Borrego and Clark valleys lies outside the state park and is vulnerable to off-road vehicles as well.

Taxonomy: The subspecies of Le Conte's Thrasher in San Diego County is the pale, long-tailed *T. l. lecontei* Lawrence, 1851.

STARLINGS — FAMILY STURNIDAE

European Starling *Sturnus vulgaris*

The European Starling has become a metaphor for the unforeseen effects of misguided introductions of foreign organisms. From 100 birds released in New York City in 1890 and 1891, the starling proliferated throughout North America. In San Diego County, it was found first as a winter visitor in the late 1940s, began breeding in 1959, and has been abundant since the mid 1960s. The most obvious effect of the starling's invasion in southern California is its competition for nest cavities with native birds such as the Acorn Woodpecker, Northern Flicker, and Purple Martin.

Breeding distribution: The European Starling now breeds over almost all of San Diego County's coastal slope. Because the birds feed largely by walking on the ground—probing for insects, worms, and snails—lawns, pastures, and dairies constitute ideal starling habitat. Thus the species is most abundant in urban and agricultural areas. As soon as the young begin fledging in May, starlings may be seen in flocks of hundreds, with up to 500 at Lake Henshaw (G17) 18 June 2000 (P. Unitt) and 1000 at Sweetwater Reservoir (S12) 28 July 1998 (P. Famolaro). But they are scarce or even absent in regions of extensive unbroken chaparral like the north slopes of Palomar Mountain (C15), Viejas Mountain (O17),

Photo by Anthony Mercieca

Otay Mountain (U15/V15), and Tecate Peak (V18). Even where there is good nesting habitat in the form of groves of oaks or sycamores inhabited by Acorn Woodpeckers and flickers, starlings may be absent if no foraging habitat is nearby, as along upper San Mateo Creek (A3/B3) and in Black Canyon (I16).

In the Anza–Borrego Desert the European Starling is confined largely to developed areas. Though it breeds along San Felipe Creek at Scissors Crossing and Sentenac Ciénaga (J22/J23), it is not confirmed breeding at other riparian oases. At Lower Willows (D23) along Coyote Creek, for example, the starling is only occasional (Massey 1998), and we recorded it only once in the breeding season from 1997 to 2001. California fan palms offer nest sites, however, and the starling uses them in the native palm oasis at Mountain Palm Springs (Massey 1998; active nest at Southwest Grove, P27, 11 May 2001, D. G. Seay), possibly at Five Palms Springs (G29; two on 19 April 1998, G. Rebstock, K. Forney).

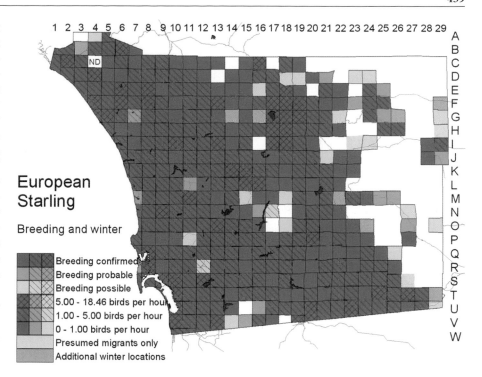

European Starling

Breeding and winter

- Breeding confirmed
- Breeding probable
- Breeding possible
- 5.00 - 18.46 birds per hour
- 1.00 - 5.00 birds per hour
- 0 - 1.00 birds per hour
- Presumed migrants only
- Additional winter locations

Nesting: The European Starling is a secondary cavity nester, commonly using woodpecker holes in trees, and sometimes ejecting other birds occupying them. Atlas observers described nests in palms, eucalyptus, and a wide variety of native trees, especially sycamores. The birds also use diverse man-made structures, such as the supports for street lamps, traffic lights, and power poles, wherever there is a pipe with an open end. They use the drain holes under box-frame bridges and any cavities in buildings, such as the spaces under roof tiles. Artificial structures may enable starlings to nest in areas where there are no trees, for example, in aircraft-warning spheres hung on power lines crossing Proctor Valley (T14).

Our observations from 1997 to 2001 show that in San Diego County starlings lay eggs mainly from mid March through early June; a few birds start as early as about 1 March.

Migration: Because the European Starling is abundant in San Diego County in both summer and winter, its migration and dispersal are not easily tracked. Single birds have been seen far from nesting sites in the Anza–Borrego Desert as late as 27 April 2001 in the Ocotillo Wells off-road vehicle area (H29; J. R. Barth) and 6 May 1998 at Carrizo Marsh (O29; P. D. Jorgensen).

Winter: In winter the European Starling's distribution in San Diego County is similar to its breeding distribution. The species may be seen in suburbs and pasture-

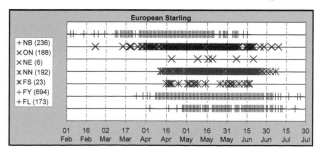

lands in large flocks, up to 1000 in Sunnyside (T12) 19 December 1998 (E. Mirsky) and in Woods Valley (H12) 2 January 1999 (C. Bingham). Even at high elevations starlings may remain in large numbers in winter, with up to 200 around 4000 feet elevation near Julian (J20) 17 December 2001 (K. J. Winter) and up to 66 around 4900 feet at San Ignacio, Los Coyotes Indian Reservation (E21) 11 December 1999 (K. L. Weaver, C. R. Mahrdt). In the Anza–Borrego Desert the starling is abundant in the Borrego Valley (up to 472 at Borrego Springs, G24, 19 December 1999, P. D. Ache et al.) and regular in smaller numbers in other developed areas but generally rare at natural oases (maximum 20 at Lower Willows 29 December 2001, F. A. Belinsky; five at Seventeen Palms, F29, 18 December 1999, G. Rebstock, K. Forney).

Conservation: The European Starling was first reported in San Diego County "in the winter of 1948 or 1949," with a flock of about 25 at Julian (Banks 1965). It was first noted in San Diego 4 February 1959 (Stott 1959) and was first recorded nesting in May 1959 (Banks 1965). In the winter of 1963–64 it arrived in numbers; on the San Diego Christmas bird count that year, the first year the starling was recorded, there were 153. Counts over the next five years show an explosive increase: 974 in 1964, 1500 in 1965, 4448 in 1966, and 7928 in 1969. But subsequently this count and others throughout the county suggest stable numbers. Urban development creates new starling habitat, but when this replaces agriculture the effect on the starling is probably negative; pavement is as useless to the starling as to any other bird. Newer buildings are designed to discourage cavity-nesting birds like starlings. Nevertheless, the starling is ineradicably established as a common resident of southern California.

The effects of the European Starling on native birds are difficult to establish conclusively, but competition with the starling for nest cavities is thought to be the primary factor in the steep decline of the Purple Martin as a nesting bird in the West (Brown 1977, 1981). Atlas participants observed starlings contesting ownership of cavities with Acorn Woodpeckers and occupying nest boxes designed for Western Bluebirds. In general, however, the smaller cavity-nesting birds, up through the size of the Western Bluebird and Nuttall's Woodpecker, are on the increase in San Diego County, so these may be making

or exploiting cavities too small for the starling. Possible negative effects should therefore be investigated with the larger cavity nesters: the Acorn and Hairy Woodpeckers, Northern Flicker, and American Kestrel.

Taxonomy: The subspecies of the European Starling in North America is *S. v. vulgaris* Linnaeus, 1758; the birds originated in England.

PIPITS AND WAGTAILS — FAMILY MOTACILLIDAE

Red-throated Pipit *Anthus cervinus*

An Old World species, the Red-throated Pipit barely crosses the Bering Strait as a breeding bird to reach the coast of western Alaska. Yet it is remarkably regular, almost annual, as a fall vagrant to California, the most frequent Asian songbird in the lower 48 states. In California, the Red-throated Pipit's habits and habitats are similar to those of the American Pipit, and it often flocks with that species.

Migration: In San Diego County, the Red-throated Pipit has been found in 21 of the 40 years from 1964, when McCaskie (1966a) first discovered it, through 2003. Almost all the birds have been in cultivated fields in the Tijuana River valley, the only exceptions being two at Point Loma (S7; 25–28 October 1981, D. Rawlins, Binford 1985; 27 September 2003, S. E. Smith), one at Kate Sessions Park (Q8; 21 October–27 November 2003, C. G. Edwards), and one in the floodplain of San Mateo Creek at San Onofre State Beach (C1; 13 October 1995, R. A. Erickson, NASFN 50:116, 1996). Occasionally multiple Red-throateds are found together; the largest numbers recorded in a year are 10 in 1966 and 1967, 12 in 1964, and 15 in 1991. Until 2003, the occurrences were clustered in an interval only 38 days long from 4 October (1994) to 11 November

Photo by Brian L. Sullivan

(1991). The three preserved specimens were collected 13 October 1964 (SDNHM 35097, MVZ 145172) and 19 October 1966 (LACM 46029).

Conservation: In California, Red-throated Pipits occur largely in agricultural fields along the coast—a land use being ousted by urbanization. In the Tijuana River valley the only habitat remaining are fields of sod, an environment sterile in comparison to the fields of alfalfa, tomato, and other crops that the birds once visited.

American Pipit *Anthus rubescens*

Breeding above timberline, the American Pipit reaches San Diego County as a winter visitor only. It is a bird of open county, visiting pastures, lawns, lakeshores, beaches, and expanses of bare dirt. In winter it is gregarious, flocks occasionally numbering in the hundreds. The pipit takes advantage of many of man's alterations of the environment: agriculture, reservoirs, city parks, ball fields, and golf courses. It is an opportunist, moving in to exploit habitats that are suitable only intermittently, like dry desert playas coaxed to life by rare winter rains.

Winter: The American Pipit is widespread on the coastal slope wherever there are large areas of its habitats. The largest numbers frequent lakeshores, with up to 750 at Sweetwater Reservoir (S12) 16 December 2000 (P. Famolaro) and 400 at Lake Henshaw (G17) 18 December

Photo by Anthony Mercieca

2000 (J. Coker). Pipits can be abundant in agricultural areas, too, with up to 200 near the Santa Margarita River mouth (G4) 28 February 1998 (P. A. Ginsburg), 300 at San Pasqual (J13) 15 January 2000 (D. and D. Bylin), and 200 in

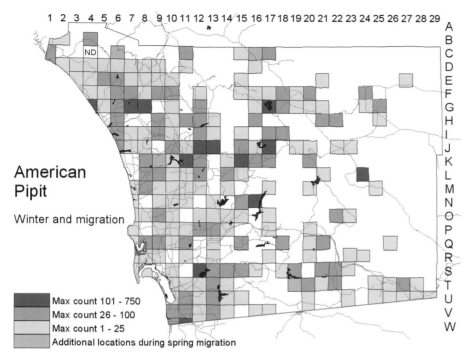

American
Pipit

Winter and migration

- ■ Max count 101 - 750
- ▨ Max count 26 - 100
- ▢ Max count 1 - 25
- ▨ Additional locations during spring migration

(1999, Sweetwater Reservoir, P. Famolaro). There are few records for May, the latest of one at Point Loma (S7) 21 May 1984 (R. E. Webster, AB 38:961, 1984). The nearest sites where the American Pipit summers are the summit of San Gorgonio Peak in the San Bernardino Mountains (Miller and Green 1987) and the high plateau of the Sierra San Pedro Mártir, Baja California (Howell and Webb 1992).

Conservation: In its winter range in southern California, the American Pipit benefits from many human activities, especially water storage, irrigation, and the clearing of scrub. Conversion of agricultural land to cities, however, is negative. San Diego County Christmas bird count results suggest no trend, just irregularity, probably due to the randomness of birders encountering flocks. The American Pipit's recent spread as a breeding bird to California's highest mountains (Miller and Green 1987) suggests an increase, though these colonizers are not the same subspecies as the pipits wintering in California.

Taxonomy: The only subspecies of American Pipit collected in San Diego County is *A. r. pacificus* Todd, 1935, which breeds in northwestern North America. In fall 1991, sightings of the more heavily streaked east Asian *A. r. japonicus* Temminck and Schlegel, 1847, were reported, from the Tijuana River valley 26 October–11 November (at least two individuals) and from Mission Bay 23 November (G. McCaskie, R. E. Webster, AB 46:151, 1991). Confirmation with a specimen is appropriate before this subspecies is added to the list of California birds. Though the lightly streaked *A. r. alticola* Todd, 1935, breeds in California's high mountains, on migration it apparently skips over southern California's lower elevations.

the Tijuana River valley (W11) 16 January 2000 (P. Unitt). In the higher mountains, we noted them fairly regularly at 5400–5500 feet elevation in Laguna Meadow (O22/O23; up to 50 on 14 January 1998, P. Unitt) and once at 4900 feet near San Ignacio on the east slope of Hot Springs Mountain (E21; two on 11 December 1999, when one to three inches of snow lay on the ground, K. L. Weaver, C. R. Mahrdt).

In the Anza–Borrego Desert, the pipit occurs mainly on lawns and at sewage ponds (up to 50 in north Borrego Springs, F24, 21 December 1997, R. Thériault). It visits other habitats there—dry lake beds and plowed fields—only rarely. In the wet winter of 1997–1998, however, large numbers occurred in Little Blair Valley (L24), up to 196 on 20 February (R. Thériault).

Migration: American Pipits arrive in San Diego County occasionally as early as mid September, in numbers in early October. They depart largely in April. During the five-year atlas period, the dates on which the species was last reported ranged from 16 to 30 April

Sprague's Pipit *Anthus spragueii*

From a breeding range in the northern Great Plains, Sprague's Pipit migrates for the winter to the south-central United States and mainland Mexico. In California it occurs primarily as a rare fall vagrant, though the introduction of Bermuda grass to the Imperial Valley as a major crop may enable small numbers to winter there, as seen in 1997–98 and 2002–03.

Migration: The California Bird Records Committee has accepted only four records of Sprague's Pipit from San Diego County. Three are from the Tijuana River valley: up to three birds in an alfalfa field 19–27 October 1974, McCaskie

Photo by John S. Luther

(1975), SDNHM 38980; one in a pasture 22 November 1974 (Luther et al. 1979); one in a field of bare dirt 22 November 1977 (Binford 1985). One is from weedy brush on Fiesta Island, Mission Bay (Q8), 19 December 1977 (Luther et al. 1983). The committee rejected two later reports.

Conservation: Like many birds of native prairie, Sprague's Pipit is on the decline. Changing land use in the Tijuana River valley has eliminated dense but low vegetation like alfalfa that Sprague's Pipits seek.

Waxwings — Family Bombycillidae

Bohemian Waxwing *Bombycilla garrulus*

A bird of the far north, the Bohemian Waxwing winters irregularly as far south as northern California. The records from San Diego County are the species' southernmost along the Pacific coast.

Winter: The three records are of two found dead and badly decomposed (not preserved) at Vallecito (M25) 29 March 1920 (Stephens 1920b), four to six at Yaqui Well (I24) 3–5 December 1972 (AB 27:664, 1973), and one at Presidio Park (R9) 3–4 December 1974 (AB 39:743, 1975). The first two occurrences were in invasion years for the species farther north in California, although the third was not.

Conservation: From 1968 to 1977 the Bohemian Waxwing reached California annually, but since then it has been much less frequent. The trend toward warmer winters may result in the species' winter range shifting north and raises the question of whether the Bohemian Waxwing will ever again make it as far south as San Diego County.

Cedar Waxwing *Bombycilla cedrorum*

Of the fruit-eaters that come to San Diego County as winter visitors, the Cedar Waxwing is perhaps the most familiar. The birds move in flocks of dozens if not hundreds and feed on the berries of ornamental plants in urban gardens at least as eagerly as they do on the fruits of wild plants. Like other wintering frugivores, their abundance varies much from year to year, on the basis of both the number arriving from the north and movements within San Diego County.

Winter: In most years, the Cedar Waxwing is most abundant in the coastal lowland, becoming less frequent at higher elevations and in drier habitats. During the field seasons for this atlas from 1997 to 2002, San Diego County missed the extremes of variation in this famously irregular species. Numbers were somewhat lower than average in 1997–98 and higher than average in 1998–99, but the number did not approach zero as in 1993–94, nor was there a massive invasion as in 1981–82 or 1983–84. The highest daily counts during the atlas period, of 245 near Ross Lake (B7) 18 February 2002 (K. L. Weaver), 260 at Kit Carson Park (K11) 30 December 2000 (P. Hernandez), and 280 at El Camino Cemetery (O9) 3 January 1999 (D. K. Adams et al.), could have been exceeded easily in an invasion year like 1983–84, when 3387 were totaled on the San Diego Christmas bird count.

Above about 2500 feet elevation the Cedar Waxwing is usually uncommon, and in the higher mountains it is rare; in the latter our maximum from 1997 to 2002 was of 20 from Julian to William Heise County Park (K20) 24 January 1999 (E. C. Hall). Nevertheless, there is great variation from year to year: in 1992–93, when the San Diego Christmas bird count yielded only 14 waxwings, its lowest total since 1962, the Lake Henshaw count yielded

Photo by Anthony Mercieca

496, its second highest since the count's inception in 1980–81.

On the Campo Plateau and in the Anza–Borrego Desert fruits suitable for the Cedar Waxwing are scarce and the birds are uncommon to absent. In these regions the highest counts are from gardens in Borrego Springs (F24; up to 45 on 21 December 1997, P. K. Nelson et al.). Cedar Waxwings rarely compete for mistletoe with the Phainopepla. During the atlas period we had no records of the waxwing from sites with abundant mistletoe such as Yaqui Well (I24), Vallecito (M25), or Agua Caliente Springs (M26), though the highest count in the Anza–Borrego State Park database is of 45 at Yaqui Well 4 April 1958 (L. Penhale).

Migration: The comings and goings of the Cedar Waxwing are as irregular as its abundance. In some years a few appear in the first week of September, but the mass of winter visitors arrives much later in the fall. During the atlas period our largest concentration of spring migrants was of 250 near Escondido (I10) 16 May 1999 (E. C. Hall), but 2500 were halted by a snowstorm around the Palomar

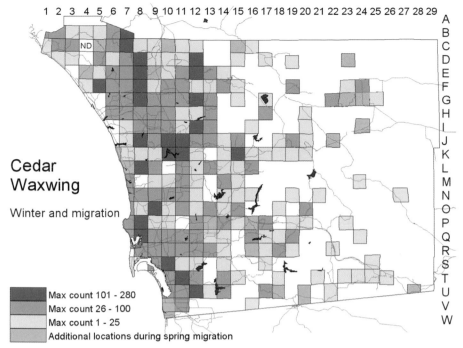

Cedar
Waxwing

Winter and migration

■ Max count 101 - 280
▨ Max count 26 - 100
□ Max count 1 - 25
▨ Additional locations during spring migration

Observatory (D15) 21 March 1983 (R. Higson, AB 37:913, 1983). In most years a few waxwings linger to mid May; after larger incursions numbers then can still be substantial. Our latest date from 1997 to 2001 was 3 June (2000; two near the south fork of San Onofre Creek, Camp Pendleton, D3, R. and S. L. Breisch). After the big invasion of 1983–84 "small numbers" remained in San Diego through "the first half of June" (AB 38:1063, 1984). In 1985 C. G. Edwards noted one at Old Mission Dam (P11) 20 June and a flock

of 35 in La Mesa (R12) 27 July. During the atlas period the only summer record for San Diego County was of eight along Roblar Creek (C5) 5 August 1998 (P. Galvin, C. Collier). The Cedar Waxwing has been recorded in summer elsewhere south of its normal breeding range and even nested successfully once in Orange County, in 1964.

Conservation: Ornamental plants offer the Cedar Waxwing many food sources lacking in natural habitats, and these have now replaced the native vegetation over wide areas that once had little to attract the birds. *Pyracantha*, *Cotoneaster*, *Liquidambar*, Peruvian and Brazilian pepper, palms, heavenly "bamboo," juniper, camphor, and fig are among the cultivated shrubs and trees on which the waxwings now rely. Some of these may even contribute to lessening the species' nomadism: some urban fig trees that fruit abundantly attract waxwings consistently year after year.

Taxonomy: Burleigh's (1963) proposal of two western subspecies of the Cedar Waxwing has not been widely supported, and the species is generally regarded as monotypic.

Silky Flycatchers — Family Ptilogonatidae

Phainopepla *Phainopepla nitens*

The Phainopepla's biology is unusual in many ways. The birds feed predominantly on berries, especially those of mistletoe, and they are a primary vector for that plant's dispersal. They are common, locally abundant, in the Anza–Borrego Desert most of the year but largely vacate it in summer. On the coastal slope they are common in oak and riparian woodland and open chaparral from late spring through summer, uncommon in winter. It seems likely that many Phainopeplas nest in both regions in the same year, but this has still not been proven.

Breeding distribution: The Phainopepla is most abundant on the desert slopes of San Diego County's mountains and at oases along their bases, where thickets of mesquite and catclaw are heavily laden with mistletoe (up to 60 at Agua Caliente Springs, M26, 13 April 1998, E. C. Hall; 100 at Vallecito, M25, 27 April 1998, M. C. Jorgensen). Away from these thickets, however, the species is less common, even absent on valley floors and in badlands where mistletoe and the plants it parasitizes are absent. Though the Phainopepla is scarce to absent in

Photo by Anthony Mercieca

coniferous woodland, it breeds essentially continuously from the desert over the mountain crest onto the coastal slope. In this region, the Phainopepla is a common summer visitor in the inland valleys and foothills, with up to 53 at Oak Grove (C16) 23 June 2001 (K. L. Weaver) and 40 on the north slope of Otay Mountain (U15) 14 June 2001 (A. P. and T. E. Keenan). Within 10 miles of the coast the

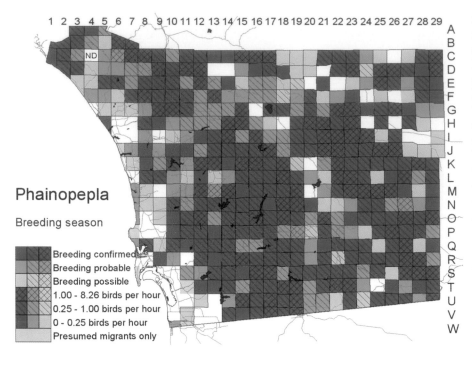

Phainopepla

Breeding season

- Breeding confirmed
- Breeding probable
- Breeding possible
- 1.00 - 8.26 birds per hour
- 0.25 - 1.00 birds per hour
- 0 - 0.25 birds per hour
- Presumed migrants only

feet from the ground, sometimes in plants that offer edible berries, sometimes not. In the Anza–Borrego Desert, we found nests in palo verde, mesquite, catclaw, lotebush, desert willow, Mojave yucca, agave (dry flower stalk), ocotillo, and snake cholla. On the coastal slope, nest sites included both native trees and shrubs like California sycamore, willow, coast live and Engelmann oak, elderberry, laurel sumac, mission manzanita, and chamise (even dead and leafless) and exotic species like eucalyptus, Peruvian pepper, pine, olive, black locust, myoporum, and giant reed. Chu and Walsberg (1999) reported that Phainopepla nests are heavily shaded by vegetation, but we found some completely exposed to the sun.

Phainopepla is much scarcer than farther inland, though some breed along the coast, with up to six, including adults feeding juveniles, at San Onofre (C1) 15 June 2000 (M. Lesinsky) and eight, including fledglings, in Tecolote Canyon (Q8) 26 June 1998 (E. Wallace). Though the birds favor the mistletoes that infest oaks, sycamores, and cottonwoods as well as mesquites and catclaws, they also feed heavily on the berries of other plants, especially blue elderberry, redberry, and desert thorn or wolfberry.

Nesting: In the Phainopepla, unlike most songbirds, the male does most of the nest building. The shallow cup nest is small for the size of the bird. The choice of nest site is unspecialized; we noted nests from 4 to over 60

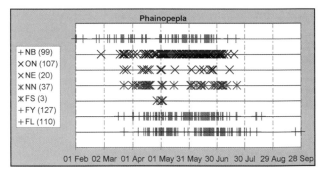

The Phainopepla's breeding season varies much with locality. In the low desert, Phainopeplas lay as early as late February, mainly from mid March through mid April. At higher elevations, along the desert edge, they continue to early June. In the coastal lowland, most begin laying in late April, some in mid April, and a few possibly as early as early April (pair courting and nest building northeast of Oceanside, F7, 31 March 2001, P. A. Ginsburg). Even at the higher elevations most Phainopeplas apparently complete their clutches by the end of June, but a few nest later, as seen by nest building as late as 21 July 2001 northeast of Santa Ysabel (I19; D. W. Au) and a pair with four fledglings in Spring Valley (R12) 22–28 September 1997 (M. and D. Hastings).

Migration: The Phainopepla's movements are among the most

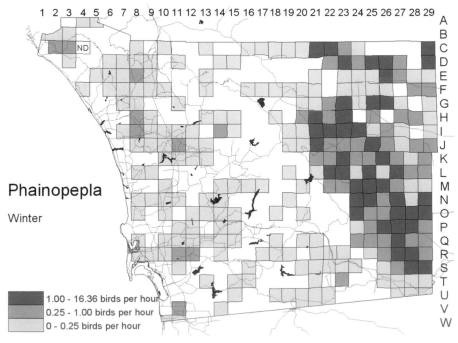

Phainopepla

Winter

- 1.00 - 16.36 birds per hour
- 0.25 - 1.00 birds per hour
- 0 - 0.25 birds per hour

complex and poorly understood of any North American bird. Three hypotheses remain to be tested: (1) that individuals breeding in the desert in early spring move to the coastal slope and breed again; (2) that the desert and coastal populations are distinct, each moving and breeding on its own schedule; (3) that the birds breeding on the coastal slope had attempted nesting in the desert but failed (Chu and Walsberg 1999). Evidence against the second hypothesis is the lack of a distinct break among the Phainopepla's habitats in San Diego County. The peak of breeding in each zone overlaps that in the neighboring zones, so most likely the birds move and breed facultatively as stimulated by multiple cues. They may remain sedentary if conditions permit.

In the low desert, the Phainopepla returns in September and departs largely in May. Late records for dry habitats are of two in Carrizo Canyon (Q27) 8 June 1997 (D. Julian) and six on Mescal Bajada (J25) 12 June 1998 (M. and B. McIntosh). At oases some birds are seen through June. Between 4 July and 15 September the only low-desert record is of one at Bow Willow (P27) 6 August 1972 (P. D. Jorgensen). At higher elevations, above about 2500 feet but still on the desert slope, as in Culp Valley (G23/H23), Phainopeplas remain in small numbers through the summer, though they are far more common in spring (M. L. Gabel in Massey 1998).

On the coastal slope, exact spring arrival dates are impossible to determine because of the number of wintering birds. Crouch (1943) reported arrival 15 April 1935. From 1997 to 2001, our first counts on the coastal slope of more than five individuals per day were on 19 April in both 1997 and 1999. On the coastal slope, there is no seasonal gap in March as I suggested previously (Unitt 1984); from 1997 to 2001 atlas observers accumulated 70 records of the Phainopepla on the coastal slope from 1 March through 14 April. Individual Phainopeplas or small flocks may be seen moving through atypical habitat through much of the year.

Winter: The Phainopepla's distribution on the desert side of San Diego County in winter is much the same as in early spring. Daily counts at sites thick with mistletoe range as high as 125 at Vallecito 14 January 2000 (M. C. Jorgensen) and 122 on the southwest-facing slope of San Felipe Valley (H21) 17 December 2001 (W. E. Haas). On the coastal slope we found the Phainopepla to be surprisingly widespread in winter, both in the lowland (up to 15 between Bonsall and Fallbrook, E8, 3 and 29 December 2000, P. A. Ginsburg; 15 in the Tijuana River valley, W11, 19 December 1998, G. McCaskie) and in the foothills (up to 12 near La Posta Microwave Station, T23, 3 February 2001, J. S. Larson; eight northeast of Lake Henshaw, F18, 29 December 1997, G. L. Rogers). Phainopeplas occur in winter occasionally as high as 4600 feet at Lake Cuyamaca (M20; three on 22 February 1999, A. P. and T. E. Keenan) and 4900 feet at San Ignacio, Los Coyotes Indian Reservation (E21; up to two on 28 December 1999, P. D. Jorgensen).

Conservation: The Phainopepla has so far been little affected by man-made changes to the San Diego County environment, and no trend in the species' numbers is evident here. Possible threats in the Anza–Borrego Desert are declining water tables, which kill mistletoe-supporting trees and shrubs, the proliferation of the exotic saltcedar, which does not host mistletoe and displaces native vegetation, and climate change leading to longer droughts. During the dry years from 1999 through 2002, we witnessed the death of many clumps of mistletoe, constricting the Phainopepla's habitat into oases. On the coastal slope, the Phainopepla has been somewhat insulated from urbanization by its more inland distribution, and small numbers breed in developed areas. An invasive exotic plant that Phainopeplas do use is the Peruvian pepper tree, but the value of this tree's berries in comparison to that of the Phainopepla's natural foods is unknown.

Taxonomy: Two subspecies of the Phainopepla are generally recognized, differing in size. The smaller *P. n. lepida* van Tyne, 1925, occupies the northwestern part of the species' range, including California.

WOOD WARBLERS — FAMILY PARULIDAE

Blue-winged Warbler *Vermivora pinus*

Of the various eastern warblers reaching California, the Blue-winged is represented disproportionately more in the desert and less on the coast. As a result, it is exceptionally rare in San Diego County. The California Bird Records Committee has accepted only two from this area—and rejected three others as inadequately or not supported.

Migration: San Diego County's well-described Blue-winged Warblers were in the Tijuana River valley 26 September 1964 (McCaskie and Banks 1966, Bevier 1990) and at Point Loma 30 September 1999 (J. C. Worley, T. Plunkett, Rogers and Jaramillo 2002). Roberson (1993) list-

Photo by Anthony Mercieca

ed the rejected records. A specimen or photograph to support the Blue-winged Warbler in San Diego County is still

lacking, though the species has been photographed once in adjacent Orange County (Heindel and Garrett 1995).

Golden-winged Warbler *Vermivora chrysoptera*

San Diego County seems to have got less than its fair share of both the Golden-winged and Blue-winged Warblers. Though the California Bird Records Committee has accepted 67 records of the Golden-winged through 2002, only three of these are from San Diego County. Yet one of the four hybrids between these species known in California was in San Diego County.

Migration: The county's first Golden-winged Warbler was photographed in a residential area on the southeast side of Mount Soledad, La Jolla (P8) 6–12 October 1984 (J. Moore, Dunn 1988). One in the Tijuana River valley (W10) 15 December 1990 (R. E. Webster, Heindel and Garrett 1995) was probably a late fall migrant rather than a winter visitor, though three Golden-winged Warblers have wintered elsewhere in coastal southern California. In spring, one was along Keys Creek near Lilac (F11) 21 May 1991 (E. R. Lichtwardt, Heindel and Garrett 1995).

Photo by Anthony Mercieca

A female photographed at Point Loma (S7) 15–19 May 2001 had some yellow on the underparts and so appeared to be a hybrid with a Blue-winged Warbler (P. A. Ginsburg, Garrett and Wilson 2003).

Tennessee Warbler *Vermivora peregrina*

From the 1960s and through the mid 1980s, the Tennessee Warbler was one of the more frequent eastern warblers reaching San Diego County as a fall vagrant, averaging about 10 per year. By the end of the century, however, that rate had dropped considerably, to about three per fall. The Tennessee Warbler also occurs in the county, though less frequently, as a winter visitor and spring vagrant.

Migration: The Tennessee, like most vagrant warblers, has been found primarily along the coast, especially at Point Loma. The only fall record more than 13 miles inland is of one at Butterfield Ranch (M23) 5 November 1978 (G. McCaskie). The species occurs mainly from mid September to late October, exceptionally as early as 27 August (1972, one in the Tijuana River valley, G. McCaskie). It is also of nearly annual occurrence in spring migration, mainly in late May and early June. Spring records range from 24 April (2000, singing male at Fallbrook Naval Weapons Station, E7, W. E. Haas) and 1 May (1985, Point Loma, E. Copper) to 21 June (1980, Coronado, AB 34:931, 1980; 1982, Point Loma, AB 36:1017, 1982) and 2 July (1970, two at Point Loma, AFN 24:718, 1970). Reports from Culp Valley in late April and early May only (Massey 1998) are unseasonal enough to suggest misidentification.

Winter: Tennessee Warblers have remained on several occasions as late as the third week of December, resulting in one record for an Oceanside Christmas bird count

Photo by Anthony Mercieca

(1979) and six for the San Diego count (1968–83), with up to three individuals in 1980 and 1983. Records later in the winter are fewer but include at least eight extending to mid January or beyond.

Conservation: Of the warblers nesting in Canada's boreal forest, some have decreased sharply as vagrants to southern California, and the Tennessee is among them. Numbers at Point Loma as high as four in a day (4 June 1977, P. Unitt) have not been approached recently, though spring 2002 yielded three (R. E. Webster). The most recent winter record for the county is of one in San Diego 18 January–25 February 1995 (R. E. Webster, NASFN 48:249, 1994).

Orange-crowned Warbler *Vermivora celata*

An inconspicuous little green bird, the Orange-crowned is second only to the Yellow-rumped as San Diego County's commonest warbler. Because of multiple subspecies and multiple seasonal roles, its status is complex. It is common throughout the county in migration. In winter it is common in the coastal lowland, less so farther inland. As a breeding species the Orange-crowned Warbler is common in coniferous, oak, and riparian woodland, less so in ornamental shrubbery and coastal chaparral. Its status as a widespread breeding bird and winter visitor appears to have evolved just in the 20th century. Like the Western Flycatcher the Orange-crowned Warbler was a stealth invader: the change in breeding and winter status went unappreciated because the process took decades and the species was always common as a migrant.

Breeding distribution: The Orange-crowned Warbler is widespread as a breeding bird in riparian, oak, and coniferous woodlands over most of the coastal slope of San Diego County, lacking only from the plateau east of Campo. The population is more concentrated along the axis of the higher mountains and in northwestern San Diego County from Camp Pendleton east to Valley Center and Bear Valley (H13). High counts are of 28 (23 singing males) along the Santa Margarita River north of Fallbrook (C8) 24 May 2001 (K. L. Weaver) and 21 in Woods Valley (H12) 19 June 1998 (W. E. Haas). There are also concentrations farther south, in canyons and on north-facing slopes, as in San Clemente Canyon (P8; 12 on 29 May 1998, C. G. Edwards) and in stands of Tecate cypress on the north slope of Otay Mountain (U15; 26 on 25 May 1999, G. L. Rogers). The breeding range only

Photo by Anthony Mercieca

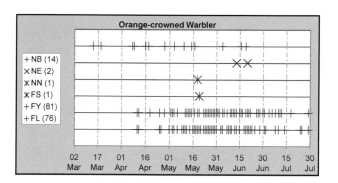

barely spills onto the east slope of the mountains where oak woodland is still thick, as at 4500 feet elevation in the middle fork of Borrego Palm Canyon (F22; two on 16 June 1999, D. C. Seals). Single birds at Lower Willows (D23) 12 June 1994 (C. Sankpill, L. Clark), 4 July 1998 (B. Getty), and 24 June 2002 (J. R. Barth) suggest the Orange-crowned Warbler is an occasional nonbreeding summer visitor at this riparian desert oasis.

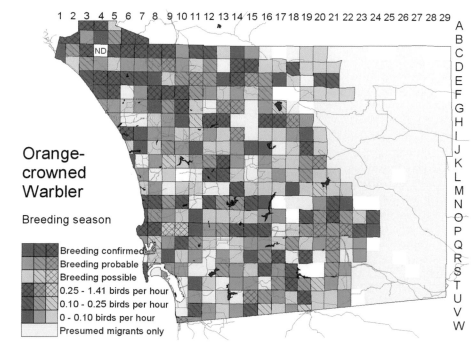

Orange-crowned Warbler

Breeding season

- ◩ Breeding confirmed
- ◪ Breeding probable
- ▨ Breeding possible
- ▦ 0.25 - 1.41 birds per hour
- ▦ 0.10 - 0.25 birds per hour
- ▨ 0 - 0.10 birds per hour
- ▢ Presumed migrants only

Nesting: Orange-crowned Warblers usually nest on the ground, screened behind dense undergrowth, often on steep slopes or banks (Sogge et al. 1994). As a result, the nests are difficult to find. The only one described by atlas observers, though along a popular trail along Doane Creek (E14) 13 June 1999 (P. Unitt et al.), was typical in being nestled in a hollow on a cut bank.

Along the coast, Orange-crowned Warblers begin nesting in mid March, with observations of nest building as early as 14 March (near the mouth of Las Pulgas Creek, E3, R. and S. L. Breisch) and fledglings as early as 11 April (Bonita, T11, P. Unitt). Four egg sets collected along the

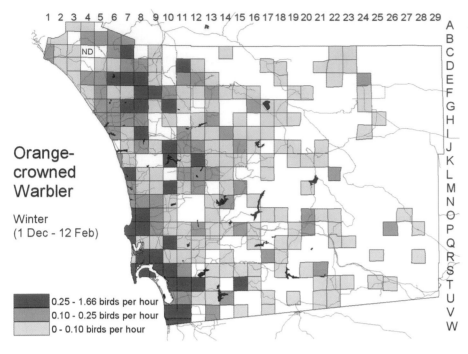

Orange-
crowned
Warbler

Winter
(1 Dec - 12 Feb)

- 0.25 - 1.66 birds per hour
- 0.10 - 0.25 birds per hour
- 0 - 0.10 birds per hour

ter counts during the atlas' term were of 42 in Coronado (S9) 15 December 2001 (R. E. Webster), 24 in Imperial Beach (V10) the same day (C. G. Edwards), and 29 at San Elijo Lagoon (L7) 22 December 2000 (G. C. Hazard). At higher elevations the species is uncommon (maximum six at Descanso, P20, 11 December 1998, P. Unitt) but occurs widely in riparian and oak woodland. Winter records extend as high as 4600–4700 feet elevation, as near Shingle Spring (D21; one on 21 December 1999, L. J. Hargrove), on the middle fork of Borrego Palm Canyon (E22; one on 19 December 1999, P. D. Jorgensen), and at Lake Cuyamaca (M20; one on 2 December 2001, C. G. Edwards). In the Anza–Borrego Desert wintering Orange-crowned Warblers are uncommon and restricted to irrigated areas and oases. In this area the maximum daily count before 15 February is of four at Bow Willow Palms (P26) 9 January 2000 (M. B. Mulrooney).

coast 1916–28 range from 26 March to 24 April. Nesting at higher elevations is later in the season, with egg laying continuing at least through mid June. Orange-crowned Warblers may nest late at low elevations, too, as attested by fledglings being fed at Point Loma (S7) 18 July 1998 (C. G. Edwards) and along the Santa Margarita River north of Fallbrook (C8) 29 July 1999 (K. L. Weaver).

Migration: The Orange-crowned Warbler is an early migrant. In spring, the birds begin moving through parts of the Anza–Borrego Desert, where they do not winter, in mid February. Early dates for these migrants are 15 February (1999, six in Smuggler Canyon, L25, R. Thériault) and 18 February (2000, seven in Sunset Wash, I26, L. J. Hargrove), possibly 13 February (2001, one near Little Clark Dry Lake, E27, R. Thériault). By late February the species can be numerous (up to 40 in Indian Canyon, O27, 25 February 1998, P. K. Nelson), and similar concentrations can be encountered at any time from then through early May when the weather compels migrants to pause. Peak migration is in April, with up to 80 at Agua Caliente Springs (M26) 7 April 1994 (Massey 1998). A fallout as large as the "thousands" grounded during a severe windstorm near Banner (K21) 22 April 1967 (G. McCaskie) has not been reported since, though regular monitoring of nearby San Felipe Valley, now known as a corridor for migrants, could detect such events. During May the last of the migrants continue north; late dates are 26 May (1998, four at Yaqui Flat, I23, P. K. Nelson) and 28 May (1999, one at Southwest Grove, Mountain Palm Springs, P27, D. G. Seay). Fall migrants become common in mid August but may be on the move as early as mid July, as in the Salton Sink (Patten et al. 2003).

Winter: Wintering Orange-crowned Warblers are concentrated in the coastal lowland, mainly in riparian woodland and ornamental trees and shrubbery. Maximum win-

Conservation: As a breeding species, the Orange-crowned Warbler has increased greatly in San Diego County, extending its range in the process. This change is due to the subspecies *V. c. lutescens* expanding south. Of this subspecies, Willett (1912) wrote that only "a few remain through the summer and breed in the cañons and on the brushy mountain sides" of southern California. He cited no specific breeding records as far south as San Diego County. Stephens (1919a) called *lutescens* an "abundant migrant," not mentioning any breeding, though he collected a specimen in the Cuyamaca Mountains 6 June 1889 (SDNHM 1349). The only eggs taken by the early collectors were from the breeding range of subspecies *sordida* on the coastal strip. In the 1970s breeding Orange-crowned Warblers were fairly common only at Point Loma, uncommon in montane coniferous woodland, and rare elsewhere (Unitt 1984). The species was not confirmed breeding on the mainland of Baja California until 1987 (Unitt et al. 1995). Thus the evidence suggests that *lutescens* has spread and increased vigorously over the past century.

While the breeding range of *lutescens* was expanding south, the winter range was expanding north. Stephens (1919a) did not mention any wintering by this subspecies, and Dawson (1923) wrote that it "apparently passes entirely beyond the state in winter." Brewster (1902), however, wrote that *lutescens* "winters as far north as San Diego," and the subspecies was collected in winter as early as 1904 (30 December; Witch Creek, J18, FMNH 148559). Now the species is locally common in winter, more widespread, and most of the birds appear to be *lutescens*.

The reasons for the Orange-crowned Warbler's expansion are still a mystery. The spread parallels that of the Western Flycatcher, a species of similar habitats but completely different nesting habits. The warbler is only rarely a host to the Brown-headed Cowbird (Sogge et al. 1994), giving it an advantage for much of the 20th century over other small insectivorous birds.

Taxonomy: Three of the Orange-crowned Warbler's four subspecies occur in San Diego County, and the fourth is a likely vagrant. *Vermivora c. lutescens* (Ridgway, 1872), bright yellow and lightly streaked, is the most common in migration, both spring and fall. It breeds in the Pacific coast district of North America, south to San Diego County or northwestern Baja California. It appears to be the widespread breeding subspecies and the most common in winter as well, though better specimen support for this statement is needed—most existing specimens are of migrants.

Vermivora c. orestera Oberholser, 1905, breeds in the Great Basin/Rocky Mountain region. Each sex considered separately, it is less yellow than *lutescens*, and the females have grayish heads. It reaches San Diego County as a migrant and winter visitor, uncommon or fairly common, at least from 21 August (1908, Cuyamaca Mountains, Grinnell and Miller 1944, MVZ 3942) to 24 April (1909, Witch Creek, FMNH 148483).

Vermivora c. sordida (Townsend, 1890) breeds on the islands off southern California and Baja California, locally on the nearby mainland. It is darker than *lutescens*, with heavier streaking below, especially on the undertail coverts. It has bred at least at Torrey Pines (N7), Point Loma (eggs collected, WFVZ), Coronado (S9; A. M. Ingersoll in Willett 1912), and canyons in San Diego

(WFVZ; nest in a "decorative hanging fern basket inside a small lath house" in Golden Hill, S9, Abbott 1926). In one of California's more unusual bird migrations, *sordida* disperses to the mainland during its nonbreeding season. Grinnell and Miller (1944) reported such migrants from mid July through March, and all 18 San Diego County specimens fit within this window, except for one from Poway Grade 29 April 1918, at that time possibly a local breeder. *Vermivora c. sordida* ranges as far inland as the San Luis Rey River 0.5 mile west of Henshaw Dam (G16; 10 September 1996, SDNHM 49614), Julian (K20; 5 August 1908, MVZ 3819), the Cuyamaca Mountains (1 September 1908, MVZ 3944), and 1.3 miles northwest of Morena Conservation Camp (S21; 14 November 1983, SDNHM 42815). With the spread of *lutescens*, however, the gap between the breeding ranges of *lutescens* and *sordida* mapped by Grinnell and Miller (1944) has closed, and it is possible that *lutescens* is swamping out *sordida* on the mainland. Specimens in known breeding condition are needed to test this hypothesis.

Vermivora c. celata (Say, 1823), breeding in the transcontinental taiga zone, is even less yellow than *orestera*; the head is always gray, and in some females the yellowish on the underparts is reduced to irregular blotches. It reaches southern California as a rare migrant and winter visitor (Grinnell and Miller 1944). One specimen from San Diego County has been reported, collected at Witch Creek (J18) 24 April 1909 (Willett 1912), but on examining this specimen I found is actually *orestera* (FMNH 148483). Nevertheless, nominate *celata* is reconfirmed elsewhere in southern California by recent specimens from the Channel Islands and Imperial Valley (SDNHM, Patten et al. 2003).

Nashville Warbler *Vermivora ruficapilla*

In spring, if the rains have been good, the desert blooms, insects proliferate, and warblers like the Nashville can stop to refuel on their way from western Mexico to the Pacific Northwest. The Nashville Warbler is primarily a spring migrant through San Diego County, most numerous on the desert slope. It is uncommon as a fall migrant and rare as a winter visitor. Our atlas effort revealed the species for the first time in summer in San Diego County, with three records of apparently unmated males on Palomar Mountain—the first summer sightings of the Nashville south of the San Bernardino Mountains.

Breeding distribution: The Sierra Nevada represents the southern end of the Nashville Warbler's traditional breeding range. It has been only since 1970 that small numbers have been found summering in the Transverse Ranges, with breeding confirmed at least in the San Gabriel Mountains (AB 37:1028, 1983) and on Big Pine Mountain, Santa Barbara County (Lentz 1993). Field work for this atlas yielded three observations on Palomar Mountain,

Photo by Anthony Mercieca

the first summer records of the Nashville Warbler for San Diego County. Two were from the confluence of Doane and Pauma creeks, elevation 4475 feet (D14), where males sang at length 24 June 1997 and 18 June 1998 (P. D. Jorgensen). The third record was of a male at Sourdough Spring, at 5725 feet 0.25 mile northeast of High Point,

Palomar Mountain (D15), 12 July 2000 (K. L. Weaver). In no case did the birds appear paired, and nesting of the Nashville Warbler as far south as San Diego County is still unconfirmed. These are the only summer records south of the San Bernardino Mountains, as no definite records for the San Jacinto Mountains have been published; "Mill Creek, San Jacinto Mountains" (AB 41:1488, 1987) is an error for the San Bernardino Mountains.

Migration: Nashville Warblers arrive in spring at the end of March or beginning of April. During the atlas period first reports ranged from 27 March (1997, two at Agua Caliente Springs, M26, E. C. Hall) to 1 April. The earliest spring date ever is 21 March (1970, Valley Center, G11, AFN 24:673, 1970). Spring migration peaks in late April. Numbers are higher in the Anza–Borrego Desert and on the east slope of the mountains than on the coastal slope, though the species is seen throughout the county. The highest count in a day during the atlas period, 20 near San Felipe (H20) 24 April 1999 (A. P. and T. E. Keenan), was from the San Felipe Valley corridor traveled by many birds following the lowest routes from the desert to the coast. By mid May most Nashville Warblers have finished passing through, and the latest spring date is 25 May (1998, one at Tamarisk Grove Campground, I24, P. D. Jorgensen).

In fall, the Nashville Warbler is uncommon in San Diego County, as it is one of those species whose primary migration route swings east, the birds avoiding Baja California and a crossing of the Gulf of California on their way to a winter range in western mainland Mexico. Fall migrants may appear as early as 29 July (2000, one along Agua Dulce Creek, Laguna Mountains, O23, J. R. Barth).

Winter: The Nashville Warbler is a rare but annual visitor along the coast. One to five individuals were reported during each winter of the atlas' five-year term, for a total of 12. The species was found on 22 of 34 San Diego Christmas bird counts 1968–2002, with up to three noted on three counts in the 1970s. In the north county wintering Nashville Warblers are much rarer than around metropolitan San Diego, with no reports on Rancho Santa Fe Christmas bird counts and only one on an Oceanside Count (two on 23 December 1980). Other reports along the north coast are of one at San Onofre (C1) 20 January 2001 (J. M. and B. Hargrove) and one in Vista (G7) 4 January 2002 (C. Andregg). There are two winter reports from farther inland, of one in Carney Canyon (H15) 2 January 1999 (M. Dudley) and two in Ballena Valley (K17) 25 February 2002 (D. C. Seals).

Conservation: Breeding in the undergrowth of coniferous forests, the Nashville Warbler may be taking advantage of the second growth that follows logging. Results of both the Breeding Bird Survey (Sauer et al. 2003) and counts of migrants on Southeast Farallon Island (Pyle et al. 1994) imply that the western subspecies *ridgwayi* is increasing on a broad scale. Numbers of Nashville Warblers observed in San Diego County 1997–2001, however, were less than could be found in the 1970s, though our protocol for this atlas did not emphasize migrants.

Taxonomy: The western subspecies, the Calaveras Warbler, has been known as *V. r. ridgwayi* since van Rossem (1929) proposed this as a substitute name. The Calaveras Warbler's original name, *V. r. gutturalis* (Ridgway, 1874), was preoccupied by *Vermivora gutturalis* (Cabanis, 1860), when the Flame-throated Warbler of Costa Rica and Panama was placed in the same genus with the Nashville. If the Flame-throated Warbler is transferred to the genus *Parula*, as in the 7th edition of the A. O. U. checklist, van Rossem's substitution is unnecessary but retained because of the provision in the latest version of the code of scientific nomenclature that conserves such changes if they happened before 1961. The eastern subspecies of the Nashville, *V. r. ruficapilla* (Wilson, 1811), is still unconfirmed in California, though all other warblers with similar ranges reach the state regularly.

Virginia's Warbler *Vermivora virginiae*

Though Virginia's Warbler breeds in the Great Basin and Rocky Mountains, it is a rare vagrant to coastal southern California, in fall almost exclusively. Since 1962, when Guy McCaskie discovered it in fair numbers in the Tijuana River valley, its frequency has decreased precipitously. By the beginning of the 21st century only two or three were being reported in San Diego County per year.

Migration: Though San Diego County is not on Virginia's Warbler's normal migration route, the species is most frequent here in September, like other western warblers, not shifted later in the season like vagrants from the east. There are many records for August, one as early as the 13th (1972, Tijuana River valley, G. McCaskie), and few later than mid October. All fall records for Virginia's Warbler in San Diego County are from the coastal low-

Photo by Anthony Mercieca

land, except for one at Jacumba (U28) 3 September 1963 (AFN 18:75, 1964).

There are three spring records, one from Encinitas (K6/K7; 29 April 1979, AB 33:806, 1979), two from Point

Loma (S7; 15 May 1988, G. McCaskie, AB 42:482, 1988; 3 May 2001, J. C. Worley).

Winter: San Diego County has seven winter records of Virginia's Warbler, all for the coastal lowland. Unitt (1984) listed three; more recent were three in January and February 1990 (AB 44:331, 1990, Rancho Santa Fe Christmas bird count) and one at La Jolla (P7) 16 March 2001 (P. K. Nelson).

Conservation: The highest number of Virginia's Warblers reported in San Diego County per fall was 35 in 1962, when McCaskie was the county's only birder searching out vagrants (McCaskie and Banks 1964). In spite of the increase in observers, by the mid to late 1970s, the rate had dropped to five to ten per year (Unitt 1984). Thus the current rate of two per year continues a 40 year trend of decline. No significant decrease has been reported in the species' breeding range, so the reason for this decrease in San Diego County is not clear.

Lucy's Warbler *Vermivora luciae*

Colonizing only in 1990, Lucy's Warbler is a recent addition to San Diego County's breeding birds. It is still rare and confirmed nesting at only one site, the thicket or bosque of mesquite in the center of the Borrego Valley. Its stay in the area is only three months, from mid March to early June. Though a few sightings elsewhere in the desert suggest that Lucy's Warbler could colonize additional stands of mesquite, the future of the bosque in Borrego Valley is clouded by continued pumping of groundwater that could lower the water table until the trees can no longer reach it.

Breeding distribution: Lucy's Warbler has one of the most limited distributions of any breeding bird in San Diego County, confined to the mesquite bosque on the floor of the Borrego Valley. Its numbers are low, the maximum count of singing males per day being seven on 8 April 1997 and 23 March and 27 April 1998 (R. Thériault). All were seen within atlas square G25, with only one singing male on the southeast side of Borrego Sink in G26 (1 May 2000, P. Unitt). Vegetation maps of the area show the habitat covering about 2500 acres, but

Photo by Anthony Mercieca

the warblers occupy it only sparsely. The total population is no more than a few dozen pairs, and probably less.

The possibility of Lucy's Warbler colonizing additional sites in the Anza–Borrego Desert is raised by one at Tamarisk Grove Campground (I24) 1 May 1997 (P. K. Nelson) and one in Vallecito Valley (M24) 5 May 2002 (J. R. Barth). Though extensive mesquite thickets suitable for the species are at both sites, in both cases the birds were evidently unmated and could not be found on subsequent dates.

Nesting: Atypically for a warbler, Lucy's usually nests in tree cavities, old Verdin nests, or behind slabs of loose bark (Johnson et al. 1997). The one certain nest found in San Diego County was being built in a cavity of a mesquite 6.5 feet off the ground 22 April 1997 (R. Thériault). On this day, four independent juveniles were foraging together near the adult female gathering nest material, suggesting the adult was starting a second nest. Another probable nest, from which a bird was flushed, was about 15 feet off the ground under a section of bark loosened by a mesquite branch that had partially broken (G26,

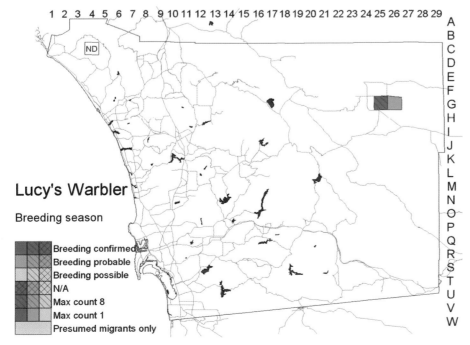

Lucy's Warbler

Breeding season

Breeding confirmed
Breeding probable
Breeding possible
N/A
Max count 8
Max count 1
Presumed migrants only

1 May 2000). Earlier observations of breeding activity include a bird carrying an insect larva 10 May 1993 and a family group the following day (P. Unitt).

Migration: Dates for Lucy's Warbler in the Borrego Valley extend from 11 March (1997, two singing males) to 4 June (1998, three singing males and one independent juvenile, R. Thériault). The arrival date agrees with that in southern Arizona (Phillips et al. 1964) and along the lower Colorado River (Rosenberg et al. 1991). The late date may not be completely representative, the birds becoming less detectable when singing ceases. But Thériault's visits to the same site on 11 and 15 June 1998 did not reveal any, and Lucy's Warbler is a famously early migrant. Johnson et al. (1997) found its numbers near Phoenix greatly diminished even by late June.

Lucy's Warbler also occurs as a rare fall vagrant near the coast, with over 50 individuals now reported. Most are found in August and September, though dates range from 19 July (1982, Tijuana River valley, R. E. Webster, AB 36:1017, 1982) to 12 November (1979, same locality, G. McCaskie). Inland, fall migrants have been found also at Borrego Springs (F24/G24; 12 October 1969, AFN 24:100b, 1970) and Jacumba (U28; two on 26 August 1967, AFN 22:91, 1968). An especially unusual record, outside the species' migration periods, was of one at Point Loma (S7) 2 June 1982 (R. E. Webster, AB 36: 895, 1982).

Winter: Lucy's Warbler is a casual winter visitor around San Diego with four records, of one at Coronado (S9) 15–20 December 1979, one in the Tijuana River valley 15–25 December 1979, one on the San Diego Christmas bird count 17 December 1983, and one in San Diego 7 January 1986 (R. E. Webster, AB 40:335, 1986).

Conservation: As a breeding species, Lucy's Warbler is a recent arrival in San Diego County, first noted in the Borrego Valley in April 1990 (J. O'Brien, AB 44:498, 1990). It is certain that the species colonized about this time, for birders had visited the site regularly in spring since the Crissal Thrasher was discovered there in the 1950s. Since the original colonization, however, the warbler's numbers have remained low. With further development of the Borrego Valley and overdraw of the water table, the mesquite bosque, a habitat unique in San Diego County, could be killed and Lucy's Warbler extirpated—just as dramatized near Tucson by Johnson et al. (1997). Throughout its range, Lucy's Warbler has had a checkered history, extirpated from the Salton Sink (Patten et al. 2003), crashing then recovering partially along the lower Colorado River (Rosenberg et al. 1991), spreading in the Grand Canyon (Johnson et al. 1997) and elsewhere in Arizona as mesquite supplanted grassland (Phillips et al. 1964).

Northern Parula *Parula americana*

Unlike many eastern warblers, the Parula occurs in San Diego County at all seasons. It is now more frequent in spring (about two per year) than in fall (about one per year). There are seven winter records, including one of a bird that returned for four successive years. Most interesting, there are over a dozen summer records, of up to three individuals, part of the species' trend toward increase and colonization of California.

Migration: In fall the Northern Parula is rather typical of eastern warblers, occurring largely along the coast, with most records for Point Loma and the Tijuana River valley. Fall dates range from 17 August (1985, Coronado, S9, E. Copper) to 16 November (1975, Tijuana River valley, AB 30:129, 1976). In spring, however, the story is different. Most spring vagrants are late, occurring in late May and early June, but records of the Parula are scattered throughout the season, with several in April, and range from 24 March (Borrego Springs, G24, 24 March 1978, AB 32:1056, 1978) to 4 June (1989, Point Loma, D. M. Parker, AB 43:538, 1989). Most spring records are from Point Loma, but there are also three for the Anza–Borrego Desert, with one 2.5 miles south of Ocotillo Wells (J28) 5 May 2000 (J. R. Barth) and another in Borrego Palm Canyon (F23) 14 May 2001 (R. Waayers).

Breeding distribution: Even though the Parula has not been confirmed breeding in San Diego County, it has nested repeatedly along the coast of northern California

Photo by Anthony Mercieca

and as near San Diego County as the San Bernardino Mountains (Patten and Marantz 1996, AB 46:1179, 1992). Since 1988, when one was near the Forest Service's San Luis Rey Picnic Ground (G16) 22 May (M. and B. McIntosh, P. Unitt), San Diego County has had at least 16 Parulas from June to mid July, all in native riparian or coniferous woodland. The species recurred along the San Luis Rey River near the Forest Service picnic ground in 2000 and 2001, with three singing males maintaining adjacent territories 10 June–4 July 2001 (W. E. Haas). A pair was along Agua Dulce Creek, Laguna Mountains (O23), 11 June–4 July 1992 (T. Clawson, AB 46:1179, 1992). Nine additional locations for single individuals are scattered around the county from the San Luis Rey River near Pala (D10; 12 July 1991, E. R. Lichtwardt, AB 45:1162, 1991; 4–7 July 2000, D. Bylin, W. E. Haas) south to Jamul

Creek (T15; 8 June 1999, P. Unitt) and east to San Felipe Creek at Scissors Crossing (J23; 5 July 2002, J. R. Barth, NAB 56:487, 2002) and La Posta Creek near La Posta Service (S23; 15 June 2000, L. J. Hargrove).

Winter: San Diego County's seven winter Parulas have all been in the coastal lowland. None was during the five-year atlas period, but one appeared the following winter at Santee (P12) 26 December 2002–2 January 2003 (M. B. Mulrooney, NAB 57:258, 2003). One returned to the San Diego Zoo (R9) for four consecutive winters 1988–91 (AB 45:322, 1991).

Conservation: Since 1972, the Northern Parula's frequency in California in spring and summer, like that of several warblers of the southeastern United States, has increased significantly. The Parula was a major participant in the irruption of southeastern warblers to California in 1992. Evidence for various factors explaining these events is still equivocal (Patten and Marantz 1996).

Yellow Warbler *Dendroica petechia*

The Yellow Warbler symbolizes mature riparian woodland, that is, streamside cottonwood, willow, alder, and ash trees that have reached their full height. It is a fairly common breeding summer resident in this habitat, though the habitat itself is scarce and patchy. Though the Yellow Warbler is recognized by the California Department of Fish and Game as a species of special concern, since the late 1980s San Diego County's population has increased, evidently in response to the widespread trapping of the Brown-headed Cowbird, which parasitizes the warbler heavily. The Yellow Warbler is also common as a migrant passing through the county. It is rare as a winter visitor, in riparian woodland near the coast almost exclusively.

Breeding distribution: The Yellow Warbler's distribution is one of the more difficult to interpret, because migrants headed north may be seen through much of the season when the local population is nesting, and in the same habitat. Males sing freely in migration, negating that clue to territoriality. The interpretation of just what sightings to designate as in "suitable habitat" thus required judgment and review in the context of the entire

Photo by Anthony Mercieca

data set. With the population expanding, some birds were pioneering into marginal habitat. Three late June records for the Anza–Borrego Desert mock any attempt to define a "safe date" after which no spring migrants are seen. The designations of breeding as "probable" and "possible" must be taken more literally for this species than for many others.

Despite these caveats, the Yellow Warbler's breeding distribution is clear: riparian corridors on the coastal slope. There is one area of known breeding on the desert slope, San Felipe Valley (J22; 50—probably including some migrants—on 21 May 1999, E. C. Hall; feeding young 13 July 2001, P. Unitt). A singing male in a cottonwood grove at San Ignacio at the headwaters of Borrego Palm Canyon 16 June 1999 (E22; P. Unitt) suggests breeding at that site.

In the coastal lowland, breeding Yellow Warblers are most widespread from Carlsbad north, more localized farther south. At low elevations the species is more confined to larger streams; in the foothills and mountains it takes advantage of narrow strips and patches of riparian trees. Surface water favors Yellow Warblers strongly but is probably not essential, as long as groundwater

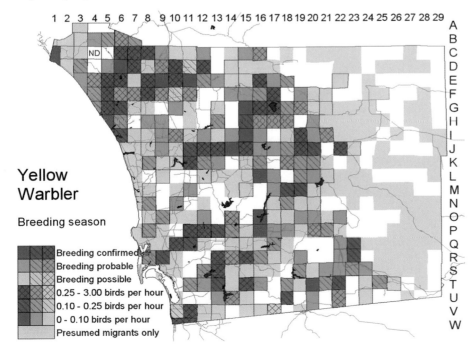

Yellow Warbler

Breeding season

- Breeding confirmed
- Breeding probable
- Breeding possible
- 0.25 - 3.00 birds per hour
- 0.10 - 0.25 birds per hour
- 0 - 0.10 birds per hour
- Presumed migrants only

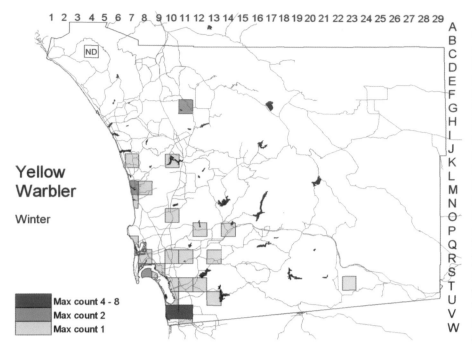

Yellow
Warbler

Winter

Max count 4 - 8
Max count 2
Max count 1

Though many Yellow Warblers arrive in March, apparently they do not begin nesting until well into April. Our dates of breeding activity are consistent with dates of 20 egg sets collected 1903–1931: 3 May–10 June; Sharp (1907) reported 20 June. The nesting schedule implied by our observations allows ample time for the birds to raise two broods. Previous studies (Goossen and Sealy 1982, Lowther et al. 1999) found the Yellow Warbler only rarely attempting two broods, but these studies were made at latitudes far to the north of San Diego. Indeed, virtually all of what has been published on the Yellow Warbler's biology comes from regions remote from southern California.

suffices to support tall trees. The Yellow Warbler's attachment to mature riparian woodland in southern California contrasts with its habitat in the more humid parts of its transcontinental range, where it inhabits lower thickets and disturbed and early successional habitats (Lowther et al. 1999).

Some sites where breeding Yellow Warblers are exceptionally numerous are the Santa Margarita River north of Fallbrook (C8; 64, including 60 singing males, 24 May 2001, K. L. Weaver), the east end of Lake Hodges (K11; 50, including 40 singing males, 18 April 1997, E. C. Hall), and the Tijuana River valley (W11; 40, including 30 singing males, 27 June 1998, P. Unitt). Away from the main rivers numbers are much smaller. Still, San Diego County appears to be one of the main population centers for the Yellow Warbler in California, along with the Santa Ynez River in Santa Barbara County and the east base of the Sierra Nevada in Mono County (S. Heath pers. comm.).

Nesting: Yellow Warblers build a cup nest, placing it typically in upright forks of twigs. One nest in Peutz Canyon (P16) was along the trunk of an alder tree, supported by a slab of loose bark (M. B. Stowe, P. Unitt). The two nests whose height our observers estimated were about 23 and 35 feet above ground—well above the average height reported by studies elsewhere (Lowther et al. 1999).

Migration: Spring arrival of the local population of the Yellow Warbler is in March, typically in the last week, sometimes in the third week. One along the Sweetwater River near Jamacha (R14) 8 March 1998 (M. and D. Hastings) was exceptionally early. Migrants headed farther north become frequent in mid April, peak in May, and occur regularly through the first week of June. Numbers of spring migrants seen in a day at nonbreeding localities may run as high as 40, as in Vallecito Valley (M24) 24 May 1999 (P. D. Jorgensen). Two at Tamarisk Grove (I24) 16 June 1998 (P. D. Jorgensen), one in Borrego Springs (F24) 20 June 1998 (M. L. Gabel), and another nearby in Borrego Springs (G24) 21 June 1998 (P. D. Jorgensen) were very late stragglers, later than any spring Yellow Warbler recorded in the Salton Sink (Patten et al. 2003).

Fall migration takes place mainly from mid August to mid October, but at least some of the local population remains on its breeding territories, the males still singing, through early September.

Winter: In winter the Yellow Warbler is a rare but annual visitor, mainly in riparian willows, also in ornamental plantings. Usually only a single individual is seen at a time, but multiple birds are regular in the Tijuana River valley, up to eight around the Dairy Mart pond (V11) 19 December 1998 (G. McCaskie). The birds can survive the winter successfully and even return to the same spot in successive years, as one has done to *Myoporum* trees at Famosa Slough (R8). Almost all records are from low elevations near the coast, inland to Valley Center (G11) and Lindo Lake (P14), with one notable exception: one near the navy's La Posta Microwave Station (T23), elevation about 3000 feet, 21 February 1998 (C. R. Mahrdt).

Conservation: The Yellow Warbler is well known throughout its range as a frequent host of the Brown-headed Cowbird—and famous for its response of flooring over parasitized nests to build a new nest atop the old.

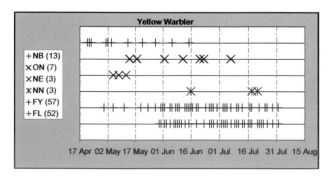

Yellow Warbler

+NB (13)
×ON (7)
×NE (3)
×NN (3)
+FY (57)
+FL (52)

17 Apr 02 May 17 May 01 Jun 16 Jun 01 Jul 16 Jul 31 Jul 15 Aug

Nevertheless, many parasitized Yellow Warblers end by raising cowbirds anyway. Like that of many other riparian songbirds, the population of the Yellow Warbler in southern California collapsed during the mid 20th century under the double onslaught of the cowbird invasion and the elimination of riparian woodland. Then, once the Least Bell's Vireo was formally listed as endangered in 1986, cowbird trapping began at many sites throughout the county, and the Yellow Warbler was among the species whose numbers resurged. Unfortunately, rigorous numerical data with which these changes in Yellow Warbler abundance could be assessed are lacking, and habitat changes, like the regrowth of riparian woodland in the Tijuana River valley, have played a role too. In 1984, I called the species only "uncommon" as a summer resident, and counts of dozens in a day along a two- or three-mile strip of river, as found at the most favorable localities now, were unknown. The species has refilled apparently all of the San Diego County range from which it retracted before 1980. From 1997 through 2002, we recorded only a single instance of cowbird parasitism on the Yellow Warbler—a female feeding a fledgling cowbird in Kit Carson Park (J11) 24 June 1998 (W. Pray).

Regulations restricting the removal of riparian woodland and channelizing of streams have been critical in slowing the loss of the Yellow Warbler's habitat. Also, the damming of rivers has largely eliminated the flooding that once knocked over large trees, allowing more woodland to mature to the point where it attracts Yellow Warblers. Continuing negative factors, though, are the proliferation of the exotic giant reed, which replaces native riparian trees, and the pumping of groundwater, which lowers the water table to the point where these trees can no longer survive.

Taxonomy: The Yellow Warblers nesting in San Diego County, and most migrants as well, are *D. p. morcomi* Coale, 1887. The few Rocky Mountain specimens I have seen do not differ consistently from California specimens, dissuading me from following Browning (1994) in resurrecting *brewsteri* Grinnell, 1903, for the California population (Patten et al. 2003). Spring males have a yellow forehead contrasting with the greenish remainder of the upperparts. Each age and sex class considered separately, *morcomi* is brighter yellow than *rubiginosa* Pallas, 1811, the darker subspecies breeding along the Pacific coasts of Alaska and British Columbia. Spring males of *rubiginosa* have the entire crown green down to the base of the bill. *D. p. rubiginosa* migrates through San Diego County in both spring and fall. Its spring migration is concentrated in the second half of May (7 of 9 SDNHM specimens for this interval), though records extend from 7 April to 1 June (Unitt 1984). Four fall specimens are from 8 to 15 October, a late one from 21 November, part of the pattern suggesting that *rubiginosa* is a late migrant in fall (Patten et al. 2003). Though no winter specimens have been collected, most or all of the Yellow Warblers occurring in winter are bright yellow, implying *morcomi*.

Chestnut-sided Warbler *Dendroica pensylvanica*

The Chestnut-sided Warbler is a regular fall vagrant to San Diego County, its recent numbers varying from one per year as in 2000 to five in 2002. There are only five records of spring vagrants. Twelve Chestnut-sided Warblers are known to have wintered in San Diego County, all since 1983, suggesting the species could be adding southern California to its winter range—there are also 12 winter records from the Salton Sink (Patten et al. 2003).

Migration: In fall the status of the Chestnut-sided typifies that of many eastern warblers. All records are for the coastal lowland, most from Point Loma (S7), from mid September to late October. One at Coronado (S9) 17 August 1985 (E. Copper) was exceptionally early. The spring records are from the Tijuana River valley 5–6 June 1965 (AFN 19:511, 1965), the Sweetwater River at Jamacha (R14) 29 May 1974 (AB 28:854, 1974), Point Loma 5 June 1977 (AB 31:1049, 1977) and 22–23 May 2001 (M. Farley, NAB 55:357, 2001), and Lower Willows (D23) 19 May 2001 (M. L. Gabel, NAB 55:357, 2001). The last is the county's only record outside the coastal lowland.

Winter: Since two Chestnut-sided Warblers were noted on the Oceanside Christmas bird count 24 December 1983, the species has been found in San Diego about every other winter. Some of the birds have been in native ripar-

Photo by Matt Sadowski

ian woodland, as at Kit Carson Park, Escondido (K11; two from 30 December 1993 to 2 January 1994, K. L. Weaver, NASFN 48:249, 1994; one on 30 December 2000, P. Unitt). Others have been in gardens or ornamental trees in heavily urbanized areas, such as one on the grounds of the Self-Realization Fellowship, Encinitas (K6), 20 March 2001 (G. C. Hazard, NAB 55:357, 2001), one in a parking lot between the Marriott and Hyatt hotels along downtown San Diego's waterfront (S9) 18 November 2001–9 March 2002 (M. M. Rogers, NAB 56:225, 2002), and one in the Little Italy neighborhood of downtown San Diego (S9) 19 November–24 December 2003 (M. Sadowski).

Magnolia Warbler *Dendroica magnolia*

The Magnolia is one of the more frequent vagrant warblers reaching San Diego County in fall. Recent annual totals have varied from two in 2002 to about 10 in 2001. There are also six records in spring and one in winter.

Migration: San Diego County records of the Magnolia Warbler are largely from the usual coastal vagrant traps, in recent years from Point Loma (S7) almost exclusively. One at Palomar Mountain (D15) 2 October 1979 (AB 34:203, 1980) was exceptional. Occurrences are concentrated from late September to mid October but range from 5 September (1986, Point Loma, R. E. Webster, AB 41:146, 1987) to 22 November (1964, Rancho Santa Fe, L8, AFN 19:81, 1985).

Of the six spring records, four are from Point Loma: 18 June 1970 (AFN 24:645, 1970), 25 May 1983 (R. E. Webster, AB 37:913, 1983), 26 May 1993 (M. B. Stowe, AB 47:454, 1993), and 6 June 2001 (R. E. Webster, NAB 55:483, 2001). One was at sea 75 miles off San Diego 5 June 1979 (AB 33:806, 1979), and one was in Cuyamaca Rancho State Park (M20) 8 June 1991 (J. F. Walters, AB 45:497, 1991).

Photo by Anthony Mercieca

Winter: The single winter record is of one at Point Loma November 1999–7 January 2000 (R. E. Webster, NAB 54:106, 222, 2000).

Conservation: Occurrences of the Magnolia Warbler in California increased significantly from 1972 to 1994, in an inverse correlation with the abundance in eastern Canada of the Cape May and Bay-breasted Warblers and their primary prey, the spruce budworm (Patten and Burger 1998).

Cape May Warbler *Dendroica tigrina*

The Cape May Warbler commutes between a breeding range mainly in central and eastern Canada and a winter range mainly in the West Indies, so California is far from its normal migration route. Vagrants here were strongly concentrated from the mid 1970s to the mid 1980s, a period when the Cape May Warbler's principal summer prey, the spruce budworm, proliferated in eastern Canada, probably leading to a spike in the warbler's population (Patten and Burger 1998). There are about 28 records for San Diego County.

Migration: Fall records of the Cape May Warbler in San Diego County are all from Point Loma, the Tijuana River valley, or Otay Mesa, except for one at Carlsbad 23 November 1962 (AFN 17:71, 1963). Fall dates range from 14 September (1991, Point Loma, R. E. Webster, AB 46:151, 1992) to 23 November. San Diego County went without a single Cape May Warbler from 1993 to 2003, when one was at Point Loma 1–14 November (D. V. Blue). There are three spring records, all from Point Loma, of a female 1–3 June 1977, a male 9 June 1977 (AB 31:1048, 1977), and a male 30–31 May 1987 (B. Florand, AB 41:489, 1987).

Photo by Brian L. Sullivan

Winter: The Cape May Warbler is known to have wintered in San Diego County twice, with one at Point Loma 10 November 1979–6 January 1980 (AB 34:308, 1980) and another in the nearby neighborhood of Loma Portal (R8) 25 December 1986–16 February 1987 (G. McCaskie, AB 41:331, 1987). The latter foraged primarily in eucalyptus trees, toward the end of its stay becoming stained almost completely black with eucalyptus pitch.

Black-throated Blue Warbler *Dendroica caerulescens*

In spite of breeding only in eastern North America and wintering in the West Indies, the Black-throated Blue Warbler is a regular visitor to California. San Diego County gets the species nearly every year, with up to 12 in 1988. The species is dispropor-

tionately scarce in spring, when there are only three records for the county. It has been found three times in winter also.

Migration: As for most vagrant warblers, San Diego County records of the Black-throated Blue are concentrated along the coast. A few, though, are scattered farther inland, as at Valley Center (G11; 11 November 1971, AB 26:123, 1972), Grable Ranch (M16; 29 September 1992, R. T. Patton), and 1.3 miles southwest of Iron Mountain (M13; struck the window of a house about 4 October 1998, SDNHM 50143). The species occurs rather late in the fall; dates range from 29 September to 6 December (1987, San Diego, P. D. Jorgensen, AB 42:323, 1988), with the winter records excluded.

The spring records are of one at Point Loma (S7) 18 May 1992 (M. B. Grossman, AB 46:482, 1992), one at Clark Dry Lake (E26) 4 June 1995 (M. L. Gabel, Massey 1998), and one in Cuyamaca Rancho State Park 9 June 1995 (J. Herried, NASFN 49:982, 1995).

Winter: San Diego County's three wintering Black-throated Blue Warblers were at Old Mission Dam (P11) 25 December 1974–5 January 1975 (AB 29:744, 1975), Oakzanita Springs (O20) 20 December 1995–1 January 1996 (at the unexpectedly high elevation of 3860 feet, D. W. Povey, NASFN 50:225, 1996), and Coronado (S9) December 1998–28 March 1999 (H. Weeks, NAB 53:210, 1999).

Photo by Anthony Mercieca

Taxonomy: The Black-throated Blue Warbler is often divided into two subspecies; only the more northern nominate *D. c. caerulescens* (Gmelin, 1789) is likely to reach California, and all of California's identifiable specimens are of it.

Yellow-rumped Warbler *Dendroica coronata*

The Yellow-rumped Warbler is probably San Diego County's most abundant winter visitor. If the White-crowned Sparrow exceeds it, it is not by much. Eucalyptus groves and other exotic trees planted in developed areas suit the Yellow-rumped Warbler at least as much as natural sage scrub, chaparral, and woodland. The birds are strongly concentrated in the coastal lowland but are found almost throughout the county, lacking only from the most rugged parts of the Anza–Borrego Desert. As a breeding species, however, the Yellow-rumped Warbler is a recent colonist, rare and confined to coniferous

Photo by Anthony Mercieca

forest on San Diego County's highest mountains. Because almost all Yellow-rumped Warblers are readily distinguished in the field as belonging to either the eastern or the western group of subspecies, and the status of each is so different, this account refers to them by their traditional names, Audubon's Warbler for the yellow-throated western birds, Myrtle Warbler for the white-throated eastern ones. See under Taxonomy for the status of the Myrtle.

Winter: San Diego County must be near the core of the Audubon's Warbler's winter range. The species is common to abundant

Yellow-rumped Warbler

Winter
(1 Dec - 20 Feb)

10.00 - 56.54 birds per hour
2.50 - 10.00 birds per hour
0 - 2.50 birds per hour

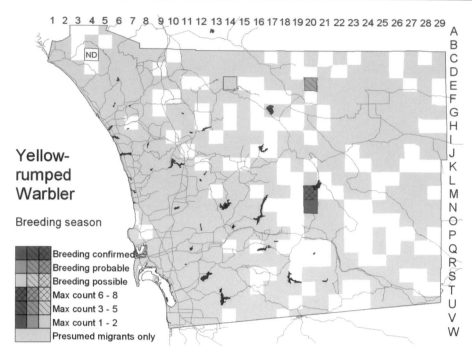

Yellow-rumped Warbler

Breeding season

Breeding confirmed
Breeding probable
Breeding possible
Max count 6 - 8
Max count 3 - 5
Max count 1 - 2
Presumed migrants only

Breeding distribution: Audubon's Warbler is another of those birds, like the Fox Sparrow, Green-tailed Towhee, and Dusky Flycatcher, whose breeding habitat lies in an elevation zone barely pierced by San Diego County's highest peaks. The warblers are now of annual occurrence in the Cuyamaca Mountains, with up to eight, including five singing males, on Middle Peak (M20) 11 June 2000 (R. E. Webster) and six on Cuyamaca Peak (M20) 5 June 2001 (M. B. Mulrooney). On Cuyamaca Peak almost all Audubon's Warblers are found on the northeast slopes, with only one report from the south slope (N20; adult with fledgling 18 June 2000, G. Hazard). On Cuyamaca Peak the birds occur above 5200 feet elevation, but on Middle Peak they go down to 4920 feet (R. E. Webster). Since 1986 Audubon's Warblers have summered at least irregularly above 6000 feet elevation near the summit of Hot Springs Mountain (E20). The maximum count there is of four, all singing males, 9 June 2001 (K. L. Weaver, C. R. Mahrdt). One on the steep north-facing slope near Doane Pond in Palomar Mountain State Park (E14) 21 May 2000 (G. Hazard) could have been a late migrant but was more likely a summering bird, as previous summer sightings from Palomar are known (Unitt 1984).

Nesting: In the higher mountains of southern California, Audubon's Warblers usually nest in the outer branches of the middle levels of conifers. A nest on Middle Peak in 2004 was in a burned canyon live oak retaining toasted leaves. Dates of fledglings range from 18 June to 14 July; sightings of adults carrying insects, possibly to young still in the nest, are as early as 27 May.

Conservation: Yellow-rumped Warblers may have benefited from urbanization, urban trees offering more habitat than sage scrub. In any case, no trends in the number of winter visitors are obvious. As a breeding bird, however, the species is a recent arrival. Though the first summer report, from Palomar Mountain, was as long

from the coast up to about 2500 feet elevation. In this region, daily counts commonly reach into the hundreds, occasionally over 1000 (1300 around Lake Hodges, K10, 22 December 2000, R. L. Barber). At higher elevations the birds become uncommon and more localized to developed areas. Above 3500 feet elevation they can be missed, and at the county's highest elevations they are rare. Above 5000 feet elevation in the Laguna Mountains, for example, we never encountered more than one individual per day. In the Anza–Borrego Desert Audubon's Warbler is abundant in the developed areas of Borrego Springs (up to 328 north of Palm Canyon Drive, F24, 19 December 1999, P. K. Nelson) but much less common in native desert habitats. It is rare to absent in the least-vegetated tracts of desert and lacking entirely from the pinyon–juniper zone of the Santa Rosa and Vallecito mountains.

Migration: In fall, Audubon's Warblers may begin arriving in the first week of September or may not show up until mid September. By the end of September they are common. The end of fall migration is governed by the weather and food supply (Terrill and Ohmart 1984). In spring, the birds are apparently on the move by late February, certainly by March (Massey 1998). Numbers as high as 36 in Blair Valley (L24) 21 February 1998 (R. Thériault) and 40 at Butterfield Ranch (M23) 26 February 2000 (E. C. Hall) had not been approached at these desert locations earlier in the winter. Audubon's Warblers depart in late April and early May; by mid May they are scarce. Stragglers are occasional even in the first week of June. From 1997 to 2001 the latest were two in Ballena Valley (K17) 5 June 2000 (O. Carter); in 1995 there was one as late as 9 June (San Diego, R. E. Webster, NASFN 49:308, 1995). There is also one unseasonal summer record far from plausible breeding habitat, of one at Blue Sky Ecological Reserve, Poway (L12), 23 June 1998 (M. and B. McIntosh, FN 52:504, 1998).

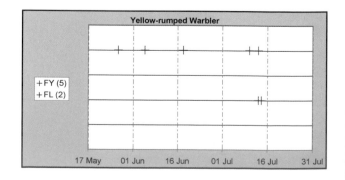

Yellow-rumped Warbler

+FY (5)
+FL (2)

17 May   01 Jun   16 Jun   01 Jul   16 Jul   31 Jul

ago as 1949, the species' breeding was not confirmed until 1986, with a pair feeding fledglings on Hot Springs Mountain 12 July (G. McCaskie, AB 40:1256, 1986). Unitt (1981) had not found the warblers on this mountain in 1980, so it is almost certain the birds first colonized about the time they were confirmed breeding. They became regular on Cuyamaca Peak only in the late 1980s as well. Thus Audubon's Warbler is part of the pattern exemplified by several breeding birds of southern California's high mountains, extending their range to the comparatively low summits of San Diego County's peaks. Sometimes, as in the case of Audubon's Warbler, this means filling in a gap between the San Jacinto Mountains to the north and the Sierra San Pedro Mártir to the south.

Taxonomy: The dominant subspecies of the Yellow-rumped Warbler in San Diego County is *D. c. auduboni* (Townsend, 1837). In the western United States, north of southeastern Arizona, Audubon's Warbler is often divided into two subspecies, smaller *auduboni* in the Pacific states, larger *D. c. memorabilis* Oberholser, 1921, in the

Rocky Mountain region. The size difference, however, needs better quantification before its ability to define a subspecies can be assessed. Breeding males of *memorabilis* tend to be blacker than those of *auduboni*, but the difference is of no help in identifying the birds in their winter plumage.

The Myrtle Warbler reaches San Diego County as an uncommon winter visitor, flocking indiscriminately with Audubon's Warblers in riparian woodland but avoiding dry scrub. Most records are from the coastal lowland, but there are some from Borrego Springs and as high as 3200 feet elevation near Warner Springs (F19; one on 18 December 2000, C. G. Edwards). The highest count during the atlas period was of 11 at Lake Hodges (K10) 22 December 2000 (R. L. Barber), but past daily tallies run as high as 30 in Tijuana River valley 17 December 1977 (P. E. Lehman). Dates for the Myrtle range from 5 October to 23 May (Unitt 1984). The Myrtle Warbler too is usually divided into two subspecies; only the larger, more western *D. c. hooveri* McGregor, 1899, has been reported from California.

Black-throated Gray Warbler
Dendroica nigrescens

William E. Haas

The handsome Black-throated Gray Warbler occurs in San Diego County primarily during migration, but even then it is only uncommon to fairly common. It is rare but regular in winter, when several are found annually, mainly in riparian woodland or ornamental trees. Historically, the species was rare in summer, though the atlas study revealed small numbers in mixed conifer–oak woodland in all of the county's higher mountain ranges. Remarkably, in the late 1990s a population burgeoned in the canyon of the San Luis Rey River just below Lake Henshaw, swelling to more than 70 pairs by 2003.

Breeding distribution: The Black-throated Gray Warbler is most widespread on Hot Springs Mountain, where it occurs uncommonly around the base as well as near the summit (up to five, including four singing males, in Lost Valley, D21, 25 June 1998, P. Unitt). It breeds more sparsely on Palomar Mountain (two family groups one quarter mile apart near the Palomar Observatory, D15, 12 July 2000, K. L. Weaver), on Volcan Mountain (H20; one on 23 or 30 May 1999, A. P. and T. E. Keenan; I20; three 30–31 May 1993, P. Unitt), in the Cuyamaca Mountains (up to six, including four singing males, at William Heise County Park, K20, 19 May 1998, E. C. Hall), and in the Laguna Mountains (up to five singing males near Oasis Spring, N23, 24 May 2001, K. J. Winter).

Completely unexpected was the Black-throated Gray Warbler's colonization of the San Luis Rey River between Lake Henshaw and La Jolla Indian Reservation (F16/ G16). Other nesting locations for the species in San Diego County are at elevations of 4200 feet and above,

Photo by Anthony Mercieca

but the section of canyon the warblers inhabit along the San Luis Rey ranges in elevation from 2300 to 2700 feet. The Black-throated Gray first appeared as a summer visitor in this area, which Haas has studied intensively since 1993, only in 1995, when it nested. The numbers soon ballooned astonishingly, reaching at least 25 pairs in 2000 and at least 70 in 2003. Elsewhere in San Diego County the species' breeding habitat is patchy woodland of pine and oak, especially the canyon live oak, at least on Palomar and Hot Springs mountains (K. L. Weaver). But along the San Luis Rey the coast live oak dominates, with velvet ash and willow trees at the water's edge.

Nesting: Haas has found 26 Black-throated Gray Warbler nests along the San Luis Rey River; all were as described by Bent (1953), built of grasses and leafy forbs, bits of cocoons, dry leaves, plant down, and hair, always with feathers woven into the interior lining. Harrison (1978) reported that nests are woven together and suspended from the branch with spider webs; E. C. Hall observed a female making repeated trips for nest material to spider

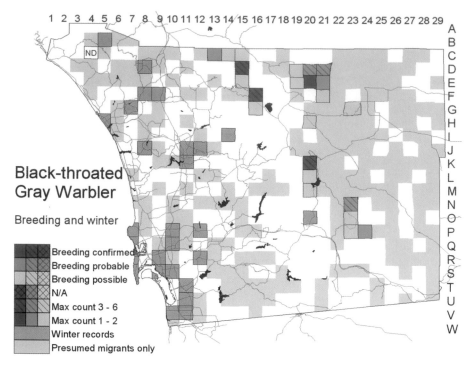

**Black-throated
Gray Warbler**

Breeding and winter

- Breeding confirmed
- Breeding probable
- Breeding possible
- N/A
- Max count 3 - 6
- Max count 1 - 2
- Winter records
- Presumed migrants only

latest records of spring migrants are of two along Vallecito Creek near Campbell Grade (M23) 20 May 1999 (R. Thériault) and one near Barrel Spring (G20) 24 May 1998 (C. G. Edwards). The birds arrive in local breeding habitat beginning in late April and remain through July. Fall migration extends mainly from 15 August (1998, one along Roblar Creek, C5, J. M. Wells) through November. Single birds along the Elephant Tree Trail (K29) 3 December 1991 (A. G. Morley) and at Tamarisk Grove (I24) 4 December 1988 were probably late migrants. Fall migrants are fewer than spring migrants, with no more than five per day and usually only one or two.

Winter: San Diego County lies at the northern edge of the Black-throated Gray Warbler's usual winter range. Countywide, about 10 were reported per year through the atlas period. Eight on the San Diego Christmas bird count 18 December 1999 was a record high for the county, though the maximum per atlas square per day was only two. Almost all wintering Black-throated Gray Warblers are in the coastal lowland, but birds near Margarita Peak (B5) 31 January 1988 (W. E. Haas) and near Oakzanita (O20) 13 and 28 January 1999 (D. W. Povey, M. B. Stowe) were at elevations up to 3900 feet in oak woodland more suited to breeding. There are also three late December records from the Borrego Valley from Anza–Borrego Christmas bird counts.

Conservation: Although the Black-throated Gray Warbler is not a common species, its numbers in San Diego County appear to be on the rise. Reasons for the sudden expansion into the oak woodlands below the Lake Henshaw dam could include displacement from forest at higher elevations following a nearby fire in 1999 and the low level of cowbird parasitism currently enjoyed by all songbirds nesting at this site. This species may be a good colonizer once it invades suitable new habitats; for example, it has colonized Vancouver Island only since 1950 (Guzy and Lowther 1997). It also responds positively to the early successional stages of forest regeneration within certain forest types (Paige et al. 1999).

webs at William Heise County Park. Nests found recently in San Diego County were built well out on lower to intermediate limbs of coast live oaks along the San Luis Rey River, in canyon live oaks on Palomar and Hot Springs mountains, in incense cedar in the Cuyamaca Mountains, and in ponderosa pine on Palomar (W. E. Haas, K. L. Weaver). All nests were 15 or more feet above the ground; two along the San Luis Rey River were over 40 feet above the ground.

Bent (1953) reported clutch sizes of three to five, with four the usual number. Along the San Luis Rey River fledglings are usually three or four per brood, with some variation from year to year, possibly related to weather and availability of prey. The Black-throated Gray Warbler is generally thought to have only one brood per year, but observations of adults with nest material into June and nests with eggs as late as July suggest double broods (Guzy and Lowther 1997). During the atlas period at least two pairs along the San Luis Rey River raised two broods per year, in 1999 and 2001 (W. E. Haas).

In San Diego County Black-throated Gray Warblers lay eggs at least from early May to mid June. Most young have fledged by mid July.

Migration: In spring, the Black-throated Gray Warbler arrives annually in late March. During the atlas period, first dates ranged from 24 to 30 March. One in Balboa Park (R9) 10 March 1998 (J. K. Wilson) had presumably wintered in the area; the earliest spring arrival date recorded is 20 March (1976, AB 30:886, 1976; 1983, AB 37:911, 1983). Migrants continuing northward pass through the county primarily in April; our largest counts were of 22 at Wilderness Gardens (D11) 5 April 1997 (V. Dineen), 28 in Carrizo Valley (O28) 19 April 2000 (D. C. Seals), and 25 at Vallecito (M25) 29 April 1997 (M. C. Jorgensen). Few are seen after the middle of May; our

Taxonomy: The Black-throated Gray Warbler is sometimes divided into two subspecies, a shorter-winged nominate *D. n. nigrescens* (Townsend, 1837) breeding west of the Cascade Range in the Pacific Northwest, south to northern California, and a longer-winged *D. n. halseii* (Giraud, 1841) with more white in the tail breeding in the remainder of the species' range. Morrison (1990) identified a difference in song between these two populations in Oregon, but adequate testing of the size and plumage differences over the entire range of the species, which would allow a decision on the subspecies' validity, has yet to be done. Migrants and winter visitors to San Diego County are presumably nominate *nigrescens*, but the identity of the local breeding population is unclear. When he proposed the division of the Black-throated Gray into two subspecies, Oberholser (1930) included southern California in the breeding range of *halseii*.

Black-throated Green Warbler *Dendroica virens*

The Black-throated Green Warbler replaces the Hermit and Townsend's east of the Rocky Mountains. Like other warblers breeding in Canada's boreal forest, however, it strays to California regularly in fall migration. One or two are reported in San Diego County in most years, with six in 1975 and 1986. There are only two records in spring. The pace of winter records has accelerated since the first in 1978: at least seven Black-throated Green Warblers have wintered in the county, some of them returning repeatedly.

Photo by Anthony Mercieca

Migration: Most of San Diego County's Black-throated Green Warblers have been along or near the coast, but two have been in the Anza–Borrego Desert, at Yaqui Well (I24) 24 October 1963 (AFN 18:75, 1964) and Clark Dry Lake (D25) 15 November 1989 (D. and M. Hastings, AB 44:164, 1990). Most occurrences are from mid September through early November; earliest was one in San Clemente Canyon (P8) 7 September 1974 (AB 29:123, 1975). The two spring records are of a male photographed near San Diego 7 June 1987 (L. Walton, AB 41:489, 1987) and one at Point Loma (S7) 27–29 May 1996 (R. E. Webster, NASFN 50:334, 1996).

Winter: Sites of San Diego County's wintering Black-throated Green Warblers are Guajome Lake (G7; returned four consecutive winters 24 December 1995–6 February 2000, P. A. Ginsburg, NAB 54:106, 222, 2000), Buena Vista Lagoon (H5; 22 December 2001, P. Unitt, NAB 56:224, 2002), Spring Valley (R12) 20 January–21 February 2002 (M. Hastings, NAB 56:224, 2002), Coronado (S9; 30 November–2 March 2002, E. Copper, NAB 56:107, 2002), National City (T11; returned seven consecutive winters 27 November 1996–19 February 2003, D. W. Aguillard, NAB 57:118, 258, 2003), and Otay Valley (V11; returned three consecutive winters 16 December 1978–15 February 1981, AB 35:336, 1981; also 18 December 1999, P. Unitt, NAB 54:222, 2000). In 1998 the bird in National City remained as late as 10 April.

Conservation: The upsurge of wintering Black-throated Green Warblers beginning in 1995 suggests an expansion of the species' winter range, as the rate of fall records has not accelerated.

Townsend's Warbler *Dendroica townsendi*

A bird of coniferous forests in its breeding range in the Pacific Northwest, Townsend's Warbler is partial to conifers as it passes through San Diego County on its way to and from its winter range in the mountains of Middle America. The species winters commonly on the coast of central California and increasingly in southern California. It is still uncommon as a winter visitor in San Diego County but uses planted conifer, alder, and eucalyptus trees more than native oaks and willows. Its spread as a winter visitor may reflect urbanization, climate change, or both.

Photo by Anthony Mercieca

Migration: Townsend's Warbler occurs in San Diego County most commonly as a spring migrant. It is less abundant than some other migrant warblers, like the Orange-crowned, Wilson's, or Yellow, but occasionally concentrations are seen, such as 50 at Vallecito (M25) 29 April 1997 (M. C. Jorgensen), 20 near Little Stonewall Creek (M21) 6 May 1999 (P. D. Jorgensen), and 25 on the ridge of the Santa Rosa Mountains just south of the Riverside County line (C27) 3 May 2000 (P. Unitt). On the last date, the birds were migrating northwest with other warblers from dawn to 9:00 AM, flying up the canyons out of the desert, stopping for only a few seconds in the pinyons on the ridge, then continuing their flight. Reflecting the origin of most of the migrants in western

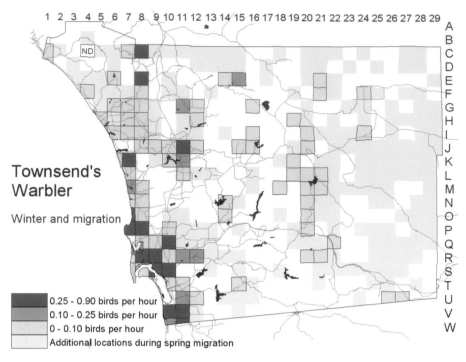

Townsend's Warbler

Winter and migration

■ 0.25 - 0.90 birds per hour
▨ 0.10 - 0.25 birds per hour
▢ 0 - 0.10 birds per hour
▢ Additional locations during spring migration

mainland Mexico, Townsend's Warblers are more numerous in spring in the eastern half of the county than along the coast. They arrive typically in mid April; 8 April (2000, one at Ocotillo Wells, I29, R. Miller) is the earliest spring date from a location where the bird probably did not winter. Migration peaks in early May, then trails off to the end of that month. From 1997 to 2001 the latest spring date reported was 31 May (1999, one at Sentenac Ciénaga, J23, R. Thériault), though stragglers have been noted in past years through the first week of June.

An unprecedented summer record was of two singing Townsend's Warblers in sycamores along the San Luis Rey River at 2600 feet elevation 0.85 mile southeast of the San Luis Rey Day Use Area (G16) 16–23 June 2000 (W. E. Haas).

Fall migrants begin arriving in August, exceptionally as early as 28 July (2001, one at Buena Vista Lagoon, H6, J. Smith et. al.). Wintering birds, however, do not seem to occupy their habitat before October.

Winter: Wintering Townsend's Warblers concentrate in a narrow strip along the coast, using both native riparian woodland and ornamental trees in parks, cemeteries, and residential areas. High counts are of 14 in Balboa Park (R9) 15 December 2001 (V. P. Johnson) and 14 in Imperial Beach (V10) 18 December 1999 (C. G. Edwards). In the inland valleys wintering Townsend's Warblers are sparser

but can be found in small numbers especially where the white alder is a major component of riparian woodland or used in landscaping. Numbers in this area range up to five along the Santa Margarita River north of Fallbrook (C8) 10 January 1999 (L. Ale), five in Kit Carson Park, Escondido (J11), 29 December 2001 (P. Hernandez), exceptionally 11 in Valley Center (G11) 28 February 2002 (S. L. and S. J. Farrow).

One unexpected revelation of the winter phase of the study was the regularity of Townsend's Warblers in the pine–oak woodland of San Diego County's mountains. The Palomar, Hot Springs, Volcan, and Cuyamaca mountains all stand out as isolated regions of Townsend's Warbler wintering. We recorded the species on 27 occasions above 3000 feet elevation, usually single birds, but up to three at Palomar Mountain (E15) 30 December 1999 (E. C. Hall) and three on West Mesa, Cuyamaca Mountains (N20), 3 January 1999 (B. Siegel). In the Anza–Borrego Desert and on the Campo Plateau wintering Townsend's Warblers are rare; during the atlas period there were only two records in each area.

Conservation: In spite of being a species of mature coniferous forest breeding in an area subject to massive logging, Townsend's Warbler appears to be expanding its breeding range in the Pacific Northwest southward, possibly at the expense of the Hermit Warbler (Rohwer and Wood 1998, Rohwer et al. 2001). Numbers on San Diego Christmas bird counts are greater now than in the 1960s, possibly because of increased area landscaped with the conifers and white alder trees preferred by wintering Townsend's Warblers. The change may be part of a trend going back decades, as Willett (1933) said that Townsend's Warbler wintered in southern California only "occasionally," and Stephens (1919a) did not mention its wintering in San Diego County at all. The species' wintering in San Diego County's mountains appears to be a recent development, possibly the result of climatic warming. Such warming is most evident in this area by an increase in winter low temperatures at higher elevations.

Hermit Warbler *Dendroica occidentalis*

One of our most attractive western warblers, in San Diego County the Hermit Warbler is also one of the least commonly seen. It is now uncommon in spring migration, rare in fall migration, and very rare in winter. There are no midsummer records; the San Bernardino Mountains are the southern tip of the

Hermit Warbler's breeding range. Reflecting their habitat preference at other seasons, migrants are often seen high in conifers, be they native or planted as landscaping in urban parks. Unfortunately, the species' numbers may be declining. Both the main breeding habitat, forests of Douglas fir in the Pacific Northwest, and the main winter habitat, pine–oak forests in the mountains of Middle America, are subject to large-scale logging. Better quantitative data are needed, but the number of migrants moving through San Diego County appears less than it did 30 years ago.

Migration: The Hermit Warbler passes quickly through San Diego County on its spring migration; the birds are strongly concentrated in late April and early May. The range of spring dates recorded during the atlas period essentially equaled that recorded previously, extending from 12 April (2000, one on the east slope of Whale Peak, L26, J. R. Barth) to 6 June (2000, one along upper La Posta Creek, P24, D. C. Seals). First spring dates from 1997 to 2001 varied from 12 to 21 April. During the atlas' five-year term, the highest daily count was of 15 near Little Stonewall Creek, Cuyamaca Mountains (M21), 6 May 1999 (P. D. Jorgensen); subsequently, 30 were around the head of Chariot Canyon (L21) 26 April 2003 (R. C. Sanger). The Hermit is widespread through San Diego County in spring migration but, like other migrant warblers, may be concentrated by headwinds as it ascends the east slope of the county's mountains. Preferring conifers, it often pauses in montane woodland.

Fall migrants are known from 19 July (1987, one on Middle Peak, M20, R. E. Webster, AB 41:1489, 1987) to early November. Some adults may pause in San Diego County's mountains in August, but the scattered individuals seen later in the fall are probably all straggling immatures. San Diego County lies astride the Hermit Warbler's spring migration route but off its fall migration route.

Winter: Far from the species' main winter range in central Mexico, small numbers of Hermit Warblers winter regularly on the coast of central California. South of Point Conception, their numbers decrease markedly. At the latitude of San Diego County the Hermit Warbler is very rare. Six individuals were reported during the five-year atlas period, at O'Neill Lake (E6, 19 December 1997, P. A. Ginsburg), near Bonsall (F8, 6 December 2000, P.

Photo by Anthony Mercieca

A. Ginsburg; 23 December 2000–12 February 2001, J. Evans), in Kit Carson Park (K11, 2 January 2001, J. D. Barr), in Mt. Hope Cemetery (S10, 19 December 1997–22 January 1998, P. Unitt, FN 52:259, 1998), and at the Dairy Mart pond, Tijuana River valley (V11, 19 December 1998–23 January 1999, G. McCaskie, NAB 53:210, 1999). Only about 20 Hermit Warblers ever have been noted wintering in the county. Interestingly, nearly half of them have been in north-coastal San Diego County, in spite of birders' more intensive coverage of the south coast, implying the species' north–south trend of winter abundance is perceptible even within San Diego County.

Conservation: The Hermit Warbler appears to be on the decline as a migrant through San Diego County. It can no longer be called "fairly common to common," as I did in 1984. Concentrations of 30 to 40 in a day, as seen occasionally in the 1960s and 1970s, are no longer encountered along the coast. Likely negative factors for this bird of mature coniferous forest are logging of both the summer and winter ranges and displacement at the northern edge of the breeding range by Townsend's Warbler (Rohwer and Wood 1998).

Blackburnian Warbler *Dendroica fusca*

In spring the Blackburnian Warbler, the male with its flaming orange throat framed in black, is one of the most spectacular warblers. In California, however, the Blackburnian is seen in fall almost exclusively, when it can be confused with the immature female Townsend's Warbler. The Blackburnian occurs in San Diego County nearly annually, typically with only one or two reported. Two winter records are surprising because the species winters mainly in South America.

Migration: The fall of 2001 was an exceptional year for the Blackburnian Warbler in San Diego County, yielding at least six individuals on Point Loma (S7). Most of the county's Blackburnians have been there or in the Tijuana River valley. The most inland fall locality is Old Mission Dam (P11; 27 September 1977, B. Cord), except for the

Photo by Brian L. Sullivan

single record for the Anza–Borrego Desert, at Agua Caliente Springs (M26; 10 October 1977, AB 32:262, 1978). The county's only spring record is of a male at Point Loma 4 June 1985 (R. E. Webster, AB 39:351, 1985).

Winter: One Blackburnian was in Santee (P12) 26 December 1988 (D. S. Cooper, AB 43:368, 1989); another was in Imperial Beach (V10) 8 December 2003–14 February 2004 (M. Sadowski).

Yellow-throated Warbler *Dendroica dominica*

The Yellow-throated Warbler is one of the scarcer eastern warblers reaching California, though 17 have been recorded in San Diego County. Most eastern warblers occur here predominantly in fall, so the Yellow-throated is unusual in that over half have been found in spring. Furthermore, though most spring vagrants show up in late May and early June, five of San Diego County's nine spring Yellow-throated Warblers were found in April.

Migration: The nine spring records range in date from 10 April (1997, Point Loma, S7, P. A. Ginsburg, Rottenborn and Morlan 2000) to 7 June (1979, Point Loma, Binford 1983). All are for Point Loma except for one for Presidio Park (R8) 23 April 1974 (Luther et al. 1979) and one for Encinitas (K6/K7) 29 April 1979 (Luther et al. 1983). The seven fall records range in date from 19 September (1973, Point Loma, AB 28:110, 1974) to 5 November (1979, Point Loma, Craig 1972). All are for Point Loma except for one for the Tijuana River valley 3 October 1976

(Dunn 1988), one for Torrey Pines State Reserve (N7) 8–9 October 1986 (Langham 1991), and one for Solana Beach (L7) 24 October 2001 (P. A. Ginsburg; Garrett and Wilson 2003).

Winter: Just six Yellow-throated Warblers have been reported wintering in California. One of these was in San Diego County, frequenting palms planted in a business park on Mira Mesa (N9) 24 January–21 March 2001 (T. R. Clawson, Garrett and Wilson 2003).

Taxonomy: Fifteen of San Diego County's Yellow-throated Warblers were of the white-lored subspecies *D. d. albilora* Ridgway, 1873. Two, however, were apparently the yellow-lored nominate *D. d. dominica* (Linnaeus, 1766), which breeds along the Atlantic coast, east of the Appalachian Mountains: at Point Loma 15 October–5 November 1969 (Craig 1972) and at Solana Beach 24 October 2001. No Yellow-throated Warbler has yet been colleted in San Diego County, though the example of nominate *dominica* at Point Loma was examined in hand and photographed.

Grace's Warbler *Dendroica graciae*

Grace's Warbler nests just across the California border in the mountains of southern Nevada and northwestern Arizona, perhaps occasionally in the mountains of the eastern Mojave Desert. But it is only a rare vagrant to southern California's coast. There are 14 well-supported records for San Diego County, 11 of fall migrants, three of winter visitors, two of which involve birds returning for successive years. Even in migration and winter Grace's Warbler has a strong preference for conifers or trees such as athel tamarisk whose foliage mimics that of conifers.

Migration: San Diego County's fall Grace's Warblers accepted by the California Bird Records Committee are all from the Tijuana River valley (four) or Point Loma

(seven). Their dates range from 8 September (1968, Point Loma, Craig 1970) to 29 October (1966, Tijuana River valley, SDNHM 36047, the only specimen). Two 1987 sightings published in *American Birds* but not submitted to the committee fall within these dates.

Winter: One was at La Jolla (P7) 13 February–3 April 1988 (R. E. Webster; Pyle and McCaskie 1992). One was in Fort Rosecrans National Cemetery, Point Loma, 20 September 2001–20 April 2002 (G. McCaskie, Garrett and Wilson 2003), evidently returning 11 September 2002–2 February 2003 and 11 September 2003; it was joined by another Grace's Warbler after 9 November 2003. One at the San Dieguito River mouth, Del Mar (M7), 9 November 2001 (E. Copper; Garrett and Wilson 2003) returned the next year, being seen 8 January 2003 (NAB 57:258, 2003).

Pine Warbler *Dendroica pinus*

Characteristic of pine forests of eastern North America, the Pine Warbler is a rare but increasing vagrant to California. The California Bird Records Committee has accepted 24 records for San Diego County, 17 for fall, six for winter, and one for spring.

Migration: San Diego County's fall Pine Warblers have all been found in the Tijuana River valley (eight) or at Point Loma (eight), except for one in Presidio Park (R8) 6 November 1988 (Pyle and McCaskie 1992). Their

dates range from 4 October (2001, Point Loma, S7, R. E. Webster; Garrett and Wilson 2003) to 10 November (1992, Point Loma, R. E. Webster, Heindel and Patten 1996). The records committee rejected the report for 18 September 1971; well-supported California records of the Pine Warbler are notably late in the fall. The single spring record is of a singing male in Torrey Pines State Reserve (N7) 5–6 June 1987 (J. O'Brien; Langham 1991).

Winter: The California Bird Records Committee has accepted one winter record for Coronado (S9), 15 December 1984–9 March 1985 (E. Copper, Bevier 1990), one for San Diego, 3–21 March 1991 (D. M. Parker,

Heindel and Garrett 1995), and three for Point Loma, 12–23 December 1983 (R. E. Webster, Roberson 1986), 6 January–12 April 1992 (P. A. Ginsburg, Heindel and Patten 1996), and 3 April 2002 (V. P. Johnson, Cole and McCaskie 2004). Two wintering Pine Warblers were found at Veterans' Park, Imperial Beach (V10), 7 December 2003–27 January 2004 (M. Billings).

Conservation: California occurrences of the Pine Warbler spiked from 1983 to 1993, perhaps reflecting a spike in the species' total population. A possible long-term change is the Pine Warbler's increasing frequency in winter; California's first winter record was in 1978, yet by 2002 winter records statewide reached 25.

Photo by Anthony Mercieca

Taxonomy: Nominate *D. p. pinus* (Wilson, 1811) is the subspecies breeding throughout the eastern United States except Florida and is the subspecies reaching California.

Prairie Warbler *Dendroica discolor*

Even though it breeds mainly in the southeastern United States and winters mainly in the West Indies, the Prairie Warbler is seen nearly annually as a fall vagrant in San Diego County. There are five records in winter but none in spring.

Migration: Fall records of the Prairie Warbler in San Diego County are mainly from Point Loma and the Tijuana River valley, with a few as far inland as Otay Mesa (V11) and O'Neill Lake (E6; 27 September 2000, P. A. Ginsburg). They are concentrated from early September to mid October but range from 16 August (1977, Tijuana River valley, AB 32:263, 1978) to 14 December (2002, Cabrillo National Monument, Point Loma, J. C. Worley). The latter bird was apparently attempting to winter, as it had been in the area continuously from 23 September.

Photo by Anthony Mercieca

315, 1991), Santee (P12) 31 March 1996 (D. Yee, NASFN 50:225, 1996), and in the Anza–Borrego Desert at Carrizo Palms (R28) 8 February 1998 (J. O. Zimmer, FN 52:259, 1998).

Winter: San Diego County's five definitely wintering Prairie Warblers were in Otay Valley (V11) 19 December 1969–24 January 1970 (AFN 24:540, 1970), Coronado (S9) 15 December 1979–6 January 1980 (when found dead, SDNHM 41418), Los Peñasquitos Canyon (N8) 3 November 1991–5 April 1992 (C. G. Edwards, AB 46:151,

Taxonomy: San Diego County specimens of the Prairie Warbler are nominate *D. d. discolor* (Vieillot, 1807), the subspecies widespread in the eastern United States.

Palm Warbler *Dendroica palmarum*

The Palm Warbler's name is a historical accident. The species nests in the taiga zone east of the Rocky Mountains and winters mainly in the southeastern United States, the Yucatan Peninsula, and West Indies, where it prefers rather open, scrubby habitats whether these have palms or not. It is a rare but regular fall migrant and winter visitor to the California coast, less frequent in San Diego County than farther north.

Migration: In San Diego County, as elsewhere in California, the Palm Warbler is seen mainly along the coast. As for other eastern warblers, Point Loma and the

Photo by Brian L. Sullivan

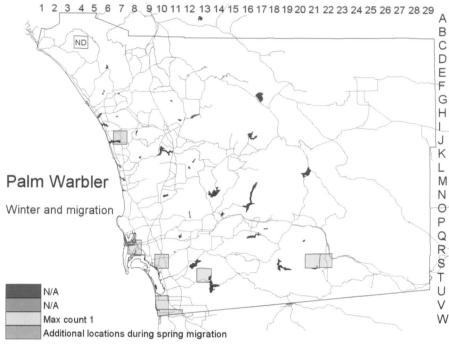

Palm Warbler

Winter and migration

- N/A
- N/A
- Max count 1
- Additional locations during spring migration

at Greenwood Cemetery (S10) to 20 April 2002 (M. Lubin). The only records more likely to represent spring migrants are from O'Neill Lake (E6) 6 May 2003 (P. A. Ginsburg), Point Loma 7 May 1982 (R. E. Webster, AB 36:895, 1982) and 7 June 2003 (D. Langhoff), and Agua Caliente Springs (M26) 4 May 1996 (G. L. Rogers, NASFN 50:334, 1996).

Winter: One or two wintering Palm Warblers are noted in San Diego County annually. The five-year atlas period, 1997–2002, yielded nine. All of the county's wintering Palm Warblers have been within 10 miles of the coast, except for one at the Morena Conservation Camp, elevation 3060 feet (S21/S22), 23 January 1999 (S. E. Smith).

Tijuana River valley account for most sightings, but the Palm Warbler has been seen at many other sites as well. Exceptionally far inland were one at Lindo Lake (O14) 31 October 1999 (M. B. Mulrooney), two at Lake Henshaw (G17) 4 October 1982 (R. Higson AB 37:225, 1983), and the three fall records for the Anza–Borrego Desert, of single birds at Tamarisk Grove (I24) 12 November 1989 (M. Green, AB 44:164, 1990) and 12 October 1996 (P. D. Jorgensen) and in Quartz Vein Wash (I25) 22 October 1996 (P. D. Jorgensen).

The Palm Warbler occurs rather late in fall migration, mainly from early October to mid November. One at Point Loma 9 September 1981 (D. Rawlins, AB 36:219, 1982) was exceptionally early. The number of Palm Warblers reported per fall in San Diego County recently has varied from only one in 2000 to about eight in 2001 and 2002.

Sightings of Palm Warblers through the end of April most likely represent wintering birds. Individuals known to have wintered have remained in the Tijuana River valley to 10 April 1983 (J. Oldenettel, AB 37:913, 1983) and

Conservation: Like some other eastern warblers, the Palm Warbler had a spike in the numbers found in San Diego County in the late 1970s. The San Diego Christmas bird count recorded its maximum of nine in the Tijuana River valley 15 December 1979. No decrease since then has been reported in the breeding range or elsewhere in California, so the apparent change may be due to local habitat changes (fewer low, damp weedy areas) or simply a change in birders' habits in fall migration (narrower focus on Point Loma, which lacks riparian scrub more appealing to Palm Warblers).

Taxonomy: As expected, it is the Western Palm Warbler, *D. p. palmarum* (Gmelin, 1789), that occurs predominantly in San Diego County. There are, however, nine records of *D. p. hypochrysea* Ridgway, 1876, even though it breeds east of Hudson Bay. Unitt (1984) listed seven through 1981; subsequently, one was at Point Loma 15 October 1985 (C. G. Edwards, AB 40:160, 1986) and one was with two Western Palm Warblers near La Jolla (O8) 16 October 1993 (G. McCaskie, AB 48:153, 1994).

Bay-breasted Warbler *Dendroica castanea*

Breeding mainly in Canada's boreal forest, the Bay-breasted Warbler fluctuates in numbers with its primary prey, the spruce budworm. Numbers of vagrants reaching California vary in tandem, so that the warbler averaged one per fall in San Diego County from the 1970s to the mid 1980s but only 0.2 per fall by the turn of the century.

Migration: Most of San Diego County's approximately 41 Bay-breasted Warblers have been at the usual sites for vagrants, Point Loma and the Tijuana River valley. None has been found farther inland than Otay Mesa (V13; 29 September 1973, AB 28:110, 1974). Fall dates range

Photo by Anthony Mercieca

from 9 September (1991, Point Loma, R. E. Webster, AB 46:151, 1991) to 20 November (1985, same location, C. G. Edwards, AB 40:160, 1986), unless one at Coronado (S9) 17–21 December 1983 (R. E. Webster, AB 38:358, 1984) is considered a late fall straggler rather than a wintering bird.

Four Bay-breasted Warblers have been noted in San Diego County in spring, at Point Loma 5–6 June 1979 (AB 33:806, 1979) and 25–28 May 1981 (E. Copper), at Coronado 15 June 1983 (E. Copper, AB 37:913, 1983), and at Pine Valley (P21) 23 June 1993 (C. G. Edwards, AB 47:1151, 1993).

Winter: The one Bay-breasted Warbler clearly wintering in the county was in the University City area of San Diego

(P8) 30 December 1983–10 April 1984 (T. and G. Quinn, AB 38:358, 1984).

Conservation: From 1973 to 1987 the Bay-breasted Warbler was found in San Diego County almost annually, with up to four in 1974 and three in 1987. Subsequently its frequency declined sharply. From 1994 through 2003 there were only two records, both from Point Loma, 26 September 1995 (G. L. Rogers, NASFN 50:117, 1996) and 20–21 September 2001 (J. C. Worley, NAB 56:108, 2002). Patten and Burger (1998) found the high correlation between numbers of the Bay-breasted Warbler reported in California and of the spruce budworm in eastern Canada second only to that for the Cape May Warbler.

Blackpoll Warbler *Dendroica striata*

In the 1960s and 1970s the Blackpoll Warbler was one of the most frequent eastern warblers seen as a fall vagrant to San Diego County, so much so that a birder searching for land birds along the coast from late September to mid October could expect to see one or two. Since then the species' abundance has decreased precipitously, so that by the beginning of the 21st century the average for the county per year was just two to three.

Migration: Recent totals for the Blackpoll Warbler in San Diego County are one in 1999, one in 2000, five in 2001, three in 2002, and two in 2003. Like other eastern warblers, the Blackpoll has been found in the coastal lowland almost exclusively. The county's only fall records elsewhere are of one at Agua Caliente Springs (M26) 4 October 1977 (AB 32:263, 1978) and one at Lake Henshaw (G17) 7 November 1980 (AB 35:228, 1982). The species' fall dates range from 3 September (1973, Otay Mesa, V13, G. McCaskie) to 26 November (1987, Tijuana River valley, E. Copper, AB 42:138, 1988) and 2 December (2003, Guajome Lake, G7, P. A. Ginsburg).

In spring, the county has seven records, three for Point Loma (S7), 21 June 1966 (McCaskie 1970b), 13 May 1982 (R. E. Webster, AB 36: 895, 1982), and 8 May 1985 (R. E. Webster, AB 39:351, 1985), one for the Tijuana River valley, 24 June 1978 (AB 32:1210, 1978), one for Solana Beach (L7), 18–21 May 1991 (P. A. Ginsburg, AB 45:497,

Photo by Anthony Mercieca

1991), one for Santa Ysabel (J18) 21 June 1998 (S. E. Smith), and one for Carrizo Marsh, Anza–Borrego Desert (O29), 18 May 1994 (P. D. Jorgensen, NASFN 48:342, 1994). One at La Jolla (P7) 16–17 July 1998 (S. E. Smith, FN 52:504, 1998) probably never made it to its breeding range.

Conservation: The Blackpoll Warbler's decline in San Diego County may reflect a change in the breeding range. Data from the Breeding Bird Survey 1996–2001 suggest a decline in the breeding population in at least the western end of the species' range, in Alaska and British Columbia (Sauer et al. 2003).

Cerulean Warbler *Dendroica cerulea*

The Cerulean Warbler is one of the rarest eastern warblers reaching the Pacific coast as a vagrant: the California Bird Records Committee has accepted just 15 for the state. Two of these are for San Diego County.

Migration: Both of the accepted records are for Point Loma in spring: one photographed 26–27 May 1979 (Luther et al. 1983) and one seen 7 June 1992 (R. E. Webster; Heindel and Patten 1996). Three reports in fall have been rejected or not submitted.

Photo by Anthony Mercieca

Conservation: The Cerulean Warbler is in serious decline. The situation is reflected in the petering out of occurrences in California: 11 from 1974 to 1988 but only three from 1989 through 2003.

Black-and-white Warbler *Mniotilta varia*

The Black-and-white Warbler differs from other warblers in its habit of creeping on trunks and large branches, like a nuthatch. Its range is largely east of the Rockies, but it is regular in small numbers in San Diego County. Seasonally, it is spread rather evenly. Annually, about four to five are reported each fall, three to four each winter, and two to three each spring. There are even a few summer records.

Winter: The Black-and-white is less concentrated along the coast than many eastern warblers; there are many reports from riparian woodland inland. In winter, however, the species is known from the coastal lowland only, inland as far as Kit Carson Park, Escondido (J11/K11), as from 3 December 1998 to 12 February 1999 (W. Pray). The atlas period from 1997 to 2002 yielded 14 wintering Black-and-white Warblers, with up to two together at the Dairy Mart pond, Tijuana River valley (V11) 19–26 December 1998 and 15 December 2001 (G. McCaskie).

Migration: In recent years, the number of Black-and-white Warblers reported in San Diego County each fall has ranged from two in 2002 to seven or eight in 2003. Thirteen Black-and-white Warblers were noted in spring 1997–2001, and the pace picked up subsequently, with six in 2002 and seven in 2003. Again, most records are for the coastal lowland, but a few are at higher elevations, such as one at Wynola (J19) 2 June 2000 (S. E. Smith). In the

Photo by Anthony Mercieca

Anza–Borrego Desert, one was in Borrego Springs (G24) 5 June 1990 (A. G. Morley, AB 44:1188, 1990), one was at Yaqui Well (I24) 23 April 1997 (P. K. Nelson), one was at Vallecito (M25) 12 May 1999 (M. C. Jorgensen), and one was at Canebrake (N27) 16 May 2002 (C. Smith).

Because the Black-and-white Warbler occurs in San Diego County at all seasons, its migration schedule can be determined only approximately. Fall migration begins by 6 September (1966, Point Loma, S7, AFN 21:79, 1967) and peaks from late September to late October. One Black-and-white Warbler near Mt. Woodson (L13) 15 April 1998 (P. M. von Hendy) was probably a spring migrant rather than wintering; the one at Yaqui Well 23 April 1997 certainly was. Spring records are scattered through June, with a few birds apparently remaining to summer. Sightings that might be considered summer records are of single birds at the east end of Lower Otay Lake (U14) 13 July–21 August 1975 (AB 29:1034, 1974), in the Tijuana River valley 17 June 1984 (G. McCaskie, AB 38:1063, 1984), in La Jolla (P8) 14 July 1986 (J. Moore, AB 40:1256, 1986), in San Diego 10–11 July 1991 (W. E. Haas, AB 45:1162, 1991), at Old Mission Dam (P11; singing male) 10 August 2000 (M. B. Stowe), on Villager Peak, Santa Rosa Mountains (C27), 17 June 2001 (R. Thériault, NAB 55:483, 2001), and near Scissors Crossing (J22) 23 June 2002 (J. R. Barth, NAB 56:487, 2002).

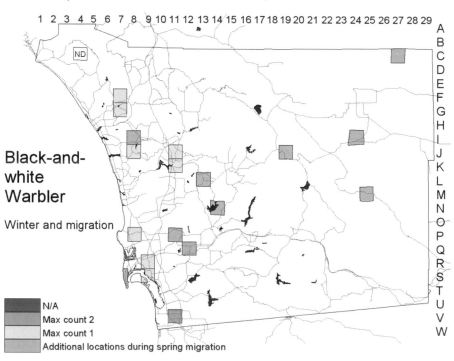

Black-and-white Warbler

Winter and migration

- N/A
- Max count 2
- Max count 1
- Additional locations during spring migration

American Redstart *Setophaga ruticilla*

The American Redstart is traditionally regarded as the most frequent of the eastern warblers in California. With scattered pairs now breeding in the northern part of the state, and small numbers wintering annually in the Imperial Valley, the redstart's label as "eastern" is wearing thin. In San Diego County the species occurs most frequently in fall migration, with several found annually. But it is also regular in winter, with an average of about four per year, and in spring migration, with an average of about one per year.

Photo by Anthony Mercieca

Winter: In San Diego County the American Redstart winters in the coastal lowland, in both ornamental trees and native riparian woodland. The number seen each year through the atlas period varied from one in 1997–98 to nine in 1998–99. The maximum per site is three, at Guajome Lake (G7) 13 December 1998 (S. Grain, P. A. Ginsburg) and at the Dairy Mart pond, Tijuana River valley (V11) 15 December 2001 (G. McCaskie).

Migration: In migration redstart records are mainly from the coastal lowland, but there are also several from the Anza–Borrego Desert, for example, of one at Scissors Crossing (J22) 8 September 2000 and one at Lower Willows (D22) 27 May 1999 (P. D. Jorgensen). Fall occurrences begin 11 August (1987, Buena Vista Lagoon, H5, M. and M. Johnson) and peak from mid September through October. Wintering birds have remained as late as 20 April (2000, Whelan Lake, G6, P. A. Ginsburg). Spring occurrences extend from 24 April (1964, Tijuana River valley, AFN 18:488, 1964) to 27 June (1987, Buena Vista Lagoon, D. B. King) and 30 June (1993, Encinitas, K7, B. E. Daniels, AB 47:1151, 1993), with a peak from mid to late May. Records later in the summer are of one at Point Loma (S7) 9 July 1967 (AFN 21:605, 1967), one at Old Mission Dam (P11) 17 July 1975 (AB 29:1086, 1975), one at Lake Henshaw (G17) 26 July 1998 (R. A. Hamilton, FN 52:504, 1998), and one that apparently returned two consecutive years to the Tijuana River valley, seen 30 July 1989 and 27 May–30 June 1990 (G. McCaskie, J. Oldenettel, AB 43:1369, 1989; 44:1188, 1990).

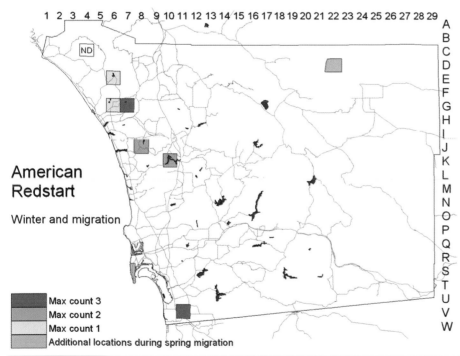

American Redstart

Winter and migration

■ Max count 3
■ Max count 2
☐ Max count 1
■ Additional locations during spring migration

Prothonotary Warbler *Protonotaria citrea*

The Prothonotary was once one of the rarest eastern warblers reaching California, but it has been one of the participants in the recent surge of species originating from the southeastern United States (Patten and Marantz 1996). Reported from San Diego County first in 1967, the Prothonotary has kept up a pace of slightly over one county record per year since 1977, to a total 34 by the end of 2003. Most occurrences are in fall, but eight are in spring, two in winter.

Migration: Most of San Diego County's Prothonotary Warblers have been at the usual sites for vagrant warblers, Point Loma and the Tijuana River valley, but a few have been found elsewhere in the coastal lowland, one as far as inland as Pauma Valley (E12, 30 September–1 October 1995, D. Rawlins, NASFN 50:117, 1996). Fall records range from 1 September (1989, La Jolla, P7, SDNHM 46026) to 4 November (1967, Point Loma, S7, AFN 22:91, 1968) with a peak in late September and early October. Two additional specimens were picked up at Olivenhain (K8) 21 October 1991 (SDNHM 47838) and in the gorilla enclosure at the

San Diego Zoo (R9) 22 September 2002 (SDNHM 50657). Spring records range from 3 May (1996, San Diego, R9, M. U. Evans, NASFN 50:334, 1996) to 7 June (1977, Tijuana River valley, Luther et al. 1983).

Winter: Though it typically winters in tropical swamps, the Prothonotary Warbler has wintered twice in San Diego County, once in San Diego's neighborhood of University Heights (R9) 25 January–20 March 1987 (R. Abnet, Roberson 1993), once in Greenwood Cemetery (S9) 12–15 December 2003 (D. W. Aguillard, J. O. Zimmer).

Photo by Anthony Mercieca

Worm-eating Warbler *Helmitheros vermivorus*

In spite of having a limited breeding range in the eastern United States, the Worm-eating Warbler is known in California from over 90 well-supported records, 13 of them from San Diego County.

Migration: Most of San Diego County's Worm-eating Warblers have been at Point Loma (S7). Other sites represented are Chula Vista (U11, 18 September 1960, SDNHM 30219, Huey 1961a—California's first Worm-eating Warbler), Otay Mesa (V13; 12 September 1971, Bevier 1990), Old Mission Dam (P11; 16–21 August 1973, Luther et al. 1979), the Tijuana River valley (10 September 1974, Roberson 1986), and Coronado (S9; 22 September 1988, E. Copper, Patten and Erickson 1994). The records range in date from 16 August to 26 October (1977, Point Loma, Luther 1980). One spring record, from Point Loma 27 May 1985 (E. Copper, AB 39:351, 1985), has not been evaluated by the California Bird Records Committee.

Photo by Anthony Mercieca

Ovenbird *Seiurus aurocapilla*

The Ovenbird is the most terrestrial of the warblers, walking inconspicuously on the ground. In spite of concerns about a population decline due to fragmentation of the forests where it breeds, the Ovenbird remains a regular vagrant to California. In San Diego County, it is recorded at a rate of about two per fall and about one every other spring. The atlas study yielded one unprecedented summer sighting of the Ovenbird on Palomar Mountain.

Migration: Fall records of the Ovenbird in San Diego County are all coastal except for a sighting of two at Agua Caliente Springs (M26) 4 October 1977 (AB 32:263, 1978). Their dates range from 17 August (1982, found dead at Ocean Beach, R7, preservable as skeleton only, SDNHM 47987) to 27 November (1982, AB 37:225, 1983), peaking from mid September through October. There are at least 25 county records in spring, most from Point Loma, the others from elsewhere in the coastal lowland, except for sightings of one at Tamarisk Grove (I24) 23 May 1977 (C. Stuteville) and one along the Azalea Glen Trail, Cuyamaca Rancho State Park (M20), 8 May

Photo by Anthony Mercieca

1999 (G. L. Rogers). Spring records range from 1 May (2003, Cabrillo National Monument, S7, S. E. Smith) to 18 June (1988, San Diego, B. and I. Mazin, AB 42:1341, 1988), with a strong concentration in late May and early June.

The unique summer record is of one along Kolb Creek, Palomar Mountain (D15), 7 July 1998 (K. L. Weaver, FN 52:504, 1998).

Winter: San Diego County has two early winter records of the Ovenbird, at Point Loma 23 December 1983 (J. M. Langham, AB 38:359, 1984) and at Western Hills Park (Q8) 26 December 2001 (T. Brashear, NAB 56:224, 2002).

Taxonomy: The two specimens for San Diego County preserved as study skins, from Point Loma 22 May 1966 (SDNHM 36029) and Bonita (T11) 17 October 1999 (SDNHM 50339), are both nominate *S. a. aurocapilla* (Linnaeus, 1766), being as dark and green as specimens from New York.

Northern Waterthrush *Seiurus noveboracensis*

The Northern Waterthrush breeds west to Alaska and winters in the coastal mangroves of Baja California. Yet it is rarely seen as a migrant and winter visitor in San Diego County. Some of this rarity is due to the species' habits: it walks on the ground in the dense understory of riparian woodland, staying close to water or hopping through branches hanging low over water. Often it reveals itself only by call, a characteristic loud "chink."

Photo by Anthony Mercieca

Winter: In San Diego County, the Northern Waterthrush is primarily a winter visitor to the coastal lowland. Since 1985 winter records have been almost entirely from the Tijuana River valley, where the species occurs annually. During the atlas period our only counts of more than a single individual were of two in the valley west of Hollister Street (V10) 18 December 1999 (W. E. Haas) and two at the Dairy Mart pond (V11) 1 January 2000 (G. McCaskie). Five were in the valley in December 1990 (R. E. Webster, AB 45:322, 1991). The Northern Waterthrush has also been seen repeatedly along the lower Otay and San Luis Rey rivers, the latter accounting for the Oceanside Christmas bird count picking up the species in 1981 and 1984.

Migration: Northern Waterthrushes wintering in the Tijuana River valley may arrive as early as 6 September (2003, G. McCaskie) and remain as late as 4 May (1980, AB 34:817, 1980). The earliest fall date recorded for the county is 13 August (1966, San Diego, AFN 21:79, 1967). Sightings of the Northern Waterthrush at the usual sites for vagrant fall warblers on Point Loma (S7) are exceptional (24 September 2002, J. K. Wilson; 6 September 2003, W. McCausland). A Northern Waterthrush in Los Peñasquitos Canyon (N8) 11 April 1999 (P. A. Ginsburg) was our only spring migrant during the atlas period. Outside the coastal lowland, the Northern Waterthrush has been recorded four times in the Anza–Borrego Desert, at Lower Willows (D23) 4 May 1980 and 18 May 1981 (the latest spring record for San Diego County, A. G. Morley), at Agua Caliente Springs (M26) 8 May 2002 (J. K. Wilson), and along Vallecito Creek at the east end of Mason Valley (M23) 2 September 1984 (SDNHM 43173).

Louisiana Waterthrush *Seiurus motacilla*

For decades, the Louisiana Waterthrush was known in California from a single specimen. Then, in 1985, this bird of forest streams from the eastern United States began participating in the upsurge of vagrancy of southeastern warblers (Patten and Marantz 1996). Through 2002, records statewide stand at 14, just one from San Diego County.

Winter: The single Louisiana Waterthrush known from San Diego County frequented a drainage ditch near the Salk Institute, La Jolla (O7), 9 February–21 March 1990 (J. O'Brien; Patten and Erickson 1994). The identification is supported by photographs.

Photo by Anthony Mercieca

Kentucky Warbler *Oporornis formosus*

The Kentucky Warbler is rare but increasing as a vagrant to California. In summer 1992 an unprecedented irruption brought at least 36 to the state's riparian woodlands, two to San Diego County, with one more the following summer. Eight of the county's 16 records are for fall, four are for spring, and one is for winter.

Migration: San Diego County's fall records of the Kentucky Warbler extend from 14 September (1990, Point Loma, S7, D. W. Aguillard; Heindel and Garrett 1995) to 16 November (1983, Del Mar, M7, D. Delaney; Roberson 1986). All are along or near the coast. At 2.5 miles from the coast, the single specimen, from Paso del Sol, Del Mar (M8), represents the fall record farthest inland (D. R. Grine, SDNHM 49223). Four spring records are all from Point Loma: 4 June 1968 (Craig 1970), 5–7 May 1987 (R. E. Webster; Langham 1991), 28 May 1995 (G. L. Rogers, NASFN 49:311, 1995), and 22 May 2001 (M. B. Mulrooney, NAB 55:358, 2001).

The incursion of summer 1992–93 was noted most in Santa Barbara and Kern counties, but it yielded three Kentucky Warblers in San Diego County: one along

Photo by Anthony Mercieca

Noble Creek (O22) 8 June 1992 (B. Cord; Heindel and Patten 1996), one along Sandia Creek (C7) 19–22 June 1992 (K. L. Weaver; Heindel and Patten 1996), and one in Green Valley, Encinitas (K7), 30 June–2 July 1993 (B. E. Daniels, D. R. Willick; Erickson and Terrill 1996).

Winter: The county's single wintering Kentucky Warbler was along Agua Hedionda Creek, Vista (I7), 15–25 March 1999 (P. A. Ginsburg, NAB 53:210, 1999).

Connecticut Warbler *Oporornis agilis*

The Connecticut Warbler breeds not in Connecticut but in Canada's boreal forest, east of the Rocky Mountains. It is a rare vagrant to California, though undoubtedly many are missed; Connecticut Warblers walk quietly on the ground, concealed under dense vegetation. There are six well-supported records for San Diego County, five in fall, one in spring.

Migration: The California Bird Records Committee has accepted two fall records of the Connecticut Warbler from the Tijuana River valley (27 September 1963, SDNHM 30776; 19 September 1974, Binford 1985), two from Point Loma (4–12 October 1980, Binford 1985; 14–15 September 1990, G. McCaskie; Heindel and Garrett 1995), and one from San Diego (14 September 1978, Luther et al. 1983). The single spring record is of a bird trapped and photographed at Point Loma 4 June 1968 (McCaskie 1970).

Mourning Warbler *Oporornis philadelphia*

A close relative of MacGillivray's Warbler, the Mourning Warbler replaces that western species in the boreal forest east of the Rocky Mountains. The Mourning is a rare vagrant to California, probably often overlooked because of its preference for dense vegetation and its similarity to MacGillivray's Warbler. The California Bird Records Committee has accepted five records of the Mourning for San Diego County.

Migration: The five records are all for late September and early October. Four are for Point Loma: 3 October 1968 (McCaskie 1970, SDNHM 36933), 8 October 1982 and 20 September 1983 (R. E. Webster; Roberson 1986), and 21–25 September 2002 (J. C. Worley; Cole and McCaskie 2004). One is for the Tijuana River valley: 21 September 1985 (G. McCaskie, Bevier 1990). No documentation was submitted for two other records published in *American Birds*. The individual at Point Loma in 2002 was remarkable for being an adult male; the vast majority of vagrant warblers are immature.

Photo by Anthony Mercieca

Taxonomy: In spite of subsequent statements that hybrid Mourning × MacGillivray's Warblers are unknown, the apparent hybrids collected in Alberta and studied by Cox (1973) are still preserved in the San Diego Natural History Museum.

MacGillivray's Warbler *Oporornis tolmiei*

A bird of dense, low vegetation, MacGillivray's Warbler is easily overlooked. As a result, it appears to be the scarcest of the western warblers in San Diego County. Nevertheless, it is a regular if uncommon migrant in both spring and fall, best found in spring at oases along the east base of the mountains. Though San Diego County is apparently off the species' main migration route, some birds do follow the pattern of many other migrant landbirds, using the canyons on the county's desert slope as routes for breaching the barrier of the mountains on their journey northwest. MacGillivray's Warbler is expanding its breeding range south, but in San Diego County so far this expansion has generated but a single summer sighting from Palomar Mountain.

Migration: In spring, MacGillivray's Warbler is seen in San Diego County most numerously on the desert flank of the mountains, the birds pausing as they seek the routes of least resistance to the coastal slope. The high count during the atlas period exemplifies this pattern (nine in Oriflamme Canyon, L22, 23 April 2001, R. Thériault), as do other high counts (25 at Banner, K21, 15 April 1978, P. Unitt; 11 near the head of Rodriguez Canyon, K21, 26 April 2003, S. D. Cameron). The species' main spring migration period is mid April to mid May, but we recorded the species twice in late March. The earliest date, 23 March (1997, one at Mescal Bajada, J25, M. and B. McIntosh), appears to be the earliest ever for San Diego County and equals the earliest for the Salton Sink (Patten et al. 2003). The latest spring date is 28 May (2000, one near White Oak Spring, A3, L. J. Hargrove), except for a specimen (SDNHM 37194) from Mount Helix (R12) dated "June 1967" with no more exact information.

Fall migrants occur primarily from mid August through mid October, rarely as late as mid November.

Winter: MacGillivray's Warbler is very rare in winter in southern California, which is well north of the main winter range in western mainland Mexico. Eleven have been recorded around metropolitan San Diego at this season, most recently in 1992. Another was reported on the Anza–Borrego Christmas bird count 29 December 1985.

Breeding distribution: The Sierra Nevada was the southern end of MacGillivray's Warbler's traditional breeding range (Grinnell and Miller 1944). In the final third of the 20th century, small numbers colonized the higher elevations of the Transverse Ranges of southern California (Lentz 1993, Dunn and Garrett 1997). In 1987 two or three

Photo by Anthony Mercieca

summered on Black Mountain in the San Jacinto range of Riverside County (R. McKernan, AB 41:1489, 1987). In San Diego County there is only one summer record, of a singing male in Doane Valley, Palomar Mountain State Park (E14), 9 June 1994 (M. B. Stowe, NASFN 48:989, 1994). There was no suggestion of breeding.

Conservation: MacGillivray's Warbler is a bird of coniferous forest, but one of the understory, not the canopy. As a result, it capitalizes on the new low growth that follows logging. Data on the trends of the species as a whole are conflicting (Pitochelli 1995), but the number of migrants passing through San Diego may be on the increase. Though Stephens (1919a) called MacGillivray's Warbler "rather common," the same term he used for Townsend's, the San Diego Natural History Museum had no specimens from the county before 1963. Now these have swelled to 22. As an understory species, MacGillivray's Warbler is liable to collision with windows and capture by domestic cats, so the upsurge in specimens may be related more to the hazards of migrating through an increasingly urban environment than to an increase in the number of birds themselves.

Taxonomy: Most specimens of MacGillivray's Warbler from San Diego County are the more brightly colored subspecies of the Pacific coast region, *O. t. tolmiei* (Townsend, 1839). The one exception known was collected in Tubb Canyon (H23) 14 April 1938 (LACM 73980). Its dull grayish-olive upperparts and small size (tail 51 mm, wing chord 57 mm) match *O. t. monticola* Phillips, 1947, or *O. t. austinsmithi* Phillips, 1947, if the latter is separable (Patten et al. 2003). It is a surprise that the one specimen of the Rocky Mountain subspecies should be so early in the spring, for the typical pattern is that spring migration of Rocky Mountain subspecies lags that of their Pacific coast counterparts (compare Wilson's Warbler, for example).

Common Yellowthroat *Geothlypis trichas*

The Common Yellowthroat is second only to the Song Sparrow as the commonest bird of San Diego County's riparian woodland. Freshwater marshes and even uplands overgrown with rank weeds like fennel or white sweet clover also offer good habitat.

The yellowthroat is common in both summer and winter but not sedentary. Wintering birds move into ornamental shrubbery and thickets of dry weeds where the species does not breed, and migrants show up occasionally even in desert scrub or chaparral. Despite its preferring wetland habitats and being a principal host of the Brown-headed Cowbird, the Common Yellowthroat has sustained its numbers in San Diego County better than have many other small insectivorous birds.

Breeding distribution: As a bird primarily of riparian woodland and freshwater marshes, the Common Yellowthroat is most numerous in the valleys of the coastal lowland. Counts in one atlas square on a single day ranged as high as 107 (70 singing males) in lower Los Peñasquitos Canyon (N8) 7 May 2000 (P. A. Ginsburg et al.). With increasing elevation the yellowthroat's habitat becomes scarcer and the birds less abundant, though they are still locally common, as near Mesa Grande (H17; 23 on 12 May 2001, C. and J. Manning) and along Buena Vista Creek in Warner Valley (G19; 25 on 24 June 2000, E. C. Hall). Yellowthroats breed up to about 4500 feet elevation in the Palomar and Cuyamaca mountains. On the desert slope they breed at riparian oases, especially Lower Willows (D23; up to 26 on 12 May 2001, B. L. Peterson) and Sentenac Ciénaga (J23; up to 33, including 26 singing males, 7 June 2000, R. Thériault), uncommonly elsewhere.

Nesting: Common Yellowthroats nest in dense, low undergrowth, sometimes on the ground. Atlas results revealed their breeding season to be broader than the 14 April–14 June attested by 23 egg sets collected from San Diego County 1902–35 (WFVZ) and even the 4 April–10 July attested by 66 from throughout California (Bent 1953). Observations of nest building along the Sweetwater River in Sunnyside (S12) 5 March 1999 (T. W. Dorman) and fledglings in Mission Valley (Q10) 12 April 1998 (P. Unitt) suggest that yellowthroats begin laying as early as mid March. Observations of nest building at the upper end of Sweetwater Reservoir (S13) 13 July 1998 and fledglings at O'Neill Lake (E6) 12 August 1998

Photo by Anthony Mercieca

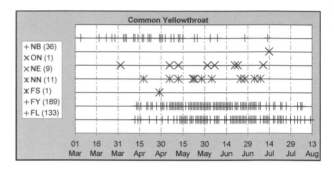

(P. A. Ginsburg) suggest they continue laying as late as mid July.

Migration: Away from sites where it breeds and winters, the Common Yellowthroat is an uncommon migrant. Seldom are more than two such migrants seen in a day, though maximum counts of them range up to eight in Borrego Springs (G24) 25 April 1998 (P. D. Ache) and seven in Rodriguez Canyon (L22) 26 April 1999 (P. Unitt). Peak spring migration is in April (30 of 46 records), but dates range from 15 March (1997, four at Borrego Springs, P. D. Ache) to 25 May (2000, one in Rodriguez Canyon, J. R. Barth). Postbreeding dispersal evidently begins as early as 10 July (1997, one at Chollas Lake, R11, C. G. Edwards).

Winter: Though Common Yellowthroats breeding farther north invade San Diego County in migration and winter, the species winters mostly in the same areas where it breeds. Wintering Common Yellowthroats are strongly concentrated in the coastal lowland, where over 100 per day can be found in marshes and riparian undergrowth (e.g., 135 at Lake Hodges, K10, 26 December 1999, R. L. Barber). Some birds use ornamental shrubbery and patches of low

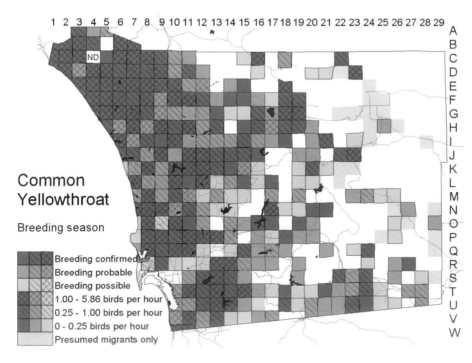

Common Yellowthroat

Breeding season

Breeding confirmed
Breeding probable
Breeding possible
1.00 - 5.86 birds per hour
0.25 - 1.00 birds per hour
0 - 0.25 birds per hour
Presumed migrants only

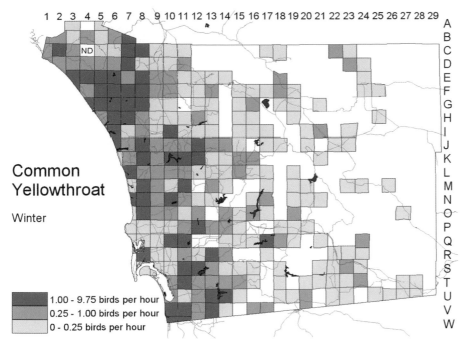

Common Yellowthroat

Winter

- 1.00 - 9.75 birds per hour
- 0.25 - 1.00 birds per hour
- 0 - 0.25 birds per hour

most frequent foster parent to the Brown-headed Cowbird in San Diego County, the Common Yellowthroat did not decrease grossly when the cowbird invaded, if one may judge from general assessments in the literature; the yellowthroat has always been common. Like other common hosts, it likely benefited from the widespread trapping of cowbirds initiated in the late 1980s.

Taxonomy: Subspecies of the Common Yellowthroat remain poorly quantified; the validity of many is uncertain. Grinnell (1901) distinguished the yellowthroats of southern California as *G. t. scirpicola* on the basis of their brighter color, more extensive yellow on the belly, and more rounded wing than in *G. t. occidentalis* Brewster, 1883, of the Great Basin. *G. t. scirpicola* has been maintained through successive editions of the American Ornithologists' Union checklist though synonymized by Ridgway (1902) and Phillips et al. (1964). Similarly, a darker subspecies *G. t. arizela* Oberholser, 1899, of the Pacific Northwest and northern California was recognized by the A. O. U. (1957) but not by Grinnell and Miller (1944) or Marshall and Dedrick (1994). Yellowthroats from the ranges of both *arizela* and *occidentalis* may be expected to reach San Diego County in migration. One subspecies universally recognized is *G. t. sinuosa* Grinnell, 1901, breeding in the salt marshes of the San Francisco Bay area and distinguished by its smaller size as well as darker color and browner flanks. It is partially migratory and known in San Diego County still from only two specimens, from San Diego 30 October 1914 (SDNHM 33397, Willett 1933) and San Diego Bay 3 March 1939 (SDNHM 18054). With the elimination of over 80% of the salt marshes around San Francisco Bay *sinuosa* has become rare (Marshall and Dedrick 1994). Presumably the numbers of birds dispersing south has been reduced proportionately, and the even greater level of habitat loss in southern California could select against migrants.

weeds away from water. The maximum count of birds wintering in nonbreeding habitat is of six at North Island Naval Air Station (S8) 18 December 1999 (R. T. Patton). Above 1500 feet elevation the species is generally uncommon, more numerous only in Warner Valley (up to 20 near Swan Lake, F18, 18 December 2000, G. L. Rogers). Winter records at exceptionally high elevations are of single birds at 4600–4650 feet at Doane Pond, Palomar Mountain State Park (E14; 27 February 2000, J. K. Wilson, A. Mauro), and Lake Cuyamaca (M20; 1 February 1999, A. P. and T. E. Keenan). In the Anza–Borrego Desert the Common Yellowthroat is a rare winter visitor to irrigated places in the Borrego Valley (up to four in the north end of the valley, E24, 19 December 1999, P. R. Pryde), with one record from a natural oasis where the species does not breed (three at Mountain Palm Springs, O27, 8 January 2000, P. K. Nelson)

Conservation: There is no strong evidence for significant changes in the numbers or status of the Common Yellowthroat through San Diego history. Even though marshes and riparian woodland have been much reduced, the yellowthroat persists in small remnants and readily recolonizes regenerated habitat. Though perhaps the

Hooded Warbler *Wilsonia citrina*

Over the last two decades of the 20th century, several warblers nesting in the Canadian taiga decreased as vagrants to California, while several others nesting in the southeastern United States increased. Preeminent among the latter is the Hooded Warbler, which irrupted from 1992 to 1994, nesting in California for the first time in Los Angeles and Kern counties in 1992. The species was first reported from San Diego County in 1967, but by 2003 at least 50 had been seen here.

Photo by Anthony Mercieca

Migration: Unlike most vagrant warblers, the Hooded is more frequent in San Diego County in spring than in fall. Fall records number 13, extending from 11 September (1988, Point Loma, S7, J. L. Dunn, AB 43:170, 1989; 2002, Oceanside, H5, S. Gustafson, NAB 57:118, 2003) to 28 November (1967, Borrego Palm Canyon, F23, McCaskie 1970). The last record is the only one for fall not along the coast.

Hooded Warbler records in spring and early summer (there is no clear division between the two) extend from 16 April (1993, Green Valley, K7, D. R. Willick, AB 47:454, 1993) to 30 June (1998, banded in West Sycamore Canyon, O12, P. A. Campbell, FN 52:504, 1998). Most at this season are along the coast, but some are well scattered inland in riparian woodland where the species might nest, as along the Santa Margarita River north of Fallbrook (C8) 5–19 June 1992 and 24 May 2001 (K. L. Weaver), along Fallbrook Creek in the Fallbrook Naval Weapons Station (D6) 1 June 2001 (P. A. Campbell), along Keys Creek near Turner Reservoir (G11) 22 May 1992 (C. G. Edwards), and along Kitchen Creek between Highway 80 and Interstate 8 (R22) 14 June 1993 (P. Unitt, AB 47:1151, 1993). Six spring records from the Anza–Borrego Desert encompass one from Culp Valley (G23; 15–16 June 1997,

R. Thériault, FN 51:1055, 1997), one from Tamarisk Grove (I24; 15 May 2003, M. B. Mulrooney), three from Agua Caliente Springs (M26), and one from Dos Cabezas Spring (S29; 11 May 1973, AB 27:822, 1973). The Hooded Warbler's irregularity continued through the atlas period with yearly totals varying from zero in 1999 and 2000 to six in spring 2001.

Winter: Four Hooded Warblers are known to have wintered in San Diego County, one at Sweetwater Dam (S12) 17 December 1977–27 January 1978 (AB 32:401, 1978), two in residential areas of Coronado (S9), 11 December 1988–18 March 1989 (G. McCaskie, AB 43:368, 1989) and 31 October 2002–7 March 2003 (E. Copper, NAB 57:118, 259, 2003), and one nearby at North Island Naval Air Station (S8) 15 December 2001 (R. T. Patton, NAB 56:224, 2002).

Conservation: The sudden upsurge in Hooded Warblers in California may represent the beginnings of a range expansion. Patten and Marantz (1996) reviewed several hypotheses such as unusual weather conditions, displacement from degraded habitat, and population increase that might account for the change. The convergence of multiple factors seems likely.

Wilson's Warbler *Wilsonia pusilla*

The intense yellow of Wilson's Warbler is a common sight in San Diego County during spring and fall migration. As a winter visitor the species is rare but annual. But as a breeding bird Wilson's Warbler has the barest toehold in the county, which lies at the southern tip of its breeding range. The known breeding population is only three or four pairs, though it could increase with continued suppression of cowbirds and preservation of riparian woodland. But the larger-scale trend is not good—the Pacific coast subspecies of Wilson's Warbler is in decline over much of its range.

Photo by Anthony Mercieca

Breeding distribution: Summering Wilson's Warblers were recorded in only two areas of San Diego County during the five-year atlas period, along the Santa Margarita River in Camp Pendleton and on Palomar Mountain. Along the Santa Margarita, all were in a 2-mile segment from just east of Rifle Range Road to the mouth of Pueblitos Canyon (F5; P. P. Beck, B. E. Kus, J. M. Wells), except for one a short distance farther downstream in Ysidora Gorge (G5) 19 June 1999 (R. E. Fischer). Never was more than a single pair or family seen on one day. At the confluence of Doane and French creeks (D14), a single male apparently summered each year 1997–2000, but the only observation of more than one bird was of a pair 28 July 1997 (P. D. Jorgensen).

Nesting: Along the California coast, Wilson's Warblers typically nest in shrubbery, in contrast to the rest of their range, where they typically nest on the ground (Ammon and Gilbert 1999). Egg records from southern California

specify that in this area they select primarily nettle and blackberry as nest sites (Ammon and Gilbert 1999), and observations from San Diego County agree with this preference. Of two nests seen being built along the lower Santa Margarita River, one was in nettle (F5; 4 May 1999, P. P. Beck), the other in blackberry (F5; 30 May 2000, J. M. Wells). The only evidence of success was a fledgling accompanying the adult female 6 July 1999. It was the result of a replacement clutch, as it was in the territory with the nest in nettle, after that nest failed (P. P. Beck).

Migration: Wilson's Warbler is common throughout San Diego County as a spring migrant. Arrival dates during the atlas period ranged from 11 to 20 March, though arrival as early as 6 March has been reported (Belding 1890). Numbers are greatest at desert oases and along the corridor from San Felipe Valley to Warner Springs. High

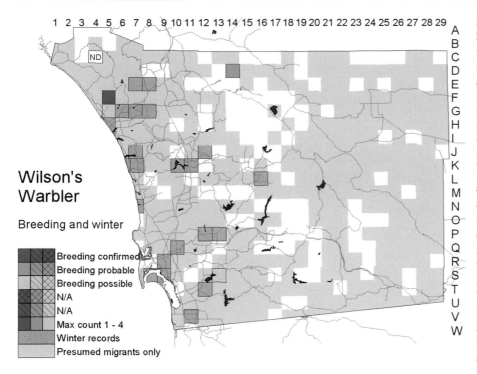

Wilson's Warbler

Breeding and winter

- Breeding confirmed
- Breeding probable
- Breeding possible
- N/A
- N/A
- Max count 1 - 4
- Winter records
- Presumed migrants only

counts during the atlas period were of 80 around Scissors Crossing (J22) 14 May 1998 (E. C. Hall), 75 at Vallecito (M25) 12 May 1999 (M. C. Jorgensen), and 65 at Agua Caliente Springs (M26) 12 May 1997 (E. C. Hall). The last migrants depart during the first week of June; the latest spring date is 7 June (1999, two at Banner, K21, P. K. Nelson). Wilson's Warbler's migration period is long in fall as well; arrival may be as early as 1 August (1998, one at Los Peñasquitos Lagoon, N7, S. Grain), and some birds seen in December may still be heading south.

Winter: Wilson's Warbler is a rare winter visitor to ornamental shrubbery and riparian woodland in the coastal lowland. Though some seen in early December could be late migrants, others have been tracked over the entire winter, such as one at Guajome Lake (G7) 13 December 1998–6 March 1999 (P. A. Ginsburg, C. C. Gorman). During the atlas period, reports averaged nine individuals per year. The maximum daily count, of four in Balboa Park (R9) 20 December 1997 (V. P. Johnson), was the only one of over two individuals. Wintering Wilson's Warblers extended inland to Bonsall (E8; up to two on 3 December 2000, P. A. Ginsburg), the Wild Animal Park at San Pasqual (J12; one on 23 January 2001, M. Farley), and Lakeside (P13; one on 8 January 1998, D. C. Seals), except for one in San Vicente Valley (L16), elevation about 1500 feet, 27 February 2000 (J. D. Barr). The last might have been a very early spring migrant, though even farther inland there is a record from a Lake Henshaw Christmas bird count (one on 27 December 1982) and another from an Anza–Borrego Christmas bird count (two on 2 January 1993).

Conservation: San Diego County is at the southern tip of Wilson's Warbler's breeding range, and the species has never been common here as a breeding bird. Previous specific

records are of a nest with eggs at San Pasqual (J12/13; Sharp 1907), reports of the species as a "summer resident" at Poway (M11) and "breeding" at Julian (K20; Belding 1890), a pair summering along Reidy Creek in 1980 (H10; K. L. Weaver), one along the Santa Margarita River 21 June 1984 (L. Salata, AB 38:1063, 1984), and two singing males, an adult female, and a fledgling along the Santa Margarita River (F5) 11 July 1995 (P. Unitt). In spite of the meagerness of these records, however, it is likely that the species once bred more commonly. Stephens (1919a) said that Wilson's Warbler "breeds in small numbers in oak forests and in willow groves" in San Diego County. For coastal southern California as a whole, Willett (1933) called it a "common summer resident." Currently, this status applies only north of Point Conception (Lehman 1994). Thus the species' breeding range has retracted out of southern California almost entirely, presumably in response to the invasion of the Brown-headed Cowbird. In southern and central California cowbirds parasitize Wilson's Warblers heavily (Friedmann et al. 1977, Ammon and Gilbert 1999). Cowbirds are likely contributing, along with degradation of riparian woodland, to the decrease in Wilson's Warbler numbers now evident all along the Pacific coast (e.g., Pyle et al. 1994). Currently, in the coastal lowland, daily counts as high as 30 are unusual even at the peak of spring migration; in the 1970s, counts of 75 in this area were not exceptional (Unitt 1984). Along the lower Santa Margarita, years of cowbird trapping have reduced the parasitism rate on all hosts in this area to practically zero, allowing locally breeding Wilson's Warblers the beginning of a recovery. But another threat to the riparian woodland in this area has arisen in the proliferation of the giant reed, which displaces native plants.

Taxonomy: The Pacific coast subspecies *W. p. chryseola* Ridgway, 1902, is the dominant subspecies of Wilson's Warbler in San Diego County. Though there are no specimens of the breeding population, it is undoubtedly *chryseola*, as is the single winter specimen, from Balboa Park (R9) 21 December 1927 (SDNHM 11646; not *pileolata* as reported originally by Abbott 1928a). In spring, the early arrivals are presumably all *chryseola*; specimens extend at least from 28 March (1904, Witch Creek, J16, FMNH 151436) to 14 May (1989, Point Loma, S7, SDNHM 47989). Fall specimens range at least from 4 August (1908, Volcan Mountain, I20, MVZ 3861) to 7 October (1966, Point Loma, SDNHM 36040).

Wilsonia p. pileolata (Pallas, 1811) breeds from the Great Basin and Rocky Mountains north to Alaska; it is a duller yellow than *chryseola* on both the underparts and upperparts. Small numbers come through in spring migration, generally after the peak of *chryseola*. The six specimens in the San Diego Natural History Museum extend from 2 May (1924, 2 miles northwest of La Mesa, Q11, SDNHM 9325) to 22 May (1961, Spring Valley, S12, SDNHM 30269). The single fall specimen of *pileolata* is also on the late side, from San Luis Rey (G6) 6 October 1962 (SDNHM 3179). The pattern of migration of the two subspecies in San Diego County is similar to that in the Salton Sink to the east (Patten et al. 2003).

Canada Warbler *Wilsonia canadensis*

Breeding east of the Rocky Mountains and wintering in South America, the Canada Warbler is a vagrant to California. It reaches San Diego County at a rate of about one per year, so far occurring only in fall migration.

Migration: About 43 Canada Warblers have been reported in San Diego County, from the first in 1967 through 2003. All have been near the coast; Otay Mesa (V13) is the site of the record farthest inland. Their dates range from 6 September (1976, San Luis Rey River, Oceanside, G6, R. Bacon) to 15 November (1969, Tijuana River valley, AFN 24:100c, 1970) with a peak from late September to mid October. The number reported per year has varied from zero, as in 1998, to four, in 2000. Since the late 1960s there has been no trend in the species' frequency.

Photo by Anthony Mercieca

Red-faced Warbler *Cardellina rubrifrons*

The Red-faced Warbler breeds in high mountains north to Arizona but is one of the rarest warblers reaching California as a vagrant, with just 13 well-supported records through 2002. The California Bird Records Committee has accepted three from San Diego County.

Migration: All three of the county's accepted records of the Red-faced Warbler are from Point Loma (S7). Two are for spring, one photographed 21–24 May 1977 (G. McCaskie et al., Luther et al. 1983) and one seen 29 May 1996 (R. E. Webster, P. A. Ginsburg, McCaskie and San Miguel 1999). One is for fall, 11–12 September 1982 (R. E. Webster et al., Morlan 1985). The records committee did not have evidence sufficient to accept the report from Old Mission Dam 26 August 1974 (AB 29:124, 1975).

Painted Redstart *Myioborus pictus*

The Painted Redstart nests in mountain forests from Arizona south through Mexico and is a vagrant to California. The nesting attempt in San Diego County's Laguna Mountains in 1974 is one of only two known for California. Most of the county's 44 records are for fall, with nine for winter, three for spring, and two for summer.

Migration: In fall the Painted Redstart is reported in San Diego County at the rate of about one per year. Except for one at Agua Caliente Springs (M26) in the Anza–Borrego Desert 1–2 October 1996 (M. Graham, NASFN 51:121, 1997), all fall reports are coastal, inland to Lakeside (O14/P14; 14 October 1991, C. M. Keller, AB 46:152, 1991). The number reported per year has varied from zero to three, as in 1986 and 1996. Fall dates range from 24 August (1993, Tijuana River valley, D. W. Aguillard, C. H. Reiser, McCaskie and San Miguel 1999) to 8 November (1987, Point Loma, S7, R. Fowler, AB 42:139, 1988).

Photo by Anthony Mercieca

The three spring records are from Borrego Springs (F24/G24) 1 April 1979 (AB 33:898, 1979), Sorrento Valley (N8) 1 May 1994 (D. K. Adams, NASFN 48:342, 1994), and Encinitas (K7) 24 May 1995 (D. W. Aguillard, NASFN 49:311, 1995).

Winter: The nine winter records are all for the coastal lowland. Unitt (1984) listed five; subsequent ones are from Point Loma 20 December 1986–22 March 1987 (R. Arn, AB 41:331, 1987), Coronado (S9) 25 November 1987–21 March 1988 (E. Copper, AB 42:139, 323, 1988), Mission Valley (R9) 30 January–27 February 1990 (M. E. Gowan, AB 44:331, 1990), and San Diego (R9) 2 February 1998 (T. Hartnett, FN 52:259, 1998).

Breeding distribution: The two summer records are of one along Jaybird Creek, Palomar Mountain (E13), 25 June–6 August 1969 (AFN 23:696, 1970) and a pair along Agua Dulce Creek, Laguna Mountains (O23), 23 May–29 July 1974. The nest of this pair, with recently hatched chicks, was found 6 July, but by 13 July the nest was deserted and the chicks were dead (Unitt 1974).

Yellow-breasted Chat *Icteria virens*

The song of the Yellow-breasted Chat, a mockingbirdlike series of repeated whistles, "chacks," and "churrs," is a characteristic sound of dense riparian woodland. Though often maddeningly difficult to see, the chat is a locally common summer visitor. Like many other riparian birds, it is a frequent host of the Brown-headed Cowbird. After a decline during the middle of the 20th century, the Yellow-breasted Chat has increased in numbers considerably since the mid 1980s, presumably in response to the widespread trapping of cowbirds.

Photo by Anthony Mercieca

Breeding distribution: Yellow-breasted Chats occur widely in San Diego County's coastal lowland wherever there is substantial riparian woodland. They are strongly concentrated, though, in the northwest, not only along the Santa Margarita and San Luis Rey rivers, but along smaller creeks too, like San Mateo, San Onofre, Las Pulgas, Aliso, and De Luz. Daily counts in this area go as high as 40 (36 singing males) along the Santa Margarita River north of Fallbrook (C8) 24 May 2001 (K. L. Weaver). Another large concentration is the San Benardo and San Pasqual valleys east of Lake Hodges. When the water level in Lake Hodges drops, the exposed basin is quickly colonized by shrubby willows offering the Yellow-breasted Chat ideal habitat (K11; maximum count 50, including 45 singing males, 3 June 1997, E. C. Hall). Farther south concentrations are along lower Los Peñasquitos Canyon (N8; up to 21, including 15 singing males, 2 May 1999, P. A. Ginsburg), the San Diego River from Mission Gorge to Santee (Q11/P11–13), the Sweetwater River from Sweetwater Reservoir to Jamacha (S13/R13–14; up to 30 in R13 on 15 May 1998, D. and M. Hastings), Jamul and Dulzura creeks from Lower Otay Lake to Pio Pico Campground (U14/T15), the Tijuana River valley (V10–11/W10–11; up to 20, including 18 singing males, along the river east of Hollister St., W11, 27 June 1998, P. Unitt), and in Marron Valley (V16/V17). Away from these areas the chat is uncommon.

Above 1500 feet elevation on the coastal slope, chats are possibly irregular. Four sites in this area emerged during the atlas' term: San Luis Rey River between Lake Henshaw and the La Jolla Indian Reservation (F16/G16; up to six near the San Luis Rey Day Use Area, G16, 24 June 2001, W. E. Haas), Buena Vista Creek near Warner's Ranch (G18–19; up to three singing males east of the old ranch house, G19, 24 June 2000, E. C. Hall), Cottonwood Creek between Lake Morena and

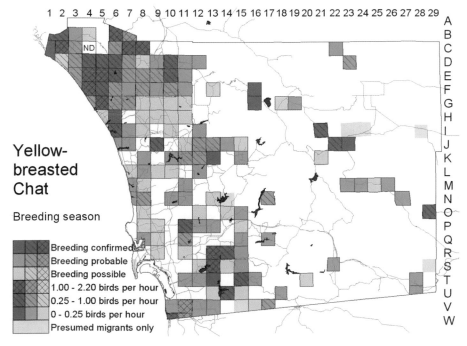

Yellow-breasted Chat

Breeding season

Breeding confirmed
Breeding probable
Breeding possible
1.00 - 2.20 birds per hour
0.25 - 1.00 birds per hour
0 - 0.25 birds per hour
Presumed migrants only

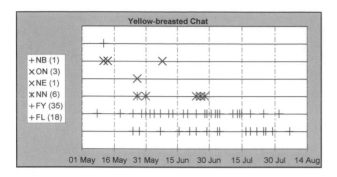

Boulder Oaks (S22; two singing males 9 May 1999, R. and S. L. Breisch), and Hauser Canyon (T20; one on 15 May and 5 June 1997, J. M. Wells).

On the desert slope, the Yellow-breasted Chat is known or suspected to breed along Coyote, San Felipe, Vallecito, and Boundary/Carrizo creeks, as well as at Agua Caliente Springs (M26; three singing males 27 April 1998, D. C. Seals), in Canebrake Canyon (N27; two singing males 25 April 1998, M. U. Evans), and at Carrizo Marsh (O29; up to six on 6 May 1998, P. D. Jorgensen). Desert numbers are largest along the larger creeks, Coyote (up to 17 at Lower Willows, D23, 12 May 2001, B. L. Peterson) and San Felipe (up to 15, including 10 singing males, in San Felipe Valley, I21, 13 June 1999, J. O. Zimmer).

Nesting: Yellow-breasted Chats hide their nests in extensive thickets of dense vegetation, making them difficult to find. Almost all evidence of breeding that atlas observers reported was sightings of fledglings or adults carrying insects. These observations correspond closely with the range of dates of the 50 egg sets collected from 1889 to 1948, 4 May–6 July. The one exception is a record of an adult carrying food to young at the east end of Sweetwater Reservoir (S13) 8 May 1998 (P. Famolaro); this date implies eggs laid by 27 April.

Migration: Yellow-breasted Chats usually return to San Diego County in the second week of April. The schedule of their arrival varies somewhat from year to year; during the atlas' five-year term dates of first reports ranged from 26 March to 17 April. Arrival of chats in March,

as observed in 1997, had not been reported previously (one at the east of Sweetwater Reservoir 26 March 1997, P. Famolaro; three along the Sweetwater River near Highway 94, R13, 31 March 1997, D. and M. Hastings). Migrants are seen only rarely away from breeding habitat, most often at desert oases. Our 12 records of such migrants during the atlas' term ranged from 17 April (1999, one at Dos Cabezas Spring, S29, A. P. and T. E. Keenan) to 17 May (1999, one at Yaqui Well, I24, P. K. Nelson). Fall migration begins by early August, as attested by one at Cabrillo National Monument (S7) 3 August 2001 (J. L. Coatsworth). Most birds depart in mid September, with only rare stragglers seen later in the fall.

Winter: There are only two records for the Yellow-breasted Chat in San Diego County as late as December, of one at Otay (V11) 2 December 1973 (AB 28:694, 1974) and one in the Tijuana River valley (V10) 16 December 2000 (W. E. Haas). Possibly these were late fall migrants rather than wintering birds.

Conservation: Stephens (1919a) called the Yellow-breasted Chat "rather common" in San Diego County; Willett (1933) called it "common" through the lowlands of coastal southern California in general. By the 1970s, however, it was uncommon, with a count of six in a day being high (Unitt 1984). The chat evidently fell into the same trap as the Willow Flycatcher and Bell's Vireo, suffering simultaneously from the widespread destruction of riparian woodland and the invasion of the Brown-headed Cowbird. The chat is known as a common cowbird host over much of its range (Friedmann 1963), including southern California (e.g., Hanna 1928). The chat's recent rebound has taken place since cowbird trapping was initiated and appears concentrated where that trapping has been focused. Nevertheless, other factors play a role too. The rate of destruction of riparian woodland slowed after the Least Bell's Vireo was designated as endangered in 1986, and some habitat has regenerated, especially in the Tijuana River valley and at the heads of reservoirs.

Taxonomy: Only the western subspecies *I. v. auricollis* (Deppe, 1830) is yet known from California.

TANAGERS — FAMILY THRAUPIDAE

Hepatic Tanager *Piranga flava*

The Hepatic Tanager enjoys a broad range, spreading from Arizona and New Mexico south to Argentina. In California, however, there are only a few breeding pairs, in the San Bernardino Mountains and the mountains of the eastern Mojave Desert. In San Diego County the species is a vagrant, with 22 reported so far, all in fall and winter.

Migration: Fourteen Hepatic Tanagers have been reported in San Diego in fall, 12 from Point Loma (S7), two from the Tijuana River valley. Dates for these are mainly in late September and October; one at Point Loma 10–18 September 1988 (J. Oldenettel, AB 43:170, 1989) was

Photo by Alan M. Craig

exceptionally early. One that returned three successive years to winter at Point Loma arrived as early as 4 October in 1985 (V. P. Johnson, AB 40:160, 1986). It also set the record for late departure, being seen as late as 8 April in 1985 (R. E. Webster, AB 39:351, 1985). Two early spring records are also of birds that possibly wintered locally: Point Loma 9 April 1966 (AFN 20:547, 1966) and Agua Caliente Springs (M26) 9 March 1974 (AB 28:694, 1974). A unique vagrant in late spring was at Point Loma 11 June 2002 (R. E. Webster, NAB 56:358, 2002).

Winter: Six Hepatic Tanagers are known to have wintered in San Diego County. At Poway (M11), one first seen 18 December 1960 was collected 31 December, providing California's first record of the Hepatic Tanager and San Diego County's only specimen (SDNHM 30257, Huey 1961b). Other sites where the species has wintered are the grounds of the Rosicrucian Fellowship, Oceanside (H5; female in three consecutive winters, 1977–79; male in four consecutive winters, 1978–81), the Mission Hills area of San Diego (R8/R9; 1967–68, AFN 22:480, 1968), Point Loma (male in three consecutive winters, 1983–86), and Bonita (T11; 1987–88, G. McCaskie, AB 42:323, 1988).

Taxonomy: *Piranga f. hepatica* Swainson, 1827, is the subspecies of the Hepatic Tanager reaching California; it ranges from Arizona south through the Sierra Madre Occidental of Mexico.

Summer Tanager *Piranga rubra*

One of the more exciting events of the San Diego County Bird Atlas' five-year term was the first discovery of the Summer Tanager nesting in the county. Though the population in the species' core California range along the Colorado River collapsed, leading to its designation as a species of special concern by the California Department of Fish and Game, the Summer Tanager has pioneered west, colonizing new sites in the Mojave Desert and on the Kern River. The tanager's arrival as a nesting bird in San Diego County is part of this trend. The western subspecies occurs as a rare and localized summer visitor only, in mature riparian woodland, but the eastern subspecies of the Summer Tanager occurs as a rare migrant and winter visitor every year, usually in ornamental trees near the coast.

Breeding distribution: The Summer Tanager inhabits mature riparian woodland, especially where Fremont cot-

Photo by Anthony Mercieca

tonwoods form a fairly continuous canopy. The largest colony in San Diego County is along San Felipe Creek, from 1.5 miles west of Scissors Crossing to Sentenac Ciénaga (J22/J23). Here, the species was first noted 20 May 1998 (E. C. Hall) and increased to seven nesting pairs in 2001, eight in 2002, then dropped to five in 2003 (P. D. Jorgensen, J. R. Barth). Thorough surveys in the last three years were made possible when the area was added to Anza–Borrego Desert State Park. Nearby were two pairs along Banner Creek near Banner (K21) in 2001 (feeding fledglings 16 July 2001, P. D. Jorgensen) and one singing male along San Felipe Creek near Paroli Spring (I21) 9 June–21 July 2000 (J. O. Zimmer, P. D. Jorgensen). Elsewhere in the Anza–Borrego Desert, the Summer Tanager occurs in Coyote Creek Canyon at both Middle Willows (C22; singing male 28 May 1998, P. D. Jorgensen) and Lower Willows (D23; only single birds 2000–2001, but at least one pair and up to four males 13 May–9 July

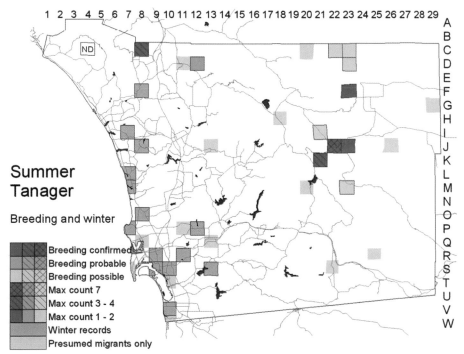

Summer Tanager

Breeding and winter

Breeding confirmed
Breeding probable
Breeding possible
Max count 7
Max count 3 - 4
Max count 1 - 2
Winter records
Presumed migrants only

2002, J. R. Barth). In Borrego Palm Canyon, near the confluence of the middle and south forks (F23), there was one individual in the summers of 1997 and 2001, a singing male and a female carrying insects 30 June–3 July 2000 (L. J. Hargrove). Along Vallecito Creek near Campbell Grade (M23), one on 11 May 2001 was on a date when the species is still migrating, but in riparian woodland similar to that where it nests elsewhere on the desert slope (R. Thériault).

Summer Tanagers colonized the Santa Margarita River north of Fallbrook (C8) in 2000. The following year there were five pairs, with at least two confirmed breeding on the basis of males carrying insects 24 July 2001 (K. L. Weaver). The only other Summer Tanager nestings known from the coastal slope of southern California are from Soledad Canyon and near San Dimas, Los Angeles County, beginning in 1995 (Los Angeles County bird atlas data). Along the Santa Margarita River the birds are associated more with tall sycamores than with cottonwoods. Along the San Luis Rey River, one Summer Tanager was near Pala (D11) 2 July 1993 (J. C. Lovio, AB 47:1151, 1993), at least one remained in Wilderness Gardens (D11/D12) 13 May–4 June 2000 (K. L. Weaver et al.), and a pair was in nearby Marion Canyon (D12), elevation 1600 feet, 18 June–17 July 2001 (K. L. Weaver). Up to three Summer Tanagers have occurred irregularly in summer along the San Diego River at Old Mission Dam (P11) since 1968 (one 8–13 August 2000, M. B. Stowe). An apparent pair of Summer Tanagers, the male singing, on Cuyamaca Peak (M20) 10–18 June 2000 (G. L. Rogers, G. Hazard) was in pine/oak woodland seemingly inappropriate for nesting. An earlier parallel record was of one at Pine Hills (K19) 22–24 June 1987 (V. P. Johnson, AB 41:1489, 1987).

Other records from April to June more likely represent late winter visitors or spring vagrants of the eastern subspecies, but some could be pioneers of the western subspecies, especially one near the confluence of Cottonwood and La Posta creeks (S22) 9 May 1998 (R. and S. L. Breisch) and one at Seventeen Palms (G29) 2 May 1997 (G. Rebstock, K. Forney). The subspecies are readily distinguished only with the bird in hand.

Nesting: Although the Summer Tanager typically builds its nest far out on the longer branches of trees, over an opening (Robinson 1996), five nests found along San Felipe Creek 2000–2002 were near the trunks or major branches of often spindly trees, cottonwood and red willow, 30–50 feet above the ground (P. D. Jorgensen, J. R. Barth). These nests were built of a dark material and so sparsely lined that light passed through them (P. D. Jorgensen).

Reflecting its name, the Summer Tanager nests in midsummer. Data from San Felipe Creek, including those from 2002 not plotted here, imply the Summer Tanager lays from early June (fledgling 29 June 2002) to early July (nest building 3 July 2002, J. R. Barth). Along the Santa Margarita River, nesting appears even later, with three observations of adults carrying insects 24 July–5 August (K. L. Weaver). The lateness there may be due to the birds

taking longer to find each other in a sparse, newly colonizing population.

Migration: Data are still skimpy, but breeding Summer Tanagers evidently arrive in late April or at the beginning of May. The earliest dates are 26 April 2003 at Scissors Crossing (J. R. Barth) and 1 May 2001 at Lower Willows (D. C. Seals). In 2002, when arrival of Summer Tanagers along San Felipe Creek was watched for almost daily, the first appeared 1 May (R. Thériault). Five were still at Scissors Crossing 8 September 2000 (P. D. Jorgensen). Along the lower Colorado River, specimens have been collected as late as 24 September (SDNHM 9990, 33708, 33718).

The eastern subspecies of the Summer Tanager follows a completely different pattern. In spring, its schedule is like that of other eastern vagrants, shifted late in the season. Records extend from at least 11 May (1992, one male found dead at Coronado, S9, SDNHM 48027) to at least 18 June (1998, one near Chollas Reservoir, R11, P. Unitt). One at Solana Beach (L7) 13 July 1991 (R. T. Patton, AB 45:1162, 1991) was most likely a vagrant from the east as well. The Summer Tanager occurs annually in spring, with nine records 1997–2001.

In fall, the eastern subspecies begins showing up definitely by 19 September (1932, one at Point Loma, S7, SDNHM 16134) and presumably by 9 September (1977, four in the Tijuana River valley, L. C. Binford; 1994, one in Borrego Springs, G24, P. D. Jorgensen). It is more numerous in fall than in spring, though still to be considered rare. There is no clear break between fall and winter records, though one at Yaqui Well (I24) 22 November 1962 (AFN 17:71, 1963) was still migrating. Winter visitors may remain into early April (one at Bonsall, F8, 7 April 2000, P. A. Ginsburg; one at Point Loma 7 April 2000, V. P. Johnson; one at El Cajon, Q13, 8 April 1998, K. Neal).

Winter: The Summer Tanager winters annually in San Diego County's coastal lowland, in much the same habitat as the Western Tanager: exotic flowering and fruiting trees, mainly in urban parks. Numbers are somewhat smaller than those of the Western Tanager, but 22 wintering individuals were reported 1997–2002. Winter records extend inland as far as Bonsall (F8; one on 17 January 2000, P. A. Ginsburg), Santee (P12; up to two from 12 January to 3 February 2001, M. B. Mulrooney), and 0.9 mile east of Dictionary Hill (S13; one from 12 to 19 January 2002, R. Norgaard). The Summer Tanager was recorded on 30 of 39 San Diego Christmas bird counts 1963–2001, with a maximum of five in 1984. It is less frequent on the Oceanside and Rancho Santa Fe counts, with up to three on the latter in 1990.

Conservation: The Summer Tanager's history in California is remarkable. In the late 19th and early 20th centuries, the species was known as a breeding bird only along the Colorado River, where it was common. In the mid to late 20th century, following the building of the dams and the nearly total elimination of the native riparian forest, the population crashed, until in 1986 only three males were known persisting on the California side (Rosenberg et al.

1991). At the same time the population along the river was in free fall, however, the Summer Tanager began colonizing riparian oases farther west (Johnson 1994). Thus forces acting at cross purposes must be controlling the population.

Even if broad-scale factors are inducing the Summer Tanager to expand its range, there must be habitat to host the pioneers. Thus maintenance and enhancement of mature riparian woodland are essential. Clearing, burning, off-road vehicles, excessive groundwater pumping, and invasion of exotic plants are all continuing threats to Summer Tanager habitat elsewhere in California. Without careful management these factors could degrade the habitat in San Diego County as well. The inclusion of most of the sites in Anza–Borrego Desert State Park and the California Department of Fish and Game's San Felipe

Valley Wildlife Area gives the Summer Tanager a head start in San Diego County.

Taxonomy: I confirmed the identity of the locally breeding population of the Summer Tanager as the western subspecies *P. r. cooperi* Ridgway, 1869, with the trapping, measuring, and electronic colorimetry of two males and one female at Scissors Crossing in 2002. All five specimens of migrants and winter visitors, however, are the eastern *P. r. rubra* (Linnaeus, 1758), which is smaller and darker in both sexes. As detailed by Rea (1972), throughout southern California nonbreeding Summer Tanagers are of the eastern subspecies prevails; only one exception is known, from Ventura County. The pattern has only been reinforced further as additional specimens have accumulated.

Scarlet Tanager *Piranga olivacea*

The Scarlet Tanager is a vagrant to California, as it nests only east of the Rocky Mountains and winters in South America. Nevertheless, there are about 35 records for San Diego County (nearly one third of all for California), three in spring, the remainder in fall.

Migration: The California Bird Records Committee has accepted 26 records of the Scarlet Tanager from San Diego County in fall; another nine have not been submitted or are still pending. The species thus averages about one per year, though with some irregularity. There were none 1970–76 but five in 2001. Most of the reports are from Point Loma (S7); six are from elsewhere near the coast, inland as far as Otay Mesa (V13). Dates of accepted records range from 5 October (2000, Point Loma, G. McCaskie; McKee and Erickson 2002) to 17 November (1969, Point Loma, Bevier 1990); unsubmitted records range from 29 September (1987, Point Loma, R. E. Webster, AB 42:139, 1988) to 30 November (1997, Tecolote Canyon, Q9, K. Radamaker, FN 52:128, 1998).

Photo by Anthony Mercieca

Howell and Pyle (1997) questioned an unseasonably early report, 24–26 August 1994 (NASFN 49:103, 1995).

The three spring records are from Point Loma 26–28 May 1979 (Binford 1983) and 29 May–2 June 1983 (L. R. Santaella; Morlan 1985) and from Coronado (S9) 7 May 1987 (E. Copper; Langham 1991).

Western Tanager *Piranga ludoviciana*

The Western Tanager's splash of color marks the peak of spring migration through San Diego County. The birds also nest in the pine–oak forests of the county's mountains, where they are generally uncommon. In fall migration the Western Tanager is less conspicuous than in spring, but adults pass through in late July and August, immatures largely in September and early October. In winter the species is rare but regular, occurring almost exclusively in urban parks. Indeed, the Western Tanager was the first species known to shift its range to take advantage of this novel habitat.

Breeding distribution: The Western Tanager's breeding distribution in San Diego County corresponds to

Photo by Anthony Mercieca

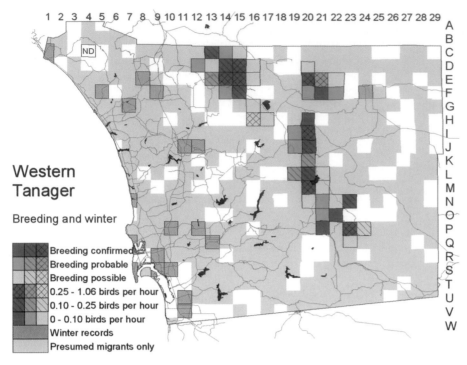

Western
Tanager

Breeding and winter

Breeding confirmed
Breeding probable
Breeding possible
0.25 - 1.06 birds per hour
0.10 - 0.25 birds per hour
0 - 0.10 birds per hour
Winter records
Presumed migrants only

Nesting: Western Tanagers typically nest in the middle to upper levels of trees, often placing the nests atop the outer branches of conifers (Hudon 1999). With the species uncommon and its nest built in the canopy, atlas observers noted few nests. The two described were in a big-cone Douglas fir and a willow, 18 to 25 feet above the ground. Most breeding confirmations were of adults carrying insects, on dates ranging from 20 May to 19 July. These and other data suggest that in San Diego County Western Tanagers lay from early May to early July, a wider spread than the 6–27 June of five egg sets collected 1915–20.

Migration: As a migrant the Western Tanager occurs county-wide. From 1997 to 2001 the

the higher mountains supporting stands of conifers and black oaks. In this habitat the birds are typically uncommon; high counts are of 28 (10 singing males) on Middle Peak (M20) 11 June 2000 (R. E. Webster), 12 (10 singing males) near the summit of Hot Springs Mountain (E20) 18 June 2000 (K. L. Weaver, C. R. Mahrdt), and 11 (8 singing males) near Palomar Observatory (D15) 1 July 1999 (K. L. Weaver). In southern San Diego County the downslope limit for breeding Western Tanagers is around 3600 feet elevation at Pine Valley (P21; two feeding young 7 July 1998, J. K. Wilson). In the northern half of the county breeding tanagers extend down to 3200 feet at the northeast base of Volcan Mountain (H20; fledglings in summer 1999, A. P. and T. E. Keenan). Apparently a few birds summer around Mesa Grande (3200–3300 feet; H16/H17), where there are many black oaks but few conifers (e.g., one tanager along Mesa Grande Road, H16, 17 June 1998, C. G. Edwards). Along the San Luis Rey River below Lake Henshaw many mountain birds extend to unusually low elevations, but the only midsummer record of a Western Tanager there is of a single male near the San Luis Rey Picnic Ground (2600 feet; G16) 3 July 1999 (W. E. Haas). In the deep canyons cutting the southwest face of Palomar Mountain, however, Western Tanagers summer down to 2000 feet, among big-cone Douglas firs (four singing males along Pauma Creek, E13, 7 June 2001, P. Unitt; two singing males along Agua Tibia Creek, D12, 18 June 2001, K. L. Weaver).

Scattered Western Tanagers, evidently nonbreeding, show up rarely at odd localities through the summer (one at Fallbrook, D8, 21 June 2000, M. Freda; one near Puerta La Cruz, E18, 23 June 2000, A. P. and T. E. Keenan; one near Warner's Ranch, G19, 24 June 2000, E. C. Hall; one at Fernbrook, M14, 24 June 2000, B. Hendricks; two at Torrey Pines State Reserve, N7, 1 July 2001, J. Lesley).

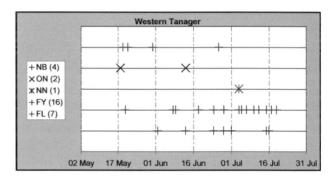

spring's first date for arriving Western Tanagers ranged from 3 to 15 April. The earliest record, of two in Boden Canyon (I14) 3 April 1999 (R. L. Barber), is exceptionally early for California. But the recurrence of early April arrivals since 1998 may foreshadow a shift in the species' migration schedule (compare also Patten et al. 2003); mid April arrival had long been the rule (Garrett and Dunn 1981). Still, spring migrants do not become common until late April, and their numbers vary from year to year. The birds occasionally concentrate in large numbers, with up to 100 at the University of California, San Diego (O8), 5 May 1999 (L. Myklebust) and 200 at Tecate (V19) 1 May 1999 (M. and B. McIntosh). Past years occasionally saw even larger numbers, up to 500 at Pauma Valley (E12) 16 May 1942 (E. Beemer) and 1000 at Bonita (T11) 1 May 1964 (AFN 18:488, 1964). Migrants are still frequent in small numbers in the first week of June, and stragglers occur through the second week. Latest, if not summering, were one near Rincon (F13) 12 June 1999 (E. Wallace) and one in Carlsbad (I7) 14 June 1998 (E. Garnica).

Adults begin heading south in mid July, possibly even early July (one at Scissors Crossing, J22, 3–6 July 2001, P. D. Jorgensen; two near Rincon, F13, 8 July 2000, M. B.

Mosher), and have all departed by the end of August. The immatures, by contrast, begin appearing at low elevations only in late August, then continue in dwindling numbers through October. In fall, adults avoid the coast; only immatures are normally seen there.

Winter: At this season the Western Tanager is confined to the coastal lowland, to parks and residential areas well wooded with exotic trees. It is most numerous in Balboa Park (R9; three west of Highway 163 on 16 December 2000, J. K. Wilson; three on the grounds of the San Diego Zoo 15 December 2001, V. P. Johnson). Wintering birds can often be heard calling from the tops of tall eucalyptus and fig trees near the San Diego Natural History Museum. The highest winter number recorded is 21 on the San Diego Christmas bird count, 19 December 1981. Elsewhere records are scattered from San Onofre (C1; one on 11 January 1999, M. Lesinsky) to the Tijuana River valley (V11; one on 16 December 2000, G.

McCaskie). The records farthest inland are from 2.5 miles east of Bonsall (F9; two on 12 December 1999, J. Evans), Kit Carson Park, Escondido (J11; two on 2 February 1999, M. B. Stowe; one on 30 December 2000 and 27–29 December 2001, K. L. Weaver), and El Cajon (Q13; one on 15 January 2001, J. R. Barth). One in Borrego Springs (F24) 1 December 1998 (M. L. Gabel) was likely a late fall migrant, though there are three winter records for the Salton Sink (Patten et al. 2003).

Conservation: No changes to San Diego County's breeding population of the Western Tanager are known; the species has always been uncommon as a breeding bird. The species' wintering came only with the planting of exotic trees that flower and fruit through that season. The first winter reports, from National City, were in the 1920s (Johnson 1922, 1928), and only since 1956 have wintering Western Tanagers been noted annually.

NEW WORLD SPARROWS AND BUNTINGS — FAMILY EMBERIZIDAE

Green-tailed Towhee *Pipilo chlorurus*

The few Green-tailed Towhees breeding high in the Cuyamaca Mountains represent an outpost well isolated from the nearest other populations, in the San Jacinto and Santa Rosa mountains to the north and in the Sierra San Pedro Mártir to the south. Like that of the Yellow-rumped Warbler, Dusky Flycatcher, and Fox Sparrow, the Green-tailed Towhee's preferred habitat of montane chaparral and young conifers is barely touched by San Diego County's highest mountains. Just as the county lies near the southern margin of the species' breeding range, it lies near the northern margin of the winter range,

Photo by Anthony Mercieca

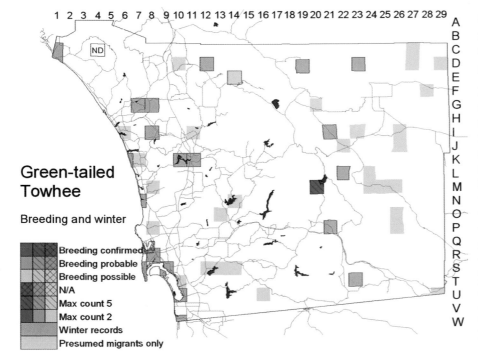

so the Green-tailed Towhee is rare in winter. Even in migration the species largely skips over San Diego County.

Breeding distribution: During the atlas period, breeding Green-tailed Towhees were seen only near the summits of Cuyamaca and Middle peaks (M20). Their distribution thus closely resembles that of the Fox Sparrow, with which they share the same habitat. On Cuyamaca Peak Green-tailed Towhees occur along the fire road above 5700 feet elevation in chaparral and bracken fern. From 1997 to 2001, the high count there was of five on 5 June 2001 (M. B. Mulrooney). On Middle Peak, the towhees have been seen on the west slope between 4600 and 5000 feet elevation, with a high count of three, including two singing males, 2 July 2000 (R. E. Webster)

The observations of up to two on Hot Springs Mountain in June 1980 (E20/E21; Unitt 1981) and one at the Palomar Observatory (D15) 24 August 1981 (C. G. Edwards) have not been repeated since.

Nesting: During the atlas period, the only confirmations of Green-tailed Towhee breeding were observations of birds building nests on Cuyamaca Peak 22 May 1998 (G. L. Rogers) and 5 June 2001 (M. B. Mulrooney). A juvenile was accompanying adults there 29 July 1978 (AB 32:1210, 1978). The nest is usually well hidden within a dense-foliaged shrub or small tree. On the Mogollon Rim of Arizona, Dobbs et al. (1998) found nests predominantly in white firs, also available in the Green-tailed Towhee's habitat in San Diego County.

Migration: The Green-tailed Towhee is recorded in its breeding habitat in the Cuyamaca Mountains from 19 May (1998, R. E. Webster) to 27 August (1978, D. W. Povey, Unitt 1984); records from elsewhere in the Green-tailed Towhee's breeding range suggest these dates could be extended three or four weeks in both directions.

In spite of breeding commonly in the Sierra Nevada and Transverse Ranges and wintering commonly in southern Baja California, the Green-tailed Towhee is rare as a migrant through San Diego County, suggesting most birds fly nonstop over southern California. Fall migration extends from early September to mid November, spring migration from early April to mid May. From 1997 to 2001 spring dates extended from 4 April (1999, one at the Paradise Creek marsh, National City, T10, W. E. Haas; 1998, two in a cowbird trap in Goat Canyon, W10, J. M. Wells) to 14 May (1998, one near Scissors Crossing, J22, E. C. Hall). Of the 31 spring records during this period, the only ones of more than a single individual were of four at Vallecito (M25) 12 May 1999 (M. C. Jorgensen) and the two in the cowbird trap (one of which was trapped again four days later). Spring migrants appear somewhat more numerous in the eastern half of the county than in the western half: 14 records in the west versus 17 in the east, in spite of nearly 50% more observer-hours in the field in the west. Massey (1998) also reported several April

records in the Anza–Borrego Desert. Near the coast, an unseasonal straggler was in a condominium complex just northeast of Kate Sessions Park (P8) 10 June 1999 (J. Moore).

Winter: The Green-tailed Towhee is rare in San Diego County at this season, though hardly more so than in migration. It does not have a clear habitat preference in winter, other than dense low shrubbery, often near water. From 1997 to 2002 we recorded about 21 individual wintering Green-tailed Towhees, 15 in the coastal lowland. Only one record is of more than a single bird: two were at Lake Hodges (K10) 23 December 1998 (R. T. Patton). Some individuals were observed repeatedly through the winter, and at least two, at Point Loma Nazarene University (S7) and the Chula Vista Nature Center (U10), returned for three consecutive years. We noted six Green-tailed Towhees farther inland, where there are only a couple of earlier records, on Lake Henshaw and Anza–Borrego Christmas bird counts. Three were in canyons draining into the desert, while three were scattered in chaparral-dominated landscapes at higher elevations: one at 2800 feet elevation near La Posta microwave tower (T23) 22 January 2000 (G. Rebstock), one at 3600 feet at Indian Flats (D19) 6 January 1999 (K. J. Burns), and one at 3700 feet at a bird feeder in Pine Valley (P21) 24 December 1998 (J. K. Wilson).

Conservation: On the scale of the species' entire range, there is no clear evidence of population change (Dobbs et al. 1998). As a bird of undergrowth and second growth, the Green-tailed Towhee colonizes logged forest (Franzreb and Ohmart 1978). Persisting continuously since its discovery on Cuyamaca Peak in 1974, the Green-tailed Towhee seems well established there, though populations so small are vulnerable to extirpation. In winter, the Green-tailed Towhee has become less frequent since the 1960s and 1970s, at least around metropolitan San Diego, the region of most early records. The maximum on a San Diego Christmas bird count, eight on 20 December 1969, is implausible today. From 1980 to 1992, the Green-tailed Towhee was recorded on 8 of 13 counts, but from 1993 to 2001 it was recorded on only one. Most likely the decrease is a result of the elimination of weedy thickets as more and more of the count circle was urbanized.

Spotted Towhee *Pipilo maculatus*

The Spotted Towhee is one of the most common birds—perhaps the most common bird—of chaparral. A study near Pine Valley comparing bird abundance in mature and recovering chaparral found the Spotted Towhee the most numerous species in stands averaging both 30 and 6 years after a fire, though the Wrentit was a close second (Cleveland National Forest data). A year-round resident, the towhee is just as common in the understory of riparian, oak, and coniferous woodland but much sparser where the shrubs are sparser, as in coastal sage

Photo by Anthony Mercieca

scrub and desert-edge scrub. Poorly adapted to urbanization, the Spotted Towhee is beginning to see its range erode as a result of habitat fragmentation.

Breeding distribution: The Spotted Towhee occurs almost uniformly over the coastal slope. High numbers have been recorded in both the mountains (up to 170 in Matagual Valley, H19, 18 June 2000, S. E. Smith, B. E. Bell) and the coastal lowland (up to 115 along the Santa Margarita River north of Fallbrook, C8, K. L. Weaver). The Spotted Towhee is somewhat less numerous along the central and southern coast of San Diego County, dominated by developed areas and sage scrub. The remnant patches of

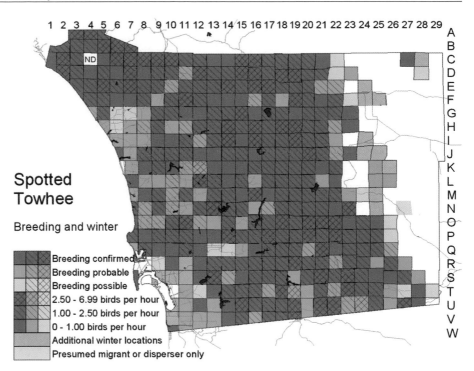

Spotted Towhee

Breeding and winter

- Breeding confirmed
- Breeding probable
- Breeding possible
- 2.50 - 6.99 birds per hour
- 1.00 - 2.50 birds per hour
- 0 - 1.00 birds per hour
- Additional winter locations
- Presumed migrant or disperser only

native habitat in the 11 atlas squares around San Diego where breeding Spotted Towhees are lacking have almost no chaparral—though some have appreciable sage scrub. The Spotted Towhee generally inhabits sage scrub only if it contains lemonadeberry or laurel sumac shrubs, in whose leaf litter the birds forage (M. A. Patten pers. comm.). On the east slopes of the mountains, the Spotted Towhee inhabits desert-edge scrub with shrubs like desert scrub oak and sugarbush and descends in riparian scrub to Lower Willows, Coyote Creek Canyon (D23; up to four on 24 May 2000, J. R. Barth), and Sentenac Canyon (J23; up to seven on 7 June 2000, R. Thériault). At some points on the eastern margin of the range the Spotted Towhee is apparently irregular: mesquite thicket near east end of Vallecito Valley (M24), two on 9 May 2001 (P. K. Nelson); Inner Pasture (N25), one on 6 April 2000 (M. B. Mulrooney); and upper end of Indian Valley (P26), one on 9 May 1998 and 30 April 2000 (P. R. Pryde). In high-desert scrub, junipers, and pinyons, the Spotted Towhee extends into San Diego County along the spine of the Santa Rosa Mountains from Rabbit to Villager Peak (C27; up to nine on 17 June 2001, R. Thériault); a few birds are isolated east of a deep chasm in the pinyon grove near benchmark Rosa (D28; up to two on 2 May 2000, L. J. Hargrove). Another isolated population lives in similar habitat in the upper elevations of the Vallecito Mountains (K25/L25/L26; maximum count seven on the east slope of Whale Peak, L26, 12 April 2000, J. R. Barth).

Nesting: The Spotted Towhee usually nests on the ground, concealing the nest in leaf litter or under low-growing plants like snowberry, skunkbrush, mugwort, California rose, or clumps of grass. Nests as high as 12 feet have been reported in Alameda County (Cohen 1899), but San Diego County bird atlas observers described no nest higher than 1 foot off the ground. Of 45 nests studied by

M. A. Patten (pers. comm.) around San Diego 2001–02, 44 were on the ground; one was 36 cm above the ground in a white sage. Patten found the nests under a variety of plants, including dead wood, but noted the birds avoided nesting deep within the cover of large shrubs, choosing instead small shrubs, herbs, grass, or the outer edge of a large shrub, where its branches hang near the ground.

Our observations suggest the Spotted Towhee begins laying around the end of March or first of April; Patten's egg dates extended from 2 April to 26 June. An egg set collected at Escondido 11 March 1900 (C. S. Sharp, WFVZ 86710) was exceptionally early. The nesting season continues into July; a nest with three eggs along Pilgrim Creek, Oceanside (F6), 8 July 2000 (B. L. Peterson) was slightly later than the 4 July date of the latest of 31 egg sets collected in San Diego County 1898–1940.

Migration: There is little evidence of Spotted Towhee migration in San Diego County. The only spring record clearly outside the breeding range is of one at Palm Spring (N27) 24–27 April 1998 (D. C. Seals, S. Peters).

Winter: The Spotted Towhee remains year round even at high elevations. In winter, a few birds disperse a short distance, resulting in records from most of the urban squares

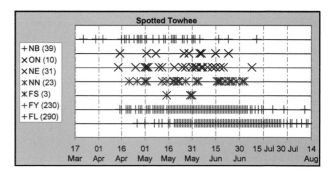

in San Diego where the species does not breed. None of these records is more than 4 miles from breeding habitat; two at the Chula Vista Nature Center (U10) 8 December 2001 (B. C. Moore) had moved the farthest. Similarly, the Spotted Towhee is a rare winter visitor to the Anza–Borrego Desert outside the breeding range. The 11 such records 1997–2002 were all of one or two individuals, and none was farther than 6 miles from breeding habitat (one at Ellis Farms nursery, F25, 17 December 2000, L. J. Hargrove, P. Unitt).

Conservation: As a ground nester, the Spotted Towhee is ill equipped to survive in the urban environment, and it is absent from heavily developed areas. Crooks et al. (2001) investigated its response to habitat fragmentation in San Diego in 1997, finding it in 17 of 30 urban canyons, consistently only in the six fragments of greater than 30 hectares. The towhee occurred in 11 of 24 fragments of 2 to 15 hectares. Two of these had been recolonized since 1987, and the towhee had disappeared from none of the fragments where it had been noted at the time of that initial study. Crooks et al. reported two Spotted Towhees in residential development 250–750 meters from Mission Trails Regional Park, revealing some capability for dispersal across unsuitable habitat, and they suggested that recolonization of habitat fragments could take place during the nonbreeding season—as attested by atlas results. Their analysis suggested that the size of a habitat fragment is the most important factor governing the likelihood of the Spotted Towhee inhabiting it, but that the time since the fragment was isolated plays a role as well. Crooks et

al. did not consider, however, another likely factor: the type of habitat within a fragment. Bolger et al. (1997), addressing the question at a somewhat coarser scale, did not identify the Spotted Towhee as strongly affected by fragmentation but did find that its abundance increased significantly with distance from development. Sensitivity to fragmentation can be measured in various ways, but the results of Crooks et al. and Bolger et al. imply that the Spotted Towhee is moderately sensitive—less so than the California Quail, Greater Roadrunner, and Rufous-crowned, Sage, and Lark Sparrows, more so than the Wrentit, Bewick's Wren, and California Towhee. Lovio (1996), studying less-isolated fragments in the Spring Valley/Jamacha region (R12/R13/R14/S12/S13), found the Spotted Towhee in 29 of 36 habitat fragments, including all nine greater than 15 hectares.

Taxonomy: Only coastal southern California's resident subspecies of Spotted Towhee, *P. m. megalonyx* Baird, 1858, is known from San Diego County. It is boldly spotted with white but otherwise represents the dark extreme of the species: the blackish parts of the female's plumage are almost as black as the male's; even her rump is almost black. The paler (female especially) subspecies *P. m. curtatus* Grinnell, 1911, from the northern Great Basin and intermountain region reaches the Salton Sink and lower Colorado River as a rare winter visitor. It is so far unknown from San Diego County but could reach the Anza–Borrego Desert; a specimen would be needed to confirm it.

California Towhee *Pipilo crissalis*

The California Towhee is one of the dominant birds of coastal sage scrub. It is also common in chaparral (especially where broken by openings), riparian scrub, high-desert scrub, and the undergrowth of riparian and oak woodland. It is famed for its sedentary nature, mated pairs remaining for life in one territory. The California Towhee adapts fairly well to urban life, readily moving into parks and residential areas wherever these offer a certain density of shrubbery for nesting and unpaved ground surface for foraging.

Breeding distribution: The California Towhee covers almost the entire coastal slope of San Diego County except the Coronado peninsula, the most densely built parts of cities, and the forested summits of the highest mountains. Even in the long-developed parts of San Diego, there remains enough habitat for the towhee in every atlas block except R7 and S8, incomplete squares that lack any native scrub. The species is distinctly more numerous in the coastal lowland than at higher elevations, but it was still found in every foothill and mountain square surveyed except D14 (Palomar Mountain), E20 (summit of Hot Springs Mountain), M20 (Cuyamaca Peak), and O23 (Mount Laguna).

Photo by Anthony Mercieca

On the east slopes of the mountains the California Towhee is uncommon but widespread even in sparse desert-edge scrub. Only in creosote bush scrub on the desert floor does it drop out completely. Mesquite thickets offer it good habitat in canyons (maximum 25 at Vallecito, M25, 27 April 1998, M. C. Jorgensen), yet it is absent from the mesquite bosque on the floor of the Borrego Valley. The birds also range into the Santa Rosa Mountains (maximum three on the east slope, C28, 2 May 2000, R. Thériault) and Vallecito Mountains (maximum seven on the east slope of Whale Peak, L26, 12 April 2000, J. R. Barth).

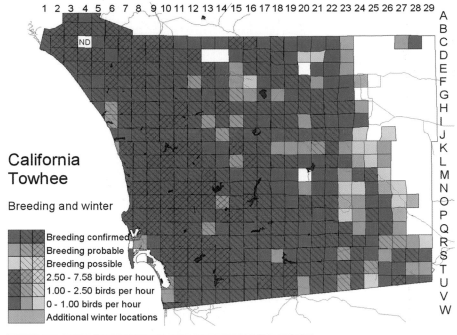

California Towhee

Breeding and winter

Breeding confirmed
Breeding probable
Breeding possible
2.50 - 7.58 birds per hour
1.00 - 2.50 birds per hour
0 - 1.00 birds per hour
Additional winter locations

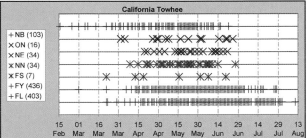

California Towhee

+NB (103)
×ON (16)
×NF (34)
×NN (34)
×FS (7)
+FY (436)
+FL (403)

15 01 16 31 15 30 15 30 14 29 14 29 13
Feb Mar Mar Mar Apr Apr May May Jun Jun Jul Jul Aug

earliest observations of court-ship behavior were 8 February 1998 (a rainy day—female solic-iting copulation in Rancho Cuca, F14, P. Unitt), of nest building 16 February 2001 (near Puerta La Cruz, E18, K. J. Winter), and of fledglings 22 March 1998 (Encanto, S11, P. Unitt).

Winter: Only two records imply winter dispersal of California Towhees out of their breeding range by the width of even one atlas square: two at Borrego Springs (F24) 19 December 1999 (P. K. Nelson) and one in Carrizo Valley east of Highway S2 (O28) 7 February 2002 (P. D. Jorgensen). There is only one record from the Salton Sink (Patten et al. 2003).

Conservation: With its ability to use nonnative habitats, the California Towhee has largely avoided the negative effects of urban sprawl that afflict many other birds that prefer sage scrub. Bolger et al. (1997) identified it as a species insensitive to habitat fragmentation in San Diego, and this is corroborated by our atlas results. High-density development can eliminate the towhee, as it has in some neighborhoods of inner-city San Diego. At the scale of our atlas grid, though, this effect is visible only in the species' absence from Ocean Beach (R7).

Taxonomy: The subspecies of the California Towhee found in coastal southern California and northern Baja California, *P. c. senicula* Anthony, 1895, is a prime exam-ple of the subspecies whose ranges define the San Diegan district of the California Floristic Province. Like the Rufous-crowned Sparrow, Bewick's Wren, Oak Titmouse, and others in this area, it is distinguished by its darker color in comparison to the other subspecies both farther north and farther south.

Nesting: Unlike the Spotted Towhee, the California Towhee seldom places its nest on the ground; more usually it builds in low shrubs, sometimes even in the outer canopy of coast live oaks. The birds commonly use ornamental shrubs and fruit trees as well as native plants. Like many other resident birds, most California Towhees begin laying in the third week of March; 31 egg sets col-lected 1891–1953 range from 16 March to 12 July. During the atlas period, we found a few birds starting two to three weeks earlier, especially in the wet year of 1998. Our

Cassin's Sparrow *Aimophila cassinii*

Cassin's Sparrow normally ranges from southeastern Arizona and the southwestern Great Plains south into mainland Mexico. Though there were small influxes to the Mojave Desert in spring 1978 and 1993, fol-lowing wet winters, the species is a rare vagrant to California. The three records for San Diego County are likely of a single bird returning to the same site.

Migration: San Diego County's one location for Cassin's Sparrow was open sage scrub along Dehesa Road 1 mile east of Granite Hills Drive, El Cajon (Q14). Here a sing-ing male appeared 15–30 May 1970, 8–11 May 1976, and 10–12 June 1978, to be photographed and tape-recorded (S. Oberbauer, M. U. Evans, Roberson 1993). The habitat has since been replaced with a housing development.

Photo by Brian L. Sullivan

Rufous-crowned Sparrow *Aimophila ruficeps*

The Rufous-crowned Sparrow is one of the characteristic birds of coastal sage scrub. Preferring this threatened habitat and sensitive to habitat fragmentation, the sparrow has seen its numbers and range reduced over much of coastal San Diego County. Yet it remains fairly common over wide areas, as it can use steep slopes that discourage development, readily colonizes burned chaparral, and persists in openings in mature chaparral. A year-round resident, the Rufous-crowned Sparrow is rarely seen even a short distance away from the habitat where it breeds.

Photo by Anthony Mercieca

Breeding distribution: The Rufous-crowned Sparrow is widespread over the coastal lowland and foothills of San Diego County in sage scrub, broken or burned chaparral, and grassland with scattered shrubs. Collins (1999) found that its average habitat in northwestern Santa Barbara County is fairly steep south-facing slopes with about 50% cover of low shrubs, and this represents the current situation in San Diego County as well. Sage scrub on gentle rolling hillsides is even more favorable but now greatly reduced and fragmented. The Rufous-crowned Sparrow avoids flat valley floors and floodplains, impenetrable chaparral, woodland, and developed areas. It ranges down to the coast where suitable habitat remains, as in Camp Pendleton, Torrey Pines State Reserve, and Point Loma. The denser populations are at low elevations, as in eastern Camp Pendleton and the Fallbrook Naval Weapons Station (D7, 36 on 4 April 2000, W. E. Haas), from Mission Trails Regional Park and Miramar east to San Vicente Reservoir (N13, 22 on 22 March 1998, C. G. Edwards) and Lake Jennings, and from Sweetwater Reservoir east to Rancho Jamul (T15, 18 on 5 April 2000, P. Unitt). The local distribution shifts with time, though, because the Rufous-crowned Sparrow quickly invades

recovering burned chaparral while it is still dominated by grasses and herbs, then drops out as the chaparral matures. At higher elevations, largely covered with thick chaparral, the species is linked to microhabitats such as rock outcrops or gabbro soil that make for openings or sparser growth. Rocks surrounded by clumps of the giant needlegrass are a frequent clue for the Rufous-crowned Sparrow in San Diego County's foothills. Man-made openings like firebreaks and small abandoned clearings also attract the species. The Rufous-crowned Sparrow largely avoids the mountain zone, being rare above 4000 feet elevation, but occurs almost continuously, though in low density, along the mountains' steep east slope. In the Anza–Borrego Desert it is a rare resident in the Vallecito Mountains (K26, pair on 3 May 2001; L26, two on 10 May 2000, J. R. Barth) and possibly the Santa Rosa Mountains, though all records in the latter are for winter.

Nesting: The Rufous-crowned Sparrow nests primarily on the ground, only rarely in low shrubs. Of 304 nests studied around San Diego by Morrison and Bolger (2002) and M. A. Patten (pers. comm.), 42% were on the ground at the base of a bunchgrass, typically the native purple needlegrass or giant needlegrass, but one pair used an exotic African fountain grass. Other nests (32%) were at the bases of small shrubs like flat-top buckwheat, white sage, and California sagebrush, and most others were among rocks or dirt clods. Only 4% of nests were above ground in low shrubs. Like most resident birds of its habitat, the Rufous-crowned Sparrow usually begins nesting in the third week of March; collected egg sets range from 11 March to 7 June. In 2001, M. A. Patten found 26 nests with eggs between 3 April and 15 June, with nestlings between 6 April and 25 June. A few individuals start earlier: pairs seen carrying insects near the Highway 94

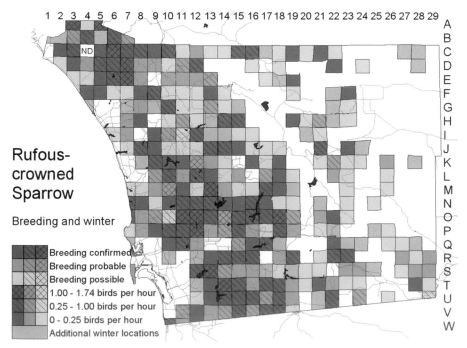

Rufous-crowned Sparrow

Breeding and winter

Breeding confirmed
Breeding probable
Breeding possible
1.00 - 1.74 birds per hour
0.25 - 1.00 birds per hour
0 - 0.25 birds per hour
Additional winter locations

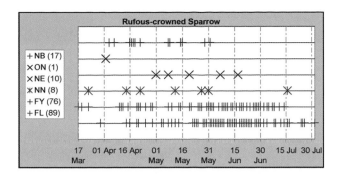

crossing of the Sweetwater River (R13) 17 March 1997 (D. and M. Hastings) and at the De Luz Road crossing of the Santa Margarita River (C7) 19 March 1997 (K. L. Weaver) must have laid in the first week of March, slightly earlier than previously reported. Likewise, a nest with eggs in Pueblitos Canyon (F5) 17 June 1999 (C. Reynolds) and one with nestlings near the summit of Mt. Woodson (L13) 16 July 1997 (P. von Hendy) demonstrate nesting somewhat later than previous records.

Migration: The Rufous-crowned Sparrow is sedentary. Studies with banded birds addressing this issue directly are lacking, but probably juveniles disperse only a few miles from the place where they hatched and adults remain in their established territories for life.

Winter: Few records of the Rufous-crowned Sparrow suggest even short-distance shifting in winter outside its breeding habitat. The birds at higher elevations remain there through the winter, e.g., one at 4290 feet on the ridge 0.5 mile north of the Indian exhibit, Cuyamaca Rancho State Park (N21), 10 February 2000 (J. Fitch) and one at 4640 feet in Scove Canyon (P22) 31 December 1998 (P. Unitt). A couple of records from isolated urban canyons in Pacific Beach (Q7, one on 22 January 2000, L. Polinsky) and East San Diego (R10, one on 20 December 1997, J. A. Dietrick) suggest occasional birds still reach habitat fragments where the species is unable to sustain itself. Other locations where the Rufous-crowned Sparrow was recorded in the winter but not the breeding season are mostly in marginal habitat where the species probably occurs in low density year round. Possible exceptions are in the northeast-draining canyons of the Santa Rosa Mountains (C27/C28/D28) and in the Alma Wash/Starfish Cove area at the east end of the Vallecito Mountains (K28). Winter visits to these areas yielded daily counts of up to five at the east base of the Santa

Rosa Mountains (C28) 20 January 2000 (R. Thériault) and four near Starfish Cove 5 December 1999 (L. J. Hargrove, J. O. Zimmer), but an equal level of effort during the breeding season yielded none. In these very marginal habitats the Rufous-crowned Sparrow may be irregular.

Conservation: The Rufous-crowned Sparrow's susceptibility to habitat fragmentation is attested by multiple studies (e.g., Lovio 1996, Bolger et al. 1997, K. L. Weaver unpubl. data) and is clear in the distribution we observed 1997–2002. The native maritime scrub on Point Loma (S7) is the only site where the species survives far isolated by development. If this is a minimum, and the population is viable indefinitely, it implies that nearly 400 hectares of habitat are necessary to support a self-sustaining population. Lovio (1996) found the Rufous-crowned Sparrow consistently only in tracts of scrub of 17 hectares or greater; the habitat fragments he studied were less isolated in both space and time than Point Loma. Morrison and Bolger (2002) reported the sparrow's abundance in small, isolated habitat fragments (1–100 hectares) to be only 2% of that in expanses over 1000 hectares. The Rufous-crowned Sparrow's apparent absence from patches of sage scrub in Oceanside and Encinitas also implies loss due to habitat fragmentation. The outlook is therefore not good for the birds persisting in smaller isolated patches like Soledad Natural Park in La Jolla (P7). The Rufous-crowned Sparrow's survival over much of the coastal lowland of San Diego County may depend on how well multiple-species conservation plans succeed in linking patches of sage scrub. Because the process of piecing together habitat reserves under these plans is gradual, their success with the Rufous-crowned Sparrow cannot yet be predicted. Even if this success is poor, and the species disappears from large areas west of Interstate 15, the Rufous-crowned Sparrow is likely to survive farther inland. Although the Rufous-crowned Sparrow is sparser here than at lower elevations, its adaptability as a fire follower seems certain to ensure its place in San Diego County's biota.

Taxonomy: The Ashy Rufous-crowned Sparrow, *A. r. canescens* Todd, 1922, is the subspecies occurring in San Diego County. It is restricted to the San Diegan District of the California Floristic Province, and its characters typify the pattern of this area's endemic birds: it is darker both above and below than the subspecies to both the north and the south, and the underparts differ from those of the other subspecies in having a gray wash.

American Tree Sparrow *Spizella arborea*

The American Tree Sparrow is a bird of the arctic and subarctic. Even in northernmost California it is a rare winter visitor. The 12 records for San Diego County are the southernmost along the Pacific coast.

Migration: All sightings of the American Tree Sparrow in San Diego County have been at Point Loma (S7), except for one in southwestern Balboa Park (S9) 13–21 December 1975 and one in Presidio Park (R8) 13 November 1976 (AB 31:225, 1977). All have been of

Photo by Richard E. Webster

single individuals (usually flocked with other sparrows), except for two at Point Loma 28–31 October 1982 (R. E. Webster, AB 37:226, 1983). The only one during the atlas period was there 4–5 November 1999 (J. C. Worley, NAB 54:107, 2000). The species' dates range from 11 October (1970, McCaskie 1973) to 21 December.

Taxonomy: No specimen has been collected in San Diego County, but specimens from elsewhere in California are *S. a. ochracea* Brewster, 1882 (McCaskie 1973).

Chipping Sparrow *Spizella passerina*

Though the Chipping Sparrow takes to man-made habitats like orchards, cemeteries, and landscaped parks, it is at best locally common in San Diego County. Its distribution is complex: it breeds primarily in the mountains among the pines, only sparingly elsewhere. In winter it is even less predictable, fluctuating with the supply of seeds in natural habitats and being most consistent in irrigated parks. The Chipping Sparrow is most widespread as a spring migrant, at this season concentrating at the east base of the mountains.

Photo by Anthony Mercieca

Breeding distribution: The Chipping Sparrow's distribution in San Diego County is curious and unique. Open pine/oak woodland with a grassy understory is the species' principal breeding habitat, so the higher mountain ranges constitute the core of the sparrow's range. Yet even here the distribution is patchy: the Chipping Sparrow is uncommon and local on Palomar Mountain and now absent from Hot Springs Mountain (previously, only a single bird seen on two of three visits in summer 1980, Unitt 1981). It is most numerous in the Julian area, with up to 20 at Wynola (J19) 17 April 1999 (S. E. Smith), 18 (all singing males) between Julian and William Heise County Park (K20) 10 June 1998 (E. C. Hall), and 12 on Volcan Mountain (I20) 28 June 2000 (A. P. and T. E. Keenan).

In oak woodland without conifers the Chipping Sparrow is very local and usually rare, with only scattered pairs. It occurs at several sites from near Santa Ysabel northwest through Mesa Grande to Pine Mountain (G15), a region also occupied by several other birds more typical of coniferous woodland. Eight in the Edwards Ranch (J18) near Santa Ysabel 25 June 2000 (S. E. Smith) was the highest count in this area. The only other substantial population in natural habitat—open Engelmann oak woodland—is in Camp Pendleton at the south end of the Santa Margarita Mountains between Roblar Creek and Case Spring (B4, C5). From 1998 to 2001 the species was consistent there, unlike the scattered ephemeral pairs or individuals at most other oak woodland sites, in numbers ranging up to 16 on 27 May 2001 (C5; L. J. Hargrove).

The Chipping Sparrow is also an uncommon and localized breeding bird in avocado and citrus orchards, mainly around Pauma Valley, Valley Center, and San Pasqual. The highest count in this habitat was of six 1.5 miles northeast of Weaver Mountain (E11) 27 May 1999 (D. C. Seals), and most reports are of scattered individuals or pairs. Yet another isolated colony, known since the 1970s, is at Point Loma (S7), where the birds occur fairly commonly both around the edges of native scrub and in the ornamental plantings

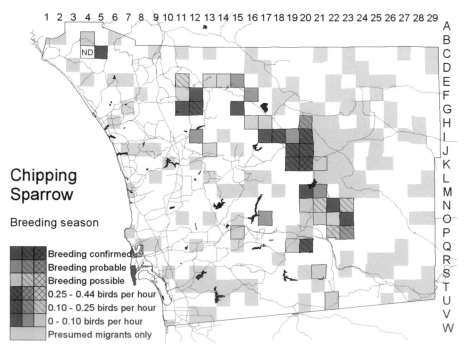

Chipping Sparrow

Breeding season

- Breeding confirmed
- Breeding probable
- Breeding possible
- 0.25 - 0.44 birds per hour
- 0.10 - 0.25 birds per hour
- 0 - 0.10 birds per hour
- Presumed migrants only

of Cabrillo National Monument and Fort Rosecrans Cemetery. The Chipping Sparrow may be colonizing La Jolla (P7) as well, where L. and M. Polinsky noted six and two on 16 and 27 May 1999, respectively.

Nesting: The Chipping Sparrow prefers to nest in conifers (Middleton 1998), a preference that may account for its concentrating in San Diego County's mountain forests. There is little information about the species' nesting in the county, though. On Point Loma the birds have been found nesting in shrubs; one early collected egg set from Palomar Mountain was in a wild rose. The schedule of breeding activity we observed was consistent with the eight egg sets

Chipping Sparrow

Winter

1.00 - 3.57 birds per hour
0.25 - 1.00 birds per hour
0 - 0.25 birds per hour

collected 1895–1920, whose dates ranged from 29 April to 21 June. Any differences in nesting schedule among the Chipping Sparrow's diverse habitats remain unknown.

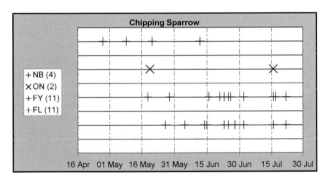

Migration: Over much of San Diego County the Chipping Sparrow occurs only as a migrant. Records far from wintering and breeding localities suggest that spring migration extends mainly from late March to mid May, with extreme dates 16 March (1998, one in Travertine Palms Wash, C29, R. Thériault) and 24 May (1999, 10 at Yaqui Well, I24, P. K. Nelson). Spring migrants are most numerous in the Anza–Borrego Desert along the east base of the mountains, with up to 59 in Blair Valley (L24) 3 April 1998 (R. Thériault), 30 near Scissors Crossing (J22) 26 April 1999 (E. C. Hall), and 30 near San Felipe Narrows (I25) 10 April 1999 (P. K. Nelson). Twenty-five at Sunshine Summit (D17) 1 May 1999 (A. Mauro) were at a concentration point for migrants crossing the mountains. Numbers of migrants elsewhere on the coastal slope were small—all counts of over 10 in a day were from sites where the species winters. Fall migration begins in late August or early September.

Winter: At this season the Chipping Sparrow is widespread but patchy. The species can be seen almost

anyplace where bare ground or short grass for foraging lies near dense shrubs or trees for refuge from predators. Wintering birds range from the coast to the low desert and up to at least 4700 feet in the mountains (15 northeast of Lake Cuyamaca, L21, 5 January 1999, J. K. Wilson). They appear to be most numerous, though, in the inland valleys. They typically flock with other wintering sparrows, especially the White-crowned and, in the desert, Brewer's. Lawns and open ground with scattered trees attract wintering Chipping Sparrows, so parks and cemeteries are the most consistent sites for them. In natural habitats, especially desert, the species is irregular, presumably according to the food supply. The numbers reported in the eastern two-thirds of San Diego were at least twice as high in 1998–99 (the winter following the wet one) than in any other of the five. By 2001–02, an exceptionally dry winter, numbers of Chipping Sparrows reported from this region were only 12% of those three years earlier.

Conservation: Although the Chipping Sparrow uses artificial landscaping, and has become a suburban bird in the eastern United States (Middleton 1998), it has not taken to residential areas in San Diego County. Breeding birds have benefited to a modest extent from the planting of orchards—and have suffered from their replacement by urban sprawl. Anecdotal observations do not imply a conspicuous change in the status of the Chipping Sparrow in San Diego County over the last third of the 20th century, but the Breeding Bird Survey implies a significant decrease in California as a whole over this period (Sauer et al. 2003). Stephens (1919a) called the species a "rather common summer resident" in San Diego County, Willett (1912) a "common resident of orchards, gardens, and parks in the foothill and mesa region, abundant in summer in coniferous forests of the mountains" of coastal southern California as a whole—evaluations that no longer apply. Brown-headed Cowbird parasitism is likely a factor in this decrease; the cowbird parasitizes the sparrow heavily, reducing its nest success (Middleton 1998).

Taxonomy: Chipping Sparrows of the western United States are now generally all listed as the pale *S. p. arizonae*

Coues, 1872. Kenneth C. Parkes identified two fall specimens from San Diego County as probably *S. p. boreophila* Oberholser, 1955, a far-northern darker-backed subspecies of uncertain validity (Unitt 1984).

Clay-colored Sparrow *Spizella pallida*

Even though it nests in eastern British Columbia and winters in Baja California Sur, the Clay-colored Sparrow is rare in San Diego County. It occurs mainly as a fall migrant, flocking with its close relative the Chipping Sparrow and seen most frequently at Point Loma.

Migration: Four or five per fall is an average number of sightings of the Clay-colored Sparrow in San Diego County. The species occurs mainly from mid September to mid November; 28 August (1968, one in the Tijuana River valley, AFN 23:112, 1969) is the earliest date. All reports are from the coastal lowland, overwhelmingly from Point Loma (S7) and the Tijuana River valley.

There are only three records of spring migrants, all from Point Loma: 19 May 1980 (AB 34:817, 1980), 29 April–1 May 2001 (J. Abernathy, P. A. Ginsburg, NAB 55:358, 2001), and 5 May 2002 (J. C. Worley).

Photo by Anthony Mercieca

Winter: The seven winter records, all from the coastal lowland, include five listed by Unitt (1984), one at Point Loma 10 January–10 April 1992 (G. McCaskie, AB 46:316, 1992), and one that returned for two years to Oak Hill Cemetery, Escondido (I12), 20–22 February 2001 and 16–24 February 2002 (M. B. Mulrooney, NAB 55:229, 2001).

Brewer's Sparrow *Spizella breweri*

Brewer's Sparrow may not be much to look at, but its song is a show-stopper: a series of trills at varying high pitches and tempos, continued at length. The birds often sing in chorus, creating a surreal sound. They sing even in their winter range—fortunately for San Diegans, because it is as a winter visitor and migrant that Brewer's Sparrow occurs primarily in San Diego County. It is overwhelmingly a bird of the Anza–Borrego Desert but occurs locally in small numbers on the coastal slope, mainly in habitats mimicking desert scrub. Field work for this atlas generated much new data on Brewer's Sparrow, recording a winter invasion on an unprecedented scale and the first confirmed breeding of the species in San Diego County.

Winter: As a winter visitor, Brewer's Sparrow is widespread in the Anza–Borrego Desert, especially in broad washes and on valley floors where there are good numbers of shrubs as well as open sandy ground. The species' abundance, though, varies greatly with rainfall. The numbers reported in the winter of 1998–99, the year after a wet El Niño, were 20 times higher than in any of the three following dry winters. The difference even from 1997–98 would have been almost as great if not for the flock of 300 northwest of Carrizo Marsh (O29) 21 January 1998 (M. C. Jorgensen). In the peak year concentrations ranged up to 231 at Borrego Springs (G24) 20 December 1998 (P.

Photo by Anthony Mercieca

D. Ache) and 200 near Yaqui Well (I24) 31 January 1999 (R. Thériault). The Anza–Borrego Christmas bird count implies substantial year-to-year variation in numbers of the Brewer's Sparrow, but the figure in 1998–99 was still at least 15 times higher than in any year back to the count's inception in 1984. In most years the species is seen inconsistently at any given site; it probably wanders nomadically.

Brewer's Sparrow also occurs in semidesert scrub on the south-facing slopes of Dameron and Oak Grove valleys, in the coastal drainage basin of the Santa Margarita River. The species was common there in 1998–99 (up to 34 in Dameron Valley, C16, 12 December 1998, K. L. Weaver) and still occurred in small numbers in later years. The only report of a large number elsewhere on the coastal slope was from near Campo (U22), site of 20 on 23 January 1999 (C. R. Mahrdt). Locations of scattered Brewer's Sparrows elsewhere on the coastal slope were mostly from pockets of exceptionally arid scrub on south-facing slopes, such as Pamo Valley (I15, three on 10 December 1998, O. Carter) and the region of Otay Lakes (four records of single birds, P. Unitt, S. Buchanan).

Migration: As a migrant, Brewer's Sparrow is as widespread in the Anza–Borrego Desert as in winter but more numerous. Exceptionally high concentrations occurred in both 1998 (up to 600 on Mescal Bajada, J25, 26 April, M. and B. McIntosh) and 1999 (up to 440 in the Borrego Valley's mesquite bosque, G25, 16 March, R. Thériault). Even in "normal" years large flocks of spring migrants are seen occasionally, such as 70 near Whitaker Horse Camp (D24) 4 April 2001 (J. O. Zimmer) and 50 along Rockhouse Trail (D25) 15 April 2000 (K. J. Winter). Also, a few are seen in spring at the places on the coastal slope where the species winters (six in Dameron Valley, C16, 10 April 1999, K. L. Weaver; two in Proctor Valley, T14, 29 April 1998, P. Unitt). Coastal migrants away from wintering areas are rare (maximum four in Rancho Jamul, S15, 21 April 2001, P. Unitt, C. Woodruff) but scattered as far northwest as Las Pulgas Canyon, Camp Pendleton (E4, one on 26 April 2001, S. Brad). Numbers decline through the first half of May; 15 May 1999 (two in Indian Gorge, O27, P. R. Pryde) may be the latest date for a migrant, close to the species' latest date of 11 May for the Imperial Valley (Patten et al. 2003). Two in Miller Valley (S24) 22 May 1999 (L. J. Hargrove) and two near Sentenac Ciénaga (J23) 28 May 1998 (R. Thériault) may have been prospective breeders, in light of the discovery of the species' nesting in 2001.

In fall, Brewer's Sparrow begins arriving in early September (4 September 1988, one along Carrizo Creek near Arsenic Spring, T28, P. Unitt). It is most frequent along the coast at this season, sometimes associating with flocks of Chipping Sparrows.

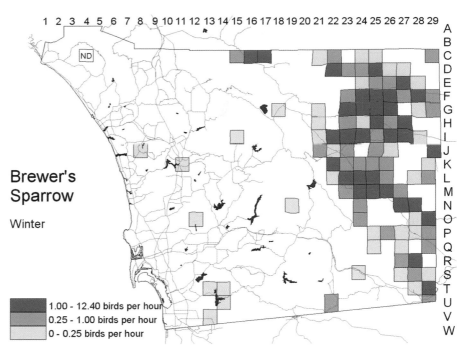

Brewer's Sparrow

Winter

- 1.00 - 12.40 birds per hour
- 0.25 - 1.00 birds per hour
- 0 - 0.25 birds per hour

Breeding distribution: Though Stephens (1919a) wrote that a few Brewer's Sparrows breed on the eastern slope of San Diego County's mountains, and collected a specimen at 6000 feet elevation in the Cuyamaca Mountains 21 May 1893 (SDNHM 1012), the first confirmation of the species' nesting in the county came in 2001. On 13 May 2001, in a stand of the big sagebrush in Montezuma Valley just southwest of Ranchita (H21), B. E. Bell, G. Rebstock, and I found a singing male, a highly agitated presumed female, and her completed but still empty nest, 1–2 feet above the ground in sagebrush. A follow-up visit on 31 May revealed the nest deserted and the birds gone from the area. Less than 1 mile to the east, in sagebrush just southeast of Ranchita, Brewer's Sparrows occurred in

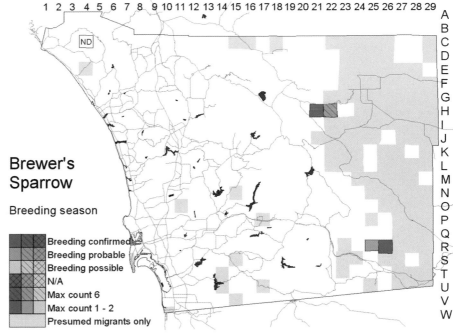

Brewer's Sparrow

Breeding season

- Breeding confirmed
- Breeding probable
- Breeding possible
- N/A
- Max count 6
- Max count 1 - 2
- Presumed migrants only

late April 1999, 2000, and 2001, with up to six, including two singing males, 29 April 2001 (P. D. Jorgensen). In the Manzanita Indian Reservation (R25), G. Rebstock and J. Determan noted a single agitated Brewer's Sparrow 6 May 2001. Less than 2 miles to the east in upper McCain Valley (R26), J. R. Barth found one carrying an insect 17 May 2001, then found two juveniles at the same site 11 and 13 June 2001. Finally, M. B. Mulrooney reported a singing male in a large patch of big sagebrush along Indian Creek in the Laguna Mountains (N22) 21 May 2002. Over 80 years later, Stephens' assessment of the Brewer's Sparrow's breeding in San Diego County has been verified, extending the species' breeding range significantly south of its previously established limit in the San Bernardino Mountains.

The only previous summer record of Brewer's Sparrow in San Diego County is of one singing at 850 feet elevation along Marron Valley Road (V17) 7 August 1991 (C. G. Edwards).

Nesting: The one Brewer's Sparrow nest known from San Diego County was typical for the species in being placed under the crown of a big sagebrush.

Conservation: Brewer's Sparrow is suffering a decline in its core breeding range in the Great Basin (Rotenberry et al. 1999) and has been extirpated from former breeding sites in the Los Angeles region (Garrett and Dunn 1981). No change is evident in the Anza–Borrego Desert, however, where the species' winter habitat is little modified and the historical record is slight. Brewer's Sparrow has been known in winter on the coastal slope since L. M. Huey collected two at San Diego 15 January 1914 (SDNHM 34563–4) but has apparently always been rare. Nevertheless, runaway urbanization threatens the sage scrub used by wintering Brewer's Sparrows both in the Proctor Valley/Otay Lakes area and in Dameron Valley.

Taxonomy: All specimens from San Diego County are *S. b. breweri* Cassin, 1856, except for one from San Luis Rey (G6) 14 February 1962 (Rea 1967, DEL 27230), the only reported California specimen of *S. b. taverneri* Swarth and Brooks 1925. This larger, darker, grayer, more heavily streaked form breeds north of nominate *breweri*, largely in northwestern Canada, and apparently winters primarily in the Chihuahuan Desert of mainland Mexico.

Black-chinned Sparrow *Spizella atrogularis*

The Black-chinned Sparrow is one of North America's least-studied birds, yet it is one of the commonest species on the steep chaparral-covered slopes so widespread in San Diego County's foothills and mountains. Rugged topography seems to be nearly as much a feature of the Black-chinned Sparrow's habitat as chaparral. The birds are inconspicuous except for the male's song, an accelerating trill with a mechanical quality unique among California's breeding birds. The Black-chinned Sparrow is a summer visitor almost exclusively, being very rare in winter and even as a migrant away from its breeding habitat.

Photo by Anthony Mercieca

Breeding distribution: The Black-chinned Sparrow occurs widely in San Diego County's foothills and mountains above 1500 feet elevation. Gaps are due to extensive grassland, as in Warner Valley, or forest, as in the Cuyamaca Mountains. The largest concentrations appear to be between 2500 and 5500 feet elevation on south-facing slopes, e.g., 60 in Noble Canyon (O22) 6 June 1997 (R. A. Hamilton), 48 on Otay Mountain (V15) 25 May 1999 (D. C. Seals), and 46 along the Pacific Crest Trail from Kitchen Creek to Fred Canyon (R23) 17 May 1998 (L. J. Hargrove). In prime habitat the population is so dense that up to four territorial males are within earshot of each other and sing in rotation (L. J. Hargrove). Though the big sagebrush is not typically defined as chaparral, and the Black-chinned Sparrow is absent from the Great Basin where this shrub dominates, in San Diego County the sparrow uses this plant commonly. The Black-chinned Sparrow's use of coastal sage scrub, though, is only marginal. Outlying sites nearer the coast

correspond to more isolated chaparral-covered hills, such as San Onofre Mountain (D3; one on 3 June 2000, R. and S. L. Breisch), the San Marcos Mountains (G8/H8; up to three on 31 May 1999, J. O. Zimmer), Frank's Peak/Mt. Whitney (J9; one on 25 May 1998, J. O. Zimmer), Black Mountain (M10; three on 9 May 1999, K. J. Winter), the western edge of steep hills on Miramar (O10; feeding young on 10 June 1998, G. L. Rogers), and Cowles Mountain (Q11; up to four on 7 and 29 April 1997, N. Osborn). The lowest elevation to which breeding Black-chinned Sparrows descend appears to be about 500 feet, as in Sycamore Canyon (O12; seven on 6 May 1999, G. L. Rogers). A few pairs edge into coastal sage scrub, occupying small patches of chamise within the sage scrub or stands of denser, leafier shrubs like redberry and laurel sumac (M. A. Patten).

Along the desert slope the edge of the Black-chinned Sparrow's breeding range tracks the edge of the chaparral closely. The notable exception is in the stunted pinyon

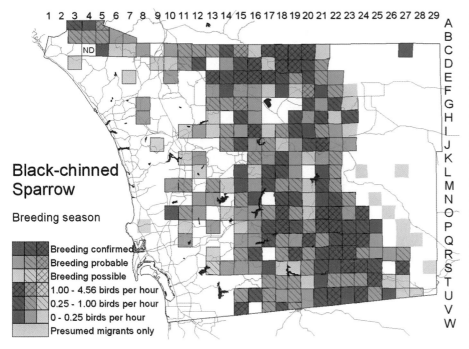

Black-chinned Sparrow

Breeding season

- Breeding confirmed
- Breeding probable
- Breeding possible
- 1.00 - 4.56 birds per hour
- 0.25 - 1.00 birds per hour
- 0 - 0.25 birds per hour
- Presumed migrants only

seen in migration away from its breeding habitat, but we recorded the species 12 times in spring in the Anza–Borrego Desert, mainly along the east base of the mountains, between 26 March (2001, two in Inner Pasture, N25, A. P. and T. E. Keenan) and 24 May (1997, one in Bow Willow Canyon, P27, D. G. Seay). Though some of these birds were singing, the observations were not repeated later in the season and were not concentrated in 1998, as would be expected if the species expanded its range during a wet year. Therefore I infer that these birds were migrants. Along the coast, the only records of migrants were of one in San Clemente Canyon (P8) 27 April 1999 (M. B. Stowe) and one at Point Loma (S7) on the very late date of 5 June 2001 (R. E. Webster, NAB 55:484, 2001). As a fall migrant the Black-chinned Sparrow is equally rare, reported away from breeding habitat from 12 August to 21 October (both records from Point Loma in 1984, R. E. Webster, AB 39:104, 1985); an even later one was at Point Loma 6–28 November 1965 (AFN 20:93, 1966).

woodland of the Santa Rosa Mountains, where the species is rare and possibly sporadic. There is one record, of a pair with three fledglings at 5700 feet elevation 1.25 miles south-southeast of Rabbit Peak (C27) 4 June 2001 (R. Thériault).

Nesting: The Black-chinned Sparrow conceals its small cup nest in the middle level of shrubs. The species of shrub appears immaterial: in San Diego County, chamise, big sagebrush, manzanita, and flat-top buckwheat have all been noted as nest sites. The nesting schedule we observed during the atlas period agrees largely with published data (91 California egg dates 21 April–7 July, J. D. Newman in Austin 1968), but the species' breeding season can extend slightly later: a clutch near Guatay (P21) hatched between 17 and 19 July 1995 (Cleveland National Forest data).

Migration: During the atlas' term, first spring dates for the Black-chinned Sparrow ranged from 16 March (1997, two at Cowles Mountain, N. Osborn) to 26 March. The earliest date ever reported is 10 March (1983, near San Diego, AB 37:911, 1983). Since 1980 spring arrival appears to have shifted a few days earlier than previously reported (cf. Unitt 1984). The Black-chinned Sparrow is seldom

Winter: Though the Black-chinned Sparrow winters commonly in central Baja California, it is very rare at this season in San Diego County. Before 1997, there were only nine records, all from Christmas bird counts; one of the birds was collected (2 miles west of Bonita, T11, 26 December 1940, SDNHM 18245, Huey 1954). Four of the records are from the San Diego circle, one from Oceanside, two from Escondido, one from Lake Henshaw, and one from Borrego Springs. During the atlas period, we added five records, three from the foothills of central San Diego County in 1999: two in the gorge of the San Diego River above El Capitan Reservoir (M17) 23 January (R. C. Sanger), one at 2200 feet elevation on the steep west slope of Lillian Hill (M18) 7 February (P. Unitt, L. J. Hargrove, NAB 53:210, 1999), and the third 1 mile southwest of El Capitan Dam (O16) 3 January (S. Kingswood). Two records were from rugged regions of the Anza–Borrego Desert in 1998: one above Angelina Spring (I22) 21 January (P. K. Nelson), the other from 2200 feet elevation 1.1 miles south of Sunset Mountain (J26) 11 January (J. Determan, FN 52:259, 1998). The last two records, in a wet winter, recall the "extraordinary flight" of the Black-chinned Sparrow to the Kofa Mountains of southwestern Arizona in 1955–56, "a time of unusually beneficial rain" (Phillips et al. 1964).

Conservation: The Black-chinned Sparrow does not adapt to urbanization, but its rugged habitat is unattractive to development, and much is conserved in areas under the jurisdiction of the Cleveland National Forest, Bureau

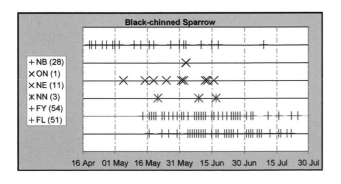

Black-chinned Sparrow

- +NB (28)
- ×ON (1)
- ×NE (11)
- ✳NN (3)
- +FY (54)
- +FL (51)

16 Apr | 01 May | 16 May | 31 May | 15 Jun | 30 Jun | 15 Jul | 30 Jul

of Land Management, and California State Parks. The sparrow readily recolonizes recovering burned chaparral. A study on national forest land near Pine Valley found no difference in Black-chinned Sparrow abundance between chaparral averaging 31 and that averaging six years since burning (Cleveland National Forest data). It is in thick old chaparral on north-facing slopes where the species is scarce or absent. Cowbird parasitism of the Black-chinned Sparrow occurs but appears light (Friedmann 1963). Of 31 Black-chinned Sparrow nests found around Pine Valley 1994–97 only one was parasitized (Cleveland National Forest data).

Bolger et al. (1997) listed the Black-chinned Sparrow as the most sensitive to habitat fragmentation of 20 species studied in northern San Diego. Their study design, though, assumed that the species addressed were uni-formly distributed over the study area before urban-ization, certainly not the case with the Black-chinned Sparrow. The sparrow's absence or scarcity along the coast is well attested by both historical data and its cur-rent anticoastal distribution in little-developed areas like Camp Pendleton.

Taxonomy: *Spizella a. cana* Coues, 1866, distinguished by its combination of dark plumage and small size, is the only subspecies of the Black-chinned Sparrow occur-ring in San Diego County. Indeed, San Diego County constitutes the core of this subspecies' range. The inland subspecies *S. a. evura* Coues, 1866, is not confirmed by specimens as a vagrant to the coast, but the individual seen on Point Loma in June may have been *evura*, which migrates later than *cana*.

Vesper Sparrow *Pooecetes gramineus*

Open grassland and sparse scrub in the inland valleys and desert sinks are home to the Vesper Sparrow during its winter stay in San Diego County. Generally uncommon, the Vesper Sparrow can be overlooked among the Savannah Sparrows that often outnumber it, but it is locally common in the most favorable places, Warner and San Felipe val-leys. The Vesper Sparrow's restriction to only large tracts of its habitat suggests that birds can suffer the effects of habitat fragmentation in their winter range as well as their breeding range.

Photo by Anthony Mercieca

Winter: The Vesper Sparrow avoids a narrow strip along the coast but otherwise occurs widely in the largest tracts of its habitats: grassland, stands of the big sagebrush, and halophytic scrub on valley floors in the Anza–Borrego Desert. In San Diego County these habitats are patchy, giving the Vesper Sparrow a patchy distribution. Sparse semidesert sage scrub was once also Vesper Sparrow habitat, but stands of this large enough to attract the birds remain only in Dameron Valley (C15; up to 10 on 6 February 1999, K. L. Weaver) and around the upper end of El Capitan Reservoir (M17/N17; up to 25 on 16 January 2002, J. R. Barth). Warner Valley and San Felipe Valley (I21/J21) offer the most Vesper Sparrow habitat, and the birds are most numerous there, with up to 35 north of Lake Henshaw (F17) 8 December 2001 (P. Unitt), 27 in the east arm of Warner Valley (G19) 10 December 2000 (R. and S. L. Breisch), and 79 in San Felipe Valley 18 December 2000 (W. E. Haas).

In the northwestern part of the county Camp Pendleton (up to 12 in San Onofre Canyon, C3, 19 January 2002, J. R. Barth), the Fallbrook Naval Weapons Station (E6, up to 12 on 11 December

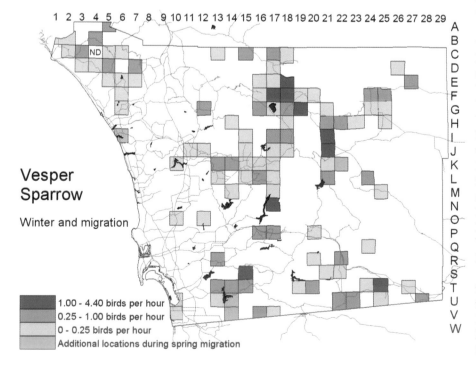

**Vesper
Sparrow**

Winter and migration

1.00 - 4.40 birds per hour
0.25 - 1.00 birds per hour
0 - 0.25 birds per hour
Additional locations during spring migration

1998, P. A. Ginsburg), and grassland around Willow Spring (A5, up to 20 on 12 December 2001, K. J. Winter) are the only areas where the Vesper Sparrow occurs currently. Other places where Vesper Sparrows concentrate are broad inland valleys like Oak Grove (C17; 15 on 9 December 2001, J. M. and B. Hargrove), Montezuma (Ranchita; H21/H22; 20 on 15 January 1999, P. Unitt), Santa Maria (Ramona; K13–15; 10 on 3 January 1998, F. C. Hall), Proctor (T13/T14; 30 on 5 December 1999, S. Buchanan), Rancho Jamul (S15/T15; 21 on 14 January 2001, P. Unitt), Marron (V16/V17; 15 on 22 January 2001, D. C. Seals), Campo (U22/U23; 16 on 3 February 1999, D. C. Seals), Hill (T25; 36 on 10 February 2001, E. C. Hall), and Jacumba (U28; 20 on 23 January 2001, F. L. Unmack). Another noteworthy site is the native grassland at Wright's Field, Alpine (P17; 20 on 9 December 2001, K. J. Winter).

In the Anza–Borrego Desert the Vesper Sparrow is usually uncommon, though the Anza–Borrego Christmas bird count on 20 December 1998 produced 48 in north Borrego Springs (F24) and 56 in the entire count circle, the only record of more than eight individuals since the count's inception in 1984. Recorded during the atlas period in the Borrego Valley and at Clark Dry Lake (D26), Little Clark Dry Lake (E27), Blair Valley (L24), and Vallecito Valley (M25), the species is localized in the Anza–Borrego Desert to poorly drained valley floors and sinks with scattered shrubs, especially saltbush.

Migration: The Vesper Sparrow begins arriving in late September and departs largely by early April. Interestingly, the six records later than 15 April are from elevations between 2500 and 4200 feet, most from stands of big sagebrush recalling the species' breeding habitat in the Great Basin. The Vesper Sparrow breeds around Baldwin Lake in the San Bernardino Mountains, 60 miles north of San Diego County, but this is an isolated colony separated by over 100 miles from the species' main breeding range still farther north. The latest San Diego County records are of three between Ranchita and Camel Rock (H22) 27 April 1999 and one near Adobe Springs, Chihuahua Valley (C18), 2 May 1999 (P. Unitt).

Conservation: The Vesper Sparrow's absence from small patches of grassland suggests it is susceptible to habitat loss through fragmentation. Specimens and published reports confirm it at places where it no longer occurs, such as National City (T10), Lake Murray (Q11; SDNHM), Poway (M11), and El Cajon (Q13; Belding 1890). Most grassland in the coastal lowland has already been urbanized, and what remains is fragmented and degraded by the proliferation of nonnative grasses and weeds. Heavy grazing and groundwater pumping affect the Warner Valley, but fortunately two other important Vesper Sparrow sites, San Felipe Valley and Rancho Jamul, have been acquired by the California Department of Fish and Game. Field work for the atlas revealed the Vesper Sparrow to be more common in San Diego County than I reported in 1984, but this is a result of better surveys of areas formerly poorly known. Christmas bird counts show no clear trend in Vesper Sparrow numbers, though this may be an artifact of coverage. In the San Diego count circle, the best habitat, in Rancho Otay (U12), was not consistently accessible before it was eliminated. The decline of the Oregon Vesper Sparrow, *P. g. affinis*, may also have contributed to a decline of the Vesper Sparrow as a whole in San Diego County (see Taxonomy).

Taxonomy: The subspecies of the Vesper Sparrow dominant in San Diego County is the pale grayish *P. g. confinis* Baird, 1858, which breeds widely in western North America east of the Cascade Range. The smaller, buffier *P. g. affinis* is known in San Diego County from two specimens from Jamacha (R14) 23 February and 1 March 1924 (SDNHM 9266 and 9270) and one from El Cajon (Belding 1890). *Pooecetes g. affinis* breeds largely in western Washington and western Oregon, where it has gone from "abundant" in the Willamette Valley (Gabrielson and Jewett 1940) to "locally uncommon to rare" (Gilligan et al. 1994). It is recognized as a bird of special concern by the California Department of Fish and Game. Though *affinis* has been collected as far south as Santo Domingo in northwestern Baja California, the San Joaquin Valley was apparently the core of its winter range (R. A. Erickson unpubl. data).

Lark Sparrow *Chondestes grammacus*

The Lark Sparrow is a characteristic bird of San Diego County's inland valleys. It is a year-round resident, but in winter its numbers are augmented by migrants, most noticeably in the Borrego Valley. The Lark Sparrow is common where there is ample grassland, pasture, or bare ground for foraging, yet also scattered trees or shrubs for nesting. It adapts to agriculture but retreats from urbanization.

Breeding distribution: The Lark Sparrow offers one of the clearest examples of an "anticoastal" distribution: a bird that is widespread except in a narrow strip along the coast. It remains at least 5 miles from the beach throughout the county. The only coastal atlas square with a Lark

Photo by Anthony Mercieca

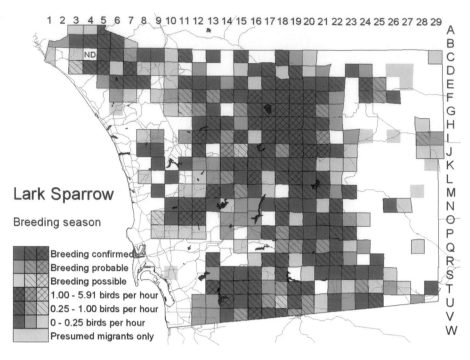

Lark Sparrow

Breeding season

Breeding confirmed
Breeding probable
Breeding possible
1.00 - 5.91 birds per hour
0.25 - 1.00 birds per hour
0 - 0.25 birds per hour
Presumed migrants only

The Lark Sparrow ranges up to San Diego County's highest elevations; mountain meadows and broken coniferous forest offer it good habitat. On the desert slope, it ranges down into San Felipe, Earthquake, and Mason valleys, then occurs in scattered patches in the Anza–Borrego Desert. Most desert locations for the Lark Sparrow are in or near orchards (north Borrego Valley) or shade trees around buildings (e.g., Ocotillo Wells). Yet, during the atlas period, the Lark Sparrow did not occupy all such habitat. It is evidently a recent colonist in the low desert. Our eight confirmations of breeding in the Anza–Borrego Desert are the first for this area (cf. Massey 1998). The earliest was in 1998, and all but two were in 2001. In the Imperial Valley just east of San Diego County, the Lark Sparrow colonized as a new breeding species in the mid 1980s (Patten et al. 2003). Among the grapefruit orchards of the northern Borrego Valley (E24), the Lark Sparrow is already fairly common, with up to 10 on 25 May 2001 (P. D. Ache).

Sparrow record during the breeding season was at the far north, along the Orange County line near San Onofre (C1), and there was only a single record even there (two on 14 June 1998, K. Lopina). Just 10 miles inland, though, the species can be common, as illustrated by 30 around lower Roblar Road in Camp Pendleton (D5) 2 July 2000 (R. E. Fischer) and 50 at Lower Otay Lake (U14) 3 July 1999 (S. Buchanan). The Lark Sparrow's center of abundance in San Diego County is the county's largest grassland, Warner Valley (G18, 107 on 19 March 1999, C. G. Edwards; G19, 65 on 25 June 2000, P. Unitt). The grasshoppers that swarm over Warner Valley in summer are the principal food Lark Sparrows feed their young.

Nesting: The Lark Sparrow may nest in a tree, in a shrub, or on the ground, usually at the base of a shrub. Atlas observers reported four nests on the ground or in grass. When the Lark Sparrow nests above ground its choice of site is unspecialized; atlas observers noted laurel sumac, eucalyptus, and tamarisk, and egg collections from the county mention lemon trees.

Lark Sparrow eggs collected from San Diego County 1887–1935 range from 27 March to 6 July, and our atlas data reflect this same schedule almost exactly, with fledglings as early as 26 April (1998, Cuyamaca College, R13, J. R. Barth) and a nest with nestlings as late as 29 July (2001, Edwards Ranch, I19, D. W. Au). On 27 March in the wet spring of 1998, though, K. L. Weaver noted exceptionally early nesting in the semidesert scrub of Dameron Valley (C15): a pair of Lark Sparrows carrying small caterpillars, evidently feeding young and implying egg laying at least 11 days earlier than the previous early nest date.

Migration: There are few data on Lark Sparrow migration in

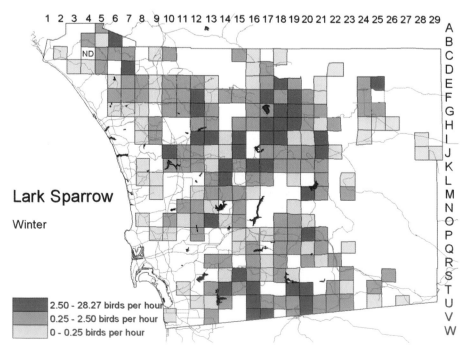

Lark Sparrow

Winter

2.50 - 28.27 birds per hour
0.25 - 2.50 birds per hour
0 - 0.25 birds per hour

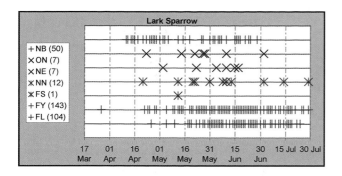

San Diego County. Away from known or probable nesting habitat in the Anza–Borrego Desert, the latest spring date is 24 April (1998, two at the east end of Clark Valley, E27, P. D. Jorgensen) or 1 May (1997, one at Tamarisk Grove—a plausible site for the species to pioneer, I24, P. K. Nelson). Near the coast our only spring records outside the breeding range were of one at Whelan Lake (G6) 18 March 1998 (D. Rorick) and one at Mt. Hope Cemetery (S10) 20 April 1997 (P. Unitt). Fall migration begins by 9 September (1977, one in the Tijuana River valley, J. L. Dunn).

Winter: In winter the number of Lark Sparrows in the Borrego Valley increases greatly. Daily counts for a single atlas square in that area run up to 75 in north Borrego Springs (F24) 17 December 2000 (N. Osborn). Totals for Anza–Borrego Christmas bird counts run as high as 154 on that same day. High numbers in the inland valleys of the coastal slope—up to 400 in a day, as in Pamo Valley (I15) 29 February 2000 (O. Carter) and at Puerta La Cruz (F18) 11 December 1999 (L. and M. Polinsky)—probably reflect both an influx of migrants from the north and the local population gathering in flocks. It seems that in winter the birds leave smaller patches of breeding habitat to flock in larger grasslands. Also, the Lark Sparrow

largely vacates San Diego County's higher elevations in winter; note the lack of winter records from the Palomar and Laguna mountains, where the species breeds. From 1997 to 2002 the Lark Sparrow occurred only rarely in the coastal strip where it is absent as a breeding species. The maximum in this area was only five, at Guajome Lake (G7) 23 December 2000 (K. L. Weaver). In the Tijuana River valley (V10), the sole winter record during the atlas period was of one 19 December 1998 (P. K. Nelson).

Conservation: The Lark Sparrow responds positively to agriculture and low-density rural development. Orchards, pastures, horse corrals, and firebreaks all offer expanses of bare dirt and low weeds where the sparrow can feed. Urban sprawl, though, eliminates the Lark Sparrow. Pavement, lawns, and landscaping disfavor it. The species' disappearance from Escondido and El Cajon, for example, is clearly the result of cities replacing farms. More curious are the coastal localities where Lark Sparrow eggs were collected 1887–1935, such as Encinitas (K6), La Jolla (P7), and National City (T10). Though these have been urbanized and no longer offer Lark Sparrow habitat, they contradict the anticoastal distribution observed in recent years, which appears unrelated to urbanization because it extends seamlessly through undeveloped areas of Camp Pendleton. Bolger et al. (1997), studying birds' response to habitat fragmentation in San Diego, identified the Lark Sparrow as a species reduced in range by fragmentation. Even in winter the Lark Sparrow is retracting inland: during the atlas period it went unrecorded in Balboa Park (R9), where it was a sporadic winter visitor until the early 1980s (D. Herron), and it is no longer seen regularly in the Tijuana River Valley, where counts once ranged as high as 100 (20 December 1975, C. Lyons).

Taxonomy: Only the paler western subspecies *C. g. strigatus* Swainson, 1827, is known from California.

Black-throated Sparrow *Amphispiza bilineata*

Few birds evoke the rugged beauty of the Anza–Borrego Desert more than the Black-throated Sparrow. Rocky bajadas graced with agaves, yuccas, cacti, and thorny shrubs are its prime habitat, and it is common there year round. It ranges upslope into the junipers and, in smaller numbers, down onto the valley floors. To the east its numbers diminish, until around the Salton Sea it is absent.

Breeding distribution: The Black-throated Sparrow occurs almost throughout the Anza–Borrego Desert but very little outside it. Its numbers are highest on well-drained slopes supporting a diversity of cacti and thorny shrubs. In such areas, searching for a day, one can reach counts as high as over 50 in Chuckwalla Wash (J24) 15 April 2001 (L. and M. Polinsky), 82 around Jacumba (U28) 20 March 1998 (C. G. Edwards), and 100, including 90 singing males, around Indian Hill (R28) 26 April 1999 (J. O. Zimmer). On valley floors, especially on alkaline soil sparsely grown with halophytic shrubs, the

Photo by Jack C. Daynes

Black-throated Sparrow is quite uncommon. Only in the Ocotillo Wells off-road vehicle area, though, does the species appear absent from an entire atlas square (H29). Altitudinally, Black-throated Sparrows range from under 200 feet near Ocotillo Wells (J29) to over 5000 feet along the ridgeline of the Santa Rosa Mountains (C27).

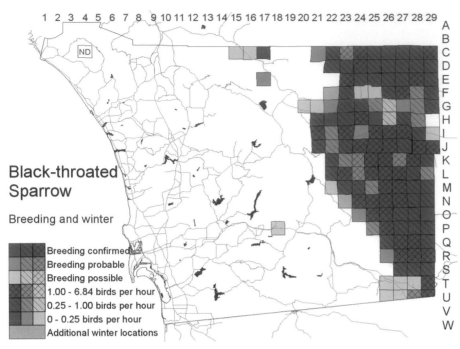

Black-throated
Sparrow

Breeding and winter

Breeding confirmed
Breeding probable
Breeding possible
1.00 - 6.84 birds per hour
0.25 - 1.00 birds per hour
0 - 0.25 birds per hour
Additional winter locations

still singing territorially 15 June (M. B. Stowe), and yet another was reported from north of Pine Valley (P21) in July 2002 (N. Ferguson). On the Pacific slope of Baja California, the Black-throated Sparrow ranges north to Sangre de Cristo and San Rafael Valley, just east of Ensenada and only about 50 miles south of the international border.

Nesting: The Black-throated Sparrow builds its cup nest in a wide variety of desert shrubs and cacti. Nest plants reported by atlas observers—desert lavender, oco-tillo, smoketree, and cholla—are all spiny enough to offer the nest substantial protection. Elsewhere Black-throated Sparrows com-monly nest in nonthorny shrubs like the creosote bush (Johnson

Toward the west, the Black-throated Sparrow drops out as chamise crowds out desert shrubs along the divide. Along the Mexican border, the Black-throated Sparrow extends west as far as Lake Domingo (U26, 21 May 1997, F. L. Unmack), still east of the Tecate Divide. In the Ranchita area, a few range a short distance onto the coastal slope west to Cañada Buena Vista (G20, one singing male 12 May 2001, A. P. and T. E. Keenan). Also on the coastal slope, a population in the Aguanga region of Riverside County extends sparsely into San Diego County in semidesert scrub on the south-facing slopes of Dameron and Oak Grove valleys, e.g., one carrying food items northeast of Oak Grove (C17) 9 June 2001 (J. M. and B. Hargrove). A tenuous linkage between Oak Grove and Ranchita is possible, implied by a report of three Black-throated Sparrows on Aguanga Ridge near Sunshine Summit (E17) 25 April 2001 (J. D. Barr).

Elsewhere on the coastal slope, the only suggestion of Black-throated Sparrow breeding before or during the atlas period was a single singing male in a patch of native needlegrass on the south slope of Poser Mountain (P18) 18 June 1999, not relocated six days later (K. J. Winter). In the record dry year of 2002, however, two appeared in burned chaparral just east of Buckman Springs (R22) in mid May (M. Sadowski, J. K. Wilson), with one

et al. 2002). Little was known of the schedule of Black-throated Sparrow nesting in San Diego County before our field work for the atlas. Rain stimulates this species to nest, and the birds may raise two broods in wetter years (Johnson et al. 2002). Our observations suggest that egg laying ranges from about 5 March to 8 July, making even three broods possible. A nest with young 2–4 days old in Palo Verde Canyon (E28) 20 March 1998 (P. D. Jorgensen) implies eggs laid about 5 March. In dry years, though, there is little nesting activity before April. A pair was still building a nest near Sentenac Ciénaga (J23) 4 July 1999 (R. Thériault), and nestlings hatched—in a nest built in a hanging basket around a house—in Borrego Springs (G24) 20 July 2000 (P. D. Jorgensen).

Migration: San Diego County's population of the Black-throated Sparrow is apparently resident, but that breeding in the northern part of the species' range is migratory. Such migrants occur rarely near the coast, most frequent-ly in fall. There are only six coastal records in spring, between 26 March (1995, Torrey Pines State Reserve, N7, S. Summers, NASFN 49:311, 1995) and 30 May (1984, Point Loma, S7, V. P. Johnson, AB 38:965, 1984). Black-throated Sparrows, still in juvenile plumage, are somewhat more frequent along the coast in the fall, with at least 21 individuals reported between 20 August (1984) and 11 October (1973 and 1984; AB 28:111, 1974; 39:104, 1985). An adult in downtown San Diego (S9) 10 July 1997 (R. Scalf, FN 51:1055, 1997) was perhaps an early fall migrant or postbreeding disperser.

Winter: The distribution and abundance of the Black-throated Sparrow in winter do not differ noticeably from those in the breeding season, though the birds flock more in winter. Maximum winter counts are similar, with up to 100 in Borrego Palm Canyon (F23) 19 December 1999 (A. DeBolt) and 72 in the Table Mountain/In-Ko-Pah area (T29) 2 February 1999 (L. J. Hargrove). Numbers

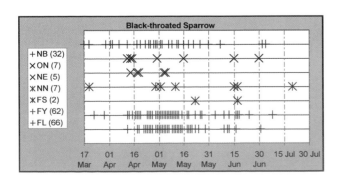

increased following the wet winter of 1997–98 but far less dramatically than in some other species of sparrows. Small numbers still occur in winter on the north sides of Dameron and Oak Grove valleys (maximum winter count two northeast of Oak Grove, C17, 31 December 2000, L. J. Hargrove). There are two coastal winter records, of one near Sweetwater Dam (S12) 21 December 1969 (AFN 24:541, 1970) and one in Coronado (S9) 11 December 1988 (J. Oldenettel, AB 43:368, 1989).

Conservation: Living largely on land conserved by Anza–Borrego Desert State Park and the Bureau of Land Management, on terrain that isolates it from human disturbance, and adapted to a harsh climate, the Black-throated Sparrow seems insulated from man-made problems. Ever longer droughts, though, could depress its population and shift its range to the west.

Taxonomy: *A. b. deserticola* Ridgway, 1898, is the only subspecies known or expected in California.

Sage Sparrow *Amphispiza belli*

Two subspecies of the Sage Sparrow occur in San Diego County, so well differentiated in plumage, habitat, and seasonal status that they are more easily discussed separately. Bell's Sparrow, the dark form, is a year-round resident in chaparral and sage scrub. The habitat must not be too dense or too encumbered by leaf litter to favor this bird that spends most of its time running on the ground. Thus chaparral partly recovered from a fire, stunted by growing on magnesium-laden gabbro soil, or growing on mesa tops or south-facing slopes most frequently offers the Sage Sparrow habitat. Though broad areas of its habitat persist in south-central San Diego County, it has been eliminated from most coastal areas—it is the shrubland bird most sensitive to habitat fragmentation. The pale subspecies, the Sage Sparrow proper, is a winter visitor to the Anza–Borrego Desert, where it seeks halophytic scrub on the valley floors.

Breeding distribution: The distribution of Bell's Sage Sparrow follows a unique pattern, though that pattern

Photo by Anthony Mercieca

is now partly obscured by urbanization. Because its low, open habitat is rather specialized, and shifts with fire, it is naturally patchy. Even during the breeding season territories seem clumped, perhaps because of social interaction. The distribution is most continuous in the extensive chaparral of the Campo Plateau, north into the south-facing slopes of the Laguna Mountains. Farther to the northwest, it becomes progressively more localized, but there are sites of concentrated populations. Some of these correspond to peaks or outcrops of gabbro-based soil, as on Otay (V15), McGinty (R15), Sycuan (R16), Viejas (O17), and Guatay (P20) mountains. In north-central San Diego County, semidesert climates as well as recovering burns and gabbro soils appear to be responsible for the more open chaparral attracting concentrations of Sage Sparrows around Ranchita (H21/H22) and in Dameron and Oak Grove valleys (C16/C17). Near Ranchita, subspecies *belli* nests in stands of the big sagebrush, the same habitat as subspecies *nevadensis* in the Great Basin. Along the crest of the mountains, the edge of the Sage Sparrow's range follows the edge of the chaparral.

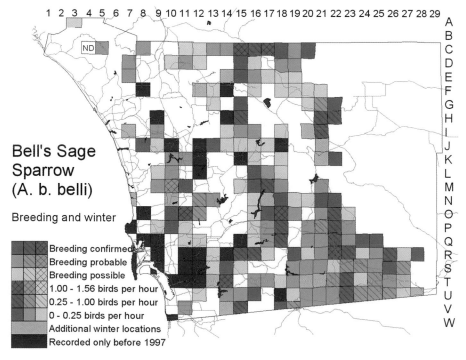

Bell's Sage Sparrow (A. b. belli)

Breeding and winter

- Breeding confirmed
- Breeding probable
- Breeding possible
- 1.00 - 1.56 birds per hour
- 0.25 - 1.00 birds per hour
- 0 - 0.25 birds per hour
- Additional winter locations
- Recorded only before 1997

In the wet spring of 1998, a pair edged slightly into the desert, seen with a fledgling at 2040 feet elevation 0.35 mile north-northeast of Indian Hill (R28) 6 May (J. O. Zimmer). Elevationally, the Sage Sparrow is not limited in San Diego County, breeding up to at least 5600 feet near High Point, Palomar Mountain (D15; pair with fledglings 12 July 2000, K. L. Weaver).

Toward the coast, Sage Sparrows are now localized. In the south county, west of Sweetwater and Otay reservoirs, where the species was once widespread, the only birds found 1997–2002 were one pair on the hill just east of San Ysidro Junior High School (V11, 10 April 1999, P. Unitt). There is a small number on Cowles Mountain (Q11/Q12), then a population in Mission Trails Regional Park merges with that in Marine Corps Air Station Miramar. The mesa of Miramar, its chaparral broken by vernal pools, supports the largest concentration of Sage Sparrows remaining near the coast. Urban sprawl has now broken the connection between this core and other sites to the north, where the sparrows survive in scattered undeveloped patches. The largest of these is on Black Mountain (M10), where Kirsten Winter counted 18, many paired, 18 April 1999 and estimated at least 50 pairs in the atlas square on the basis of the extent of burned chaparral. The vicinity of Lake Hodges (K10) offers substantial habitat and one of the few remaining sites where the Sage Sparrow occurs in sage scrub rather than chaparral (maximum count eight on 28 May 1999, R. L. Barber). A pair feeding young about 0.7 mile southwest of the San Marcos landfill (J8) 31 May 1997, a pair just southeast of Fuerte Park, Carlsbad (J8) 15 May 1999 (J. O. Zimmer), and six, including four singing males, in black sage just northeast of Palomar College, San Marcos (I9) 2 April 1997 (K. L. Weaver) were our northernmost in coastal San Diego County during the breeding season. Farther north, the Sage Sparrow is scarce, local, and

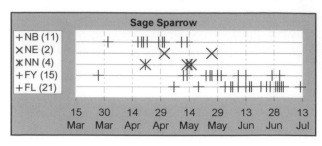

restricted to the Fallbrook Naval Weapons Station (D7/E7) and foothills of the Santa Margarita Mountains, well away from the coast.

Nesting: Sage Sparrows nest typically in shrubs, well below the canopy, occasionally on the ground. Nest sites atlas observers noted were chamise, Cleveland sage, big sagebrush, and on the ground amid broken-down branches of big sagebrush. Our observations of breeding activity were consistent with the 25 March–18 June spread of known San Diego County egg dates, except for nest building 1 March 1997 and feeding young 27 March 1997 in Dameron Valley (C15/C16, K. L. Weaver). The habitat here resembles that in western Riverside County, where Martin and Carlson (1998) reported nest building beginning in mid February and egg laying beginning 11 March.

Migration: Bell's Sage Sparrow is sedentary, though in the nonbreeding season the birds cease maintaining their territories and often form loose flocks. A juvenile in residential Fallbrook (D7) in early October 1992, at least 1 mile from breeding habitat in the naval weapons station, demonstrates some dispersal across unsuitable terrain by young birds (K. L. Weaver).

Subspecies *nevadensis*, by contrast, is largely migratory. Most arrive in San Diego County probably in September (earliest date around the Salton Sea 27 August, Patten et al. 2003) and depart around the first of March. The latest date is 17 March (2000, one south of Clark Dry Lake, E26, K. L. Weaver).

Winter: The few squares on the coastal slope and desert edge where we recorded Bell's Sage Sparrow in winter but not the breeding season are presumably sites where the species is resident in small numbers but was missed during the spring and summer. A probable exception is at Torrey Pines State Reserve (N7; one on 7 February 1998, K. Estey), a site well isolated from known populations and well covered during the breeding season. One near Agua Hedionda Creek at the east edge of Carlsbad (I7) 22 December 2001 (E. Garnica, S. Walens) may represent another small remnant population in north coastal San Diego County.

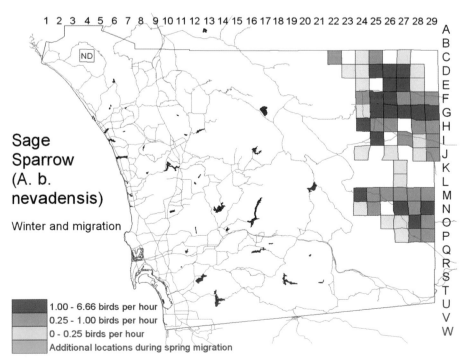

Sage
Sparrow
(A. b.
nevadensis)

Winter and migration

1.00 - 6.66 birds per hour
0.25 - 1.00 birds per hour
0 - 0.25 birds per hour
Additional locations during spring migration

The winter range of subspecies *nevadensis* is completely separated from the year-round range of *belli* by steep mountain slopes. Stands of saltbush and iodine bush on valley floors and in sinks are the Sage Sparrow's most typical winter habitat, but the birds can also be common in broad sandy washes with more diverse shrubs. Unexpectedly, we found the Sage Sparrow as a rare winter visitor in the open pinyon woodland of the Santa Rosa Mountains (C27/D28, maximum count two, 20–21 January 2000, L. J. Hargrove). The blackbush, though, is more numerous than the pinyons on these mountains, and forms stands of a low open scrub recalling the Great Basin. The highest counts of *nevadensis* recorded during the atlas period, 127 in San Felipe Creek near San Felipe Narrows (I25) 10 January 1998 (A. Mauro) and 72 in the Borrego Sink (G25) 9 February 1998 (R. Thériault), coincided with rain in a wet year. Overall numbers of the Sage Sparrow in the Anza–Borrego Desert, though, varied less dramatically in response to rain than those of some other wintering sparrows. They remained fairly steady from 1997 to 2001 and plummeted only in the record dry winter of 2001–02.

Conservation: Lovio (1996) found Bell's Sparrow to be the most sensitive to habitat fragmentation of 31 species nesting in southwestern San Diego County. The smallest tract of habitat in which he found the species was 160 hectares. K. L. Weaver (unpubl. data) had similar results in the north county, though recording the species in one patch of only 13 hectares. He has found the birds persisting over time in a 26-hectare patch near Palomar College (I9). On the basis of a study ranging from Tecolote and Rose canyons to Miramar, Bolger et al. (1997) also found Bell's Sparrow highly sensitive to fragmentation. On the Fallbrook Naval Weapons Station Bell's Sparrows occupy rather small patches of sage scrub amid a mosaic of grassland and weeds, so apparently they do not perceive the grassy areas between the scrub patches to be barriers like housing developments. In the coastal lowland they are now restricted to the last large blocks of brushland, and their prospects in this area are dubious since many of these areas are subject to further development. Smaller tracts may not accommodate enough opportunity for the birds to shift among recovering burned chaparral and older stands that have become too dense for them. Away from the Santa Margarita Mountains, Bell's Sparrow could easily be eliminated west of Interstate 15. Even farther inland extensive habitat degradation through fragmentation is possible. Fire-management practices that lead to infrequent colossal fires instead of frequent small ones also likely disfavor the Sage Sparrow.

Taxonomy: Patten and Unitt (2002) found too much overlap between *A. b. nevadensis* (Ridgway, 1873) and *A. b. canescens* (Grinnell, 1905) for the latter to be distinguished. Synonymizing *canescens* leaves only one pale migratory subspecies and eliminates the apparent but unlikely scenario that these two subspecies have the same winter range. We found no significant difference in bill length between *A. b. belli* (Cassin, 1850) and the supposedly longer-billed *A. b. clementae* Ridgway, 1898, of San Clemente Island, so we synonymized the latter, leaving only one dark subspecies of the Sage Sparrow.

Lark Bunting *Calamospiza melanocorys*

Though the Lark Bunting migrates southwest from the northwestern Great Plains to winter commonly in Baja California, it is rare in Alta California. Historically, records for San Diego County were concentrated along the coast in the fall, though there were also several winter and spring records, some of the latter of flocks. The more uniform coverage of the county achieved by field work for this atlas, however, suggests the Lark Bunting's primary role here is as a rare spring migrant through the Anza–Borrego Desert.

Migration: In fall, the Lark Bunting is reported in San Diego County less than annually, with no more than three birds together. Aside from one in Mason Valley (M23) 13 September 1913 (SDNHM 1851) and one at Lake Henshaw (G17) 18 November 1978 (P. Unitt), all have been in the coastal lowland, most in the Tijuana River valley. Fall dates are 6 September and later, except for 22 July 1996, when an exceptionally early migrant was at Chula Vista (U10; D. and M. Vanier, NASFN 50:998, 1996).

In spring the Lark Bunting is notably sporadic, occasionally occurring in small flocks. It is most likely in the

Photo by Anthony Mercieca

Anza–Borrego Desert after wet winters, as illustrated in 1983 and 1998. In the latter year, one was near Seventeen Palm Springs (F29) 4 April (C. Hagen), 10 were near Five Palms Spring (G29) 11 April (G. Rebstock, K. Forney), 10 were near the Volcanic Hills (Q29) 25 April (R. Thériault), and five were near the Borrego Air Ranch (H27) 27 April (M. L. Gabel). The Lark Bunting has occurred in the desert in normal to dry years, too, for example, one or two at Agua Caliente Springs (M26) 4 April–1 May 1990 (R. Thériault, AB 44:498, 1990) and one at the north end of Clark Valley (C25) 7 May 2001 (D. C. Seals). Desert records extend from 30 March (1999, one at Ocotillo Wells, I29, P. Unitt) to 9 May (1983, one in Earthquake Valley, K23, R. L. McKernan, AB 37:914, 1983).

There are also a few spring records for the coastal slope, clumped in a few wet years, especially 1884 and 1978, following the wettest and third wettest winters in San Diego County history. In the former year, the birds were seen in flocks at Campo (U23) and National City (T10). On 25 May, from National City, Holterhoff (1884) wrote, "they are everywhere abundant on the mesas, and apparently breeding." No proof of breeding followed, however. The Lark Bunting has been confirmed nesting in California only in the Lanfair Valley of the Mojave Desert in spring 1978 (AB 32:1210, 1978). The only spring Lark

Bunting on the coastal slope during the atlas period was in Proctor Valley (T14) 29 April 1998 (P. Unitt). With 1884 excluded, spring records for the coastal slope extend from 4 April (1977, Campo, AB 31:1049, 1977) to 20 May (1978, Horno area, Camp Pendleton, D3, A. Fries).

Winter: There are 10 winter records of the Lark Bunting in San Diego County, all of one or two individuals and all from the coastal lowland. Since Unitt (1984) listed eight, the only ones have been at Chula Vista 5–24 March 1989 (R. Reinke, AB 43:368, 1989) and about 0.5 mile northwest of the mouth of Las Flores Creek (E3) 16 February 1998 (R. and S. L. Breisch).

Savannah Sparrow *Passerculus sandwichensis*

Belding's Sparrow, the nonmigratory subspecies of the Savannah Sparrow endemic to the coast of southern California and northern Baja California, is narrowly restricted to coastal marshes dominated by pickleweed. Recognized as endangered by the California Department of Fish and Game, Belding's Sparrow has been censused statewide five times, most recently in 2001. These results suggest that the bird is holding its own, with a county population of 1105 pairs, but many threats to its habitat persist. Three other subspecies of the Savannah Sparrow, breeding to the north, come to San Diego County as winter visitors only. These subspecies are locally common in open grassy or weedy areas throughout the county and invade the Belding's Sparrow's habitat. Small numbers of yet another subspecies, the Large-billed Sparrow, breeding around the head

Photo by Anthony Mercieca

of the Gulf of California, visit the coast in fall and winter.

Breeding distribution: Thanks to the work of Richard Zembal and Barbara Massey, the distribution of Belding's Sparrow in California is known exhaustively. Field work for the atlas did not reveal any sites beyond the ones they have surveyed. The most recent census is that for 2001 (Zembal and Hoffman 2002). It recorded one territory at the Aliso Creek mouth (F4), 172 at the Santa Margarita River estuary (G4), 6 at Buena Vista Lagoon (H6), 22 at Agua Hedionda Lagoon (I6), 66 at Batiquitos Lagoon (J6/J7), 75 at San Elijo Lagoon (L7), 40 at the San Dieguito River lagoon (M7), 129 at Los Peñasquitos Lagoon (N7), 38 at Kendall–Frost Reserve, Mission Bay (Q8), 4 at the FAA island in Mission Bay (Q8), 26 at the San Diego River flood-control channel (R8), 7 at the Paradise Creek marsh, National City (T10), 93

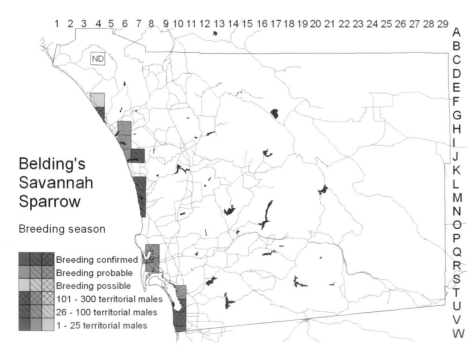

Belding's Savannah Sparrow

Breeding season

Breeding confirmed
Breeding probable
Breeding possible
101 - 300 territorial males
26 - 100 territorial males
1 - 25 territorial males

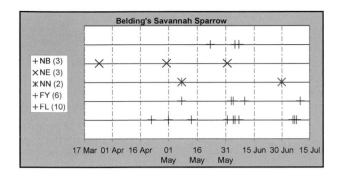

at the Sweetwater River marsh, Chula Vista (U10), 9 at the marsh on the south site of F Street (Lagoon Drive), Chula Vista (U10), 26 at the South Bay Marine Biology Study Area (U10/V10), 102 in the south San Diego Bay salt works (U10/V10), and 289 in the Tijuana River estuary (V10/W10).

Nesting: Belding's Sparrow places its nest in dense marsh vegetation, on or near the ground, concealed from above. Pickleweed, shore grass, and saltwort are recorded as nest plants (Collier and Powell 1998). Nesting success is higher where the marsh plants are denser and taller (Powell and Collier 1998). With 221 sets taken from 1887 to 1952, Belding's Sparrow was one of the species whose eggs were most avidly sought by the early collectors. The breeding activity we observed from 1997 to 2001 was entirely consistent with the dates of the collected sets, 15 March–2 July.

Migration: Belding's Sparrow is sedentary; Collier and Powell (1998) did not find population exchange even between the F Street and Sweetwater marshes, separated by only a quarter mile. Habitat fragmentation is thus a serious concern for this subspecies.

The northern subspecies of the Savannah Sparrow occur in San Diego County mainly from mid or late August to late April. By the first week of May they are rare; the latest was one 0.3 mile north of Indian Hill (R28) 6 May 1998 (J. O. Zimmer). The Large-billed Sparrow's season is shifted earlier. Its current seasonal status is still encompassed by the dates of older specimens, 8 August (1914, National City, T10, SDNHM 34223) to 23 February (1930, Silver Strand, T9, SDNHM 34215).

Winter: In winter the subspecies that come from the north spread widely over San Diego County in grassland (whether it retains any native plants or not), pastures, farmland, weedy open areas, and salt marshes. These visitors are common along the coast and in the inland valleys, with up to 285 in the

San Dieguito River valley east of Lake Hodges (K11) 29 December 2001 (E. C. Hall) and 255 at Sweetwater Reservoir (S12) 18 December 1999 (P. Famolaro). The beds of reservoirs exposed by low water offer Savannah Sparrows habitat: e.g., 60 on the dry floor of upper El Capitan Reservoir (N17) 31 January 2001 (J. R. Barth). In the mountains the Savannah Sparrow is uncommon; maximum counts are only 12, 2–3 miles north of Julian (J20) 27 December 1999 (R. T. Patton), and 10 northeast of Lake Cuyamaca (L21) 27 January 2000 (J. K. Wilson). In the desert it is common only in the Borrego Valley, in agricultural areas or halophytic scrub, where it may flock with Sage, Brewer's, and Vesper Sparrows. Numbers of Savannah Sparrows in the Anza–Borrego Desert did not swing so widely over the atlas' five years as did those of some other sparrows, but they were higher in the first two years of the period than in the three dry later ones. High counts in the desert ranged up to 56 in north Borrego Springs (F24) 20 December 1998 (R. Thériault) and 50 in Sleepy Hollow (H26) 9 February 1998 (M. L. Gabel).

The Large-billed Sparrow is strictly coastal and often mixes in the salt marshes with Belding's. But it occurs just as readily on jetties and beaches among driftwood and kelp. During the atlas period high counts were seven at the Del Mar jetty in Camp Pendleton (G4) 15 November 2001 (P. A. Ginsburg), six near Zuñiga Point on North Island (S8) 11 January 2002, six in the south San Diego Bay salt works (U10) 15 December 2001 (D. C. Seals), and nine at Imperial Beach (V10) 16 December 2000 (C. G. Edwards). Other reported locations include the San Luis Rey River mouth (H5) and the San Diego River flood-control channel (R8). The subspecies could be expected anywhere along the coast of San Diego County.

Conservation: With the elimination of at least 75% of southern California's salt marshes, the range of Belding's Sparrow contracted greatly, especially around Mission

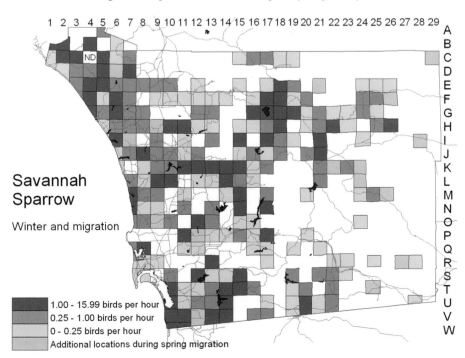

Savannah Sparrow

Winter and migration

- 1.00 - 15.99 birds per hour
- 0.25 - 1.00 birds per hour
- 0 - 0.25 birds per hour
- Additional locations during spring migration

and San Diego bays. Only 1182 hectares of salt marsh are left in San Diego County, some of it seriously degraded, and the birds fill the remaining suitable habitat to capacity. Now, fortunately, most of the Belding's Sparrow's remaining sites are designated as wildlife refuges of various kinds. But, in the delicate balance of its habitat, Belding's Sparrow still walks a tightrope. Nesting success in small, isolated marshes like that at F Street is low to none, so these sites probably act as population sinks (Powell and Collier 1998). The marshes must be flooded regularly enough to sustain the pickleweed and prevent the invasion of upland plants but not so deeply or for so long the birds are precluded from nesting. Belding's Sparrow's primary habitat is the upper marsh zone that is flooded by the tide only infrequently. The birds nest only in this zone (Powell 1993), though they range outside it to forage. Because this is the part of a marsh that is most easily filled and developed, the fraction of its habitat Belding's Sparrow has lost is even greater than the fraction of total coastal wetland lost. Currently, at Santa Margarita, Buena Vista, and Los Peñasquitos, the lagoons' mouths are often or continuously blocked from the tides. Thus the pickleweed may dry out for long periods, then be flooded for long periods by winter rain. Restoration of consistent tidal flow at Batiquitos and San Elijo allowed the numbers of Belding's there to increase (Zembal and Hoffman 2002). Blockage of lagoon mouths comes with accelerated sedimentation of the lagoons, a consequence of their watersheds being stripped of vegetative cover during development. Another factor is that tidal flow into most lagoons is constricted by the berms built for roads and train tracks. Sedimentation converts salt marsh into nonsaline uplands, as has happened on a large scale at Los Peñasquitos. Sediment and debris washing in from Tijuana threaten the Tijuana River estuary, site of San Diego County's largest Belding's Sparrow colony. Techniques for salt-marsh restoration have been established but have not yet been carried out on a scale large enough to be of significant benefit to Belding's Sparrow. Restored habitat takes over four years to reach a structure beneficial to the birds (Keer and Zedler 2002). The low numbers at several sites and the lack of dispersal between these sites raise concern for the long-term genetic viability of the population (Zembal et al. 1988). Finally, invasion of nonnative predators, disturbance by domestic dogs, and trampling of the marshes by people are continuing problems.

The career of the Large-billed Sparrow is one of the most interesting of California's birds. It is all the more mysterious because it has been viewed largely in ignorance of what has happened in the subspecies' breeding range. At the turn of the last century the Large-billed Sparrow was common in marshes and on beaches, wharves, and even city streets along the coast of San Diego County. By the 1940s it was on the decline, and 1954 saw the last report for 23 years (Unitt 1984). After one seen in 1977 and one in 1987, the Large-billed Sparrow invaded in fall 1988 (AB 43:170, 1989) and 1989; 37 were reported on the San Diego Christmas bird count, 17 December 1988, and over 50 were around south San Diego Bay in September 1989 (C. G. Edwards, AB 44:165, 1990). Subsequently the numbers have not been so large, but the subspecies has continued to occur as a rare but annual winter visitor. Presumably the fluctuations are due to habitat changes in the Colorado delta and possibly to changes in sparrow's adaptability to them.

Even the northern subspecies of the Savannah Sparrow are not immune to habitat change. With the conversion of much farmland and grassland to urban development the habitat available to winter visitors has been reduced. The thousands recorded on San Diego Christmas bird counts in the 1960s and early 1970s, primarily in the Tijuana River valley, are no longer found.

Taxonomy: Belding's Sparrow, *P. s. beldingi* Ridgway, 1885, is recognized by its heavily black-streaked underparts and dark olive-tinged upperparts. The three subspecies occurring as winter visitors from the north are paler above and have narrow crisp brown streaks on the underparts. Not safely distinguishable from each other in the field, the three comprise *P. s. anthinus* Bonaparte, 1853, rich brown above and breeding widely in Alaska and northwestern Canada, *P. s. nevadensis* Grinnell, 1910, grayer with broad silvery-white streaks on the back, breeding in the Rocky Mountains and Great Basin, and *P. s. brooksi* Bishop, 1915, similar in color to *nevadensis* but slightly smaller, breeding in the Pacific Northwest. Restudy of 178 San Diego County specimens of the Savannah Sparrow reveals that *anthinus* and *nevadensis* are about equally common, with 35 and 32 specimens, respectively (P. A. Campbell, P. Unitt). With only four specimens *brooksi* is much scarcer, as might be expected with San Diego near the southern tip of its winter range. On the basis of existing specimens, both *anthinus* and *nevadensis* are widespread in the county with no difference in seasonal status, though the earliest fall specimen was collected only on 6 October and by spring the plumage of some individuals is so badly worn as to leave them unidentifiable. The Large-billed Sparrow, *P. s. rostratus* (Cassin, 1852), differs grossly, in its large size, brown-streaked underparts, inconspicuously streaked gray upperparts, and thick bill. It looks almost as much like a female House Finch as a Savannah Sparrow.

Grasshopper Sparrow *Ammodramus savannarum*

The Grasshopper Sparrow is San Diego County's bird most restricted to native grassland—one of southern California's most threatened habitats. The habitat, dominated by bunchgrasses of the genus *Nassella*, was once widespread in the inland valleys. Now it has been much diminished and degraded by overgrazing, groundwater pumping, invasion of exotic plants, conversion to agriculture, and urban sprawl. As a result, the Grasshopper Sparrow is localized and generally uncommon; it has been designated a species of special concern by the California Department of Fish and Game. Yet at a few sites it persists in numbers even where the native grass has been replaced totally by nonnative species. Because the species is so difficult to find and identify except when singing (mainly March–July), its seasonal status is still not clear. Nevertheless, atlas observers generated enough winter records to demonstrate that in San Diego County the Grasshopper Sparrow is at most a partial migrant.

Breeding distribution: The Grasshopper Sparrow's range in San Diego County is now reduced to five main blocks and a few other scattered colonies. Camp Pendleton supports the largest area of contiguous habitat and probably the largest population, with single-day counts of up to 20 around Case Spring (B4) 30 June 1998 (P. A. Ginsburg) and 18 in Piedra de Lumbre Canyon north of Pulgas Lake (D4) 29 May 1999 (P. Unitt, B. O'Leary, J. Asmus). Both the abundance of clay soil and frequent fires favor native grassland on the base. In central coastal San Diego County the original broad distribution of grassland is much fragmented, and most of what remains is threatened by urbanization. The sites of the largest counts in this region are from the only two large areas not subject to urban sprawl: Los Peñasquitos Canyon Preserve (N8; up to 20 on 3 June 2001, B. Siegel) and Marine Corps Air Station Miramar/Mission Trails Regional Park (up to 12 in West Sycamore Canyon, O12, 24 March 1999, P. Unitt). In the southern part of the county Grasshopper Sparrow habitat is now narrowly wedged between the cities of San Diego and Chula Vista and the higher chaparral-covered mountains, McGinty and Otay. Even though the site is former agricultural land, much of which is

Photo by Anthony Mercieca

now vegetated with exotic grasses only, Rancho Jamul, now acquired by the California Department of Fish and Game, appears to host the key population in this region (S15/T15; up to 47 on 22 April 2001, M. and B. McIntosh, V. Marquez). The Ramona grasslands are also important to the Grasshopper Sparrow, though poor access impeded our quantifying this. The site of our largest count in this region, northeast of Ramona (K15; 23 on 25 May 1998, M. and B. McIntosh), had houses built on it the following year.

In the mountains, from Dyche and Love valleys (F16) southeast of Palomar Mountain to Lake Cuyamaca (M20), Grasshopper Sparrow habitat is discontinuous and the birds appear less numerous and more irregular than at lower elevations. The highest counts were of 16 at Wynola (J19) 2 July 1999 (S. E. Smith) and nine at Lake Henshaw (G17) 12 May 2001 (R. and S. L. Breisch). Of the more isolated colonies, by far the most important is that around Willow Spring (A5), with counts of up to 20 on 25 May and 10 June 1999 (K. J. Winter).

The Grasshopper Sparrow's grassland habitat usually has some shrubs typical of coastal sage scrub, and some of its sites are shrubby enough to have been mapped as scrub rather than as grassland. Wet winters that stimulate the spread of grass stimulate the Grasshopper Sparrow to move into marginal habitat. Its sensitivity to rainfall variation is dramatized by figures from West Sycamore Canyon in Miramar, monitored annually 1997–2002. The same area that had up to 12 territorial males in 1998 and 1999 had no more than two during the drought of 2002 (P. Unitt). After the wet winter of 1983–84, Roger Higson reported up to 30 in summer 1984 at Lake Henshaw and one at the Palomar Observatory (D15) 5 May 1984 (AB 38:1063, 1984). An atypical site for the Grasshopper Sparrow

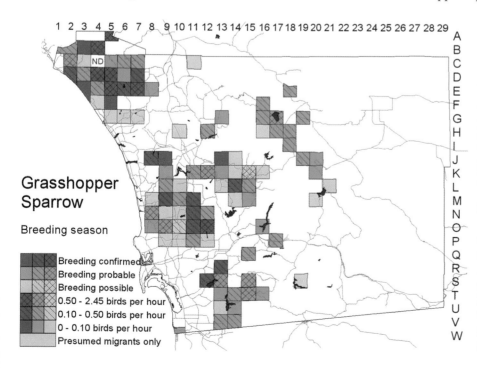

Grasshopper Sparrow

Breeding season

- Breeding confirmed
- Breeding probable
- Breeding possible
- 0.50 - 2.45 birds per hour
- 0.10 - 0.50 birds per hour
- 0 - 0.10 birds per hour
- Presumed migrants only

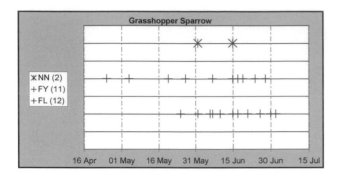

is Border Field State Park (W10), where on 23 May 2000 three birds had established territories in former salt marsh still dominated by pickleweed, now degraded by silt washed in from Tijuana (W. E. Haas). Dawson (1923) mentioned a nest near Escondido in an alkaline meadow covered with saltgrass, but no significant stands of such habitat remain inland.

Nesting: Hidden on the ground under clumps of grass, screened from above by a dome, Grasshopper Sparrow nests are notoriously hard to find. Only three were reported during the atlas period. The dates of breeding behavior we observed imply egg laying from the second week of April to the last week of May.

Migration: Records of winter visitors south to Cabo San Lucas demonstrate that the Grasshopper Sparrow is migratory, but in San Diego County the species is very rarely seen away from its breeding habitat. There are no records of such migrants in spring. The three records from Point Loma (S7) coincide in late fall: 25 October–1 November 1984 (R. E. Webster, AB 39:104, 1985), 30–31 October 1986 (R. E. Webster, AB 41:146, 1987), 22 October 1989 (M. A. Patten, AB 44:165, 1990).

Winter: Our field work for this atlas generated 55 winter records of the Grasshopper Sparrow, far more than expected and far more than reported previously. Excluding eight records from the last week of February, when the birds may begin singing, still leaves 47. By the end of the project it became clear that the species could be found consistently in its summer habitat, at least at low elevations, with persistent searching. Winter counts, excluding those in late February, ranged up to six, near Pilgrim Creek, Camp Pendleton (E7), 4 December 1998 (P. A. Ginsburg). Even the birds at higher elevations may be resident, with three as high as 3430 feet in Love Valley (G16) 22 January 2001 (W. E. Haas). The most notable winter records were from San Felipe Valley (I21, one on 8 February 2000; J21, two on 14 December 1999, P. K. Nelson), in grassland but on the desert slope where the species is not known in summer. Two at Campo (U23) 14 January 2001 (D. S. and A. W. Hester) were also in suitable habitat but at a site where no breeding birds were found.

Conservation: Dependent on a threatened habitat, the Grasshopper Sparrow's outlook in San Diego County is dim. Most habitat is privately owned and subject to intense pressure for development. Conservation of all grasslands under multiple-species conservation plans is relatively poor (around 31% under the plan for the north county), and little native grassland remains in the areas covered by these plans. As a result, the Grasshopper Sparrow was excluded from the list of species "covered" by San Diego's plan.

Conservation of the Grasshopper Sparrow will require action on multiple fronts. Maintaining grassland's value as habitat may require control of invasive weeds and enhancement, possibly through burning, to give native species an advantage over exotics. In Warner Valley, San Diego County's largest grassland, where the birds are now confined to patches around seeps, recovery will require that grazing and groundwater pumping be reduced. The largest tracts of Grasshopper Sparrow habitat currently lie on military bases and water-district lands set aside for purposes other than wildlife conservation. It is far from certain that existing parks and reserves, mainly Los Peñasquitos, Mission Trails, and Rancho Jamul, covering only a small fraction of the Grasshopper Sparrow's habitat, will suffice to ensure the species' survival in San Diego County.

Taxonomy: Only the western subspecies *A. s. perpallidus* has been collected in California. It is paler and drabber than the other Grasshopper Sparrows of North America.

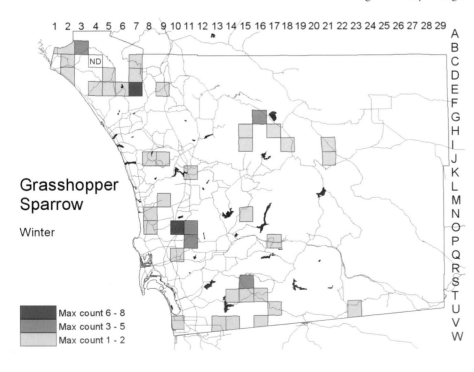

Grasshopper
Sparrow

Winter

Max count 6 - 8
Max count 3 - 5
Max count 1 - 2

Baird's Sparrow *Ammodramus bairdii*

A scarce and declining bird of the northern Great Plains, Baird's Sparrow winters regularly as far west as southeastern Arizona. But there are only three records for California, two from Southeast Farallon Island and one from San Diego County.

Migration: Southern California's single known Baird's Sparrow was a juvenile photographed at Fort Rosecrans Cemetery, Point Loma (S7), 5–10 October 1981 (G. McCaskie, Binford 1985).

Photo by Herb Clarke

Nelson's Sharp-tailed Sparrow *Ammodramus nelsoni*

Most of the population of Nelson's Sharp-tailed Sparrow migrates from central Canada to the Gulf of Mexico, but a few birds reach the coast of California. Here they are found in coastal salt marshes almost invariably. The birds seldom expose themselves outside the cover of dense vegetation, especially pickleweed. Birders have learned to look for them as they look for rails, during the winter's highest tides, when high water floods them out and forces them to the marsh's edge.

Photo by Anthony Mercieca

Winter: There are just 13 records of Nelson's Sharp-tailed Sparrow in San Diego County, and some of these likely represent the same individuals returning in successive years. Locations are a freshwater marsh near Oceanside (H5) 11 October 1992 (R. R. Veit, AB 47:151, 1993), Kendall–Frost Marsh, Mission Bay (Q8), 31 December 1986–27 February 1987 and 8 October 1987–18 January 1988 (E. Copper, AB 41:331, 1987; 42:139, 323, 1988), the Sweetwater River estuary, Chula Vista (U10), 8 December 1987 (S. J. Montgomery, AB 42:323, 1988) and 2–17 December 1994 (V. P. Johnson, NASFN 49:200, 1995), and the Tijuana River estuary (V10). The six records for the last site encompass the only specimen, collected 2 November 1963 (McCaskie et al. 1967c, SDNHM 30788), the highest count (three from 22 December 1991 to 16 February 1992,

A. Mercieca, AB 46:316, 1992), and the only reports during the atlas period, of two 21–22 January 2000 (D. K. Adams, NAB 54:222, 2000) and 9 January 2001 (E. Wallace, NAB 55:229, 2001).

Migration: Extreme dates for this species in San Diego County are 8 October and 27 February.

Taxonomy: The split of the Sharp-tailed Sparrow into two species (AOU 1995) has still left Nelson's with three component subspecies. Nominate *A. n. nelsoni* Allen, 1875, is the one occurring in California. See Sibley (1996) for details on its identification.

Fox Sparrow *Passerella iliaca*

The Fox Sparrow is a common winter visitor in the chaparral that blankets San Diego County's foothills and mountains—one of the most common winter birds in this habitat. Yet it easily passes unnoticed, foraging quietly on the ground, screened from view by dense shrubbery. Only when the birder "squeaks" or "pishes" to stimulate the birds' curiosity do Fox Sparrows reveal their true abundance, rising to the tops of the shrubs to look around and call, "smack" or "chink." San Diego County appears central to the winter range of two or three subspecies of the Fox Sparrow, and it hosts at least eight subspecies—more than of any other species of bird. The county is mar-

Photo by Anthony Mercieca

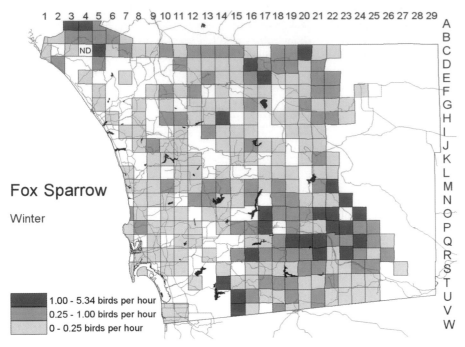

Fox Sparrow

Winter

1.00 - 5.34 birds per hour
0.25 - 1.00 birds per hour
0 - 0.25 birds per hour

Migration: Wintering Fox Sparrows depart gradually through March and April. No peaks or concentrations of migrants are known or expected, given that northwestern Baja California marks the southern end of the species' winter range. By 1 May the Fox Sparrow is rare. The only records of spring migrants after 3 May during the atlas period were of one at Yaqui Well (I24) 24 May 1999 (P. K. Nelson) and one at Camp Horno, Camp Pendleton (D3), 27 May 2000 (P. A. Ginsburg), and these appear to be the latest ever. Fall migrants begin returning in the third week of September.

The migration schedule of the Fox Sparrows nesting in San Diego County's mountains is still not known. The birds have been reported on Cuyamaca Peak only from 23 May to 6 August. Data from elsewhere in California suggest arrival in April and departure in September or early October.

ginal, though, to the Fox Sparrow's breeding range. Only a few birds summer, near the summit of the county's highest mountains.

Breeding distribution: Cuyamaca Peak (M20) is the Fox Sparrow's principal breeding site in San Diego County, occupied annually since D. W. Povey first discovered the species there in 1978. Thickets of bracken fern and Palmer's ceanothus between Deer Spring and Cherry Flat, 5600 to 6200 feet elevation, are the birds' habitat. The maximum count in this area, 1997–2002, was five on 13 July 2000 (J. R. Barth), less than the high of 16 reported in 1980 (AB 34:931, 1980). Fox Sparrows have also colonized the west slope of nearby Middle Peak (M20), where R. E. Webster had two singing males 11 June 2000 and an adult with a fledgling 2 July 2000.

During the first opportunity for an ornithologist to visit Volcan Mountain (I20) in many years, I found Fox Sparrows in small numbers (five singing males) 30–31 May 1993. During the atlas period, only a single individual was found there, 22 July 1999 (L. J. Hargrove). Summering Fox Sparrows were found for the first time in the Laguna Mountains in 2000. C. H. Reiser reported one on Garnet Peak (N23) 26 June 2000, then G. L. Rogers reported another near Pine Mountain (N22) 30 June 2001. Roger Higson located three or four pairs around the Palomar Observatory (D15) in summer 1979 (AB 33:898, 1979), but the birds have not returned there since.

Nesting: No nests of the Fox Sparrow have yet been found in San Diego County, and the observations of fledglings on Middle Peak 2 July 2000 (R. E. Webster) and on Cuyamaca Peak 8 and 13 July 2000 (G. L. Rogers, J. R. Barth) appear to be the first confirmation of the species' nesting here. The nest may be either in or under dense shrubs; of eight nests Pierce (1921) described in the San Bernardino Mountains, three were on the ground, five were in ceanothus bushes.

Winter: The Fox Sparrow is widespread over the coastal slope of San Diego County, most concentrated in extensive stands of mature chaparral. In northern San Diego County the Santa Margarita Mountains, the north slope of Palomar Mountain, and the Indian Flats/Bucksnort Mountain region emerge as regions of greatest abundance. In central and southern San Diego County the Fox Sparrow is common almost continuously from Viejas (O17), McGinty (R15), and Sycuan (R16) mountains east to the Lagunas. Our high counts, of up to 70 near Thing Valley (Q24) 7 January 2001 (J. R. Barth) and 55 along Miner's Road (O21) 5 January 1999 (P. Unitt), could be duplicated easily in this region by an observer focusing his effort on Fox Sparrows.

The Fox Sparrow occurs in coastal sage scrub and riparian scrub but is uncommon in those habitats, and it is lacking in grassland and developed areas, making its distribution patchy. It can still be fairly common even right along the coast, though, where conditions are suitable, as around Onofre Hill (D2; 12 on 21 January 2002, P. Unitt) and Torrey Pines City Park (O7; 10 on 16 January 2002, D. G. Seay). At the desert's edge, the Fox Sparrow drops out quickly as the chaparral begins to break up. On the desert floor the Fox Sparrow is very rare, recorded twice in Borrego Springs (G24, one on 14 January 1991, A. G. Morley; F24, one on 20 December 1998, R. Thériault) and seven times at Yaqui Well and Tamarisk Grove (I24; ABDSP database).

Conservation: Whether the small numbers of Fox Sparrows in San Diego County's mountains represent a recent range extension or a discovery (as a result of better coverage) of birds long present remains unknown.

Because the numbers are so small, the population is vulnerable to disruptions like fire or prolonged drought, but the Fox Sparrow's chaparral habitat regenerates quickly after fire. Broad-scale climate change, though, could push the birds' preferred habitat to an elevation zone above the county's highest peaks. Urbanization has rendered a chunk of the Fox Sparrow's winter range unusable, but the core of this range is inland from the coastal regions where the cities are spreading. The Cleveland National Forest encloses the areas of the Fox Sparrow's greatest winter density, so it seems likely the species will remain common in winter indefinitely.

Taxonomy: The Fox Sparrow offers one of the prime examples of the application of subspecies, because its subspecies enable us to identify the regions where these winter visitors originate. The largest numbers come from the Sierra Nevada and Cascade Range, but other major sources are southwestern and/or south-central Alaska and the Rocky Mountains, in both Canada and the contiguous United States.

Swarth (1920) divided the Fox Sparrow into three groups of subspecies: the gray or *schistacea* group, with plain gray crown and back, the brown or *unalaschcensis* group, with plain brown crown and back, and the red or *iliaca* group, with a red-streaked gray crown and back. This arrangement has been supported by genetic studies, leading to the proposal that each group be considered a species in its own right (Zink 1986, 1994, Rising 1996). Nevertheless, there are specimens intermediate between the groups, whole subspecies intermediate between the gray and red groups, and no known differences in the birds' winter ecology. The Fox Sparrows most common in San Diego County are of the *schistacea* group, having gray heads and backs contrasting with more rufous wings and tails and black spots on the underparts. This group can be divided into three subspecies on the basis of bill thickness. The heaviest-billed birds, the subspecies *P. i. stephensi* Anthony, 1895, are those breeding in the high mountains of southern California, including San Diego County. No specimens of the local breeding population, however, have been collected yet. Mailliard (1918) named the large-billed Fox Sparrows breeding in the inner Coast Ranges of northwestern California from the Trinity River to Snow Mountain as *P. i. brevicauda*, and Swarth (1920) supported this, distinguishing *brevicauda* from *stephensi* by its supposedly browner color, shorter tail, and more bulbous bill. The color difference is not evident in specimens now so was presumably based on comparison of specimens of different ages—the Fox Sparrow is a prime exemplar of foxing, the tendency of feather color to drift from gray to brown to rusty as a bird skin sits in the museum. The shorter tail is a poor character because these ground-dwelling birds' tails wear so quickly; hardly any specimens collected during the breeding season have a tail intact enough to yield a valid measurement. There is a slight average difference, insufficient to diagnose a subspecies (male *brevicauda* mean 85.0, *n* = 20 in MVZ and CAS, standard deviation 4.01; male *stephensi* mean 89.2, *n* = 5 in MVZ and SDNHM, standard deviation

2.93). Zink (1986) found no difference between the populations in the length of the outermost rectrix. Bill shape varies much among individuals, and the width of the maxilla of *stephensi* actually averages greater than that of *brevicauda* (male *brevicauda* mean 9.47, *n* = 60; male *stephensi* mean 9.58, *n* = 38). Therefore, despite the two populations' ranges being so disjunct, *brevicauda* cannot be distinguished from *stephensi* and must be considered a synonym of it. Including *brevicauda*, *stephensi* is uncommon as a winter visitor in San Diego, with six specimens (4 miles southwest of Ramona, L14; Old Mission Dam, P11; Flinn Springs, P15; 3 miles south of Alpine, Q17; Otay Mountain, V12).

The Fox Sparrows breeding in the southern Cascade Range and northern and central Sierra Nevada, *P. i. megarhynchus* Baird, 1858, are gray like *stephensi* but have a smaller bill, though the bill is still larger than in the remaining subspecies of the Fox Sparrow. The difference in bill thickness is adequate to support *megarhynchus* and *stephensi* as subspecies by the criteria of Patten and Unitt (2002) (Table 8). Fox Sparrows averaging smaller billed, intermediate toward the small-billed birds of the Great Basin, occur on the east slope of the Cascade Range in Oregon, on northeastern California's Modoc Plateau (*P. i. fulva* Swarth, 1918), and in and near Mono County, California (*P. i. monoensis* Grinnell and Storer, 1917). These populations' differences from *megarhynchus*, though, are insufficient to support their recognition as subspecies; both must be synonymized with *megarhynchus* (Table 8). Zink (1986) made the same recommendation. He proposed merging *stephensi* and *brevicauda* with *megarhynchus* as well, while saying "there might be a basis for recognizing two groups, *stephensi* plus *brevicauda* vs the other three" (i.e., *megarhynchus*, *fulva*, and *monoensis*). Data in Table 8 show that the Fox Sparrows in the largest-billed subspecies' core ranges are adequately differentiated to merit another name. Defined to include *fulva* and *monoensis*, *megarhynchus* is the most numerous subspecies of the Fox Sparrow in San Diego County, represented by 83 of 124 SDNHM specimens (67%). These specimens range from La Jolla (P7) and Point Loma (S7) on the coast east to Oriflamme Canyon (M22) and the Laguna Mountains (P23), on dates extending from 7 October to 11 April.

Passerella i. schistacea Baird, 1858, the Fox Sparrow of the Great Basin and Rocky Mountains north to southwest-

Table 8   Bill depths of males of gray subspecies of the Fox Sparrow[a]

Nominal subspecies	N	Mean	Range	Standard deviation
stephensi	50	14.14	12.8–15.2	0.53
brevicauda	59	13.65	12.5–14.5	0.44
megarhynchus	53	11.90	11.3–13.0	0.41
monoensis	25	11.72	10.8–12.6	0.49
fulva	98	10.83	9.1–12.2	0.59
schistacea	51	9.53	8.7–10.6	0.41

[a]All specimens from the breeding range; bill depth measured by Swarth's (1920:83) technique.

ern Alberta, is gray too but has a small bill, like that of the brown and rusty subspecies. It includes as synonyms *P. i. canescens* Swarth, 1918, and *P. i. swarthi* Behle and Selander, 1951. Specimens of *schistacea* from eastern Nevada are well differentiated from those of *megarhynchus* on the west slope of the Sierra Nevada (Table 8). *P. i. schistacea* is much less common than *megarhynchus* but appears more prevalent in semidesert chaparral. Of the 15 SDNHM specimens from San Diego County eight are from the east slope of the mountains at the edge of Fox Sparrow habitat. Others, though, are from as close to the coast as 4 miles north of San Marcos (H9) and Escondido (J10).

The Fox Sparrows of the Washington Cascades and south-central British Columbia are an intermediate step between *schistacea* and the browner subspecies *altivagans* to the north. This subspecies, *P. i. olivacea* Aldrich, 1943, appears to reach San Diego County in small numbers. Four specimens from San Diego County meet the description of *olivacea* or intergrades between *olivacea* and *altivagans*: Point Loma, 16 December 1970 (SDNHM 37751), Highland Valley (K12), 9 October 1950 (SDNHM 29877), 1 mile north of Cibbets Flat (Q23), 11 December 1989 (SDNHM 46484), and 0.95 mile north of Los Pinos Mountain (R20), 13 March 1984 (SDNHM 42942).

All along the Pacific coast from Unalaska Island in the Aleutians to the Olympic Peninsula of Washington nest the seven brown or sooty subspecies of the Fox Sparrow. These subspecies have the entire upperparts almost uniform, the wings and tail hardly more rufous than the back, brown spots on the underparts, and a distinctly yellow base to the mandible. These subspecies are famed for their leapfrog pattern of migration: the southernmost migrating little or none, the northernmost migrating the farthest, that is, to San Diego. The three northernmost subspecies, *P. i. unalaschcensis* (Gmelin, 1789), breeding in the eastern Aleutian Islands and Alaska Peninsula, *P. i. insularis* Ridgway, 1901, breeding on Kodiak Island, and *P. i. sinuosa* Grinnell, 1910, breeding in south-central Alaska, are closely similar. Willett (1933) implied that they are better combined, but Gibson and Kessel (1997), with specimens from the breeding range, continued to recognize them. With 22 of 124 SDNHM specimens, *unalaschcensis* is less numerous in San Diego County than *megarhynchus*, but it is still common and widespread. The specimens range from Point Loma to the Cottonwood Campground in the In-Ko-Pah Mountains (Q25), near the east edge of the chaparral.

Coastal Fox Sparrows from farther southeast in Alaska reach San Diego County only rarely. Bishop (1905) reported that H. C. Oberholser identified three of 13 Fox Sparrows taken at Witch Creek (J18) on 12 December 1904 as *P. i. annectens* Ridgway, 1900, a somewhat darker brown subspecies breeding in the Yakutat area of Alaska. There is only one county specimen of *annectens* in the SDNHM collection (46485), from 1 mile north of Cibbets Flat 11 December 1989 (T. Ijichi). Still darker birds, sooty brown on the upperparts and very thickly spotted on the underparts, breed in southeastern Alaska and on the Queen Charlotte Islands—*P. i. townsendi* (Audubon, 1838). One specimen of *townsendi* has been collected in San Diego County, 2 miles east of Descanso (P20) 16 November 1924 (SDNHM 34697). These are the southernmost specimens known of both *annectens* and *townsendi*—their main winter ranges lie farther north.

In interior British Columbia and the northern Rocky Mountains of Alberta breed Fox Sparrows that bridge the *schistacea* and *iliaca* groups, the subspecies *P. i. altivagans* Riley, 1911. It has brown spots on the underparts and brown upperparts, often with a hint of the rufous streaking characteristic of the *iliaca* group. Swarth grouped *altivagans* with *iliaca*; Zink (1994) and Rising (1996) grouped it with *schistacea*. Toward the coast of British Columbia it apparently intergrades with the dark subspecies of the *unalaschcensis* group as well (Swarth 1920). Specimens of *altivagans* lacking any back streaking resemble the geographically disjunct *sinuosa*, differing most clearly in their brighter rufous, more contrasting uppertail coverts. Distinguishing *altivagans* in the field from the paler subspecies of the *unalaschcensis* group may not be possible unless there are differences in calls or bill color, still inadequately explored. *P. i. altivagans* is an uncommon or fairly common winter visitor in San Diego County, with 13 SDNHM specimens scattered from Point Loma to the Laguna Mountains. Another specimen from Ames Valley in the Laguna Mountains (P23) 14 November 1983 (SDNHM 42692) appears to be an intergrade between *altivagans* and *P. i. fuliginosa* Ridgway, 1899, the darkest subspecies of the brown group.

Finally, *P. i. zaboria* Oberholser, 1946, the western representative of the boldly patterned rufous-and-gray *iliaca* group, reaches San Diego County very rarely. There is one specimen of *zaboria*, from Point Loma 18 November 1968 (SBCM 4423), and four sight records, from Agua Caliente Springs (M26) 25 February 1973 (G. McCaskie), Tijuana River valley 8 March 1974 (G. McCaskie), near Green Valley Falls Campground (N20) 11 January 1992 (K. L. Weaver), and Santee (P12) 12 February 2002 (M. B. Mulrooney, NAB 56:225, 2002).

Song Sparrow *Melospiza melodia*

The Song Sparrow is the most abundant bird in San Diego County's riparian woodlands. Freshwater marshes, low rank vegetation in disturbed areas, shrubbery in parks, coastal chaparral, and any dense vegetation near water offer it habitat too. Though making little use of heavily built-up areas, the Song Sparrow on balance benefits from human modification of the southern California environment, taking advantage of agriculture, irrigated landscaping, and urban runoff. A year-round resident, it is seen only very rarely in desert areas outside its breeding range.

Breeding distribution: Though the Song Sparrow lives mainly around water, its habitat needs are generalized enough that on the scale of our atlas grid its distribution appears almost uniform over the coastal slope. The few gaps correspond to large stands of chaparral and/or coniferous forest. Concentrations correspond to squares with much riparian woodland (especially northwestern San Diego County), lagoons, and lakes. In prime habitat daily counts of Song Sparrows can be in triple digits, e.g., 226 in lower Los Peñasquitos Canyon (N8) 3 May 1997 (L. D. and R. Johnson et al.), 125 in Daley Ranch (H11) 31 May 1998 (C. G. Edwards).

On the desert slope the Song Sparrow occurs in all canyons where there is permanent water: Coyote Creek (C22/D23), Borrego Palm (F23), Hellhole (G23), Sentenac (J23), Vallecito Creek (M23–25), Canebrake (N27/O27), Bow Willow (P26), and Carrizo (Q27/R27). It also inhabits the oases of Agua Caliente Springs (M26, up to four on 4 June 1998, E. C. Hall) and Carrizo Marsh (O29, up to eight on 17 April 1998, M. C. Jorgensen). It has colonized plant nurseries on the floor of the northern Borrego Valley (maximum 16 at Ellis Farms, F25, 13 May 2001, P. D. Ache), outside its historic breeding range but in parallel with the spread of the coastal subspecies *heermanni* on the floor of the Coachella Valley in Riverside County (Patten 2001).

Nesting: Song Sparrows usually build their cup nest in or under dense low vegetation. The nest is occasionally higher, such as one 10 feet up in a saltcedar in Vallecito Valley (M24). It is often over or near water, as implied by atlas observers' reports of nests in cattails, hedge nettle, and debris left by a flood. Some nests are in drier places, and some are in entirely man-made habitats, such as one in rosemary in a garden and another in a potted shrub in a nursery.

Photo by Anthony Mercieca

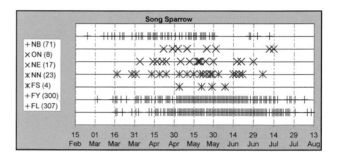

Song Sparrows are prolific, often raising three, rarely four broods per year (M. M. Nice in Austin 1968). In San Diego County they usually nest from March to July. A few birds begin even in mid February, as implied by two fledglings at the east end of Lake Hodges (K11) 17 March 1999 (E. C. Hall), adults carrying insects at Sentenac Ciénaga (J22) 3 March 1997 (L. Allen), and an egg set collected at Encinitas (K6) 16 February 1939 (WFVZ).

Migration: The local population of the Song Sparrow appears practically sedentary. In the Anza–Borrego Desert, migrants occur rarely away from sites where the species is resident: south Borrego Springs (G24), one on 7 March 1998 (P. D. Ache); Borrego sewage ponds (H25), one on 4 April 1997 (H. L. Young, M. B. Mosher); Yaqui Well (I24), one on 18 March 1997 (P. K. Nelson); Arroyo Seco del Diablo (N28), one on 14 March 1998 (R. and S. L. Breisch). Massey (1998) also reported single spring sightings from Clark Dry Lake (D26/E26) and Indian Valley (O27). These records more likely represent wanderers or pioneers of the local subspecies *heermanni* rather than migrants headed farther north: *heermanni* occasionally reaches the Imperial Valley (Patten et al. 2003).

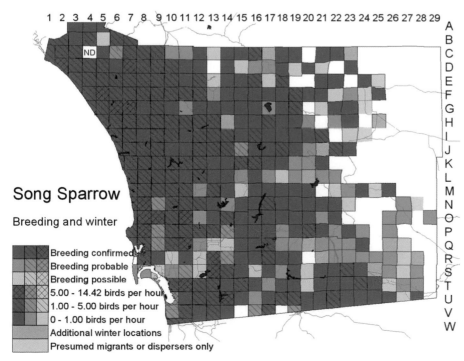

Song Sparrow

Breeding and winter

Breeding confirmed
Breeding probable
Breeding possible
5.00 - 14.42 birds per hour
1.00 - 5.00 birds per hour
0 - 1.00 birds per hour
Additional winter locations
Presumed migrants or dispersers only

Winter: In San Diego County, the only site outside the Song Sparrow's breeding range where the species appears even somewhat regular in winter is the Borrego sewage ponds, with three records 1997–2002, of up to two on 16 January 1999 (P. D. Jorgensen) and 16 December 2001 (L. D. and R. Johnson). The few other winter records from atlas squares where no Song Sparrows were noted during the breeding season are adjacent to squares where it breeds; they may represent sites where it is resident in small numbers.

Conservation: Although primarily a species of riparian woodland and scrub, many of whose birds have suffered declines, the Song Sparrow continues to thrive. Though a principal host for the Brown-headed Cowbird, the Song Sparrow remained common in San Diego County in spite of the cowbird's invading. Importation of water and irrigation allowed the sparrow to colonize areas formerly unsuitable, compensating for loss of riparian habitat. Urban runoff yields enough water to turn small canyons within the cities into Song Sparrow habitat. Although sparse in older residential areas, the Song Sparrow colonizes the ornamental shrubbery around new office parks and in landscaped housing developments. Low rank weeds often suffice: after a restoration attempt at the San Dieguito River estuary (M7), a sandy island intended as a Least Tern site was soon overgrown with weeds, and Song Sparrows moved in. The amount of habitat needed to support a pair may be quite small—Song Sparrows can usually be found in the patch of ornamental shrubbery, measuring about 50 by 30 feet, on the northeast side of the San Diego Natural History Museum.

Taxonomy: Though the Song Sparrow has differentiated into a remarkable number of subspecies—25 even after Patten's (2001) revision dispensed with some inadequately defined ones—only two of these are known from San Diego County. The resident subspecies, characterized by its heavy black streaking below and tricolor (black, brown, and olive gray) streaking above, is *M. m. heermanni* Baird, 1858, from which *cooperi* Ridgway, 1899 (type locality San Diego) is not well differentiated (Patten 2001). Although *heermanni* hybridizes with the small pale rusty *fallax* of the desert Southwest in the Coachella Valley of Riverside County (Patten 2001), the Song Sparrows at even the easternmost sites in San Diego County, Borrego Valley and Carrizo Marsh, appear typical of *heermanni*.

Some other subspecies breeding to the north of San Diego County are migratory, but their winter ranges do not extend quite this far south. The only specimen of one of these migrants is *M. m. merrilli* Brewster, 1896, collected by L. M. Huey at Yaqui Well (I24), where *heermanni* is absent, 13 October 1936 (SDNHM 17255). *M. m. merrilli* has moderate rufous streaking on its underparts and muted streaking on its upperparts—it would be readily noticed in the field as different from *heermanni*. The specimen from Yaqui Well is too pale and crisply streaked for subspecies *morphna* of the Pacific Northwest, as Huey (1954) reported it. *M. m. merrilli* originates in the intermountain area of eastern Washington, southeastern British Columbia, northern Idaho, and northwestern Montana. The next winter records north of San Diego County are from Los Angeles County (Grinnell and Miller 1944).

Lincoln's Sparrow *Melospiza lincolnii*

Though often overlooked, hidden in dense, low vegetation, Lincoln's Sparrow is not rare. It is uncommon, even fairly common, in riparian scrub, riparian edges, and damp weedy areas. One must learn its juncolike "tup" and buntinglike buzz calls to appreciate Lincoln's Sparrow's actual numbers. Lincoln's Sparrow occurs in San Diego County as a migrant and winter visitor only. Though the southern tip of its breeding range is as close as the San Jacinto Mountains of Riverside County, there is only one summer record for San Diego County.

Winter: Lincoln's Sparrow is widespread in the coastal lowland, where the damp thickets the birds prefer are most frequent. During the atlas period, daily counts ran to a maximum of 35 at the south base of Cerro de las Posas, San Marcos (J8), 24 December 1997 (J. O. Zimmer) and 26 in the San Pasqual Valley (K12) 2 January 2000 (C. G. Edwards). In wet years even higher numbers occur in the thick ruderal vegetation along Santa Ysabel Creek in the San Pasqual Valley (K. L. Weaver). Seldom, though, are more than 10 individuals counted in a day, even in good habitat. And the species was missed entirely in a few atlas squares with substantial riparian habitat where it

Photo by Anthony Mercieca

should be expected. Other gaps at low elevations are due to dearth or lack of habitat. At higher elevations, in more rugged terrain, wintering Lincoln's Sparrows become progressively scarcer and more localized. A few individuals occur as high as 5300 feet elevation, such as one near the Palomar Fire Station (D15) 4 December 1998 (K. L. Weaver) and two at Cuyamaca Lake (M20) 22 February 1999 (A. P. and T. E. Keenan).

In the Anza–Borrego Desert, Lincoln's Sparrow is uncommon at oases and in developed areas with irrigated

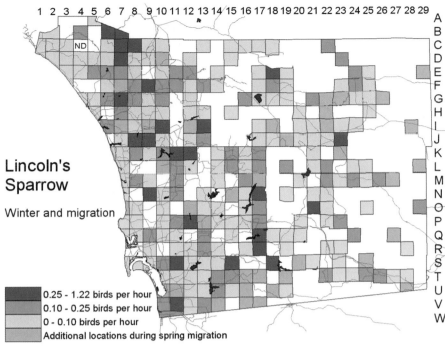

Lincoln's
Sparrow

Winter and migration

- 0.25 - 1.22 birds per hour
- 0.10 - 0.25 birds per hour
- 0 - 0.10 birds per hour
- Additional locations during spring migration

State Park (E14), 7 July 1986 (K. L. Weaver, E. J. McNeil)—the wet meadow at this site is the closest approximation to Lincoln's Sparrow's breeding habitat in San Diego County.

Conservation: No trend in Lincoln's Sparrow numbers in San Diego County is obvious. Christmas bird count results suggest much variability from year to year, but, among the county's six counts, these variations do not run in phase. Importation of water benefits Lincoln's Sparrow; even the weedy dry beds of reservoirs exposed during droughts are good Lincoln's Sparrow habitat. But the development of floodplains—channelizing, landscaping, paving—disfavors this bird so partial to uncontrolled dense undergrowth.

shrubbery. Desert numbers range up to 21 in Borrego Springs (F24) 20 December 1998 (R. Thériault), six at Lower Willows (D23) 19 December 1999 (P. R. Pryde), and five at Agua Caliente Springs (M26) 28 January 1998 (E. C. Hall). We noted only five scattered individuals in dry desert habitats, and three of these were in the wet winter of 1997–98.

Migration: Lincoln's Sparrows arrive in mid to late September, then depart in April. Scattered birds are seen in late March and April at locations where the species does not winter, rarely even in sparsely vegetated desert. By the first of May the species is rare. The only spring records after 5 May are of single birds near Puerta La Cruz (E18) 12 May 2001 and near Angelina Spring (I22) 16 May 1999 (both P. K. Nelson). The single summer record is of one along Doane Creek, Palomar Mountain

Taxonomy: Two subspecies of Lincoln's Sparrows are generally recognized, *M. l. gracilis* (Kittlitz, 1858), breeding in southeastern Alaska and coastal British Columbia, and *M. l. lincolnii* (Audubon, 1834), breeding in the rest of the species' transcontinental range. The two still need to be better defined; the characters of *gracilis*, small size and heavier black streaking on the upperparts, are not always correlated. As might be expected from its much wider range, nominate *lincolnii* is the common subspecies in San Diego County, but some examples of *gracilis* (core winter range central and northern California) reach us as well. Of the 30 Lincoln's Sparrow specimens in the San Diego Natural History Museum, three appear to qualify as *gracilis* on both characters: National City (T10) 10 January 1924 (SDNHM 9216), Tijuana River valley 25 October 1974 (SDNHM 38983), and Point Loma (S7) 19 March 1990 (SDNHM 46540).

Swamp Sparrow *Melospiza georgiana*

The Swamp Sparrow lives mainly east of the Rocky Mountains but is a regular rare fall migrant and winter visitor to California. It is well named, for it seeks freshwater marshes and the undergrowth of riparian woodland.

Winter: The Swamp Sparrow is an annual visitor to San Diego County. The atlas period 1997–2002 was rather meager for the species, with only seven reported. Three per year is more typical. All wintering Swamp Sparrows have been found in the coastal lowland except for one at Lake Henshaw (G17) 20 February 1979 (AB 33:317, 1979). Typical sites are San Elijo Lagoon (L7; 1 April 2000, M. B. Mulrooney), San Dieguito Valley (M8; 28 December 1997, P. Unitt), Santee Lakes (P12; 9 February

Photo by Kenneth Z. Kurland

2000, J. C. Worley), Lindo Lake (P14; 17 January–18 February 2002, M. B. Mulrooney), and the Dairy Mart Pond, Tijuana River valley (V11; 1–11 January 2000, G. McCaskie). The maximum seen in one area is four in the Tijuana River valley 18 January 1964 (G. McCaskie); nine were seen countywide that winter. December 1990 yielded two on the Oceanside Christmas bird count and five on the San Diego count.

Migration: Fall migrants have been noted a few times in atypical habitat such as Point Loma (S7). The only record for the Anza–Borrego Desert is of one at the Borrego sewage ponds (H25) 9 November 1997 (P. D. Jorgensen). Dates for the Swamp Sparrow in San Diego County

extend from 13 October (1957, near Lakeside, P14, AFN 12:60, 1958) to 11 April (1975, O'Neill Lake, E6, A. Fries), except for the single known spring vagrant, singing along the San Diego River in Mission Valley (R9) 30 May 1992 (P. Unitt, AB 46:482, 1992).

Taxonomy: The two specimens from San Diego County, from the east end of Sweetwater Reservoir (S13) 4 November 1943 (SDNHM 18759) and the Tijuana River valley 12 February 1964 (SDNHM 35080), are *M. g. ericrypta* Oberholser, 1938, which breeds in the northern part of the species' range, through the boreal forest of Canada.

White-throated Sparrow *Zonotrichia albicollis*

The White-throated Sparrow is a rare but regular winter visitor to San Diego County. The five-year atlas-study period generated about five sightings per year. The White-throated Sparrow is often found with the more common species of *Zonotrichia* but prefers the cover of dense vegetation, much like the Golden-crowned Sparrow. It avoids the open scrub and grassland where the White-crowned Sparrow is often abundant.

Winter: In San Diego County the White-throated Sparrow occurs widely through the coastal slope. Its locations during the atlas period were all at 2600 feet elevation or lower, but earlier records go as high as 4600 feet at Lake Cuyamaca (M20). There are only a few

Photo by Anthony Mercieca

records from the Anza–Borrego Desert, of birds picked up dead at the Borrego airport (F25) 7 and 19 December 1984 (SDNHM 44445 and 44498), one in Borrego Springs (G24) 30 December 1990–16 March 1991 (A. G. Morley), and one at Agua Caliente Springs (M26) 28 January 1998 (E. C. Hall). Seldom is more than one White-throated seen at a time, though it flocks with other sparrows. The maximum is three, as at Fort Rosecrans Cemetery, Point Loma (S7), 2 March 2002 (D. V. Blue).

Migration: The White-throated Sparrow occurs in San Diego County mainly from November to March, but dates range from 10 October (1974, Point Loma, J. L. Dunn) to 12 May (1988, same location, R. E. Webster, AB 42:483, 1988).

White-throated Sparrow

Winter

Max count 3
Max count 2
Max count 1
Additional location during spring migration

Harris' Sparrow *Zonotrichia querula*

Breeding in the central Arctic of Canada, Harris' Sparrow winters mainly on the southern Great Plains of the United States. In California it is a rare winter visitor, and in San Diego County, through 2003, there are 24 records. When Harris' Sparrow shows up in the county, it often flocks with the abundant White-crowned Sparrow.

Photo by Kenneth Z. Kurland

Winter: Records of Harris' Sparrow in San Diego County are well scattered through the coastal lowland from Fallbrook (D15; one from 16 December 1984 to 8 January 1985, L. Bevier, AB 39:211, 1985) to the Tijuana River valley (four records). Although the species commonly winters in regions with a climate far harsher than any San Diego County has to offer, only one Harris' Sparrow has been seen in the county above 1500 feet elevation: at about 2500 feet in Dameron Valley (C15; 6 February 1999, K. L. Weaver). It was also the only one reported 1997–2001. Other recent sightings are from Guajome Lake (G7) 29 December 1996 (K. L. Weaver, Oceanside Christmas bird count), San Elijo Lagoon (L7) 28 November–13 December 2003 (J. Benton), and the Sweetwater County Park campground (T13) 14 December 2002 (S. Walens, NAB 57:259, 2003). All reports are of single individuals, except for one of two birds in the Tijuana River valley 16 December 1972–20 January 1973 (G. McCaskie).

Migration: San Diego County's records of Harris' Sparrow extend from 22 November (1970, Tijuana River valley, AB 25:112, 1971) to 10 May (1976, Coronado Cays, T9, AB 30:893, 1976).

White-crowned Sparrow *Zonotrichia leucophrys*

In winter, the White-crowned Sparrow is one of San Diego County's most abundant birds. Some grass, weeds, or open ground for foraging, and nearby shrubbery or trees for refuge from predators, are all it needs for habitat at this season. Thus coastal sage scrub, broken chaparral, woodland edges, desert-edge scrub, desert washes and sinks, urban parks, and disturbed weedy areas all are home to the White-crowned Sparrow during its seven-month stay in San Diego County. White-crowned Sparrows often gather in large flocks and patronize bird feeders, making them seem even more numerous.

Photo by Anthony Mercieca

Winter: As an abundant winter visitor, the White-crowned Sparrow seems to be everywhere. On the coastal slope it is indeed almost ubiquitous, being scarce or lacking only at the highest elevations. The largest numbers are near the coast and in the inland valleys, with reports as high as 940 in the Tijuana River valley 18 December 1999 (W. E. Haas) and 700 at Sweetwater Reservoir (S12) 20 December 1997 (P. Famolaro). Large numbers sometimes occur even as high as 5000 feet (572 near Julian, J20, 27 December 1999, E. Post; 253 near San Ignacio, Los Coyotes Indian Reservation, E21, 11 December 1999, K. L. Weaver, C. R. Mahrdt). In the Anza–Borrego Desert the White-crowned Sparrow is abundant around oases and irrigated developed areas, with counts as high as 1053 in north Borrego Springs (F24) 20 December 1998 (R. Thériault et al.). In dry natural desert habitats, though, its numbers vary with rainfall. White-crowned Sparrow numbers in the desert outside Borrego Springs were greatest during the atlas' first year, the wet winter of 1997–98. Daily counts in creosote bush scrub ran as high as 300 on Mescal Bajada (J25) 11 January 1998 (M. and B. McIntosh) and near Indian Hill (R28) 8 February 1998 (J. O. Zimmer). The following three years White-crowned Sparrows remained fairly steady at a level less than half that in the wet year. In the atlas' final winter, the record dry winter of 2001–02, their numbers dropped even further. During the drought, the sparrows became so sparse over so much desert that they were missed in 16 atlas squares not covered in 1997–98.

Migration: In fall, the White-crowned Sparrow arrives punctually in the third week of September and is common by the end of that month. The earliest date is 7 September with one near Lake Murray (Q11; N. Osborn) and two near Los Peñasquitos Lagoon (N7; D. K. Adams) in 2003. In spring, the sparrow's numbers decrease through April and early May. By the end of April the

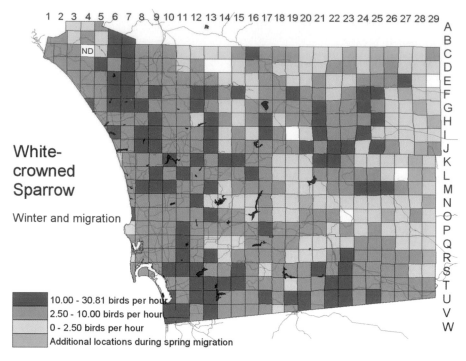

White-
crowned
Sparrow

Winter and migration

■ 10.00 - 30.81 birds per hour
▨ 2.50 - 10.00 birds per hour
□ 0 - 2.50 birds per hour
▨ Additional locations during spring migration

north in little-disturbed subarctic regions, so the White-crowned Sparrow seems secure as a dominant bird of San Diego County's winter landscape.

Taxonomy: Of the White-crowned Sparrow's five subspecies, three are known from San Diego County. *Z. l. gambelii* (Nuttall, 1840), with its pink bill, gray and rufous back stripes, and white eyebrow extending through the lores to the base of the bill, is the abundant winter visitor, representing 84 of 87 SDNHM specimens.

Zonotrichia l. pugetensis Grinnell, 1928, with its yellowish bill, brown-and-black back stripes, and white lores, breeds in the Pacific Northwest. It reaches the southern tip of its winter range in San Diego County. Specimens have been reported from San Luis Rey (G6), San Marcos (I9), La Jolla (P7), and Nestor (V10/11), on dates ranging from 19 October to 10 April (Grinnell 1928b, Grinnell and Miller 1944, Rea 1967, Unitt 1984). Rea (1967) also reported that "during the period 1958–63 several other White-crowns of this race were banded by us at the Old Mission [San Luis Rey], leading me to believe that the race has largely been overlooked." But the scarcity of *pugetensis* in the SDNHM collection (only one of 87 county specimens), the lack of further sight reports, and the lack of records farther south attest to the rarity of the subspecies here.

Zonotrichia l. oriantha Oberholser, 1932, with its pinkish bill, gray-and-rufous back stripes, and black lores, occurs in San Diego County mainly as a rare spring migrant. Most birds must overfly the county, since the subspecies is a common breeding bird in the Sierra Nevada and a common winter visitor in southern Baja California. It is more common even in the Imperial Valley than in San Diego County. Dates extend from 8 April (1904, Witch Creek, J18, Bishop 1905) to 5 May (1885, San Diego, Belding 1890); the bird noted 2–11 June 1975 was also black-lored. Apparently there is still only one good record of a fall migrant, of one at Point Loma (S7) 20 September 1973 (J. L. Dunn). Just as San Diego County is the southern tip of the winter range of *pugetensis*, it is the northern tip of the winter range of *oriantha*. Bishop (1905) reported an immature collected at Volcan Mountain (I20) 3 December 1904, and there are a few other winter specimens from elsewhere in southern California (Grinnell and Miller 1944).

species is uncommon, though large numbers remained in the Anza–Borrego Desert into late April after the wet winter of 1997–98: 150 on Mescal Bajada 26 April 1998 (M. and B. McIntosh), 30 at Vallecito (M25) 27 April 1998 (M. C. Jorgensen). By mid May the White-crowned Sparrow is rare, and the only records after 20 May during the atlas period were of single birds at Lower Willows (D23) 21 May 2001 (M. L. Gabel), in La Jolla (P7) 22 May 1999 (L. and M. Polinsky), along the Pepperwood Trail (P25) 22 May 2000 (L. J. Hargrove), and one at the De Luz Campground (B6) 29 May 2000 (K. L. Weaver). Ill health accounts for some of these stragglers; for example, the bird on the Pepperwood Trail had a tumor over one eye. The only later record published is of one in East San Diego (S10) 2–11 June 1975 (AB 29:912, 1036, 1975).

Breeding distribution: There is only one record of the White-crowned Sparrow breeding in San Diego County, of a pair with three juveniles near the Palomar Observatory (D15) 18 July 1983 (R. Higson, AB 37:1028, 1983). This is far outside the species' normal breeding range, which extends south only to Mt. San Gorgonio, and the small colony even there is an outlier from the main range of subspecies *oriantha* in the high Sierra Nevada. The record at Palomar, though, came after the wet El Niño winter of 1982–83, the event most likely to induce such a bizarre occurrence.

Conservation: The White-crowned Sparrow is less common in heavily urbanized areas than where much open ground remains, whether the latter is natural or disturbed. But no trend in its winter numbers is obvious. The breeding range of our principal subspecies, *gambelii*, is far to the

Golden-crowned Sparrow *Zonotrichia atricapilla*

Less conspicuous than its familiar relative the White-crowned Sparrow, the Golden-crowned is actually more numerous in montane chaparral and the shady undergrowth of oak woodland. Manzanita, snowberry, California coffeeberry, and poison oak offer the Golden-crowned Sparrow prime habitat. In drier, more open chaparral, in sage scrub, and in riparian scrub the Golden-crowned Sparrow occurs at a much lower density. The Golden-crowned Sparrow is a winter visitor to San Diego County, occurring generally from the first week of October to the first week of May.

Photo by Jack C. Daynes

Winter: The Golden-crowned Sparrow occurs widely over the coastal slope of San Diego County. Its abundance is not uniform over this area but concentrated in two zones. The zone of greatest concentration is the higher mountains, where counts can range as high as 113 around High Point of Palomar Mountain (D15) 21 December 1999 (K. L. Weaver) and 100 along upper La Posta Creek (P24) 19 December 2001 (E. C. Hall, J. O. Zimmer). Within 15 miles of the coast, in the shadier canyons and on north-facing slopes, the Golden-crowned Sparrow is also common. Daily counts there range up to 80 around Torrey Pines City Park (O7) 25 January 2002 (D. G. Seay) and 66 around Batiquitos Lagoon (J7) 22 December 2001 (R. and A. Campbell). Between these zones, the species is only fairly common and can be missed where favorable habitat is sparse. On the Campo Plateau it is quite uncommon, and in the canyons draining into the Anza–Borrego Desert it is usually rare, with the only report of more than two individuals being of five in Box Canyon (L23) 13 February 1998 (D. Lantz). On the desert floor, our only winter records were during an unusual influx

of several species of sparrows in response to rain (or, in the case of the Golden-crowned, possibly to snowstorms at higher elevations): four near San Felipe Narrows (I26) 10 January 1998 (A. Mauro) and eight in lower Carrizo Valley (O28) 11 January 1998 (P. D. Jorgensen).

Migration: In San Diego County, the Golden-crowned Sparrow is no more numerous in migration than in winter, as one might expect with the county's lying near the southern tip of the main winter range. Migrants occur rarely, though, at places in the Anza–Borrego Desert where the species does not winter. Our only such record during the atlas period was of one at Agua Caliente Springs (M26) 27 April 1998 (D. C. Seals), but Massey (1998) reported a few others, including two in spring far out on the desert in Hawk Canyon (H27). Fall arrival is in early October, exceptionally very late September. Spring departure takes place in late April and early May. In the first week of May, the Golden-crowned Sparrow can still be seen in small numbers, e.g., up to 12 near Adobe Springs (C18) 2 May 1999 (A. Mauro, J. R. Barth). From 1997 to 2001, however, the only record later than 6 May was of two near the Palomar Observatory (D15) 14 May 1999 (K. L. Weaver). Later stragglers occur rarely, even into the first week of June: Tijuana River valley, 3 June 1978 (AB 332:1057, 1978), and Point Loma (S7), 7 June 1984 (R. E. Webster, AB 38:965, 1984). There remains only a single San Diego County record of a Golden-crowned Sparrow in summer, 1000 miles south of the species' breeding range: one at Old Mission Dam (P11) 14 August 1974 (AB 29:124, 1975).

Conservation: The Golden-crowned Sparrow occurs in residential areas planted heavily with thick shrubbery but is less numerous there than in natu-

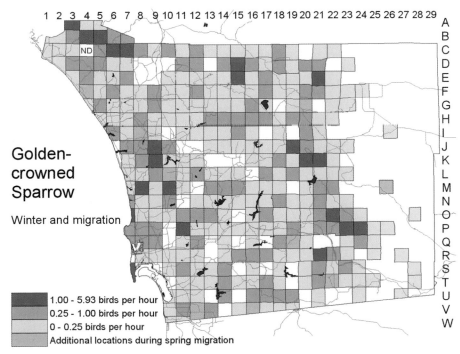

Golden-
crowned
Sparrow

Winter and migration

1 2 3 4 5 6 7 8 9 10 11 12 13 14 15 16 17 18 19 20 21 22 23 24 25 26 27 28 29

A B C D E F G H I J K L M N O P Q R S T U V W

ND

■ 1.00 - 5.93 birds per hour
▨ 0.25 - 1.00 birds per hour
□ 0 - 0.25 birds per hour
▦ Additional locations during spring migration

---

ral habitats. Thus development of the coastal lowland degrades the sparrow's habitat in its secondary zone of concentration. But the primary zone lies in deep canyons and rugged mountains farther inland, suggesting that the

Golden-crowned Sparrow should long remain common in San Diego County. Christmas bird count results vary much from year to year, but the variations are not parallel among the counts, and there is no long-term trend.

Dark-eyed Junco *Junco hyemalis*

The Dark-eyed Junco is one of the most common breeding birds in the woodlands of conifers and black oaks in San Diego County's mountains. In winter, it is even more abundant, as visitors from much of western North America flock into the county. At that season they occur in oak woodland, chaparral, high-desert scrub, parks, and well-vegetated residential areas as well as coniferous woodland. Subspecies *J. h. thurberi* of the Oregon Junco dominates, but two more subspecies of the Oregon, two of the Slate-colored, the Pink-sided, and the Gray-headed all occur regularly, especially in the mountains. As a breeding species the junco is spreading to lower elevations in live oak groves and orchards. Its colonizing the University of California campus in La Jolla reveals its surprising potential as an urban adapter.

Breeding distribution: Montane coniferous woodland remains the heart of the junco's range in San Diego County, and it is here where the species' numbers are highest: up to 175 in Matagual Valley (H19) 18 June 2000 (S. E. Smith), to 100 on Volcan Mountain (I20) 28 June 2000 (A. P. and T. E. Keenan). But field work for the atlas revealed considerable spread of breeding juncos into other habitats at lower elevations. As a result, at the scale of an atlas square, the distribution appears continuous from Palomar to the Laguna Mountains, though between

Photo by Anthony Mercieca

1500 and 3500 feet elevation the birds are confined to oak woodlands in canyons, largely in the northern half of the county. In Boden Canyon (J14) they descend as low as 1000 feet (two, one building a nest, 2 May 1997, C. R. Mahrdt). Breeding juncos are locally common in foothill canyons, with up to 25 at 2400–2600 feet elevation along Temescal Creek (G15) 1 June 2001 (K. J. Winter) and 20 at 1100–2000 feet in upper Boden Canyon (I14) 24 April 2000 (R. L. Barber). The southernmost site known, and thus the southern tip of the breeding range of subspecies *thurberi*, is Hauser Canyon (T20), elevation 1700–1800 feet (four on 18 May 2000, J. M. Wells).

The small isolated population in the Santa Margarita Mountains (B4/B5/C5) is in oak woodland (up to eight singing males around the Sky Ranch, B5, 19 May 2001, J. M. and B. Hargrove), as were three around Live Oak Park, Fallbrook (D8) 17 July 1999 (M. Freda) and occasional birds near Long's Gulch (M15) in summer 1999 (C. H. Reiser). But two in an avocado orchard 2.25 miles west-southwest of Pauma Valley (F12) 12 June 1999 (M. Sadowski, J. R. Barth) and one in northwest Escondido (I10) 5 June 1999 (E. C. Hall) suggest adaptation to nonnative habitats.

By far the most dramatic example of the junco's adapting to a new environment is its colonization of the campus of the University of California, San Diego (O7/O8). Here the birds live in the eucalyptus trees and ornamental shrubbery scattered among the buildings. The birds first colonized in 1983; by 2000,

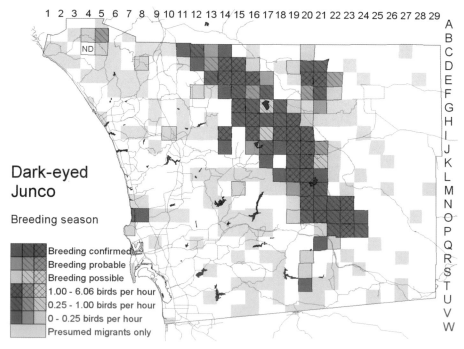

Dark-eyed Junco

Breeding season

- Breeding confirmed
- Breeding probable
- Breeding possible
- 1.00 - 6.06 birds per hour
- 0.25 - 1.00 birds per hour
- 0 - 0.25 birds per hour
- Presumed migrants only

the population reached a fairly stable level of about 130, covering an area of slightly less than 1 square mile (P. Yeh), east to the University Town Center shopping mall (O8, one singing 14 July 1998, D. G. Seay). The population barely extends into surrounding La Jolla (P7), where we recorded the species three times, including two individuals banded on the campus and seen 3.2 miles away 20 June 2000 (M. Hinton). An even more notable recovery of a junco banded on the UCSD campus was of a juvenile found 9.5 miles away in the neighborhood of Loma Portal (R8) 16 August 2000 (SDNHM 50446). A pair was feeding young in Torrey Pines State Reserve (N8) 22 July 1989 (J. R. Jehl, Jr., AB 43:1369, 1989),

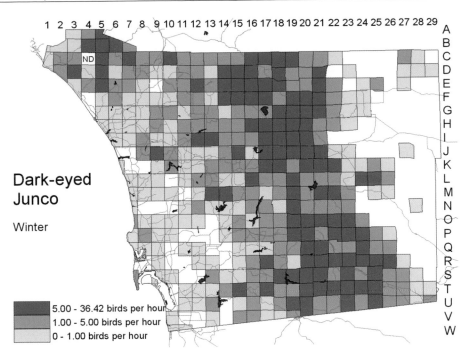

Dark-eyed
Junco

Winter

5.00 - 36.42 birds per hour
1.00 - 5.00 birds per hour
0 - 1.00 birds per hour

but the birds have not remained there, in spite of the site's nearness to UCSD and the resemblance of the Torrey pine groves to the species' typical habitat.

Nesting: The Dark-eyed Junco usually nests on the ground, the nest hidden by grass, herbs, ferns, low shrubs, or leaf litter. All nests that atlas observers described were in such situations. Elsewhere in the species' range, nests in trees or other elevated situations are known but rare (J. H. Phelps, Jr., in Austin 1968).

In the mountains, the junco's nesting season extends from late April to mid July. With observations of nest building 18 April, feeding young 13 May, and fledglings 23 May, egg laying evidently begins about 10 days earlier than the 5 May–13 July spread of nine collected egg sets. At UCSD, however, the junco enjoys a much longer breeding season. There the birds start singing in January, build nests in February, and fledge their last chicks in August and September (P. Yeh). The scattered early records visible on the chart of the species' breeding schedule are all from UCSD.

Migration: The juncos breeding in San Diego County are presumably nonmigratory, and this has been confirmed by studies of banded birds for the population at UCSD (P. Yeh). The local population is greatly augmented in the

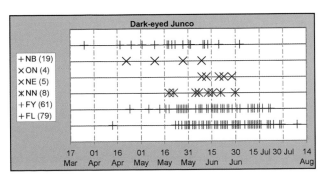

winter by migrants from the north, which begin arriving between mid September and mid October. In spring, wintering birds remain fairly common until the third week of April, then depart quickly. The latest records of apparent migrants are of one near Melrose Ranch (I13) 9 May 2001 (O. Carter) and one near Harper Flat (K26) 10 May 2000 (D. C. Seals). A couple of individuals in extreme northwestern San Diego County later in the spring could have been pioneers of the local population: one at San Onofre (C1) 26 May 2001 (M. Lesinsky) and one in San Mateo Canyon, elevation 500 feet (B3), 28 May 2001 (P. Unitt). On rare occasions migrants are seen in sparsely vegetated desert unsuitable for wintering birds (e.g., one near the Elephant Knees, M29, 1 May 2001, J. R. Barth).

Winter: In winter, juncos are abundant throughout San Diego County's mountains and foothills. Flocks of dozens and daily counts over 100 are frequent. Counts run as high as 700 north of Julian (J20) 27 December 1999 (E. Post) and 551 in Cañada Verde (F20) 12 December 2000 (M. Bache). The junco's pattern of winter abundance resembles that of resident birds of oak woodland: common near the coast in northwestern San Diego County, then decreasing, with the zone of abundance retracting inland, toward the south. Nevertheless, juncos can be common at favored spots even in south-coastal San Diego County, with up to 75 at Fort Rosecrans Cemetery, Point Loma (S7), 18 December 1999 (M. W. Klein) and 61 on the west side of Lower Otay Lake (U13) 19 January 2001 (M. and B. McIntosh). In high-desert scrub (juniper, Mojave yucca, desert apricot, desert scrub oak, etc.) the junco is irregularly common too, with up to 55 on the east slope of Whale Peak (L26) 15 February 2001 (J. R. Barth) and 45 in the Santa Rosa Mountains (C27) 9 January 2002 (P. Unitt). Numbers high as 225 one to two miles north of Vallecito (L25) 22 January 1998 and 115 in Little Blair Valley (L24) 20 February 1998 (both

544

R. Thériault) occurred only in the one wet winter of the atlas period. In the low desert, the junco is much scarcer, occurring mainly in the cultivated parts of the Borrego Valley (maximum 30 at Roadrunner Tree Farm, E25, 17 December 2000, L. J. Hargrove).

Conservation: The lack of reports of breeding juncos from low to moderate elevations before the 1980s suggests that the spread is recent and the species is doing well. It was first noted summering in Boden Canyon in 1994 (C. R. Mahrdt). Though parks, college campuses, and well-vegetated residential areas offer the junco foraging habitat, its nesting on the ground is a strike against it as a prospective urban adapter.

Taxonomy: The juncos breeding in San Diego County, including those at UCSD, are *J. h. thurberi*, with black-headed males, gray-headed females, and the back tinged pinkish in both sexes. *Junco. h. thurberi*, whose breeding range stretches from San Diego County north through the Sierra Nevada, is also the dominant wintering subspecies in San Diego County, accounting for 80 of 116 winter specimens in the San Diego Natural History Museum. Two other subspecies of Oregon Juncos, differing from *thurberi* mainly in back color and not readily identifiable in the field, reach San Diego County as winter visitors in smaller numbers. *Junco. h. simillimus* Phillips, 1962 [= *J. h. shufeldti* Coale, 1887, of Miller (1941) and AOU (1957)], has a darker chocolate-brown back than *thurberi* and originates in the Pacific Northwest. It is apparently uncommon but probably regular, represented by six specimens collected on dates ranging from 9 October (1993, Volcan Mt., SDNHM 48585) to 23 March (1944, Point Loma, SDNHM 18855). Two further specimens are apparently intergrades between *simillimus* and *thurberi* or *shufeldti. Junco h. shufeldti* Coale, 1887 [= *J. h. montanus* Ridgway, 1898, of Miller (1941) and AOU (1957)], differs from *thurberi* and *simillimus* by having the back a drab grayish-brown and the male's head being dark slaty-gray rather than black. It breeds in the northern Rocky Mountains. In San Diego County it is uncommon or fairly common, represented by nine specimens collected between 6 November (1984, Cibbets Flat, Q23, SDNHM 43474) and 1 March (1931, 4 miles southwest of Ramona, L14, SDNHM 14143). *Junco h. shufeldti* may be more prevalent in the Anza–Borrego Desert, as it is the most numerous subspecies of junco in the Salton Sink (Patten et al. 2003).

The Pink-sided Junco, *J. h. mearnsi* Ridgway, 1897, has a back even grayer than in *shufeldti* but a gray head in both sexes (black lores in the male) and broader cinnamon-pink on the sides, often extending across the breast. Immature females, though, are readily distinguished from *shufeldti* only in the hand. Only two specimens have been collected (18 December 1930, 4 miles southwest of Ramona, SDNHM 14117; 6 November 1984, Troy Flat, Laguna Mountains, Q23, SDNHM 43452), but sight records imply the subspecies occurs annually in small numbers. It is rare along the coast but more numerous in the mountains, with maximum counts possibly as high as

seven (near Julian, J20, 27 December 1999, E. Post; upper San Felipe Valley, H20, 17 December 2001, A. P. and T. E. Keenan). More specimens are desirable to support numbers this high.

The Gray-headed Junco, *J. h. caniceps* (Woodhouse, 1853), with its bright rufous back and gray sides, differs grossly from the Oregon and Pink-sided Juncos, though intergrades are known and have even been given a subspecies name of their own. The Gray-headed Junco breeds in the mountains of the Great Basin and in the Rockies from southern Wyoming to northeastern Arizona. In San Diego County the status of the Gray-headed is similar to that of the Pink-sided: rare along the coast, rare to uncommon in the mountains. The Gray-headed may be somewhat more frequent than the Pink-sided, or the apparent difference may be due to the Gray-headed's being more conspicuous in the field. Maximum counts are five near the San Luis Rey Day Use Area (G16) 22 January 2001 (W. E. Haas) and eight in Thing Valley (Q24) 2 February 1999 (P. Unitt). There are now five specimens, and sight records extend from 25 September (1960, one at Palomar Mountain State Park, D14/E14, AFN 15:78, 1960) to 19 April (2001, one in the middle fork of Borrego Palm Canyon, F22, J. R. Barth). Completely unprecedented in coastal southern California was a summer sighting of the Gray-headed Junco, of an apparent pair on Volcan Mountain 16 June 2000 (A. P. and T. E. Keenan). Parallel records must be sought among other species, such as the Red-naped Sapsucker that hybridized with the Red-breasted on Palomar Mountain or the Plumbeous Vireos colonizing the San Bernardino and San Jacinto mountains.

Two subspecies of the Slate-colored Junco also reach San Diego County, *J. h. cismontanus* Dwight, 1918, and *J. h. hyemalis* (Linnaeus, 1758). With six county specimens each in SDNHM they appear to be of roughly equal abundance—both uncommon. Sight records are a poor guide because in the field males of *hyemalis* stand out conspicuously while females of *cismontanus* could be overlooked among female Oregon Juncos. *Junco. h. cismontanus* has the concave border of the hood that distinguishes the Slate-colored from the Oregon Junco but the flanks have a variable amount of brown and the back is distinctly browner than the head. It breeds mainly in the interior of British Columbia. In *J. h. hyemalis* (Linnaeus, 1758) the males are all gray and white; the females may be brownish but no more so on the back than on the head. This subspecies has a transcontinental breeding range in the taiga from Alaska to Newfoundland. In San Diego County, seldom are more than three or four Slate-colored seen in a single large flock of juncos, but an exceptional 21 were in northeast Ramona (K15) 30 December 2000 (D. and C. Batzler). Sight records of Slate-colored Juncos in San Diego County extend from 19 October to 2 April (Unitt 1984).

Rea (1967) reported *J. h. oreganus* (Townsend, 1837) from San Luis Rey (G6) 17 January 1962, but the specimen (SBMNH 127), which I reexamined, is actually *simillimus*; the back is not dark and rusty enough for *oreganus*, and the flanks are not as extensively dark as in most specimens of *oreganus*.

There appears to be no difference in winter biology among the many subspecies of the Dark-eyed Junco; the rarer subspecies are usually found among the commoner ones in mixed flocks.

McCown's Longspur *Calcarius mccownii*

Though an annual rare winter visitor to the Imperial Valley, McCown's Longspur is only casual in San Diego County, the least frequent of the three longspurs recorded here. It has not been seen in the county since 1991, probably as a result of the elimination, especially in the Tijuana River valley, of the plowed fields the species seeks.

Migration: Ten of the 11 fall records of McCown's Longspur for San Diego County are from the Tijuana River valley, scattered from 1965 to 1991. Their dates range from 19 October (1969, AFN 24:100d, 1970) to 6 December (1975, AB 30:770, 1976). One was at Otay Mesa (V13) 6 November 1971 (AB 26:124, 1972).

Winter: The only McCown's Longspurs found in San Diego County in winter were two near Lake Henshaw (G17) 3–11 January 1987 (D. B. King, AB 41:331, 1987).

Photo by Brian L. Sullivan

Lapland Longspur *Calcarius lapponicus*

The Lapland Longspur nests in the Arctic; in the New World, it winters mostly in the northern contiguous United States. San Diego County is well to the south of its main winter range. Like the other longspurs, the Lapland seeks fields of short grass or bare dirt. With such places becoming ever fewer, longspurs are becoming less and less frequent in San Diego County.

Migration: The Lapland Longspur occurs in San Diego County mainly as a rare migrant in late fall, from mid October to mid December. Most records are of single birds with flocks of Horned Larks; the county's maximum was 10 Lapland Longspurs in the Tijuana River valley 22–27 November 1975. The earliest record, of one collected at Mission Bay (Q8) 2 October 1909 (Stephens 1910, SDNHM 917) was the first for San Diego County and tied as first for California. The only spring record is of one at Mission Bay 21 March 1987 (J. White, AB 41:490, 1987). Most of the county's Lapland Longspurs have been found in the Tijuana River valley; there are also a few from Otay Mesa (V13), Point Loma (S7), and Lake Henshaw (G17).

Winter: San Diego County records of the Lapland Longspur that could be considered to represent wintering birds are from the Tijuana River valley 3 January 1965 (AFN 19:334, 1965) and 13 January 1978 (AB 32:402, 1978) and from Lake Henshaw 29 December 1977 (AB

Photo by Richard E. Webster

32:402, 1978), 3–22 December 1983 (R. Higson, AB 38:359, 1984), and 3–11 January 1987 (D. B. King, AB 41:332, 1987).

Conservation: In San Diego County, like all the longspurs, the Lapland has decreased in frequency since the 1970s with the decline in agriculture. Possibly the trend toward warmer winters drives fewer longspurs as far south as San Diego. The only county records since 1996 are of single birds at the Tijuana River valley sod farm (W11) 23 October 1998 (E. Copper) and 20 October 1999 (G. McCaskie) and at Point Loma 24 October–5 November 2002 (G. McCaskie).

Taxonomy: California specimens of the Lapland Longspur are *C. l. alascensis* Ridgway, 1898.

Chestnut-collared Longspur *Calcarius ornatus*

The main winter range of the Chestnut-collared Longspur lies east of the Colorado River. In southern California, the species is rare and perhaps sporadic in fall and winter, occurring in dry grassland and agricultural fields. Since the 1970s, it has become much less frequent, as a result of loss of habitat locally, in the breeding range, or both.

Migration: In San Diego County, the Chestnut-collared, like the other longspurs, has been reported most often from the Tijuana River valley. Other fall locations include Point Loma (S7) and Lake Henshaw (G17). The species occurs primarily from mid October to late November; 9 October (1974, one at Point Loma, J. L. Dunn) is the earliest date.

Winter: There is no clear distinction between fall and winter records of the Chestnut-collared Longspur. Reports for January and February are of one at Lake Henshaw 9 January 1977 (AB 31:375, 1977), up to 20 there 7–13 January 1978 (AB 32:402, 1978), 25 at Whelan Lake (G6) 6 February 1977 (AB 31:375, 1977), and one at Lake Cuyamaca (M20) 8 February 1987 (J. O'Brien, AB 41:332, 1987). The flocks at Henshaw and Whelan were the largest ever reported in the county.

Photo by Anthony Mercieca

Conservation: With the development of most sites where the Chestnut-collared Longspur formerly occurred in coastal southern California, the species has gone from regular if uncommon to casual or absent. In San Diego County the only records 1997–2003 were from the sod farm in the Tijuana River valley (W11), of three 16–20 October 1999 (G. McCaskie), one 17 October 2000 (J. A. Martin), and one 19 October 2000 (E. Copper).

Little Bunting *Emberiza pusilla*

One of the least expected vagrants ever to reach San Diego County was the Little Bunting, an Asian species that is only a casual vagrant even in the western Aleutian Islands. The Little Bunting at Point Loma was the only one known for North America outside Alaska until another arrived on Southeast Farallon Island off San Francisco in September 2002 (Cole and McCaskie 2004).

Migration: San Diego County's Little Bunting was photographed at Fort Rosecrans Cemetery, Point Loma (S7), 21–24 October 1991 (AB 46:169, McCaskie 1993, Patten et al. 1995b).

Cardinals, Grosbeaks, and Buntings — Family Cardinalidae

Pyrrhuloxia *Cardinalis sinuatus*

Pretty birds of primarily Mexican distribution pose an increasing problem to birders in San Diego County. What is the likelihood that, when seen north of the border, they are vagrants all the way from the species' natural range versus escapees from captivity in Baja California? The California Bird Records Committee has accepted one Pyrrhuloxia from San Diego County and rejected another, though the circumstances of both were similar.

Migration: Although Guy McCaskie wrote that a Pyrrhuloxia at Encinitas (K6/K7) 26–27 May 1983 was "best considered an escapee" (AB 37:914, 1983), the California Bird Records Committee accepted it as a vagrant (Bevier 1990). But it questioned the natural origin of one at Point Loma (S7) 10 June 1998; it "appeared ragged" (Erickson and Hamilton 2001). Yet another San

Photo by Anthony Mercieca

Diego County report (AB 42:483, 1988) was rejected as inadequately supported, and another (AB 40:525, 1986) was not submitted.

Rose-breasted Grosbeak *Pheucticus ludovicianus*

Among the vagrants from eastern North America reaching San Diego County, the Rose-breasted Grosbeak is one of the most frequent. A few are seen annually in both spring and fall. Winter records average about one per year, and there are even a few records in mid summer.

Photo by Anthony Mercieca

Migration: Unlike many vagrants, the Rose-breasted Grosbeak is more numerous in spring than in fall. The spring of 2001 was exceptional, with at least 13. That year the species was seen at Point Loma (S7) continuously from 27 April to 7 June with up to three individuals per day. Most spring records are from mid May through mid June, but birds that were more likely spring migrants than winter visitors have been seen at Tamarisk Grove or Yaqui Well (I24) as early as 6–13 April (1986, B. Knaak, A. G. Morley) and 15 April (1990, A. G. Morley). During the atlas period, 1997–2001, our latest spring record was of one found dead in Chula Vista (T11) 24 June 1998 (SDNHM 50601), but there are at least six records for July, and one of a bird that remained in El Cajon (Q13) to 10 August 1969 (AFN 23:696, 1969).

Fall records are usually two to four per year, though 1986 had an exceptional 18. Fall dates are concentrated from late September to early November but range from 18 August (1986, Tijuana River valley, G. McCaskie) to 6 December (2001, Borrego Palm Canyon, F23, J. Determan) and 6–11 December (1987, Borrego Palm Canyon campground, R. Thériault).

Winter: Wintering Rose-breasted Grosbeaks average about one per year, so the atlas period was typical with five over its five years. Three of these, however, were on the grounds of the San Diego Zoo (R9) 15 December 2001 (M. B. Stowe, V. P. Johnson). The maximum in a

winter was five in 1982–83 (AB 37:347, 1983). Most of the county's wintering Rose-breasted Grosbeaks have been found in the parks and residential areas of metropolitan San Diego, but a few have been in the lowlands of the north county, such as one near Fallbrook (E7) 20 December 1998 (J. Ginger, P. A. Ginsburg) and one in Bonsall (F9) 1–15 January 1999 (J. Evans). Two records from the Anza–Borrego Desert, from the Roadrunner Club, Borrego Springs (F24), 16 March 1985 and Vallecito (M25) 16 March 1983, apparently represent winter visitors (ABDSP database).

Breeding distribution: The Rose-breasted Grosbeak is not known to nest in California, but occasional hybridization with the Black-headed Grosbeak is likely. A male at Pine Hills (K19) 14 June 1994 was paired with a female Black-headed (R. T. Patton), and a male along the Sunset Trail, Laguna Mountains (O22), 8 June 1997 was associating with a nesting pair of Black-headeds (P. Unitt). The June specimen from Chula Vista was in breeding condition with enlarged testes.

Black-headed Grosbeak *Pheucticus melanocephalus*

A common summer visitor, the Black-headed Grosbeak is one of the characteristic birds of oak and riparian woodland. It is also locally common in mature chaparral, mainly on north-facing slopes. But it is rare, though possibly increasing, as a breeding species in developed areas. As a migrant it is seen throughout the county, including deserts and cities. In winter it is very rare—much rarer than its eastern counterpart, the Rose-breasted Grosbeak.

Breeding distribution: At the scale of our atlas grid, the Black-headed Grosbeak is distributed almost uniformly over San Diego County's coastal slope. It is most common in oak and riparian woodland, with up to 30, including 20 singing males, in Moosa Canyon (F9) 18 May 1999 (J. Evans) and up to 27, including 20 singing males, along the Santa Margarita River north of Fallbrook (C8) 24 May 2001 (K. L. Weaver). Mature chaparral often offers good habitat as well, as on the north slope of Otay Mountain (U15; 46 on 25 May 1999, G. L. Rogers). Certain types

Photo by Anthony Mercieca

of chaparral, such as those dominated by scrub oak or Tecate cypress, may be more favorable than others, such as those dominated by chamise or redshank. The Black-headed Grosbeak is also numerous in montane pine/oak woodland (up to 25 at Palomar Mountain, E15, 3 July 2000, E. C. Hall) but over 6000 feet elevation begins to thin out; the maximum daily count near the summit of

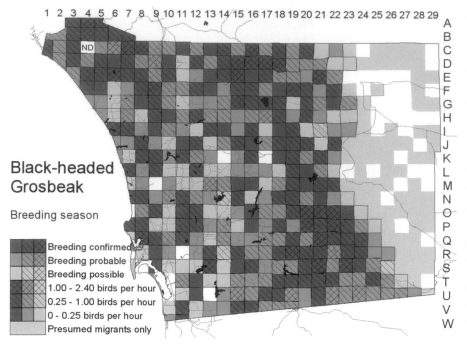

Black-headed Grosbeak

Breeding season

- Breeding confirmed
- Breeding probable
- Breeding possible
- 1.00 - 2.40 birds per hour
- 0.25 - 1.00 birds per hour
- 0 - 0.25 birds per hour
- Presumed migrants only

Migration: The Black-headed Grosbeak is one of San Diego County's most punctual migrants, the first birds normally returning in the last few days of March. From 1997 to 2001 the first reported date varied only from 27 March to 1 April, except for a report of one at Butterfield Ranch (M23) 17 March 1999 (H. and K. Williams). The only earlier published date is 16 March 1986 (one male at Point Loma S7, J. Oldenettel, AB 40:525, 1986). San Diego County is evidently on the grosbeak's main spring migration route from western Mexico to the Pacific coast, taking advantage of the comparatively low elevation of the county's mountains to cross from the desert to the coast. As for many other species, San Felipe Valley (I21) is evidently the center of the corridor, with at least 620 migrating northwest there 24 April 1999 (W. E. Haas) and 100 a short distance farther upstream (H20) the same day (A. P. and T. E. Keenan). The route apparently continues from the head of San Felipe Valley across Warner Valley to Sunshine Summit (D17) at the east base of Palomar Mountain, where A. Mauro noted 50 in migrating flocks 1 May 1999. Many individuals follow other paths. Numbers of migrants drop through May; from 1997 to 2001 24 May 1999 (six at Yaqui Well, I24, P. K. Nelson) was the latest spring date outside the breeding range. Previous late spring dates for Point Loma run as late as 3 June (1974, J. L. Dunn). Fall migrants pass through mainly from late July through mid September, exceptionally to mid October.

Hot Springs Mountain (E20) was only three on 19 May 2001 and 15 July 2000 (K. L. Weaver, C. R. Mahrdt).

The distribution hardly extends over the crest of the mountains to the desert slope, however. Records of apparently breeding birds along the east edge of the range are of one at Lower Willows in Coyote Creek Canyon (D23) 20 June 1998 (B. L. Peterson), four, including a pair, in Hellhole Canyon (G23) 7 July 1998 (M. L. Gabel), a pair in Grapevine Canyon (I23) 11 May 1998 (P. K. Nelson), and a pair at Jacumba (U28) 1 July 2000 (P. Unitt). Note that most of these marginal records followed the wet winter of 1997–98. In dry years Scissors Crossing along San Felipe Creek (J22) is probably the farthest into the desert breeding Black-headed Grosbeaks extend.

Nesting: Female Black-headed Grosbeaks build a flimsy open-cup nest of twigs and other plant material, placing it in the outer branches of a tree or shrub. Atlas observers reported nests in willows (5), Engelmann, black, and coast live oak. Nest building begins in the third week of April, egg laying in the fourth week of April, and hatching in the second week of May, in agreement with past data (California egg dates 23 April–10 July, Bent 1968). The birds continue far into the summer, making the Black-headed Grosbeak one of San Diego County's later-nesting species, with fledglings reported as late as 16 August.

Winter: Of the 14 winter records for the county, only two are since 1983, of one at Point Loma 8 January 1991 (D. and M. Hastings, AB 45:322, 1991) and one at a feeder in Oceanside (H5) winter 1996–97. Thus the Black-headed Grosbeak is much less frequent in winter than the Rose-breasted, and the disparity is growing. All other winter records are from parks and residential areas around San Diego, except two reports (possibly of one individual) wintering at Pauma Valley (E12) 1953–55 (Unitt 1984).

Conservation: The Black-headed Grosbeak's ability to adapt to the urban environment is so far modest. The species persists uncommonly in San Diego's largest canyons (San Clemente, Tecolote, Mission Valley), with a maximum of 16, including 10 singing males, in Tecolote Canyon (Q8) 15 June 1999 (J. C. Worley). In small urban canyons and residential areas, as a breeding species, it is rare. For example, in La Jolla (P7) a pair with two fledglings came to a feeder 27 June 1999 (L. Polinsky), in a La Mesa (Q11) canyon a pair had a nest 29 May–4 June 2002 in a laurel sumac within 20 meters of backyards (M. A. Patten), a pair nested in a pepper tree along I Avenue in Coronado (S9) in 1997 and 1998 (J. Guilmette), and

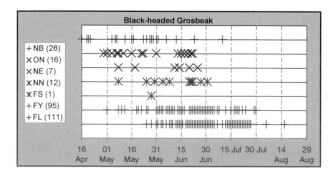

in East San Diego (R10) the only record outside migration periods is of one in Talmadge Park Canyon 30 June 1997 (J. A. Dietrick). At least one pair began summering in eucalyptus groves in Fallbrook (D7) in 2000 (K. L. Weaver).

Taxonomy: Specimens from San Diego County, migrants and breeders (none yet for winter), are *P. m. maculatus* (Audubon, 1837), occurring all along the Pacific coast and smaller billed than the nominate subspecies of the Rocky Mountain region.

Blue Grosbeak *Passerina caerulea*

Lush, low plants, growing in damp swales, offer prime habitat for the Blue Grosbeak. The grosbeak is primarily a summer visitor to San Diego County, locally common at the edges of riparian woodland and in riparian scrub like young willows and mulefat. Blue Grosbeaks can also be common in grassy uplands with scattered shrubs. Migrants are rarely seen away from breeding habitat, and in winter the species is extremely rare.

Breeding distribution: The Blue Grosbeak has a distribution in San Diego County that is wide but patchy. Areas of concentration correspond to riparian corridors and stands of grassland; gaps correspond to unbroken chaparral, forest, waterless desert, and extensive development. Largely insectivorous in summer, the Blue Grosbeak forages primarily among low herbaceous plants, native or exotic. So valley bottoms, where the water necessary for the vegetation accumulates, provide the best habitat. Grassland is also often good habitat, as can be seen on Camp Pendleton (the species' center of abundance in San Diego County) and from Warner Valley south over Mesa Grande to Santa Ysabel Valley. Blue Grosbeaks take advantage of grassland invaded by nonnative plants, using stands of mustard. Because of its preference for herbaceous undergrowth, the Blue Grosbeak is more widespread after wet winters than after dry ones. It is primarily a species of low to middle elevations but probably

Photo by Anthony Mercieca

breeds up to 4100 feet elevation north of Julian (J20; up to nine on 1 July 1999, M. B. Stowe) and to 4600 feet at Lake Cuyamaca (M20; up to five on 10 July 2001, M. B. Mulrooney). A male near the Palomar Observatory (D15) 11 June–21 July 1983 (R. Higson, AB 37:1028, 1983) was exceptional—and in an exceptionally wet El Niño year. In the Anza–Borrego Desert the Blue Grosbeak is confined as a breeding bird to natural riparian oases.

Nesting: The Blue Grosbeak places its cup nest in herbaceous vegetation, shrubs, or trees, with no one type of site apparently favored. The nest is usually hidden in dense vegetation, and difficult to find, accounting for atlas observers' reporting only eight. The one whose situation was described was 3 to 4 feet above the ground in coyote brush.

After wet years, Blue Grosbeaks enjoy a long breeding season. Then they pair, build a nest, and lay within a week of arriving. Nests with nestlings along the San Diego River near Lakeside (P13) 30 April 1998 (W. E. Haas), at Goodan Ranch County Park (N12) 3 May 1998 (W. E. Haas), and fledglings at the Wild Animal Park (J12) 11 May 1998 (D. and D. Bylin) must have come from clutches laid around the earliest recorded date for eggs of the Blue Grosbeak in California, 18 April (Austin 1968). The season ran late that year too, with young being fed at Lake Henshaw (G17) 5 September 1998 (C. G. Edwards). Raising of

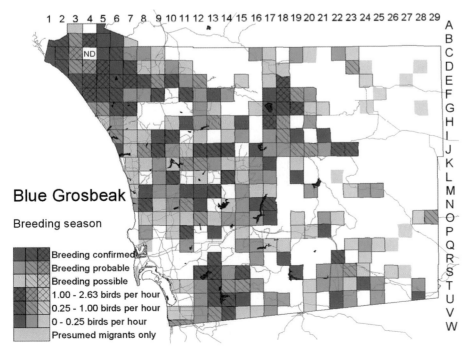

Blue Grosbeak

Breeding season

- Breeding confirmed
- Breeding probable
- Breeding possible
- 1.00 - 2.63 birds per hour
- 0.25 - 1.00 birds per hour
- 0 - 0.25 birds per hour
- Presumed migrants only

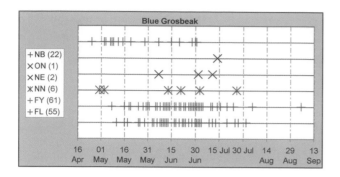

second broods is apparently common (Ingold 1993) but probably more so after wet years than dry ones.

Migration: In spring, Blue Grosbeaks begin arriving in mid April. From 1997 through 2001 we recorded earliest dates ranging from 11 April (1998, two in Oriflamme Canyon, L22, D. and C. Batzler; 2001, one along San Mateo Creek, C2, S. Brad) to 16 April. No earlier dates appear in the literature. A report from Otay Valley (V12) 22 March 1998 (P. Walsh) is so much earlier than other spring dates it more likely represents a wintering bird. In migration, Blue Grosbeaks are rare away from their breeding habitat. From 1997 through 2001 we recorded only about 15 such migrants in spring. The latest of these was at Point Loma (S7) 17 May 1997 (C. G. Edwards). In fall, migrants pause little in San Diego County. By late September the species is very rare, and 1 November (1984, one at Point Loma, R. E. Webster, AB 39:104, 1985) is the latest recorded fall date.

Winter: During the atlas period, one was near Moretti's Junction (H18) at the surprisingly high elevation of 2800 feet on 12 December 2000 (P. Unitt, M. G. Mathos), and

another was at the Dairy Mart pond in the Tijuana River valley (V11) on 9 December 2001 (G. McCaskie). The only previous records are from Escondido (I10) 20–22 February 1957 (AFN 11:291, 1957), Otay Mesa (V12) 29 January 1964, Solana Beach (L7) 22 February–13 March 1964 (McCaskie et al. 1967c), and the Sweetwater River in National City (T10) 12 December 1979 (AB 34:308, 1980).

Conservation: As a species primarily of undergrowth, the Blue Grosbeak shows no ability to cope with urbanization. Occurrences in isolated patches of suitable habitat within heavily developed areas are rare (one in Tecolote Canyon, Q8, 14 June 1999, J. C. Worley; one singing male near the mouth of the Sweetwater River, T10, 30 June 1999, P. Unitt). Loss of riparian habitat to agriculture, golf courses, and sand mining have undoubtedly taken their toll, but the Blue Grosbeak never experienced population collapse on the scale of some other riparian songbirds. The Blue Grosbeak has been subject to heavy parasitism by the Brown-headed Cowbird in Orange County (7 of 7 nests parasitized in 1949, Bleitz 1956), but the effect on the grosbeak's population is unclear; it may have been able to sustain the parasitism better than smaller birds. Yet the Blue Grosbeak is not represented among 38 cowbird-parasitized egg sets collected in San Diego County 1915–52.

Taxonomy: San Diego County specimens are all *P. c. salicaria* (Grinnell, 1911), with a smaller bill than the subspecies east of the Colorado River. The inclusion of the Blue Grosbeak in the genus *Passerina*, so strongly suggested by the birds' calls, songs, posture, behavior, and plumage, is now supported by mitochondrial DNA as well (Klicka et al. 2001).

Lazuli Bunting *Passerina amoena*

The male Lazuli Bunting is one of San Diego County's most colorful birds, but the species is of interest for more than just pretty plumage. Typical of riparian woodland edges and mountain meadows, the Lazuli Bunting is also a fire follower. It colonizes burned chaparral in recovery, during the stage when wildflowers—and insects that feed on them—can proliferate before the resprouting shrubs take over again. The Lazuli Bunting is common in San Diego County as both a breeding bird and a migrant, but it is absent in winter.

Breeding distribution: Though not linked to oak woodland, the Lazuli Bunting has a distribution similar to that of several species characteristic of this habitat. That is, the bunting is widespread as a breeding bird over the coastal slope but not along the coast itself. The distribution approaches the coast in the north, then retreats inland toward the south. Macario Canyon near Agua Hedionda Lagoon (I6) is the southernmost known nesting site near the coast (active nest 4–11 May 1999, W. E. Haas). In the

Photo by Anthony Mercieca

southern half of the county, a pair in Los Peñasquitos Canyon (N8) 6 June 1999 (M. Baumgartel) and eight individuals in Tecolote Canyon (Q8) 10 June 1999, dropping to one four days later (J. C. Worley), are outliers. On the east slope of the mountains, Lazuli Buntings breed possibly at 2200 feet elevation in Borrego Palm Canyon (F23; singing male 5–8 July 2001, L. J. Hargrove), definitely along San Felipe Creek, in wet years probably down to the mouth of Sentenac Canyon (I23, pair 26 May 1998, P. K. Nelson), and probably east to near Bankhead Springs (U27, pair regular in April and May 1997, F. L. Unmack). Any breeding east of Campo (U22), though, is tenuous; all records there are within the period of spring migration.

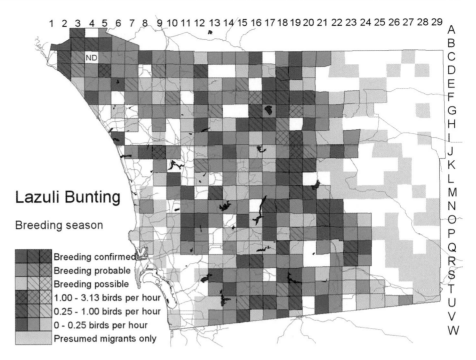

Lazuli Bunting

Breeding season

▨	Breeding confirmed
▨	Breeding probable
▨	Breeding possible
▨	1.00 - 3.13 birds per hour
▨	0.25 - 1.00 birds per hour
▨	0 - 0.25 birds per hour
▨	Presumed migrants only

Lazuli Buntings are usually most abundant in the inland valleys and lower mountains where low herbs grow near thick shrubbery. Daily counts of breeding birds run very exceptionally up to 150, as in the Nature Conservancy's Edwards Ranch northeast of Santa Ysabel (I19) 30 June 2001 (D. W. Au, S. E. Smith). The species' distribution is rather patchy, though, and somewhat irregular from year to year. This irregularity arises in part because one of the Lazuli Bunting's prime habitats in San Diego County is successional: recovering burned chaparral in which low herbaceous growth still dominates. Its preference for low herbaceous growth also means that more habitat will be suitable after wet years than after dry ones. Michael A. Patten (pers. comm.) found the bunting widespread as a breeding species in sage scrub on the periphery of San Diego in 2001, when rainfall was near average, but virtually absent in 2002, when rainfall was at a record low. Perennial habitats are riparian woodland and scrub and mountain meadows, especially where there are thickets of California rose.

Nesting: The Lazuli Bunting usually hides its cup nest in dense, low vegetation. Atlas observers described or inferred four nests in rose thickets, two in white sage, two in California sagebrush, one in San Diego sunflower, one in a willow, and one in a laurel sumac in a burned area. Clearly the buntings recognize the ability of rose thorns to deter predators.

Lazuli Buntings generally begin nesting in late April or early May. In the wet spring of 1998, they apparently began a bit early. Observations of adults carrying insects

that year began as early as 3 May in Sycamore Canyon (O12; I. S. Quon), of fledglings, as early as 15 May (J9; J. O. Zimmer), implying egg laying no later than 21–23 April. Adults fed fledglings far into July, even to 8 August in Cuyamaca Rancho State Park (N21) in 2000 (P. D. Jorgensen). Early or failed breeders, though, depart earlier, in mid July.

Migration: Spring arrival of the Lazuli Bunting is typically in early April. From 1997 to 2001, the first report of the spring varied only from 27 March (1997, one at Upper Willows, Coyote Creek Canyon, C22, P. D. Jorgensen) to 3 April. Arrival even a day or two before 1 April, however, is rare. Migrants are widespread throughout the county, including coastal and desert areas where the species does not nest. High concentrations of migrants run up to 40 around Scissors Crossing (J22) 13 April 1998 (E. C. Hall) and 25 at Carrizo Marsh (O29) 4 May 1999 (P. D. Jorgensen). In most years, migrants headed farther north have continued on by the third week of May; our latest such date 1997–2001 was 23 May 2000 (two in Goat Canyon, W10, W. E. Haas). In other years, stragglers have been seen as late as 15 June (1977, Point Loma, S7, P. Unitt). Fall migration takes place primarily in August and early September. By late September the Lazuli Bunting is rare; 4 November (1962, one in the Tijuana River valley, G. McCaskie) is still the latest known date.

Winter: Although the Lazuli Bunting winters regularly as close to California as southeastern Arizona and southern Baja California, there are no well-supported winter records for San Diego County.

Conservation: The Lazuli Bunting does not adapt to urbanization. A few holes in its distribution are likely due to habitat loss, as around Vista, San Marcos, Escondido, and El Cajon. The core of its range in San Diego County, though, is at higher elevations little threatened by devel-

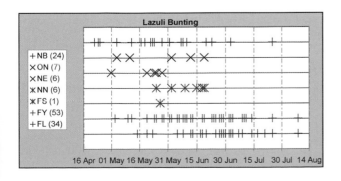

Lazuli Bunting

+NB (24)	
×ON (7)	
×NE (6)	
×NN (6)	
×FS (1)	
+FY (53)	
+FL (34)	

16 Apr 01 May 16 May 31 May 15 Jun 30 Jun 15 Jul 30 Jul 14 Aug

opment. In some parts of its range the Lazuli Bunting is parasitized heavily by the Brown-headed Cowbird (Greene et al. 1996). In San Diego County cowbird parasitism seems not to have been a significant factor, as implied by the bunting's not clearly decreasing after the cowbird's invasion, the lack of cowbird eggs among

collected sets of the bunting, and atlas observers' not reporting any parasitism 1997–2001. The inevitability of fire in chaparral implies that the Lazuli Bunting will persist, shifting from burn to burn, as long as chaparral dominates San Diego County's landscape.

Indigo Bunting *Passerina cyanea*

In the 1960s the Indigo Bunting was just another vagrant from the eastern United States. But the front of its expanding breeding range has now almost reached the Pacific coast. Today this brilliant bird, though still rare, is becoming ever more frequent as a summer visitor to San Diego County's inland valleys and foothills. A noticeable upswing in occurrences coincided with the arrival of the new millennium.

Breeding distribution: The Indigo Bunting is a recent colonist in San Diego County, as elsewhere in southern California (Rowe and Cooper 1997). Until 2002, all known nestings were of mixed pairs, Indigo and Lazuli, or the identity of the female was ambiguous. The first likely hybridization took place in Spring Canyon (P11) in 1973, when a male Indigo was seen paired with a female Lazuli 2–10 June and the female was later seen with fledglings (P. Unitt, AB 29:920, 1973). Since then, summer records have become ever more frequent, too frequent to list individually. Subsequent records of apparent or definite breeding have been 22 May–3 July 1991 near Lake Cuyamaca (M20), where a male Indigo was paired with a Lazuli and feeding a fledgling on latter date (R. Ford, C. G. Edwards, AB 45:1162, 1991), 28 May 1993 near Ramona (K15), where a male was paired with female Lazuli (C. G. Edwards, AB 47:1151, 1993),

Photo by Anthony Mercieca

16 July 2000 at Pine Hills (K19), where an unidentified female and/or juvenile bunting were near a male Indigo (J. R. Barth), and 21 June 2001 in Peutz Valley (P16), where a male was calling agitatedly as well as singing territorially (M. B. Stowe, P. Unitt). On 24 June 2001, along Kitchen Creek near Cibbets Flat (Q23), an agitated female Indigo, with male Lazuli Buntings singing nearby, had two probable fledglings (C. G. Edwards). On 28 June 2001, in Cañada Verde near the Warner Springs fire station (F19), an apparent first-year male Indigo (some irregular white on belly) was associated with a female Indigo and a hybrid fledgling (streaking heavier than in a juvenile Lazuli; M. B. Stowe, P. Unitt). On 13 July 2001, near the confluence of San Felipe and Banner creeks (J22) a male Indigo was paired with a female Lazuli, and a mixed pair nested twice at the same site in summer 2002 (J. R. Barth), the first apparent return of an Indigo, another step toward establishment of a population. Outside the Lazuli Bunting's observed breeding range, a male Indigo at Jacumba (U28) 28 June–1 July 2000 was paired with an ambiguous female; she was with a fledgling on the first date and went into a copulation-solicitation posture when the male few over her on the latter date (J. K. Wilson, P. K. Nelson, P. Unitt).

Though records of territorial Indigo Buntings are still scattered, they range from the inland

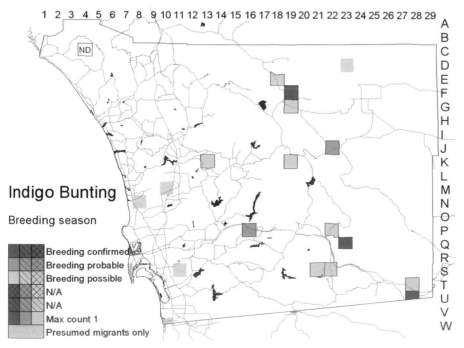

Indigo Bunting

Breeding season

Breeding confirmed
Breeding probable
Breeding possible
N/A
N/A
Max count 1
Presumed migrants only

valleys to the desert edge but exclude the coastal strip and the desert floor. The birds' habitat is not too specialized: riparian woodland and edges, oak woodland edges, and even an abandoned avocado orchard.

Nesting: Like the Lazuli, the Indigo Bunting places its nest in dense low, often thorny vegetation, usually within 3 feet of the ground. The nest is screened from above by leaves (Payne 1992). A female Indigo paired with a first-year male Indigo was building a nest, later abandoned, near Scissors Crossing (J22) 7 July 2002 (J. R. Barth). The nest was about 2 feet off the ground in a thicket of mugwort.

Migration: In San Diego County, the Indigo Bunting has been recorded primarily from mid May through July, when the males stop singing. From 1997 through 2001 the earliest date was 12 May (2001, one at Lower Willows, D23, B. L. Peterson; one in Los Peñasquitos Canyon, N8, P. Lovehart). Records as early as 11–12 April (1992, one at Point Loma, S7, G. McCaskie, AB 46:482, 1982) and 15 April (1987, one at Vallecito, M25, B. Andeman, AB 41:490, 1987) are exceptional. Spring vagrants may be seen at least as late as 21 June (1997, one at Widman Park, Encanto, S11, P. Unitt). The latest summer record is of an adult male in the Tijuana River valley 7 August 1976 (G. McCaskie). The Indigo Bunting is now more frequent in spring and summer than in fall but still occurs regularly as a vagrant in September and October, exceptionally as late as 22 November (1975, Balboa Park, R9, J. L. Dunn).

Winter: Still only two records, of one in Balboa Park 10–23 December 1967 (AFN 22:480, 1968) and one in San Marcos (I9) 9 March 1976 (AB 30:770, 1976).

Conservation: Despite heavy cowbird parasitism in its breeding range, being trapped as a cage bird in its winter range, and failing to adapt to urbanization anywhere (Payne 1992), the Indigo Bunting continues to spread.

Taxonomy: A borderline case as species or subspecies, the Indigo and Lazuli Buntings hybridize wherever they occur together. Yet differences in song, molt, females' mate preference, and the persistence of the parental phenotypes in the zone of overlap imply that mechanisms isolating the two have taken hold.

Painted Bunting *Passerina ciris*

The most popular cage bird in Baja California, the Painted Bunting occurs in San Diego County mainly as an escapee from captivity. On the basis of records of immatures well north of the international border, however, the species also reaches California as a natural vagrant, at least in fall migration. The California Bird Records Committee has accepted 15 Painted Buntings as vagrants to San Diego County, but identifying any particular individual as a vagrant rather than escapee is now impossible.

Photo by Anthony Mercieca

Migration: Of San Diego County's 15 committee-endorsed records of the Painted Bunting, eight are from the Tijuana River valley, five are from Point Loma, one is from San Diego (4 September 1992, N. Whelan, Garrett and Singer 1998), and one is from Encinitas (K7; 21–22 October 2000, K. Aldern, Garrett and Wilson 2003). The 14 fall records range in date from 24 August (1993 or 1994, Tijuana River valley, D. W. Aguillard, McCaskie and San Miguel 1999) to 3 December (1995, same locality, G. McCaskie, Garrett and Singer 1998). Even though the evidence for spring vagrancy of the Painted Bunting to California is much weaker, the committee has also accepted one spring record from San Diego County, of a female at Cabrillo National Monument (S7) 16 May 2001 (G. C. Hazard, T. Plunkett, Garrett and Wilson 2003).

In northern Baja California, Hamilton (2001) found the Painted Bunting to be the cage bird offered for sale most abundantly by far. Females are sold as much as males. Escapees are seen at all seasons; at least 13 were reported in San Diego County during the atlas period 1997–2002. They can often be identified by injuries around the bill, damage to the flight feathers, and, in adult males, by the faded red of the underparts. Even some of the accepted records from San Diego County may represent escapees. At least the five Painted Buntings in the Tijuana River valley 1962–63 (McCaskie et al. 1967c), however, were almost certainly vagrants, as they predated the explosive growth of Tijuana's human population.

Taxonomy: Thompson (1991) discounted the long-maintained division of the Painted Bunting into two subspecies.

Dickcissel *Spiza americana*

The Dickcissel breeds largely in the prairie region of the central United States and winters largely in the llanos of Venezuela, in immense flocks. Its frequency as a vagrant to San Diego County is on the decline, reaching about one every other fall by the beginning of the 21st century. Responsible factors likely include both overall population decline and local habitat changes, in the form of loss of the agricultural fields in the Tijuana River valley where the species had been found most often.

Photo by Richard E. Webster

Migration: All of San Diego County's fall records of the Dickcissel are from the Tijuana River valley, Otay Mesa (V12/V13), and Point Loma (S7), except for one at Camp Pendleton 3 October 1964 (AFN 19:82, 1965). Their dates range from 7 September (1980, Tijuana River valley, AB 35:228, 1982) to 2 November (1968, Otay Mesa, AFN 23:112, 1969).

Winter: The county's single winter record of the Dickcissel is of one that frequented a feeder on Kearny Mesa (P9) 2 December 1963–16 March 1964 (McCaskie et al. 1967c).

Conservation: The maximum annual count of Dickcissels in San Diego County was 12 in 1963 (McCaskie et al. 1967c). By the mid to late 1970s the species was occurring at a rate of one to four per year (Unitt 1984). From 1993 through 2003, however, only four were reported. The Dickcissel's concentration on the Venezuelan llanos in huge winter roosts renders the species vulnerable to mass killing, especially as it is regarded there as an agricultural pest.

New World Blackbirds and Orioles — Family Icteridae

Bobolink *Dolichonyx oryzivorus*

When the Tijuana River valley was covered with alfalfa fields, the Bobolink was a regular fall visitor there. When these fields were abandoned, sightings of the Bobolink in San Diego County almost ceased. Bobolinks reaching the coast of California, however, may all be misoriented immatures; even the birds breeding in eastern Washington and eastern Oregon apparently head far to the east before turning south toward the winter range in South America.

Photo by Anthony Mercieca

Migration: In San Diego County, the great majority of Bobolinks have been seen in the Tijuana River valley. There are only a few records from other sites in the coastal lowland and only one from the Anza–Borrego Desert, of up to two at the Borrego sewage ponds (H25) 13–25 September 1997 (P. D. Jorgensen, FN 52:129, 1998). The Bobolink is, or was, most frequent in late September and early October; fall dates range from 3 September (1973, Tijuana River valley) to 13 November (1976, same location, G. McCaskie).

There are also four records in late spring and summer, one from Point Loma (6 June 1974, AB 28:854, 1974), three from the Tijuana River valley (3 June 1977, AB 31:1049, 1977; 25–26 July 1976, AB 30:1005, 1976; 24 June 1995, NASFN 49:983, 1995).

Conservation: In the 1960s and 1970s the Bobolink was irregularly common in the Tijuana River valley, with up to 60 between 26 September and 18 October 1969 (AFN 24:100c, 1970). In the 1980s the numbers dropped abruptly. From 1997 through 2003 the only record, besides that at the Borrego sewage ponds, was of three in a small tomato field in the Tijuana River valley (V11) 15 October 2001, with one remaining to 22 October (G. McCaskie).

Red-winged Blackbird *Agelaius phoeniceus*

Probably no bird is more common in freshwater marshes across North America than the Red-winged Blackbird. Even San Diego County, in spite of the aridity of its climate, has enough wetlands to support the Red-winged as a common if localized permanent resident. Creation of reservoirs has created new blackbird habitat, and the birds' gathering in large flocks in winter gives the impression that they are doing well. But breeding Redwings need open uplands for foraging as well as marshes for nesting. Urbanization eliminates this habitat, and the blackbirds' retreat from development is already evident in San Diego.

Photo by Anthony Mercieca

Breeding distribution: Though most characteristic of freshwater marshes, the Red-winged Blackbird takes advantage of small isolated creeks, scattered ranch ponds, and thick stands of mustard. As a result, it is widely distributed over San Diego County's coastal slope, recorded as at least a possibly breeding species in 78% of atlas squares outside the Anza–Borrego Desert and confirmed nesting in 58% of them. Gaps correspond mainly to rugged terrain covered largely by chaparral, such as Aguanga Ridge (D15/D16/E16) and Otay Mountain (U15/V15). The intensively developed area of metropolitan San Diego is a conspicuous gap. Larger concentrations correspond to marshes near grassland or pastures where large numbers of blackbirds can forage. Such sites lie in Warner Valley (up to 350 in the east arm of the valley, G19, 25 June 2000, P. Unitt), the Mesa Grande area (up to 275 southeast of Mesa Grande, I17, 5 May 1999, D. C. Seals), Santa Maria Valley (up to 300 northeast of Ramona, K15, 25 May 1998, M. and B. McIntosh), Los Peñasquitos Lagoon and lower canyon (up to 260 at the lagoon, N7, 2 May 1999, D. K. Adams), and from Sweetwater Reservoir

south to Otay Mesa (up to 375 at Upper Otay Lake and north end of Lower Otay Lake, T13, 14 April 2000, T. W. Dorman).

As long as habitat is available, the Red-winged Blackbird does not appear limited in San Diego County by elevation; it nests up to 5400 feet in Laguna Meadow (O23; 60, including fledglings being fed by adults, 24 July 1998, E. C. Hall, J. O. Zimmer). In the Anza–Borrego Desert the Red-winged Blackbird breeds along San Felipe Creek east to Sentenac Ciénaga (J23; up to 83 on 14 June 1998, R. Thériault), in some years probably down to the mouth of Sentenac Canyon (I23; three on 23 May 1997, P. K. Nelson). Other desert sites of confirmed or probable Red-winged Blackbird nesting are in the agricultural area of the northern Borrego Valley (E24; 16, with adults feeding young, 15 April 2001, P. D. Ache), at the Borrego sewage ponds (H25; 12, with adults building nests and feeding young, 25 May 1998, P. D. Jorgensen), Vallecito (M25; up to eight, including pairs, 27 April 1998, M. C. Jorgensen), Carrizo Marsh (O29; four, including pairs, 25 April 2001, M. C. Jorgensen), and springs in Carrizo Gorge (R27; six, with up to three singing males, 29 April and 14 May 2000, G. Rebstock, L. J. Hargrove; S28; 12, with four singing males, 6 May 2001, R. Breisch). Nesting at most desert locations is probably irregular; Massey (1998) reported a fledgling at Lower Willows (D23) in 1994, but from 1997 to 2001 we had only a single record there (two on 25 April 1998, B. L. Peterson). The birds in Carrizo Gorge may need to commute out of the gorge to McCain and Jacumba valleys to feed.

Nesting: In San Diego County Red-winged Blackbirds nest usually in marshes of cattail or bulrush, anchoring the nest to

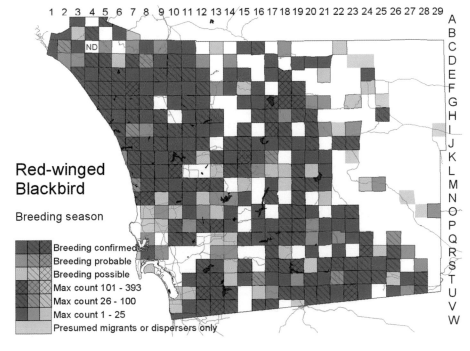

Red-winged
Blackbird

Breeding season

Breeding confirmed
Breeding probable
Breeding possible
Max count 101 - 393
Max count 26 - 100
Max count 1 - 25
Presumed migrants or dispersers only

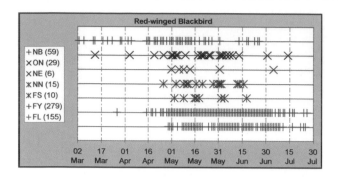

several vertical leaves. Other substrates are common too, including black mustard over dry ground. Atlas records indicate that most Red-winged Blackbirds begin laying in the first week of April. A few lay earlier, as early as mid March, as implied by observations of nest building as early as 3 March 1997 at Scissors Crossing (J22; L. Allen), an occupied nest 13 March 2001 at Rancho Santa Fe (L8; A. Mauro), and adults feeding young 27 March 1998 in Dameron Valley (C15; K. L. Weaver). Egg laying probably continues to the end of June, as implied by observations of nest building as late as 26 June 1999 at Potrero (U20; R. and S. L. Breisch), a nest with eggs 5 July 1997 near San Luis Rey (G6; M. R. Smith), and an occupied nest 14 July 1997 at Sweetwater Reservoir (S13; P. Famolaro). Thus the season is slightly longer than implied by the 20 March–18 June spread of 38 egg sets collected 1911–36.

Migration: There is evidence for only occasional long-distance movement of Red-winged Blackbirds in and out of San Diego County (see Taxonomy). Rather, most of the birds appearing away from breeding locations are making short-distance movements. Our only spring records of Red-winged Blackbirds more than one atlas square away from where the species likely breeds were from the Anza–Borrego Desert, of one at Canebrake (N27) 18

April 1999 (R. and S. L. Breisch) and one at Ocotillo Wells (I29) 1 May 2000 (P. Unitt).

Winter: The Red-winged Blackbird appears more abundant in winter than during the breeding season because many birds then gather into large flocks (up to 1200 in San Marcos, J8, 26 December 1998, D. and C. Batzler; 840 in Escondido, J10, 22 December 2000, W. E. Haas; 620 in the Tijuana River valley, V10, 18 December 1999, W. E. Haas). But the winter distribution of the Red-winged Blackbird in San Diego County differs little from the breeding distribution. Only sporadically do small flocks invade the urban area of San Diego at any distance from where the birds breed (up to 13 at Seaport Village in downtown San Diego, S9, 13 December 1998, Y. Ikegaya). Large numbers may remain as high as 5400 feet elevation at Big Laguna Lake (O23; up to 62 on 21 January 2002; E. C. Hall, J. O. Zimmer). In the Anza–Borrego Desert the species leaves the more isolated oases, becoming localized in winter to San Felipe, Earthquake, and Borrego valleys (up to 68 at Ram's Hill, H25, 20 December 1998, R. Halford; 75 at Sentenac Ciénaga, J23, 11 January 1998, P. Unitt).

Conservation: The Red-winged Blackbird has proven more adaptable than many marsh birds. Its ability to nest as scattered pairs has saved it from the fate of the colonial Tricolored Blackbird. The installation of reservoirs and ponds has been a positive factor that has compensated in part for loss of habitat to stream channelization and urbanization. It can take quick advantage of changes in its favor: in 1984, when the mouth of the Tijuana River estuary was blocked, hundreds colonized and nested, departing again once the estuary mouth was open and the tides returned (P. D. Jorgensen). But the Red-winged Blackbird's adaptability has its limits, as can be seen in the species' absence over most of central San Diego. Over this area the blackbirds nest only along the San Diego River in Mission Valley (R8, R9, Q10) and at the mouth of Rose Canyon at the northeast corner of Mission Bay (Q8; up to 20, nests probable, 15–30 May 1999, E. Wallace). Even if marshes suitable for nesting remain within the city, surrounding developed uplands do not offer the abundance of insects needed for the blackbirds to raise their young.

Taxonomy: The resident subspecies of the Red-winged Blackbird in southwestern California is *A. p. neutralis* Ridgway 1901 (type locality Jacumba, U28). It has the bill thick, the female's underparts wholly and heavily streaked with dark, her upperpart feathers edged with pale chestnut and yellow-buff, and the male's epaulet broadly edged with buff. Only four of the 76 San Diego County Red-winged Blackbird

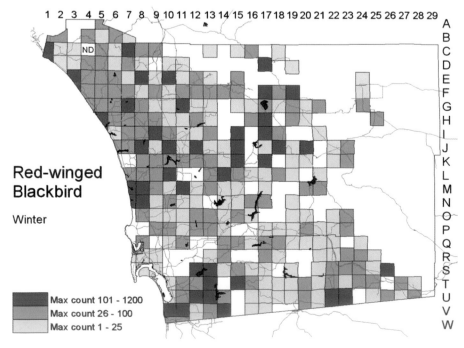

Red-winged Blackbird

Winter

Max count 101 - 1200
Max count 26 - 100
Max count 1 - 25

specimens in the San Diego Natural History Museum demonstrate migration from outside the range of *neutralis*. These four females are *A. p. nevadensis* Grinnell, 1914, from the Great Basin/intermountain region, as indicated by their more rusty, fewer buff fringes on the upperpart feathers: National City (T10) 4 January 1914 (SDNHM 33498) and 28 January 1921 (SDNHM 33545), Jamacha (R14) 4 January 1924 (SDNHM 2783), and Bonita (T11) 6 January 1929 (SDNHM 12328). *Agelaius p. nevadensis* is partially migratory and has been reported previously as close to San Diego County as San Timoteo Canyon, Riverside County (Grinnell and Miller 1944) and Bard, Imperial County (Patten et al. 2003).

Van Rossem (1926) reported a male collected at Witch Creek (J18) 13 April 1904 as *A. p. californicus* Nelson, 1897, breeding in the Central Valley, in which the female has the belly blacker than in *neutralis* and the male has less or no buff edge on the epaulet. Two females collected 15 October 1923 at Jamacha (SDNHM 2801, 2806; van Rossem 1926) have the more narrowly streaked underparts of *A. p. sonoriensis* Ridgway, 1887, from the desert Southwest, but they have the thicker bill of *neutralis*. No specimens from the Anza–Borrego Desert are available to test whether the Red-winged Blackbirds in this area could be *sonoriensis*, which breeds commonly in the Salton Sink.

Tricolored Blackbird *Agelaius tricolor*

The Tricolored Blackbird is one of California's amazing natural treasures: a songbird whose biology follows the model of a colonial seabird. Tricolored Blackbirds nest in large, dense colonies, usually in freshwater marshes, and forage in nearby grassland, pastures, or agricultural fields. Colonies once ranged up to 200,000 nests, but elimination of marshes and development of surrounding uplands has reduced the population greatly, especially in southern California. The Tricolored Blackbird is recognized as a highest-priority species of special concern by the California Department of Fish and Game. The San Diego County population is probably 5000–8000 birds, concentrated in 20–30 colonies. In spite of the Tricolored Blackbird's demanding requirements for breeding, in the nonbreeding season it forages readily in artificial habitats like dairies, lawns, garbage dumps, and parking lots.

Photo by Anthony Mercieca

Breeding distribution: Tricolored Blackbird colonies in San Diego County are now so few that they can be listed individually (Table 9). They are concentrated in two areas: north-central San Diego County from Dameron Valley and Oak Grove south to Ramona and Santa Ysabel, and the Campo Plateau from Potrero to Jacumba. The roster is not exhaustive; a few colonies undoubtedly passed undetected on private ranches or water-district lands we were unable to reach; such properties are the sites of most of the known colonies. Unconfirmed colonies are likely especially in La Jolla Valley (L10; 20 on 7 May 2000, K. J. Winter), at Miramar Lake (N10; 50 on 23 June 1999, K. J. Winter), Merigan Ranch, Descanso (P20; 15 on 18 April 1997, P. Unitt), Lake Murray (Q11; up to 30 on 9 June 2000, N. Osborn), La Posta Valley (S23; up to 20, males displaying, 11 April 1999, L. J. Hargrove), and McCain Valley (R26; 12 on 11 May 1999, L. J. Hargrove). Some colonies may remain active for years; that at

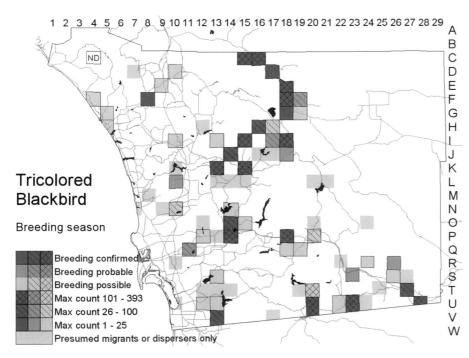

Tricolored Blackbird

Breeding season

- Breeding confirmed
- Breeding probable
- Breeding possible
- Max count 101 - 393
- Max count 26 - 100
- Max count 1 - 25
- Presumed migrants or dispersers only

TABLE 9   Known Tricolored Blackbird Colonies in San Diego County, 1997–2001

Colony	Square	Years Known Active	Maximum Count	Observers
Dameron Valley	C15	1997, 1998	200	K. L. Weaver
Oak Grove	C16	1998, 1999	840	K. L. Weaver
Sunshine Summit	D17	1999, 2000	25	P. Unitt
Puerta La Cruz	E18/F18	2000, 2001	250	P. K. Nelson, P. Unitt, M. G. Mathos
Swan Lake	F18	2000, 2001	1000	P. Unitt, M. G. Mathos, P. K. Nelson
Warner Ranch	G18	1999, 2000	18	P. K. Nelson, J. K. Wilson
Bonsall	F8	2000	20	J. Evans
Mesa Grande NW	H16	1999	12	E. C. Hall, J. O. Zimmer
Pamo Valley	I15	2000	1280	W. E. Haas
Mesa Grande SE	I17	2000	160	W. E. Haas
Santa Ysabel Ranch	I18	2000	260	S. E. Smith
Boden Canyon	J14	1999, 2000, 2001	40	C. R. Mahrdt, R. L. Barber, O. Carter, L. Comrack
Ramona W. D. Pond	K13	1998, 2000	1000	P. von Hendy, W. E. Haas, P. Unitt
East Ramona Pond	K15	1998, 1999	400	M. and B. McIntosh
Lindo Lake	P14/O14	1997, 1998, 2000	220	M. B. Stowe
Viejas Casino	P18	1999, 2000	600	K. J. Winter
Tule Lake	T27	2000	30	J. K. Wilson, F. L. Unmack
Twin Lakes	U20	1999, 2000, 2001	150	R. and S. L. Brelsch
Campo	U23	1997, 1998, 1999, 2000, 2001	1000	D. S. and A. W. Hester, P. Unitt
Jacumba	U28	1997, 1998, 1999, 2000	300	F. L. Unmack
La Media Rd.	V13	1998, 1999, 2000, 2001	100	P. Unitt

Jacumba has been used continuously since at least the 1970s. But others shift from year to year (a predator-avoidance strategy in many colonial birds), and others become unusable if the nesting marsh is trimmed or cut completely (as at the pond at Magnolia Ave. and Highway 78 in Ramona, K15) or the surrounding uplands are developed. The paucity of colonies in the coastal lowland where marshes are more numerous suggests that foraging habitat sufficient to support a large colony, not availability of nesting sites, has become the most important factor limiting the population.

Nesting: Most colonies are in cattail marshes, but Tricolored Blackbirds also nest in blackberry thickets (as in Santa Ysabel Valley, I18) or stands of black mustard (as on Otay Mesa, V13). Like the Red-winged Blackbird, the Tricolored attaches its nest to several usually vertical stems or leaves. But the male Tricolored defends a territory of as little as 1.8 square meters, and as many as six females build nests within one square meter (Beedy and Hamilton 1999). Nesting within a colony is often synchronized, so that all young may hatch and fledge within a few days of each other. Large colonies may include one or more successive waves of peripheral settlement. But different colonies are often unsynchronized, some establishing themselves up to nine weeks after others. The birds may shift to a second site and renest in the same season (Hamilton 1998). The schedule of Tricolored Blackbird nesting we observed in San Diego County 1997–2001 fits within that reported from the Central Valley by Beedy and Hamilton (1999), though with nest building at Twin Lakes, Potrero (U20), 19 June 1999 (R. and S. L. Breisch) it runs later than known from egg sets collected in the county 1890–1962 (latest 26 May).

Migration: Tricolored Blackbirds wander nomadically when not breeding, and some are seen sporadically away from nesting habitat through the breeding season. Some of these, such as 85 at a dairy 1.9 miles south of Ramona (L15) 22 April 2000 (P. Unitt), were within a few miles of known colonies. But others, such as eight at the east end of the basin of Lake Cuyamaca (L21) 13 April 1999 (J. K. Wilson), six along the Kelly Ditch Trail in the Cuyamaca Mountains (L20) 14 July 2000 (E. C. Hall), and two in Marron Valley (V17) 16 May 2000 (P. Beck), were far from any suspected colony. Particularly unusual were seven flying over a chaparral-covered ridge 1 mile east of Mount Laguna (O24) 16 June 2001 (P. Unitt) and the only recent records for the Anza–Borrego Desert, of 13 caught and released from a cowbird trap at

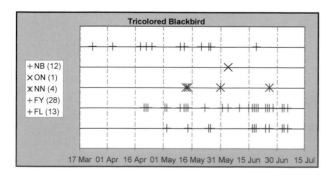

Whitaker Horse Camp (D24) 24 April 2002 (N. Collin) and one feeding in horse corrals at Borrego Springs (G24) 11 May 2002 (K. and P. D. Jorgensen). Old records from the desert slope are of specimens collected by Frank Stephens at "Palmetto Spring" (i.c., Palm Spring, N27) 1 April 1895 (SDNHM 792) and in San Felipe Valley near Scissors Crossing (J22) 4 April 1895 (SDNHM 793).

Winter: Though Tricolored Blackbirds may leave their breeding colonies in the winter, they still prefer to roost in marshes. In San Diego County it appears that most of the population does not shift a great distance. Sometimes large flocks are seen in winter at nesting colonies: up to 700 at Swan Lake 10 December 2000 (M. G. Mathos, J. R. Barth) and 500 at Oak Grove 26 February 2000 (K. L. Weaver). Some large winter flocks elsewhere could represent undiscovered nesting colonies: 300 in Lawson Valley (R17) 1 December 2001 (M. B. Stowe), 250 near Dulzura (T16) 31 January 2001 (D. W. Povey), 400 in Japatul Valley (Q18) 17 January 2001, and 525 in Hill Valley (T25) 4 February 2001 (P. Unitt). In north-coastal San Diego County wintering Tricolored Blackbirds are generally inconsistent (most regular around Bonsall and in the San Dieguito Valley), but the numbers may be much larger than are known to breed in this area (up to 200 in Rancho Santa Fe, L8, 28 December 1997; 190 at the Hollandia Dairy, San Marcos, I9, 27 February 1999, W. E. Haas). In south-coastal San Diego County a few still winter around Mission Bay and the San Diego River mouth, where they forage on lawns (maximum 20 at Robb Field, R7, 1 March 1999, V. P. Johnson). Considerable numbers wintered at the Otay dump (U12) until 1998 (135 on 19 December 1998, W. E. Haas), and Santee Lakes (P12) remains a regular wintering site, possibly for birds originating from the Lindo Lake colony (up to 70 on 19 December 1997, E. Post—fewer since). But over most of metropolitan San Diego the Tricolored Blackbird is now rare even as a winter visitor.

Conservation: The history of the Tricolored Blackbird in San Diego County has been one of continuous decline. In the early 1860s, J. G. Cooper (in Baird 1870) considered the Tricolored Blackbird "the most abundant species near San Diego." Neff (1937) listed five colonies in San Diego County's coastal lowland in 1935 and 1936, of up to 1000 nests. None of these persists today. The Dairy Mart pond in the Tijuana River valley (V11; Unitt 1984) is no longer a colony. San Diego Christmas bird count results show a sharp decline from the mid 1980s through 2001, with only a single Tricolored Blackbird reported in the latter

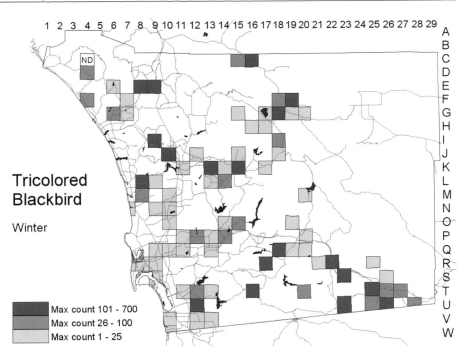

Tricolored Blackbird

Winter

■ Max count 101 - 700
■ Max count 26 - 100
□ Max count 1 - 25

year. The pattern on the Oceanside count is similar: the Tricolored Blackbird was formerly abundant in the lower San Luis Rey River valley, but a 95% drop from 1990 to 1991 was never reversed; the species was missed on the count for the first time in 2001.

Elimination of marshes undoubtedly contributed to the Tricolored Blackbird's population collapse, but loss of foraging habitat to development probably played an even greater role. For the species to nest successfully, it may need large colonies for proper social stimulation (Orians 1980). And a large colony requires a considerable habitat with abundant prey like grasshoppers. The critical mass for the population to be self sustaining is doubtless larger for the Tricolored Blackbird than for species that live as dispersed pairs.

Can the decline be arrested or reversed? Critical questions that still need to be answered include the extent of foraging habitat needed to support a viable colony and the number of alternative colony sites needed to support a viable population. Only one of the colonies, in Boden Canyon, lies on land devoted primarily to conservation, but the water in the pond was taken to fight a fire in August 2001; the pond did not refill in the following year of drought, and the blackbirds abandoned the colony in 2002 (L. Comrack). The only colony on public parkland, that at Lindo Lake, is already surrounded by development. Sustaining the Tricolored Blackbird will require the cooperation of water districts and private landowners. Can new colonies be attracted to restored or artificial marshes put near foraging habitat? Even though it lasted only two years, a colony formed in 1990 in a revegetation project in Mission Valley (R9) the first year after artificial islands were installed in the San Diego River. But the Tricolored Blackbird likely poses one of the most difficult conservation problems among North American birds.

Western Meadowlark *Sturnella neglecta*

Grassland is the Western Meadowlark's most typical habitat, but coastal marshes, open sage scrub, disturbed weedy areas, and even desert sinks also host the species. The Western Meadowlark is fairly widespread and common as a breeding species but is even more widespread and common as a winter visitor, when it gathers into flocks. The meadowlark survives cattle grazing and replacement of native grasses with exotics, but it does not adapt to urbanization and is susceptible to the ill effects of habitat fragmentation. Though heard all over the coastal mesas a century ago, in most of the city of San Diego the meadowlark's song has now fallen silent.

Photo by Anthony Mercieca

Breeding distribution: Western Meadowlarks concentrate in San Diego County's remaining large tracts of grassland. The largest numbers of breeding birds were reported from Warner Valley (up to 75 near Puerta La Cruz, E18, 12 May 2001, P. K. Nelson), Ballena Valley (K17; 60 on 12 June 2000, D. C. Seals), and Santa Maria Valley (up to 106 northeast of Ramona, K15, 26 April 1999, M. and B. McIntosh). Other areas important to the species are Camp Pendleton, Santa Ysabel Valley, Air Station Miramar, Proctor Valley, Rancho Jamul, Otay Mesa, and Campo Valley. Western Meadowlarks are widely but patchily distributed elsewhere: many atlas squares that are largely developed or covered largely by chaparral lack them. Along the coast they inhabit coastal wetlands (up to 20 at San Elijo Lagoon, L7, 14 May 1997, A. Mauro; 20 in the Tijuana River estuary, V10, 16 May 1998, B. C. Moore). A few persist around Mission Bay on weedy bayfill (e.g., two on the south shore, R8, 31 May 1998, C. B. Hewitt). In the Anza–Borrego Desert the Western Meadowlark is fairly common at Sentenac Ciénaga (J23; up to 16 on 14 June 1998, feeding young

in an extensive area of yerba mansa, R. Thériault) but uncommon to rare on valley floors elsewhere. Some birds advertise territories but apparently find the habitat insufficient and move on in the middle of the breeding season. Nevertheless, a few remain and nest at least irregularly, both in the agricultural area of the Borrego Valley (E24; three, including fledgling, 31 May 2001, J. Fitch) and in sinks (Clark Dry Lake, D26; three, including feeding young, in a weed patch amid mesquite and tama-

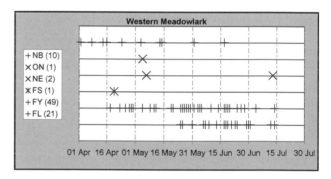

risk 30 April 2001, J. R. Barth). These records are the first of Western Meadowlarks breeding in the Anza–Borrego Desert (cf. Massey 1998), though the species breeds fairly commonly in the agricultural lands of the Coachella and Imperial valleys (Patten et al. 2003).

Nesting: Western Meadowlarks nest on the ground in dense grass or other low vegetation. The birds often build a dome or roof over the nest, screening it from above and making it difficult to locate. Atlas observers reported only three. Though egg collections demonstrate that Western Meadowlarks lay in San Diego County as early as 11 March, atlas observations reveal

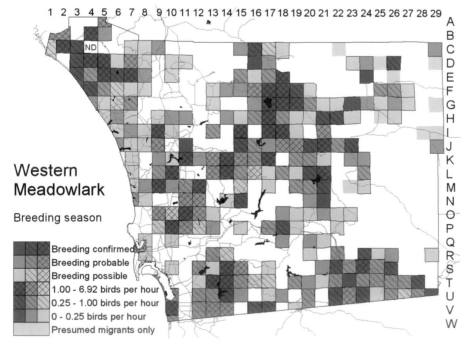

Western Meadowlark

Breeding season

- Breeding confirmed
- Breeding probable
- Breeding possible
- 1.00 - 6.92 birds per hour
- 0.25 - 1.00 birds per hour
- 0 - 0.25 birds per hour
- Presumed migrants only

that early April to late June is the principal season for meadowlark nesting in San Diego County. Reports of nest building near Warner's Ranch (G19) 17 June 2000 (J. D. Barr) and a nest with eggs near Dyar Spring, Cuyamaca Rancho State Park (N21) 13 July 2000 (S. Martin) are later than previous egg dates (to 15 June, Sharp 1907) but from elevations higher than most collected sets. We noted no winter nesting, as reported by Sechrist (1915b) and Abbott (1927c) during relatively wet winters.

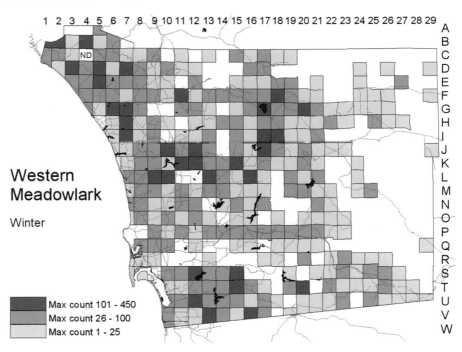

Western
Meadowlark

Winter

Max count 101 - 450
Max count 26 - 100
Max count 1 - 25

Migration: During migration and winter Western Meadowlarks spread into habitats like open desert and sparsely vegetated disturbed areas unsuitable for their breeding. In spring, migrants or winter visitors occur in such areas to mid April (11 April 1998, one near Five Palms Spring, G29, G. Rebstock, K. Forney; 20 April 1997, four near Greenwood Cemetery, S10, P. Unitt). Later scattered records from marginal desert habitat may be of birds scouting for possible breeding territories but unable to attract a mate (e.g., one near Middle Willows, C22, 14 May 1997, P. D. Jorgensen).

Winter: At this season the Western Meadowlark is considerably more abundant than during the breeding season. Maximum daily counts range up to 250 at Lake Henshaw (G17) 27 December 1999 (D. Aklufi), 368 between Poggi Canyon and Otay Valley (U12) 20 December 1997 (W. E. Haas), and 450 in Rancho Jamul (S15) 14 January 2001 (P. Unitt). The winter distribution is similar to the breeding distribution, though, with rather little spread into areas where breeding birds are absent. Among these latter areas are open spaces within the city of San Diego (up to 50 around the radio towers at Emerald Hills Park, S11, 12 December 1999, P. Unitt). The Western Meadowlark occurs irregularly even at high elevations through the winter (up to 40 at 4600 feet in the upper basin of Lake Cuyamaca, L21, 5 January 1999, J. K. Wilson; 32 at 4700 feet near Dyar Spring, N21, 20 January 2002, R. C. Sanger; 10 at 5400 feet in Laguna Meadow, O23, 6 December 1999, D. S. Cooper). In the Anza–Borrego Desert wintering Western Meadowlarks occur mainly on golf courses and on sandy valley floors (up to 30 near Little Clark Dry Lake, E27, 7 December 2000, R. Thériault; 30 at Vallecito, M25, 25 February 1999, M. C. Jorgensen).

Conservation: The Western Meadowlark has survived heavy grazing of its grassland and replacement of native

plants by foreign weeds, though these factors likely depressed the population. The meadowlark forages as readily in disturbed areas as in pristine habitat. But as a ground-nesting and ground-foraging species it has no ability to adapt to urbanization. As a result, there are now large gaps in what was once undoubtedly a nearly continuous distribution though the coastal lowland. Bolger et al. (1997) reported the Western Meadowlark to be susceptible to the effects of fragmentation, and this is implicit in the atlas results as well. Nesting birds are highly sensitive to human disturbance (Lanyon 1994). Disturbed grassland constitutes much of the meadowlark's remaining habitat in San Diego County but has been given low priority in habitat-conservation plans. Large areas of former meadowlark habitat, as around the eastern fringe of Chula Vista (T13/U12/U13), were developed and eliminated during the five-year atlas period. On the positive side are acquisition as wildlife habitat of San Felipe Valley and Rancho Jamul by the California Department of Fish and Game and part of the Ramona grasslands by the Nature Conservancy.

Taxonomy: The two described subspecies of the Western Meadowlark, *S. n. confluenta* Rathbun, 1917, and *S. n. neglecta* Audubon, 1844, are said to intergrade in San Diego County (AOU 1957). *S. n. confluenta* is darker, with heavier black barring on the upperparts and larger spots on the sides and flanks; it breeds in the Pacific Northwest and possibly south through coastal California. Nominate *neglecta* occurs farther south and east. The difference between the subspecies is obscured in worn plumage, and Lanyon (1994) considered them poorly differentiated.

Yellow-headed Blackbird
Xanthocephalus xanthocephalus

San Diego County lies at the southwestern margin of the Yellow-headed Blackbird's breeding range, so the species occurs here mainly as a rare migrant and winter visitor. Colonial, the Yellow-headed Blackbird has probably nested in the county irregularly, but the first colony described in any detail was discovered in 2000 at Tule Lake near Boulevard. Like that other colonial blackbird, the Tricolored, the Yellow-headed has suffered population decline in California, and it is recognized as a species of special concern by the California Department of Fish and Game.

Photo by Anthony Mercieca

Breeding distribution: Only one nesting colony was confirmed during the atlas' five-year term, within a private ranch near Boulevard at Tule Lake (T27). On 20 April 2000, F. L. Unmack and J. K. Wilson discovered 15 adults at a marsh within the lake, the males displaying and the females building nests. On 6 June at least three nests had nestlings, and at least one young had fledged. The colony was still active with more fledglings (20 individuals total) on 21 June. In 2001 the numbers were larger, with 50 adults and nests with nestlings on 6 June and 20 individuals, including fledglings, on 27 June (J. K. Wilson).

Other possible nestings were in nearby McCain Valley (R26), with four on 11 May 1999 (L. J. Hargrove), and near Rangeland Road northwest of Ramona (K13), with two and a suspected nest 26 May 2000 (P. M. von Hendy). The marsh in McCain Valley was dry in 2001, hosting a few Red-winged but no Yellow-headed or Tricolored Blackbirds. Sightings of the Yellow-headed elsewhere during the atlas period most likely represent migrants, though 20 southwest of Ramona (L14) 24 April 1999 (F. Sproul) suggest the possibility of another colony in the Santa Maria Valley.

Nesting: The Yellow-headed has the narrowest requirements of any of North America's blackbirds: it nests in deeply flooded freshwater marshes only (Twedt and Crawford 1995). Like those of the Red-winged and Tricolored, the nests of the Yellow-headed are usually wrapped around several vertical leaves of cattail or tule. Though colonial, and often polygynous, the Yellow-headed Blackbird seems to be more successful in small colonies than the Tricolored, and small colonies can get by with less foraging habitat surrounding the colony. The site at Tule Lake is typical.

Migration: As a spring migrant, the Yellow-headed Blackbird occurs most consistently in the Borrego Valley, sometimes in small flocks. Reported numbers range up to 35 at the Borrego sewage ponds (H25) 3 May 1997 (H. L. Young) and 20 at Borrego Springs (G24) 30 April 1997 and 19 April 1999 (P. D. Ache). Also of note in the desert were 13 at Agua Caliente County Park (M26) 4 May 2000 (D. C. Seals). Along the coastal slope numbers are much smaller, with a maximum of seven at Sweetwater Reservoir (S12) 4 May 1998 (P. Famolaro).

Spring migration of the Yellow-headed Blackbird takes place largely in April and early May. During the atlas period, spring records ranged from 1 April (2001, one at Borrego Springs, P. D. Ache) to 13 May (1998, one in the San Dieguito Valley, M8, J. Lesley) and 14 May (1998, one at Borrego Springs, M. C. Jorgensen). There are a few later records of nonbreeding summering individuals: one at Lake Cuyamaca (M20) 28 May 1998 (A. P. and T. E. Keenan); one at San Elijo Lagoon (L7) 12 July 1998 (B. C. Moore); one at Discovery Lake (J9) 17 July 1998 (J. O. Zimmer). Yellow-headed Blackbirds seen by early August

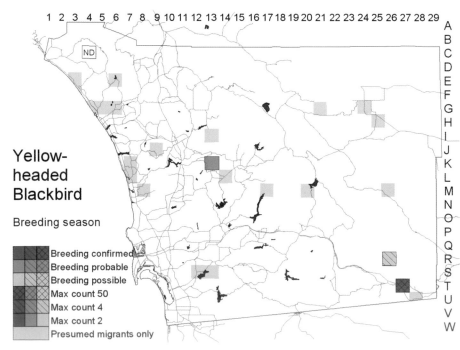

Yellow-headed Blackbird

Breeding season

Breeding confirmed
Breeding probable
Breeding possible
Max count 50
Max count 4
Max count 2
Presumed migrants only

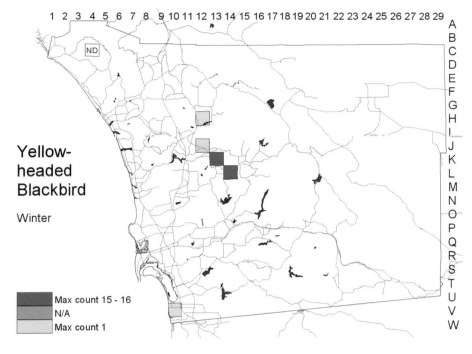

Yellow-headed Blackbird

Winter

Max count 15 - 16
N/A
Max count 1

Lake in 2000 notwithstanding, the trend of the Yellow-headed Blackbird's numbers in recent years has been sharply downward. It is likely that the species bred at least irregularly in the past. Refuse excavated from the nineteenth-century stage station at Carrizo Marsh (O29) contained numerous bones of both male and female Yellow-headed Blackbirds (S. Arter, P. Unitt). Albert M. Ingersoll (in Willett 1912) believed the Yellow-headed Blackbird "probably breeds at Warner's Ranch" (G19). Stephens (1919a), while providing no details and never collecting a specimen, said that it bred "in small colonies in tule marshes." Sams and Stott (1959) wrote "a few records of breeding locally (Murray Res.)." The Yellow-headed Blackbird summered at the Dairy Mart pond in the Tijuana River valley (V11) in 1979 and 1981 (Unitt 1984).

The species has become much scarcer since the late 1970s. In the lower San Luis Rey River valley (at Guajome and Whelan lakes and nearby dairies, G6/G7), the flocks of the 1960s and 1970s (Unitt 1984) dwindled to single digits in the early 1980s. Since 1984, the Oceanside Christmas bird count has recorded only a single individual. On the San Diego count the Yellow-headed Blackbird was found on 7 of 11 counts in the 1960s, with a maximum of 21 in 1963, but its frequency declined thereafter, with only a single individual noted since 1990.

Local factors, especially the urbanization of farm and pasture land, are undoubtedly contributing to the Yellow-headed Blackbird's decline in San Diego County. But factors operating on a broader scale, closer to the species' population centers, are probably more important. Threats identified by A. Jaramillo (unpubl. data) are loss of nesting habitat to drainage of marshes and pesticide contamination; the species feeds predominantly in agricultural areas.

(one at O'Neill Lake, E6, 6 August 1997, P. A. Ginsburg) are probably fall migrants; Phillips et al. (1964) reported such migrants arriving in southern Arizona in July. Migrants are occasionally seen in flocks in the Borrego Valley in fall as well as spring, with up to 25 at Ram's Hill (H25) 12 October 1998 (P. D. Jorgensen).

Winter: The Yellow-headed Blackbird has become rare as a winter visitor to San Diego County. Atlas observers recorded the species only six times at this season 1997–2002. Three of these records were from the Santa Maria Valley: 16 along Rangeland Road (K13) 20 February 1999 and five there 2 January 1999 (P. M. von Hendy); 15 southwest of Ramona (L14) 11 December 1998 (F. Sproul). Three were from scattered other locations: one along Woods Valley Road (H12) 2 January 1999 (C. Bingham), one in San Pasqual Valley (J12) 14 December 1998 (P. A. Ginsburg), and one in the Tijuana River valley (V10) 15 December 2001 (L. and M. Polinsky). Yellow-headed Blackbirds have deserted their former area of winter concentration in the lower San Luis Rey River valley.

Conservation: The discovery of the colony at Tule

Rusty Blackbird *Euphagus carolinus*

The Rusty Blackbird nests in the taiga zone of Alaska and Canada and winters mostly in the southeastern quadrant of the United States. It is a rare visitor to California in fall and winter. The six records for San Diego County are almost the southernmost along the Pacific coast, as there are just two records for northern Baja California and one from northwestern Sonora.

Winter: Sefton (1926) collected one at the former Monte Vista Ranch, Jamacha (R13), 14 November 1925 (SDNHM

Photo by Brian L. Sullivan

10163). Sight records are of one at Borrego Springs (F24/ G24) 27 November 1964 (AFN 19:81–82, 1965), one at Point Loma (S7) 9–10 November 1974 (AB 29:124, 1975), two in the Tijuana River valley (W11) 11–28 February 1981 (P. Unitt, AB 35:337, 1981), one there 28 October 1983 (G. McCaskie, AB 38:248, 1984), and one

near Oceanside (G6) 22 February–20 March 1987 (G. McCaskie, AB 41:332, 1987).

Conservation: The lack of reports since 1987 reflects a downturn in the Rusty Blackbird's rate of occurrence throughout California.

Brewer's Blackbird *Euphagus cyanocephalus*

Another colonial icterid, Brewer's Blackbird was one of southern California's early urban adapters. It became a common resident in city parks and shopping centers and capitalized on the clearing of chaparral for ranchettes in the countryside. But it remains common in the less-developed regions of the county where ponds, low grass, and open ground offer foraging. For nesting, exotic dense-foliaged vegetation suits it even better than native trees. Around rural houses, Italian cypresses attract Brewer's Blackbirds the way fan palms attract Hooded Orioles. Brewer's Blackbird is a recent colonist at Borrego Springs. Yet in spite of these adaptations to civilization, something in the urban environment is not right, for Brewer's Blackbird is disappearing from many of its former haunts in San Diego.

Breeding distribution: Brewer's Blackbird is fairly widespread over the coastal slope. The larger gaps in its distribution correspond mainly to areas thickly covered with chaparral and little open country or water. Some smaller gaps, though, include considerable suitable habitat. Colonial habits lead to a patchy distribution. The greatest numbers of breeding birds are along the Highway 79 corridor from Oak Grove (C16) south

Photo by Anthony Mercieca

through Warner Valley to Santa Ysabel (J18), in the Santa Maria Valley, and on the Campo Plateau. Daily counts of Brewer's Blackbirds during the breeding season range up to 200 around Warner's Ranch (G19) 17 June 2000 (J. D. Barr) and 302 in Ramona (K15) 25 May 1998 (M. and B. McIntosh). Numbers along the coast can also be large: up to 150 at La Costa (J7) 8 July 1998 (C. C. Gorman) and 70 at Los Peñasquitos Lagoon (N7) 1 August 1998 (S. Grain).

On the desert slope, breeding Brewer's Blackbirds extend down San Felipe Valley and Banner Canyon to Earthquake Valley (J23/K23; up to 30 on 13 June 2001, R. Thériault). The species also breeds at Butterfield Ranch in Mason Valley (M23; 25, plus active nests, 22 May 2001, P. K. Nelson). Elsewhere in the Anza–Borrego Desert, Brewer's Blackbirds breed only in the developed and agricultural areas of the Borrego Valley, where they are recent colonists. Though first reported breeding at the Roadrunner Club (F24) only in 1995 (M. L. Gabel in Massey 1998), Brewer's Blackbirds are now common around irrigated developments, with up to 40, plus nests with nestlings, at Club Circle (G24) 15 April 2001 (L. and M. Polinsky).

Nesting: Brewer's Blackbirds build their bowl-shaped nest in

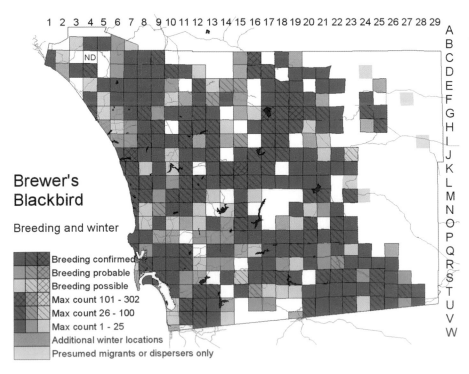

Brewer's Blackbird

Breeding and winter

- Breeding confirmed
- Breeding probable
- Breeding possible
- Max count 101 - 302
- Max count 26 - 100
- Max count 1 - 25
- Additional winter locations
- Presumed migrants or dispersers only

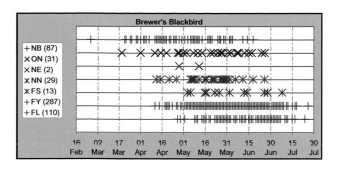

a wide variety of situations: in trees, shrubs, or on the ground. The common theme is that the nest is screened from view behind thick vegetation. The Italian cypress, an exotic ornamental growing as a narrow column, offers just this kind of screening. It appears that in San Diego County Brewer's Blackbirds often select the Italian cypress preferentially, and eight of 16 Brewer's Blackbird nests whose sites atlas observers described were in this single species of tree. Eight of 24 sites described by egg collectors were also cypresses, so this preference was established decades ago. Other elevated sites reported by atlas observers included, of native plants, California rose, and, of ornamental plants, pine, podocarpus, bottlebrush, Natal plum, oleander, and ivy growing over the wall of a shopping center. Ground sites were on a creek bank in the Cuyamaca Mountains and under a bed of baby sun rose iceplant separating a gas station from a street.

Atlas records indicate that Brewer's Blackbirds usually begin nest building in late March, begin laying about 1 April, and continue to lay until about 26 June. Exceptional early nesting is attested by a bird gathering nest material at the Camp Pendleton golf course (F6) 26 February 1999 (B. E. Bell) and an occupied nest in Encinitas (K6) 19 March 2000 (J. Ciarletta). This pattern is practically identical to that of 26 egg sets collected in San Diego County 1897–1934: range 31 March–28 June, except for one dated 5 March 1932.

Migration: Brewer's Blackbird migration is noticeable only in parts of the Anza–Borrego desert where the species does not nest. There were six spring records during the atlas period, from 20 March (2001, nine at Whitaker Horse Camp, D24, K. L. Weaver) to 1 May (1999, six near Font's Point, F27, G. Rebstock, K. Forney). Massey (1998) also reported Brewer's Blackbird as a rare spring migrant in the Anza–Borrego Desert's natural habitats. Previous desert records extend as late in the spring as 20 May (Unitt 1984). Fall migration is less well known, but a few Brewer's Blackbirds have been noted at nonbreeding locations beginning 26 September (1998, one at Tamarisk Grove, I24, P. D. Jorgensen).

Winter: Where foraging is good, Brewer's Blackbirds gather into large flocks in winter, up to 1400 southwest of Ramona (L14) 3 January 1998 (W. E. Haas) and 1000 in the San Pasqual Valley (J12) the same day (M. and S. Cassidy). But the species' distribution in winter differs

little from that during the breeding season. Even in urban areas its dispersal away from breeding colonies seems slight; for example, from 1997 to 2002 we never recorded Brewer's Blackbird at Greenwood, Mount Hope, and Holy Cross cemeteries (S10) and only once even at Point Loma (S7), so often visited by birders. Brewer's Blackbird may be irregular in winter at the higher elevations, where snow covers the ground for days. We had no winter records for San Ignacio at 4900 feet elevation on the east flank of Hot Springs Mountain (E21), where counts during the breeding season ranged as high as 18 per day. But at Laguna Meadow (O23), 5400 feet elevation, wintering Brewer's Blackbirds were found repeatedly, in numbers as high as 28 on 24 December 2001 (P. Unitt).

Conservation: Brewer's Blackbird seems ideally adapted to an urban lifestyle. Shade trees and ornamental shrubbery offer it better nest sites than native vegetation. It forages readily on lawns, disturbed open areas, and even parking lots. Furthermore, the importation and management of water have created lakes and ponds that offer breeding habitat in many areas where once there was none. It seems likely that Brewer's Blackbird's population in San Diego County increased with settlement and irrigation, though all the early writers already described it as common. Now, however, the trend appears to be heading into reverse. Some colonies persist in heavily urbanized areas, as on the campus of City College (S9) and at Colina del Sol Park (R11). But Brewer's Blackbird now appears absent from Point Loma, where it occurred during the breeding season as recently as 1995. In western and central Balboa Park (R9) our only record during the breeding season was of three birds nesting 14 May 1997 (J. K. Wilson), none have been noted subsequently. The species was formerly common there. Brewer's Blackbird is now absent from the campus of San Diego State University, where it was once common too. Totals of over 1000 on the San Diego Christmas bird count, routine from the 1960s to the early 1980s, are no longer reached. The totals for Oceanside 2000–02 were the lowest for that count since 1976. Why should Brewer's Blackbird be going into decline? One possible factor is a disease of the feet that leads to loss of toes and ultimately the entire foot. This condition has been common among Brewer's Blackbirds in San Diego for decades.

Taxonomy: No new information on geographic variation in Brewer's Blackbird has come to light since Rea (1983) tentatively recognized three subspecies based largely on variation in the females. Specimens from San Diego County, as elsewhere in coastal California, are *E. c. minusculus* Oberholser, 1920, with short wings, thin bill, and pale gray female. An exception is one female from La Mesa Heights (R12) 2 October 1926, larger and browner and so apparently a migrant of *E. c. cyanocephalus* (Wagler, 1829) from the Great Basin and Rocky Mountains (Unitt 1984).

Common Grackle *Quiscalus quiscula*

The Common Grackle occurs mainly east of the Rocky Mountains but is gradually increasing as a vagrant to California. Since the first in 1967, records in the state have accelerated to total 61 by 2002. The California Bird Records Committee has accepted just four for San Diego County.

Migration: Of the county's four committee-endorsed records of the Common Grackle one is for fall, one is for winter, and two are for spring. The fall record is the first for California, of one collected along La Cresta Road between El Cajon and Crest (Q14/Q15) 20 November 1967 (SDSU 2092, Roberson 1993). Unfortunately, the original label was apparently lost between the early 1980s and the early 1990s, before the specimen was catalogued, so the identification of SDSU 2092 as the specimen from La Cresta Road is only by inference. The spring records are of one at Point Loma (S7) 23 April 1992 (V. P. Johnson, B. Jones, Heindel and Patten 1996) and one photographed at Butterfield Ranch (M23) 14 April 2000 (J. E. Solis, J. E. Hunter, G. C. Hazard, McKee and Erickson 2002). Another spring report, of one "seen in flight" at Point Loma, was apparently not submitted to the records committee (FN 51:929, 1997).

Photo by Anthony Mercieca

Winter: One at Carlsbad (I6) 9 February–26 March 1977 was photographed (Luther 1980).

Taxonomy: All of California's Common Grackles have been Bronzed Grackles, *Q. q. versicolor* Vieillot, 1819, expected because it is the migratory subspecies widespread across the northern part of the species' range.

Great-tailed Grackle *Quiscalus mexicanus*

Otherworldly shrieks, brazen demeanor, and a tail that defies the laws of aerodynamics made the arrival of the Great-tailed Grackle in San Diego County impossible to miss. Few other birds have spread in North America so aggressively. Invading from the Imperial Valley, Arizona, and Sonora, the Great-tailed Grackle was first recorded in San Diego County in 1977 and first noted nesting in 1988. After that it increased rapidly, by the new millennium becoming a locally common resident around lakes and marshes. Though largely a wetland species, usually nesting over or near water, the Great-tailed Grackle is almost a commensal of man. It forages on lawns, around livestock, and in the food courts of shopping centers as long as these are within commuting distance of marshes.

Breeding distribution: As a newly colonizing species, the Great-tailed Grackle has a distribution that is still patchy, though quickly filling in. The patches or colonies are scattered throughout the county at low to moderate elevations. Current regions of concentration in the coastal lowland are as follows: along the San Luis Rey River from Oceanside (H5) to Pala (D10), with up to 50 in the San Luis Rey valley near Interstate 15 (E9) 14 May 2000 (C. and D. Wysong); Lake Hodges/San Pasqual Valley, with up to 40 at the lake (K10) 14 June 1999 (R. L. Barber); from Santee to Lakeside, with up to 20 at Santee Lakes (P12) 10 May 1998 and 21 March 1999 (B. C. Moore); Lower Otay Lake (U13), with up to 50 on 11 April 2001

Photo by Kenneth W. Fink

(T. W. Dorman); and the Dairy Mart pond in the Tijuana River valley (V11; 20 on 12 March 2000, P. Unitt). Higher in the foothills the species is sparser, but substantial colonies are in San Vicente Valley (L16; up to 20 on 27 June 2000, J. D. Barr) and at Sunshine Summit (D17), where the grackles nest at ponds in a mobile-home park (up to 40 on 3 June 2001, P. K. Nelson). At 3310 feet elevation the latter is highest colony in the county. Great-tailed Grackles nest also at lakes, ponds, and marshes on the Campo Plateau, from Potrero (U20) to Jacumba (U28). In this region they are still in small numbers except at Jacumba (up to 25 on 21 April 1999, F. L. Unmack). In the Anza–Borrego Desert the grackle is confined as a breeding species to developed areas, in the Borrego Valley (up to 24 at Club Circle, Borrego Springs, G24, 15 April 2001, L. and M. Polinsky), at Ocotillo Wells (I28/I29; up to 13 on 26 April 2001, J. R. Barth), and at Butterfield Ranch (M23; up to 25 on 22 May 2001, P. K. Nelson). Only single grackles were seen at other desert locations (Earthquake Valley, Vallecito, Agua Caliente County Park), though the species could colonize them too.

Nesting: The Great-tailed Grackle is flexible in its choice of nest site, often in stands of cattails, as at Sunshine Summit, Lower Otay Lake, and Jacumba, but also in willows, as in the Tijuana River valley, palms, as in the Heart of Africa exhibit at the Wild Animal Park, and

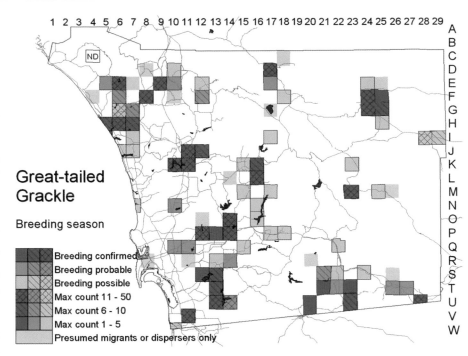

Great-tailed Grackle

Breeding season

Breeding confirmed
Breeding probable
Breeding possible
Max count 11 - 50
Max count 6 - 10
Max count 1 - 5
Presumed migrants or dispersers only

ornamental shade trees, as in the schoolyard at Borrego Springs. Like those of the smaller marsh blackbirds, the nest is supported from the side by several leaves or stems. The birds are colonial and frequently polygynous (Johnson et al. 2001).

Atlas results constitute the first significant body of information on the Great-tailed Grackle's nesting schedule in San Diego County. Nest building starts as early as 29 March (1997, along the San Diego River near Lakeside, P13, D. C. Seals), but no observations of adult females carrying food items suggest egg laying earlier than 25 April. The birds continue to lay until at least 1 July, as implied by a nest with eggs at the upper end of Sweetwater Reservoir (S13) 14 July 1997 and a nest with nestlings there 28 July 1997 (P. Famolaro). Fledglings may still be following their

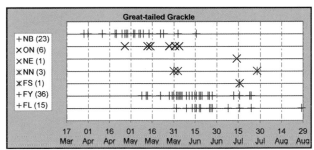

mothers late in the summer, as at the Roadrunner Club, Borrego Springs (F24), 28 August 2000 (P. Unitt).

Migration: The Great-tailed Grackle's schedule of movement in and out of the higher elevations where it does not winter is still poorly known. Our earliest date for these areas is 12 March (2000, one in San Vicente Valley, L16, J. D. Barr). Grackles are seen occasionally away from breeding colonies even in June (two in Chihuahua Valley, C18, 2 June 2001, J. M. and B. Hargrove; one in Corte Madera Valley, R20, 20 June 1998, J., E., and K. Berndes).

Winter: At this season, the Great-tailed Grackle's distribu-

tion in the coastal lowland is similar to that in the breeding season. The birds vacate elevations above 1000 feet almost completely, however, disappearing from Sunshine Summit, the Ramona area, and the Campo Plateau except

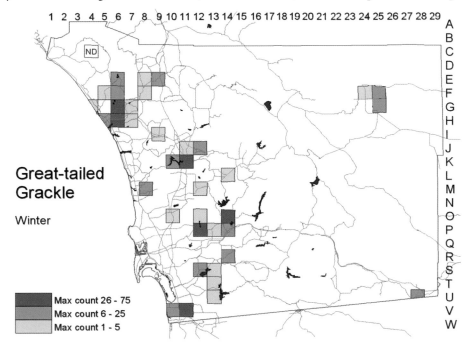

Great-tailed Grackle

Winter

Max count 26 - 75
Max count 6 - 25
Max count 1 - 5

Jacumba (up to eight on 1 February 2000 and 23 January and 16 February 2001, F. L. Unmack). In the Anza–Borrego Desert, wintering grackles are known only from developed areas around Borrego Springs, where their numbers may be somewhat smaller than in the breeding season (maximum count 13 on 30 December 1998, P. D. Ache). In the coastal lowland, occasional individuals or small flocks wander some distance from known colonies (e.g., six in San Dieguito Valley, M8, 23 December 2001, P. Unitt); presumably this is how new colonies are pioneered.

Conservation: Over much of San Diego County, the Great-tailed Grackle population appeared to be entering its exponential growth phase in the late 1990s. The species was first recorded in the county at Sweetwater Reservoir (S12) 5 February 1977 (AB 31:375, 1977) but not again until November 1981. After that, however, sightings increased rapidly. The first recorded breeding was in July 1988, at the Dairy Mart pond in the Tijuana River valley (V11), when two pairs fledged young (G. McCaskie, AB 42:1341, 1988). This colony grew quickly, and new ones soon formed elsewhere. In the Tijuana River valley, however, grackle numbers peaked in 1993, when the total

on the San Diego Christmas bird count hit 200. Smaller numbers since suggest the colony may be limited by lack of foraging habitat. In spite of the Great-tailed Grackle's ready use of man-made environments, urban development offers little habitat to a large bird that feeds its young principally on insects taken from the ground.

Taxonomy: The first Great-tailed Grackles reaching California arrived from Sonora or southern Arizona. The earliest specimens were *Q. m. nelsoni* (Ridgway, 1901), the smallest of the subspecies, in which the females are pale—honey blonde on the breast when in fresh plumage. By the late 1980s some specimens closer to the larger *Q. q. monsoni* (Phillips, 1950), with dark females, had invaded the Imperial Valley, after colonizing central Arizona from the Chihuahuan Desert and blending with *nelsoni* (Rea 1969, Patten et al. 2003). The two specimens so far available from San Diego County, one picked up in a residential area two blocks from the Dairy Mart Road colony 12 July 1999 (SDNHM 50303), the other from Camp Del Mar in Camp Pendleton (G4) 30 June 2001 (S. M. Wolf, SDNHM 50569), are both juveniles; in juvenile plumage *nelsoni* and *monsoni* are not well differentiated.

Bronzed Cowbird *Molothrus aeneus*

Like its better-known relative the Brown-headed Cowbird, the Bronzed Cowbird invaded southern California from the southeast. Unlike that of the Brown-headed, though, the pace of the Bronzed Cowbird's invasion has been glacial. Though the Bronzed was first recorded in San Diego County in 1973, 30 years later it is still rare, with only 17 records. Most of these are from or near the Anza–Borrego Desert, and some resulted from efforts to trap Brown-headed Cowbirds. Like the Brown-headed, the Bronzed Cowbird is a brood parasite, laying its eggs in the nests of other usually medium-sized songbirds.

Breeding distribution: The Bronzed Cowbird was not confirmed breeding in San Diego County 1997–2001, though likely it did breed. A male was displaying to two females 2.9 miles west of Jacumba (U27) in spring 1997 (F. L. Unmack), then an apparent independent juvenile (no red evident in eyes) was in the agricultural area of the north Borrego Valley (E24) 11 June 2001 (P. D. Jorgensen). The only previous confirmation of the species' reproducing in the county was the juvenile seen with Brewer's Blackbirds at Jacumba (U28) 13 July 1974 (J. L. Dunn). But all three specimens from the Anza–Borrego Desert are males in breeding condition with enlarged testes.

Nesting: Though Brewer's Blackbird is the only host of the Bronzed Cowbird known in San Diego County, other suitable species are readily available. Lowther (1995) listed the Northern Mockingbird and Hooded Oriole, common in San Diego County, as the birds most frequently reported parasitized by the Bronzed Cowbird. Lack of

Photo by Anthony Mercieca

suitable hosts is no block to the Bronzed Cowbird's further increase.

Migration: The Bronzed Cowbird is primarily a spring and summer visitor to southern California. With two exceptions, San Diego County records extend from 13 April (1991, one at Lower Willows, D23, P. D. Jorgensen) to 17 July (1974, pair at Jacumba, AB 28:951, 1974). Of San Diego County's 17 Bronzed Cowbird records, eight are from the Borrego Valley, one from Tamarisk Grove Campground (I24) 10 May 2003 (P. D. Jorgensen), and five from the Jacumba area (one in 1997, four in consecutive years 1973–76). There are three records from the coastal slope, only one on an expected date (6 May 1999, one at Dehesa, Q15, W. E. Haas). The other two coastal records are among the few winter records of the Bronzed Cowbird for California.

Winter: Two records, of immature males at Whelan Lake (G6) 28 February–21 April 1987 (J. O'Brien, AB

41:332, 490, 1987) and in a cowbird trap in the Tijuana River Valley (V10) 1 December 1998 (J. Wells, J. Turnbull, SDNHM 50154).

Conservation: The Bronzed Cowbird was first noted in San Diego County 3 June 1973, at Jacumba. The rate of occurrence is increasing only slowly, with gaps between records 1977–86 and 1992–96. The species' history in southeastern California, where it arrived in 1951 but is still scarce, suggests it does not have the Brown-headed Cowbird's capacity to increase explosively and threaten a broad spectrum of hosts.

Taxonomy: Bronzed Cowbirds from southern California are *M. a. loyei* Parkes and Blake, 1965, well differentiated from the other two subspecies in its comparatively large size and thick bill, gray not black female, and violet-rumped silky-plumaged male. For San Diego County this identification is attested by three specimens trapped in the Anza–Borrego Desert, two from Whitaker Horse Camp (D24; 23 June 1990, SDNHM 46772; 28 April 1997, SDNHM 49914) and one from Circle K Ranch (G25; 3 June 1998, SDNHM 50058), as well as the December specimen from the Tijuana River Valley.

Brown-headed Cowbird *Molothrus ater*

As the only brood parasite common in southern California, the Brown-headed Cowbird plays a major role in the community of birds. It is native to North America but a rather recent immigrant to San Diego County, arriving in numbers about 1915. It is highly migratory but found in the county year round. Conversion of scrub and woodland to agriculture and cities enhanced the habitat for a bird that feeds on the ground, often among livestock. As the cowbird's population increased, that of some hosts decreased, some nearly to extirpation. With the formal listing of the Least Bell's Vireo as endangered, trapping of cowbirds became a tool for recovering the vireo. How this trapping should be carried out over the long term has become one of the major questions in San Diego County wildlife management.

Breeding distribution: The Brown-headed Cowbird is widespread as a breeding bird in San Diego County,

Photo by Anthony Mercieca

lacking only in sparse desert scrub or mountains thickly covered in forest or chaparral. But currently, over most of the county, the species is only fairly common. Of over 1300 records in the atlas database from late April through July, only nine are of more than 15 individuals. The highest numbers among these are 35 in northwest Escondido (I10) 16 May 1999 (E. C. Hall) and 33 near Mt. Gower (L17) 30 May 1999 (R. C. Sanger). High numbers earlier in the season are likely of flocks of migrants or lingering winter visitors. Some gaps in the observed distribution, as in parts of Camp Pendleton, Mission Gorge (P11), and along the Sweetwater River above Sweetwater Reservoir (S13) appear due to trapping, carried out at Camp Pendleton since 1983, at Mission Gorge intermittently since 1985, and along the Sweetwater intermittently since 1986. Conversely, there appears to be a somewhat greater concentration in the inland valleys from Fallbrook and Rainbow south to Escondido and Valley Center, from Ramona to Mesa Grande and Warner Springs, and near Vallecito. But over much of San Diego County the cowbird's

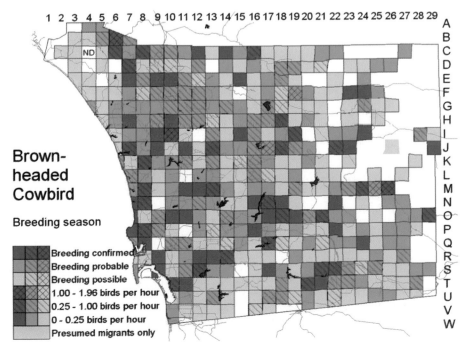

Brown-headed Cowbird

Breeding season

- Breeding confirmed
- Breeding probable
- Breeding possible
- 1.00 - 1.96 birds per hour
- 0.25 - 1.00 birds per hour
- 0 - 0.25 birds per hour
- Presumed migrants only

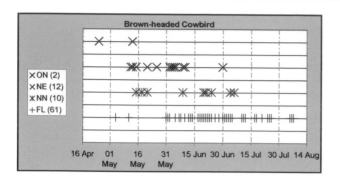

abundance seems fairly uniform, implying that trapping is reducing the cowbird's population on the scale of the entire county, not just within some limited radius of the traps. Yet the trap operators report that the numbers of cowbirds caught have remained constant over time. The areas of trapping could be acting as a population sink.

Nesting: The Brown-headed Cowbird is a brood parasite, laying its eggs in the nests of a wide variety of small insectivorous songbirds. Atlas observers recorded 16 species that the cowbird parasitized successfully, as judged by nestlings or fledglings being tended by foster parents: Common Yellowthroat (10 times), Song Sparrow (6), Hooded Oriole (6), Hutton's Vireo (6), Bell's Vireo (5), Blue-gray Gnatcatcher (3), Wrentit (3), Western Flycatcher (3), Black-tailed Gnatcatcher (2), and Yellow Warbler, Dark-eyed Junco, Red-winged and Brewer's Blackbirds, California Towhee, Western Wood-Pewee, and Phainopepla (once each). Further records of cowbird eggs in nests and observations of female cowbirds entering nests—attempts at parasitism whose success was uncertain—involve Bell's Vireo (5 times) and the Common Yellowthroat, Lark Sparrow, Warbling Vireo, Black-chinned Sparrow, Black-tailed Gnatcatcher, California Gnatcatcher, Verdin, and Lesser Goldfinch

(once each). All of these are suitable hosts except the Lesser Goldfinch, which feeds its young on regurgitated seeds rather than insects. Additional hosts represented among 38 egg sets collected 1915–52 are the Willow Flycatcher, now rare, and the American Goldfinch, an unsuitable host for the same reason as the Lesser. Bell's Vireo has long been a favored host, though the number of recent records of parasitism of it may be disproportionately high because of the intensive monitoring directed at this endangered species.

Atlas records suggest that cowbirds generally begin laying in late April. The schedule we observed thus accords with the schedule of 38 egg sets collected 1915–1952, which range from 27 April to 30 June. Thus host species that nest early in the spring, mainly sedentary residents, may be able to raise a brood before cowbirds begin laying. Most summer visitors, starting later in the spring, do not have this opportunity. Two early May records of cowbird fledglings from the Anza–Borrego Desert, however, demonstrate that a few cowbirds begin laying in early to mid April (Vallecito Valley, M24, 4 May 2001, B. Siegel; Agua Caliente Springs, M26, 11 May 1998, E. C. Hall).

Migration: The Brown-headed Cowbird is highly migratory, and at least in spring San Diego County's breeding and wintering populations overlap considerably. A few cowbirds appear in riparian woodland surrounded by chaparral-covered mountains, far from wintering concentrations in open valleys, in early March. But most of the breeding population does not arrive until early April. Meanwhile, wintering flocks may remain until late April (100 southwest of Ramona, L14, 24 April 1999, F. Sproul). The Great Basin subspecies *M. a. artemisiae* visits San Diego County, and its schedule helps illustrate the cowbird's long-distance migrations (see Taxonomy).

Winter: At this season the Brown-headed Cowbird is much less widespread than in summer. And it is much more concentrated—around cows. Some wintering birds forage on lawns, at garbage dumps, and on disturbed open ground, but the large flocks occur most often at dairies and in pastureland. Winter numbers run as high as 500 near El Monte Park (O15) 15 January 2000 (D. C. Seals), 420 at a dairy in San Marcos (I9) 27 February 1999 (W. E. Haas), and 350 at the Otay dump (U12) 19 December 1998 (W. E. Haas). Most of the winter records are from the coastal lowland, but concentrations occur regularly as high as 3600 feet elevation, as in Hill Valley (T25; up to 210 on 22 January 2000, R. B. Riggan). At higher elevations atlas results show the cowbird localized in winter to pastoral

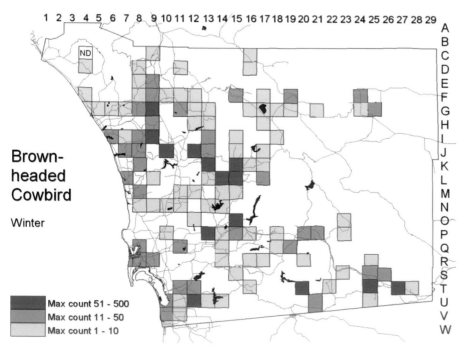

Brown-headed Cowbird

Winter

Max count 51 - 500
Max count 11 - 50
Max count 1 - 10

valleys like Warner, Descanso (P20), Japatul (Q18), and Round Potrero (T20). We recorded the cowbird on only four occasions in winter between 3600 and 5400 feet elevation, but these included a flock of 20 at Pine Valley (P21) 8 January 1998 (J. K. Wilson) and a single bird at Laguna Meadow (O23; 5400 feet) 21 January 2002 (E. C. Hall). In the Anza–Borrego Desert wintering cowbirds are localized to developed and agricultural areas in the Borrego Valley, where numbers range up to 35 in Borrego Springs (F24) 24 January 1999 (P. D. Jorgensen).

Conservation: Before 1915, the Brown-headed Cowbird occurred in San Diego County only as an occasional migrant. In that year, the front of the species' expanding range, moving west and north, hit San Diego (Laymon 1987, Rothstein 1994). A population explosion ensued. In 1919 Frank Stephens was still calling the cowbird a "rare straggler" in the county, but 14 years later, Willett (1933) wrote, for all coastal southern California, that the cowbird "is well established throughout our district, frequenting the willow regions in large numbers in summer and found commonly around farms and in parks at other seasons of the year." By the 1970s the cowbird's more susceptible host species, the Willow Flycatcher, Bell's, Cassin's, and Warbling Vireos, Blue-gray Gnatcatcher, and Yellow Warbler had declined, but the more resilient ones remained common, sustaining the cowbird's numbers.

The formal listing of the Least Bell's Vireo as endangered in 1986 opened the way to management by cowbird trapping. Since then, areas trapped most consistently have been Camp Pendleton, the lower San Luis Rey River valley, San Pasqual Valley, Mission Trails Regional Park, the Sweetwater River from Jamacha to Bonita, the Tijuana River valley, and Anza Borrego Desert State Park. According to data compiled by the Least Bell's

Vireo/Southwestern Willow Flycatcher Working Group, in 2003, 6391 trap-days in San Diego County yielded 1235 cowbirds (P. Famolaro unpubl. data).

Taxonomy: The breeding subspecies of the Brown-headed Cowbird in San Diego County, as elsewhere in southern California, is the Dwarf Cowbird, *M. a. obscurus* (Gmelin, 1789), small, with the bill tapered, the female pale, and the nestling with a yellow gape. It is also the dominant subspecies in winter and migration. *Molothrus a. artemisiae* Grinnell, 1909, breeding in the Rocky Mountain region, is larger and also has a tapered bill, but fresh-plumaged females are darker and nestlings have a white gape. It is apparently uncommon in San Diego County, occurring at least as a spring migrant and represented by three specimens, one from Borrego Springs 30 April 1896 (SDNHM 768), one trapped at Whitaker Horse Camp, Anza–Borrego Desert (D24), 8 April 1988 (SDNHM 45604), and one given to wildlife rehabilitators from an unknown location in northern San Diego County in May 1979 (SDNHM 41375). *Molothrus a. artemisiae* undoubtedly occurs in fall and winter as well; L. M. Huey collected a specimen on Los Coronados Islands within sight of San Diego 5 September 1914 (SDNHM 33654). Fleischer and Rothstein (1988) found *obscurus* invading the range of *artemisiae* and intergrading with it in the Sierra Nevada of Mono County. Thus with the secondary contact of *artemisiae* and *obscurus* the distinction of these formerly well-differentiated subspecies is being blurred, and southern California is likely in the path of these intergrades' migration. Finally, one specimen of the eastern subspecies *M. a. ater* (Boddaert, 1783) has been picked up in San Diego County, at Coronado (S9) 1 March 1978 (SDNHM 40587; Unitt 1984). It is identified by its more bulbous, not smoothly tapered, maxilla.

Orchard Oriole *Icterus spurius*

Two species of oriole breed in eastern North America, the Baltimore and the Orchard. The Orchard is the less frequent as a vagrant to California but still reaches San Diego County in fall at the rate of about one every other year. There are about 20 records for winter and two for spring. Because the Orchard and Hooded Orioles are so similar in the female and immature plumages, the Orchard must be identified in southern California with caution.

Migration: San Diego County's fall records of the Orchard Oriole are all from the coastal lowland, except for one from Santa Ysabel (J18), of an adult male 10 October 1987 (W. McCausland, AB 42:139, 1988). Fall dates range from 28 August to 6 December (Unitt 1984) but are concentrated from mid September through late October. The maximum reported per fall is five in 1964 and 1982. During the atlas period 1997–2002, four Orchard Orioles were recorded from San Diego County in fall, all at Point Loma (S7).

Dates of birds known to have wintered range from 5 November (1983, San Diego, L. Zarins, AB 38:248, 966,

Photo by Anthony Mercieca

1984) to 21 April (1985, Point Loma, C. G. Edwards, AB 39:351, 1985). The two spring records are from Point Loma 22 May 1980 (AB 34:817, 1980) and near Rincon (F13) 30 April 1989 (F. S. Armstrong, AB 43:538, 1989).

Winter: San Diego County's winter records of the

Orchard Oriole are largely from metropolitan San Diego, though two have been found on Oceanside Christmas bird counts, 26 December 1982 and 22 December 1990. As with the Baltimore Oriole, the winter records are from ornamental trees in parks, cemeteries, and residential areas. February 1984 had three wintering Orchard Orioles (AB 38:359, 1984), but the five-year atlas period had only

one, in Greenwood Cemetery (S10) 11–19 January 2002 (M. B. Mulrooney, NAB 56:225, 2002).

Taxonomy: All Orchard Orioles north of the Mexican border, including the single specimen from San Diego County (Tijuana River valley, 19 October 1962, SDNHM 30472), are nominate *I. s. spurius* (Linnaeus, 1766).

Hooded Oriole *Icterus cucullatus*

The southern California lifestyle suits few birds more than it does the Hooded Oriole. The iconic palm trees are the oriole's primary nest site and source of nest material. Where palms are absent, the orioles turn readily to eucalyptus. They patronize hummingbird feeders eagerly. They are far more numerous along palm-lined streets and in eucalyptus groves than in their primitive habitats of desert palm oases and riparian sycamores. Though adapted to the urban landscape, the Hooded Oriole keeps tightly to its schedule of migration. In San Diego County it is common in spring and summer but very rare in late fall and winter.

Photo by Anthony Mercieca

Breeding distribution: The Hooded Oriole occupies two main zones of San Diego County: the coastal lowland and lower foothills and the canyons draining into the Anza–Borrego Desert. On the coastal slope, the oriole is most common below 2500 feet elevation in suburbs and agricultural valleys. It spreads uncommonly as high as 3500 feet only where palms or eucalyptus trees are planted around buildings. In this zone there are substantial areas where the birds are rare or absent, as on Otay and Tecate mountains and between Potrero and Campo. Between 3500 and 4600 feet there are few records: near Julian (J20), six, including adults feeding young, 26 June

2001 (O. Carter et al.); at Lake Cuyamaca (M20), a pair 28 May 1999 and one bird 2 July 1999 (A. P. and T. E. Keenan); at Pine Valley (P21), one on 17 May 1997 (J. K. Wilson); near Yellow Rose Spring (R23), one on 13 May 1997 and two the following day (L. J. Hargrove). Only the last were in natural habitat, and the birds at the last two locations were most likely migrants.

One of the surprises of the atlas effort was persistence of Hooded Orioles in small numbers in sycamores away from palms and eucalyptus groves. This was most noticeable in northern Camp Pendleton and the San Mateo Canyon Wilderness, the only region of the coastal lowland where entire atlas squares still lack any development other than a few dirt roads and trails. Daily counts in this area ranged as high as seven in San Mateo Canyon (B3) 27 May 2001 (P. Unitt).

In the Anza–Borrego Desert, the Hooded Oriole's distribution traces the lower east slope of the mountains where oases of California fan palms dot the canyons. There are usually only two or three pairs of orioles in each grove (Massey 1998), but counts ran as high as 10 at Carrizo Palms (R28) 6 May 1998 (J. O. Zimmer) and 20 at Agua Caliente County Park (M26) 4 June 1998 (E. C. Hall). Smaller numbers use riparian woodland without palms, e.g.,

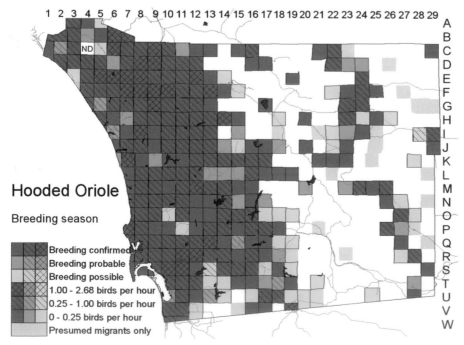

Hooded Oriole

Breeding season

- Breeding confirmed
- Breeding probable
- Breeding possible
- 1.00 - 2.68 birds per hour
- 0.25 - 1.00 birds per hour
- 0 - 0.25 birds per hour
- Presumed migrants only

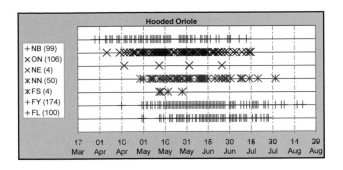

six near Banner (K21) 16 April 1999 (P. K. Nelson) and three at Sentenac Ciénaga (J23) 14 June 1998 (R. Thériault). The Hooded Oriole is uncommon to fairly common in orchards, nurseries, and developed areas around Earthquake Valley, Borrego Springs, and Ocotillo Wells but rare and irregular at native palm oases away from the base of the mountains (birds themselves never seen but old nest in palm in Travertine Palms Wash, C29, 24 January 2000, R. Thériault). Hooded Orioles at Seventeen Palms and Five Palms Spring (G29; two or three on 5 April 1997, one on 11 April 1998, G. Rebstock, K. Forney) were migrants only.

Nesting: The Hooded Oriole's predilection for nesting in palms has been known for a century (e.g., Wheelock 1904). It is so familiar to southern California birders that atlas participants seeking to confirm the species' nesting targeted palms. The birds strip the fibers from the leaves, weave a pouch, and sew it to the underside of a leaf. Twenty-eight of 39 nests whose site atlas observers described were in fan palms (the Mexican as well as the California); only one was in a Canary Island date palm. Nests in eucalyptus trees are also common (atlas observers described three), placed within a cluster of leaves that forms a canopy over the nest. Near the De Luz Fire Station (C6) 5 June 1999, K. L. Weaver found Hooded Orioles nesting almost colonially in eucalyptus trees with Bullock's Orioles, about six pairs of each species in a small grove. Four nests were in sycamores, presumably the species' original nest site in coastal San Diego County (two of these were in mistletoe clumps within a sycamore, one under a Red-shouldered Hawk nest). The Hooded Oriole's preference for a canopy occasionally leads to its suspending the nest from man-made structures, as reported by Bent (1958) and Hardy (1970). In San Diego County, one nest was attached under the eave of a house, one was under a building's second-story deck, and one with nestlings was under the shade of a light fixture in a campground.

Hooded Orioles begin building nests in early April, with one record for 29 March. Nestlings are heard from about 1 May to 1 August, suggesting laying mainly from mid April to mid July. The 42 egg sets collected 1895–1936 range from 21 April to 4 August. Adults carrying insects at Banner 16 April 1999 (P. K. Nelson) imply occasional laying in the first few days of April. The prevalence of Hooded Oriole nesting in June and July suggests the birds raise two broods in a season in coastal southern California, as elsewhere (*contra* Pleasants and Albano 2001).

Migration: Hooded Orioles return to San Diego during March; they are rare during the first half of the month, common by the end. From 1997 to 2001 first arrival dates ranged from 26 February to 18 March. Adult males precede females. Arrival in the last few days of February is exceptional; no dates earlier than 26 February are known (2000, one at Borrego Springs, F24, M. L. Gabel; one at Agua Caliente County Park, M26, E. C. Hall). Records of spring migrants far from nesting habitat in the Anza–Borrego Desert peak in late April and extend as late as 9 May (2000, one at Split Mountain, L29, J. R. Barth). In fall, adult males depart in August, the young of the year largely in the second week of September. Stragglers occur rarely through October.

Winter: The Hooded Oriole has been slower than many species to respond to the newly available winter habitat offered by urban trees. At this season it remains rare; some winters, like 1999–2000, pass with no records at all. Wintering birds are usually single (though sometimes with other wintering orioles). The maximum winter numbers reported were three on the San Diego Christmas bird count 21 December 1968 and five at Point Loma (S7) during the winter of 1963–64 (AFN 18:289, 1964), but the possibility of the Orchard Oriole may not have been fully appreciated at the time. From 1997 to 2002, 10 individual

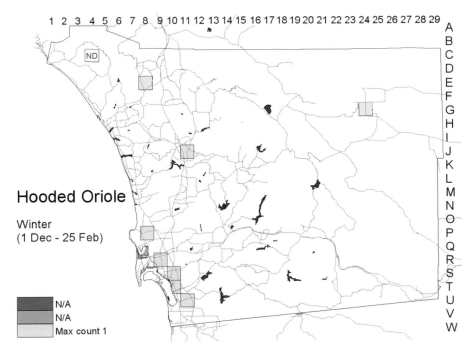

Hooded Oriole

Winter
(1 Dec - 25 Feb)

N/A
N/A
Max count 1

wintering Hooded Orioles were reported in San Diego County. Most of these were within 5 miles of the coast, but two were somewhat farther inland, one in San Luis Rey Heights (E8) 3 December 2000 (P. A. Ginsburg) and a female in Kit Carson Park (J11) 23 February 1999 (W. Pray). The only previous winter record so far inland was of one on the Escondido Christmas bird count 1 January 1993. One in Borrego Springs (G24) 23 January 1999 (M. C. Jorgensen) was the first in winter in the Anza–Borrego Desert, though the species occurs nearly annually in winter in the Salton Sink (Patten et al. 2003).

Conservation: In California the Hooded Oriole has become practically a commensal of man, expanding its range considerably with settlement and urbanization, so one would hardly think it a conservation problem. Along the middle Gila River and lower Rio Grande, however, the population has declined (Rea 1983, Pleasants and Albano 2001). The Hooded Oriole is a frequent host of the

Brown-headed Cowbird; in 1975, S. I. Rothstein found that 16 of 23 nests around Santa Barbara had been parasitized (Friedmann et al. 1977). The Hooded Oriole is one of the more likely birds to be affected by the spread of the American Crow; atlas observers noted crows depredating Hooded Oriole nests. Suspending their nests from the lowest leaves of urban palms renders the birds vulnerable to tree trimming during the nesting season. Yet the local population is vigorous, colonizing new habitat as soon as it becomes available. For example, in Mission Valley (R9) in 1991, the orioles nested in a condominium complex within the first year after it was built and landscaped with transplanted full-grown fan palms (P. Unitt).

Taxonomy: The only subspecies of the Hooded Oriole in California is *I. c. nelsoni* Ridgway, 1885. Males are paler, with less black on the face, than the subspecies of southern Texas and eastern Mexico; females have the flanks yellowish rather than gray.

Streak-backed Oriole *Icterus pustulatus*

The Streak-backed Oriole is a primarily Mexican species that is spreading gradually north, first confirmed nesting in Arizona in 1993 (Corman and Monson 1995). The California Bird Records Committee has accepted six records of vagrants to California, three for San Diego County.

Migration: Huey (1931a) collected the first Streak-backed Oriole known in the United States, at the Lake Murray dam (Q11) 1 May 1931 (SDNHM 14521). McCaskie saw one in the Tijuana River valley 22 September 1962 (McCaskie and Banks 1964). The records committee rejected two other sightings there in 1962 and 1963 (Roberson 1993).

Winter: The county's one wintering Streak-backed Oriole was in a residential area of Pacific Beach (Q7; slightly south of La Jolla as originally reported) 10 December 1984–29 April 1985 (Dunn 1988). The identification is supported by photographs.

Conservation: The specter of escapees hangs over sightings of the Streak-backed Oriole as for many other Mexican species. Hamilton (2001) did not report the Streak-backed Oriole among the many cage birds he saw in shops in northern Baja California, but I saw one for sale on the streets of Tijuana in the mid 1980s.

Taxonomy: The specimen is the expected subspecies of northwestern Mexico, *I. p. microstictus* Griscom, 1934.

Bullock's Oriole *Icterus bullockii*

Open woodland, woodland edges, and scattered trees are home to one of San Diego County's most colorful birds, Bullock's Oriole. Riparian edges, sycamore groves, and oak woodland were the species' primitive habitat, and the birds are still common there. Bullock's Oriole also takes full advantage of eucalyptus and other exotic trees in rural areas, where its characteristic baglike nest can be found easily—even long after the birds themselves have headed south. The species is primarily a summer visitor and migrant in San Diego County; only a few individuals are found each winter.

Breeding distribution: Bullock's Oriole breeds over practically the entire coastal slope of San Diego County. The largest numbers are in the inland valleys; there are fewer right along the coast, and the species is absent as a breeding bird from Point Loma and Coronado. The zone of greatest concentration appears to extend from Wynola (J19) and Santa Ysabel (J18) north through Mesa Grande

Photo by Anthony Mercieca

(H17) and Warner Valley to Lake Henshaw (G17) and Warner Springs (F19), where the orioles are common both on the valley floors and in the wooded hills (31 around Mesa Grande 12 May 2001, C. and J. Manning; 30 at Lake Henshaw the same day, R. and S. L. Breisch). Even small oak groves or scattered ranches offer enough habitat for a few pairs, so the distribution appears almost uniform at the scale of the atlas grid. There were few atlas squares (D18, V15, V18) so completely covered with treeless chaparral that the orioles were absent. Bullock's Oriole is sparse at the higher elevations, above 5000 feet, but is lacking only near the summit of Hot Springs Mountain (E20), the county's highest peak.

On the desert slope, Bullock's Oriole breeds in the riparian woodland along Coyote and San Felipe creeks and where trees are irrigated around buildings, as at Tamarisk Grove (I24), in Earthquake Valley (K23), and at Butterfield Ranch (M23). In the low desert Bullock's Oriole breeds uncommonly in the Borrego Valley (maximum count of breeding birds four, including one building a nest, at Ellis Farms nursery, F25, 13 May 2001, P. D. Ache). Near Ocotillo Wells (J28) the closest suggestion of breeding was an apparent pair 5 May 2000 (J. R. Barth). In southern San Diego County breeding Bullock's Orioles extend into the desert no farther than Vallecito (M24/ M25; six on 11 June 2002, J. R. Barth et al.). The gap in the range is the result of lack of habitat; Bullock's Oriole is a common breeding bird in the cultivated areas of the Salton Sink (Patten et al. 2003).

Nesting: Bullock's Oriole builds its nest in the middle to upper levels of trees and large shrubs, often at edges or hanging over an opening. The nests are thus easy to see if not to reach, so atlas observers reported many. Described sites were in coast live oak (10), syca- more (6), eucalyptus (6), willow (3), mistletoe (2), mulefat (1), catclaw (1), mesquite (1), and deodar cedar (1), at heights of 7 to 60 feet. The pensile nests are woven of a variety of filaments: observers described nests built predominantly of grass, horse- hair, dodder, and fishing line.

Twenty-eight egg sets of Bullock's Oriole collected 1889– 1935 range in date from 22 April to 18 June, but atlas records imply a somewhat wider spread, from early April to early July. The two records suggesting lay- ing as early as the first week of April were both in the wet spring of 1998 (adults carrying

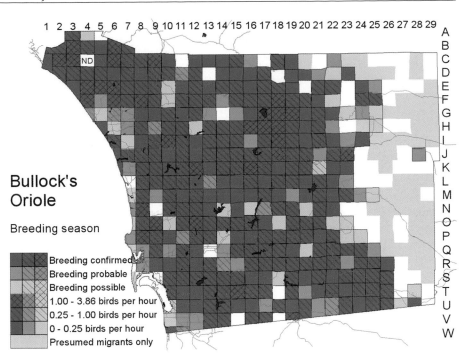

Bullock's Oriole

Breeding season

- Breeding confirmed
- Breeding probable
- Breeding possible
- 1.00 - 3.86 birds per hour
- 0.25 - 1.00 birds per hour
- 0 - 0.25 birds per hour
- Presumed migrants only

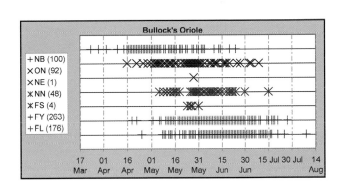

Bullock's Oriole

+NB (100)
×ON (92)
×NE (1)
×NN (48)
×FS (4)
+FY (263)
+FL (176)

17 Mar / 01 Apr / 16 Apr / 01 May / 16 May / 31 May / 15 Jun / 30 Jun / 15 Jul / 30 Jul / 14 Aug

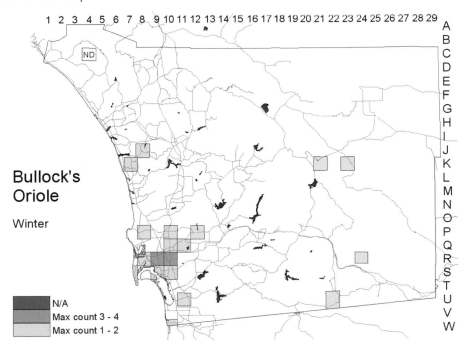

Bullock's Oriole

Winter

- N/A
- Max count 3 - 4
- Max count 1 - 2

insects near Upper Otay Lake, T13, 19 April, J. F. Walters; fledgling at La Costa, J7, 25 April, M. Baumgartel).

Migration: Bullock's Oriole occurs throughout the county as a spring migrant, moving commonly through desert habitats where it does not breed. It arrives typically in mid March. From 1997 to 2001 dates of first arrivals ranged from 11 to 18 March. The earliest date reported for San Diego County is 5 March (1982; AB 36:893, 1982), possibly 1 March (Cooper 1880). The locally breeding population presumably arrives first, with migrants headed farther north coming through mainly in April, then in decreasing numbers through May. Records for places in the Anza–Borrego Desert where the species does not breed extend as late as 17 May (2001, one in Carrizo Valley, O28, D. C. Seals). In fall, the local population departs in July and August, and migrants after 1 September are rare.

Winter: Bullock's Oriole is a rare winter visitor, regular in urban parks and well-wooded residential areas in San Diego, occasional in riparian woodland elsewhere in the coastal lowland. The maximum daily count in a single atlas square during the atlas period was four in Balboa Park (R9) 1 December 1998 (J. K. Wilson), but the San Diego Christmas bird count 19 December 1998 totaled five, and earlier Christmas bird counts have gone as high as 14 in San Diego 17 December 1988 and 6 in Oceanside 27 December 1981. The atlas effort generated the first winter records for the Bullock's Oriole in San Diego County outside the coastal lowland, of single birds at Banner (K21) 16 January 1999 (M. B. Stowe), Earthquake Valley (K23) 23 December 1999 (G. P. Sanders), Simmons Canyon (R24) 22 January–7 February 2000 (A. P. and T. E. Keenan, J. Larson), and Campo (U22) 31 January 2000 (C. R. Mahrdt, E. C. Hall). Still farther inland Bullock's Oriole is a casual winter visitor in the Salton Sink (Patten et al. 2003).

Conservation: There has been no obvious change in the abundance of breeding Bullock's Orioles through San Diego County history. The species takes readily to low-density development and has probably spread with the planting of shade trees around rural ranches. Trash like ribbon and string offers it nest material superior to natural substances. But intensive urbanization disfavors it; in the inner city it is found mainly in parks and around school campuses planted with sycamores or eucalyptus, or in eucalyptus trees bordering open areas. Conversely, wintering of Bullock's Oriole is largely a result of human modification of the landscape—the planting of exotic trees, especially eucalyptus, on whose flowers the orioles feed. Wintering of Bullock's Oriole was first recorded in San Diego County in 1957, except for Cooper's (1880) mention of one in San Diego 1 March (1862?).

Taxonomy: Bullock's Oriole is usually divided into two subspecies, *I. b. parvus* van Rossem, 1945, breeding mainly in California and western Arizona, and the slightly larger *I. b. bullockii* (Swainson, 1827), over the rest of the species' range. The difference is most pronounced in wing length, but even on this basis the distinction is only marginally valid. Comparison of 19 breeding males of *parvus* (type locality Jacumba, U28) from San Diego and Imperial counties (mean wing chord 95.2, standard deviation 1.95; Patten et al. 2003) with samples from British Columbia (Okanagan), Colorado (Greeley), and southern Idaho (from Rising and Williams 1999) yields adequate separation by the 75% standard as quantified by Patten and Unitt (2002). But the same comparison with samples from Kansas (Elkhart), Oklahoma (Boise City), and northern Nevada does not, so Bullock's Oriole is best considered monotypic.

Baltimore Oriole *Icterus galbula*

Originating in eastern North America, the Baltimore Oriole is a rare migrant and winter visitor in California. Around the turn of the millennium, reports from San Diego County were averaging one to two per fall and one every other winter. Records of spring migrants may number as few as eight total. Wintering of the Baltimore Oriole in southern California, like that of some other orioles and tanagers, is linked to ornamental flowering trees, especially eucalyptus.

Migration: The Baltimore Oriole is most frequent in San Diego County in fall, mainly from late September through October. The earliest date is 9 September (1991, Point Loma, S7, R. E. Webster, AB 45:323, 1991). Nine in 1974 is still the record total for one fall. Wintering birds have stayed as late as 24 April (1968, Point Loma, AFN 22:577, 1968), so seven Baltimore Orioles discovered from late March to April may have been wintering rather than spring migrants. The eight records later in the spring

Photo by Anthony Mercieca

range from 11 May (1986, Point Loma, J. Oldenettel, AB 40:256, 1978; 1994, Torrey Pines State Reserve, N7, M. B. Stowe, NASFN 48:342, 1994) to 27 May (1967, Point Loma, AFN 21:542, 1967). Only one of the latter was during the atlas period (18 May 2001, Point Loma, J. C. Worley, NAB 55:358, 2001). All records are from the coastal lowland.

Winter: San Diego County's winter records of the Baltimore Oriole are scattered from near Fallbrook (D7; 30 January 1995, I. S. Quon, NASFN 49:200, 1995) to Coronado (S9/T9; three records), but many are from Balboa Park (R9). Flowering eucalyptus trees there were largely responsible for the winter maximum, seven on the San Diego Christmas bird count 18 December 1982. The atlas period had three wintering Baltimore Orioles,

at Coronado (T9) 19 December 1998, at Balboa Park 15 December 2001 (R. E. Webster), and at Greenwood Cemetery (S10) 16 December 2001 (G. McCaskie).

Taxonomy: The Baltimore and Bullock's Orioles hybridize regularly in a narrow zone in the Great Plains. One hybrid has been seen in San Diego County, at Point Loma 26–28 April 2000 (M. Lubin, P. A. Ginsburg).

Scott's Oriole *Icterus parisorum*

No bird symbolizes high desert more than Scott's Oriole, and few birds are as strongly linked to specific plants in San Diego County as Scott's Oriole is to the desert agave and Mojave yucca. The birds are distributed sparsely even in prime habitat, so they are uncommon over most of their range: the mountains and bajadas of the Anza–Borrego Desert and arid chaparral of the Campo Plateau. A few birds are scattered farther west. Scott's Oriole is mainly a summer visitor, but the species winters in small numbers as well, mainly at lower elevations in the Anza–Borrego Desert and in a few large stands of prickly pear on the coastal slope.

Breeding distribution: In San Diego County Scott's Oriole's distribution centers on the rim of the Anza–Borrego Desert: the east slope of the Peninsular Ranges mainly between 1000 and 5000 feet elevation. Even there the species is generally uncommon; maximum daily counts are 10 in lower Grapevine Canyon (I23) 7 April 1998 (P. K. Nelson) and 12 between Table Mountain and In-Ko-Pah County Park (T29) 16 April 1999 (D. C. Seals).

Field work for the atlas revealed nesting Scott's Orioles extending in smaller numbers into low desert on alluvial slopes and washes, rarely into gardens on valley floors

Photo by Jack C. Daynes

(single singing males in Borrego Springs, G24, 11 June 1999, R. Thériault, and at the Borrego Air Ranch, H26, 12 July 1998, M. L. Gabel). The orioles may be able to spread to lower elevations only after wet winters; in the drought-plagued later years of the atlas' term we found only old nests in low desert.

Another surprise was that Scott's Oriole breeds in small numbers on the Campo Plateau, especially in patches of semidesert habitat like Miller Valley (S24; pair, female collecting yucca fiber, 22 June 2000, L. J. Hargrove). A few pairs are scattered in chaparral with chaparral yucca but no Mojave yucca, as along the Noble Canyon Trail 1.8 miles north-northeast of Pine Valley (P22) 24 April–16 May 1997 (R. A. Hamilton). A few extend west of Pine Valley and Campo, south of Interstate 8, as far as Lee Valley (S16; one coming to hummingbird feeder 15 June 1999, J. R. Barth) and near Dulzura between Marron Valley Road and Dulzura Summit (U17; apparently two pairs 17 May–20 July 1998, D. W. Povey).

Two other small populations on the coastal slope correspond to enclaves of semidesert habitat.

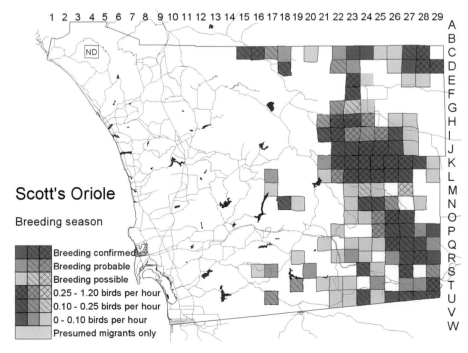

Scott's Oriole

Breeding season

- Breeding confirmed
- Breeding probable
- Breeding possible
- 0.25 - 1.20 birds per hour
- 0.10 - 0.25 birds per hour
- 0 - 0.10 birds per hour
- Presumed migrants only

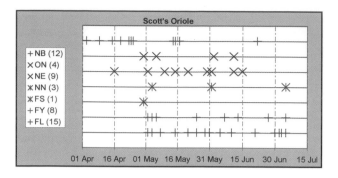

One is in the gorge of the San Diego River above El Capitan Reservoir (L17/M17; up to two singing males 22 May 1999, R. C. Sanger), extending southeast to near Tule Springs (N18; six, including fledglings, 2 July 2001, E. C. Hall) and upper Conejos Creek (N19; singing male 27 June 2001, J. R. Barth). The other is presumably an extension from the Aguanga area of Riverside County, running from Dameron and Oak Grove valleys (C15/C16/C17) to Chihuahua Valley (C18) and Rocky Mountain (D18). In this region the birds are rare except in Dameron Valley (C16; maximum seven on 27 June 1998, K. L. Weaver).

Nesting: Scott's Oriole's baglike nest resembles that of the Hooded and Bullock's Orioles. Most commonly, Scott's Oriole attaches its nest under the leaves of a Mojave yucca, at the base of the clump of living leaves. Eighteen of 30 nests atlas observers described were in yuccas. Paul Jorgensen notes that the birds typically select the tallest Mojave yucca in their territory as a nest site. Yucca fibers are the staple nest material. Where agaves offer good foraging but there are no yuccas, the orioles nest in a variety of other plants, selecting sites that offer the greatest shelter and concealment. Such sites were in mistletoe clumps in paloverde (3), catclaw (2), mesquite (1), smoketree (2), indigo bush, jojoba, and California fan palm (1 each). Where there is no yucca, vine tendrils provide nest material.

Because only one set of Scott's Oriole eggs was ever collected from San Diego County, atlas data provide the best information to date on the species' nesting schedule in this area. The nine dates of nests with eggs range from 16 April to 15 June. A fledging at Hapaha Flat (L26) 2 May 2001 (D. C. Seals) indicates egg laying can take place as early as the first week of April, while the female nest building in Miller Valley 22 June 2000 suggests it can take place as late as the last week of June. Very likely there is substantial variation in the timing of breeding with local conditions of vegetation, rainfall, and elevation.

Migration: The schedule of Scott's Oriole migration is now clouded by birds wintering in breeding habitat. From 1997 to 2001, arrival dates varied from 27 February to 16 March, though the earliest of these records, of a singing male near Yaqui Well (I24) 27 February 1997 (P. K. Nelson), was from a site where the species winters occasionally. Scott's Oriole may be a short-distance facultative migrant, moving to take advantage of seasonal food supplies, rather than a longer-distance calendar-driven migrant like the Hooded and Bullock's Orioles. September and October reports from Culp Valley (G23/H23; Massey 1998) mean that some birds occur in breeding habitat at an elevation of 3000 feet in every season of the year. The schedule of wintering birds is still poorly known; they may arrive by 3 November (1999, one in Borrego Springs, G24, R. Thériault) and depart as late as 18 April (1998, one in north Borrego Valley, E24, P. K. Nelson), though there are few reports from the Borrego Valley after 1 March. On the coastal slope, at sites where the species is not known to breed, there were no records during the atlas period after 27 February (2000, one at Rancho Cuca, F14, P. Unitt), yet in the 1970s in Pauma Valley (E12) Eleanor Beemer noted Scott's Orioles repeatedly as late as mid May (Unitt 1984). Again, substantial annual variation seems likely.

Along the coast Scott's Oriole is very rare, as both a migrant and winter visitor. The only ones noted 1997–2001 were along the south side of the Tijuana River valley (W11, one on 12 March 2000, P. Unitt; W10, one 9 April–16 July 2000, G. Hazard; W10, one on 22 April 2001, P. R. Pryde).

Winter: Scott's Oriole winters uncommonly in the Anza–Borrego Desert, mainly in date palms and ornamental shrubbery around houses (up to nine in Borrego Springs, G24, 14 December 1997, P. D. Ache; seven at Canebrake, N27, 8 January 2000, R. and S. L. Breisch; four at Ocotillo Wells, I28, 20 December 1999, P. Unitt) and at native palm oases (up to seven at Carrizo Palms, R28, 6

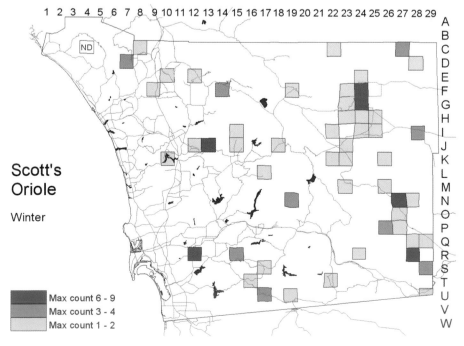

Scott's Oriole

Winter

Max count 6 - 9
Max count 3 - 4
Max count 1 - 2

January 2000, J. O. Zimmer; four at Mortero Palms, S29, 25 February 1999, A. Young). In typical breeding habitat with yucca and agave, wintering Scott's Orioles are rare but recorded as high as 5350 feet elevation in the Santa Rosa Mountains 1.2 miles north-northwest of Villager Peak (C27; three on 19 January 2000, P. Unitt). Totals on Anza–Borrego Christmas bird counts have ranged from 4 to 23 (2 January 1993). On the Lake Henshaw count, which extends into desert scrub in San Felipe Valley, the species is irregular with only one or two per year, except on 20 December 1993 when there were 26. Atlas data reveal substantial annual variability as well: more than three times as many Scott's Orioles were reported in the winter of 1999–2000 than in any other winter of the project's five-year term.

On the coastal slope south of Interstate 8, Scott's Oriole is rare in winter (11 records 1997–2002). At least some of the birds were at the same sites as those in the breeding season and probably year-round residents (e.g., up to three near Dulzura Summit, U17, 5 February 2001, D. W. Povey). Others were taking advantage of temporary food sources like prickly pears near Bancroft Point (R12; six on 12 January 2000, N. A. Inman) or flowering eucalyptus in North Jamul (R15; three on 1 January 2000, P. Unitt). On the coastal slope north of Interstate 8, winter occurrences appear even more strongly tied to fruiting prickly pears. The primary site there is the grounds of the Wild Animal Park and adjacent San Pasqual Battlefield State Historical Monument (J12/J13), where the thickets of prickly pears are large. The maximum count in a single atlas square 1997–2002, nine on 2 January 2000 (J13; K. L. Weaver), was also the highest total for the area on an Escondido Christmas bird count. Other cactus-dominated sites of more than a single wintering Scott's Oriole include the Fallbrook Naval Weapons Station (D7; four on 11 February 2000, K. L. Weaver), Pauma Valley (E12; two on 15 February 2001, K. Fischer), Rancho Cuca (F14; up to four on 27 December 1999, S. Berg), Pamo Valley (I15/J15; two on 2 January 2000, W. E. Haas), and Sherilton Valley (N19; three on 17 and 18 December 1999, G. and R. Wynn). Where the supply of fruit was small, as in Sherilton Valley, the birds moved on after exhausting it. Wintering Scott's Orioles often occur in small flocks.

Conservation: Most of Scott's Oriole's breeding habitat in San Diego County lies in rugged wildernesses conserved in Anza–Borrego Desert State Park or under the jurisdiction of the Bureau of Land Management. In Dameron Valley, however, the habitat is privately owned and undergoing piecemeal development, possibly eliminating not only the Scott's Orioles but also one of the most biogeographically interesting sites in San Diego County, a patch of semidesert scrub with many desert plants and animals isolated on the coastal slope. Scott's Orioles once bred to some extent in the coastal sage scrub now replaced by metropolitan San Diego. Only two locations were reported, Balboa Park (R9/S9; several spring/summer records 1901–15, K. Stephens 1906, Grey 1915, Stephens 1915) and Telegraph Canyon (U11/U12/T13; nest 16 May 1890, Browne 1891), but the Mojave yucca was once common on south-facing slopes.

The regularity of Scott's Oriole in winter became clear only in the 1980s, more likely as a result of the establishment of the Escondido and Anza–Borrego Christmas bird counts than from a change in status. The historic winter range of Scott's Oriole lies not far south of San Diego—both Anthony (1894) and Huey (1926a) found it in January and February near San Quintín, just 150 miles south of the border. The date palms and gardens in the Borrego Valley are a new habitat that the birds only recently learned to exploit. But the palm oases and prickly pear thickets are native habitats, and records for each dating back to 1968 and 1947, respectively (Unitt 1984), suggest that Scott's Orioles occurred but were seldom noticed. On the coastal slope, cacti have been much reduced, along with the coastal sage scrub of which they are usually a part. Conservation of the remaining stands, so critical to the San Diego Cactus Wren, would favor wintering Scott's Orioles too.

FINCHES — FAMILY FRINGILLIDAE

Purple Finch *Carpodacus purpureus*

The Purple Finch has long been known as a fairly common resident of the coniferous woodlands of San Diego County's mountains. It still plays that role, but atlas observers also discovered an unexpected new one, as an uncommon and newly established resident of oak and riparian woodland at low elevations in northwestern San Diego County. Yet another role, this one traditional, is as an irregular winter visitor all over the county's coastal slope to woodland and dense chaparral with fruiting shrubs like toyon and California coffeeberry. In this role, however, the Purple Finch seems to be on the decrease. How changes in habitats and climate may

Photo by Anthony Mercieca

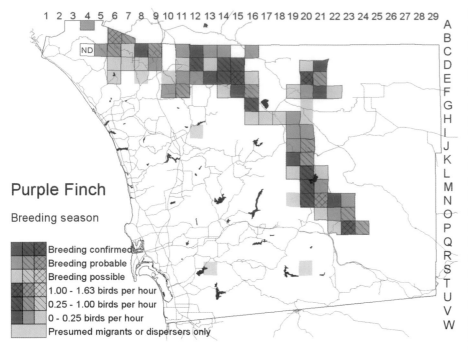

Purple Finch

Breeding season

- Breeding confirmed
- Breeding probable
- Breeding possible
- 1.00 - 1.63 birds per hour
- 0.25 - 1.00 birds per hour
- 0 - 0.25 birds per hour
- Presumed migrants or dispersers only

Finch has colonized woodland of sycamores and coast live oaks at low elevations in northwestern San Diego County. We noted the species during the breeding season on 76 occasions in 19 atlas squares where no elevation covered exceeds 2000 feet. The area colonized extends from the Santa Margarita Mountains east through Fallbrook to Valley Center and Palomar Mountain. In this zone, the birds were most concentrated along De Luz Creek (B6/C6), with ten, all singing males, in B6 on 10 July 2000 and seven, including six singing males, in C6 on 26 June 1999 (K. L. Weaver). The record nearest the coast was of one singing male near O'Neill Lake (E6), elevation barely over 100 feet, 18 May 1999 (P. A. Ginsburg). Breeding

be contributing to these seemingly contradictory changes in status is unclear.

Breeding distribution: The Purple Finch occurs in all of the larger stands of coniferous forest in San Diego County's mountains, being more common in denser stands of bigcone Douglas fir, incense cedar, and canyon live oak than in open groves of Jeffrey or Coulter pine. Seldom does one find more than a dozen birds in a morning even in prime habitat, but counts occasionally run as high as 25 from 0.25 to 1.5 miles south of Burnt Rancheria Campground, Laguna Mountains (P23), 23 June 2000 (E. C. Hall, J. O. Zimmer), 30 on Palomar Mountain (E15) 3 July 2000 (C. R. Mahrdt, E. C. Hall), and 40 on Middle Peak, Cuyamaca Mountains (M20), 11 June 2000 (R. E. Webster). Between Palomar and Volcan mountains, Purple Finches inhabit a narrow band of oak woodland with few or no conifers around Mesa Grande and in the gorge of the San Luis Rey River below Lake Henshaw. In this band the species is generally uncommon, but W. E. Haas noted 11, including a mist-netted female with a brood patch, near the San Luis Rey Day Use Area (G16) 3 July 1999.

One of the biggest surprises generated by the field work for this atlas was the discovery that the Purple

confirmations at low elevations were observations of nest building and feeding young at 840 feet in Fallbrook (C8) May 1998 (L. Ale), an occupied nest (female apparently incubating) at 1900 feet between Magee Creek and Castro Canyon (C12) 30 April 2000 (J. Determan), and nest building at 1600 feet in Marion Canyon (D12) 18 June 2001 (K. L. Weaver). Two singing males along Temecula Creek about 2600 feet elevation (C16) 10 April 1999 (K. L. Weaver) suggest spread north as well as west from Palomar Mountain.

Nesting: Before field work for this atlas began in 1997, no specific data on Purple Finch nesting in San Diego County had been published, and no eggs of the species had been collected. Of the seven nests reported since 1997, one was in a Jeffrey pine, one in a Coulter pine, one in a sycamore, and four in coast live oaks. Most were rather high in the trees, at heights of 28 to 45 feet, but one along the San Luis Rey River at Prisoner Creek (G16) 4 June 2001 (W. E. Haas) was barely over 3 feet above the ground in a coast live oak.

Our observations suggest the birds begin nesting in late April (occupied nest in Lost Valley, D20, 28 April 2000, W. E. Haas; adult feeding young along Nate Harrison Grade, E13, 18 May 1997, C. Sankpill). Most nesting activity concludes in mid July, but Maxine Dougan noted nest building as late as 18 July 2000 west of Dyche Valley (F15) and V. S. Moran noted fledglings as late as 2 August 2000 on North Peak, Cuyamaca Mountains (L20).

Migration: The Purple Finch's colonizing low elevations as a breeding species complicates tracking the species' dispersal. For example, four in Couser Canyon (E10) 4 April 1998 (K. Aldern, M. Bache) could well have been pioneers rather than late winter visitors. During the atlas period the latest observation far from a likely breeding location was of two in Oak Hill Cemetery, Escondido (I12), 13 April 1999 (C. Rideout), and that was the only

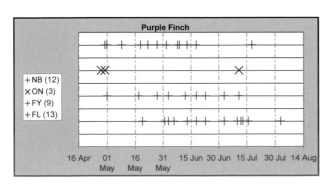

Purple Finch

+NB (12)
×ON (3)
+FY (9)
+FL (13)

16 Apr   01   16   31   15 Jun 30 Jun 15 Jul 30 Jul 14 Aug
    May   May   May

one after 4 April. Extreme dates in previous years range from 5 November (1972, five at Point Loma, S7, G. McCaskie) to 18 April (1975, two at Live Oak Park, D8, J. L. Dunn).

Winter: The Purple Finch is well known as an irruptive species in winter, but this irregularity was not well featured during the five-year atlas period. Numbers were low in 1997–98 and 2001–02 in comparison to the three intervening winters, but there was no broad-scale invasion as in 1974–75 or 1987–88. Coinciding with an invasion of Cassin's Finch, the highest winter counts of the Purple were in 2000–01: 52 in Palomar Mountain State Park (E14) 28 December 2000 (J. D. Barr), 79 around the Palomar Observatory (D15) the same day (K. L. Weaver), and 55 at Oak Grove (C16) 24 February 2001 (K. L. Weaver). Few observations during the atlas period were far from the breeding range, though past winter records were from as far from it as Point Loma. There was only one winter report from the Anza–Borrego Desert 1997–2002, of two at Agua Caliente Springs (M26) 26 February 1999 (J. L. Coatsworth). There are only about four earlier records from the desert floor, somewhat more from desert-edge locations like Culp Valley (H23) and Chariot Canyon (K21) (Massey 1998, ABDSP database).

Conservation: The Purple Finch's invasion of northwestern San Diego County just happened to coincide with the initiation of field work for this atlas. In spite of 20 years of field experience in the Fallbrook area, in areas covered well for the atlas, Kenneth L. Weaver had not found Purple Finches summering there before 1998. At low elevations in northwestern San Diego County, both the total number and the number reported per hour increased every breeding season of the five-year term. The reason

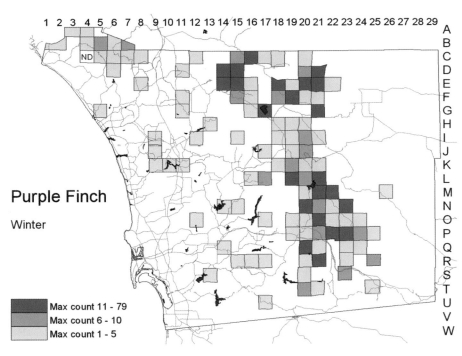

Purple Finch

Winter

■ Max count 11 - 79
▨ Max count 6 - 10
▢ Max count 1 - 5

for this spread is still a mystery. The avocado orchards widespread in this area give it a more forested aspect than it would have naturally, but the Purple Finches are using native woodland almost entirely.

In contrast to this trend during the breeding season, the Purple Finch seems to be on the decline as a winter visitor. It has not invaded San Diego County on any large scale since 1987–1988. It was noted on all 11 of the San Diego Christmas bird counts from 1965 to 1975, but on the 11 counts from 1991 to 2002 it was noted on only two, in 1992 and 2002. Trends on the Rancho Santa Fe, Oceanside, and Escondido counts are similar, if not quite so stark. Could climatic warming be obviating the need for this facultative migrant to move south?

Taxonomy: Only the western subspecies of the Purple Finch, *C. p. californicus* Baird, 1858, is known from San Diego County, though there are a few sight records and one specimen of the more eastern *C. p. purpureus* (Gmelin, 1789) from elsewhere in southern California (Patten et al. 2003).

Cassin's Finch *Carpodacus cassinii*

Cassin's Finch is another of those high-mountain birds whose breeding range skips over San Diego County's comparatively low mountains. It breeds in the San Jacinto and Santa Rosa Mountains to the north and in the Sierra San Pedro Mártir to the south, but in San Diego County there is only a single summer record. Some winters pass with no records of Cassin's Finch either—the species is quite irregular. On rare occasions, though, Cassin's Finches invade, and flocks of dozens can be seen, mainly in the mountains. One of these incursions took place in the winter of 2000–01, because of the

Photo by Anthony Mercieca

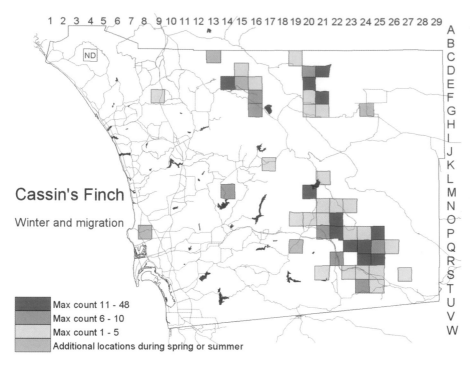

1 2 3 4 5 6 7 8 9 10 11 12 13 14 15 16 17 18 19 20 21 22 23 24 25 26 27 28 29

A B C D E F G H I J K L M N O P Q R S T U V W

ND

Cassin's Finch

Winter and migration

Max count 11 - 48
Max count 6 - 10
Max count 1 - 5
Additional locations during spring or summer

atlas the best documented Cassin's Finch invasion in San Diego County history.

Winter: In most winters, Cassin's Finch is a rare visitor to San Diego County's mountains, especially the Laguna Mountains, which offer more of the open dry pine forest that resembles the species' breeding habitat. In some years there are none, in some substantial incursions. The atlas' five-year term captured the full range of this variation. The annual total was 0 in 1997–98, 15 in 1998–99, 0 in 1999–2000, 503 in 2000–01, and 4 in 2001–02. The invasion of 2000–01 may have been the largest in San Diego County history, rivaled only by that of 1975–76, when B. Cord counted 103 in the Laguna Mountains 26 January. In 2000–01, numbers in pine-dominated woodland ranged up to 45 around Crouch Valley (P22) 7 January (P. Unitt) and 38 in Lost Valley near Shingle Spring (D21) 23 December (L. J. Hargrove). The birds spread into oak and riparian woodland as well, however, sometimes in numbers

just as large: 48 in Thing Valley (Q24) 7 January (J. R. Barth) and 36 in the Manzanita Indian Reservation (R25) 10 February (K. J. Winter, A. Mauro). Few birds strayed from the mountains; the only records below 2500 feet elevation were of one near Bonsall (F9) from December to 18 February (J. Evans) and eight at Fernbook (M14) 10 February (B. Hendricks). Lowland records were rare during past incursions as well.

Migration: As expected in an irruptive species, Cassin's Finch does not follow a regular migration schedule. With one exception, dates for San Diego County extend from 3 October (1987, three at Point Loma, S7, J. L. Dunn, AB 42:139, 1988) to 17 May (1997, two at Pine Valley, P21, J. K. Wilson). The winter preceding initiation of field work for this atlas, 1996–97, was also an invasion year for Cassin's Finch, as for several other mountain birds, so spring 1997 generated several late records, most notably of one in the Clairemont area of San Diego (P8) 10 April 1997 (C. G. Edwards). After the incursion of 2000–01 the latest sightings were from Panawatt Spring, Los Coyotes Indian Reservation (F21), of nine on 5 May and one on 6 May (J. Hargrove).

The first summer record of Cassin's Finch for San Diego County was of a single singing male on Birch Hill, Palomar Mountain (E15), 3 July 2000 (C. R. Mahrdt, E. C. Hall). Curiously, this sighting followed a winter in which no Cassin's Finches reached San Diego County.

Conservation: No strong trends in Cassin's Finch numbers have been reported, but these numbers fluctuate at some places even in the species' core range (Hahn 1996), making long-term changes difficult to detect.

House Finch *Carpodacus mexicanus*

The House Finch is the most abundant bird in San Diego County, and the field work for this atlas only supported this statement further. A year-round resident, the House Finch occupies all terrestrial habitats, from the coastal strand to montane coniferous woodland and sparse desert scrub. Most of man's modifications of the environment favor the House Finch: buildings and bridges offer nest sites, and disturbed weedy areas offer foraging habitat. The House Finch is a leading patron of bird feeders—of both seeds and sugar water.

Breeding distribution: The House Finch is San Diego County's most widespread breeding bird. It is most

Photo by Anthony Mercieca

abundant in the coastal lowland (up to 335 in lower Los Peñasquitos Canyon, N8, 2 July 2000, D. R. Grine) and around oases and developed areas in the Anza–Borrego

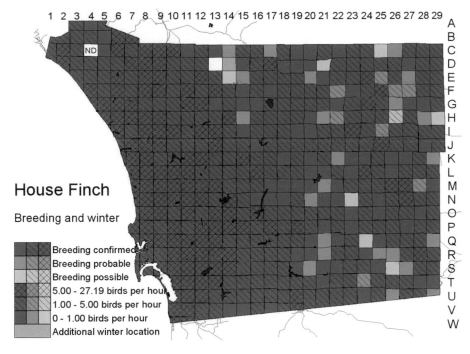

House Finch

Breeding and winter

Breeding confirmed
Breeding probable
Breeding possible
5.00 - 27.19 birds per hour
1.00 - 5.00 birds per hour
0 - 1.00 birds per hour
Additional winter location

inflorescences of the chaparral yucca appear to be the preferred nest site. With 26 of 145 records, however, the most frequently described nest sites were cholla and prickly pear cacti, from the Anza–Borrego Desert to the cactus garden in Balboa Park. House Finches nest colonially in stands of the teddy-bear or jumping cholla. They evidently recognize the ability of cactus spines to deter predators.

House Finches may begin laying in San Diego County as early as the end of February, as attested by observations of nest building as early as 19 February, occupied nests on 27 February, nests with nestlings on 15 March, and fledglings on 21 March. They continue into July, with young still in the nest as late as 29 July. These dates extend the season known from 33 egg sets collected in San Diego County, 30 March–29 June, but agree with the 28 February–7 August spread of egg dates from California as a whole (R. S. Woods in Austin 1968).

Desert (up to 300 around Carrizo Palms and Indian Hill, R28, 6 May 1998, J. O. Zimmer). But it occurs throughout the county, being uncommon only in montane coniferous forest and in sparsely vegetated desert miles from water. During the breeding season, the House Finch was missed from only one well-covered atlas square, D14 on Palomar Mountain.

Nesting: With close to 1500 records, the House Finch was the bird we confirmed nesting most frequently. Many confirmations are of more than one nest; the House Finch sometimes nests colonially where good nest sites are scarce, as at desert oases with California fan palms. The House Finch has been said to nest "anywhere" (Adams 1899), but scanning atlas participants' descriptions of nest sites reveals quickly that the birds prefer placing the nest on as solid a surface as possible, accounting for the abundance of nests on buildings. A covered situation is also desirable, leading the birds to nest in drain holes, under roof tiles, inside the hollow arms of power poles, behind slabs of buckled cottonwood bark, and in old nests of Black Phoebes, Cliff Swallows, and Hooded Orioles. If the birds nest in trees, the trees are usually ones that offer dense screening foliage, especially cultivated trees like orange and Italian cypress. In treeless chaparral, the

Migration: After breeding, House Finches gather into large flocks and move nomadically, searching for good foraging. But they do not engage in regular migration, and their distribution's uniformity masks seasonal shifts, if any.

Winter: The House Finch's distribution in San Diego County in winter differs little from that in the breeding season, being concentrated at low elevations, sparser in the mountains and in regions of extensive unbroken chaparral. Flocks may be larger in winter than in the breeding season (up to 690 in and near June Wash, M27, 10 January 1998, R. Thériault). Numbers in the Anza–Borrego Desert varied positively with rainfall, increasing in 1998, decreasing thereafter. But the magnitude of the fluctuation was less than with other seed-eating birds. The total in 2001–02 was still 43% of that in 1998–99.

Conservation: The House Finch has been abundant in San Diego County since the earliest naturalists reported on the county's birds. There is no evidence for significant recent change in the species' numbers. Nevertheless, buildings, disturbed openings, irrigation, and bird feeders are all continuing changes to the environment that favor House Finches in man-modified habitats more than in natural ones.

Taxonomy: *Carpodacus m. frontalis*, widespread on the mainland of western North America, is the only subspecies of the House Finch in San Diego County.

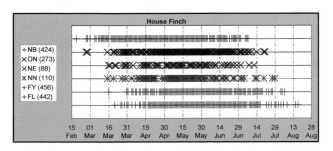

Red Crossbill *Loxia curvirostra*

Many members of the finch family migrate irregularly, as demanded by the irregularity of their food supply. The crossbills, with their unique specialization and dependence on conifer seeds, take this irregularity to an extreme. With only small areas forested in conifers, San Diego County cannot support a population of the Red Crossbill, so the species is a sporadic visitor here, though it has attempted nesting in the county at least once. Studies of morphology, genetics, and voice suggest the Red Crossbill, with its great variation across North America in size and bill shape, may consist of multiple cryptic species.

Photo by Anthony Mercieca

Winter: The winters of 1966–67, 1984–85, and 1996–97 saw the biggest incursions of the Red Crossbill known in the history of San Diego County. Thus the 5-year atlas period 1997–2002 began with the winding down of an incursion in which small flocks were seen through much of the county, such as 10 at the Vineyard Golf Course, Escondido (K11), 17 February 1997 (E. C. Hall). The Oceanside Christmas bird count yielded the maximum of 24 on 29 December 1996, and up to 10 occurred even at Borrego Springs (F24) that winter (M. L. Gabel, NASFN 51:119, 1997). The irruption of 1966–67 yielded up to 150 at Point Loma in November 1966 (AB 21:80, 1967), that of 1984–85, up to 25 there in March 1985 (AB 39:351, 1985).

The remainder of the atlas period was more typical. In the five winters following 1996–97 no crossbills were noted in San Diego County at all, except in 2000–01, which yielded four occurrences, three of them in conifer-wooded mountains, with a maximum of eight birds in Lower Doane Valley, Palomar Mountain State Park (D14), 22 December 2000 (P. D. Jorgensen).

Migration: The movements of the Red Crossbill are famously unpredictable, with little correspondence to the calendar. Nevertheless, in San Diego County, the birds seldom if ever arrive before late October. After larger invasions they may remain quite late in the spring, being recorded at Point Loma as late as 4 June in 1967 (AFN 21:542, 1967) and 3 June in 1985 (AB 39:351, 1985). In 1997 the latest report was of two near Descanso (O19) 13 May 1997 (R. A. Hamilton).

Breeding distribution: The crossbill's only breeding activity noted in San Diego County was at Point Loma in late March 1967, when some birds were paired, carrying nest material, and engaging in apparent courtship feeding. No fledglings were seen subsequently. The species occurs rarely in San Diego County's mountain forests in summer, and not only in summers following irruptions.

The maximum number in such a role was up to 15 in the Laguna Mountains in late July 1993 (G. L. Rogers, P. A. Ginsburg, AB 47:1152, 1993). From 1997 to 2001 the only such reports were from Middle and Cuyamaca peaks (M20), with one on 19 May 1998 and one or two 23–24 June 2001 (S. Peterson, D. Holway).

Conservation: The crossbills breeding in the southwestern quadrant of the contiguous United States have bills adapted to feed on the seeds of pines. Prolonged drought, as seen at the beginning of the 21st century, brings death to large numbers of pines by way of bark-beetle attack or forest fire. The Red Crossbill, being so specialized, is thus one of the most likely of the coniferous forest birds to suffer the effect of a drying climate.

Taxonomy: The Red Crossbill presents a taxonomic conundrum unique in North America. Various populations differ to a greater or lesser degree in size, bill shape, learned calls, genetic makeup, and specialization for certain conifers. The breeding ranges of these populations overlap to varying and still uncertain degrees. In spite of considerable study (Groth 1993, Benkman 1993), the proper interpretation and categorization of this variation is far from clear (DeBenedictis 1995). All but one of the eight specimens from San Diego County in the San Diego Natural History Museum, including three from the irruption of 1996–97, are of the medium-large size prevalent in the pine forests of western North America. That is, they are of size class III of Phillips (in Monson and Phillips 1981) or call types 2, 5, or 7 of Groth (1993), for which the oldest name is *L. pusilla* Gloger, 1834, or *L. c. bendirei* Ridgway, 1884. The exception is SDNHM 873, collected at Campo (U23) 6 March 1877. It has the very large bill identifying it as *L. c. stricklandi* Ridgway, 1885, which breeds in the mountains of mainland Mexico, north to southeastern Arizona, and in the mountains of northern Baja California.

Pine Siskin *Carduelis pinus*

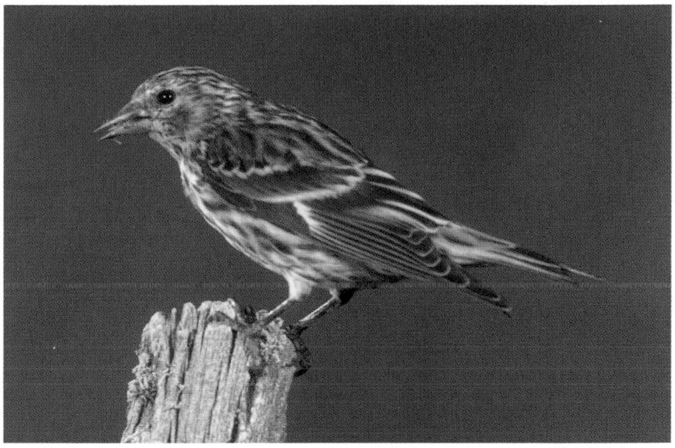

Photo by Anthony Mercieca

In its breeding range, the Pine Siskin is indeed a bird of pines, as well as other conifers. But in San Diego County, where it occurs primarily as a winter visitor, the siskin is just as likely to be seen in riparian woodland, where it feeds on the catkins of willows and alders. Its abundance varies enormously from year to year. In some winters flocks are common; in other years there are hardly any. Though the Pine Siskin breeds regularly south to the San Jacinto Mountains, Riverside County, in San Diego County's mountains there are only five summer records, one of a juvenile with a flock of adults.

Winter: In general, the Pine Siskin is most numerous in the mountains, becoming less so at lower elevations toward the coast. Nevertheless, variation from year to year is much greater than that from site to site. There was a substantial irruption in 1996–97, so that the first spring of the five-year atlas period yielded fair numbers of siskins, but in the next five winters the numbers were average to low. In the winter of 2001–02 the species was almost absent, with only three individuals reported. By far the largest count made during the atlas period was of 235 around North Peak, Cuyamaca Mountains (L20) 6 February 1999 (R. Breisch), but this could have been equaled easily in years of big invasions, such as 1975–76, 1981–82, 1984–85, 1987–88, and 1992–93. The highest number on any of the county's Christmas bird counts was 553 on the Lake Henshaw count 29 December 1981.

At lower elevations, during the atlas period, no Christmas bird count yielded more than 29, and high numbers in one atlas square were of 49 at Oak Hill Cemetery (I12) 16 March 2001 (C. Rideout) and 30 at Guajome Lake (G7) 8 December 2000 (G. C. Hazard). But totals of lowland Christmas bird counts during irruptions are as high as 182 in Oceanside 27 December 1981, and G. McCaskie noted 800 in Presidio Park (R8) 17 November 1963.

No siskins were found in the Anza–Borrego Desert during the atlas period, but small numbers reach there during major irruptions, with up to 20 at Lower Willows (D23) 20 December 1987 (A. G. Morley) and 29 in the north Borrego Valley (F24) 2 January 1993 (Christmas bird count).

Migration: Like other erratic winter visitors, the Pine Siskin has no regular migration schedule. Early November to mid April is its principal season, but it has been noted in fall as early as 9 September (1963, Tijuana River valley, G. McCaskie; 1992, Borrego Palm Canyon, F23, R. Thériault). During the atlas period, our latest spring date was 10 May (1999, 10 in Lost Valley, D20, J. M. and B. Hargrove), except for a remarkably late straggler, the latest ever in southern California's lowlands, at the Dairy Mart pond, Tijuana River valley (V11), 6 June 1999 (G. McCaskie).

Breeding distribution: No nests of the Pine Siskin have ever been found in San Diego County, and there are only five records in the county's mountains from late spring and summer. One of these, however, was of a juvenile, probably raised locally, with four adults on Middle Peak, Cuyamaca Mountains (M20), 19 July 1987 (R. E. Webster, AB 41:1489, 1987). Of the other records, two are from Palomar Mountain [one on 19 July 1966, AFN 20:600, 1966; one at Bailey's Meadow (E14) 28 May 1999, C. R. Mahrdt, E. C. Hall, J. O. Zimmer], one from the Cuyamaca Mountains (one on 9 July 1967, G. McCaskie),

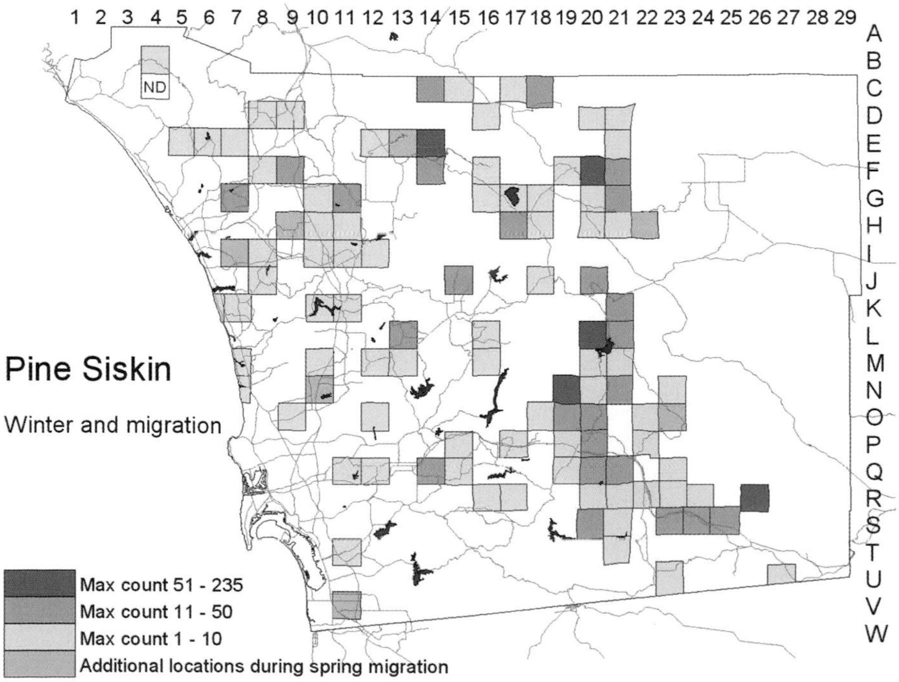
1 2 3 4 5 6 7 8 9 10 11 12 13 14 15 16 17 18 19 20 21 22 23 24 25 26 27 28 29
A B C D E F G H I J K L M N O P Q R S T U V W
ND
Pine Siskin
Winter and migration
Max count 51 - 235
Max count 11 - 50
Max count 1 - 10
Additional locations during spring migration

and one from the Laguna Mountains (one near Laguna Campground, O23, 13 June 1998, C. G. Edwards).

Conservation: Pine Siskins feed on the seeds of some common ornamental trees and so take advantage of areas that once had little to offer them. The white alder, a native riparian tree used frequently in landscaping, is one of the

siskins' favorite seed sources. Gander (1929) commented on their feeding on eucalyptus seeds in Balboa Park.

Taxonomy: Pine Siskins in San Diego County, like those throughout the United States, are of the small subspecies *C. p. pinus* (Wilson, 1810).

Lesser Goldfinch *Carduelis psaltria*

The Lesser Goldfinch is one of San Diego County's most widespread birds. It is a year-round resident and a habitat generalist, taking advantage of any weedy area for foraging. Nesting birds need shrubs or trees for nest sites and water for drinking within an easy commute of the foraging habitat. Our most interesting discovery about the Lesser Goldfinch was its response to El Niño: following the wet winter of 1997–98, the birds spread over the Anza–Borrego Desert, some nesting far from the oases to which they are usually restricted there. When drought returned, the spread proved as ephemeral as the bloom of desert wildflowers.

Breeding distribution: The Lesser Goldfinch is almost ubiquitous in San Diego County. It is especially abundant in the inland valleys, where as many as 150 have been counted during a day in the breeding season, as near Monserate Mountain (D9) 19 May 1999 (E. C. Hall), in lower Boden Canyon (J14) 1 June 1999 (C. R. Mahrdt), and near Ramona (K15) 18 June 1999 (M. and B. McIntosh). Because male Lesser Goldfinches defend only a small area around the nest, the species may breed semicolonially; Weaver (1992) recorded 11 territories in one 11.7-acre study plot along the Santa Margarita River north of Fallbrook (C8). Large numbers occur also in the

Photo by Anthony Mercieca

mountains (up to 125 in Matagual Valley, H19, 18 June 2000, S. E. Smith) and in the Borrego Valley (up to 65 in the north end of the valley, E24, 12 March 2000, P. D. Ache). The Lesser Goldfinch occurs in heavily urbanized areas though less commonly than where development is sparse or none; we did not find it in the breeding season in the two most completely developed atlas squares, R7 (Ocean Beach) and S8 (North Island).

Only in the remoter waterless reaches of the Anza–Borrego Desert do we see large holes in the distribution of this species that must drink regularly. Even there the Lesser Goldfinch is surprisingly widespread. The lack of nesting confirmations from many desert areas, however, suggests that many of the goldfinches there during the breeding season are not nesting. It was primarily in the wet year 1998 that Lesser Goldfinches spread over the Anza–Borrego Desert and were confirmed nesting in washes far from oases. Only two nestings in such dry habitats were noted in the other four years of the study (nest building on the northeast slope of the Santa Rosa Mountains, C28, 2 May 2000, R. Thériault; occupied nest along Fish Creek Wash at Split Mountain, L29, 11 April 2000, J. R. Barth).

Nesting: The Lesser Goldfinch usually builds its nest in a dense-foliaged shrub or tree, generally placing the nest toward the tip of a limb in a situation where it will be shaded at least part of the day (Linsdale 1957, Dawson 1923).

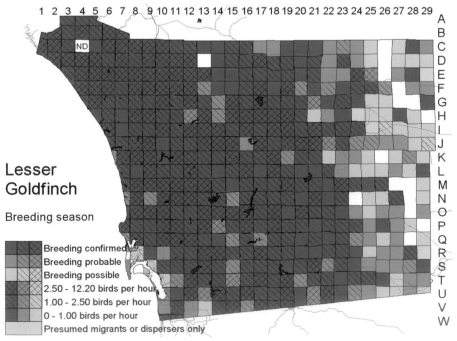

**Lesser
Goldfinch**

Breeding season

- Breeding confirmed
- Breeding probable
- Breeding possible
- 2.50 - 12.20 birds per hour
- 1.00 - 2.50 birds per hour
- 0 - 1.00 birds per hour
- Presumed migrants or dispersers only

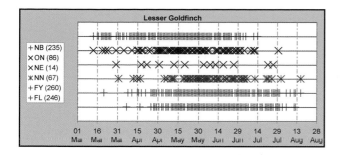

Of 29 nests atlas observers described, nine were in coast live oaks; others were in Engelmann oak, sycamore, willow, cottonwood, pine, ash, eucalyptus, avocado, mulefat, laurel sumac, coyote brush, and Chinese weeping elm. Clearly, the Lesser Goldfinch is a generalist when it comes to nesting.

We observed quite a bit of nesting activity beginning in mid March, especially in the wet year 1998. An occupied nest as early as 13 March 1998 (near Lake Murray, Q11, N. Osborn), an adult feeding a nestling as early as 21 March 1998 (Lower Willows, D23, B. Peterson), and a fledging as early as 7 April 1998 (west end of Batiquitos Lagoon, J6, M. Baumgartel) all imply egg laying in the second week of March, and therefore earlier than the 6 April attested by collected egg sets from San Diego County or 22 March from all of California. The season winds down in late July and early August (nest with nestlings in Poway, L12, as late as 16 August 1999, K. J. Winter). But the Lesser Goldfinch is also known to nest in the fall, in San Diego County (Sharp 1908, Carpenter 1919) as elsewhere. During the atlas period we noted fall nesting twice, with an adult male feeding a fledgling in the Rolando neighborhood of San Diego (R11) 3 December 1998 (F. Shaw) and a nestling found fallen

out of a nest on the campus of San Diego State University (Q11) 20 October 2000 (SDNHM 50489).

Migration: The Lesser Goldfinch does not undertake any regular migration in San Diego County. Nonbreeding birds, however, flock and wander. In open desert scrub, where few if any Lesser Goldfinches nest, small flocks have been seen as late as 7 April (1998, eight at Yaqui Meadows, H24, P. K. Nelson).

Winter: The distribution of the Lesser Goldfinch in San Diego County in winter differs little from that during the breeding season. The species' flocking in winter leads occasionally to counts as high as 293 east of Chula Vista (U12) 19 December 1998 (W. E. Haas) and 207 at Sentenac Ciénaga (J23) 16 February 1998 (R. Thériault). There is some shifting downslope from the highest elevations; we did not find the species in winter near the summits of Hot Springs Mountain (E20) and the Laguna Mountains (O23), where it occurs in summer. The Lesser Goldfinch is scattered over the Anza–Borrego Desert in winter but more sparsely than in spring. Probably the difference is due to the birds being able to take greater advantage of the desert when spring growth follows the rains.

Conservation: The Lesser Goldfinch benefits from many of man's alterations of the southern California environment. It feeds heavily on introduced weeds like the common sow-thistle and yellow star-thistle (Beal 1910, Linsdale 1957). Rural ranches offer disturbed open areas for foraging, shade trees for nesting, and water sources for drinking lacking in undeveloped native chaparral. The widespread use of the native white alder in landscaping puts another of the goldfinch's favored seed sources in many places where it does not grow naturally. These factors likely outweigh negative ones like overgrazing, overpumping of groundwater, and landscaping so intensive it eliminates weedy edges.

Taxonomy: The subspecies of the Lesser Goldfinch resident in San Diego County is the Green-backed Goldfinch, usually called *C. p. hesperophilus* (Oberholser, 1903). There are at least two sight records of black-backed males elsewhere in southern California (Patten et al. 2003), apparently nominate *C. p. psaltria* (Say, 1823). Such birds could be escapees from captivity, however, rather than vagrants or variants. The black-backed subspecies is widespread in mainland Mexico, the source of many escaped cage birds.

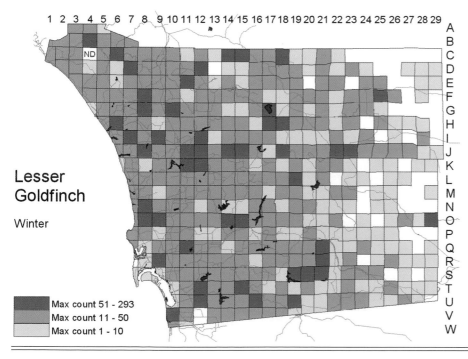

Lesser Goldfinch

Winter

Max count 51 - 293
Max count 11 - 50
Max count 1 - 10

Lawrence's Goldfinch *Carduelis lawrencei*

Though found in San Diego County year round, Lawrence's Goldfinch is notoriously nomadic, exploiting food sources that are abundant but ephemeral. In summer, these are seeds of wild-flowers of the family Boraginaceae, especially the fiddleneck, which grows in scattered meadows, often in disturbed soil. In winter, the goldfinches shift to gleaning seeds from the dried flowers of chamise, the shrub dominating San Diego County's chaparral. Nevertheless, the bird's irregularity in winter is even greater than in summer. Lawrence's Goldfinch responded to El Niño rains of 1997–1998, capitalizing on the bloom of desert wildflowers. Lawrence's, like the other goldfinches, must drink regularly, making long flights to water sources scattered through its arid habitat.

Breeding distribution: In San Diego County, Lawrence's Goldfinches are concentrated in the mountains. For suitable habitat, a meadow, a creek, and a grove of oaks is the ideal combination. In such areas, one may occasionally encounter concentrations as high as 50 in Chariot Canyon (L21) 16 June 1999 (J. K. Wilson), 56 on East Mesa, Cuyamaca Mountains (N21), 8 July 1999 (D. C. Seals), and 60 along upper Pine Valley Creek (O21) 4 July 1997 (P. Unitt). Even in this core range, however, the species is patchy and irregular, often lacking. At lower elevations, toward the coast, it becomes ever more so, though numbers as high as 40 in Pauma Valley (E12) 13 May 2000 (P. Unitt) and 20 along the San Diego River in Santee (P13) 24 June 1997 (D. C. Seals) may still occur in the middle of the breeding season in the inland valleys. Along the coast, Lawrence's Goldfinch is rare, especially as a breeding bird. Susan E. Smith noted two coastal nest-

Photo by Anthony Mercieca

ings, one barely more than 1 mile from the beach near the intersection of Interstate 5 and Del Mar Heights Road (N7), where apparently three pairs nested in Canary Island pines planted around an apartment complex; nestlings were visible in one nest 8 May 1999. The other was 0.3 mile from the beach near the University of California (O7), where a male fed a female on a nest in a eucalyptus 9 May 2000.

In the Anza–Borrego Desert Lawrence's Goldfinch's irregularity is accentuated further. Of the atlas period's five years, the wet 1998 saw by far the greatest numbers; in other years there were few to none. Butterfield Ranch in Mason Valley (M23) is the only desert location where Lawrence's Goldfinch is even moderately regular. All our desert confirmations of Lawrence's Goldfinch nesting were in 1998, except at the desert-edge locations of Earthquake Valley (K23), Mason Valley, and In-Ko-Pah (T29), where the birds nested in 2001 as well. Lawrence's Goldfinch nesting in the Anza–Borrego Desert was unknown before 1998 (Massey 1998).

Nesting: Lawrence's Goldfinch's strategy of opportunism results in its being the most colonial of San Diego County's finches. Several pairs may nest simultaneously in a small grove of trees. In addition to coast live and Engelmann oaks, sycamores, and pines, reported nest sites included deodar cedar and Italian cypress. Evidently the dense screening foliage of these exotic trees makes them especially attractive. An atypical apparent nest site was in a rotted out cavity in a horizontal willow branch, from which I flushed a pair near Moretti's Junction (H18) 12 May 2001.

The timing of Lawrence's Goldfinch nesting varies with the rains and food supply as well.

Lawrence's Goldfinch

Breeding season

- Breeding confirmed
- Breeding probable
- Breeding possible
- 1.00 - 4.58 birds per hour
- 0.25 - 1.00 birds per hour
- 0 - 0.25 birds per hour
- Presumed migrants or dispersers only

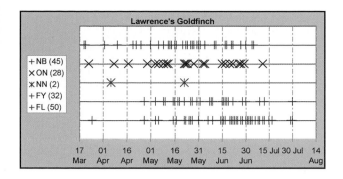

Most nesting takes place from April to July, as shown by the 7 April–9 July spread of 12 collected egg sets. After the wet winter of 1997–1998, however, Lawrence's Goldfinches began nesting exceptionally early, as attested by an occupied nest in Culp Valley (H23) 23 March 1998 (M. L. Gabel), a nest with nestlings at Stelzer County Park (O14) 4 April 1998 (M. B. Mulrooney), and a fledgling at the Roadrunner Club, Borrego Springs (F24), 25 March 1998 (M. L. Gabel). The last implies eggs laid at the end of February, apparently the earliest the species' nesting has ever been reported. On the late side, Lawrence's Goldfinches were still building nests in Pine Valley (P21) 5 July 1997 (J. K. Wilson) and at Lake Morena (T21) the same day (R. and S. L. Breisch).

Migration: Lawrence's Goldfinch is an irregular, partial migrant, a variable fraction of the population moving east of the Colorado River for the winter. In San Diego County, migrants are most notable in March and April, when flocks are seen occasionally and the birds show up more frequently in the Anza–Borrego Desert and along the coast. Such flocks may be as large as 60 at Lower Otay Lake (U14) 2 April 2000 (S. Buchanan), 350 in the Borrego Valley's mesquite bosque (G25) 10 April 1995 (Massey 1998), and "hundreds" in Santee (P12) 24 March 2001 (W. McCausland). In a nomadic, opportunistically nesting species like Lawrence's Goldfinch the notion of a migration schedule is fuzzy. Especially in 1998 we noted occasional pairs or flocks in habitat atypical for breeding in late spring and summer: pair near Sunset Mountain (J26) 19 April 1998 (F. L. Unmack, R. Orr); pair at Azalea Park, East San Diego (R10) 28 May 1998 (J. A. Dietrick); 10 on the east side of Chula Vista (U12) 24 June 1998 (T. W. Dorman).

Winter: In winter opportunism rules Lawrence's Goldfinch's behavior and distribution even more strongly. The birds descend on a source of seeds, exhaust it, and move on. They are concentrated at this season between 1500 and 4500 feet elevation and most widespread in south-central San Diego County, where the chamise on which they feed covers vast areas. During the atlas period the largest winter flocks noted were 236 east of Corte Madera Valley (R21) 20 February 1999 (W. E. Haas), 200 near Corral Canyon (S20) 30 January 1999 (D. C. Seals), and 150 near Swan Lake (F18) 29 December 1997 (G. L. Rogers). We found the species rare along the coast in winter, with a maximum of six in Torrey Pines State Reserve (N7) 23 December 2001 (S. Walens). The irregularity of Lawrence's Goldfinch is exemplified by the results of the Escondido Christmas bird count: species recorded on 10 of 17 counts, mean 22, standard deviation 71, maximum 224.

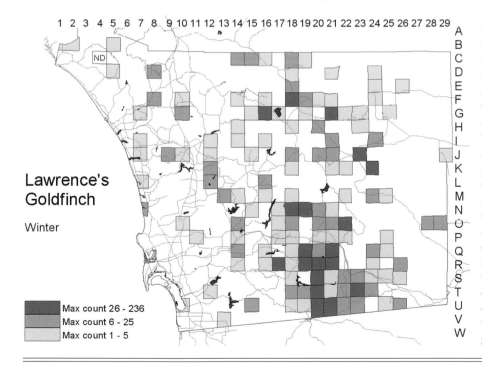

Lawrence's Goldfinch

Winter

- Max count 26 – 236
- Max count 6 – 25
- Max count 1 – 5

Conservation: Lawrence's Goldfinch's irregularity means that much more information is needed for trends to be identified in this species than in most others. No trends are evident yet, though the flocks of hundreds noted occasionally in the Tijuana River valley in the 1960s did not recur during the atlas period. The planting of exotic conifers and the irrigation of rural ranches enhance Lawrence's Goldfinch habitat, but intensive development, obliterating meadows and weedy fields, eliminates it. Another likely negative factor is the proliferation of foreign weeds that have so largely displaced the native wildflowers that provide the staples of the goldfinch's summer diet.

American Goldfinch *Carduelis tristis*

The American is the most widespread of the three goldfinches in North America but the most restricted in San Diego County, which is virtually at the southern tip of the bird's range. As implied by the names of the California subspecies, the Willow Goldfinch, *C. t. salicamans*, the American is a riparian species in this region. It is a common resident in northwestern San Diego County but common in only a few places elsewhere. During the nonbreeding season flocks readily depart riparian woodland to forage on seeds of plants like sunflowers and the great marsh evening primrose.

Photo by Anthony Mercieca

Breeding distribution: As a breeding bird, the American Goldfinch is closely tied in San Diego County to riparian woodland. By far the largest numbers are found along the Santa Margarita River in Camp Pendleton, where daily counts in a single atlas square ran as high as 120 near the confluence of De Luz Creek (D6) 20 July 1999 (D. C. Seals) and 100 between Rifle Range Road and Ysidora Basin (F5) 16 May, 13 June, and 11 July 1998 (R. E. Fischer). The species is common elsewhere in the lowlands of northwestern San Diego County (24 along the Santa Margarita River north of Fallbrook, C8, 16 July 1999, W. Pray; 50 along the San Luis Rey River near Gird Road, E8, 26 April 1999, P. A. Ginsburg) and found along small creeks as well as the Santa Margarita and San Luis Rey rivers. Farther south the American Goldfinch becomes more and more localized to the major riparian corridors but is still common in a few places, especially along the Sweetwater and Tijuana rivers (up to 50 along the Tijuana River east of Hollister Street, W11, 27 June 1998, P. Unitt). Above 1500 feet elevation the American Goldfinch is sparse and possibly irregular at any particular site. During the atlas period, the only place in this

zone where the species was found repeatedly was along Buena Vista Creek in Warner Valley (G18/G19; up to 20 near Warner's Ranch, G19, 17 June 2000, J. D. Barr). The species is absent from southern San Diego County east of Descanso and Potrero. On the desert slope the American Goldfinch occurs in San Felipe Valley but not consistently. Near Paroli Spring (I21) there were 10, including multiple singing males and pairs, 26 April 1999, but on 13 June 1999 there was only a single bird (J. O. Zimmer). Farther downstream, near Scissors Crossing (J22), there were two on 14 May 1998 (E. C. Hall), but intensive coverage of this area May–July 2002 did not reveal any.

Nesting: Unsurprisingly for a species so closely linked to riparian woodland, the American Goldfinch nests primarily in willow trees. Of 18 collected egg sets whose site was described, 15 were in willows. Other known sites in San Diego County are cottonwood, cypress, orange trees, and goldenrod. Thus the American Goldfinch may nest high or low. In the eastern United States, the American Goldfinch is famed for nesting late in the summer, but in southern California its nesting season is typical of that of other riparian woodland birds. Dates of 33 egg sets collected 1889–1940 range from 21 April to 6 July, and the nesting activity we observed during the atlas period was largely consistent with this. The exception was at the upper end of Sweetwater Reservoir (S13) in 1997, when P. Famolaro noted nest building as early as 26 March, an occupied nest as early as 10 April, and fledglings as early as 30 April.

Migration: The American Goldfinch is not as nomadic as some members of its family, but occasional birds show up in nonbreeding habitat even in the middle of the breeding season (e.g., one at the Chula Vista Nature Center,

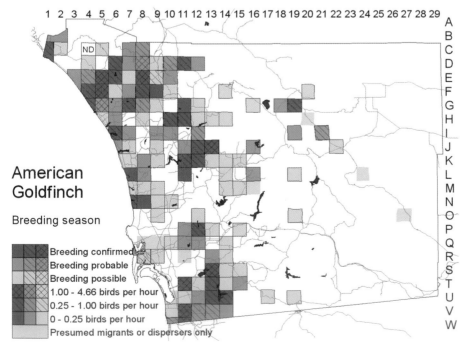

American Goldfinch

Breeding season

- Breeding confirmed
- Breeding probable
- Breeding possible
- 1.00 - 4.66 birds per hour
- 0.25 - 1.00 birds per hour
- 0 - 0.25 birds per hour
- Presumed migrants or dispersers only

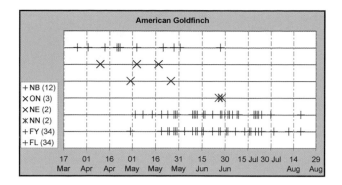

U11, 30 May 1999, B. C. Moore). The species is a very rare wanderer to the Anza–Borrego Desert, recorded from 19 September (1991, three in Culp Valley, H22, M. L. Gabel) to 22 April (1957, two at Yaqui Well, I24, ABDSP database). The only spring migrants reported from the desert 1997–2001 were three at Mountain Palm Springs (O27) 22 March 1998 (S. V. Fukuman) and one in Blair Valley (L24) 13 April 1998 (G. P. Sanders). Note that these records were in the wet spring of 1998 that induced the Lesser and Lawrence's Goldfinches to spread into the desert.

Winter: At this season the American Goldfinch loosens its attachment to extensive riparian woodland and takes advantage of weedy areas along minor creeks and even alder and liquidambar trees planted in parks and residential areas. The pattern of winter records, though,

suggests that few birds move more than a few miles. High counts in winter were of 60 at the east end of Lake Hodges (K11) 31 December 1997 (E. C. Hall), 50 in Reidy Canyon (H10) 12 December 1999 (D. and D. Bylin), and 50 near the upper end of Sweetwater Reservoir 31 January 2002 (T. W. Dorman). A few American Goldfinches were reported in southeastern San Diego County, east to Live Oak Springs (S25; three on 21 January 2001, W. Dallas) and as high as 5200 feet elevation along La Posta Creek (P24; two on 19 December 2001, E. C. Hall, J. O. Zimmer). The latter is the only winter record above 4000 feet elevation. During the atlas period we noted the species twice in the Anza–Borrego Desert, one in the northern Borrego Valley (E24) 17 February 1999 (J. E. Fitch), eight at Agua Caliente Springs (M26) 1 December 1997 (E. C. Hall). The American Goldfinch has been recorded on only three of 18 Anza–Borrego Christmas bird counts 1984–2001, maximum eight on 28 December 1986. The winter irregularity of so many cardueline finches is not typical of the American Goldfinch in southern California, but the 262 reported on the Lake Henshaw Christmas bird count 3 January 1987 far exceeded the count's second highest total of 18.

Conservation: The range of the American Goldfinch may have retracted over the 20th century in Baja California. Currently, it is only a rare visitor south of the Tijuana River, despite its abundance along this river on the U.S. side of the border (Erickson et al. 2001). Within San Diego County, although much riparian woodland has been lost, the American Goldfinch has sustained its numbers in the habitat that remains. Cowbird trapping may benefit the American Goldfinch, as the goldfinch is a frequent victim of the cowbird in California (Friedmann 1963). With its vegetarian diet, however, the goldfinch is not a good host for the cowbird. Cowbird parasitism may reduce the goldfinch's nest success significantly even if it fails to increase the cowbird's.

Taxonomy: The only subspecies of the American Goldfinch known from southern California is the one breeding locally, the Willow Goldfinch, *S. t. salicamans* Grinnell, 1897.

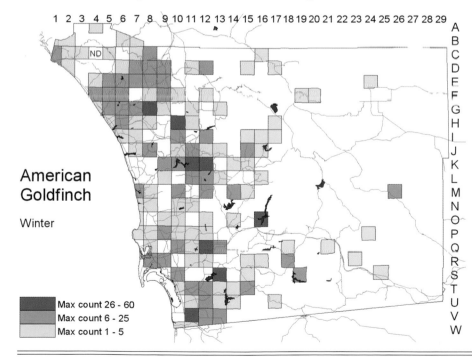

American Goldfinch

Winter

Max count 26 - 60
Max count 6 - 25
Max count 1 - 5

Evening Grosbeak *Coccothraustes vespertinus*

A denizen of boreal forests, the Evening Grosbeak breeds in the Sierra Nevada but not in southern California. In San Diego County it is a rare and sporadic visitor, mainly to the mountains in winter.

Winter: Most reports of the Evening Grosbeak in San Diego County are from Palomar Mountain (up to 40 on 9 February 1987, K. L. Weaver, AB 41:332, 1987), the Cuyamaca Mountains (up to eight on 11 November 1997, P. A. Ginsburg, NASFN 51:119, 1997), and the Laguna Mountains (up to 20 from 2 to 18 January 1987,

B. McCausland, AB 41:332, 1987). There are only 12 records below 1500 feet elevation, one as far southwest as the Tijuana River valley (20–22 October 1966, AFN 21:80, 1967).

Like many members of the finch family, the Evening Grosbeak is irregular in its movements. Years may pass with no reports for San Diego County, then, as in 1955–56, 1972–73, 1984–85, or 1986–87, there is a small irruption, often coinciding with irruptions of other finches. During the atlas period, there were no records of the grosbeak between 1997, when an irruption the preceding winter yielded a spring straggler in Noble Canyon, Laguna Mountains (O22), 15 May (R. A. Hamilton, FN 51:927, 1997), and 2001, when at least five were at Paso Picacho Campground, Cuyamaca Rancho State Park (M20), 6 January–4 February (G. C. Hazard, M. B. Mulrooney).

Migration: San Diego County records of the Evening Grosbeak extend from 9 October (1972, one at Palomar Mountain, AB 27:125, 1973) to 13 February (1985, two at San Diego, R. E. Webster, AB 39:211, 1985) and from 26 April (2001, one at Paso Picacho Campground, R. Thériault) to 25 May (1971, three at Palomar Mountain, AB 25:804, 1971). The eight spring records include the only desert or desert-edge records, from Yaqui Well (I24) 16 May 1964 (AFN 18:488, 1964) and Jacumba (U28) 30 April 1978 (AB 32:1057, 1978).

Photo by Anthony Mercieca

Taxonomy: In lack of a specimen, the subspecies of the Evening Grosbeak reaching San Diego County is not definitely known. But all specimens from elsewhere in California, migrants as well as breeding birds, have been ascribed to *C. v. brooksi* (Grinnell, 1917), which breeds from British Columbia south through the western United States to central Arizona. Shorter-billed nominate *C. v. vespertinus* (Cooper, 1825), breeding in Canada, has reached as far as Arizona, however, as attested by two specimens collected during the invasion of 1955–56 (Phillips et al. 1964).

OLD WORLD SPARROWS — FAMILY PASSERIDAE

House Sparrow *Passer domesticus*

No bird on earth is as completely a commensal of man as the House Sparrow. A native of Eurasia, it was introduced repeatedly from England to the United States in the 19th century, then transplanted within this country. Transplantation to San Francisco allowed the birds to spread to southern California; they arrived in San Diego in 1913 and quickly proliferated. Now few clusters of buildings of any consequence lack House Sparrows, but in southern California the birds seldom spread into undeveloped natural habitats.

Breeding distribution: The House Sparrow's distribution in San Diego County follows the limits of built-up areas almost exactly. Even isolated desert communities and campgrounds have their colonies; indeed, numbers in such places can be quite large (75 at Ocotillo Wells, I28, 26 April 2001, J. R. Barth). The Anza–Borrego Desert also furnished our largest one-day estimate of House Sparrow numbers in the breeding season, 200 in the Club Circle area of Borrego Springs (G24) 15 April 2001 (L. and M. Polinsky). The apparent gaps in a few squares with appreciable urban development were likely due to atlas observers' concentrating on natural habitats at the expense of developed areas. The sparrows are lacking around some scattered rural ranches, however, though they inhabit

Photo by Anthony Mercieca

even many of these. House Sparrows are largely absent above 4500 feet elevation, although there may be buildings that would attract them elsewhere.

Nesting: House Sparrows most typically nest in a crevice in buildings, filling the cavity with grass and trash. In southern California, the birds commonly use the gaps under curved Spanish roof tiles, so much so that builders now attempt to exclude House Sparrows—not always successfully—by blocking these gaps with strips or sections of material called birdstops. Other common nest

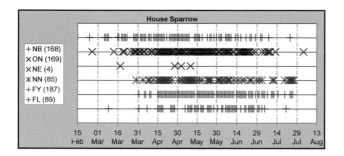

sites include street lamps, old Cliff Swallow nests, and the spaces between the bases of palm leaves. Many pairs may nest colonially in a single palm, as at Club Circle, Borrego Springs, or Kimball Park, National City (T10). Sometimes House Sparrows build ball-shaped nests with side entrances, placing them in exposed situations in trees, especially thorny ones. Even eucalyptus trees occasionally host colonies of such nests.

Because House Sparrows may maintain their nests year round, observations of nest building and occupied nests convey less information about breeding than they do with most songbirds. A female with a brood patch

trapped at Point Loma (S7) 18 March 1997 (V. P. Johnson) and the 30 March–27 July spread of nests with nestlings demonstrate that in San Diego County House Sparrows lay from mid March to early July.

Migration: The House Sparrow is nonmigratory, adults often roosting in their nest cavities and guarding them year round. Only a fraction of the juveniles disperse from their natal colonies (Lowther and Cink 1992).

Winter: The House Sparrow's winter distribution in San Diego County does not differ materially from its breeding distribution. The site of concentration that emerges most conspicuously from winter atlas data is the San Diego Zoo in Balboa Park (R9), where the sparrows capitalize on animal feed as well as human food waste. Estimates from the zoo ranged up to 300 on 15 January 2000 (J. R. Barth).

Conservation: The House Sparrow may be expected to spread further in San Diego County with continued urban development, but its exponential growth phase is long over. Christmas bird counts over the final third of the 20th century show no clear trend. The population may decline as buildings are engineered to preclude the birds' nesting. Conversion of land from agriculture to urban uses disfavors the House Sparrow because even if more buildings mean more nest sites, suburbs probably offer less food, especially the insects fed to the young. America's shift from the horse to the automobile is generally credited for a decline in House Sparrow numbers in the eastern U.S. A more recent sharp decline in several European countries has not yet been paralleled in California. But the more sterile, the more rigorously managed our environment, the more it discourages all wildlife, even the lowly House Sparrow.

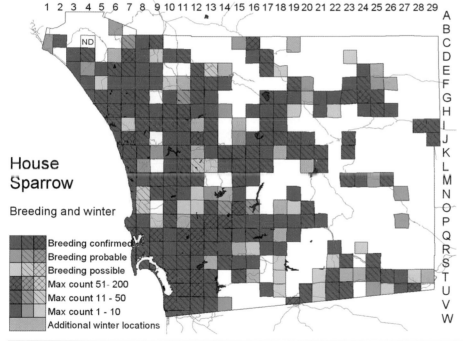

House
Sparrow

Breeding and winter

Breeding confirmed
Breeding probable
Breeding possible
Max count 51- 200
Max count 11 - 50
Max count 1 - 10
Additional winter locations

Taxonomy: The north Eurasian *P. d. domesticus* is the subspecies introduced to North America.

EXOTIC AND HYPOTHETICAL SPECIES

The following section addresses species that have been observed in San Diego County since 1984 but are not native and do not (yet) have a well-established self-sustaining population in the wild. Probably or undoubtedly their occurrence in the county is based on escapees from captivity. They range from more or less domesticated birds with little chance of establishing themselves to others, such as the Black-throated Magpie-Jay and Northern Cardinal, well on their

way to becoming naturalized. Eight introduced species (Ring-necked Pheasant, Wild Turkey, Domestic Pigeon, Eurasian Collared Dove, Spotted Dove, Red-crowned Parrot, European Starling, House Sparrow) that have been considered established, at least in the past, are covered with the native species on the main list. Observers for this atlas reported still more escaped cage birds than are listed here, such as the Golden-fronted Leafbird (*Chloropsis aurifrons*) and

Rufous Treepie (*Dendrocitta vagabunda*); this section addresses only species seen repeatedly, species possibly establishing themselves elsewhere in North America, and species given some consideration by the California Bird Records Committee as prospective natural vagrants.

Also in this section are species reported in *North American Birds* or its predecessors that have been discounted by the California Bird Records Committee. Hypothetical species addressed in my 1984 *Birds of San Diego County* are not repeated here.

Black-bellied Whistling-Duck
Dendrocygna autumnalis

Two in the Tijuana River estuary (V10) 24 May 1986 were probably escapees from captivity (R. T. Patton, Langham 1991). Nevertheless, the frequency of natural vagrants in the Salton Sink is increasing, with 19 records for that area by 2002 (Patten et al. 2003). Thus the Black-bellied Whistling-Duck could join the Painted Bunting as a species of which both vagrants and escapees are likely in San Diego County.

Photo by Anthony Mercieca

Mute Swan *Cygnus olor*

Native to Eurasia, the Mute Swan has been introduced in North America as an ornamental waterfowl. Semidomesticated, the swan has increased in the suburban landscape and spread to the point where it is considered a nuisance in some states. In San Diego County the Mute Swan population is still small, possibly not yet self sustaining.

Breeding distribution: Mute Swans were released at the lake within the Del Mar racetrack (M7) sometime before 1997, where they have been fed by racetrack officials, nested repeatedly, and increased (A. Mauro). This source is presumably responsible for the swans seen in the adjacent San Dieguito River estuary (two from 22 April to 10 June 2000, A. Dempsey, D. R. Grine) and at San Elijo Lagoon (L7; up to two on 8 July 1998, A. Mauro, and 22 April 2000, R. T. Patton). Mute Swans elsewhere in the county may be the result of independent introductions. The only site of more than three and of confirmed nesting is Lake San Marcos (I8/J8), with up to 12, including cygnets, 14 May and 8 June 1997 (J. O. Zimmer).

Winter: In winter as in the breeding season, Lake San Marcos was our principal site for the Mute Swan, with up to 11 on 27 December 1997 and 9 on 2 February 1999 (J. O. Zimmer). The least-expected site was a pond at the Roadrunner Club, Borrego Springs (F24), where there was one Mute Swan 28 February 1999 (P. D. Jorgensen).

Photo by Anthony Mercieca

Conservation: This account is the first published report of the Mute Swan's occurrence and nesting in San Diego County. The species was not reported on any Christmas bird count in the county before 1997, though it may have been seen but dismissed as an escapee from captivity. Because of its history of establishing feral populations, the Mute Swan should not be ignored.

Possible negative effects of the Mute Swan's increase include its depleting the food supply for native waterfowl. In Maryland, Mute Swans have trampled eggs and chicks of the Least Tern (Ciaranca et al. 1997). Another threat is the last thing the Least Tern needs in San Diego County.

Ruddy Shelduck *Tadorna ferruginea*

Native to Eurasia and north Africa, the Ruddy Shelduck is a popular ornamental waterfowl. Birds kept at the La Jolla Beach and Tennis Club (P7) are apparently responsible for repeated sightings around La Jolla, including the Torrey Pines golf course, Black's Beach, and Southwest Fisheries Science Center (O7). One found near the La Jolla Beach and Tennis Club 23 January 2000 is preserved as SDNHM 50468. No more than two were reported during the atlas period 1997–2002, but eight flew by the Southwest Fisheries Science Center 20 April 2004 (S. E. Smith). In April 2003, an apparent pair were entering and exiting a cave in the cliff face above Black's Beach, suggesting a possible nest site (S. E. Smith). Six were at Crown Point, Mission Bay (Q8), 2 November 2002 (M. A. Faulkner), and one was at a pond just north of Imperial Beach (V10) 31 March 2003 (R. Bledsoe).

Photo by Anthony Mercieca

Mandarin Duck *Aix galericulata*

As one of the world's most exquisite and popular waterfowl, the Mandarin Duck is kept commonly in captivity. Thus reports from seven locations during the atlas period were not a surprise. All were of single individuals, except at a pond along Buena Creek 2.7 miles southeast of downtown Vista (H8). Here J. O. Zimmer noted a pair on 13 May 1999 and up to eight on 3 January 2000. The Mandarin Duck is not established as a feral bird in California, but such establishment becomes ever more likely with the spreading provision of nest boxes for Wood Ducks. In Fallbrook (D8) in 2003, rehabilitator Terri Halverson reported at least three breeding pairs and a brood of six chicks found when their nest tree was chopped down.

Photo by Anthony Mercieca

Band-rumped or Harcourt's Storm-Petrel *Oceanodroma castro*

The California Bird Records Committee once accepted a sighting of this difficult-to-identify species 25 miles west of San Diego 12 September 1970 (McCaskie 1990), but it later reversed itself (Garrett and Singer 1998). There are no well-supported records near California.

Red-tailed Tropicbird *Phaethon rubricauda*

The California Bird Records Committee has accepted a sighting 145 nautical miles west-southwest of San Diego 16 August 1980 (Roberson 1993), but this location is closer to Mexico than to San Diego.

Nazca Booby *Sula granti*

One came aboard a boat 50 nautical miles west of Punta Banda, Baja California, 27 May 2001, and rode the boat as it came into San Diego Bay. Therefore, the bird's occurrence in San Diego was clearly not natural, and the California Bird Records Committee did not add the species to the list of California birds (Garrett and Wilson 2003). A sibling species of the Masked Booby, the Nazca Booby nests largely on the Galapagos and Malpelo islands, with only a few nesting on Mexico's San Benedicto Island, possibly on the Alijos Rocks (Pitman and Jehl 1998).

Darter *Anhinga melanogaster*

The seemingly simple identification of the Anhinga has now been complicated by local sightings of that species' counterpart in the Old World, the Darter. Free-flying Darters in the Western Hemisphere are undoubtedly escapees from captivity; the species is raised at the San Diego Wild Animal Park and San Diego Zoo. In southern California and Baja California at least two Darters have been reported from the Imperial Valley, one near Ensenada. In San Diego County one was at Barrett Lake (S18) 2 February and 7 April 2001 (R. and S. L. Breisch, J. Hannan) and one, probably a Darter rather than an Anhinga, flew over the San Carlos area of San Diego (Q12) 7 April 2002 (J. Morris).

Crested Caracara *Caracara cheriway*

The Crested Caracara is resident as far northwest as central Baja California and southern Arizona, where its numbers are declining. But the status of at least 10 reports of caracaras in California is clouded by the question of whether the birds were escapees from captivity. One was photographed in San Diego County near the edge of the Sweetwater River estuary (U10) 9 February 1995 (R. Christie, B. C. Moore; Garrett and Singer 1998).

Photo by Anthony Mercieca

Red-necked Stint or Rufous-necked Sandpiper *Calidris ruficollis*

The record of a juvenile photographed in the Tijuana River valley 10 August 1980 (AB 35:226, 1981) was not accepted by the California Bird Records Committee (Roberson 1986). All nine of the species' well-supported occurrences elsewhere in California are of birds in the more easily identified adult breeding plumage.

Black-headed Gull *Larus ridibundus*

The report of one at Point Loma (S7) 23 January 1990 (AB 44:329, 1990) was not accepted by the California Bird Records Committee. Nevertheless, there are 20 well-supported winter records elsewhere in California, south to Huntington Beach, Orange County.

Photo by Anthony Mercieca

Ringed Turtle-Dove *Streptopelia risoria*

The Ringed Turtle-Dove, the domesticated form of the African Collared Dove (*S. roseogrisea*), was one of the first birds to be domesticated. It remains one of the most popular cage birds. Escapees are seen in San Diego County from time to time (two reported by atlas observers), but no nesting in the wild has been confirmed here, and no feral population has established itself anywhere in California.

Photo by Anthony Mercieca

Cockatiel *Nymphicus hollandicus*

The Cockatiel is native to Australia and very popular as a cage bird in San Diego County. Thus occasional escapees are to be expected; atlas observers reported them twice. Unlike some less-frequently held species of the Psittaciformes, the Cockatiel shows no evidence of establishing a feral population in southern California and is not confirmed to have nested here in the wild.

Budgerigar *Melopsittacus undulatus*

Native to Australia, the Budgerigar is bred commercially in captivity and known generally in America simply as the "parakeet." It has established a feral population in Florida but not in California. Atlas observers reported escapees in San Diego County twice.

Rose-ringed Parakeet *Psittacula krameri*

The Rose-ringed Parakeet, of Old World origin, is establishing itself in metropolitan Los Angeles (population at least 60, Garrett 1997) and Bakersfield (population about 500, A. Sheehey unpubl. data). In San Diego County its nesting is not yet confirmed. In spring 1998, J. A. Martin saw up to four at a communal parrot roost near Point Loma High School (R8), then no more until May 2002, after which he saw single individuals or pairs in Ocean Beach (R7) irregularly into 2004. He has seen the birds feeding on the flowers of bottlebrush and the fruits of the Canary Island date palm. An apparent pair was at Famosa Slough (R8) 15 July 2000 (A. E. Klovstad).

Moustached or Red-breasted Parakeet *Psittacula alexandri*

The Moustached Parakeet, of Asian origin, is a frequent cagebird, and one escapee was reported from Poway (M11). This species has been seen in urban areas elsewhere in southern California but has not been naturalized (Garrett 1997).

Blue-and-yellow Macaw *Ara ararauna*

Up to two were seen around Ocean Beach and Point Loma (R7/S7) from at least 1992 through February 2001 (V. P. Johnson). These represent at least three individuals, as one was found contaminated with oil and died in 1998 (B. Kenk), yet a pair was copulating, tearing pieces off a billboard, and entering a cavity behind the billboard 13 June 1999 (J. C. Worley). After 2001, a single bird remained in Ocean Beach into 2004, feeding on loquats and the fruits of other ornamental trees and associating with a captive bird kept in an outdoor yard (J. A. Martin). In summer 1992, a Blue-and-yellow Macaw hybridized with a Red-and-green Macaw (*A. chloroptera*) on Point Loma, raising one young in a cavity at the top of a dead palm tree along Hill Street (R. E. Webster, AB 46:1180, 1992). Another Blue-and-yellow showed up at Morena Village (T22; R. and S. L. Breisch); escapees of this much-loved South American species could be anywhere.

Photo by Kenneth W. Fink

Blue-crowned Parakeet *Aratinga acuticaudata*

Atlas observers reported the Blue-crowned Parakeet, a native of South America, on several occasions from Pacific Beach (Q7), Ocean Beach (R7/R8), and Point Loma (S7). The birds were often in flocks, the largest being 25 at Point Loma 9 February (J. C. Worley). From 2001 to 2004, J. A. Martin noted 4 to 20 daily in Ocean Beach, with a pair investigating a cavity in a vent on the side of a house 13 April 2001 and a pair feeding two fledglings 18 August 2001. Paul Jorgensen noted two at Borrego Springs (F24) 21 February 1999, and I saw small flocks coming repeatedly to my home in North Park (R10) in the summers of 1993 and 1994, feeding on the fruits of the Catalina cherry trees I had planted there. The Blue-crowned Parakeet may be more numerous in San Diego than in metropolitan Los Angeles, where Garrett (1997) estimated the population at less than 50 birds.

Mitred Parakeet *Aratinga mitrata*

The Mitred Parakeet is the most common naturalized conure in the Los Angeles region, where Garrett (1997) estimated a population of 680. In the Point Loma area of San Diego, however, the similar Red-masked Parakeet predominates. Atlas observers reported a maximum of only two of the Mitred, at Point Loma (S7) 13 and 20 April 1998 (V. P. Johnson). The Mitred can easily be overlooked, however, as it is entirely green except for variable, irregular, and often inconspicuous red markings on the head. The species is native to the Andes of Peru, Bolivia, and northern Argentina.

Red-masked Parakeet *Aratinga erythrogenys*

The Red-masked Parakeet, known to aviculturists as the Cherry-headed Conure, has only a small native range in southwestern Ecuador and northwestern Peru. It has become a popular cage bird, and escapees have established themselves in San Diego County in Ocean Beach (R7) and Point Loma (S7), with a pair also noted in Tecolote Canyon (Q8) 10 June 1999 (J. C. Worley).

The largest flock yet reported was 29 near Point Loma Nazarene University 9 February 2000 and 7 May 2001 (J. C. Worley, M. Billings). The species has nested probably since 1997 and definitely since 1998, when an adult was feeding two fledglings at Point Loma on 9 April (V. P. Johnson). John A. Martin saw an adult feeding a fledgling at Ocean Beach in spring 1999.

Black-hooded Parakeet or Nanday Conure *Nandayus nenday*

This South American species may be established in several areas of metropolitan Los Angeles, where Garrett (1997) estimated a population of at least 180. But in San Diego County our only sighting during the atlas period was of three in El Cajon (Q13) 17 September 1997 (D. C. Seals).

Lilac-crowned Parrot *Amazona finschi*

The status of the Lilac-crowned Parrot in San Diego County is somewhat unclear; it is reported occasionally but is easily overlooked among the more numerous Red-crowned Parrots, with which it often flocks. Sightings since 1997 have all been in the same areas where the Red-crowned Parrot concentrates, Mission Bay/Ocean Beach/Point Loma (Q7/Q8/R7/R8/S7) and El Cajon (Q13/Q14). High counts are of about 40 in a mixed roost of parrots at Point Loma High School (R8) 31 January 1998 (J. A. Martin), 12 along Lomaland Drive, Point Loma (S7), 24 May 2003 (J. C. Worley), and three in east El Cajon (Q14) 8 July 1999 (K. Neal). One was shot in Borrego Springs (F24) 3 April 1996 (SDNHM 49500). Since 1998 the Lilac-crowned has followed the same seasonal pattern in Ocean Beach as the Red-crowned (J. A. Martin). In Los Angeles as in San Diego the Red-crowned is the predominant species of *Amazona*, though in the early 1980s the Lilac-crowned was imported in greater numbers—at least the numbers imported legally known to the U.S. Fish and Wildlife Service (Garrett 1997). The Lilac-crowned Parrot

Photo by Kenneth W. Fink

is widespread in western mainland Mexico, ranging north to the southeastern corner of Sonora.

Yellow-crowned Parrot *Amazona ochrocephala*

The Yellow-headed Parrot (*Amazona oratrix*) persists in small, possibly declining numbers in Los Angeles and Orange counties, with nesting confirmed at least twice (Gallagher 1997, Garrett 1997). But in San Diego County, during the atlas period, our closest thing to a sighting of this species was one of the closely related Yellow-crowned Parrot in Poway (M12; K. J. Winter), presumably an escapee from captivity. On 4 May 2003 J. A. Martin and S. Lynn noted a free-flying Yellow-headed in Ocean Beach (R7).

Northern Pygmy-Owl *Glaucidium gnoma*

Though reported in San Diego County repeatedly, back to Sharp (1907) and Willett (1933), the Northern Pygmy-Owl has never been collected or photographed in California south of the San Bernardino Mountains. The lack of conclusive sightings of this largely diurnal species during the atlas period, when all other resident birds were observed repeatedly, convinced me that the Northern Pygmy-Owl does not occur in San Diego County. All reports are hearsay, based on poor views, or based on calls only, which can be confused easily with calls of the Northern Saw-whet Owl, Mountain Quail, or Merriam's Chipmunk. When presented with the evidence that the pygmy-owl is in fact absent from San Diego County, most of the few living observers who had claimed the species in the county readily recanted their previous claims.

Broad-tailed Hummingbird *Selasphorus platycercus*

The Broad-tailed is the common hummingbird of the Rocky Mountains, but San Diego County lies well outside its normal migration route. None of the four records is supported by a photograph or specimen, so the species' inclusion on the county's bird list is dubious. Though adult males can be identified easily if the characteristic trilled whine of their wings is heard, there is plenty of opportunity for misidentification of this species, as with all hummingbirds.

Guy McCaskie now questions his report of a male in the Tijuana River valley 8 September 1968 (AFN 23:109, 1969). Other published records are of a male attracted to red balloons at a birthday party near the Palomar Observatory (D15) 11–12 July 1978 (R. Higson, AB 33:218, 1969), a male at Point Loma (S7) 14 September 1982 (R. E. Webster, AB 37:224, 1983), and a female at Point Loma 10 May 1986 (R. E. Webster, AB 40:524, 1986).

Black-throated Magpie-Jay *Calocitta colliei*

William E. Haas

A creature that could have sprung from the mind of Dr. Seuss, this bizarre long-tailed corvid is establishing itself in riparian woodlands in southwestern San Diego County. The Black-throated Magpie-Jay is endemic to mainland Mexico, residing in open deciduous woodlands at low elevations of the Pacific slope from southern Sonora to northern Jalisco. Its occurrence in San Diego County is not natural but the result of the pet trade in nearby Tijuana, where the species is popular (Hamilton 2001). The species is kept in aviaries in San Diego County as well; escapees from these presumably account for sightings in northern San Diego County.

Photo by Anthony Mercieca

Breeding distribution: The Black-throated Magpie-Jay nested successfully at two locations during the atlas period, both in the Tijuana River valley (W10). The first nesting was by a group of three in Goat Canyon in 2000; they continued through 2002. Drought then killed the willow trees in which the birds had nested; after the trees fell, the family moved a short distance east to Smuggler Gulch. A different pair has nested successfully along the Tijuana River just west of Hollister Street since 2001, shifting to a new tree annually (W. E. Haas). At least two Black-throated Magpie-Jays have remained along the Sweetwater River near the Plaza Bonita shopping mall, Bonita (T11), since 1997 (P. Famolaro). They were first confirmed nesting there in 2002, fledging two young (W. E. Haas).

Black-throated Magpie-Jays seen at Jamul (S15) in 2000 and at Point Loma (S7) in 1999 and 2000 (P. A. Ginsburg, S. E. Smith) were probably escapees from local aviaries, although the possibility that these were dispersing individuals from Bonita or the Tijuana River valley should not be dismissed. The species is becoming popular in private collections in the United States as well as in Mexico. Since 2002, I have noted captive magpie-jays at several San Diego County locations, including Jamul, Escondido, and Fallbrook.

Nesting: Typical of the family Corvidae, Black-throated Magpie-Jays build untidy, bulky nests of twigs lined with mosses and lichens. They nest socially, all adults in the family group contributing to the gathering of nest material and nest building. The breeding female then

rearranges the material to her liking. In 2000 the Goat Canyon family had one helper and raised two fledglings; in 2001 it had three helpers and raised three fledglings. Helpers, however, are not necessary to nest success—the Tijuana River clan, which fledged two offspring in 2001, consisted of just a pair.

All nests (Goat Canyon 2000–2001; Tijuana River 2001; Bonita 2002) were in arroyo willows between 5 and 10 meters above the ground. Nests required almost a month to build; building proceeded slowly at first, then the rate increased gradually to completion, presumably through the time the female was ready to lay. For three nests observed, the incubation period lasted approximately 18–20 days. The female rarely left the nest, even when her mate and any helpers approached and fed her.

The nesting season in San Diego County extends from March to July, although breeding records from Mexico suggest the species may breed from November to July (Howell and Webb 1995). The two periods follow seasonal rains respective to each area.

Winter: San Diego County's Black-throated Magpie-Jays move only short distances from their breeding habitat to feed in nearby agricultural fields and residential neighborhoods. Winter records during the atlas period all come from the vicinity of breeding sites, with up to four in Bonita 15 December 2001 (J. A. Martin) and eight in the southwest quadrant of the Tijuana River Valley the same day (G. L. Rogers). Guy McCaskie has noted groups of up to 10 foraging in backyard fruit trees in Imperial Beach (V10), about 1.5 miles from the nearest nest.

Conservation: Despite its attractive appearance and intriguing behaviors, the Black-throated Magpie-Jay is an exotic species. Its behavior to date does not suggest that it is becoming an invasive pest. Corvids, however, are notoriously hardy and have the potential to wreak havoc on agriculture. They are important nest predators of native passerines. And they are the primary carriers of the West Nile virus. The Black-throated Magpie-Jay could thus affect native riparian birds, especially the endangered Least Bell's Vireo, for which the Tijuana River valley is now a major population center. The magpie-jay's potential to increase is exemplified by the survivorship of the Goat Canyon clan—all individuals fledged from 2000 to 2002 persisted through 2003.

Taxonomy: There are two magpie-jays in the genus *Calocitta*, the Black-throated and the White-throated (*C. formosa*). Although they have sometimes been considered conspecific (e.g., Blake and Vaurie 1962), studies of mitochondrial DNA suggest they are separate species (Saunders and Edwards 2000).

Green Jay *Cyanocorax yncas*

Yet another Mexican corvid seen occasionally as an escapee in San Diego County is the Green Jay. For example, one was in La Mesa (R12) 21 January 2002 (J. Spain).

Purplish-backed or Beechey's Jay *Cyanocorax beecheii*

Originating from western mainland Mexico, this black-and-blue jay with a golden eye is seen occasionally in the Tijuana River valley. Like the Black-throated Magpie-Jay, it undoubtedly arrived as a cage bird escaping in Tijuana, then flying across the border. Free-flying Purplish-backed Jays have been seen in Tijuana at Parque Morelos (M. A. Patten). Unlike the magpie-jay, it is not known to have nested on the U.S. side, though two were together along the Tijuana River (W11) 8 December 1998 (P. Unitt). The similar San Blas Jay (*Cyanocorax sanblasianus*), another Mexican species, may also occur there as an escapee.

Photo by Kenneth W. Fink

Gray Silky-flycatcher *Ptilogonys cinereus*

The Gray Silky-flycatcher resides in the mountains of Mexico and Guatemala, ranging no farther northwest than southeastern Sonora. Sightings in southern California presumably represent escapees from captivity, especially since some have appeared ragged from cage wear. The species is sold in Baja California (Hamilton 2001, pers. obs.), and there are no acceptable records from Arizona. From San Diego County, the California Bird Records Committee has received one report from Poway (M11/M12; 10–12 March 1994, Howell and Pyle 1997) and three from Point Loma (S7; 4 June 1983, Rottenborn and Morlan 2000; 24 May 1993, McCaskie and San Miguel 1999; 16 June 1999, Rogers and Jaramillo 2002). Supposing there is some chance the species could reach California as a natural vagrant, the committee has included the Gray Silky-flycatcher on its "supplemental list" (Rogers and Jaramillo 2002).

Oriental White-eye *Zosterops palpebrosus*

In the early 1980s this Asian species multiplied in San Diego after several escaped from the San Diego Zoo. But the county department of agriculture considered them a prospective pest and exterminated them in 1983.

White-collared Seedeater *Sporophila torqueola*

The White-collared Seedeater occurs primarily in Central America and mainland Mexico, north on the Pacific side only to Sinaloa. It is a frequent cage bird in Baja California (Hamilton 2001), and escapees flying across the border presumably account for the repeated sightings in the Tijuana River valley (V11/W11). The birds have not yet been reported nesting there, but up to three individuals have been seen, as on 9 December 2001 (G. McCaskie). The White-collared Seedeaters seen in the Tijuana River valley are of the west Mexican subspecies *torqueola* or *atriceps*, in which the males are more boldly patterned in black, white, and buff than in the northeast Mexican subspecies *sharpei*, the subspecies reaching southern Texas and illustrated in North American field guides.

Northern Cardinal *Cardinalis cardinalis*

The cardinal reaches San Diego County not from the east but from the south—as an escapee from captivity, flying across the border. Hamilton (2001) found it to be one of the most commonly sold cagebirds in northern Baja California. Since the mid 1990s, the cardinal has established itself as an uncommon resident in the Tijuana River valley, nesting successfully (e.g., adults feeding young in Goat Canyon, W10, 23 May 2000, W. E. Haas). Our highest counts were of no more than two per day, but several pairs may be scattered through the valley. We also noted the species on six occasions elsewhere in the county, north to Valley Center (G11; V. Dineen). There is no evidence of the small population of the eastern subspecies established in Los Angeles County spreading south.

One specimen, a male from eastern Otay Mesa (V14)

11 December 2000 (SDNHM 50492), is either *C. c. seftoni*, native to central Baja California, or *C. c. affinis*, native to western mainland Mexico from southern Sonora south through Sinaloa. The pattern of black on the face and gray edges on the feathers of the back match the subspecies of western Mexico and the southwestern United States. It is too small (wing 96 mm, tail 110 mm) for *superbus* of Arizona and does not have the bill as bulbous as in *igneus* of southern Baja California. How *seftoni* and *affinis* may differ is not clear; Huey (1940) did not compare them in his original description of *seftoni*. In any case, the bird's subspecies confirms an origin in Mexico. This individual must have escaped just before being picked up by an agent of the Border Patrol; the plumage was still spattered with excrement.

Black-backed Oriole *Icterus abeillei*

One was in Smuggler's Gulch, Tijuana River valley (W10), 9 April–1 July 2000, 28 April–4 July 2001, and 2–13 January 2002, at least (J. E. Hunter, Garrett and Wilson 2003). The species is endemic to central Mexico, ranging north only to central Durango. Although Hamilton (2001) did not find it being sold as a cage bird in northern Baja California, he did see other orioles for sale. Most likely the

bird escaped from captivity in Tijuana and flew across the border; its site in Smuggler's Gulch is less than a half mile north of the line. Nevertheless, the California Bird Records Committee expressed some ambivalence about the bird's origin by placing the Black-backed Oriole on its "supplemental list" with other species given some small chance of reaching the state unaided (Cole and McCaskie 2004).

Orange Bishop *Euplectes franciscanus*

The Orange Bishop, a cage bird of African origin, is establishing itself in flood-control basins and along the concrete-lined rivers of the Los Angeles region. By the late 1990s it was occurring in flocks of up to 100 birds (Garrett 1998). The species has colonized Phoenix, Arizona, as well, nesting in cattails and feeding on the exotic Johnson grass (Gatz 2001). In San Diego County the first report was from Agua Hedionda Lagoon (I6) 8 September 1999 (R. Gransbury). Since then, a few individuals have been

seen at scattered locations in the coastal lowland. So far the only site with more than one report and more than one individual is Famosa Slough (R8), with two on 30 August 2003 (B. J. Peugh). When in breeding plumage the male Orange Bishop can be confused only with other species of the genus *Euplectes*; the sparrowlike striped female may be confusing but differs from any North American species by its pinkish bill. For more details, see Garrett (1998).

Nutmeg Mannikin *Lonchura punctulata*

Long a popular cage bird, the Nutmeg Mannikin is becoming naturalized in southern California. By the beginning of the 21st century it was locally common in Los Angeles and Orange counties (Garrett 2000). But in San Diego County sightings to date have been only sporadic. Nesting is possible in the Tijuana River valley (V11), where the species has been seen repeatedly since at least December 1999 (up to six on 30 December 1999, G. McCaskie), and probable in Tecolote Canyon (Q8), where the species occurred

regularly at least from June 1999 to February 2002 (up to eight, including five immatures, on 17 February 2002, H. E. Stone). Atlas observers reported single individuals from Fallbrook (E8), the upper end of Lake Hodges (K11), and San Elijo Lagoon (L7). This member of the family Estrildidae is native from India east and south to the Philippines and Indonesia. The adult is easily recognized by the fine scaly pattern on its breast and belly; for identification of the plain brown juvenile, see Garrett (2000).

Appendix 1

Species and Subspecies of San Diego County Birds

This list includes all birds occurring in San Diego County naturally plus well-established nonnative species. Birds covered in the species accounts under Exotic and Hypothetical Species are excluded. The total is 493 species, including the Cackling Goose, distinguished at the species level from the Canada Goose by the American Ornithologists' Union Check-list Committee in 2004, a decision made too late to be reflected in the species account for the Canada Goose. The list includes 87 additional subspecies for a total of 580 taxa of birds known from San Diego County. Subspecies enclosed in brackets are inferred, not based on identification of specimens or characteristics discernable in the field. English names for subspecies are not standardized and drawn from various sources.

Breeding status: B, breeding confirmed; B*, breeding confirmed only before 1997 (sporadically breeding or extirpated species); P, breeding probable or possible; I, introduced (not native).

Regulatory status (as of 2004): E, endangered; T, threatened; SC, species of special concern; 1, first priority; 2, second priority; 3, third priority; US, U. S. Fish and Wildlife Service; CA, California Department of Fish and Game.

Documentation: SDNHM, specimen perseved in San Diego Natural History Museum. If a specimen has been preserved only in another museum, that museum is cited. CSULB, California State University, Long Beach; DEL, Delaware Museum of Natural History, Greenville; FMNH, Field Museum of Natural History, Chicago; LACM, Natural History Museum of Los Angeles County, Los Angeles; MVZ, Museum of Vertebrate Zoology, University of California, Los Angeles; SBCM, San Bernardino County Museum, Redlands; UCLA, University of California, Los Angeles; UMMZ, University of Michigan Museum of Zoology, Ann Arbor; USNM, National Museum of Natural History, Smithsonian Institution, Washington, D. C.; WFVZ, Western Foundation of Vertebrate Zoology, Camarillo; ph., photograph; ph.*, photograph published in this atlas; sr, sight record only.

		Breeding status	Regulatory status	Documentation
Family Anatidae				
Fulvous Whistling Duck	*Dendrocygna bicolor*	B*	SC1 (CA)	SDNHM
Greater White-fronted Goose	*Anser albifrons frontalis*			SDNHM
Snow Goose	*Chen caerulescens caerulescens*			SDNHM
Ross's Goose	*Chen rossii*			SDNHM
Brant	*Branta bernicla*			
Black Brant	*B. b. nigricans*		SC3 (CA)	SDNHM
Atlantic Brant	*B. b. hrota*			sr
Canada Goose	*Branta canadensis moffitti*	B		SDNHM
Cackling Goose	*Branta hutchinsii*			
Cackling Goose	*B. h. minima*			SDNHM
Aleutian Cackling Goose	*B. h. leucopareia*			ph.
Tundra Swan	*Cygnus columbianus columbianus*			SDNHM
Wood Duck	*Aix sponsa*	B		SDNHM
Gadwall	*Anas strepera strepera*	B		SDNHM
Eurasian Wigeon	*Anas penelope*			ph.
American Wigeon	*Anas americana*			SDNHM
Mallard	*Anas platyrhynchos platyrhynchos*	B		SDNHM
Blue-winged Teal	*Anas discors*			FMNH, LACM
Cinnamon Teal	*Anas cyanoptera septentrionalium*	B		SDNHM
Northern Shoveler	*Anas clypeata*	B*		SDNHM
Northern Pintail	*Anas acuta*	P, B*		SDNHM
Green-winged Teal	*Anas crecca*			
American Green-winged Teal	*A. c. carolinensis*	B*		SDNHM
Eurasian Green-winged Teal	*A. c. crecca*			ph.
Canvasback	*Aythya valisineria*			SDNHM
Redhead	*Aythya americana*	B	SC2 (CA)	SDNHM
Ring-necked Duck	*Aythya collaris*			SDNHM
Tufted Duck	*Aythya fuligula*			ph.*
Greater Scaup	*Aythya marila nearctica*			SDNHM
Lesser Scaup	*Aythya affinis*			SDNHM
King Eider	*Somateria spectabilis*			ph.*

(continued)

		Breeding status	Regulatory status	Documentation
Harlequin Duck	*Histrionicus histrionicus*		SC1 (CA)	ph.*
Surf Scoter	*Melanitta perspicillata*			SDNHM
White-winged Scoter	*Melanitta fusca deglandi*			SDNHM
Black Scoter	*Melanitta nigra americana*			ph.
Long-tailed Duck	*Clangula hyemalis*			SDNHM
Bufflehead	*Bucephala albeola*			SDNHM
Common Goldeneye	*Bucephala clangula americana*			SDNHM
Barrow's Goldeneye	*Bucephala islandica*		SC (CA)	sr
Hooded Merganser	*Lophodytes cucullatus*			SDNHM
Common Merganser	*Mergus merganser americanus*			SDNHM
Red-breasted Merganser	*Mergus serrator*			SDNHM
Ruddy Duck	*Oxyura jamaicensis rubida*	B		SDNHM
Family Phasianidae				
Ring-necked Pheasant	*Phasianus colchicus*	IP		SDNHM
Wild Turkey	*Meleagris gallopavo*	IB		SDNHM
Family Odontophoridae				
Mountain Quail	*Oreortyx pictus confinis*	B		SDNHM
California Quail	*Callipepla californica californica*	B		SDNHM
Gambel's Quail	*Callipepla gambelii gambelii*	B		SDNHM
Family Gaviidae				
Red-throated Loon	*Gavia stellata*			SDNHM
Pacific Loon	*Gavia pacifica*			SDNHM
Common Loon	*Gavia immer*		SC (CA)	SDNHM
Family Podicipedidae				
Pied-billed Grebe	*Podilymbus podiceps podiceps*	B		SDNHM
Horned Grebe	*Podiceps auritus*			SDNHM
Red-necked Grebe	*Podiceps grisegena [holboellii]*			sr
Eared Grebe	*Podiceps nigricollis californicus*	B		SDNHM
Western Grebe	*Aechmophorus occidentalis occidentalis*	B		SDNHM
Clark's Grebe	*Aechmophorus clarkii transitionalis*	B		SDNHM
Family Diomedeidae				
Laysan Albatross	*Phoebastria immutabilis*			SDNHM
Black-footed Albatross	*Phoebastria nigripes*			SDNHM
Short-tailed Albatross	*Phoebastria albatrus*		E (US), SC (CA)	SDNHM
Family Procellariidae				
Northern Fulmar	*Fulmarus glacialis rodgersii*			SDNHM
Cook's Petrel	*Pterodroma cookii*			sr
Pink-footed Shearwater	*Puffinus creatopus*			SDNHM
Flesh-footed Shearwater	*Puffinus carneipes*			SBCM
Buller's Shearwater	*Puffinus bulleri*			SDNHM
Sooty Shearwater	*Puffinus griseus*			SDNHM
Short-tailed Shearwater	*Puffinus tenuirostris*			SDNHM
Manx Shearwater	*Puffinus puffinus*			sr
Black-vented Shearwater	*Puffinus opisthomelas*			SDNHM
Family Oceanitidae or Hydrobatidae				
Wilson's Storm-Petrel	*Oceanites oceanicus* ssp.?			UCLA
Fork-tailed Storm-Petrel	*Oceanodroma furcata plumbea*		SC1 (CA)	SDNHM
Leach's Storm-Petrel	*Oceanodroma leucorhoa leucorhoa <> chapmani*			SDNHM
Ashy Storm-Petrel	*Oceanodroma homochroa*		SC2 (CA)	SDNHM
Black Storm-Petrel	*Oceanodroma melania*		SC3 (CA)	SDNHM
Least Storm-Petrel	*Oceanodroma microsoma*			SDNHM
Family Phaethontidae				
Red-billed Tropicbird	*Phaethon aethereus mesonauta*			SDNHM
Family Sulidae				
Masked Booby	*Sula dactylatra* ssp.			ph.*
Blue-footed Booby	*Sula nebouxii nebouxii*			SDNHM
Brown Booby	*Sula leucogaster brewsteri*			SDNHM
Red-footed Booby	*Sula sula* ssp.			ph.
Family Pelecanidae				
American White Pelican	*Pelecanus erythrorhynchos*		SC1 (CA)	SDNHM
Brown Pelican	*Pelecanus occidentalis californicus*		E (US, CA)	SDNHM
Family Phalacrocoracidae				
Brandt's Cormorant	*Phalacrocorax penicillatus*	B		SDNHM
Double-crested Cormorant	*Phalacrocorax auritus albociliatus*	B		SDNHM
Pelagic Cormorant	*Phalacrocorax pelagicus resplendens*			SDNHM

		Breeding status	Regulatory status	Documentation
Family Anhingidae				
Anhinga	*Anhinga anhinga [leucogaster]*			ph.
Family Fregatidae				
Magnificent Frigatebird	*Fregata magnificens*			SDNHM
Family Ardeidae				
American Bittern	*Botaurus lentiginosus*	B		SDNHM
Least Bittern	*Ixobrychus exilis exilis*	B	SC3 (CA)	SDNHM
Great Blue Heron	*Ardea herodias wardi*	B		SDNHM
Great Egret	*Ardea alba egretta*	B		SDNHM
Snowy Egret	*Egretta thula candidissima*	B		SDNHM
Little Blue Heron	*Egretta caerulea*	B		SDNHM
Tricolored Heron	*Egretta tricolor ruficollis*			SDNHM
Reddish Egret	*Egretta rufescens [dickeyi]*			SDNHM
Cattle Egret	*Bubulcus ibis ibis*	B		SDNHM
Green Heron	*Butorides virescens anthonyi*	B		SDNHM
Black-crowned Night-Heron	*Nycticorax nycticorax hoactli*	B		SDNHM
Yellow-crowned Night-Heron	*Nyctanassa violacea bancrofti*			SDNHM
Family Plataleidae or Threskiornithidae				
White Ibis	*Eudocimus albus*			SDNHM
White-faced Ibis	*Plegadis chihi*	B		SDNHM
Roseate Spoonbill	*Platalea ajaja*			sr
Family Ciconiidae				
Wood Stork	*Mycteria americana*		SC1 (CA)	SDNHM
Family Vulturidae or Cathartidae				
Turkey Vulture	*Cathartes aura meridionalis*	B		SDNHM
California Condor	*Gymnogyps californianus*	B*	E (US, CA)	SDNHM
Family Accipitridae				
Osprey	*Pandion haliaetus carolinensis*	B		SDNHM
White-tailed Kite	*Elanus leucurus majusculus*	B		SDNHM
Mississippi Kite	*Ictinia mississippiensis*			ph.
Bald Eagle	*Haliaeetus leucocephalus alascanus*			
Northern Bald Eagle	*H. l. alascanus*		E (CA), T (US)	MVZ
Southern Bald Eagle	*H. l. leucocephalus*	B*	E (CA), T (US)	WFVZ (eggs)
Northern Harrier	*Circus cyaneus hudsonius*	B	SC2 (CA)	SDNHM
Sharp-shinned Hawk	*Accipiter striatus velox*			SDNHM
Cooper's Hawk	*Accipiter cooperii*	B		SDNHM
Northern Goshawk	*Accipiter gentilis atricapillus*	B*	SC3 (CA)	SDNHM
Harris's Hawk	*Parabuteo unicinctus harrisi*	B	SC2 (CA)	SDNHM
Red-shouldered Hawk	*Buteo lineatus elegans*	B		SDNHM
Broad-winged Hawk	*Buteo platypterus platypterus*			SDNHM
Swainson's Hawk	*Buteo swainsoni*	B*	T (CA)	SDNHM
Zone-tailed Hawk	*Buteo albonotatus*			SDNHM
Red-tailed Hawk	*Buteo jamaicensis*			
Western Red-tailed Hawk	*B. j. calurus*	B		SDNHM
Fuertes' Red-tailed Hawk	*B. j. fuertesi*			SDNHM
Harlan's Hawk	*B. j. harlani*			sr
Ferruginous Hawk	*Buteo regalis*			SDNHM
Rough-legged Hawk	*Buteo lagopus [sanctijohannis]*			sr
Golden Eagle	*Aquila chrysaetos canadensis*	B		SDNHM
Family Falconidae				
American Kestrel	*Falco sparverius sparverius*	B		SDNHM
Merlin	*Falco columbarius*			
Taiga Merlin	*F. c. columbarius*			SDNHM
Richardson's or Prairie Merlin	*F. c. richardsoni*			SDNHM
Black Merlin	*F. c. suckleyi*			SDNHM
Peregrine Falcon	*Falco peregrinus*			
American Peregrine Falcon	*F. p. anatum*	B	E (CA)	SDNHM
Peale's Peregrine Falcon	*F. p. pealei*			SDNHM
Prairie Falcon	*Falco mexicanus*	B	SC3 (CA)	SDNHM
Family Rallidae				
Yellow Rail	*Coturnicops noveboracensis*		SC2 (CA)	SDNHM
Black Rail	*Laterallus jamaicensis coturniculus*	B*	T (CA)	SDNHM
Clapper Rail	*Rallus longirostris levipes*	B	E (US, CA)	SDNHM

(continued)

		Breeding status	Regulatory status	Documentation
Virginia Rail	*Rallus limicola*	B		SDNHM
Sora	*Porzana carolina*	B*		SDNHM
Purple Gallinule	*Porphyrio martinica*			SDNHM
Common Gallinule or Moorhen	*Gallinula chloropus cachinnans*	B		SDNHM
American Coot	*Fulica americana americana*	B		SDNHM
Family Gruidae				
Sandhill Crane	*Grus canadensis* ssp.?			sr
Family Charadriidae				
Black-bellied Plover	*Pluvialis squatarola*			SDNHM
American Golden-Plover	*Pluvialis dominica*			SDNHM
Pacific Golden-Plover	*Pluvialis fulva*			sr
Snowy Plover	*Charadrius alexandrinus nivosus*	B	T (US), SC (CA)	SDNHM
Wilson's Plover	*Charadrius wilsonia beldingi*			MVZ
Semipalmated Plover	*Charadrius semipalmatus*			SDNHM
Killdeer	*Charadrius vociferus vociferus*	B		SDNHM
Mountain Plover	*Charadrius montanus*		SC1 (CA)	SDNHM
Family Haematopodidae				
American Oystercatcher	*Haematopus palliatus frazari*			MVZ
Black Oystercatcher	*Haematopus bachmani*	P		SDNHM
Family Recurvirostridae				
Black-necked Stilt	*Himantopus mexicanus mexicanus*	B		SDNHM
American Avocet	*Recurvirostra americana*	B		SDNHM
Family Scolopacidae				
Greater Yellowlegs	*Tringa melanoleuca*			SDNHM
Lesser Yellowlegs	*Tringa flavipes*			SDNHM
Spotted Redshank	*Tringa erythropus*			ph.
Solitary Sandpiper	*Tringa solitaria cinnamomea*			SDNHM
Willet	*Catoptrophorus semipalmatus inornatus*			SDNHM
Wandering Tattler	*Heteroscelus incanus*			SDNHM
Spotted Sandpiper	*Actitis macularius*	B		SDNHM
Upland Sandpiper	*Bartramia longicauda*			ph.*
Whimbrel	*Numenius phaeopus hudsonicus*			SDNHM
Long-billed Curlew	*Numenius americanus*			SDNHM
Bar-tailed Godwit	*Limosa lapponica*			ph.*
Marbled Godwit	*Limosa fedoa fedoa*			SDNHM
Ruddy Turnstone	*Arenaria interpres interpres*			SDNHM
Black Turnstone	*Arenaria melanocephala*			SDNHM
Surfbird	*Aphriza virgata*			SDNHM
Red Knot	*Calidris canutus roselaari*			SDNHM
Sanderling	*Calidris alba*			SDNHM
Semipalmated Sandpiper	*Calidris pusilla*			ph.
Western Sandpiper	*Calidris mauri*			SDNHM
Least Sandpiper	*Calidris minutilla*			SDNHM
Baird's Sandpiper	*Calidris bairdii*			FMNH
Pectoral Sandpiper	*Calidris melanotos*			SDNHM
Sharp-tailed Sandpiper	*Calidris acuminata*			SDNHM
Dunlin	*Calidris alpina pacifica*			SDNHM
Curlew Sandpiper	*Calidris ferruginea*			ph.
Stilt Sandpiper	*Calidris himantopus*			ph.
Buff-breasted Sandpiper	*Tryngites subruficollis*			ph.*
Ruff	*Philomachus pugnax*			SDNHM
Short-billed Dowitcher	*Limnodromus griseus*			
Pacific Short-billed Dowitcher	*L. g. caurinus*			SDNHM
Inland or Prairie Short-billed Dowitcher	*L. g. hendersoni*			SDNHM
Long-billed Dowitcher	*Limnodromus scolopaceus*			SDNHM
Wilson's Snipe	*Gallinago delicata*			SDNHM
Wilson's Phalarope	*Phalaropus tricolor*			SDNHM
Red-necked Phalarope	*Phalaropus lobatus*			SDNHM
Red Phalarope	*Phalaropus fulicarius*			SDNHM
Family Laridae				
South Polar Skua	*Stercorarius maccormicki*			CSULB
Pomarine Jaeger	*Stercorarius pomarinus*			SDNHM
Parasitic Jaeger	*Stercorarius parasiticus*			SDNHM
Long-tailed Jaeger	*Stercorarius longicaudus*			SDNHM
Laughing Gull	*Larus atricilla*			ph.

Franklin's Gull	*Larus pipixcan*			SDNHM
Little Gull	*Larus minutus*			SDNHM
Bonaparte's Gull	*Larus philadelphia*			SDNHM
Heermann's Gull	*Larus heermanni*			SDNHM
Belcher's Gull	*Larus belcheri*			ph.*
Black-tailed Gull	*Larus crassirostris*			UMMZ
Mew Gull	*Larus canus brachyrhynchus*			SDNHM
Ring-billed Gull	*Larus delawarensis*			SDNHM
California Gull	*Larus californicus californicus*			
California Gull	*L. c. californicus*			SDNHM
Alberta Gull	*L. c. albertaensis*			SDNI IM
Herring Gull	*Larus argentatus smithsonianus*			SDNHM
Thayer's Gull	*Larus thayeri*			SDNHM
Iceland Gull	*Larus glaucoides* ssp.?			ph.
Lesser Black-backed Gull	*Larus fuscus graellsii*			ph.*
Yellow-footed Gull	*Larus livens*			SDNHM
Western Gull	*Larus occidentalis*			
Southern Western Gull	*L. o. wymani*	B		SDNHM
Northern Western Gull	*L. o. occidentalis*			SDNHM
Glaucous-winged Gull	*Larus glaucescens*			SDNHM
Glaucous Gull	*Larus hyperboreus barrovianus*			SDNHM
Sabine's Gull	*Xema sabini*			SDNHM
Black-legged Kittiwake	*Rissa tridactyla pollicaris*			SDNHM
Gull-billed Tern	*Sterna nilotica vanrossemi*	B	SC1 (CA)	SDNHM
Caspian Tern	*Sterna caspia*	B		SDNHM
Royal Tern	*Sterna maxima maxima*	B	SC3 (CA)	SDNHM
Elegant Tern	*Sterna elegans*	B	SC3 (CA)	SDNHM
Sandwich Tern	*Sterna sandvicensis* [*acuflavida*]			ph.
Common Tern	*Sterna hirundo hirundo*			SDNHM
Arctic Tern	*Sterna paradisaea*			SDNHM
Forster's Tern	*Sterna forsteri*	B		SDNHM
Least Tern	*Sterna antillarum browni*	B	E (US, CA)	SDNHM
Sooty Tern	*Sterna fuscata* [*crissalis*]	B		SDNHM
Black Tern	*Chlidonias niger surinamensis*		SC3 (CA)	SDNHM
Black Skimmer	*Rynchops niger niger*	B	SC3 (CA)	SDNHM
Family Alcidae				
Common Murre	*Uria aalge californica*			SDNHM
Pigeon Guillemot	*Cepphus columba eureka*			SDNHM
Marbled Murrelet	*Brachyramphus marmoratus*		E (CA), T (US)	ph.
Kittlitz's Murrelet	*Brachyramphus brevirostris*			SDNHM
Xantus's Murrelet	*Synthliboramphus hypoleucus*		SC2 (CA)	
Northern Xantus's Murrelet	*S. h. scrippsi*			SDNHM
Guadalupe Xantus's Murrelet	*S. h. hypoleucus*			SDNHM
Craveri's Murrelet	*Synthliboramphus craveri*			SDNHM
Ancient Murrelet	*Synthliboramphus antiquus*			SDNHM
Cassin's Auklet	*Ptychoramphus aleuticus aleuticus*		SC2 (CA)	SDNHM
Parakeet Auklet	*Aethia psittacula*			USNM
Rhinoceros Auklet	*Cerorhinca monocerata*			SDNHM
Horned Puffin	*Fratercula corniculata*			SDNHM
Tufted Puffin	*Fratercula cirrhata*			SDNHM
Family Columbidae				
Rock Pigeon	*Columba livia*	IB		SDNHM
Band-tailed Pigeon	*Patagioenas fasciata monilis*	B		SDNHM
Eurasian Collared-Dove	*Streptopelia decaocto*	I		sr
Spotted Dove	*Streptopelia chinensis*	IB*		SDNHM
White-winged Dove	*Zenaida asiatica mearnsi*	B		SDNHM
Mourning Dove	*Zenaida macroura marginella*	B		SDNHM
Inca Dove	*Columbina inca*			ph.*
Common Ground-Dove	*Columbina passerina pallescens*	B		SDNHM
Ruddy Ground-Dove	*Columbina talpacoti* [*eluta*]			ph.
Family Psittacidae				
Red-crowned Parrot	*Amazona viridigenalis*	IB		ph.
Family Cuculidae				
Yellow-billed Cuckoo	*Coccyzus americanus*	B*	E (CA)	SDNHM
Greater Roadrunner	*Geococcyx californianus*	B		SDNHM
Family Tytonidae				
Barn Owl	*Tyto alba pratincola*	B		SDNHM

(continued)

		Breeding status	Regulatory status	Documentation
Family Strigidae				
Flammulated Owl	*Otus flammeolus*	P		SDNHM
Western Screech-Owl	*Megascops kennicottii bendirei*	B		SDNHM
Great Horned Owl	*Bubo virginianus*			
Pacific Horned Owl	*B. b. pacificus*	B		SDNHM
Pallid Horned Owl	*B. b. pallescens*	B		SDNHM
Burrowing Owl	*Athene cunicularia hypugaea*	B		SDNHM
Spotted Owl	*Strix occidentalis occidentalis*	B	SC3 (CA)	SDNHM
Long-eared Owl	*Asio otus wilsonianus*	B	SC2 (CA)	SDNHM
Short-eared Owl	*Asio flammeus flammeus*	B*	SC2 (CA)	SDNHM
Northern Saw-whet Owl	*Aegolius acadicus acadicus*	B		SDNHM
Family Caprimulgidae				
Lesser Nighthawk	*Chordeiles acutipennis texensis*	B		SDNHM
Common Nighthawk	*Chordeiles minor* ssp.			sr
Common Poorwill	*Phalaenoptilus nuttallii*			
Dusky Poorwill	*P. n. californicus*	B		SDNHM
Nuttall's Poorwill	*P. n. nuttallii*	P		SDNHM
Whip-poor-will	*Caprimulgus vociferus vociferus*			ph.
Family Apodidae				
Black Swift	*Cypseloides niger borealis*			MVZ
Chimney Swift	*Chaetura pelagica*			SDNHM
Vaux's Swift	*Chaetura vauxi vauxi*		SC3 (CA)	SDNHM
White-throated Swift	*Aeronautes saxatalis saxatalis*	B		SDNHM
Family Trochilidae				
Broad-billed Hummingbird	*Cynanthus latirostris [magicus]*			ph.
Xantus's Hummingbird	*Hylocharis xantusii*			sr
Violet-crowned Hummingbird	*Amazilia violiceps [ellioti]*			ph.*
Magnificent Hummingbird	*Eugenes fulgens*			ph.*
Black-chinned Hummingbird	*Archilochus alexandri*	B		SDNHM
Anna's Hummingbird	*Calypte anna*	B		SDNHM
Costa's Hummingbird	*Calypte costae*	B		SDNHM
Calliope Hummingbird	*Stellula calliope*	P		SDNHM
Rufous Hummingbird	*Selasphorus rufus*			SDNHM
Allen's Hummingbird	*Selasphorus sasin*			
Migratory Allen's Hummingbird	*S. s. sasin*			SDNHM
Nonmigratory Allen's Hummingbird	*S. s. sedentarius*	B		SDNHM
Family Alcedinidae				
Belted Kingfisher	*Ceryle alcyon*	B		SDNHM
Family Picidae				
Lewis's Woodpecker	*Melanerpes lewis*			SDNHM
Acorn Woodpecker	*Melanerpes formicivorus bairdi*	B		SDNHM
Gila Woodpecker	*Melanerpes uropygialis [uropygialis]*		E (CA)	ph.
Williamson's Sapsucker	*Sphyrapicus thyroideus*			ph.*
Yellow-bellied Sapsucker	*Sphyrapicus varius*			sr
Red-naped Sapsucker	*Sphyrapicus nuchalis*			SDNHM
Red-breasted Sapsucker	*Sphyrapicus ruber*			
Sierra Red-breasted Sapsucker	*S. r. daggetti*	B		SDNHM
Northwestern Red-breasted Sapsucker	*S. r. ruber*			SDNHM
Ladder-backed Woodpecker	*Picoides scalaris cactophilus*	B		SDNHM
Nuttall's Woodpecker	*Picoides nuttallii*	B		SDNHM
Downy Woodpecker	*Picoides pubescens turati*	B		SDNHM
Hairy Woodpecker	*Picoides villosus*			
Cabanis' Hairy Woodpecker	*P. v. hyloscopus*	B		SDNHM
Modoc Hairy Woodpecker	*P. v. orius*			SDNHM
White-headed Woodpecker	*Picoides albolarvatus gravirostris*	B		SDNHM
Northern Flicker	*Colaptes auratus*			
Monterey Red-shafted Flicker	*C. a. collaris*	B		SDNHM
Interior Red-shafted Flicker	*C. a. canescens*			SDNHM
Northern Yellow-shafted Flicker	*C. a. luteus*			SDNHM
Family Tyrannidae				
Olive-sided Flycatcher	*Contopus cooperi*			
Greater Olive-sided Flycatcher	*C. c. majorinus*	B	SC2 (CA)	SDNHM
Lesser Olive-sided Flycatcher	*C. c. cooperi*		SC2 (CA)	SDNHM
Greater Pewee	*Contopus pertinax [pallidiventris]*			ph.

Common name	Scientific name			
Western Wood-Pewee	*Contopus sordidulus*			
Western Wood-Pewee	*C. s. veliei*	B		SDNHM
Alaska Wood-Pewee	*C. s. saturatus*			SDNHM
Yellow-bellied Flycatcher	*Empidonax flaviventris*			ph.*
Willow Flycatcher	*Empidonax traillii*			
Southwestern Willow Flycatcher	*E. t. extimus*	B	E (US, CA)	SDNHM
Northwestern Willow Flycatcher	*E. t. brewsteri*		E (CA)	SDNHM
Least Flycatcher	*Empidonax minimus*			SDNHM
Hammond's Flycatcher	*Empidonax hammondii*			SDNHM
Gray Flycatcher	*Empidonax wrightii*			SDNHM
Dusky Flycatcher	*Empidonax oberholseri*	B		SDNHM
Western or Pacific-slope Flycatcher	*Empidonax difficilis difficilis*	B		SDNHM
Black Phoebe	*Sayornis nigricans semiatra*	B		SDNHM
Eastern Phoebe	*Sayornis phoebe*			sr
Say's Phoebe	*Sayornis saya*			
Rocky Mountain Say's Phoebe	*S. s. saya*	B		SDNHM
San José Say's Phoebe	*S. s. quiescens*	B		SDNHM
Vermilion Flycatcher	*Pyrocephalus rubinus flammeus*	B		SDNHM
Dusky-capped or Olivaceous Flycatcher	*Myiarchus tuberculifer [olivascens]*		SC3 (CA)	ph.
Ash-throated Flycatcher	*Myiarchus cinerascens*	B		SDNHM
Great Crested Flycatcher	*Myiarchus crinitus*			sr
Brown-crested Flycatcher	*Myiarchus tyrannulus [magister]*	B		ph.
Sulphur-bellied Flycatcher	*Myiodynastes luteiventris*			ph.
Tropical Kingbird	*Tyrannus melancholicus satrapa*			SDNHM
Cassin's Kingbird	*Tyrannus vociferans*	B		SDNHM
Thick-billed Kingbird	*Tyrannus crassirostris*			ph.*
Western Kingbird	*Tyrannus verticalis*	B		SDNHM
Eastern Kingbird	*Tyrannus tyrannus*			SDNHM
Scissor-tailed Flycatcher	*Tyrannus forficatus*			SDNHM
Family Laniidae				
Loggerhead Shrike	*Lanius ludovicianus*			
Grinnell's Loggerhead Shrike	*L. l. grinnelli*	B		SDNHM
California Loggerhead Shrike	*L. l. gambeli*	B		SDNHM
White-rumped Loggerhead Shrike	*L. l. excubitorides*			SDNHM
Family Vireonidae				
White-eyed Vireo	*Vireo griseus [noveboracensis]*			ph.*
Bell's Vireo	*Vireo bellii*			
Least Bell's Vireo	*V. b. pusillus*	B	E (US, CA)	SDNHM
Arizona Bell's Vireo	*V. b. arizonae*		T (CA)	SDNHM
Gray Vireo	*Vireo vicinior*	B	SC1 (CA)	SDNHM
Yellow-throated Vireo	*Vireo flavifrons*			ph.
Plumbeous Vireo	*Vireo plumbeus plumbeus*			SDNHM
Cassin's Vireo	*Vireo cassinii cassinii*	B		SDNHM
Blue-headed Vireo	*Vireo solitarius solitarius*			sr
Hutton's Vireo	*Vireo huttoni*			
Oberholser's Hutton's Vireo	*V. h. oberholseri*	B		SDNHM
Parkes' Hutton's Vireo	*V. h. parkesi*			SDNHM
Warbling Vireo	*Vireo gilvus swainsonii*	B		SDNHM
Philadelphia Vireo	*Vireo philadelphicus*			SDNHM
Red-eyed Vireo	*Vireo olivaceus olivaceus*			SDNHM
Yellow-green Vireo	*Vireo flavoviridis hypoleucus*			SDNHM
Family Corvidae				
Steller's Jay	*Cyanocitta stelleri frontalis*	B		SDNHM
Western Scrub-Jay	*Aphelocoma californica obscura*	B		SDNHM
Pinyon Jay	*Gymnorhinus cyanocephalus*			SDNHM
Clark's Nutcracker	*Nucifraga columbiana*			SDNHM
American Crow	*Corvus brachyrhynchos hesperis*	B		SDNHM
Common Raven	*Corvus corax clarionensis*	B		SDNHM
Family Alaudidae				
Horned Lark	*Eremophila alpestris*			
California Horned Lark	*E. a. actia*	B	SC3 (CA)	SDNHM
Island Horned Lark	*E. a. insularis*			SDNHM
Yuma Horned Lark	*E. a. leucansiptila*	B		SDNHM
Mojave Horned Lark	*E. a. ammophila*			SDNHM
Family Hirundinidae				
Purple Martin	*Progne subis subis*	B	SC1 (CA)	SDNHMv
Tree Swallow	*Tachycineta bicolor*	B		SDNHM

(continued)

		Breeding status	Regulatory status	Documentation
Violet-green Swallow	*Tachycineta thalassina thalassina*	B		SDNHM
Northern Rough-winged Swallow	*Stelgidopteryx serripennis*			
Pale Rough-winged Swallow	*S. s. psammochrous*	B		SDNHM
Dark Rough-winged Swallow	*S. s. serripennis*			SDNHM
Bank Swallow	*Riparia riparia riparia*	B*	T (CA)	SDNHM
Cliff Swallow	*Petrochelidon pyrrhonota tachina*	B		SDNHM
Barn Swallow	*Hirundo rustica erythrogaster*	B		SDNHM
Family Paridae				
Mountain Chickadee	*Poecile gambeli baileyae*	B		SDNHM
Oak Titmouse	*Baeolophus inornatus affabilis*	B		SDNHM
Family Remizidae				
Verdin	*Auriparus flaviceps acaciarum*	B		SDNHM
Family Aegithalidae				
Bushtit	*Psaltriparus minimus melanurus*	B		SDNHM
Family Sittidae				
Red-breasted Nuthatch	*Sitta canadensis*	B		SDNHM
White-breasted Nuthatch	*Sitta carolinensis aculeata*	B		SDNHM
Pygmy Nuthatch	*Sitta pygmaea*			
White-naped Pygmy Nuthatch	*S. p. leuconucha*	B		SDNHM
Black-eared Pygmy Nuthatch	*S. p. melanotis*			SDNHM
Family Certhiidae				
Brown Creeper	*Certhia americana zelotes*	B		SDNHM
Family Troglodytidae				
Cactus Wren	*Campylorhynchus brunneicapillus*			
San Diego Cactus Wren	*C. b. sandiegensis*	B	SC1 (CA)	SDNHM
Desert Cactus Wren	*C. b. anthonyi*	B		SDNHM
Rock Wren	*Salpinctes obsoletus obsoletus*	B		SDNHM
Canyon Wren	*Catherpes mexicanus conspersus*	B		SDNHM
Bewick's Wren	*Thryomanes bewickii*			
Sooty Bewick's Wren	*T. b. charienturus*	B		SDNHM
San Joaquin Bewick's Wren	*T. b. drymoecus*			SDNHM
Vigors' Bewick's Wren	*T. b. spilurus*			SDNHM
House Wren	*Troglodytes aedon parkmanii*	B		SDNHM
Winter Wren	*Troglodytes troglodytes* ssp.			ph.•
Marsh Wren	*Cistothorus palustris*			
Mary Clark's Marsh Wren	*C. p. clarkae*	B	SC2 (CA)	SDNHM
Palouse Marsh Wren	*C. p. pulverius*			SDNHM
Western Marsh Wren	*C. p. plesius*			SDNHM
Family Cinclidae				
American Dipper	*Cinclus mexicanus unicolor*	B		WFVZ (eggs)
Family Regulidae				
Golden-crowned Kinglet	*Regulus satrapa*			
Northwestern Golden-crowned Kinglet	*R. s. olivaceus*			SDNHM
Arizona Golden-crowned Kinglet	*R. s. [apache]*	B		sr
Ruby-crowned Kinglet	*Regulus calendula*			
Pale Ruby-crowned Kinglet	*R. c. calendula*			SDNHM
Sitka Ruby-crowned Kinglet	*R. c. grinnelli*			SDNHM
Family Sylviidae				
Blue-gray Gnatcatcher	*Polioptila caerulea obscura*	B		SDNHM
California Gnatcatcher	*Polioptila californica californica*	B	T (US), SC (CA)	SDNHM
Black-tailed Gnatcatcher	*Polioptila melanura lucida*	B		SDNHM
Family Turdidae				
Northern Wheatear	*Oenanthe oenanthe [oenanthe]*			sr
Western Bluebird	*Sialia mexicana occidentalis*	B		SDNHM
Mountain Bluebird	*Sialia currucoides*			SDNHM
Townsend's Solitaire	*Myadestes townsendi townsendi*			SDNHM
Gray-cheeked Thrush	*Catharus minimus*			ph.
Swainson's Thrush	*Catharus ustulatus*			
Northern Russet-backed Thrush	*C. u. ustulatus*			SDNHM
California Russet-backed Thrush	*C. u. oedicus*	B	SC3 (CA)	SDNHM
Hermit Thrush	*Catharus guttatus*			
Alaska Hermit Thrush	*C. g. guttatus*			SDNHM
Dwarf Hermit Thrush	*C. g. nanus*			SDNHM
Vancouver Hermit Thrush	*C. g. vaccinius*			SDNHM

Monterey Hermit Thrush	*C. g. slevini*			SDNHM
Sierra Hermit Thrush	*C. g. [sequoiensis]*	B		sr
Wood Thrush	*Hylocichla mustelina*			SDNHM
Rufous-backed Robin	*Turdus rufopalliatus [rufopalliatus]*			ph.
American Robin	*Turdus migratorius propinquus*	B		SDNHM
Varied Thrush	*Ixoreus naevius*			
Northern Varied Thrush	*I. n. meruloides*			SDNHM
Coast Varied Thrush	*I. n. naevius*			SDNHM
Family Timaliidae				
Wrentit	*Chamaea fasciata henshawi*	B		SDNHM
Family Mimidae				
Gray Catbird	*Dumetella carolinensis*			SDNHM
Northern Mockingbird	*Mimus polyglottos polyglottos*	B		SDNHM
Sage Thrasher	*Oreoscoptes montanus*			SDNHM
Brown Thrasher	*Toxostoma rufum [longicauda]*			ph.
Bendire's Thrasher	*Toxostoma bendirei*	B*	SC1 (CA)	SDNHM
Curve-billed Thrasher	*Toxostoma curvirostre [palmeri]*			sr
California Thrasher	*Toxostoma redivivum redivivum*	B		SDNHM
Crissal Thrasher	*Toxostoma crissale [coloradense]*	B	SC1 (CA)	sr
Le Conte's Thrasher	*Toxostoma lecontei lecontei*	B		SDNHM
Family Sturnidae				
European Starling	*Sturnus vulgaris vulgaris*	IB		SDNHM
Family Motacillidae				
Red-throated Pipit	*Anthus cervinus*			SDNHM
American Pipit	*Anthus rubescens pacificus*			SDNHM
Sprague's Pipit	*Anthus spragueii*			SDNHM
Family Bombycillidae				
Bohemian Waxwing	*Bombycilla garrulus*			sr
Cedar Waxwing	*Bombycilla cedrorum*			SDNHM
Family Ptilogonatidae				
Phainopepla	*Phainopepla nitens lepida*	B		SDNHM
Family Parulidae				
Blue-winged Warbler	*Vermivora pinus*			sr
Golden-winged Warbler	*Vermivora chrysoptera*			ph.
Tennessee Warbler	*Vermivora peregrina*			SDNHM
Orange-crowned Warbler	*Vermivora celata*			
Lutescent Orange-crowned Warbler	*V. c. lutescens*	B		SDNHM
Rocky Mountain Orange-crowned Warbler	*V. c. orestera*			SDNHM
Dusky Orange-crowned Warbler	*V. c. sordida*	B		SDNHM
Nashville Warbler	*Vermivora ruficapilla ridgwayi*			SDNHM
Virginia's Warbler	*Vermivora virginiae*			SDNHM
Lucy's Warbler	*Vermivora luciae*	B	SC3 (CA)	SDNHM
Northern Parula	*Parula americana*			ph.
Yellow Warbler	*Dendroica petechia*			
Western Yellow Warbler	*D. p. morcomi*	B	SC2 (CA)	SDNHM
Alaska Yellow Warbler	*D. p. rubiginosa*			SDNHM
Chestnut-sided Warbler	*Dendroica pensylvanica*			SDNHM
Magnolia Warbler	*Dendroica magnolia*			SDNHM
Cape May Warbler	*Dendroica tigrina*			SDNHM
Black-throated Blue Warbler	*Dendroica caerulescens*			SDNHM
Yellow-rumped Warbler	*Dendroica coronata*			
Audubon's Warbler	*D. c. auduboni*	B		SDNHM
Alaska Myrtle Warbler	*D. c. hooveri*			SDNHM
Black-throated Gray Warbler	*Dendroica nigrescens*	B		SDNHM
Black-throated Green Warbler	*Dendroica virens*			SDNHM
Townsend's Warbler	*Dendroica townsendi*			SDNHM
Hermit Warbler	*Dendroica occidentalis*			SDNHM
Blackburnian Warbler	*Dendroica fusca*			SDNHM
Yellow-throated Warbler	*Dendroica dominica*			
Sycamore Warbler	*D. d. albilora*			sr
Yellow-throated Warbler	*D. d. dominica*			ph.
Grace's Warbler	*Dendroica graciae graciae*			SDNHM
Pine Warbler	*Dendroica pinus pinus*			SDNHM
Prairie Warbler	*Dendroica discolor discolor*			SDNHM
Palm Warbler	*Dendroica palmarum*			
Western Palm Warbler	*D. p. palmarum*			SDNHM
Yellow Palm Warbler	*D. p. hypochrysea*			SDNHM

(continued)

		Breeding status	Regulatory status	Documentation
Bay-breasted Warbler	*Dendroica castanea*			SDNHM
Blackpoll Warbler	*Dendroica striata*			SDNHM
Cerulean Warbler	*Dendroica cerulea*			ph.
Black-and-white Warbler	*Mniotilta varia*			SDNHM
American Redstart	*Setophaga ruticilla*			SDNHM
Prothonotary Warbler	*Protonotaria citrea*			SDNHM
Worm-eating Warbler	*Helmitheros vermivorum*			SDNHM
Ovenbird	*Seiurus aurocapilla aurocapilla*			SDNHM
Northern Waterthrush	*Seiurus noveboracensis*			SDNHM
Louisiana Waterthrush	*Seiurus motacilla*			ph.*
Kentucky Warbler	*Oporornis formosus*			SDNHM
Connecticut Warbler	*Oporornis agilis*			SDNHM
Mourning Warbler	*Oporornis philadelphia*			SDNHM
MacGillivray's Warbler	*Oporornis tolmiei*			
Pacific MacGillivray's Warbler	*O. t. tolmiei*			SDNHM
Mountain MacGillivray's Warbler	*O. t. monticola*			LACM
Common Yellowthroat	*Geothlypis trichas*			
Western Yellowthroat	*G. t. occidentalis*	B		SDNHM
San Francisco Yellowthroat	*G. t. sinuosa*		SC1 (CA)	SDNHM
Hooded Warbler	*Wilsonia citrina*			ph.
Wilson's Warbler	*Wilsonia pusilla*			
Golden Wilson's Warbler	*W. p. chryseola*	B		SDNHM
Pileolated Wilson's Warbler	*W. p. pileolata*			SDNHM
Canada Warbler	*Wilsonia canadensis*			ph.*
Red-faced Warbler	*Cardellina rubrifrons*			ph.
Painted Redstart	*Myioborus pictus pictus*	B*		SDNHM
Yellow-breasted Chat	*Icteria virens auricollis*	B	SC3 (CA)	SDNHM
Family Thraupidae				
Hepatic Tanager	*Piranga flava hepatica*			SDNHM
Summer Tanager	*Piranga rubra*			
Cooper's Summer Tanager	*P. r. cooperi*	B	SC1 (CA)	ph.
Eastern Summer Tanager	*P. r. rubra*			SDNHM
Scarlet Tanager	*Piranga olivacea*			ph.
Western Tanager	*Piranga ludoviciana*	B		SDNHM
Family Emberizidae				
Green-tailed Towhee	*Pipilo chlorurus*	B		SDNHM
Spotted Towhee	*Pipilo maculatus megalonyx*	B		SDNHM
California Towhee	*Pipilo crissalis senicula*	B		SDNHM
Cassin's Sparrow	*Aimophila cassinii*			ph.
Rufous-crowned Sparrow	*Aimophila ruficeps canescens*	B		SDNHM
American Tree Sparrow	*Spizella arborea [ochracea]*			ph.*
Chipping Sparrow	*Spizella passerina arizonae*	B		SDNHM
Clay-colored Sparrow	*Spizella pallida*			SDNHM
Brewer's Sparrow	*Spizella breweri*			
Brewer's Sparrow	*S. b. breweri*	B		SDNHM
Timberline Sparrow	*S. b. taverneri*			DEL
Black-chinned Sparrow	*Spizella atrogularis cana*	B		SDNHM
Vesper Sparrow	*Pooecetes gramineus*			
Western Vesper Sparrow	*P. g. confinis*			SDNHM
Oregon Vesper Sparrow	*P. g. affinis*		SC2 (CA)	SDNHM
Lark Sparrow	*Chondestes grammacus strigatus*	B		SDNHM
Black-throated Sparrow	*Amphispiza bilineata deserticola*	B		SDNHM
Sage Sparrow	*Amphispiza belli*			
Bell's Sparrow	*A. b. belli*	B		SDNHM
Sage Sparrow	*A. b. nevadensis*			SDNHM
Lark Bunting	*Calamospiza melanocorys*			SDNHM
Savannah Sparrow	*Passerculus sandwichensis*			
Belding's Sparrow	*P. s. beldingi*	B	E (CA)	SDNHM
Nevada Savannah Sparrow	*P. s. nevadensis*			SDNHM
Western Savannah Sparrow	*P. s. anthinus*			SDNHM
Dwarf Savannah Sparrow	*P. s. brooksi*			SDNHM
Large-billed Sparrow	*P. s. rostratus*		SC2 (CA)	SDNHM
Grasshopper Sparrow	*Ammodramus savannarum perpallidus*	B	SC2 (CA)	SDNHM
Baird's Sparrow	*Ammodramus bairdii*			ph.*
Nelson's Sharp-tailed Sparrow	*Ammodramus nelsoni nelsoni*			SDNHM

Fox Sparrow	*Passerella iliaca*			
Stephens' Fox Sparrow	*P. i. stephensi*	B		SDNHM
Thick-billed Fox Sparrow	*P. i. megarhynchus*			SDNHM
Slate-colored Fox Sparrow	*P. i. schistacea*			SDNHM
Washington Fox Sparrow	*P. i. olivacea*			SDNHM
Shumagin Fox Sparrow	*P. i. unalaschcensis*			SDNHM
Yakutat Fox Sparrow	*P. i. annectens*			SDNHM
Townsend's Fox Sparrow	*P. i. townsendi*			SDNHM
Alberta Fox Sparrow	*P. i. altivagans*			SDNHM
Yukon Fox Sparrow	*P. i. zaboria*			SBCM
Song Sparrow	*Melospiza melodia*			
Heermann's Song Sparrow	*M. m. heermanni*	B		SDNHM
Merrill's Song Sparrow	*M. m. merrilli*			SDNHM
Lincoln's Sparrow	*Melospiza lincolnii*			
Lincoln's Sparrow	*M. l. lincolnii*			SDNHM
Forbush's Sparrow	*M. l. gracilis*			SDNHM
Swamp Sparrow	*Melospiza georgiana ericrypta*			SDNHM
White-throated Sparrow	*Zonotrichia albicollis*			SDNHM
Harris's Sparrow	*Zonotrichia querula*			sr
White-crowned Sparrow	*Zonotrichia leucophrys*			
Gambel's White-crowned Sparrow	*Z. l. gambelii*			SDNHM
Puget Sound White-crowned Sparrow	*Z. l. pugetensis*			SDNHM
Mountain White-crowned Sparrow	*Z. l. oriantha*	B*		SDNHM
Golden-crowned Sparrow	*Zonotrichia atricapilla*			SDNHM
Dark-eyed Junco	*Junco hyemalis*			
Sierra Oregon Junco	*J. h. thurberi*	B		SDNHM
Shufeldt's Oregon Junco	*J. h. simillimus*			SDNHM
Montana Oregon Junco	*J. h. shufeldti*			SDNHM
Pink-sided Junco	*J. h. mearnsi*			SDNHM
Gray-headed Junco	*J. h. caniceps*			SDNHM
Cassiar Slate-colored Junco	*J. h. cismontanus*			SDNHM
Boreal Slate-colored Junco	*J. h. hyemalis*			SDNHM
McCown's Longspur	*Calcarius mccownii*			SDNHM
Lapland Longspur	*Calcarius lapponicus alascensis*			SDNHM
Chestnut-collared Longspur	*Calcarius ornatus*			SDNHM
Little Bunting	*Emberiza pusilla*			ph.
Family Cardinalidae				
Pyrrhuloxia	*Cardinalis sinuatus ssp.*			sr
Rose-breasted Grosbeak	*Pheucticus ludovicianus*			SDNHM
Black-headed Grosbeak	*Pheucticus melanocephalus maculatus*	B		SDNHM
Blue Grosbeak	*Passerina caerulea salicaria*	B		SDNHM
Lazuli Bunting	*Passerina amoena*	B		SDNHM
Indigo Bunting	*Passerina cyanea*	B		SDNHM
Painted Bunting	*Passerina ciris*			SDNHM
Dickcissel	*Spiza americana*			SDNHM
Family Icteridae				
Bobolink	*Dolichonyx oryzivorus*			SDNHM
Red-winged Blackbird	*Agelaius phoeniceus*			
San Diego Red-winged Blackbird	*A. p. neutralis*	B		SDNHM
Nevada Red-winged Blackbird	*A. p. nevadensis*			SDNHM
California Red-winged Blackbird	*A. p. californicus*			
Tricolored Blackbird	*Agelaius tricolor*	B	SC1 (CA)	SDNHM
Western Meadowlark	*Sturnella neglecta neglecta <> confluenta*	B		SDNHM
Yellow-headed Blackbird	*Xanthocephalus xanthocephalus*	B	SC2 (CA)	SDNHM
Rusty Blackbird	*Euphagus carolinus*			SDNHM
Brewer's Blackbird	*Euphagus cyanocephalus*			
Brewer's Blackbird	*E. c. minusculus*	B		SDNHM
Brewer's Blackbird	*E. c. cyanocephalus*			SDNHM
Common Grackle	*Quiscalus quiscula versicolor*			ph.
Great-tailed Grackle	*Quiscalus mexicanus ssp.*	B		SDNHM
Bronzed Cowbird	*Molothrus aeneus loyei*	B*		SDNHM
Brown-headed Cowbird	*Molothrus ater*			
Dwarf Cowbird	*M. a. obscurus*	B		SDNHM
Nevada Cowbird	*M. a. artemisiae*			SDNHM
Eastern Cowbird	*M. a. ater*			SDNHM
Orchard Oriole	*Icterus spurius spurius*			SDNHM
Hooded Oriole	*Icterus cucullatus nelsoni*	B		SDNHM

(continued)

		Breeding status	Regulatory status	Documentation
Streak-backed Oriole	*Icterus pustulatus microstictus*			SDNHM
Bullock's Oriole	*Icterus bullockii*	B		SDNHM
Baltimore Oriole	*Icterus galbula*			SDNHM
Scott's Oriole	*Icterus parisorum*	B		SDNHM
Family Fringillidae				
Purple Finch	*Carpodacus purpureus californicus*	B		SDNHM
Cassin's Finch	*Carpodacus cassinii*			SDNHM
House Finch	*Carpodacus mexicanus frontalis*	B		SDNHM
Red Crossbill	*Loxia curvirostra*			
Medium-large Red Crossbill	*L. c. pusilla*	B*		SDNHM
Mexican Giant Crossbill	*L. c. stricklandi*			SDNHM
Pine Siskin	*Carduelis pinus pinus*			SDNHM
Lesser Goldfinch	*Carduelis psaltria hesperophilus*	B		SDNHM
Lawrence's Goldfinch	*Carduelis lawrencei*	B		SDNHM
American Goldfinch	*Carduelis tristis salicamans*	B		SDNHM
Evening Grosbeak	*Coccothraustes vespertinus [brooksi]*			sr
Family Passeridae				
House Sparrow	*Passer domesticus domesticus*	IB		SDNHM

APPENDIX 2
Scientific Names of Plants Mentioned in Species Accounts

Agave, American: *Agave americana**
Agave, desert: *Agave deserti*
Alder, white: *Alnus rhombifolia*
Apricot, desert: *Prunus fremontii*
Ash, velvet: *Fraxinus velutina*
Avocado: *Persea americana**
Baccharis, broom: *Baccharis sarothroides*
Bamboo, heavenly: *Nandina domestica**
Bedstraw: *Galium* spp.
Bee plant, California: *Scrophularia californica*
Birch: *Betula* sp.*
Blackberry, California: *Rubus ursinus*
Blackbush: *Coleogyne ramosissima*
Bluecurls, woolly: *Trichostema lanatum*
Bottlebrush: *Callistemon* spp.*
Bougainvillea: *Bougainvillea spectabilis**
Buckwheat, flat-top: *Eriogonum fasciculatum*
Bugler, scarlet: *Penstemon centranthifolius*
Camphor: *Cinnamomum camphora**
Catclaw: *Acacia greggii*
Cattail: *Typha* spp.
Ceanothus, cupleaf: *Ceanothus greggii*
Ceanothus, Palmer's: *Ceanothus palmeri*
Cedar, deodar: *Cedrus deodara**
Cedar, incense: *Calocedrus decurrens*
Cedar, salt: *Tamarix ramosissima**
Chamise: *Adenostoma fasciculatum*
Cherry, Catalina: *Prunus lyonii**
Cholla, cane: *Cylindropuntia californica* var. *parkeri*
Cholla, coast: *Cylindropuntia prolifera*
Cholla, jumping: *Cylindropuntia bigelovii*
Cholla, pencil: *Cylindropuntia ramosissima*
Cholla, snake: *Cylindropuntia californica* var. *californica*
Cholla, teddy bear: *Cylindropuntia bigelovii*
Chuparosa: *Justicia californica*
Clover, white sweet: *Melilotus albus**
Coffeeberry, California: *Rhamnus californica*
Cordgrass: *Spartina foliosa*
Cottonwood, Fremont: *Populus fremontii*
Coyote brush: *Baccharis pilularis*
Creosote bush: *Larrea tridentata*
Cypress, Italian: *Cupressus sempervirens**
Cypress, Tecate: *Cupressus forbesii*
Deerweed: *Lotus scoparius*
Dodder: *Cuscuta* spp.
Eelgrass: *Zostera marina*
Elderberry, blue: *Sambucus mexicana*
Elephant tree: *Bursera microphylla*
Elm, Chinese weeping: *Ulmus parvifolia**
Eucalyptus: *Eucalyptus* spp.*
Fennel: *Foeniculum vulgare**
Fern, bracken: *Pteridium aquilinum*
Fiddleneck: *Amsinckia menziesii*
Fig: *Ficus* spp.*
Fir, big-cone Douglas: *Pseudotsuga macrocarpa*
Fir, white: *Abies concolor*
Goldenrod: *Solidago californica, S. confinis*
Grape, wild: *Vitis girdiana*
Grapefruit: *Citrus paradisi**
Grass, cord: *Spartina foliosa*
Grass, fountain: *Pennisetum setaceum**
Grass, giant needle: *Achnatherum coronatum*

Grass, pampas: *Cortaderia selloana**
Grass, purple needle: *Nassella pulchra*
Grass, salt: *Distichlis spicata*
Grass, shore: *Monanthochloe littoralis*
Hemlock, poison: *Conium maculatum**
Honeysuckle: *Lonicera* spp.
Honeysuckle, cape: *Tecomaria capensis**
Iceplant, baby sun rose: *Aptenia cordifolia**
Iceplant, crystalline: *Mesembryanthemum crystallinum**
Indigo bush: *Psorothamnus schottii*
Iodine bush: *Allenrolfea occidentalis*
Ironwood, desert: *Olneya tesota*
Ivy: *Hedera helix**
Jojoba: *Simmondsia chinensis*
Juniper: *Juniperus californica*
Larkspur, scarlet: *Delphinium cardinale*
Lavender, desert: *Hyptis emoryi*
Lemonadeberry: *Rhus integrifolia*
Lettuce, sea: *Ulva* spp.
Liquidambar: *Liquidambar styraciflua**
Locust, black: *Robinia pseudoacacia**
Lotebush: *Ziziphus parryi*
Mahogany, mountain: *Cercocarpus betuloides, C. minutiflorus*
Manzanita: *Arctostaphylos* spp.
Manzanita, mission: *Xylococcus bicolor*
Maple, silver: *Acer saccharinum**
Mesquite, honey: *Prosopis glandulosa*
Mistletoe: *Phoradendron* spp.
Monkeyflower, wide-throated yellow: *Mimulus brevipes*
Mugwort: *Artemisia douglasiana*
Mulefat: *Baccharis salicifolia*
Mustard, black: *Brassica nigra**
Myoporum: *Myoporum laetum**
Nama, sticky: *Turricula parryi*
Needlegrass, giant: *Achnatherum coronatum*
Needlegrass, purple: *Nassella pulchra*
Nettle, hedge: *Stachys ajugoides*
Nettle, stinging: *Urtica dioica*
Nolina, Parry's: *Nolina parryi*
Oak, black: *Quercus kelloggii*
Oak, canyon live: *Quercus chrysolepis*
Oak, coast live: *Quercus agrifolia*
Oak, cork: *Quercus suber**
Oak, desert scrub: *Quercus cornelius-mulleri*
Oak, Engelmann: *Quercus engelmannii*
Oak, poison: *Toxicodendron diversilobum*
Oak, scrub: *Quercus berberidifolia, Q. dumosa*
Ocotillo: *Fouquieria splendens*
Oleander: *Nerium oleander**
Olive: *Olea europaea**
Orange: *Citrus sinensis**
Palm, California fan: *Washingtonia filifera*
Palm, Canary Island date: *Phoenix canariensis**
Palm, date: *Phoenix dactylifera**
Palm, Mexican fan, *Washingtonia robusta**
Palo verde: *Cercidium floridum*
Penstemon, showy: *Penstemon spectabilis*
Penstemon, yellow bush: *Keckiella antirrhinoides*
Pepper tree, Brazilian: *Schinus terebinthifolius**
Pepper tree, Peruvian: *Schinus molle**
Pickleweed, *Salicornia virginica, S. subterminalis*

Pine, Canary Island: *Pinus canariensis**
Pine, Coulter: *Pinus coulteri*
Pine, Jeffrey: *Pinus jeffreyi*
Pine, ponderosa: *Pinus ponderosa*
Pine, Torrey: *Pinus torreyana*
Pinyon: *Pinus monophylla, P. quadrifolia*
Plum, Natal: *Carissa macrocarpa**
Podocarpus: *Podocarpus* spp.*
Poplar: *Populus nigra**
Prickly-pear: *Opuntia* spp.
Primrose, great marsh evening: *Oenothera elata*
Pyracantha: *Pyracantha coccinea**
Redberry: *Rhamnus crocea*
Redshank: *Adenostoma sparsifolium*
Redwood: *Sequoia sempervirens**
Reed, giant: *Arundo donax**
Rose, California: *Rosa californica*
Rosemary: *Rosmarinus officinalis**
Sage, black: *Salvia mellifera*
Sage, Cleveland: *Salvia clevelandii*
Sage, white: *Salvia apiana*
Sagebrush, big: *Artemisia tridentata*
Sagebrush, California: *Artemisia californica*
Saltbush: *Atriplex* spp.
Saltgrass, *Distichlis spicata*
Saltcedar: *Tamarix ramosissima**

Saltwort: *Batis maritima*
Semaphore, slope: *Mimulus brevipes*
Skunkbrush: *Rhus trilobata*
Smoketree: *Psorothamnus spinosus*
Snowberry: *Symphoricarpos mollis*
Sugarbush: *Rhus ovata*
Sumac, laurel: *Malosma laurina*
Sunflower, San Diego: *Viguiera laciniata*
Sycamore, western: *Platanus racemosa*
Tamarisk, athel: *Tamarix aphylla**
Thistle, cobwebby: *Cirsium occidentale*
Thistle, common sow: *Sonchus oleraceus**
Thistle, yellow star: *Centaurea melitensis**
Thorn, desert, *Lycium* spp.
Tobacco, tree: *Nicotiana glauca**
Toyon: *Heteromeles arbutifolia*
Tule: *Scirpus* spp.
Tumbleweed: *Salsola tragus*
Vinegar weed: *Trichostema lanceolatum*
Willow, arroyo: *Salix lasiolepis*
Willow, desert: *Chilopsis linearis*
Willow, red: *Salix laevigata*
Wolfberry: *Lycium* spp.
Yerba mansa: *Anemopsis californica*
Yucca, chaparral: *Hesperoyucca whipplei*
Yucca, Mojave: *Yucca schidigera*

*Nonnative or cultivated species.

APPENDIX 3
Photographs in Species Accounts

Fulvous Whistling-Duck: Captives at Sea World (A. Mercieca).

Greater White-fronted Goose: Fall migrants at sod farm in the Tijuana River valley, 2002 (A. Mercieca).

Snow Goose: Wintering flock at the south end of the Salton Sea, Imperial Co. (A. Mercieca).

Ross's Goose: On San Diego Bay shore at Chula Vista (A. Mercieca).

Brant: On San Diego Bay shore at Chula Vista (A. Mercieca).

Canada Goose: Captive at Sea World (A. Mercieca).

Tundra Swan: Captive at Sea World (A. Mercieca).

Wood Duck: Male at Santee Lakes (A. Mercieca).

Gadwall: Male at El Cajon (A. Mercieca).

Eurasian Wigeon: Captive male at Sea World (K. W. Fink).

American Wigeon: Male at Wild Animal Park (A. Mercieca).

Mallard: Female with ducklings at Santee Lakes (A. Mercieca).

Blue-winged Teal: Male at Famosa Slough (A. Mercieca).

Cinnamon Teal: Pair at Wild Animal Park (A. Mercieca).

Northern Shoveler: Male at Santee Lakes (A. Mercieca).

Northern Pintail: Male at Wild Animal Park (A. Mercieca).

Green-winged Teal: Male at Wild Animal Park (A. Mercieca).

Canvasback: Male at San Diego Zoo (A. Mercieca).

Redhead: Male at Mission Bay (A. Mercieca).

Ring-necked Duck: Male at Wild Animal Park (A. Mercieca).

Tufted Duck: Male at Miramar Lake, 1992 (A. Mercieca).

Greater Scaup: Male in Alaska (A. Mercieca).

Lesser Scaup: Male at Wild Animal Park (A. Mercieca).

King Eider: Adult male at Imperial Beach, December 1982 (M. B. Stowe).

Harlequin Duck: Male at Mission Bay (A. Mercieca).

Surf Scoter: Male in San Diego Bay at Chula Vista (A. Mercieca).

White-winged Scoter: Captive female at Sea World (A. Mercieca).

Black Scoter: Female at Salton Sea, Imperial County (K. Z. Kurland).

Long-tailed Duck: Immature at south San Diego Bay (A. Mercieca).

Bufflehead: Male at San Diego Zoo (A. Mercieca).

Common Goldeneye: Captive female at Sea World (A. Mercieca).

Barrow's Goldeneye: Captive female at Sea World (A. Mercieca).

Hooded Merganser: Pair at Wild Animal Park (A. Mercieca).

Common Merganser: Captive female at Sea World (A. Mercieca).

Red-breasted Merganser: Female or immature in Tijuana River estuary (A. Mercieca).

Ruddy Duck: At San Diego Wild Animal Park (A. Mercieca)

Ring-necked Pheasant: Captive male at San Diego Zoo (A. Mercieca).

Wild Turkey: Captive male at Arizona–Sonora Desert Museum (A. Mercieca).

Mountain Quail: Adult at Idyllwild, Riverside County, April 2002 (J. C. Daynes)

California Quail: Male at Lakeside (A. Mercieca).

Gambel's Quail: Male near Tucson, Arizona (A. Mercieca).

Red-throated Loon: Winter-plumaged bird at Mission Bay (A. Mercieca).

Pacific Loon: Winter-plumaged bird at Mission Bay (A. Mercieca).

Common Loon: Winter-plumaged bird at San Diego Bay (A. Mercieca).

Pied-billed Grebe: Winter-plumaged bird at Mission Bay (A. Mercieca).

Horned Grebe: Winter-plumaged bird at San Diego Bay (A. Mercieca).

Eared Grebe: Winter-plumaged bird at Mission Bay (A. Mercieca).

Western Grebe: Pair at Sweetwater Reservoir (A. Mercieca).

Clark's Grebe: At Sweetwater Reservoir (A. Mercieca).

Laysan Albatross: In eastern tropical Pacific (P. Unitt).

Black-footed Albatross: Near San Clemente Island (R. E. Webster).

Northern Fulmar: Captive at Sea World (K.W. Fink).

Pink-footed Shearwater: Near San Clemente Island (B. L. Sullivan).

Flesh-footed Shearwater: Off Fort Bragg, Mendocino Co., 17 August 2002 (B. L. Sullivan).

Buller's Shearwater: On ocean off California (R. E. Webster).

Short-tailed Shearwater: On ocean off San Diego (R. E. Webster).

Black-vented Shearwater: On ocean off La Jolla, January 2002 (B. L. Sullivan).

Black Storm-Petrel: Flock on ocean off San Diego (M. B. Stowe).

Masked Booby: Subadult at La Jolla, January 2002 (A. Mercieca).

Brown Booby: Subadult at Shelter Island 17 November 1997 (A. Mercieca).

American White Pelican: Flock soaring over Salton Sea, Imperial Co. (A. Mercieca).

Brown Pelican: Adult at La Jolla (A. Mercieca).

Brandt's Cormorant: Adult at La Jolla (A. Mercieca).

Double-crested Cormorant: Adult at La Jolla (A. Mercieca).

Pelagic Cormorant: Adult at La Jolla (A. Mercieca).

Magnificent Frigatebird: Immature over south San Diego Bay (A. Mercieca).

American Bittern: Bird held in captivity for rehabilitation at Sea World (A. Mercieca).

Least Bittern: Adult male at Wild Animal Park, 24 July 2004 (D. Furseth).

Great Blue Heron: Pair at nest at Point Loma submarine base (A. Mercieca).

Great Egret: At Wild Animal Park (A. Mercieca).

Snowy Egret: At Mission Bay (A. Mercieca).

Little Blue Heron: Adult at Mission Bay (A. Mercieca).

Tricolored Heron: At Chula Vista Nature Center (A. Mercieca).

Reddish Egret: At Salton Sea, Imperial Co. (K. Z. Kurland).

Cattle Egret: Adult at Wild Animal Park (A. Mercieca).

Green Heron: Adult at Wild Animal Park (A. Mercieca).

Black-crowned Night-Heron: Adult retaining some immature plumage at Mission Bay (A. Mercieca).

Yellow-crowned Night-Heron: Adult at Sea World, 3 April 1979 (A. Mercieca).

White Ibis: Immature in Florida (A. Mercieca).

White-faced Ibis: Immature at Whelan Lake, December 2002 (J. C. Daynes).

Roseate Spoonbill: Immature in Imperial Co. (K. Z. Kurland).

Wood Stork: Adult at Wild Animal Park (A. Mercieca).

Turkey Vulture: Adult at Ramona (A. Mercieca).

California Condor: Captive pair at Wild Animal Park (A. Mercieca).

Osprey: Over Mission Bay (A. Mercieca).

White-tailed Kite: Adult and nestlings in Texas (A. Mercieca).
Mississippi Kite: Adult in Colorado (A. Mercieca).
Bald Eagle: Captive adult at San Diego Zoo (A. Mercieca).
Northern Harrier: Adult female and nestlings in Saskatchewan (A. Mercieca).
Sharp-shinned Hawk: Immature at Chula Vista (A. Mercieca).
Cooper's Hawk: Adult at Poway, October 2003 (J. C. Daynes).
Northern Goshawk: Falconer's bird in captivity (A. Mercieca).
Harris's Hawk: Recently fledged juvenile at Boulevard, 12 July 2000 (A. Mercieca).
Red-shouldered Hawk: Adult in San Diego (A. Mercieca).
Broad-winged Hawk: Adult in Costa Rica (A. Mercieca).
Swainson's Hawk: Light-morph adult in Arizona (A. Mercieca).
Zone-tailed Hawk: Adult at Oak Hill Cemetery, Escondido (A. Mercieca).
Red-tailed Hawk: Adult female at nest, Indian Gorge, Anza–Borrego Desert State Park (A. Mercieca).
Ferruginous Hawk: Injured adult held in captivity for rehabilitation (A. Mercieca).
Rough-legged Hawk: At Lower Klamath National Wildlife Refuge, Oregon, December 2002 (J. C. Daynes).
Golden Eagle: Adult and nestlings near Jacumba (A. Mercieca).
American Kestrel: Male at Lee Vining, Mono Co. (A. Mercieca).
Merlin: Falconer's bird in captivity (A. Mercieca).
Peregrine Falcon: Adult at Point Loma (A. Mercieca).
Prairie Falcon: Pair at nest in Anza–Borrego Desert State Park (A. Mercieca).
Yellow Rail: Female found moribund in Santee 16 December 1998, now SDNHM 50186 (J. Melli).
Black Rail: Bird found in Imperial Valley, held for rehabilitation in San Diego, later released back in Imperial Valley (A. Mercieca).
Clapper Rail: Adult in Tijuana River estuary (A. Mercieca).
Virginia Rail: Adult at San Elijo Lagoon (A. Mercieca).
Sora: Adult in Tijuana River estuary (A. Mercieca).
Common Gallinule: Adult at Wild Animal Park (A. Mercieca).
American Coot: Adult and chick at Santee Lakes (A. Mercieca).
Sandhill Crane: At Bosque del Apache National Wildlife Refuge, New Mexico (A. Mercieca).
Black-bellied Plover: Molting adult at La Jolla (A. Mercieca).
American Golden-Plover: Migrant in coastal Texas (A. Mercieca).
Pacific Golden-Plover: Adult in Hawaii (A. Mercieca).
Snowy Plover: Incubating adult at Border Field State Park (A. Mercieca).
Wilson's Plover: Adult in coastal Texas (A. Mercieca).
Semipalmated Plover: Adult in Alaska (A. Mercieca).
Killdeer: Incubating adult at Proctor Valley (A. Mercieca).
Mountain Plover: In Imperial Valley, Imperial Co. (K. Z. Kurland).
American Oystercatcher: Pair in Baja California (K. W. Fink).
Black Oystercatcher: At La Jolla (A. Mercieca).
Black-necked Stilt: Incubating adult near Susanville, Lassen Co. (A. Mercieca).
American Avocet: Incubating adult at Bear River, Utah (A. Mercieca).
Greater Yellowlegs: In winter plumage at Mission Bay (A. Mercieca).
Lesser Yellowlegs: In Montana (A. Mercieca).
Spotted Redshank: Captive in winter plumage at San Diego Zoo (A. Mercieca).
Solitary Sandpiper: In Texas (A. Mercieca).
Willet: In winter plumage at Mission Bay (A. Mercieca).
Wandering Tattler: In winter plumage at La Jolla (A. Mercieca).
Spotted Sandpiper: In winter plumage at La Jolla (A. Mercieca).

Upland Sandpiper: Immature in the Tijuana River valley, October 1999 (J. W. Schlotte).
Whimbrel: At La Jolla (A. Mercieca).
Long-billed Curlew: At Mission Bay (A. Mercieca).
Bar-tailed Godwit: Immature at Coronado, November 1981 (A. Mercieca).
Marbled Godwit: At San Diego Bay (A. Mercieca).
Ruddy Turnstone: Fall migrants at south San Diego Bay, July 2003 (J. C. Daynes).
Black Turnstone: In winter plumage at La Jolla (A. Mercieca).
Surfbird: In winter plumage at Mission Bay (A. Mercieca).
Red Knot: In winter plumage at south San Diego Bay (A. Mercieca).
Sanderling: In winter plumage at La Jolla (A. Mercieca).
Semipalmated Sandpiper: Juvenile at Mono Lake (R. E. Webster).
Western Sandpiper: Juvenile on San Diego Bay at Chula Vista (A. Mercieca).
Least Sandpiper: In winter plumage at La Jolla (A. Mercieca).
Baird's Sandpiper: Juvenile at Bosque del Apache, New Mexico, September 2003 (J. C. Daynes).
Pectoral Sandpiper: Juvenile at San Clemente Island, 22 September 2002 (B. L. Sullivan).
Dunlin: In winter plumage on San Diego Bay at Chula Vista (A. Mercieca).
Stilt Sandpiper: In winter plumage at the Salton Sea, Imperial Co. (K. Z. Kurland).
Buff-breasted Sandpiper: Juvenile at sod farm, Tijuana River Valley, September 2002 (A. Mercieca).
Ruff: Adult in winter plumage on San Diego Bay at Chula Vista (A. Mercieca).
Short-billed Dowitcher: Juvenile at Mission Bay (A. Mercieca).
Long-billed Dowitcher: Juvenile at San Clemente Island (B. L. Sullivan).
Wilson's Snipe: In Tijuana River valley (A. Mercieca).
Wilson's Phalarope: Female in breeding plumage at Bear River, Utah (A. Mercieca).
Red-necked Phalarope: Pair at Churchill, Manitoba (A. Mercieca).
Red Phalarope: In winter plumage at south San Diego Bay (A. Mercieca).
South Polar Skua: In Antarctica (J. R. Jehl, Jr.)
Pomarine Jaeger: Adult in Alaska (K. W. Fink).
Parasitic Jaeger: Adult in Alaska (K. W. Fink).
Long-tailed Jaeger: Over Pacific Ocean off Ventura (R. E. Webster).
Laughing Gull: Captive in winter plumage at San Diego Zoo (A. Mercieca).
Franklin's Gull: Adult in nonbreeding plumage in Montana (A. Mercieca).
Little Gull: Immature in captivity at Sea World, after having been captured in fishing line at Oceanside, 27 December 1981 (K. W. Fink).
Bonaparte's Gull: Immature over Mission Bay (A. Mercieca).
Heermann's Gull: Adult at La Jolla (A. Mercieca).
Belcher's Gull: At the Tijuana River mouth, August 1997 (A. Mercieca).
Black-tailed Gull: Adult in Virginia, December 1998 (B. L. Sullivan).
Mew Gull: Winter-plumaged adult at Coronado (A. Mercieca).
Ring-billed Gull: Winter-plumaged adult at San Diego (A. Mercieca).
California Gull; Winter-plumaged adult at Mission Bay (A. Mercieca).
Herring Gull: Winter plumaged adult at Mission Bay (A. Mercieca).
Thayer's Gull: First-winter immature at Salton Sea, Imperial Co. (R. E. Webster).

Lesser Black-backed Gull: Winter-plumaged adult at Oceanside, February 1996 (J. W. Schlotte).

Yellow-footed Gull: Adult at Otay dump, February 1981 (R. E. Webster).

Western Gull: Adult and fledglings at La Jolla (J. C. Daynes).

Glaucous-winged Gull: First-winter immature at Mission Bay (A. Mercieca).

Glaucous Gull: First-winter immature at Otay dump (with immature Western Gull; R. E. Webster).

Sabine's Gull: Adult in breeding plumage at Del Mar (R. E. Webster).

Black-legged Kittiwake: Immature at La Jolla (K. W. Fink).

Gull-billed Tern: Adult at south San Diego Bay, July 2003 (J. C. Daynes).

Caspian Tern: Adults and chick at salt works, south San Diego Bay (A. Mercieca).

Royal Tern: Incubating adult at salt works, south San Diego Bay, May 2003 (J. C. Daynes).

Elegant Tern: Adults and chick at salt works, south San Diego Bay, May 2003 (J. C. Daynes).

Sandwich Tern: Adult in breeding plumage in coastal Texas (A. Mercieca).

Common Tern: Immature on San Diego Bay, August 2003 (J. C. Daynes).

Arctic Tern: Adult at Churchill, Manitoba (A. Mercieca).

Forster's Tern: Incubating adult at salt works, south San Diego Bay (A. Mercieca).

Least Tern: Incubating adult at Naval Amphibious Base, Coronado (A. Mercieca).

Sooty Tern: Courting pair at Santa Margarita River mouth, 7 July 1996 (B. Foster).

Black Tern: Winter-plumaged adult in Montana (A. Mercieca).

Black Skimmer: Incubating adult at salt works, south San Diego Bay (A. Mercieca).

Common Murre: In winter plumage off San Diego (R. E. Webster).

Pigeon Guillemot: In Oregon (K. W. Fink).

Xantus's Murrelet: Subspecies *S. h. scrippsi* on ocean off San Diego (R. E. Webster).

Craveri's Murrelet: At San Benito Islands, Baja California (J. R. Jehl, Jr.).

Ancient Murrelet: On ocean off California (J. R. Jehl, Jr.)

Cassin's Auklet: In captivity at Sea World (K. W. Fink).

Parakeet Auklet: In breeding plumage in Alaska (K. W. Fink).

Rhinoceros Auklet: Captive in winter plumage at Sea World (A. Mercieca).

Horned Puffin: Captive in winter plumage at Sea World (K. W. Fink).

Tufted Puffin: Captive in breeding plumage at Sea World (A. Mercieca).

Rock Pigeon: At San Diego (A. Mercieca).

Band-tailed Pigeon: At Palomar Mountain (A. Mercieca).

Eurasian Collared Dove: In Imperial Valley, Imperial Co. (K. Z. Kurland).

Spotted Dove: Captive in San Diego Zoo (A. Mercieca).

White-winged Dove: At Big Bend National Park, Texas (A. Mercieca).

Mourning Dove: Adult and nestlings at Chula Vista (A. Mercieca).

Inca Dove: At Spring Valley, February 1997 (A. Mercieca).

Common Ground-Dove: Near Falcon Dam, Texas (A. Mercieca).

Ruddy Ground-Dove: Pair at Arizona–Sonora Desert Museum (A. Mercieca).

Red-crowned Parrot: Captive at San Diego Zoo (K. W. Fink).

Yellow-billed Cuckoo: In Texas (A. Mercieca).

Greater Roadrunner: Incubating adult at Bonita. Site was destroyed for development before young fledged (A. Mercieca).

Barn Owl: Adult at nest, Sycuan Indian Reservation (A. Mercieca).

Flammulated Owl: Injured bird held in captivity for rehabilitation (A. Mercieca).

Western Screech-Owl: In Cuyamaca Mountains (A. Mercieca).

Great Horned Owl: Nestlings at Del Mar (A. Mercieca).

Burrowing Owl: Family of fledglings at Bonita. Site subsequently destroyed for development (A. Mercieca).

Spotted Owl: Adult near Wynola (A. Mercieca).

Long-eared Owl: Adult at Tamarisk Grove Campground, Anza–Borrego Desert State Park (A. Mercieca).

Short-eared Owl: In Montana (A. Mercieca).

Northern Saw-whet Owl: In Montana (A. Mercieca).

Lesser Nighthawk: Incubating adult at Lower Otay Lake (A. Mercieca).

Common Nighthawk: Adult near Reno, Nevada (A. Mercieca).

Common Poorwill: Adult at Descanso (A. Mercieca).

Whip-poor-will: In Saskatchewan (A. Mercieca).

Chimney Swift: Adult at Santa Barbara, June 1970. Originally published by P. Devillers, 1970, Chimney Swifts in coastal southern California, Calif. Birds 1:147–152. Reproduced by permission of Western Field Ornithologists.

White-throated Swift: In Montana (A. Mercieca).

Broad-billed Hummingbird: Male in Madera Canyon, Arizona (A. Mercieca).

Violet-crowned Hummingbird: At the home of Frank and Betty Scheible, Carlsbad, November 1996 (A. Mercieca).

Magnificent Hummingbird: Immature male at Kate Sessions Park, October 2003 (M. Sadowski).

Black-chinned Hummingbird: Female at nest at Sweetwater Reservoir (A. Mercieca).

Anna's Hummingbird: Female at nest at Chula Vista (A. Mercieca).

Costa's Hummingbird: Female at nest, Anza–Borrego Desert State Park (A. Mercieca).

Calliope Hummingbird: Female in Montana (A. Mercieca).

Rufous Hummingbird: Male visiting sap wells at Lee Vining, Mono Co. (A. Mercieca).

Allen's Hummingbird: Male at Tarzana, Los Angeles Co. (A. Mercieca).

Belted Kingfisher: Male in Manitoba (A. Mercieca).

Lewis's Woodpecker: At Cabin Lake, Oregon (A. Mercieca).

Acorn Woodpecker: At Cuyamaca Rancho State Park (A. Mercieca).

Williamson's Sapsucker: Female at Paso Picacho Campground, Cuyamaca Rancho State Park (A. Mercieca).

Yellow-bellied Sapsucker: Adult female in Texas (A. Mercieca).

Red-naped Sapsucker: Male at Paso Picacho Campground, Cuyamaca Rancho State Park (A. Mercieca).

Red-breasted Sapsucker: At Paso Picacho Campground, Cuyamaca Rancho State Park (A. Mercieca).

Ladder-backed Woodpecker: Male at Green River, Arizona (A. Mercieca).

Nuttall's Woodpecker: Male at nest hole at Poway, May 2003 (J. C. Daynes).

Downy Woodpecker: Female at Poway, July 2003 (J. C. Daynes).

Hairy Woodpecker: Male at nest at Yuba Pass, Sierra Co. (A. Mercieca).

White-headed Woodpecker: Male at Cabin Lake, Oregon (A. Mercieca).

Northern Flicker: Male at Cabin Lake, Oregon (A. Mercieca).

Olive-sided Flycatcher: In Santa Rosa Mountains, Riverside Co., June 2003 (J. C. Daynes).

Western Wood-Pewee: Adult at nest at Pine Valley (A. Mercieca).

Yellow-bellied Flycatcher: Juvenile at Fort Rosecrans Cemetery, Point Loma, 29 September 2003 (M. Sadowski).

Willow Flycatcher: Adult and nestlings along the upper San Luis Rey River (A. Mercieca).

Least Flycatcher: Adult in Manitoba (A. Mercieca).

Hammond's Flycatcher: At Bonita (A. Mercieca).

Gray Flycatcher: Adult at nest at Cabin Lake, Oregon (A. Mercieca).

Dusky Flycatcher: Adult at nest in Sierra Nevada (A. Mercieca).

Western or Pacific-slope Flycatcher: At Poway, March 2002 (J. C. Daynes).

Black Phoebe: Adult and nestlings at San Pasqual (A. Mercieca).

Eastern Phoebe: At San Jacinto Wildlife Area, Riverside Co., 5 January 2003 (D. Furseth).

Say's Phoebe: At Chula Vista (A. Mercieca).

Vermilion Flycatcher: Adult male along the Verde River, Arizona (A. Mercieca).

Dusky-capped or Olivaceous Flycatcher: In Cave Creek Canyon, Arizona (A. Mercieca).

Ash-throated Flycatcher: In Santa Rosa Mountains, Riverside Co., May 2003 (J. C. Daynes).

Great Crested Flycatcher: At Padre Island, Texas (A. Mercieca).

Brown-crested or Wied's Crested Flycatcher: In Guadalupe Canyon, Arizona/New Mexico (A. Mercieca).

Sulphur-bellied Flycatcher: At El Descanso, Baja California, October 2002—a first for Baja California; see N. Am. Birds 57:121 (B. L. Sullivan).

Tropical Kingbird: In Costa Rica (A. Mercieca).

Cassin's Kingbird: Adult and nestlings at Lower Otay Lake (A. Mercieca).

Thick-billed Kingbird: At Bonita, 26 December 1966 (J. M. Sheppard).

Western Kingbird: At Lower Otay Lake (A. Mercieca).

Eastern Kingbird: In Montana (A. Mercieca).

Scissor-tailed Flycatcher: In Texas (A. Mercieca).

Loggerhead Shrike: Adult and nestlings in Proctor Valley (A. Mercieca).

White-eyed Vireo: Along Sweetwater River above Sweetwater Reservoir, July 2000 (A. Mercieca).

Bell's Vireo: Adult and nestlings along Sweetwater River above Sweetwater Reservoir (A. Mercieca).

Gray Vireo: On ridge east of Buckman Springs (A. Mercieca).

Yellow-throated Vireo: On Padre Island, Texas (A. Mercieca).

Plumbeous Vireo: In Cave Creek Canyon, Arizona (A. Mercieca).

Cassin's Vireo: In Santa Rosa Mountains, Riverside Co., August 2004 (J. C. Daynes).

Blue-headed Vireo: On Padre Island, Texas (A. Mercieca).

Hutton's Vireo: Adult and fledgling at Sweetwater Reservoir (A. Mercieca).

Warbling Vireo: At Bonita (A. Mercieca).

Philadelphia Vireo: At Padre Island, Texas (A. Mercieca).

Red-eyed Vireo: At Padre Island, Texas (A. Mercieca).

Yellow-green Vireo: At Point Reyes National Seashore, Marin Co., September 1988 (P. LaTourrette).

Steller's Jay: Adult and nestling near Agua Dulce Campground, Laguna Mts. (A. Mercieca).

Western Scrub-Jay: At Chula Vista (A. Mercieca).

Pinyon Jay: At Cabin Lake, Oregon (A. Mercieca).

Clark's Nutcracker: At Crater Lake, Oregon (A. Mercieca).

American Crow: At Wild Animal Park (A. Mercieca).

Common Raven: At Ramona (A. Mercieca).

Horned Lark: Adult and nestlings at Lower Otay Lake (A. Mercieca).

Purple Martin: Female at San Benito, Texas (A. Mercieca).

Tree Swallow: At Lee Vining, Mono Co. (A. Mercieca).

Violet-green Swallow: At Lee Vining, Mono Co. (A. Mercieca).

Northern Rough-winged Swallow: Adult at nest hole, El Capitan Reservoir (A. Mercieca).

Bank Swallow: In Alaska (A. Mercieca).

Cliff Swallow: At Chula Vista (A. Mercieca).

Barn Swallow: Recently fledged juvenile at south San Diego Bay, June 2003 (J. C. Daynes).

Mountain Chickadee: At Paso Picacho Campground, Cuyamaca Rancho State Park (A. Mercieca).

Oak Titmouse: In Laguna Mts. (A. Mercieca).

Verdin: Adult and nestlings in Indian Gorge, Anza–Borrego Desert State Park (A. Mercieca).

Bushtit: Female at nest, Lower Otay Lake (A. Mercieca).

Red-breasted Nuthatch: In Ontario, Canada (A. Mercieca).

White-breasted Nuthatch: Male at Paso Picacho Campground, Cuyamaca Rancho State Park (A. Mercieca).

Pygmy Nuthatch: At Mt. Pinos, Ventura Co. (A. Mercieca).

Brown Creeper: At Lee Vining, Mono Co. (A. Mercieca).

Cactus Wren: Adult and nestlings at Bonita (A. Mercieca).

Rock Wren: In Anza–Borrego Desert State Park, March 2003 (J. C. Daynes).

Canyon Wren: In Sierra San Francisco, Baja California Sur (S. I. Bond).

Bewick's Wren: Adult at Poway, June 2003 (J. C. Daynes).

House Wren: Adult at nest hole, Sierra Nevada (A. Mercieca).

Winter Wren: At Point Loma, 19 October 1967 (A. M. Craig).

Marsh Wren: Winter visitor of subspecies *Cistothorus palustris plesius* at Tijuana River estuary (A. Mercieca).

American Dipper: Along Lee Vining Creek, Mono Co. (A. Mercieca).

Golden-crowned Kinglet: In Tijuana River valley (S. Streit).

Ruby-crowned Kinglet: Male at Paso Picacho Campground, Cuyamaca Rancho State Park (A. Mercieca).

Blue-gray Gnatcatcher: Adult female and nestlings at Spring Valley (A. Mercieca).

California Gnatcatcher: Adult female and nestlings at Spring Valley (A. Mercieca).

Black-tailed Gnatcatcher: Adult female and nestlings in Indian Gorge, Anza–Borrego Desert State Park (A. Mercieca).

Western Bluebird: Male at Wynola (A. Mercieca).

Mountain Bluebird: Male at Lee Vining (A. Mercieca).

Townsend's Solitaire: Adult in Santa Rosa Mountains, Riverside Co., June 2003 (J. C. Daynes).

Gray-cheeked Thrush: On Padre Island, Texas (A. Mercieca).

Swainson's Thrush: Migrant at Cabrillo National Monument, Point Loma (A. Mercieca).

Hermit Thrush: Winter visitor at Paso Picacho Campground, Cuyamaca Rancho State Park (A. Mercieca).

Wood Thrush: On Padre Island, Texas (A. Mercieca).

American Robin: Female at Cabin Lake, Oregon (A. Mercieca).

Varied Thrush: At Fort Rosecrans Cemetery, Point Loma, 23 November 2002 (D. Furseth).

Wrentit: Adult and nestlings at Bonita (A. Mercieca).

Gray Catbird: On Padre Island, Texas (A. Mercieca).

Northern Mockingbird: Adults and nestlings at Bonita (A. Mercieca).

Sage Thrasher: Near Littlefield, Arizona (A. Mercieca).

Brown Thrasher: In Pawnee National Grassland, Colorado (A. Mercieca).

Bendire's Thrasher: Near Tucson, Arizona (A. Mercieca).

Curve-billed Thrasher: Near Tucson, Arizona (A. Mercieca).

California Thrasher: Adult at nest, Bonita (A. Mercieca).

Le Conte's Thrasher: At Mesquite Spring, Death Valley (J. Oldenettel).

European Starling: At Chula Vista (A. Mercieca).

Red-throated Pipit: At San Clemente Island, 1 October 2002 (B. L. Sullivan).

American Pipit: In Tijuana River valley (A. Mercieca).

Sprague's Pipit: In Tijuana River valley, 19 October 1974 (J. S. Luther).

Cedar Waxwing: At Chula Vista (A. Mercieca).

Phainopepla: Adult female and nestlings in Indian Gorge, Anza–Borrego Desert State Park (A. Mercieca).

Blue-winged Warbler: On Padre Island, Texas (A. Mercieca).

Golden-winged Warbler: On Padre Island, Texas (A. Mercieca).

Tennessee Warbler: On Padre Island, Texas (A. Mercieca).

Orange-crowned Warbler: Subspecies *lutescens* at Chula Vista (A. Mercieca).

Nashville Warbler: At Cabrillo National Monument, Point Loma (A. Mercieca).

Virginia's Warbler: At Guadalupe Canyon, Arizona (A. Mercieca).

Lucy's Warbler: At Guadalupe Canyon, Arizona (A. Mercieca).

Northern Parula: At Padre Island, Texas (A. Mercieca).

Yellow Warbler: Male in spring migration at Chula Vista (A. Mercieca).

Chestnut-sided Warbler: Immature Female in Little Italy area of downtown San Diego, December 2003 (M. Sadowski).

Magnolia Warbler: Male at Padre Island, Texas (A. Mercieca).

Cape May Warbler: Female at San Clemente Island, 20 October 2001 (B. L. Sullivan).

Black-throated Blue Warbler: Male at Point Pelee, Ontario (A. Mercieca).

Yellow-rumped Warbler: At Chula Vista (A. Mercieca).

Black-throated Gray Warbler: Female and nestlings at Yuba Pass, Sierra Co. (A. Mercieca).

Black-throated Green Warbler: Female at Point Pelee, Ontario (A. Mercieca).

Townsend's Warbler: Female at Chula Vista (A. Mercieca).

Hermit Warbler: At Cabrillo National Monument, Point Loma (A. Mercieca).

Blackburnian Warbler: At San Clemente Island, October 2003 (B. L. Sullivan).

Pine Warbler: Male in Louisiana (A. Mercieca).

Prairie Warbler: Male on Padre Island, Texas (A. Mercieca).

Palm Warbler: At San Clemente Island, 24 October 2002 (B. L. Sullivan).

Bay-breasted Warbler: Male on Padre Island, Texas (A. Mercieca).

Blackpoll Warbler: Immature in Alaska (A. Mercieca).

Cerulean Warbler: Male on Padre Island, Texas (A. Mercieca).

Black-and-white Warbler: Female on Padre Island, Texas (A. Mercieca).

American Redstart: Female at Point Pelee, Ontario (A. Mercieca).

Prothonotary Warbler: At Laguna Atascosa, Texas (A. Mercieca).

Worm-eating Warbler: At Laguna Atascosa, Texas (A. Mercieca).

Ovenbird: At Padre Island, Texas (A. Mercieca).

Northern Waterthrush: At Laguna Atascosa, Texas (A. Mercieca).

Louisiana Waterthrush: Near the Salk Institute, La Jolla, February 1990 (A. Mercieca).

Kentucky Warbler: Male at Padre Island, Texas (A. Mercieca).

Mourning Warbler: Male at Long Point, Ontario (A. Mercieca).

MacGillivray's Warbler: Male at Chula Vista (A. Mercieca).

Common Yellowthroat: Female and nestlings along the Sweetwater River at Jamacha (A. Mercieca).

Hooded Warbler: Female at Padre Island, Texas (A. Mercieca).

Wilson's Warbler: At Cabrillo National Monument, Point Loma (A. Mercieca).

Canada Warbler: Immature male at Chula Vista, October 1988 (A. Mercieca).

Painted Redstart: In Cave Creek Canyon, Arizona (A. Mercieca).

Yellow-breasted Chat: Adult and nestlings along the Sweetwater River near Jamacha (A. Mercieca).

Hepatic Tanager: Female at Point Loma, 2 December 1966 (A. M. Craig).

Summer Tanager: Male in Big Bend National Park, Texas (A. Mercieca).

Scarlet Tanager: Female at Padre Island, Texas (A. Mercieca).

Western Tanager: Male at Coronado (A. Mercieca).

Green-tailed Towhee: Along Verde River, Arizona (A. Mercieca).

Spotted Towhee: Adult male and nestlings at Bonita (A. Mercieca).

California Towhee: Adult and nestlings at Bonita (A. Mercieca).

Cassin's Sparrow: At San Clemente Island, 2 November 2001 (B. L. Sullivan).

Rufous-crowned Sparrow: Adult and nestlings along the Sweetwater River near Jamacha (A. Mercieca).

American Tree Sparrow: At Point Loma (R. E. Webster).

Chipping Sparrow: Adult at Cabin Lake, Oregon (A. Mercieca).

Clay-colored Sparrow: Fall vagrant at Chula Vista (A. Mercieca).

Brewer's Sparrow: At the Arizona–Sonora Desert Museum (A. Mercieca).

Black-chinned Sparrow: Male near Buckman Springs (A. Mercieca).

Vesper Sparrow: At the Arizona–Sonora Desert Museum (A. Mercieca).

Lark Sparrow: Adult and nestlings at Lower Otay Lake (A. Mercieca).

Black-throated Sparrow: Near Landers, San Bernardino Co., February 2003 (J. C. Daynes).

Sage Sparrow: Adult and nestlings at Lower Otay Lake (A. Mercieca).

Lark Bunting: Female in Pawnee National Grassland, Colorado (A. Mercieca).

Savannah Sparrow: Subspecies *Passerculus sandwichensis rostratus* (Large-billed Sparrow) in San Diego Bay salt works (A. Mercieca).

Grasshopper Sparrow: Adult and nestlings at Medicine Lake, Montana (A. Mercieca).

Baird's Sparrow: Juvenile at Fort Rosecrans Cemetery, Point Loma, October 1981 (Herb Clarke).

Nelson's Sharp-tailed Sparrow: At the Tijuana River estuary (A. Mercieca).

Fox Sparrow: At Cabrillo National Monument, Point Loma (A. Mercieca).

Song Sparrow: Adult and nestlings at Lower Otay Lake (A. Mercieca).

Lincoln's Sparrow: In the Tijuana River valley (A. Mercieca).

Swamp Sparrow: In Imperial County (K. Z. Kurland).

White-throated Sparrow: At Pacific Beach, December 2001 (A. Mercieca).

Harris's Sparrow: In Imperial County (K. Z. Kurland).

White-crowned Sparrow: Adult at Chula Vista (A. Mercieca).

Golden-crowned Sparrow: Immature at Sacramento National Wildlife Refuge, Glenn Co. (J. C. Daynes).

Dark-eyed Junco: Male at Chula Vista (A. Mercieca).

McCown's Longspur: At San Clemente Island, October 2002 (B. L. Sullivan).

Lapland Longspur: At Fort Rosecrans National Cemetery, Point Loma, 23 October 1984 (R. E. Webster).

Chestnut-collared Longspur: Female and nestlings at Benton Lake National Wildlife Refuge, Montana (A. Mercieca).

Pyrrhuloxia: Male near Tucson, Arizona (A. Mercieca).

Rose-breasted Grosbeak: At Cabrillo National Monument, Point Loma (A. Mercieca).

Black-headed Grosbeak: Male near Lakeside (A. Mercieca).

Blue Grosbeak: Male and nestlings in Proctor Valley (A. Mercieca).

Lazuli Bunting: Female and nestlings in Proctor Valley
    (A. Mercieca).
Indigo Bunting: Male at Padre Island, Texas (A. Mercieca).
Painted Bunting: Male at Padre Island, Texas (A. Mercieca).
Dickcissel: Immature in Tijuana River valley, October 1982
    (R. E. Webster).
Bobolink: Female at Medicine Lake, Montana (A. Mercieca).
Red-winged Blackbird: Female and nestlings on Otay Mesa
    (A. Mercieca).
Tricolored Blackbird: Male at Miramar Lake (A. Mercieca).
Western Meadowlark: Adult and nestlings in Proctor Valley
    (A. Mercieca).
Yellow-headed Blackbird: Male at Bear River, Utah
    (A. Mercieca).
Rusty Blackbird: At San Clemente Island, 24 October 2002
    (B. L. Sullivan).
Brewer's Blackbird: Female and nestlings at Lower Otay Lake
    (A. Mercieca).
Common Grackle: At Rondeau Park, Ontario (A. Mercieca).
Great-tailed Grackle: Female at San Diego Wild Animal Park
    (K. W. Fink).
Bronzed Cowbird: Male near Patagonia, Arizona
    (A. Mercieca).
Brown-headed Cowbird: Female at Chula Vista (A. Mercieca).
Orchard Oriole: Female at Padre Island, Texas (A. Mercieca).
Hooded Oriole: Female at Chula Vista (A. Mercieca).
Bullock's Oriole: Pair at Lower Otay Lake (A. Mercieca).
Baltimore Oriole: Female at Padre Island, Texas (A. Mercieca).
Scott's Oriole: Male in Anza–Borrego Desert State Park, April
    2003 (J. C. Daynes).

Purple Finch: Male near Julian (A. Mercieca).
Cassin's Finch: Male at Cabin Lake, Oregon (A. Mercieca).
House Finch: Male and nestlings at Lower Otay Lake
    (A. Mercieca).
Red Crossbill: Male at Arizona–Sonora Desert Museum
    (A. Mercieca).
Pine Siskin: At Portal, Arizona (A. Mercieca).
Lesser Goldfinch: Pair at nest at Lower Otay Lake
    (A. Mercieca).
Lawrence's Goldfinch: Male at William Heise County Park
    (A. Mercieca).
American Goldfinch: Pair at nest at Lower Otay Lake
    (A. Mercieca).
Evening Grosbeak: Female in Saskatchewan (A. Mercieca).
House Sparrow: Female at San Diego Zoo (A. Mercieca).
Black-bellied Whistling-Duck: In Texas (A. Mercieca).
Mute Swan: Adult and cygnets at Long Point, Ontario
    (A. Mercieca).
Ruddy Shelduck: Captive at Sea World (A. Mercieca).
Mandarin Duck: Captive male at San Diego Zoo (A. Mercieca).
Crested Caracara: At Laguna Atascosa, Texas (A. Mercieca).
Black-headed Gull: Captive at San Diego Zoo (A. Mercieca).
Ringed Turtle-Dove: Captive at San Diego Zoo (A. Mercieca).
Blue-and-yellow Macaw: Captive at San Diego Zoo (K. W.
    Fink).
Lilac-crowned Parrot: Captive at San Diego Zoo (K. W. Fink).
Black-throated Magpie-Jay: In Tijuana River valley
    (A. Mercieca).
Purplish-backed or Beechey's Jay: Captive at Arizona–Sonora
    Desert Museum (K. W. Fink).

LITERATURE CITED

Abbott, C. G. 1926. Peculiar nesting site of a Dusky Warbler. Condor 28:57–60.

Abbott, C. G. 1927a. American Dipper established as a breeding species in San Diego County. Condor 29:117–118.

Abbott, C. G. 1927b. Notes on the nesting of the Band-tailed Pigeon. Condor 29:121–123.

Abbott, C. G. 1927c. Mid-winter nesting in southern California. Condor 29:160.

Abbott, C. G. 1927d. Western Bluebird nesting in the city of San Diego. Condor 29:165.

Abbott, C. G. 1927e. Elegant Terns at San Diego. Condor 29:171.

Abbott, C. G. 1928a. Bird notes from San Diego County. Condor 30:162–163.

Abbott, C. G. 1928b. American Goshawk in San Diego County, California. Condor 30:192–193.

Abbott, C. G. 1930. Urban Burrowing Owls. Auk 47:564–565.

Abbott, C. G. 1931. Wood Ibises summering in San Diego County, California. Condor 33:29–30.

Abbott, C. G. 1935. Another invasion of Wood Ibises in southern California. Condor 37:35–36.

Abbott, C. G. 1938. An exceptional influx of Wood Ibises into southern California. Condor 40:257.

Abbott, C. G. 1940. Mountain Plover at San Diego, California. Condor 42:125–126.

Abbott, C. G. 1941. Notes from San Diego County, California. Condor 43:77.

Adams, E. 1899. House Finches again. Bull. Cooper Ornithol. Soc. 1:24.

Ainley, D. G. 1995. Ashy Storm-Petrel, in The Birds of North America (A. Poole and F. Gill, eds.), no. 185. Acad. Nat. Sci., Philadelphia.

Ainley, D. G., Sydeman, W. J., Hatch, S. A., and Wilson, U. W. 1994. Seabird population trends along the west coast of North America: Causes and the extent of regional concordance. Studies Avian Biol. 15:119–133.

Ainley, D. G., Veit, R. L., Allen, S. G., Spear, L. B., and Pyle, P. 1995. Variations in marine bird communities of the California Current, 1986–1994. Calif. Coop. Fish. Invest. Rep. 36:72–77.

Ainley, D. G., Nettleship, D. N., Carter, H. R., and Storey, A. E. 2002. Common Murre, in The Birds of North America (A. Poole and F. Gill, eds.), no. 666. Birds N. Am., Philadelphia.

Aldrich, J. W. 1968. Population characteristics and nomenclature of the Hermit Thrush. Proc. U. S. Natl. Mus. 124:1–33.

Altman, B., and Sallabanks, R. 2000. Olive-sided Flycatcher, in The Birds of North America (A. Poole and F. Gill, eds.), no. 502. Birds N. Am., Philadelphia.

American Ornithologists' Union. 1957. Check-list of North American Birds, 5th ed. Am. Ornithol. Union, Baltimore.

American Ornithologists' Union. 1995. Fortieth supplement to the American Ornithologists' Union Check-list of North American Birds. Auk 112:819–830.

American Ornithologists' Union. 1997. Forty-first supplement to the American Ornithologists' Union Check-list of North American Birds. Auk 114:542–552.

American Ornithologists' Union. 1998. Check-list of North American Birds, 7th ed. Am. Ornithol. Union, Washington, D.C.

Ammon, E. M., and Gilbert, W. M. 1999. Wilson's Warbler, in The Birds of North America (A. Poole and F. Gill, eds.), no. 478. Birds N. Am., Philadelphia.

Anderson, C. M., Roseneau, D. G., Walton, B. J., and Bente, P.

J. 1988. New evidence of a Peregrine migration on the west coast of North America, in Peregrine Falcon Populations: Their Management and Recovery (T. J. Cade, J. H. Enderson, C. G. Thelander, and C. M. White, eds.), pp. 507–516. Peregrine Fund, Boise.

Anderson, D. W. 1988. Dose–response relationship between human disturbance and Brown Pelican breeding success. Wildlife Soc. Bull. 16:339–345.

Anderson, D. W., and Anderson, I. T. 1976. Distribution and status of Brown Pelicans in the California current. Am. Birds 30:3–12.

Anonymous. 1935. San Diego Nat. Hist. Mus. Bull 108:1.

Anthony, A. W. 1894. Icterus parisorum in western San Diego County, California. Auk 11:327–328.

Anthony, A. W. 1895. The St. Lucas Flycatcher in California. Auk 12:390.

Anthony, A. W. 1922. The Sharp-tailed Sandpiper in southern California. Auk 39:106.

Anthony, A. W. 1924. The raided rookeries of Laysan, a belated echo. Condor 26:33–34.

Arnold, J. R. 1935. The changing distribution of the Western Mockingbird in California. Condor 37:193–199.

Arnold, J. R. 1980. Distribution of the Mockingbird in California. W. Birds 11:97–102.

Asay, C. E. 1987. Habitat and productivity of Cooper's Hawks nesting in California. Calif. Fish and Game 73:80–87.

Atwood, J. L. 1988. Speciation and geographic variation in black-tailed gnatcatchers. Ornithol. Monogr. 42.

Atwood, J. L. 1993. California Gnatcatchers and coastal sage scrub: The biological basis for endangered species listing, in Interface between Ecology and Land Development in California (J. E. Keeley, ed.), pp. 149–169. S. Calif. Acad. Sci., Los Angeles.

Atwood, J. L., and Bolsinger, J. S. 1992. Elevational distribution of California Gnatcatchers in the United States. J. Field Ornithol. 63:159–168.

Atwood, J. L., and Bontrager, D. R. 2001. California Gnatcatcher, in The Birds of North America (A. Poole and F. Gill, eds.), no. 574. Birds N. Am., Philadelphia.

Atwood, J. L., and Massey, B. W. 1988. Site fidelity of Least Terns in California. Condor 90:389–394.

Atwood, J. L., Bontrager, D. R., and Gorospe, A. L. 1998. Use of refugia by California Gnatcatchers displaced by habitat loss. W. Birds 29:406–412.

Austin, J. E., and Miller, M. R. 1995. Northern Pintail, in The Birds of North America (A. Poole and F. Gill, eds.), no 163. Acad. Nat. Sci., Philadelphia.

Austin, O. L., ed. 1968. Life histories of North American cardinals, grosbeaks, towhees, finches, sparrows, and allies (part 1). U. S. Natl. Mus. Bull. 237.

Bailey, E. R., and Mock, P. J. 1998. Dispersal capability of the California Gnatcatcher: A landscape analysis of distribution data. W. Birds 29:351–360.

Bailey, F. M. 1902. Handbook of the Birds of the Western United States. Houghton Mifflin, Boston.

Baird, S. F. 1858. Explorations and surveys for a railroad route from the Mississippi River to the Pacific Ocean, vol. 9. Birds. Part II—General report upon the zoology of the several Pacific railroad routes. War Dept., Washington, D.C.

Baird, S. F. 1870. The Birds of North America; the Descriptions of Species Based Chiefly on the Collections in the Museum of the Smithsonian Institution. J. B. Lippincott, Philadelphia.

Bakus, G. J. 1962. Early nesting of the Costa Hummingbird in southern California. Condor 64:438–439.

Balda, R. P. 2002. Pinyon Jay, *in* The Birds of North America (A. Poole and F. Gill, eds.), no 605. Birds N. Am., Philadelphia.

Baltosser, W. H. 1989. Costa's Hummingbird: Its distribution and status. W. Birds 20:41–62.

Bancroft, G. 1929. A new Pacific race of Gull-billed Tern. Trans. San Diego Soc. Nat. Hist. 5:283–286.

Banks, R. C. 1964. An experiment on a Flammulated Owl. Condor 66:69.

Banks, R. C. 1965. The nesting Starling population in San Diego County, California. Bull. S. Calif. Acad. Sci. 65:11–15.

Banks, R. C. 1967. Recent records of water birds in the desert. Bull S. Calif. Acad. Sci. 66:125–128.

Banks, R. C. 1986a. Subspecies of the Glaucous Gull, *Larus hyperboreus* (Aves: Charadriiformes). Proc. Biol. Soc. Washington 99:149–159.

Banks, R. C. 1986b. Subspecies of the Greater Scaup and their names. Wilson Bull 98:433–444.

Banks, R. C., and Browning, M. R. 1995. Comments on the status of revived old names for some North American birds. Auk 112:633–648.

Banks, R. C., Cicero, C., Dunn, J. L., Kratter, A. W., Rasummen, P. C., Remsen, J. V., Jr., Rising, J. D., and Stotz, D. F. 2002. Forty-third supplement to the *American Ornithologists Union Check-list of North American Birds*. Auk 119:897–906.

Barhoum, D. N., and Burns, K. J. 2002. Phylogenetic relationships of the Wrentit based on mitochondrial cytochrome *b* sequences. Condor 104:740–749.

Bartholomew, G. A., Howell, T. R., and Cade, T. 1957. Torpidity in the White-throated Swift, Anna Hummingbird, and Poorwill. Condor 59:145–155.

Bates, J. M. 1992. Frugivory on *Bursera microphylla* (Burseraceae) by wintering Gray Vireos (*Vireo vicinior*, Vireonidae) in the coastal deserts of Sonora, Mexico. Southwest. Nat. 37:232–258.

Beal, F. E. L. 1910. Birds of California in relation to the fruit industry, part 2. U.S. Dept. Agric. Biol. Surv. Bull. 34.

Beattie, M. H. 1994. Endangered and threatened wildlife and plants; 1-year finding for a petition to list the Pacific coast population of the Cactus Wren under the Endangered Species Act. Federal Register 59:45659–45661.

Bednarz, J. C. 1995. Harris' Hawk, *in* The Birds of North America (A. Poole and F. Gill, eds.), no. 146. Acad. Nat. Sci., Philadelphia.

Beedy, E. C., and Hamilton, W. J., III. 1999. Tricolored Blackbird, *in* The Birds of North America (A. Poole and F. Gill, eds.), no 423. Birds N. Am., Philadelphia.

Beemer, E. 1949. Winter Wren in San Diego County, California. Condor 51:233.

Behle, W. H. 1942. Distribution and variation of the Horned Larks (*Otocoris alpestris*) of western North America. Univ. Calif. Publ. Zool. 46:205–316.

Behle, W. H. 1973. Clinal variation in White-throated Swifts from Utah and the Rocky Mountain region. Auk 90:299–306.

Belding, L. 1890. Land birds of the Pacific district. Occ. Pap. Calif. Acad. Sci. 2:1–174.

Belding, L. 1892. Geese which occur in California. Zoe 3:96–101.

Bell, D. A. 1996. Genetic differentiation, geographic variation, and hybridization in gulls of the *Larus glaucescens–occidentalis* complex. Condor 98:527–546.

Bell, D. A. 1997. Hybridization and reproductive performance in gulls of the *Larus glaucescens–occidentalis* complex. Condor 99:585–594.

Bemis, C., and Rising, J. D. 1999. Western Wood-Pewee, *in* The Birds of North America (A. Poole and F. Gill, eds.), no. 451. Birds N. Am., Philadelphia.

Benkman, C. W. 1993. Adaptation to single resources and the evolutions of crossbill (*Loxia*) diversity. Ecol. Monogr. 63:305–323.

Benson, L. 1969. The Native Cacti of California. Stanford Univ. Press, Stanford, CA.

Bent, A. C. 1938. Life histories of North American birds of prey, part 2. U. S. Natl. Mus. Bull. 170.

Bent, A. C. 1939. Life histories of North American woodpeckers. U. S. Natl. Mus. Bull. 174.

Bent, A. C. 1942. Life histories of North American flycatchers, larks, swallows, and their allies. U. S. Natl. Mus. Bull. 179.

Bent, A. C. 1946. Life histories of North American jays, crows, and titmice. U. S. Natl. Mus. Bull. 191.

Bent, A. C. 1948. Life histories of North American nuthatches, wrens, thrashers, and their allies. U. S. Natl. Mus. Bull. 195.

Bent, A. C. 1949. Life histories of North American thrushes, kinglets, and their allies. U. S. Natl. Mus. Bull. 196.

Bent, A. C. 1950. Life histories of North American wagtails, shrikes, vireos, and their allies. U. S. Natl. Mus. Bull. 197.

Bent, A. C. 1953. Life histories of North American wood warblers. U. S. Natl. Mus. Bull. 203.

Bent, A. C. 1958. Life histories of North American blackbirds, orioles, tanagers, and allies. U. S. Natl. Mus. Bull. 211.

Bevier, L. 1990. Eleventh report of the California Bird Records Committee. W. Birds 21:145–176.

Beyers, J. L., and Wirtz, W. O. 1997. Vegetative characteristics of coastal sage scrub used by California Gnatcatchers: Implications for management in a fire-prone ecosystem, *in* Proceedings of a conference held at Coeur d'Alene, Idaho, November, 1995 (J. M. Greenlee, ed.), pp. 81–89. Int. Assoc. Wildland Fire, Fairfield, WA.

Binford, L. C. 1983. Sixth report of the California Bird Records Committee. W. Birds 14:127–145.

Binford, L. C. 1985. Seventh report of the California Bird Records Committee. W. Birds 16:29–48.

Binford, L. C. 1989. A distributional survey of the birds of the Mexican state of Oaxaca. Ornithol. Monogr. 43.

Binford, L. C., and Johnson, D. B. 1995. Range expansion of the Glaucous-winged Gull into interior United States and Canada. W. Birds 26:169–188.

Bishop, L. B. 1905. Notes on a small collection of California birds with description of an apparently unrecognized race of Hutton's Vireo. Condor 7:141–143.

Black, C. D., Henry, T. W., and Henry, A. E. 1997. Breeding colonies of Great Blue Herons, Snowy Egret, and Little Blue Herons at Mission Bay, California, 1997. Hubbs–Sea World Res. Inst. Tech. Rep. 97-276.

Blake, E. R., and Vaurie, C. D. 1962. Family Corvidae, *in* Check-list of Birds of the World (E. Mayr and J. C. Greenway, eds.), vol. 15, pp. 204–282. Mus. Comp. Zool., Cambridge, MA.

Blanco, G., and Rodriguez-Estrella, R. 1999. Reduced sexual dimorphism in Opsreys from Baja California Sur, Mexico. Ibis 141:489–506.

Bleitz, D. 1956. Heavy parasitization of Blue Grosbeaks by cowbirds in California. Condor 58:236–238.

Bloom, P. H. 1994. The biology and current status of the Long-eared Owl in coastal southern California. Bull. S. Calif. Acad. Sci. 93:1–12.

Bloom, P. H., McCrary, M. D., and Gibson, M. J. 1993. Red-shouldered Hawk home-range and habitat use in southern California. J. Wildlife Mgmt. 57:258–265.

Boarman, W. I., and Heinrich, B. 1999. Common Raven, *in* The Birds of North America (A. Poole and F. Gill, eds.), no. 476. Birds N. Am., Philadelphia.

Boekelheide, R. J., Ainley, D. G., Morrell, S. H., and Lewis, T. J. 1990. Brandt's Cormorant, *in* Seabirds of the Farallon Islands

(D. G. Ainley and R. J. Boekelheide, eds.), pp. 163–194. Stanford Univ. Press, Stanford, CA.

Boersma, P. D., and Silva, M. C. 2001. Fork-tailed Storm-Petrel, *in* The Birds of North America (A. Poole and F. Gill, eds.), no. 569. Birds N. Am., Philadelphia.

Bolger, D. T., Scott, T. A., and Rotenberry, J. T. 1997. Breeding bird abundance in an urbanizing landscape in coastal southern California. Cons. Biol. 11:406–421.

Bond, M., and Bradley, C. 2004. Impacts of the 2003 southern California wildfires on four species listed as threatened or endangered under the federal Endangered Species Act. Center for Biological Diversity, Idyllwild, CA.

Bontrager, D.R. 1991. Habitat requirements, home range requirements, and breeding biology of the California Gnatcatcher (*Polioptila californica*) in south Orange County, California. Report to Santa Margarita Company, Rancho Santa Margarita, CA.

Bontrager, D. R., Erickson, R. A., and Hamilton, R.A. 1995. Impacts of the 1993 Laguna fire on California Gnatcatchers and Cactus Wrens, in Brushfires in California Wildlands: Ecology and Resource Management (J. E. Keeley and T. A. Scott, eds.), pp. 69–76. Int. Assoc. Wildland Fire, Fairfield, WA.

Both, C., and Visser, M. E. 2001. Adjustment to climate change is constrained by arrival date in a long-distance migrant bird. Nature 411:296–298.

Bourne, W. R. P., and Jehl, J. R., Jr. 1982. Variation and nomenclature of Leach's Storm-Petrels. Auk 99:793–797.

Boyce, D. A., Jr., Garrett. R. L., and Walton, B. J. 1986. Distribution and density of Prairie Falcons nesting in California during the 1970s. Raptor Res. 20:71-74.

Braden, G. T. 1992. California Gnatcatchers (*Polioptila californica*) at three sites in western Riverside County. Report to Metropolitan Water District, Los Angeles.

Braden, G. T., McKernan, R. L., and Powell, S. M. 1997. Effects of nest parasitism by the Brown-headed Cowbird on nesting success of the California Gnatcatcher. Condor 99: 858–865.

Brennan, L. A., Block, W. M., and Gutiérrez, R. J. 1987. Habitat use by Mountain Quail in northern California. Condor 89:66–74.

Brewster, W. 1902. Birds of the cape region of Lower California. Bull Mus. Comp. Zool. 41:1–241.

Briggs, K. T., Tyler, W. B., Lewis, D. B., and Carlson, D. R. 1987. Bird communities at sea off California: 1975 to 1983. Studies Avian Biol. 11.

Brisbin, I. L., Jr., and Mowbray, T. B. 2002. American Coot, *in* The Birds of North America (A. Poole and F. Gill, eds.), no. 697. Birds N. Am., Philadelphia.

Brown, C. R. 1977. Purple Martins versus Starlings and House Sparrows in nest-site competition. Bull. Tex. Ornithol. Soc. 10:31–35.

Brown, C. R. 1981. The impact of Starlings on Purple Martin populations in unmanaged colonies. Am. Birds 35:266–268.

Brown, C. R. 1997. Purple Martin, *in* The Birds of North America (A. Poole and F. Gill, eds.), no. 287. Acad. Nat. Sci., Philadelphia.

Brown, C. R., and Brown, M. B. 1995. Cliff Swallow, *in* The Birds of North America (A. Poole and F. Gill, eds.), no. 149. Acad. Nat., Sci., Philadelphia.

Brown, D. E., Hagelin, J. C., Taylor, M., and Galloway, J. 1998. Gambel's Quail, *in* The Birds of North America (A. Poole and F. Gill, eds.), no. 321. Birds N. Am., Philadelphia.

Brown, P. W., and Frederickson, L. H. 1997. White-winged Scoter, *in* The Birds of North America (A. Poole and F. Gill, eds.), no. 274. Acad. Nat. Sci., Philadelphia.

Browne, F. C. 1891. Scott's Oriole in California. Auk 8:238.

Browning, M. R. 1974. Comments on the winter distribution of the Swainson's Hawk (*Buteo swainsoni*) in North America. Am. Birds 28:856–867.

Browning, M. R. 1977. Geographic variation in Dunlins, *Calidris alpina*, of North America. Can. Field-Nat. 91:391–393.

Browning, M. R. 1994. A taxonomic review of *Dendroica petechia* (Yellow Warbler; Aves; Parulinae). Proc. Biol. Soc. Washington 107:27–51.

Browning, M. R., and Cross, S. P. 1999. Specimens of birds from Jackson County, Oregon: Distribution and taxonomy of selected species. Ore. Birds 25:62–71.

Brua, R. B. 2002. Ruddy Duck, *in* The Birds of North America (A. Poole and F. Gill, eds.), no. 696. Birds N. Am., Philadelphia.

Buckley, P. A., and Mitra, S. S. 2002. Three geese resembling "Gray-bellied Brant"/ "Lawrence's Brant" from Long Island, New York. N. Am. Birds 56:502–507.

Buehler, D. A. 2000. Bald Eagle, *in* The Birds of North America (A. Poole and F. Gill, eds.), no. 506. Birds N. Am., Philadelphia.

Bull, E. L., and Cooper, H. D. 1991. Vaux's Swift nests in hollow trees. W. Birds 22:85–91.

Bull, E. L., and Hohmann, J. E. 1993. The association between Vaux's Swifts and old-growth forests in northeastern Oregon. W. Birds 24:38–42.

Burleigh, T. D. 1963. Geographic variation in the Cedar Waxwing (*Bombycilla cedrorum*). Proc. Biol. Soc. Washington 76:177–180.

Burness, G. P., Lefevre, K., and Collins, C. T. 1999. Elegant Tern, *in* The Birds of North America (A. Poole and F. Gill, eds.), no. 404. Birds N. Am., Philadelphia.

California Department of Fish and Game. 1993. 5-year status review: Swainson's Hawk (*Buteo swainsoni*). Calif. Dept. Fish and Game, Wildlife Mgmt. Div., Nongame bird and mammal program, Sacramento.

California Department of Fish and Game. 1995. Draft mitigated negative declaration for the release of Wild Turkeys on the Descanso Ranger District of the Cleveland National Forest. Calif. Dept. Fish and Game, Sacramento.

Campbell, K. F., Erickson, R. A., Haas, W. E., and Patten, M. A. 1998. California Gnatcatcher use of habitats other than coastal sage scrub: Conservation and management implications. W. Birds 29:421–433.

Cannings, R. J., and Angell, T. 2001. Western Screech-Owl, *in* The Birds of North America (A. Poole and F. Gill, eds.), no. 597. Birds N. Am., Philadelphia.

Cardiff, E., and Cardiff, B. 1953. Records of the Coues Flycatcher and Chestnut-sided Warbler for California. Condor 55:217.

Carpenter, N. K. 1917. Western Belted Kingfisher nesting in San Diego County, California. Condor 19:22.

Carpenter, N. K. 1918. Observations in a swallow colony. Condor 20:90–91.

Carpenter, N. K. 1919. An early or late nesting of the Green-backed Goldfinch? Condor 21:86.

Carter, H. R., Sowls, A. L., Rodway, M. S., Wilson, U. W., Lowe, R. W., McChesney, G. J., Gress, F., and Anderson, D. W. 1995. Population size, trends, and conservation problems of the Double-crested Cormorant on the Pacific coast of North America. Colonial Waterbirds 18 (spec. publ. 1): 189–215.

Chu, M., and Walsberg, G. 1999. Phainopepla, *in* The Birds of North America (A. Poole and F. Gill, eds.), no. 415. Birds N. Am., Philadelphia.

Ciaranca, M. A., Allin, C. C., and Jones, G. S. 1997. Mute Swan, *in* The Birds of North America (A. Poole and F. Gill, eds.), no. 273. Acad. Nat. Sci., Philadelphia.

Cicero, C. 2000. Oak and Juniper Titmouse, *in* The Birds of North America (A. Poole and F. Gill, eds.), no. 485. Birds N. Am., Philadelphia.

Cicero, C., and Johnson, N. K. 1995. Speciation in sapsuckers (*Sphyrapicus*): III. Mitochondrial-DNA sequence divergence at the cytochrome-B locus. Auk 112:547–563.

Cody, M. L. 1998. California Thrasher, *in* The Birds of North

America (A. Poole and F. Gill, eds.), no. 323. Birds N. Am., Philadelphia.

Cody, M. L. 1999. Crissal Thrasher, *in* The Birds of North America (A. Poole and F. Gill, eds.), no. 419. Birds N. Am., Philadelphia.

Cohen, D. A. 1899. Nesting and other habits of the Oregon Towhee. Bull. Cooper Ornithol. Soc. 1:61–63.

Cole, L. W., and McCaskie, G. 2004. Report of the California Bird Records Committee: 2002 records. W. Birds 35:2–31.

Collins, C. T. 1997. Hybridization of a Sandwich and Elegant Tern in California. W. Birds 28:169–173.

Collins, C. T., and Garrett, K. L. 1996. The Black Skimmer in California: An overview. W. Birds 27:127–135.

Collins, C. T., and Landry, R. E. 1977. Artificial nest burrows for Burrowing Owls. N. Am. Bird Bander 2:151–154.

Collins, C. T., Schew, W. A., and Burkett, E. 1991. Elegant Terns breeding in Orange County, California. Am. Birds 45:393–395.

Collins, P. W. 1999. Rufous-crowned Sparrow, *in* The Birds of North America (A. Poole and F. Gill, eds.), no. 472. Birds N. Am., Philadelphia.

Connors, P. G., McCaffery, B. J., and Maron, J. L. 1993. Speciation in golden-plovers, *Pluvialis dominica* and *P. fulva*: Evidence from the breeding grounds. Auk 110:9–20.

Conover, M. R. 1983. Recent changes in the Ring-billed and California Gull populations in the western United States. Wilson Bull. 95:362–383.

Conway, C. J. 1995. Virginia Rail, *in* The Birds of North America (A. Poole and F. Gill, eds.), no. 173. Acad. Nat. Sci., Philadelphia.

Cooper, J. G. 1868. Some recent additions to the fauna of California. Proc. Calif. Acad. Sci. 4:3–13.

Cooper, J. G. 1870. Geological Survey of California. Ornithology. "Published by Authority of the Legislature."

Cooper, J. G. 1874. Animal life of the Cuyamaca Mountains. Am. Nat. 8:14–18.

Cooper, J. G. 1880. On the migrations and nesting habits of west-coast birds. Proc. U. S. Natl. Mus. 2:241–251.

Corman, T., and Monson, G. 1995. First United States nesting records of the Streak-backed Oriole. W. Birds 26:49–53.

Cox, G. W. 1973. Hybridization between Mourning and MacGillivray's Warblers. Auk 90:190–191.

Cox, G. W. 1981. Pollination ecology of the Cleveland sage. Environment Southwest 494:15–19.

Craig, A. M. 1970. Two California records of Grace's Warbler. Calif. Birds 1:77–78.

Craig, A. M. 1972. Two fall Yellow-throated Warblers in California. Calif. Birds 3:17–18.

Craig, J. T. 1970. Kentucky Warbler in San Diego. Calif. Birds 1:37–38.

Craig, J. T. 1971. Eastern Whip-poor-will in San Diego. Calif. Birds 2:37–40.

Cramp, S., and Simmons, K. E. L., eds. 1977. The Birds of the Western Palearctic, vol. 1. Oxford Univ. Press, Oxford, England.

Crooks, K. R., Suarez, A. V., Bolger, D. T., and Soulé, M. E. 2001. Extinction and colonization of birds on habitat islands. Cons. Biol. 15:159–172.

Crouch, J. E. 1943. Distribution and habitat relationships of the Phainopepla. Auk 60:319–332.

Crouch, J. E. 1959. Vermilion Flycatcher nesting in San Diego County, California. Condor 61:57.

Cullen, S. A., Jehl, J. R., Jr., and Nuechterlein, G. L. 1999. Eared Grebe, *in* The Birds of North America (A. Poole and F. Gill, eds.), no. 433. Birds N. Am., Philadelphia.

Cuthbert, F. J., and Wires, L. R. 1999. Caspian Tern, *in* The Birds of North America (A. Poole and F. Gill, eds.), no. 403. Birds N. Am., Philadelphia.

Davis, J. 1952. A second November nest of the California Thrasher. Condor 54:116.

Davis, J. N. 1995. Hutton's Vireo, *in* The Birds of North America (A. Poole and F. Gill, eds.), no. 189. Acad. Nat. Sci., Philadelphia.

Davis, T. A., Platter-Rieger, M. F., and Ackerman, R. A. 1984. Incubation water loss by Pied-billed Grebe eggs: Adaptation to a hot, wet nest. Physiol. Zool. 57: 384–391.

Davis, W. E., Jr., and Kushlan, J. A. 1994. Green Heron, *in* The Birds of North America (A. Poole and F. Gill, eds.), no. 129. Acad. Nat. Sci., Philadelphia.

Dawson, W. L. 1923. The Birds of California. South Moulton Co., San Diego.

DeBenedictis, P. A. 1995. Red Crossbills, one through eight. Birding 27:494–501.

DeJong, M. J. 1996. Northern Rough-winged Swallow, *in* The Birds of North America (A. Poole and F. Gill, eds.), no. 234. Acad. Nat. Sci., Philadelphia.

Delacour, J., and Ripley, S. D. 1975. Description of a new subspecies of the White-fronted Goose, *Anser albifrons*. Am. Mus. Nov. 2565.

Delacour, J., and Zimmer, J. T. 1952. The identity of *Anser nigricans* Lawrence 1846. Auk 69:82–84.

Devillers, P. 1970a. Identification and distribution in California of the *Sphyrapicus varius* group of sapsuckers. Calif. Birds 1:47–76.

Devillers, P. 1970b. Chimney Swifts in coastal southern California. Calif. Birds 1:147–152.

Devillers, P. 1972. The juvenal plumage of Kittlitz's Murrelet. Calif. Birds 3:33–38.

Devillers, P., McCaskie, G., and Jehl, J. R., Jr. 1971. The distribution of certain large gulls (*Larus*) in southern California and Baja California. Calif. Birds 2:11–26.

Diamond, A. W., and Schreiber, E. A. 2002. Magnificent Frigatebird, *in* The Birds of North America (A. Poole and F. Gill, eds.), no. 601. Birds N. Am., Philadelphia.

Dickerman, R. W. 1973. The Least Bittern in Mexico and Central America. Auk 90:689–691.

Dickerman, R. W., and Parkes, K. C. 1997. Taxa described by Allan R. Phillips, 1939–1994: A critical list, *in* The Era of Allan R. Phillips: A Festschrift (R. W. Dickerman, compiler), pp. 211–234. Horizon Communications, Albuquerque.

Dixon, J. 1906. Land birds of San Onofre, California. Condor 8:91–98.

Dixon, J. 1912. The Costa Hummingbird. Condor 14:75–77.

Dixon, J. 1916. Mexican Ground Dove, Western Grasshopper Sparrow, and California Cuckoo at Escondido, San Diego County, California. Condor 18:83–84.

Dixon, J. 1921. A specimen of the Black Swift from San Diego County, California. Condor 23:168–169.

Dixon, J. B. 1928. Life history of the Red-bellied Hawk. Condor 30:228–236.

Dixon, J. B. 1937. The Golden Eagle in San Diego County, California. Condor 39:49–56.

Dixon, J. B., Dixon, R. E., and Dixon, J. E. 1957. Natural history of the White-tailed Kite in San Diego County, California. Condor 59:156–165.

Dobbs, R. C., Martin, P. R., and Martin, T. E. 1998. Green-tailed Towhee, *in* The Birds of North America (A. Poole and F. Gill, eds.), no. 368. Birds N. Am., Philadelphia.

Dolton, D. D. 1993. Mourning Dove breeding population status 1993. U.S. Fish and Wildlife Service, Laurel, MD.

Drilling, N., Titman, R., and McKinney, F. 2002. Mallard, *in* The Birds of North America (A. Poole and F. Gill, eds.), no. 658. Birds N. Am., Philadelphia.

Drost, C. A., and Lewis, D. B. 1995. Xantus' Murrelet, *in* The Birds of North America (A. Poole and F. Gill, eds.), no. 164. Acad. Nat. Sci., Philadelphia.

Dunlap, E. 1988. Laysan Albatrosses nesting on Guadalupe Island, Mexico. Am. Birds 42:180–181.

Dunn, E. H., and Agro, D. J. 1995. Black Tern, *in* The Birds of North America (A. Poole and F. Gill, eds.), no. 147. Acad. Nat. Sci., Philadelphia.

Dunn, J. L. 1988. Tenth report of the California Bird Records Committee. W. Birds 19:129–163.

Dunn, J. L., and Garrett, K. L. 1997. A Field Guide to Warblers of North America. Houghton Mifflin, Boston.

Eadie, J. M., Mallory, M. L., and Lumsden, H. G. 1995. Common Goldeneye, *in* The Birds of North America (A. Poole and F. Gill, eds.), no. 170. Acad. Nat. Sci., Philadelphia.

Earnheart-Gold, S., and Pyle, P. 2001. Occurrence patterns of Peregrine Falcons on Southeast Farallon Island, California, by subspecies, age, and sex. W. Birds 32:119–126.

Ellison, W. G. 1992. Blue-gray Gnatcatcher, *in* The Birds of North America (A. Poole and F. Gill, eds.), no. 23. Acad. Nat. Sci., Philadelphia.

Ely, C. R., and Dzubin, A. X. 1994. Greater White-fronted Goose, *in* The Birds of North America (A. Poole and F. Gill, eds.), no 131. Acad. Nat. Sci., Philadelphia.

Emerson, W. C. 1887. Ornithological observations in San Diego County. Bull. Calif. Acad. Sci. 2:419–431.

Engelmoer, M., and Roselaar, C. S. 1998. Geographical Variation in Waders. Kluwer Acad. Publ., Dordrecht, the Netherlands.

England, A. S., and Laudenslayer, W. F., Jr. 1989. Distribution and seasonal movements of Bendire's Thrasher in California. W. Birds 20:97–123.

Enkerlin-Hoeflich, E. C., and Hogan, K. M. 1997. Red-crowned Parrot, *in* The Birds of North America (A. Poole and F. Gill, eds.), no. 292. Acad. Nat. Sci., Philadelphia.

Erickson, R. A., and Hamilton, R. A. 2001. Report of the California Bird Records Committee: 1998 records. W. Birds 32:13–49.

Erickson, R. A., Hamilton, R. A., González-Guzmán, S., and Ruiz-Campos, G. 2002. Primeros registros de anidación del pato friso (*Anas strepera*) en México. Anal. Inst. Biol., Univ. Nacl. Autónoma Méx., Ser. Zool. 73:67–71.

Erickson, R. A., Hamilton, R. A., and Howell, S. N. G. 2001. New Information on migrant birds in northern and central portions of the Baja California Peninsula, including species new to Mexico. Am. Birding Assoc. Monogr. Field Ornithol. 3:112–170.

Erickson, R. A., and Terrill, S. B. 1996. Nineteenth report of the California Bird Records Committee: 1993 records. W. Birds 27:93–126.

Erickson, R. A., and Wurster, T. E. 1998. Confirmation of nesting in Mexico for four bird species from the Sierra San Pedro Mártir, Baja California. Wilson Bull. 110:118–120.

Erwin, C. A., Rozell, K. B., and DeCicco, L. H. 2004. Update on the status and distribution of Wilson's Phalarope and Yellow-bellied Sapsucker in Alaska. W. Birds 35:42–44.

Evens, J., and Page, G. W. 1986. Predation on Black Rails during high tides in salt marshes. Condor 88:107–109.

Evens, J. G., Page, G. W., Laymon, S. A., and Stallcup, R. W. 1991. Distribution, relative abundance and status of the California Black Rail in western North America. Condor 93:952–966.

Everett, W. T. 1991. Breeding biology of the Black Storm-Petrel at Islas Los Coronados, Baja California, Mexico. M. S. thesis, Univ. San Diego.

Everett, W. T., and Ainley, D. G. 2001. Black Storm-Petrel, *in* The Birds of North America (A. Poole and F. Gill, eds.), no. 577. Birds N. Am., Philadelphia.

Everett, W. T., and Anderson, D. W. 1991. Status and conservation of the breeding seabirds on offshore Pacific islands of Baja Calfornia and the Gulf of California, *in* Seabird status and conservation: A supplement (J. Croxall, ed.), pp. 115–139. ICBP Tech. Publ. 11.

Famolaro, P., and Newman, J. 1998. Occurrence and management considerations of California Gnatcatchers along San Diego County highways. W. Birds 29:447–452.

Fleischer, R. C., and Rothstein, S. I. 1988. Known secondary contact and rapid gene flow among subspecies and dialects in the Brown-headed Cowbird. Evolution 42:1146–1158

Foerster, K. S., and Collins, C. T. 1990. Breeding distribution of the Black Swift in southern California. W. Birds 21:1–9.

Fortiner, J. C. 1920. Clark Nutcracker and White-winged Dove in southern California. Condor 22:190.

Franzreb, K. E. 1987. Endangered status and strategies for conservation of the Least Bell's Vireo (*Vireo bellii pusillus*) in Calfornia. W. Birds 18:43–49.

Franzreb, K. E., and Ohmart, R. D. 1978. The effects of timber harvesting on breeding birds in a mixed coniferous forest. Condor 80:431–441.

Friedmann, H. 1946. The birds of North and Middle America. U. S. Natl. Mus. Bull. 50, part 10.

Friedmann, H. 1963. Host relations of the parasitic cowbirds. U. S. Natl. Mus. Bull. 233.

Friedmann, H., Kiff, L. F., and Rothstein, S. I. 1977. A further contribution to knowledge of the host relations of the parasitic cowbirds. Smithsonian Contr. Zool. 235:1–75.

Fyfe, R. W., Risebrough, R. W., Monk, J. G., Jarman, W. M., Anderson, D. W., Kiff, L. F., Lincer, J. L., Nisbet, I. C. T., Walker, W., II, and Walton, B. J. 1987. DDE, productivity, and eggshell-thickness relationships in the genus *Falco*, *in* Peregrine Falcon Populations: Their Management and Recovery (T. J. Cade, J. H. Enderson, C. G. Thelander, and C. M. White, eds.), pp. 319–335. Peregrine Fund, Boise.

Gabrielson, I. N., and Jewett, S. G. 1940. Birds of Oregon. Ore. State College, Corvallis.

Gaines, D. 1974. Review of the status of the Yellow-billed Cuckoo in California: Sacramento Valley populations. Condor 76:204–209.

Gaines, D., and Laymon, S. A. 1984. Decline, status and preservation of the Yellow-billed Cuckoo in California. W. Birds 15:49–80.

Galati, R. 1991. Golden-crowned Kinglets: Treetop Nesters of the North Woods. Iowa State Univ. Press, Ames.

Gallagher, S. R. 1997. Atlas of Breeding Birds, Orange County, California. Sea and Sage Audubon Press, Irvine, CA.

Gallup, F. 1963. Southward extension of breeding range of Forster Tern on Pacific coast. Condor 65:246.

Gallup, F., and Bailey, B. H. 1960. Elegant Tern and Royal Tern nesting in California. Condor 62:65–66.

Galvin, J. P. 1998. Breeding and dispersal biology of the California Gnatcatcher in central Orange County. W. Birds 29:323–332.

Gamble, L. R., and Bergin, T. M. 1996. Western Kingbird, *in* The Birds of North America (A. Poole and F. Gill, eds.), no. 227. Acad. Nat. Sci., Philadelphia.

Gander, F. F. 1929. Notes on the food and feeding habits of certain birds. Condor 31:250–251.

Gander, F. F. 1930. A Black Rail leaves the salt marsh. Condor 32:211.

Gardali, T., and Jaramillo, A. 2001. Further evidence for a population decline in the western Warbling Vireo. W. Birds 32:173–176.

Gardner, L. L. 1959. Gila Woodpecker in San Diego County, California. Condor 61:435.

Garrett, K. L. 1997. Population status and distribution of naturalized parrots in southern California. W. Birds 28:181–195.

Garrett, K. L. 1998. Field separation of bishops (*Euplectes*) from North American emberizids. W. Birds 29:231–232.

Garrett, K. L. 2000. The juvenile Nutmeg Mannikin: Identification of a little brown bird. W. Birds 31:130–131.

Garrett, K., and Dunn, J. 1981. Birds of Southern California: Status and Distribution. Los Angeles Audubon Soc., Los Angeles.

Garrett, K. L., and Molina, K. C. 1998. First record of the Black-tailed Gull for Mexico. W. Birds 29:49–54.

Garrett, K. L., Raphael, M. G., and Dixon, R. D. 1996. White-headed Woodpecker, *in* The Birds of North America (A. Poole and F. Gill, eds.), no 252. Acad. Nat. Sci., Philadelphia.

Garrett, K. L., and Singer, D. S. 1998. Report of the California Bird Records Committee: 1995 records. W. Birds 29:133–156.

Garrett, K. L., and Walker, R. L. 2001. Spotted Dove, *in* The Birds of North America (A. Poole and F. Gill, eds.), no. 586. Birds N. Am., Philadelphia.

Garrett, K. L., and Wilson, J. C. 2003. Report of the California Bird Records Committee: 2001 records. W. Birds 34:15–41.

Garrison, B. A. 1993. Distribution and trends in abundance of Rough-legged Hawks wintering in California. J. Field Ornithol. 64:566–574.

Garrison, B. A., and Bloom, P. H. 1993. Natal origins and winter site fidelity of Rough-legged Hawks wintering in California. J. Raptor Res. 27:116–118.

Garrison, B. A., Humphrey, J. M., and Laymon, S. A. 1987. Bank Swallow distribution and nesting ecology on the Sacramento River, California. W. Birds 18:71–76.

Gatz, T. A. 2001. Orange Bishops breeding in Phoenix, Arizona. W. Birds 32:81–82.

Gazzaniga, K. T. 1996. Overwintering of Black Skimmers in California: Site fidelity and inter-site movements. W. Birds 27:136–142.

Gedney, P. L. 1900. Nesting of the Condor on the slope of the Cuyamacas, San Diego Co., Cal. Condor 2:124–126.

Gee, J. M. 2003. How a hybrid zone is maintained: Behavioral mechanisms of interbreeding between California and Gambel's Quail (*Callipepla californica* and *C. gambelii*). Evolution 57:2407–2415.

Gibbs, J. P., Melvin, S., and Reid, F. A. 1992. American Bittern, *in* The Birds of North America (A. Poole, P. Stettenheim, and F. Gill, eds.), no. 18. Acad. Nat. Sci., Philadelphia.

Gibson, D. D., and Kessel, B. 1997. Inventory of the species and subspecies of Alaska birds. W. Birds 28:45–95.

Gill, R. E., McCaffery, B. J., and Tomkovich, P. S. 2002. Wandering Tattler, *in* The Birds of North America (A. Poole and F. Gill, eds.), no. 642. Birds N. Am., Philadelphia.

Gill, R. E., and Mewaldt, L. R. 1983. Pacific coast Caspian Terns: Dynamics of an expanding population. Auk 100:369–381.

Gilligan, J., Smith, M., Rogers, D., and Contreras, A. 1994. Birds of Oregon. Cinclus, McMinnville, OR.

Gilman, M. F. 1909. Among the thrashers in Arizona. Condor 11:49–54.

Gilman, M. F. 1915. A forty-acre bird census at Sacaton, Arizona. Condor 17:86–90.

Goguen, C. B., and Curson, D. R. 2002. Cassin's Vireo, *in* The Birds of North America (A. Poole and F. Gill, eds.), no. 615. Birds N. Am., Philadelphia.

Goldwasser, S., Gaines, D., and Wilbur, S. 1980. The Least Bell's Vireo in California: A de facto endangered race. Am. Birds 34:742–745.

Good, T. P., Ellis, J. C., Annett, C. A., and Pierotti, R. 2000. Bounded hybrid superiority in an avian hybrid zone: Effects of mate, diet, and habitat choice. Evolution 54:1774–1783.

Goossen, J. P., and Sealy, S. G. 1982. Production of young in a dense nesting population of Yellow Warblers, *Dendroica petechia*, in Manitoba. Can. Field-Nat. 96:189–199.

Gould, G. I., Jr. 1977. Distribution of the Spotted Owl in California. W. Birds 8:131–146.

Gratto-Trevor, C. L. 2000. Marbled Godwit, *in* The Birds of North America (A. Poole and F. Gill, eds.), no 492. Birds N. Am., Philadelphia.

Greaves, J. M. 1987. Nest-site tenacity of Least Bell's Vireos. W. Birds 18:50–54.

Greaves, J. M., and Labinger, Z. 1997. Site tenacity and dispersal of Least Bell's Vireos. Trans. W. Sect. Wildlife Soc. 33:18–23.

Greene, E., Muehter, V. R., and Davison, W. 1996. Lazuli Bunting, *in* The Birds of North America (A. Poole and F. Gill, eds.), no. 232. Acad. Nat. Sci., Philadelphia.

Gress, F., Risebrough, R. W., Anderson, D. W., Kiff, L. F., and Jehl, J. R., Jr. 1973. Reproductive failures of Double-crested Cormorants in southern California and Baja California. Wilson Bull. 85:197–208.

Grey, H. 1913a. Harris Hawk in California. Condor 15:128.

Grey, H. 1913b. American Egret in San Diego County. Condor 15:129.

Grey, H. 1915. Bird notes from British Columbia and southern California. Condor 17:59.

Grey, H. 1916. Mexican Ground Dove at San Diego. Condor 18:83.

Grey, H. 1925. Some unusual birds at or near San Diego. Condor 27:37.

Grinnell, J. 1900. Early nesting of the Pasadena Thrasher. Condor 2:19.

Grinnell, J. 1901. The Pacific coast Yellowthroats. Condor 3:65–66.

Grinnell, J. 1911. Distribution of the Mockingbird in California. Auk 28:293–300.

Grinnell, J. 1913. The outlook for conserving the Band-tailed Pigeon as a game bird of California. Condor 15:25–40.

Grinnell, J. 1915. A distributional list of the birds of California. Pac. Coast Avifauna 11.

Grinnell, J. 1928a. Notes on the systematics of west American birds. I. Condor 30:121–124.

Grinnell, J. 1928b. Notes on the systematics of west American birds. III. Condor 30:185–189.

Grinnell, J., Bryant, H. C., and Storer, T. I. 1918. The Game Birds of California. Univ. of Calif. Press, Berkeley.

Grinnell, J., and Miller, A. H. 1944. The distribution of the birds of California. Pac. Coast Avifauna 27.

Grinnell, J., and Swarth, H. S. 1913. An account of the birds and mammals of the San Jacinto area of southern California with remarks upon the behavior of geographic races on the margins of their habitats. Univ. Calif. Publ. Zool. 10:197–406.

Grishaver, M. A., Mock, P. J., and Preston, K. L. 1998. Breeding behavior of the California Gnatcatcher in southwestern San Diego County, California. W. Birds 29:299–322.

Groth, J. G. 1993. Evolutionary differentiation in morphology, vocalizations, and allozymes among nomadic sibling species in the North American Red Crossbill (*Loxia curvirostra*) complex. Univ. Calif. Publ. Zool. 127:1–143.

Groves, D. J., Conant, B., King, R. J., Hodges, J. I., and King, J. G. 1996. Status and trends of loon populations summering in Alaska, 1971–1993. Condor 98:189–195.

Guinan, J. A., Gowaty, P. A., and Eltzroth, E. K. 2000. Western Bluebird, *in* The Birds of North America (A. Poole and F. Gill, eds.), no. 510. Birds N. Am., Philadelphia.

Gutiérrez, R. J., and Pritchard, J. 1990. Distribution, density, and age structure of Spotted Owls on two southern California habitat islands. Condor 92:491–495.

Gutiérrez, R. J., Franklin, A. B., and LaHaye, W. S. 1995. Spotted Owl, *in* The Birds of North America (A. Poole and F. Gill, eds.), no. 179. Acad. Nat. Sci., Philadelphia.

Gutiérrez, R. J., Verner, J., McKelvey, K. S., Noon, B. R., Steger, G. N., Call, D. R., LaHaye, W. S., Bingham, B. B., and Senser, J. S. 1992. Habitat relations of the California Spotted Owl, *in* The California Spotted Owl: A technical assessment of its current status (J. Verner, K. S. McKelvey, B. R. Noon, R. J. Gutiérrez, G. I. Gould, Jr., and T. W. Beck, tech. coords.), pp. 79–98. Gen. Tech. Rep. PSW-GTR-133, U.S. Forest Service, Albany, CA.

Guzy, M. J., and Lowther, P. E. 1997. Black-throated Gray Warbler, *in* The Birds of North America (A. Poole and F. Gill, eds.), no. 319. Birds N. Am., Philadelphia.

Haas, W. E., and Campbell, K. F. 2003. Report of Coastal California Gnatcatcher juvenile dispersal across Interstate 8 at the MSCP southern Lakeside archipelago lands, San Diego County, California. Report to County of San Diego Department of Parks and Recreation, San Diego.

Hagen, Y. 1965. The food, population fluctuations, and ecology of the Long-eared Owl (*Asio otus* [L.]) in Norway. Nor. State Game Res. Pap. Ser. 2, 23.

Hahn, T. P. 1996. Cassin's Finch, *in* The Birds of North America (A. Poole and F. Gill, eds.), no. 240. Acad. Nat. Sci., Philadelphia.

Hainebach, K. 1992. First records of Xantus' Hummingbird in California. W. Birds 23:133–136.

Hamilton, R. A. 2001. Appendix D. Records of caged birds in Baja California. Am. Birding Assoc. Monogr. Field Ornithol. 3:254–257.

Hamilton, R. A., and Willick, D. R. 1996. The Birds of Orange County, California: Status and Distribution. Sea and Sage Press, Irvine.

Hamilton, W. J., III. 1998. Tricolored Blackbird itinerant breeding in California. Condor 100:218–226.

Hancock, J., and Kushlan, J. 1984. The Herons Handbook. Harper & Row, New York.

Hanna, W. C. 1928. Notes on the Dwarf Cowbird in southern California. Condor 30:161–162.

Hanna, W. C. 1933. Nesting of the Crissal Thrasher in Coachella Valley, California. Condor 35:79.

Hardy, J. W. 1970. Duplex nest construction by Hooded Oriole circumvents cowbird parasitism. Condor 72:491.

Hardy, P. C., Morrison, M. L., and Barry, R. X. 1999. Abundance and habitat associations of Elf Owls and Western Screech-Owls in the Sonoran Desert. Southwest. Nat. 44:311–323.

Harrington, B. A. 2001. Red Knot, *in* The Birds of North America (A. Poole and F. Gill, eds.), no. 563. Birds N. Am., Philadelphia.

Harrison, C. 1978. A Field Guide to the Nests, Eggs and Nestlings of North American Birds. Collins, Glasgow, Scotland.

Hatch, J. J., and Weseloh, D. V. 1999. Double-crested Cormorant, *in* The Birds of North America (A. Poole and F. Gill, eds.), no. 441. Birds N. Am., Philadelphia.

Haug, E. A., Millsap, B. A., and Martell, S. M. 1993. Burrowing Owl, *in* The Birds of North America (A. Poole and F. Gill, eds.), no. 61. Acad. Nat. Sci., Philadelphia.

Hayslette, S. E., and Hayslette, B. A. 1999. Late and early season reproduction of urban White-winged Doves in southern Texas. Tex. J. Sci. 51:173–180.

Heermann, A. L. 1859. Explorations and surveys for a railroad route from the Mississippi River to the Pacific Ocean, part IV. Routes in California, to connect with the routes near the thirty-fifth and thirty-second parallels, explored by Lieut. R. S. Williamson, Corps of Top. Eng., in 1853. Zoological Report, no. 2. Report upon birds collected on the survey, pp. 29–80. War Dept., Washington, D.C.

Heindel, M. T. 1999. The status of vagrant Whimbrels in the United States and Canada with notes on identification. N. Am. Birds 53:232–236.

Heindel, M. T., and Garrett, K, L. 1995. Sixteenth annual report of the California Bird Records Committee. W. Birds 26:1–33.

Heindel, M. T., and Patten, M. A. 1996. Eighteenth report of the California Bird Records Committee: 1992 records. W. Birds 27:1–29

Helmuth, W. T., III. 1939. Oldsquaw and American Scoter in San Diego region. Condor 41:167.

Herzog, S. K. 1996. Wintering Swainson's Hawks in California's Sacramento–San Joaquin River delta. Condor 98:867–879.

Hill, D. K. 1995. Pacific warming unsettles ecosystems. Science 267:1911–1912.

Hill, J. R. 1988. Nest-depth preference in pipe-nesting Northern Rough-winged Swallows. J. Field Ornithol. 59:334–336.

Hobson, K. A. 1997. Pelagic Cormorant, in The Birds of North America (A. Poole and F. Gill, eds.), no. 282. Birds N. Am., Philadelphia.

Hodges, J. I., King, J. G., Conant, B., and Hanson, H. A. 1996. Aerial surveys of waterbirds in Alaska 1957–94: Population trends and observer variability. U.S. Dept. Interior, Natl. Biol. Serv., Inf. Technol. Rep. 4.

Hoffman, S. W., and Smith, J. P. 2003. Population trends of migratory raptors in western North America, 1977–2001. Condor 105:397–419.

Hoffman, W., Elliott, W. P., and Scott, J. M. 1975. The occurrence and status of the Horned Puffin in the western United States. W. Birds 6:87–94.

Hoffman, W., Wiens, J. A., and Scott, J. M. 1978. Hybridization between gulls (*Larus glaucescens* and *L. occidentalis*) in the Pacific Northwest. Auk 95:441–458.

Hohmann, W. L., and Eberhardt, R. T. 1998. Ring-necked Duck, *in* The Birds of North America (A. Poole and F. Gill, eds.), no. 329. Birds N. Am., Philadelphia.

Holroyd, G. L., Rodríguez-E., R., and Sheffield, S. R. 2001. Conservation of the Burrowing Owl in western North American: Issues, challenges, and recommendations. J. Raptor Res. 35:399–407.

Holterhoff, G. 1884. *Calamospiza bicolor* in southern California. Auk 1:293.

Houston, C. S., and Brown, P. W. 1983. Recoveries of Saskatchewan-banded White-winged Scoters, *Melanitta fusca*. Can. Field-Nat. 97:454–455.

Howell, S. N. G., and Pyle, P., 1997. Twentieth report of the California Bird Records Committee: 1994 records. W. Birds 28:117–141.

Howell, S. N. G., and Webb, S. 1992. Noteworthy bird observations from Baja California, Mexico. W. Birds 23:153–163.

Howell, S. N. G., and Webb, S. 1995. A Guide to the Birds of Mexico and Northern Central America. Oxford Univ. Press, Oxford, England.

Hubbard, J. P., and Crossin, R. S. 1974. Notes on northern Mexican birds. Nemouria 14:1–41.

Hudon, J. 1999. Western Tanager, *in* The Birds of North America (A. Poole and F. Gill, eds.), no. 432. Birds N. Am., Philadelphia.

Huey, L. M. 1915. Two birds new to California. Condor 17:57–58.

Huey, L. M. 1916. The Farallon Rails of San Diego County. Condor 18:58–62.

Huey, L. M. 1924. Notes from southern and Lower California. Condor 26:74–75.

Huey, L. M. 1926a. Notes from northwestern Lower California, with the description of an apparently new race of the Screech Owl. Auk 63:347–362.

Huey, L. M. 1926b. Two unrecorded occurrences of the Richardson Pigeon Hawk in California. Condor 28:102.

Huey, L. M. 1927. Observations on the spring migration of *Aphriza* and *Gavia* in the Gulf of California. Auk 44:529–531.

Huey, L. M. 1928a. Some bird records form northern Lower California. Condor 30:158–159.

Huey, L. M. 1928b. A mid-winter Anthony Green Heron. Condor 30:251.

Huey, L. M. 1931a. *Icterus pustulatus*, a new bird to the A. O. U. check-list. Auk 48:606–607.

Huey, L. M. 1931b. Notes on two birds from San Diego County, California. Auk 48:620–621.

Huey, L. M. 1933. Southernmost record of the Horned Puffin. Condor 35:233.

Huey, L. M. 1936. Noteworthy records from San Diego, California. Condor 38:121.

Huey, L. M. 1939. Fork-tailed Petrels from the coast of San Diego County, California. Condor 41:215–216.

Huey, L. M. 1940. A new cardinal from central Lower California, Mexico. Trans. San Diego Soc. Nat. Hist. 9:215–218.

Huey, L. M. 1954. Notes from southern California and Baja California. Condor 56:51–52.

Huey, L. M. 1960. Notes on Vaux and Chimney Swifts. Condor 62:483.

Huey, L. M. 1961a. Two unusual bird records for California. Auk 78:260.

Huey, L. M. 1961b. Two noteworthy records for California. Auk 78:426–427.

Huey, L. M. 1962. Purple Galinule [*sic*] strays to southern California. Auk 79:483.

Hughes, J. M. 1996. Greater Roadrunner, *in* The Birds of North America (A. Poole and F. Gill, eds.), no. 244. Acad. Nat. Sci., Philadelphia.

Hunsaker, D., II, O'Leary, J., and Awbrey, F. T. 2000. Final report: Habitat evaluation, home range determination, and dispersal study of the coastal California Gnatcatcher (*Polioptila californica californica*) on Marine Corps Air Station Miramar. Report to MCAS Miramar and Southwest Division, Naval Facilities Engineering Command, San Diego.

Huntington, C. E., Butler, R. G., and Mauck, R. A. 1996. Leach's Storm-Petrel, *in* The Birds of North America (A. Poole and F. Gill, eds.), no. 233. Acad. Nat. Sci., Philadelphia.

Ingersoll, A. M. 1895. Wilson's Plover in California. Nidiologist 2:87.

Ingersoll, A. M. 1909. The only known breeding ground of *Creciscus coturniculus*. Condor 11:123–127.

Ingersoll, A. M. 1918. Second occurrence of Wilson Plover in California. Condor 20:187.

Ingold, J. L. 1993. Blue Grosbeak, *in* The Birds of North America (A. Poole and F. Gill, eds.), no. 79. Acad. Nat. Sci., Philadelphia.

Jay, A. 1911. Nesting of the California Cuckoo in Los Angeles County, California. Condor 13:69–73.

Jehl, J. R., Jr. 1973. Late autumn observations of pelagic birds off southern California. W. Birds 4:45–52.

Jehl, J. R., Jr. 1977. An annotated list of birds of Islas Los Coronados, Baja California, and adjacent waters. W. Birds 8:91–101.

Jehl, J. R., Jr. 1985. Hybridization and evolution of oystercatchers on the Pacific coast of Baja California. Ornithol. Monogr. 36:484–504.

Jehl, J. R., Jr. 1988. Biology of the Eared Grebe and Wilson's Phalarope in the non-breeding season: A study of adaptations to saline lakes. Studies Avian Biol. 12.

Jehl, J. R., Jr. 1996a. Changes in saline and alkaline lake avifaunas in western North American in the past 150 years. Studies Avian Biol. 15:258–272.

Jehl, J. R., Jr. 1996b. Mass mortality events of Eared Grebes in North America. J. Field Ornithol. 67:471–476.

Jehl, J. R., Jr. 2001. The abundance of the Eared (Black-necked) Grebe as a recent phenomenon. Waterbirds 24:245–249.

Jehl, J. R., Jr., and Bond, S. I. 1975. Morphological variation and species limits in murrelets of the genus *Endomychura*. Trans. San Diego Soc. Nat. Hist. 18:9–24.

Jehl, J. R., Jr., and Bond, S. I. 1983. Mortality of Eared Grebes in winter of 1982–1983. Am. Birds 37:832–835.

Jehl, J. R., Jr., and Everett, W. T. 1985. History and status of the avifauna of Isla Guadalupe, Mexico. Trans. San Diego Soc. Nat. Hist. 20:313–336.

Jehl, J. R., Jr., and McKernan, R. L. 2002. Biology and migration of Eared Grebes at the Salton Sea. Hydrobiologia 473:245–253.

Jehl, J. R., Jr., Henry, A. E., and Bond, S. I. 1999. Flying the gantlet: Population characteristics, sampling bias, and migration routes of Eared Grebes downed in the Utah desert. Auk 116:178–183.

Johnson, K. 1995. Green-winged Teal, *in* The Birds of North America (A. Poole and F. Gill, eds.), no. 193. Acad. Nat. Sci., Philadelphia.

Johnson, K., Du Val, E., Kielt, M., and Hughes, C. 2001. Male mating strategies and the mating system of Great-tailed Grackles. Behav. Ecol. 11:132–141.

Johnson, M. J., van Riper, C., III, and Pearson, K. M. 2002. Black-throated Sparrow, *in* The Birds of North America (A. Poole and F. Gill, eds.), no. 637. Birds N. Am., Philadelphia.

Johnson, N. K. 1970. Fall migration and winter distribution of the Hammond Flycatcher. Bird-Banding 41:169–190.

Johnson, N. K. 1974. Montane avifaunas of southern Nevada: Historical change in species composition. Condor 76:334–337.

Johnson, N. K. 1994. Pioneering and natural expansion of breeding distributions in western North American birds. Studies Avian Biol. 15:27–44.

Johnson, N. K. 1995. Speciation in vireos. I. Macrogeographic patterns of allozymic variation in the *Vireo solitarius* complex in the contiguous United States. Condor 97:903–919.

Johnson, N. K., and Johnson, C. B. 1985. Speciation in sapsuckers (*Sphyrapicus*): II. Sympatry, hybridization, and mate preference in *S. ruber daggetti* and *S. nuchalis*. Auk 102:1–15.

Johnson, N. K., Remsen, J. V., Jr., and Cicero, C. 1998. Refined colorimetry validates endangered subspecies of the Least Tern. Condor 100:18–26.

Johnson, N. K., and Zink, R. M. 1983. Speciation in sapsuckers (*Sphyrapicus*): I. Genetic differentiation. Auk 100:871–884.

Johnson, R. R., Glinski, R. L., and Matteson, S. W. 2000. Zone-tailed Hawk, *in* The Birds of North America (A. Poole and F. Gill, eds.), no. 529. Birds N. Am., Philadelphia.

Johnson, R. R., Yard, H. K., and Brown, B. T. 1997. Lucy's Warbler, *in* The Birds of North America (A. Poole and F. Gill, eds.), no. 318. Acad. Nat., Sci., Philadelphia.

Johnson, T. F. 1922. An unknown near San Diego. Condor 24:135–136.

Johnson, T. F. 1928. Western Tanager in winter at San Diego. Condor 30:325–326.

Keer, G., and Zedler, J. B. 2002. Salt marsh canopy architecture differs with the number and composition of species. Ecol. Appl. 12:456–473.

Keitt, B. S., Tershy, B. R., and Croll, D. A. 2003. Breeding biology and conservation of the Black-vented Shearwater *Puffinus opisthomelas*. Ibis 145:673–680.

Kennedy, E. D., and White, D. W. 1997. Bewick's Wren, *in* The Birds of North America (A. Poole and F. Gill, eds.), no. 315. Birds N. Am., Philadelphia.

Kent, W. A. 1944. Rare birds seen in southern California. Condor 46:129–130.

Kenyon, K. W. 1937. Two sea-bird records for southern California. Condor 39:257–258.

Kenyon, K. W. 1942. Notes on the occurrence of some pelagic birds off San Diego County, California. Condor 44: 232–233.

Kenyon, K. W. 1943. Birds found dead on the beach in San Diego County, California. Condor 45:77.

Keppie, D. M., and Braun, C. E. 2000. Band-tailed Pigeon, *in* The Birds of North America (A. Poole, and F. Gill, eds.), no. 530. Birds N. Am., Philadelphia.

Kiff, L. F., and Paulson, D. R. 1997. Northern Goshawk breeding records from San Diego County, California. W. Birds 28:113–114.

King, D. B., Jr., Baumgartel, M., De Beer, J., and Meyer, T. 1987. The birds of San Elijo Lagoon, San Diego County, California. W. Birds 18:177–208.

King, D. [B., Jr.], Hastings, D., and Hastings, M. 1988. Communal winter roosts of Ferruginous Hawks in San Diego County, California. W. Birds 19:170–171.

Kingery, H. E. 1996. American Dipper, *in* The Birds of North America (A. Poole and F. Gill, eds.), no. 229. Acad. Nat. Sci., Philadelphia.

Kingery, H. E., and Ghalambor, C. E. 2001. Pygmy Nuthatch, *in* The Birds of North America (A. Poole and F. Gill, eds.), no. 567. Birds N. Am., Philadlephia.

Kirk, D. A., and Mossman, M. J. 1998. Turkey Vulture, *in* The Birds of North America (A. Poole and F. Gill, eds.), no. 339. Birds N. Am., Philadelphia.

Kirven, M. 1969. The breeding biology of Caspian Terns (*Hydroprogne caspia*) and Elegant Terns (*Thalasseus elegans*) at San Diego Bay. Master's thesis, San Diego State College.

Kjelmyr, J., Page, G. W., Shuford, W. D., and Stenzel, L. E. 1991. Shorebird numbers in wetlands of the Pacific Flyway: A summary of spring, fall, & winter counts in 1988, 1989, and 1990. Point Reyes Bird Observatory, Stinson Beach, CA.

Klicka, J., Fry, A. J., Zink, R. M., and Thompson, C. W. 2001. A cytochrome-*b* perspective on *Passerina* bunting relationships. Auk 118:611–623.

Knopf, F. L. 1996. Mountain Plover, *in* The Birds of North America (A. Poole and F. Gill, eds.), no. 211. Birds N. Am., Philadelphia.

Kochert, M. N., Steenhof, K., McIntyre, C. L., and Craig, E. H. 2002. Golden Eagle, *in* The Birds of North America (A. Poole and F. Gill, eds.), no. 684. Birds N. Am., Philadelphia.

Koenig, W. D. 1991. The effects of tannins and lipids on the digestibility of acorns by Acorn Woodpeckers. Auk 108:79–88.

Koenig, W. D. 2001. Synchrony and periodicity of eruptions by boreal birds. Condor 103:725–735.

Koenig, W. D., and Heck, M. K. 1988. Ability of two species of oak woodland birds to subsist on acorns. Condor 90:705–708.

Koenig, W. D., and Knops, J. M. H. 2001. Seed-crop size and eruptions of North American boreal seed-eating birds. J. Animal Ecol. 70:609–620.

Koenig, W. D., and Mumme, R. L. 1987. Population Ecology of the Cooperatively Breeding Acorn Woodpecker. Princeton Univ. Press, Princeton, NJ.

Koenig, W. D., Stacey, P. B., Stanback, M. T., and Mumme, R. L. 1995. Acorn Woodpecker, *in* The Birds of North America (A. Poole and F. Gill, eds.), no. 194. Acad. Nat. Sci., Philadelphia.

Koford, C. B. 1953. The California Condor. Natl. Audubon Soc. Res. Rep. 4:1–54.

Korpimäki, E., and Norrdahl, K. 1991. Numerical and functional responses of Kestrels, Short-eared Owls, and Long-eared Owls to vole densities. Ecology 72:814–826.

Krutzsch, P. H., and Dixon, K. L. 1947. The White-winged Dove in San Diego County, California. Condor 49:37.

Kus, B. E. 1998. Use of restored riparian habitat by the endangered Least Bell's Vireo (*Vireo bellii pusillus*). Restoration Ecol. 6:75–82.

Kus, B. E. 1999. Impacts of Brown-headed Cowbird parasitism on productivity of the endangered Least Bell's Vireo. Studies Avian Biol. 18:160–166.

Kus, B. E. 2000. Distribution, abundance, and breeding activities of the Southwestern Willow Flycatcher at Marine Corps Base Camp Pendleton, California, in 2000. Final report prepared for Assistant Chief of Staff, Environmental Security, Marine Corps Base Camp Pendleton, CA.

Kus, B. E. 2002. Fitness consequences of nest desertion in an endangered host, the Least Bell's Vireo. Condor 104:795–802.

Kus, B. E., and Beck, P. P. 1998. Distribution and abundance of the Least Bell's Vireo (*Vireo bellii pusillus*) and the Southwestern Willow Flycatcher (*Empidonax traillii extimus*)

at selected southern California sites in 1997. Report to California Department of Fish and Game, Sacramento, CA.

Kus, B. E., Beck, P. P., and Wells, J. M. 2003a. Southwestern Willow Flycatcher populations in California: Distribution, abundance, and potential for conservation. Studies Avian Biol. 26:12–21.

Kus, B. E., Evans, D., Langan, B., and Mulrooney, M. B. 2003b. Status and distribution of the Least Bell's Vireo and Southwestern Willow Flycatcher at the Cleveland National Forest in 2002. Final report to USDA Forest Service, Cleveland National Forest, San Diego, CA.

Kus, B. E., and Miner, K. L. 1989. The use of non-riparian habitats by Least Bell's Vireos (*Vireo bellii pusillus*), in California riparian systems conference: Protection, management, and restoration for the 1990s (D. L. Abell, ed.), pp. 299–303. Forest Serv. Gen. Tech. Rep. PSW-110.

Kus, B. E., and Sharp, B. L. 2002. Neotropical migratory bird monitoring study at Marine Corps Base Camp Pendleton, California. Seventh annual progress report, 2001. Report to U.S. Marine Corps, Environmental and Natural Resources Office, Camp Pendleton, CA.

LaHaye, W. S., Gutiérrez, R. J., and Akçakaya, H. R. 1994. Spotted Owl metapopulation dynamics in southern California. J. Animal Ecol. 63:775–785.

Lamberson, R. H., B. R. Noon and M. L. Farnsworth. 2000. An incidence function analysis of the viability of the southwestern willow flycatcher. Report prepared for the Bureau of Reclamation.

Langham, J. M. 1991. Twelfth report of the California Bird Records Committee. W. Birds 22:97–130.

Lanyon, W. E. 1994. Western Meadowlark, *in* The Birds of North America (A. Poole and F. Gill, eds.), no. 104. Acad. Nat. Sci., Philadelphia.

LaRue, C. T., Dickson, L. L., Brown, N. L., Spence, J. R., and Stevens, L. E. 2001. Recent bird records from the Grand Canyon region, 1974–2000. W. Birds 32:101–118.

Laudenslayer, W. F., Jr., England, A. S., Fitton, S., and Saslaw, L. 1992. The *Toxostoma* thrashers in California: Species at risk? Trans. W. Sect. Wildlife Soc. 28:22–29.

Laymon, S. A. 1987. Brown-headed Cowbirds in California: Historical perspectives and management opportunities in riparian habitats. W. Birds 18:63–70.

Laymon, S. A., and Halterman, M. D. 1987. Can the western subspecies of the Yellow-billed Cuckoo be saved from extinction? W. Birds 18:19–25.

Leachman, B., and Osmundson, B. 1990. Status of the Mountain Plover: A literature review. U.S. Fish and Wildlife Service, Golden, CO.

Lee, C.-T. A. 1995. More records of breeding Barn Swallows in Riverside, California. W. Birds 26:155–156.

Lee, D. T. 1967. Winter breeding of the Western Grebe. Condor 69:209.

Lee, M. H. 1921. A unique visitor. Condor 23:37–38.

Lehman, P. E. 1994. The Birds of Santa Barbara County, California. Vert. Mus., Univ. Calif., Santa Barbara.

Lentz, J. E. 1993. Breeding birds of four isolated mountains in southern California. W. Birds 24:201–234.

Leopold, A. S., and Smith, R. H. 1953. Numbers and winter distribution of Pacific Black Brant in North America. Calif. Fish and Game 39:95–101.

LeSchack, C. R., McKnight, S. K., and Hepp, G. R. 1997. Gadwall, *in* The Birds of North America (A. Poole and F. Gill, eds.), no. 283. Acad. Nat. Sci., Philadelphia.

Lethaby, N., and Bangma, J. 1998. Identifying Black-tailed Gull in North America. Birding 30:470–483.

Lewis, D. B., and Tyler, W. B. 1978. First record of the Blue-faced Booby from the Pacific coast of the United States. W. Birds 9:175–176.

Lincer, J. L. 1975. The effects of dietary DDE on eggshell-thinning in the American Kestrel: A comparison of the field situation and laboratory results. J. Appl. Ecol. 12:781–793.

Lincer, J. L., and Steenhof, K., eds. 1997. The Burrowing Owl, its biology and management. Raptor Res. Rep. 9.

Lincoln, F. C. 1936a. Recoveries of banded birds of prey. Bird-Banding 7:38–45.

Lincoln, F. C. 1936b Returns of banded birds: Second paper. Bird-Banding 7:121–128.

Linsdale, J. M. 1957. Goldfinches on the Hastings Natural History Reservation. Am. Midland Nat. 57:1–119.

Littrell, E. E. 1986. Mortality of American Wigeon on a golf course treated with the organophosphate Diazinon. Calif. Fish and Game 77:122–124.

Lovio, J. C. 1996. The effects of habitat fragmentation on the breeding-bird assemblage in California coastal sage scrub. M.S. thesis, San Diego Sate Univ.

Lowther, P. E. 1995. Bronzed Cowbird, in The Birds of North America (A. Poole and F. Gill, eds.), no. 144. Acad. Nat. Sci., Philadelphia.

Lowther, P. E. 2000a. Nuttall's Woodpecker, in The Birds of North America (A. Poole and F. Gill, eds.), no. 555. Birds N. Am., Philadelphia.

Lowther, P. E. 2000b. Pacific-slope Flycatcher and Cordilleran Flycatcher, in The Birds of North America (A. Poole and F. Gill, eds.), no. 556. Birds N. Am., Philadelphia.

Lowther, P. E., Celada, C., Klein, N. K., Rimmer, C. C., and Spector, D. A. 1999. Yellow Warbler, in The Birds of North America (A. Poole and F. Gill, eds.), no. 454. Birds N. Am., Philadelphia.

Lowther, P. E., and Cink, C. L. 1992. House Sparrow, in The Birds of North America (A. Poole and F. Gill, eds.), no. 12. Acad. Nat. Sci., Philadelphia.

Luther, J. S. 1980. Fourth report of the California Bird Records Committee. W. Birds 11:161–173.

Luther, J. S., McCaskie, G., and Dunn, J. 1979. Third report of the California Bird Records Committee. W. Birds 10:169–187.

Luther, J. S., McCaskie, G., and Dunn, J. 1983. Fifth report of the California Bird Records Committee. W. Birds 14:1–16.

Mabb, K. T. 1997. Nesting behavior of *Amazona* parrots and Rose-ringed Parakeets in the San Gabriel Valley, California. W. Birds 38:209–217.

Macdonald, K. B., Ford, R. F., Copper, E. B., Unitt, P., and Haltiner, J. P. 1990. South San Diego Bay enhancement plan. Resources atlas, vol. 2. Birds of San Diego Bay: Historical data and 1988–89 surveys. Report to San Diego Unified Port District, San Diego, and California State Coastal Conservancy, Oakland.

Maender, G. J., Bailey, S., and Hiett, K. L. 1996. Nesting Anna's Hummingbirds (*Calypte anna*) in urban Tucson, Arizona. W. Birds 27:78–80.

Mailliard, J. 1918. The Yolla Bolly Fox Sparrow. Condor 20:138–139.

Mallek, E. J., Platte, R., and Stehn, R. 2003. Aerial breeding pair surveys of the arctic coastal plain of Alaska—2002. U.S. Fish and Wildlife Service, Waterfowl Management, Fairbanks, AK.

Manning, J. A. 1995. Waterbirds of central and south San Diego Bay 1994–1994. Coastal Ecosystem Program, U. S. Fish and Wildlife Service, Carlsbad, CA.

Manning, J. A. 1997a. Breeding biology and status of the Turkey Vulture in San Diego County, California. Report to San Diego County Fish and Wildlife Advisory Commission.

Manning, J. A. 1997b. Habitat characteristics of Turkey Vulture nests in San Diego County, California. Report to San Diego County Fish and Wildlife Advisory Commission.

Marks, J. S., Evans, D. L., and Holt, D. W. 1994. Long-eared Owl, in The Birds of North America (A. Poole and F. Gill, eds.), no. 133. Acad. Nat. Sci., Philadelphia.

Marshall, J. T., Jr. 1967. Parallel variation in North and Middle American screech-owls. W. Found. Vert. Zool. Monogr. 1.

Marshall, J. T., Jr. 1988. Birds lost from a giant sequoia forest during fifty years. Condor 90:359–372.

Marshall, J. T., and Dedrick, K. G. 1994. Endemic Song Sparrows and Yellowthroats of San Francisco Bay. Studies Avian Biol. 15:316–327.

Marti, C. D., and Marks, J. S. 1989. Medium-sized owls [status report], in Proceedings of the Western Raptor Management Symposium and Workshop (B. G. Pendleton, ed.), pp. 124–133. Natl. Wildlife Found. Sci. Tech. Ser. 12.

Martin, D. J. 1973. Burrow digging by Barn Owls. Bird-Banding 44:59–60.

Martin, J. W., and Carlson, B. A. 1998. Sage Sparrow, in The Birds of North America (A. Poole and F. Gill, eds.), no. 326. Birds N. Am., Philadelphia.

Marzluff, J. M., Kimsey, B. A., Schueck, L. S., McFadzen, M. E., Vekasy, M. S., and Bednarz, J. C. 1997. The influence of habitat, prey abundance, sex, and breeding success on the ranging behavior of Paririe Falcons. Condor 99:567–584.

Massey, B. W. 1981. A Least Tern makes a right turn. Nat. Hist. 90(11):62–71.

Massey, B. W. 1998. Guide to Birds of the Anza–Borrego Desert. Anza–Borrego Desert Nat. Hist. Assoc., Borrego Springs, CA.

Massey, B. W., and Atwood, J. L. 1981. Second-wave nesting of the California Least Tern: Age composition and reproductive success. Auk 98:596–605.

Massey, B. W., Bradley, D. W., and Atwood, J. L. 1992. Demography of a California Least Tern colony including effects of the 1982–1983 El Niño. Condor 94:976–983.

Massey, B. W., and Evans, M. U. 1994. An eight-year census of birds of Vallecito Creek, Anza–Borrego Desert, California. W. Birds 25:178–191.

Massey, B. W., Zembal, R., and Jorgensen, P. D. 1984. Nesting habitat of the Light-footed Clapper Rail in southern California. J. Field Ornithol. 55:67–80.

Mayer, A. L., and Wirtz, W. O. 1995. Effects of fire on the ecology of the California Gnatcatcher (*Polioptila californica*) and associated species, in the coastal sage scrub community of southern California, in Brushfires in California Wildlands: Ecology and Resource Management (J. E. Keeley and T. A. Scott, eds.), pp. 77–90. Int. Assoc. Wildland Fire, Fairfield, WA.

McCaskie, R. G. 1963. The occurrence of the Ruff in California. Condor 65:166–167.

McCaskie, R. G. 1964. Three southern herons in California. Condor 66:442–443.

McCaskie, R. G. 1965. The Cattle Egret reaches the west coast of the United States. Condor 67:89.

McCaskie, R. G. 1966. The occurrence of Red-throated Pipits in California. Auk 83:135–136.

McCaskie, R. G. 1968a. A Broad-winged Hawk in California. Condor 70:93.

McCaskie, R. G. 1968b. Noteworthy vireo records in California. Condor 66:442–443.

McCaskie, G. 1970. Occurrence of the eastern species of *Oporornis* and *Wilsonia* in California. Condor 72:373.

McCaskie, G. 1971. The Wood Thrush in California. Calif. Birds 2:135–136.

McCaskie, G. 1973. A look at the Tree Sparrow in California. W. Birds 4:71–76.

McCaskie, G. 1975. The Sprague's Pipit reaches California. W. Birds 6:29–30.

McCaskie, G. 1990. First record of the Band-rumped Storm-Petrel in California. W. Birds 21:65–68.

McCaskie, G. 1993. A Little Bunting reaches California. W. Birds 24:95–97.

McCaskie, G. 2003. Ruddy Ground-Dove breeding in California. W. Birds 34:171–172.

McCaskie, G., and Banks, R. C. 1964. Occurrence and migration of certain birds in southwestern California. Auk 81:353–361.

McCaskie, G., and Banks, R. C. 1966. Supplemental list of the birds of San Diego County, California. Trans. San Diego Soc. Nat. Hist. 14:157–168.

McCaskie, G., and Cardiff, E. A. 1965. Notes on the distribution of the Parasitic Jaeger and some members of the Laridae in California. Condor 67:542–544.

McCaskie, G., and San Miguel, M. 1999. Report of the California Bird Records Committee: 1996 records. W. Birds 30:57–85.

McCaskie, G., Stallcup, R., and DeBenedictis, P. 1967a. The occurrence of certain flycatchers in California. Condor 69:85–86.

McCaskie, G., Stallcup, R., and DeBenedictis, P. 1967b. The distribution of certain Mimidae in California. Condor 69:310.

McCaskie, G., Stallcup, R., and DeBenedictis, P. 1967c. The status of certain fringillids in California. Condor 69:429–429.

McChesney, G. J., Carter, H. R., and McIver, W. R. 1998. Population monitoring of seabirds in California: 1997 surveys of breeding colonies of Double-crested, Brandt's, and Pelagic Cormorants in southern California. Report to Calif. Dept. Fish and Game, Office of Oil Spill Prevention and Response, Sacramento, and U.S. Navy, Naval Air Weapons Station, Point Mugu.

McChesney, G. J., Carter, H. R., and Whitworth, D. L. 1995. Reoccupation and extension of southern breeding limits of Tufted Puffins and Rhinoceros Auklets in California. Colonial Waterbirds 18:79–90.

McClure, H. E. 1992. The collapse of a local population of Spotted Doves in southern California. N. Am. Bird Bander 16 (2): 34–36.

McCrary, M. D., and Bloom, P. H. 1984. Lethal effects of introduced grasses on Red shouldered Hawks. J. Wildlife Mgmt. 48:1005–1008.

McDonald, P., Booth, C., and Snover, S. 2000. Status of the heronry at Naval Air Station North Island, San Diego, in 1999. Report to Southwest Division, Naval Facilities Engineering Command, Naval Air Station North Island, San Diego.

McGillivray, B. 1988. Breeding of the Rock Dove, *Columbia livia*, in January at Edmonton, Alberta. Can. Field-Nat. 102.76–77.

McGowan, J. A., Cayan, D. R., and Dorman, L. M. 1998. Climate–ocean variability and ecosystem response in the northeast Pacific. Science 281:210–217.

McGrew, C. A. 1922. City of San Diego and San Diego County: The Birthplace of California. Am. Hist. Soc., Chicago.

McKee, T., and Erickson, R. A. 2002. Report of the California Bird Records Committee: 2000 records. W. Birds 33:175–201.

Mead, G. H. 1952. Robin breeding in San Diego, California. Condor 54:64.

Meadows, D. 1933. California Condor in San Diego County. Condor 35:234.

Mellink, E., and Rea, A. M. 1994. Taxonomic status of the California Gnatcatchers of northwestern Baja California, Mexico. W. Birds 25:50–62.

Merkel and Associates, Inc. 1997. Batiquitos Lagoon enhancement project long-term monitoring and pilot vegetation program: 1997 annual report. Report to Board of Harbor Commissioners, city of Los Angeles, and city of Carlsbad.

Michael, C. W. 1935a. Nesting habits of cormorants. Condor 37:36–37.

Michael, C. W. 1935b. The Lesser Yellowlegs near San Diego in winter. Condor 37:42–43.

Middleton, A. L. A. 1998. Chipping Sparrow, *in* The Birds of North America (A. Poole and F. Gill, eds.), no. 334. Birds N. Am., Philadelphia.

Miller, A. H. 1930. Two new races of the Loggerhead Shrike from western North America. Condor 32:155–156.

Miller, A. H. 1941. Speciation in the avian genus *Junco*. Univ. Calif. Publ. Zool. 44:173–434.

Miller, A. H. 1951. An analysis of the distribution of the birds of California. Univ. Calif. Publ. Zool. 50:531–644.

Miller, A. H., and Stebbins, R. C. 1964. The Lives of Desert Animals in Joshua Tree National Monument. Univ. of Calif. Press, Berkeley.

Miller, J. H., and Green, M. T. 1987. Distribution, status, and origin of Water Pipits breeding in California. Condor 89:788–797.

Miller, L. 1936. Some maritime birds observed off San Diego, California. Condor 38:9–16.

Mock, P. J. 1993. Population viability analysis for the MSCP study area. Report to the city of San Diego MSCP Program.

Mock, P. J. 1998. Energetic constraints to the distribution and abundance of the California Gnatcatcher. W. Birds 29:413–420.

Mock, P. J., and Bolger, D. T. 1992. Ecology of the California Gnatcatcher at Rancho San Diego. Technical appendix to the Rancho San Diego Habitat Conservation Plan. Report to Home Capital Development Corp., San Diego.

Mock, P. J., and Preston, K. L. 1995. Phase III Report: Amber Ridge California Gnatcatcher Study. Report to Weingarten, Siegel, Fletcher Group, Inc., San Diego.

Mock, P. J., Preston, K., and Mann, M. D. 1994. Waterbird survey: North and central San Diego Bay, 1993. Report to U. S. Department of the Navy, Naval Air Station North Island [original and additional data not printed in report supplied by P. J. Mock].

Moffitt, J. 1938 Eighth annual Black Brant census in California. Calif. Fish and Game 24:341–346.

Moffitt, J. 1943. Twelfth annual Black Brant census in California. Calif. Fish and Game 29:19–28.

Molina, K. C. 2000. The recent breeding of California and Laughing Gulls at the Salton Sea, California. W. Birds 31:106–111.

Molina, K. C. 2004. Breeding larids of the Salton Sea: Trends in population size and colony site occupation. Studies Avian Biol. 27:92–99.

Molina, K. C., and Marschalek, D. A. 2003. Foraging behavior and diet of breeding Western Gull-billed Terns (*Sterna nilotica vanrossemi*) in San Diego Bay, California. Calif. Dept. Fish and Game, Habitat Conservation and Recovery Program Rep. 2003-01.

Monroe, B. L., Jr. 1955. A gull new to North America. Auk 72:208.

Monroe, B. L., Jr. 1956. Observations of Elegant Terns at San Diego, California. Wilson Bull. 68:239–244.

Monson, G., and Phillips, A. R. 1981. Annotated Checklist of the Birds of Arizona. Univ. of Ariz. Press, Tucson.

Morlan, J. 1985. Eighth report of the California Bird Records Committee. W. Birds 16:105–122.

Morley, A. G. 1959. Notes on occurrences of birds in San Diego County, California. Condor 61:302.

Morrison, M. L. 1990. Morphological and vocal variation in the Black-throated Gray Warbler in the Pacific Northwest. Northwest. Nat. 71:53–58.

Morrison, S. A., and Bolger, D. T. 2002. Lack of an urban edge effect on reproduction in a fragmentation-sensitive sparrow. Ecol. Appl. 12:398–411.

Mowbray, T. B. 2002. Canvasback, *in* The Birds of North America (A. Poole and F. Gill, eds.), no 659. Birds N. Am., Philadelphia.

Mowbray, T. B., Ely, C. R., Sedinger, J. S., and Trost, R. E. 2002.

Canada Goose, *in* The Birds of North America (A. Poole and F. Gill, eds.), no. 682. Birds N. Am., Philadelphia.

Muller, M. J., and Storer, R. W. Pied-billed Grebe, *in* The Birds of North America (A. Poole and F. Gill, eds.), no. 410. Birds N. Am., Philadelphia.

Neff, J. A. 1937. Nesting distribution of the Tricolored Red-wing. Condor 39:61–81.

Newman, D. L. 1961. House Wren and Bewick's Wren, northern Ohio. Wilson Bull. 73:84–86.

Nisbet, I. C. T. 2002. Common Tern, *in* The Birds of North America (A. Poole and F. Gill, eds.), no 618. Birds N. Am., Philadelphia.

Norris, R. A. 1958. Comparative biosystematics and life history of the nuthatches *Sitta pygmaea* and *Sitta pusilla*. Univ. Calif. Publ. Zool. 56:119–300.

Oberholser, H. C. 1912. A revision of the forms of the Great Blue Heron (*Ardea herodias* Linnaeus). Proc. U. S. Natl. Mus. 43:531–559.

Oberholser, H. C. 1930. Notes on a collection of birds from Arizona and New Mexico. Sci. Publ. Cleveland Mus. Nat. Hist. 1:83–124.

Oberholser, H. C. 1974. The Bird Life of Texas. Univ. of Tex. Press, Austin.

Oedekoven, C. S., Ainley, D. G., and Spear, L. B. 2001. Variable responses of seabirds to change in marine climate: California Current, 1985–1994. Mar. Ecol. Prog. Ser. 212:265–281.

Omland, K. E., Tarr, C. L., Boarman, W. I., Marzluff, J. M., and Fleischer, R. C. 2000. Cryptic genetic variation and paraphyly in ravens. Proc. Royal Soc. London B 267:2475–2482.

Orians, G. H. 1980. Some Adaptations of Marsh-Nesting Blackbirds. Princeton Univ. Press, Princeton, NJ.

Oring, L. W., Gray, E. M., and Reed, J. M. 1997. Spotted Sandpiper, *in* The Birds of North America (A. Poole and F. Gill, eds.), no 289. Acad. Nat. Sci., Philadelphia.

Page, G. W., and Stenzel, L. E. (eds.). 1981. The breeding status of the Snowy Plover in California. W. Birds 12:1–40.

Page, G. W., Stenzel, L. E., Shuford, W. D., and Bruce, C. R. 1991. Distribution and abundance of the Snowy Plover on its western North American breeding grounds. J. Field Ornithol. 62:245–255.

Page, G. W., Warriner, J. S. and J. C., and Paton, P. W. C. 1995. Snowy Plover, *in* The Birds of North America (A. Poole and F. Gill, eds.), no. 154. Acad. Nat. Sci., Philadelphia.

Paige, C. (revised by M. Koenen and D. W. Mehlman). 1999. Wings Info Resources/ Species Information and Management Abstracts: Black-throated Gray Warbler (*Dendroica nigrescens*). The Nature Conservancy. Edition date: 1999-10-20.

Palacios, E., and Mellink, E. 2000. Nesting waterbirds on islas San Martín and Todos Santos, Baja California. W. Birds 31:184–189.

Palacios, E., and Mellink, E. 2003. Status distribution, and ecology of nesting larids in western Mexico, with emphasis on *vanrossemi* Gull-billed Terns and Caspian Terns. Final report to U.S. Fish & Wildlife Service, Division of Migratory Birds and Habitat Programs, Portland, OR.

Panza, R. K., and Parkes, K. C. 1992. Baja California specimens of *Parus gambeli baileyae*. W. Birds 23:87–89.

Parker, J. W., and Ogden, J. C. 1979. The recent history and status of the Mississippi Kite. Am. Birds 33:119–129.

Parkes, K .C. 1952. Geographic in the Horned Grebe. Condor 54:314–315.

Parnell, J. F., Erwin, R. M., and Molina, K. C. 1995. Gull-billed Tern, *in* The Birds of North America (A. Poole and F. Gill, eds.), no. 140. Acad. Nat. Sci., Philadelphia.

Patten, M. A. 2001. The roles of habitat and signaling in speciation: Evidence from a contact zone of two Song Sparrow (*Melospiza melodia*) subspecies. Ph. D. dissertation, Univ. Calif., Riverside.

Patten, M. A., and Burger, J. C. 1998. Spruce budworm outbreaks and the incidence of vagrancy in eastern North American wood-warblers. Can. J. Zool. 76:433–439.

Patten, M. A., and Campbell, K. F. 1994. Late nesting of the California Gnatcatcher. W. Birds 25:110–111.

Patten, M. A., and Campbell, K. F. 1998. Has brood parasitism selected for earlier nesting in the California Gnatcatcher? W. Birds 29:290–298.

Patten, M. A., and Campbell, K. F. 2000. Typological thinking and the conservation of subspecies: The case of the San Clemente Island Loggerhead Shrike. Diversity and Distributions 6:177–178.

Patten, M. A., and Erickson, R. A. 1994. Fifteenth report of the California Bird Records Committee. W. Birds 25:1–34.

Patten, M. A., and Erickson, R. A. 2000. Population fluctuations of the Harris' Hawk (*Parabuteo unicinctus*) and its reappearance in California. J. Raptor Res. 34:187–195.

Patten, M. A., and Marantz, C. A. 1996. Implications of vagrant southeastern vireos and warblers in California. Auk 113:911–923.

Patten, M. A., and Unitt, P. 2002. Diagnosability versus mean differences of Sage Sparrow subspecies. Auk 119:26–35.

Patten, M. A., Unitt, P., Erickson, R. A., Campbell, K. F. 1995a. Fifty years since Grinnell and Miller: Where is California ornithology headed? W. Birds 26:54–64.

Patten, M. A., Finnegan, S. E., and Lehman, P. E. 1995b. Seventeenth report of the California Bird Records Committee: 1991 records. W. Birds 26:113–143.

Patten, M. A., McCaskie, G., and Unitt, P. 2003. Birds of the Salton Sea: Status, Biogeography, and Ecology. Univ. Calif. Press, Berkeley.

Pavelka, M. A. 1990. Peregrine Falcons nesting in San Diego, California. W. Birds 21:181–183.

Payne, R. B. 1992. Indigo Bunting, *in* The Birds of North America (A. Poole, P. Stettenheim, and F. Gill, eds.), no. 4. Acad. Nat. Sci., Philadelphia.

Peterson, B. L. 2002. A multi-scale approach to nest predation of the Least Bell's Vireo (*Vireo bellii pusillus*). Master's thesis, San Diego State University.

Peterson, B. L., Kus, B. E., and Deutschman, D. H. 2004. Determining nest predators of the Least Bell's Vireo through point counts, tracking stations and videophotography. J. Field Ornithol. 75:89–95.

Phillips, A. R. 1962. Notas sistematicas sobre aves mexicanas. II. Anal. Inst. Biol. México 33:331–372.

Phillips, A. R. 1975. The migrations of Allen's and other hummingbirds. Condor 77:196–205

Phillips, A. R. 1986. The Known Birds of North and Middle America, part 1. A. R. Phillips, Denver.

Phillips, A. R. 1991. The Known Birds of North and Middle America, part 2. A. R. Phillips, Denver.

Phillips, A., Marshall, J., and Monson, G. 1964. The Birds of Arizona. Univ. Ariz. Press, Tucson.

Pierce, W. M. 1921. Nesting of the Stephens Fox Sparrow. Condor 23:80–85.

Pierotti, R. J., and Annett, C. A. 1995. Western Gull, *in* The Birds of North America (A. Poole and F. Gill, eds.), no. 174. Acad. Nat. Sci., Philadelphia.

Pitman, R. L. 1988. Laysan Albatross breeding in the eastern Pacific—and a comment. Pac. Seabird Group Bull. 15:52.

Pitman, R. L., and Jehl, J. R., Jr. 1998. Geographic variation and reassessment of species limits in the "Masked" boobies of the eastern Pacific Ocean. Wilson Bull. 110:155–170.

Pitochelli, J. 1995. MacGillivray's Warbler, *in* The Birds of North

America (A. Poole and G. Gill, eds.), no. 159. Acad. Nat. Sci., Philadelphia.

Pleasants, B. Y., and Albano, D. J. 2001. Hooded Oriole, *in* The Birds of North America (A. Poole and F. Gill, eds.), no. 568. Birds N. Am., Philadelphia.

Post, P. W., and Lewis, R. H. 1995. The Lesser Black-backed Gull in the Americas: Occurrence and subspecific identity. Part I: Taxonomy, distribution, and migration. Birding 27:282–290.

Powell, A. N. 1993. Nesting habitat of Belding's Savannah Sparrows in coastal salt marshes. Wetlands 13:210–223.

Powell, A. N., and Collier, C. L. 1998. Reproductive success of Belding's Savannah Sparrow in a highly fragmented landscape. Auk 115:508–513.

Powell, A. N., and Collier, C. L. 2000. Habitat use and reproductive success of Western Snowy Plovers at new nesting areas created for California Least Terns. J. Wildlife Mgmt. 64:24–33.

Powell, A. N., Fritz, C. L., Peterson, B. L., and Terp, J. M. 2002. Status of breeding and wintering Snowy Plovers in San Diego County, California, 1994–1999. J. Field Ornithol. 73:156–165.

Power, D. M., and Ainley, D. G. 1986. Seabird geographic variability: Similarity among populations of Leach's Storm-Petrel. Auk 103:575–585.

Pranty, B., and Garrett, K. L. 2002. The parrot fauna of the ABA area: A current look. Birding 35:248–261.

Pravosudov, V. V., and Grubb, T. C., Jr. 1993. White-breasted Nuthatch, *in* The Birds of North America (A. Poole and F. Gill, eds.), no. 54. Acad. Nat. Sci., Philadelphia.

Preston, K. L., and Mock, P. J. 1995. Waterbird survey: Central San Diego Bay, 1994. Report to U. S. Dept. of the Navy, Naval Air Station North Island, San Diego.

Preston, K. L., Mock, P. J., Grishaver, M. A., Bailey, E. A., and King, D. F. 1998. California Gnatcatcher territorial behavior. W. Birds 29:242–257.

Pryde, P. R. 2004. San Diego: An Introduction to the Region, 4th ed. Pearson Custom Publ., Boston.

Pyle, P. 2001. Age at first breeding and natal dispersal in a declining population of Cassin's Auklet. Auk 118:996–1007.

Pyle, P., and McCaskie, G. 1992. Thirteenth report of the California Bird Records Committee. W. Birds 23:92–132.

Pyle, P., Nur, N., and DeSante, D. F. 1994. Trends in nocturnal migrant landbird populations at southeast Farallon Island, California, 1968–1992. Studies Avian Biol. 15:58–74.

Rand, A. L., and Traylor, M. A. 1950. The amount of overlap allowable for subspecies. Auk 67:169–183.

Ratti, J. T. 1979. Reproductive separation and isolating mechanisms between sympatric dark- and light-phase Western Grebes. Auk 96:573–586.

Ratti, J. T. 1981. Identification and distribution of Clark's Grebe. W. Birds 12:41–46.

Rea, A. M. 1967. Some bird records from San Diego County, California. Condor 69:316–318.

Rea, A. M. 1969. Interbreeding of two subspecies of Boat-tailed Grackle, *Cassidix mexicanus nelsoni* and *Cassidix mexicanus monsoni*, in secondary contact in central Arizona. M.S. thesis, Ariz. State Univ., Tempe.

Rea, A. M. 1972. Status of the Summer Tanager on the Pacific slope. Condor 72:230–233.

Rea, A. M. 1983. Once a River: Bird Life and Habitat Changes on the Middle Gila. Univ. Ariz. Press, Tucson.

Rea, A. M., and Weaver, K. L. 1990. The taxonomy, distribution, and status of coastal California Cactus Wrens. W. Birds 21:81–126.

Rechnitzer, A. B. 1954. Status of the Wood Ibis in San Diego County, California. Condor 56:309–310.

Reed, A., Ward, D. H., Derksen, D. V., and Sedinger, J. S. 1998. Brant, *in* The Birds of North America (A. Poole and F. Gill, eds.), no. 337. Birds N. Am., Philadelphia.

Remsen, J. V. 1978. Bird species of special concern in California. Calif. Dept. Fish and Game, Wildlife Mgmt. Branch Admin. Rep. 78-1.

Ridgway, R. 1902. The birds of North and Middle America. U.S. Natl. Mus. Bull. 50, part 2.

Ridgway, R. 1904. The birds of North and Middle America. U.S. Natl. Mus. Bull 50, part 3.

Ridgway, R. 1907. The birds of North and Middle America. U.S. Natl. Mus. Bull. 50, part 4.

Ridgway, R. 1914. The birds of North and Middle America. U.S. Natl. Mus. Bull 50, part 6.

Risebrough, F. S., Reiche, P., Peakall, D. B., Herman, S. G., and Kirven, M. N. 1968. Polychlorinated biphenyls in the global ecosystem. Nature 220:1098–1102.

Rising, J. D. 1996. A Guide to the Identification and Natural History of the Sparrows of the United States and Canada. Academic Press, San Diego.

Rising, J. D., and Williams, P. L. 1999. Bullock's Oriole, *in* The Birds of North America (A. Poole and F. Gill, eds.), no. 416. Birds N. Am., Philadelphia.

Roach, J. D. 1989. The influence of vegetation structure and arthropod abundance on the reproductive success of California Black-tailed Gnatcatchers, *Polioptila californica californica*. M. S. Thesis, San Diego State Univ.

Roberson, D. 1986. Ninth report of the California Bird Records Committee. W. Birds 17:49–77.

Roberson, D. 1993. Fourteenth report of the California Bird Records Committee. W. Birds 24:113–166.

Robertson, R. J., Stutchbury, B. J., and Cohen, R. R. 1992. Tree Swallow, *in* The Birds of North America (A. Poole, P. Stettenheim, and F. Gill, eds.), no. 11. Acad. Nat. Sci., Philadelphia.

Robinson, W. D. 1996. Summer Tanager, *in* The Birds of North America (A. Poole and F. Gill, eds.), no. 248. Acad. Nat. Sci., Philadelphia.

Roemich, D., and McGowan, J. A. 1995. Climatic warming and the decline of zooplankton in the California Current. Science 267:1324–1326.

Rogers M. M., and Jaramillo, A. 2002. Report of the California Bird Records Committee: 1999 records. W. Birds 33:1–33.

Rohwer, S., and Wood., C. S. 1998. Three hybrid zones between Hermit and Townsend's Warblers in Washington and Oregon. Auk 115:384–310.

Rohwer, S., Bermingham, E., and Wood, C. 2001. Plumage and mitochondrial DNA haplotype variation across a moving hybrid zone. Evolution 55:405–422.

Romagosa, C. M., and McEneaney, T. 1999. Eurasian Collared-Dove in North America and the Caribbean. N. Am. Birds 53:348–353.

Root, R. B. 1969. The behavior and reproductive success of the Blue-gray Gnatcatcher. Condor 71:16–31.

Rosenberg, K. V., Ohmart, R. D., Hunter, W. C., and Anderson, B. W. 1991. Birds of the Lower Colorado River Valley. Univ. Ariz. Press, Tucson.

Rotenberry, J. T., Patten, M. A., and Preston, K. L. 1999. Brewer's Sparrow, *in* The Birds of North America (A. Poole and F. Gill, eds.), no. 390. Birds N. Am., Philadelphia.

Rothstein, S. I. 1994. The cowbird's invasion of the far west: History, causes, and consequences experienced by host species. Studies Avian Biol. 15:301–315.

Rothstein, S. I., Verner, J., and Stevens, E. 1980. Range expansion and diurnal changes in dispersion of the Brown-headed Cowbird in the Sierra Nevada. Auk 97:253–267.

Rottenborn, S. C., and Morlan, J. 2000. Report of the California Bird Records Committee: 1997 records. W. Birds 31:1–37.

Rowe, S. P., and Cooper, D. S. 1997. Confirmed nesting of an Indigo with a Lazuli Bunting in Kern County, California. W. Birds 28:225–227.

Russell, R. W. 2002. Pacific Loon and Arctic Loon, *in* The Birds of North America (A. Poole and F. Gill, eds.), no. 657. Birds N. Am., Philadelphia.

Russell, R. W., and Lehman, P. E. 1994. Spring migration of Pacific Loons through the Southern California Bight: Nearshore flights, seasonal timing, and distribution at sea. Condor 96:300–315.

Russell, S. M. 1996. Anna's Hummingbird, *in* The Birds of North America (A. Poole and F. Gill, eds.), no. 226. Acad. Nat. Sci., Philadelphia.

Russell, S. M., and Monson, G. 1998. The Birds of Sonora. Univ. of Ariz. Press, Tucson.

Ryan, T. P., and Collins, C. T. 2000. White-throated Swift, *in* The Birds of North America (A. Poole and F. Gill, eds.), no 526. Birds N. Am., Philadelphia.

Ryder, J. P. 1993. Ring-billed Gull, *in* The Birds of North America (A. Poole and F. Gill, eds.), no. 33. Acad. Nat. Sci., Philadelphia.

Ryder, J. P., and Alisauskas, R. T. 1995. Ross' Goose, *in* The Birds of North America (A. Poole and F. Gill, eds.), no. 162. Acad. Nat. Sci., Philadelphia.

Salvadori, T. 1895. Catalogue of the Birds in the British Museum, vol 27. Br. Mus. (Nat. Hist.), London.

Sams, J. R. 1959. Ground Doves nesting in San Diego County. Condor 61:155.

Sams, J. R., and Stott, K., Jr. 1959. Birds of San Diego County, California: An annotated checklist. Occ. Pap. San Diego Soc. Nat. Hist. 10.

Sargent, G. T. 1940. Observations on color-banded California Thrashers. Condor 42:49–60.

Sauer, J. R., Hines, J. E., and Fallon, J. 2003. The North American Breeding Bird Survey, Results and Analysis 1966–2002. Version 2003.1, U. S. Geol. Surv. Patuxent Wildlife Res. Center, Laurel, MD.

Saunders, H. 1896. Catalogue of the Birds in the British Museum, vol. 25. Br. Mus. (Nat. Hist.), London.

Saunders, M. A., and Edwards, S. V. 2000. Dynamics and phylogenetic implications of mtDNA control region sequences in New World jays (Aves: Corvidae). J. Molec. Evol. 51:97–109.

Schaffner, F. C. 1981. A Sandwich Tern in California. W. Birds 12:181–182.

Schaffner, F. C. 1982. Aspects of the reproductive ecology of the Elegant Tern (*Sterna elegans*) at San Diego Bay. Master's thesis, San Diego State Univ.

Schaffner, F. C. 1985. Royal Tern nesting attempts in California: Isolated or significant incidents? W. Birds 16:71–80.

Schaffner, F. C. 1986. Trends in Elegant Tern and Northern Anchovy populations in California. Condor 88:347–354.

Schlorff, R. W., and Bloom, P. H. 1983. Importance of riparian systems to nesting Swainson's Hawks in the Central Valley of California, *in* California Riparian Systems (R. B. Warner and K. M. Hendrix, eds.), pp. 612–618. Univ. of Calif. Press, Berkeley.

Schorger, A. 1952. Introduction of the Domestic Pigeon. Auk 69:462–463.

Scott, C. D. 1936. Who killed the condors? Nature Magazine 28:368–370.

Scott, T. A. 1984. Breeding bird census 132. Tall willow woodland. Am. Birds 38:105–106, 1984.

Scott, T. A. 1985. Human impacts on the Golden Eagle population of San Diego County. Master's thesis, San Diego State Univ.

Scott, T. A. 1994. Irruptive dispersal of Black-shouldered Kites to a coastal island. Condor 96:197–200.

Sealy, S. G., Banks, A., and Chace, J. F. 2000. Trends in response to cowbird eggs by two subspecies of the Warbling Vireo. W. Birds 31:190–194.

Sechrist, E. E. 1915b. Western Meadowlark. Oologist 32:91.

Sedgwick, J. A. 1993. Dusky Flycatcher, *in* The Birds of North America (A. Poole and F. Gill, eds.), no. 78. Acad. Nat. Sci., Philadelphia.

Sedgwick, J. A., 2001, Geographic variation in the song of Willow Flycatchers. I. Differentiation between *Empidonax traillii adastus* and *E. t. extimus*. Auk 118:366–379.

Sefton, J. W., Jr. 1926. A third Rusty Blackbird to be recorded in California. Condor 28:99.

Sefton, J. W., Jr. 1936. An American Egret roost. Condor 38:41–42.

Sefton, J. W., Jr. 1938. Another California record of the Red-billed Tropicbird. Condor 40:40.

Sefton, J. W., Jr. 1939. Oldsquaw taken at San Diego, California. Condor 41:83.

Serie, J. R., and Bartonek, J. B. 1991. Population status and productivity of Tundra Swans *Cygnus columbianus columbianus* in North America, *in* Proceedings of the Third IWRB International Swan Symposium (J. Sears and P. J. Bacon, eds.), pp. 172–177. Wildfowl, suppl. 1.

Sharp, C. S. 1902. Nesting of Swainson Hawk. Condor 4:116–118.

Sharp, C. S. 1906a. Unusual breeding records at Escondido. Condor 8:75.

Sharp, C. S. 1906b. Nesting of the Red-bellied Hawk. Condor 8:144–148

Sharp, C. S. 1907. The breeding birds of Escondido. Condor 9:84–91.

Sharp, C. S. 1908. Late nesting of the Green-backed Goldfinch. Condor 10:237.

Sharp, C. S. 1919. Nesting of the Band-tailed Pigeon in San Diego County, California. Condor 21:40–41.

Sheppard, J. M. 1996. Le Conte's Thrasher, *in* The Birds of North America (A. Poole and F. Gill, eds.), no. 230. Acad. Nat. Sci., Philadelphia.

Shields, M. 2002. Brown Pelican, *in* The Birds of North America (A. Poole and F. Gill, eds.), no. 609. Birds N. Am., Philadelphia.

Short, L. L., Jr. 1971. Systematics and behavior of some North American woodpeckers, genus *Picoides* (Aves). Bull Am. Mus. Nat. Hist. 145:1–118.

Short, L. L., Jr. 1982. Woodpeckers of the World. Del. Mus. Nat. Hist., Greenville, DE.

Shuford, W. D., and Ryan, T. P. 2000. Nesting populations of California and Ring-billed Gulls in California: Recent surveys and historical status. W. Birds 31:133–164.

Shuford, W. D., Hickey, C. M., Safran, R. J., and Page, G. W. 1996. A review of the status of the White-faced Ibis in winter in California. W. Birds 27:169–196.

Shuford, W. D., Humphrey, J. M., and Nur, N. 2001. Breeding status of the Black Tern in California. W. Birds 32:189–217.

Shuford, W. D., Page, G. W., and Stenzel, L. E. 2002. Patterns of distribution and abundance of migratory shorebirds in the intermountain West of the United States. W. Birds 33:134–174.

Sibley, D. 1996. Field identification of the Sharp-tailed Sparrow complex. Birding 28:197–208.

Sidle, J. G., Koonz, W. H., and Roney, K. 1985. Status of the American White Pelican: An update. Am. Birds 39:859–864.

Siegel-Causey, D. 1988. Phylogeny of the Phalacrocoracidae. Condor 90:885–905.

Small, A. 1994. California Birds: Their Status and Distribution. Ibis Publ. Co., Vista, CA.

Smith, M. R. 1999. First Sooty Tern nest in the contiguous western United States. W. Birds 30:121–122.

Snell, R. R. 2002. Iceland Gull and Thayer's Gull, *in* The Birds of North America (A. Poole and F. Gill, eds.), no. 699. Birds N. Am., Philadelphia.

Snyder, N. F. R., and Schmitt, N. J. 2002. California Condor, *in* The Birds of North America (A. Poole and F. Gill, eds.), no. 610. Birds N. Am., Philadelphia.

Snyder, N. F. R., and Snyder, H. A. 2000. The California Condor, a Saga of Natural History and Conservation. Academic Press, London.

Snyder, N. F. R., Snyder, H. A., Lincer, J. L., and Reynolds, R. T. 1973. Organochlorines, heavy metals, and the biology of North American accipiters. Bioscience 23:300–305.

Sockman, K.W. 1997. Variation in life-history traits and nest-site selection affects risk of nest predation in the California Gnatcatcher. Auk 114:324–332.

Sogge, M. K., Gilbert, W. M., and van Riper, C., III. 1994. Orange-crowned Warbler, *in* The Birds of North America (A. Poole and F. Gill, eds.), no. 101. Acad. Nat. Sci., Philadelphia.

Soulé, M. E., Bolger, D. T., Alberts, A. C., Sauvajot, R. S., Wright, J., Sorice, M., and Hill, S. 1988. Reconstructed dynamics of rapid extinctions of chaparral-requiring birds in urban habitat islands. Cons. Biol. 2:75–92.

Spear, L. B., and Ainley, D. G. 1999. Migration routes of Sooty Shearwaters in the Pacific Ocean. Condor 101:205–218.

Stadtlander, D. 1993. Breeding activity of colonial nesting birds and Western Snowy Plovers at the Western Salt Works, San Diego Bay, California. Preliminary report, Bay and Estuary Program, U. S. Fish and Wildlife Service, Carlsbad, CA.

Stadtlander, D., and Konecny, J. 1994. Avifauna of South San Diego Bay: The Western Salt Works. Unpublished report by Coastal Ecosystem Program, U.S. Fish and Wildlife Service, Carlsbad, CA.

Stedman, S. J. 2000. Horned Grebe, *in* The Birds of North America (A. Poole and F. Gill, eds.), no 505. Birds N. Am., Philadelphia.

Steenhof, K. 1998. Prairie Falcon, *in* The Birds of North America (A. Poole and F. Gill, eds.), no. 346. Birds N. Am., Philadelphia.

Steenhof, K., Kochert, M. N., and Roppe, J. A. 1993. Nesting by raptors and Common Ravens on electrical transmission line towers. J. Wildlife Mgmt. 57:271–281.

Stenzel, L. E., Warriner, J. C. and J. S., Wilson, K. S., Bidstrup, F. C., and Page, G. W. 1994. Long-distance breeding dispersal of Snowy Plovers in western North America. J. Animal Ecol. 63:887–902.

Stephens, F. 1878. *Vireo vicinior* in California. Bull. Nuttall Ornithol. Club 3:42.

Stephens, F. 1909. Notes on the California Black Rail. Condor 11:47–49.

Stephens, F. 1910. The Alaska Longspur in California. Condor 12:44.

Stephens, F. 1915. Scott Oriole at San Diego in the fall. Condor 17:69.

Stephens, F. 1919a. An annotated list of the birds of San Diego County, California. Trans. San Diego Soc. Nat. Hist. 3:142–180.

Stephens, F. 1919b. Unusual occurrences of Bendire Thrasher, Forked-tailed Petrel, and Western Goshawk. Condor 21:87.

Stephens, F. 1920a. A swan hunt. Condor 22:77.

Stephens, F. 1920b. Bohemian Waxwing in San Diego County. Condor 22:159.

Stephens, K. 1906. Scott Orioles at San Diego. Condor 8:30.

Sterling, J. C. 1999. Gray Flycatcher, *in* The Birds of North America (A. Poole and F. Gill, eds.), no. 458. Birds N. Am., Philadelphia.

Sterling, J., and Paton, P. W. C. 1996. Breeding distribution of Vaux's Swift in California. W. Birds 27:30–40.

Stiles, F. G. 1972. Age and sex determination in Rufous and Allen Hummingbirds. Condor 74:25–32.

Stiles, F. G. 1973. Food supply and the annual cycle of the Anna Hummingbird. Univ. Calif. Publ. Zool. 97:1–109.

Storer, R. W., and Nuechterlein, G. L. 1992. Western and Clark's Grebes, *in* The Birds of North America (A. Poole, P. Stettenheim, and F. Gill, eds.), no. 26. Acad. Nat. Sci, Philadelphia.

Stott, K., Jr. 1959. The Starling arrives in San Diego, California. Condor 61:373.

Stott, K., Jr., and Sams, J. R. 1959. Distributional records of the Common Goldeneye and Crissal Thrasher in southeastern California. Condor 61:298–299.

Suffel, G. S. 1970. An Olivaceous Flycatcher in California. Calif. Birds 1:79–80.

Swarth, H. S. 1920. Revision of the avian genus *Passerella*, with special reference to the distribution and migration of the races in California. Univ. Calif. Publ. Zool. 21:75–224.

Swarth, H. S. 1933. Peale Falcon in California. Condor 35:233–234.

Terp, J. M., and Pavelka, M. 1999. Summary of colonial seabird nesting at Western Salt Company, San Diego Bay, California: 1998 season. Coastal Program, U.S. Fish & Wildlife Service, Carlsbad, CA.

Terrill, S. B., and Ohmart, R. D. 1984. Facultative extension of fall migration by Yellow-rumped Warblers (*Dendroica coronata*). Auk 101:427–438.

Thompson, C. W. 1991. Is the Painted Bunting actually two species? Problems determining species limits between allopatric populations. Condor 93:987–1000.

Todd, W. E. C. 1963. Birds of the Labrador Peninsula and Adjacent Areas. Univ. Toronto Press, Toronto.

Toochin, R. 1998. A Xantus' Hummingbird in British Columbia: A first Canadian record. Birders' J. 6:293–297.

Torrey, B. 1909. The Golden Plover at Coronado. Condor 11:207.

Torrey, B. 1913. Field-days in California. Houghton Mifflin, Boston.

Twedt, D. J., and Crawford, R. D. 1995. Yellow-headed Blackbird, *in* The Birds of North America (A. Poole and F. Gill, eds.), no. 192. Acad. Nat. Sci., Philadelphia.

Tweit, R. C., and Tweit, J. C. 2000. Cassin's Kingbird, *in* The Birds of North America (A. Poole and F. Gill, eds.), no. 534. Birds N. Am., Philadelphia.

U.S. Fish and Wildlife Service. 1996. Biological opinion 1-6-93-F-37R1 on the effects of implementing the 4(d) rule for the coastal California Gnatcatcher. U.S. Fish and Wildlife Serv., Carlsbad, CA.

U. S. Fish and Wildlife Service. 1998. Draft recovery plan for the Least Bell's Vireo. U.S. Fish and Wildlife Serv., Portland, OR.

Unitt, P. 1974. Painted Redstarts attempt to breed in California. W. Birds 5:94–96.

Unitt, P. 1981. Birds of Hot Springs Mountain, San Diego County, California. W. Birds 12:125–135.

Unitt, P. 1984. The birds of San Diego County. San Diego Soc. Nat. Hist. Memoir 13.

Unitt, P. 1986. Another hybrid Downy × Nuttall's Woodpecker from San Diego County. W. Birds 17:43–44.

Unitt, P. 2000. Gray Vireos wintering in California elephant trees. W. Birds 31:258–262.

Unitt, P., and Rea, A. M. 1997. Taxonomy of the Brown Creeper, in The Era of Allan R. Phillips: A Festschrift (R. W. Dickerman, compiler), pp. 177–185. Horizon Publ., Albuquerque.

Unitt, P., Rea, A. M., Palacios, E., Mellink, E., Alfaro, L., and Gonzalez, S. 1995. Noteworthy records of birds in northwestern Baja California. W. Birds 26:144–154.

Unitt, P., Messer, K., and Théry, M. 1996. Taxonomy of the Marsh Wren in southern California. Proc. San Diego Soc. Nat. Hist. 31.

URS Corporation. 2004. Summary of biological monitoring surveys for California gnatcatcher, Caltrans construction projects 12-0C9414 and 12-0C9444, State Route 73 (San Joaquin Hills Toll Road). Report to Calif. Dept. Transportation, San Diego.

Van Rossem, A. J. 1926. The California forms of *Agelaius phoeniceus* (Linnaeus). Condor 28:215–230.

Van Rossem, A. J. 1929. A new name necessary for the Calaveras Warbler. Proc. Biol. Soc. Washington 42:179.

Veit, R. R., Pyle, P., and McGowan, J. A. 1996. Ocean warming and long-term change in pelagic bird abundance within the California Current system. Mar. Ecol. Prog. Ser. 139:11–18.

Verbeek, N. A. M. 1993. Glaucous-winged Gull, *in* The Birds of North America (A. Poole and F. Gill, eds.), no. 59. Acad. Nat. Sci., Philadelphia.

Verbeek, N. A. M., and Caffrey, C. 2002. American Crow, *in* The Birds of North America (A. Poole and F. Gill, eds.), no. 647. Birds N. Am., Philadelphia.

Verner, J. 1965. Breeding biology of the Long-billed Marsh Wren. Condor 67:6–30.

Verner, J., and Ritter, L. V. 1983. Current status of the Brown-headed Cowbird in the Sierra National Forest. Auk 100:355–368.

Verner, J., Gutiérrez, R. J., and Gould, G. I. 1992. The California Spotted Owl: General biology and ecological relations, *in* The California Spotted Owl: A technical assessment of its current status (J. Verner, K. S. McKelvey, B. R. Noon, R. J. Gutiérrez, G. I. Gould, Jr., and T. W. Beck, tech. coords.), pp. 55–78. Gen. Tech. Rep. PSW-GTR-133, U.S. Forest Service, Albany, CA.

Voelker, G., and Rohwer, S. 1998. Contrasts in scheduling of molt and migration in eastern and western Warbling Vireos. Auk 115:142–155.

Von Bloeker, J. C., Jr. 1931. *Perognathus pacificus* from the type locality. J. Mammal. 12:369–372.

Wallace, E. A. H., and Wallace, G. E. 1998. Brandt's Cormorant, *in* The Birds of North America (A. Poole and F. Gill, eds.), no. 362. Birds N. Am., Philadelphia.

Walton, B. J., Thelander, C. G., and Harlow, D. L. 1988. The status of Peregrines nesting in California, Oregon, Washington, and Nevada, *in* Peregrine Falcon Populations: Their Management and Recovery (T. J. Cade, J. H. Enderson, C. G. Thelander, and C. M. White, eds.), pp. 95–104. Peregrine Fund, Boise.

Ward, D., and Smith, J. N. M. 2000. Brown-headed Cowbird parasitism results in a sink population in Warbling Vireos. Auk 117:337–344.

Weathers, W. W. 1983. Birds of Southern California's Deep Canyon. Univ. Calif. Press, Berkeley.

Weaver, K. L. 1990. Breeding bird census 3. Coast live oak woodland. J. Field Ornithol. 61 (suppl.):39–30.

Weaver, K. L. 1992. Breeding bird census 2. Riparian woodland. J. Field Ornithol. 63 (suppl.):35.

Weaver, K.L. 1998a. Coastal sage scrub variations of San Diego County and their influence on the distribution of the California Gnatcatcher. W. Birds 29:392–405.

Weaver, K. L. 1998b. A new site of sympatry of the California and Black-tailed Gnatcatchers in the United States. W. Birds 29:476–479.

Wellicome, T. I., and Holroyd, G. L. 2001. The second international Burrowing Owl symposium: Background and context. J. Raptor Res. 35:269–273.

Wells, J. M., and Kus, B. E. 2001. Least Bell's Vireo surveys and nest monitoring at Anza–Borrego Desert State Park in 2000. U.S. Geol. Surv., W. Ecol. Res. Center, San Diego.

Wells, J. M., and Turnbull, J. 1998. Final report. 1997 Tijuana River valley Least Bell's Vireo monitoring and territory mapping program. Report to International Boundary and Water Commission, El Paso.

Wells, S., and Baptista, L. F. 1979. Breeding of Allen's Hummingbird (*Selasphorus sasin sedentarius*) on the southern California mainland. W. Birds 10:83–85.

Wheelock, I. G. 1904. Birds of California. A. C. McClurg, Chicago.

Whelchel, A. W., Keane, K. M., and Josselyn, M. N. 1996. Establishment of a new Black Skimmer colony in southern California. W. Birds 27:164–167.

White, C. M. 1968. Diagnosis and relationships of the North American tundra-inhabiting Peregrine Falcon. Auk 85:179–191.

White, C. M., Clum, N. J., Cade, T. J., and Hunt, W. G. 2002. Peregrine Falcon, *in* The Birds of North America (A. Poole and F. Gill, eds.), no 660. Birds N. Am., Philadelphia.

Wilbur, S. R. 1978. The California Condor, 1966–76: A look at its past and future. N. Am. Fauna 72.

Wildlife Research Institute. 2004. Year 2 final report for NCCP raptor monitoring project (January 1–December 31, 2002). Report to Calif. Dept. Fish and Game, San Diego.

Willett, G. 1912. Birds of the Pacific slope of southern California. Pac. Coast Avifauna 7.

Willett, G. 1933. A revised list of the birds of southwestern California. Pac. Coast Avifauna 21.

Williams, B. D. C. 2001. Low-elevation nesting by Calliope Hummingbirds in the western Sierra Nevada foothills. W. Birds 32:127–130.

Williams, B. D. C. 2002. Purple Martins in oak woodlands, in Proceedings of the symposium on oaks in California's changing landscape, fifth symposium on oak woodlands; 22–25 October 2001, San Diego. Gen. Tech. Rep. PSW-GTR-xxx. USDA Forest Service, Pacific Southwest Research Station, Berkeley, CA.

Williams, L. 1942. Display and sexual behavior of the Brandt Cormorant. Condor 44:85–104.

Wilson, W. H. 1994. Western Sandpiper, *in* The Birds of North America (A. Poole and F. Gill, eds.), no. 90. Acad. Nat. Sci., Philadelphia.

Winter, J. 1974. The distribution of the Flammulated Owl in California. W. Birds 5:25–44.

Winter, K. J., and McKelvey, S. D. 1999. Cowbird trapping in remote areas: Alternative control measures may be more effective. Studies Avian Biol. 18:282–289.

Wires, L. R., and Cuthbert, F. J. 2000. Trends in Caspian Tern numbers and distribution in North America: A review. Waterbirds 23:388–404.

Wirtz, W. O., Mayer, A. L., Raney, M. M., and Beyers, J. L. 1997. Effects of fire on the ecology of the California Gnatcatcher, *Polioptila californica*, in California sage scrub communities, *in* Proceedings of a conference held at Coeur d'Alene, Idaho, November 1995 (J. M. Greenlee, ed.), pp. 91–96. Int. Assoc. Wildland Fire, Fairfield, WA.

Wolf, B. O. 1997. Black Phoebe, *in* The Birds of North America (A. Poole and F. Gill, eds.), no 268. Acad. Nat. Sci., Philadelphia.

Wolf, B. O., and Jones, S. L. 2000. Vermilion Flycatcher, *in* The Birds of North America (A. Poole and F. Gill, eds.), no. 484. Birds N. Am., Philadelphia.

Woodbridge, B., Finley, K. K., and Seager, S. T. 1995. An investigation of the Swainson's Hawk in Argentina. J. Raptor Res. 29:202–204.

Zedler, P. H., Gautier, C. R., and McMaster, G. S. 1983. Vegetation change in response to extreme events: The effect of a short interval between fires in California chaparral and coastal scrub. Ecology 64:809–818.

Zembal, R., Fancher, J. M., Nordby, C. S., and Bransfield, R. J. 1985. Intermarsh movements by Light-footed Clapper Rails indicated in part through regular censusing. Calif. Fish and Game 71:164–171.

Zembal, R., and Hoffman, S. M. 2002a. A survey of the Belding's Savannah Sparrow (*Passerculus sandwichensis beldingi*) in California 2001. Final report to California Department of Fish and Game, San Diego.

Zembal, R., and Hoffman, S. M. 2002b. Light-footed Clapper Rail Management, Study, and Translocation, 2002. Report to Natural Resources Management Office, Naval Base Ventura County, Point Mugu, CA.

Zembal, R., Kramer, J., Bransfield, R. J., and Gilbert, N. 1988. A survey of Belding's Savannah Sparrows in California. Am. Birds 42: 1233–1236.

Zembal, R., and Massey, B. W. 1981. A census of the Light-footed Clapper Rail in California. W. Birds 12:87–99.

Zimmerman, D. A. 1973. Range expansion of Anna's Hummingbird. Am. Birds 27:827–835.

Zink, R. M. 1986. Patterns and evolutionary significance of geographic variation in the *schistacea* group of the Fox Sparrow (*Passerella iliaca*). Ornithol. Monogr. 40.

Zink, R. M. 1994. The geography of mitochondrial DNA variation, population structure, hybridization, and species limits in the Fox Sparrow (*Passerella iliaca*). Evolution 48:96–111.

Zink, R. M., Barrowclough, G. F., Atwood, J. L., and Blackwell-Rago, R. C. 2000. Genetics, taxonomy, and conservation of the threatened California Gnatcatcher. Cons. Biol. 14:1394–1405.

INDEX